Gun Digest

29th Anniversary

1975 Deluxe Edition

EDITED BY JOHN T. AMBER

DIGEST BOOKS, INC. NORTHFIELD, ILL.

This year's covers, front and back, honor two of the world's best known and best loved gunmakers—Browning and Winchester. Both of these great companies have, in the past several years, become truly international in scope.

The top gun on our front cover is a Winchester you probably won't see. An over-under double rifle, no less, it is made in Belgium by a specialist gunmaker, its caliber the German 9.3x74R. Below it is the excellent new Winchester Super X Model 1, a gas-operated autoloading shotgun—specially engraved for the GUN DIGEST*—that was five years in the development stage.*

The upper gun on our back cover—again custom engraved for this issue—is Browning's single shot rifle, made in Japan.

The shotgun below it is the latest Browning, the Model 2000, also a gas-functioning autoloader, its left-side loading system and general design engineered by Val Browning.

The man who did these brilliant drawings is the inimitable James M. Triggs.

Townsend Whelen Award

Our 9th presentation honoring the late Colonel Townsend Whelen goes to Mr. Wallace Labisky for his comprehensive and detailed report on modern Browning shotguns.

This annual $500 award is given to the author who, in the opinion of our judges, made the best contribution to the literature of firearms, as published in this edition. The criteria are originality, clarity, readability and lasting value.

Our thanks to Mr. Labisky and our sincere congratulations.

MEMBER OF THE
NATIONAL
SHOOTING SPORTS
FOUNDATION
INC

Manuscripts, contributions and inquiries, including first class return postage, should be sent to the Gun Digest Editorial Offices, 540 Frontage Rd., Northfield, Ill. 60093. All material received will receive reasonable care, but we will not be responsible for its safe return. Material accepted is subject to our requirements for editing and revisions. Author payment covers all rights and title to the accepted material, including photos, drawings and other illustrations. Payment is made at our current rates.

Printed in U.S.A.

ISBN-0-695-80498-7 Library of Congress Catalog #44-32588

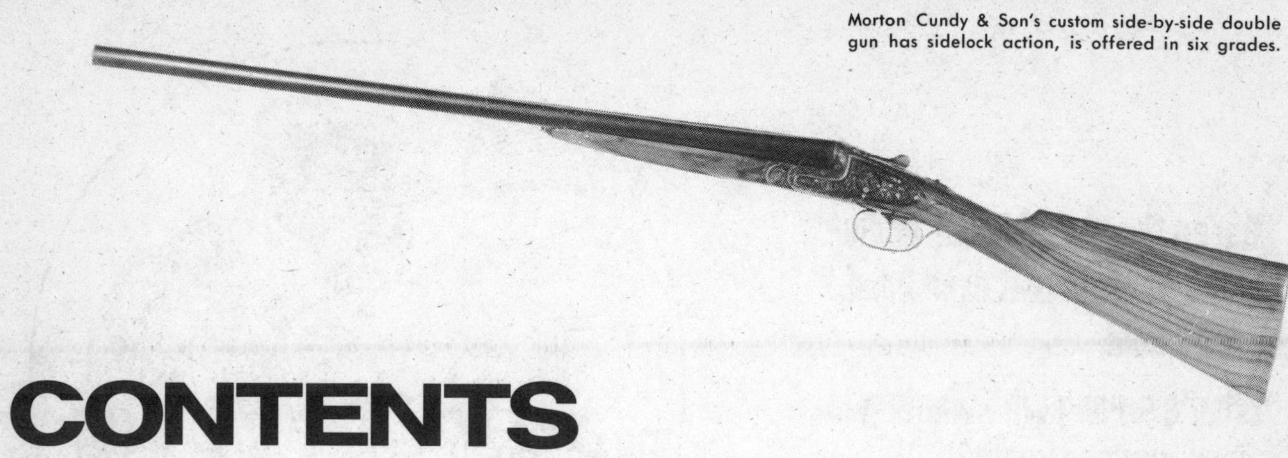

Morton Cundy & Son's custom side-by-side double gun has sidelock action, is offered in six grades.

CONTENTS

"You're the most famous maker of rifle barrels that ever lived," Joe Hill said,

"What's wrong with wanting to learn what you know?"

J. M. Pyne hesitated—could he trust this young fellow?

Illustrations by Lisle Reedstrom

The Secret of THE OLD MASTER

by LUCIAN CARY

JOE HILL had two target rifles in cases of canvas and leather hanging from his shoulders as he walked down a factory-lined street in Jersey City of a hot Saturday afternoon in August.

He guessed, after half a mile, that he had come to the right corner. There was the little red-brick saloon across the street and here beside him was the outside stairway sheathed in corrugated iron.

He eased the rifles off his shoulders. They weighed fourteen or fifteen pounds apiece. He sat down on the curbstone and stood the guns upright between his knees. He wanted to rest. But mostly he wanted a minute or two in which to get up his courage. He had sat up all night and all morning in a day couch. He had slept at times, but he had awakened always to the same anxiety. Somehow he had to impress the old man, and by all accounts the old man was not easily impressed.

A hot breeze came down the street between the gray-brown walls of the factory buildings. The cobblestones shimmered in the heat. He knew how bad the mirage would be on a day like this. You would think you were looking at the target through running water. You wouldn't know where the bull really was.

He wiped his face with his handkerchief. He could feel the water running down his chest. He could see where the sweat had turned his blue work shirt a darker blue. He got up presently and hung the rifles on his shoulders and tried the door at the bottom of the stairway. The door was locked. He walked across the street into the saloon. The place was empty, except for the bartender.

"Where is J. M. Pyne's shop?" he asked.

"You mean the old man who fixes the guns?" The bartender pointed through the open door. "Up that stairway. Fourth floor."

"The street door is locked."

"When it's after hours you have to yell for him to come all the way down and open up the door for you."

Joe hesitated. It didn't seem right that he should yell to a man as famous as J. M. Pyne to come down three flights of stairs and let him in.

"They all yell for him when they come to see him," the bartender said.

Joe walked out into the middle of the street and looked up at the fourth story. The window nearest the corner was open at the top.

"Hey, Pyne!" he called out.

There was no answer.

"Hey, Pyne!" he yelled as loud as he could.

The window he was watching went up and an old man with a white beard and a black engineer's cap peered out. He pointed to the stairway.

Joe waited at the door. He heard the old man's slow footsteps. The moment he had worked and waited and saved his money for was coming.

The door opened and the old man stood there, in a sleeveless undershirt and pants, looking over his spectacles at Joe. The old man had

brown eyes. His nose was finely molded. *You'd know,* Joe thought, *that he was somebody, even if you didn't know who he was.*

"Mr. Pyne," he said, "my name is Hill – Joe Hill."

"Come in," the old man said, and held the door wide.

Joe walked up the stairs while the old man climbed wearily after him. The air was hot and dead under the iron roof of the stairway and the rifles dragged at Joe's shoulders. But he was happy. He was going to see the place he had dreamed of.

The room he went into was fifty feet long and thirty feet wide, and so full of things that only a narrow gangway remained. He walked toward the bench that ran clear across the room under the bank of windows at the far end, guessing that the long narrow boxes standing on end contained rifles waiting for Pyne barrels, noting a drill press, no longer in use, and what looked like a lathe, but wasn't. He took another look over his shoulder as he passed the machine. It seemed too light and too simple. But it must be the machine from which, for fifty years, those barrels, so smooth inside, so even, so beautifully rifled, had come.

There was so little room in front of the bench that he paused to let the old man pass him. Except for a small clear space around the vise, the bench was piled three feet deep with open cigar boxes and cartons and letters and tools.

"Take off your coat," J. M. Pyne said. "It's warm."

Joe took off his coat and hunted for a place to put it. He laid it across a rack of barrel stock.

"Mr. Pyne," he said, "I've got one of your guns here."

He opened one of his cases and took out a 22-caliber rifle of the sort that is made for offhand shooting when there are no restrictions as to weight or trigger pull or sights. It had a long barrel as thick as a crowbar and a Ballard action with double-set triggers.

The old man opened the vise and dropped clamps of sole leather inside the iron jaws. Joe put the heavy barrel in the vise. The old man opened the gun and picked up a steel rod that stood against the bench, and a pledget of absorbent cotton.

He put two pledgets through the bore to get the oil out and held the gun up to the light and looked through it. He let the gun down and studied the open breech. "Who cut it off?" he demanded.

"I did."

"What for?" The old man's eyes were no longer friendly as he looked at Joe.

"The chamber had been rubbed several thousandths out of round at twelve o'clock, so it wouldn't shoot any more."

"They will do that," the old man said. "They won't take the trouble to push a cleaning rod straight, so it doesn't rub."

The old man pushed the lever back and forth, studying the extractor, which was of the kind that travels parallel to the bore in a T slot. Joe knew that extractor was a nice job. But the old man said nothing. He closed the action. The lever made a distinct snap as it passed dead center and the block came home, the way the lever of a falling-block rifle should.

"The action was in tough shape when I got it," Joe said. "Made new pins for the lever and the link."

The old man took the forearm off the gun and looked at the numbers stamped on the under side of the barrel. Then he got an old notebook out of a drawer under the bench and leafed through it.

"I made that barrel in 1923. I didn't put it on a Ballard action."

"The fellow wanted to keep the action it was on."

"What did you do about the firing pin?"

Joe picked up a screw driver and took the block out and handed it over.

The old man studied the face of the block with his magnifying glass.

"Where did you get the idea of that circular plate?"

"From one of your guns."

Joe knew his work was good. But he could guess what the old man was thinking. Maybe he was bored.

J. M. Pyne walked down to the other end of the bench and got cigarettes. He offered Joe a cigarette. Joe said he didn't smoke. The old man lit his cigarette deliberately. "What's your trade?" he asked.

"I'm a toolmaker."

"How old are you?"

"Twenty-six."

The old man looked at him sharply. "They used to say that it took twenty years to make a toolmaker out of a good mechanic."

"I'm still learning."

"So am I," J. M. Pyne said.

He took a cigarette paper and laid it across the breech of the barrel and raised the lever. He had to force it a little. But he closed the gun. He opened it again. The cigarette paper was torn away where the block had met the breech. The block was so closely fitted that it wouldn't quite accept the cigarette paper, yet it worked freely.

The old man picked up his micrometer and measured the thickness of the paper. It came to an even thousandth of an inch.

"Do you know how much your head space is?"

"Forty-three thousandths."

J. M. Pyne looked down at the gun. "I don't see anything the matter with it," he said. "How does it shoot?"

"Not as well as a Pyne barrel should. I've tried every kind of match ammunition in it. I haven't found anything that will average better than an inch and three eighths for fifty shots at a hundred yards."

The old man went down to the far corner of his shop and turned on a light and put up a card about five by eight inches in front of a small steel plate. He handed Joe a pair of field glasses.

"If you sit on that stool and rest your elbows on the lathe bed so you can hold the glasses steady, you can see," J. M. Pyne said.

He took the gun to the other corner of the room and put it in a machine rest. A little telescope was mounted beside the rest. Joe saw, watching everything J. M. Pyne did, that he had a clear line of fire past the rack of barrel stock between the legs of the rifling machine, and under a stepladder.

J. M. Pyne began to shoot, firing five shots, and moving the rest a little and firing another five shots. Joe Hill saw that the first group was ragged; the second group closed up, as the gun warmed. But he did not know what to expect of a rifle at such a short distance.

J. M. Pyne paused after twenty-five shots and studied a fired case with his magnifying glass. He handed the case and the glass to Joe.

"Your pin is too big," he said. "It's hitting too far out over the rim."

He took the firing pin out of the breech block and fastened it in the vise.

"Take this stone and the glass," he said. "Reduce it a little at twelve o'clock, but don't make it any shorter."

Joe worked cautiously with the oil stone. When he paused for a moment the old man took the glass and looked at the rounded end of the pin and nodded to Joe to go on. Joe felt the sweat dripping down his body as he worked. It was hot in the shop. But he would have sweated anyway, doing a job like that with J. M. Pyne watching him.

"All right," the old man said at last.

He put the firing pin back and tried a fired case in the gun. He turned the case about under his magnifying glass.

"That may help it," he said. "The area is reduced, so it's hitting deeper and in the right place."

He put the gun back in the rest and fired five more groups of five shots each. Joe could see that they were closer than the previous groups. J. M. Pyne went down and got the card and brought it back. The groups were only a trifle bigger in diameter than a 22 caliber bullet.

"That gun is all right," J. M. Pyne said.

"Can you really tell—at fifty feet?"

"Oh, yes. You should get some groups under an inch at a hundred yards. I'd guess it will average an inch and an eighth when everything is going right and there's no wind. It won't do it day in and day out, of course. It'll pick up a bit of lead or hard fouling now and then, like any twenty-two, that'll make it throw wide ones until it shoots out."

Joe knew the moment had come to say what he had come all the way from Indiana to say. How could he say it? Now that he was here he felt how out of line it would sound.

He thought of showing J. M. Pyne the other gun he'd brought along. But it was a Springfield bull gun to which he had fitted a factory-rifled blank. There was nothing about it that would interest the old man.

"I guess," he said—"I guess I've taken enough of your time."

J. M. Pyne smiled. "I'm old and I'm tired and I ache all over. My eyes are no good. I can't shoot any more. But I've always had time for anybody who was interested in rifles. What do you want to know?"

"Mr. Pyne——" Joe began, and for a moment the presumption of what he was going to ask overcame him. He knew he was a good workman. But who was he to propose himself as successor to the old master of them all? "Mr. Pyne," he began again, "couldn't you use a helper?"

The old man shook his head. "I've had two or three helpers in the last thirty years. They got underfoot."

Joe Hill waited.

"Besides," J. M. Pyne said, and Joe could feel that he was softening the blow, "making fine shooting rifles isn't a paying business. I can't afford a helper."

"I wouldn't expect to be paid," Joe said. "I've saved some money."

He had $229 in his pocket. He knew that a man could live four or five months on that if he wanted to.

The old man turned on him then. His eyes blazed as he spoke. "Why," he asked, "do you want to work for me for nothing?"

Joe could not dodge the question. He had to tell the truth.

"I want to learn the secret of Pyne barrels," he said.

The old man nodded grimly. "I thought so," he said. "You—and a lot of others."

"You're the most famous maker of rifle barrels that ever lived. What's wrong with wanting to learn what you know?"

"And setting up shop in competition with me."

"I wouldn't do that unless you said I could."

J. M. Pyne looked off into the dimming corner of the shop. When he spoke, he seemed to be talking to himself. "I gave a fellow the run of my shop once. I told him all I knew. And he started out making rifles. I wouldn't have cared if he'd done a good job. The more fine shooting rifles there are in this country the better. But he didn't make fine shooting rifles. He chambered guns without a pilot on the reamer, so the chamber wasn't concentric with the bore. He botched everything he touched. Time after time men came in here with guns he had made and I had to fix them."

Joe wondered why he'd felt he had to fix the guns his rival had spoiled. He thought he knew. It was part of the old man's passion for fine shooting guns.

"Mr. Pyne— —" Joe began. But it really wasn't any use. You couldn't argue with an old master who didn't choose to give you his secret lest you abuse it.

"You come back tomorrow," the old man said. "You come back tomorrow and I'll show you how to fix the triggers on that offhand gun of yours, so the front one won't kick. Leave your guns here tonight."

II

Joe went back to New York by the Hudson Tube and found his way to the Grand Central, where he'd checked his suitcase and his kit of tools. He carried the double load down 42nd Street to Eighth Avenue. He got a room in a small hotel for a dollar. The little room was hot, without a breath of air. He went out and walked back across 42nd Street until he came to Fifth Avenue.

He had never seen Fifth Avenue before. He felt he ought to be thrilled by it. He got on a Fifth Avenue bus and rode down to Washington Square and back. It was almost cool on top of the bus. And there was something about rolling down Fifth Avenue of a summer night, when the biggest city you had ever known was Richmond, Indiana. But for him the magic was in a cluttered, dusty room, four stories up, in a gray factory building across the river, where for so many years J. M. Pyne had done the work no one in all the world could match.

He awoke at dawn the next morning and remembered then that it was Sunday. J. M. Pyne must have forgotten that it was Sunday, when he'd said to come. But perhaps he hadn't. Joe took his kit of tools. He might need it, and he didn't dare leave it where it might be stolen. He couldn't take a chance on a set of micrometer calipers and a micrometer depth gauge and the chambering reamers and gauges and counterbores and milling cutters he had made for himself through the spare time of several years.

He was sitting on the curbstone close to the locked door of the outside stairway when he saw the old man coming toward him.

"Good morning, Joe," he said. "I'm sorry to be late. I try to sleep on Sunday mornings. I seldom get here before half past eight . . .

"The trouble with those factory triggers," J. M. Pyne said, when he had taken off his Sunday clothes, "is they're on small pins. The least bit of wear and they wobble from side to side. They want to be on trunnions. And I put in a kind of recoil block, so the front trigger doesn't kick."

Joe Hill worked for hours, under the old man's direction, remaking the triggers of the offhand gun. Toward three in the afternoon J. M. Pyne remembered that they hadn't eaten. He got out a paper bag of sandwiches and two cans of beer, which he cooled a bit under the tap. They sat opposite each other, eating corned-beef sandwiches and drinking half-warm beer, and the old man grew expansive, and told stories of the days when he had made world records with a rifle. Joe Hill asked himself if it was really he, sitting there in friendly conversation, as if he were an equal, with J. M. Pyne.

They went back to work then. They worked until the light failed and J. M. Pyne turned on the powerful electric bulbs over his lathe and bench. Joe thought the job was done at nine o'clock that night. But the old man, trying the triggers, shook his head.

"They're too light," he said. "Maybe you could shoot them in weather like this. But they would never do in the Election Day match. You can't feel a light trigger when your finger is cold. We'll have to make a new spring."

It was nearly midnight when Joe finished the spring. He drew the temper in a gas flame while the old man watched the color. He put the spring in place. The old man tried the triggers.

He looked up at Joe Hill, smiling. "I could shoot those triggers myself," he said. "Let's go home."

Joe picked up his kit of tools.

"What do you want to carry that for?" the old man asked. "Why don't you leave it here?"

"I will," Joe said.

They paused in Exchange Place. The old man was taking a bus and Joe was taking the Hudson Tube.

Joe waited, hoping the old man was going to say he could hang around the shop as long as he wanted to. But J. M. Pyne was looking up at the sky, where the quarter of a moon gave some light behind the haze.

"Two more weeks of dog days," he said.

Joe Hill was sitting on the curbstone again the next morning when the old man arrived. He hardly spoke. The old man got out a piece of barrel stock and set it up in the lathe. Joe didn't know what to do with himself, so he sat in a corner and watched J. M. Pyne turn the stock to size.

When he had done that he put the barrel in the drilling and rifling machine and got out a drill with a shank longer than the barrel.

"Come over here, Joe," he said.

It was the first time he had spoken in three hours.

"This is my drill," he said. "It's better than any other I ever saw. It takes a smaller chip, so it doesn't choke itself."

Joe studied the odd shape of the cutting surfaces. He could see how well designed it was to drill a deep hole without choking itself. He watched with what care the old man set everything up before he started the machine and the drill began to bite into the rapidly revolving stock.

When everything was going to his satisfaction, the old man asked, "Can you file?"

"Some," Joe said. He knew the things old-timers could do with files. Few living toolmakers could do them.

J. M. Pyne picked up a malleable-iron casting with a curve to take each finger except the trigger finger.

"That's a blank for a Pyne lever. You ought to have one on your off-hand gun."

There was a lot of stock to take off. Joe filed on that lever for two days and a half, trying all through the last day to make the contours perfect.

That was the pattern of the days that followed. Week after week he went to the shop every morning, seven days a week, and stayed until the old man left, which was sometimes at six o'clock and sometimes at midnight. He saw, several times over, the process by which the old man made a rifle barrel—drilling the blank, reaming it, rifling it, fitting it to the action, chambering it, polishing it with a lead lap cast in the muzzle and pushed out just enough so it could be coated with oil and emery and drawn back, and finally testing it in the machine rest.

But watch as he would, he could not guess the secret.

He suspected that the old man put him to work on some simple job when he came to that part.

III

The money he had saved was almost gone by Christmas. He was lucky enough to sell his Springfield bull gun for a hundred dollars. He lived in a tenement where he got a room for four dollars a week. He did not smoke and he had no time for the movies. He got coffee and rolls for ten cents every morning. The big sandwich he ate for lunch cost fifteen cents and his dinner at a cafeteria was forty cents. He figured he could make a hundred dollars last ten weeks.

The old man came down the street one bitter morning in February, and Joe knew that he was sick. His long overcoat hung almost to the ground as he bent against the wind and felt for a footing with his stick. It took him a long time to climb the stairs.

"I've got a heck of a cold," he said, when they reached the shop. "I think I'd better lie down for a while."

He spent that day and the next lying on an old couch in a corner. He had a cough that racked him, and when he got up and walked across the shop he staggered like a drunken man.

Joe offered to get a doctor.

"Nonsense," J. M. Pyne said, "I've been my own doctor for forty years."

Joe took his arm when they left that night, and went with him on the bus and saw him safely to his room.

But he didn't stay home. He came staggering down the street the next morning the same as ever.

"I had to come," he said. "I had a letter from Paul French yesterday, saying he'd be in today. His old barrel won't shoot. He wants a new one for the Metropolitan Championship."

The old man lay on the couch, coughing as if he were turning himself inside out, until there was a rap at the door.

"That's Paul," the old man said, and staggered to his feet.

Joe opened the door to a solidly built man of fifty with a rifle in a case over his shoulder.

"How are you, Johnny?" the solid man asked J. M. Pyne.

"I'm sick," the old man said. "But I'll be all right in a couple of days."

The solid man took his rifle out of its case. It was an exceptionally heavy gun on a Ballard action.

"The barrel's gone," he said.

"Why wouldn't it be," J. M. Pyne said. "You've been shooting it ten years."

The solid man said he wanted the barrel in a hurry, the match was only two weeks away. J. M. Pyne said he would get the barrel out.

He went back to his couch again when the solid man had left. He lay there the rest of the day. He let Joe take him home again.

"I've got to get that barrel out," he said to Joe. "He's about the best all-round shot there is. He's got to have a new barrel."

Joe walked up and down the street the next morning in a snowstorm, waiting for the old man. He didn't come at nine o'clock. Joe kept on pacing back and forth, trying to keep warm, for another hour. Then he went back to Exchange Place and took a bus to the old man's house.

J. M. Pyne sat up in bed. "I couldn't make it this morning." A spell of coughing interrupted him. "My keys are in my pants there."

He wouldn't have a doctor. He insisted that all he needed was to rest until he got over the cold. Joe took the keys and went back to the shop. He measured the barrel of Paul French's rifle. It was thirty-two inches long and slightly bigger than a No. 4. He found a piece of barrel stock long enough and set it up in the lathe and began to turn it to size.

He knew a sixty-fourth of an inch more or less in outside diameter would make no difference that the man who shot the gun would ever know. But he did the job to a thousandth.

When he called on the old man that night he could see that he was feverish and a little out of his head. He thought he'd better not mention the piece of barrel stock he'd turned to size.

Joe went on with the barrel the next day. He set the barrel up and got everything ready. He checked and rechecked the setup. He wanted that hole to come out at the other end to within a thousandth of dead center, the way it did when the old man drilled it.

It took all the nerve he had to start the machine. But he did it. He stood there anxiously, watching everything. If the drill struck a hard spot in the stock, it would probably break before he could stop it.

When the hole was drilled he took the barrel out and wiped it clean and looked through it at the light, watching the shadow line. It seemed to him that the hole was straight, and as smooth as a hole drilled by J. M. Pyne.

He got out the six-sided reamers that the old man used, and measured until he found the one that was right. He set the barrel up in the lathe and reamed it, watching it every minute, and putting on the oil with a brush the way J. M. Pyne did.

When the reaming was done, he upset a soft lead slug in the bore and pushed the slug through and measured it. The diameter was right.

That night the old man said he felt better. He said he would be around in the morning. Joe said nothing, feeling that if he urged him not to come, the old man would resent it.

Joe went back to the shop at daylight the next morning and hunted out the rifling head. He knew the cutter had to be stoned just so. Sharpening it was the toughest part of the job. It was hard enough to cut glass. And if the old man came in while he was working on that cutter, he'd be furious. What if he spoiled it?

The old man had said that nowadays he had to have bright sunlight softened by the dirty window panes of his shop to make a rifling cutter. It took days to make one, even when the sun shone. And in winter you might not get two hours of sun in a week.

Joe waited until after ten o'clock before he dared take the chance that J. M. Pyne might come in. He worked so cautiously that it took him all day to hone the cutter.

The old man was sure that night that he would be around in the morning. Joe caught himself hoping he wouldn't be.

Joe rifled the barrel the next day, running the rifling head back and forth by hand, the way the old man did, and making a mark with chalk on the head of the machine for each pass, and indexing the head for the next cut. It took forty passes of the rifling head to cut one groove two and a half thousandths deep. There were eight grooves to cut, three hundred and twenty passes. He finished the job toward six o'clock and took the barrel out and wiped it clean inside.

He took a soft lead slug out of the drawer and upset it in the bore and pushed it through. He thought it felt pretty even – without any loose places where the slug jumped ahead or any tight places either. But his hands were trembling so that he couldn't be sure it was as good as he hoped it was.

Then he held the barrel up to the light. He could see minute tool marks. But then, of course, you always could – even when J. M. Pyne had rifled a barrel. The tool marks came out when you polished with the lead lap.

Joe finished the barrel the next day and fitted it to the action. But he wasn't ready to test what he had done. The old Ballard action was loose. The lever didn't snap up. It took a whole day to get that right.

The old man looked a lot better that night. He would be there in the morning. Joe would have liked to stay away. But he couldn't. He had the key to the shop.

He got there at half past seven the next morning. He took the gun out of the vise and looked through it against the light. It looked good to him. But what did looks amount to? He had made it just the way the old man made his barrels – except that he didn't know the ultimate secret of a Pyne barrel. The old man had never said a word about that since the first time Joe had talked to him when he had said he didn't want a helper. Joe put the gun back in the vise. He guessed that was the best way to tell the old man what he had done – to let him see it.

J. M. Pyne knocked on the door at nine o'clock. Joe let him in. The old man walked down the narrow gangway and paused at the vise. He looked hard at the gun in the vise and went on to the corner where he hung his overcoat.

Joe sat down on the couch in the corner. The old man got into his working clothes and went back to the vise. He took the gun out of the vise and looked through it. He put it back and took a lead slug out of the drawer and pushed it through and caught it in his cap. He picked up his micrometer and measured the slug.

Without a word, he took the gun and put it in the machine rest. Joe got up and found the field glasses with which he had so often sat watching the old man shoot.

"Joe," J. M. Pyne said, "what did you do about those triggers you were going to fix on that 32-40?"

"Why," Joe said, "I haven't done anything."

He'd forgotten all about them.

"You'd better get to work," J. M. Pyne said.

Joe got out the triggers. The old man began to shoot from the machine rest. Joe's back was to the target as he worked and he could guess that was what J. M. Pyne intended.

The old man shot the gun all morning, firing five five-shot groups on a card and putting up a new card, while Joe worked on the triggers in an agony of curiosity. He guessed that the old man had fired four hundred shots when he took the gun out of the rest and put it in the vise and cleaned it.

The old man said nothing and Joe didn't dare say anything.

There was a rap on the door.

"That'll be Paul," J. M. Pyne said. "How are those triggers coming?"

"All right," Joe said.

"You'd better do something else for a while, so you'll be out of my way. You go back there and read some of the old copies of *Shooting and Fishing*. You can learn a lot from those old files of thirty or forty years ago."

Joe went back to the far corner where the piles of *Shooting and Fishing* lay, while the old man went to the door. He heard Paul French say, "Johnny, I just stopped by to see how you were coming with that barrel."

"It isn't done yet," J. M. Pyne said.

They moved down to the vise at the far end of the shop and Joe couldn't hear the rest of their talk. He could only sit there and open one old copy of *Shooting and Fishing* and look through it and take up another. When he couldn't stand it any longer, he sat up and looked over the boxes between him and the old man and Paul French.

J. M. Pyne had a sheaf of targets in his hand. He was always showing targets to customers. They might be targets he'd shot ten or twenty or thirty years ago. But as he watched, the old man laid the targets down. The gun was in the vise. And now the old man was hunting in the drawer under the bench. Joe saw that he had some small tool in his left hand. He was picking up a hammer with his other hand. And now he was holding the small tool on top of the barrel.

It couldn't be anything but the stamp that cut "J. M. Pyne" in small Roman capitals on a barrel.

Joe leaned forward, staring, and the old man struck with the hammer.

Paul French was turning to go. J. M. Pyne walked down the gangway with him. He paused at the door.

"It'll take a few days to brown that barrel," J. M. Pyne said.

"I know," French said. "I'll be in Saturday to get it."

The old man shut the door and walked wearily back to the vise. Joe got up and went down there. It was true. Cut in the polished steel was the mark of J. M. Pyne.

The old man got a cigarette and lit it with unnecessary deliberation. Then he picked up the sheaf of targets he had been showing French. He leafed through them until he found the one he wanted. He took that one out, and laid the others down and picked up a 22 cartridge. He let the bullet gently into the round hole of the first group.

"You see," he said, "it sticks."

He tried the others. The bullet stuck in all of them.

J. M. Pyne looked up at Joe. "So," he said, "I put my name on it."

"But the secret," Joe said. "I don't know the secret of a Pyne barrel."

The old man shook his head.

"There isn't any secret." He looked at Joe Hill over his spectacles and his eyes were friendly. "Except that you have to know what nice work is and you have to be willing to take the pains to do it. You knew that when you came here—else I wouldn't have bothered with you." •

"The Secret of the Old Master" was first published in the October 5th, 1940 issue of the *Saturday Evening Post*. It was one of an irregular series written about J. M. Pyne—a thin disguise for famed barrelmaker H. M. Pope. We are pleased indeed to reprint another of these heart warming stories.

Lucian Cary died on September 7, 1971. He was 85 years old.

There is rewarding information in Pope Rifle Barrels, even after the passage of 75 years. True, the groups guaranteed by Pope — 2½"-3" at 200 yards — would hardly excite today's 22 caliber bench-rest shooters, but try to beat them with 32 caliber lead bullets.

The original catalog measures 5½" by 7", and consists of 28 pages, including blank pages and covers. Page 2 shows only the printer's mark, nothing else, in the original. Page 26 shows a 5-shot group at 200 yards, made with a Pope 32 caliber barrel, that measures under 9/16". This we show in enlarged scale on page 25, underprinted.

CATALOGUE AND PRICE LIST OF

Pope Rifle Barrels

POPE SPECIAL BULLET MOULDS

REAR WIND GAUGE SIGHTS : LUBRICATING PUMPS

DOUBLE LOADING FLASKS

MACHINE RESTS : ETC.

H. M. POPE

59 ASHLEY STREET : HARTFORD CONNECTICUT

MARCH 1, 1899

PLIMPTON PRINT, HARTFORD, CONN.

PREFACE.

IN presenting this catalogue to your attention, the writer, making no pretence to a literary character, asks your indulgence for any shortcomings of such a nature, but, understanding his subject well, asks also your careful attention to the points brought forward, and to descriptions of the various articles of his manufacture, which he has tried to describe as plainly as possible. These points of superiority have been demonstrated by infinite labor and experiment, and are, so far as known, absolutely true.

By profession, I am a mechanical engineer and a skillful workman; for recreation and by preference, a "rifle crank." I first made a barrel (entirely on a foot lathe) because I could not buy what I wanted; *i. e.*, a .25 cal., which I made in 1887, before this size was manufactured. My first charge was a straight shell holding 25 grs. powder and a 100 gr. bullet, then a shorter one with 20 or 21 grs. powder and 85 gr. bullet. Finding the making of a sufficient number of these shells on a foot lathe an arduous task, I rechambered and swaged down a 32–20 shell. I used this shell for some time, but on making my first muzzle loader, I swaged down a 38 ex. long c. f. holding 30 grs. and using bullets up to 120 grs. With this rifle I did my best shooting under N. R. A. rules. Being troubled with bursting shells, I finally swaged down 32–40 everlasting shells, using 35 grs. This did good work muzzle loading, but had passed the limit for accuracy for breech loading with black powder. In these shells you will find the prototype of nearly every .25 cal. shell now made. Shortly after this I accidentally injured my barrel and abandoned this rifle for a 13 lb. rifle with set trigger, the state of my pocketbook at prize matches giving an unanswerable argument that this gave better results than the lighter arm, and later experience fully bears this out, and I find that I can still shoot a "practical" rifle with the rest, some "arms over your head" cranks to the contrary. (Proof, five dead deer with five cartridges, standing and running, all in thick woods at usual distances). The conditions of target shooting and field shooting bear no resemblance to one another, the most difficult change being not the change in arm, but the change from the deliberate aim at target to the snap shot at game. Therefore, *when you shoot at target use every refinement known to increase your scores*, as almost every refinement known for target use is impracticable in the field or woods.

During the period above mentioned I became interested in and thoroughly convinced that the so-called Schalke system, devised by Wm. Hayes and Geo. Schalke, possessed advantages for off-hand shooting that placed it far in advance of any other method of loading. This system I adopted, improving on Mr. Schalke's method of manufacture and altering somewhat the form of cut, though retaining the essential features. The above-mentioned heavy rifle, as well as the last .25 cal., were so made. Their performance was so good that I had to fit out my intimate shooting friends, and their improvement in shooting was so marked that I began to be besieged by outside parties to make barrels for them. This, for a long time, I refused to do, but finally these enquiries became so numerous, and Mr. Schalke's death occurring about this time, I consented, with the result that my barrels are now in the hands of the most expert off-hand shots in the country and are making scores that are unsurpassed, and *every man who shoots a Pope improves his scores*. Don't believe me, but watch the papers and see if this is not so.

4

The Pope System,

so-called, is, as previously stated, nearly the same as the Schalke, the difference being in the shape of the cut and that my barrels are cut to correct shape, while Mr. Schalke's were leaded. Mr. Schalke's rifling had eight flat grooves and eight narrow lands, with sharp corners to grooves. My rifling is shown here. It has eight wide grooves, which are on a radius about three times the radius of the bore, and has the corners rounded out, so dirt is easier removed, and it is cleaner in use. This groove is cut just deep enough to clean the bore in centre and gives a depth at corners of about .004″, which is about one-half the depth of the Schalke, but which is of ample depth, and works cleaner, and leaves less to depend on on upset of bullet, and is therefore more reliable. The lands are very narrow (about one-fifth to one-sixth the groove).

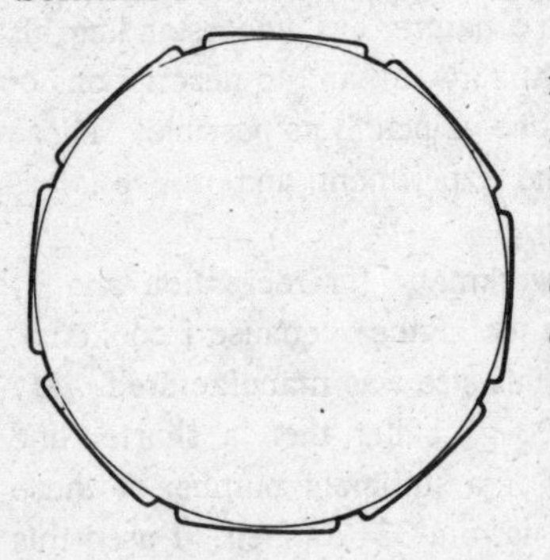

The bullet is made with a base large enough to fill grooves completely, and the body of practically the same diameter as the bore. This gives a form that is gas tight, loads very easily (being assisted in this by the narrow lands and choke bore) and on upset, instead of the body of bullet meeting only sharp lands and these cutting into the body more or less unequally, it is immediately held to place by the nearly flat centre of the broad grooves, and swells out into grooves equally and perfectly central; consequently it is accurate.

In this system a false muzzle and starter are used, and the lubricated bullet

5

seated from the muzzle, the shell with powder being afterward inserted in the ordinary way. In doing this the labor is very light, as the shooter has to handle nothing over a few ounces weight, the rifle standing in the loading stand. By the simple act of pushing the bullet home the sharp flat base of the bullet cuts the dirt down behind it, and does so *exactly alike*, each time giving a *uniformly clean barrel without the labor of cleaning*. The result of these things is that we attain *all the accuracy of patched bullets*, and in ordinary hands more, *without the labor of cleaning*. This is also less labor than the ordinary way of seating a greased bullet in the breech, having to invert the rifle and generally sustaining its weight while so doing.

Other things being equal, *the man who tires himself least does the best shooting* in the long run, and if this is accompanied by increased accuracy of the rifle, he has a great advantage over his fellows who do otherwise.

A properly made barrel, loaded in this way, will shoot 10 shot groups at 200 yards that will average about 1¼ or 1½ inches less diameter than the same or an equally good barrel shot dirty, bullet seated from the breech, while one using bullets seated in the shell is so far out of the game as to have no chance whatever on a string of any considerable number of shots, if otherwise he is an even match for his competitors.

1¼ to 1½ inches does not sound much, but on the fine ringed targets now in use it means *points*. I have before me a good muzzle-loading group, .32 cal., 10 shots, 200 yards. On German ring target it counts 250. Another group shot breech-loading, bullet seated in breech, same load, is but 1 inch larger diameter and is the *best* group I ever saw shot under these conditions. It counts 245. On the

6

Columbia target the scores are respectively 12 and 21; on Standard American, 120 and 115. The difference between *average* groups is still more marked, averaging fully 7 or 8 points on German ring target. On this, no comment is necessary.

For steadiness of shooting, I have fired 130 consecutive shots in 10 shot strings, measuring from centres of groups 104″, an average of exactly .8″ per shot. The largest group was 3.75″ across from centre to centre of outside shots, and measured $9\frac{11}{16}$″. The smallest group was 1.8″ across and measured 6″. All but two of the shots would cut into a 3-inch circle.

An advantage a bullet loaded from the muzzle will always have over one loaded from the breech is shown in this cut. This is an enlarged view of a .32 cal. bullet seated from the muzzle. Notice the perfect base, as the lands *cutting forward* into the bullet left it nearly perfect. Contrast it with a bullet seated in breech with a bullet seater in the ordinary way (see cut, next page). Here the lands *cutting backward* into the bullet *drag out burrs behind, leaving an uneven and serrated base*. If this bullet

7

is not perfectly centred these burrs will be *longer on one side* than on the other. As these burrs leave the muzzle, the gas escapes first from the short side, tipping the bullet to the opposite side, in which it is assisted by the longer burrs holding the bullet back; the result is an uneven, wobbling flight. *The greatest essential for perfect shooting is to deliver the bullet perfectly from the muzzle;* that being done, atmospheric conditions and gravity alone govern its flight; the result is accurate shooting. To so deliver the bullet, it must have a perfect base, and be perfectly centred, and have uniform velocity.

To illustrate, a group was shot at 200 yards, machine rest, with as perfect bullets as I could select, another on same holding with bullets very badly mutilated at the point; these two grouped closely, a 3-inch circle holding all. Another group was then shot with bullets very slightly filed on one edge of the base, but otherwise perfect; this caused imperfect delivery, and the group was *8 inches* in diameter. Weather conditions were good.

The base band of my bullets is broad and sharp, and of full size; the starter

8

centres it perfectly, and fits it to rifling with a perfect base; the shape of grooves holds it central on upset, and it delivers perfectly from the muzzle. No other method will do this.

My barrels are all (unless specially ordered) cut with a gain twist, and are so bored and rifled as to have a slight, but gradual, taper from breech to muzzle. This, beside keeping bullet perfectly under control, in connection with the narrow lands (which cut through the bullet easily), makes loading very easy, and very materially increases accuracy. A bullet pushed through from the breech is tight all the way, there are *no loose places,* and this result is attained by close, careful workmanship, no emery being used; the result is a barrel with a long life. Wherever practicable I chamber and make all crosscuts before rifling; I then fit a bushing to chamber and bore and rifle it with the barrel and false muzzle. As the rifling is then the last cut made in the barrel, I am *absolutely certain* that there can be no burrs across the grooves, a very common fault.

The advantages of the gain twist are two: 1st—The twist being less at the breech, gives less friction to the bullet; it therefore starts easier and quicker, giving the powder less time to burn on in front of chamber, which therefore fouls less than in a barrel of uniform twist at the same necessary muzzle pitch. 2nd—The slight change in angle of rifling, in connection with choke boring, effectually shuts off any escape of gas and prevents gas cutting, which is another cause of imperfect delivery.

9

The Advantages of the Pope System

are briefly summed up as follows:

1—Accuracy. 2—Light labor. 3—Seating the bullet centrally without deforming the base, and fitting it perfectly to the bore. 4—The shape of the grooves holding bullet centrally on upset. 5—Non-burning on qualities of the gain twist. 6—Perfect workmanship. 7—Ability to load from either breech or muzzle, and to clean and inspect from the breech. 8—The ability to shoot any charge desired by inserting shell first and loading both powder and bullet from the muzzle.

Workmanship.

To produce the quality of work that I do, the methods employed in factories producing work in large quantities are impossible; that is to say, that this method of interchangeable parts must leave some leeway for slight inaccuracies, to insure parts assembling. In my work such looseness of fit would be fatal to the results attained. False muzzles, for instance, it is utterly impossible to make *perfectly* interchangeable, neither is it possible for automatic machinery to produce the same quality of work as a skilled workman with *brains* behind. The automatic machine does more, and does it cheaper, but the quality is not there. Therefore I do *all nice work by hand*, in the very best manner I know how. Nothing is slighted. This is slow work and takes expensive men. Naturally I can not compete with factory work in price, but, *quality considered*, my price is very low. The half tones I show you give but a faint idea of the quality of the work; this must be seen and handled to be appreciated.

The Pope Muzzle-Loading Outfit

consists of barrel, false muzzle, starter, ramrod, Pope special muzzle-loading mould, and lubricating pump. A cut of false muzzle and starter is here shown (cuts of the

mould and pump will be found later with descriptions of these articles). Barrels will be furnished of almost any weight and length, within about 3 to 6 oz. limit of variation up to about 8 lbs. 2 oz. for a 32 inch, No. 4 oct., .32 cal. barrel; longer or heavier barrels, also barrels to exact weight specified, at special prices. I consider for offhand 200 yard work, a barrel of about 7¾ lbs., 30 inch, oct., as the best adapted. This I consider my standard, and recommend it as giving the best average results. For calibre for offhand work I prefer a .28, .32 or .33.

The price for this outfit includes fitting the barrel to your action, and fitting to it your extractor, forearm and sights, where they can be used. If new ones are necessary, they will be charged at cost.

The price of above, untested, is	$35.00
The same, but tested at 200 yards from machine rest, I guaranteeing to furnish a 10 shot group on 3-inch circle, or closer, is	40.00
The same, but 2½-inch group, or closer, guaranteed	45.00

In these there is absolutely no difference in the quality of barrels or workmanship. I have a long trip to make to test, and in my guarantee have to make allowance for adverse weather conditions, sometimes having to make several trips to secure the desired results. I never alter a barrel in testing, it is a matter of ammunition wholly. If tested, you see what has actually been accomplished with fine appliances and know exactly what load did it. If untested, you, unless very expert, can hardly expect to equal at once the results of my machine rest, and may have to do some experimenting (when you become accustomed to the system, not before), to determine the best temper of bullets, etc. You are as liable to get as close a group on one guarantee as on another, as it is largely a matter of weather conditions. If weather is good, I get close groups; if weather is cold and wind tricky, they are not so good. It is perfectly obvious that I can not guarantee to furnish as close a group as the barrel is capable of shooting, though I might happen to do so. I believe all my barrels are capable of shooting closer than 2-inch groups, with favorable conditions.

Recutting to Pope System.

I recut rifles of other makes to larger sizes with the same outfit and guarantees as for a new barrel.

Price, untested	$25.00
" 3-inch guarantee	30.00
" 2½-inch "	35.00

12

CALIBRES AND WEIGHTS.

CALIBRE.	POWDER.	M. L. BULLET.	B. L. BULLET.	200 YD. GUARANTEE.
.25	26 grs.	98 grs.	86 grs.	3½ and 3
.28	30 "	118 and 138 "	108 "	3 " 2½
.32	47 "	180 " 200 "	165 or 185 "	"
.33	47 "	195 " 218 "		"
.38	55 "	277 " 330 "	255 "	"
.39	55 "	265 " 343 "		"

The weight of powder charges are the drawn shell full. This can be decreased by the use of everlasting or special shells, or by using less powder and an air space. Weights of B. L. bullets are those intended to seat in shell. Barrels are cut with a pitch correct for the bullet they are intended to use. Shorter bullets can be used in a barrel cut for the long one, but not the reverse. It is oftentimes better to use the lighter bullet. Unless specially ordered I shall use my own judgment in cutting the barrel.

Breech-Loading Barrels.

I cut barrels for breech loading in the same style as for muzzle loading. A mould for same bullet is recommended as giving better results than the ordinary B. L. bullet. The price for new barrel of same sizes and weights as given under the Muzzle-Loading Outfit, fitted to your action and to your extractor, forearm and sights, is $16.00.

Testing and guaranteeing same prices as there given, but the size of group guaranteed is 1¼ inches larger.

13

.22 Calibre Barrels.

I am now prepared to furnish .22 cal. barrels, with the same quality of workmanship used on my muzzle loaders. These can be furnished for .22 short or long rifle cartridges, up to 30-inch, No. 3 oct., weight about 6 to 6¼ lbs.

Price, fitted to your action, etc., and tested at 25 yards, $18.00.

Pope Special Muzzle-Loading Mould.

As previously shown, a bullet with a perfect base is essential for the finest work. To meet this requisite the mould shown above was designed. It differs from all

others in having a cut-off with a bottom plate rigidly connected to it and swinging with it. These plates, with the joint pin and dowels, hold the two halves of mould perfectly in position; bullets from it average within .0005″ of being round, which is practically perfect. No other mould does such work. The bullet is poured from the point, bringing imperfections to this end. When sprue is cut off, both plates swing entirely clear of bullet, which easily falls out. Great pains are taken to have each half of mould of equal depth, to avoid sticking. This mould is part

of the muzzle-loading outfit. It is also recommended as being the best for breech-loading work, shooting dirty with bullet seated in the barrel.

Moulds can be ventilated, if desired. This consists of cutting air passages from each groove and from point and base in the mould to allow air to escape freely. It is a little advantage where one works so slowly that mould is apt to be too cool, but not otherwise.

All moulds are broken in ready for use. Keep them dry and use no oil. Wax joints in use when necessary to keep them free.

I have a large number of cherries of various sizes and styles. Moulds can be made from any of these at regular prices. I make special sizes, to order, at $3.00 extra, retaining the cherry as my own property.

Price of Pope Special mould	$3.50
" Moulds cutting off at base	1.50
" Ventilating, extra	.50
" Double mould, extra	.50

The Pope Lubricating Pump.

The construction is clearly shown in cut. It holds enough to grease 180 to 300 of my bullets, according to size. By its use, using grease cold, one greases bullets perfectly as fast as fifteen to twenty-five per minute, according to skill; rightly used, it just fills the grooves and no more, leaving the bands bare. This is essential for fine work, for if there be more grease on one side of bullet than on the other, it displaces that bulk of lead on upset, throwing the bullet out of balance. If the mould is round, as mine are, no wiping of bullet is necessary. Dies are made interchangeable, so any number of different ones may be had, each bullet requiring a different die.

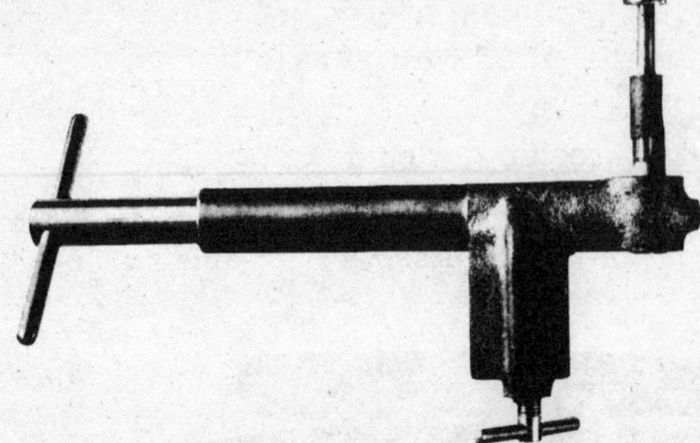

It is used as follows. It is best filled by removing forcing screw and pouring in melted lubricant; this excludes air better than by other methods of filling, and makes it work better. Do this some time before you want to use it, so grease will be cold; preferably fill it immediately after use, so it will be ready for next time. Grease can be jammed in cold if so desired, but the operation is not so good. Clamp pump onto corner of table, or onto a projecting stick fastened to bench or held in a vice, insert a bullet, hold it firmly in, turn forcing screw just enough to fill grooves (a very little practice will enable you to do this accurately), turn screw

16

back about one-fourth turn to relieve pressure on grease and prevent its oozing out, and expel bullet with plunger.

This is an indispensable tool for the nicest work; it forms part of the muzzle-loading outfit.

In ordering, send several samples of each size bullet it is intended to grease, and pack these carefully, so they can not be bruised in transportation.

Price..$3.00
Extra Dies, each.. .75

The Pope Rear Wind Gauge and Elevating Sight.

The cut shows this plainly. I claim it to be the neatest, safest, most convenient and accurate sight made. Wind and elevating movements are entirely separate, so moving one can not also disturb the other. One hole movement of either elevating nuts or wind screw equals *1 inch on 200 yard target*. The two elevating nuts are operated by the small lever pin, which can be carried in the head of sight as shown, or worn upon the watch chain, as preferred. These nuts bind against *opposite* sides of the solid frame, therefore looseness of fit from wear *can not affect the accuracy* of adjustment. These nuts are usually set firmly, so they can not be accidentally moved, but may be left so as to move with the fingers if desired. The wind screw differs from the ordinary construction by passing through a bearing at both ends of frame and

17

by having a shoulder on one end and a jam nut on the other; when wear occurs, all that is necessary to correct it is to screw the nut up a little firmer, filing off a trifle from end of screw if necessary.

The key to the operation of this sight is found in the following: "Turn your sight the way you want your shot to go." To shoot to the *right*, turn wind screw to the *right*, and *vice versa*. One hole or one-fourth turn of screw equals 1 inch; one turn or one graduation equals 4 inches on 200 yard target. To shoot *higher*, first move the *upper* nut the required amount, then tighten the lower one, turning from you (holding muzzle to left, sight folded). You can not turn these the wrong way if you put pin in the correct nut, as that tightens the nut instead of loosening it. To shoot *lower*, first move *lower* nut, then tighten upper one, turning both toward you.

In ordering, send me your old sights if practicable, set on 200 yards elevation; give make of rifle, and, if old sights are not sent, state height of present front sight above top of barrel to centre of disc, also diameter of muzzle.

The advantages of this sight are its *safety*, convenience and accuracy; also, one does not have to remove front sight to carry rifle in case; the result is that the sights are always on the rifle, and you do not go to the range and forget your wind gauge. Who has not done this?

Price, without base, fitted to any base sent me	$5.00
Price, with base, complete	6.50
Globe Sight, with interchangeable disc	1.00

The Pope Loading Flask.

This is an improvement on my previous flask in several ways, the principal one being that it is adjustable for charge, without having to exchange the charger. It loads a nitro priming and black body or a full charge of black at one operation, and is very quick and the most accurate flask made. For use in a regular place, the supporting bar on back is slotted so it can be slid over two screws permanently placed on a projecting bar, such as the rod rack or a wall timber; this gives plenty of hand room and brings it to a convenient height. Where this is not convenient, it is supported in the same way from a small metal spider (not shown) which can be screwed into the wall or post (no screw driver being necessary); this gives the necessary hand room and, being removable, does not enlarge the flask so as to make it unnecessarily large to carry. The operation is very simple. The operating lever has a loose knurled sleeve upon it; holding this against the forward stop and twisting it locates the nitro charger properly and shakes the powder down uniformly into it; lever is then pushed to back stop and again twisted; this empties the nitro into shell, and settles the black into charger, which is then drawn forward and rattled, emptying every particle of black into the shell. Changing the charge is effected by loosening the clamp screw on lower

Tube 8 inches long

body, then turning this up or down, setting the slot to line and reclamping. One turn equals one grain of black powder. The flask holds enough for about 125 charges of 47 grs. The charge varies from 28 grs. bulk to 60 grs. where nitro priming is used, and from 22 grs. to 60 grs. using all one kind, or by using double or treble charges of one kind any required amount may be loaded. This flask covers all charges used regularly in my barrels. Special size for smaller charges will be made to order.

In carrying the flask, the loading tube is unscrewed, and the small thumb screw, shown behind it, screwed up, the lever being in front position. This prevents charger turning and spilling powder through it, when being carried in a horizontal position.

Price, complete, $5.00.

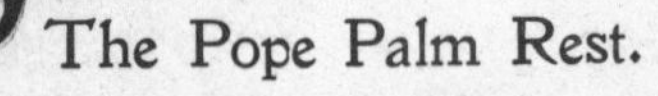

The Pope Palm Rest.

This is made so the shank is easily unscrewed for carrying, without changing the adjustment. It swings away from the lever for loading, and from recoil (can be put on the reverse way, if desired). The shank is adjustable for length by the telescoping tube and taper nut, and for position to or from the body, by changing the position of the check nuts on the shank, so as to allow the shank to come against the stop at different angles, thus affecting the distance. Price, $4.00.

20

The Pope Double or Machine Rest.

Shown complete in cut, with all attachments, should be owned by every club

for testing purposes. More information can be derived from its use in a few hours, than can be had by ordinary rest shooting by an ordinary shooter in as many

21

weeks, as, if at all carefully used, it has no ***human errors*** of holding and pulling. The results, therefore, are those due to rifle, ammunition and weather; the man is out of it, except so far as his loading of the rifle and judgment of wind are concerned.

This rest is made in various styles. That shown is the best and consists of the No. 1 rear rest, No. 3 front rest, with sliding telescope mountings, stop, and telescope sight. These mounts are all adjustable and clamp to the barrel, no screw holes or marring of barrel being necessary; they take barrels of all ordinary sizes, without change. Forearm is removed while testing.

In use, two stout posts are set deeply in the ground, the firmer the better; these are braced together, and a smooth, level plank fastened on top; both posts are firmly braced in two directions, stop is fastened on top plank in proper position and rear rest to rear post so as to give approximately the correct elevation. Front rest and scope mountings are clamped to barrel, the same loaded and slid gently to stop; to sight on, I prefer four black pasters placed at the corners of a square about 2½ inches on a side; adjust your rest or telescope or perhaps both, so gun points where you wish, cross hairs being between each pair of pasters; let the rifle rest naturally, hold right hand about 6 inches behind the butt, touch set trigger with left hand and catch the rifle on recoil. If the gun has a heavy pull, pinch the trigger and guard with thumb and forefinger so as not to disturb the rifle in the rest. In setting up, it is often convenient to set the rest, so the rifle will point on the target before the telescope is mounted, using the ordinary sights, then mount the scope and adjust it to your pasters, and shoot your group, then move rest a fair amount, that depending on how close the gun will shoot, then bring your scope again to the pasters and shoot again. It very seldom pays to try to

22

get the rifle to shoot at any given spot in testing. Hold in one spot, and get your group wherever it happens to fall.

A telescope sight is not a necessity in double rest shooting, though it is a great convenience. With it you can shoot from a bench that is not firm, as the sight gives you a chance to correct the aim each time; for all that an absolutely firm bench is best, and if you shoot from double rest without a scope, it is an absolute necessity. "Shooting and Fishing," Aug. 25, 1898, contains an illustrated article on double rests. Price of complete double rest and scope, as shown, $25.00.

No. 1 rear rest is the best and most compact, has a collar screw for elevating and depressing, giving a positive movement both ways; shank is securely fastened by the clamp screw and lever. The wind adjustment is by two tension screws operating against each other, permitting the most exact adjustment and locking firmly. Price, $8.50.

No. 2 rear rest is the same as No. 1, except that the three adjusting screws are set screws. These necessarily project much further than in No. 1, and are therefore a little more likely to accidental movement, also elevation depends wholly on the weight of rifle following up the movement of the screw, taking, therefore, a little more care in handling. This construction avoids the necessity of careful lining up of parts, and makes fewer parts necessary, thus cheapening its construction. Price, $6.00.

No. 3 rear rest has no adjusting screws at all; the elevation is held by the clamp, as in Nos. 1 and 2, the cross movement by a set screw and shoe against the V block. It is all right for group shooting on one setting, but does not permit of adjustment for wind or close setting. Price, $4.00.

23

No. 1 front rest. This is the simplest and lightest possible; it consists of the lower part of front rest shown in cut. It is fastened to the barrel by one screw, tapped into it. It is the best for permanent double rest work, but not so convenient for various arms, as all barrels used with it must have a screw hole in them. Price, with stop, $1.00.

No. 2 front rest. This has a cap and clamp screws. Its size is such that it takes barrels of all ordinary dimensions without necessity of screw holes. Price, with stop, $1.50.

No. 3 front rest is the same as No. 2, with the addition of front mounting for sliding telescope sight. With this is also included the rear telescope mounting, also clamping to barrel, and with adjustments for both wind and elevation. Price of all, $6.50.

Telescope sight. I have a special sight made for me by John W. Sidle for this work. It is ¾″ diameter, 28″ long, steel tube, browned, 14 power, fine cross hairs, with cross hairs and object glass both adjustable for focus. Price, $10.00.

Set of castings and blue print for double rest for those who wish to make their own rest, $1.50.

Rifles.

I do not make complete rifles, but can furnish any standard make at reasonable prices. These I can generally have come to me unrifled, when I can bore, rifle and fit my outfit to them at the price given for reboring. This gives the slight advantage of standard sizes on these arms, and the ability to use factory ammunition in them if desired. It takes usually three or four weeks to get such a rifle from the factory, before I can do much work on it. Write for prices.

24

Winchester barrels are interchangeable, and are the only ones, to my knowledge, that are so. To any one wishing such, and who will give me the necessary time, as given above for rifles, I can furnish a blank barrel from them at same discount I give on rifles, and charge, beside, my price for recutting. I can buy these blanks as cheaply as I can make a new barrel; and as I save myself the work of fitting to action, slotting, etc., I am thus enabled to furnish a barrel at a little less than my regular price. This applies to *no* other make and to these only where the necessary time is given me. I also do not, on this, need your action to fit to and test from.

Read This.

From all parties having new barrels fitted, I require the old barrel where possible, as well as the action, as this is of much assistance to me in fitting the new barrel. Make the case you ship in large enough to contain both barrels, together with the new outfit. Prepay express charges and mark box plainly, Paid. I will not waste my time, as I have done, in rectifying express company's mistakes; where collections are made on both ends (in one case it took me six months and cost me in time nearly $10 to collect a double charge of $1.35), if box is not plainly marked, and the express company charge me, I charge you, and you pay the bill. If I succeed in collecting the bill, I will remit to you; otherwise not. Therefore prepay the express and mark it PAID.

Terms.

My terms from parties unknown to me are 25 per cent. with order, the balance upon notification of completion of work, or C. O. D. and return charges. I consider a rifle sent to be recut or for other work equivalent to a deposit.

Prices are subject to change without notice.

25

The Wild Sheep of North America

by JACK O'CONNOR

How and where to hunt them, their habits and characteristics—from the desert rams of the Southwest and old Mexico to the big horns and thin horns of the great Northwest. An entertaining and instructive account—with sage advice on choosing a sheep rifle. This is O'Connor at his excellent best.

RAY HAD BEEN back into the mountains with a fishing party during August, and he had seen the big bunch of rams then. It was September now, but as yet no snow had fallen in the high country and he was convinced that if we were the first outfit in we'd find them not too far from where he'd seen them last.

Our main camp was to be on one of the many "Sheep Creeks" that are found wherever wild sheep make their home, just as there are "Ram Creeks" and "Bighorn Creeks." It was a hard 5-day pack from the railroad but we made it on schedule. The next morning Ray and I left the cook and the horse wrangler camped in the timber beside a lively little creek and headed for the ram basins. We had our two saddle horses, a packhorse with our bedrolls, some grub, and a little tent.

Late that afternoon we pitched our tent 12 or 15 miles away from the main camp and possibly 4,000 feet above it. Up there in the Canadian Rockies we were well above timberline. We had to do our cooking with the dry branches of stunted arctic willow that grew there in the basin. Because we didn't want to disturb the sheep, Ray picketed the horses instead of hobbling and belling them.

It was sheepy country, this—big empty basins, gray limestone cliffs and slide rock, little silver streams, basins filled with the lush grass that wild sheep love. Early in September it was a land of frosty nights with big close stars glittering coldy in a black sky, days that were voluptuously warm in the sunshine, bitter chill in the shade and on the lofty windswept ridges.

Frost had already painted the willows along the little meandering creeks yellow and tiny arctic plants patterned the still-green grass with red and orange, brown and yellow, giving an effect as softly glowing as an oriental rug.

This not only looked like sheep country; it *was* sheep country. In bare spots in the sand by the tinkling creek I could see big blunt ram tracks, and my sheep hunting experience told me that the droppings, rock hard from dryness but still jet black and glazed, were those of mature rams and had been made since the last rain or probably within 10 days.

Ray was a great horse lover. As a youth he had been a cowboy and it made him nervous to be without a horse for company, so the next morning when we set out to find rams we were leading our horses. As it turned out we were to drag them up and down the mountains most of the day.

The most useful skill a sheep hunter can have is the ability to use a binocular, to pick a neutral-colored sheep up out of neutral-colored surroundings at long range. Because the wild sheep is an animal of the mountains it is usually possible for the hunter to approach from behind a ridge and take a fairly easy shot. It is the finding that is difficult.

Climbing for Altitude

Since sheep are best approached from above, the first thing Ray and I did that morning was to gain altitude. We led our horses up a steep, shaley ridge, where patches of lichens, ground juniper, and high-altitude grasses struggled to live and where, occasionally, we could see the elongated depressions that sheep had pawed out so they could lie down. Old sheep trails that had been used by generations of bighorns ran around the steep slopes. Some of them were wide enough and had such an easy grade that a bicycle could have been ridden on them. At one point we hit beds so fresh that the droppings that peppered the ground could be squeezed with the fingers, and we could smell the sweetish, musty odor of the mountain ram.

Just under the crest of the main ridge we tied our horses to each other, head to tail. Then we wormed our way up to the top on our bellies and peeked over. When we could make out no sheep with the naked eye, we searched the country with glasses. We were right at the crest of the Rockies, the top of the world. Basin after basin, without number and without end, stretched out before us. High peaks, cliffs, and shale slides, patches of last winter's snow, marched endlessly north. This was really sheep country. As I glassed there on that freezing windswept ridge, I lay in an old sheep bed and around me rose the rich exciting odor of sheep.

But no animals were in sight. A lone eagle floated just under a little white cloud high in the polished sky. In the basin below we could see a couple of hoary marmots watching us, and we could hear the rusty creak of their clear wild whistles. A grizzly had been at the village of the whistlers recently, one end of it torn up as if by a bulldozer, a jumble of rocks and loose soil and uprooted grass.

We led our horses around the basin and to another ridge. We had hardly got our heads over the top when we both saw an enormous herd of ewes and lambs and young rams. Long years before the last of the hunting Indians had moved out of this area and, as the only hunters who ever penetrated it were after trophies, the ewes were not wary. Some of the sheep were lying down, some were feeding. A couple of lambs were nursing. There were a few young rams in the herd, too—youngsters who hadn't as yet gone off to join the bachelors' club.

The way we had planned to go was blocked now. We didn't want to take any chance of scaring the ewe herd and having them stampede the big rams we knew were somewhere in the area. We had to drop around to our left and, because we had horses with us, we lost a lot of altitude. Finally, though, we managed to drag our heaving, slipping, laboring steeds up and around the steep shaley slopes so we could glass the next basin without spooking the ewes.

The Magic Word

Ray had hardly got his glass to his eyes when he uttered that word which is magic to the sheep hunter: *Rams!*

In a moment I saw them myself, a dozen brown specks lying in gray-brown shale under the ridge and about

O'Conner shot this 37-inch Stone ram in 1973 when he was 71. Jack says a horse did most of the climbing!

a mile away, clear across the basin. I had carried a 20-power prismatic spotting scope in a rucksack with me. Now I set it up on a little stand to look the rams over.

A good deal of mirage was running then and the rams showed little and wavy, blue with the haze of distance, grainy and indistinct like an enlargement blown up too much from a poor negative. Now and then the mirage would lift a bit and we could get a pretty good look at the heads. Two of the rams, high and to the left of the bunch, were dillies, but the one we decided was the best was an old-timer with heavy massive horns that came up a bit above the bridge of his nose. From that distance it looked as if the horns were broomed off about three or four inches wide at the tips.

"Son of a gun ought to go 40," Ray grunted. "Maybe over! Let's go get him!"

Again our horses delayed us. If we hadn't taken them along we could have cut around just under the ridge, but it was too steep and too slippery for our horses. Again we lost altitude. Finally we got so boxed in that we had to tie our animals at the bottom of a deep canyon and climb out again until we were just under the ridge that had been about 1,500 feet above us.

At long last we were clear around to the spot where we had planned to shoot from and I lay on my belly, just under the ridge. A few minutes before I had worked the bolt to slip a cartridge into the chamber. Now the rifle was on safe.

The time for the payoff had now come. If our luck had held, I'd be within easy range of the rams. However, it had been well over an hour since we'd seen them. If our luck was bad they might have been spooked by a prowling wolf or a grizzly, or they might have moved out of range by getting up to feed. The shadows were lengthening and it was getting to be about dinner time for them. Too, they might have decided that the shale was softer somewhere else.

All this I thought of as I crawled forward, pushing my binocular and my little scope-sighted 270 ahead of me. I made a mental note not to get excited and to look the heads over carefully even if the rams saw me immediately and took off. I remembered the time on another sheep hunt when I had stalked a bunch of 7 rams, after carefully picking out the best head from a half-mile away. There had been stunted timberline trees on the ridge I came over. I had apparently made some noise as I came through

them and the moment I broke out into view the sheep started to run. I shot the ram near the dead whitebark pine where I had marked him. It was the wrong ram, a good one but not the Old-Timer himself.

But this day luck was with me. The dozen big rams lay in their beds in the shale below me, not much over a hundred yards away. They were big and dark and blocky, wide of back and rump. Seven of them were big trophy rams so dark brown they were almost black, heavy of horn, burly of neck. These were the true bighorns, old *Ovis canadensis canadensis* himself, no offshoot, no subspecies, one of the grandest trophy animals that walks the face of this earth. Most of the rams had very close curls with horns that came up close to the eye and, like all wild sheep no matter where found, those that had found their horns blocking their vision had rubbed them down against rock until they looked as if the points had been filed off. One of the old rams had horns more slender than those of the others. They flared out away from his face and did not block his view. The points were perfect and I am sure the horns would have measured over 40 inches around the curve. Such heads are more common among Stone and Dall sheep, those northern relatives of the bighorn, but both types of heads are found in all species of sheep from Mexico to the arctic circle. The youngest of the rams were full-grown animals from 7 to 9 years old and the patriarchs from 10 to 13 – which is about as long as a wild sheep lives.

Every Wrinkle

I have never had a better chance to look rams over. I focused my glasses so sharp on them that I could count every wrinkle, every nick in their horns. The best one for my money was the big fellow over to the left and below – the one we had picked out clear across the canyon. Ray punched me and pointed at the ram. He was getting impatient. It was time to shoot.

The big boy was partially concealed by another ram, so I whispered to Ray to throw out a stone. When it clattered into the shale every ram was immediately on his feet. My ram was in the clear. The intersection of the crosswires came to rest just behind his shoulder and I squeezed off the shot. When the 130-gr. open-point 270 bullet struck him, he simply collapsed.

For a few seconds not a ram moved. They all gazed right into our eyes with shocked disbelief. One moment they had been alone in the emptiness except for a soaring eagle and a couple of marmots, but now two men were looking down their throats. Then they whirled and ran, strung out single file along a sheep trail below. They fled clear around the basin and then stopped, watching us for a minute or so. When we got up to inspect the dead ram, they took off once more, humping up the steep shale slide on the other side of the basin. We saw them climb out, hit a rocky cliff, and then disappear over the skyline, their horns cutting circles against the sky.

The head of my old ram was a fine one – heavy, massive, close of curl, broomed so badly on one side that the core of the horn peeped through. The longest horn was just short of 40 inches and the bases were just under 16. So much growth had been broomed off that an exact count of the annual rings was impossible, but we guessed that his battered old horns had started growing about 13 years before.

An old ram is a lazy creature. During the brief, lush summer in those subarctic basins, the old rams eat, drink, lie around. They get very fat and, since they come through the winter lean and gaunt, their flesh is

mostly new. It is succulent, tender, the best meat in the mountains, more like corn-fed beef than mutton. We skinned the hide off the shoulders and the neck, cut the head off just back of the skull. I took the heavy head and both backstraps. Ray carried the massive hindquarters. Lurching under our burdens like drunken men, our lungs heaving from the altitude, we slowly worked our way around the ridge and down to our patient horses.

When we were at last guided to camp by the desperate whinnying of our lonely packhorse it was long after dark. A drink of Scotch diluted with freezing creek water was good. Over our little fire of willows we fried bacon, then cooked a whole pan full of little filets of backstrap in the hot grease. Ray made another frying pan full of bannocks. We ate the meat and the hot, greasy, delicious bread soggy with butter, drank tea, and smoked. A late moon rose over the ragged black sheep mountains. By its misty light we could see the frost glittering whitely on the grass.

With a little liquor and a lot of food and tea in my belly I was suddenly and overwhelmingly weary. I staggered to the little tent, ripped off my clothes and fell into my down bag. Vaguely I remembered Ray's hitting the sack but I was asleep so quickly I didn't even hear him begin to snore.

Tough sheep hunt? No, that was an easy one—and a lucky one. Usually the hunter must work far harder for a trophy ram. Once on a 60-day trip in a far wild part of the great province of British Columbia I did not fire a shot at sheep until I had been out 45 days. Another time I climbed every day for 10 days in ghastly weather, returning to a miserable little timberline jack camp every night so beat that it took a husky jolt of Scotch to give me enough energy to start cooking.

But I loved it. Finally recovered, I ate everything in sight, slept like a baby, and every morning my weary legs had regained their spring.

The Lure of Sheep Hunting

I have long been fascinated by sheep hunting and so have many others. I have often wondered why. I think it is the combination of being in high, beautiful country, of breathing pure and untainted air, of hunting a rare and beautiful animal. Another ingredient, I believe, is the long suspense, the sustained excitement of sheep hunting. You may glass shootable rams one day but not be able to fire a shot for a week. You may start a stalk early in the morning yet not be in position to shoot until late afternoon. Or you may be within a few hundred yards of your ram when, in the final stages of the stalk, the rams are spooked by a sudden shift of the wind, the advent of a wandering grizzly, or the mischance of encountering and frightening an unsuspected bunch of sheep.

Sheep hunting gets into the blood. I shot my first ram in Sonora many years ago. By 1946 I had taken at least three examples each of all four subspecies of North American sheep. At least a half-dozen times I have gone on "my last sheep hunt." Yet I shot my last ram, a good Stone, in 1971 when I was 69. I'll probably go again. If I should drop dead up on a sheep mountain within sight of noble rams and with the hoary marmots on a nearby rockslide whistling my requiem I can imagine worse fates. An old friend with whom I hunted Dall sheep in the White River country of the Yukon, a long generation ago, had a stroke which left him lame and weak. Yet every fall he hired a pack outfit and went back into the lovely Yukon wilderness. He had to be helped onto a horse and he could walk only with the greatest difficulty, but he loved the sound of the water in little tinkling rills, the fragrance of spruce and fir, the melody of the horse bells. He spent hours with binoculars and spotting scope watching sheep on distant hillsides. "If I die up there," he told me, "I'll die happy." But fate was not that kind to him. He died one winter afternoon in a chair in his Ohio trophy room.

To me the head of a good mature ram, at least 10 years old, stalked fairly and shot cleanly, is the finest of all North American trophies and one of the great trophies of the world. I have shot rams that went into the record book. I have shot several that went over 40 inches, the figure that traditionally denotes a ram of the very highest class. But any *old* ram, no matter what his measurements are, is a fine trophy. One of the heads I cherish most is of an old ram that would go nowhere near the record book. His horns are broomed and broken. He was a dwarf sheep and, when I shot him, he was all alone, an exile from his clan. When I squeezed off the shot I thought he was much larger than he measured. But I'll always cherish that head for the memory of a long tough stalk during a dark, miserable afternoon of low clouds and snow flurries, of the final exciting minutes when the snow hid the ram and I wondered if he was still there, of the relief when the curtain of snow lifted and he was revealed still in his bed, and of a clean, one-shot kill!

The Emigrant Sheep

Like the American Indian, the elk, the moose, and the caribou, North American wild sheep are immigrants from Asia. As good a theory as any is that some of the sheep were driven south by the glaciers of the ice age but some were able to survive in the mountains of the arctic, where the snow was dry and light and did not form glaciers. Those that went south developed into the brown bighorns. They worked north as the ice receded and occupied suitable ranges in the northwestern United States and southwestern Canada and south into the desert mountains of Arizona, Nevada, California, and northwestern Mexico. In the meantime, this theory goes, the sheep that had survived in the arctic spread south to develop into the snow-white Dall sheep and the black-bodied, gray-faced Stone sheep. The two races never united after the ice age, as south of the Peace and Skeena rivers in British Columbia there is a belt of relatively low, heavily wooded mountains of heavy snowfall—country unsuitable for sheep.

Another theory is that the bighorn and the so-called thinhorn sheep (Stone and Dall) are derived from two separate migrations from Asia—that the bighorns came first and were driven south by the ice, and that the thinhorns came across during another epoch.

American scientists put the various subspecies of the brown sheep into one species *(Ovis canadensis)* and the thinhorns into another *(Ovis dalli)*. The British lump them all into one species *(Ovis canadensis)* and throw into it the wild sheep of northeastern Siberia—the Kamchatka sheep and Clifton's bighorn. I am inclined to agree with the British. I have seen many Stone sheep heads which, except for the lighter color of the horns, are indistinguishable from those of the bighorn. Once when I was in London I spent a morning at the British Natural History Museum in Kensington going over the world's finest collection of Asiatic sheep heads. I found that the average sheep hunter like me would not be able to distinguish between the skull and horns of an Alaskan Dall sheep and those of a Kamchatka ram. All these sheep which the British put together as *canadensis* are essentially alike, and all are very different from the other wild sheep of the world—the argali, urial, blue sheep, audad, and mouflon.

The Rocky Mountain bighorn is one of the world's largest sheep. Much has been written about the "enormous" sheep of Central Asia. The famous *Ovis poli* has very long horns (up to 6 *feet* in length) but he is not a heavy sheep. The great Siberian argali has very long and heavy horns and stands taller than a large bighorn, but he isn't much heavier. All the argali are running animals which live in relatively rounded, smooth mountains, and they escape wolves and snow leopards by their speed. They are slenderly built and have long legs. The North American wild sheep, on the other hand, are stout big-boned fellows built for jumping and climbing, and they escape their enemies by taking refuge in rocks and cliffs.

A small band of younger bighorn rams, seemingly calm, unafraid and curious.

The Wild Sheep

Rocky Mountain and desert bighorns are chunky, blocky brown sheep with relatively short, powerful legs. Rams tend to get darker with age. An old trophy ram from 10 to 13 years old is often so dark that, at a distance and under certain light conditions and against some backgrounds, he may appear almost black. Ewes and young rams are a lighter brown. In the late spring, after months of bleaching from brilliant sun against snow, the winter coats fade to a light yellowish brown that sometimes appears almost white. Both albinism and melanism occur. A few years ago an albino desert bighorn was shot in Nevada, and once I did my darndest to collect a coal black desert ram. He was as black as ink, blacker than any Stone sheep I have ever seen, so black that against the hair of his neck and jaw his dark brown horns looked yellow. I have a color photograph of a desert bighorn shot in Arizona that *is* black.

The Northern sheep range from rams in the southern part of the Stone range that have black bodies with black necks, gray faces and white rumps to Dall rams that are pure white. The two subspecies of *Dalli* interbreed where their ranges overlap. It can be said that the farther south one goes the darker the sheep get and the farther north the more nearly white. In the southern part of the Cassiar district of British Columbia the sheep are very dark. Light gray heads and necks are rare. Farther north near the Yukon border many rams have white heads and necks, and north of the chain of large lakes that runs more or less along the British Columbia/Yukon border and west of the Yukon River the sheep are pretty much pure white. Some have black tails, a sprinkling of black hairs in the saddle, around the eyes, and on the bridge of the nose.

Just as North American wild sheep vary a great deal in color they also vary in size. They not only vary from subspecies to subspecies but from region to region. The desert bighorns of the Southwestern United States and northern Mexico average the smallest and the bighorns of western Montana, southwestern Alberta and southeastern British Columbia the largest. I believe the heaviest desert bighorn ever weighed in Arizona field dressed at 165 pounds, but the heaviest old Alberta bighorn rams will field dress on occasion at over 300 pounds. Generally it can be said that the average mountain ram will weigh about like a buck mule deer except that his heavier horns add to the total weight.

Because mountain sheep are generally shot in high, rough country, where it is difficult or impossible to get the whole carcass out, I have weighed very few of them. However, I have measured many. The average large buck mule deer in good condition shot in the Northwest will have antlers with 5 points (including brow points) to the side, will measure about 18 inches on a straight line from the top of the shoulder to the bottom of the brisket, and will weigh field dressed from 185 to 195 pounds. The average mature Northern ram of whatever species will measure somewhat larger. He is a blockier animal with a broader back than a deer. Viewed from above an old ram looks as broad as a beef steer.

The last ram I shot as I write this was a 9-year-old Stone. His shoulder-brisket measurement was 19 inches. From chest to rump in a straight line he measured 39 inches. His teeth were going and he was not very fat. I would guess his weight as around 180-185 pounds. A very large, fat, heavy Stone with a 41½-inch head I shot in 1946 measured 22 inches and 42 inches, the same measurements of a very large Dall I took on Pilot Mountain in the Yukon in 1950. A 44-inch Dall my wife shot in 1963 in the Ruby Range of the Yukon was only slightly smaller. I am sure that any of these rams would have field dressed at over 250 pounds. The late Bert Rigall, dean of the Alberta bighorn guides, who hunted in the area where the North American mountain sheep reach their optimum size, told me that just at the beginning of the rut in the last week in November he shot a very large, fat ram near his ranch, carried it to his ranch house on a packhorse and weighed it. The weight, he said, was 365 pounds. As I recall it was dressed weight, but it may have been weighed entire. In that case the ram would have weighed about 315 field dressed. Rams weighing 300 pounds field dressed are as rare as buck mule deer weighing that much, but both occur.

The Habits of Wild Sheep

Rams vary enormously in size, weight, and horn measurement with the area in which they live and the food they eat. Some of the largest and some of the smallest sheep I have ever seen have been Stones. In one area in northwestern British Columbia the mountains were made of schist rock and the topsoil was thin and apparently sterile. I estimated the 9- and 10-year-old rams we shot dressed out

to about 125-130 pounds, smaller than desert sheep. By way of contrast the Stone rams of the limestone country around the head of the Prophet River are large and heavy. An occasional ram will measure 24 inches on a straight line between the top of the shoulder and the bottom of the brisket when the measurement is taken from hair to hair of the fall coat. This is about the chest depth of a spike bull elk. The sheep are not so long, of course, and not as heavy.

Artists are fond of depicting mountain sheep standing alert on rocky cliffs spotted with snow. In such country a sheep would starve to death. Actually the wild sheep is by nature a grazer who loves the tender grass of mountain meadows and the weeds and forbs that grow along with it. The sheep is an adaptable animal, much more so than the wild goat, and where grass is in short supply, as it is in the Southwest, he can get along by browsing almost entirely.

To survive sheep need feed and escape areas of cliffs, slides, and rocky hillsides so they can elude their enemies. When the first American pioneers came west they found sheep in the brakes of the Missouri and other rivers, on little rocky buttes far out in the great plains of Montana and Wyoming. The badlands of the Dakotas were great sheep country. In most of this country sheep have been extinct for generations, but they have been restored in the Missouri brakes.

The wild sheep is North America's handiest animal in getting around in the rocks. He knows it and so do the predators. I have seen sheep stand on slide rock and watch wolves below them not over 50 yards away. I once saw a grizzly make a clumsy rush at a pair of young Dall rams, but he gave up and turned back the instant they hit the rocks.

In many refuge areas sheep are easy for a rifleman to get since those who do not know man the rifleman feel safe from anything if they are up in the rocks. I once shot a fine old Stone ram when I was riding at the head of a packtrain. He lay calmly on a ledge on the wall of a rocky canyon about 200 yards away, watching me and chewing his cud contemplatively. At my shot he tumbled about 200 feet into the creek.

The canyon of the Little Colorado in northern Arizona was full of sheep in the 1920s, but they were easily shot out because a hunter could ride along the rim on a horse, get off and shoot sheep below him.

The first Rocky Mountain bighorn I ever shot was lying on a ridge above a little side canyon that ran into Chocolate Creek in Alberta. I had spotted him with binoculars from a mountainside about two miles away. My guide and I came down off the mountain to the Muddywater River, turned up into Chocolate Creek, climbed up a draw so I could shoot from the ridge opposite the ram. He was not over 150 feet above the waters of Chocolate Creek. I dragged him down to the creek bed while my guide went for the horses. Many times I have seen sheep in little canyons in northern British Columbia and the Yukon. Sheep often feed up on the top of a plateau and then seek refuge and bed down in cliffs and on slide rock below. This is the situation in some of the sheep areas in Arizona adjacent to the Grand Canyon.

The best sheep areas are fairly dry, as sheep do not like cold rains, deep snow, and heavy timber. They can get along without open water almost indefinitely if there is sufficient moisture in their feed. In Sonora much of the best sheep country has no open water. The sheep get their moisture from dew, the sap of plants, and from water-bearing cactus. In times of severe drought these desert sheep break open barrel cactus *(bisnaga)* and girdle *saguaros* (giant cactus).

This 38-inch Stone ram, shot by O'Connor in northern British Columbia in 1971, just missed making the book.

Sheep Hunting

Sheep are found in many different types of terrain. I have hunted in the low rocky hills of decomposed granite along the Sonora coast, on the cinder cones and lava fields of Sonora's Pinacate Mountains, in the higher mountains of limestone and of solid granite farther inland in the Sonora desert. I have hunted sheep in the lava mountains of the Yukon's River country, on plateaus as flat as billiard tables in the Cassiar district of British Columbia, in great open basins lush with grass and sprinkled by bright flowers. I have hunted them in hills so gentle and rounded that I could ride almost anywhere on a horse and I have hunted them in country so steep and rough that a horse would break his neck before he had climbed 50 feet.

Sheep hunting is primarily stalking—and stalking simply means that the hunter sees the game before it sees him, and then keeps out of sight as he sneaks up within range. The sheep hunter's most useful tool is a good binocular that he knows how to use. A spotting scope will enable him to judge heads at long range, and will save the hunter from many fruitless stalks on rams with inferior heads. The binocular should be relatively light and compact. Incidentally, few white guides and no Indian guides bring good binoculars. A prismatic spotting scope of 20-25x is about right. It should always be used with a tripod.

The use of binoculars in sheep hunting is an art which I cannot go into at this time. However, the primary ingredient is patience. Sheep are not as easy to locate as it might seem. The white Dalls against green grass are the easiest to see. I have picked them up 10 and 12 miles away. The brown Rocky Mountain and desert bighorns are the most difficult to locate, for they're often found on rock and soil of about the same color.

Wherever they are found wild sheep have similar habits. When the rams are not concerned with the rut they go off by themselves and tend to form groups of about the same age. The last ram I shot was with two younger rams. However, I saw a big herd of stone rams in 1967 that were all from 7 to 9 years old. My wife's 13-year-old Dall with a 44-inch head was with two other old-timers equally ancient.

In late summer and early fall the rams are in bunches, apart from the ewes. In the north they generally summer in higher and rougher country, but this is not always the case. I have seen big rams in low country in northern Canada and clear down on the bank of the Middle Fork of the Salmon River in Idaho.

Prior to the onset of the rut the rams like to find a spot where the feed is good and they can feel safe from their enemies. They are up feeding at first light. They usually feed until mid-morning. Then they bed down where they can look out over a lot of country. Favorite spots are on points, the heads of basins, open slopes where they cannot be approached from any direction.

Around midday sheep and most herbivorous animals like to get up, browse a few minutes to a half-hour, then lie down again. Generally they'll stay near their original beds until they get up to feed again in late afternoon. Sometimes, however, they will move a short distance to a more comfortable spot—to get out of a chill wind, to find a cooler or warmer place, to escape gnats. For this reason anyone stalking rams should not take it for granted that they never move.

I like to locate rams, decide with the spotting scope if one has a shootable head, and then, unless I can complete a stalk within a half-hour or so, to wait until the rams bed down. Sometimes sheep will bed down a considerable distance from where they feed, and it is a disconcerting experience to arrive at the spot where you plan to shoot and find the ram gone!

The last stages of a stalk should be handled carefully. Sometimes in the bunch there is a nervous ram that has been shot at or chased by a wolf. He may get up to take a look around and bump into the stalker. As I have said, the bedded rams sometimes move to a more comfortable spot. Sometimes a bunch of sheep the stalker has not previously seen will move into his path. For these reasons he should approach every new prospect with extreme caution.

The wild sheep's main defense are his eyes and his legs. He can see moving objects about as far away as man can see them with a good 6x or 8x binocular. But stationary objects don't mean much to the sheep—or to most other mammals other than apes and men. If you and a sheep blunder into each other freeze. Don't move a muscle or bat an eye. I have had sheep walk up within a few yards and pay no attention to me because I didn't move and they didn't get my wind.

Generally, though, it is possible to stalk within 200 yards of rams and, if the stalk is well executed, shots at rams are generally not difficult. I have shot more rams at under 200 yards than over, and I have shot several at less than 50 yards. Now and then the sheep hunter is forced to take a fairly long shot, but if there is a chance of missing or wounding him the hunter should refrain from shooting and come back another day. For sheep hunting I prefer a rifle weighing about eight pounds with a 4-power scope and a 22-inch barrel.

Trophy Rams

It takes 9 or 10 years to grow a trophy sheep head, generally 12 or 13 to grow one that will make the record list. The ¾-curl rule of many game departments for legal rams means nothing. I have seen such rams with heavily-broomed horns that were fine trophies, but most ¾-curl rams are youngsters, some as young as 4 years old. These should never be shot.

In general there are three types of sheep horns—the close curl, where the horns stay close to the head and come up close to the eyes; the wide spread, where the horns flare out away from the head; and the "argali" type, where the horns come in close and then flare out. All three types are found in all species of North American sheep. The close curl is characteristic of the Rocky Mountain and the desert bighorns. For this rea-

Three of Herb Klein's great sheep. From left—a desert ram from Sonora, Mexico, and No. 7 in the Boone & Crockett Record Book. Center, a Dall from the Yukon, No. 80 B&C. Last, a Stone sheep from northern British Columbia, No. 7 B&C.

excited and didn't wait for the bunch of rams to finish feeding and lie down. They changed positions while I was stalking them and saw me first. They started to run and I opened up. I shot at them 11 times off-hand. I thought I hit one of them and found a lot of blood when I got over to where they had been. I followed the blood but lost it. I found the ram a week later. I was crossing a creek to climb the mountain and see if I could find another ram when I smelled something awful. I went to see what it was and it was the ram I had shot at. I had hit him in the rump and the wound was full of maggots. He was so weak he couldn't get up. I shot him again."

His story made me so sick I couldn't eat dinner. ●

The Sheep Rifle

I don't think the caliber of the sheep rifle is particularly important. I have shot more sheep with 270 rifles than with any other caliber, but I've also shot a good many with a 30-06. I have used the 7x57, the 257 Roberts, and the rather unsuitable 348 Winchester. The late Charlie Ren, my mentor on desert sheep, used a Waffenfabrik Mauser in 7x57 and a 300 Savage. Old Charlie had little use for the 270 or the 30-06. He said they made too much noise, kicked too much, and tore up too much meat. Another old sheep hunter, a sometime prospector who poached sheep in southwest Arizona and in Sonora, swore by an iron-sighted 94 Winchester 25-35 carbine. Prince Abdorreza Pahlavi, the most experienced sheep hunter living today, and who has hunted in more different sheep areas than any hunter who has ever lived, has settled on the 270. He has a matched trio of pre-1964 270 Winchesters, all scope sighted, restocked, and engraved. I have been told that the King of Afghanistan likewise uses a 270. So does Alex Firouz, an American-educated civil engineer who heads the Iranian game department.

Sheep are not large animals and they are not tenacious of life. If the sheep hunter knows his business he usually gets an easy shot at a stationary target. I've never wounded and lost a North American sheep, and about 95% of those I have shot were killed stone dead in their tracks with one shot. Those that required more than one bullet were not hit right.

In many sheep areas grizzly bears may be encountered, and for that reason I'd prefer a rifle of the 270—30-06 class. The sheep hunter also stands a good chance of bumping into moose and caribou and sometimes Rocky Mountain goats.

The sheep rifle should not be too heavy nor too long of barrel. If climbing has to be done in rocks and cliffs even a 24-inch barrel is awkward at times. I like a 22-inch barrel, and my pet pair of 270 sheep rifles have such barrels. They weigh 8 pounds on the button with 4x scopes. A 22-inch barrel doesn't reduce velocity enough to make any difference in the field. Shorter barrels give considerable velocity loss and increased muzzle blast. I have a Winchester 70 "Mannlicher" with a 19-inch barrel. A handload that produces 3,140 fps my 270's 22-inch barrels shows less than 2,900 in the short barrel.

Prince Abdorreza, whose opinion I have regard for, likes a 3-9x variable scope on his 270 sheep rifles. I have always found 4x scopes sufficient. In fact, all my early sheep hunting was done with a 2½x scope, and I thought it was a dandy. J. O'C.

son a very high proportion of the old brown rams have heavily-broomed horns. As the horns grow up to block side vision the rams rub the points against rocks to keep the view clear. Often the rams will work particularly on the horn on one side. Rams with wide spreads and argali-type horns generally have perfect points because horns of this type do not interfere with their side vision. Many of the record heads, even of Rocky Mountain bighorns, are of the argali type. My best Dall is an example of this type.

In my trophy room I have examples of all species of North American sheep. No matter what the species the close-curl heads are all broomed. Rams also broom their horns through fighting and from accidents. The big 44-inch Dall my wife shot in 1963 had apparently taken a bad tumble not long before it was killed. About four inches of one horn was so badly cracked it was about to fall off, and on the same side the ram's ribs were cracked and broken, the flesh terribly bruised. Rams also break their horns in fighting, and often big chunks knocked out expose the core.

See the ram first. Size him up and decide if you want him. If you do, look the country over carefully and decide on a route that will keep you out of sight and with the wind favorable. Before you begin the stalk be patient enough to wait until the ram beds down so you can count on his staying put for a while. Then approach carefully from above, take your time and squeeze off the shot for a clean one-shot kill.

This is the formula for a good ram hunt. I gave it to a young man who had been lucky enough to draw a permit in a Western state. He had scouted an area and had a bunch of rams located. He asked me for advice.

When the season was over he called me up. "Well," he said, "I got my ram!"

"Congratulations," I said. "Did you follow my script?"

"Well, not exactly," he said. "I got

This Dall ram was shot at more than 440 yards with a 300 Winchester Magnum, the 180-gr. Nosler bullet backed by a husky charge of 4831. Both rifle and bullet are capable of this kind of shooting if you do your part, but it is doubtful that shooting beyond another 100 yards is justified. *Bob Hagel photo.*

Pellet Pistol Phizzles

by LADD FANTA

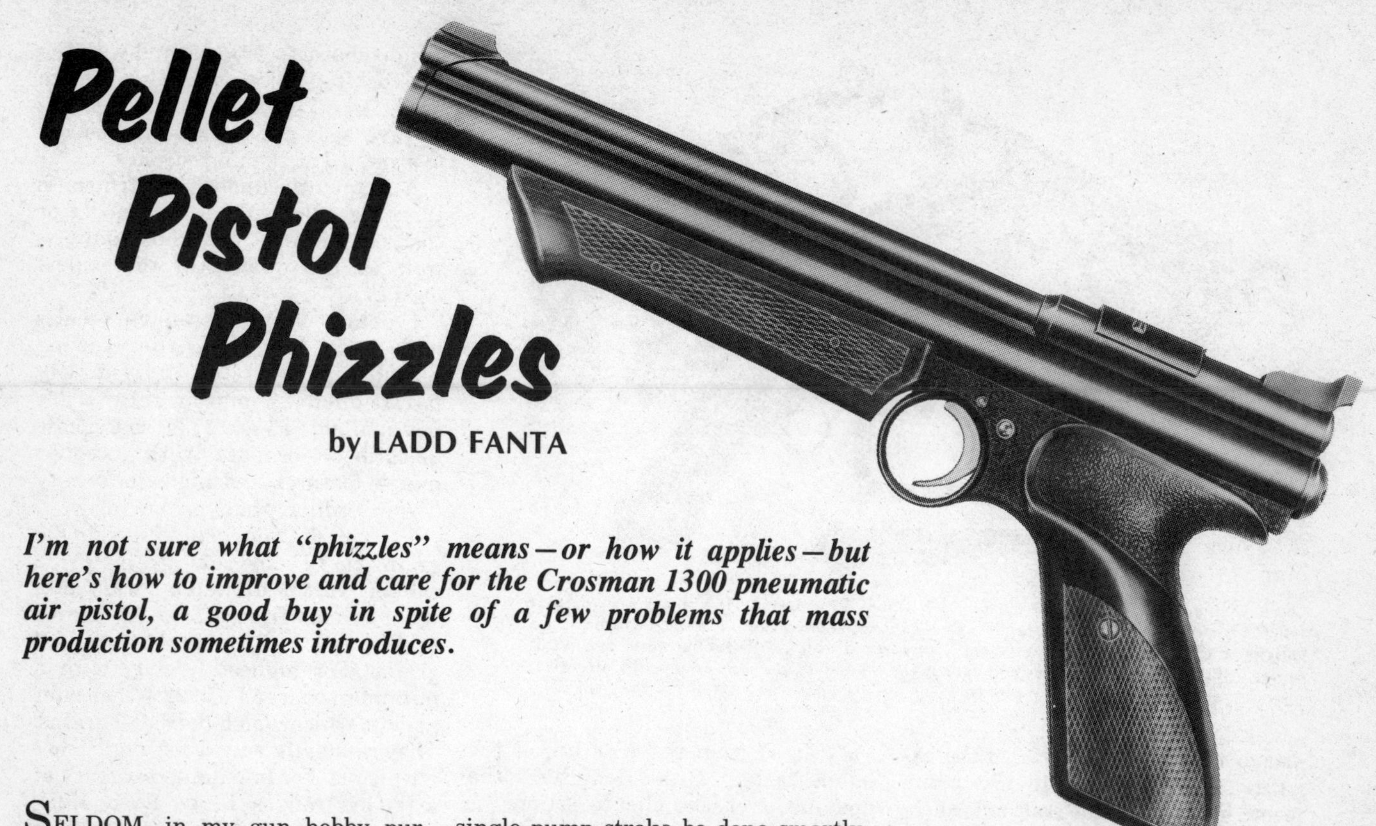

I'm not sure what "phizzles" means—or how it applies—but here's how to improve and care for the Crosman 1300 pneumatic air pistol, a good buy in spite of a few problems that mass production sometimes introduces.

The Crosman 1300, Medalist II, is an improved version of the earlier Crosman 130 pneumatic pistol. Why "Medalist II"? Historically there was a little-known earlier Crosman "Medalist," a limited production pistol powered by CO^2. This chrome-finish, target-type Model 150 Medalist came in plush lined "heirloom" wooden case and was guaranteed for life. General configuration was strikingly similar to the Model 1300 despite different propulsion system.

SELDOM, in my gun hobby pursuits, has a simple modification produced such gratifying results as the bail-type pump handle installed on my Crosman 1300 pneumatic air pistol.

The idea isn't entirely new. Something similar has appeared, at times, on earlier pneumatic air arms. The closed-loop pump handle prevents hand pinching, it vastly improves charging efficiency, and it serves as a barrel weight. Linkage and handle snap firmly under the pump tube via strong toggle action.

Pumping the pneumatic air arm for every shot is, perhaps, the least popular feature inherent to that type. Most pneumatic air rifles deliver useful short-range power with only 2 or 3 strokes but, because of greatly reduced size, pneumatic air pistols require their recommended minimum of 6 strokes. This is one reason why 5 U.S. manufacturers produce pneumatic rifles, but only two of them make pneumatic pistols.

Some might decry upsetting the pistol's esthetic lines with an ignoble pump handle. If such relatively expensive and sophisticated models as the Walther LP III match pistol can have an unorthodox pump handle in front of the grip, then the addition of a robust handle on my Crosman 1300 should be forgiven. The LP III is frequently called a "recoilless" pistol, which it is, but it's not spring-powered, as is often stated or implied. The LP III is an unusual pneumatic type, and the maker stresses that the single pump stroke be done smartly and always in same manner. Knowledgeable pneumo-buffs know that rhythm or cadence in pumping any pneumatic air arm is very important for equally-powered shots. To this end, my handy pump handle allows not only consistent, but rapid charging, letting me readily maintain the normal firing pace and plinking accuracy of those shooting other kinds of air pistols.

The Handle

The original pump lever grip is removed by driving out two ⅛″ roll pins. Save the pins and the plastic grip for possible refitting in the future.

The variety of handles one might substitute is limited only by the imagination. My first one consisted of a scrap piece of U-shaped aluminum channel, the inside ¼″ wide by ½″ deep and 4¾″ long, this the base for the 4¼″ handle. The handle, a ¼″ diameter round solid rod used for electronic panels, has 8-32 internal threaded ends. This was bent to the form pictured. To fatten and enhance the "feel," a piece of ¼″ I.D. black rubber hose was forced onto the handle from one end before assembly. Use ⅝″ machine screws, with lock nuts, to

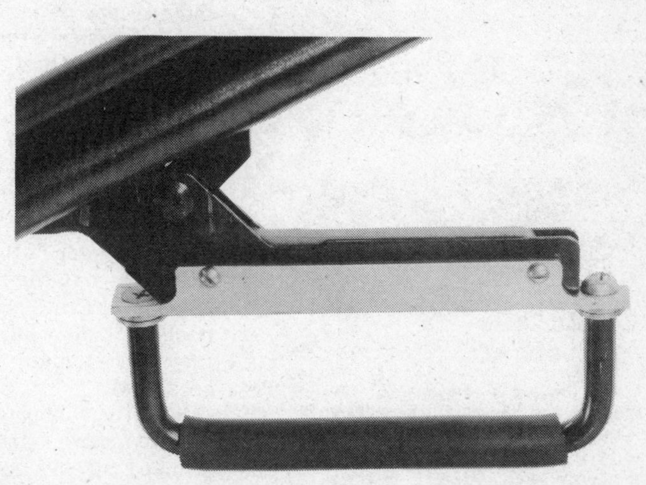

Detail of author's first pump handle installation. Note solid rubber bumper lengthwise within pump link.

Three variations of handles on the author's Model 1300 pistols. The shiny, semi-circular handle is made from 1/2"-dia. stainless steel tubing. Although very robust, it proved to be slippery and thereby the least efficient until covered with 1/2" ID rubber hose. Version at upper right is handle style described in text. These handles, perhaps esthetically offensive, provide much better pumping capability.

attach the channel—through the existing roll-pin holes—to the pump lever link. The illustration clearly shows how I filed the channel ends and fitted the handle.

Among other minor details, a worthwhile finishing touch is to fit a bumper, which reduces contact noise during the pumping operation.

Cementing a thin rubber or felt cushion to the bottom of the pump tube didn't work for long. A better way is to stuff a solid rubber strip edgewise into the topside of the pump link, leaving a small protruding margin to serve as a buffer.

Loading and Sights

A desirable aspect of most single shot CO^2 and pneumatic air arms is a breechbolt projection which, when thrust forward to the closed position, automatically seats the pellet.

On the Model 1300 this projection rather limits the loading port clearance for fast reloading. Filing 1/16" or so from the *rear* lip on the outer loading sleeve lengthens the opening for easier pellet insertion.

Outer loading sleeve lip (A) can be filed shorter, providing more access for pellet loading. To remove outer sleeve for filing remove screw (B), slide the outer sleeve forward over the barrel and lift off.

Stamped metal parts normally have one side more rounded than the other. Check the rear sight blade insert to see which way it was assembled. For better sight picture definition let the sharper edge face the shooter. Lock the adjustable rear sight blade in level position with the top edge of the rear sight proper, thus presenting to the eye a broad, unbroken horizontal line to help prevent canting. If needed, adjust elevation by shimming (paper can be used) or by filing the flat bottom of the rear sight base, held by one screw. This special Crosman screw (Part #1934-10) must be checked to make sure that its shoulder does not limit secure tightening. If so, place a small washer under the screw head.

It is important that front sight and rear sight assembly are in the same vertical plane. The front sight blade should appear perfectly straight up and down within the rear sight notch. If it does not, shim under the low side of the rear sight to align. There's not much that can be done with the moulded front blade.

Triggers and Pellets

The surprisingly light and crisp M1300 trigger pull usually needs no attention, but the addition of a trigger shoe to the very narrow trigger itself is beneficial. The No.5 "Ace" fits well enough, but needs longer set screws.

Sensitive shooters may detect slightly harder trigger pull as the pumped strokes increase. This is a design characteristic normal with the self-cocking, "blow-off" valve system used. At 6-7 pumps the trigger let-off averages 2.5 pounds, increasing to around 3 at 10 pump strokes.

A frequently underrated truism is this: regardless of caliber, model or cost, an air arm can shoot only as well as the quality of the pellets used in it.

I obtain very impressive results with the 22 caliber Medalist II firing match-type pellets. Individually partitioned 22 match pellets are not available as are 177s, so I choose 22-caliber brands with similar match features and high uniformity despite ordinary bulk packaging.

Typical diabolo pellets weigh 8.0 grains in 177 and 14.0 grains in 22 caliber. However, weights vary between brands from 7.1 to 9.5 grains in 177 and in 22 from 11.9 to 15.3 grains! For highest velocity with a minimum charge I use 22 Winchester pellets, which weigh only 12.0 grains. They're ideally suited for single shot air pistols. For maximum accuracy at extended ranges I use RWS Meisterkugeln 22s, which average 13.5 grains.

Critique

The relatively low-cost Crosman

Trigger spring (A) should not be over-lightened. When weakened below charge-holding level, premature "pop-offs" (air charge release) will occur while pumping. If more spring pressure is ever needed, it is better to add washers under the spring (B) instead of stretching the spring. Space within lower handle area (C) can be used to add weight, as here.

1300 has the basic essentials to make highly accurate air pistol shooting a reality. By virtue of its surge-free pneumatic power supply and key match-type features, it can be the "poor man's recoilless pistol." Good rifling, sights, trigger pull and well-shaped target grips are important ingredients.

At today's $30.95, the mass-produced 1300 can't be expected to have the perfection in details found on sophisticated match pistols at 5 or 6 times higher cost. There are inevitable slips in quality control. Among the author's three new 1300 pistols the following faults were found and corrected:

All 3 pistols—a large burr in rear of slot on aluminum sear-spring head, left from machining operation. This source of potential trouble was easily removed with a small file.

A heavily rusted sear spring on one pistol was replaced. The 6-32 grip threads were cross-threaded on both sides. Chasing with a 6-32 tap remedied the condition, allowing secure grip tightening.

On another pistol the corker was what at first appeared to be loose locking of the loading sleeve. Closer examination disclosed excessive headspace clearance, created by the barrel not having been fully pressed home into the receiver. This small gap also shaved lead from the flat-headed edge of match type pellets, and caused them to hang up when being chambered. Ordinary round-nose Diabolo pellets fed normally. The fix was classic—a few good smacks on the muzzle with a soft hammer, with the receiver rear solidly bucked.

Incidentally, in writing to Crosman about the above guns, it took months for an answer. A replacement barrel assembly, when received, likewise had the barrel insufficiently pressed into the receiver.

Dominant Don'ts

Don't loan your pneumatic gun to strong armed friends bent on seeing how much "power" they can pump into it. Exceeding manufacturer's recommendations is foolish, reduces accuracy and can be expensive.

Don't lubricate your pneumatic gun with just any old oil or even with high grade gun oil. Crosman's siliconized pellet gun oil is cheap insurance.

Don't over-oil your pneumatic gun. Even with the proper oil, there's such a thing as overdoing it.

Don't shoot without some form of eye protection.

Don't load first. For greatest safety always charge first (or cock, in the case of spring guns), then load last.

Don't get discouraged if you can't shoot like a movie hero. Put utility before vanity and use two hands. This can open new found pistol accuracy for you, as it has for me.

Accuracy

As an inveterate plinker, I shoot paper targets only for necessary zero finding and group testing. Otherwise, it's safe targets of opportunity, fun targets. One example is using an expended 8.5-gram CO^2 cylinder with the neck tightly forced into a 5/16" I.D. piece of extension spring (soldering or rubber cementing is optional). The other end of the spring is pressed onto a rod or dowel to be pushed into the ground or otherwise anchored.

At close range you'll see that, when struck dead center, the cylinder swings straight back. With off-center hits on the left side the cylinder bobs to the right, and vice versa. Hits produce a distinct "clink," adding to shooter enjoyment and interest.

With a hillock as a back stop, for several years one such maintenance-free target has been set up in my back yard facing a door that's 47 measured feet away. I can shoot from indoors, comfortable and unobtrusive. Intended as a challenge for open sight air rifles, the ¾"x2" cylinder does look small at 47 feet. Happiness is hitting it with the accurized Model 1300 as regularly as I can with match pistols of many times the cost! ●

Open rear sights with an adjustable insert can detract from accuracy by the "steps" created when the insert adjustment falls above or below the main sight body line. With the insert locked in level position, the greater total sight width makes for faster, accurate, cant-free aim.

Bulk-pack quality extremes. Importance of pellet quality cannot be over-emphasized. A relatively lower-priced air arm with good ammunition will frequently perform better than a fine one with indifferent ammunition.

New Locking Substance

The barrel-receiver gap fix mentioned earlier turned out to be temporary. After some use the loading sleeve lock-up again loosened and the gap reappeared. This time I used a relatively new industrial locking-sealing viscous coating called VC-3. This was applied with a toothpick into the crevice and the barrel once more rapped home into its recess. Excess fluid was carefully wiped off and the gun put away to cure for 48 hours. The repair has been positive; the gun received considerable use and deliberate mis-use over many months, with no hint of further loosening. VC-3 should be available in good hardware or automotive stores.

VC-3 may well become another useful gunsmith tool a la Loc.Tite. Though VC-3 may parallel Loc-Tite in many uses, there is a big difference. Loc-Tite is "anærobic," which means it hardens in the absence of air, as when a threaded assembly is completed. For optimum results it requires a catalyst-primer or at least through degreasing. VC-3 (made by the Ny-Lok-Detroit Corp., the people who make Ny-Lok self-locking screws) is not a cement, nor does it ever "set." No primers are needed and pre-cleaning of parts is normally not required, although I habitually try to clean them off. The parts need only be wiped off if there are visibly excess oils. It adheres to ferrous and non-ferrous metals, platings, wood and plastic. Screws coated with VC-3 do not lose their locking feature; they can be used over again.

However, VC-3 must be dry to lock. Dry *before* assembly. If assembled wet, it takes days before dryness and locking occur. You fill threads about 80% with VC-3, let air dry from 6 to 24 hours. Or oven heat at 200°-300°F for 3 to 10 minutes. A quickie way (factory approved) for drying VC-3 on a screw thread is to burn off solvents with a match or lighter. After flaming stops, you continue heating until bubbling stops. The part is ready for immediate use.

I find VC-3 excellent for locking troublesome gun screws, sights, shifting scope mounts on spring rifles, etc. Applications are almost limitless.

Charter Arms Bulldog - THE 44 SPECIAL REVIVED

Light at a scant 19 ounces, the newest member of the Charter Arms family offers big performance in a compact package. The author's tailored handload makes the Bulldog even more potent.

by GEORGE C. NONTE, JR.

THERE WAS once a Hammond "Bulldog" pistol, and the name bulldog has been stamped on a few bureau-drawer specials in the dim and distant past. But neither the long-defunct Hammond nor those two-dollar revolvers bear any but the most rudimentary resemblance to the latest Bulldog. In price, design, quality, power, and genuine utility, it stands far above the long-ago guns.

"Bulldog" is an apt name for Charter Arms' latest offering from the inventive mind and capable hands of Doug McClenahan, President of the company. The name implies tenacity, perseverance and strength—all of which are characteristics of the basic Charter revolver design. But the new gun possesses more than that—it's powerful; it's accurate; it's attractive; and it gives one an indefinable feeling of security or invincibility when it is in hand.

If the name Bulldog isn't the best, I can't think of one that serves the gun better.

At first, it might appear that Charter Arms' metal cutters just squeezed five 44 chambers into the 6-shot 38 Undercover frame, and screwed in a 44 barrel.

44 Bulldog New

I want to allay, completely, the comment snorted by one would-be handgunner that "Hell, they just put a new cylinder and barrel on the old gun."

It didn't happen that way. While basic frame length and width remain the same, height has increased 0.170"

Charter Arms' newest offering, shown here on author's small paw, is very nearly hand-size.

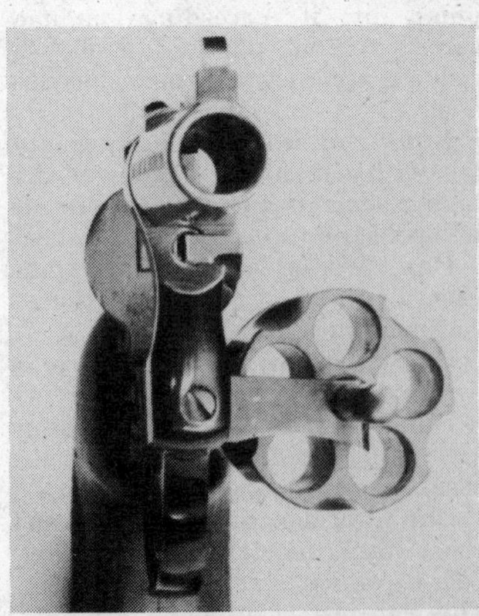

Barrel walls at muzzle are relatively thin but amply strong for any reasonable 44 Special load. Chamber walls *look* thin, but are really as thick as on some older guns in large calibers, and they contain much better material.

to 2.045", and the barrel boss is enlarged to 0.770", up 0.095" from the 38. The cylinder recess is also increased 0.055" in length and 0.140" in height.

As a result the frame is dimensionally new, along with the crane or yoke. Grip frame and trigger guard appear to be interchangeable—as are hammer, trigger, latch, and some other parts—between the Bulldog and the Undercover.

Instead of being just a rechambered and rebarreled Undercover, the Bulldog is a completely new gun, though sharing the basic design—and some parts interchangeability—with the Undercover. In that respect its relationship to the Undercover is the same as that of a S&W M27 to the smaller-framed M14.

The main thing going for the Charter Bulldog is this—it is the largest-bore *practical* pocket revolver yet to see the light of day. It was designed with the sole purpose of fitting a 44-caliber gun into the dimensional envelope of the typical 38 Special snub-nose. The only pocket-style guns previously produced in such large caliber were simply round-butted, short-barreled Colt New Service sixguns, made in limited quantity before WW II. For those guns to be considered "pocket size" requires damned big britches and pockets. Weighing nearly twice as much as the Bulldog, and half again as big in all other dimensions, they were built on the largest of American DA revolver frames. In short, Colt simply took its biggest gun and whittled off the edges to make it *look* little. It wasn't.

McClenahan took the opposite approach. He selected the basic dimensional container of existing small-frame, snub-nosed 38 Special revolvers and then fitted into it a 5-shot cylinder chambered for the ever-popular 44 S&W Special cartridge. He combined this with the current version of his "Undercover" revolver—the simplified, swing-out design with which we have become so familiar since 1964.

Major and minor—last of the big-gun 44 Special double action revolvers was built on Smith & Wesson's N-frame (top). The small 5-shot gun below is the latest Charter Arms design, the 18.5-oz. Bulldog.

Compactness and light weight are the result in the Bulldog—with a cylinder diameter of 1.45", a 3" barrel, 4⅝" height, and 7½" length, it weighs a mere 18½ ounces, though some brochures have said 19. In addition the frame, barrel, cylinder, and all working parts, are made of modern steels especially selected for each job and function.

Even though the cylinder and frame are substantially smaller than anything previously chambered for the 44 Special, their strength is more than adequate. The specially heat-treated 1.45" diameter cylinder is the key to it all. It measures 1.575" long, and its five chambers are on a 72-degree spacing. This 5-hole arrangement permits the strongest cylinder construction possible within a given diameter because the cylinder bolt locking cuts are located *between* the chambers.

44 Bulldog Amply Strong

Minimum cylinder-wall thickness of .055" occurs at the outer edge of the chambers, while the section between chambers measures .065". These dimensions may look thin in print, but they are actually equal to, or greater than, the comparable thicknesses for some currently-produced 38 Special revolvers, guns which are regularly used with ammunition producing chamber pressures *double* that of the factory 44 Special load. The minimum thickness at the outer edge of the chambers is at least as great as is found on some calibers of the Colt Single Action Army revolver. In addition to these comparisons, consider the fact that the "hoop strength" of the chambers has been determined to be far in excess of any reasonable 44 Special load that one might ever wish to shoot in so light a gun.

The chambers are laid out on a .440" radius, and rims are not countersunk. Rims are exposed between cylinder and recoil shield when the gun is loaded. This presents no hazard whatever. In fact, the "recessed safety chamber" of even magnum revolvers is generally just a promotional gimmick. Modern solid-head centerfire cases are no more likely to rupture when the rim is exposed than when it is enclosed. Only rimfire cases really benefit from this treatment.

When loaded, the view from the rear is a bit unusual, in that about ⅓ of the case heads protrude beyond the recoil shield, virtually flush with the perimeter of the cylinder. In this gun,

Small-diameter Bulldog cylinder is only 5-shot, but those five 44 Special cartridges fill it to the brim . . . er, rim. That 6th round? It's in there to help hold the cylinder open for photo purposes.

you see a hell of a lot more brass from the shooting position than with any other I know.

The barrel is equally sturdy. The tenon measures .530″, the shoulder abutting the frame .730″, and the muzzle .600″. Comparatively speaking, those dimensions are quite within normal revolver design practice.

While precise figures and test results have not yet been released—and may not be—we do know, from discussions with the designer of the gun, that extensive firing has been conducted with high-pressure loads to insure that an adequate safety margin exists in the cylinder. Of course, the 44 Special Bulldog is proof-fired with industry-standard 44 Special proof loads before leaving the factory. Nevertheless, it should be pointed out that *no* handgun manufacturer recommends—or even condones—handloads exceeding factory-load pressures.

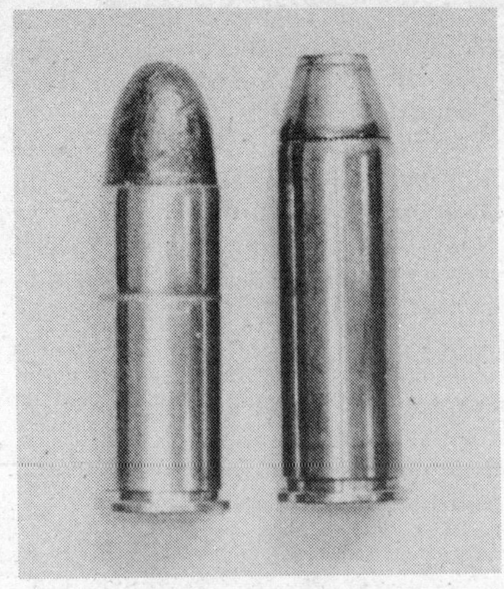

Bulldog is chambered **only** for 44 Special cartridge, at left; under no circumstances should chambers be deepened to take the high pressure (40,000 psi) 44 Magnum at right.

44 Special Ammo

The principal reason I'm emphasizing the safety and strength aspect of this particular cylinder is that probably more high-performance handloads have been recommended for the 44 Special than for any other sixgun cartridge. While factory standard pressures for this cartridge are in the vicinity of 12 to 14,000 psi, many commonly-used and highly-recommended handloads generate pressures in the 20 to 25,000 psi range. Many of these loads were developed at a time when pressure-testing equipment was not generally available, and were worked up in the big-frame Colt and S&W revolvers, guns at least *thought* to be very strong. Most of these older recommended loads (before the advent of the 44 Magnum) do not produce pressures as great as was believed at the time. In fact, Elmer Keith's classic load of 18.5 grains of Hercules 2400 with a 250-gr. cast bullet in balloon-head cases produces slightly under 21,000 psi—while its counterpart of 17.5 grains of the same powder in solid-head cases develops just under 23,000 psi. Since these pressures actually exceed 44 Special proof-load pressures slightly, it would appear that one should proceed cautiously with them in this small, light handgun.

While the factory 44 Special cartridge appears unimpressive on paper—770 fps with a 246-gr. round nosed lead bullet, muzzle energy 322 foot pounds—the load has a quite favorable reputation as a man stopper. It is noted for being an ideal combination of light recoil with good stopping effect. However, that light recoil relates to guns weighing 36 ounces or more, and in this lightweight Bulldog, of half that heft, the recoil sensation is a good bit different. Heavy, yes, but not one whit worse than modern high-performance ammunition fired in the typical two-inch 38 Special snubnose. A good deal of credit for this is due to the hand-filling Bulldog grip supplied on the new gun.

Those who feel the standard 44 Special load isn't as effective as they would like are quite likely to handload it with some of those older loads. The Keith load (cited earlier) drives a 250-gr. semi-wadcutter lead bullet at about 1200 fps from a 6-inch barrel. That gives it a 125% gain in energy over the standard load, which is increased further in stopping power and wound-channel size by the sharp-edged profile of the SWC bullet.

This being the load, we thought,

Charter Arms' hammer safety design. With trigger forward, hammer is fully blocked by safety bar, cannot reach firing pin. Safety bar is not raised to permit firing until trigger is pulled all the way rearward or hammer is thumbed to full-cock position.

which the 44 devotee might want to use in the new Charter lightweight, we brewed up a fresh batch of it—17.5 grains of 2400 in modern solid-head W-W cases. Our sample gun took them in stride—which is more than I can say for my hand. The gun showed no ill effects whatever from firing a number (limited!) of these 23,000 psi loads, but the gun becomes difficult to control with them, and the cylinder latch thumbpiece begins to chew up my thumb. Not one handgunner in a thousand—*machismo* be damned—will want to shoot this load a second time in the Bulldog.

Therein lies the main stumbling block to producing a genuinely high-performance load for use in this gun. Recoil becomes quite sharp and gun control becomes difficult, especially in fast double-action work—and this happens before a load level that might prove damaging to the gun is reached. Frankly, we had intended running enough of Keith's load through this gun to determine whether extensive use might produce damage or excessive wear. At the moment, that project is cancelled—or at least postponed—until I can find three or four willing assistants, who don't mind having their shooting hands chawed a bit. Wanna see a checkered right mitt?

We then backed off to another load—240/245-gr. lead bullet (Lyman 429352) and 7.5 to 8.0 grains of Hercules Unique—which in past experience has produced 930-950 fps in 6½-inch revolver barrels. To date we've had no chance to run velocity tests on this load in the Bulldog—but no matter, since it represents about the limit in recoil for the typical shooter.

This load, which really isn't uncomfortable to shoot, yet offers a substantial increase in velocity and energy over the factory cartridge, plus the more damaging effect of its semi-wadcutter shape. In fact, still using 6-inch barrels for the sake of uniformity in comparison, this load is fully as effective as the factory 45 Colt load, and will actually produce deeper penetration.

Only the round-nosed bullet (left) is available in factory 44 Special loads; cast bullets in numerous other shapes, as at right, may be handloaded.

Charter Arms revolvers use unbreakable, lifetime Beryllium copper firing pins.

What we've accomplished by upgrading the 44 Special to this particular level, for use in this particular gun, is to make it equal to the 45 Colt under similar conditions. That is no mean accomplishment for an 18½-ounce gun, one that can be slipped neatly into the hip pocket.

All of this, mind you, with a load not at all uncomfortable to shoot, and one that produces less than 13,000 psi chamber pressure—a figure within industry standards for the 44 Special. Most significant, there's a sizeable increase in power and effectiveness over the factory load without exceeding maximum allowable factory pressures. Actually, typical factory 44 Special loads of today produce less than 10,000 psi chamber pressure. We have exceeded that by a sizeable margin, but we have not exceeded acceptable *standard* pressures, therefore we haven't shaved the safety margin normally built into a new gun.

We had hopes of developing an expanding-bullet load that would be genuinely effective, that is, drive the bullet fast enough from this short, 3-inch tube to produce reliable and consistent expansion at reasonable range—while staying within the same general pressure range. However, existing 44 expanding bullets are intended primarily for the 44 Magnum, with velocities in the 1300-1500 range. Their construction is too strong to produce reasonable expansion at the velocities obtainable with our self-imposed pressure/recoil limits and the Bulldog's 3-inch barrel.

We could have made up special jackets and dies and cranked out almost any bullet design we wanted. Maybe we will some day, but not just now. Instead, we chose to drive a cast lead wadcutter of light weight as fast as possible. The first choice was Lyman bullet 429348, a full wadcutter type weighing 180 grains, and 8.0 grains of Unique. This looked good—accuracy was acceptable and recoil was quite manageable. Unfortunately, while it did blast a rather big hole

With the advent of the new 44 Bulldog, Charter Arms now offers revolvers for 5 cartridges, left to right: 22LR, 32 S&W Long, 38 Special, 357 Magnum and 44 Special.

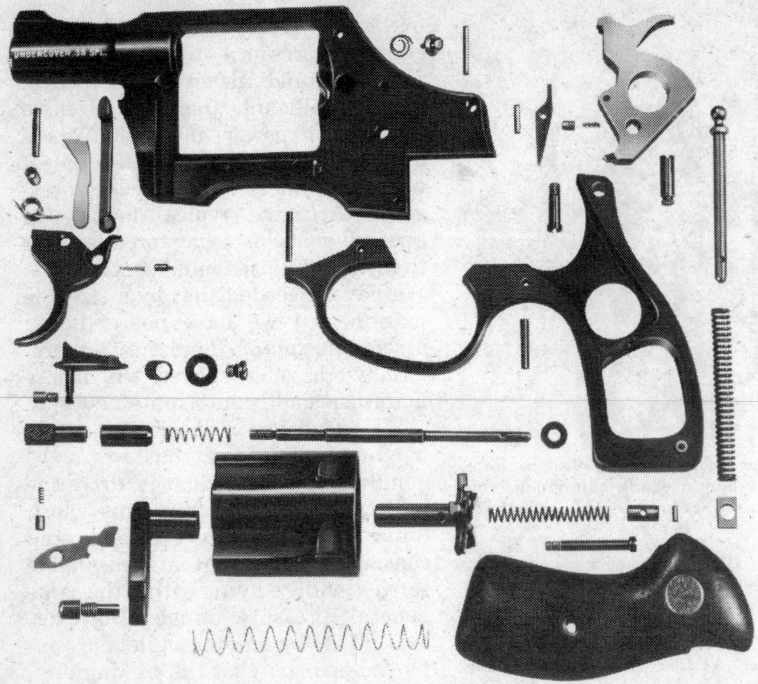

Component parts of the Charter Arms "Undercover" revolver. Essentially the same parts —except for dimensional differences—are used in the new 44 Bulldog.

in Duxseal blocks, no significant expansion was obtained except when the bullet was cast of almost pure lead, and that produced undesirable bore leading.

Special Handload Developed

The next choice was Lyman bullet 429352, another wadcutter design weighing 245 grains, according to the catalog. Far too heavy for what we had in mind, but we intended to alter it anyway. Lacking swaging dies suitable for the purpose, this bullet was cast and then slipped into an expanded, cut-off case neck and chucked in a Unimat miniature lathe. The broad, flat nose was then drilled with a 3/16" bit to a depth of 3/8". A triangular forming tool was then substituted for the bit, and used to cut a large conical cavity, similar to that found in hollow-base 38 wadcutters. When all this was done, we had a bullet weighing under 200 grains and, when seated conventionally, it gave the appearance of an *inverted* HB wadcutter in 38 Special—a load noted for its effectiveness from short-tubed six-guns.

We were able to push this bullet fast—using the same 8.0-gr. Unique charge—enough to expand well without exceeding reasonable pressures and recoil.

This load not only *looks* wicked, it is! When fired into Duxseal at 10 feet the bullet expands consistently to 60 caliber, creating a massive wound channel with relatively low penetration. Even so, with this greatly increased effectiveness, the 18½-ounce Bulldog remains comfortable to shoot and reasonably docile in fast, double-action work.

I'd dislike very much being on the receiving end of one of those gaping HP wadcutters. Based on its performance in Duxseal, it will blast a bigger wound than any 38, 357 or 45 load currently available—and runs a close second (very) to 41 and 44 Magnum loads shot from 4" barrels.

With this 8.0 Unique/200-gr. reworked bullet load, the new Charter Arms Bulldog represents the most potent pocketsize handgun in existence. That is more than enough recommendation for it to displace a great many hip-pocket and waistband 38 snubbies, and will doubtless cause it to sell like peppered firewater at a trapper's rendezvous.

Faults are Few

It's not all roses, though, and we do have a couple of minor complaints.

First is the propensity of the rear cylinder-latch to bite one's thumb when firing heavy loads—hold the digit up and it's ball gets gouged; curl it down, and the inside of your knuckle gets split. In a gunfight, I don't think it would matter.

Second is an occasional binding of the cylinder caused by case rims jamming against the frame lug (which holds the cylinder forward when it is swung out) and interfering with extraction or reloading. Rotating the cylinder a fraction of a turn to place the lug *between* chambers eliminates the problem—which occurs only with some lots of cases. No big thing, really, but one should be aware of it and check that cases to be carried don't exhibit this problem.

Those are the only faults I can find in the new Charter Arms Bulldog. At the announced price of $110, it's altogether one hell of a good buy. The planned offering of the Bulldog later in 357 Magnum caliber will only enhance its desirability. ●

Charter Arms Table of Dimensions

	44 Bulldog	38 Undercover
Cylinder dia.	1.45"	1.295"
Cylinder length	1.575"	1.510"
Frame height	2.045" (at trigger)	1.875"
Cylinder recess	1.680x1.470"	1.625x1.330"
Ejector-rod stroke	0.650"	0.600"
Frame width	0.530" (at top strap)	0.530"
Frame length	4.100" (grip top to front)	4.100"
Barrel breech dia.	0.740"	0.640"
Barrel muzzle dia.	0.600"	0.520"
Barrel tenon dia.	0.525" (behind frame)	0.450"
Barrel boss	0.770"	0.675"
Throat dia.	.430-.431"	.357-.359"
Groove dia.	.432"(at muzzle)	.355"
Weight	18¼ oz.	16½ oz.
Over-all length	7½"	7½"
Over-all height	4½"	4⅜"
Number of shots	5	5
Rifling	8-groove, RH	8-groove, RH
Sights	Fixed, open	Fixed, open
Stocks	Wraparound, combat, walnut check'ed	Wraparound, combat walnut, check'ed
Finish	Blue only	Blue or nickel
Trigger pull, SA	3 lbs. (sample gun)	3½ lbs.
Trigger pull, DA	9½ lbs. (sample gun)	9 lbs.
Price	$110.00	$87.00

For over a half-century only two Browning shotguns were offered—the old original autoloader and the great Superposed, both still going strong. Today, though, there are four others from which to choose—described here in detail—if you want to go...

Shotgunning with Browning

by WALLACE LABISKY

THE FIRST of several patents covering what is known as the Automatic-5 shotgun was granted to John M. Browning in the year 1900 and, shortly thereafter, manufacturing arrangements were concluded with Fabrique Nationale d'Armes de Guerre (FN) in Liege, Belgium. Introduced to the U.S. market in 1903, this gun has been continuously produced by FN ever since. Then, in 1931, the Browning Superposed made its appearance, and this pace-setting over-under was followed in 1954 by the Double Automatic, a gun of the short-recoil type which was designed by Val Browning, JMB's son. Thus there was a period of 51 years during which the Browning shotgun line was comprised of just two guns.

Today it is very much a different story. The turning point seems to have been the introduction of the BT-99, a single-barrel trap gun which came forward in 1970. Since then there has been a beehive of activity, with the Browning firm affixing its signature to what may seem like a half acre of new scatterguns.

In 1974, and for many years to come, we'll still be seeing a great many of the old reliables—the venerable A-5 and the much-copied Superposed. Great guns, these two. But we'll also be seeing in ever-increasing numbers those newcomers which include the B-S/S (a side-by-side double), the Liege and the Citori (both O-U guns), and the long-awaited gas-operated autoloader, to be known as the B/2000.

At this juncture, there are only two fields which haven't been turned by the Browning plow—the slide-action repeater and the low-cost, top-break single barrel for knock-about use. But please don't ask whether these guns are currently in the works, or whether Browning is even toying with the idea, because I honestly don't know. I'm merely speculating that if the Browning people decide to further expand their shotgun line-up, this would seem the logical way to go.

But for right now, let's see what the new guns are like...

Browning B-S/S Double

Browning's first side-by-side gun made its debut in 12 gauge in 1972, followed a year later by the 20-ga. version. I've had an opportunity to burn powder in both bore sizes. The 12 was used for busting something like half a hundred crows, and the 20 these past months for informal clay target and pest-bird shooting. Both guns handled extremely well for me, and both exhibit the high-quality craftsmanship we've come to expect from Browning.

The usual number of rumbles preceded the appearance of the B-S/S. Browning's strong right arm, FN, was already building for the European market a side-by-side gun known as the Anson Hammerless and, according to one story, the Browning name would simply be stamped on this FN gun. Another version was that the FN gun was in reality a Browning project and, when the time was right, it would be introduced on these shores.

But as any GI can attest, rumors are not taken seriously. The B-S/S was designed at Browning's Utah facility and turned over to Miroku, a leading Japanese gunmaker already doing a first-class job with the BT-99 trap gun. A factor which may have influenced this move is that skilled European labor doesn't come as cheaply as it once did and, if the B-S/S were to be produced in Belgium, it might well wear a stiffer price tag.

The only thing European about the B-S/S, and then only in a roundabout way, is that its boxlock action is patterned after the much-copied Anson & Deeley design; and that the breech lock-up follows the Purdey approach in that a sliding underbolt engages both barrel lumps.

The 20-ga. B-S/S received by GUN DIGEST for test purposes was carefully checked for bolt fit and it was found that contact with the lug cuts is excellent. The bolt takes an adequately deep bite and it bears evenly across both locking surfaces. Since the gun is without supplementary top lock, there is no rib extension to clutter up the barrel breech area and interfere with loading and unloading.

Browning's design engineers added some modern innovations to the basic A&D-type action. For one thing, the hammers are driven by powerful coil springs. The firing pins are bushed and thus accessible through the action face. A husky longitudinal through-bolt securely joins the buttstock to the action. Complementing these features are selective ejectors and a non-selective single trigger. The safety is the usual thumbslide located on the top tang, the automatic type which returns to "safe" when the top lever is actuated.

The B-S/S ejector system is pretty much conventional in both design and operation. The ejector hammers, sears and coil springs are attached to the fore-end hardware, the sears being triggered by the forward end of the cocking levers. If, for example, only the right-hand barrel is fired, then only the right-hand ejector mechanism will be actuated to release the ejector hammer as the action comes fully open. The hammer then falls, striking the ejector leg which, in turn, ejects the spent shell from the chamber. The shell in the opposite barrel will only be lifted to a slightly elevated position. If both barrels have been fired, then both empties will, of course, be ejected. If neither barrel has been fired, then both shells will simply be elevated (called primary extraction) when the action is opened. You old hands are quite familiar with this, but beginners are often somewhat hazy about selective ejectors and this brief explanation of how they work is strictly for their benefit.

The B-S/S 20-ga. test gun ejected in a no-nonsense way, flipping the empty hulls a good 6-7 feet away, with no failures to function during the firing of about 200 rounds of assorted ammo in both paper and plastic cases. Almost invariably the two hulls would land within a few inches of one another, indicating not only a perfectly timed action, but also ejector springs that are well matched for strength.

A camming stud fixed at the center of the frame knuckle handles primary extraction, the lift amounting to ⅛"—somewhat shallow, but still sufficient to permit the removal of unfired shells, though if gloves are worn there could be a few fumbles. This camming stud serves a double purpose in that it cocks the ejector hammers upon closing the action.

Being of the non-selective type, the B-S/S single trigger limits the barrel firing sequence to right/left. Unless the two barrels are choked alike I've always considered a fixed firing order as something of a liability, one that detracts from the versatility of a two-barreler.

This trigger system is also of the mechanical type, meaning that recoil is not needed to accomplish the shift to the other sear. Opinions differ, but I've always regarded the mechanical trigger as holding some advantage over the inertial type, because if, for whatever reason, the first pull fails to fire the righthand barrel, the simple expedient of releasing the trigger and pulling it again will bring that second barrel into play.

The trigger on the test gun functioned perfectly throughout my "shakedown" shooting. The pull for the right barrel weighs 4½ pounds, the let-off being preceded by a small amount of smooth travel. The second pull requires nearly 6 pounds of pressure, but this let-off is completely without travel. On a rifle, pulls this heavy would come in for some cussing,

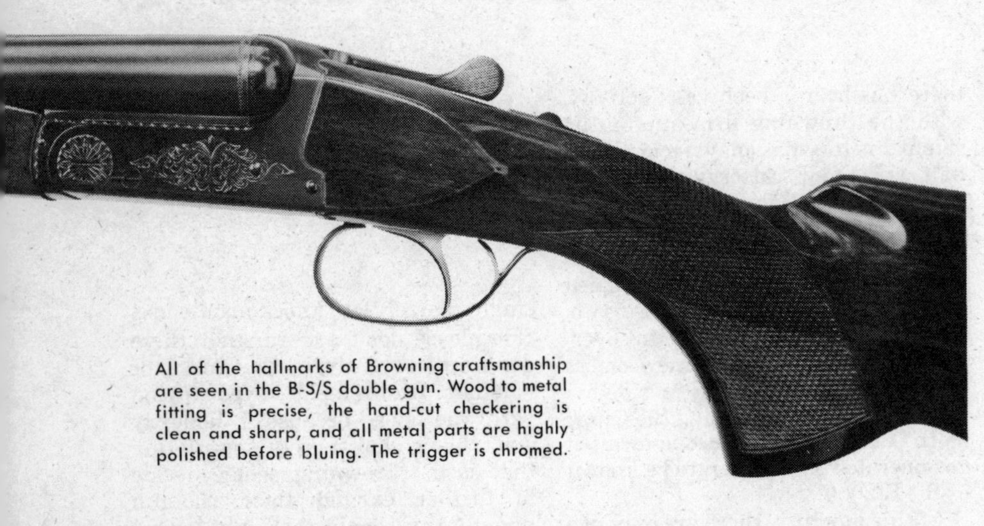

All of the hallmarks of Browning craftsmanship are seen in the B-S/S double gun. Wood to metal fitting is precise, the hand-cut checkering is clean and sharp, and all metal parts are highly polished before bluing. The trigger is chromed.

Introduced in 1973, the B-S/S 20 gauge is chambered for the 3-inch Magnum shell. The barrel lengths offered are 28 inches (Mod/Full), and 26 inches (Mod/Full and IC/Mod). Weight runs around 6¾ pounds for the 26-inch barreled gun.

Selective automatic ejectors are standard on the B-S/S gun. The trigger, however, is non-selective, meaning that the firing sequence cannot be changed. The first pull on the single trigger always fires the right-hand barrel, the second pull fires the left barrel. • This view also reveals the hand-cut engraving found on the B-S/S—scroll work on the frame bar and the hinge pin, plus simple lines cut at the borders of the standing breech, the barrel breech and the fore-end iron.

but on a shotgun they are not at all difficult to live with. The trigger itself, by the way, wears a chromed finish.

This shotgunner is thankful that Browning did not vote for a ventilated rib on the B-S/S, because on a side-by-side gun it's a real chore to get one absolutely dry following a session in the rain. The solid top rib on both the 12 and 20-ga. guns provides a dead-level sighting plane. It stands about 1⁄16" above the barrels at the breech, and just a wee bit below them at the muzzles. The flat surface is cut with closely-spaced wavy lines that form a ripple pattern to eliminate reflected light. The rib also tapers slightly. For the 20-ga. gun, width at the breech end is .325"; at the muzzle it measures .250". As such, it gives the illusion of a longer sighting plane.

A squint through the bores of the B-S/S brings tears of pure joy. Chambers, forcing cones and all else are superbly finished, being glassy smooth and mirror bright. A bore diameter of .615" has long been considered the standard for a 20-ga. gun.

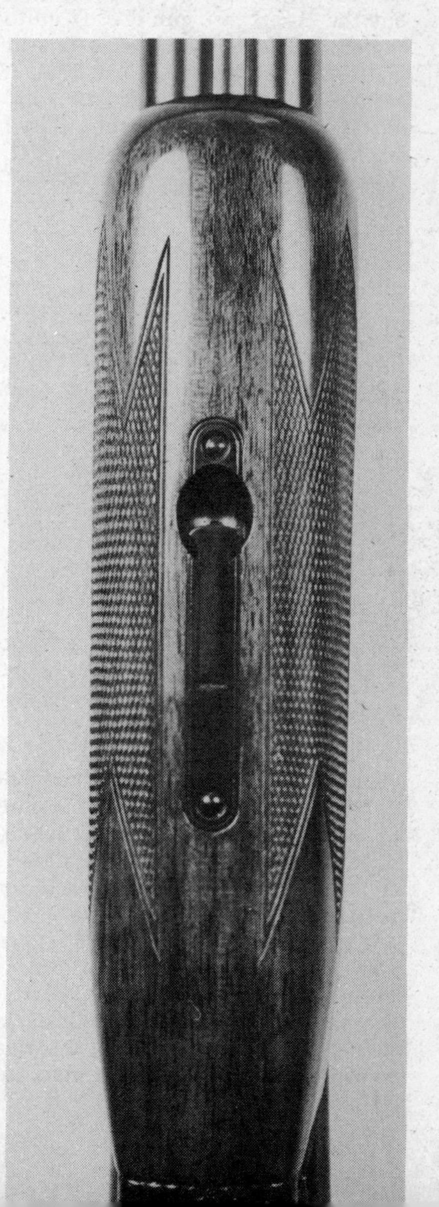

Described by Browning as a "full grip" beavertail, the B-S/S fore-end has a reverse taper that places the maximum width at the forward end—a design that enhances gun control during recoil. The taper is actually more pronounced than this photo shows.

The B-S/S firing pins are bushed and accessible through the action face. The action is patterned after the time-tested Anson & Deeley design, with the cocking levers and an ejector-camming stud protruding from the knuckle of the frame.

Not that it's of any great importance, but the B-S/S test gun doesn't quite conform. The bores checked out at .619" for the right-hand barrel (at a point 5 inches from the muzzle), and at .626" for the left-hand tube. Based on these bore diameters, the Imp. Cyl. tube (right barrel) carries .008" of choke constriction, while the Mod. tube (left barrel) has .017". The chokes are of the conical-parallel design. Roundness at the muzzle is excellent, this staying within .001" for both barrels.

The B-S/S 20 ga. with its 26" tubes was given only a token workout at the pattern board. For the IC barrel, the patterning was carried out at 30 yards. In view of the boring, this was considered a more realistic distance than the usual 40-yard stretch.

With the Browning 35 Power 2½x 1x8 shotshell loading, all patterns opened to roughly 48" and delivered an average efficiency of almost 53%. (See pattern summary table.) If we take that old rule of thumb which fixes density loss a 9% for each additional 5 yards of range, then this barrel/load combination could be expected to print a 35% average at 40 yards. This would meet the Browning standard of 35% to 45% for an Imp. Cyl. choke.

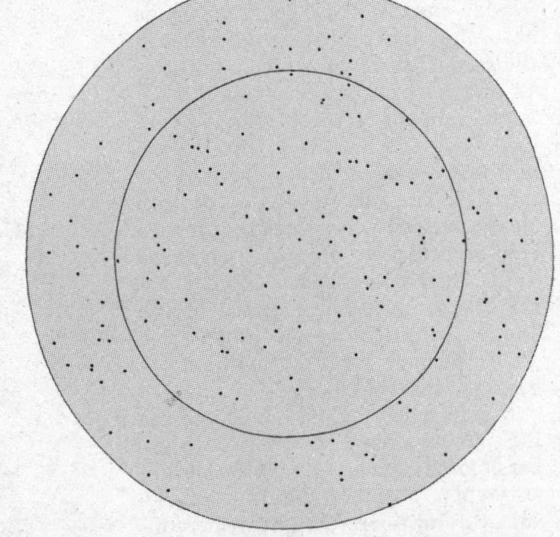
The modified-choke barrel of our B-S/S 20-ga. test gun averaged 56% at 40 yards with Browning's 3-inch 45 Power load—1½ ozs. No. 6 shot. This pattern, with a slightly dense center, has a 164 count (56.9%) for the 30-inch circle. Browning's standard for a modified choke is 45 to 55 percent.

Moving back to the 40-yard marker, the Mod. tube was checked out with the 3-inch 45 Power load containing 1¼ ozs. of 6's. This gave a 5-shot average of 56%, and slightly exceeds Browning's cataloged performance bracket of 45% to 55% for a Mod. barrel.

Barrel alignment for the B-S/S 20 was right on the money, with no significant cross-shift in pattern centers. In other words, the right barrel didn't throw left, nor the left tube to the right. In the vertical plane, the gun was found to center perfectly with a down-the-rib sight picture and with the front bead covering the small (2½") aiming marker. In the field, therefore, one could cheek the stock less firmly so as to see a small amount of rib, and by "floating" the bird over the front bead, the pattern would arrive dead-on.

Double-gun buffs who feel that all side-by-sides should wear one of those starved fore-ends of 19th century

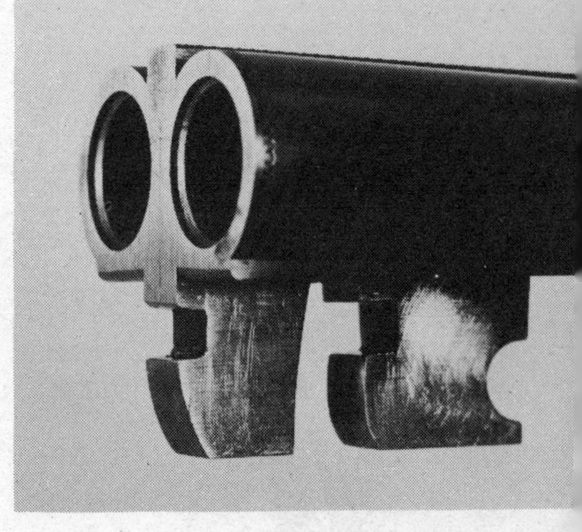
Top-breech lock-up on the B-S/S double is handled by sliding under-bolt which engages both barrel lumps. This bolting system leaves the breech area free and uncluttered.

Below—This view shows the extractors in a backed-out position. Metal-to-metal fitting here is done with hair-line precision. When shooting, unfired shells are elevated for manual removal; fired shells are automatically thrown clear of the gun.

vintage will probably flip when they see the front handle on the B-S/S. Racy it isn't, but functional it is—and highly so. The reverse taper design gives greater width at the front than at the rear. On the B-S/S 20, maximum forward width is 2¼", while the rear is 3/16" narrower. This reverse taper provides better up-front control, both in pointing and in preventing the gun from being driven back through the left hand during recoil. You'll appreciate this design innovation if you're shooting a lot of 3-inch Magnums, and Browning is to be congratulated for its intestinal fortitude in breaking away from the traditional.

Total length of the fore-end wood is 8⅞" for the 20-bore gun, and the release is a spring-loaded lever of the Deeley type. The hand-cut checkering, very well done, runs 20 lpi.

Pattern Tests—Browning B-S/S 20 Gauge
(Average of 5 Shots)

Barrel	Range/Yds.	Load	D. 20" circle	D. 30" circle	E. 30" circle	EDV 30" circle
Imp Cyl.	30	35 Power 2½x1x8 (387)	106	204	52.9%	50/12.9%
Mod.	40	45 Power Max.x1¼x6 (288)	90	162	56.2%	36/12.5%

Remarks: Barrels, 26". Imp. Cyl. barrel has a bore diameter of .619", with .008" of choke. The Mod. barrel runs .626", with .017" of choke.
EDV = Extreme spread in pellet count between individual patterns. D = Density. E = Efficiency.

The butt area of the B-S/S 20-ga. stock measures 1⅝x5⅛ inches, these dimensions being man-sized and quite adequate for good distribution of recoil forces. In keeping with conventional practices, the buttplate is of plastic.

The buttstock on the 20 is man-sized, the wood a select grade of close-grained walnut, but with no figure to speak of. The stock comb, quite full, is attractively fluted. In keeping with Browning practices, the pistol grip is left uncapped. Although the butt of the grip strikes the writer as appearing a bit robust, it nonetheless feels as comfortable as an old shoe. Total grip length runs 5", measured from the trigger, and the maximum circumference at the rear of the trigger guard is 4¼".

Checkering on the grip is also a 20-line-inch job and, when viewed under 2½ magnification, no miscues of any consequence were noted. The wood-to-metal fit cannot be faulted, though at the stock jaws the wood does stand slightly above the frame—a rather common practice nowadays, from what I've seen. The stock finish is a high-luster modern type which Browning says is hand rubbed.

While the workmanship is generally excellent, one thing in particular that impressed me is the extremely "clean" metal work. Some manufacturers will skimp a little here and there by not polishing parts that will be hidden to the eye when the gun is fully assembled—as when the barrels are covered by the fore-end. But when you pull the fore-end off the B-S/S, you'll see that the Miroku people (and Browning) don't believe in cutting corners. It's a slick job all around.

The B-S/S doubles are offered in Grade I only, and this means minimal engraving. There is a small amount of scroll work on the bar of the frame, on the hinge pin ends, on the top lever and the trigger guard. There is also some simple line work around the edges of the frame, on the fore-end iron and on the barrels at the breech. That's it; perhaps a bit Spartan for some tastes, but still a nice touch.

Stock dimensions for the B-S/S are identical for both the 12 and 20-bore at 14¼" x 1 9/16" x 2½"; most shooters should be able to adapt nicely to these measurements. As for weight distribution, the point of balance for the 20-ga. gun with 26" tubes (6¾ pounds, empty) occurs at the front edge of the hinge pin, or 4⅝" ahead of the trigger. This results in just a very slight weight-forward feeling that imparts a measure of steadiness to the muzzles and, in turn, enhances accurate pointing. Muzzle-light guns, with a point of balance behind the hinge pin, will point like lightning, but not always precisely where you want them to—at least that's been my experience.

Based on the fair amount of shooting I've done with the B-S/S in both 12 and 20, I think Browning has struck just the right chord when they say that "hunting is its middle name."

Specifications
Browning B-S/S 20 Gauge Shotgun

Action Type: Boxlock, top-break side-by-side double with selective ejectors, double under-lugs
Chambers: 3"
Barrels & Chokes: 26", IC/M
Trigger: Non-selective single
Sights: Front bead only, nickel silver, .120" dia.
Safety: Top tang slide, automatic
Weight: 6¾ lbs. with 26" bbls. (empty)
Over-all: 42¾" (26" bbls.)
Buttstock & Fore-end: Select European walnut; fluted comb; pistol grip; beavertail fore-end reverse taper; hand-cut checkering; hand-rubbed glossy finish; plastic buttplate
Stock Measurements (Test Gun): Length of pull 14¼"; drop at comb 1 9/16"; drop at heel 2½"; pitch 2"; zero cast-off
Price: $257.50
Mfr: Made by Miroku (Japan) to Browning specs.
Remarks: Offered in Grade I only. Mod./Full choke also available in both 26" and 28" barrels.

Browning's 2000 Gas Autoloader

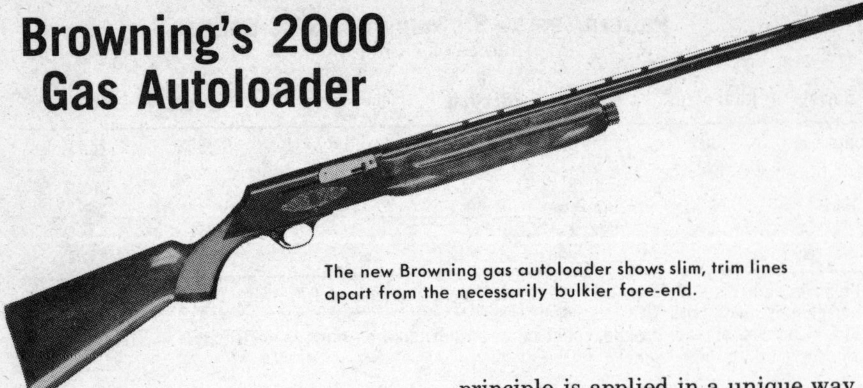

The new Browning gas autoloader shows slim, trim lines apart from the necessarily bulkier fore-end.

There can be no doubt that the biggest piece of news from Browning this year (1974) is the introduction of the Model 2000 gas-operated autoloading shotgun. Many of us knew for quite some time that Browning had a gas gun in the works, and this scribe had expected to be shooting one during the '73 hunting season. But, alas, there were delays. Not that the design hadn't been painstakingly perfected to the Nth degree, but rather the problem was on the manufacturing end. Whatever the specific kinks, these were ironed out in time for the gun to be formally announced at the most recent N.S.G.A. show in Chicago.

From buttplate to muzzle, the B-2000 represents the labor of Val A. Browning. This gun, I am told, has been largely his personal project all the way, from design inception to the production stage. Like the Automatic-5 (A-5), it is being manufactured by Fabrique Nationale in Herstal (Liege), Belgium.

There is a rather strong family resemblance, outwardly, between the new B-2000 and the old A-5. Yes—the square-sterned receiver. This, however, has been modified to a considerable degree on the B-2000, the lines being smoothed out and held closer to what we see on the Browning Automatic Rifle. Some shooters, I suppose, are going to weep and wail and wonder why the old look wasn't completely abandoned in favor of a perfectly streamlined receiver. Personally, I'm glad that things are just the way they are. Anybody who has shot an A-5 for a season or two can attest to the fact that the square stern serves as an excellent visual aid, one that tends to promote highly accurate pointing. I suspect that this is one of the reasons why the A-5 has always been so tremendously popular on the waterfowling front.

The B-2000 gas system is not necessarily unique in principle, but the principle is applied in a unique way. The system, tucked away *inside* the magazine tube, is less susceptible to wet weather, grit and other assorted crud. Like most gas-operated shotguns, powder gas is bled off through a barrel port(s) that coincides with the location of the barrel ring. The B-2000 barrels chambered for 2¾" shells have twin ports about 11¾" ahead of the breech.

The extreme forward portion of the magazine tube itself acts as a gas chamber. The gas enters through a ¼-inch opening on the top side, acting against a piston which, in turn, transmits the force to an inertia piece (collar). The latter connects to twin action bars which are hooked to the bolt slide. This inertia piece, along with the action bars and the action spring for returning the bolt to battery, are all located *outside* the magazine tube.

The gas piston itself travels only a short distance (¹¹⁄₁₆"). Contact with the inertia piece is by means of a gas piston bar positioned crosswise through the magazine tube. The tube is slotted for a short distance at this point to permit the necessary movement of the gas system parts. By means of a valve within the gas piston, excess gas is cleanly vented off forward through the end of the magazine cap.

Self Compensating System

This is a self-compensating system, meaning that absolutely no adjustments are necessary when switching from light to heavy loads, or vice versa. I've fed the GUN DIGEST test gun (a 2¾" chambered barrel) a varied diet ranging from 2¾ DE target loads to 1½-oz. short magnums and not once has this B-2000 complained. All loads, light and heavy, have been digested in stride.

All gas-operated shotguns do a pretty decent job of taming recoil, but in my opinion the B-2000 is really superb in this department. Target loads are a pure joy to shoot, producing only a token buttstock nudge. With field and high-velocity fodder, the apparent recoil is genuinely *soft*, and if baby magnums are your cup of tea you'll find that the B-2000 gas system chops the "tiger" roughly in half. If anybody flinches with this gun, it will be only because of the bang—certainly not the buttstock punch.

It is of special interest to note that the system is buffered by shock-absorbing units to prevent, as Browning puts it, steel from slamming against steel. These units are in the form of thick nylon washers and the gas system has two of them—one in the magazine cap and the other within the gas piston immediately behind the valve. A third unit of block-like configuration is located at the rear of the receiver where it serves to cushion the breech bolt and the slide as these action parts end their rearward travel. Not only do the buffers help to eliminate wear of vital parts, they contribute also to quietness of operation.

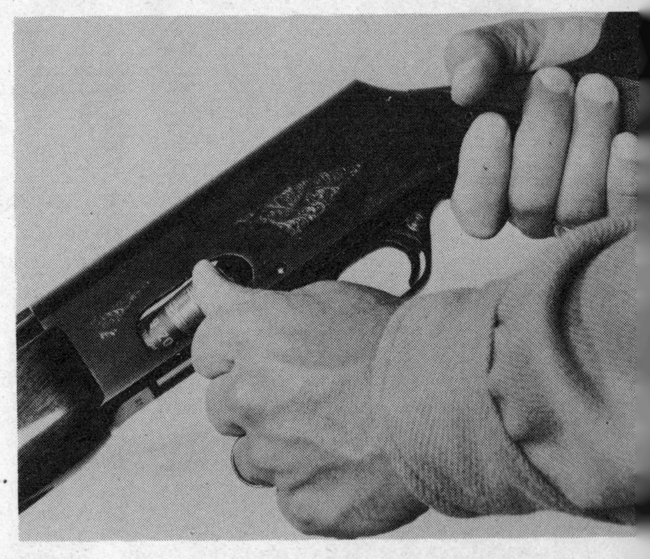

Speed loading the B-2000 is simplicity itself—just shove a shotshell into the port side opening, remove your thumb and Zip!—the mechanism feeds the round into the chamber, closing the bolt.

The gas system is pretty much self-cleaning. Both the gas piston and a companion piece called the gas cylinder plug have surface ridges designed to scrub the walls of the magazine tube. This scrubbing action prevents carbon deposits from accumulating and causing sluggishness. Additionally, the gas is sealed off so that it cannot work to rear and foul the various action parts.

Stripping the gas system is not complicated—with the bolt locked open and the barrel and fore-end removed, the first step is to remove the gas piston bar which extends through the magazine tube. The 6-piece gas system will then be free to move forward out the end of the magazine tube. But watch it here, as the parts are under spring tension, and you'll also want to carefully note the order in which the various parts emerge.

A powder solvent works well for cleaning the parts. However, both the gas piston and the gas cylinder plug are made of bronze, so don't use a steel brush. Use a brass bore brush or an old toothbrush. The parts should be replaced without lubrication, as oil tends to collect foreign matter and may lead to functioning foul-ups.

Browning 2000 Takedown

Disassembly of the B-2000's receiver parts is much less complicated than in the case of the A-5. The receiver contains no screws. There is just one crosspin and when this is removed it frees the trigger group and the whole shootin' match, so to speak. So—stripping the receiver after exposure to wet weather, or at the end of a season of heavy use, takes about one minute's time. The only tool needed is a drift punch or something similar.

One of the B-2000's more exciting design features, in my estimation, and a highly practical approach, too, is that converting a 2¾" chambered gun to handle 3" Magnum loads requires only that the shooter buy an extra interchangeable barrel—not a whole new gun. The basic action functions with either length of shell with no need for alteration; and, as we have already seen, the gas system requires no adjustments for different loads. This, I think you'll agree, amounts to a very large slice of versatility.

The B-2000 bolt locks up at the rear of the barrel extension, the latter being integral with the barrel. The extension is U-notched at the rear to mate with an aligning "finger" positioned on the receiver roof. The bolt carries a single hook-type extractor, while the ejector is simply a shallow shoulder machined into the rear of the barrel extension.

The safety is a conventional cross-bolt design located in the rear of the trigger guard, with the usual red band showing when in the "fire" position. It can be reversed for a left-handed shooter, but Browning suggests turning this task over to a qualified gunsmith.

The ventilated rib represents a departure from past Browning designs in that the support posts are fastened directly to the barrel, there being no base piece. This is more pleasing to the eye—at least to mine—and there is the added bonus of greater space between the rib and the barrel for better dissipation of barrel heat. Perhaps this isn't so awfully important in a field gun, but it's a nice touch just the same.

Browning has always leaned toward rather narrow ribs on their field guns and this one is no exception, its rib width not quite ¼-inch. It's a level rib, its flat surface finely knurled in a crosshatch pattern to suppress glare. Combined with the grooved receiver, even a 26-inch barreled B-2000 offers a sighting plane of 32½". Up front there is a white metal bead of .158" diameter.

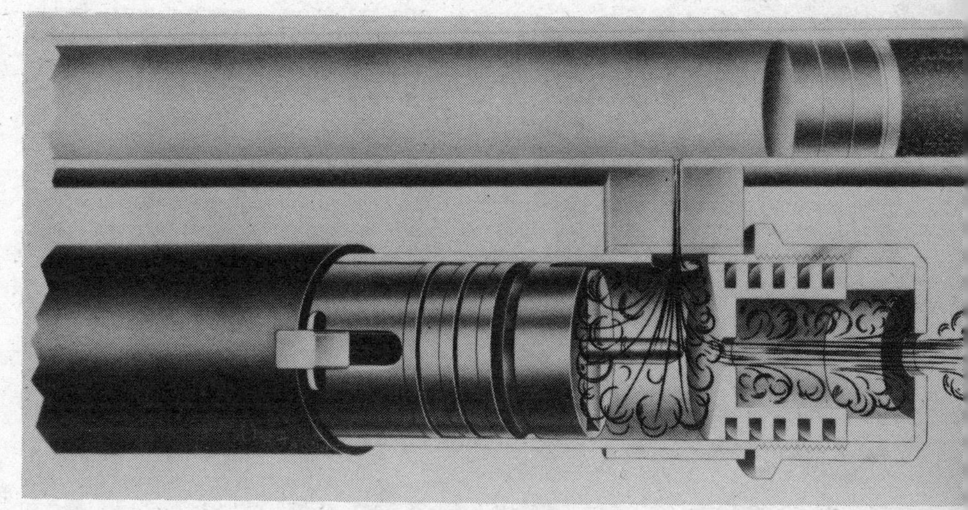

The B-2000 has a self-cleaning gas system. Special ribs, machined into the gas piston and gas-cylinder plug, scrub the walls of the magazine tube, helping to prevent carbon build-up.

Speed Loading System

The B-2000 has a speed-loading system much like that found on the earlier Browning Double Automatic, wherein the loading port is in the left side of the receiver. With the breech bolt locked open, the first shell is shoved into this port-side port and smartly released, whereupon it is instantly transported into the chamber. The magazine is then filled in the usual manner by individually thumbing each shell into the loading port.

But don't get all shook up if the last shell doesn't want to enter the magazine—it's not supposed to! It will remain almost fully exposed to view in the loading port, a position in which it will neither rattle nor fall out, despite appearing somewhat insecurely retained.

There are, of course, two alternate methods of loading the B-2000, both quite conventional practices. A round can be dropped directly into the chamber, the bolt eased down, and the magazine then charged. Or, starting with an empty chamber and a closed bolt, the magazine can be loaded first and a shell chambered by manually cycling the bolt.

But the speed system is a lot faster, more convenient, and there will be situations where it can be used to good advantage. Let's say, for example, that a flock of ducks has just made a pass over the decoys and you have emptied your B-2000, putting two birds down. One, however, only winged, is rapidly swimming to safety. You simply slap a shell into the side loading port and the gun does the rest. You're ready to deal with that cripple—right now!

The bolt release is at the bottom center of the receiver, just forward of the guard. Though diminutive, being only ¼" wide and about ⅛" high, it operates easily and can be quickly found by feel. It will probably take a bit of practice before you're completely at home with it, however.

One thing that may produce a few frowns is the non-ferrous alloy used for the trigger and guard. These parts, however, are beautifully polished and carry a black finish that closely matches the deeply blued receiver.

The trigger pull on the test gun is very good, letting off at 4½ pounds and possessing only a tiny amount of smooth travel. The trigger face is smooth.

Hand Fitted Parts

All critical working parts are said to be hand fitted to insure super-smooth functioning. Except for the breechbolt, operating handle, shell carrier and shell cut-off (which are finished bright), all exposed metal is deeply blued, and the receiver (cold forged from high-grade steel) wears about the same amount of handcut scroll engraving as found on the standard grade A-5.

Barrel metallurgy apparently remains unchanged, with the familiar old "Special Steel" marking that has graced Browning barrels for many decades. The test gun is marked as having a bore diameter of 18.4mm (.724") and my measurements are in close agreement at .725". The choke is of the conical-parallel type, the taper beginning about 3" behind the muzzle and the parallel section roughly 1⅛" long. Muzzle constriction for this 28" full-choke barrel checks out at .034". Pattern testing had to be cancelled in order to meet the deadline for this issue, but what shooting I've done thus far indicates that the tube is performing as marked.

The B-2000 can be taken apart in a minute—a small drift punch is the only tool needed. Barrel, fore-end, the gas system, the double-bar assembly, bolt and bolt slide, trigger group are all removed in this single operation. All parts are fully exposed for a thorough end-of-season cleaning.

With the wooden plug removed, the B-2000 magazine holds four 2¾" shells or three 3" shells, for a total capacity of 5 and 4 rounds respectively. Installation of the magazine plug (or its removal) is handled through the bottom of the receiver and requires removing trigger group first. The plug is then simply pushed through an opening in the magazine follower. To replace the plug, push an empty shell against the follower. This forces the split end of the plug back through the follower opening far enough so that it can be grasped and withdrawn. This is, I must add, one of the easiest magazines to unload I've ever come across among autoloaders, largely because of free access to the shell stop, which pivots down from the center of the bolt slide.

Stock and Fore-end

Tight-grained French walnut is used for stocking the B-2000, with the wood given a scratch and weather-resistant finish said to be hand rubbed for an attractive, high-luster look, which is certainly the case. The pistol grip (not capped) and the hand-filling fore-end are checkered in the double-border style, and I make this out to be 22 lines per inch. The work is of good quality, there being no miscues that I can spot, but I would prefer to have the diamonds pointed up rather than being the flat-topped style they are.

The B-2000 fore-end shows a bit more fullness than does the A-5, made necessary by the inertia piece and the double action bars on the magazine tube. The length is 11⅞" and the wood extends back over the receiver sides a distance of ¼". The bottom is roundish and extensively covered with checkering, while the upper half sweeps inward to provide a wide and comfortable concave area for the thumb and fingers.

The front of the fore-end is reinforced inside with a metal liner, and there is also a rubber bushing which makes contact with the barrel ring. Projecting from the inside rear of the fore-end is a pair of metal tabs, these mating with recesses in the receiver walls to insure proper positioning and anchoring. There is no way this fore-end can shift about or rattle once the magazine cap is tightened down.

As on the A-5, the magazine cap is fully exposed. But, unlike the A-5, there are no receiver tangs extending back into the grip of the stock, since stock joining on the B-2000 is handled by a longitudinal through-bolt.

Stock measurements for the Field gun we are trying run 14⅜"x1½"x2¼", with a downpitch of only ¾" for the 28" barrel. These dimensions don't quite jibe with what the Browning catalog says, but they are reasonably close. The comb is left unfluted and, although it is not a knife-edge comb by any stretch of the imagination, it is definitely less robust than the combs on the Liege and Citori O-U guns. Both the Field and Magnum models are fitted with a hard-rubber buttplate.

B-2000's with vent-rib barrels will range from 7½ pounds for a 26" barrel to 7¾ pounds for a 32" tube. Guns with plain barrels can be expected to run about 3 ounces less.

At this point my shooting with the B-2000 has been limited to busting crows (is there a better test?) and, in my judgement, the gun handles and points in a first-class way. The functioning has been absolutely flawless. The point of balance (for a 28" barrel) occurs one inch forward of the receiver, and I believe most shooters will be satisfied with the weight distribution.

B-2000 Options

At present the B-2000 is offered only in 12 gauge. Although Browning hasn't said so, I think there is probably a good chance that a 20-gauge version will be offered about a year from now. The 2¾" Field model with a plain barrel is $269.50, and $289.50 with a vent-rib barrel. The 3" Magnum model (vent-rib barrels only) also carries a $289.50 tag.

Browning offers a wide choice of interchangeable barrels for the B-2000. Those chambered for the 2¾" shell range from a 26" Cyl to a 32" Full choke, either in plain barrel style (matted sighting plane) or with a vent rib. In the 3" chambering, a Full choke is offered in 28", 30" and 32" lengths, and a Mod choke in 28" only. The plain barrels will sell for $67.50, the vent-rib jobs at $87.50.

Additionally, there will be a 24" Buck Special barrel, fitted with rifle sights, and offered with either a 2¾" or 3" chamber. As this is written, the price has not been announced.

Claybirders, too, will soon be having their innings with the B-2000, as Browning has announced that trap and Skeet guns will become available about mid-1974. These will have specially designed recoil pads, special stock dimensions, beavertail fore-ends, and front and center ivory beads. Prices haven't as yet been firmed up.

Right about now many of you are probably wondering about the future of the recoil-operated A-5, now that the new B-2000 is waltzing down the pike. I put this question to Ted Collins, late chief of Browning's public relations division, and was told that the A-5 will be kept in production. But Ted didn't say for how long, so if you want one for your collection, now's the time to act. Val Browning's Double Automatic was retired a few years back, and it wouldn't surprise me to see the A-5 turned out to pasture by the time this decade takes its curtain call.

BROWNING *Liège*

When I showed Browning's new Liege (pronounced Lee-áge) to a small gathering of shotgunners last summer, one of them persisted in referring to the gun as a "junior grade" Superposed. He was both right and wrong—in terms of outward appearance, the Liege is almost a mirror image of its famous stablemate, but behind that familiar profile and beneath that high-grade fit and finish there are a great many differences—some major, some minor. So it would be much more correct to say that the Liege represents a new design, than to label it as a modification of the Superposed.

Produced in Belgium by FN and introduced to these shores in 1973, the Liege came about because of Browning's desire to market a high-quality O-U at a more palatable price. The Superposed is costly to make; its current retail base price is, indeed, a sobering one. With Grade I guns starting at $780, ('74 prices), it is mostly only those Bwana types who can really afford one.

If Browning was to meet its goal, then manufacturing shortcuts would have to be implemented, but to do so without sacrificing quality and operational excellence in any way meant that there would have to be sweeping changes in design. The Liege is the culmination of all this, but I rather doubt that the final price tag represents all that Browning had hoped for. The Liege was introduced at $472.50, with an increase to $494.50 shortly thereafter.

Lest there be any misunderstanding, the Liege is *not* intended as a replacement for the Superposed. The latter will remain very much in production, and in its present form.

Some design differences between the two guns are immediately discernible; others are not. One of the most obvious involves the take-down. The Superposed breaks down into two units, with the fore-end remaining attached to the barrels. The Liege is more conventional—the fore-end disengages from the barrels for a 3-piece take-down. The Liege fore-end release, also different, is a rotary-type latch recessed into the belly of the wood, and one that obviates the need for precision inletting.

Another obvious difference is that the Liege frame is fully enclosed on the bottom side. In other words, there are no "windows" to accommodate the barrel lumps, nor is there a "trapdoor" opening in connection with the cocking system.

Like the Superposed, the Liege is built around a boxlock action, and the breech lock-up is similarly handled by an under-bolt which moves longitudinally to engage the rear barrel lump. But a difference in the cocking system between the two guns necessitated a change in the width of the locking bolt and a minor change in the rear lump. Instead of a single centrally-positioned cocking arm, the Liege employs individual cocking rods (which also actuate the ejector sears), these rods flanking the bolt along the bottom of the frame and thus limiting bolt width to 5/8". The rear lump is of matching width, and bolt contact is a 100% proposition because the center of the locking surface does not have to be cut away to make room for the cocking lever as is the case with the Superposed.

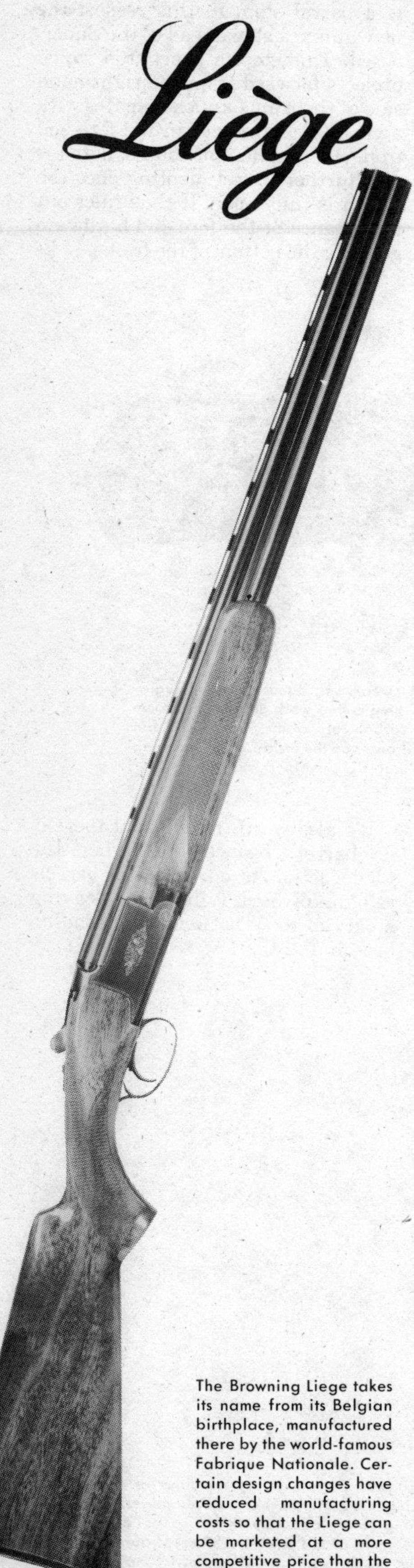

The Browning Liege takes its name from its Belgian birthplace, manufactured there by the world-famous Fabrique Nationale. Certain design changes have reduced manufacturing costs so that the Liege can be marketed at a more competitive price than the Browning Superposed.

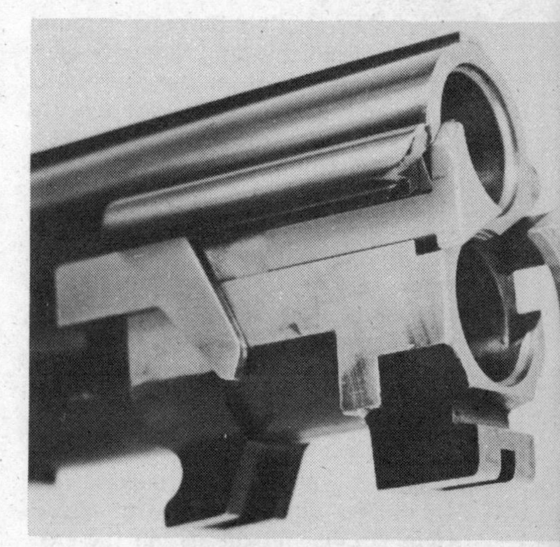

Like the famous Superposed, the Liege is an under-bolted gun, the bolt engaging a cut in the rear barrel lump. But on the Liege (shown here) the rear lump is less wide, made necessary because of a different cocking system. The Liege ejectors are of 2-piece design, but the camming surfaces on the forward section are shaped differently from those on the Superposed.

Despite these differences in the cocking and bolting system, frame dimensions are practically the same for these two Browning stack-barrel guns. The Liege frame depth at the standing breech is 2 11/16"; width is 1 9/16".

Still another major difference between the two guns, and one that doesn't readily come to light, involves the joining of the barrels at the breech. The Superposed lumps are integral with the lower barrel, the two tubes held together by soft solder. Barrel joining for the Liege, on the other hand, can be described as a semi-monoblock approach.

The breech end of the under barrel is inserted into a sleeve-like unit of which the two lumps are an integral part. The upper surface of this unit is a flat-bottomed, V-shaped channel which cradles the top barrel. At this critical point the barrels are silver soldered. The side ribs, however, are attached with soft solder. Why this modified system won approval over regular monoblock construction I do not know. Perhaps it makes the job of barrel alignment a bit less of a chore.

A small difference is seen in the stock joining. The Liege buttstock is, of course, retained by a husky longitudinal through-bolt which mates with a vertical post between the frame tangs, this post being an integral part of the frame. For the Superposed, the post is not integral, being held in position between the tangs by a pair of screws.

Another small difference is found in the ejector system. Selective ejectors are standard on the Liege O-U and their design and operation are basically the same as for the Superposed, with the two-piece ejectors traveling in dovetail slots in the barrel flats. The design variation involves the forward part of the ejector, which works against camming surfaces on the frame wall to give primary extraction and to cock the ejector hammers. These camming sections are simply of a different shape, with corresponding changes in the camming shoulders within the frame.

The Liege ejectors elevate the shells 5/32" during primary extraction. On closing the action the ejectors are seated by camming action so that they do not drag down against the action face. As with the Superposed, the ejector hammers, sears and coil springs are housed within the fore-end and, should tuning or cleaning become necessary, these parts and their framework can be easily removed as a single unit. Simply turning out two screws completely frees the unit from the forearm.

Like the Superposed, the Liege has a selective single trigger, the barrel selector switch being the same for both guns; this is incorporated with the thumbslide safety on the top tang. The triggers differ in type, however, with an inertial system used on the Superposed and a mechanical system on the Liege, the latter not being dependent on recoil to shift from one sear to the other.

The trigger pulls for the test gun are very good, these weighing 3½ and 3¾ pounds regardless of the barrel firing order. Both, however, have just a very small amount of smooth travel preceding let-off.

An interesting feature of the Liege is a barrel stop; in this respect the new gun is a step ahead of the Superposed. This stop, a short stud which projects forward from the right-hand side of the frame knuckle, mates with a closed-end channel in the fore-end iron. It's function, of course, is to arrest further barrel pivoting once the action is fully open. It thus rules out any chance of the fore-end hardware gouging the bottom of the frame.

The Liege O-U (offered in Grade I only) wears only a touch of scroll engraving on the sides of the frame, plus simple line work around the frame edges. Outwardly, it is pretty much a carbon copy of the Superposed, but there are a number of mechanical differences on the inside. The checkering is nicely done, well laid out, the grip curve not overtight.

It's also worth noting that there is no barrel "bounce-back" when the Liege action is opened. The barrels remain pivoted fully down, leaving plenty of room between the standing breech and the lower barrel for easy

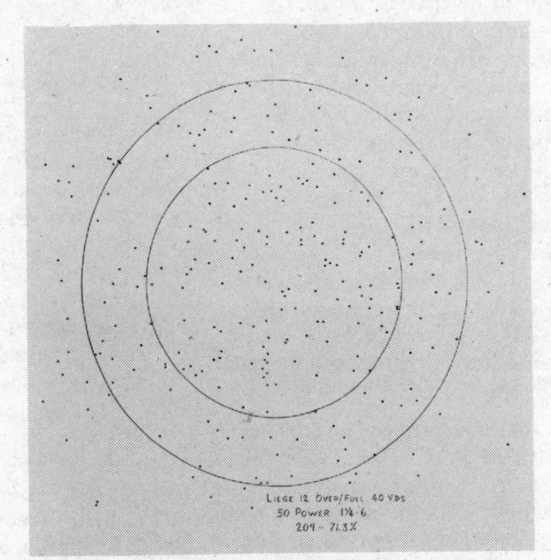

Pattern width at 40 yards ranged from 40" to 44" when the Liege full-choke barrel was teamed with the Browning 50 Power load—1¼ ozs. No. 6. The average was 68.8%, with all patterns showing dense centers such as this one (71.3%); the 20" core contains 39 more hits than the 5" annular area.

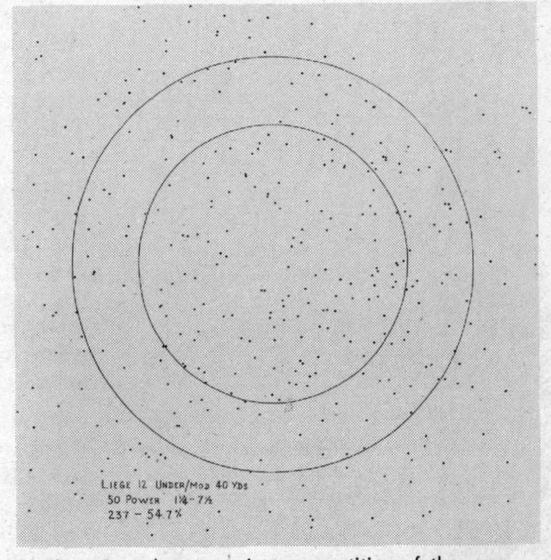

This 40-yard pattern is representitive of the way the Liege modified-choke barrel digested the Browning Power loading with 1¼ ozs. of No. 7½. The 20" core of this 54.7% (237 count) spread has slightly higher density (31 pellets) than the 5" annular area. The average for 5 shots was 56%.

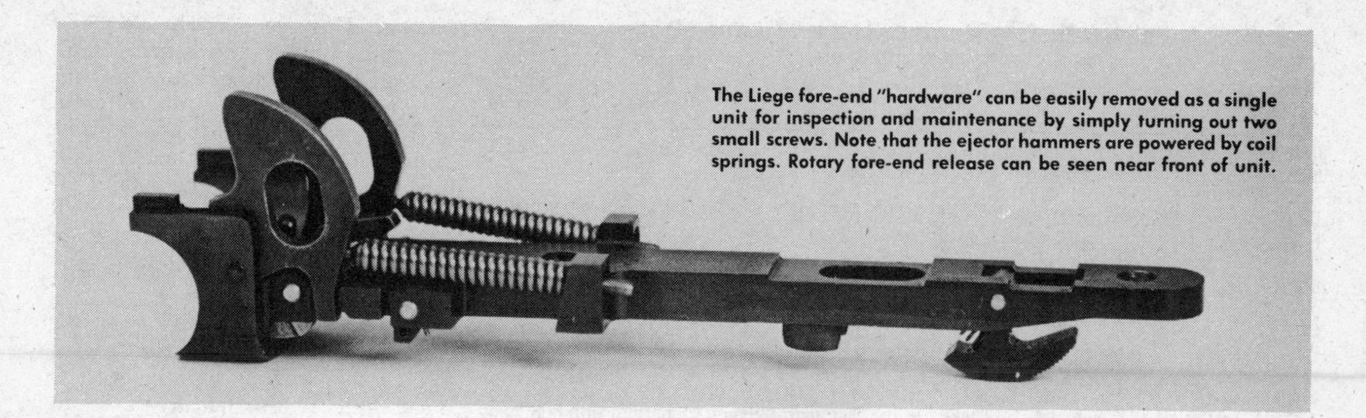

The Liege fore-end "hardware" can be easily removed as a single unit for inspection and maintenance by simply turning out two small screws. Note that the ejector hammers are powered by coil springs. Rotary fore-end release can be seen near front of unit.

loading and unloading.

Like the Superposed, the Liege has wooden "spacers" that are screw-fastened to each side rib to fill the gutter openings at the tip of the fore-end.

The Liege is currently available only in 12 gauge and only as a Grade I gun, and it's not likely that this situation will change. There is a Magnum 12 model chambered for 3" shells and equipped with a recoil pad. Barrel length for the Magnum is limited to 30" and the choke combinations are Full/Full and Mod/Full.

The Field model has 2¾" chambers, a plastic buttplate, and barrel lengths of 26½" or 28". Both barrel lengths are offered with Full/Full, Mod./Full or I.C./Mod. choke combinations.

A ventilated rib is standard on both the Magnum and Field guns, offering a dead-level sighting plane. The flat surface is cut with closely-spaced wavy lines that do a very good job of knocking out reflected light. The rib has no taper, the width running .275" or about 9/32", breech to muzzle. The openings between the rib supports are 1⅜".

One of the differences between the Liege and the Superposed is seen in the fore-end release. The recessed release for the Liege, here pictured, is a spring-loaded rotary-type latch with deep serrations for ease of operation. Rearward rotation releases the fore-end.

Our test gun is a Field Model with 28" barrels bored Mod./Full. Empty, it weighs 7⅝ pounds, which is some 3 ounces heavier than Browning's cataloged weight. With 26½" tubes the Liege is said to run 7¼ pounds; the Magnum model is listed at 7⅞ pounds.

Browning shotgun bores traditionally run on the tight side of standard, and the Liege is no exception. The tubes are marked as having bore diameters of 18.4mm (.724"). Measurements taken with an internal dial caliper gauge at two points (5" from the breech and 5" from the muzzle) were in complete agreement with the barrel markings. I also found muzzle roundness to be excellent for both bores, the variation not exceeding .001". Forcing cone length is about one-half inch.

Browning has always been a stickler for spit and polish and their shotgun bores certainly reflect this policy. They're smooth, gleamingly bright

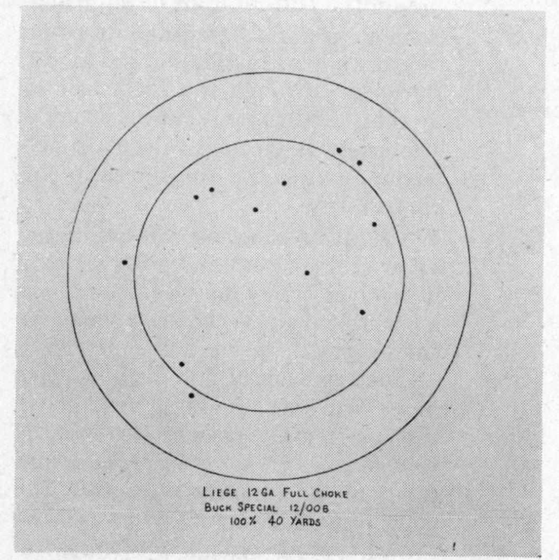

Using the Liege full-choke barrel, the average 40-yard dispersion for 5 shots with the Buck Special 00B loading was 25½". This 100 percent pattern is typical of its pellet distribution. Here the main cluster of 33-caliber pellets printed just above the point of hold.

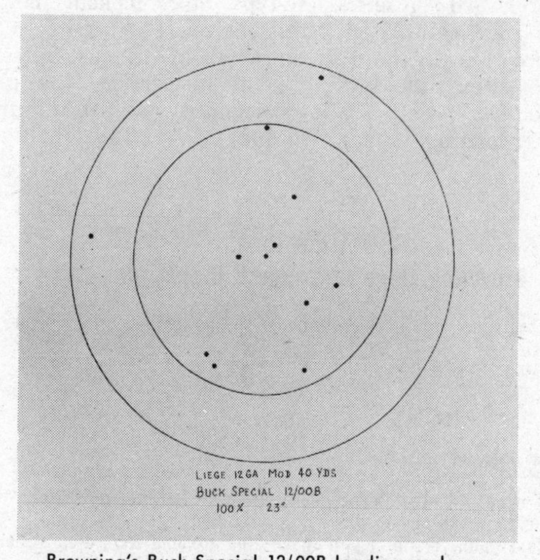

Browning's Buck Special 12/00B loading made an excellent showing out of the Liege O-U. Shown here is a 100% pattern fired at 40 yards from the modified-choke barrel. Note the deadly cluster of 6 hits in the center and very close to the point of hold. All 12 pellets stayed within 23".

Pattern Tests—Browning Liege 12 Gauge O-U

(Average of 5 Shots)

Barrel	Range/Yds.	Load	D. 20" circle	D. 30" circle	E. 30" circle	EDV 30" circle
Under Mod.	40	50 Power Max.-1¼-7½ (433)	137	242	56.0%	54/12.5%
Over Full	40	50 Power Max.-1¼-6 (293)	118	201	68.8%	30/10.2%
Under Mod.	40	Buck Spl 12/00B	---	11.4	95.0%	1/ 8.4%
Over Full	40	Buck Spl 12/00B	---	11.8	98.3%	1/ 8.4%

Remarks: Barrels, 28". Mod. barrel has a bore diameter of .724", with .020" of choke. Full barrel has a bore diameter of .724", with .042" of choke. For the Mod. barrel, the 40-yd. pattern with 00B loads averaged 27.3", maximum 33", minimum 20.5". The Full barrel with 00B averaged 25.5", maximum 34.5", minimum 21.25".
EDV = Extreme spread in pellet count between individual patterns. D = Density. E = Efficiency.

and above criticism. The Liege chokes are of the conical-parallel type, with the taper beginning about 2⅝" behind the muzzle for both barrels of the test gun. Choke constriction for the Mod. (under) barrel amounts to .020", while that for the Full (over) barrel is .042".

Barrel alignment was checked simultaneously with patterning; shooting from a sandbagged rest minimized possible human error in pointing. Using a down-the-rib sight picture, the under barrel was absolutely dead-on at 40 yards; the top barrel, same distance, centered its spread some 3-4 inches higher. Both tubes were on the nose in the horizontal plane.

Teaming the under barrel with Browning's 50 Power 3¾x1¼x7½ loading, the average for a 5-shot string at 40 yards was 56% (see pattern summary table). This, of course, meets the Browning standard of 45% to 55% for a Mod-choke barrel. All patterns showed slightly higher pellet density in the 20" core than in the 5" annular area, the actual difference averaging just under 4%.

With the 50 Power loading, 1¼ ozs. No. 6, the tightly-choked over barrel averaged 68.8% for a 5-shot test at 40 yards. These patterns opened from 40" to 44" and were characterized by a 6% difference in pellet density between the 20" core and the 5" annular area—the greater number of hits printing in the center, of course.

I'll have more to say later about the Browning shotshell line, but for now I'd just like to point out that the Liege test gun showed a strong liking for the Buck Special loading—12 pellets of #00 Buck. Averaging 95% at 40 yards, the Mod. tube held the big 33-caliber pellets to a 27.3" spread, while the Full tube went 98.3% for an average dispersion of 25½". Strong medicine, indeed, for thick-cover whitetails!

Like all Browning scatterguns, the Liege is nicely stocked. The wood is straight-grained French Walnut, dressed up with 22-line-inch hand-cut checkering, the finish a modern glossy-type. Stock measurements for the test gun are 14¼" x 1½" x 2½", and there's about 3/16" cast-off.

Oval in section, the pistol grip (not capped) has a minimum circumference of 5". The "medium" curve feels good to the hand but, equally important it keeps one's second finger from crowding the rear of the trigger guard where it might get painfully banged when firing heavy loads. The comb of the stock is left quite full, and that's good. The comb fluting, however, is not particularly well done, to my thinking. But this, of course, is purely a cosmetic thing.

Browning describes the Liege fore-end as a "sure grip" field type. It's somewhat flattish across the bottom, then tapers inward slightly over its upper half. It also features a slight upsweep at the forward end. At 10½" long and a maximum depth of 2⅛", there's plenty of wood to fill the hand; both sides are well covered with checkering. All in all, it's a good front handle, though this shooter would have preferred less checkering on the sides and more on the bottom.

As for fit and finish in general, I see no need to belabor matters with a big song and dance. It is enough to say that Browning has a huge reputation to uphold, and they are not about to jeopardize this position with penny-pinching craftsmanship.

Being of Grade I social stature, the Liege is not smothered with ornamentation. The engraving consists of a small amount of nicely executed scroll work on the sides of the frame, on the trigger guard and on the top lever. The hinge-pin faces are covered with a floral pattern.

The top lever thumbpiece is checkered, and the thumbslide safety/barrel selector is serrated for non-slip control. In addition to the usual barrel markings, the name *Liege* appears in script-like lettering above *Browning* on the bottom front of the frame.

As a check on handling and pointing, as well as functioning, 250 rounds were shot through the Liege at clay targets—without one iota of trouble! The selective ejectors worked to perfection, and so did the selective single trigger.

All of this shooting was done from a low-gun position and a big share of it involved tricky doubles tossed from a portable trap. My scores, though far from perfect, were consistently good, and on the basis of this the Liege gets more than just a passing grade from this quarter. Others who also shot the test gun are in close agreement that the gun is a natural pointer. The point of balance with 28" barrels, by the way, occurs roughly ⅜" ahead of the hinge-pin center, contributing a touch of muzzle steadiness; this I believe, is a good compromise when the gun may see duty both in the game fields and on the clay-target range.

Specifications
Browning Liege 12 Gauge O-U Shotgun

Action Type: Boxlock, break-action over-under with under bolting and selective ejectors
G Chambers: 2¾" and 3"
Barrels & Chokes: 28", Mod. (U) & F (O)
Trigger: Selective single
Sights: Front bead only, nickel silver, .155" dia.
Safety: Top tang slide; non-automatic
Weight: 7⅝ lbs. with 28" bbls. (empty)
Over-all: 45" (28" bbls.)
Buttstock & Fore-End: French walnut; fluted comb; pistol grip; full fore-end; hand-cut checkering; hand-rubbed glossy finish; plastic buttplate
Stock Measurements (Test Gun): Length of pull 14¼"; drop at comb 1½"; drop at heel 2½"; down pitch 2 3/16"; cast-off 3/16"
Price: $494.50 (all models)
Mfr: Made in Belgium by FN
Remarks: The Liege is offered in 12 ga. and Grade I only. The Magnum model (for 3" shells) has a recoil pad and 30" barrels choked F/F or M/F. The Standard model (2¾" chambers) is offered with 26½" or 28" barrels, the choke options F/F, M/F or IC/M.

Browning Citori Over-Under

In 1973 we had Watergate, but history of note was made on other fronts as well. The Liege, appearing early in the year, had hardly been assigned space in gunshop racks before the Citori came along in late summer, asking for equal rights. It's a story of East meeting West under the same banner, for the Citori is made not in Belgium, but in Japan by Miroku, manufacturers of the B-S/S double gun.

As viewed from this quarter, it appears that Browning has finally brought about that long-sought happy marriage of good quality and within-reach price. Surely the Citori is destined for great things, like cutting a wide swath through enemy lines, because the $325 ticket won't send the prospective O-U buyer to bed with a case of the galloping chills.

When introduced, the Citori was offered only as a 12-ga. Field model with a choice of 26", 28" and 30" barrels. Although not designated a Magnum model, the 30" barreled gun had 3-inch chambers, the choke combinations being Full/Full and Mod/Full. The 26" and 28" barreled guns carried standard 2¾" chambers, and either could be had with Mod./Full or I.C./Mod. chokes.

This year (1974), and largely because of the way the Citori quickly captured shooter acceptance, other models and gauges are being offered. Trap and Skeet guns in 12 gauge will become available about mid-year, as will a 20-ga. Field model. Also, all 12-ga. Field guns will now have 3-inch chambers. As before, all guns, 12s and 20s alike, will have a White Line recoil pad by Pachmayr.

Although the Citori test gun was a magnum model with 30" tubes, the author found it handled well for long-range upland shooting. Many sharptails and China birds were collected with this newest Browning over-under.

As this is written full particulars on these '74 additions haven't been released. We do know, however, that the Citori trap gun will have a specially-dimensioned Monte Carlo stock and that its recoil pad will be of trap styling. The 30" ventilated-rib barrel will wear ivory beads front and center, and there will be three choke combinations—(Full/Full, I.M./Full and Mod./Full). The price will run $335.

Tagged at $5 less, the Skeet model will have 26" and 28" barrels, specially bored for this clay-target game. It will also have front and center ivories on the vent rib, and it will carry a Skeet-style recoil pad.

According to a Browning representative, the Citori Field model 20 is a gun that "will steal your heart away." Not having seen one as yet, I'll have to take his word. At any rate, the 20 will have 3-inch chambers, barrel lengths of 26" and 28" and a choice of Mod./Full and I.C./Mod. chokes. The price, $325.

I don't know what your reaction will be, but in my book the Citori is a helluva lot of shootin' iron for the money. It's crafted from high-strength steels and quality wood; its lines are as functional as they are attractive; it's not lacking in the area of fit and finish; and certainly it's built around a time-tested action known for operational excellence. If I seem to be waxing enthusiastic, it's not because I'm bucking for sergeant. I've lived with the Citori for a few months, have shot a fair amount of game with the gun and, frankly, I'm impressed.

In many ways the Citori is pure Superposed—a close pattern in terms of basic design. It has inherited the Superposed bolting system, the cocking system, the same open-bottom type frame, the inertia-type single trigger, the ejector system, and the combination manual safety and barrel selector. Even the barrel joining is the same. This is not to say that parts are interchangeable between the two guns, but there is certainly no question as to its ancestry. We can truly say, in this instance, that the

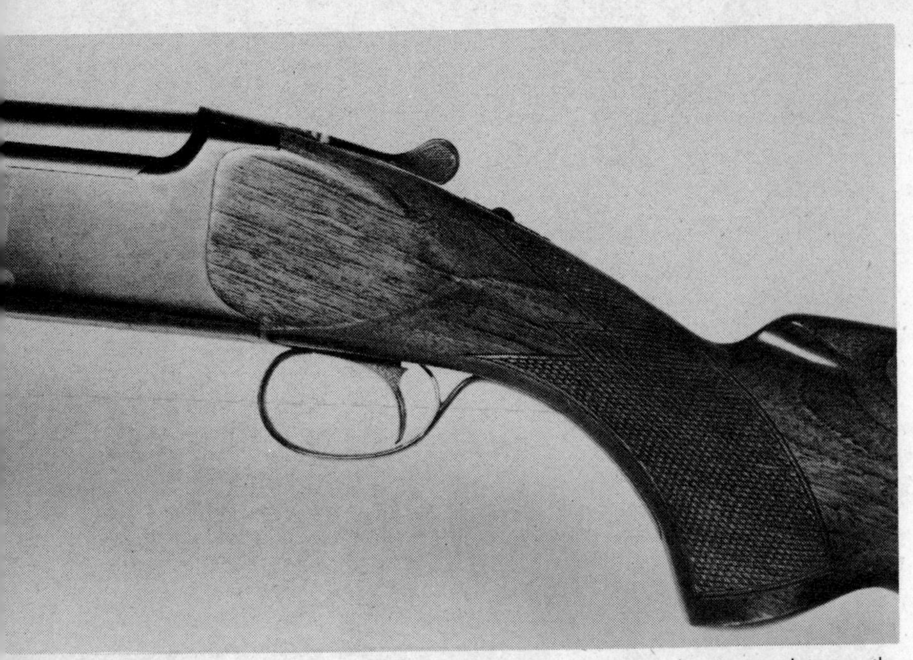

The Citori's pistol grip is comfortably shaped and it's dimensioned to accommodate even the ham-handed shooter. But if you're looking for engraving, you're out of luck. The frame is strictly Plain Jane. The hand-cut checkering on the Citori is of excellent quality—clean and deep, the diamonds nicely pointed. Running 16 lines per inch on the pistol grip, and 18 lines on the fore-end, the work is both decorative and highly functional. The comb-nose fluting is well handled.

gun is a "junior grade" Superposed.

That the Citori evolved as such isn't really surprising. After all, Miroku had already logged many years of building stack-barrel guns in the image of Browning's famous Belgian-made O-U. With this background in mind it's likely that only a few changes in extant tooling were necessary to get the Citori into production.

There are, however, a number of differences between the Citori and its upper-crust cousin. The Citori frame is a bit shorter—about 5/16". You'll also notice on the Citori that the rear of the fore-end is fully shod so that all contact with the frame is a steel-to-steel proposition.

The Citori has bushed and spring-loaded firing pins, accessible through the action face, which the Superposed doesn't. If a firing pin should break, or if the firing pin hole should enlarge after extensive use, replacement of these parts is no big deal.

In the fired position the hammers remain at rest against the firing pins, holding them slightly above the action face more or less in contact with the indented primer. Such a situation has been known to cause a problem—that of the action being "sticky" on opening. But apparently the Citori firing pins are set at an angle that totally precludes this, as no trouble of this nature was experienced with the test gun.

A not-so-small difference between the Citori and other Browning O-Us involves fore-end styling. In Browning's words it's a "hunting beavertail," which description really doesn't do justice to the splendid design. As on the B-S/S double, it has a reverse taper, broadening from 1¾" near the rear to a full 2" up front. The belly is slightly flattish, the upper sides "sculptured" with finger grooves measuring a full inch wide. The lower sides and bottom are almost completely wrapped in cleanly cut checkering. Superb control during pointing and recoil are its biggest assets.

The Citori fore-end release parallels that found on the Superposed, being a finger-lift, lever-type latch. Take-down, on the other hand, follows the Liege, with the fore-end disengaging from the barrels. Nor does the Citori have those wooden "spacers" to close the gap between the fore-end tip and the barrels—a small loss at best.

A ventilated rib is standard on the Citori and, on my 30" barreled Field gun, the width is 5/16". Offering a dead-level sighting plane, it has a flat surface which is cut with fine-line crosshatching to reduce glare—and no burrs or rough edges here. The

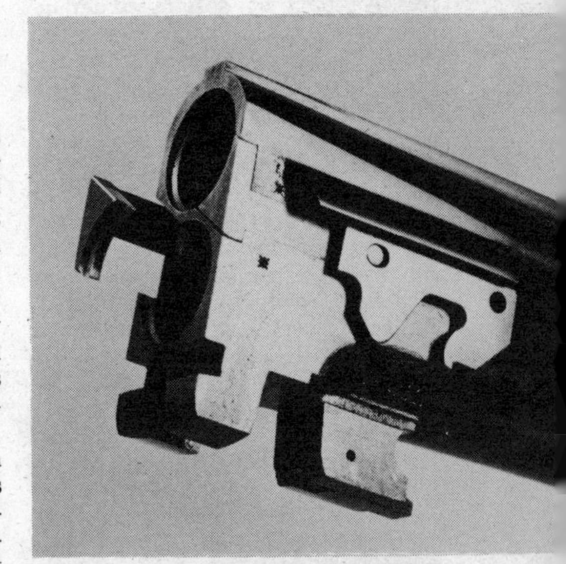

In many ways the relationship between the Citori and the Superposed is a close one. Basically, the ejectors are of the same design, and the rear lump is divided below the locking-bolt cut so as to clear the cocking lever. Even the method of barrel joining at the breech parallels the Superposed.

supports, 1 7/16" apart on centers, are integral with the top and bottom portions of the rib. Soft solder ties it all together. It will be interesting to see what the rib variations will be, if any, on the forthcoming Trap and Skeet models.

The Citori shows very good hand-cut checkering, which I make out to be a 16-line-inch job on the pistol grip, and with 16 or 18 lines on the fore-end. At any rate, it's cleanly cut and the diamonds are nicely

Pattern Tests—Browning Citori 12 Gauge O-U
(Average of 5 Shots)

Barrel	Range/Yds.	Load	D. 20" circle	D. 30" circle	E. 30" circle	EDV 30" circle
Under Full	40	60 Power Max.-1⅞-4 (250)	133	199	79.6%	11/ 4.4%
Under Full	40	60 Power Max.-1⅞-2 (166)	84	128	77.5%	23/13.9%
Over Full	40	60 Power Max.-1⅞-4 (250)	126	197	78.8%	23/ 9.2%
Over Full	40	60 Power Max.-1⅞-2 (166)	73	122	73.8%	34/20.5%

Remarks: Barrels, 30", 3" chambers. The Under barrel has a bore diameter of .724", with .034" of choke. The Over barrel bore runs .726", with .034" of choke.
EDV = Extreme spread in pellet count between individual patterns. D = Density. E = Efficiency.

pointed up for a sure-grip surface. However, there is a runover here and there between the double borders but, quite honestly, these slip-ups are hard to spot without magnification.

The gun, stocked with good, tight-grained walnut, is sealed with a weatherproof (glossy) finish that promises to stand up well to field-use knocks. The comb of the stock is left quite broad and it is attractively fluted—much more so than on the Liege. Stock measurements for the test gun are 14¼"x1⅝"x2⅜" with about ⅛" of cast-off.

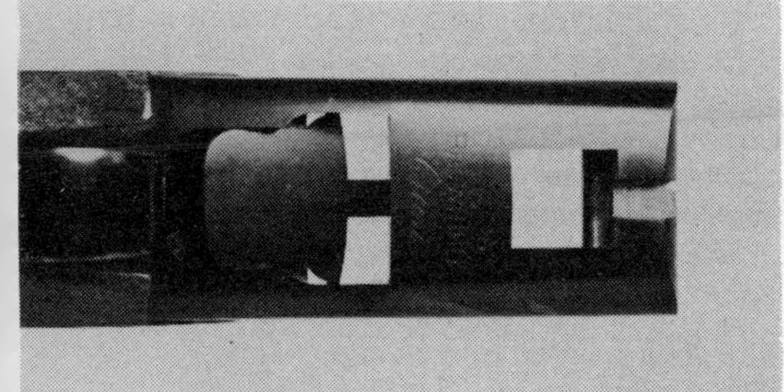

This bottom view of the Citori frame shows another way in which the Superposed design is followed. The front "window" accommodates the forward or hinge-pin lump, while the other opening takes the rear lump. The "trapdoor" at the rear is part of the cocking system.

Most any size hand should find the Citori pistol grip comfortable. Its circumference at midpoint is 5", and its length along the bottom of the curve from trigger to butt is also 5". Happily, the curve does not hook too sharply, and in this respect it strikes me as being near perfect for a single-trigger gun.

A through-bolt ties the buttstock to the action and the wood-to-metal fit cannot be faulted. But in keeping with what seems a common practice nowadays, the wood is left noticeably higher than the frame sides, rather than being a flush fit. This draws criticism from some, but when you consider that after long and hard use the stock might be in need of refinishing, then a little surplus wood isn't really such a bad idea. Too, in certain cases, the wood might shrink a bit.

The Citori's barrels and frame are richly blued, and it's obvious that Miroku, prior to this operation, expends a lot of elbow grease in cleaning up the metal and polishing it. But brace yourself—the frame is totally without engraving. This barebones approach is one way, I suppose, that helps Browning keep the price tag competitive.

Chrome-moly steel is used for barreling the Citori, and the chambers and bores have a finish that's fully up to Browning standards. Slick! In checking out the test gun's 30" F/F barrels, inside measurements at the muzzles disclosed a difference of .002", but because of a like difference in bore diameters (.724" and .726"), both tubes carry .034" of choke.

The chokes, of the conical-parallel type, start roughly 3¾" behind the muzzles. The forcing cones just ahead of the 3-inch chambers are approximately 11/16" long. Muzzle roundness again earns a triple-A rating, with less than .001" variation in inside diameter.

As part of the Citori test program, I had in mind a good bit of duck and goose shooting, so the patterning tests were carried out at 40 yards using Browning's heaviest loading—the 60 Power 3-incher with 1⅞ ozs. of shot. Five rounds each of 4s and 2s were put through both barrels.

This particular gun shows a preference for 4s, but the next like-bored Citori off the shelf might do its best work with 2s. With the 1⅞x4 loading the under barrel printed a very tight 79% average; the over barrel did about the same, averaging a fraction over 78%. (See pattern summary table.) All patterns showed strong pellet density in the center of the spread. The under barrel, for example, put 53% into the 20" core, while the over barrel placed 50% in the same area.

These strong dense-center patterns would be a disadvantage for any shooting under 50 yards but, beyond that distance, say for long-range pass shooting, this kind of pellet distribution really pays off.

The Citori under barrel did quite well with the 1⅞x2 loading, printing a 40-yard average of 77%, with 50% clustering in the 20" core. The over barrel, on the other hand, dropped to 73% and pellet distribution was on the erratic side, ranging from a balanced spread to a strong center density.

Both barrels shot to pretty much the same point of hold. Firing with the fore-end hand resting on a sandbag, the downstairs tube centered its pattern dead-on with the eye seeing about 1/16" of rib and the front bead covering the 2½" aiming marker. As was expected, the top barrel registered just a few inches higher with the same sight picture. This small difference is of absolutely no consequence in the field.

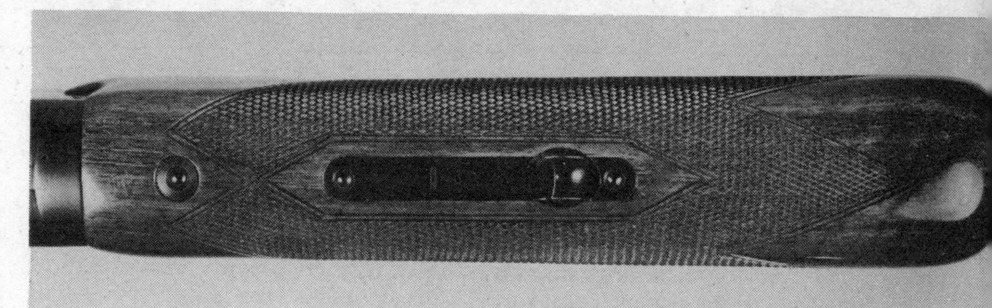

The Citori fore-end is described by Browning as a "hunting beavertail." Like that for the B-S/S double, it has a reverse taper which helps the left hand absorb some of the recoil. The fore-end release is similar to that found on the Superposed.

With the test gun weighing 7⅞ lbs. (empty), apparent recoil while pattern testing with the 1⅞-oz. blockbusters was quite stiff. But in the field, hammering at passing mallards,

Specifications

Browning Citori 12 Gauge O-U Shotgun

Action Type: Boxlock, break-action over-under with under-bolting and selective ejectors
Chambers: 3" for Field model; 2¾" for trap and skeet models
Barrels & Chokes: 26", 28", and 30"; Field model with F/F, M/F, IC/M; Trap model F/F, IM/F, M/F; Skeet model with special Skeet boring
Trigger: Selective single
Sights: Field model, nickel silver front bead only; trap and skeet models have ivory beads front and center
Safety: Top tang slide; non-automatic
Weight: 7⅞ lbs. (Field model with 30" bbls.)
Over-all Length: 47" for 30" bbls.
Buttstock & Fore-end: Select, tight-grained walnut; pistol grip; fluted comb; beavertail fore-end; hand-cut checkering; high-luster weatherproof finish; "White Line" recoil pad
Stock Measurements (test gun): Length of pull 14¼"; drop at comb 1⅝"; drop at heel 2⅜"; down pitch 2⅛"; cast-off ⅛"
Price: Field model $325; Skeet $330; Trap $335
Mfr: Made by Miroku (Japan) to Browning specs.
Remarks: Vent. rib standard on all models. Skeet and trap models have specially dimensioned buttstocks and specially styled recoil pads. A 20-ga. Field model with 3" chambers will become available by mid-1974.

recoil with these same loads seemed mild in comparison. I would say that even a recoil-sensitive shooter should be able to hack this 30″ barreled Citori with the less authoritative 1⅝-oz. loads.

Although I'd intended to do a lot of waterfowling with the Citori, as it turned out I did more shooting on the upland species. In mid-September, for example, I spent a few days gunning for sharp-tailed grouse in western South Dakota. The Citori went along, intended only as a spare gun, because weather and cover conditions at the start of the season usually result in close-flushing birds that can easily be handled with an I.C./Mod. boring. But the weather did an about-face. A chilly north wind teamed up with overcast skies, and the birds, instead of sticking to the brush pockets, moved out into the open grass where they were as spooky as the proverbial March hare. With kill distances averaging close to 50 yards, the Citori with its tight chokes saved the trip. In fact, the gun handled and pointed so nicely that I stuck with it for our third day of shooting when both the weather and the birds had settled down to normal.

Later, as the season wore on, the Citori accounted for a variety of ducks, a few geese, and quite a number of pheasants that got in my way while I was prowling favored wetlands. During this workout in the field, using a variety of Browning ammo and handloads, the selective single trigger never once balked. The pulls, by the way, weigh 5 and 5¾ pounds for the under-over firing order. For the reverse sequence, they weigh an even 5/5.

Nor was there any problem with the ejector system. Fired hulls were tossed well clear of the gun, while primary extraction of live rounds amounts to a 3/16″ lift. As mentioned previously, the action opened freely, with no tendency for the firing pins to hang in the primer indentations.

With 30″ barrels, the point of balance occurs 6½″ ahead of the trigger, or 1½″ ahead of the hinge pin, all of which results in a moderate weight-forward situation that serves well in taking the kinks out of one's swing on high-balling waterfowl. This point of balance would, with the shorter 26″ and 28″ tubes, shift to the rear, closer to the hinge pin, and would be more in line with what some shooters prefer for upland work.

The only thing about the Citori that ruffles my feathers, and then only in a subjective way, is the non-automatic (manual type) safety. I can well appreciate the advantage of a manual system on a gun that's to be chiefly used for trap or skeet, but on an over-under or side-by-side bonafide field gun my vote goes to the automatic type. I suppose that in the final analysis it boils down to what each individual shooter has become accustomed to, and apparently Browning, in opting for the manual safety, felt that the majority would be pleased. You can't really blame 'em for that.

Power Rated Shotshells

For over 70 years Browning shotguns have accepted a wide and varied diet without so much as making a wry face. It mattered little whether the shells were red, blue or green in color; whether they came off a factory production line here or abroad, or were given a new life on some handloader's bench. All were digested in stride, and surely this will continue in much the same vein. But if you're the sort of chap who favors wearing a pair of pants that goes well with the coat, then you'll want to take a close look at the new Browning shotshell line.

Long ago it occurred to this gun nut that if Browning wanted to expand its horizons, the logical step would be into the cartridge field. This has finally happened, though why it took so long, I cannot say. The initial move came in 1971 with the introduction of centerfire rifle and handgun ammo, with 22 rimfires appearing the following year. Then, in 1973, the Power Rated shotshell line was ushered in.

In GUN DIGEST No. 28, we presented an explanation of Browning's Power Rated Index (PRI), but it might be well to run through this again, briefly. Some will probably say that the PRI is largely a sales gimmick, but there is really more to it than that. It is, essentially, an attempt by Browning to simplify load selection, to phase out the dated and sometimes confusing matter of drams equivalency and such.

The PRI is based on a calculation involving the weight of the shot charge and its velocity, and accordingly each Browning load has been assigned a so-called energy rating ranging from 35 to 60 Power which can be *roughly* taken as the maximum effective range in yards. The purpose of this new concept in ammo merchandising is to enable the shooter (particularly the fellow who isn't thoroughly oriented in such matters) to quickly rate one loading against another and thus help answer the question of what is suitable for his specific needs.

While the PRI is a step in the right direction, and is probably as close as any system can ever come in meeting such a goal, the shooter still has to consider such factors as choke constriction and the balancing of shot size to target size. As an obvious example, a 12-ga. 55 Power load (baby magnum with 1½ ozs. of shot) carrying 4s wouldn't gather in many ducks at 55 yards if fired in an Imp. Cyl. barrel—pellet energy to do the job would be there, but pattern density would be sorely lacking. So the system is not infallible. It still has to be seasoned with a little shooter experience or knowledge.

For those old hands who prefer to select shells on the basis of drams equivalent velocity, this information is printed on every box of Browning shells, along with the shot charge weight and pellet size. No problem there.

The Power Rated line includes 22 different loads ranging from a 2½″ 410 shell, with ½-oz. of shot, through the 12-ga. 3″ Magnum shell with a 1⅞-oz. payload. The entire line, however, is aimed exclusively at the hunter. You won't find a Browning shell that's billed specifically as a target load. There is, of course, a 12-ga. field load (45 Power) that pushes a 1⅛-oz. load at a 3¼ dram-equivalent velocity, and with No. 8 shot this will meet the new ISU regulation for International-style claybird busting. There are also 20 and 28 field loads that could be pressed into service for domestic Skeet, but beyond this the cupboard is bare.

All Browning 12, 16 and 20 loads, standard and magnum lengths alike, are put together in plastic-bodied hulls, and thus slick feeding properties and resistance to wet weather are insured. The 28 and 410 loads, on the other hand, are assembled in paper-tube shells. Except for the rifled-slug loads, all of the plastic-bodied shells are crimped with a 6-pt. fold closure that has a heat-fused center "plug." The 28-ga. paper-tube load is also fold crimped (6-pt.), but the 410 shells are closed with an overshot card and a roll crimp. All have cannelured brass heads; the headstamp shows the gauge and the Browning name.

In keeping with current practices, these Power Rated shells are color coded to help eliminate hazardous mix-ups, such as dropping a 20-ga. round into a 12-ga. chamber. Twelve-gauge shells are black with the tube markings in yellow, while the 20s are yellow with black tube markings. Our test samples did not include 16-ga. shells, but my guess is that these are probably some shade of purple. The paper-bodied 28-ga. and 410 loads are a dark red in color.

The plastic-bodied shell which Browning has adopted is the type known in handloading circles as a poly-formed case. This ribbed-surface hull is of built-up construction, consisting of three component parts—the plastic tube, a paper basewad and the brass head.

The basewad has a cup-style paper overlay, designed to prevent the powder gases from working rearward between the basewad and the shell tube. From a functional standpoint this overlay represents an excellent design. It eliminates excessive brass expansion, thus guaranteeing easy extraction of fired cases. Handloaders, however, have never been deliriously happy with a basewad of this type; the overlay has a tendency to loosen and to deteriorate quite rapidly, hence case life is therefore shortened. The 28-ga. paper-tube shell, by the way, has this same style of basewad, while that for the 410 shell is without the overlay.

Regardless of gauge or shot charge weight, all of the Browning shotshells are powered by progressive-burning Ball-type powders. Ignition in all instances is handled by a 209-size primer, and though it probably doesn't need saying, this "sparkplug" incorporates the very latest technical advances in primer manufacture.

Browning voted nay on the unit-type or one-piece plastic column. Approval was given, instead, to a multi-wad approach, one which is used for *all* Power Rated loads. It starts, at the powder end, with a cupped paper wad. The "umbrella" wad, actually an old, time-tested design, expands readily for an excellent gas seal, both in the shell and in the bore. The shot charge, cushioned by conventional fiber filler wads, is protected from damaging bore contact by a plastic cup which Browning calls the "Escort'R." Quite conventional in type, it has 4 slits extending to within about ⅛" of the cup's floor, facilitating immediate release of the shot load once it exits the muzzle.

Breaking down various Browning loads, it was found in some instances that the shot cup does not fully accommodate the charge. Looking at the 12-ga. 60 Powder with 1⅞ ozs. of shot, for example, the nominal cup capacity is only 1 9/16 ozs. In the 20-ga. 45 Power with 1¼ ozs., nominal capacity is roughly 1 1/16 ozs.

My calling attention to this is not a matter of criticism, for the practice is pretty much standard throughout the ammo industry. When extra-heavy shot charges are used, case capacity almost invariably dictates a sacrifice in wad column length, and the remedy is usually a two-pronged move. Along with filler wads of less thickness, the holding capacity of the shot container is also reduced.

Browning's Slug Special and Buck Special loads don't use the Escort'R shot cup, nor is it used for the 28-ga.

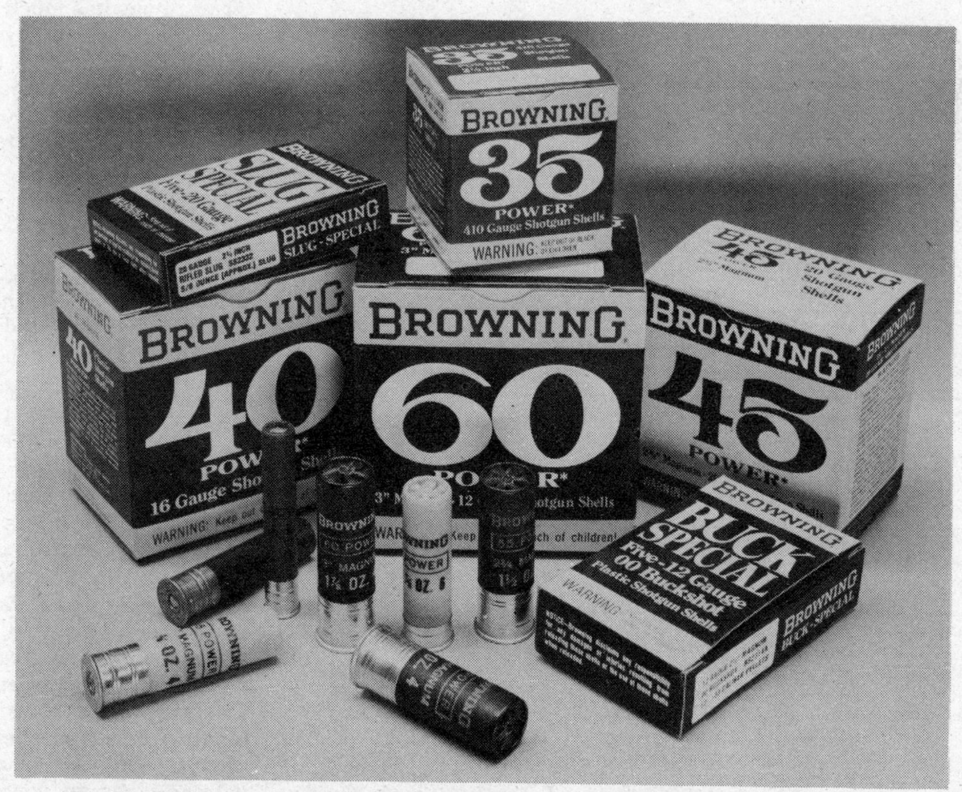

Browning's Power Rated shotshell line covers the field from 2½" 410 through 12-ga. 3" Magnum. Twelve, 16 and 20-ga. loads are in plastic-bodied shells. Buckshot and rifled slug loads, also loaded in plastic cases, come in handy 5-round boxes.

and 410 loads. The latter two are "straight" loadings, which is to say that the wad column consists only of the paper O/P cup topped by fiber fillers.

Only one Buck Special load is offered, this being a 12-ga. short magnum recipe with 12 pellets of #00 buckshot (33 cal.). The load shot like a million bucks in my Liege test gun, at times placing highly lethal clusters of 3 to 6 pellets close to the point of hold. Planting one of these multi-pellet clusters in the lung area of a white-tailed buck would mean venison for sure.

The 12-pellet load is stacked in 4 tiers of 3 pellets each, and a very thin (.008") plastic wrapper is used to prevent pellet abrasion during bore travel. In conjunction with this collar (which, by the way, does not enclose the top layer of pellets), a filler material of granulated polyethylene occupies the rather voluminous interstice area. This filler, not the plastic collar, is the real key to high-density pattern performance. It greatly reduces the pellet deformation that occurs as the pellets jam against one another when the powder gases first begin to move the load. Because the buckshot pellets remain more round, they fly more truly, and dispersion is greatly reduced.

Being a dedicated handloader, the filler material was of special interest to me. It is of more coarse granulation than that used in other brands of buckshot loads, being comprised of ball-like particles which appear to be fused together into clusters of varying size. The amount used in the 12/00B load is just a bit short of 25.0 grains.

The situation is more encompassing for the Slug Special loads, with 12, 16 and 20-ga. missiles being offered. The omission of the 410 in this instance will hardly cause tears of woe, as this pipsqueak slug lacks enough energy to have any really useful application in the hunting field.

Browning's rifled slug is of conventional Foster-type, with the usual diagonal lands and grooves and a big base cavity. The 12-ga. slug is cataloged as being a 1-oz. projectile, but on the Slug Special box the weight is given as being about ⅞-oz. However, a sample slug checked out at 401.5 grs., or very close to 15/16 oz. Like the Buck Special, these slug loads are packaged in handy pocket-sized 5-round boxes.

I had hoped to include a few remarks on the accuracy level of the Browning slug load, but somehow a range session never materialized. I did take a careful look at the wad column and it left me somewhat aghast—the slug is in direct contact with the soft-fiber filler wadding! This violates that generally accepted rule that a hard card wad of about .200" thickness be used for topping off the wad column. The function of the card wad is to improve accuracy (that is, the ability to group tightly) by preventing the wadding from being driven forward into the slug's cavity, where it creates an imbalance. But as I've said, I haven't sent any of these Slug Special loads downrange, so I'm going to button my lip. Speculation is a damn poor substitute for actual test firing.

The shot used in the Power Rated loads is of excellent quality. I've examined, under magnification, a number of charges in the various pellet sizes without spotting any misshapen or flat-sided pellets, and only very occasionally one that was slightly dimpled. In reply to my inquiry about pellet hardness (antimony content), Browning was a little vague. But I gathered that those loads with a Power Rating of 40 or less carry shot of standard hardness, whereas the higher rated loads contain extra-hard pellets.

Speaking of shot, there are a couple of highly useful pellet sizes not currently offered in any U.S. produced factory load, and I think Browning may have missed a profitable turn by not including these. No. 7 shot, for example, has much to recommend it for ducks over decoys and for moderately long shots on the larger upland birds. No. 3 shot is excellent medicine for all goose shooting, maintaining adequate penetration out to about 80 yards or thereabouts, and providing much better pattern density than that given by an equal charge weight of 2s. In the 12-ga. 3" Magnum, as an example, 1⅝x3 loading will do everything that a 1⅞x 2 loading will do, and with less cost and less recoil. I hope Browning is listening.

Using Browning's Citori O-U, as well as other guns in my battery, I gave the Power Rated loads a good workout in the field. Because my shotgunning revolves around such species as prairie grouse, Huns, pheasants and waterfowl, I used mostly those loads rated 45 Power and higher, and they performed in a very business-like way. In fact, they did as good a job as any factory load I've ever used. The 12-ga. loads, being dressed as they are in that ultra-conservative black color, won't win any beauty contest, but don't let outward appearances throw you. It's what's inside that counts. ●

Browning
Power Rated Shotgun Shells

Gauge	Shell/ins.	P.R.	D.E.	Shot/ozs.	Shot/No.
12	3" Mag.	60	Max.	1⅞	2, 4
12	3" Mag.	60	Max.	1⅝	4, 6
12	2¾' Mag.	55	Max.	1½	2, 4, 5, 6
12	2¾"	50	Max.	1¼	4, 5, 6, 7½
12	2¾"	45	3¼	1¼	8
12	2¾"	45	3¼	1⅛	6, 7½, 8
12	2¾"	40	3¼	1	6, 8
16	2¾" Mag.	50	Max.	1¼	4
16	2¾"	45	3¼	1⅛	4, 6, 7½
16	2¾"	40	2¾	1⅛	6, 7½, 8
20	3" Mag.	45	Max.	1¼	2, 4, 6
20	2¾" Mag.	45	Max.	1⅛	4, 6
20	2¾"	40	Max.	1	4, 5, 6, 7½
20	2¾"	35	2½	1	6, 7½, 8
20	2¾"	35	2½	⅞	6, 8
28	2¾"	35	Max.	¾	6, 7½, 9
410	3"	35	Max.	11/16	4, 6, 7½
410	2½"	35	Max.	½	6, 7½
12	2¾" Mag.	Buck Spl	Max.	12*	00 Buck
12	2¾"	Slug Spl	Max.	⅞	Slug
16	2¾"	Slug Spl	Max.	⅘	Slug
20	2¾"	Slug Spl	Max.	⅝	Slug

Remarks: P.R. = Power Rating. D.E. = Drams Equivalent of powder charge. * indicates 12 pellets in charge.

The Art of TURKEY HUNTING

The pursuit of *M. gallopavo* is indeed an art—the ability to successfully hunt our grandest wild bird calls for painstaking, studied efforts if he is to be outwitted. The author points the way.

by James C. Gates

TURKEY HUNTING is an art. This simple and plain statement sums up totally one of the most demanding sports on the American continent. There are more dangerous, more plentiful types of hunting, but none can rival the complexness of turkey shooting.

I once asked a now-departed dean of turkey hunting to sum up the art. His answer was: "Predict the unpredictable and have the hunting ability to carry out your prediction." It was years, and many turkeys later, before I fully realized the truth in this old sage's words.

My career as a turkey hunter began one cold December morning. A lanky and gangling teenager, I, with two smaller brothers, a Winchester pump shotgun and an English setter left my father and grandfather at the camp house to fill our game bag. I had seen fresh killed turkeys being displayed by successful hunters in front of the stores downtown, but I had never come to face with this wily old bird.

This morning the three of us left the camp house and traveled along the edge of a great oak hammock running along a creek. We'd gone about a half-mile when my setter began to trail what I assumed to be a covey of quail. She worked gingerly along the fringe of palmettos and got well ahead of us. We watched intently, shotgun ready and loaded with low-base 6's. She froze into one of her stone-like points and I, trailed by my younger brothers, moved in for the covey rise. Instead of quail buzzing out of the palmettos, we were met with the most heart-stopping flock rise of turkeys any three boys could ever wish to see. Instinctively, I swung onto an obviously larger, darker bird. The familiar jolt from the Winchester was followed by the inspiring sight of an out-of-control, death-dealt turkey. As it fell crashing into the palmettos, our ears were still ringing from the shot and heavy wingbeats of the retreating flock. The little setter did all she could by trying to drag out the prize to us while we all stood in dumb disbelief. We finally regained our senses, sat down and gently caressed the bronze-black feathers of an 18-pound butter-fat gobbler. That was the beginning of a long addiction to the glorious sport of turkey hunting.

The Turkey

The wild turkey has inhabited the North American continent at least as long as man has. Turkey bones, a little larger than those of today's birds, have been dug up from the lower levels of prehistoric Indian mounds. Some I've seen must have been in the 30-pound plus class. The early Indian inhabitants, though placing some degree of divinity on turkeys, hunted and ate them.

The Spaniards found turkeys delectable, introducing them throughout their colonies and Spain. Domestic strains were spread throughout Europe and brought back to the North American continent in a variety of colors and sizes.

The wild and domestic strains can be crossbred, but this hybrid is too nervous for captivity, and too uninstinctive for wild habitation.

The wild turkey's diet is mainly acorns and various seeds. If available he relishes peanuts, corn, or any grain crops. It takes about a pint and a half of food a day to keep the average turkey in good shape. The scratching area in oak hammocks is readily seen after a flock of 15 or so birds pass through. Turkeys are creatures of habit and, once established on a range, their movements are predictable. Only man's over-hunting breaks up this habit. He is a large bird with a thinner, more prominent breast bone, a narrower, deeper body and longer legs than his domestic cousin. The table qualities of the wild turkey are even better than tame turkeys; there's no gamy taste but rather a nut-like sweetness.

Normally wild turkeys roost in secluded and remote areas, high in a cypress or oak. It is incorrect that turkeys always roost over water. That habit would help them hear approach-

ing danger, but in dry areas they sometimes roost in high pines or the like. They leave the roost at daybreak and glide into a relatively open area that is adjacent to or is a feed area. They glide in singly or in doubles, never altogether, then reorganize amidst turkey small talk that sounds like "pert, pert, pert." The flock immediately begins feeding in the open grain or back into the oak hammock. They can make a lot of noise, hence novices are often deceived as to their alertness. One strange noise or movement makes them instinctivly scatter, run or fly. Wily old tom turkeys feed on the border of a flock, never in the midst, using the hens and younger birds as a cover. To seek him out you must first outsmart the protective shield of his flock.

The flock feeds until around 1 o'clock, then the birds begin their dusting and preening, which lasts until about 3. By then they will have completed about half of the day's circle from the roost, the morning feed will be partly digested, and they'll begin their afternoon feeding. They move leisurely back to the roost, filling the craw for the night's inactivity. About 30 minutes before sunset they take off singly and in pairs to the roost. Once in the roost trees they move around getting comfortable. The old tom sometimes roosts alone in a neighboring tree.

If bad weather develops they won't leave the roost all day. The first day after a foul one is the best possible time to hunt turkeys. Ravished with hunger, they'll be a little, just a little, less alert. If the weather clears by noon the birds will leave the roost and feed as far around their route as light allows. Caught by a passing rain, they take cover and wait it out. If the weather closes in for the day, they will move on to the roost. They react to the weather regardless of the temperature, and cold, crisp weather seems to sharpen their reflexes.

Speaking now of their instinctive reflexes, a turkey can see no better than man, but reacts to sudden or strange movements more quickly than man. His sense of smell is no higher developed than man's. The turkey's great attribute is his sense of hearing, some 7 times as acute as a human's. His ultra-keen hearing can distinguish a footfall in leaves at phenomenal distances. Smoking doesn't seem to bother him, but the sudden flare of a match or cigarette lighter in the early hours of dawn will ruin your chances for any turkey that spots it.

Another fallacy much believed in by novice hunters is that the turkey won't wade water. He will until it gets deep enough to start wetting his belly feathers. This is pretty deep because of his long legs. I've seen a full flock wading around trying to get acorns.

A peculiar thing I've seen is dusting bowls made in large ant beds. Whether because of a lack of dry sand elsewhere or for some other reason, I don't know. By the way, count the number of dust bowls and you have the number of birds in the flock.

If undisturbed by man a flock usually averages up to 20 birds before nature, through the old tom's inadequacy, allows the young toms to break it up. It is rare indeed, however, to see this many except in wilderness or protected areas. A large flock usually consists of an old tom, a few young toms, and the rest hens, living throughout the year in a compatible togetherness until about the last of March. It is then that the great Architect of the Universe causes strange and beautiful instincts to surge forth. The gobblers get irritable and restless. Spring begins to arrive and it is mating time. The old tom starts first by running off all the young toms. These last, unable to secure hens, band together and spend all day trying to prove to each other their wasted virility. By early April the older toms have their harems secure from the younger males and are now watching for encroachments from other older toms. The air is punctuated with gobblings and challenges sent ringing through the majestic swamp and lonely hammocks. If an old tom is

This hunter collects his reward for an early morning hunt—a fat Tom turkey.

Eleven calling devices in Don Shiner's collection. Origin ranges from Pennsylvania to Florida and westward to Texas.

killed the young toms take over and there may be as many as four new flocks. An old tom's flock will lay only 5 or 6 eggs, so the population is fairly stable. If a flock is broken up the hens lay 10 or so eggs and each individual flock is built up to about the original number. Things quiet down while the hen sets, and, when the poults are hatched, she remains aloof from the flock of young toms, old hens, and the old tom. After the birds have their feathers the flock comes together again, usually by July.

The great enemy of young turkeys is weather. Heavy spring rains or an exceptionally dry summer causes more deaths than wildcats or other predators. The young birds grow quickly. By November they're hard to tell from the older ones.

The wild turkey's beard is a much-sought-after trophy and its length governs its value. A first-year tom will have a very short beard, not showing out of the breast feathers. By the second year the beard will be 3 or maybe 4 inches long, and his feathers are now a bronze-black instead of the hen's lighter brown. His spurs start developing and he'll begin to gobble. By the third year he is a heavy and tough customer. If the harem master doesn't put the fear into him, he'll usurp the old boy. It's a beautiful circle of events.

Arms and Ammo

For successful turkey hunting, nothing is so important as the selection of firearms and loads. The 45-yard positive killing range handicaps the shotgun, for the average range that turkeys can be taken, some 75 yards, calls for a rifle.

The turkey is a fairly large target over-all, but the vital area where a bullet must be placed to avoid destroying fine eatng meat is only 5″—6″ long and two inches deep. This area lies along the bird's back, from just in front of the wingbutts to above the thighs. When the turkey is facing you this vital area is reduced to 3″x2″ wide from the V in the wishbone to the top of the back.

During my years of turkey hunting I tried everything from full-jacketed military 30-06s to 22 rimfires, some of them failing badly. For most turkey hunters these requirements must be met in a turkey rifle: An accurate rifle (2 moa minimum) with both iron and telescopic sights, firing a cartridge that kills quickly and humanely without destroying excess meat.

I soon found that any well-made factory or custom bolt action would suffice, but only two pump actions. The second requirement was easily answered, but the third gave me trouble. Finally, the following loads filled the requirement for a 40- to 80-gr. bullet with fairly heavy jacket at a velocity between 2,000 and 2,400 feet per second. This velocity may seem low, but if you go any higher your bird will be blasted to tatters.

1. 22 rimfire magnum—2000 fps.
2. 22 Hornet—55-gr. Speer or Hornady, 9 grains 2400. 2300 fps.
3. 218 Bee—55-gr. Speer or Hornady, 10 grains 2400, 2300 fps.
4. 256 Magnum—60-gr. Speer, 15.5 grains 2400. 2300 fps.
5. 25-20—60-gr. Hornady, 11 grains 2400. 2200 fps.
6. 32-20—80-gr. Rem. H.P. (.310″), 13 grains 2400. 1900 fps.

These loads have killed many turkeys for me, but in the same bullet weight-velocity brackets, many other cartridges might suffice.

A very good load for the 30-06 is the military 152-gr. bullet ahead of 24/2400 for about 2000 fps. In a 1-10 twist, the bullet is stabilized well, but in custom 1-12 and 1-14 twists, stability is marginal. In the 22 WMR, which is loaded with a thin-skinned 40-gr. bullet, I suggest pulling the factory bullet and replace it with the heavier-jacket 40-gr. Speer spire point. Only a negligible amount of pressure increase is experienced.

I have killed 13 turkeys with this excellent load. Exchanging the bullets is simple, and extra cost is nothing compared with the gain in efficiency.

For the hunter seeking economy, there are various gas-check cast bullets available in the same calibers. Cast these bullets hard and 2000 fps can be approached with relatively accurate results. With higher velocities accuracy suffers. However, a turkey load is not a simple plinking or squirrel load, and the opportunity to kill a trophy class tom turkey comes seldom. Why handicap yourself with a cheap round? I'd gladly pay a dollar a round, if necessary, to know that I had the best medicine for these much-sought-after, seldom-killed prizes.

Rifles

Over the years I've tried about every rifle practical for turkey hunting. I now have three long guns and one revolver, the essence of all my trials, these suitable for all the ranges and situations I have run up against: A Winchester 61 in 22 WMR, a 54 Winchester bolt action in 22 Hornet, an Ansley Fox 12-ga. double, with full and modified tubes, and, surprisingly, a Smith & Wesson Masterpiece in 22 Rem. Jet.

The 61, now discontinued, would be my choice above all comers in a turkey rifle if I had to select only one rifle. Even the thin-skin factory loads are excellent. With my substitute-bullet loads this is just about a perfect turkey rifle. It is astonishingly accurate for a light rifle, consistently shooting 2 moa bench groups with my loads. I have a bright 2¾ Redfield scope on it, mounted with blocks instead of the poor dovetail type mounts for its grooved receiver. The reticle is a post-crosshair. Sighted-in for 125 yards, this gives a midrange trajectory of about 2 inches at 65 yards. I have killed turkeys out to about 130 yards with this combination.

My other turkey rifle is a beautiful 54 Hornet with a Redfield 4x scope, again with a picket post. I use it exclusively when scouting new country, when I'm not familiar with the feeding spots of new flocks, and for shots at longer ranges. Such shots call for the steadiness of a heavier rifle, more power in the scope, and a little more velocity. Groove diameter of this Hornet mikes .2235", allowing use of the heaviest jacketed 50- and 55-gr. .224" bullets. It has a Lyman 48 micrometer rear sight. I have to remove the slide to mount the scope, but I always carry it as insurance against a damaged scope. This rifle with my handloads groups consistently into a minute of angle, from the bench. It has never let me down.

I never use anything in my 12-gauge Fox but Mark 5, 2¾ magnums. The quick two shots available are good medicine for flushing birds in heavy cover, or birds flying onto or off the roost. Shots are taken at 45 yards maximum; aimed at the neck areas, they're consistent killers. Never use shot heavier than number 2s and 4s are preferable. Buckshot patterns are patchy and pellet energy low; don't use them.

Lastly, on those rare occasions when the ultra-sportsmanship bug bites me, I hunt turkeys with the 22 Jet Magnum. To do this successfully hunting techniques must be perfect, and shots held under 75 yards. This is tough hunting, and I try not to be disheartened at misses!

Despite factory propaganda, true velocity of the 22 Jet is about 1800 fps, not the advertised 2400, but still good on turkeys if you use the proper bullet. The early 22 Jet cartridges had bullets that broke up at around 2000 fps. At 1800 they peeled back into perfect mushrooms on turkeys. Then came a thin-skinned bomb with a lot of lead exposed which fouled up those who hunt turkey with this handgun. Bore dimensions of the Jet were designed, for some unexplained reason, for .222" bullets. To get a bullet with adequate jacket thickness I swage 40-gr. Sierra Hornet bullets (.223") to .222". With this bullet and 10.5 grains of 2400, I surpass factory ballistics safely, and have an excellent short-range cartridge. I also use the revolver, sighted in for 100 yards, when I take someone out to get his Christmas turkey. There isn't enough room in a properly built turkey blind for two hunters with long guns, so I do the calling and back the friend's shotgun. (I never allow a novice to use anything but a shotgun, and I call his shot when I get the birds in range.) This way I have less cripples and more satisfied friends.

Among currently-made and older rifles I might suggest: the 54 or 70 Winchester in 22 Hornet (if you can find one), or 225, the Sako 22 Hornet, the Remington 700 in 222 and 22-250, the Krico Hornet (on special order), and custom jobs built around such cartridges and loads. Maybe a 243 as well, with handloads, but the 25s and the like are sometimes hard to get working well at the 2000-2400 fps required because of the fast twist. Stability falls off.

In shotguns nothing beats a well-made double or over-under 12-gauge with tight chokes. They are practically weatherproof, quiet and quick. The excellent 101 Winchester is reasonably priced for the quality. My second choice would be a pump or auto 12 with a full-choke tube. There are, of course, many makes and models to choose from—let your pocket book be your guide.

Hunting Techniques

Generally, regardless of hunting terrain, the methods of turkey hunting are more or less the same. Old time turkey hunters call him a "fringe fowl," which means he's found in areas providing protective cover, yet open enough for feeding.

In the deep South, and in parts of the West, hunting from a blind located at the feed area is the chief method. Ideally, the blind is so-positioned that the rising sun will be behind the hunter, giving him good light on his target and puts the sun in the birds' eyes.

A one-man blind should be at least 6x6 feet. This will give the hunter ample room to move if necessary without hitting the walls of the blind. Try to place the blind so that heavy cover is behind you when you face the feeding area. This not only puts you in a shaded area but helps break your silhouette. Of course, the reverse direction is faced if you are hunting and afternoon feed area. Only close observation of the birds' habits will show whether the scratching was made in the morning or afternoon. A good way to determine this is by inspecting the scratching when it has rained during a known time of the day.

After selecting your blind's spot, take careful note of surrounding vegetation, for you must build the blind of this local material. Begin by cleaning all loose material from the blind's floor area, removing all small sticks and vines, then carefully arrange the vegetation in a horseshoe shape. A favorite material here in Florida is palm fronds. These give maximum concealment without the blind looking like a rubbish pile. Don't, like so many novice hunters do, build a blind you can't even see out of, much less shoot from! As you arrange your material go out and get a turkey's eye view. As soon as your blind will absorb the shape of a man, stop. I know you'll feel your blind is full of holes when you're inside, but don't worry—it's easier for you to look out then it is for the turkey to look in.

If possible, wait a few days after the blind is built before taking your turkeys. This will let them get used to it, especially if you've been a little careless in its construction. The day your hunt is planned, if it is a morning hunt, be in position by daylight or a little before. Get in a comfortable shooting position, stop fidgeting, and begin your vigil.

If you are using a shotgun, a trick taught me by an old turkey hunter will help. Take a small roll of toilet paper with you, and tear a few sheets into about one-inch squares. Pace off 45 yards, in about four or five directions from your blind, and stick one of these little squares on the grass. They'll give you something to judge distance by. Turkeys don't seem to be bothered by a few small pieces of paper.

When your turkeys appear and start feeding, stay calm. If you are using a rifle the above suggestions still hold true, but you should build your blind where the entire feed area can be covered by the longer-range capabilities of your rifle.

An old tom is usually the last one

on the field and, if he is your meat, use extreme care not to excite or flush the birds that feed out ahead of him.

There is no need to use a call on fall mornings unless a flock has been scattered. At that time turkeys respond only to the reassemble call, a series of semi low-pitched yelps. They don't gobble except during the mating season.

If your birds are accidentally scattered, stay in the blind. After about 30 minutes, if you don't hear their reassembly calls, begin discreetly with spaced calls. Most calls can be tuned for pitch, so if you hear the birds beginning to assemble and you are familiar with your caller, tune it to their pitch. If you aren't an experienced caller or haven't practiced before season, forget it.

The blind system only works in areas where the birds are not heavily hunted and their habits can be predicted. In areas where a wilderness turkey is not, one of the best techniques is for the hunter to ramble slowly through areas where turkeys have been previously seen. He should be alert to such signs as scratching, tracks, or dusting. If he sees these, he should slowly continue his search, hoping he'll be lucky enough to get a long shot or flush the birds, whereby his caller can be brought into play.

In bygone days this system, used with a turkey dog, was so effective it decimated the turkey population in many states. When the dog flushed them the turkeys flew but a short distance. The hunter then called in his dog, built a rough blind and, after a while called the birds back.

The rambling system, less the dog, still kills a lot of birds. A rifle is a must for this system because of the varying and sometime long-range shooting. I use this system until I learn a flock's daily feeding route, then I switch to the blind system.

In the spring the turkey hunter's dream comes true, at least in those states that wisely allow the hunter to pick off old toms. Such states have seen a marked increase in turkey population because of the greater vigor of the young toms that take over.

Spring time can be most exciting. The hunter should use a call that produces the throaty gobble. He should begin hunting at daylight, using the rambling system. Every quarter-mile he should give forth with a couple of real challenging gobbles. If there is an old tom and his flock within hearing distance, rest assured he's going to be interested. When the hunter hears the return gobble he should immediately select a place of concealment. He has ample time to quickly prepare his blind while the old tom gets his flock buttoned down. Gobble only, from now on, as an answering challenge to the old tom. If you are careful and use your call right, a prize is yours for the taking.

I have covered three basic systems that take turkeys successfully. These systems, backed by simple logic and experience, will allow the turkey hunter to consistently take turkeys. There are others, of course, based on differing terrain, etc.

Callers and their Manufacturers

Turkey callers are legion. I have seen callers as simple as a pipe stem; with the lip held just right, a sucking-in action made an acceptable assembly call. At the other extreme was a lead-like washer covered with thin rubber material, held in the mouth. This curious gadget made good calls but never appealed to me.

In between there are many different varieties and pitches of turkey callers. All, except for a simple few, emit delicate puts, whines, and yelps suitable for only the most special circumstances. Only the most adept turkey caller should ever even attempt these specialized calls.

There is only one caller that I can honestly recommend for either novice or experienced turkey hunters. This is a big box caller, Model 102, made by M. L. Lynch, 306 Edgewood Blvd., Birmingham, Ala. 35209, and it produces all the known variations except the extra high pitch small talk of first year turkeys. It has two lips and is one of the few caller that can produce the gobble of the gobbler in the spring.

A tuning peg, wedged between the lips, varies the pitch from very high, as in young birds, to the throaty call of older birds. This produces the best gobble I have ever heard from a manual caller. Mr. Lynch includes a booklet on the different calls, but for the learner the only calls for him to worry about are the assembly call, lost-hen call, and gobble. Leave the specialized calls for the experienced.

Fall hunting calls for very little use of a caller except when the birds have been flushed. This will bring comments from the experts, I know, but I still stand firm on the statement that more turkeys have been run off by so-called experts, running through their ritual of calls, than have ever been brought to the gun. Many overly-enthusiastic beginners think that owning a caller makes them turkey hunters. Forget the caller and spend more time learning turkey habits. In the spring, however, even the novice, with a little care in calling, will get a response.

Clothes for the Turkey Hunter

Clothing worn by the turkey hunter is not only important for his comfort but also to his success in killing birds. Certain colors spook turkeys more than others. The worst seems to be blue, followed by black, and white, red, or yellow would be ridiculous. The best, of course, is camouflage material. Next best are dark tan, full grey, or fatigue green. I have found that only mud-stained camoulflage really works where a wise old tom is concerned. Unstarched material is preferred; a reflective sheen is all-too-noticeable from starched material, and it is noisy. Rough-dried clothes, though not the neatest looking, are best.

Turkey hunting, except in the most temperate areas, is at times a cold and bone-chilling experience. The hunter, however, must be able to move around without a lot of heavy clothes binding him up. I use Navy thermal long johns, an athletic sweat suit under a full suit of heavy camouflage, and wool boot socks. These are adequate except in extremely cold weather; then heavy insulated underwear and jackets are necessary. For boots I find a pair of 8″ quail hunter's boots are best in warmer weather. Some Florida hunters use low-cut sneakers, but in cold weather they are rough. The main thing, in any case, is maximum concealment.

Conclusion

I began this article with the killing of my first turkey. I tried to portray the thrill of taking one of these majestic birds. The wheels of time have ground on and I haven't had the opportunity to revisit that memorable spot.

This year I managed to fill my fall and spring bag limit, and the sheer thrill hasn't left me. In a secluded spot joining the fabled St. Johns swamp, the climax of a two-year hunt came to an unforgettable end this year. Here fell one of the toughest-to-kill old tom turkeys I've ever hunted.

I had been taking turkeys from his flock for two years, and now and then I'd get a glimpse of one of the biggest toms I had ever seen. I would set up a blind, hoping to get a crack at him, but the flock would approach without the old tom and I'd decide he was a figment of my imagination. I would kill a young tom and go home. I was flushing the old tom when scouting the flock's movement. He was flanking the main flock, a trait which protected him, but I decided that somehow I would take him. Thus began a series of unlucky hunts where I tried every trick I knew.

Each time, before I got a crack at him, the main flock would flush or something else would go wrong. Once I was lying by a fallen log, well-concealed, my Hornet and the Lynch caller handy. The main flock had been scattered from the roost the previous night by a predator. I had walked quietly into my position by the light of a full moon. I had lain motionless for two hours, the mosquitoes humming around by head, doused with insect repellent. In the early light I heard the small talk of several turkeys trying to reassemble. In the grey light of dawn I watched them move cautiously out onto the field, very alert. I then saw a solitary bird land some 200 yards from me, then quickly dash into the fringe at the edge of the field. It happened so fast I felt I must have imagined it. I slowly began a series of deep-throated assembly calls and the birds responded. It reaffirmed my theory that the old tom was the leader of this flock. When the birds moved to within 100 yards of me I heard the old tom start talking. The flock momentarily seemed confused, but I couldn't match the authenticity of his calls and the flock moved away.

I now knew what I had to do. For the next two weeks I watched the habits of the main flock. When they re-established their feed cycle I selected the location of my blind, setting it up on the east side of a field, where they fed through in the mornings. When I left the blind, I filled my pockets with dirt from the site. That night I smeared my camouflage suit with mud made from this dirt, doused a square of camouflage netting in the mud, and let them dry. My Model 61 rifle was checked, then loaded with cartridges carefully selected for their perfect bullet points.

I was up at 4 o'clock, the temperature about 30 degrees. It was around 5:30 when I reached the blind. The woods stood in icy stillness. In the black darkness I smoked my last cigarette; I could dare none in the next critical hours. I lay down, spreading the camouflage net over me and then leaves over that. The rifle, lying ahead of me, was covered with pine needles. Concealment now complete, the waiting began.

I lay perfectly still for about an hour and then the woods and swamp begin the waking-up ritual hunters have heard for ages. Light began creeping out onto the field, pushing back the darkness. A robin landed not four feet from my rifle muzzle, then went about his feeding. Now I could see the approaching flock, moving cautiously onto the field. I hardly dared to breathe. As the sun lifted behind my back I saw the light beams play over the chocolate brown of the hens' feathers and the black-brown of four young toms. I counted 19 birds scattered over the field—feeding, scratching, and watching. They seemed to look directly at me. A squirrel was playing in the tree directly above. If he saw me and fussed I knew my hope of getting the tom would be over. I lay motionless while he cut an acorn, the giblets falling on me. He moved on, to my relief.

The pressure of watching the feeding flock was intense. I began telling myself that the big tom was not coming, that I should take a young one. There was a hen not 15 yards from me, so it was only a matter of moments until one would discover me.

Then I saw him. He stood like a statue about 150 yards from me. He didn't move a feather for at least 15 minutes. Very carefully I pulled the glove from my right hand, slowly pushing the rifle's safety off as I watched the closest hen.

Now the big tom moved slowly down the shadows of the fringe on the opposite side of the field, his long beard almost dragging on the ground. When he approached to about 90 yards, I slowly inched the rifle into position. I could see the picket post of the scope resting on his wingbutt. Damn, he was a sight! The cold steel of the rifle cut into my numbing hands, and I could smell the earthly odor of the muddy camouflage. As the turkey began to turn toward me I started my trigger squeeze. He suddenly stepped into the sun light and every black-bronze feather was highlighted. He was such a grand spectacle that I momentarily froze in sheer awe of his majesty. My years of conditioning then took over, and the stillness of the woods was shattered by the sharp crack of the rifle. The old tom fell backwards onto his fanned-out tail, rolled over and regained his feet. The rest of the astonished flock had scattered in mass confusion. I jacked another round into the chamber as the old tom took a few strides. The picket post fell again on the wingbutts and, as I began my squeeze, I saw his wing tips fall. He pitched forward dead. The only sound now was the fading wingbeats of the flock as they headed for the safety of the deep swamp.

The author and the smart old gobbler responsible for the events concluding this story.

For minutes I lay there, looking out across the now deserted field at a spot of black. Time seemed to stop. As I slowly arose on cold, numbed legs, I knew that years would roll by before another tom this great would fall to my rifle. As I approached him, I could see that he was fully as large as I had suspected. I gently picked him up, feeling the warmth of his body and experiencing that bittersweet feeling of happiness in my success and remorse at the death of this grand old bird.

He tipped the scale in town at 23 pounds, his beard a good 10⅝ inches, his spurs 1¾ inches long. ●

THE RUGER 220 SWIFT– an instant success!

by JIM HORTON

Launched in the face of a shortage of cartridges, the limited edition Swifts produced in 1973 were swept from the dealers' shelves very quickly. Take heart, though—the Swift will be included in the regular Ruger line for 1974.

The Ruger M77 in 220 Swift, the scope a Unertl 10x Varmint type. A trim, graceful and workmanlike rifle.

INTRODUCED in the mid-1930s, the 220 Swift was a bombshell—literally and figuratively. Shooters of that era were more or less content with cartridges that gave velocities in the low 3000 foot seconds (fps) area but, almost overnight, here was a cartridge that went well over 4000 fps. Today that would be like one of the gun and ammunition makers announcing a new cartridge with a muzzle velocity of over 5000 fps.

The new cartridge was the 220 Swift and what a cartridge it was. It still is, even today for that matter, although circumstances have changed a bit.

The Swift case evolved from the old 6mm Lee Navy; though redesigned for extra strength, it kept the semi-rim case design of the Lee Navy. Exactly why the 6mm Lee case was chosen remains a mystery.

Introduced by Winchester in their Model 54 bolt action rifle, early Swift rifles had a 1/16″ twist. A short time later this rate was changed to 1/14″ twist to better handle bullets of over 50 grains with sharp points.

At one time or another four different bullets were loaded for the Swift:

46-gr. hollow point	4140 fps
48-gr. soft point	4140 fps
55-gr. soft point	3720 fps
56-gr. soft point	3690 fps

Over the years all of these were dropped in favor of the 48-gr. loading, its velocity reduced slightly to 4110 fps.

The Swift went right along in the lineup when the Model 54 was dropped in favor of the Model 70, and it stayed in the line until 1964 when the Model 70 was changed—and for the worse rather than better, Model 70 lovers are wont to say. Both the old style Model 70 and the Swift chambering were dropped in 1964, but the cartridge was made available for a few more years until it, too, was discarded. Which may have been a big mistake on Winchester's part.

It wasn't too long before Winchester and Remington brought out new centerfire cartridges. Remington's offering really wasn't a new cartridge in that they merely legitimized the old 22/250, a long-popular wildcat, sometimes called the Varminter. This is nothing more than the 250/3000 cartridge necked to 22 caliber, and a hell of a fine varmint cartridge it was and is. The Winchester offering, called the 225, was a completely new semi-rim design from top to bottom. But neither cartridge had the steam of the Swift. The Swift is about 100 to 200 fps faster than the 22/250 and the 225 Winchester trails the 22/250 by another 100 fps. Too bad Winchester didn't keep the 220 Swift in their line-up, as the ad wars might have made interesting reading comparing the Swift to the 22/250.

Purported Problems

Much prose has been written about the Swift, both good and bad but, sadly, most of it seemed to be on the debit side. To understand why this was so you should remember that the Swift was a high pressure load, developing over 50,000 psi chamber pressure—in the mid-'30s this was hot stuff indeed, while today there are many cartridges loaded to such pressure levels. Cases with gentle tapers, as the Swift has, tend to let the brass flow forward. This can cause the case to grow longer and the case mouths to thicken, or so it was charged. In neither instance is this dangerous if you understand what is happening and how to keep on top of the problem. If cases stretch then all you have to do is trim more often. To check on thickening of the case mouth try a bullet in a fired case; if it's a tight fit then that case needs to be reamed.* A little warning: most modern actions have a strong ejector spring that pushes the case mouth against the side of the chamber and action during ejection. This will bend the case mouth a tiny bit, resulting in a tight bullet fit when checking for thickness of the case mouth. The cure is to hold the case against the ejector spring so that it can't drag. If you want the highest velocity possible you may have to work a little harder to achieve it.

Here's the Canjar single set trigger, shown in set mode.

be in the 3200 fps area, which is on a par with the 222 Remington. In fact, muzzle velocities in the 3600-3800 fps bracket usually show the best accuracy in many 220 Swift rifles.

Many Swift owners could hardly wait to try it on such larger game as deer, a use it was never intended for. The Swift was and is a varmint cartridge, say up to the coyote in size, and as such it was the *ultra* 22 varmint load, in my opinion. For my money, it has no peers. But for larger game, the Swift is a no-no! I'm not saying that the Swift hasn't killed a lot of deer and, possibly, larger game in the right hands; when conditions are right it can and has been very, very good. But for every hunter who knew the limitations of the Swift there were ten or more that didn't. The Swift bullet, although made with a heavy jacket, just wasn't designed for the deep penetration needed for larger game and this is where the Swift came in for a lot of bad publicity.

Barrel diameters also had no little bit to do with the bad press relations of the Swift. In those days the then popular 22 Hornet used a barrel diameter of .223" or less—some were made up with .222" tubes! Now .001" may not sound like much, and it really isn't when working at lower pressure levels, but in the 50,000 psi range and over that little .001" undersized barrel will really scoot pressure upwards. Some early Swift barrels were cut on the tight side, too.

It was often alleged that the 220 Swift had to be loaded to top velocity and pressure levels to be accurate. This is an old wives tale, pure and simple, as one of the most accurate loads in my Ruger Swift happens to

Many a Swift barrel was cursed and condemned for its failure to maintain high accuracy. That did happen, no question, but it needn't have. Too much rapid fire and too little bore scrubbing were the main causes of lost accuracy. The boxed material on Barrel Cleaning with this article tells the sad story.

Top—Ruger M77 220 Swift with flat-top receiver and original bolt handle style. Round-top 257 Roberts shown, below, has latest bolt handle.

Whatever the causes the Swift chambering was dropped from the Winchester line in 1964 and, a few years later, ammunition and cartridge cases were also dropped. But Winchester did re-instate the cases the next year and Norma still furnishes both loaded ammunition and cases, so the Swift fan is still in business. However, reloading is the only way to get the most out of the Swift, or most other centerfire cartridge for that matter.

Rumors From Ruger

Early in 1973 I heard, via the grapevine, that Ruger would bring out the Model 77 in 220 Swift, but unaware at the time if this would be with a sporter weight barrel or, possibly, in a heavier varmint weight. Whatever the style, I wanted a Swift, and no time was wasted in placing my order. Fully expecting a delay of 6 months or more I was surprised when the Ruger Swift arrived, less than 3 months after placing the order.

I had first been introduced to the Swift in 1947 or '48 by a cousin who had a Swift built on a military Mauser action. The barrel had once been a car axle as at that time barrel steel was still scarce. That barrel, left heavy, would today be called a bull barrel; with a target type stock and topped with a 10x Unertl target scope it was a heavy outfit, not one easily carried over hill and dale. Accuracy was pretty good for those days. Five-shot groups would stay under a quarter-dollar at 100 yards with factory ammunition. In my teens in those days, I watched that Swift owner bust many a groundhog and crow—he even allowed me to send a few crows to their Happy Cawing Grounds. After my first dead center shot on a rather stupid crow at 150 yards, I vowed that someday I'd own a Swift, but that day was a long time comin'. 20 years to be exact.

That was too long a wait, in fact, because the Model 70 Swift had long since been dropped. My Swift would have to be a custom rifle, but this was

*As a matter of proven fact, case mouth thickening in the 220 Swift doesn't seem to occur. Bob Hagel recently made extensive tests in this area, finding that case mouth walls actually shrink a little! See his article in the *Rifle* for Jan.-Feb., 1974.

no problem as I had latched onto a G33/40 Mauser action, a small-ring cousin of the Model 98. With a Douglas No. 5 barrel and one of Flaig's Pennsylvania walnut varmint stocks, the scope a Unertl 10x Varmint glass, this rifle could be depended on to group right at ½" when fed a diet of 38.8 grains of Norma 203 and the Sierra 53-gr. flat-base match bullet. But too much paper punchin' burnt the barrel out, so this rifle now carries a 25-06 barrel.

The Ruger Swift Appears

Ruger's offering is in their varmint grade, which means a rather heavy barrel and, in this case, 26" long rather than their standard length of 24". While this rifle is tapped for target scope bases, they are not supplied. However, included with the rifle is a pair of Ruger's 1" scope rings. These rings fit notches cut into the integral receiver bases, so nothing else is needed to mount a hunting type scope. This particular rifle, with a Leupold 10x scope, tips the scales at 10 pounds 3 ounces empty. A fine weight for those long range shots from a good rest, but the rifle also hangs well in the offhand position.

The stock is very straight grained, with just a touch of figure. I prefer such wood in my stocks as opposed to those with a lot of figure, especially when the grain runs in the wrong direction!

The workmanship of the stock is very, very good. Metal to wood fit is as good, if not better, than you'll see on many custom stocked rifles. The checkering—while not profuse—is also quite nicely done and it's sharp; every time I pull it from the case there's lint stuck to the checkering.

The well-proportioned, oblong diamonds run in straight lines, and there are no borders to hide overruns—of which there are none on this handcut checkering pattern. Which is a pleasant change from the impressed or machined checkering found on some other factory firearms.

The stock finish is neither flat nor of a high gloss. Praise be, too, it isn't one of the plastic finishes so popular with many gunmakers, and the pores are well filled. Most plastic finishes leave me a little cold; they either have an extremely thick coat or one that's too thin, with open pores plainly visible.

Neither does Ruger install white line spacers or fore-end caps, both of which cheapen a stock, at least to my mind's eye. Nor does Ruger use a cheap plastic buttplate. Instead there's a red rubber butt pad, which adds a margin of safety when leaning the rifle against something. That soft rubber plate makes it less likely to slip and fall down, and it also helps to hold the gun securely against your shoulder. While Ruger deserves a pat on the back for his choice of buttplates, I'd have preferred one in a brown or walnut color.

As I've already noted, the Ruger 220 Swift is tapped for target scope bases, but the bases aren't supplied with the rifle. These bases are impossible to find in a small farm town, and they're not always easy to come by in larger towns, either. But $8 sent to Unertl, along with a note on your wants, will get you a set and pay the postage too.

However, the scope I intended to use was a Leupold 10x and no time was lost in mounting this scope in the Ruger rings. But when the ring screws were tightened the objective lens housing touched the barrel. However, a thin cardboard shim placed in the lower half of the front ring allowed the scope to clear the barrel.

Canjar Trigger Fitted

The trigger pull, at 5¾ pounds, was a tad heavy, at least for my tastes. Adjusting the trigger per Ruger instructions helped a bit, but 5 pounds was still too heavy. No problem this time, though—I have another Ruger 77, chambered for the 257, which also suffered from a heavy pull. Its trigger was replaced by one of Canjar's single set triggers, which was removed from the 257 and installed on the Swift. Fitting these Canjars is a snap, although the trigger opening in the guard does have to be opened a bit. A few minutes with a file quickly cured this little snag, but there was just enough difference in the two receivers so that the Canjar trigger had to be completely readjusted. However, these triggers come with complete and clear instructions for this, so no trouble was experienced. I now had a pull of 2 pounds unset and with the trigger in the set mode, a very, very few ounces touches her off. An excellent trigger in all respects, this Canjar, and with no creep or backlash I could detect. Two pounds might be a little light for some shooters, but it's the weight I prefer, not only for hunting and varmint use but for test shooting also. Most of my test shooting of the Ruger Swift has been done using the set trigger. I know, many shooters don't like set triggers, and they aren't for those who shoot maybe three or four times a year. Set triggers take some

Top—bolt handle shape used with round-top M77 Ruger receiver. Bottom bolt is from flat-top Ruger M77.

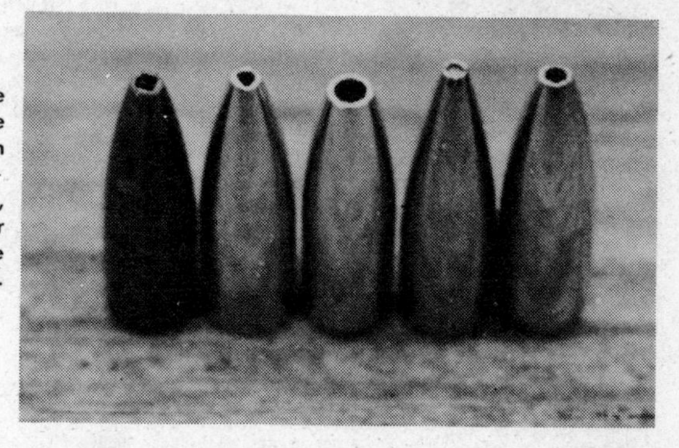

This view shows the considerable differences between the size of the hollow point openings in several 22 bullets. From left—Remington 52-gr., Sierra 53-gr., Speer (new) 52-gr. Silver Match, Hornady 53-gr. and the Nosler 52-gr. (non-match).

getting used to, of course, for the slightest touch of the untrained finger and off they go. Certainly they're not ideal for any and all shooting conditions, but I'm convinced that those who actively dislike them haven't given set triggers a fair trial.

One of these days Ruger will, I hope, re-design his triggers so that the added expense of a new system won't be required if a lighter pull is desired. But this is the one and only area where I can fault the Ruger and, considering all the good features, it's a small price to pay.

Before getting the rifle I'd ordered 100 new W-W cases, with instructions to sub Normas if W-W weren't available. I wasn't unhappy on receiving the Norma cases; in the past I've used many of these with perfect results. The cases were run through the RCBS size die to true up the cases mouths, then shaved on a Forster case trimmer to remove any high or low spots and to give a uniform length.

Primers used were Remington 9½s, a favorite of mine for several years. Seating was done with the compact and sensitive Lee priming tool. The first 20 cases were filled with 38.5 grains of 4064 and the Sierra 53-gr. flat base match bullet. This load had shot very well in my other Swift, but not quite as good as had 38.8 grains of N-203. However, my supply of N-203 was very low, as none has been imported for well over a year and there just wasn't any to be had. Too, I wanted to wait until I had the Swift in top notch shooting form before using any of my tiny supply of N-203.

Readying the Rifle

Before firing the first shot I gave Ruger's barrel a good cleaning with Hoppe's No. 9, leaving the bore well coated with it overnight to see if there was any jacket fouling remaining in the barrel. A clean patch pushed through the barrel next day didn't show a trace of fouling; any such residue would have spotted the patch a light to dark green, according to how heavy the fouling was. The barrel was then cleaned with Rice's XF-10, followed by a coat of Rice's XF-20, applied to the bore with a patch. This was allowed to stand in the barrel until arrival at the range, when a clean and dry patch was run down the bore. During all firing of this rifle the bore was cleaned after every 12 shots with XF-10, using one of his special swabs for this purpose, and then given a coating of XF-20 and wiped dry. Whether the use of these products have had any bearing on accuracy, I can't really say, at least with any degree of certainty, but it is a fact that fouling of the bore has been held to a minimum, much less than in any of my other centerfire 22s. As we shall see later on, accuracy has been outstanding. It is an indisputable fact, well known to benchresters and other accuracy addicts, that heavy bore fouling has a detrimental effect on accuracy—even *light* fouling can widen groups.

The rifle was bore sighted at 50 yards and the first shot, at the same distance, was ¾" high. That seemed to be a favorable omen, as I generally consider it good when the first shot, after bore sighting, is within 3" of my aiming point. Four more shots were then fired at 100 yards to insure that the zero was 1½" high and to condition the bore. The rifle was then set aside to cool; at no time have more than 5 shots been fired without letting the barrel cool. It's senseless to rush a lot of ammo through any barrel, unless barrel life is of no or little importance, for nothing shortens barrel life quicker than extended rapid fire. This is especially true with such cartridges as the Swift, which have a high powder charge/bore diameter ratio.

First Firings

The first test loads were all pushed by 38.5 grains of 4064 and 5 each using Remington, Hornady and Sierra flat base 52/53-gr. match bullets and the Sierra 55-gr. spitzer. These first 4 groups averaged .61" on centers; the Remington bullets made the smallest group, just under ½", but were pushed hard by the 53-gr. Sierras. The Sierra 55-gr. spitzer came in 3rd, the Hornady 4th.

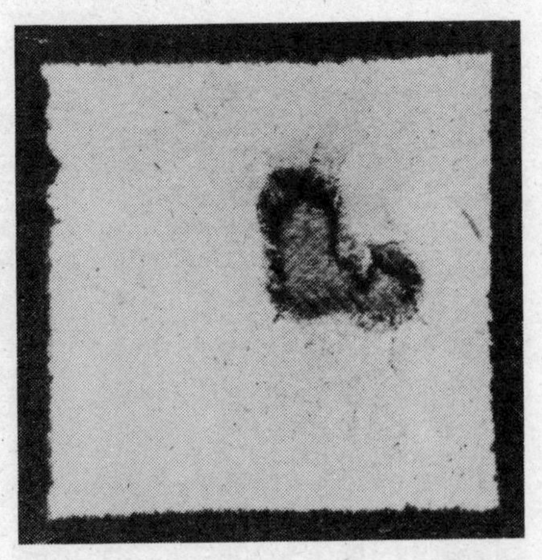
The smallest group shot with the untuned, unaltered Ruger 220 Swift measured .269" on centers for 5 shots at 100 yards. The scope was a Leupold 10x AO.

For the next session the same bullets were used, but this time the powder was 4320, 39.5 grains. Results were almost the same but there was a slight shift in the order of accuracy. Remington was again first at just under ½" but the Sierra match also came in under ½"; the Hornady match bullet was 3d, the Sierra 55-gr. last. For these eight 5-shot groups the average was a flat 6". At this point, even if I found no other loads that would shoot under ¾", I was well ahead of the game. However, Remington bullets had to be dropped from the testing; my supply was now exhausted and none could be had from any of my suppliers. It seems I wasn't the only one who knew about their shooting qualities, for Remington is heavily back ordered on these, a several week's or month's wait being "normal."

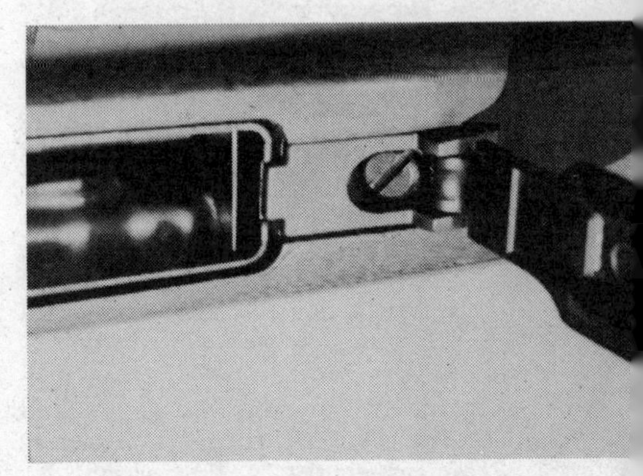
The M77 angled front guard screw, patented by Ruger, pulls barrel back and down.

I must admit that during both of the above shooting sessions conditions were ideal. Once, on the way to the range, a light rain fell and the temperature dropped several degrees. At the range not a breath of air was stirring nor was any mirage to be seen. When conditions are like this, you just have to shoot your best.

Since those first two shooting sessions the weather has been against me, with temps in the low 90's and mirage running all over the place, but even at that, among others, two outstanding groups were shot with the Speer 70-gr. bullet. Rather blunt in profile, this bullet has been a star performer when backed by 44.0 grains of 4831. Would you believe groups under ½"? That's true, though, and its shooting qualities are such that this bullet can be considered match grade in accuracy.

To date no bullet or load has grouped larger then .75" and most will group well under that. This is one crazy shooting rifle.

Second Ruger 220 Tested

About the time I finished most of the test shooting with my Ruger Swift a friend bought one, and he also mounted a Leupold 10x AO scope on it. As was the case with both of my Rugers we also had to replace his rifle's trigger with one of Canjar's in order to get a decent pull. Because he had done very little shooting from a bench his groups were running around the 1" mark. I then sat down and fired a group using the ammo he'd loaded — 39.5 grains of 4320 and the 53-gr. Sierra flat base match HP — which measured just under .41". But for the grand finale I then shot my rifle and the same load (his) and fired a group that measured just under .27", my smallest to date. For this shooting, though, on my rifle I'd mounted a 10x Unertl Varmint scope. With its smaller crosshair I figured I might be able to squeeze group size down a bit. However, in spite of this braggin' size .269" group, over-all testing didn't show any significant difference between groups shot with the two scopes.

It is very rare, at least in my experience, to find a rifle that will handle so many different bullet styles or weights, in this case from 50 to 70 grains. None of the other centerfire rifles I've owned over the years would do it, hence this Ruger is a jewel. Now that the test shooting is over with, very, very little shooting at targets will be done with it. Instead the barrel will be reserved for serious varmint shooting.

Nosler Match Boat-Tails

The Nosler Match HPBT 52-gr. bullets arrived near the end of January. Shooting conditions weren't good but, considering the time of the year, they could have been a hell of a lot worse. The temperature was 25 degrees and what wind there was came out of the north but, as the range faces south, this was no problem.

For testing 12 rounds were loaded with 39.5 grains of 4320, 12 with 38.5/4064 and 12 more with 42/4831, all in Norma cases and with Remington 9½ primers. The Ruger rifle was cleaned after each 10 shots and two shots of each 12 were fired to condition the bore.

The first loads shot were those using 4320 as this had been the most accurate load with all of the other match bullets. The first group measured .958" but one was high and the other 4 were in .298". The second group measured .542".

The 4064 loads fared a little better at .532" and .613", again with one or two shots away from the rest.

I had high hopes for the 4831 loads as these have always shown top notch accuracy, but groups were larger than expected at .898" and .635", again with one or two shots going wide.

Grand average of the 6 groups was on the order of .69", which is very close to the average of the Nosler regular HPBT bullets. Though I was a little disappointed in the results with the match grade Noslers, I must point out that all of my previous shooting, with all other bullets, had been done in much better conditions. Yet, in my shooting, the flat-base bullets have performed better than the Sierra and Nosler boat-tails in the Ruger Swift.

While waiting for the above Noslers to arrive I'd borrowed some early-production Nosler — 52-gr. match grade HPBTs in polished and unpolished form — and some first-run Remington match bullets of 53-gr. type.

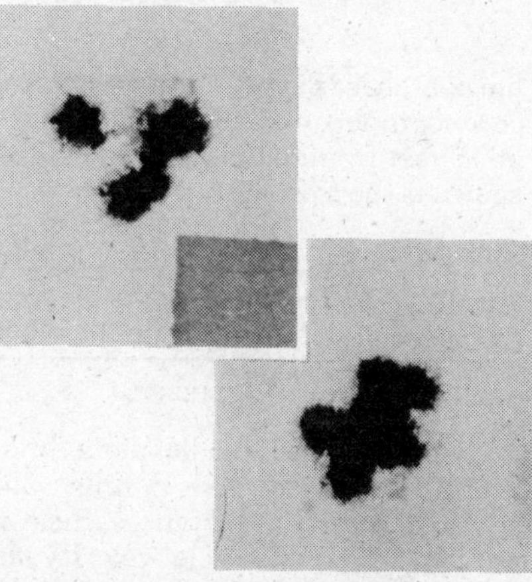

70-gr. Speers shot well in the Ruger 220. These are 5-shot 100-yd. groups; .376" (left) and .426", the load 44/4831/9½ primers.

Accordingly 12 of each were loaded with 39.5/4320, primers Remington 9½ in Norma cases. Two of these were to be used as foulers and the other 10 to be fired for group, 5 shots each.

The day these were fired left a lot to be desired; the temp was 33° with a rather chilly wind blowing, and there was a heavy overcast.

First group with the unpolished Noslers measured .867" with 4 touching and one out. The next measured a flat .9" with only two shots touching each other. Next up were the polished Noslers, the first group .898"; all strung up and down but 3 were in a very tight cluster. The last group measured 1.071", again strung up and down, but also 3 together.

The first Remington group gave a rather large group of .887". I say "rather large" because these will generally average, and note I said average, under ½" for 5 shots. Four shots were touching, but the one wild shot shows an elongated hole as if the bullet had tipped. The next group measured .459", which is more in line with what the bullet will usually do in the Ruger Swift.

Test Notes

Both of the Ruger Swifts have good chambers and long throats. The 53-gr. Sierra flat base match bullet can be seated to an over-all length of 2.84" and, obviously, both barrels must be top notch in view of the accuracy that both can and do give.

The front guard screw on the Ruger 77 rifles is angled, a radical (and U.S. patented) departure, as all other bolt action rifles use a vertical front screw. The barrel is free floating, except for the last inch or so at the muzzle, which has full contact with the fore-end. Nothing was done to change or even check the bedding otherwise and, except for installing the Canjar trigger, the wood and metal have never been apart. Believe me, I ain't about to change anything, not the way it shoots now!

All loading was done with full-length RCBS dies, but backed off so that only half of the neck was sized; these were set up in the RCBS Rockchucker press. Primer pockets were cleaned using the new RCBS brush type primer pocket cleaner which is a little whiz for this work. Powder charges were thrown with the RCBS measure, but a few tenths light and then brought up to par using an old Redding powder scale. As already mentioned, primer seating was done using the Lee priming tool. Cases were checked or trimmed after each shot on a Forster trimmer as the Swift case does tend to lengthen when loaded to near-top or top pressure/velocity levels.

For best accuracy the 52/53-gr. match grade bullets are *it!* However, the Speer 70-gr. bullet is an exception. You will pay more for the match grade bullets, but if you want the best in accuracy then this is the way to go. While the Remington match HPs gave a little better accuracy in this Swift than did the Sierras, there was very little practical difference, none really as far as field performance is concerned. The other match grade bullets were also good performers and the improved Speer Silver match bullet is very good. This has a much larger HP than the older version.

Following my mixed-bullet testing session, I managed to get out to the range again — in spite of the bad weather—and four 5-shot groups with the new Speer Silvers went into another .6″-.65″ average. The older Speer Silvers hovered around the 1-inch mark.

For some reason the boat-tail design—Sierra match or Nosler regular BT—doesn't perform quite as well in this Swift as do the flat-based versions; your rifle, though, might prefer the BT bullets. Still, accuracy of .6″ to .65″ with the BT bullets is a damned fine performance for a bullet moving over 3800 fps. The new Nosler match grade bullet was unavailable for testing as this is written due to production difficulties.

One thing can certainly be said about Bill Ruger and his crew—they've got intestinal fortitude! Can you see Remington or Winchester bringing out rifles for the 7x57 Mauser, the 257 Roberts, 22 Hornet, 30-40 Krag and last, but by no means least, the 220 Swift. Norma is the only company still loading Swift ammunition, which makes Ruger's move even more surprising. This takes guts, even if some of the chamberings named will be limited editions.* But it hasn't been too many years ago that "they" said Ruger's Single Action Revolvers wouldn't sell, either. That outfit at Ruger's is crazy—like a fox that is. More power to them!

High Velocity Check

I wanted to see if the Ruger Swift could show good accuracy with higher muzzle speeds, and here's what the chronograph revealed, velocity taken at 10 feet from the muzzle.The speed shown is the average of 10 shots.

Bullet/grs.	Powder/grs.	V/fps
Sisk 45 Sp	3031/39.0	4087
Sierra 50 Sp	3031/38.0	3992

Norma cases, Rem. 9½ primers.

Using the NRA Handloader's Guide tables formula for determining velocity loss over short distances, the correction for true muzzle velocity for the two bullets fired comes to about 37 and 30 respectively, thus MV can be read as about 4124 for the Sisk bullet and about 4022 for the Sierra.

*At this time—mid-winter 1973-74, Ruger's 257, 7x57 and 220 Swift rifles have been made in limited quantities (a few thousand of each) and all have been parceled out to the trade. Few remain on dealers' shelves. Bill Ruger told me that the 220 Swift rifles had sold exceptionally fast, and that he planned to add this chambering to his regular Model 77 calibers in 1974. J.T.A.

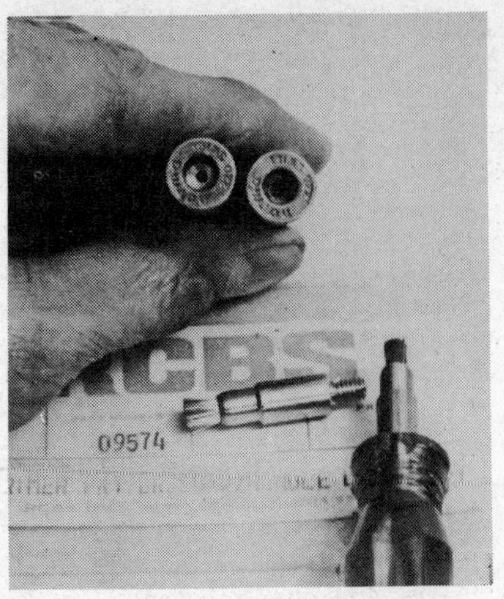

The new RCBS stainless steel brush-type primer pocket cleaner is quick and easy to use.

Marble and Walther 220/22 Adaptors

Having bought one of these obsolete adaptors at a gun show, I gave it a trial in the M77 Ruger Swift.

Accuracy was only fair. Fifty-yard groups as small as ¾-inch were rare, and drop was considerable—Winchester T-22s printed 4.2 inches low from my 100-yd. zero with full power loads. Another brand, match velocity ammo, dropped some 6 inches.

If you find one of these Marble adaptors—for the 220 Swift or any other centerfire 22—try several brands or types of 22 rimfires. One or two are almost certain to shoot much better than the rest.

The Walther (German-made) 220/22 adaptor—imported and sold by Harry Owen, Sport Specialties, Box 774, Sunnyvale, CA 94088—gave a quite poor performance in the Ruger Swift. I tried 5 brands of 22 L.R. cartridges, but no two shots were within 3½ inches of each other! As a check, I shot 5 rounds through the Marble unit and got a 0.79-inch group. I found this puzzling, too, because a Walther 222/22 adaptor did quite well in a Remington 700—1″-1¼″ for 5. ●

Barrel Cleaning

Much of the bad press the Swift received related to cleaning—or to the failure to clean properly. In the 1930s the necessity to scrub the barrel ceased—non-corrosive primers and gilding metal bullet jackets were introduced, and cleaning the bore declined, at least to a considerable degree. Unknown then was the fact that powder and jacket material could build up in the bore to a degree—however slight relatively—that could seriously affect accuracy.

Such conditions developed in many Swift rifles—their accuracy fell off, of course, but the true cause lay undiscovered for many years. Instead it was charged that their ultra velocity was the culprit, that the bores become eroded unduly fast, that barrel life was as little as a few hundred or so rounds, *ad infinitum*.

We know better today—as we should. The benchresters have led the way in discovering that frequent and careful bore cleaning is an absolute must operation if accuracy levels are to be retained.

Moral—if you own or intend to buy an accurate rifle, run a tight brass or bronze bristle brush through it after each 10 or 15 shots, using Hoppe's or another reliable powder solvent. Tedious and time consuming? Sure, but you'll keep that barrel shooting.

If you have a rifle that seems to have lost some of its performance, try J-B Compound as directed on the label. It cannot do any harm, and it could help greatly. This treatment won't rescue a barrel that never was a good performer, of course. J.T.A.

220 Swift Loading Data

Bullet	Weight/grs.	Powder	Weight/grs.	MV/fps
Sierra	50 SP	3031	37.0	3960
Remington	52 Match	4320	39.5	3876
Sierra	53 Match	4064	38.5	3846
Hornady	53 Match	H-414	42.5	3721
Nosler	52 HP/BT	R-21	39.5	3843
Sierra	55 SP	4350	44.5	3809
Remington	52 Match	4831	41.0	3163
Speer	53 HP	4895	39.0	3889
Hornady	60 HP	H-380	40.5	3535
Speer	70 SP	N-205	45.0	3417
Speer	70 SP	4831	44.0	3263

All loads above were chronographed using an ITCC instrument. All were assembled in once-fired Norma cases with Remington No. 9½ large rifle primers. Many of the above loads are maximum or nearly so, and starting loads should be reduced at least 5% using the same components, more if components cited are changed.

JAPANESE AUTOLOADING PISTOLS

. . . a Comprehensive History

by John L. Moss

Japanese semiautomatic pistols have been common in America since the end of World War II, but printed material on them is scanty and public reaction has been scornful. Most don't deserve such cavalier treatment, claims this long-time student. Get the facts in this full-length, definitive article

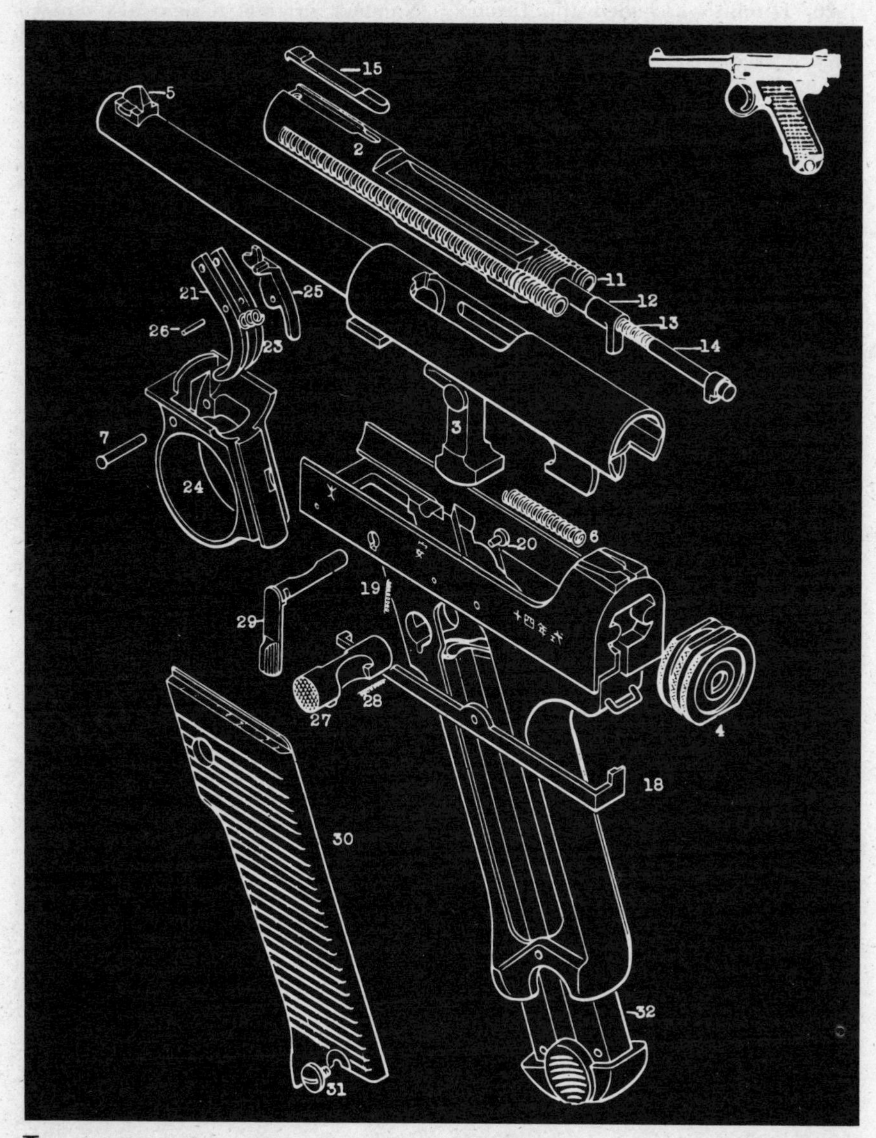

Parts List

1. Barrel
2. Breechbolt
3. Lock/block
4. Bolt nut
5. Front sight
6. Lock block spring
7. Trigger axle
11. Recoil spring
12. Firing pin
13. Firing pin spring
14. Firing pin guide
15. Extractor
16. Ejector
17. Frame
18. Sear
19. Sear spring
20. Sear pin
21. Trigger
23. Trigger spring
24. Trigger guard
25. Trigger lever
26. Trigger lever pin
27. Magazine catch
28. Magazine catch spring
29. Safety
30. Grip
31. Grip screw
32. Magazine

Japanese Pistol, Model 1925, reproduced from *The Firearms Handbook* by Shelley Braverman (Athens, N.Y., 1960), through the courtesy of the author, from whom the various parts are available.

IN 1945, AFTER YEARS of bitter fighting, the Rising Sun of Nippon finally set. Returning American fighting men brought back thousands of Japanese semiautomatic pistols as souvenirs of the Pacific conflict. Despite the large number of these pistols in America, however, little has been written about them.

Semiautomatic pistols of the basic Nambu design were the standard service handguns of Japan from 1914 until the termination of WW II. These pistols have been objects of much scorn, evolving from a general lack of knowledge about Japanese weapons and a poor reputation derived from those specimens of poor materials and poorer workmanship produced in the closing days of the war. This scorn is not deserved, for most Japanese pistols were well made of good materials, and quite acceptable as military weapons.

Kijiro Nambu was a field grade officer in the Imperial Japanese Army when he first produced his "Type Nambu" pistol. He evidently designed the weapon around the turn of the century, as the Japanese High Command authorized its purchase by officers as early as 1904. Since a weapon is rarely adopted or recognized by

The author gratefully acknowledges the assistance of the following individuals in the preparation of this article: Roy A. Brayton; Kirk Kellogg; John Lappin; Leslie McCleary, and Al Moss, his brother. Without their help, the completion of this article would not have been possible.

any government until it has undergone official trials, or commercial sales and public use, it stands to reason that the Type Nambu pistol was no exception. Therefore, it is reasonable to assume that specimens of Nambu's design were in existence prior to 1904, perhaps as early as 1899.

It has been suggested that the Nambu is a copy of the Italian Glisenti 9mm pistol, to which it bears some similarity. Certain information, however, tends to discredit this belief. The original Glisenti pistol was patented in Italy on June 30, 1905, by the Societa Siderurgica Glisenti, of Carcina, Italy, one year after the Type Nambu pistol was authorized for purchase by Japanese officers. Thus, there seems little doubt that the Nambu was an original Japanese design.

Model Designations

The Japanese method of assigning model designations has been the source of some confusion. A brief explanation of these systems, as related to automatic pistols, should clear this up.

The bulk of perplexity centers around the designation of the original Nambu design, often referred to in the U.S. as the Papa Nambu. Some sources have called it the Model 1904 Nambu, others the Model 1914 Nambu. Officially, the Japanese government called it only the Shiki Nambu Kenju, or Type Nambu Pistol. Even though the government sanctioned its purchase by officers in 1904, enlisted men armed with a handgun were still required to carry the regulation sidearm, the Type 26 revolver. Nambu's pistol was not officially adopted by the Japanese service until 1914. This explains why it has been referred to as the Type Nambu, the Model 1904, and the Model 1914. None of these designations is completely erroneous, but Type Nambu is most correct.

The Baby Nambu, as the cal. 7mm Type Nambu pistol is often called, was also known merely as Type Nambu Pistol, and evidently never had an official year-model designation. It seems to have appeared in the first decade of the 20th century, not long after the 8mm Type Nambu, and production probably continued on a limited basis into the 1920s.

The first Japanese semiautomatic pistol to bear an official numerical designation was the Type 14 (Model 1925), an improvement of the original Nambu design. Most equipment adopted by the Japanese military prior to 1926 was named for the year of the Emperor's reign in which it was adopted. The Type 14 pistol was adopted in the fourteenth (final) year of Taisho, the reign of Emperor Yoshihito, that being the Julian calender year 1925.

After 1926, designations were based on the assumed date of the founding of the Japanese Empire. Thus, the Model 1934 Pistol, known as the Type 94 in Japan, was adopted in the Japanese year 2594 and derives its designation from the last two digits of that date. This explains the seeming disparity in nomenclature between the Type 14, adopted in 1925, and the Type 94, selected only nine years later.

Another area of interest is the method of dating actual manufacture as found on Type 14 and Type 94 pistols. 1925 saw the end of the Taisho Reign in Japan. With the death of his father, Yoshihito, on December 25, 1926, Hirohito ascended the throne, thus beginning the Showa (Enlightened Peace) Era. In the Japanese dating system, the year an Emperor comes to the throne is considered the first year of his reign. Therefore, even though Hirohito was Emperor less than a week during 1926, that year is considered the first year of his reign. 1926, then, is Year One of the Showa Era. Dates of manufacture found on Type 14 and Type 94 pistols are expressed in the year of the Reign of Showa, followed by a decimal point and the numerical designation of the month. Thus, a pistol marked "12.1" was manufactured in the twelfth year of Showa during the first month, or January, 1937. All Type 14 and Type 94 pistols examined by the author have been dated in this fashion.

In passing, it might be of interest to translate the markings found on Japanese pistols, character by character. See Table I.

For an explanation of arsenal markings that will be encountered on Japanese semiautomatic pistols, see Table II.

Most other markings found on these pistols are either Arabic numerals showing the date of manufacture and the serial number, or Japanese characters expressing proof marks or perhaps an inspector's initials or markings. The latter are extremely difficult to translate, and of little importance.

Now that some of the background has been discussed, let us examine each of the basic Japanese semiautomatic pistol models in greater detail.

8mm Type Nambu

The Type Nambu pistol, Kijiro Nambu's original design, also known as Papa Nambu, Model 1904, and Model 1914, will be encountered in two major variations, differing somewhat in construction, and in several minor ones, which differ merely in details of machining and markings. Only the major variations need be discussed in detail here. Of eleven 8mm Type Nambu pistols examined by the author, only one was of the first variation. On this early model, the magazine bottom piece is of wood; those produced later are metal. The lanyard ring on the first variation is a fixed, U-shaped protrusion, similar to that on Luger pistols, while the loop on the rear of the second variation is a ring linked through a fixed stud. Also, the shape of the cocking knob is somewhat different between the two variations.

The first variation Papa Nambu in the author's collection is cut along the back grip strap for the attachment of a shoulder stock. Of the 10 second variation pistols examined, 5 had never been cut for a stock; on the remaining 5 the stock slot had been

The 7mm Type Nambu pistol, often referred to as the "Baby" Nambu. These beautifully made little pistols are seldom encountered. They were carried primarily by staff officers of the Japanese armed forces. Note that trigger section is identical to that on the first variation 8mm Papa Nambu. Author's collection.

Cal.: 7mm Nambu	Mag. cap.: 7 rounds
Bbl.: 3¼"	Grooves: 6
Over-all: 6¾"	Twist: 1/11, right hand
Wgt.: 20½ ozs.	

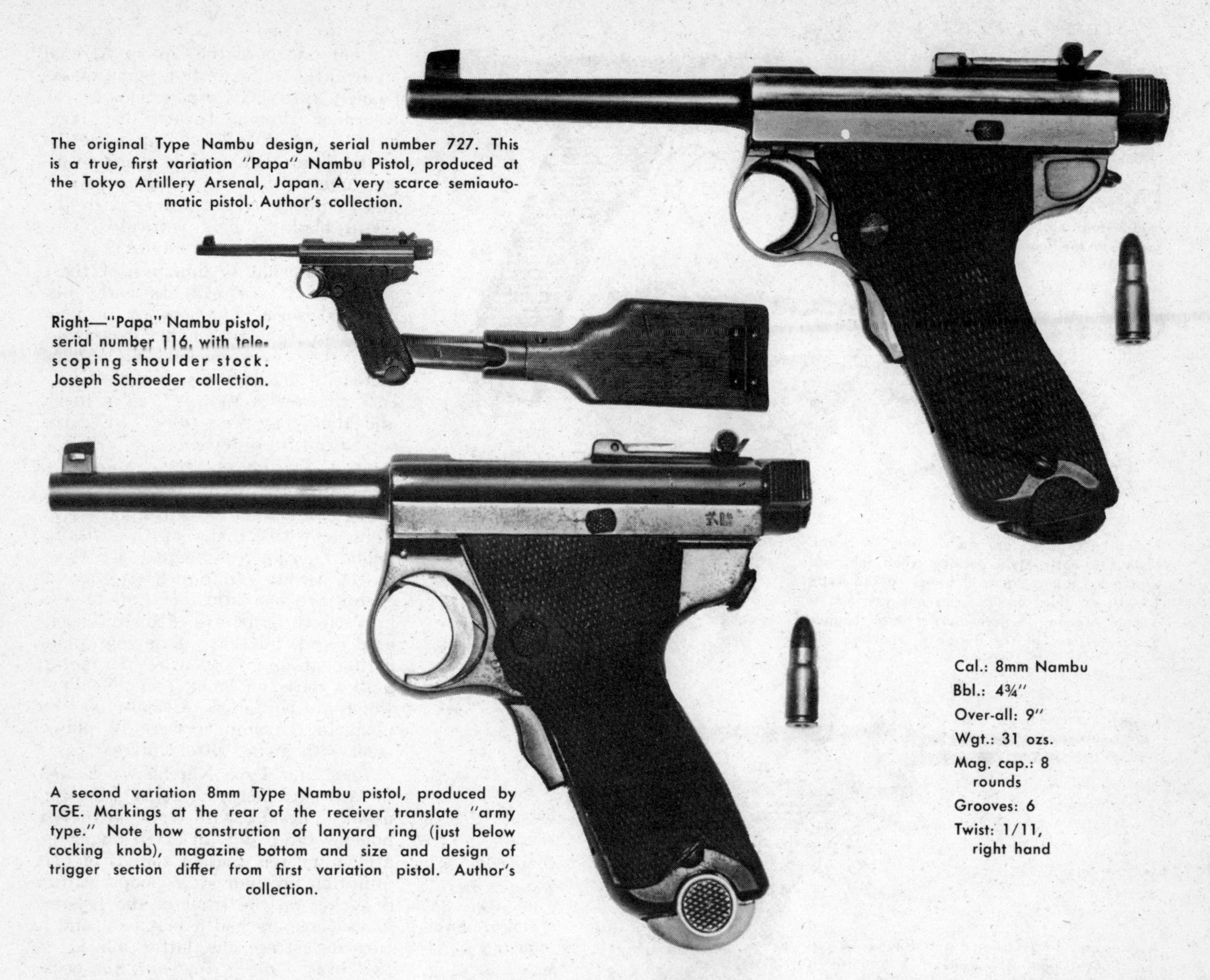

The original Type Nambu design, serial number 727. This is a true, first variation "Papa" Nambu Pistol, produced at the Tokyo Artillery Arsenal, Japan. A very scarce semiautomatic pistol. Author's collection.

Right—"Papa" Nambu pistol, serial number 116, with telescoping shoulder stock. Joseph Schroeder collection.

A second variation 8mm Type Nambu pistol, produced by TGE. Markings at the rear of the receiver translate "army type." Note how construction of lanyard ring (just below cocking knob), magazine bottom and size and design of trigger section differ from first variation pistol. Author's collection.

expertly filled in, apparently many years ago. The reason for filling these slots, and where and when it was done, is unknown to the writer.

The shape of the stock cut on the first variation pistol indicates that the stock-attaching lug was similar in construction to that used with German Mauser pistols of the 1896 type, but the exact nature of the stock itself can be seen above. The first picture of a Nambu pistol stock ever seen by the author appeared in *Special Series Number 19, MID 461,* "Japanese Infantry Weapons," dated December 31, 1943. This is a manual prepared by the Military Intelligence Division of the U.S. War Department. Shown is a second variation Type Nambu pistol equipped with a holster-stock apparently fabricated of wood, much like those issued with Mauser pistols, but with a telescoping extension. The illustration appears to be a drawing, so its accuracy may be open to question.

Papa Nambu Variations

Perhaps the most significant difference between the first and second variation Papa Nambus is in the construction of the trigger section. In the original design much of the trigger bar, directly above the trigger, is exposed. This is the identical mechanism noted on all Baby Nambu pistols. Type Nambus made later have a trigger section positioned slightly lower on the front grip strap, which encloses the entire mechanism save for the trigger itself. The trigger guard on second variation pistols is much larger than on the original design, as is the trigger itself, and bears a closer similarity to the Type 14 pistol than to the first variation Papa Nambu.

All 8mm Type Nambus encountered have been equipped with tangent-type rear sights adjustable in 50-meter steps to 500 meters. All had grip safety devices on the front grip strap, directly below the trigger guard. This is the only safety found on Papa Nambu pistols. The checkered button on the left side of the receiver above the grip is not a safety, as some sources have stated. It has to do with disassembly, which will not be discussed here. Both variations of the Type Nambu are mechanically similar, and use the same short-recoil locking system. Grips on all noted specimens have been of checkered wood.

Of the 11 Type Nambus examined, three had the intertwined-circle trademark of the Tokyo Artillery Arsenal over the chamber, 7 were marked TGE, and one specimen, in one of the finest Japanese pistol collections in the country, for reasons unknown was marked TGE over the chamber and yet had the Tokyo Arsenal mark on the right-rear of the receiver. Several had an anchor stamped on the right-rear of the receiver, indicating issue by the Japanese navy. It is interesting that these pistols, marked for navy property, nevertheless bore the characters for "Army Type" on the left-rear of the receiver.

Some mystery surrounds the so-called TGE trademark. This is believed by many collectors to stand for Tokyo Gas and Electric, but this interpretation does not seem valid. Although the manufacturer's monogram is in Arabic letters, rather than Japanese characters, it seems doubtful that the words represented by these initials would be English words as well, as Type Nambu pistols were never exported to an English-speaking country. Indeed, it is strange enough that Arabic letters were used at all. More likely, these letters are a translitera-

The small trigger guard Type 14 pistol, adopted in 1925 by the Japanese government. This model does not have the magazine retaining spring in the lower-front grip strap. Author's collection.

An early large trigger guard Type 14 pistol. Note the early style cocking knob identical with those found on small trigger guard Type 14s. Upper third of the grips not grooved — a style peculiar to these earlier large trigger guard versions of the Type 14. Author's collection.

A late issue large trigger guard Type 14 pistol. Construction is excellent, but finish is rather crude. Note checkered cocking knob — much easier to produce than the early grooved type. Grips are grooved from top to bottom in the manner of the early, small trigger guard Type 14 Pistols. Author's collection.

Cal.: 8mm Nambu
Bbl.: 4⅝″
Over-all: 9-/16″
Wgt.: 32 ozs. (large guard; 31¾ ozs., small guard)
Mag. cap.: 8 rounds
Lands and grooves: 6
Twist: 1/11, right hand

tion of Japanese characters (and words) into Arabic letters. Since the transliteration of the characters for Tokyo Gas and Electric would, phonetically, be "Tokyo Gasu Denki," resulting in the initials "TGD," the Tokyo Gas and Electric theory does not seem reasonable. Further, as written on the pistols, the trademark actually reads GTE, not TGE. True, the T is the dominant letter and, therefore, could be interpreted as the first letter of the initials. It would seem that the actual meaning of this marking is still unknown and further research is warranted.

All Papa Nambus examined have been of high quality manufacture and finish, but most have shown hard use and many reflect a lack of proper care. This is in marked contrast to the cal.-7mm Type Nambu, popularly called the Baby Nambu, discussed next. Almost all of these encountered have been not only of the highest quality of fit and finish, but also in excellent condition, reflecting little use and much care.

7mm Type Nambu

For many years the existence of the 7mm Type Nambu was nothing more than a rumor. Even as late as the early days of WW II, some U.S. ordnance authorities denied its existence. Indeed, the previously mentioned Military Intelligence Division manual, published in late 1943, makes no mention of either the pistol or its cartridge. However, after the war these little sidearms began to find their way to American shores, and while still a rather scarce weapon, they are common in advanced arms collections. The author has seen a dozen or so in local collections and at gun shows, and does not believe them nearly so scarce as original 8mm Type Nambu (Papa) pistols.

Among specimens examined, no variation whatsoever has been observed, except for arsenal markings. All but one bore the Tokyo Arsenal trademark, the exception being of extremely rare TGE production. At the Aberdeen Proving Ground in Maryland is one probably unique variation of the 7mm Nambu. This pistol forms the handle of a samurai-type sword, and is presented for firing when the sword blade is held vertically. This weapon's history is unknown.

It is unusual to find one of these attractive little pistols with mismatched serial numbers or in poor condition. It is reasonable to assume, since they were owned and carried primarily by high-ranking staff officers, that few were ever fired in anger, and that they were diligently cared for by dutiful orderlies.

Mechanically, the Baby Nambu is virtually identical to the first variation Papa Nambu, except for the rear sight and the shape of the cocking knob. This knob is shaped like those on the second variation Papa Nambu. Sights are non-adjustable, all have a grip safety, grips are of finely checkered wood, but have a narrow, plain border around the entire perimeter, unlike those on 8mm Type Nambus, which are borderless. All Baby Nambu magazines examined were of plated steel with metal bottom pieces.

The 7mm Type Nambu was issued in an extremely compact holster, usually pigskin, with provision for housing the pistol, an extra magazine, a cleaning rod, and 14 rounds of ammunition in individual loops within a pocket on the front of the holster. These holsters had a belt loop and a carrying strap, the latter affixed to two brass "dee" rings on the back. The cleaning rod is plated steel, with a slotted tip. The tip also forms a screwdriver, apparently for removal of the grips, as no other screws are used in the construction of the 7mm and 8mm Nambus.

The Baby Nambu is often considered unique because it is a true miniature of the earlier 8mm. Actually, many arms manufacturers have produced series of pistols of identical design, but varying in size proportionate to the cartridge utilized. Among notable examples are the Bergmann and Astra lines of automatics. The 5mm Bergmann is almost identical to the 6.5mm, except much smaller. Another, perhaps more common, example is found in the Spanish Astra line. The Model 400, in 9mm Bayard caliber, has two duplicates, each progressively smaller. The Model 600, in 9mm Parabellum caliber, is only slightly smaller than the Model 400, while the Model 300 Astra is smaller than either, but still mechanically identical, and fires the 32 or 380 ACP cartridges. In revolver-automatics, the truly unique Webley-Fosbery was made primarily in 44 caliber, but there is also a smaller duplicate in 38 caliber.

The year 1925 saw considerable improvement of the original design of Kijiro Nambu, which resulted in the government's adoption of the Type 14 semiautomatic pistol. These improvements, and the pistol which resulted, bear careful examination, as the Type 14 is the Japanese pistol most often encountered.

8mm Type 14 Pistol

After 21 years of military use, the Type Nambu pistol was finally improved, and officially was superseded in the Japanese armed forces by the Type 14, in the 14th year of Taisho (1925). It must be reiterated that the designation Type 14 has nothing whatsoever to do with the fact that the original Type Nambu pistol has been popularly called the Model 1914 in the U.S. Sources have attributed the designation to the fact that it is an improvement of the original Type Nambu pistol, which they have termed the Model 1914 Nambu. This is, of course, erroneous. The Papa Nambu was never officially known as the Model 1914, and the Type 14 derives its designation solely from the date of its adoption. As this was 1925, the pistol is sometimes known as the Model 1925.

The Type 14 incorporated many design changes. The single recoil spring, housed in a tube milled into the left side of the Type Nambu's receiver, making it somewhat lopsided in appearance and considerably wider than necessary, was eliminated. In its place were dual recoil springs housed within recesses on either side of the barrel extension and bolt, giving the Type 14 a generally sleeker appearance than the Papa Nambu, and perhaps a more positive action. The grip safety of the Type Nambu was eliminated in favor of a rotating safety catch located on the left front of the receiver. The catch rotates 180° and is on safe when turned to the rear. Although far more positive than the grip safety, which has a weak leaf spring, this rotating catch is poorly positioned and almost impossible to disengage with the hand gripping the weapon.

American theory has always held that a handgun, to be useful in emergencies, must be capable of being drawn from the holster, having the safety disengaged, and fired in the shortest possible time. Even the American issue holster, with its leg thong and exposed grip, is designed for fast draw. In fairness to the Type 14's safety device, it must be said that the Japanese patterned their military practices somewhat after European armies, whose practices dictate that the pistol be carried in hand, ready for firing, whenever there is the faintest possibility that it will be needed. This would minimize, for the Japanese, the need for a safety that could be disengaged with the shooting hand. From an American viewpoint, however, it's a poor design.

Magazine Disconnector

In addition to the safety catch, the Type 14 has a magazine disconnector, a device not found on the original Type Nambu. With the magazine removed, the pistol cannot be fired even though loaded and cocked and the manual safety disengaged. Again, this is a feature quite popular on European pistols and some American commercial designs, but frowned upon by American military concepts. It can be reasoned validly that if the magazine of a pistol equipped with a magazine disconnector is lost, the weapon is useless, even if loose cartridges are at hand. Type 14 pistols with dates of manufacture ranging from February, 1928, through June, 1945, were examined, and were found, without exception, to be equipped with magazine disconnectors. Competent authorities have written that early Type 14s were manufactured without this feature, but the author has yet to see one.

All Type 14s were manufactured with fixed sights of rather good design for fast combat shooting. The front sight is of pyramid shape, while the rear sight is a notch slightly wider at the bottom than at the top, thereby complementing the front one. The author found this sighting arrangement quite satisfactory in test firing, the sights aligning quickly.

Many variations exist in the Type 14 series. The two basic ones are the Small Trigger Guard and the Large Trigger Guard types. Other than in markings, the author has encountered no significant differences among the small-guard variety. The same cannot be said for the later Type 14 pistols. Those with large guards will be found to have many differences, depending primarily on when they were manufactured.

The greatest single variation in mechanical detail of the Type 14 is found

Cal.: 8mm Nambu
Bbl.: 3¾"
Over-all: 7½"
Wgt.: 27½ ozs.
Mag. cap.: 6 rounds
Grooves: 6
Twist: 1/11, right hand

The Type 94 8mm pistol. Note the unusual shape of the grip. Author's collection.

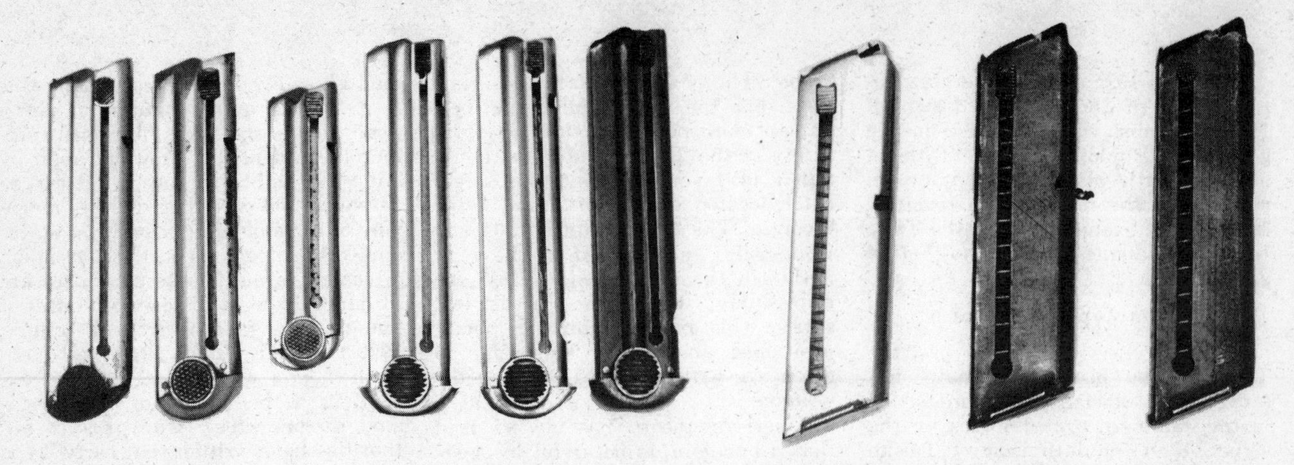

Japanese semiautomatic pistol magazines. From left: first variation Papa Nambu; second variation Papa Nambu; 7mm Baby Nambu; small trigger guard Type 14; early large trigger guard Type 14; later large trigger guard Type 14. The first five magazines are chrome plated, the sixth is blued. The fourth and fifth are identical, except the fifth has a hole in the bottom-front edge for the magazine retaining spring found on large trigger guard Type 14s. Right-hand photo shows Type 94 pistol magazine variations. Magazine at left is chrome plated and has a rectangular, grooved follower button. Center magazine, of blued steel, has similar follower button. The one on the right is blued and has a round, checkered follower button.

in the firing pins and bolt-locking pieces. All small-guard and earlier large-guard versions examined have had firing pins approximately 3″ long which, when released from the sear, stop short of the bolt-locking piece engaged in a notch in the bolt. Shortly after 1940, the firing pin was shortened to about 2½″, and the bolt-locking piece was deeply notched to allow passage of the firing pin on its longer fall. This shorter firing pin, with resultant longer firing pin fall (and lock time), was evidently adopted to lessen the chance of misfire due to insufficient indentation of hard primers. While long lock time is not desirable in a target weapon, it certainly is more positive on a military handgun where greater variation in ammunition characteristics may be expected.

Another significant variation between early and later Type 14 pistols is in the shape of the cocking knob. Small-guard pistols, and the earlier run of the large-guard model, have cocking knobs with three narrow, checkered flanges separated by two deep, wide grooves. Pistols produced after the beginning of the war between Japan and the U.S. usually have cocking knobs which are checkered, but ungrooved. One specimen, produced late in 1945, had an absolutely smooth knob on the end of the bolt. That particular pistol was the crudest Japanese firearm ever viewed by the author.

At approximately the same time the large, elongated trigger guard was adopted, apparently for easy handling of the pistol with winter gloves, another addition was made to the Type 14. This was a piece of spring steel riveted to the lower front grip strap and passing through a slot into the magazine well. This spring serves two purposes, only one of which seems understood by the majority of those familiar with the Type 14. First, the spring prevents the magazine from falling out if the release button is accidentally depressed. This is important in a pistol having a magazine disconnector, where loss of the magazine completely inactivates the weapon. Magazines for pistols provided with this spring have a piece cut out of the lower front edge. When the follower is depressed to its lowest position, the lip on its front end catches in this hole and holds the follower down. This makes the insertion of cartridges much easier than if they are pushed in one at a time against the follower spring's tension. However, with the follower locked down, there is no spring force to feed the cartridges upward once the magazine is filled. This is where the second function of the friction spring comes in. When the magazine is inserted, the tongue of the friction spring, passing through the front grip strap, bears on the tongue of the magazine follower locked in the magazine hole. It forces the follower to the rear, freeing it from the magazine recess and releasing the spring tension against the follower. While the practical military value of this device is open to question, it is quite handy and original. No other semiautomatic pistol known to the author has such a feature.

Early magazines, found primarily in small-guard Type 14s, are plated, while those of later manufacture are blued. Plated magazines have been examined which had the recess and were made for use in the earlier large-guard pistols. No blued magazines without this cut have been seen by the author. Magazine followers are provided with a rectangular, grooved button for depressing the follower. No variation in this button's size, shape or position have been noted. All Type 14 magazines have a metal alloy bottom piece, held to the magazine box by two pins. These bottom pieces have large, circular finger grips, with deep horizontal grooves. All Type 14 magazines examined, including those of the latest wartime manufacture, have been sturdy and well made, although they vary in finish, as do the pistols themselves.

One feature of the Type 14 remained constant throughout its 20 years of production — the trigger pull. All pistols have good trigger take-up, regardless of how finely or crudely finished the weapon is. The pull is uniform and light, if a bit long, and does not vary appreciably from one pistol to another. This, its rather good sights, and its light recoil all combine to make the Type 14 an enjoyable firearm to shoot.

With the exception of one extremely early specimen, dated February, 1928, which was replete with toolmarks, all pre-war Type 14s examined showed a high degree of attention to polish and fitting. Wartime pistols range from good finish and excellent fitting to crude finish and sloppy assembly. They are, however, no cruder than the infamous Volksturm weapons produced by the Nazis in the closing days of the European conflict. There is no truth to the myth that most Japanese weapons were crude and dangerous to fire. This is a misconception born from examination of only those specimens produced after Japan's major industries had been pounded to rubble by American air raids — the same situation that caused the Germans, noted for fine precision weapons, to produce some of the poorest, crudest firearms ever assembled.

There is no general rule for the type of finish found on Type 14 pis-

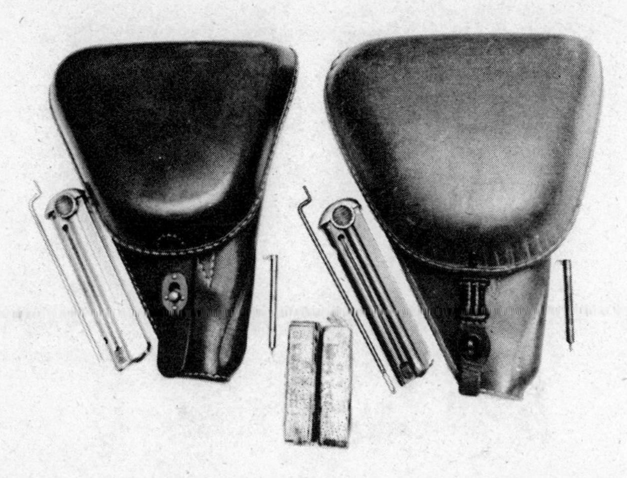

Type 14 pistol holsters. Holster at left is the early leather design, while the one at right is made of rubberized canvas. Identical in design, each is shown with cleaning rod, extra magazine and extra firing pin, which were carried in the holsters. At bottom-center are two original boxes of cartridges which were carried in a pocket on the front of the holster.

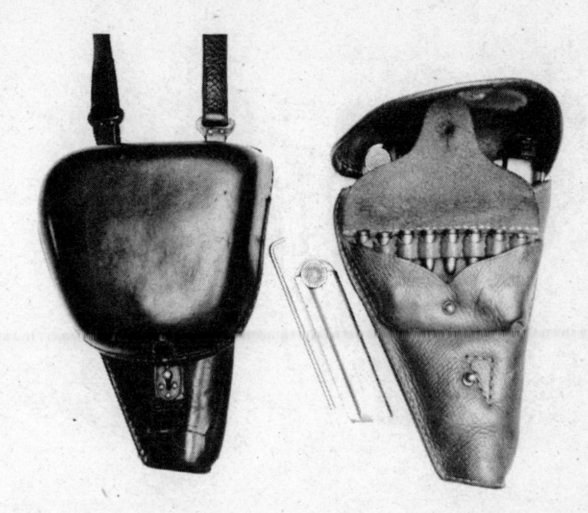

Original issue holsters for the 7mm Baby Nambu, shown with an original cleaning rod and extra magazine. Holster at right is open to show the pocket containing 14 cartridges carried in individual loops within the pocket. From the collections of the author and Roy A. Brayton.

tols. All of the small-guard variety examined have had a good finish, the major components being a light charcoal blue, with small parts heat-treated to a nice straw color. Early large-guard models also have this finish, while those produced during the war have no straw-colored parts and a finish which ranges from only fair to extremely crude.

Type 14s had wood grips, many with horizontal grooves covering most of the surface, although on some the upper third of the grips is plain. Pistols made in the closing days of the war normally have crude and poorly fitted smooth wood grips.

Most Type 14 pistols examined carried the mark of either the Nagoya Arsenal or its southern branch, although one had the intertwined-circle trademark of the Tokyo Artillery Arsenal. The latter was a small-guard version produced in 1929, undoubtedly made in Kokura after the transfer of the Tokyo Arsenal to that city in 1923.

Type 14s were issued with an excellent holster made either of leather or rubberized canvas. Some have said the leather ones were issued to officers, the others to enlisted men. More likely, the leather holster represents early manufacture, the canvas style probably being produced during the war.

Both are of the same general design, with a large, moulded flap, held shut by a tongue which snaps over a metal stud. Under this flap, on the front of the holster, is a large pocket which holds two 15-round boxes of ammunition. These are held in place by the pocket's own small flap, which also is held shut by a metal stud. Along the front edge of this pocket is a small, tubular pocket which holds an extra firing pin. Within the holster itself are compartments for a cleaning rod and extra magazine. These holsters are extremely compact rigs which eliminate the need for accessory pouches on the belt. The holster has a belt loop and two "dee" rings for a shoulder strap.

Early cleaning rods provided with the Type 14 pistols are plated, those issued later being blued steel. One end of these rods is slotted to take a cleaning patch, while the other is bent to form a pin punch. This punch fits the hole found on the right side of Type 14 magazine followers directly under the follower depressor button. As no other reason for this hole can be determined, it would seem that the end of the cleaning rod was intended to be inserted and used to depress the follower for loading, as well as for use as a pin punch during disassembly.

Although underpowered by our standards, the Type 14 is nevertheless an excellent pistol, and does not deserve the poor reputation it seems to have acquired since World War II.

8mm Type 94 Pistol

In 1934, 2,594 years after the assumed year of the founding of the Japanese Empire, another semiautomatic pistol appeared on the Japanese scene. Originally intended as a commercial weapon, probably primarily for export, the Type 94 pistol, named from the last two digits of the Japanese year 2594, was to see service with the Japanese armed forces. (It is also known as the Model 1934, for its year of adoption.)

This rather peculiar looking weapon became general issue, primarily in the Air Force, although it saw some use with naval landing parties, often erroneously referred to as "Japanese Marines." It was popular with pilots, probably because it is much smaller and lighter than the Type 14.

While a Japanese design, the Type 94 is not based on the Type Nambu, as is the Type 14 pistol, nor is it nearly so good a weapon as the latter. Early specimens of good quality manufacture are mediocre pistols at best, and those produced late in the war are very poor. Major faults are poor balance, an inadequate locking system for the best and safest performance, and too small a grip. The last criticism may be valid only from a Western standpoint, as the Oriental hand generally is smaller than the Caucasian. The grip, nevertheless, is poorly shaped for any size hand.

The only improvement over the Type 14 is in the position of the safety catch, a lever located at the left-rear of the receiver, thus easily manipulated by the thumb of the shooting hand. The Type 94 also has a magazine disconnector, hence cannot be fired with the magazine removed.

One extremely poor feature of the Type 94 is the completely exposed sear bar. The weapon may be accidentally discharged without any trigger movement if the sear bar is inadvertantly depressed. This dangerous feature, further, tends to negate the disconnector safety, which merely blocks the trigger when the magazine is removed. Even with the magazine removed, the sear bar may be depressed and the weapon fired.

No significant variations have been encountered among Type 94 Pistols. All had fixed sights, similar to those found on the earlier Japanese pistols. Finish ranges from good to crude, depending on the date of manufacture. Grips on early Type 94s are of black, checkered plastic, while those on pistols produced late in the war are of smooth wood. Three magazine variants have been noted. The earliest are chrome plated and have a rectangular, grooved follower button. Sec-

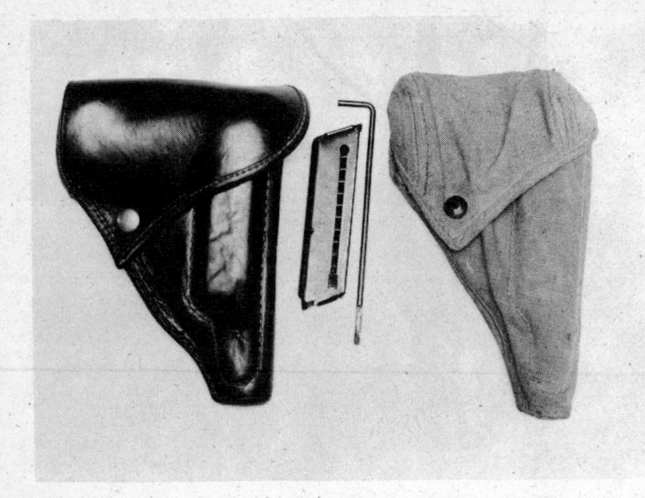

Original issue holsters for the Type 94 pistol. Holster on left is made of leather, while that at right is the extremely scarce soft canvas holster. Both are identical in design. The extra magazine and cleaning rod were carried in the pocket on the front of the holster.

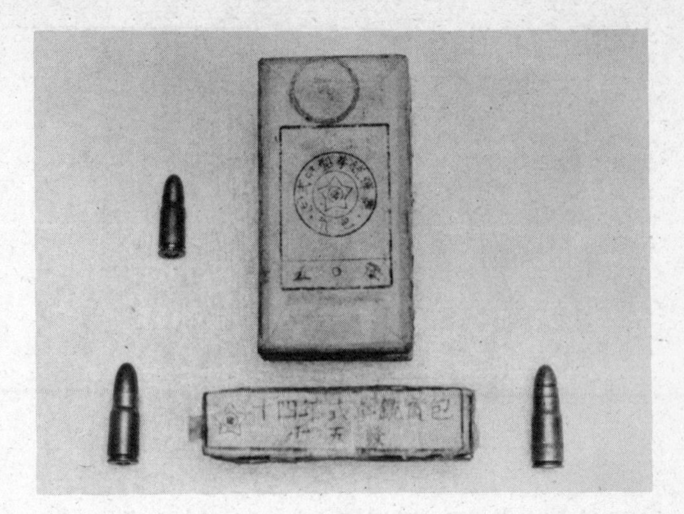

Top: original 50-round box for 7mm Nambu cartridges and an original 7mm Nambu cartridge. Bottom: original, 15-round box of 8mm Nambu cartridges for the Type 14 pistol, flanked by an original ball 8mm cartridge, left, and an original 8mm Nambu factory dummy round.

ond and third variation magazines are identical, except they are of blued steel, and the latter has a smaller depressing button on the follower, round in shape and checkered. All Type 94 magazines examined have been sturdy and well made, although those of late manufacture are crudely finished.

Type 94s were issued in two types of holsters, leather and canvas. The latter are soft, similar to British issue holsters, not the hard, moulded, rubberized canvas common to Type 14 pistol holsters. Both Type 94 holsters are identical in size, shape and design. They hold the pistol, an extra magazine and a cleaning rod, the accessories being contained in a common pocket on the front. The holster fastens with a snap. It has a belt loop and two "dee" rings for the attachment of a shoulder strap. The cleaning rod has a slotted tip, ground to screwdriver shape. All cleaning rods encountered have been of blued steel.

While a rather poor pistol, the Type 94 is nevertheless unusual in appearance and an interesting example of a native Oriental design.

Japanese Nambu Cartridges

No firearm can be any more effective than the cartridge for which it is chambered, nor can any discussion of a firearm be complete without some mention of the ammunition utilized. This is especially true of Japanese semiautomatic pistols, for the scarcity and marginal quality of their issue ammunition has been one of the main causes for the unfavorable opinion of Japanese pistols held by a majority of weapons enthusiasts.

With the exception of the 7mm Baby Nambu, all Japanese pistols previously mentioned are chambered for the 8mm Nambu cartridge. This is a bottlenecked rimless cartridge resembling the 7.65mm Luger cartridge. All specimens of original Japanese manufacture have brass cases, without headstamp markings of any kind. All are Berdan primed. Bullets are of two kinds, cupro-nickel or copper, both with lead cores. Bullets are seated approximately 3/8″ into the case and held by three stab crimps, spaced equidistant around the case neck.

Because of scarcity and value of original 8mm Nambu cartridges, it was not economical to disassemble more than one of each type to study the components. The cartridge with the cupro-nickel bullet contained 4.7 grains of a green powder of medium-coarse granules. Bullet weight was 100.8 grains. The copper colored bullet weighed 99.5 grains, and was backed by 4.9 grains of the same powder. Although all source books researched indicate the official weight of the 8mm Nambu bullet as 102 grains, an average of these two specimens suggests the intended weight was 100 grains. Measurement of only two specimens, however, is far from conclusive.

Japanese issue cleaning rods. Top to bottom: Baby Nambu, chrome plated; early Type 14, chrome plated; late Type 14, blued; Type 94, blued. Rods issued with the Baby Nambu and the Type 94 have screwdriver tips. Type 14 rods have handles bent to form pin punches.

The only other type of cartridge known for the 8mm Japanese pistols is the dummy round. The specimen in the author's collection has a plain cannelure on the bullet and a knurled cannelure around the case, approximately 1/4″ above the base, to identify it as a dummy.

Ball ammunition was issued in 15-round cardboard boxes, labeled in Japanese characters which usually read: 14th Year Type Pistol Ball Ammunition, 15 Rounds. Labels of all boxes seen by the author have carried the "star" trademark of the Tokyo Artillery Arsenal. Two boxes were carried in the large pocket on the front of Type 14 pistol holsters.

Published ballistics for the 8mm Nambu cartridge generally show a muzzle velocity of approximately 950 fps. A test by the H. P. White Laboratory, reported in *Centerfire Metric Pistol and Revolver Cartridges*, by H. P. White and B. D. Munhall (Washington, D. C., 1948), yielded an instrumental velocity at 15 feet of 1065 fps using a 4 9/16″ barrel. Muzzle energy of the 8mm Nambu is usually rated at 202 fp. While not in a class with our 45 ACP in stopping power, the 8mm Nambu is certainly as adequate as the 380 ACP, which was a

Table I

On the Papa and Baby Nambu pistols, the nomenclature markings found on the right-rear of the receiver are read from right to left. These characters read **Nambu Shiki,** and translate to Type Nambu, thus:	式 部 南
Characters on the left-rear of the receiver of second variation Papa Nambu pistols, right to left, read **Riki Shiki,** which translates to Army Type, as shown:	式 陸
Type 94 pistols are also read right to left. These markings, on the left side of the receiver above the trigger, mean **Kyoyon Shiki,** which translates as 94 Type as shown:	式 四 九
On Type 14 pistols, the nomenclature reads **Shiki Juyonen,** or Type 14th Year. These markings are found on the left-rear of the receiver:	十 四 年 式
Ideographs located at the safety lever on Type 14 and Type 94 pistols are:	火 安

Table II

Tokyo Artillery and Small Arms Arsenal (Kokura Arsenal after 1923). Found on Papa and Baby Nambu pistols on the receiver above the chamber.	
Allegedly the trademark of the "Tokyo Gas and Electric Company." Found on Papa and, in rare instances, Baby Nambu pistols, on the receiver above the chamber.	
Nagoya Arsenal. Found on Type 14 and Type 94 pistols on the receiver.	
Southern Branch of Nagoya Arsenal. Found on Type 14 and Type 94 pistols manufactured at that facility.	
Tokyo Arsenal ammunition marking. Found on cardboard ammunition containers.	
Navy property mark. Found on some Papa Nambu pistols, usually on the right-rear of the receiver.	

standard military and police cartridge in many European countries during both World Wars.

As mentioned, the Baby Type Nambu was the only standard Japanese semiautomatic pistol not chambered for the 8mm Nambu cartridge. It used a special 7mm bottlenecked, rimless cartridge which looks like a reduced-scale 8mm round, much as the pistol is a scaled-down version of the 8mm Type Nambu. Its scarcity prevented the destruction of even one specimen for study. Published data give a bullet weight of 56 grains, backed by 3 grains of fine, green powder, yielding approximately 1250 fps velocity and about 196 fp energy at the muzzle. Cases are of brass, Berdan primed. All cartridges encountered have been without headstamp, loaded with cupro-nickel type bullets and packed in cardboard boxes holding 50 rounds.

The 7mm Nambu is superior to the 32 ACP, the favorite cartridge in pistols carried by European army staff officers.

Until recently it was thought that the end of World War II had rung down the curtain on semiautomatic pistols bearing the name Nambu. However, two new automatic pistols and one revolver being currently produced in Japan, although of general Browning or Smith & Wesson pattern, have been named "New Nambu," a fitting tribute by a country grateful to its foremost automatic weapons designer, General Kijiro Nambu. ●

Bibliography

Anonymous, "Exploded Drawings — 7mm Nambu (Baby Nambu)," *The Gun Digest*, (Chicago, 1953), p. 151.

Anonymous, "Japanese Infantry Weapons," *War Department Special Series Number 19, MID 461,* Washington, D.C., United States Government Printing Office, 1943.

Berkin, Gerald L., "Old Name—New Guns," *Guns Magazine*, (June, 1962), pp. 28-29, 61, 64, 66.

Braverman, Shelley, *The Firearms Encyclopedia,* Athens, N.Y., Shelley Braverman, 1959, Inserts No. 606, 608.

Hoffschmidt, E. J., "Nambu Type 14 Pistol," *The American Rifleman*, (Sept., 1958), pp. 24-25.

Hoffschmidt, E. J., "Pistol Magazines — 7mm Baby Nambu," *The American Rifleman*, (Nov., 1958), p. 22.

"Pistol Magazines — Type 14 Pistol," *The American Rifleman*, (Oct., 1955), p. 39.

"Pistol Magazines — Type 94 Pistol," *The American Rifleman*, (July, 1955), p. 41.

Johnson, G. B. and Lockhoven, H. B., *International Armament, Volume I*, Cologne, International Small Arms Publishers, 1965, pp. 108-114.

Mathews, J. Howard, *Firearms Identification, Volume I,* Madison, Wis., University of Wisconsin Press, 1962, pp. 99, 108, 128, 139, 211-214, 348.

Firearms Identification, Volume II, Madison, The University of Wisconsin Press, 1962, pp. 91, 157-158, 288, 365, 384, 392.

Smith, W. H. B., *The Book of Pistols and Revolvers,* Harrisburg, Pa., The Stackpole Co., 1962, pp. 41, 206, 325, 210-217, 206.

Small Arms of the World, Harrisburg, Pa., The Stackpole Co., 1960, pp. 201, 498-503, 700.

Strengholt, Roy D., "The Baby Nambu," *The Gun Digest,* (Chicago, 1963), pp. 158-160.

White, H. P. and Munhall, B. D., *Centerfire Metric Pistol and Revolver Cartridges,* Washington, D. C., Infantry Journal Press, 1948, pp. 17-18, 36-37, 47.

CHECKERING WITH POWER

by JIM CARMICHEL

FEW PEOPLE PAID much attention to good hand checkering until, a few years ago, the major arms manufacturers began stamping their shotgun and rifle stocks with a rather bland, semi-serviceable type of "checkering." Sure, the patterns of this "impressed" checkering are attractive enough, but the non-slip grip and esthetic appeal of the hand-cut variety are sorely missed.

The move to impressed checkering was simply a matter of production economics. There just aren't enough skilled checkerers to keep up with production demands. Too, the time involved in producing even a simple hand-cut pattern can add considerably to the cost of the finished firearm. This is further complicated by the fact that training a person to be even moderately competent with a checkering tool can be a matter of weeks or even months. In fact, the singular requirements of attitude, dexterity and determination needed to master the art of the checkering tool eliminates a large segment of the population. However, those who do acquire the skill can pretty much write their own ticket so far as hours and wages go. For example, the cost of a nice quality custom stock with a moderate amount of well done checkering is largely determined by the checkering. Order yourself a truly top quality stock with lots of high grade checkering, and you can be pretty sure that at least half, if not more, of the total cost will be for the checkering. Yet some gunsmiths and stockmakers contend that the high prices they must charge for checkering still aren't enough. In short—checkering is hell on the eyes, muscles, nerves and one's general disposition.

An acquaintance of mine, whose name will remain unrevealed, was able to pay his way through college with checkering jobs he picked up. By his third year in college his reputation for high quality checkering had grown to the point that he could ask—and get—as much as $75 for one of his fancy patterns. That was pretty good money in those days. As a full time professional, he could have made a very respectable living at checkering, but on graduation day he unceremoniously dumped his tools in the campus fish pond, and announced to the world in no uncertain terms that his checkering days were at *an end*!

What this all boils down to is that if you have a hankering for fine hand-cut checkering, you're going to have to (a) spend a lot of miserable hours learning the skill or (b) shell out a lot of hard earned dollars paying someone to do it for you.

A Third Choice

Fortunately, there is a third and brighter alternative being offered by Bob Brownell of Brownell's, Incorporated, Montezuma, Iowa, in the form of a remarkable little gadget that cuts checkering which is absolutely indistinguishable from that cut with hand tools. In fact the Miniature Machine Company tool is a hand tool, but it features a tiny buzz saw which cuts

Here's the high-revving little V-cutter that does the job, taking the drudgery out of checkering.

The MMC checkering tool at work. Note the tiny wood particles kicked out by the high speed cutter, in motion here and hence blurred.

a sharp, clean full depth V-groove as fast or faster than you can guide it along.

Powered by a Foredom electric motor or similar power source the precision built little checkering tool can complete a terrific looking checkering job in a fraction of the time required with conventional hand powered tools. Too, once you get the hang of the gadget the quality of your checkering will be at least as good as your best efforts with conventional tools – if not better! For those who have never mastered the skills of checkering, the

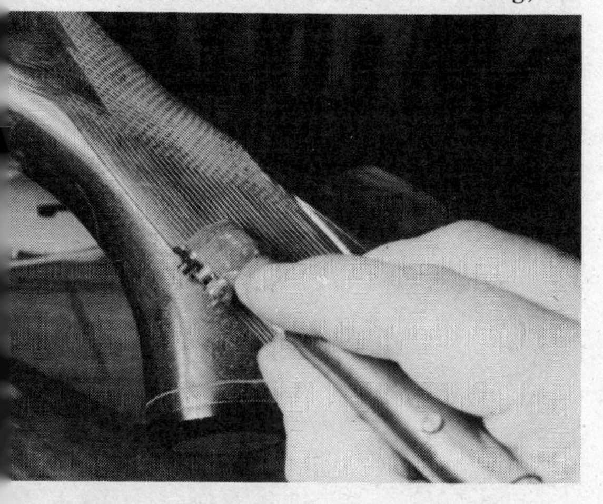

At work with the MMC checkering tool.

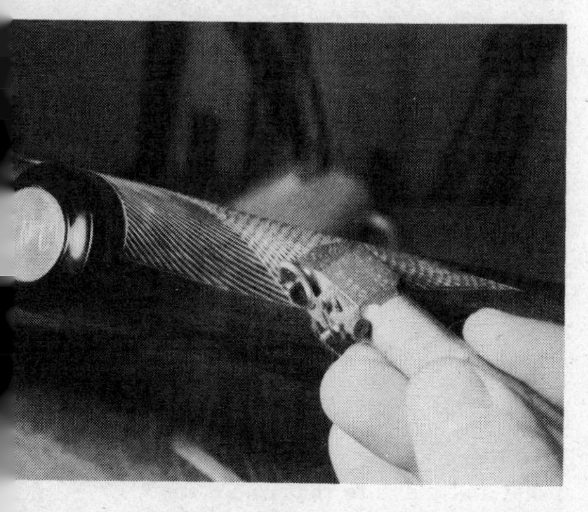

Working in tight places like this is quite difficult with hand tools, but there's no problem with the MMC power tool.

MMC tool offers a darn good reason for taking it up, whether on a professional, a part time or amateur basis.

The MMC tool is a remarkably compact and lightweight (4⅞ inches long and under 2½ ounces) instrument which, despite its relatively simple appearance, represents an enormous amount of development and perfecting by machine wizard Bob Sconce. The cutter is a ½-inch diameter bevel-edged saw which spins so fast that a perfect 75° V-groove is cut with no fuzzing, tearing or shattering, regardless of the wood being cut. What's more, the edges of the cut are perfectly smooth with absolutely no sign of tool marks!

Spacing is accomplished by a blade-like guide which has adjustments for both depth and spacing of cut. The click-ball spacing adjustment may be set anywhere from 16 to 22 lines to the inch. With a special narrow cutter checkering as fine as 32 l.p.i. is possible.

A 36" flexible shaft connects the cutting head with the 1/10 h.p. Foredom motor. With the motor suspended somewhat above and to the rear of the operator the cutter can be manipulated with complete freedom and ease, though the sensation is somewhat awkward at first for those accustomed to hand tools.

Terrifying Trial

One's first experience with the MMC checkering tool can either be pleasant or terrifying – depending on what you're expecting. Never having seen the tool demonstrated, previously, my reaction was closer to fright! Laying out a nice straight pair of master lines, I pressed the rheostat foot pedal and carefully laid the tool against the wood. The result was an angry snarl and a shower of powdered wood. This is ridiculous, I thought, who can do precision checkering with something scaring the hell out of him. A few more passes, however, and I was soothed – and solid.

One of the first concerns one might have about using a power tool for such work is that the cutter, in the manner of many saws, might tend to chatter, dig out soft spots or lead with the grain. Such, however, is not the case. The Foredom motor produces up to 14,000 r.p.m.'s and, at such speeds as this, the tiny buzz saw of a cutter is totally oblivious to the texture of the wood or direction of the grain. The tool head simply glides along on its path with a minimum of effort on the part of the user. In fact, the real trick in mastering the tool is learning to let it, not you, do the work. Once one gets the "feel" of the MMC tool, checkering can become a real pleasure.

Laying out a pattern to be checkered with the power tool is done exactly the way one might do layout work for conventional tools: The outlines are scribed or marked, then the master lines are marked and cut with a single line cutter or "V" tool or, better yet, use a layout tool or "riffler," which is also available from Brownell's. A pleasant alternative to the tedious and sometime downright aggravating job of laying out the pattern is to use the checkering decals available in a wide assortment of designs from Brownell's.

With the master lines cut one simply steps on the rheostat, and the power head buzzes into action. Spacing with the tool is the conventional right-to-left, line-by-line process, only this time you start the tool at one border and push or pull the tool along in one smooth, continuous motion to the opposite border. The line is cut several times as fast as with a hand powered tool, and the groove can also be cut to full depth!

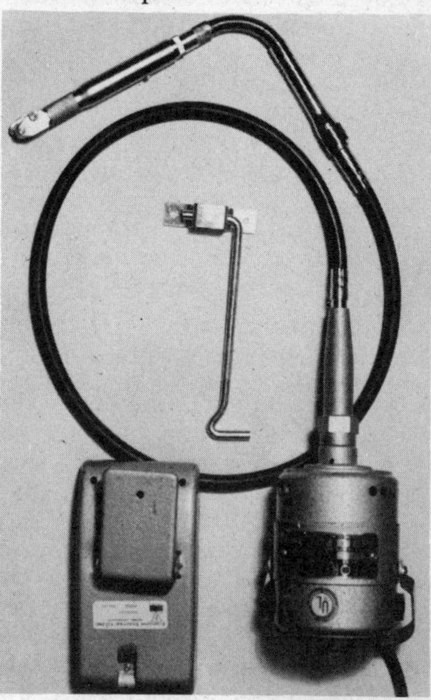

Complete checkering rig (available from Brownell's Inc., Montezuma, Iowa), includes Foredom 14,000 RPM motor, foot rheostat, flexible shaft and handpiece, MMC checkering head. The bill for everything is about $250, but cost can be recovered in 5-10 checkering days. Too, the Foredom tool has hundreds of other uses.

Close to the Edges

With a little practice one can come extremely close to the edge of the pattern. So close, in fact, that a final hand touch up around the edges may not be required. A good technique for cutting a trim, borderless edge without runovers is to scribe only a light line around the pattern, then on each lining pass run the tool up so that it only lightly nicks the scribed line. When the panel is fully checkered deepen the edge line with a "V" tool or riffler. This removes the necks and leaves a neat edge with no runovers and clean, full depth checkering running right up to the edges.

One's first judgement of the maneuverability of the MMC tool might be that it would be O.K. for broad, flat patterns, but would necessarily need to be augmented by hand tools in tight corners or on tricky contours. In practice the opposite is likely. A typical example is the inside curve of the pistol grip on "down and under" patterns. Unless the masterlines are at the right, bottom corner on the right grip panel (which is impractical) one soon faces a situation where he has to cut spacing lines from left to right—an awkward task for many checkerers. Coming in from the other side is mainly impossible because the stock gets in the way. With the MMC tool, however, one just tilts the tool a little higher and checkers, right to left, to a fair-thee-well. (See illustration)

On first acquaintance with the power tool one has the impression that he cannot feel the wood as he can with hand tools. This is true only to the extent that one cannot feel the effort required to plow through the wood. With a little experience, however, one develops a surprisingly sensitive "feel" and "ear" for the tool. When the wood toughens up and r.p.m.'s begin to drop, the foot seems to automatically press harder on the rheostat. Likewise, one learns to accurately judge the correct cutting pace to best suit wood conditions.

The ideal depth of cut is that which will bring each row or "ridge" just to a sharp crest. Cutting the grooves too deep will cause the crests to be lower than they should and low spots will result. On the other hand, not cutting the grooves deep enough will cause the ridges and diamonds to be flat topped. The beginner may prefer to leave ridges slightly flat topped, then bring the diamonds to a point with a once over pass with the hand tool. This is a safe way of doing it, and perhaps a pretty good idea during the learning period. With practice, however, one can cut perfect rows of perfect diamonds with only one pass. This is where checkering gets to be fun and, if you're in the business for a living, this is where the profits show a sharp gain.

Checkering Quality Excellent

The quality of checkering that's possible with the MMC power tool is equal to the very best hand work. From the standpoint of appearance there is no way that anyone can tell the difference between work done with the power tool or with hand tools. A well done pattern with the power cutter commands as much admiration, respect and price as any hand labor.

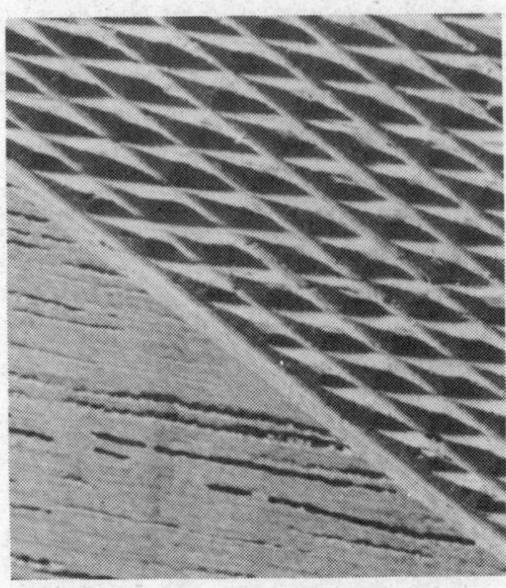

This view shows how close the powered checkering can be brought to the border without runovers. This extremely fine-line checkering enlarged here offers no obstacle to the MMC tool. Note grain of wood for a size comparison.

According to the manufacturer maintenance is virtually nil except for resharpening the cutter. The fine bearings are packed with a special lubricant which lasts several years. When the lubricant shows signs of failing (if it ever does) the tool is returned to the factory where the gearbox is repacked and the whole tool given a thorough going over.

The cutters will become dull after a certain amount of use (depending on type of wood and stock finishes) and must be returned to the factory for resharpening. Cost for this service is $3.00. Just how long a cutter will last between sharpenings I can't really say—the tool submitted for tests has so far checkered two extensively covered stocks, and the equivalent of about two more in practice, with no signs of needing resharpening. So we know that, at most, the MMC tool will cost no more to operate than the cost of buying new cutters for hand tools.

The initial cash investment in the power checkering tool and necessary equipment hits the pocketbook a fairly sharp clout. Prices as listed by Brownell's, the exclusive distributor are: Checkering head $164; Foredom 1/10 h.p. motor, flexible shaft, handpiece and rheostat total $79.25 for a grand total of $243.25. Just how long it might take to recover this investment by saving the cost of work you would otherwise have to farm out or, by speeding up your present checkering output depends, of course, on just how much checkering you intend to do. However, a fairly complex pattern which might cost $75 to $125 (one that could ordinarily take the better part of 3 days) can be completed in a single working day with no sweat. With this in mind the initial cost is recovered in 5 to 10 checkering days. From there on out the time saved is all gravy.

Naturally the home hobbiest is not necessarily interested in profit, but he is concerned with his time investment; the MMC tool can certainly save him a lot of time, hours which can be usefully spent in the shop or out at the range showing off his checkering. In addition to this there's the pride and pleasure that comes from owning and operating a fine piece of precision equipment—not to mention the same satisfaction felt on completing good work. Don't forget, too, the Foredom motor, shaft and tool holder have a thousand other uses!

Perhaps you're wondering just how fast the MMC checkering tool works? The only careful time log kept was of a fully checkered wrap-around fore-end panel involving some 26 square inches of checkered area and 17 points! Checkering was done 22 lines to the inch. Total elapsed time from the moment the tool touched the wood until oil was brushed into the checkering was *one hour and 55 minutes!* ●

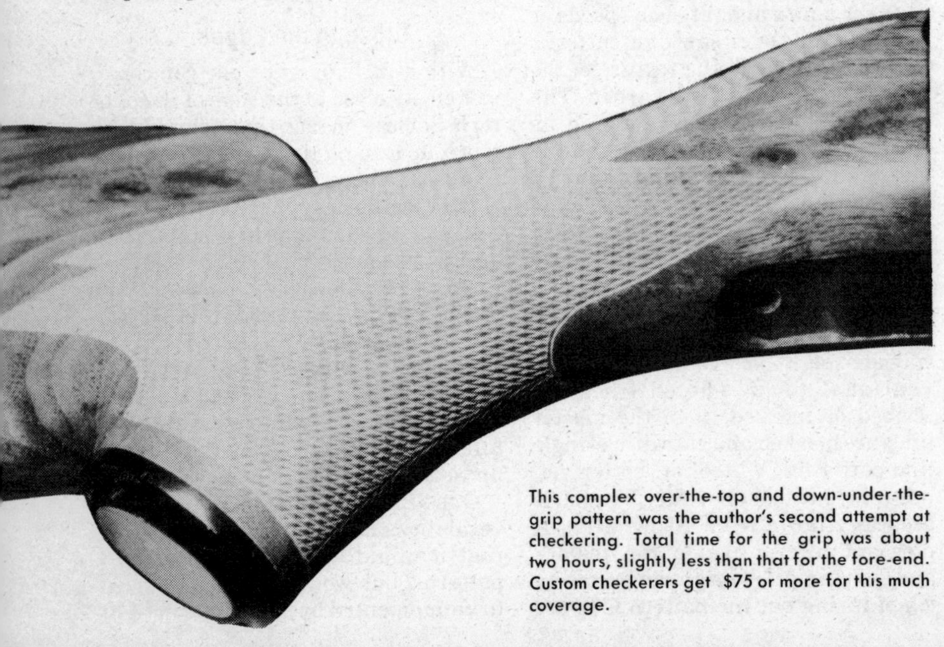

This complex over-the-top and down-under-the-grip pattern was the author's second attempt at checkering. Total time for the grip was about two hours, slightly less than that for the fore-end. Custom checkerers get $75 or more for this much coverage.

Wildcats and Wildcatters

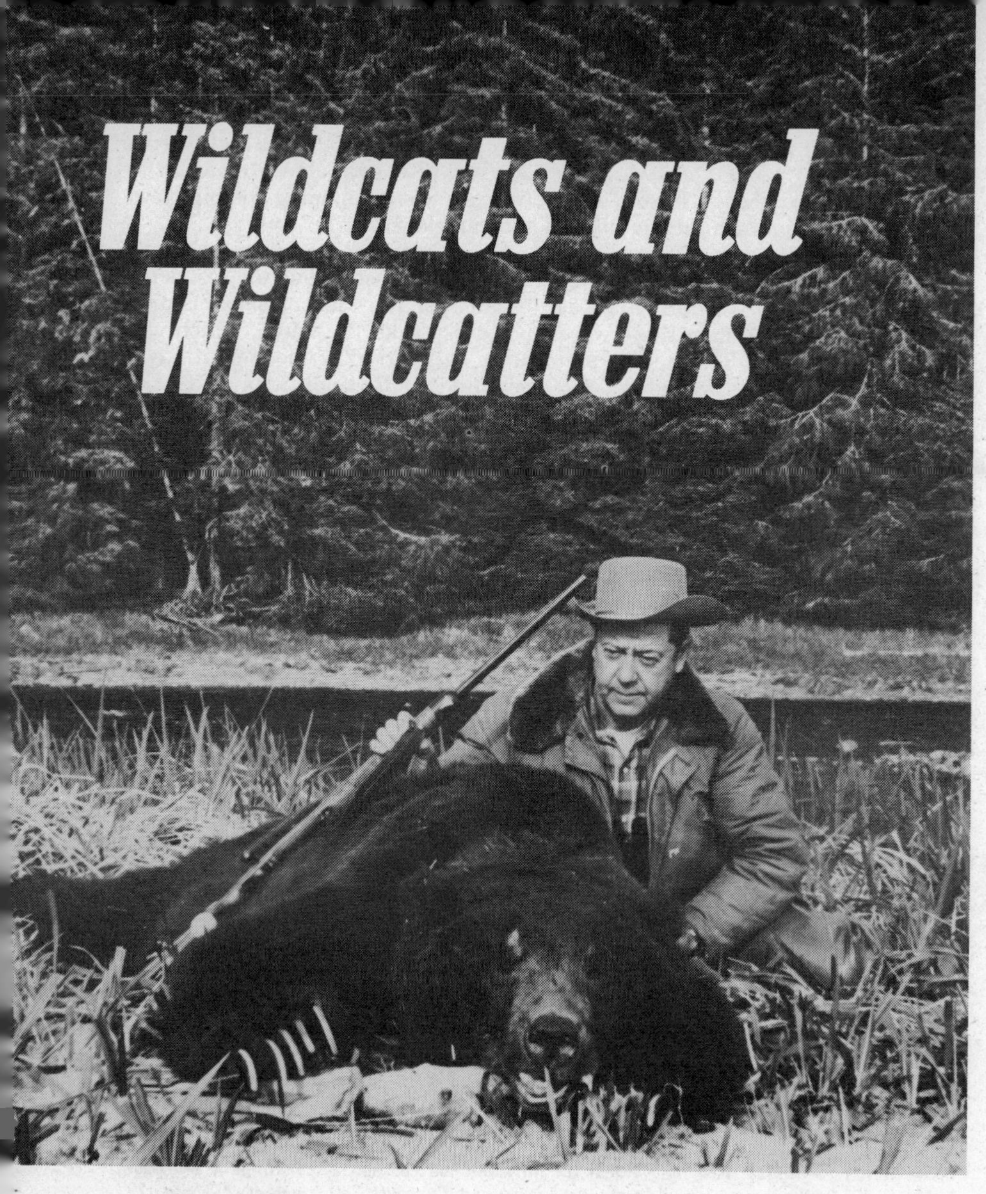

Perhaps more wildcat cartridges have been designed and used for shooting the big Alaskan brown bears than for most other hunting. This Admiralty Island brownie was shot by the writer with a 340 Weatherby, not a wildcat. It was, however, built on a Model 70 Winchester action, has a Hobaugh barrel, is chambered without the Weatherby free-bore, and is handloaded with a 250-gr. Bitterroot Bonded Core bullet—maybe it is some kind of wildcat.

by BOB HAGEL

The wildcatter isn't as prevalent as he once was, and with good reason, most would say. Fair enough, yet many of today's most popular and useful factory cartridges were, long years ago, the wildest of wildcats.

WILDCAT CARTRIDGES have stirred up a great deal of controversy over the past few years. They have been maligned by many who feel they have no useful purpose, especially nowadays; that they're inferior to similar factory offerings, and that they're not as reliable as the factory rounds. Some have even insisted that they are dangerous. Also, it has been intimated that the wildcatter—the fellow who dreams up these offbeat cartridges—is something of a social misfit, or at least has a couple of cogs that don't always mesh.

This wasn't always so. Not so many years ago, the wildcatter was considered something of a hero by most of the brotherhood of gun bugs; a fellow who had more gun savvy and ability than average.

In all fairness to the thinking of yesteryear, and to many of the thoughts advanced by some present generation shooters, we'll have to admit that changes have come about. There simply isn't the need for wildcat cartridges today that there was even 20 years ago. Gaps in the cartridge line-up have gradually been filled until there is little room for either caliber changes or velocity levels that stray far from the commercial offerings.

But take a close look at the cartridges that have filled those holes in the commercial line, and you'll find that most of them were originally wildcats; the fruit of some wildcatter's imagination, and ingenuity. Some have been changed slightly to conform to an engineer's idea. Which brings up another fact of life: many of the cartridges that were changed during the transition from wildcat to commercial production fell flat on their faces, and were later replaced by the wildcat that sired them. The 220 Swift and the 22-250 are one example. This isn't to say the 22-250 is a better cartridge than the Swift, but it does prove the point.

Just how old wildcatting is or who started it, is impossible to say.* There

*If anyone might be singled out as our first wildcatter, the honors would fall on Frank Wesson—a brother of Daniel B. and the maker, in a small way, of unusual single shot rifles in the 1860-1890 period. Among the high quality centerfire target rifles made by Wesson there is a fair number with chambers decidedly different in form from those then standard. Calibers of 42 are not uncommon, and it remains a puzzle as to just how Frank Wesson supplied some of his rifle buyers with cartridges or cases. He was not, it is generally agreed, a maker of cartridges. For a detailed report on Frank Wesson's weird chamberings see *More Single Shot Rifles* (J. J. Grant, N.Y. 1959), pp. 52-87.

Perhaps Charles H. Herrick of Winchester, Massachusetts, should be considered an early wildcatter. Around 1895 or so he designed the 28-30 cartridge, our first 7mm caliber. The 28-30 was adopted by Stevens Arms & Tool Co., in 1900. Mr. Herrich was also the designer of the 22-15-60 cartridge, offered by Stevens as early as 1896.

About 1897, according to an early Ideal Hand Book, one Capt. W. L. Carpenter (U.S. Army) designed the 25-25 cartridge, and Ideal made the first case for him from solid brass bar stock. The 25-25, soon after offered by Stevens in the 44-actioned rifles, became a fairly famous cartridge. J.T.A.

is little information to show that much if anything was done with black powder cartridges in general, and then not at the time when they were being used. One exception might be the 22 Hornet, which was based on the 22 Winchester Center Fire case, but there was no case form change, However, this was not done until the late 1920s, when Col. Townsend Whelen and Grosvenor Wotkyns, among others, developed the Hornet.

Early Wildcatters

Long before that time, in the early years of the century or before, wildcatting got under way with smokeless powder cases. It has been said that the 30-40 Krag case was one of the earliest cartridges to be wildcatted, when it was necked to 25. This first 25 Krag wildcat has been credited to Charles Newton, but so many different men worked with the 25 Krag that this point is a little hazy. A.O. Niedner, also credited with the development of the 25-06, also worked with the 25 Krag, and many custom gunsmiths, including Griffin & Howe, chambered rifles for it.

Ned Roberts doubtless experimented with the 25 Krag, as he did with so many other case configurations in 25 caliber, before his 257 Roberts was adopted by Remington.

But whether Newton was the first to work with the 25 Krag or not, he was certainly one of the earliest and most prolific of the wildcatters. He also saw more of his brainchilds turn into commercial numbers than any other wildcatter. Of course a great deal of Newton's work was done with a commercial cartridge in mind because he designed the cartridge and then made rifles in which it was chambered, or designed it for rifles he already had going. However, he also designed many cartridges that were eventually made by various ammunition companies. Some of these, the 256, 30 and 35 Newton were loaded by the Western Cartridge Co. until the late 1930s, but were never chambered in any commercial rifle that I know of except the various Newtons. Other Newton developments, the 22 Savage High Power and the 250-3000 Savage, were chambered not only in Savage rifles but by many other companies as well. The 22 Savage Imp, which was .228-inch diameter instead of .224-inch, and in factory form used a 70-gr. bullet, faded out of the cartridge picture without becoming overly popular, but the 250-3000 is still with us. Dropped from chambering by Savage in 1960 in the various Model 99 rifles, it was reintroduced in the Savage 99-A in 1971.

Debt to Newton

In addition to those Newton cartridges that became commercial numbers, several more were designed that may not have been commercially chambered even in Newton rifles, at least in quantity. Among these were the 22 Newton, the 33 Newton, and the 40 Newton. There was also a 280 Newton, according to some sources, but I don't recall ever seeing it listed in Newton ballistic tables. It is almost certain, however, that Newton did come up with several wildcats during his many years of cartridge development that were never given much publicity.

While today's magnum cartridges are based on the H&H belted case design, the recent trend is back to the Newton design of a short, fat case with even more powder capacity than the original Holland & Holland cases have. Modern shoulder design also leans toward Newton's thinking. The big Newton cases that derived from the 30 Newton had shoulder angles of about 23 degrees, while the 300 H&H has an angle of 8.30 degrees and the 375 H&H case has 12.45 degrees. Modern magnum cases are mostly made with 25-degree shoulders. Certainly we owe much of our modern case design and efficiency to Newton developments, designs that originally sprang from a wildcat cartridge based on an 11mm Mauser case, which later became the famous and efficient 30 Newton.

Here in the U.S. we would undoubtedly have been using the modern magnum cartridge many years before they became popular if slow, progressive powders like 4350, 4831 and Norma 205 had been available when Charles Newton was developing the big Newton cartridges.

Even those who worked mostly with smaller cases were severely restricted because of the lack of slow-burning powders. Take the 25-06, which was often called the 25 Niedner; it never reached its full potential with the heavier bullets until slow powders arrived. But here again, a wildcat cartridge that was developed sometime before 1920 was bypassed by the arms companies until Remington gave it commercial status in 1970. It took the arms companies over 50 years to realize what a hell of a good cartridge it was!

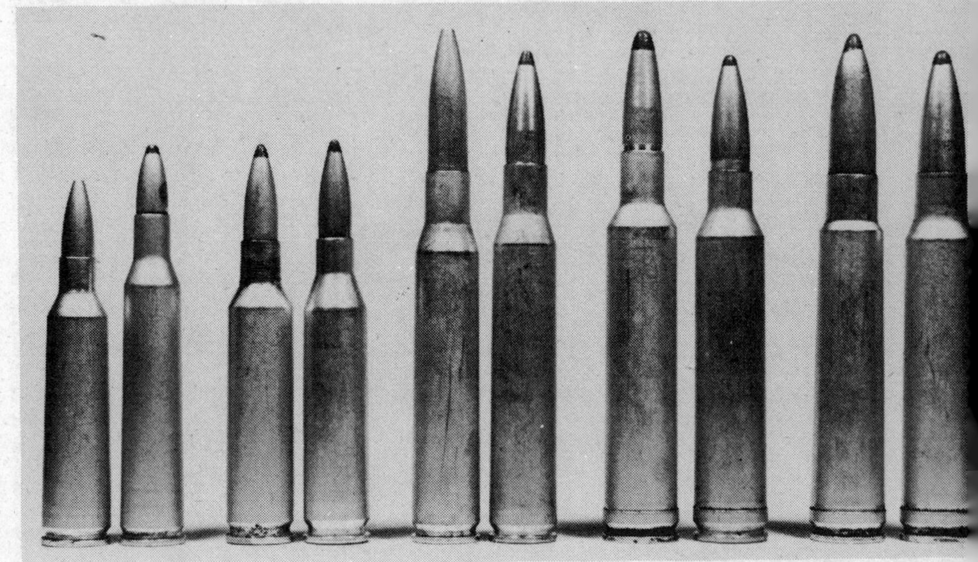

These paired cartridges show the wildcat (at left) and the commercial cartridge it preceded. From left—22-250 (now commercial in identical form) and 220 Swift; 240 Page and 243 Win.; 285 OKH and 280 Rem.; 7mm Mashburn Super Magnum and 7mm Rem. Mag.; 333 OKH Belted and 338 Win. Mag.

Other early day wildcatters were also frustrated by the lack of slow-burning powders. The 276 and 280 Dubiel magnums would certainly have done better with today's powders. But, once again, we probably owe John Dubiel, and his early attempts with a magnum seven, at least some credit in the development of the modern 7mm magnums.

The OKH Line

Another wildcat line that undoubtedly contributed a great deal to the development of some of today's cartridges were those by OKH (O'Neil-Keith-Hopkins). Elmer Keith and Don Hopkins had a big hand in the ideas and development of many of the OKH cartridges, but many were also the products of Charlie O'Neil's fertile mind and endeavors. Some of these cartridges, a 25 on the 30 Newton case, a 6mm on the 300 H&H case, and a 7mm on the full-length 375

Many wildcat 17s appeared before the 17 Remington became a commercial reality. From left—the Mach IV on the 221 Fireball case, the 17-222, 17-222 Magnum and 17 Remington.

Some wildcats were never very popular, others were never more than experimental. From left—240 Gibbs on the 30-06 case with body blown out and shoulder pushed forward, gained some popularity. A 6mm on the 300 H&H shortened case, a 25 on the 30 Newton Case, and a 7mm on the full-length 375 case, all three by Charley O'Neil, but experimental only.

H&H case, were not practical or successful with the powders available even during the mid-'30s. They would have done much better with propellants like Hodgdon's H-870 and H-570. Far from ideal—and far overbore capacity—even with those slow powders, they did lead to more practical developments.

O'Neil was one of the more prolific wildcatters but, though none of his cartridges ever went commercial in identical form, there is little doubt that the various 333 caliber OKH cartridges had a great deal to do with the popular and potent 338 Winchester Magnum being available today. The 285 OKH is almost identical to the 280 Remington, with the only difference being that Remington decided to push the shoulder of their ill-fated 7mm forward a wee bit. The 280 Remington—or 7mm-06 if you prefer—would likely have gained a great deal more popularity had it appeared several years before it did. But by the time it came out at least two commercial 7mm magnums (the 7x61 S&H and the 7mm Weatherby Magnum) and many wildcats had appeared, all of them apparently holding more appeal and long range potential.

Very few wildcats have ever become factory-loaded cartridges without some changes being made by factory engineers—ballistic or production. About the only exceptions known to me are: the 22-250 Remington, which has the same dimensions as the 22 Varminter as Jerry Gebby finally settled on it; the 25-06 Remington, which is identical to the Niedner, and probably the 22 Hornet, which was based on the 22 WCF case. This is, of course, the main reason why many wildcatters never gain recognition for their work. Their cartridges may have had a great deal of influence on later factory rounds with very similar ballistics, but few of the people who use the factory round ever know of or about these unsung men.

P.O. Ackley, probably the most prolific wildcatter of all time, has come up with some very useful and efficient cartridges. However, as far as I know, none of his cartridges has been commercialized in identical form. It is fairly certain, however, that his work with shortened belted cases in various calibers, especially 30, has influenced our modern short magnums.
magnums.

Similarly, Art Mashburn came up with several wildcats that were very useful and extremely potent, but none of them ever made factory-loaded status. I feel fairly certain that the Mashburn 7mm Super Magnum did have a great deal of bearing on the decision of Remington to develop the 7mm Remington Magnum. Most of the credit for that decision is, I believe, due to the efforts of Warren Page and his many hunting successes with Art Mashburn's big 7.

Warren Page and Fred Huntington

It is also certain that we owe Page a big thank you for the fact that the 243 Winchester was ever born. This cartridge is mostly due to his wildcatting of the military T-65 (later brought out as the 308 Winchester) to take the 6mm bullet. Here again, when Winchester decided to bring out the 243 they couldn't quite bring themselves to duplicate the 240 Page as it was. Instead, they used the 20-degree shoulder of the 308 case instead of the 30-degree angle of Page's 6mm. The Page cartridge also offered the advantage of a longer neck for the same over-all case length.

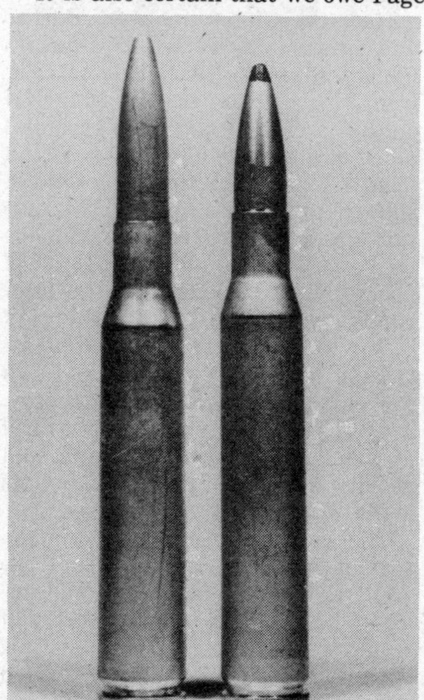

The 285 OKH or 7mm-06 (left) and its commercial counterpart, the 280 Remington.

Fred Huntington of RCBS wildcatted the 257 Roberts case (which itself was wildcatted from the 7x57 Mauser case by Ned Roberts before Remington chambered it, and which, incidentally, was not used in its original wildcat form) to 6mm, and it became the 244-6mm Remington. But here Remington decided to come up with a happy medium and used a 26-degree shoulder instead of either the 20.45-degree shoulder of the 257 or the 32-degree shoulder of the Huntington Rockchucker.

With both of these 243-caliber cartridges the arms companies were able to see the light sooner than is normal for them, and they brought out factory cartridges which, for all practical purposes, were identical in performance with their wildcat predecessors. The quick and lasting success of these 243 and 6mm cartridges should be ample proof of at least one thing—that the brainchild of someone who does a lot of shooting and hunting pretty well knows his stuff when he wildcats a case. Remington apparently got the message, though belatedly, because they decided to chamber the 22-250 and 25-06 with no dimensional changes!

There are, probably, times when the changes made by the arms and/or cartridge companies are improvements over the wildcat cartridge that preceded it, but there are also many times when it is hard to see the logic behind their thinking. I have always thought that two prime examples of this are the 7mm Remington Magnum and the 300 Winchester Magnum.

The Factory Approach

In the case of the 7mm Remington simply necked the 264-338 Winchester case to 7mm with no other changes. In order to do this they were stuck with the overly short neck—which is a pain in the neck to anyone using the many makes, styles and weights of 7mm bullets available for handloading. But I've always felt that the one big mistake they made—and one that could have been taken care of, even if they did intend to use the short neck—was this: the 7mm Remington was brought out simultaneously with the Model 700 rifle, whose action was long enough to handle 300-375 S&H cartridges. There was little reason why Remington couldn't have A) used a longer neck, similar to the 7mm Mashburn or B) throated out the chamber so that the heavier bullets could have been seated out, far enough forward so that they don't hang far down into the powder space. No reason why the original factory 150- and 175-gr. bullets couldn't have been seated with bullet bases about flush with the base of the case neck. A longer neck would have been an even better solution, because several bullet weights could have been seated to give the same bullet-to-land distance without any of them intruding into the boiler room.

Winchester did the same thing with their 300 Magnum, only worse as far as the handloader is concerned. They made a case with a head to shoulder length far longer than the 338 has, cut the neck to the bare minimum, then loaded it to an over-all length only a little longer than the 338's. The result is that many bullets of 180/220-gr. weight have to be seated below the full diameter of the bullet's shank, which causes them to drive back into the case under recoil. None of the wildcat 30s gave this trouble that I know of.

It has often been asked why anyone wants to fool with a wildcat cartridge when so many factory cartridges are available that one of them would certainly serve. This is a good question in many instances because there actually isn't, in most cases, any need for the dozens of wildcats that have been conjured up. Many of these wildcats were simply the product of someone who wanted his "own" cartridge to shoot. Many people feel a huge sense of satisfaction, a big degree of personal pride, in hunting and taking game with a cartridge they've dreamed up, even though it may actually be inferior to some factory round of the same caliber. But the best and most popular wildcats have come about because of a need for something not already offered in factory-loaded ammunition.

The 333 OKH cartridges were prime examples of this. O'Neil wanted a cartridge that would deliver heavy-weight bullets similar to those used in the 35 or 375, yet of better sectional density and ballistic coefficient for long range shooting and deep penetration on large game. Looking at the ballistics of all of the great big-game cartridges used throughout the world, he noticed that the 333 Jeffery retained more energy at extreme ranges than any other cartridge that fitted his needs. The 333 Jeffery was not readily available in this country, so it was much more logical to work with that bullet diameter in domestic cases. Bullets in 333 caliber were first imported, then later made by Barnes and Speer. Cases were made from 30-06 brass, simply necked to 333, or from 375 H&H brass. The 333 OKH on the '06 case kicked a 250-gr. bullet along at about 2600 fps, but with full length 375 brass the same bullet showed around 2900 fps from 26" barrels. The later 330 OKH Belted, made on a shortened 300-375 H&H case of about the same length as the later 338 Winchester, gave 2750 fps.

With these cartridges O'Neil attained his goal, which has been proven by the 338 and 340 Weatherby. They deliver energy at the same level as the 375, but have better sectional density and shoot flatter with bullets of the same weight.

The same situation is true of the various wildcat predecessors of the 7mm Remington Magnum. The fellows who designed and used the 7mm wildcats for hunting did so with a special purpose in mind: they wanted a cartridge that would handle a fairly small caliber bullet of great sectional density and high ballistic coefficient at velocities of well over 3000 fps for the longest practical ranges of big game shooting. Such a bullet, if properly designed, would retain energy and velocity at the longest ranges for easier vital hits, more terminal energy, and deeper penetration on large animals. They found it in the big sevens with 150/175-gr. bullets at velocities of 3000-3200 fps. These cartridges, in wildcat or commercial form, have proven to be great performers for long range shooting of all kinds of American hoofed game.

Many wildcat cartridges spring from a special need that isn't necessarily of any great value to anyone except the fellow who originally worked it up. One such cartridge was the 300 Winchester case expanded to take 338 bullets that I wildcatted and used because it had an intermediate case capacity between the 338 Winchester and 340 Weatherby cartridges. It was a good cartridge, more potent than the 338, and only slightly less powerful than the 340, but certainly not the ultimate 338 cartridge. But it gave me the information I needed. (See the 1969 GUN DIGEST.)

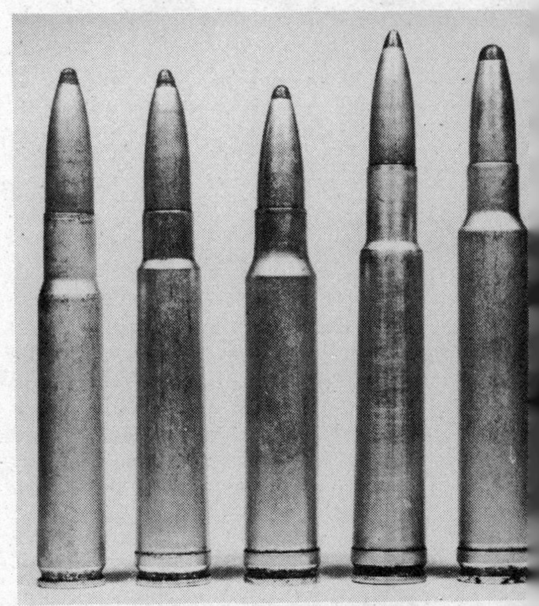

333/338 cartridges, wildcat and factory rounds. From left—333 OKH, 333 OKH Belted, 338 Winchester, 334 OKH and 340 Weatherby. These cartridges were intended to give energy near the 375 H&H, but with bullets of better sectional density and ballistic coefficient for long range shooting of heavy game. They do this well.

Wildcats and Credibility

One thing that has caused many shooters to doubt the validity of wildcatters and wildcat cartridges is the fact that many wildcatters have made some pretty ridiculous claims for their cartridges. Sometimes they have

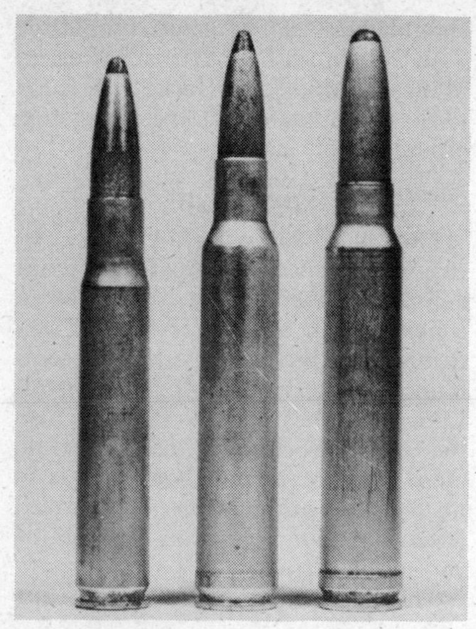

Some wildcats are "special purpose" rounds, calibers that are in no way superior ballistically to factory cartridges, but which serve a particular need for the fellow who uses them. Three of these are shown here: From left—the 338-06, successor to the 333 OKH, and used by those who like a mild 338; a 30 caliber made from 300 H&H brass brought to 300 Winchester dimensions but with a long neck for a better grip on all bullet lengths, by Fred Huntington; and a 338 on 300 Winchester brass, designed by the writer and used to test velocity with a case of that capacity.

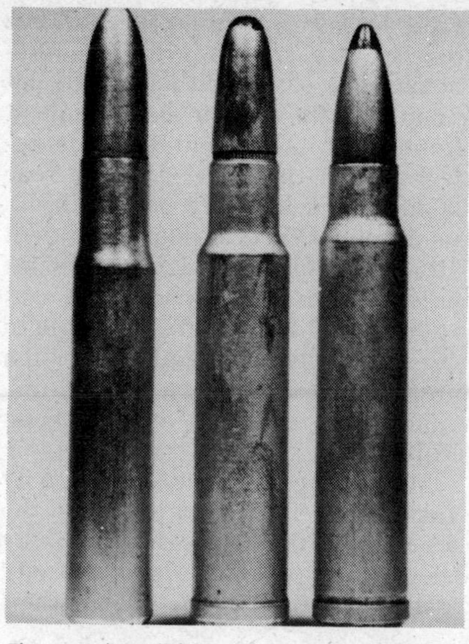

There might well be some use for a magnum 35 cartridge, loaded and chambered by American companies. From left—the popular 35 Whelen wildcat on the 30-06 case, the Mashburn short 35 Magnum on H&H brass, and the 358 Norma Magnum, a factory-loaded round but not loaded in America, and stocked by few American dealers.

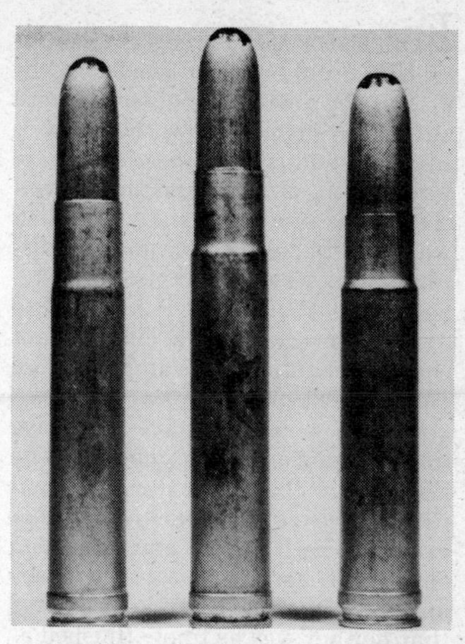

Perhaps the biggest hole in the American cartridge line appears between the 375 and 458. Logically, this hole could be filled by a big 40 cartridge. Here are some 40-cal. wildcats. From left—the short 424 OKH, with the long version at center; these handed .423" diameter bullets. At right is a 416-338 on the 458 Winchester case, a project of Carl Jacobsen's and the writer, which pushes a 400-gr. bullet at 2440 fps.

only overestimated the velocity their pride and joy produces because they didn't have it clocked, but at other times they load it to pressures that are far above the safety point.

One fellow, who made up wildcats in several calibers from blown-out 30-06 brass, claimed velocities considerably higher than those obtainable with belted brass of a great deal more capacity. In trying to verify this I found it impossible to get anything out of the wildcatter. I knew where he had run some of his velocity tests, so I questioned the lab ballistician about the velocities and pressures. He told me that when the chronographing was being done the wildcatter insisted on doing it himself, and all the lab man got to see were figures on the chronograph and a case that he managed to steal a peek at. The ejector-slot mark on the case head stood out like a headlight, so you can bet the primer was ready to fall out. No wonder velocity was high!

Here's something to remember—when someone tells you that his wildcat creation gives higher velocity than much larger cartridges do because of some idea he has incorporated in the design, don't believe it! There is no magic in cold, hard ballistics. The cartridge of a given caliber that burns the most powder, provided you use the right powder for the case, caliber and bullet weight, will give the highest velocity. It may not be the most efficient from the energy-per-grain standpoint, but it will still give the highest velocity.

Needs Today

Today there are few holes left in the caliber-cartridge line that need filling to fulfill a specific need, so while wildcatters continue to wildcat every new case that appears, both up and down, they really aren't accomplishing much that hasn't been done before, or isn't being done by some commercial cartridge. There are, however, a couple of holes left in the factory line in American cartridges that may be filled sometime in the future, and it will be up to wildcatters to fill them until the arms-ammunition companies see fit to follow suit.

One of these is for a big 35 cartridge, and the other is a magnum 40. When it was rumored that Remington was going to unveil a 35 a few years back, many of us thought it would be on something like the 338 or 300 Winchester case. But the 350 Remington Magnum they unwrapped was little more potent than the never-popular 358 Winchester, and not quite as good in many respects as the wildcat 35 Whelen. There is still room for a magnum 35 that will kick a .358-inch 250-gr. bullet along at about 3000 fps, or better yet, a 275/300-gr. at a bit lower velocity for deep penetration on the heaviest game, here or where legal in Africa.

There is also room for a big 40, mostly for African use. Several gun buffs have shown a good deal of interest in this caliber of late, and at least three wildcats have been made up. One by none other than Winchester for Robert Chatfield-Taylor, another by John Amber on a rimmed 2¾-inch case and the third by the writer and Carl Jacobson, with barrel and chamber job by Bill Hobaugh. The Jacobson-Hagel creation is based on a 458 Winchester case necked to take 416-caliber bullets. It will kick a Colorado Custom 400-gr. bullet along at 2440 fps to deliver a muzzle energy of over 5300 foot pounds. It should make an elephant whomper of the first water.

For details of the 416 that Clayton Nelson made for Amber on a big Farquharson single shot, see the 27th ed./1973 GUN DIGEST, pp. 54-55. This 416 A.C. should also deliver velocities in the 2350-2400 fps area with 400-gr. bullets.

The big trouble today with 35 and 40 magnum wildcats is that few good bullets are available. However if factory rounds appear in those calibers in magnum persuasion, this will change rapidly.

In brief summation, it doesn't matter whether you have a high opinion of wildcat cartridges or not, just remember that you owe a big thanks to some wildcatter for developing many of the finest, most useful factory rounds. ●

New SIG-Sauer Pistols

by J. B. WOOD

Two of them, in fact, the P-220 and P-230, both designed for utilitarian service. Production samples functioned and shot well in Switzerland.

FOR THE PAST 25 years the beautiful SIG P-210 has been considered by many to be the most finely made of all automatic pistols. Now the Schweizerische Industrie Gesellschaft of Neuhausen, Switzerland, has developed two new pistols, to establish what will surely become a distinguished series. Both pistols, designated the P-220 and P-230, are so recently produced that it was not possible to obtain test samples before publication time.

We do, however, have extensive information on them, obtained by Editor John T. Amber during a visit to Neuhausen last year. Mr. Amber examined both models, and fired them on the SIG range. He says their performance was flawless. He also noted that neither was as finely finished as the P-210. Two possible good reasons for this: Intended for combat-military and personal-police use respectively, their utilitarian finish and less costly construction may help to keep the price within reason. Their old stable mate, the P-210, is expensive.

The new pistols are to be a cooperative effort, in association with the old and respected firm of J. P. Sauer & Sohn of Eckernforde, West Germany, who will actually manufacture the guns. To reflect this combination of design and production skills, the pistols will be marketed under the name "SIG-Sauer."

SIG P-220

The P-220 is the larger, combat-type pistol. It has an unusual feature, a de-cocking lever, located at the top forward edge of the left grip panel. This is similar to the system used on the Sauer Model 38H pistol but, unlike the Sauer, the P-220 lever is for lowering the hammer only.

The firing pin has an automatic block which is moved only by the last fraction of trigger pull. Thus, when using the de-cocking lever, there is no chance of accidental firing, even if the thumb slips. There is also a wide safety-step on the hammer at normal rest position. Between these two systems, the P-220 will be safe even if dropped on the hammer, say the SIG people. There is *no* manual safety, and on this point the Swiss engineers are in complete agreement with this writer. On a double action pistol with an external hammer, who needs it?

The P-220 has an aluminum-alloy grip frame and plastic grips. The magazine release is a bottom-of-handle type. The location of the slide stop, at top center of the left grip panel, is perfect. Sights are the Stavenhagen-patent "contrast" type, these said to allow quick alignment, even in low-light conditions. These consist of a white-outlined square-notch rear sight, with a white dot inlaid into the rear surface of the post front sight. The front sight is integral with the slide, and the rear is adjustable laterally by drifting in its dovetail. Vertical adjustment will also be possible by changing rear sight units—5 sizes will be made.

The SIG P-220 will be available in 45 ACP, with optional conversion units for 38 Super, 9mm Parabellum, 7.65mm Parabellum, and 22 Long Rifle.

Magazine capacity is listed at only 7 rounds in 45 ACP, 9 rounds in the other centerfires. One wonders why they didn't use a larger capacity magazine, such as the one in their experimental SP 44/16, the forerunner of the P-210.

There is one constructional element of the new P-220 which, like the de-cocking lever, is similar to the old Sauer 38H arrangement. The breechlock is a separate part, secured in the slide shell by a heavy top lug at its forward end, and by a cross-pin. The front strap of the trigger guard is shaped to afford a good rest for a finger of the other hand when using the two-hand hold, a feature which has previously been available only on custom-made combat alterations. The unique features and cartridge options of the P-220 should make it a good competitor with the Walter P-38, Smith & Wesson M39 and M59, and Heckler & Koch P9S—the other double action pistols of comparable size.

SIG P-230

The SIG P-230 will, in the U.S., be considered a pocket pistol for personal defense. In Europe, it will have some consideration as a police pistol. Externally it bears a striking resemblance to the Beretta Model 90 pistol. Like its big brother, the P-220, it also has the de-cocking lever. The slide stop is not external, however—it is an internal automatic type, released from last-shot hold-open by a slight retraction of the slide.

The double action P-230 also has the hammer-step and firing-pin-block safety systems of the larger pistol, an external hammer, Stavenhagen sights and an alloy frame and plastic grips. Basic chambering will be for a new loading called the "9mm Police," with optional conversions to 9mm Short (380 ACP), 7.65mm Browning (32 ACP) and 22 Long Rifle. We have no dimensional data on the "9mm Police," but its muzzle velocity is listed at 1110 feet per second, which is comparable to the old 9mm Browning Long. I note, however, that a different magazine is not required for conversion to the other centerfire rounds, so perhaps it is only a slightly-lengthened 380, like the Russian 9mm Makarov, which also has comparable ballistics.

To handle the increased power of the new special cartridge, the slide used with that chambering is 2.47 ounces heavier than the one on the standard 380 model. The P-230 slide is one-piece, with an integral breechblock. In its size and price range, the pistol will be compared with the Walther PPK-S, Beretta Model 90, and Mauser HSc. It should be a strong sales contender, especially in the "9mm Police" version.

Though not as costly as the celestial P-210, the new pistols are relatively expensive. The P-220 lists at 640 Swiss francs, the smaller P-230 at 580. At early 1974 exchange rates this comes to $192 and $174 respectively. Whether these are European prices or the cost in the U.S. is not known at this time. I doubt that they include the import tax. SIG-Sauer have set the approximate availability dates as follows:

P-230	7.65mm (32 ACP)	Oct., 1974
	9mm kurz (380 ACP)	Nov., 1974
	"9mm Police"	March, 1975
P-220	9mm Parabellum	Aug., 1975

Considering their features, and the two names they bear, these two should be worth waiting for! ●

Specifications

SIG-Sauer P-230		SIG-Sauer P-220	
Weight:	460 grams - 16.23 oz. (380 ACP)	Weight:	830 grams - 29.29 oz. (9mm Parabellum)
Length:	168mm - 6.61 in.	Length:	198mm - 7.79 in.
Height:	119mm - 4.68 in.	Height:	143mm - 5.62 in.
Width:	31mm - 1.22 in.	Width:	34mm - 1.34 in.
Barrel:	92mm - 3.62 in.	Barrel:	112mm - 4.40 in.

Left-side view of SIG-Sauer P-220.

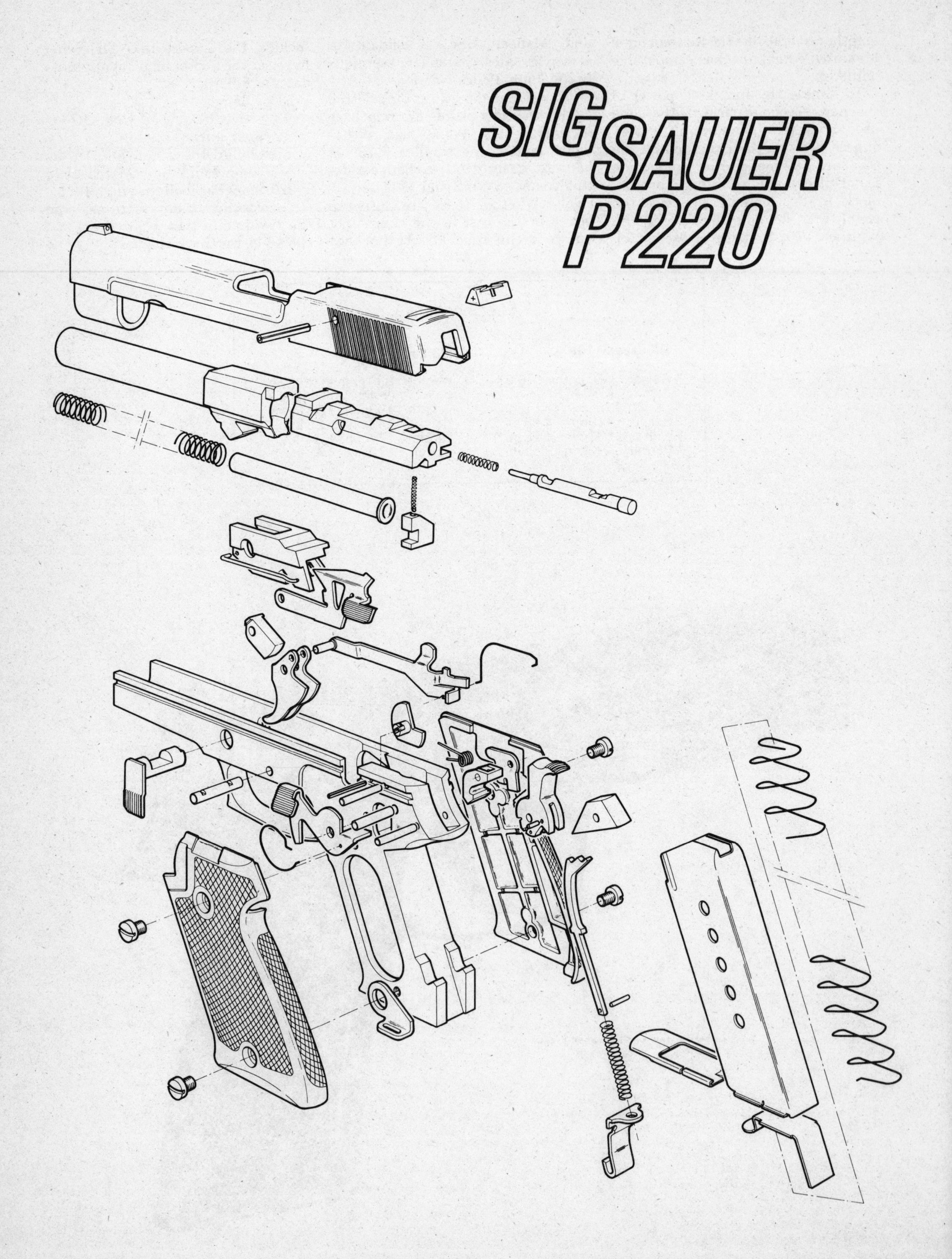
SIG SAUER
P 220

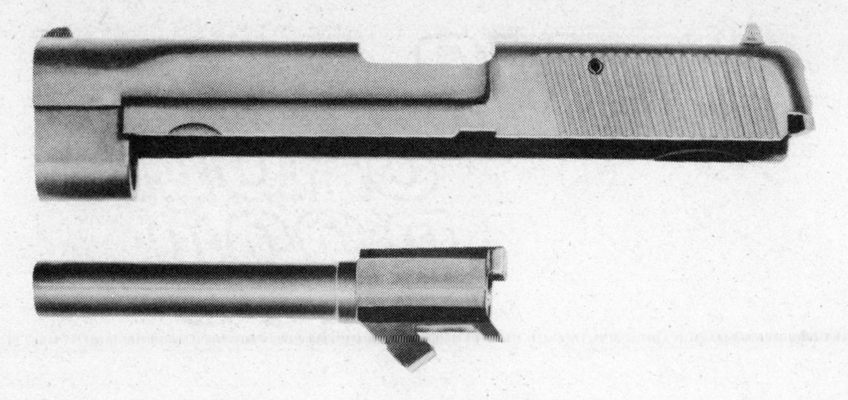

SIG/Sauer P-220 Operational Data

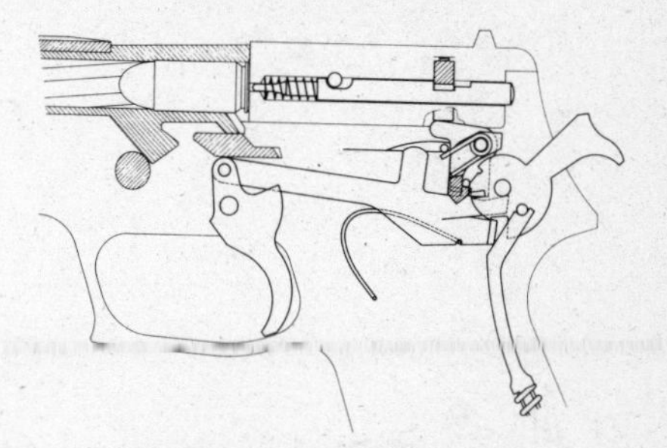

Double-Action Triggering

If the loaded pistol is not cocked, the shot can be fired by way of double-action. The trigger is squeezed, cocking the hammer via the trigger rod, and the safety lever is pressed against the lock pin. The sear is moved away from the hammer and the firing pin released by the lock pin. Further pulling of the trigger lifts the hammer out of register and fires the shot.

SIG/Sauer P-220 field stripped.

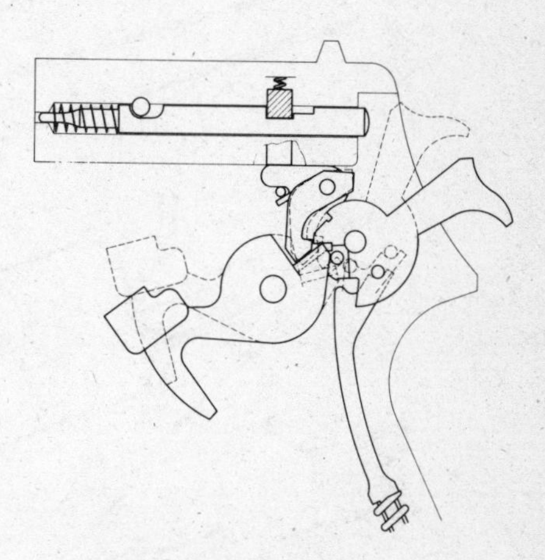

De-cocking Lever and Hammer Safety Notch

The de-cocking lever permits lowering of the hammer into the safety notch so that the loaded gun can be safely carried. The safety notch is the rest position of the hammer. The firing pin is always blocked during and after de-cocking.

Operating Principles to the SIG/Sauer P-220

With the pistol loaded the first shot is fired by pulling the trigger double action. The trigger moves the trigger rod, which lifts the sear out of the hammer notch.

At the same time, the trigger rod moves the safety lever, which takes the lock pin out of engagement with the firing pin, releasing the firing pin just before the shot is fired. The hammer is swung forward by the hammer spring to strike the firing pin, firing the cartridge.

Recoil from the fired cartridge operates the system (comprising the slide and barrel) back against the recoil spring. After recoiling about 3mm, the lock between the barrel and slide is released, the barrel swinging down and being held in place. The slide continues its backward motion, cocks the hammer, extracts and ejects the empty case, and compresses the recoil spring. The slide recoil stroke is limited by a stop on the frame. The recoil spring now forces the slide forward, stripping a cartridge from the magazine into the chamber. Just before reaching battery position, the barrel is again locked to the slide. The trigger rod can now engage the sear and the gun is ready for single action firing (hammer cocked.)

After firing the last shot the slide is caught by the slide stop, actuated by the magazine follower. The slide stop is so-located that it can be used with the thumb of the shooting hand without shifting the gun from the line of fire as a loaded magazine is inserted.

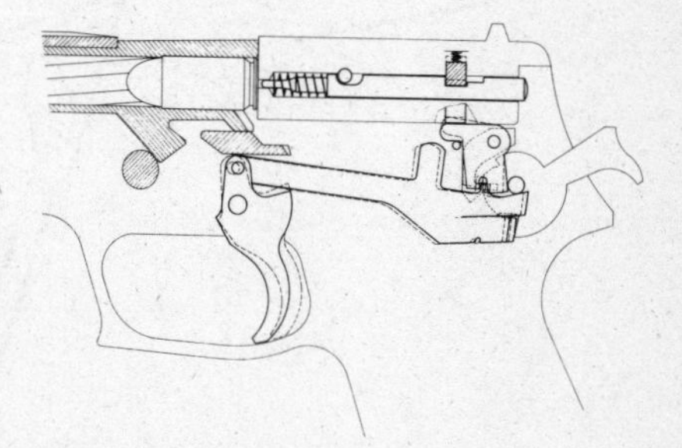

Firing Pin Safety Catch

For maximum safety, the firing pin is locked. It is released automatically by trigger action without manipulation of any lever. The catch is not released until the shot is about to be willfully fired.

SIG SAUER P230

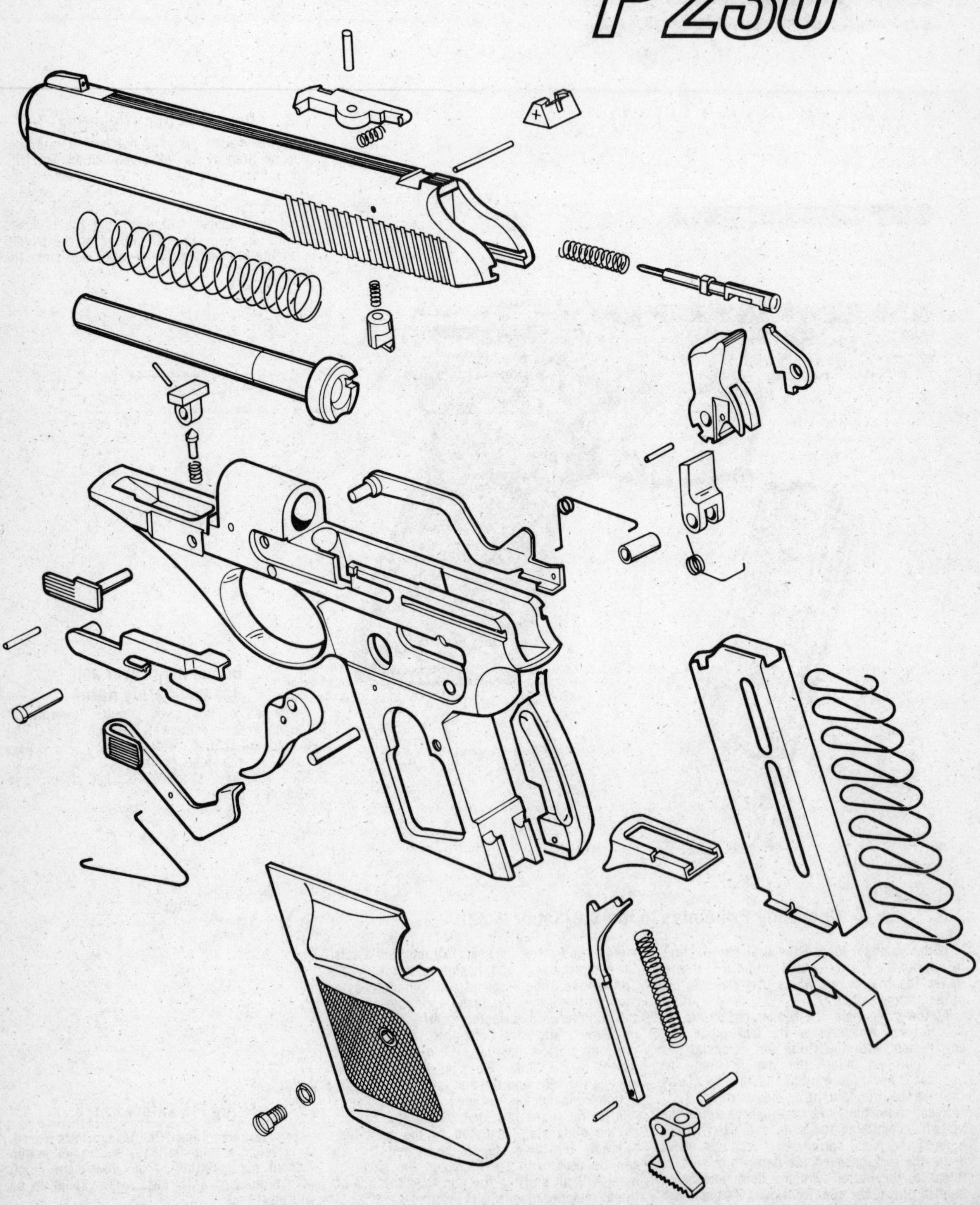

SIG/Sauer P-230 field stripped.

Operating Principles of the SIG/Sauer P-230

With the pistol loaded the first shot is fired by squeezing the trigger double action. The trigger moves the trigger rod, lifting the sear out of the hammer notch.

At the same time the trigger rod moves the safety lever, taking the lock pin out of engagement with the firing pin and releasing the firing pin just before the shot is fired. The hammer is swung forward by the hammer spring to strike the firing pin, firing the cartridge.

The forces of recoil push the slide back against the recoil spring, cocking the hammer, extracting and ejecting the spent case. The slide recoil stroke is limited by a stop on the frame. The compressed recoil spring now pushes the slide forward, stripping a cartridge from the magazine into the chamber. With the slide in battery position the trigger rod again engages the sear, readying the gun for firing.

After firing the last round the slide is held open by the slide stop, actuated by the magazine follower.

SIG/Sauer P-230 right-side view.

SIG/Sauer P-230 Operational Data

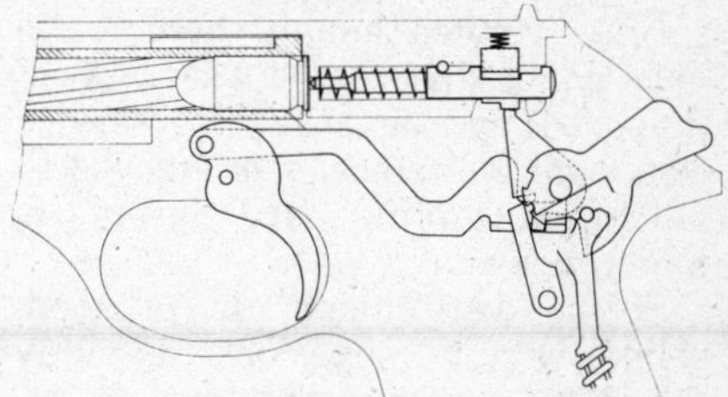

Double-Action Triggering

If the hammer is not cocked, the shot can be fired double-action. The trigger is squeezed, cocking the hammer via the trigger rod, which also presses the safety lever against the lock pin. The sear is moved away from the hammer and the firing pin is released by the lock pin. Completing the trigger pull lifts the hammer out of register and fires the shot.

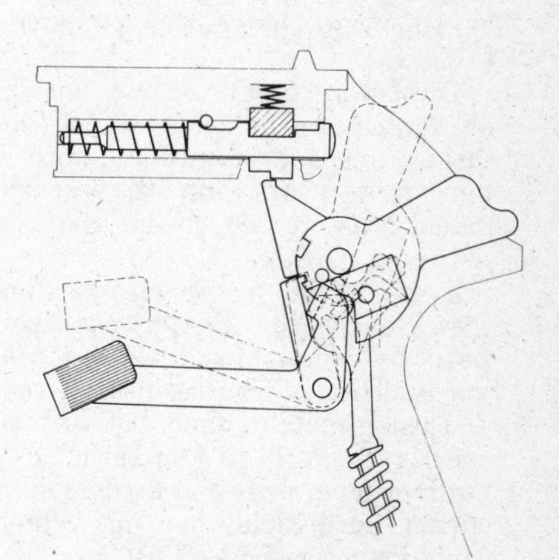

De-cocking Lever and Hammer Safety Catch

The de-cocking lever permits lowering of the hammer into the safety notch so the loaded pistol can be safely carried. The safety notch is the rest position for the hammer. The firing pin is always blocked during and after de-cocking.

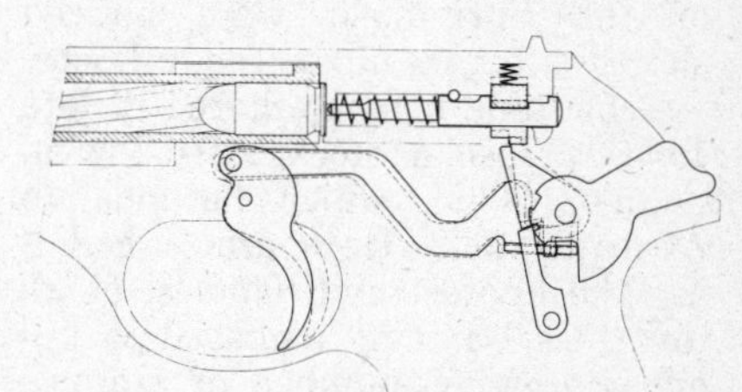

Firing Pin Safety Catch

Because of the automatic firing-pin safety catch, the pin is locked until just before the hammer is released. The safety catch is not released until the shot is intentionally fired. Even if dropped with the hammer cocked, the gun will not fire.

The 1903

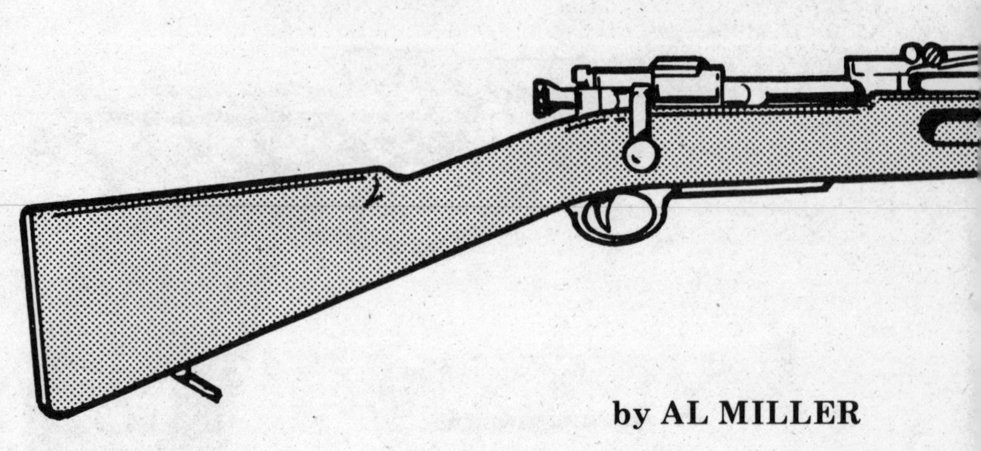

by AL MILLER

WHETHER OR NOT the Springfield 03 was the best military rifle of its time is still open to argument; Mausers, Lee-Enfields—each has its protagonists. Regardless of their respective virtues though, there can be little doubt that the 03 was the best prepared and finished. No service arm, before or since, ever enjoyed so much painstaking care during its manufacture.

Stocks were made out of good, solid walnut, superior to many found on commercial sporters today. Although machine-inletted, the marriage of wood to metal was unbelievably close, especially on those rifles fashioned between the wars when quality, not time, was the watchword. Metal fittings, all machined from forgings, were carefully polished before bluing. Bolt heads were knurled, triggers serrated. For a while, even buttplates were machine-checkered. Tool marks were rare. Each rifle was a "finished" product when it left the armory.

They were accurate, too. National Match Springfields ruled the target ranges both here and abroad for many years and the service model was no slouch in that department, either.

Every 03 in my racks, including the World War II versions, will keep five shots inside 2½" at 100 yards. This, of course, from a rest and using match ammo, but with issue sights. Perhaps I've been lucky but I've never owned or fired an inaccurate Springfield; nor one which could be described as "just so-so."

The oft-repeated charge that the 03 made a better sporter than a military arm may have some justification. Many of its design features—the excellent finish, the close tolerances—hint of a conception by riflemen, target shots and hunters, rather than by soldiers.

The inherent sporting qualities of the Springfield were noticed shortly after its birth. Teddy Roosevelt had one armory-altered in late 1903, a special stock fitted (serial number 0009), which he took to Africa in 1909. He characterized it as "the lightest and handiest of all my rifles," and he managed to kill an impressive number of animals with it, including both hippo and rhino, using the original 150-gr., full-patch bullet at 2700 fps.

Stewart Edward White, the sportsman-novelist, was another of the early Springfield users. He collected upwards of 400 African trophies using one or another of his 03 sporters, among others, and judged the new rifle-cartridge combination ideal medicine for lions.

White's first Springfield sporter was made up by Louis Wundhammer about 1910, this first rifle one of four that had been ordered by Capt. E. C. Crossman.* Later, Owen, Griffin & Howe, Hoffman, Linden and several others made them. These were handsome rifles, a bit heavy by modern standards but each a thing of beauty: choice wood, tasteful engraving and checkering—and if they were not too well used, still capable today of formidable accuracy. Until the middle 'thirties, when Winchester brought out their Model 70, Springfield sporters set the standards by which other hunting and target rifles were judged.

For years, the 03 was this nation's official service rifle. It lost that title to the Garand in 1935, but with the advent of World War II the 03 and its descendants, the A3 and A4, saw active duty as late as the 1950s. The Springfield's battle honors include campaigns in the Phillipines, Central America, the Caribbean, Mexico, the Western Front during World War I, every theater in World War II and, finally, Korea.

Turned out to pasture, the Springfield's career is far from over. During the past two decades, thousands have found their way into the hands and gunracks of American sportsmen. The NRA offered them, via the Director of Civilian Marksmanship, to its members at bargain rates over the years; surplus stores sold them; every sporting goods store of any stature at all tallied some in its inventory. Today these veterans, most civilianized by fancy stocks, scopes and professional blue jobs, can be seen by the score each fall when the redcoated hordes invade mountain and forest. The 03 isn't dead yet.

But they're getting scarce; at least, the "as issued" specimens are—and the gun collecting fraternity is becoming aware of it. During the past year, Springfield prices have soared. If a man has any ambition to collect them, the time to start is now.

The Early Models

"Sired by Mauser, out of Krag" is the way one wag described the Springfield. Its official birthday was June 18, 1903 when the Chief of Ordnance accepted it, the official designation: *U.S. Magazine Rifle, Model of 1903, Caliber .30.* It came with a 24" barrel, rod bayonet, ramp type rear sight and an odd looking blade with two large holes drilled through it for a front sight. The bolt handle was curved but wasn't swept back. The forward barrel band was located right at the nose of the stock.

The 1903 cartridge, which came into being at the same time, was

*The first Stewart Edward White rifle, serial number 166,346, has a Rock Island arsenal barrel dated February, 1910. Made by Louis Wundhammer of Los Angeles, it is one of four such Springfield 1903 sporters ordered by Capt. E. C. (Ned) Crossman. One was for Capt. Crossman, the other two for Robert C. Rogers and John Colby. See Crossman's *Book of the Springfield* (Georgetown, S. C., 1951) or the GUN DIGEST, *15th edition.*

Springfield

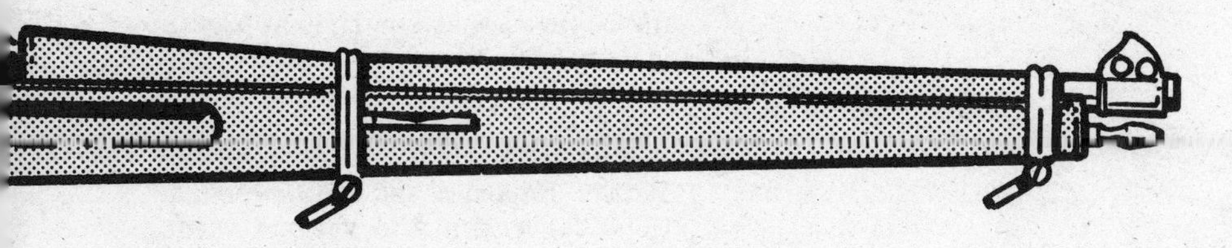

An interesting and detailed account of the most famous military rifle in United States history—including the numerous variations made since its birth.

slightly longer than the current '06 round and fired a 220-gr., full-jacketed round nose bullet at 2200 fps.

In 1905, the rod bayonet was shunted aside in favor of the knife type and, about the same time, an improved leaf rear sight, resembling that used on the Krag, was mounted in place of the unsatisfactory ramp.

Meanwhile, the ever-busy Germans had opened their bag of tricks again, surprising the shooting world by introducing a radical pointed bullet they called *spitzgeschoss*. This new pointed shape enabled them to send the 154-gr. bullet from their 8mm service round at the then astonishing speed of 2800 fps. Quick to see the advantages of the new design, our ordnance people got busy in their ballistics labs and whipped up the now famous 30-06 cartridge.

Pushing a 150-gr. pointed bullet out of the muzzle at 2700 fps, the 06 case was reduced to 2.49" long, necessitated by the 03 case having been too long for the new spitzer bullet by .070". Several thousand 1903 rifles had been produced by this time but, rather than re-barrel them, it was decided, in the interests of economy, to shorten and re-chamber the existing barrels. Two-tenths inch (.200") was shaved off the breech, the chambers altered for the new cartridge, and the threads cut two turns deeper. This operation left the barrels 23.79" long (chamber and bore) and all Springfield 03 barrels made since then have measured the same. Over-all barrel length became 24.006".

The next major change took place in 1918 when the steel used to make receivers and bolts was strengthened. Those critical parts were double heat treated, a process which made the surface metal extremely hard while allowing the core steel to remain relatively soft. Actions fabricated in this manner have weathered test rounds developing pressures of 125,000 psi without a whimper. The tough surface not only wears well but with a little use, cams and runways smooth to a mirror-like glaze, making those particular actions the slickest Springfield ever built.

Despite the time, effort and expense which must have been spent creating the new process, nobody bothered to record the exact point when the change was instituted. Authorities agree it took place somewhere around receiver No. 800,000, but nobody's really sure. Nevertheless, 800,000 is the magic number, it being generally accepted that actions made subsequently are the stronger. Although "low numbered" Springfields, that is, those with serial numbers under 800,000, are regarded as weaker and less desirable, it should be remembered that each was subjected to 70,000 pound test loads, and that these were the same rifles which created the Springfield's reputation in the wars and on the game fields. Nevertheless, it is true that the shattering of several of the earlier case-hardened actions brought on the change in heat treatment in early 1918.

Rock Island 03s received the improved double heat treatment starting with receiver No. 285,507. From No. 319,921 on some R.I. receivers were made of a nickel steel similar to that used later in producing the wartime A3s and A4s. Springfield Armory didn't adopt nickel steel until 1928 but again, no one there in Massachusetts noticed the exact time of the changeover. In all probability rifles produced after No. 1,290,266 boasted nickel steel actions.

Variations in the quality of steel are primarily of interest only to purists. It goes without saying that any high-numbered 03—always assuming good condition—will accomodate modern loads with perfect safety.

The Pedersen Device

To back up slightly: Shortly after the U.S. declared war on Germany in 1917, a well known arms designer of the day, one J. D. Pedersen, approached the War Department with an intriguing invention. The Pedersen Device, as historians call it, was essentially an automatic pistol mechanism with a stubby, integral barrel which could be slipped into the 03's receiver in place of the regular bolt. Once locked in place—this was accomplished by a flip of the magazine cutoff to "Off"—a long box magazine containing 40 cartridges resembling the 32 ACP was inserted into the right side of the bolt and—presto! The Springfield was converted into an instant semi-automatic rifle!

Only three alterations to the rifle were necessary: an ejection port had to be cut into the left side of the receiver; the magazine cutoff had two grooves milled in it, and a small "kicker" was added to the sear. None of these modifications prevented the rifle from using the regular service round when the original bolt was in place.

Although the pistol-sized cartridge fired an 80-gr. bullet at a mere 1300 fps, General Pershing recognized its lethal potential and ordered 100,000 Pedersen units. Some 65,000 had been completed when Armistice Day arrived but none were ever issued to troops. A few years after the war, most of the devices were destroyed. A few, as usual, managed to escape the crushers and are now eagerly sought after by collectors.

It's easy to recognize the 03s

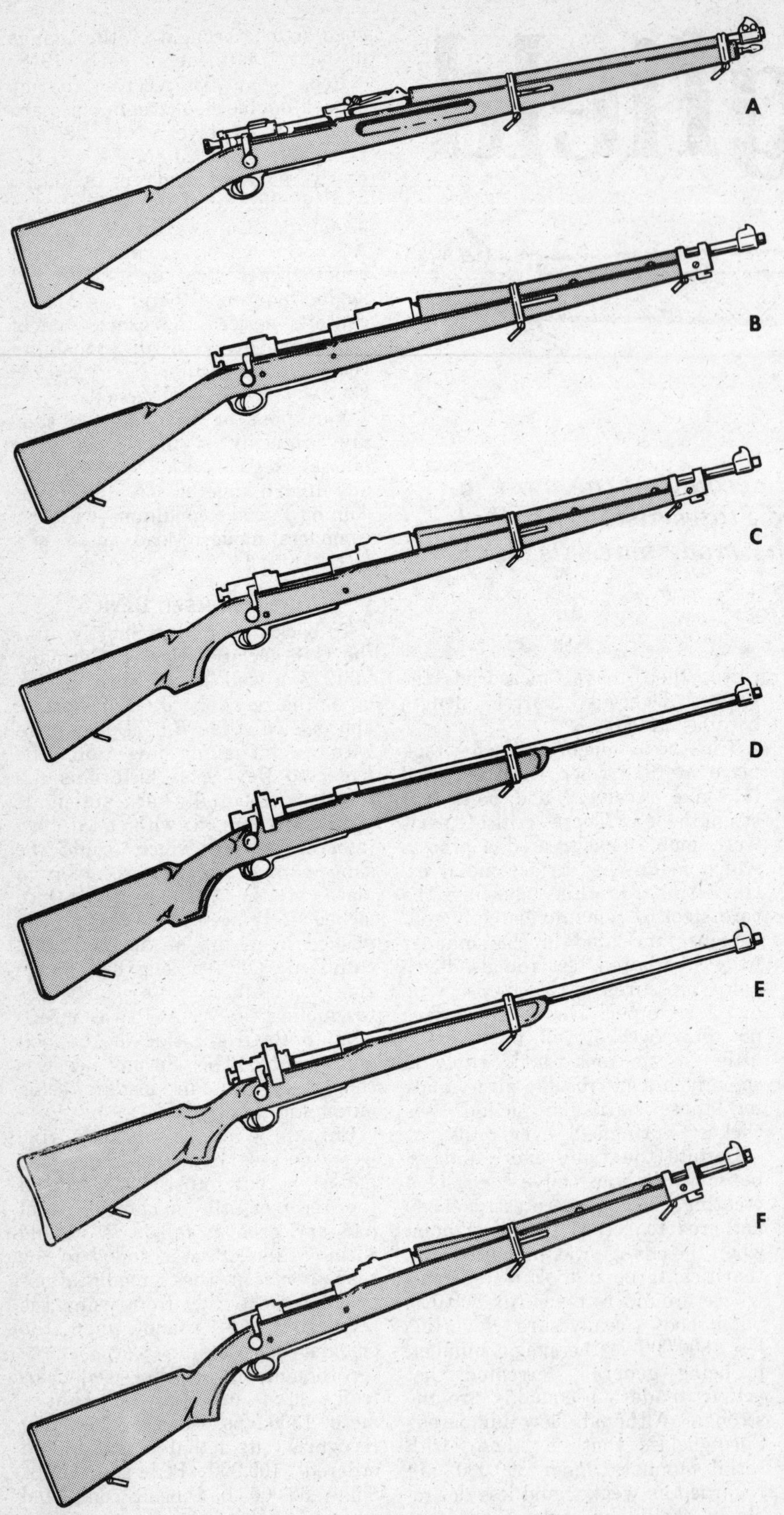

A—Original Model 1903. When it was accepted by the Army in 1903, the Springfield was equipped with a ramp-type rear sight and a rod bayonet. Note that the bolt handle turns straight down. B—The Type S stock was supplied with the service model 03 until it was supplanted by the Type C in 1929. C—The Model 1922 M1 stock was supplied on National Match 03s issued to Service Teams. D—The Model 1922 M1 issue stock (caliber 22). Note how this oversized pistol grip stock differs from *NRA* stock on the same action-barrel. E—The Model 1922 M1 stock (caliber 30). This was commonly called the NRA or Sporter stock. F—The Type C stock was adopted in 1929. Rifles so equipped were designated Model 1903A1.

modified for the Pedersen unit. There is a small, lozenge-shaped ejection port on the left side of the receiver, and to quell any further doubts the legend, *U.S Springfield Armory Model 1903 Mark I* is inscribed on the receiver. Records concerning this variation are sketchy but it's believed that one rifle, appropriately modified, was produced for each of the Pedersen devices manufactured.

When World War I ended, the Battle Reports and recommendations concerning the various weapons used were reviewed. The 03 came through with flying colors. Complaints were few and suggested changes even fewer. One, that was accepted, concerned the bolt handle. It was angled backwards slightly to bring it more in line with the trigger.

The Marine Corps, always marksmanship oriented, altered the sights of their rifles: the width of the front blade was increased to .10" and undercut, while the diameter of the rear peep was doubled. In addition, the triangular-shaped open sight in the rear leaf was dispensed with. 03s with Marine Corps sights are very much in demand by collectors.

Type C Stocks

After a considerable amount of experimentation, a new service stock, the Type C was chosen in 1928. The original Type S stock had been criticized for its abrupt drop at the heel and because many felt it was too short. The new stock was straighter, its buttstock contour reminiscent of those found on good shotguns. A hand-filling integral pistol grip had been added and the finger grooves, so pronounced on the old S stock, were deleted. Rifles with the new stock were designated Model 1903A1s.

Although the semi-automatic M1 was chosen to succeed the 03 in 1935, almost a year passed before the last bolt action rolled off the production line at Springfield Armory. A few more were assembled in 1937 and another handful, the last, were produced in 1939. With receiver No. 1,532,878, the 03 became just another obsolete military rifle—or so everyone believed at the time.

Just before production ceased, a second gas escape port was drilled through the forward receiver ring. Up to this point, only one port, about ⅛" diameter, had pierced the ring on the right. Why an additional hole was put on the left is anyone's guess. I've only noticed a handful of 03s so made, all with serial numbers above 1,500,000. When the wartime A3s and A4s appeared, only one port was evident, this time on the left side.

Late in 1941, sensing the hot breath of war and unable to supply our rapidly expanding military forces sufficiently with the new M1, the War Department issued a contract to the Remington Arms Company to begin production of the 03. Except for the name Remington and the serial numbers, which started with No. 3,000,000, this version of the 03 was a faithful replica of the Armory model in every respect.

With an eye toward increasing production, Remington's engineers took a critical look at the old design. After a few months of fiddling with slide rules and hand-made prototypes, they came up with the *U.S. Rifle, Caliber .30, Model of 1903A3.*

Why not A2? Because a Model A2 had already been approved and was in service. Not really a rifle, it was simply a modified barreled action, altered to fit inside the breech of a tank cannon and used for practice to reduce training expenses.

Old-timers howled in anguish when the first A3 appeared. Barrel bands, floorplate and trigger guard were made of stamped metal. To add insult to injury, the barrels, most still bearing lathe scars, had only two grooves instead of the traditional four. Critics admitted that the rear-mounted receiver sight might offer some advantages but most insisted that the rifle would never stand up under battle conditions.

Despite the outraged cries and dire predictions, the A3 performed creditably throughout World War II, seeing service in every theater and adding new luster to the name Springfield. It was sturdy, as dependable as its famed forefather, and just about as accurate.

This last surprised everyone. The ability of a 4-grooved barrel to group better than a two-groover, if any, must be slight. From a rest, my 03s and A3s deliver the same accuracy: 2″ to 2½″ at 100 yards with match ammo. The life of a 2-grooved tube is reputedly shorter than the four if AP ammunition is

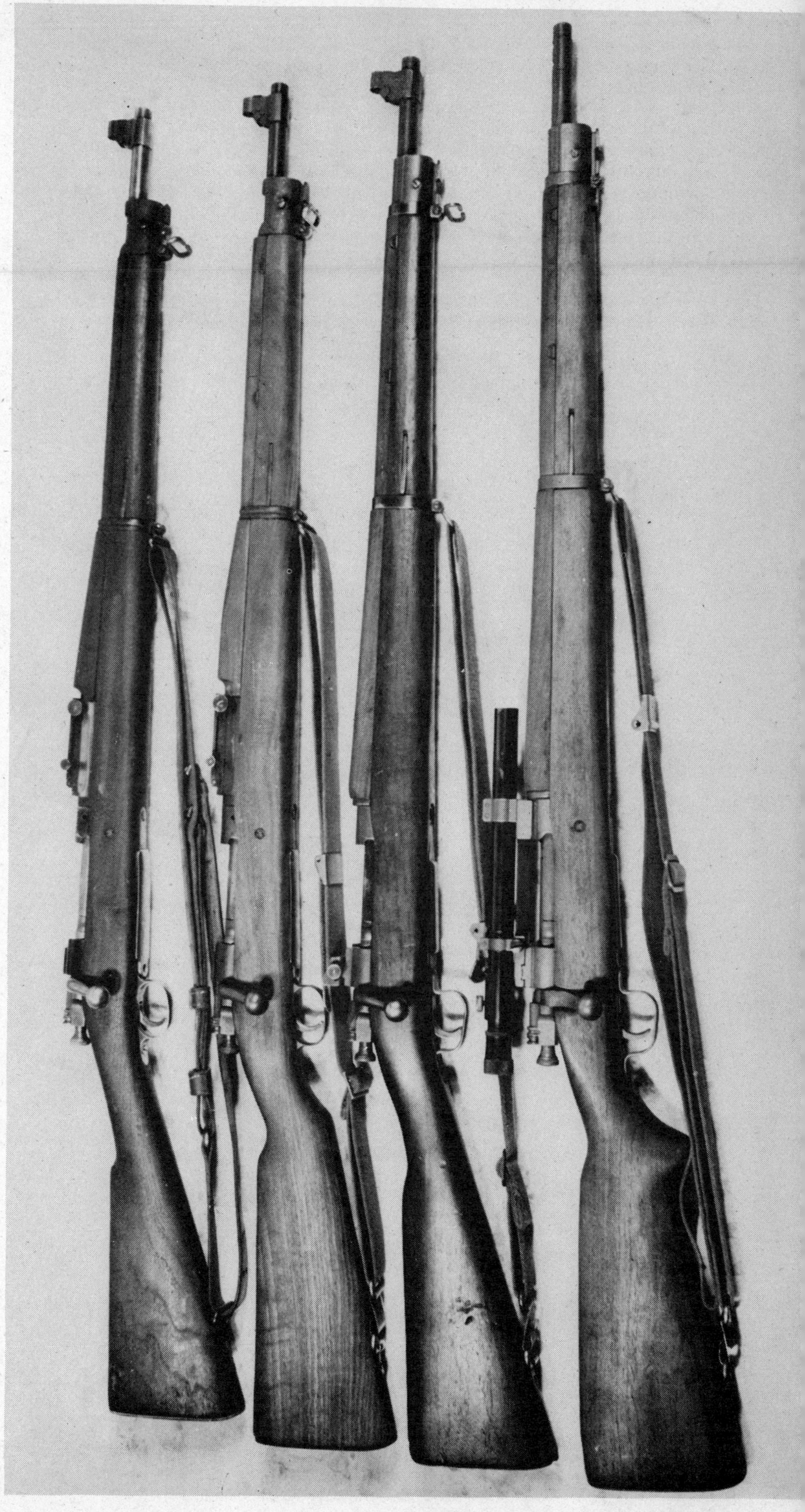

1903 Service. Left to right: 1903 with S stock; 1903A1 with WW II semi-pistol-grip stock; 1903A3; 1903A4, the sniper's model with a modified Type C stock.

used, but evidently the Army felt the difference in longevity was more than offset by lower manufacturing costs and greater production.

A—The 1903 Springfield in early standard-issue forms. It has the original S stock with grasping grooves and greater drop, at heel. B—The 1903A1 was simply the standard 03 mounted in a Type C stock. C—1903A1 in a wartime C stock. Notice the blunted pistol grip, the general absence of clean stock lines. D—The 1903A3. The World War II version of the 03 has a receiver peep sight and is characterized by the use of stamped parts and a two-groove barrel. E—The 1903A4. The sniper's model is equipped with a Weaver 2½X scope in Redfield Jr. mounts and the Type C stock. No iron sights were fitted.

Two Million A3s

Remington turned out most of the two million A3s but Smith-Corona also added another 200,000 or so to the total. A number of the latter will be found with 4-groove and, occasionally, 6-groove barrels which were supplied by High Standard, Savage and several other sub-contractors.

The A4, the sniper's model, made its bow in 1943. It was simply an A3 equipped with a Weaver 330C telescopic sight (the Army called it the M73B1 carried in a Redfield Jr. mount. The bolt handle was altered to clear the scope and no iron sights were fitted.

To the best of my knowledge, Remington took no special pains with bedding or action but the A4 sniper standing in my rack is blessed with what must surely be one of the smoothest actions ever made. Its condition indicated that it had never been issued yet the trigger is crisp and light—almost too light—and the rifle will consistently group all shots within 1¼".

The number of A4s produced was very small, something on the order of 28,000 all told. Few were issued before 1944 but many were still in action as late as the early 1950s. The Marines used them in Korea, mounting 8- and 12-power target scopes on them.

There's no way of knowing how many survived but the number must be small. The rarest of all have serial numbers beginning with a "Z" prefix; fewer than 2900 were made.

Of all the Springfields produced, the cream were the target and sporter rifles which trickled out of the Armory during the quiet years between wars. Less than 2000 ever saw the light of day in any given year but each was a handcrafted marvel.

Assembled from carefully selected parts, with cocking cams, bolts, sight leaves, extractors and runways polished, stocks fashioned from first-class, straight-grained black walnut, equipped with star gauged barrels and target sights, the National Match Springfields, NRA Sporters and the other limited edition models represented the Armory's finest achievements. Little wonder they dominated the target ranges for so many years.

When I was a boy, the word

"star gauged" had a magic ring. This interesting device was a feeler gauge used at the Armory to measure the uniformity of a barrel's bore. If land and groove measurements were within one ten-thousandths of an inch (.0001") from chamber to muzzle the barrel was judged match grade, and a small "star mark" was stamped on the lower edge of the muzzle crown. In U.S. shooting circles a star gauged barrel was regarded as the ultimate.

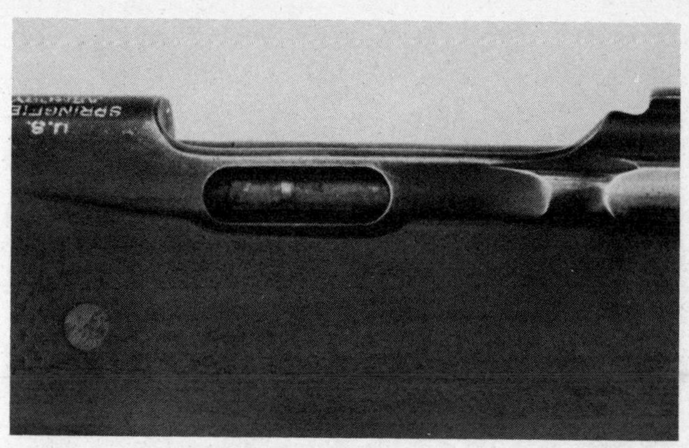

An ejection port on the Mark I Springfield allowed the small Pedersen-designed cartridge cases to escape the semi-automatic bolt. Note the slight stock cutaway beneath the port.

Target-Sporter Models

More than a dozen different match, target and sporting models were created by Springfield Armory between 1921 and 1940. (Some 1000 or fewer National Match versions of the A3 rifle, purportedly equipped with Redfield micrometer rear sights, were produced from about 1953 through 1956, but I haven't been able to find a photograph of one of these or a specimen.) Some were designed exclusively for service teams; most were made available to NRA members. In addition, a series of full-fledged 30-caliber target rifles was issued. They were characterized by long, heavy barrels, micrometer sights on the receiver, globe sights at the muzzle, mounting blocks for telescopic sights —some were even decorated with adjustable buttplates and other match-rifle equipment. These remarkable rifles, weighing from 12 to 13 pounds, were just about unbeatable on the range.

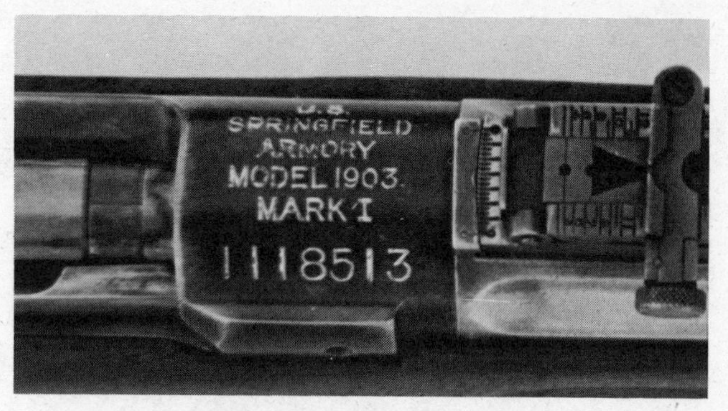

Those Mark I 03s modified to accept the Pedersen device were plainly marked as such on the receiver ring.

During one period, the Armory even made up a few "free rifles" for the International Teams. These had longer, heavier barrels, set triggers, long hook buttplates and palm rests. They were about as good as anything Europe had to offer, and they tipped the scales at a hefty 14 pounds.

Mark I parts. Top, sear and cutoff from a standard 03; bottom, sear and cutoff from a Mark I Springfield modified to accept the Pedersen device.

Some of those old rifles are still floating around, most of them pretty worn now. I'd never pay extra money for one myself unless it is accompanied by the original Ordnance Dept. bill of sale and its star gauging record.

Needless to say, a clever gunsmith can counterfeit a National Match model without too much trouble. A bit of judicious polishing, a close fitting stock, a homemade star mark on the muzzle, the rifle's serial number engraved on the bolt —as always, it pays to be prudent when purchasing a used firearm.

Chances are, if you do run across one of those old specials, it will be an NRA Sporter. Several thousand were made and quite a few, relatively speaking, seem to have survived.

The Sporter, like the other specials, was put together from near-perfect parts and given the same care as a National Match rifle during production. The barrel—star gauged, of course—was slightly tapered; a Lyman 48 receiver sight was mounted on the bridge but the standard service blade was retained up forward; the stock contour was distinctly different from the service style, resembling those on commercial rifles.

While on the subject, it should be noted that the Armory developed several different stocks. The S and C stocks, which have already been mentioned, were relegated to the service rifles, including the N.M. models, but there were various other supplied for the specials.

The Model 1922 or NRA Model

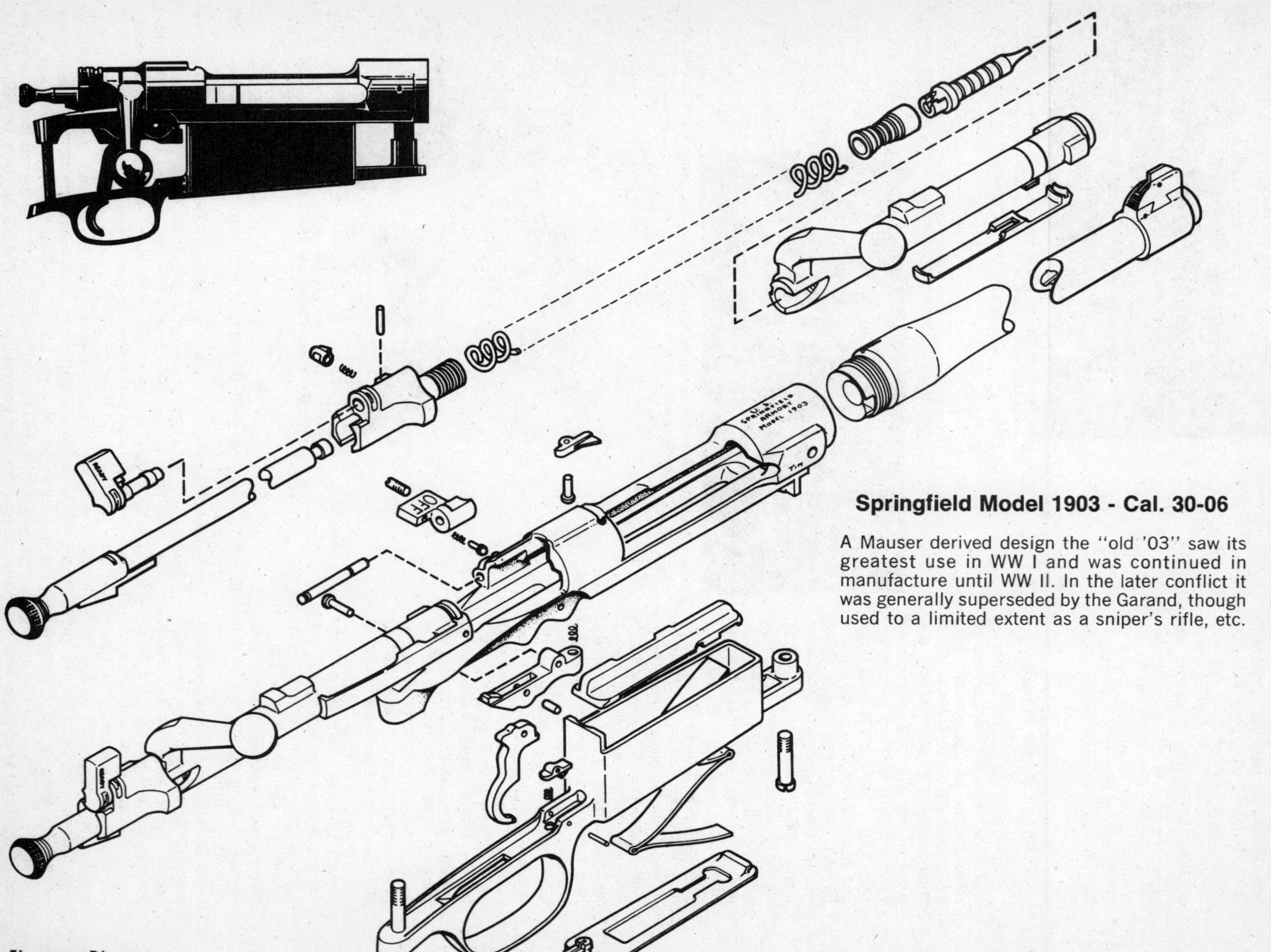

Springfield Model 1903 - Cal. 30-06

A Mauser derived design the "old '03" saw its greatest use in WW I and was continued in manufacture until WW II. In the later conflict it was generally superseded by the Garand, though used to a limited extent as a sniper's rifle, etc.

Firearms Directory

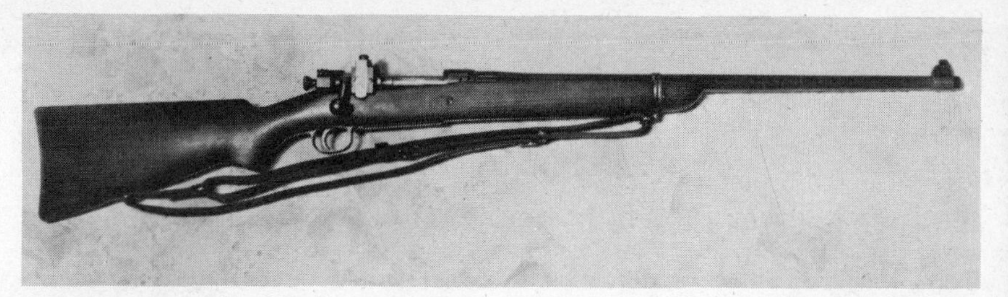

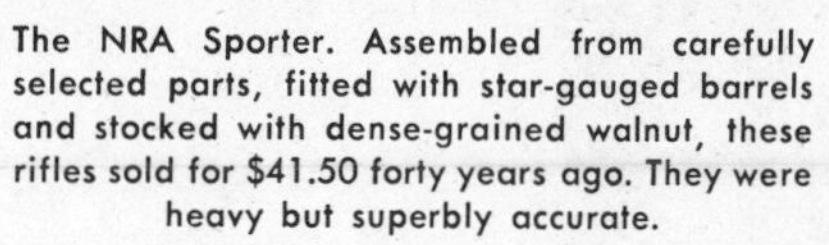

The NRA Sporter. Assembled from carefully selected parts, fitted with star-gauged barrels and stocked with dense-grained walnut, these rifles sold for $41.50 forty years ago. They were heavy but superbly accurate.

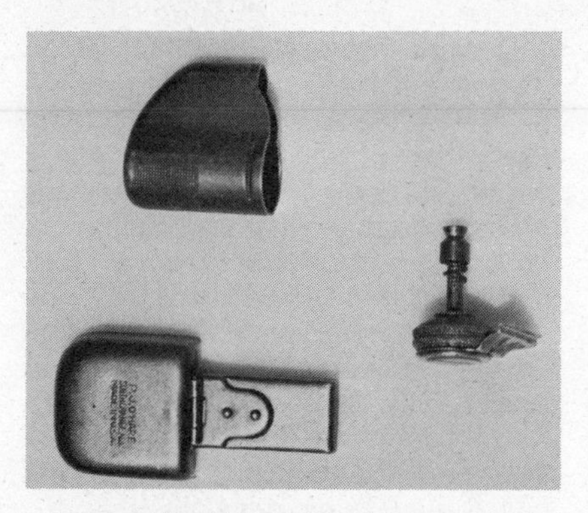

Curiosa. Relics of the days when the 03 ruled the target range. Top, front sight protector; lower left, rear sight protector; right, rear sight micrometer adjuster.

Micrometer sight adjustor. One of the accessories offered the serious competitor of the early 1920s when the 03 dominated the ranges. These tools permitted accurately controlled small changes in elevation.

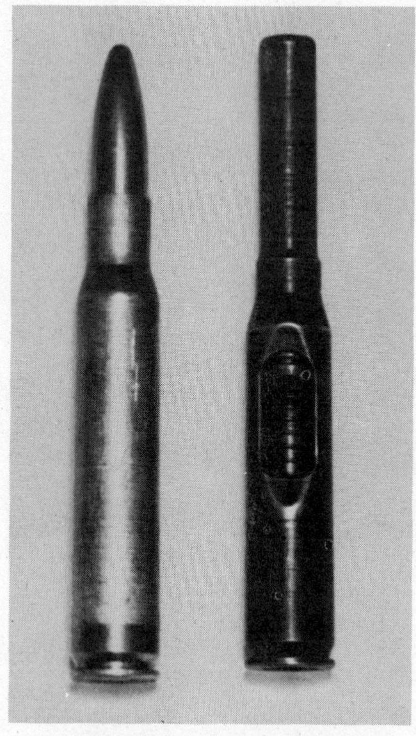

22 Short cartridge adaptor (right), used in the Gallery Practice Rifle of 1907. A 30-06 Military round is shown for comparison.

as it was popularly known, featured a shotgun-style butt, a well-turned pistol grip and short, sporter style fore-end. This was used on the 22 rimfire Springfields and on the 30-06 Sporters when these (and other later versions) were sold for civilian use through the DCM.

This same M1922 NRA stock—except for having finger grooves—was used on the 1922 "Match Springfield," a 30-cal. rifle introduced that year. This rifle was a fore-runner of the "Style T" Match 03 rifle first offered in late 1929 and made in limited numbers for a few years.

The M1922 M1 stock, in its NRA form, differed little from the M1922 stock, but the "issue only" version was considerably different—while a half- or sporter stock, the fore-end had finger grooves, the pistol grip profile showed a flatter angle, and the rear of the buttstock looked like the service rifle or S stock in drops, dimension and form.*

The Springfield Sporter

To get back to the Sporters: They're heavy by today's standards, scaling pretty close to 9 pounds. Weighty though they may be, those I've fired were very accurate with actions as smooth as silk. A great number served as the basis for some of the classics turned out by such people as Niedner, Shelhamer, Griffin & Howe and Stoeger during the 1920s and the early '30s.

The first 22 practice rifle based on the 03 action was a single shot. It was fitted with a 24-inch barrel bored off-center at the breech so that the regular firing pin would hit the rim of the small case. The cartridge, by the way, was a special 22 Long Rifle featuring a Pope-designed bullet. It was manufactured by Peters for a limited time and called the "22 Stevens-Pope Armory." Only a few of these arms were produced. Except for the bores, their appearance was indistinguishable from the service rifle.

Another chip off the old block was the Gallery Practice Rifle, Model 1903. Except for chamber and barrel, it too was a duplicate of the issue rifle. Although some of its design features smacked of genius, its accuracy left much to be desired.

Rather than fashion a new bolt or firing pin assembly, Springfield engineers (Majors J. E. Hoffer and J. T. Thompson) created an adaptor cartridge. Made entirely of steel, they were deliberately made shorter than the standard 06 round to prevent one of the latter from being chambered by mistake. Each adaptor contained an integral firing pin and a tiny slot in the side which permitted a 22 Short cartridge to be inserted. The devices could be loaded into the magazine, worked through the action and extracted exactly like the service cartridge. From a training standpoint, the approach was ideal, especially for those ROTC and National Guard units located far from regular outdoor ranges. It meant that the troops could train with a rifle of standard size and weight, shoot from all positions and even practice rapid-fire on indoor ranges.

Clever as the idea was, the adaptors proved impractical. When fired, the bullet enjoyed about half an inch of free travel before it struck the rifling. After a few rounds, lead and grease built up at

*There were numerous other stock styles over the years, some experimental, others of limited production. For full and complete information on all of these—and for the finest account of Springfield rifles extant, see *The '03 Springfield*, by Clark S. Campbell, published by Ray Riling Arms Books Co., 6844 Gorsten St., Philadelphia, Pa. 19119.

A "long-slide" Lyman 48 micrometer sight, here seen on a Sedgeley sporter.

this point. Accuracy suffered accordingly. In addition, the adaptors tended to rust in short order, requiring an exasperating amount of maintenance to keep them in operating condition. Most aggravating of all—as far as the shooters were concerned—was the fact that unloading the spent 22 cases was a miserable and frustrating chore.

Despite these shortcomings, it wasn't until 1919 that plans for a new 22 trainer were started. More like the target rifles we know today, its bolt was two-piece and a 5-shot magazine jutted below the floorplate. It still looked in 1920 like the issue rifle except for a Lyman 48 micrometer sight mounted on the receiver. Chambered for the regular 22 Long Rifle cartridge, these prototype versions were the first really accurate 22s that Ordnance had ever developed.

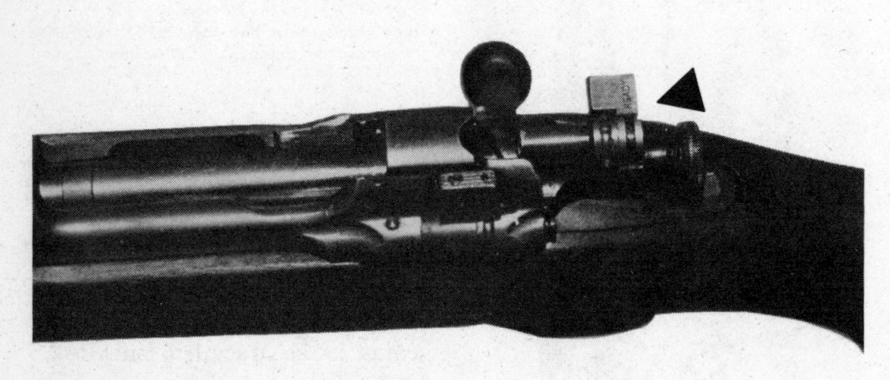

The reversed safety on the above rifle (arrow) must have been taken from a match rifle, for the serial number on the bolt doesn't match that on the receiver. It pays to be cautious when shopping for collector's items.

The Model 1922

Two years later (in June of 1922) a refined version, called the *U.S. Rifle, Caliber .22, Model 1922,* was issued. It was the first Springfield to have the half-stock style that was soon to become famous as the "Sporter" stock. By mid-1924 some 2000 M1922 rifles had been made, their price just over $39.

The improved-mechanism Model 1922 M1 which followed also had—in its "as issued" form—a half-stock with an oversize flat-angle pistol grip. These had an excessive amount of drop at the heel. The NRA version had the graceful Sporter stock, as before. Bolt travel was still as long as that of the standard 03, a full 3.3 inches, but chamber dimensions were better, the 5-shot magazine was now flush, and the Lyman 48 C receiver sight had ½-minute clicks.

Below—This 1903A4 Sniper rifle has a 2½X Weaver telescopic sight in a Redfield Jr. mount, saw active duty as late as the Korean conflict. Note the altered bolt handle.

The 1922 M2s, introduced in late 1932, wore a new stock. While a half-stock, it was not the Sporter NRA style used earlier; instead, it had finger-grooves in the fore-end and a buttstock profile about like the N.M. stock. These M2s had a short bolt throw, speed lock ignition and provision for headspace adjustment. That last was incorporated in the locking lug assembly on the final production models.

M2s can still be found hard at work on small bore ranges around the country. Many carry the letters "A" or "B" after their serial numbers. Those markings signify that the rifles were originally issued as M1922s or M1922s M1s and later arsenal modified to M2 specifications.

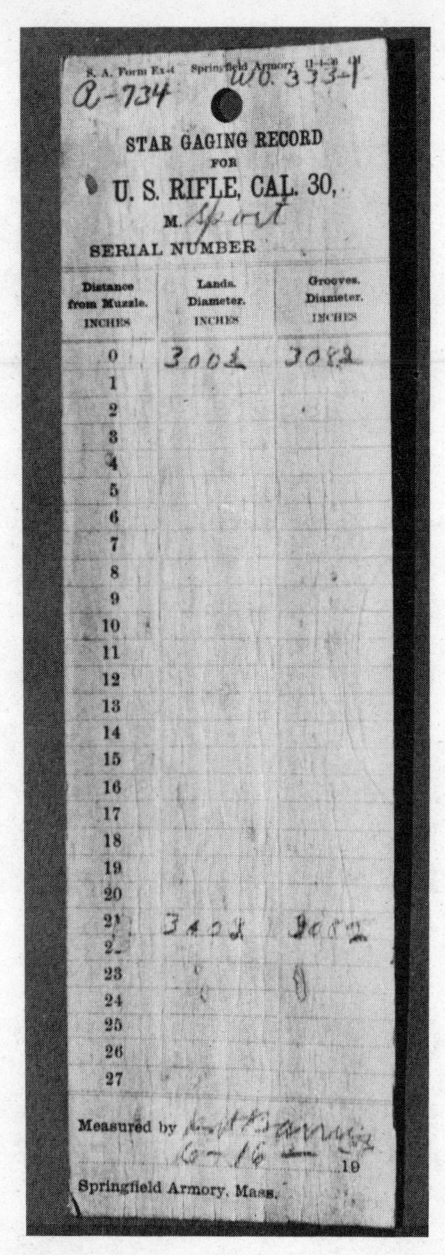

S. A. Form Ex-4 Springfield Armory 11-4-20

Q-734 WO. 333-1

STAR GAGING RECORD

FOR

U. S. RIFLE, CAL. 30,

M. Sport

SERIAL NUMBER

Distance from Muzzle. INCHES	Lands. Diameter. INCHES	Grooves. Diameter. INCHES
0	3002	3082
1		
2		
3		
4		
5		
6		
7		
8		
9		
10		
11		
12		
13		
14		
15		
16		
17		
18		
19		
20		
21	3402	3082
2[illegible]		
23		
24		
25		
26		
27		

Measured by [illegible]

6-16 19

Springfield Armory, Mass.

Left—"Star Gaging Record" card used to indicate bore and groove dimensions of selected 03 barrels.

The *International Match Rifle, Caliber 30, Model 1924*, carried a checkered pistol grip stock, a hooked buttplate, a ball-type palm rest, a Lyman 48 receiver sight and a heavy 30″ barrel. These also had double-set triggers of one type or another (see Campbell's book). An identical rifle was made in 22 Long Rifle, using the Model 1922 M1 action, for our successful U.S. International teams, but with the action considerably re-designed. Twelve of the 1924 match Springfields in 22 caliber were made in 15 days, the result of a last-minute order for them!

The old 03 wasn't perfect. Its sights were too delicate for battle conditions; the two-piece firing pin, which failed on occasion, affected lock time adversely; the high bridge made for an overly tall sighting plane and the Springfield action could never cope with escaping gas as well as the Mauser. Nonetheless, it was the best rifle that ever came out of the Armory—and it could shoot. The average 03 was more accurate than any of its contemporaries. Regardless of its shortcomings it looms high on the list of the world's great rifles.

The 03 helped make a lot of history during the first half of this century; on target ranges, battle ground and game fields. More than four million were produced but age, wear and tear, combat, lend-lease and sporterizing have taken their toll. The 03, in military dress, is rapidly disappearing from the scene.

Tribute and Epitaph

But not entirely. A handful are still on active duty. While watching General Eisenhower's funeral, I noticed the familiar silhouettes when the Presidential color guard hove into view. Sure enough, they were armed with the old bolt actions. Some months ago I saw the Army Drill Team in action. They too were equipped with 03s. I've no idea why they carried them but it was a nostalgic sight to a guy who learned to shoot and run through the Manual of Arms with one.

I remember crossing the English Channel one gray day in June of '44. The ship rolled sluggishly as the helmsman threw the wheel hard over to avoid a floating mine. Several of the troopers broke out their M1s and emptied them at the shiny, dark globe without result. A lanky, tobacco-chewing sergeant muttered an apology as he elbowed up to the rail, cradling a weather-beaten 03 tenderly in his arms. Balancing easily against the ship's gentle heave, he slid into the leather sling and sighted carefully for what seemed to be an eternity. The Springfield's bark was lost in the dull boom of the exploding mine and, as the echoes lost themselves over the tortured water, the marksman cast a scornful glance at the M1s. "Firepower, hell! I'll stick to my 03!"

If the 03 ever needs an epitaph, that should do as well as any. ●

Below—Sighting tube. A small number of "sighting tubes" made at Springfield Armory and issued to service rifle teams. The minimum sight setting was 600 yards.

Lynton McKenzie and Richard Hodgson

This classic treatment of a Ruger No. 1 Single Shot rifle is the combined work of Richard Hodgson, the gunsmith of Boulder, Colorado, and Lynton McKenzie, the ex-Purdey gun engraver of New Orleans—and who may well be the finest engraver in the world.

Hodgson, relatively a newcomer to the field of custom metalsmithing for firearms, is very much an artist in his imaginative and innovative treatment of steel—barrels, graceful guards, scope and metallic sight bases, rings, subtle changes in receiver contours and profiles. At the same time, Hodgson is a stockmaker of the first rank, and a master at checkering.

Hodgson machined the barrel shown here from the full round to form a tapered octagon with an integral rib. It is to be fitted with Hodgson's folding express sights and quick-detachable scope mounts, double lever operated. He restocked this Ruger beautifully in fine French walnut, and fitted it with a Purdey style safety. The steel buttplate is finely engraved by McKenzie, and in a restrained treatment. The buttplate will be protected by a removable padded leather shoe or boot—a thin pad will be used when heavy clothing is worn, a thick one for use when the shooter is lightly dressed. This is an

Right side of the Ruger rifle—see caption for the other side.

Gun Engravers and Gunsmiths

On this page—and on other pages that follow or appear elsewhere in this edition—you will be reading about several of our first flight artisans, engravers, stockmakers and metal workers, all striving to achieve and create in the highest tradition of their chosen crafts.

The GUN DIGEST is pleased indeed to present here, for your enjoyment and edification, a glimpse of the important works these individuals are doing.

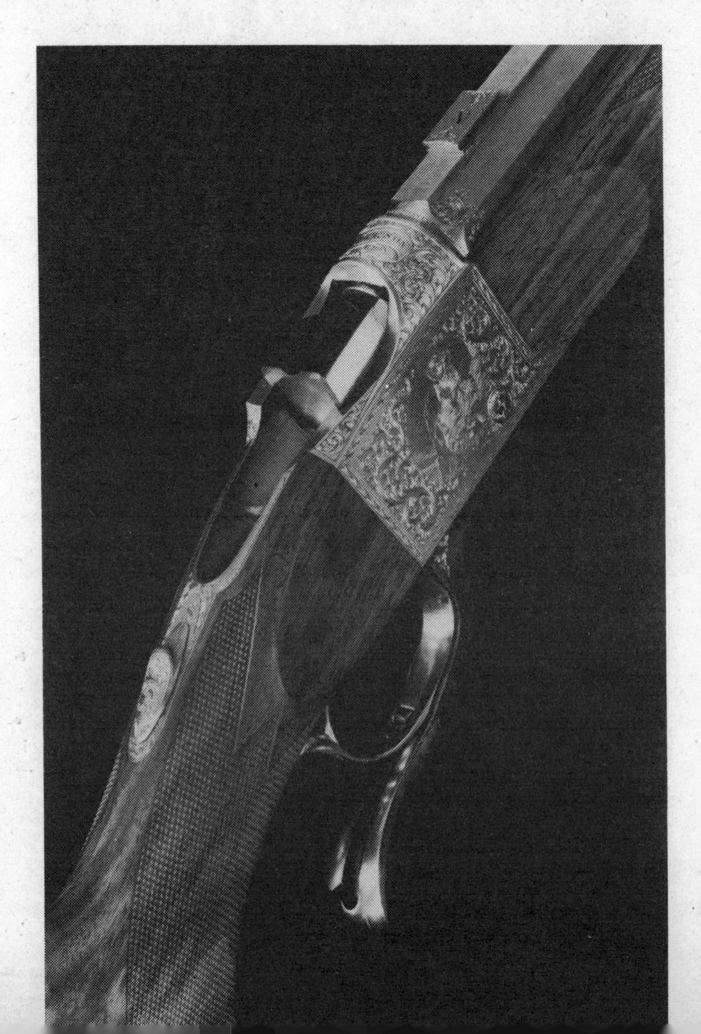

Note new tang safety fitted to Hodgson-McKenzie rifle, and the dovetail scope base let into the raised rib of the octagon barrel.

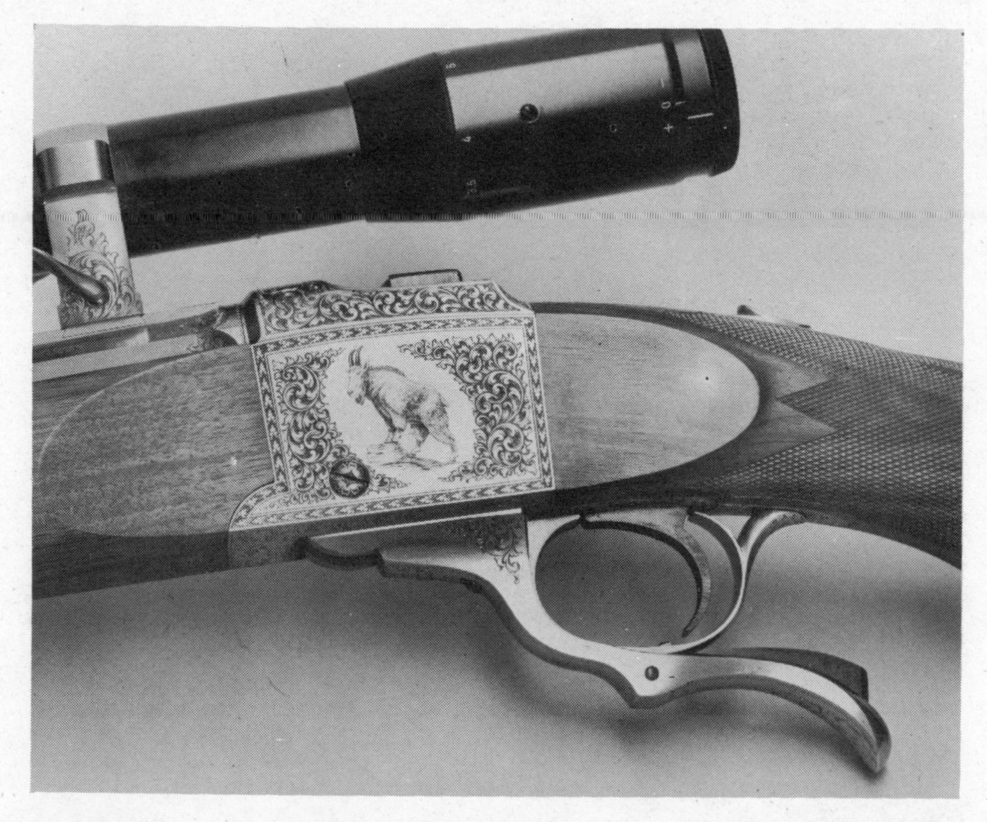

This clear view of the Ruger rifle reveals several interesting aspects of the work done by Hodgson and McKenzie. Outstanding, of course, is the superb engraving of the receiver, the Rocky Mountain goat beautifully cut within its cartouche. Note also the custom scope rings, quickly detachable via levers front and rear from the bases dovetailed into the barrel rib. In that same area can be seen the graceful and radiused flowing of the barrel flats out of their round beginnings. Now, moving to the right, see the crisp edging of the panel behind the action and the equally sharp, long-aspect diamonds of the checkering—borderless and without run-overs. The right-side closeup shows a big-horn sheep, well-modeled and brilliantly carved, alive and moving.

Photograph by Ron Wright

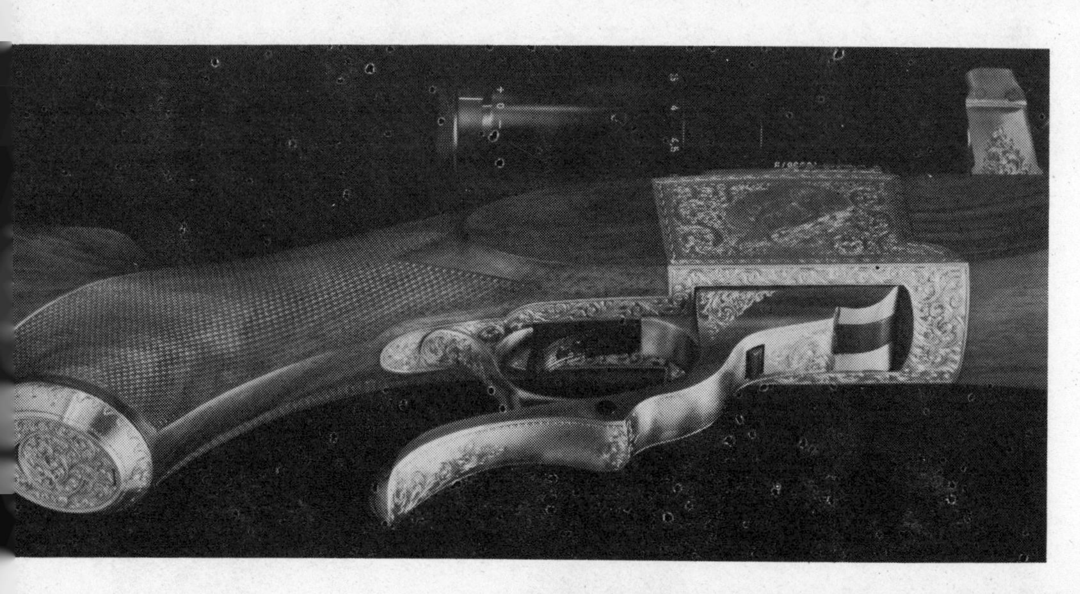

The handsome engraving found on the top and sides of the Ruger single shot rifle is continued underneath, as well as on the lever and the trapped grip cap.

The special scope mount bases on the Ruger's octagon barrel are screwed and dovetailed into the file-cut rib.

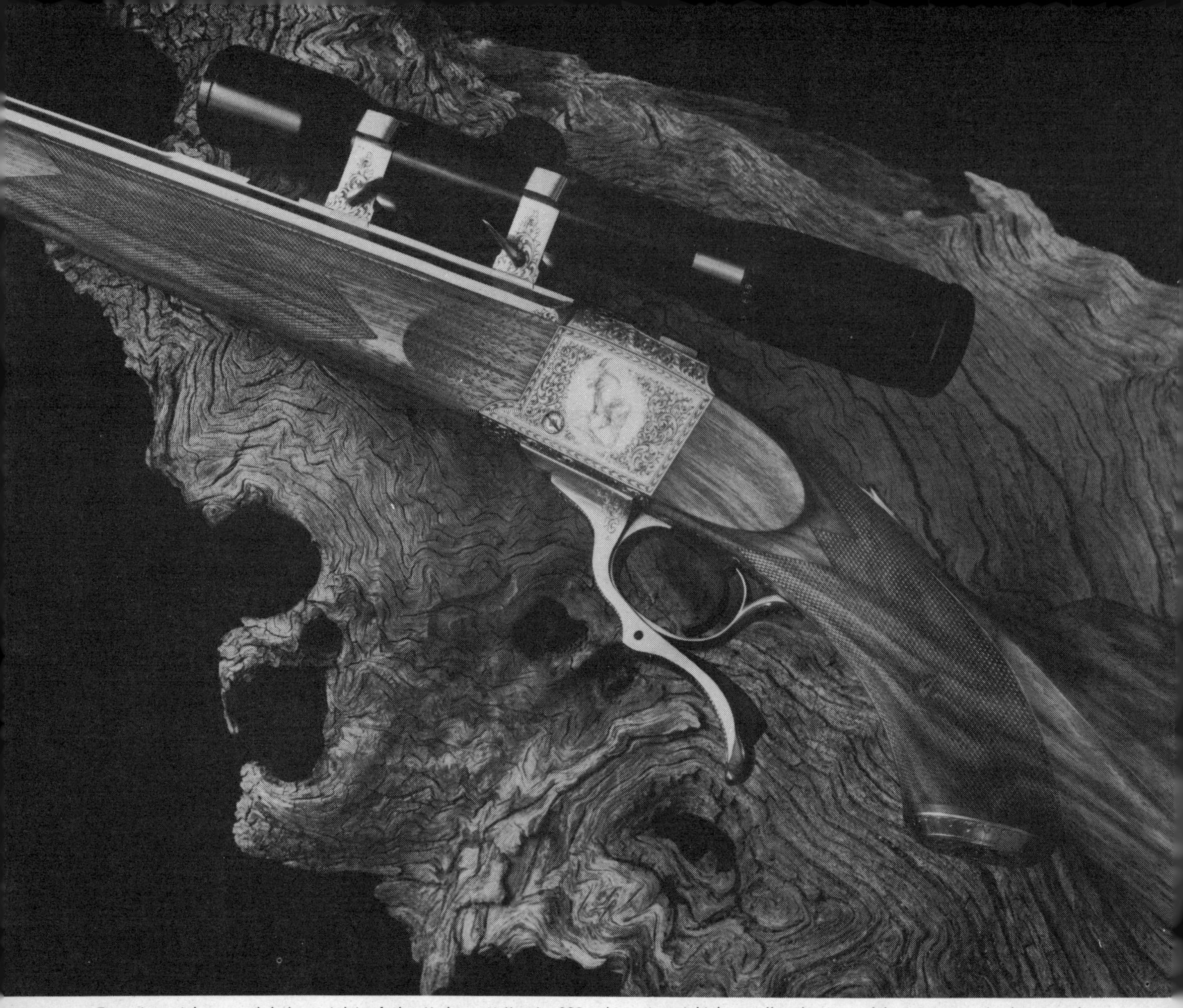

Two views (above and below, right) of the Hodgson-McKenzie 338 Ruger rifle. The scope is a big Zeiss Diavari Variable, hence the rather high base-rings. I think a smaller glass, one of the 1.5-4x straight objective tube scopes would be better suited, making for a lower, more compact profile.

The Ruger rifle's grip cap is made with a hinged trapdoor, meant to hold a spare front sight, or firing pin. Such trapped caps are often found on quality British rifles.

Photograph by Ron Wright

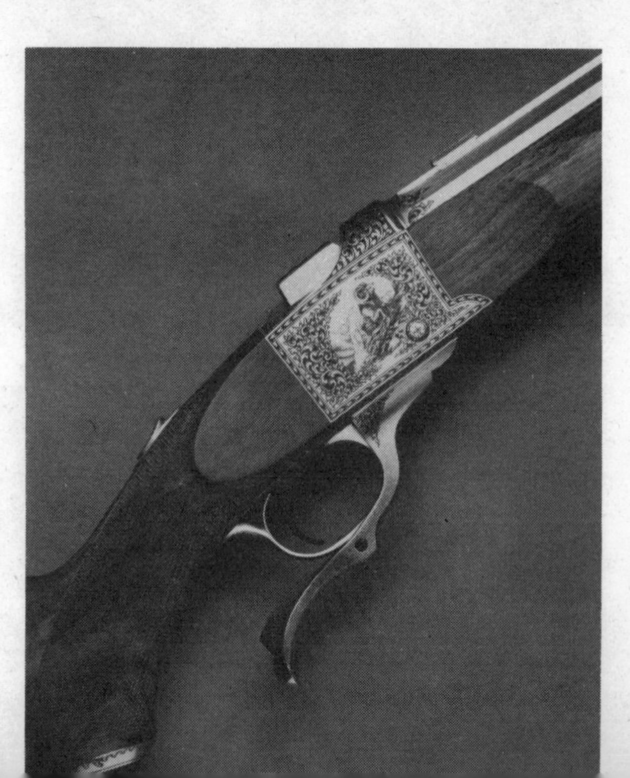

Photograph by Ron Wright

old British touch seldom seen over here.

Spare sight elements are stored in the trapped grip cap—a hinged lid covers a small well, as on some early English double rifles. The barrel and the scope mounts will be rust blued in the traditional manner, slowly, and the action will carry the Purdey "old silver" finish. This shows the engraving off to the best effect. The rifle scope mounts are lavishly covered with the best British-type medium scroll engraving, the background made black for high contrast. The delicately treated scenes show a complete mastery of the tough and hard Ruger receiver.

Both Hodgson and McKenzie are so far behind in their work that, for us all, unfortunately, neither man is likely to accept your order. They pick a job they want to do, plan it out for best effect, then do their finest possible work. When finished, they tally up what it cost them, then offer it for sale. Their production is very limited but extremely choice.

Your chances of ever owning one of McKenzie's exhibition pieces is very slim. Today his plans include fewer jobs, but these with more involved and extensive treatment. Although he has worked here for 4 years with the New Orleans Arms Company, not one of his jobs, once sold, has been offered for re-sale. McKenzie won't duplicate a job so they're all one-of-a kind pieces. When he displayed the Ruger No. 1 pictured here for one day at the NRA show in Atlanta, he turned down 37 jobs on Rugers alone!

I'm delighted to see a brilliant gunsmith like Hodgson teamed up with McKenzie. Their work speaks for itself. J.T.A.

Above, the steel buttplate of the Ruger single shot rifle shows clearly the mastery of Lynton McKenzie—the scrolling strong yet delicate, the design laid out with restraint.

Right, Lynton McKenzie engraving the guard of a Purdey shotgun. The Gravermeister vise, a freely-rotating type, was designed especially for such demanding free hand work.

Lynton McKenzie

This James Purdey and Sons 12 bore double gun, serial number 26599, demonstrates clearly the great and remarkable abilities of Lynton McKenzie. What he says about Churchill's work applies equally to his own efforts—look at these pictures with a good magnifying glass. Note the grace and natural flight rendering of the birds, their anatomical excellence. The photograph doesn't show it, but those bands at the breech ends of the barrels are inlaid gold.

Winston Churchill

Despite the name he bears, young Churchill—he's 32—is a native Vermonter. Apart from a 4-year or so stint at Griffin & Howe/Abercrombie & Fitch, under the demanding eye of Joseph Fugger, Winston Churchill has had no formal training in engraving as such.

Joseph Fugger, well known indeed for his fine engraving, learned his craft in the school at Ferlach (Austria). Then, on coming to the U.S., he worked here for three years with the great Rudolph Kornbrath, who had gone to the same school. Kornbrath had, in fact, been responsible for bringing Fugger to this country. Fugger's work, understandably, appears to be greatly influenced by his time with Kornbrath.

Joe Fugger in his turn has helped to train Winston Churchill, who well may turn out to be the finest American-born gun engraver of all time.

I've said that Churchill had no formal schooling in engraving firearms—or metal of any kind—and that's quite true. But Winston Churchill springs from a very long line of self-sufficient Vermont countrymen, men who had to make do, in the wilderness that early Vermont was, with what came to hand.

Now, from a lengthy letter to his good friend and mentor, Lynton McKenzie—of whom more later—I'm going to put down here some of Churchill's autobiographical notes. These have been edited a bit for brevity, but in essence they're Winston Churchill's words—and frequently they're his comments verbatim. They were penned after he and his wife returned to Vermont from 4½ years in New York.

"I was born and brought up on a Vermont farm. I come from a long line of country folk. We still own the land where my great-great-great-great-grandfather settled just after the Revolutionary War. It was just wilderness then, and it's almost grown up to wilderness again. And these old farmers were craftsmen too. They built their own houses, made their furniture, their implements and their clothes. Hardly anything was imported from the outside. My own grandfather made his own ox yokes, bending the bows in sugaring time after steaming them above the boiling vat of maple sap. For a little extra money, he also made watering tubs and buckets and wove excellent grain baskets from strips of ash. All in addition to the main business of small farm agriculture.

"I grew up with a thirst to create things.

Gold tie clip

I was about 14 when Gramp let me have an old single barreled Damascus shotgun. My uncle had clubbed a suddenly reviving woodchuck over the head with it, and the stock had suffered severely through the pistol grip. So I made a new stock from a piece of white ash plank. Bloody hard carving, but the inletting came out quite well. The old gun began gathering in an occasional rabbit and I was proud as punch.

"From 15 to 19 I served an apprenticeship as a patternmaker. Although this was not creative work in an artistic sense, the years were not by any means wasted, as it was excellent training in discipline and craftsmanship. Made of either mahogany or sugar pine, our patterns were perfectly fitted and joined, and held to extremely close tolerances.

"While at this task, I saw my first proper gunstock made. An old patternmaker (a gunsmith at heart) was building a rifle stock—each noon advancing the work a bit. I hung around looking over his shoulder and was absolutely fascinated by what was taking shape before my eyes. Old Dave, as I grew to call him, asked if I'd like to make up a rifle too. He gave me a piece of walnut plank and set me to work on a Springfield after rebarreling the action and considerably altering the other metalwork. I made a trigger guard out of a solid piece of steel and made a blind magazine in the wood. This first rifle took an ungodly length of time. I finished the wood with all the tender loving care I could muster up; lavished a fancy fleur-de-lis checkering job on it similar in

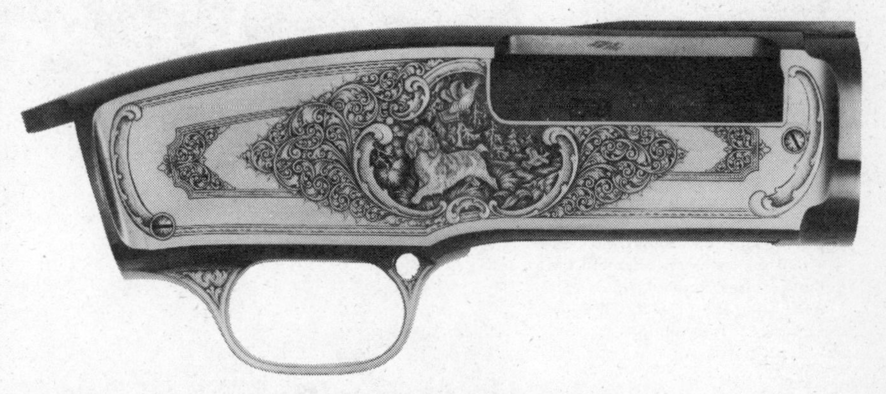

An unusual paneled design for a Winchester Model 12 shotgun. As Lynton McKenzie suggests, look at this work with a glass.

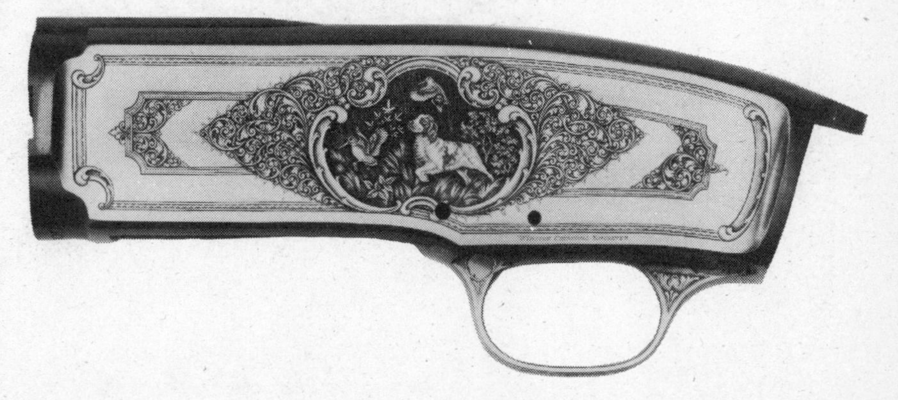

Gold money clip

appearance to Tom Shelhamer's "Rex O Dell" pattern. I was about 17 at the time.

"This is the gun I still hunt with and I'm not ashamed to be seen anywhere with it.

Toward the end of my patternmaker apprenticeship, Uncle Sam began to long for my presence, so I enlisted in the Navy as a patternmaker. I served most of my time relief carving the various ship insignias onto mahogany placques.

"Soon after I got out of the Navy, Fran and I were married and came to live in Vermont. Most of our furniture was of the early attic period, but we slowly replaced it with antique reproductions I was able to make. I favored the American Chippendale designs and made them up out of native wild black Cherry that we had cut on our farm. I'd always loved to work with wood, but soon metal fashioning took over.

"I think it was around 1965 when I got my hands on a copy of L. D. Nimschke's* pattern book. I was overwhelmed by such beauty in cold steel. I began engraving as a hobby. Soon after, Fran got me E.C. Prudhomme's book, *Gun Engraving Review*. This fanned the flames higher. I think the greatest benefit of this book is its exposure to the viewer of a great variety of engraving—both good and bad. Soon one learns to differentiate between the two, and to emulate the good.

"I saw work by Joe Fugger in this book and, while visiting in New York, I went to Abercrombie and Fitch (with fear and trembling) in hopes of meeting the máster. He was on vacation, but Leo Martin, the vice president and gun department manager, showed a real interest in me,

L. D. Nimschke, Firearms Engraver (Teaneck, N. J. 1965)

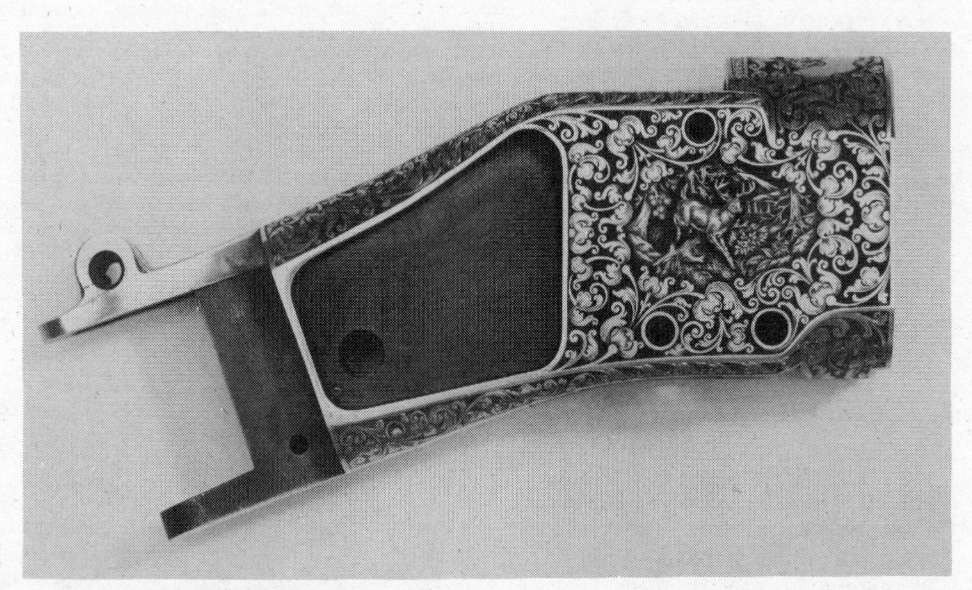

Extensive and brilliant coverage of an original Sharps Borchardt paneled action—minus the panels at the moment. Churchill did these raised animal figures, in gold, in a superbly life-like fashioning.

looked at the piece of work I'd brought, talked of employment, and told me to come again.

"The next year I did, bringing my wares.

"This time I got to meet Old Joe. He greeted me politely, wrung my hand, crammed another pinch of snuff up his nose and proceeded to tear my scrollwork apart. But he did have some encouraging words to say for the game scenes I had put on the sides on a Winchester highwall. "Good snoot, good tail," and so on, he said in his Germanic accent, concerning a buffalo I'd engraved.

"They hired me and we moved to New York. Old Joe treated me kindly for the most part and we got along famously.

"After a year or so, Joe let me help him on some major jobs that he'd been putting off—in some cases 6 or 8 years! Joe designed the scroll and roughly laid it out, but I did all the actual cutting. It was mostly of the beautiful leaf and flower work that the German and Austrian folks are so proficient at. I had to learn to do some real fine shading then—microscopic, it seemed like—but that's the only way Fugger would have it. Joe did the gold inlaid scenes himself. Soon after, I began to do gold inlaid scenes on my own work and loved (and sweated) every minute of it. My technique for getting the gold into the steel took a great leap forward when I met you. What Joe had taught me was a bit backward—using different chunks for the various parts of the gold figure.

"After I had been there about 3½ years, Old Joe retired. I moved down to his bench and tried to fill his shoes as best I could. In addition to the engraving, I did all of the stock checkering for Griffin & Howe.

"About this time also, I began to get gold jewelry to engrave with wildlife game scenes and dogs. This has been good experience. Each scene was an original, and knowing that it would be the sole focus of attention demanded the very best that I could produce.

"From here on, Lynton, you pretty much know the story: I longed for more of an identity as an individual craftsman, and for the freedom and beauty of my Vermont birthplace. Fran and I had pretty much decided to make the move when you came along. You built a bonfire under me, as you have ever since. Until that time I'd had almost no fellowship with engravers of my own generation. Then, suddenly, to be sharing things with two of the world's best—yourself and Kenny Hunt—opened up whole new realms to me.

"To sum up what I feel about our trade, I might say that I love beauty in all of its forms and think that firearms making has embodied one of the greatest—if not *the* greatest—expressions of beauty. We take cold metal and wood and form into it and cover it with life and beauty—both with the swing and flow of our scroll work and with the vivid protrayal, in their natural habitats, of birds and animals and sometimes humans.

"In short, it's an extremely satisfying occupation and I'm grateful to be in it; and grateful to those who have inspired me along the way." *Winston Churchill*

Most of Churchill's great work is done under a magnifying glass, which is a heavy burden on the eyes. To fully appreciate the beauty of this delicate work you, too, must use a glass. The cuff links and money clips he has engraved are gems. At present his work greatly resembles that of his teacher. It will no doubt slowly evolve along his own lines.

He has returned to the beauty of Ludlow, Vermont, where he does free-lance engraving. To examine his work is to marvel at its beauty. Joe Fugger should be very proud.

Lynton McKenzie.

Gold cuff links

A different and well-handled treatment of a floorplate—most attractive.

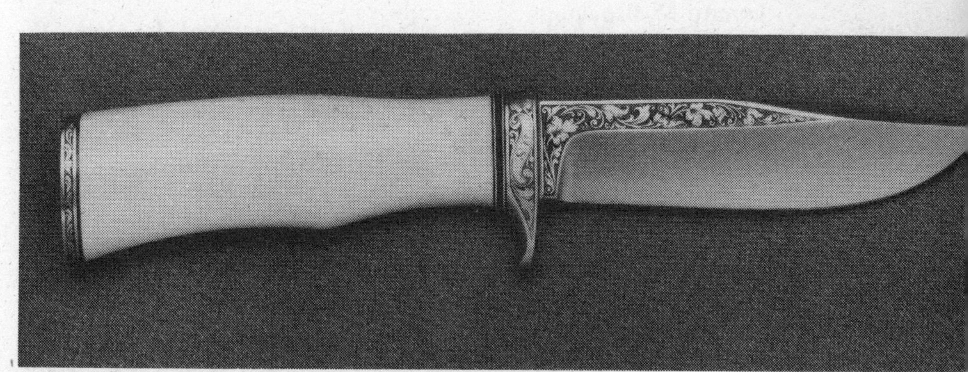

A well-shaped and functional knife, engraved in a chaste and restrained treatment.

Gene Clark

A native of Pagosa Springs, Colorado, Clark has steadily worked his way to the top. He is now regarded as this country's leading action and ejector man on best British single shot and double rifles, on pre-war Continental double guns, combination guns and drillings.

His normal, everyday work could frighten most gunsmiths—he'll quite calmly remove the ribs of a valuable double gun, then make his corrections and put it all back together. Clark will next hand polish the barrels, then re-blue them, via the old and slow rust-blue technique. The results are faultless.

If the gun is engraved, any needed refurbishing is done by Lynton McKenzie, formerly a Purdey engraver, who works in the next room.

Most of Clark's time is spent on action and ejector work, as noted above. His replacement parts have the clean precision of the best pre-war work. That's not so surprising when you learn that his hobby is clocks and miniature work. He also makes and installs the best old style quick-detachable scope mounts on high grade British double rifles. These mounts, made individually to insure the lowest possible siting, are generally soldered to the tubes and then slowly rust-blued.

All of Clark's work is fairly expensive, but it's so well done as to be indistinguishable from the "best quality" craftsmanship done in pre-war England. He's also done a lot of work on good quality drillings (3-barrel guns), and he's got literally thousands of original pre-war parts for them. Too, in case he doesn't have the particular part needed, there is virtually no complicated part that he cannot make to perfection. Also, and quite often, he'll make up or fit the old German style detachable scope mounts to a rifle—but *not* to a British double rifle!

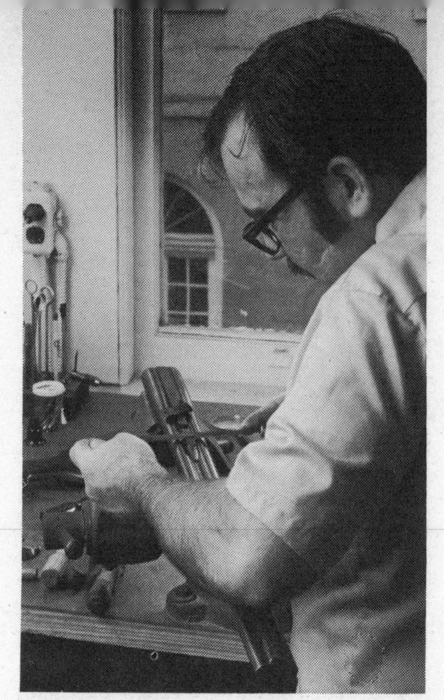

Gene Clark fitting replacement express sights to an H&H double rifle.

He rebrowns Damascus barrels and can do a beautiful French Grey or Purdey Old Silver finish.

All in all, Clark is a remarkable craftsman. It is little wonder that those owners of Purdeys, Bosses, Woodwards and Holland & Hollands on which he has worked would like to keep him out of the limelight. His work, especially on antiques, has always been of a confidential nature.

It's a great pleasure to me—and gratifying—to have a gunsmith of such considerable skill working in the United States. But for the grace of God... J.T.A.

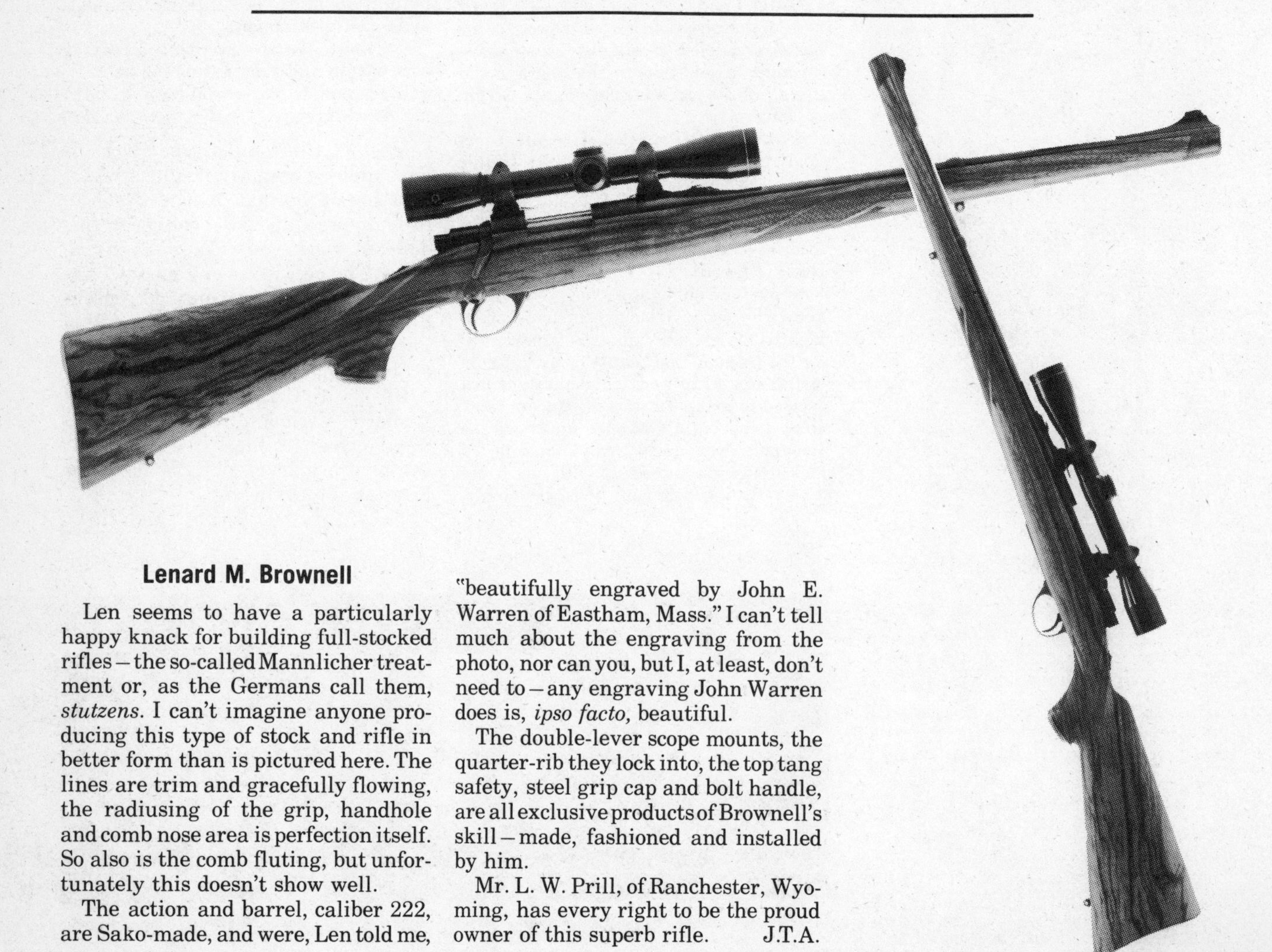

Lenard M. Brownell

Len seems to have a particularly happy knack for building full-stocked rifles—the so-called Mannlicher treatment or, as the Germans call them, *stutzens*. I can't imagine anyone producing this type of stock and rifle in better form than is pictured here. The lines are trim and gracefully flowing, the radiusing of the grip, handhole and comb nose area is perfection itself. So also is the comb fluting, but unfortunately this doesn't show well.

The action and barrel, caliber 222, are Sako-made, and were, Len told me, "beautifully engraved by John E. Warren of Eastham, Mass." I can't tell much about the engraving from the photo, nor can you, but I, at least, don't need to—any engraving John Warren does is, *ipso facto*, beautiful.

The double-lever scope mounts, the quarter-rib they lock into, the top tang safety, steel grip cap and bolt handle, are all exclusive products of Brownell's skill—made, fashioned and installed by him.

Mr. L. W. Prill, of Ranchester, Wyoming, has every right to be the proud owner of this superb rifle. J.T.A.

Dale Goens and Lester Womack

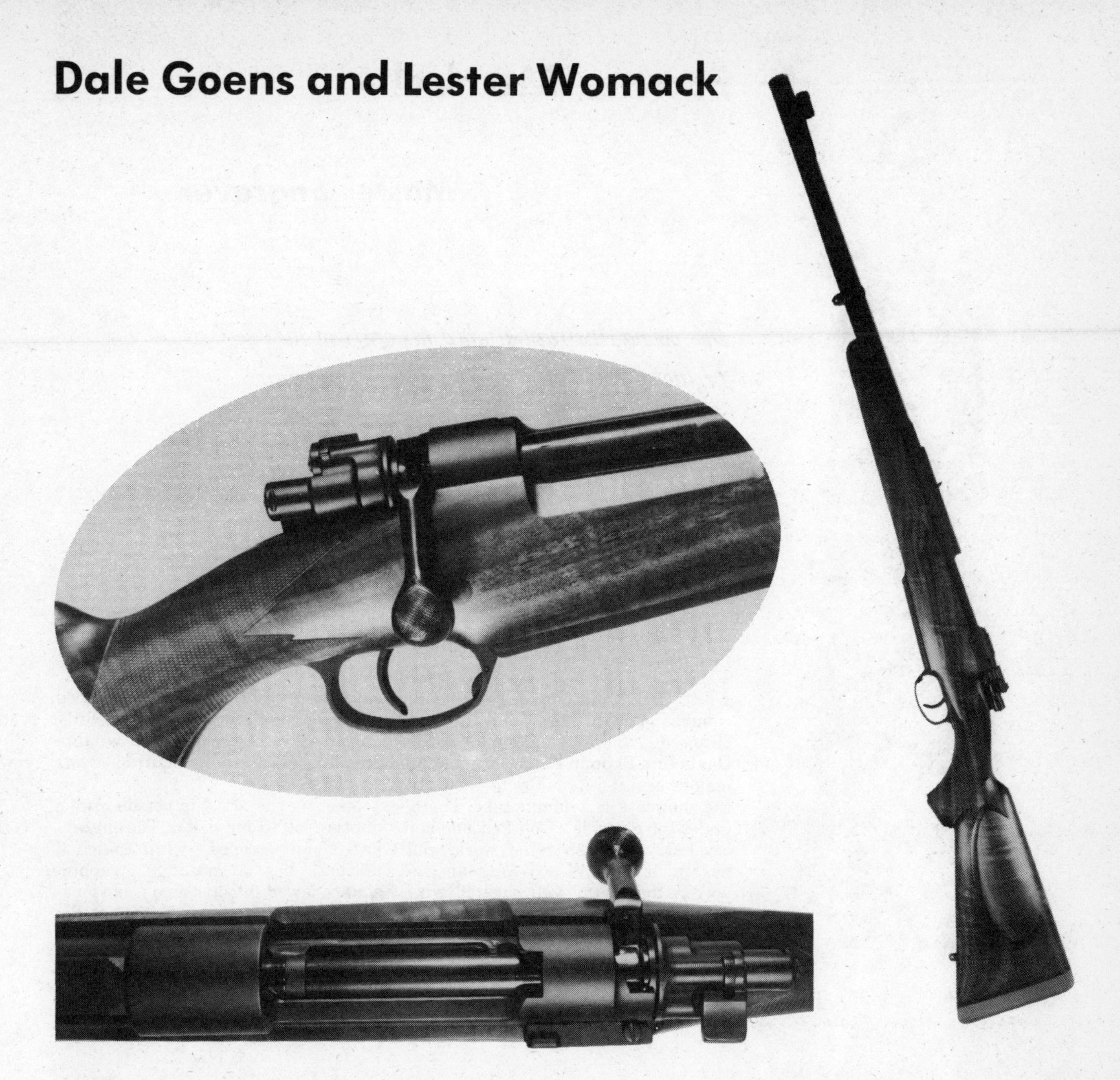

Brutus-Brevex No. 1. Why Brutus? For "brute," I imagine, in that the Brevex Mauser action is a big one indeed. Anyway, that's what Lester Womack nicknamed this big 416 Weatherby Magnum rifle, and at 13 pounds-plus it's hardly a featherweight. Certainly a little extra heft helps in taming the recoil of that powerhouse load. Womack—a long-time custom gunsmith—and Dale Goens collaborated in building this big rifle. Womack handled all the metal work and Goens made the stock—the latter deliberately styled to produce a rifle looking much like a Rigby, Jeffrey or Gibbs of a generation or more ago. I think they succeeded very well—note the cheekpiece treatment, the bulkier magazine, the shorter fore-end, the checkering design and that parade of folding-leaf open rear sights on the Douglas Premium grade 22-inch barrel.

Goens used a nice piece of California English walnut, the grain travel selected for best strength, in stocking the rifle and, as the photos show, kept it all simple and elegant. Womack, by the way, made the photos and, except for the full length view, they're quite good. I wish there'd been a little more light on the barrel and fore-end.

The owner of this rifle (who prefers anonymity) had a stroke of luck! Brevex actions have not been made for some time, but Mr. I.W. Walentiny of Tradewinds, Inc.—which company marketed the Brevex earlier—found one. Serial No. 1, of all things and, apart from possible pre-production pieces, the very first Brevex made.

Womack went all out on metalsmithing—in addition to three recoil bolts in the stock, there's a fourth lug on the barrel, below the sight base. Sights and base are modeled after a 416 Rigby. The original FN extractor was lengthened and a new bolt handle—shaped like a Mauser Werke magnum—was made and fitted by Womack. A grooved trigger was newly-made, and a floorplate release button installed in the guard. The matte blue was achieved by "particle" blasting the metal before hot blueing—it looks like a fine rust blue but it isn't. The recoil pad is a Pachmayr presentation type.

In toto, an impressive rifle, and a tribute to the high skills and craftsmanship of Lester Womack and Dale Goens. J.T.A.

Franz Marktl—

Master Engraver

This young Austrian studied his craft at the Ferlach School of Firearms for over six years. He left there with the degree of graveur – a master engraver. Today Marktl is one of our top flight practitioners of this delicate and demanding craft.

IT IS QUITE uncommon for a small suburban gunshop to display fine gun engraving, and a casual visitor to the Davis Gun Shop in Falls Church, Va., may be excused if his first glance into the showcase is a double take. There, under the glass, is a Colt Peacemaker covered with high relief work, and next to it a S&W 357 Magnum revolver, the metal well covered with delicate scrollwork and with raised animal figures inlaid in gold as well. A Mauser floorplate depicts a lifelike African elephant against a Kilimanjaro backdrop.

Across the aisle in its own glass case there's a Browning Superposed, elegantly stocked and tastefully engraved, with gold inlaid wildlife scenes. This is the domain of *Franz Marktl, Graveur*.

Meeting the artist in person brings another jolt to our visitor. The engraver is no stooped, white-thatched ancient, but a smiling, strapping, square-jawed 6-footer who is obviously on the sunny side of 30. Yet his youth is deceiving – Franz is the product of 6 years' intensive training to which he has added nearly a decade of solid professional experience. It shows in his work.

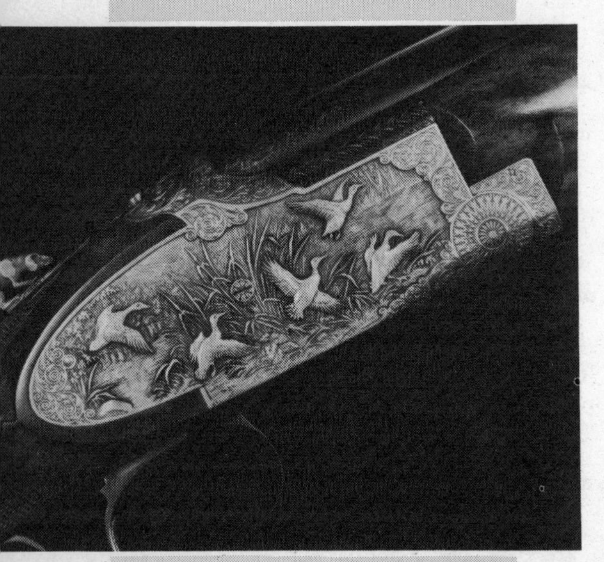

Excellent rendering of the Saint Hubertus legend, both figures handsomely portrayed.

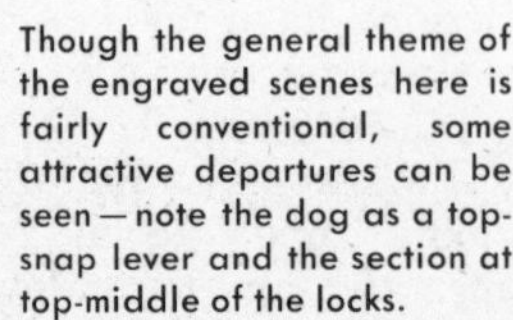

Though the general theme of the engraved scenes here is fairly conventional, some attractive departures can be seen — note the dog as a top-snap lever and the section at top-middle of the locks.

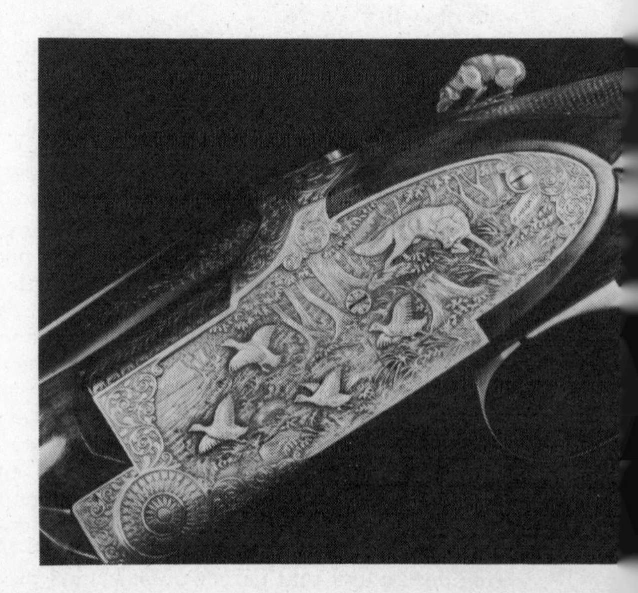

As a youngster of 14, Marktl enrolled at the Ferlach Technical School of Firearms in his native Austria. Five years later he graduated with the title of *Graveur* (the *summa cum laude* of engraving) and promptly signed up for some postgraduate work. During the next several years, he did custom engraving for many of Europe's most prominent gunmakers.

A chance meeting in 1970 with an American gun collector changed Franz' life dramatically. The collector, Alfred Guarente, was impressed with Marktl's work, and suggested that Franz emigrate to the U.S. Because Franz had no U.S. "connections," and little of value besides his skill, Guarente offered to sponsor the engraver's immigration, guarantee his income for several months, and help establish him as an independent businessman. The deal was too good to turn down; Franz is now an up-and-coming U.S. gun decorator, and Guarente is the proud owner of a Marktl-engraved gun collection.

Franz works in close association with the Davis shop. Fred Davis and his capable associates handle all the disassembly and (after Franz has done his part), the rebluing and reassembly. This cooperative arrangement allows Franz full time for the exercise of his engraving talents.

The process of engraving looks deceptively simple when Marktl does it. The work is held between the padded jaws of a ball-foot vise. Franz quickly sketches on the polished surface whatever design he and the client have agreed upon. Then he attacks it with his graving tools, aided occasionally by a well-used hammer. Generally he works with hand pressure alone, gouging out tiny scraps of metal until the pattern is complete. On especially hard steel, however, the hammer provides an assist. Some extremely hard surfaces must be annealed before they will accept engraving.

The gravers are like small-ended chisels; Franz shapes and hardens them himself. Different tools are used for different parts of the job. Tool selection is also guided by the hardness of the material to be worked, and by the fineness and type of engraving required. Undercut recesses are prepared for precious metal inlays, which are hammered into place, then engraved. All of Marktl's work is done by hand but that's not to disparage such motorized tools as the Gravermeister that another good engraver, John Rohner, offers to the trade.

Franz tries to work as quickly as possible; he is paid by the amount and quality of his work, not by the time it consumes. He works carefully, though. This has to be a "zero defects" business; an engraver cannot afford to ruin a valuable firearm.

Although Franz Marktl has been working in the U.S. for only a few years, his reputation is already widespread. Knowledgeable gun buffs and custom gunsmiths send him work from all over the world. Pictures of his engraving have appeared in the Gun Digest before this and on the covers of gun magazines. He has been commissioned to do presentation pieces for heads of state and the top officers of major firearms manufacturers.

Good engraving is not cheap, but because Franz' work was relatively unknown until recently, Franz' prices were relatively low until recently! Today, with a good backlog of orders, his fees have increased. Even so, a Marktl engraving job is still priced moderately for such top grade work; his charges in future will doubtless go up, the times and inflation being what they are.

Franz will send his price list free on request, and for 50 cents he'll include an illustrated brochure of his work. His address is listed in our Directory of the Arms Trade, farther along in this volume. *Dave Lombard*

Marktl lost little time in learning to engrave American game figures. These turkeys show very good modeling treatment.

Davis Gun Shop had a booth at the 1974 NRA meeting in Atlanta (GA), with Franz Marktl in attendance and showing examples of his striking engraving. Other engravers at the same meeting were Lynton McKenzie of New Orleans, Winston Churchill (a native Vermonter, in fact) and John Rohner. These exhibits of first class engraving were among the top attractions at Atlanta.

Our long-time readers know that the Gun Digest began to illustrate the work of engravers many years ago. We wanted to acquaint readers everywhere with the art of the engraver, with what was being done to decorate and embellish firearms—much of it excellent, some of it not so good.

I'm delighted to see this growing interest in engraving, and even more so to watch these young men working hard and becoming such superb artists—McKenzie and Churchill are both in their 30s, like Franz Marktl. It's immensely gratifying, too, to know that this resurgence of high craftsmanship is by no means confined to the carving and chiseling of metal. We have today, in this country, more master-class stockmakers and creative metalsmiths than ever before.

In this age of the machine, this period when plastics predominate, there appears to be a surprisingly strong urge to development of the manual skills. I'm more than pleased. J.T.A.

The several figures delicately cut into these big expanses of metal are depicted with a high degree of fidelity and a fine economy of space. All are well drawn, lifelike in response and action.

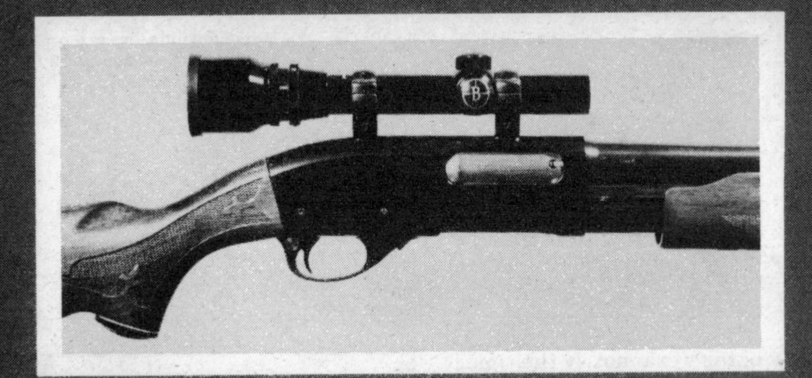

For checking the accuracy of his 16-ga. rifled-slug handloads, the author used a Remington M-870 pump gun with a 26" Improved Cylinder barrel. The gun was equipped with a Bushnell Ix shotgun scope in Bushnell Universal mounts, which increased gun weight by exactly one pound.

Deer Stoppers for the 16 Gauge

IF CONTROVERSY is your favorite dish, you're going to have to shop elsewhere, because this essay will occupy neutral ground. It is not going to hit you with a generous serving of razzmatazz that extolls the virtues of the 16-bore as a slug gun—or, conversely, with a studious critique of its shortcomings. First and foremost, the objective is to arm the 16-gauge *aficionado* with the basics necessary for turning out hand-crafted slug loads that will cause the factory-loaded round to sit up and take notice.

Sixteen-gauge slugs of various designs are currently available for handloading purposes. Certainly the best known of these is the Foster type, with its large base cavity and shallow "rifling." Introduced back in the 1930s, it is being used to this day in all 16-ga. factory slug ammo loaded in the U.S. and Canada, and in essentially its original form. The German-designed Brenneke, with its attached wad column and deeper, rib-style rifling (available for handloading through Stoeger Arms Corp.), has seen only comparatively limited use here, though it is an excellent projectile. Lesser known is the French-made Balle Blondeau, an all-steel design that has a pair of lead bearing rings for bore protection. Top-drawer accuracy is claimed for the Blondeau, its rather bizarre shape using air flow for stabilization in flight.

In this article, however, we will concern ourselves only with the Brenneke and Foster designs, the latter specifically with the Meyer Bros. (M-B) version, which features a modification in the form of a hollow-point nose. The M-B version is, in fact, the only Foster-type slug commercially available to handloaders. Lyman, of course, offers a 16-ga. mould that will cast a smooth-sided slug, and this approach is a good bet for those who already have basic bullet casting equipment.

But a word of caution: The loading data shown in the accompanying table for the M-B slug is not to be used interchangeably for the Lyman hand-cast slug. The latter is about ⅛-ounce heavier, and the same powder charges will result in higher chamber pressure. The *Lyman Shotshell Handbook* contains a smattering of load data for the smooth-sided slug.

Ammo catalogs optimistically list the 16-ga. Foster-type slug as weighing ⅞-oz., but most I've pulled from various factory rounds run about 355 grs., or some 25 to 30 grs. under the advertised weight. The M-B design weighs slightly less and for all practical purposes can be classed as a ¾-oz. projectile. A sampling of 25 averaged 337 grs., with an extreme variation of 15.6 grs. This reduced weight is partly because of the hollow-point, partly to other but minor design modifications.

Meyer Bros. Slugs

Here are the vital statistics for the M-B 16-ga. slug. Over-all length is .733", maximum outside diameter (at the base) is .630". Since the nominal bore diameter of the 16-ga. gun is .670", this considerably sub-caliber slug will rattle through the tightest full choke with space to spare.

The M-B slug has 14 grooves, these being cut on a shallow diagonal angle. Groove depth is about the same as found on slugs taken from factory rounds. The base cavity has a depth of .385", and the wall thickness at the base is .090".

The most interesting facet of design is the hollow-point nose, this frontal cavity being .175" in diameter and .260" deep. Extending outward from the hollow-point are three evenly-spaced fine-line cuts that go completely through the ogive. Their purpose is to induce slug break-up following penetration, thereby causing much additional tissue and other internal damage for more effective killing power. The manufacturer claims that a deer will drop almost instantly when zapped with the M-B slug, even with a marginal hit; and he further says that "Normally wood will not trigger slug break-up, assuring good performance through brush."

Incidentally, Meyer Bros. (Wabasha, Minn. 55981) also offers this same hollow-point slug in 12 and 20

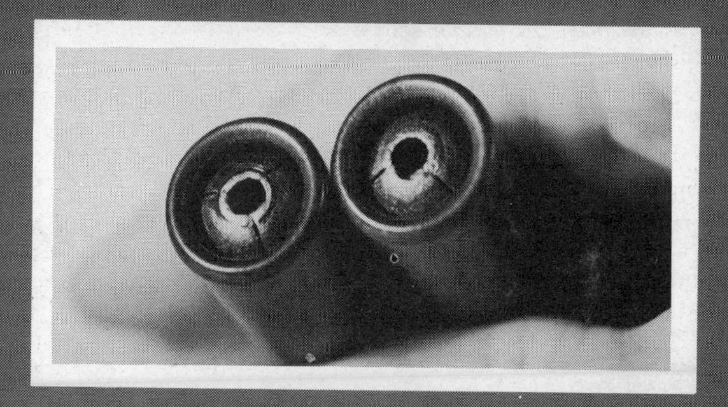

The roll crimp is complete when the turnover is deep enough to firmly hold the slug in a centered position. Shown here are Federal paper-tube shells, the wad column built to leave a crimp space of 5/16″. This properly positions the nose of the slug about 1/16″ below the mouth of the finished crimp.

Here's all you need to know on loading the neglected 16 bore with rifled slugs. The M-B and Brenneke projectiles are treated at length, with important notes on achieving accurate results. A big load table is included.

by WALLACE LABISKY

ga., though the latter bore size may now be discontinued. At any rate, packaging is in boxes of 50 slugs, and the last time I looked the price tag said $4.85. Rifled slugs, by the way, are subject to the provisions of the Gun Control Act of 1968, and interstate shipment can be made only to federally-licensed dealers.

Now that we've taken a look at the projectile, let's turn our attention to the other components involved. Where the 16 gauge is concerned the best policy is to start with virgin hulls, because the slug load demands a roll-crimp, and previously fired fold-crimp cases simply will not take a satisfactory turnover. Used plastic shells which were originally roll crimped are okay for practice loads, but for either hunting or accuracy testing a new shell in either paper or plastic is advised. It will contribute appreciably to more uniform ballistics, primarily because variations in tube diameter and crimp strength will be minimal. Uniform ballistics will, in turn, result in a tighter-grouping load.

Choice of Cases

The 16-ga. cases usually preferred by the writer are the Federal low-brass (Monark) paper-tube and the Alcan low-brass (LP-7) plastic shell. These large-capacity hulls will easily accomodate the lengthy, built-up wad columns that are required for best results.

The Remington SP plastic shell (field type) has a skived mouth and partly because of this a slightly deeper turnover is needed to center the slug in the shell and to snugly retain it in that position. Also, the plastic itself seems more resistant than other brands. This poses no problem with power roll-crimping equipment, but with the Lyman Easy tool the number of press strokes to complete the turnover is almost double that usually needed with other shells.

Aside from this, the Remington hull represents a good choice. A circumferential "ridge" will show on the tube surface for each nitro card used and, additionally, a slight "flare out" will show at the mouth of the finished crimp, since the plastic doesn't "shape" as readily as paper. But both of these conditions are strictly cosmetic and won't give rise to chambering problems. The same appearances, by the way, will be seen with the Federal plastic shell (virgin cases not available for handloading), and to a lesser extent with the Alcan LP-7 offering.

Powder Selection

There is fairly good latitude when it comes to powder selection for the 16-ga. slug load. Some of the so-called "fast" powders and most of the "medium" propellants are useful, though the latter will produce higher velocities when loaded to the same chamber pressure.

Factory rounds give us a goal to aim for. Five Remington Express slug loads routed through the Smith & Wesson ballistic lab gave an average velocity (instrumental at 15 feet) of 1,543 fps (feet per second), while the chamber pressure averaged 10,100 lup (lead units of pressure). So if we establish the maximum pressure for our handload as to not exceed 11,000 lup (certainly a safe level provided strong, new cases are used and the loads fired in a gun of modern manufacture), we can come fairly close to matching the factory velocity with the medium-burning powders.

These include AL-5, Herco, HS-5, SR-7625, 500HS, HP-164 and N-2020. All should burn efficiently in 26″ or longer barrels. These fuels may not deliver any better accuracy than the faster powders such as Top Mark, AL-120, PB, Unique, HP-162 and Green Dot, but the velocity/pressure ratio will be in better balance—and the faster that slug can be pushed without any great sacrifice in accuracy, so much the better. The ballistic table shown elsewhere on these pages will provide charge-weight guidelines for some of the powders listed above. Powder charge weight should, of course, be reduced for those loads which give a chamber pressure in excess of 11,000 lup.

As for primer choice, one can hardly go wrong in matching the case brand. Bear in mind, however, that primers with an *open flash hole* should not be used with the spherical or ball-type powders marketed by Hodgdon and Winchester.

Wad Column Problems

This brings us around to the wad column which, to my thinking, is not only the most important part of the slug load in terms of accuracy, but also the least understood. In short, the wad column built to deliver high percentage patterns with shot loads will not give first-class accuracy with the rifled slug. Some cushioning is required to regulate chamber pressure with the slug, of course, but the column must possess a greater degree of rigidity and the reason will become clear as we go along.

The first wad-column rule calls for *total and consistent sealing off* of the propellant gases. Escaping gas means a change in velocity and if the load-to-load loss occurs in varying amounts, the accuracy potential of the load is seriously undermined. As an obturator the nitro card cannot compete with the plastic over-powder cup. In 16 gauge the choice is limited to the Alcan PGS, and the ballistic table offers proof that it does a commendable job.

Looking at the extreme spread in velocity (based on 5 shots), it will be noted that our handloads were second to the factory load only once, and even then the difference was a mere 2 fps. In most instances, the handloads delivered velocities markedly more uniform than the factory loads gave.

The next step in building the wad column is the filler wad, and if we simply place the slug on top of the filler and crimp, we will have a load that shoots, but not the way we want it to. During the acceleration thrust, the soft filler wad will be driven into the slug's base cavity. This will set up an imbalance that plays hob with in-flight travel and, again, accuracy suffers.

To combat this tendency for the filler wad to flow forward, the slug has to be placed on a relatively stiff platform, and here is where we find use for the time-honored nitro card. One card of at least .200" thickness should be used over the filler wad. Two cards are even better if case capacity will permit.

As a rule of thumb, the filler wad used should have a minimum thickness of ⅜"—certainly no less than 5/16". When the filler is of the conventional fiber type, I like to sandwich it between stiff card wads; in other words, I use an extra nitro card placed directly over the PGS. But when using the somewhat less resilient Ljutic Mono-Wad (an excellent choice for cushioning slug loads), I can see no advantage in using a card wad between it and the over-powder cup.

The Meyer Bros. hollow-point projectile is the only 16-ga. slug of the Foster type commercially available to handloaders. M-B slugs are heavily graphited to reduce lead fouling. Packaging is in boxes of 50.

Crimping

A roll crimp with M-B slugs is mandatory for two reasons: it not only retains the slug in the shell, it also keeps the slug concentric with the bore—not always precisely, but usually reasonably so. This, too, makes a contribution to accuracy.

Don't use just any type of wad over the slug. A "B" or over-shot card, for example, could be easily overridden by the slug and a bulged barrel might very well result.

The roll crimp does not require as much crimping space as the fold-type closure. Ideally, crimp space should

A Lyman Easy shotshell tool with a roll-crimping attachment was used for turning out the writer's test loads. A Federal paper-tube shell is shown here in the process of being roll crimped. Several press strokes are required to complete the turnover.

be such that by the time the hollow-ground crimping head makes contact with the slug's nose, there is already enough turnover to securely hold the slug in the centered position. The slug's nose will then be positioned about 1/16" below the flush line of the finished crimp.

For the 16-ga. M-B slug in Federal paper-tube shells, a crimp space of 5/16" will be close to perfect. For most plastic shells, an extra 1/16" will be necessary, because more turnover will be needed to grip the slug firmly—this due to thinner tube walls for the plastic shells.

As all shotshell handloaders know, crimp space is controlled by the height of the wad column. When working up a slug load, the best way I know to avoid those time-consuming and temper-testing errors is to use the following procedure: with the powder charge in the shell, seat the over-powder wad and place a slug on top of it. Then, using a wooden dowel of suitable diameter, measure the distance from the nose of the slug to the mouth of the shell and subtract the crimp space that will be needed. The difference will be the proper wad column height, and this method usually proves accurate to within 1/16".

An important fact to keep in mind is that variations in crimp depth will have an effect on both interior and exterior ballistics. A heavy turnover will offer more resistance than a shallow one, with a consequent change in the pressure/velocity picture. So care should be taken to crimp all slug loads to the same over-all length. Doing so will pay off in accuracy.

Slug Load Tools

"Tooling up" for slug loads is not necessarily costly. If you already own equipment for turning out fold-crimp shot loads for the gauge in question, your only concern revolves around the roll crimp. All 16-ga. loads detailed here were crimped on the Lyman Easy shotshell press, for which roll-crimping die sets are available. Additionally, Lyman offers a low-cost roll-crimping head (all gauges), complete with an adapter, for use in an electric hand drill or a drill press.

I prefer to weigh all powder charges for slug loads, though they can be thrown from a bench-type measure or dropped from a shotshell tool bushing. But a powder scale will be necessary for setting the measure and for verifying the charge bar or bushing, and I cannot imagine anybody trying to handload without a good scale on the bench.

Another quirk of mine regarding slug loads is that I like to insert the wads by hand, this to preclude any possible wad-guide damage. Also, when applying seating pressure, I like to use a wooden dowel with a diameter which matches that of the wads, or nearly so. The typical loading tool wad ram, or drop tube, tends to "dish" the wads slightly, and this condition is something we can do nicely without.

The M-B rifled slug has a trio of fine-line cuts which evenly divide the nose into three sections. The purpose of these cuts, along with the hollow point, is to induce slug break-up following penetration and transmit greater shock to deer-sized game.

A very slight belling at the mouth of the shell will facilitate inserting wads by hand. For this you can use the tapered end of a priming punch that is one gauge larger in size—that is, a 12-ga. punch for 16-ga. shells, and so on. Simply rotate the punch by hand, simultaneously applying pressure. With the Alcan LP-7 plastic shell, I found that slightly belling the case mouth in this manner seemed to condition the plastic and make for less effort in crimping.

Bore Fouling

The Foster-type slug, being made from pure, soft lead, is notorious for fouling the bore; the factory rounds have always been particularly bad offenders in this respect. Even a barrel which has been smoothed through much shooting with birdshot will usually become fouled after as few as 5 shots with slugs, the heavier deposits generally occurring just ahead of the forcing cone, a lesser amount near the muzzle. It would probably be a good idea for all slug-gun barrels to be chrome lined; not that this would eliminate lead fouling, but it would certainly facilitate cleaning.

When the M-B rifled slug first came on the market several years ago, the manufacturer recommended filling the slug grooves with bullet lube as a solution to the problem of leading. I tried this method at the time, using M-B 12-ga. slugs, but the results were not encouraging; there was only a very minor improvement. Later on, the people at M-B hit on the idea of heavily coating the slugs with graphite, and this approach does get results.

When running accuracy tests with our 16-ga. M-B handloads (see table), lead fouling was almost non-existent. The Remington M-870 barrel was carefully checked for deposits following each 5-shot string, then scrubbed hound's-tooth clean with solvent and extra-fine steel wool before going on to the next string.

The AL-5 and Herco loads using the Ljutic Mono-Wad left absolutely no lead fouling behind, while the AL-120/Mono-Wad load deposited just a light touch here and there. Both the AL-5 and AL-120 loads with a fiber filler in the wad column left a few faint streaks just ahead of the forcing cone, and I am not being the least bit charitable in describing them as such.

This is in sharp contrast to what takes place when factory loads are put through this same barrel. Lead deposits build up almost as fast as snow on a December night, and this heavy fouling hurts accuracy.

Accuracy of Slugs

Here again I've made reference to *accuracy,* so perhaps it would be in order to briefly enlarge on this term as it relates to the shotgun slug and its use, and to spell out the performance level that the handloader should strive for.

First of all, let's review a basic concept, this being that the rifled slug was never intended to compete on a head-to-head basis with the centerfire deer rifle. Essentially, the slug's reason for being is to convert the shotgun into an effective weapon for taking big game (principally deer) at short range. Opinions are quite divided on this, but I believe that the maximum effective range of the Foster-type slug on deer, whether fired from a 12- or 16-ga. gun, can be reasonably fixed at no more than 75 yards.

At this distance, and thinking in terms of a rib-cage shot, we obviously do not need rifle accuracy—that is, accuracy on the order of one-and-a-half to two minutes of angle, which is generally regarded as adequate for the deer rifle. Even if this level of accuracy were required of the slug load, we could not attain it with the Foster-type projectile. The slug's surface rifling does not impart rotational spin of any consequence (if any at all) so as to provide in-flight stabilization, and the smoothbored barrel certainly doesn't make any contribution in this respect. It is only the weight-forward principle that keeps the slug on course in a nose-forward attitude. In comparison with the inherent advantages held by the rifle bullet, it's a wonder that the slug can be made to group as well as it does.

The rifle-slug load, then, that will stay within a 6-inch circle at 75 yards (and this will approximate 4 inches at 50 yards) provides adequate accuracy if we try only for the whitetail's largest vital area—the chest cavity. In general, when using open sights or a scope of 1x power on the shotgun, it will be a struggle for the factory round to meet this accuracy requirement. With handloads, it can be easily met.

Although the handload that will print a 6-inch group at maximum effective range is adequate, that's about all that can be said for it, because it does not leave much margin to compensate for an error in holding—and when the chance to hang meat on the pole presents itself, most of us will manage to introduce plenty of aiming error. What it all boils down to is simply this: the handloader should not settle for merely adequate accuracy, he should take all that he can possibly get.

At a test range of 50 yards, 5-shot groups measuring as small as two inches, measured on centers, are not unheard of with handloads employing the Foster-type slug, but I would say that such groups are very closely approaching the ultimate level. Any load printing, say, a 3-inch group at this distance can be rated as very good, indeed, for out at the 75-yard marker it will stay within 4½-5 inches.

A glance at the accompanying accuracy table will show that 3-inch, 50-yard groups are definitely within reach through careful handloading. This shooting was done with an off-the-shelf bird-gun barrel—a 26" Imp

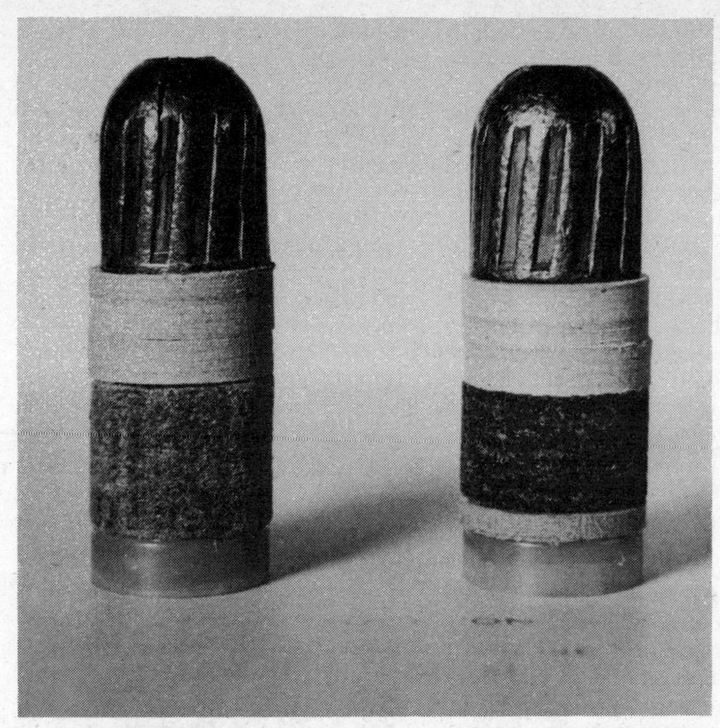

The rifled-slug load calls for a built-up wad column, and the best accuracy results when there is a rigid "platform" directly under the slug. The column at left consists of a PGS plastic over-powder cup, a ½" Ljutic Mono-Wad and, finally, one each .135" and .200" nitro cards. Column at right starts with a PGS and .080" card wad, then a ⅜" Feltan-Bluestreak filler topped by .135" and .200" nitro cards.

Cyl tube—aided by the excellent Bushnell 1x shotgun scope. Most of these loads meet the "adequate" requirement; some are truly excellent. All are what can be honestly labeled as a first-trial combination, which is to say that they are not the end product of a great deal of component tinkering.

Considering that most of us will fire only a couple of handfuls of slug loads each year, zeroing-in and hunting combined, the justification for handloading (if you must have one) is not one of economics. In the long run it probably won't cost a bit more to shoot factory ammo; it may even cost less. But by now it should be clearly evident that the benefits of handloading greatly outweigh any monetary values. There is the improved performance to consider, primarily in terms of accuracy, as well as the great personal satisfaction one derives from producing a load that gives top-drawer results. For me, at least, that clinches the knot.

Loading the Brennekes

The world-famous Brenneke slug has gone through various stages of design; the most successful of these is apparently the Model 1930, currently available in factory-loaded ammo (RWS/Rottweil) and in handloading form. Somewhere I still have an old A. F. Stoeger catalog (*circa* 1931) which touted the Brenneke projectile as being effective to 100 yards on deer-sized game; and to 70 yards on such ill-tempered and dangerous stuff as buffalo, lion, bear, boar and tiger. As a wide-eyed kid whose field experience was primarily that of lobbing 22 Shorts and Longs at trusting ground squirrels, I was greatly impressed. I often daydreamed of knocking off all sorts of big game with the German-made shotgun slug. But several decades marched past before I got around to taking a really close look at the fruit of Herr Brenneke's labor.

For something like 40 years, Stoeger Arms Corporation was the exclusive importer of the Brenneke slug, but now Interarms (10 Prince Street, Alexandria, Virginia 22313) is serving in this capacity. Interarms offers factory rounds, and can also supply the Brenneke slug in gauges 12, 16 and 20 for handloading purposes.

Gauge for gauge, the Brenneke slug is heavier than the U.S.-designed Foster type. Thus the German-made slug delivers more energy if loaded to the same velocity, or equal energy if loaded to a lesser velocity. The 16-ga. Brennekes I got from Stoeger Arms a couple of years ago averaged 419 grains, with an extreme variation of only 5.2 grains for a random sample of 10. This places the 16-bore Brenneke very close to the one-ounce level and, as such, it runs slightly heavier than a 12-ga. Foster-type slug, most of these being only ⅞-oz. projectiles.

Much of what was said above regarding wad column requirements with the M-B hollow-point slug does *not* apply to the Brenneke. As sold for handloading, the Brenneke carries its own wadding, screw-attached to the slug's base. The 16 ga. wad column consists of a ⅜″ hard felt wad sandwiched between two thin card wads. Total wad column length is one-half inch. In addition to providing improved sectional density, the attached wadding contributes to in-flight stability and prevents the slug from keyholing. However, the slug will reach the target with some yaw at ranges of 50 yards and beyond, but the amount is small.

Without its wad column, the 16-ga. Brenneke has a length of .681″. There is a base cavity, but much of this is occupied by an integral post which takes the screw for the wadding. The diameter of the slug across the ribbed section at the nose end is a nominal .655″, this increasing to .670″ across the annular ring at the base, so the projectile is very close to bore diameter. But despite this full diameter, the Brenneke is said to be perfectly safe for use in full-choke barrels.

As for other details of design, the 16-ga. Brenneke has 12 angular ribs spaced .100″ apart. These ribs are about .055″ wide and with a matching height. Whether they contribute to accuracy by imparting rotational spin is open to question. Judging from their "fingerprints" in heavy target paper at 50 yards, the spin, if any exists at all, is extremely slow. Probably the most important function of the angular ribs is that they will crush down and thus enhance passage of the slug without damage to barrels with heavy choke.

While the attached wadding simplifies handloading in one respect, it tends to complicate matters in other ways. The Brenneke factory loads carry a roll crimp, this turnover being exceptionally deep with the nose of the slug positioned far below the mouth of the crimped shell. The handloader could probably duplicate this heavy turnover on a paper-tube shell if he had power equipment, but with a plastic hull it would doubtless prove a difficult task. It is for this reason that Stoeger Arms strongly recommended a fold-type crimp for Brenneke handloads. But when a fold crimp is used, an over-slug retainer is necessary. These are included with each box of Brenneke slugs sold for handloading.

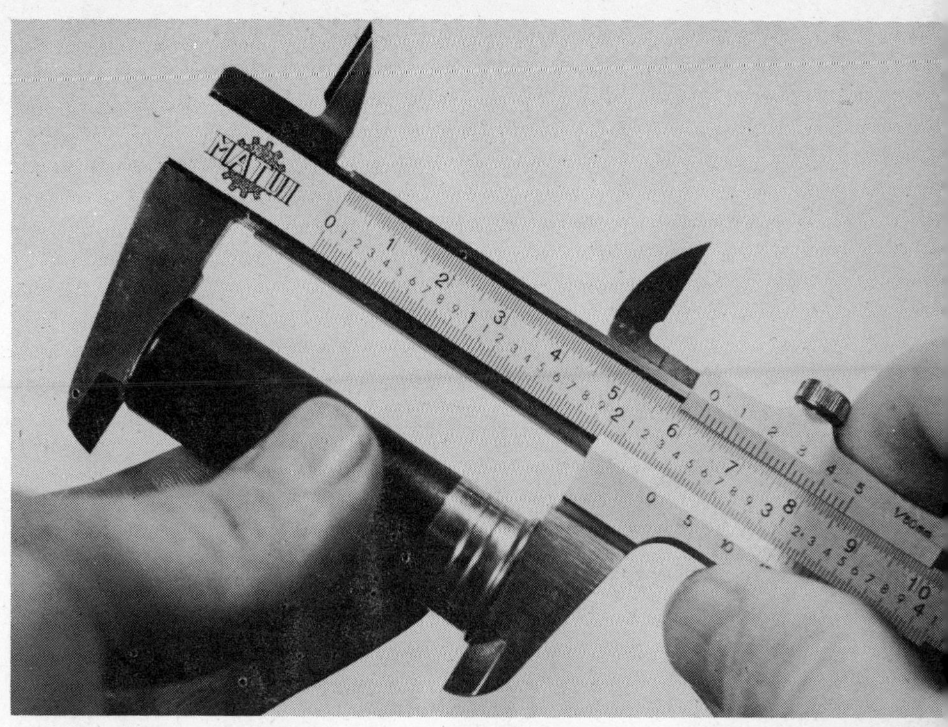

If turnover depth varies appreciably from load to load the ballistics will not be uniform and, in turn, accuracy will suffer. Care should be taken, therefore, to roll crimp the handloads to a matching length.

The plastic retainer consists of a pair of half-moon pieces. Once the slug is seated on the powder charge, this two-piece retainer is placed over the nose of the slug so as to bear against the radiused shoulder. After the crimp is finished, its perimeter should bear firmly against the upper part of the retainer. Upon firing, the retainer falls away from the slug as soon as it clears the muzzle.

Although this fold-crimp route has merit, if only because conventional loading equipment will handle the job, it is by no means a problem-free approach to handloading the Brenneke slug. The pinch is that case capacity must be precisely matched to powder charge and slug displacement.

An example: for the 16-ga. Brenneke, the Stoeger recommendation is either 27/Herco or 31/SR-4756 in a 2¾″ plastic shell with the Remington 57 Star primer. These powder charges, incidentally, are listed as producing muzzle velocities of 1,411 and 1,412 fps (feet per second), respectively. The chamber pressure shown for Herco is 10,420 lup (lead units of pressure), 10,780 lup for SR-4756. The Stoeger charge table does not identify the plastic shell as to brand or type, but it is assumed to be the Remington SP plastic field type.

Dummy rounds with inert primers were made up using both Herco and SR-4756 in the Remington SP hull, but the fold crimps turned out to be complete disasters. Nearly ¾″ of crimp space remained *after* the over-slug retainer was in place, an amount far in excess of what was needed. The 6-point closure turned completely down, much in the manner of a roll crimp. Perhaps the low-brass (high basewad) Winchester-Western field-load paper hull might have worked out for fold crimping (the powder recommendation in this instance being 30/Herco or 31/SR-4756), but this hull was not within reach at the time.

Next, a dummy round was made up using the Federal paper-tube shell (virgin tube) and applying a roll crimp. In order to get around the matter of excessive case capacity, a ⅜″ Ljutic Mono-Wad was first seated on the powder charge (31/SR-4756), followed by the 16-ga. Brenneke with its attached wadding. The required turnover was about two-thirds as deep as for the Brenneke factory loads, and the Lyman Easy tool handled this task with no difficulty. Over-all length of the crimped round was 2 7/16″, with the nose of the slug recessed about 1/16″. It was a beautiful job.

But when discussing this method of loading with the Stoeger people, I was urged to abandon the idea. I was told that when additional wads of any type were used between the powder and the slug unit, the chamber pressure would be adversely affected and that accuracy would go to pot. The reason given for the accuracy loss was that the supplementary wadding would attach itself to the head of the slug screw and produce an imbalance. So the idea was dropped—at least for the moment.

The next move was to investigate what could be described as a modified roll-crimp approach. Earlier I had found that in the Remington SP plastic shells (virgin tubes), the Brenneke unit gave an extremely tight fit. In fact, it required 80 to 100 pounds of seating pressure just to put the slug in contact with the powder charge and the outside of the tube walls were distinctly imprinted by the slug's ribs and wadding. My thinking was that if the slug did not migrate forward under recoil while in the magazine of a pump gun or autoloader, then this might prove to be a simplified method of handloading the Brenneke. A shallow roll crimp would be applied, its sole purpose being to insure trouble-free feeding in a maga-

Ballistic Tests

Meyer Bros. 16-Ga. Hollow-Point Rifled Slug (average weight = 337.0 grs.)

Case/Primer	Powder/Grs.	Wad Column	Roll Crimp Over-All	Velocity @ 15'	Chamber Pressure	Velocity Variation
Fed. Hi-Power Plastic/Fed. 209	28.0/Herco	PGS + .135" NC + 3/8" FBS + .135" + .135" NC	2 3/8"	1,422 fps	7,000 lup	61 fps
Fed. Hi-Power Plastic/Fed. 209	27.0/Herco	PGS + 1/2" Mono-Wad + .135" + .200" NC	2 3/8"	1,384 fps	7,100 lup	42 fps
Fed. Hi-Power Plastic/Fed. 209	21.0/Top Mark	PGS + .135" NC + 3/8" FBS + .200" + .200" NC	2 3/8"	1,338 fps	10,200 lup	26 fps
Fed. Hi-Power Plastic/Fed. 209	20.5/Top Mark	PGS + 9/16" Mono-Wad + .200" + .200" NC	2 3/8"	1,318 fps	10,100 1 up	48 fps
Rem. SP Plastic Field/G57F	20.0/Top Mark	PGS + .080" NC + 1/2" Mono-Wad + .200" NC	2 5/16"	1,323 fps	10,700 lup	27 fps
Rem. SP Plastic Field/G57F	20.0/Top Mark	PGS + .080" NC + 1/4" + 1/4" FBS + .200" NC	2 5/16"	1,312 fps	9,200 lup	43 fps
Fed. Monark Paper/Fed. 209	30.0/AL-5	PGS + 1/2" Mono-Wad + .135" + .200" NC	2 7/16"	1,425 fps	8,700 lup	35 fps
Fed. Monark Paper/Fed. 209	30.0/AL-5	PGS + 1/2" Mono-Wad + .080" + .200" NC	2 3/8"	1,440 fps	8,700 lup	25 fps
Fed. Monark Paper/Fed. 209	31.0/AL-5	PGS + 3/8" FBS + .200" + .200" NC	2 3/8"	1,475 fps	9,000 lup	31 fps
Fed. Monark Paper/Fed. 209	27.0/Herco	PGS + 1/2" Mono-Wad + .135" + .200" NC	2 3/8"	1,426 fps	8,900 lup	29 fps
Fed. Monark Paper/Fed. 209	28.0/Herco	PGS + .135" NC + 3/8" FBS + .135" + .200" NC	2 3/8"	1,456 fps	9,500 lup	54 fps
Fed. Monark Paper/Fed. 209	26.0/AL-120	PGS + .135" NC + 5/16" FBS + .135" + .200" NC	2 3/8"	1,506 fps	12,100 lup	11 fps
Fed. Monark Paper/Fed. 209	25.0/AL-120	PGS + 3/8" Mono-Wad + .200" + .200" NC	2 3/8"	1,478 fps	12,200 lup	16 fps
Alcan Type LP-7 Plastic/220 Max-Fire	26.0/AL-120	PGS + .080" NC + 3/8" FBS + .200" NC	2 3/8"	1,522 fps	10,700 lup	17 fps
Alcan Type LP-7 Plastic/220 Max-Fire	25.0/AL-120	PGS + 3/8" Mono-Wad + .080" + .200" NC	2 3/8"	1,487 fps	11,000 lup	29 fps
Alcan Type LP-7 Plastic/220 Max-Fire	30.0/AL-5	PGS + 3/8" Mono-Wad + .080" + .200" NC	2 3/8"	1,441 fps	8,500 lup	33 fps
Alcan Type LP-7 Plastic/220 Max-Fire	20.0/Top Mark	PGS + 1/2" Mono-Wad + .135" + .200" NC	2 3/8"	1,332 fps	10,300 lup	28 fps
Remington Express	Factory	Factory		1,543 fps	10,100 lup	59 fps

Abbreviations: Mono-Wad = Filler wad (Ljutic Industries)
fps = feet per second
lup = lead units chamber pressure
PGS = Alcan Plastic Gas Seal
FBS = Alcan Feltan-Bluestreak filler wad
NC = Nitro Card

Notes on ballistic tests:
The velocities and pressures shown represent an average for 5 shots; the velocity variation shows the extreme spread between individual loads. All loads tested were assembled in new cases, and the roll crimps were turned on the Lyman Easy shotshell press. Wad-seating pressure for Herco powder was 100 lbs.; 40 lbs. for Top Mark; 60 lbs. for AL-5 and AL-120. Test firing was done by the Ballistic Research Department, Smith & Wesson, Inc.

zine gun. In no way would the crimp serve as an aid to powder ignition and initial combustion, since the turnover would not even come close to bearing against the slug.

Trial loads were put together using 26/Herco and 30/SR-4756, both powders being one grain under the Stoeger recommendations. The slug was seated with 125 pounds of pressure for both propellants, and this force was held for several seconds to be certain that trapped air had a chance to fully vent off. The loads were roll crimped to an over-all length of 2½" and then set aside for several days, at which time it was noticed that the shallow turnover had a tendency to unfurl in places. Crimping deeper to a 2⁷⁄₁₆" over-all cured this problem.

Remington's translucent plastic permitted the slug position to be precisely marked on the outside of the hull. Two loads, carefully so-indexed, were kept in the magazine of the Remington M-870 pump gun during the firing of 10 Brenneke factory rounds. This amount of recoil produced not one iota of change in slug position, so the decision was made to go ahead with handload accuracy tests using this modified roll-crimp system.

Before doing so, however, there was an accuracy session with factory-loaded Brennekes, these loads being in the RWS/Rottweil black paper-tube shell (current loads, I believe, are in plastic shells). The shooting was done from sandbag rest using the M-870 pump gun with a 26" improved cylinder barrel. Bore diameter of this barrel is .675" and choke constriction is .005". The gun was equipped with a Bushnell 1x shotgun scope.

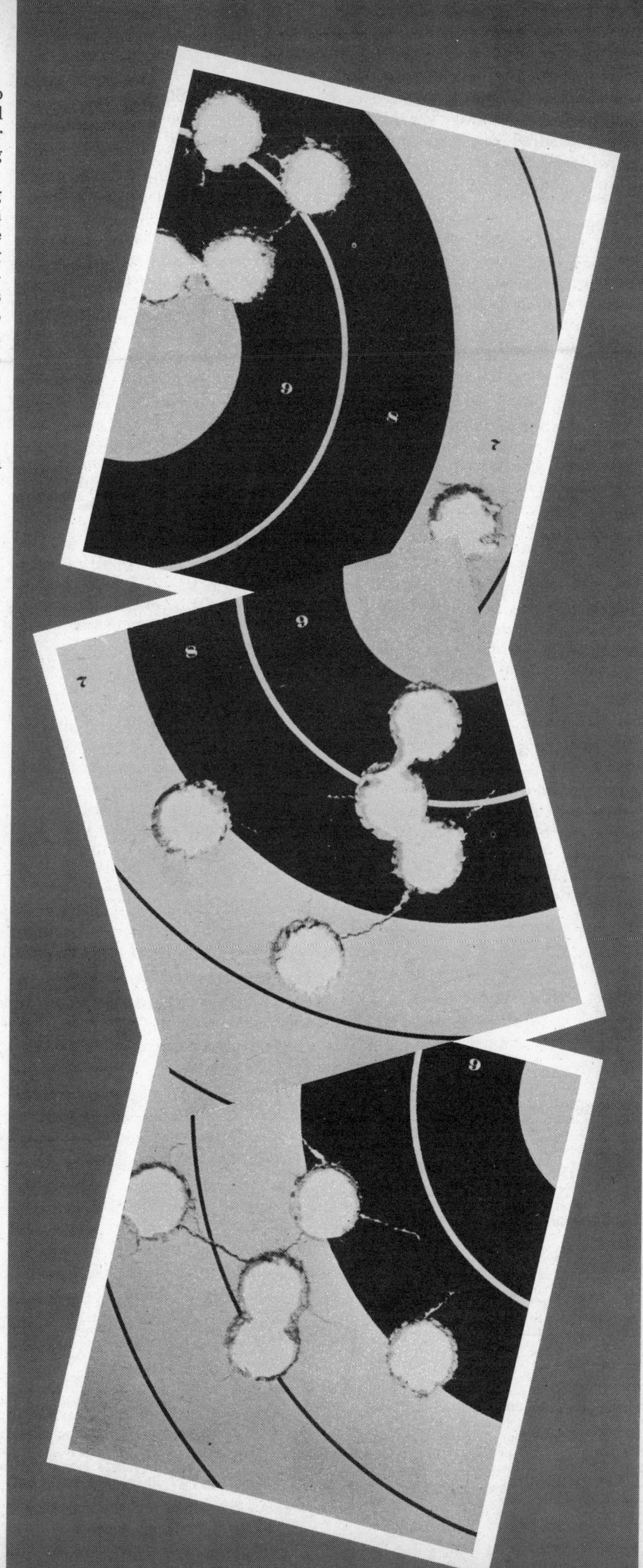

The Remington M-870 with 26-inch Imp. Cyl. barrel printed very good 50-yd. groups with all of the range-tested 16-ga. rifled-slug handloads. A powder charge of 31.0 grs. AL-5 with PGS and Mono-Wad (approximately 1,500 fps) delivered this 5-shot group, which measures 4⅛ inches on centers; four slugs printed in 1⅝ inches. The wide hit was the first shot from a clean, dry bore and is considered coincidental.

Accuracy was excellent with Alcan's AL-120 powder behind the 337-gr. hollow-point M-B projectile, also using the PGS and Ljutic Mono-Wad. A 24.5-gr. charge gives over 1,400 fps. This 5-shot group on the 100-yd. smallbore rifle target, fired at 50 yards, measures just 2¼ inches on centers.

A charge of 28.0 grs. Herco behind the Meyer Bros. hollow-point 16-ga. slug gave this 2¾-inch group at 50 yards. Muzzle velocity with the PGS and Mono-Wad is estimated at close to 1,500 fps. Sighting equipment for this and all other loads tested was a Bushnell 1x shotgun scope.

Seven 5-shot groups were fired at 50 yards and the average spread was 6.69" (measured center-to-center of the widest hits). In almost every instance the horizontal dispersion was markedly greater than the vertical dispersion. All groups except one were fired under calm winds. The smallest group ran 3", the largest 9¾". Usually there was one slug in the 5-shot string that printed wide of the rest. The big group, for example, had a nice tight cluster of four in 4". Another group of 5⅝" had four printing in 2¼".

At about this same time eight 5-shot groups were fired with the same gun using Remington factory-loaded rifled slugs. These printed precisely one inch smaller clusters than did the Brenneke, the average group size at 50 yards leveling off at 5.59". As with the Brenneke loads, the bore was thoroughly cleaned following each 5-shot string, and it was noted that the Foster-type slug in the Remington loads leaded the bore (ahead of the forcing cone and also in the choke area) much more heavily than did the Brenneke.

Accuracy with my Brenneke-slug handloads, using the slug as issued and the modified roll-crimp method outlined above, did somewhat better than the factory rounds. Average grouping at 50 yards for four 5-shot strings with varied powder charges was 4.96". I might point out again that all handloads were put together in new Remington SP plastic field hulls with the 57 Star primer.

A charge of 26/Herco was chosen as a starting load and the 5 Brennekes clustered into 4½". Increasing the charge one-half grain gave a group size (on centers) of 4⅜". Boosting the powder charge to 27/Herco gave a rather disappointing spread of 6⅛". However, four slugs did print in 3⅜", with three of these cutting one ragged hole. A final group was shot using 30/SR-4756, this one running 4⅞" on centers.

An average group size at 50 yards of roughly 5 inches isn't the worst accuracy, but it's not the best either. I felt the Brenneke was capable of doing somewhat better than this and the only alternative (other than using the over-slug retainer in conjunction with a fold crimp) was to take steps to improve the gas seal. With my supply of slugs down to 10, it was decided to supplement the Brenneke wadding with the PGS plastic over-powder wad. This, of course, was in conflict with the advice passed along by the Stoeger people.

But rather than seating the PGS on the powder and then the slug unit over that, I attached the plastic wad directly to the Brenneke wad column. The screw was removed, the PGS wad placed in position and the screw then replaced. In order to do so, it was necessary to first slightly enlarge the existing center hole in the PGS, and special care was taken to insure that the PGS was concentric with the other wads.

Since the PGS would increase the efficiency of the propellant charge, a reduction in charge weight was mandatory. Stoeger's recommended top loading with Herco is 27.0 grs., so for the first trial group I cut back to 25.5 grs. The results at the target were outstandingly good—these 5 slugs grouped into 2½" on centers!

For the remaining 5 slugs (with the PGS attached), I increased the charge to 26/Herco. Four clustered in 2⅝", while a wild one (which I'm certain was my fault) opened the spread to 5".

Although only two groups involving the PGS wad were fired, I believe the excellent results serve to once again demonstrate that the better the gas seal, the better the accuracy. It all accrues, of course, through more uniform ballistics. As seen from this quarter, supplementing the Brenneke wadding with a plastic over-powder cup is the only way to travel.

And what about chamber pressure with these 25.5 and 26/Herco loadings with the PGS wad? A careful examination of the fired hulls revealed no evidence that dangerous pressures were being generated. But lacking lab tests, I can only offer a "guesstimate" that the 25.5/Herco charge should be considered *max* (it may even be a bit on the *hot* side—over 11,000 lup) and is not to be exceeded regardless of the case, primer or type of crimp. As I've said, the loads appear to be safe ones, but no guarantee can be offered to that effect. ●

Bench Rest Accuracy Tests—50 Yards Range

(Meyer Bros. 16-Ga. Hollow-Point Rifled Slug)

Gun: Remington Model 870 Wingmaster slide-action; barrel: 26" Imp. Cyl., bore .675", choke .005". Sights: Bushnell 1x shotgun scope.

(5-shot groups measured on centers)

Case	Primer	Powder/Grs.	Wad Column	Roll Crimp Over-All	Group Size
Federal Monark Paper	Fed. 209	31.0/AL-5	PGS + ½" Mono-Wad + .080" + .200" NC	2⅜"	4⅛" (4 in 1⅝")
Federal Monark Paper	Fed. 209	31.5/AL-5	PGS + ⅜" FBS + .200" + .200" NC	2⅜"	5¼"/4⅝" (4 in 1¾")
Federal Monark Paper	Fed. 209	28.0/Herco	PGS + ½" Mono-Wad + .135" + .200" NC	2⅜"	2¾"4"
Alcan Type LP-7 Plastic	220 Max-Fire	25.5/AL-120	PGS + .080" NC + ⅜" FBS + .200" NC	2⅜"	3⅞"/3⅜" (4 in 2¼")
Alcan Type LP-7 Plastic	220 Max-Fire	24.5/AL-120	PGS + ⅜" Mono-Wad + .080" + .200" NC	2⅜"	2¼"/2½"

Comments:
Each 5-shot string was started with a clean, dry bore. Group size was measured center-to-center of widest hits. Eight 5-shot strings, fired with Remington Express factory slug loads, gave an average group size of 5½". The factory loads produced rather heavy lead fouling in the bore. Lead fouling with these handloads ranged from a light trace just ahead of the forcing cone for those with the FBS filler wad, to none at all for those with the Mono-Wad. For the AL-5 and Herco loads the powder charge was increased over that shown in the ballistic table, while the charges for the AL-120 loads were decreased.

The history and evolution of a dedicated and incurable...

CHUCK HUNTER!

Starting with a simple 22 rimfire rifle, the author was laid low with woodchuck fever at an early age. Never fully cured, he went from one cartridge to another, his longest love the mighty Swift. Big Medicine!

Photos by Helen Lewis

by Don LEWIS

THE INK was hardly dry on my army discharge papers in early 1946 when I began to grow restless—I had a malady suffered from boyhood. That particular springtime—cold and windy, with flash snow storms and hard rains—kept me confined. I was so bothered I found it nearly impossible to contain myself. With the first signs of summer I was scouting neighboring farm lands in search of a cure. You see, I'm a chuck hunter, first last and always, and chuck fever can be pretty awful.

Strange, isn't it, that a man who had just completed over three years of military service—and had a wife and child—could get so enthralled about getting back to matching wits with the wily chuck? Yet, in spite of a constant stream of invective tossed at me by so-called big game hunters, I made no attempt to deny I was just a simple groundhog hunter.

The author shot this hefty woodchuck—it weighed 16½ pounds—with the Model 77 Ruger, caliber 220 Swift. Range was 275 yards.

As a young boy living in a remote back area, I had little diversion except playing along the tiny creeks and waging a constant war against the intrepid chipmunks who challenged my ability with a homemade slingshot. When I was 8 I began to accompany my older brothers in their hunting. Thrilled with every aspect of the outdoors, I yearned for the day I could carry a hunting gun. I secretly made a hundred promises to myself that I'd become the best rabbit and grouse shot my area had ever produced. I pictured myself making doubles on grouse, never missing a rabbit, and even downing fast running deer.

Finally the time came when I was allowed to carry a 22 rifle, the Model 60 Winchester single shot for use on pests and rats around our farm buildings. Not permitted a shotgun for my first hunting season, I did manage to shoot several dumb rabbits; they made the mistake of sitting, instead of running ahead of the dog. Through the rest of that winter I trapped for weasels and shot red squirrels for bait. Reading every chance I got with the aid of a kerosene lamp, I devoured hunting and shooting magazines as fast as they hit the house. An article on chuck hunting with the 22 rifle poisoned my bloodstream, and the first pains of my malady were born.

I wish I could remember the author's name since I owe him a debt of gratitude. Through the remainder of the winter I read the article many times and waited patiently for the warm winds of summer. Serious illness kept me home during spring, however, but the first day I was allowed out I went chuck hunting.

Venturing to a nearby creek, I crawled through weeds, brush and briars to get within shooting range of an old coal mine where I'd earlier seen several chucks. Long forgotten, the old mine had caved in and only a small opening remained. For 30 years or more it had been the home of foxes, skunks and chucks.

A half-hour later I thought all my hard work had been in vain. Nothing showed around the mine except swarms of mosquitoes and sweat bees. It was late in the evening and I rose to leave. Suddenly a large chuck appeared! Caught flat-footed, and face to face with my first chuck, I was uncertain what to do. Sweat filled my eyes and the bugs rained on me as I raised the 22. It wasn't more than a hundred feet away, but with my blood pressure near boiling and my body trembling, it took all the strength I could muster to freeze the open sights on the chuck's head and pull the trigger.

First Chuck

To my dismay the chuck never moved. I stared in frustration. Seconds later the chuck slid down the dusty bank toward the creek while I watched, my mouth wide open. I had shot my first chuck! I remember as if it were today how I raced along the creek to the chuck. Waves of exhilaration swept over me and every fiber of my body tingled. The chuck probably didn't weigh over 10 pounds but, to my eyes, it looked like a grizzly. Although I'd shot squirrels, rabbits and pests, nothing before had shaken me so completely. At that moment a dedicated chuck hunter was born.

Strange how things change in a hurry. My dream to become the best game shot faded. Now my bloodstream was saturated with a malady that would find no cure, and temporary relief would be found in lonely vigils in quest of the simple woodchuck. So it's been for 40 years.

Ignorant of the outside world except for what I could gather from books and magazines, my chuck hunting equipment was limited to one lowly open sighted single shot 22. Distance was a hazard rather than a challenge. I became so adept at sneaking along a fence row to within 20 yards of an unsuspecting chuck that the odds were all in my favor. More than once I wriggled through briars and weeds, flat on my belly, without the chuck ever knowing his longevity was growing short. That's how I thought chuck hunting should be done.

Over the years I shot a few chucks with a variety of 22 rimfire rifles. I also used a friend's 25-20 several times, which filled me with awe as I connected on shots up to 125 yards. Eventually, though, a vintage 22 Hornet found its way into my hands. I was the happiest chuck hunter alive and, when I managed to get an inexpensive 4x scope, a new dimension in varmint hunting opened for me. With distance no longer a significant factor, quantity became my goal, and few chucks were safe within 200 yards.

With the war behind me, I came back to resume civilian life, but the old malady was as strong as ever. First it was a new Hornet, then a 218 Bee plus several homemade outfits, and finally a nearly new Remington Model 722 in 222 with an 8x Unertl target scope. I soon discovered that my old outfits couldn't hold a candle to the little 222. I was nearly speechless when distances grew to 250 yards.

222 and 220

The 222 Remington proved easy to handload. My wife and I burned hundreds of rounds from a makeshift benchrest. I had at last found the one and only chuck rifle, and I'd have been perfectly satisfied the rest of my life if I hadn't agreed to correct a mechanical problem for a new resident's Model 54 Winchester, being something of a gun tinkerer. What I didn't know was that the Model 54 was a 220 Swift, scoped with a dandy 10x Fecker target scope.

The newcomer, leaving two boxes of ammo with me, told me to try the 220 from the bench after repairing it. I took the rifle to my crude bench and, though I'd thought the 222 pretty noisy, I nearly jumped out of my boots when the Swift cracked. In the settling dusk I could see the vivid ball of flame spouting from the muzzle. I was so transported I shot several rounds just to see the muzzle blast! Despite the fading light, I still managed to shoot a group, 4 shots touching and one flyer, the spread just over an inch. Leaving my bench with mixed emotions, I knew I'd have to find out how the Swift acted in the field.

A few evenings later, creeping to the top of a hill, I viewed a rolling terrain that stretched more than 600 yards away. Halfway across the tattered remains of an old log building loomed up, a prime spot for chucks, I knew. Before long I saw a fat chuck sunning himself on the very tip of a protruding log. I'd sighted the Swift to print two inches high at 100 yards, and I was satisfied no elevation guesswork would be necessary.

Digging into a comfortable prone position, I rested the Model 54 on my binocular case, froze the crosshair on the chuck's head and gently squeezed the trigger. The chuck literally flew from the log. I thought he'd jumped until I heard the resounding thud of the 50-gr. bullet. Still not sure if I'd hit the chuck or the log, I was tense until I picked up the frantic gyrations of his tail. My bullet had found its mark.

I haven't forgotten that shot of two decades ago, nor have I lost any admiration for what I consider to be the finest chuck cartridge ever to hit the market in 224 caliber. Naturally, I mean the fearsome 220 Swift.

Views on Hunting

Over the many years my whole chuck hunting philosophy has changed. The common 22 rifle that reigned as the farmer's main standby for everything from butchering to pest shooting had been pushed aside by an influx of speedier centerfires.

The author is checking some of his handloads through the Ruger 220 Swift in this photograph, the chronograph an Avtron. It was a cold, raw day.

During the late 1940s the Hornet and Bee made a slight comeback in Winchester's Model 43 bolt action. I shot both and, since most of my previous experiences had been with rimfires, I was impressed.

The advent of Remington's new 222 brought death to both. Chuck shooting, 'way back, had been done simply to rid the fields of the hole diggers, and it was not considered a genuine hunting sport. That's mostly why I drew so many snide remarks when I made no bones about being a dyed-in-the-wool chuck hunter. There's no question in my mind that the impact of the 222 did more to enhance varmint shooting than any other cartridge. Perhaps it was because of its new design, its extra velocity or the fact it came along just at the right time that made the new creation so appealing to thousands of hunters. In any case the 222 was an overnight success, and it cast the eyes of a multitude of big game hunters toward the pasture fields in search of woodchucks. Best of all, it brought to light what many of us had known for years; chuck hunting is a very intriguing and demanding sport requiring the best from the hunter and his rifle.

My admiration for the 222 Remington didn't diminish when I knocked that chuck from a log at better than 300 yards, but I recognized instantly that the 220 Swift was in a class by itself in centerfire 22s. It would serve no purpose to tell about the number of Swifts I've handled, field tested or bench shot except to say that my admiration grew with each one used.

Perhaps I'm a biased partisan of the Swift. I don't deny other cartridges have plenty to offer. I know the 222 is an exceptional varmint cartridge, and I also know the 22-250 Remington can be loaded to nearly duplicate the Swift's muzzle velocity. I have a 219 Donaldson-Wasp that will cut ⅝" groups with ease.

Shooting hundreds of varmint rifles in my work, in all calibers, I have a fairly comprehensive knowledge of them. Because of that background, when it comes to selecting *the* chuck cartridge, I'll stick with the 220 Swift. For one thing, I'm in complete disagreement with many other chuck hunters over choice of caliber. I may be wrong but I have always considered chuck shooting especially compatible with the .224" bullets. This must not be taken to mean that all of my chuck hunting has been done with the .224 caliber only, since I've shot hundreds of chucks with 6mms, 257s, the 7mm Magnum and even larger bullets. I'm quick to admit that, on a windy day at 300 yards, there's no better cartridge than the Remington 25-06 or one of the 6mms. On the other hand, I have strong feelings about ranges and cartridges in proportion to the size of the species hunted.

In any event, after 40 years of chuck shooting, I feel the best bullet size is .224", and ranges should be under 350 yards. I'm not one to fire wildly at chucks scattered over the surrounding terrain. I try to calculate the yardage as closely as possible and stay within the limits of my rifle. An occasional hit at 500 yards doesn't impress me. The chuck hunter should be precise and methodical. For me the 220 Swift has a considerable edge on the other .224" cartridges. It doesn't have an impressive benchrest record, certainly, but it was never designed for such shooting.

Like the wild cow ponies of the old West, the Swift is a hellbender in its own right. From its inception the Swift was hated, condemned, and finally relegated to the ranks of the unwanted. No other cartridge I can think of created the furor that raged around the Swift.

The Detractors

Unlike Remington's 222 and its immediate acceptance by varmint hunters across the land, the 220 was ripped wide open. The writing fraternity in particular poured out a steady stream of criticism, yet the Swift was innocent of most charges. Was it, perhaps, ahead of its time?

The advent of the Hornet signalled the decline, in good part, for the reliable 22 rimfire rifle that had stood behind every farmhouse door. Winchester's 22 WRF offered a little improvement, but the Hornet's 2,600 fps surpassed both rimfires by a considerable margin, and in hitting power as well. Varmint shooting began to take on a new look.

With rifle shooters becoming speed conscious, the 220 ought to have got the red carpet treatment. Truth is, it was almost the complete opposite. Maybe the Swift had too much speed for varmint hunters who were just getting used to the Hornet. Although Savage brought out the 250-3000 'way back in 1915, its muzzle velocity 3,000 fps with the 87-gr. bullet, it never caught the fancy of many varmint shooters.

We must remember that barrel life was a main concern between the wars, so the blistering 4,000 fps the Swift offered would throw the fear of a charging wildcat into many hunters. Knowing these things, I don't find it difficult to understand why the shooters of that period believed implicitly in 90% of the rubbish written about the 220.

The advent of WW II really didn't contribute significantly to the decline of the 220 Swift since it was reportedly a bad actor right from the start. The hunting and shooting magazines of that era had a tremendous impact on the shooting public. In my small community, though nearly every male was a hunter, we waited patiently and trustingly each month for certain magazines, accepting with a pure innocence what their gun writers were saying.

Influence of Writers

In those days I'd never seen a chronograph or a loading press, nor did I know anyone with a private testing range. Before a new gun was bought every scrap of data was gathered and many evenings were spent around a coal burning fireplace discussing the pros and cons of a cartridge or gun. We relied greatly on the opinions of certain writers. With little or no testing equipment available to most of us then, the success —or failure—of a new cartridge depended a good bit on the writers. Since the Swift's virtues were not extolled by many gun writers, it came to an ignominious end.

Many of the charges against the Swift had no basis in fact. Its adversaries said that Swift pressures jumped unaccountably, that case necks stretched and thickened unduly, that full power loads were a must for accuracy, and that a Swift consumed cases faster than a toad picks bugs off a rock. Probably the most damaging charges leveled against the caliber were a very short barrel life, perhaps of only a few hundred rounds, and an element of danger because of its high chamber pressures.

There's a bit of truth in some of these claims, since maximum loads do generate high pressures, causing case necks to stretch and sometimes thicken. That can happen in any caliber. However, it is quite untrue that maximum loads are needed in the Swift, for it can be loaded down to whatever level desired. With normal loads Swift cases act no differently than other cartridges with similar characteristics and neck angles.

Reliability and Longevity

I'm against maximum loads in any rifle, and I found the Ruger Swift gave its best performance when I held velocities under 4,000 or more fps. I ran the gamut of bullet weights, from 45 to 70 grains, and I had no accuracy problem until I began increasing the velocity. Everyone thinks about the Swift in terms of sheer speed, and this shouldn't be.

As for case consumption, I get more than average life from Swift brass. Several times during the past 10 years I've kept accurate records on a specific number of 22 cases, and I've always got 10 to 20 loadings out of each one. The Swift has a very strong case, one that will last longer than believed when loaded a few grains under maximum.

I've had two actions rupture under my nose during the years I've been shooting, but neither was a Swift. I don't advocate screwing a 220 barrel into just any action, and I've seen a few homemade Swifts I had no hankering to shoot. In my opinion the Swift is just as safe in the factory actions as any other cartridge.

Bore life? That depends a lot on the owner. During the years I was a gunsmith I saw more barrels ruined by neglect than from excessive shooting. There is no formula for determining how long a barrel will remain consistently accurate. I've discussed this several times with leading barrel makers without reaching a conclusive

Ruger M-77V/ 220 Swift
Velocities and Groups

Powder/grs.	Bullet/grs.	Velocity*	Groups/ins.		
3031/32	63 Sierra Semi-Point	3253	1⅜	1⅛	1¼
3031/35	55 Sierra Spitzer	3676	⅝	¾	⅝
3031/37	50 Hornady Spire Point	3866	⅓	⅝	⅝
3031/37	52 Speer HP Silver Match	3963	⅝	¾	¾
3031/37	55 Nosler Spitzer	3927	¾	1	⅞
3031/38	50 Sierra Spitzer	4109	1	⅞	1
4064/36½	55 Nosler Spitzer	3692	1	1⅛	1¼
4064/40½	45 Sierra Spitzer	4195	1¼	1¼	1
4064/40	52 Speer HP Silver Match	4076	¾	9/16	¾
4064/41	50 Sierra Spitzer	4201	1⅛	1¼	1⅛
4064/42	40 Speer Spire Point	4385†	1¼	1⅛	1½
4064/42	45 Sierra Spitzer	4347†	1½	1¼	1½
4320/37	52 Speer Silver Match	3529	9/16	⅜	½
4320/37	53 Detsch Handmade HP	—	⅜	7/16	½
4320/39	52 Nosler Match HP	3896	⅞	¾	¾
4320/40	45 Sierra Spitzer	3917	1⅛	1¼	1⅛
4320/38	70 Speer Semi-Spitzer	3610	⅞	1⅛	1¼
4320/41	52 Speer HP Silver Match	4049	1⅛	1	⅞
4320/42	50 Sierra Spitzer	4172	1	⅞	¾
4320/43	40 Speer Spire Point	4310†	1¾	1½	1½
4320/43	45 Sierra Spitzer	4288†	1⅞	1¼	1½
4350/39	52 Speer Silver Match	3393	⅝	⅝	¾
4350/39	63 Sierra Semi-Point	3269	1⅛	1¼	1⅛
4350/40	70 Speer Semi-Spitzer	3156	1⅛	1	1
4350/42	53 Sierra Bench Rest HP	3615	⅝	9/16	⅝
4350/43	70 Speer Semi-Spitzer	3703	1⅛	1	1⅛
4895/35	52 Speer H-P	3565	⅝	¾	¾
4895/37	52 Nosler Match HP	3855	⅝	½	¾
4895/38	55 Sierra Spitzer	3958	¾	1	¾
4895/39	50 Sierra Spitzer	4110	1⅛	1⅛	1
4895/40	45 Sierra Spitzer	4262	1¼	1½	1¼
4895/41	52 Nosler Spitzer	4177	⅝	⅞	⅝
4895/41	55 Nosler Spitzer	4115	1	1⅛	1⅛
4831/43	70 Speer-Semi Spitzer	3440	1⅛	1	1¼

* Instrumental Velocity at 15 feet. Range 100 yards, 5-shot groups. Remington 9½ primers. K-233 Avtron Chronograph

†Maximum loads—approach with caution.

Factory rifle (untouched) with 26″ targetweight barrel. All cases new Winchester-Western, full length resized after each firing. After first firing each case neck reamed inside.

Scopes: Chronographing - Redfield 1¾ to 5 Variable
Group shooting - Redfield Model 3200 - 20 & 24
Hunting - Redfield Model 3200 - 16 & 12

Here are some of the rifles Don Lewis uses—or has used—for his Pennsylvania varmint hunting, which means woodchucks. Too numerous to describe in detail, this array of 19 rifles and one T/C Contender includes calibers from 17 to 284 Winchester, among them the 243, 6mm Remington and 25-06. Most, however, are 224s—Hornets, Varminters, Swifts, et al. Apart from a No. 1 Ruger single shot in 22-250, the rest are bolt action rifles—factory and custom, of varied makes and models.

Don Lewis shooting his Ruger M77 in 220 Swift caliber from the new Belding & Mull portable rest. Made of aluminum alloy and steel, it weighs only 2½ pounds—the padded fore-end rest piece locks in any position, the adjustable tripod legs offer excellent stability.

answer. Varmint hunters in particular worry over shooting out a barrel, but there's little basis for this concern. Even a few maximum loads fired during a season will not signal the end for a fine barrel.

I believe the Swift barrels will last just as long as those on the 22-250, 25-06, or one of the 6mms, if common sense is used during the loading process—and that the barrel is cleaned well and often! I have one Swift that's been fired hundreds of times, but it still shoots inch groups at 100 yards consistently. Barrel life is the least of my worries, even with the Swift.

Loads and Groups

I got the best results with the 52-gr. factory match and handmade bench-rest bullets, but the M-77V gave impressive results with most of the rest. I had little luck with the 63-gr. bullets, and when Speer sent me a box of 70-gr. semi-spitzer bullets I had some reservations about accuracy. To my surprise, I made groups below the inch mark on several occasions, and averaged just over an inch for 8 five-shot groups.

The M-77 is too well known to need detailing here. It's most significant feature is the angled recoil-lug screw, which draws the barrel/receiver assembly both downward and to the rear. The diagonal force eliminates any movement of the barrel and action, offering a greater potential for accuracy.

The Ruger Swift has a 26″ medium-heavy barrel. The rifle, at just over 9 pounds, makes it an ideal varminter. The M-77V receiver has Ruger's integral scope bases to take the one-inch steel scope rings supplied with the rifle. Also, the M-77V barrel is tapped for target scope bases. From my close association with the M-77, I easily agree that the rifle meets Ruger's classification of the model as "The Performance Rifle." Adding the famous 220 Swift to this line, especially one with a semi-heavy barrel, is truly giving the ol' timer a real chance for recognition.

I depend quite a bit on my chronograph to help determine top loads. Since I'm not interested in sheer speed, the K-233 Avtron eliminates a lot of pure guesswork in the velocity column. However, even before chronographing, I like to smooth out a "green" barrel with a couple of boxes of mild handloads. Using 36½ grains of 4064 behind a 55-gr. bullet held velocity to just under 3,700 fps.

Having a real affinity for 4895 powder, I used it as a starter—37 grains of it behind a 52-gr. Nosler hollow point gave an instrumental velocity at 15 feet of 3,855. For a beginning load, this one worked very well; the first two groups, at 100 yards, measured ⅝″ and ½″. Knowing that many shooters want the extra speed, I upped the powder weight to 39 grains behind a 50-gr. Sierra spitzer. Velocity, at 4,110, fell more into line with what the Swift is supposed to do, but only one group hit the inch mark.

Throughout all the shooting I stuck with 9½ Remington primers and new Winchester-Western cases, and I kept a sharp eye for case stretching and neck thickening. I found nothing unusual when the 40 new cases had been fired 5 times each.

One mild load I enjoyed shooting was 35/3031 with the 55-gr. Sierra spitzer. Instrumental velocity was 3,676, and groups averaged between ⅝″ and ¾″. Adding two more grains of 3031 behind the 50-gr. Hornady Spire Point pushed velocity to 3,866 and put the groups in the super-accurate class. The first three groups fired were under ¾″.

The Nosler 52-gr. match bullet dropped one group into ⅜″, using 37/4320. With velocity averaging 3,529 fps, this load would be my pick for benchrest work since all the groups were well under one inch at 100 yards.

Detsch Bullets

I mentioned handmade bullets. When 37/4320 gave such superb results with the 52-gr. Nosler match bullet, I had to try some of Clarence Detsch's homemades. Detsch is one of the best bullet makers in the country.

When I'm attempting super accurate shooting, I always use a bullet spinner. This little device, really a miniature lathe, uses a dial indicator instead of a cutting tool. The operator hand turns the bullet in the spindles while watching the DI, mine reading in "tenths" or 0.0001″. From thousands of bullets checked, the runout in concentricity is mostly from .0003″ to .0008″ on factory match bullets. This isn't bad since the average is around .0005″. Most competitive shooters yearn for bullets that have a runout of .003″ or less.

I checked every Clarence Detsch bullet and all stayed .0002″ or under! However, Detsch is concerned with more than concentricity; he thinks that squareness of the bullet's base is vitally important. If the base is not truly square, gas escapes unequally during the millionth of a second the base is leaving the muzzle. Since it's next to impossible to make a flat base bullet perfectly square, Detsch puts a tiny radius on the base, a miniature boat-tail.

Using utmost care, I assembled 15 rounds of 37/4320 with the 53-gr. Detsch handmade bullet, had a cup of coffee, and asked the Ruger Swift to do its stuff. It really did. In fact, I almost wish these three groups were the only ones I'd ever fired, since it was the only time a mass-produced factory rifle cut three straight one-holers! To me, that is real shooting. Remember, too, that this rifle was untouched, untuned or whatever.

No rifle can give top results without good sights. For years I've been fortunate in having a variety of target scopes available to me. During all the shooting I did for this article, I used 4 Redfield 3200 scopes in 12x, 16x, 20x and 24x. I reached the conclusion that the 20x and 24x models should be used exclusively for bench-rest and target shooting. After three hunting trips for chucks using both the 12x and 16x Redfields, I have to recommend the 12x as the better choice for the hunter.

When all the field testing and bench shooting ended, it only proved what I had known for years; the old Swift is a darned good cartridge. Some still may think the Swift eccentric, cantankerous, and downright temperamental, but they're 'way off base. The new Ruger Swift warmed my heart and filled my bloodstream with an invigorating tonic that will hold my incurable malady in check until next springtime. The only other thing I want to say about the Ruger Swift is, welcome back Ol' Timer. ●

Ducks Unlimited

You'll discover here what a membership in DU means, and how vital your help and participation is to its waterfowl conservation programs.

THE PURPOSE of Ducks Unlimited is to perpetuate and increase the waterfowl population of the North American continent by conserving and creating breeding habitat in the nesting grounds of Canada, where 80% of the continent's waterfowl originate.

The program is carried out by Ducks Unlimited, Inc., in the United States, whose purpose is to raise the funds for this far reaching conservation program, and Ducks Unlimited (Canada) which has the task of carrying out the program in the wetlands north of the border. In addition, in 1969 a new affiliate, Ducks Unlimited de Mexico, was formed with the long-range goal of protecting and preserving the wintering grounds south of the U.S. border. Thus, DU has become a truly international cooperative effort.

A Total Program

To practically any species of wildlife, water is a critical element of survival. This, Ducks Unlimited's water impoundments represent a total environmental improvement program. Estimates are that over 300 wildlife species directly benefit from our habitat improvement projects, including many types of shorebirds and fur bearers.

This is a program that we have carried on for over 35 years, since we were incorporated in 1937 in Washington, D.C.

DU prides itself on the fact that it offers to its members a vehicle through which they can directly affect the environment of this continent. In fact, historically nearly 80c out of every dollar received by DU has actually been put to work for project construction in Canada. Moreover, *no money* is used to buy land. Land is obtained through long-term free easements from individual land owners, and from the Canadian Federal and Provincial Governments.

Available Memberships

Generally speaking, the minimum contribution is $10. For this, the member receives a membership card, an automobile decal and a year's subscription to *Ducks Unlimited Magazine* (6 issues). Those who contribute $20 or more receive a special publication direct from Canada, reporting on up-to-date habitat conditions. This, of course, is in addition to the regular member benefits.

Ducks Unlimited also maintains a special Sponsor Program for those contributing $200 or more annually, which includes a special hand-lettered certificate suitable for framing, a special Sponsor auto decal and membership card, a special Sponsor pin and individual listing in the colorful "Annual Report to Sponsors."

We also invite individuals, foundations and other groups to inquire about the possibility of having a Canadian DU wildlife conservation project dedicated in their name.

We hope that those who share our concern for the environment and the wildlife resources of the continent will take advantage of the membership information on this page.

Wills, Trusts, Bequests, Etc.

One vehicle by which our programs can be perpetuated is by remembering Ducks Unlimited, Inc., in wills, bequests, trusts or life insurance policies. For more information, contact your attorney or Ducks Unlimited's National Headquarters office.

GUN DIGEST believes wholeheartedly in the DU program — or we wouldn't be carrying this message—and we strongly urge our readers to contribute what they can to this far-reaching, important and vital cause.

Send your membership application —with your check for $10 or more, to Ducks Unlimited, Inc., P. O. Box 66300, Chicago, IL 60666. Canadian contributions should be mailed to Ducks Unlimited (Canada), 1495 Pembina Hy., Winnepeg, Manitoba R3T 2E2, Canada. ●

Borders for Wildlife

"One of the fundamental rules of game management is that wildlife is a product of borders and edges, according to Ted McCawley of Remington Arms Company, Inc. "Whether or not they have ever consciously thought about it, hunters recognize this principle every time they go afield in search of upland game. If you don't believe this, just watch how a savvy bird dog works. He doesn't waste much time on big open fields. Rather, he checks the hedges, brushpiles and woodland borders.

"It's really not hard to figure out why game favors these areas. All the things they find necessary for existence are located there. Sure they'll go out into the middle of a newly picked grain field to eat because it offers plenty of food, and they may like dense woods because of the protection they offer. But edges and borders give the advantage of both habitats and given their druthers, that's where most critters like to live.

"Of course this fact of wildlife is also why small patch farms are more productive of game than some of the big consolidated operations. All too often, the big operators farm 'clean' and don't leave sufficient brushy borders to provide necessary food and cover for game. Such practices are really not necessary, however, since the clean fence lines don't really produce much in the way of crops. With a little cover, however, they can be home to many wild creatures including both song and game birds.

"One of the main thrusts of modern game management is to try to convince people to increase and improve the edge areas on agricultural land. In large areas of open fields, this might call for fence row plantings of shrubs and trees to add cover. In big timber stands, it could mean creating openings where food producing shrubs and grasses could be planted. Obviously the formula will differ depending on the types of country and game involved. However, regardless of the area, giving wildlife an edge to live in will help give them an edge in numbers."

Sporting Arms of the World

Perhaps the totality of major firearms introduced over the past year isn't as great as it has been in recent times, but there are many new and interesting products reported on here. Arms, cartridges and accessories are described in detail. Two strong trends continue—the return to the used-to-be past by way of single shot and caplock firearms, and the increasing interest in first class craftmanship and craftsmen. There are, today, more great stockmakers, metalsmiths and engravers working than ever before.

The Remington and Winchester Seminars

FOR YEARS NOW, come fall, gun writers and editors can be seen streaming into various meeting places or hunting sites for the annual get-togethers hosted by two old-line companies, Remington and Winchester. Depending upon what is on tap, they may arrive in fairly civilized-looking groups at places like Washington, D.C. or New York, or they may stagger off creaky, prop-driven antiques, garbed in boots and parkas, in places like Roswell, N.M.

Wherever and however they arrive, the goal is the same—to view, examine and shoot or otherwise use the new products which the host company will be introducing the following year. Occasionally these seminars are scheduled back-to-back—not too far apart in time—so that the sometimes strange-looking entourage moves en masse directly from one to the other. In the waning of 1973, however, the two were well apart in both time and distance—like Long Island and New Mexico.

At the Roswell, N.M. airport, the descending scribes were met not only by Dick Dietz and Ted McCawley of Remington, but by John Goodwin and other members of the New Mexico Game & Fish Department, who had assisted in setting up the meeting at the Mescalero Indian Reservation nearby; near the town of Ruidoso, well known for its track and the richest horse race in the world.

Part of the reason for this location was that the Mescalero tribe is now developing part of its hundreds of square miles of fine game territory for paid hunting—and partly because Remington always tries to give us a day or two of good shooting along with its new products. The combination was a good one, with meetings at the new Indian Community Center, and hunting deep in the mountains with experienced Apache guides; among them was, incidentally, Geronimo's grandson.

The mule deer shooting was superb but only George Nonte succedded in nailing a whitetail. It was, too, one of the few times in history when the entire group of writers and company

---

Winston Churchill

No, this is another man, not the Sea Lord—this Churchill is very much a first class stockmaker and engraver, to my knowledge, and I imagine he's also a skilled metalsmith. This makes an unusual combination of crafts, but not a unique one—John Warren, the Cape Cod worker, is another who's equally adept at these three branches of the gunmaker's art.

Winston Churchill made the handsome stock seen top left, the wood an unusually attractive piece of *Juglans regia* from New Zealand via Ernie Paulson of Chinook, Montana. As is all too common, the photograph doesn't reveal the dark, honey-blond color of this walnut, and only faintly can the chocolate-brown and black streaks flowing through it be discerned. Pity.

The 270-caliber barreled action is a left-hand Weatherby. The checkering—28 lines to the inch—shows Churchill's variations on the fleur-de-lis cum ribbon theme. The bolt knob is carved in a variant of Purdey hinge-pin design, the pistol grip cap and screw heads scroll engraved. Dave Petzel of *Field & Stream,* the inordinately proud owner of this confection, plans to have the floorplate chiseled by Churchill when and if he saves up the scratch. J.T.A.

Earl Milliron

The 7mm Remington Magnum pre-1964 rifle seen above is based on a pre-1964 Model 70 Winchester action, stocked in traditional classic form—witness the well-formed cheekpiece, without Monte Carlo, the graceful radiusing of the capped pistol grip, and the multi-point pattern of the checkering. Famed metalsmith Tom Burgess did all of the metal work, including a deeper magazine to hold 5 cartridges. Note that the wood is brought up to the mid-line of the barrel and action, and the treatment at the bolt-release button position. J.T.A.

Top—the 1973 Remington "One of 1,000" over-under was a trap gun. This year the limited-issue 3200 is a Skeet model • The Remington Model 700 bolt action rifle now has cut checkering, other changes and improvements • Remington's 40-XC rifle, here in National Match Course type, caliber 7.62 NATO (308), has international style competition stock. The 40-XR model, a rimfire rifle, is nearly identical in form.

people achieved 100% success on big game—34 guys took 34 deer! Remington M700 rifles in 7mm Magnum, topped with Leupold scopes were used, with exceedingly fine results—though one or two unkind guests made remarks about "magnum overkill." The result was probably a couple of tons of prime venison shipped back to various homes.

The part of the Reservation I hunted, guided by old Geronimo's grandson, was beautiful country. Once we got above the sagebrush and buckbrush country lower down, we traveled through big Ponderosa pine forests and rolling mountain meadows. We left well before sunup, and by the time we reached the high country, a couple of hours later, we'd seen 49 or 50 mule deer!

Quietly parking the pickup we moved into a thicket and, not even ten minutes later, there stood a buck some 100 yards or so away. All I could see was the sun-dappled body, so dense was the brush. I found a fairly clear line of sight to the deer, but I was a little worried that the 150-gr. bullet might bust up. I was lucky—leaning against a tree for support, I fired and it was all over. A small rack, true, but some very good ones were taken by others.

But the new products are the real basis for such meetings, as nice as the shooting and camaraderie might be.

A Skeet version of the 1973 "One of One Thousand" M3200 over-under is now offered. It's identical, except in stocking and boring, to the trap model offered last year. No question that it's a damn well made shotgun, and in general a highly attractive gun—but it's got a couple or so minuses, too, in my opinion. The trigger guard is needlessly big and not as well shaped as it could easily have been, which applies to all the 3200s, of course. Also, for a gun costing so much—some $1050—the engraving isn't well planned. It has a scattered-about appearance, and the subsequent polishing rounds the edges off so much that it looks like rolled engraving.

Also in the shotgun line, we were shown the new "RXP-20" load, assembled with Power-Piston RXP wad, No. 97* primer, and yellow, color-coded case. The case borrows all the RXP-12's features and promises long reloading life, combined with superb performance. Remington even recommends a handload for this case; 16.0 grains of Unique (not even a DuPont product; how about that?), RXP-20 wad, 209 or 97* primer, and the standard Skeet shot charge.

The highly-regarded M700 rifle has been fitted with a new anti-cramp system. A slender guide rib, built into the right receiver rail, engages a corresponding slot in the right locking lug. There's been little complaint about bolt bind in the earlier M700, but this feature eliminates it completely. The magazine follower is now stainless steel, and the bolt knob is shifted forward a bit to prevent recoil-induced skinned knuckles. The stock has undergone subtle styling changes, and checkering is now machine-cut in what I feel is an improved pattern—multi-point. A sealed recoil pad is now standard on magnum calibers, and rear-sight elevation adjustment is considerably improved.

Target rifle stocks—centerfire and rimfire—have been radically altered to the "military match" configuration, a style first offered in this country by Winchester a few years ago. The very deep buttstock belly and steeper grip angle look much more massive.

Handgunners will probably appreciate the new R-P 185-gr. JHP load for the 45 auto. The light bullet with its gaping nose cavity is driven at 950 fps for 370 ft. lbs. of energy at the muzzle. This puts it in the "high-performance" class—though recoil energy is said to remain the same as the standard 45 ball round. At 50 yards, velocity drops to 900 fps, energy to 335 ft. lbs.—yet at 100 yards the bullet is still traveling as fast as the 230-gr. ball does at the muzzle!

There were, of course, other minor improvements and face-liftings in various other products, but to describe them all in detail would take more room than I've got. It has been an "off" year in that Remington didn't introduce any genuinely new guns or cartridges—but I suspect they'll make up for that next year.

Hunting mule deer on the beautiful Mescalero Apache Reservation lands couldn't have been better—34 riflemen took that many deer. This is indeed a Happy Hunting Ground.

Winchester Western

Winchester-Western gathered up its crew of guests at Kennedy airport in New York, and bussed them—and the kind of busing set up by Johnny Falk and Jim Rikhoff must be experienced to be believed—out to famous Sag Harbor for its 15th consecutive seminar—the longest series of them all. I was at the first one, too, as well as all the rest. There the commercial festivities were livened up with a bit of bird shooting. The scene for that shotgunning was the Spring Farm Shooting Preserve, while the more formal activities took place at the old Mashomack Club. Quail, chukar, and pheasant fell to the writers' Winchesters with fair regularity.

The location and shooting was appropriate, for Winchester's big news was the long-awaited, gas-operated, autoloading shotgun now designated "Super-X Model 1". Most of us had seen samples of the gun a year earlier, but had been sworn to secrecy—at least to the degree of secrecy that can exist about such matters.

The Winchester boys made no secret of the fact that the new S-X1 is aimed directly at getting back a big chunk of the scattergun market lost to the Remington M1100 over the past decade. At the same time they attempted, with reasonable success, to copy the feel, handling, and style of the long-favored Model 12 pump gun. The similarity is instantly visible in the lines and paneling of the steel receiver, and in the buttstock—the fore-end doesn't quite make it. Further—perhaps still smarting from some past experiences—they decided not to use any light, sheet-metal stampings in the new gun.

Aside from that the S-X1 is not of unusual design—gas-operated, it uses an annular piston riding on the magazine tube, driving a short rod which strikes a massive bolt carrier, giving it momentum to cycle the action. As it moves rearward, the carrier retracts a tipping locking member out of engagement in the barrel extension roof, then carries the bolt rearward. Quite conventional in basic form, but highly refined in detail and function. The rest of the gun—fire control, feed mechanism, and the like—is also of a sophisticated, normal form.

Apparently the checkering battle has been won at New Haven, for the S-X1's wood adornment is precisely machine-cut on tape-controlled equipment. Very neatly done, too.

The Super-X Model 1 isn't cheap, at about $250, nor will it replace the Winchester M1400 auto that's been around quite a few years. It's made only in 12 gauge at the moment, with 20s coming later (probably in late '75), and with trap and Skeet models to follow when enough field guns have been produced.

I've got a longer story on the S-X1 elsewhere in this edition, this one covering the gestation and birth of the new auto.

The Model 101 over-under shotgun line has been enhanced by a rather handsome "Pigeon Grade" variation with a distinctive matte-finish silver gray receiver—which is also commented on in greater detail at another place in the book.

In the rimfire field Winchester has followed its highly successful M9422 with a new autoloader based on the same design philosophy behind the S-X1. Called the M490, it's a dead ringer for the M100 centerfire auto rifle in appearance.

It's an all steel, man-sized rifle, at 6½ pounds. Certainly it's miles above the Winchester 200-series of tinny 22s of a few years back, and should find wide acceptance at the planned $100-plus price.

Winchester-Western, still pushing its handloading program, has added a very slow-burning powder (for big magnums) to last year's new Ball-powder line. This powder is certainly needed, but as of May we still haven't received a sample to test. Several match-quality rifle bullets were announced, delivery to be in '74, calibers to be 22, 6mm, and 30, but there's no solid information on them yet.

Weaver is a part of Olin and thus tied to Winchester, so these days the time-tested Weaver scopes are a part of the seminars. The Weaver plant had problems last year, what with slow delivery of tooling and materials, so it wasn't until late in '73 that the new 3x-9x variables began to be available; other new-in-'73 models were equally late. As a result, the '73 Weavers are appearing in '74, and nothing newer is forecast any time soon.

These industry-hosted seminars for writers and editors have become a standard and almost indispensable feature of the shooting industry scene. Without them, we'd have a mighty hard time gathering all the latest information in time to tell readers about new products early. Even other companies—Ruger and Ithaca, to name a couple—have held a few such meetings, gathering momentum in the wake of Winchester and Remington. Maybe next year there will be a half-dozen such affairs for us to attend, giving us that much more information for you, the guys who make the whole business go around.

J.T.A.

Top—Winchester's new Model 490, 22 Long Rifle, a man-sized autoloader • Middle—the new Winchester Super-X Model 1 Trap gun is available with 30-inch vent-rib barrel, modified or full choke and regular or Monte Carlo style stock of selected American walnut, and wide fore-end. It has an engraved receiver, a red bead front sight and black rubber recoil pad • The S-X1 Skeet gun (bottom) has a 26-inch vent-rib barrel in Skeet choke, otherwise it is like the Trap gun.

Winchester's Super-X Autoloader

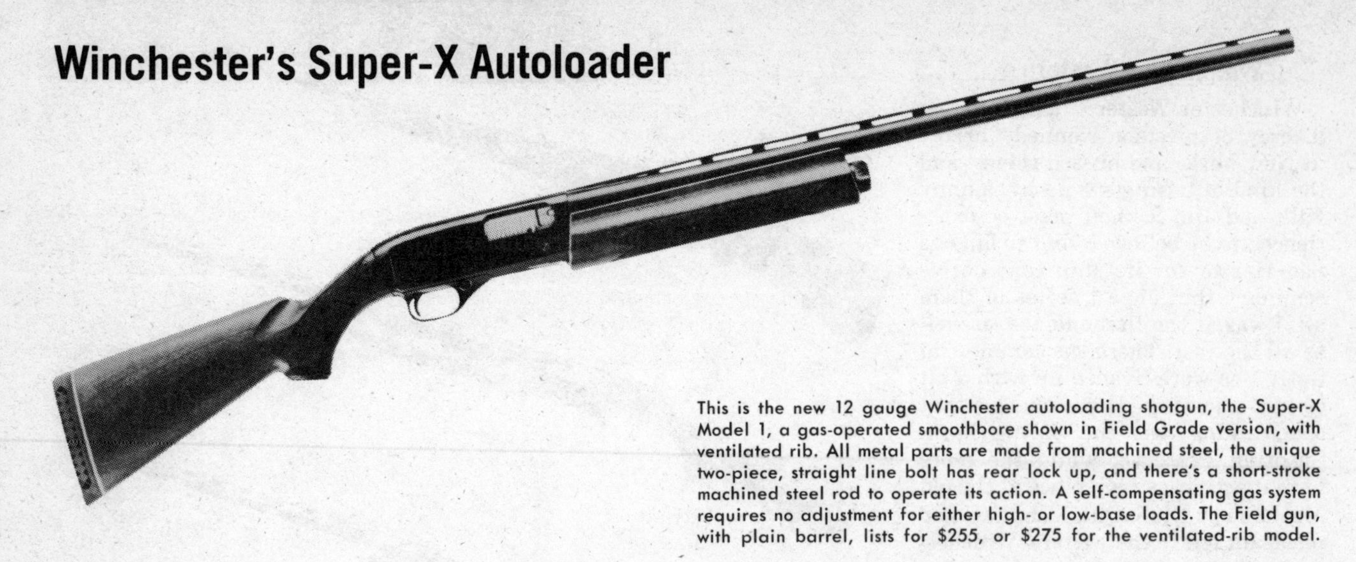

This is the new 12 gauge Winchester autoloading shotgun, the Super-X Model 1, a gas-operated smoothbore shown in Field Grade version, with ventilated rib. All metal parts are made from machined steel, the unique two-piece, straight line bolt has rear lock up, and there's a short-stroke machined steel rod to operate its action. A self-compensating gas system requires no adjustment for either high- or low-base loads. The Field gun, with plain barrel, lists for $255, or $275 for the ventilated-rib model.

The new Winchester Super-X Model 1 shotgun is the culmination of a concept that began over 5 years ago. Instructions to Winchester engineers in 1968 were simple—design and produce an autoloading shotgun with the look, feel and performance reliability of the well-loved Winchester Model 12 pump gun.

Directives are easy—execution was something else. The standards posed for the new shotgun far exceeded those of any semiautomatic shotgun previously manufactured. The designers asked for a really solid gun, one built for endurance, one "that would look better, handle better and shoot better than any comparable model."

With these tough goals in mind the Winchester engineers decided from the outset that all metal parts of the gun would be made of high-quality, precisely-machined alloy steel. No stampings, no plastics, nothing *ersatz*. The stock and fore-end would be made of high-grade American walnut, and would have genuinely cut checkering—not upside-down impressions. A special feature of the checkering machine used on the new shotgun, by the way, is a sensing device which assures uniform depth of checkering, a patented system unique to Winchester-Western. As for its total looks, that directive was also easy—the Super-X should bear a strong resemblance to the Model 12.

Two years ago, when Winchester began making the Model 9422 lever action rifle, the engineers designed for that rifle a wholly new manufacturing-inspection, and assembly-testing plant, one containing the most modern machinery and processes available. It was decided that this same facility would serve to produce the Super-X Model 1. Many of the complex machines used in making the Model 9422 would work as well for the new autoloader. There was also ample room for the additional machinery required to make the new shotgun.

Another advantage in using this facility was its access to the quality control and final inspection checkpoints used for the Model 9422. Total and continuous testing, from raw material to final assembly, assures uniformity and satisfactory functioning of every part of the gun. At final assembly, head space and trigger pull are checked, and proper functioning is tested with dummy ammunition. At this point the gun is also inspected for scratches or other imperfections. At final inspection it is proofed and test-fired for perfect mechanical function.

In developing the new Super-X Model 1, Winchester engineers have already fired three prototypes for 63,000, 67,000 and 83,000 rounds. All of this testing indicates an average malfunction rate of hardly 0.7 per cent. I make that to be 7 failures per thousand rounds, which I suppose is a good performance.

All Super-X metal parts are made from machined steel, the barrel and barrel extension made from the same manganese-chrome-moly steel used for Model 12 barrels.

Machined from a solid block of alloy steel, the new gun's receiver houses a unique 2-piece, straight-line bolt, with rear lock up, that operates on a straight plane, level with the barrel. Since the bolt is always flush and square against the shell head when fired, the shell head distortion that often results with a swing-up type bolt is eliminated, leaving a perfect hull for the reloader.

The heart of the Super-X is its patented new-design, self-compensating gas system. In place of the action bars found on most auto shotguns, a short-stroke steel rod operates the action. This new system uses more gas to work the gun's action, substantially reducing recoil, and makes any adjustment for high- or low-base loads unnecessary.

Fast and easy loading is a big feature of the Super-X, which has a 5-round capacity with factory-installed plug removed and one shell

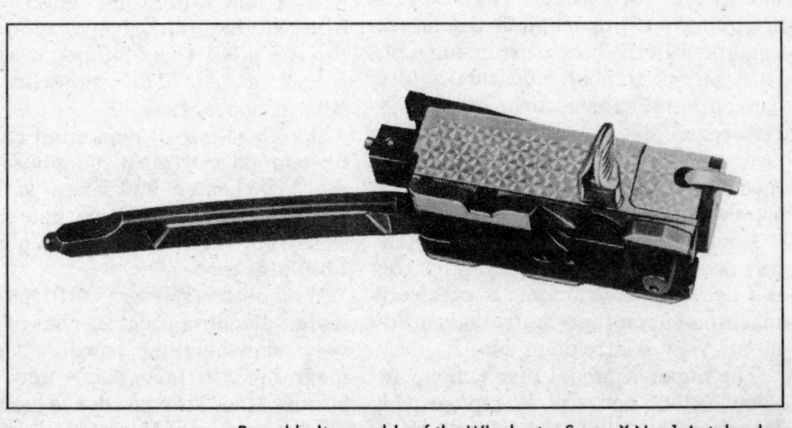

Breechbolt assembly of the Winchester Super X No. 1 Autoloader.

in the chamber. After chambering, the magazine is filled by depressing the carrier release button and inserting shells through the bottom of the receiver. When the carrier is pushed upward and the carrier release button is released, the carrier locks in the upward position for ease of loading. Then, a touch of the release button drops the carrier down into the locked position, where it remains until the gun is fired. The carrier then unlocks, feeds another shell and locks again, thus assuring more positive feeding and less possibility of jamming.

Winchester engineers, with good reason, are proud of their new shotgun, a company spokesman reported. "They've achieved their original goal—an autoloading shotgun with the look, feel and performance reliability of the classic Model 12."

Well, I'd tend to agree that the Super-X will prove a reliable performer, and as autoloaders go it is a good looking gun, cleanly designed and trim. The sample gun I shot during Winchester's 15th seminar, held far out on Long Island (N.Y.), functioned perfectly in all respects for 100 or so shots. Some members of the party had a spate of feeding problems, but my Super-X showed none.

I like the Super-X and the way it handles. There's a good between-the-hands feel, it comes up well, and its recoil is truly minimal, thanks to the excellent gas system.

I can't agree that it looks much like a Model 12—that rearward-extending fore-end, with its angled back line, hardly brings the Model 12 to mind—at least not to mine. On the other hand, those finger ledges each side of the fore-end offer good control, better pointability.

Full model specs and prices are shown in our catalog pages, so I won't set those down here.

It is high time that Winchester has a well-functioning autoloading shotgun and, as a long-time fan of the big red W, I hope indeed that it's successful. Much may hinge, it is rumored, on whether the Super-X hacks it or not. Time, to coin a phrase, will tell. J.T.A.

The product prices mentioned in these review pages were correct at presstime, but may be higher when you read this.

Among the most important men in the production of the Super-X shotgun are quality control inspectors. They check continuously everything from raw material to final assembly to insure uniform, perfect functioning of every component. Barrel extensions are being inspected here.

Here's the 4-axis numerically-controlled machine that cuts the checkering on the stock and fore-end of the Winchester Super-X Model 1 shotgun. A sensor foot assures uniform checkering depth.

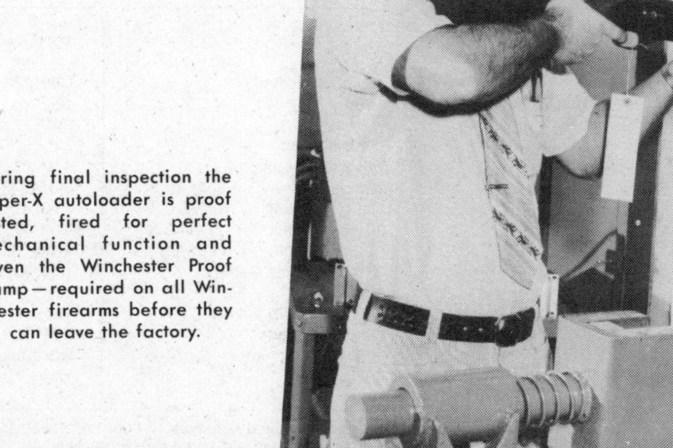

During final inspection the Super-X autoloader is proof tested, fired for perfect mechanical function and given the Winchester Proof stamp—required on all Winchester firearms before they can leave the factory.

New Winchester Pigeon Grade Trap gun differs in several ways from standard Model 101s—new checkering, all hand done, appears on panel behind receiver, the latter in silver gray finish and showing a new engraving design. The fore-end, a semi-beavertail, is well checkered below the smoothly cut finger ledges. Skeet and field versions in Pigeon Grade are also available.

Winchester's New Pigeon Grade

The Model 101 over-under shotgun was introduced just over 10 years ago. To celebrate its 10th Anniversary, there's a new—and very, very nice—Pigeon Grade 101. These will be made in limited numbers, in Skeet, trap and field versions, but all will be in 12 gauge only, at least for now. The usual array of barrel lengths and chokes will be offered, and there'll be two buttstock treatments of the trap guns—regular stock or Monte Carlo form.

As our picture(s) show—I hope—the most obvious differences are external. The receiver sides are tastefully engraved in a new pattern, the scrolling nicely done and attractively laid out. There's a modest bit of like-styled engraving at other areas, too—top lever, tangs, fences and barrel breech area (the ledges over the ejector-housings). A pigeon—looking a little immature, I thought—decorates the receiver bottom, as does the word "Winchester." The receiver, by the way, is satin-grey finished, all other metal deeply blued. Engine turning covers much of the internal breech parts, readily visible when the action is opened.

Trap and Skeet models have a new 15mm-wide ventilated rib, providing an improved sighting plane and a knurled, non-slip single trigger of inertial design. The field version—except for lacking the new rib and in having a single trigger of mechanical type—is styled just like its companions. That also includes specially selected genuine walnut stocks and fore-ends, high luster finished, and hand cut checkering of both to a new and improved design—the panels behind the receiver are fully checkered, as is the bottom of the new semi-beavertail fore-end—which has smoothly flowing finger ledges or fluting for better hand control. I like the changed fore-end tip treatment, too—it is gracefully radiused on these Pigeon guns.

An unusual aspect of all Pigeon Grade guns is this—chambers and bores are chrome-plated *except* in the choked sections, which mean that custom reworking of the chokes can be readily done. Skeet and trap shooters frequently want to alter chokes, always hoping that the change will add a few percentage points to their averages.

All in all, the new Pigeon Grade 101s look very good, a welcome upgrading—at added cost, of course—of Winchester's over-under line.

Cost of the Pigeon Grades? The Skeet and regular-stock trap guns list at $665, the Monte Carlo stocked trap version $10 more. We're reproducing full specs on the three types. J.T.A.

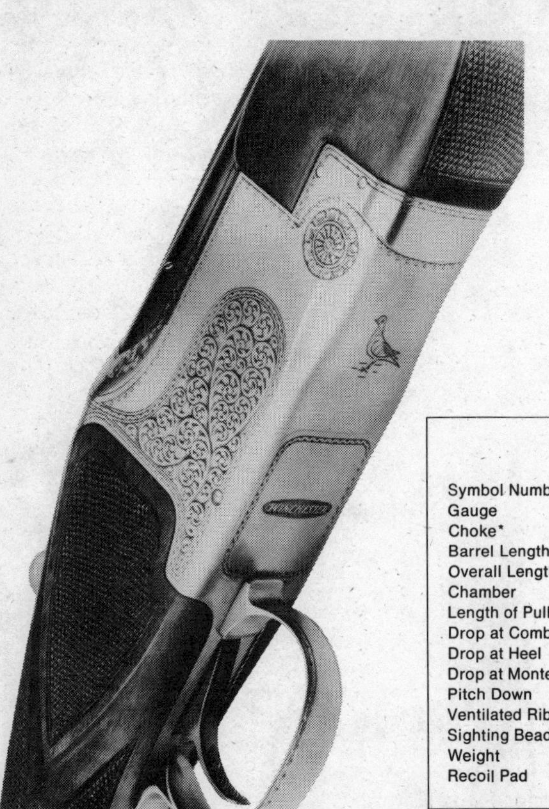

Pigeon Grade 101 shotguns have new engraving design decorating the silver gray receivers, a checkered trigger and handcut checkering on the specially-selected walnut—note panel behind receiver.

Winchester Pigeon Grade Guns

	TRAP		SKEET		FIELD
	Monte Carlo Stock	Regular Stock			
Symbol Number	G30162	G30161	G3017	G30110	G3013
Gauge	12	12	12	12	12
Choke*	IM/F	IM/F	SK/SK	SK/SK	M/F
Barrel Length	30"	30"	26"	28"	28"
Overall Length	47-1/8"	47-1/8"	42-15/16"	44-15/16"	44-15/16"
Chamber	2-3/4"	2-3/4"	2-3/4"	2-3/4"	2-3/4"
Length of Pull	14-3/8"	14-3/8"	14-3/16"	14-3/16"	14-3/16"
Drop at Comb	1-13/32"	1-13/32"	1-1/2"	1-1/2"	1-1/2"
Drop at Heel	2-1/8"	1-3/4"	2-1/2"	2-1/2"	2-1/2"
Drop at Monte Carlo	1-13/32"	-	-	-	-
Pitch Down	1"	1"	2"	2"	2"
Ventilated Rib Width	15mm	15mm	15mm	15mm	8mm
Sighting Beads**	F-M	F-M	F-M	F-M	F
Weight	8-3/8 lbs.	8-3/8 lbs.	7-3/8 lbs.	7-3/4 lbs.	6-7/8 lbs.
Recoil Pad	Yes	Yes	No	No	No

* IM=Improved Modified; F=Full; SK=Skeet; M=Modified.
** F-M=Front and Middle; F=Front only.

Colt

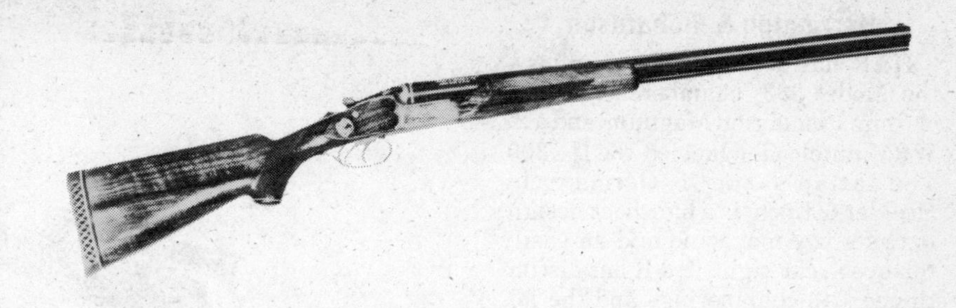

Last year the Colt-Sauer rifle was introduced in standard and magnum calibers. In early 1974 a short action model was brought out. Chambered for the 22-250, 243 or 308, the latest version is ¾" shorter than the standard model and about a half-pound lighter. Otherwise it is basically the same rifle, including the $450 price.

There have been some additions to the handgun line, but the only other new item in the long arm lineup is a Colt-Sauer drilling. Priced at $1650, this is a 3-barrel combination of side-by-side 12 gauge barrels over a 30-06 rifle barrel. The barrels measure 25", giving an over-all length of 41¾". The weight is about 8 pounds, depending on the density of the oil-finished American walnut buttstock and fore-arm. A thumb-actuated device on the tang raises and lowers the rear sight for use of the rifle barrel, and also activates the forward trigger mechanism for firing the rifle barrel. With the tang selector in the rear position the double triggers are used to fire the shotgun barrels. The safety button is on the left side of the stock for convenient operation with the thumb, in the style of some old Greener double guns.

The drilling examined handled well, with the sight perfectly aligned when the butt touched my shoulder. Workmanship was very good, and although the price is steep, this drilling may be welcomed by deer hunters in areas where a shotgun or rifle can be used for hunting. Florida turkey hunters, take note! L.S.S.

Garcia

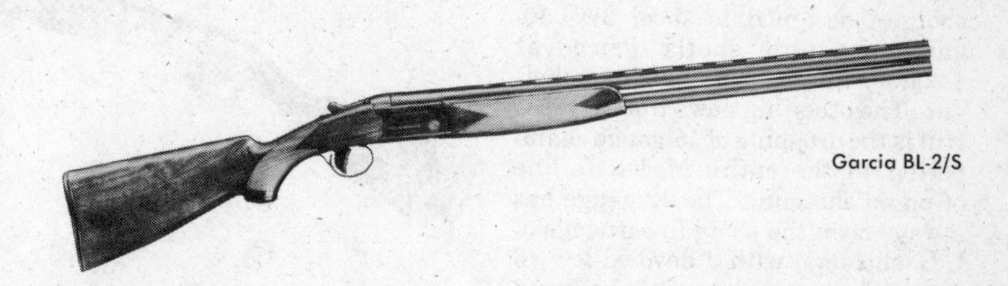

Garcia BL-2/S

The Sako M72 rifle, reported on here last year, has now been renamed the M74. It's available in sporter and heavy-barrel versions, with more hand checkering, detachable swivel studs; without open sights, two new calibers—300 and 338 Winchester Magnum—have been added. There is also a De luxe Sporter M74, with selected wood and finishing. The Golden Anniversary model is also still available. The F.N. Supreme Mauser line has been trimmed by dropping three chamberings—270, 7mm Remington Magnum and 300 Winchester Magnum. Barreled actions are available in the same calibers, and of course the actions are available.

The Bronco 22 and 410 models are still going strong, as is the excellent Gallery rifle by Rossi. The Star Rolling Block is advertised, but seldom seen...maybe one of these days. The Rossi Overland is available only in the "Coach Gun" model with 20" barrel and only in 12 or 20 gauge. The hammerless Rossi is available in 12 or 20 gauge with 26" or 28" barrels. The AL-1 autoloader with plain barrel has been discontinued, and the AL-2 is now available chambered for 3" shells. The Beretta TR-2 single barrel trap gun has also been discontinued, along with the GR-2, GR-3, and GR-4 12 and 20 gauge side-by-side shotguns. The rest of the shotgun line remains unchanged, but there is an addition—the BL-2/S, an over-under with a unique barrel selector-trigger.

Available only in 12 gauge at present with a choice of 26", 28" or 30" (3" chambers) barrel, the BL-2/S retains the slim action designs of other Beretta over-under shotguns, and the careful wood-to-metal fit, ventilated rib, and hand checkered stock and fore-end. There are some differences—there are no side ribs on the barrels, to permit rapid cooling, and the double-crescent shaped trigger is pivoted in the middle! In the normal firing sequence, the shooter simply pulls the top part of the trigger, lets his finger slide down past the pivot point, and pulls the bottom part of the trigger for his second shot. The trigger is the barrel selector—top part for bottom barrel and the bottom part for the top barrel—there is no separate thumb-activated selector on the upper tang. The concept is interesting, having been used previously on at least one submachine gun and it should find a lot of field use. Price—expected to be in the low- to medium-priced bracket—had not been set in late February, 1974. L.S.S.

Jana

This firm still handles the Parker-Hale line of Mauser-actioned rifles, plus the handsomely done Enfield muzzle-loading carbines—and now rifles—Laurona and Lames O-U shotgun, Lucio Loyola side-by-side shotguns in 4 different gauges, a host of black powder revolvers and assorted items related to shooting. But they now have another new item that should create a lot of interest among the black powder clan. This gun, an authentic reproduction of the 54-caliber Gallagher carbine used during the Civil War, has an underlever-operated action; the barrel moves forward and tips up for loading the chamber like a shotgun, using a brass cartridge case that is handloaded. Priced at $250, this reproduction has a polished blue barrel and action, a walnut stock, and comes with a powder measure, spare cartridge case, nipple wrench and a cleaning kit. The carbine examined was very well finished, operated smoothly, had a barrel length of just over 22 inches. Length over-all is about 39 inches, weight about 7¼ pounds—about right for the caliber—and should find a big demand among black powder deer hunters. L.S.S.

Harrington & Richardson

H&R has a couple of new rifles—the Model 333, chambered in 30-06 or 7mm Remington Magnum, and a 22 WRM autoloader labeled the HK300. The latter, made in Germany by Heckler & Koch, is a blowback design. It has a box magazine and an easily removed rear sight. H&R has discontinued 243 chamberings and the following models: left hand version of the Model 361, the 370 Medalist rifle, the 175 DL, Springfield Stalker rifle, the 440 and 442 pump action shotguns, as well as the HK-4 autoloading pistol. L.S.S.

H&R Model 333

Ithaca

The big news is the Mag-10, a Jim Tollinger-designed American-made gas-operated semi-automatic shotgun designed to shoot 3½" 10-gauge magnum shells. Priced at $424.95, this is one whale of a shotgun. The other big news from Terrace Hill is the dropping of 16-gauge chambering in the entire Model 37 line of pump shotguns. The 12 gauge has always been the shotgun cartridge of U.S. shooters, with a devoted few 16 gauge users—in Europe it is reversed—but the 20 gauge has been catching up in recent years. Whether decreasing sales made it a wise move economically, or Ithaca saw the handwriting on the wall, the discontinuance of the 16 gauge chambering is a surprise... or maybe it isn't. The 20 gauge Model 51 Deerslayer has also been dropped from the line.

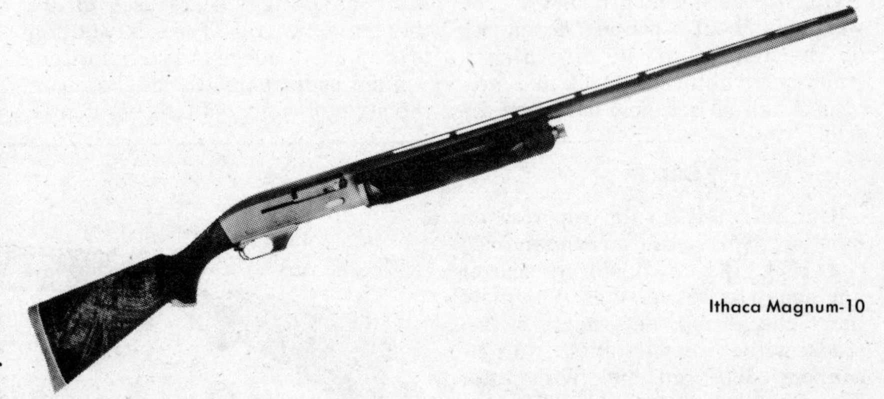

Ithaca Magnum-10

A de luxe version of the Model 72 Saddlegun has been added. Priced at $149.95, this one has an engraved silver-colored frame, 18½" octagonal barrel, and a semi-fancy oil-finished European walnut stock.

The Mitchell line of shooting glasses has been expanded with a couple of models, the gun case line shows 6 new models, including a Gun Glove with side zipper. Other new Ithaca products include the Track line of handcrafted outdoor knives in 13 models, and two air rifles—177 and 22—from BSA of England. The knives range in price from $38.95 to $67.95, and the air rifles go for $34.95 and $75.95 respectively. L.S.S.

Interarms

The "One of One Thousand" Churchill rifles, Walther rifles and handguns, Mauser handguns, and the Mark X line of bolt action sporting rifles are still mainstays at Interarms, but there are some additions. There is now a Whitworth Express bolt rifle available chambered for the 7mm Remington, 375 H&H or 458 Winchester Magnum cartridges. This rifle has the Mark X Mauser action, a classic oil-finish English design stock of European walnut with hand checkering, triple-leaf British Express rear sight on a quarter rib, a hooded ramp front sight, non-ventilated rubber recoil pad, and quick-detachable sling swivels with the front swivel mounted on a barrel band. Two other Mark X bolt rifles have been added—the Cavalier with a selected walnut stock with roll-over cheekpiece, rosewood fore-end tip and grip cap, and it has no swivels.

Interarms Whitworth

The Viscount has a plainer walnut stock without fore-end tip, but with swivels. Both rifles use Williams adjustable rear sights, and hooded ramp fronts.

A semi-automatic military-styled model of the Finnish version of the AK-47 is available as the Valmet M-62S (cal. 7.62x39) with choice of metal or wood buttstock. A similar gun—the M-72S—is chambered for the 223 cartridge. Interarms also distributes the Sako line of ammunition, Brenneke rifled shotgun slugs, Mauser riflescopes, the Arsenal line of revamped military rifles, various accessories, the Hammerli "Virginian" single action revolvers and the latest—the Mauser Parabellum P-08 pistol. L.S.S.

Sturm, Ruger

The Mini-14 military-type rifle isn't available in any quantity, but the No. 1 and No. 3 single shots are in demand, as is the excellent Model 77. Ruger has done wonders for some of the old calibers by chambering a limited number of the various models for them, such as the 220 Swift, 22 Hornet, 257 Roberts, 7x57mm and 30-40 Krag. There may be some more later, such as the No. 1 for one or more of the big Sharps cartridges, and this writer would like to see the Model 77 chambered for the 256 Newton. The Ruger 77 comes closer to the classic lines of the Newton rifle than anything manufactured since, and the 256 was a darn good cartridge; factory brass isn't available, but it is easily formed from 30-06 brass, and there are many excellent 6.5mm bullets to be found today.

The stainless steel Security Six and Single Six revolvers were not available in early 1974, and it will be late 1974 at the earliest before the stainless steel Old Army sees much action. L.S.S.

There should be good news for shotgunners next year (1975) when the long - awaited Ruger over - under smoothbore reaches the market. Near-production versions of these new stack-barrel guns—both 12s and 20s—were shown to dealers during the NSGA show at Chicago. Their reaction was enthusiastic to a man, and the orders placed were many and in generous numbers.

Bill Ruger, in the fall of 1973, invited several writers and editors to his New Hampshire place for a look at his over-under shotgun. Though that's a prototype I'm holding, I don't think the production guns will be markedly different in general appearance or treatment. The sample guns shown to us were shooting pieces, not mockups. They functioned, handled and shot well.

Bill Ruger and George Nonte look over the prototype over-under.

This latest Ruger is a attractively styled, well-balanced over-under—the receiver is a modern, low-profile type, trim enough even in 12 gauge that it's easily grasped and covered by the hand.

I shot the new Rugers (in about the same form as those appearing at the NSGA) at Ruger's New Hampshire place in the fall of 1973, as did several other writers there for the same reason. The several sample guns performed flawlessly—I wish I could say the same for myself—throughout the shooting of some 500 shotshells, mostly at Skeet. Their pointing quality is first class, and about neutral—neither muzzle heavy nor light, though the 12 shows a bit more heft forward than does the 20. I felt that the over-under 20 would make a near-ideal gun for thick-cover birds. I'm anxious to see the full production guns, and I think they're going to prove exciting for shotgunners.

However, in a talk today with Steve Vogel at Southport, we learned that stainless steel Single Six revolvers in all 4 barrel lengths, are being shipped, now, in mid-April.

Vogel also said that, as far as he knew, Bill Ruger still intended to make up the No. 1 Single Shot rifle in long range, Creedmoor style, now that the RCBS 45-3¼ cases are available. When? I won't guess. J.T.A.

Keith Stegall

I think the G33-40 Mauser-actioned rifle pictured here is one of the best—and best looking—custom stocks that Stegall has done to date—the over-all view is impressive in its elegance, the smooth and clean sweep of its lines and curves impeccable.

The beautiful stock started out as a thick blank of genuine Circassian walnut—Stegall bought a big batch from Russia! The 24-line checkering I find especially attractive, but then I'm prejudiced in favor of multi-point patterns. Still, note the treatment of the pistol grip's rear area—as well as the inlaid black diamond—and the panel in the fore-end's bottom (if you can see it).

Stegall fitted a hinged floorplate, the release in the guard, to this lightweight 270 sporter, and two nameplates, one in the stock toe-line, the other in the fore-end, underneath. The latter carries Stegall's name, as the owner requested. Buttplate and grip cap are the excellent checkered steel types made by Al Bisen.

Keith told me the owner (Palmer Faltz of Columbus, Ohio) found the rifle highly accurate—the first groups made ½-inch or less at 100 yards.

The Hiptmayers

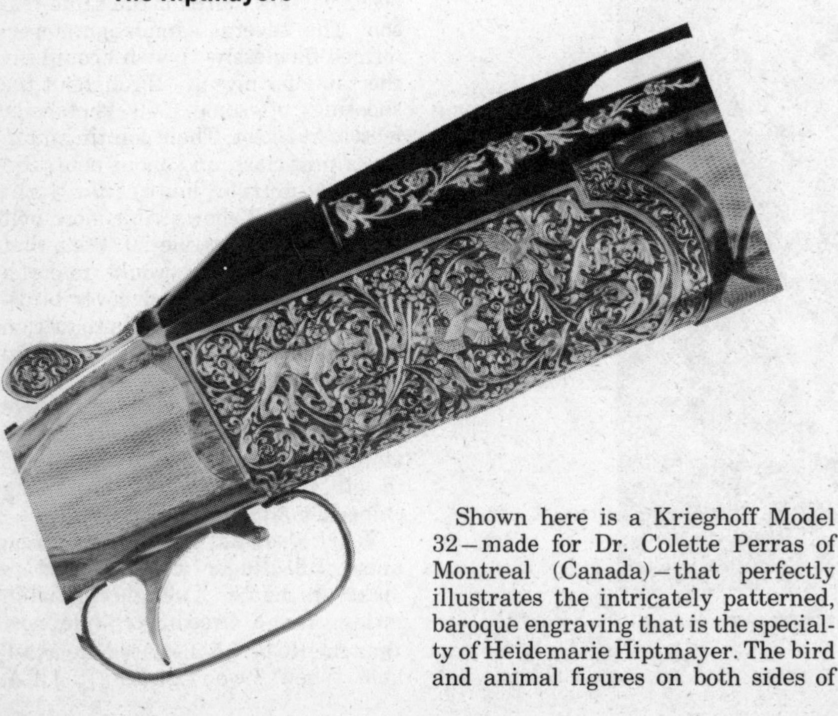

Shown here is a Krieghoff Model 32—made for Dr. Colette Perras of Montreal (Canada)—that perfectly illustrates the intricately patterned, baroque engraving that is the specialty of Heidemarie Hiptmayer. The bird and animal figures on both sides of the receiver are inlaid in 24K gold, each chiselled in full rounded relief. The bottom of the receiver (not shown) and the guard continue the pattern seen here, with another bird inlaid in gold. Unfortunately, these reproductions in black and white cannot show the brilliant appearance of the gold figures that a color photograph would reveal.

The relief inlays on the barrel, of sterling silver and gold, carry out the fanciful and convoluted floriation displayed on the receiver.

Klaus Hiptmayer, the woodworking member of the team (Box 136, Eastman, Que., Canada), stocked this Krieghoff in Circassion walnut. Not much of the fancy-figured wood can be seen in these views (the full length picture of the gun didn't do it justice, either) because the grain is concealed, to a degree, by the extensive checkering—32 lines per inch.

Klaus told me that almost 700 hours were spent on this shotgun, mostly on the engraving, I gather. Study our pictures with a glass and you can believe it. I do. J.T.A.

Savage Arms

Although labeled new, this firm's latest arms are really refinements of current designs. The Model III Chieftain bolt action rifle at $184.50 is the Model 110 clip-magazine rifle with a better select-wood stock, hooded ramp front sight and improved adjustable rear sight, sling swivels with adjustable sling, and white-line spacers at the buttplate and pistol grip cap, plus a rakish teardrop-shaped bolt handle and a new headspace sleeve for the barrel. The calibers are the same except that the 300 Winchester Magnum has been dropped in the entire Model 110 line. The Model 170 pump action rifle is now offered in a carbine version with 18½″ barrel—same price as the rifle, $105.10. The Anschutz 1432 rifle is virtually the same as the Anschutz Model 54 Sporter, but chambered for the 22 Hornet cartridge in a 24″ barrel, and priced at $298.50. There is also a Model 1408-ED "Super" Running Boar rifle, in 22 Long Rifle, on special order only, at $385, and Match grade 54 barreled actions are available at $158-$212. Surprisingly, they mean just that—the barrel and the action only (receiver and bolt), but no trigger mechanism.

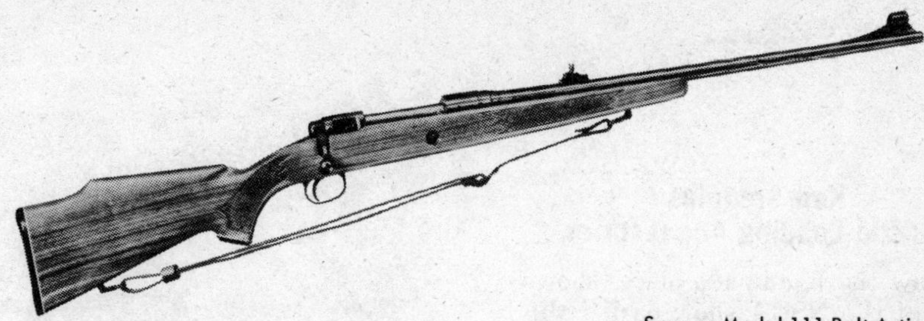

Savage Model 111 Bolt Action Rifle

It's interesting, I think, that Savage apparently sees sales possibilities for the 22 Hornet, especially at that price. Apart from Ruger listing the Hornet as one of the No. 3 Single Shot carbines chamberings—though I don't believe any have been delivered—this is the first reintroduction of the cartridge that created such a furor some 44 years ago. Certainly the new Anschutz is the first bolt action repeater so chambered.

A couple of years ago Savage advertised 93 basic models in production. Not any longer; they have really trimmed the line. The following models are no longer listed, although they may still be available from some dealers: Model 99-DL, Model 99-F, Model 110-EL, Model 74 Little Favorite, Model 46, Model 34-M, Model 65, and Model 88. This includes 3 centerfire rifles and 5 rimfire rifles, with the last of the Savage/Stevens rimfire autoloading rifles (Model 88) among them. In the scattergun line, the Model 30T pump gun is gone, as is the Model 550 side-by-side double, the Model 58 bolt action in 12 and 20 gauges, and the 6-shot 410 Model 59 with tubular magazine. It's doubtful they will be reintroduced. L.S.S.

Savage-Anschütz Hornet

As an early 22 Hornet shooter—I bought one in 1937 in a Model 70 Winchester, and still have it—I was saddened to see the little load all but disappear, at least in the U.S. It has not, however, vanished in Europe. Now, with a revived interest in the old, Savage has included a 22 Hornet among its 1974 offerings, made by Anschütz in West Germany.

Our sample rifle reached us too late for a full-blown test, but I managed about an hour's shooting with the rifle on a pretty good day—clear, bright, little wind and a pleasant 62 degrees.

Having recently cleaned a batch of Hornet cartridges—most must be 10 years or more old—I used some of these Winchester 45-gr. HPs to start off, to break the new barrel in and condition it. The only scope usable at the moment was a 22 rimfire type Redfield used to make—a 4x with coarse crosshairs. The receiver top of the Anschütz Hornet is the same as their old 514 sporter—narrow longitudinal dovetails that take some tipoff mounts, but tapped as well for scope bases. Redfield had once made this type, a sort of saddle form, but I couldn't locate a pair until too late.

In spite of the low-power glass and its big wires, the first 5 shots (for record) at my 100-yard bench, went into a surprisingly small cluster—11/16″, with 3 touching each other for 7/16″. The next 5 made 7/8″, still quite good for the conditions, but then things got worse. Impacts started to string up and down to the point that two more 5-shot groups averaged almost 1½″—I suspect that old ammo, but it might be the bedding, for though the fore-end wood at the top is free, the barrel seems to be bedded full length along the bottom. I'll check this, and I'll mount a higher powered scope if the bases reach me in time. This 22 Hornet rifle acts like it wants to shoot, and I'll try some fresh handloads later on, as well as some late factory loads, if I can locate any.

The new Anschütz Model 1432 Hornet is very nicely put together—metal and wood are carefully mated, and both are well finished. Styling is in the modern manner—rollover Monte Carlo comb-cheekpiece, grip and fore-end with skipline checkering, and comfortable—there's a palm swell for right-handed shooters. White spacers at grip and buttplate, *natürlich*, but none at the schnabel-shaped fore-end tip. Sling eyes are installed, but no sling swivels are supplied.

The sample rifle has a quite crisp trigger pull, once a little creep is got by, its 3½ pounds seeming a bit lighter. Firing pin fall is short, about ¼″, and nicely dead—there's almost no vibration as it drops.

Iron sights consist of a bead front, on a graceful hooded ramp, and a folding leaf rear sight—elevation-only adjustable—that looks rather like a Lyman No. 6. The detachable single-column box magazine holds 5 rounds; the chamber can be single loaded, but not easily. The 24″ barrel is round and tapered, muzzle diameter .590″. Weight, without scope or mounts, is 7 pounds. This Anschütz Hornet isn't cheap, not at $298.50! For that reason, and because I hardly think there are really all that many guys anxious to buy a 22 Hornet, I don't suppose many of these will be sold. Damn inflation and cheap dollars. J.T.A.

Ken Steggles
Muzzle-Loading Accessories

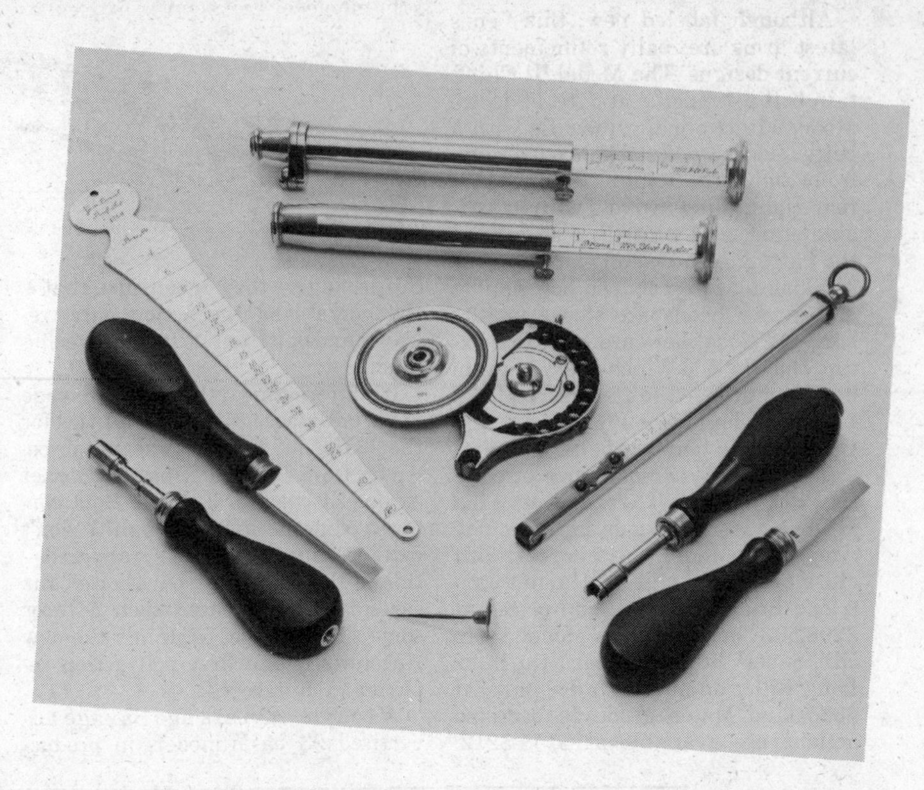

I saw the handmade pieces shown here at the NSGA show earlier this year, and they are beautiful—there's no ther word for their traditional styling, treatment and craftsmanship. Their detailing is so correct, so well done, that a master workman of the 1850s might have made them.

The materials used are traditional, too—brass in good part for many things, African Blackwood for nipple keys and turn screws (otherwise wrenches and screwdrivers), these latter with polished steel blades and shafts. Any of these accessories would grace a cased set of guns and be fully worthy of them. If the owner of such a set has an item missing—and can furnish details or a like tool, Mr. Steggles can copy it perfectly.

I was particularly impressed with the meticulous and period style lettering found on such accessories as the powder measures (the two at top in the photograph) and the bore gauge at left. All handsome stuff indeed, but beyond that serviceable and functional, too.

Inexpensive they're not—Mr. Steggles says he'll continue to make them by hand, a slow and non-productive way, but he couldn't maintain the quality otherwise. Good man!

Here are some representative prices, all postpaid to the U.S. The powder measures (one for drams and grains, the other for grains only) are $18.00 and $21.50 each. The round brass capper is $28.50, the bar capper $11.00. The nipple keys, each of which has a steel pricker (attached to a knurled brass head), are made to handle various cone sizes, and they're $17.00.

A handsewn best leather shot flask (not illus.) has a 2-gate all-brass dispenser, made to throw 1-1¼ or 1¼-1½ ounces, whichever is ordered. This top screws into the flask body—which holds 3½ pounds of shot—for easy filling. Price, about $45.00.

Write to Ken Steggles (77 Lower Eastern Green Lane, Coventry, CV5 7DT, England) for his brochure. J.T.A.

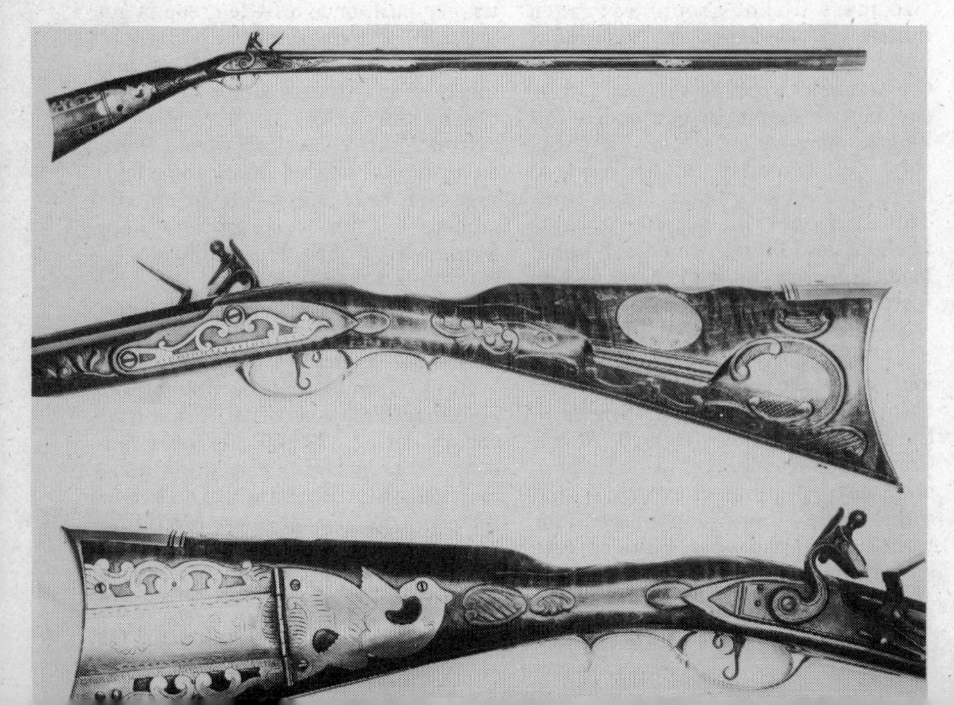

Wm. Bankard

Our picture shows a graceful and handsomely carved "Kentucky" rifle made by "Granny" Bankard, as he is better known. He makes complete rifles in flint or caplock, and also does excellent restorations or replicas. Bankard can furnish an early rifle, of 1750 type, with brass furniture, a single patchbox (sliding or side opening) and some incised carving for about $1,000. An elaborate "Golden Age" rifle of the 1800-1825 period could run to $5,000.

The rifle pictured here is an excellent example of Bankard's skills. He not only makes the entire rifle, but the tools used in creating the rifle as well.

Artistic Arms

It doesn't seem that long, but it was 2 years ago (p. 56, GD 27) that I pictured and described, at some length, the then new single shot rifle—a very close copy of the Sharps Borchardt, Model 1878—manufactured by Leland L. Metheny's company in Hoagland, Indiana.

That rifle had an early, semi-production version of the S-B action, the barrel 26" long and medium heavy, and the trigger a copy, as well, of the original S-B type. In spite of a heavy pull, the rifle, in 225 Winchester, shot well, giving about .75-MOA groups at 100 yards.

Recently—and too late for a shooting test, Mr. Metheny sent us another specimen (also in 225 caliber and perhaps the same barrel, I hope) of his Borchardt-actioned rifles. The latest one, however, shows some changes—there's a special Canjar trigger now, complete with its own safety, and the lever has been modified into one that follows the curve of the pistol grip, all the way to the end, and it's finished off with a round-section bar for easier grasping.

The new and adjustable trigger is very good. Letoff is 2¼ pounds and crisp—no creep and virtually no after travel. The checkered safety-thumbpiece sticks up a little above the top of the action wall, the safety lever below it a flat steel bar about ¼' wide. A recess in the right side of the breechblock and another one cut into the inside of the receiver wall provide room for the safety lever.

The stock and fore-end are of fiberglass, made by Brown Precision, and similar to those now found on a fair number of benchrest rifles—which stocks have been working very well. Fred Sinclair (1200 Ashbury Dr., New Haven, IN 46774) is a specialist in fitting these Brown stocks, and he did this one, including the finishing—which looks like automobile lacquer, the color a metallic brown! Still, handsome is . . . , I guess, and I'm sure this latest Artistic Arms rifle is going to shoot well. Cost of the rifle here, fiberglass stock included, is about $460. Barreled actions, I believe, run around $250, and walnut-stocked rifles will be available later, I'm told.

The Artistic Arms near-replica of the 1878 Sharps Borchardt action, barreled to 225 Winchester caliber, the stock one of Brown's fiberglass models.

Metal work isn't as good as it could be—all except the barrel is polished steel, but the polishing failed to remove various surface scratches and nicks in the exterior receiver walls. The bottom of the breechblock and its sides—as well as the top of the lever—show machining roughness and inadequate polishing.

The action screws are flat headed—with several screw slots chewed up—rather than the oval-head type usually found in firearms.

On the other hand, surfaces, corners and edges that would look better if left sharp and crisp, appear to have been too zealously—if not carelessly—polished and rounded off.

The left side wall of the action is stamped "ARTISTIC ARMS HOAGLAND IND" in two lines, the letters hit one at a time, I'd guess, each line looking a bit ragged.

I think a better place for this name stamping would be the bottom of the action, in front of the guard, using a one-piece stamp, professionally done, and made with smaller letters. Some of these actions are sure to be used by custom gunsmiths and some would be engraved—for an example, see our comments on Jay Frazier and his use of this A.A. action elsewhere in this issue. Try to imagine what an engraver might say on first seeing that bold stamping on the receiver!

The 1878 Sharps Borchardt was, in its better grades, a handsomely executed action, strong and reliable, a favorite with such famed riflesmiths as Schoyen and Zischang. Mr. Metheny's action, made with modern steels and a better technology, is just as sturdy—and it deserves to be as well turned out.

Artistic Arms' latest version of the 1878 Sharps Borchardt action, here in polished steel. A special Canjar trigger is installed, its safety arm seen at the side of the breechblock.

The new Artistic Arms rifle didn't shoot as well as the earlier one, both in 225 Winchester. Two 100-yard groups of 5 made 1½" and 2⅜", using fresh W-W 55-gr. PSP loads. I'd mounted a Unertl BV-20 scope, and conditions were nearly perfect, too.

The earlier rifle—with the *same* barrel—shot into well under an inch, though with handloads, but I found ignition erratic with the new rifle—in shooting the 10 shots I got 5 misfires. The primer indentation seems rather shallow, certainly, in those that didn't let go, but it could be the ammo, I suppose. There were no other lots on hand. J.T.A.

Hermans-Atlas Custom Guns

The Model 12 Winchester shown here was stocked by Bob Williams—coordinator and chief gunsmith for Hermans-Atlas—in a very attractive piece of Claro walnut. The checkering—which really doesn't show all that well—is cut to a fleur de lis pattern, 24 lines-per-inch.

Metal work at this Washington shop is by Dave Cook—he can furnish handmade guards, scope mounts, express sights, full- or quarter-rib barrels, etc.

All phases of custom gunsmithing are available, and it's Williams' job as well to see that the finished job is all that it should be. J.T.A.

Stock by Bob Williams

The product prices mentioned in these review pages were correct at presstime, but may be higher when you read this.

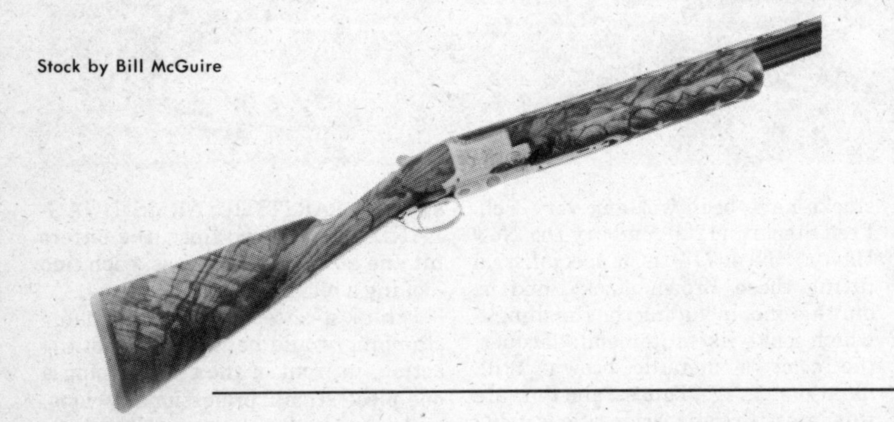

Stock by Bill McGuire

Bill McGuire, Inc.

As a strong admirer of McGuire's topnotch custom gun work—particularly his fine hand with shotguns—I'm glad to be able to show an example of his recent efforts, as I do here. Still, I'm afraid the photograph furnished us (among several others) won't do justice to the handsome job it really is—which I can see by the aid of a magnifying glass!

The photo shows an all-gauge Browning Superposed, the barrels here seen in 410. The stock is a terrific piece of European walnut, beautifully grained and full of colorful contrast. The checkering is a combination of intricately sculptured borders and fleur de lis design elements.

McGuire has a new address—10324 Valmay Ave. N.W., Seattle, WA 98177.

Above, from left—Squires Bingham M20D, seen with magazine removed, and the M15 chambered for the 22 WRM • At right—Squires Bingham M30 pump shotgun in 12 gauge, M14 rimfire rifle, and their M16—the latter uses the same barreled action as the M20, but with a 1-piece mahogany stock painted black, and aluminum carrying handle, front sight, and grip area to resemble the Colt AR-15 (M16).

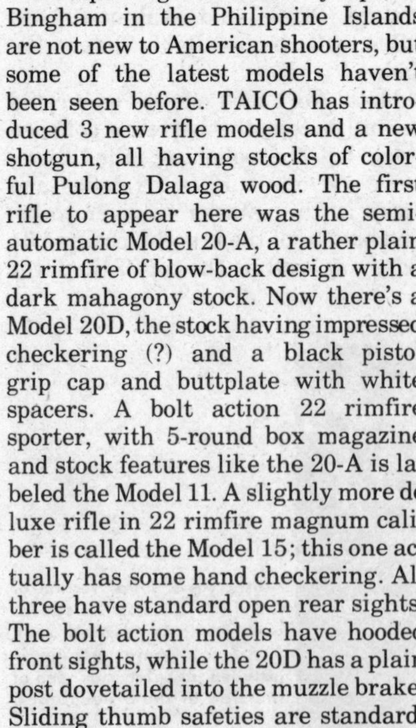

American Import

The sporting arms made by Squires Bingham in the Philippine Islands are not new to American shooters, but some of the latest models haven't been seen before. TAICO has introduced 3 new rifle models and a new shotgun, all having stocks of colorful Pulong Dalaga wood. The first rifle to appear here was the semiautomatic Model 20-A, a rather plain 22 rimfire of blow-back design with a dark mahagony stock. Now there's a Model 20D, the stock having impressed checkering (?) and a black pistol grip cap and buttplate with white spacers. A bolt action 22 rimfire sporter, with 5-round box magazine and stock features like the 20-A is labeled the Model 11. A slightly more de luxe rifle in 22 rimfire magnum caliber is called the Model 15; this one actually has some hand checkering. All three have standard open rear sights. The bolt action models have hooded front sights, while the 20D has a plain post dovetailed into the muzzle brake. Sliding thumb safeties are standard, and all 3 rifles have dovetailed receivers for low scope mounting. The fourth new arm is the M30—a 12-gauge pump shotgun chambered for the standard 2¾″ shell. L.S.S.

Smith & Wesson

Last year this Springfield firm added two shotguns to their line. The M1000 autoloader is available in 12 gauge with 26″, 28″ or 30″ ventilated rib barrel and a choice of chokes. It's gas-operated, looks similar to the Remington Model 1100, is priced at $229.95, and weighs just over 7 pounds with a 28″ barrel. Made in Japan to S&W specs, it has an alloy receiver with scroll etchings on the sides, and uses a pressure-compensating gas system to permit use of trap and field loads without adjustment. The second shotgun—the M916—is the result of taking the old Noble pump action model and upgrading it with the addition of a sliding tang safety, and other minor changes. The receiver is of chrome molybdenum steel, the stock and fore-end American walnut, as on the Model 1000. It is available in 12, 16, and 20 gauge, with choice of 26″, 28″ or 30″ barrel, plain or with ventilated rib, and improved, modified, or full choke. The 12 weighs, with 28″ plain barrel, 7⅜ pounds, the price $104.95. Adding a ventilated recoil pad ups the price $5 and, with a recoil pad and ventilated rib barrel, the tab goes to $125.95. The 1000 has hand checkering on the pistol grip and fore-end, the 916 is uncheckered, but does have a finger-grooved fore-end.

S&W has also added a 5-caliber rifle cartridge line—243, 270, 30-30, 30-06 and 308—in slim, see-through plastic "10-Pack" containers. Some additional handgun loadings are now on hand, and there is a new high-density polymer "Hunter's Pack" to hold 4 boxes of 12 gauge shotshells. They've had leather goods for several years, but now a line of 6 sportsman's knives—two for fishermen and 4 hunter models, including a couple with hollow handles to house matches, fish hooks, or other emergency items—has been added. Designed by Blackie Collins, and made of modified stainless steel, with Wessonwood or rosewood handles, the knives will be priced in line with corresponding quality brands. L.S.S.

F.I.E.

This Florida firm has handled a line of handguns, knives, and leather goods for a number of years, plus some long arms from time to time. Currently they offer 4 shotgun models, all products of Brazil. The two single shot models are made in 12, 20 or 410 bore, as is the side-by-side double, with 26″ and 28″ barrels. The over-under Model OUI2—is made only in 12 gauge, but in Skeet and field grades with 26″ or 28″ barrels also. The single shot guns average around 6 pounds, the double over 6½, and the O-U about 7¾ pounds. None of the guns examined were de luxe quality (one of the single shots was even rather crude), but they appear to be very serviceable arms that can withstand a lot of rough field use. L.S.S.

Shilen Rifles

Shilen barrels and action sleeves for benchrest shooters have been well and favorably known for several years, but now there is a complete Shilen rifle. Made in a classic field style or as a benchrest type, the rifle uses what is called a single shot Model DGA action. The new rifle has a solid top and bottom for maximum stiffness and bedding stability, a shrouded bolt head and enclosed speed-lock firing pin, 3-way adjustable trigger and slide safety. The DGA action is barreled with a stainless steel Shilen barrel chambered for the cartridge of your choice. Prices start at $475. The field model, which has a laminated walnut stock with high straight comb, full pistol grip, and wide pear-shaped beavertail fore-end, has been the most popular, but thumbhole styles are also available, as is a host of extras. L.S.S.

Navy Arms/Replica Arms

With the acquisition of Replica Arms last year, Val Forgett has one of the largest black powder and reproduction arms firms in the business. Almost everything—arms, accessories, et cetera—of any note is available, from a 1776 Brown Bess Musket to a Remington Rolling Block Buffalo rifle. Need a Model 1803 Harpers Ferry flintlock rifle, or a "One of One Thousand" M1873 engraved lever action in 44-40 caliber? Navy Arms has them. Just starting to arrive in early 1974 was a Rolling Block "Baby Carbine" with 20″ octagon barrel in 22 L.R., 357 Magnum or 44-40. Val said it would be available later in 22 Hornet. The Siamese 45-70 Mauser rifle mentioned last year is available in a carbine model with 18″ barrel and straight grip stock—mighty handy for buck or bear. The big rolling blocks, calibers 45-70 or 444 Marlin—have barrels of 18, 26, or 30″, as is the case with the Martini Target rifle. The Mauser, Rolling Block, and Martini actions are available separately, or as barreled actions, and "pre-straightened" barrels may be obtained in 45, 50 or 58 calibers. Besides the other accessories, there is also a line of beautiful engraved long arms and handguns, and a buck sent to the firm will get you a full color catalog showing all. L.S.S.

Ljutic

This firm has been building custom shotguns for a number of years. Al Ljutic started breaking claybird records back in the 1930s, and his wife Nadine is no slouch either—she *may* even be better than Al. At present prices on Ljutic shotguns range from $895 for the Dyn-A-Trap up to $3500 for the Bi Gun. Of the 5 models available, 3 are single shot models, one is an over-under (Bi Gun) and one is a 2-shot autoloader—the Bi-Matic. Only 12-gauge models are available, all over 8 pounds, and all feature solid steel receivers. Barrel lengths vary from 28 to 32 inches, depending on the model, with 33 inches being standard, and all sport a wide hollow-milled ventilated rib that extends onto the receiver. The single shot and over-under models have a push button opening mechanism on front of the trigger guard, while the Bi-Matic uses a one-piece actuating rod and one-piece bolt with conventional handle for retraction. The walnut stocks and fore-ends are oil finished, hand checkered, and built to the customer's specifications. The metal finish is a sand-blasted blue for non-glare, and workmanship on the shotguns examined was near perfection, with excellent wood-to-metal fit. Extra fancy wood, release triggers, extra barrels, etc., are available—at extra cost. L.S.S.

Iver Johnson

This old line firm has been bought by L. A. Distributors, with the Cattleman line of single action revolvers being distributed from Fitchburg now. The big news is an over-under shotgun, made in Italy to I.J. specs. Labeled the Silver Shadow, this shotgun is furnished only in 12 gauge with a single non-selective trigger, 28″ barrels choked modified and full, and a boxlock action. A ventilated rib and a semi-beavertail fore-end are standard. (Some of the first production had double triggers, and a U-shaped front handle.) Priced at $229.95, this import is probably competitive for the quality, but this writer would like to see I.J. bring out a double barrel of the quality of their "Skeeter" of many years ago. L.S.S.

Browning M78/SS Rifle

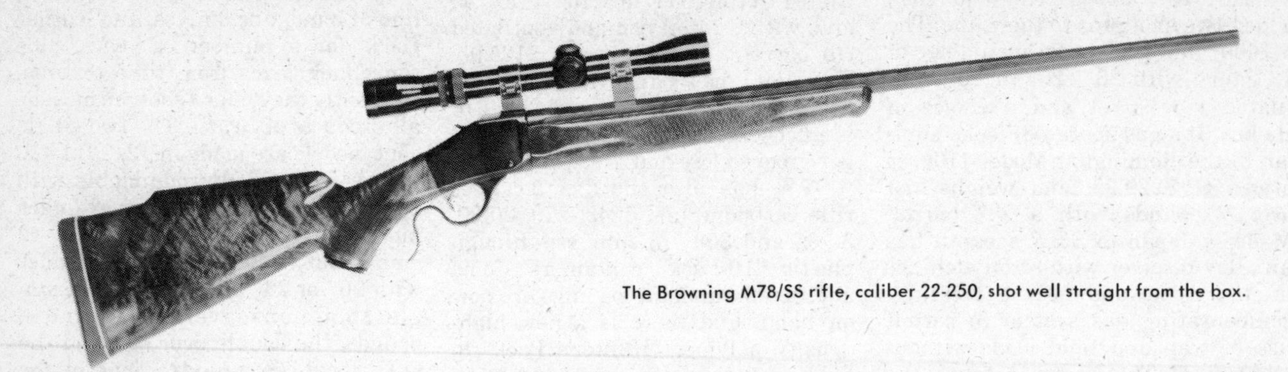

The Browning M78/SS rifle, caliber 22-250, shot well straight from the box.

My first test of the new Browning M78/SS rifle, cal. 22-250, was made on a good day. This attractive varminter, serial No. 705W37, carried a wide view 5x Browning scope with medium cross-hair in Browning mounts. The temperature was 70°, the sun bright, and there was almost no wind. Shooting was done over my 100-yd. Creedmoor Range, the time 2:00 to 4:00 P.M., Sept. 23, 1973.

The first ammo used was an old box of Norma 55-gr. semi-pointed soft points (Index 231, lot 0/727). The very first 5 rounds, *including the first shot* from the cold, clean- but slightly oily barrel, went into 3/4" (5 shots), with 4 in 7/16"! Now that is something quite unexpected, not to say gratifying, but was it a fluke, not to be duplicated? I'd soon find out.

The rifle has a very nice piece of fiddle-back walnut in the buttstock, all the way from action juncture to the butt. The rather shallow-curved pistol grip is checkered, and in a quite good amount. Diamonds, however, are rather flat, particularly at the 2-groove borders of the multi-point design. A black grip cap, with a white metal inset (which would initial well), is attached to the squared-off grip, without white spacers. A black rubber recoil pad, about ½" thick at the center, attaches via a white-line spacer. This rifle type plate is slightly curved for a good shoulder fit.

A Monte Carlo comb-cheekpiece is quite well done—the front of the cheekpiece flows slightly upward as it approaches the grip checkering, but does not enter the checkered area. The comb nose (both sides) is correctly fluted and not over large. The comb nose flows down at a graceful radius, the handhole picking up the same radius in reverse. The handhole—and the pistol grip—is long, the p.g. on a relatively shallow radius, a la shotguns. But because there is no tang at the top of the action, and only a short one (¾") at the bottom, a closely curling grip could easily be managed, as well as a reduced-length handhole.

The fore-end matches the color of the buttstock, but is without the fiddle-back grain. The checkering is in three panels (one on either side, and one underneath), each ending in points back and front. The quality is like that on the pistol grip. The fore-end tip is simple and plain, with a nicely rounded schnabel tip. Semi-beavertailed from side-to-side, it shows a straight-line profile. The fore-end sides are flatted at the rear, these faring into the action front gracefully.

The top of the action, at the rear, holds a fired-case deflection device. Coin-slotted, this may be rotated to throw cases left or right (wherein southpaws get a break), or it may be positioned to prevent the empties from being ejected. Handloaders will like that, lefties or not.

The M78 Action

The Browning M78 is, of course, a near-duplicate of the 1878-patented design sold to Winchester, and which was marketed by the New Haven firm for some 50 years. The new Browning looks like the "high wall" version, which Winchester made first and in a very wide range of calibers throughout its long life—not to mention dozens of models and grades. The M78 Browning is unlike the Winchester "low wall," a model form made later by Winchester.

Apart from all but eliminating the tangs just mentioned, Browning has modified the original 1878 design in other ways as well. The trigger is adjustable for pull weight by the owner, an Allen screw being furnished for rotating a screw set into the short lower tang. Minimum weight is given as 3½ pounds, maximum listed as around 4½. The white metal trigger on our sample rifle was adjusted to give about 3½ pounds. The trigger pull is not as crisp and clean as it might be; there's a soft take-up felt, this occuring after the initial free play, some 3/16" or so, is gone through. That preliminary, almost effortless movement is soon got used to, I found, but I'd like to see a crisp, 2-lb. trigger on this varmint rifle.

The Model 78's trigger is factory-adjusted for take-up, backlash and sear engagement. The adjusting screws (two) are factory sealed; the owners manual warns against moving these screws except by an authorized Browning Repair Station.

The action's extractor-ejection system works well. The extractor hook, lying at 6:00 o'clock, is rather wide, making for positive case removal. When the operating lever is fully open, the extractor hook lies well out of its recess; on pushing a loaded round into the chamber, the extractor stays in this outward position. Then, as the lever is closed, the extractor moves forward and *under* the case head, snapping into the extraction groove firmly.

M78 rifles are furnished with Redfield-type scope bases. The rear base mounts on the receiver ring, the front base to the barrel, center-to-center separation about 4½ inches. The M78 Owners Manual says that "The heavy target barrel is drilled and tapped to accept a longer mounting system for target scopes," but the regular-barrel M78 sent to us did not have these tapped holes. No metallic sights are furnished or available, as far as I can learn; because there is no top tang, a folding-style tang sight would hardly be feasible except by screwing a base to the wood—and that's not a satisfactory arrangement usually.

Low-profile sling-swivel bases, made by Pachmayr Gun Works, are let into the wood fore and aft. Sling swivels for use with these spring-loaded bases are available from Browning dealers, but none come with the rifle. Browning sent a pair to me a bit later, and they work well. They're easily removed or restored, and they're quite silent when in use.

The M78 barrel is exactly 26 inches long from the muzzle to the face of the breechblock, its diameter at the muzzle 0.693"; it measures 1.170" across at the receiver ring. Rifling is 6-groove, of normal style (so-called Enfield, for which read Metford), and with a rate of right-hand twist of one turn in 13½ inches! Yes, several trials gave me 13½", but I may be getting some slippage, of course, even though the fit of the patches (2) was quite tight. The muzzle is rather deeply recessed, a good idea for obviating damage. The bore feels nicely smooth and free of loose or tight spots, using a tight patch.

Because of the factory-attached 2-piece scope bases, I measured the stock dimensions from the line of bore. These are: ½" at the comb nose, ⅜" at the rear of the Monte Carlo comb, and ⅞" at the heel. It is 13⅜" from the trigger to the middle of the recoil pad, which is 5³⁄₁₆" deep and 1⅝" at its broadest.

About 1⅝" can be added to the drop figures above for the Browning scope and bases, thus practical figures become 2⅛"x2"x2½". Over-all length of the M78 Browning is 41¾ inches, a fairly compact figure for a 26" barreled rifle. With the 5x scope and its bases the M78 in 22-250 weighs 9 lbs. 3 ozs.

J.T.A.

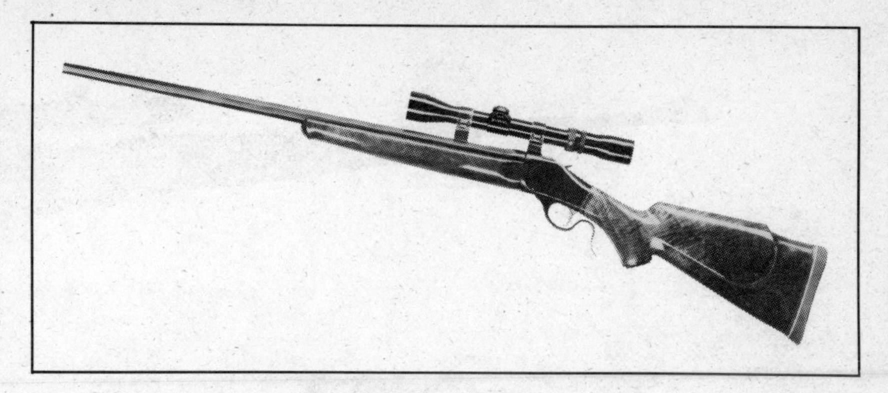

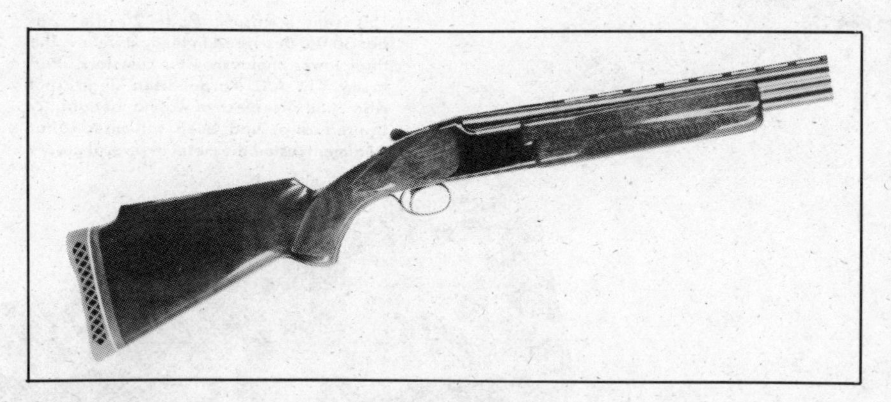

Above — Browning M78 Single Shot rifle. Below — The new Citori over-under by Browning, seen here in trap grade.

Browning

Last year the Browning-78 single shot rifle was introduced followed by the field grade Citori over-under shotgun in 12 gauge. Now 12 gauge Skeet and trap grade Citori models have been added at $335 and $330 respectively, plus a field grade Citori in 20 gauge at $325. The trap gun has 30" barrels, the Skeet gun 26" or 28" barrels, as does the Citori 20 gauge. The Citori 20 and 12 field guns are chambered for 3" shells.

The long awaited Browning 2000 gas-operated shotgun is now available. Only 12 gauge hunting models were ready in early 1974, but barrels can be switched to permit the use of standard 2¾" or 3" magnum shells. Magazine capacity is 5 rounds, and loading is through a port on the *left* side of the receiver—much like the old Browning Double Automatic. Barrels are available plain or with ventilated rib. The 2000 with 28" vent rib barrel lists at $289.50, or with the plain barrel model $20 less.

Other new Browning items for shooters include some additional shotshells, hearing protectors, sling swivels, and rimfire magnum cartridges, plus 3 new rifle scopes. In general, a pretty impressive array of quality items, and all shown in their 1974 catalog—send for it.

L.S.S.

Uncle Mike's Swivels

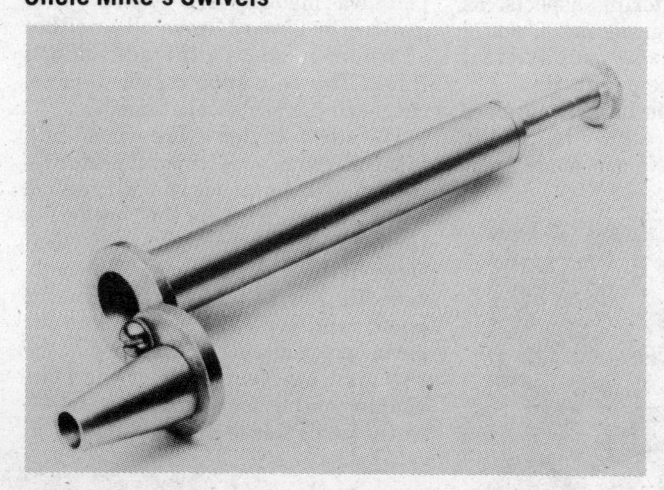

Michaels of Oregon offer this all-brass black powder measure, calibrated in grain increments and with a 120-gr. capacity. The non-spill pouring spout is a handy item. Cost, $8.95.

The QD115RGS quick detachable (and MP130WS non-detachable) swivels offered by Michaels of Oregon will fit the fore-end of virtually every bolt action rifle made. A special ½" wood screw now makes these popular swivels adaptable to fore-ends as thin as ⅝". Easily and quickly installed without taking down the gun, they'll withstand almost 500 pounds of pull without tearing loose from the wood. They're also usable on bolt action shotguns and others with non-sliding wooden fore-ends. Cost, $3.75. Want more dope on these and the many other Uncle Mike products for shooters, write to Michaels of Oregon, P.O. Box 13010, Portland, OR 97213.

This is the handsome Model 70 rifle, caliber 30-06, described in the text below. The three lower photos show the new stock fitted to my 416 A.C. Farquharson single shot rifle — the first piece of walnut, beautifully figured also, had been salt-cured. That treatment rusted the metal in several places.

The fore-end tip treatment of the 416 AC rifle — unusual and graceful.

Nelson's checkering on the 416 AC grip shows resemblance to British patterns.

Clayton Nelson

The rifle shown here is, in my opinion, the very essence of the classic form. I see no way that the stock can be faulted or the rifle as a whole criticised. I don't imply, of course, that variations and differing aspects, as practiced by other gunmakers, would suffer in comparison — such detail differences are to be expected.

The basis for this handsome piece is a Winchester pre-1964 Model 70, the caliber 30-06. Nelson made for it a new, flush-type floorplate and trigger guard, plus fitting his own custom scope bases, a sling swivel band on the barrel, and a new band-type ramp front sight. The checkered steel buttplate was made by Al Biesen, the steel grip cap by Lenard Brownell — neither of whom needs an introduction, I think. The bolt knob carries 3-panel checkering, very nicely done.

The stock, in dense French walnut, is checkered in a multi-point pattern — the fore-end diamonds run full around, and I particularly like the checkering layout for the pistol grip — that straight line at the rear. The comb-nose fluting is perfect. Last, if the photo reproduction permits, note the clean, crisp cutting of the wood below the loading-ejection port, and the shaping of the stock — and its height — in the bolt release area. J.T.A.

The 416 A.C. Farquharson rifle, stocked by Clayton Nelson in nicely figured walnut.

Steyr-Mannlichers from Law Enforcement Supplies

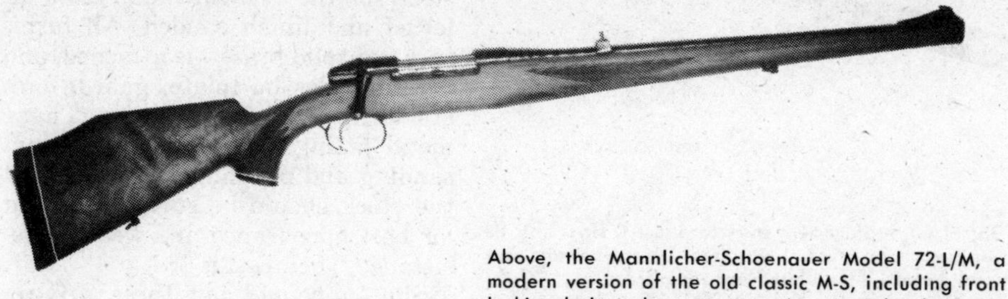

Above, the Mannlicher-Schoenauer Model 72-L/M, a modern version of the old classic M-S, including front locking bolt and rotary magazine. At right, the Steyr-Mannlicher Model S and, at far right, the Model L.

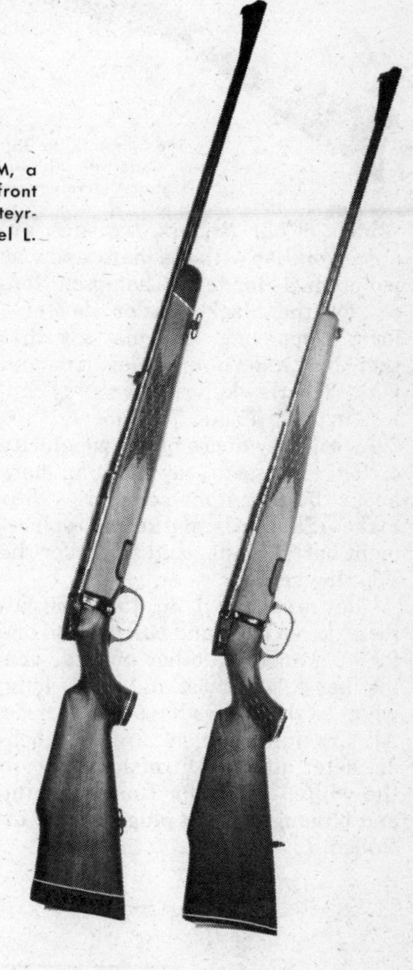

Austrian-made Steyr hunting and military arms have been around for over a century, and various models have been available for about a third of that time through Stoeger in New York. Now, an Illinois firm is handling distribution of the Steyr sporting rifles. That old favorite—the now-classic Mannlicher-Schonauer hunting carbine chambered for the 6.5mm M-S cartridge—is no more, having been discontinued in 1971, but two "improved" versions are available.

The Steyr-Mannlicher is made in 5 models—S, M, L, S/T, and SL, differing mainly in action length—and two target versions. Among the various models are chamberings for 27 different cartridges. Stock types include a modern sporter with Monte Carlo, and a full length (Mannlicher) type with skip-line checkering, fore-end tips on the sporter and, of course, swivels, pistol grip caps, etc. Using a bolt with 6 symetrically arranged locking lugs that seat behind the magazine, the bolt handle is now right above the trigger, which may be a double set or a standard single. The most obvious feature of this particular rifle is the detachable box magazine of Makrolon; coupled with the rather large trigger guard of the same material, it gives the rifle an unusual appearance.

The Mannlicher-Schonauer M-72 rifle—available in L/M, S, and S/T models—is a modern version of the old M-S complete with front locking bolt and rotary magazine. Stock styles are the same as the Steyr-Mannlicher, but the checkering is regular diamond form—not skip. The bolt handle is now behind the receiver bridge, instead of in front as on the old M-S, and the safety is a hooded type which rotates around the bolt sleeve. The M-72 is chambered only for 16 cartridges, but that's plenty as they range from the 22-250 to the 458 Win. Magnum. L.S.S.

Thompson/Center

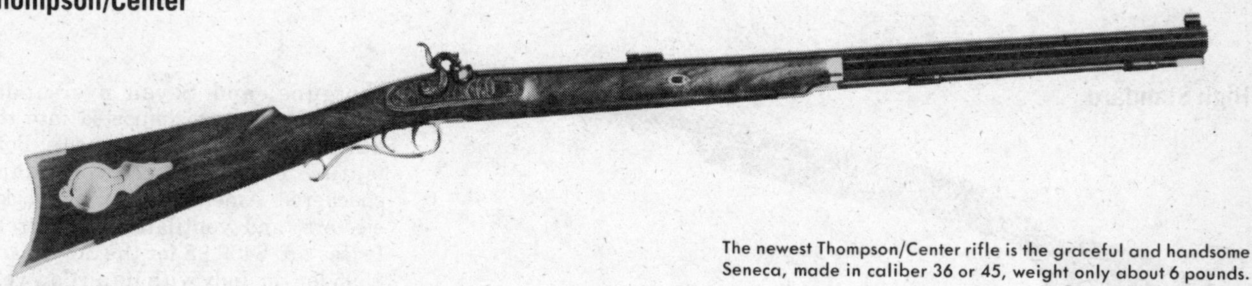

The newest Thompson/Center rifle is the graceful and handsome Seneca, made in caliber 36 or 45, weight only about 6 pounds.

This up-and-coming firm is best known for the Contender pistol, but almost every year sees a new arm added to the T/C line. The latest is the Seneca—a lightweight percussion muzzle-loading rifle in either 36 or 45 caliber. Weighing only 6 pounds, it has to be the trimmest rifle of its kind available today. Listing at $195, it comes with a 27" octagon barrel, color case-hardened lock, hooked breech, double set triggers, solid brass fittings, open sights with the rear adjustable for windage and elevation, and a fiberglass ramrod. The Seneca has the grace of a Kentucky, but with all the quality of its heavier big brother—the T/C Hawken. GD's editor named the new rifle, by the way.

Now, if T/C will just introduce a breech-loading single shot rifle similar to a prototype I saw a few years back. Oh yes, T/C now has a catalog—No. 1— listing all their products. The first catalog from T/C will probably become a collector's item. L.S.S.

Sharon Rifle Barrel Co.

The Sharon Rifle Barrel Co. replacement stock for the T/C Hawken rifle is made with a lower comb nose, thus permits use of lower front and rear sights. All furniture, solid brass, is included in the $54 price.

Most of our readers, I'm sure, are quite familiar with the many and varied products made by Thompson/Center for the black powder shooter—for the moment, let's just say that their best known and oldest long gun is the T/C Hawken rifle, a sturdy caplock made in 45 and 50 calibers.

As some evidence of the popularity of T/C rifles—to say nothing here about the numerous accessories they make—Sharon is marketing replacement barrel blanks and stocks for the T/C Hawken.

They are made in 36, 45 and 50 calibers, three for round ball use and one for 45 Minies or other bullets. This last has a 1-22 twist and is 28" long, whereas the others have 32" barrels. All are full octagon, are 15/16-inch-diameter, and are furnished only "in the white," ready for final polishing and blueing. Breech plugs are *not* included.

The 36-caliber barrels have 1-48 twist, the 45 and 50 calibers a turn in 72 inches. These 3 barrels are $34.50 each.

Two other Sharon barrels to fit the T/C are produced—one is a true cylinder 20-gauge half-octagon smoothbore barrel, 28" long, this one fully blued and ready to install. This 20-gauge barrel, by the way, is bored slightly oversize—0.620" instead of standard 0.615", so modern shotshell components—wads, plastic or not, et cetera—fit the bore well, an added convenience in loading for many.

The other and last barrel is 10" long, made with a 1-22 twist, and is 13/16-inch diameter. This is also a blank, in the white, and threaded for a breech plug, as are the other blanks. Sharon's standard threading is 5/8-18, but other sizes can be furnished. The shotgun barrel sells for $45, the pistol barrel, made for the T/C Contender frame, is $15.

Sharon also supplies a replacement stock for the T/C Hawken, 100% inletted and finish sanded. All furniture—of solid brass—is attached, and this includes buttplate, guard, forestock tip and escutcheons. These metal fittings do require some final sanding and polishing, however, and the stock should be surface finished for best appearance and weather resistance. Their cost is $54.

Sharon bought out these T/C replacement items to meet a demand for longer, slower-twist barrels, a lot of shooters apparently wanting to shoot round balls in them. Sharon also says that many shooters found the T/C Hawken stocks too high at the comb nose and the sights too high as well. The Sharon replacement stock, therefore, is lower at the comb nose, and will work best with lower sights fitted to the T/C barrel—and those are just the kind of sights seemingly wanted by this group.

Sharon makes their barrels with a slightly wide underlug, which means that the T/C stock has to be opened a bit to receive the Sharon barrel's underlug. The Sharon lugs are soldered to their barrels, which are made without transverse dovetails, and Sharon says this makes for a considerably stronger setup. The T/C barrels are dovetailed, their underlugs a little narrower. J.T.A.

High Standard

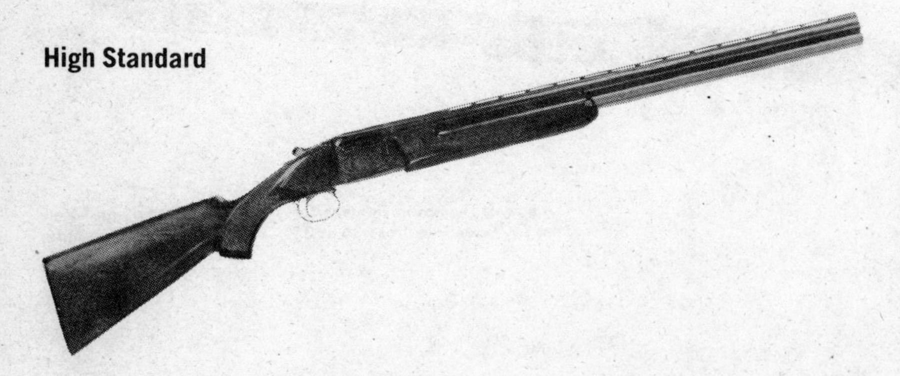

This firm is really forging ahead. There's a new steel framed Sentinel revolver in 22 Rimfire and magnum calibers, plus a new "Arms of the Confederacy" line of black powder revolvers, including the Griswold & Gunnison and Leech & Rigdon types, plus the Hopkins & Allen line of black powder rifles and shotguns. The finish—metal and wood—on the Supermatic autoloading shotguns has been improved still further to give these arms an almost custom appearance, and they now have a ventilated recoil pad, as do the Flite King pump shotguns.

Another welcome addition to the H-S line is the Shadow line of shotguns—Indy, Seven, and Automatic. The Shadow Indy (one of my favorite shotguns) and Seven over-under smoothbores were imported into the States a couple of years back. Both feature engraved receivers, hand checkered American walnut stocks, ejectors, and ventilated rib barrels. Prices are $499.95 for the Seven, and $595 for the Indy with its airflow ventilated rib. The Shadow automatic, at $264, is new to these shores, but it is going to make some other autos take notice. Available in 12 or 20 gauge, it is gas-operated, and features an octagonal bolt, a takedown barrel with the wide airflow ventilated rib common to the Indy O-U, and an American walnut stock and fore-end. Barrels range from a 26" Skeet to a 30" trap (28" Full for the 20 gauge), and the 20 gauge tubes accept 3" shells. The 12 gauge may also be had with a 3" chamber, but only in the 30" Full choke version. L.S.S.

Falling Block Works

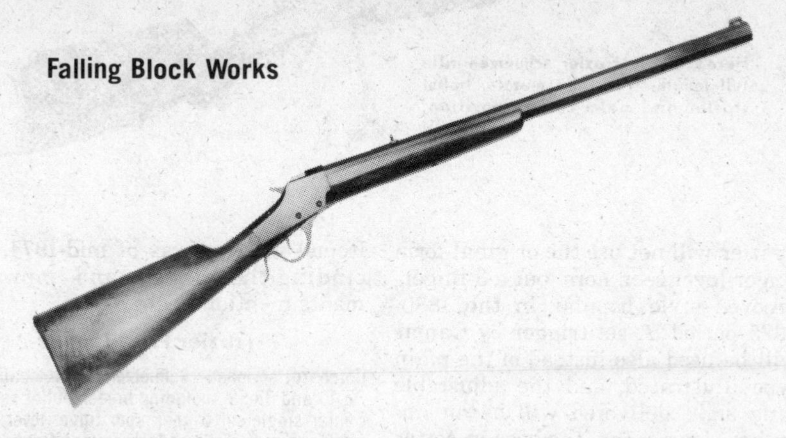

A then-new single shot action was pictured and described in our 28th edition (p.89). That well-machined Model H action, tangless and with an octagon-topped receiver section, has been joined by another falling block action—the one pictured here in both assembled and take-down state. This new action, called the Model J, differs from the earlier action in appearance—chiefly in profile—and treatment, yet both are the same, or nearly so, in internal design and ruggedness.

The Model J appears much like a Winchester High Wall action of the "thick wall" type generally (the action shown last year did not), and it functions like one as well—the vertically-dropping block has about the same dimensions as the old Winchester, as does the mortise, of course. The finger lever, sturdy and gracefully formed, is quite similar to the High Wall's lever in standard grade, and an improvement, I believe, over the lever on the earlier FBW action.

I was glad to see, also, that the action screws in the Model J are smaller-headed and of traditional type—those 3 big flat-head screws used in the Model H looked out of place, too obtrusive.

I was also pleased to see an octagon top used, a nice nostalgic touch, but I like, too, the lack of tangs top and bottom—a strong through bolt is used, and furnished. This design will easily permit pistol grip stocks to be closely curled, if desired; that couldn't be done with the 1879-85 Winchester unless the lower tang was bent considerably. The pistol grips on factory High Walls were long, shallowly-radiused treatments, something like a shotgun grip.

The FBW action differs inside, too—the breechblock face carries a round bushing, the small-diameter firing pin a snug fit in it. A shotgun type twin-pin spanner is required to remove the bushing. The trigger/sear engagement is direct, with a weight-of-pull adjusting screw at the back of the hammer, and accessible without taking the action down.

Dropping the lever lowers the breechblock—the top of which is radiused to form a loading tray, in effect. On raising the lever, the centrally-hung hammer is brought to half-cock, not full—a good safety factor in the design.

I'm impressed by the dimensioning, to close tolerances, of this strong action—there is virtually no movement of the breechblock in its mortise in any direction, and the lever is without play in any position. All machining is crisp and sharp-edged, the walls and other planes smooth and flat. Polishing and finishing has been well done—all metal except the bright breechblock is blued to a soft, low-luster sheen, highly attractive. Each action is factory proof tested.

The new action weighs 2 pounds, not including the through bolt. The action thickness is 1.366", its length 4.578". Thickness of the walls in the mortise cut is .165"; behind the block, at the top, it is .285", but at .640" down from the top, the wall increases to .516". The receiver is V-threaded 14 TPI, designed to take a barrel shank .990" long and of 1.000" diameter. The thick wall Winchester's average dimensions are .850" and .925" respectively, cut for a 16 TPI V-thread. Obviously the FBW action accepts a shank longer and thicker.

This action thickness is the same as the Winchester High Wall had in its thick wall version, whereas the latter had an average wall thickness, behind the block, of .190", a bit larger there than the Model J FBW action shows.

The FBW action, designed to take calibers from 22 Hornet to 45-70 head size, is furnished with a "blank" extractor, hence the gunsmith will need to form it for the caliber selected. Only rimmed cartridges can be accommodated by the standard extractor, but doubtless a good gunsmith could adapt it for rimless or belted brass.

The breechblock is 1.000" wide, depth front to rear is .750", and the front face is beveled back, the bevel starting about .235" below the top. There could be, therefore, some camming action imparted to a sticky cartridge, but, at a guess, not very much. This cut is a flat bevel, too, its bottom edge sharply defined.

Retail cost of the FBW Model J action is $120, and there's a dealer price available also. The Model H action will continue, its price $99. J.T.A.

The Falling Block Works Model J action, taken down. Apart from the receiver, only 15 parts are used, including screws (2), pins (3) and coil springs (2). A simple, sturdy action, excellently finished and held to close tolerances.

Jay Frazier—Schuetzen Rifles

Here's the J. Frazier schuetzen rifle full length, with false muzzle, bullet starter and palm rest in position.

This young man is, I'm glad to report, another gunmaker dedicated to building custom rifles of the best quality, rifles that display excellent craftsmanship and a high degree of professional competence in design and construction.

Frazier's main efforts, however, are devoted to making rifles in a style that was highly popular some 75 or more years ago—the schuetzen rifle, made in the style of Pope, Schoyen, Zischang and a relative handful of others in that long ago period, and made then also by Ballard and Stevens, Winchester and Remington.

Frazier can, of course, make custom rifles in the modern fashion, bolt action sporters in classic style, and he does, but the rather heavy rifle pictured here is the type he prefers to make—and shoot!

Made with the traditional deeper-bellied buttstock and high comb, the wood in this pilot version is a fancy-figured piece of black walnut. The checkering on the well-shaped pistol grip and schnabel-tipped fore-end is hand cut in a multi-point pattern. The comb-height is just right for me with the Vernier folding tang sight and windgauge front globe fitted.

The action used is the modern replica of the Model 1878 Sharps-Borchardt made by Artistic Arms, Inc., in Hoagland, IN 46745. However, Frazier will not use the original-form finger lever seen here, but a 3-finger-grooved style popular in the 1880-1925 period. A set trigger by Canjar will be used also instead of the plain type illustrated, and the adjustable tang sight delivered will be an improved, longer one, the base in better keeping with the rest of the rifle.

Barrels—in 32-40 and 38-55 calibers only for now—will be 30/32 inches long and round full length or half-octagon optionally. False muzzles—the bullet-seating device once called the "patent muzzle"—will be a standard option, with a piston-type bullet starter furnished, of course. The adjustable palm rest is a standard fitting as well.

As a one-time and enthusiastic shooter of schuetzen rifles, I find this Frazier counterpart a well made, handsome and functional effort. Regrettably, I found no time to shoot it—I couldn't keep it long enough, and deadlines wouldn't have permitted a report anyway—but it *looks* like it should perform well.

Here is what the rifle (and optional items) will cost, as of mid-1974, including the changes and improvements mentioned above:

Frazier Price List

Borchardt-actioned Schuetzen Rifle, calibers 32-40 and 38-55, including breech bullet seater, Canjar single set trigger, spur finger lever, Vernier tang rear sight and windgauge front, palm rest and Helm type buttplate. American or French walnut will be used in the buttstock and fore-end, both well checkered.
Weight, 12¼-13 lbs........................$750.00
Selected Walnut (U.S. or French) stock and fore-end from................................ 40.00
False Muzzle and Bullet Starter, add...... 30.00
Matching wood receiver panels, a la special Sharps-Borchardts 30.00
Spirit Level (for front sight)................ 15.00

Borchardt-actioned Creedmoor-styled rifle, caliber 45/3¼" (or shorter chambers). Pistol grip stock in classic or traditional "long range rifle" form, checkered at grip and fore-end. Base for back-position sight at stock heel, and skeletonized steel butt-plate, inside area checkered. Same sights as Schuetzen rifle.....$750.00

Even at the figures quoted the time and material it has to take to hand make this kind of rifle—and in the high quality easily evident in our sample—I can't see Jay Frazier getting rich.

J.T.A.

Dale Goens-Jack Prudhomme

At very long last it looks like that silver mounted rifle I've had in the works for some years (like 10) will soon be finished.

Jack Prudhomme has been in poor health for a long time, which accounts for about all of the delay, but he recently completed the floorplate and trigger guard—the only metal that hadn't been engraved—and Goens has all of the pieces now.

Jack did a handsome job on these elements—the deer is crisply cut and lifelike, the bordering floriation flows well, and the initialing on the guard is imaginative, the background recessed and darkly shaded. Gold is inlaid all around the floorplate borders, but it won't be revealed, really, until the blueing is done.

Dale Goens will reshape the FN bolt and its knob to a more graceful form, and he'll also alter the safety lever, perhaps putting a silver head on it.

J.T.A

Champlin Firearms

Being in Enid, Oklahoma, last fall for the Big Grand National Quail Hunt, I snatched a few hours out of an otherwise tight schedule to visit the Champlin shop. As a long-time admirer of Champlin rifles—and the precise way they're put together—I'd wanted to get a first-hand look. I called George Caswell, who manages the Champlin operation, and invited myself over.

I wasn't a bit disappointed—the spacious showroom was filled with fine rifles and shotguns, too, for Champlin is now the U.S. importer-distributor for the famed Merkel shotguns.

I next spent some time in the metalsmithing room, where at the moment Mike Desbian was working on a full octagon barrel. He was fitting a set of the folding-leaf rear sights that are made in the Champlin shop.

My next stop was the big, airy upstairs room, the wood shop, where Maurice Ottmar was hard at work on two stocks. No, not at the same time! But like other craftsmen I've known, Maurice spelled himself now and then by leaving the inletting job and doing something else, like checkering.

He's a meticulous and critical woodworker, it was easy to see—he had the barreled action in and out of the block several times as I watched, carefully scraping away tiny shavings of wood to get the bedding just right. Ottmar's checkering was just as skilful, too—I looked with a good glass at a recessed job he'd completed and it was perfect. Not a bobble or runover anywhere.

I wish I had enough space to tell you more about other pieces I saw, and to show more of the photos Hal Swiggett made for me, but I'm running out of time, too.

The handsome double rifle pictured here, caliber 458 only so far, will be available soon, perhaps as you read this.

Made in West Germany exclusively for Champlin Firearms—and designed by Champlin to suit the needs and taste of American sportsmen, this 10½-pound double has an Anson & Deely type action—double underlugs and a Kersten-type crossbolt. Two triggers (the front one hinged) are standard, and the tang safety is *non*-automatic, as it should be. Auto ejectors are also standard.

The 24-inch barrels are of best quality Böhler steel. The fixed, single-leaf rear sight is on at 100 yards, and scope mounting via the quarter-rib will be offered later on.

The receiver shows excellent engraving, and so well-jointed are the dummy or false back plates that the line between them and the action can hardly be seen.

The stocking is in French walnut, straight-grained for strength but of good contrast.

Price as shown, $3500; without the dummy plates, about $3200.

Champlin sales of Merkel shotguns are growing fast—Merkel has agreed to supply over a 400% increase in models for 1975-76. J.T.A.

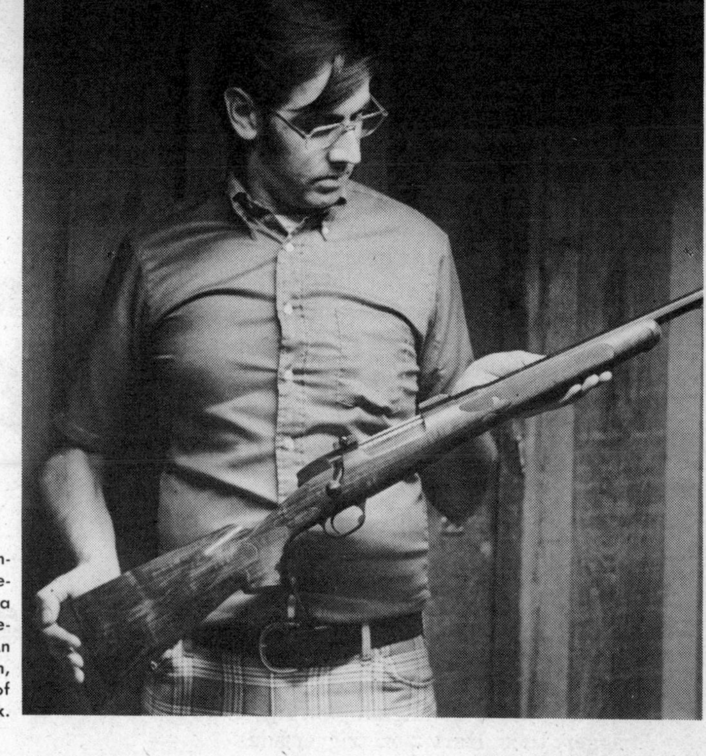

George Caswell, manager of Champlin Firearms gunshop, holds a heavy-caliber rifle recently completed. An elegantly simple design, worthy of a place of honor in any gun rack.

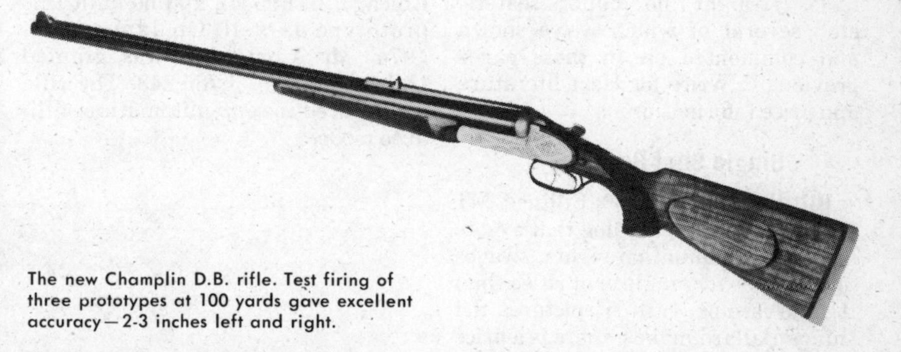

The new Champlin D.B. rifle. Test firing of three prototypes at 100 yards gave excellent accuracy—2-3 inches left and right.

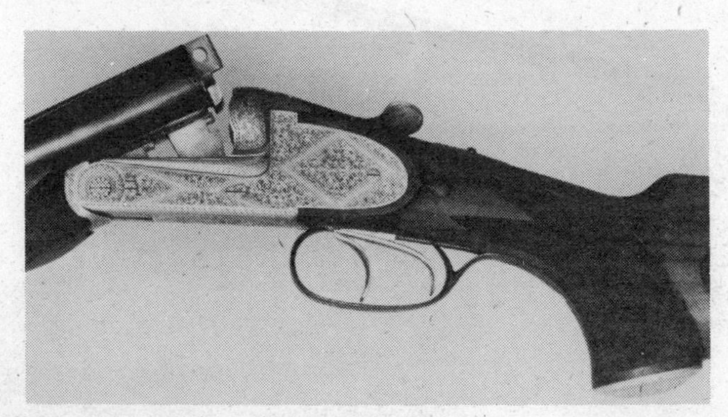

The Champlin double rifle shows tasteful engraving. Note domed grip, also engraved.

Checkering at Champlin's is also done by stockmaker Maurice Ottmar, here working on a multipoint pattern, and excellent work it is.

Robert W. Hart & Son (401 Montgomery St., Nescopeck, PA 18635) is a name to conjure with among bench shooters—and lots of them do. Their rifles have won many matches for many shooters, and here is what Bob Hart did last year, using the rifle we illustrate—he entered ten 100-200 yard Heavy Varmint matches and won the grand aggregate in 6 of them, his MOA figures running from .3105 to .4125. In a 200-300 yard BR Championship match, he won with .4890!

The rifle pictured goes 13½ lbs., has a heavy 22" barrel, and the action is the new Hart Model 1-A, in single shot form with a sleeve extension big enough inside (1.300") to let a 1.250" barrel breech be fitted. The scope shown is a Lyman 20xBR, receiver mounted. The No. 1A action sells for $230 with a Remington 40XB trigger; their Hart 2-oz. trigger adds $45 to the price. Write for quotes on complete rifles. Other and lighter actions, intended for Light Varmint and Sporter class matches, are offered as well.

The Harts make benchrest items, too—bullet spinners, neck-turning tools, straight-line bullet seaters, etc., several of which we've shown and commented on in these pages previously. Write for Hart literature and price information.

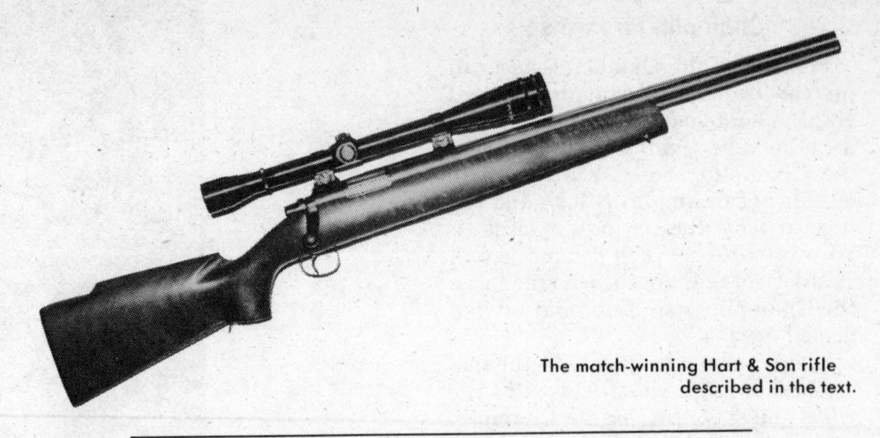

The match-winning Hart & Son rifle described in the text.

Single Shot Rifle Tools

Bill Ballard (Box 656, Billings, MT 59103) has a new catalog that's more of a small manual on sights, swages and moulds for single shot rifles than it is a catalog. Still, it pictures the things Ballard makes, there is a price list, and it holds interesting advice. 25c, plus a 10c stamped envelope with your name and address on it. J.T.A.

Thomas F. White

Best known, perhaps, for his superbly done powder horns, White is also a builder of Kentucky rifles that anyone would be proud to own. As our illustrations show, White's rifles are handsome pieces—graceful yet sturdy, and excellent examples of traditional styling and treatment.

The rifle butt shown, the wood a reddish-brown tiger-striped maple with raised carving, carries furniture and inlays of brass, silver and ivory. This grade is $750; similar rifles, with raised carving but not as richly inlaid, are $550, and those with incised carving are $450.

White also supplies hunting bags and other products for muzzleloaders. J.T.A.

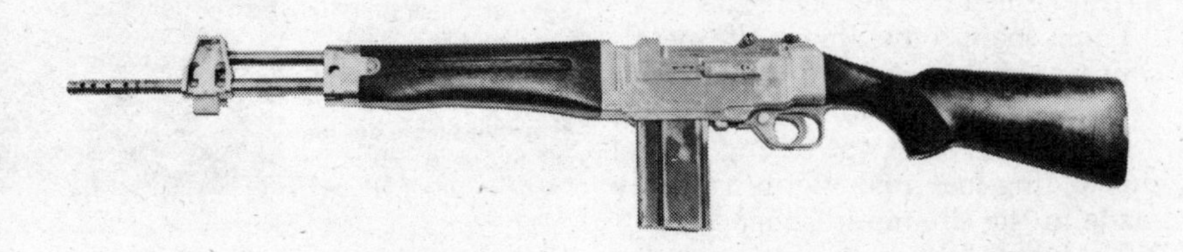

Christakos Assault Rifle

The new gas-operated military-styled combat rifle shown here, caliber 223, is the invention of Nicolas C. Christakos (of 2832 N. Austin Ave., Chicago, IL 60634), and he built this prototype as well. On January 15, 1974, Mr. Christakos was granted U.S. patent No. 3,785,243. The rifle can be fired in semi-automatic or full-auto mode.

The rifle strips down and re-assembles quickly into essentially two component groups, and maintenance-repair is said to be simple and readily done. Lockup is via a vertically-rising block, and in the specimen examined the various parts appeared rugged and well machined.

Mr. Christakos is, I understand, desirous of finding someone interested in manufacturing the Sparta Dog, as he has named his invention. J.T.A.

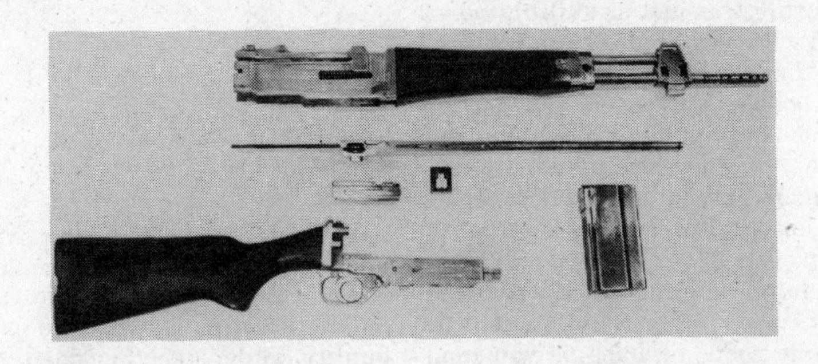

Jerry Fisher, Stockmaker

Fisher is all that the title implies, too—he makes some of the finest rifle stocks in the land, which is to say in the world nowadays. Until the advent of World War II—and perhaps for a while after its end—British rifle stocks and rifles were excellent in virtually all respects. Not so today—I've looked over nominally top class sporting rifles in London several times in recent years and, with too few exceptions, they weren't nearly as well done, as clean of line and grace, as our better U.S. stockmakers produce.

The rifle shown here is one of a closely-matched pair, these made for S.M. McCollum who, as it happened, supplied the exhibition grade French walnut used by Fisher for the handsome stock treatment. The checkering is 26-line in a fleur-de-lis pattern, the fore-end tip is ebony, and the custom metal work was done by Tom Burgess, with exceptions to be noted.

Fisher fitted his own-make skeletonized steel buttplate and new grip—of which more later—and did as well the soft matte rust blueing and engine turning or damascening.

Fisher's new grip cap is also illustrated, in this case showing the excellent engraving of Robert Swartley. The engraving seen is about $40 extra, the price of the unadorned cap being $14.95. Fisher machines these well-formed grip caps from solid steel, and I'm afraid you'd have to have one in your hand to really appreciate its excellence.

J.T.A.

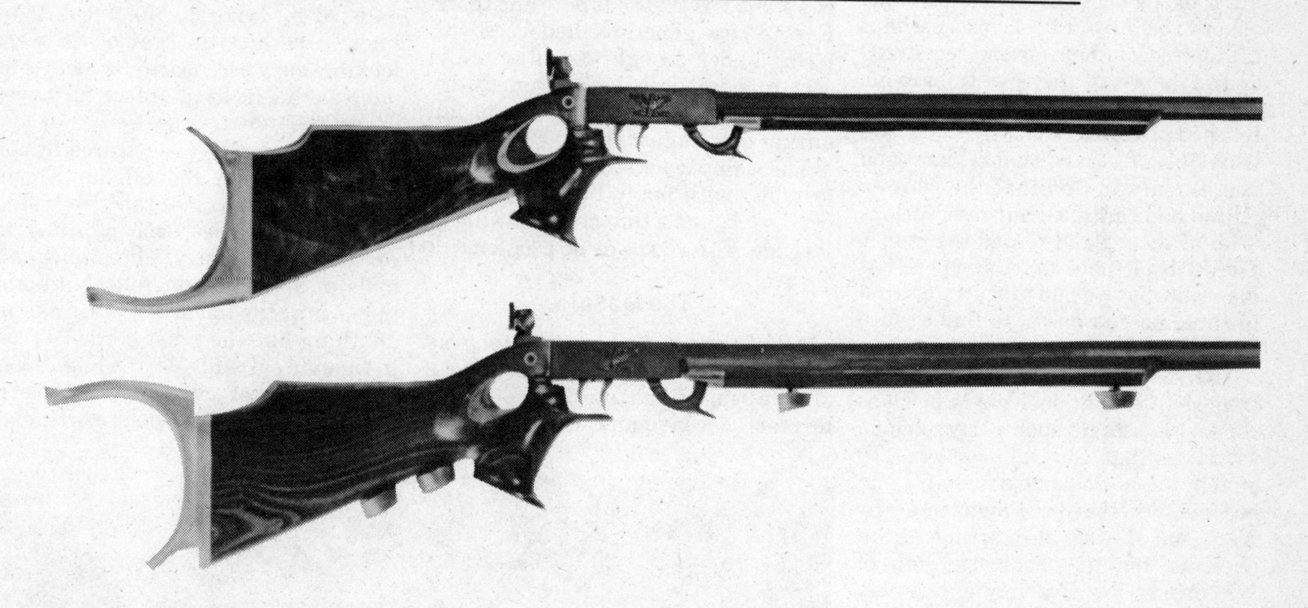

Clark K. Frazier (RFD 1, Rawson, OH 45881) builds muzzle-loading competition rifles that are decidedly different—as the photo shows, there's little traditional about their design. They're meant to shoot—and they do. These Matchmate rifles, as Frazier calls them, have won the National Championship and the Crosley Cup three times each, these big prizes among many lesser wins.

Here's how Frazier describes the Matchmate offhand rifle: Underhammer action, double set triggers, thumb-hole stock with adjustable hook buttplate, Douglas premium barrels in several diameters, lengths (26″ to 38″) and calibers—32, 36, 40, 45, 50 or 54. These specs hit only the highlights—Frazier's catalog tells all. Such rifles start at $600. His bench rifles are essentially the same, but have heavier barrels and the underside of the buttstock is made with a "duckfoot" or flattened section for resting on the bench. Same price range as above.

Atkinson Gun Co.

Bill Atkinson has a new Price List ready. Full details are given on his barrel making, rifle and shotgun, reboring and re-rifling, etc. Atkinson actually makes the barrels he supplies, as he does the very broad range of chembering reamers in his stock. He makes barrels in calibers from 17 to 50, with almost all other diameters between, and he can cut twists as tight on a turn in 5½ inches!

J.T.A.

Kenya, France and Italy

Stalking a rhino had its exciting moments, but all came out well at the end. Our European editor and I next spent an enjoyable and instructive week visiting the great Laporte works and viewing some remarkably handsome guns in Brescia, thanks to the signore Gamba and Abbiatico.

by JOHN T. AMBER

Nairobi

We reached the Kenya capitol airport—some 75 of us—at about 2:00 A.M., nearly 5 hours late out of Munich. Most of the customs people and the police had gone to bed. I suppose it could be called "orderly" chaos, but it took a hectic and frenetic couple of hours before our firearms—perhaps a hundred of them—were registered and on their way to a local strongroom. The worst was yet to come—we reached Nairobi about 4:30 A.M., traveling in taxis, safari cars and busses, only to find that the Nairobi Hilton had cancelled our reservations—all of them—and rented the rooms! They'd been paid for, too, our KLM man said, but we had to scurry around town, almost at dawn, to find a place to sleep.

The African First Shotters had arranged this hunt in Kenya, perhaps the largest single such party to go on safari in that country's history. To enable me to do some shooting I had become, necessarily, a member of the AFS, but I was also acting as an observer for the Compass Club of Wisconsin—for a variety of business reasons that needn't be gone into here. In the big group were a number of women—some of whom hunted—and men who would view the sights and take pictures. The rest, 34 of us, went off into various parts of Kenya, some of the camps quite remote from Nairobi and each other.

I hadn't hunted in Kenya before, though my first safari in Africa—many years ago—had been in neighboring Tanganyika, as it was then called. I hadn't been among the Masai people much on that long-ago trip, but this time we would be.

Our camp was a few miles beyond a small town called Narok, some 120 air kilometers west by north from Nairobi and beyond the Rift wall—we were, in fact, in the Rift Valley, our elevation about 7500 feet. A rolling, often hilly area, much of it vast and rather barren plains, but with numerous scrub forest stands here and there. East Africa generally had been suffering under drought conditions, and certainly our area was extremely dry and dusty—nor did any rain fall during our August stay.

The camp was spacious and comfortable, with many big trees on the perimeter, and a thin creek flowing at its edge. Firewood was no problem.

The Masai

All of the territory we hunted was Masai country. Wherever we drove—and we usually had to go 30 or 40 miles to reach decent game land—we saw the Masai and their cows and donkeys. Some herds were small, a dozen or so head, but many others numbered in the hundreds.

I greatly enjoyed the chance to see and visit with these people. They're warm and friendly, invariably good natured and, at least seemingly, pleased to see a strange face.

Men and women are usually tall and lithe, often handsome in their way, and they are tough and sturdy—as well they must be to survive. They've been described as dirty and shiftless, of course, but such charges are ill founded. True, they are often covered with dust—and flies—but how could they be otherwise? Water is scarce, even at the best of times, and their *manyattas* or walled villages are built in open country for protection of their herds against animals and marauders—cattle stealing by other tribes still occurs. I admire their attitude toward the flies—they can't do a damn thing about them, so they accept them! They don't have the money to buy protective products, besides which they're often scores of miles from any source of supply.

The Masai, naturally, are great trackers—their help was frequently enlisted by Mike or Mohamed. They knew whether the game we were looking for were nearby or not, thus often saving us long, unfruitful drives or walks.

Game generally was scarce in our section—59A on the official Kenya Hunting Map. As I've said, we had to travel many miles each morning to reach better country. The plains animals were fairly numerous, but nothing as large as in earlier years, nor in anything like the great herds I'd seen in Uganda or Zambia in the late 1960s. Mike said that even lions had been found a year or two before within a

KIFALU!

My rhino, front horn about 19 inches. That's Mohamed Nawaz, 475 No. 2 Jeffrey double in hand, and his trackers. The Masai at right had found the small band of rhinos the morning of the first day.

few hundred yards of our camp. None of us, I think, ever saw one during our hunt in the Narok area, and only one elephant was seen and successfully pursued.

Four hunters were assigned to each camp, generally, with one professional hunter for two people. There had been some difficulty finding enough professionals, understandably. Though a nominal 21-day safari, our actual hunting days numbered about a dozen on average, what with the usual time out for travel and assorted delays.

The two PHs in our camp were Kenyan-born Pakistanis, Mohamed Nawaz and Mike Khan—Mike was the good guy. In my camp, too, was old friend Pat Snook, another observer and a photographer for Compass Club. Pat, though nominally a non-hunter, was going to use my licenses for whatever game offered, apart from a rhino. I held a rhino ticket, as did some few others, and I'd decided that old *kifalu* was all I wanted to shoot.

The African First Shotters, formed several years ago, now has some scores of members, I believe. The principles and tenets of the AFS are high. Each member signs a solemn pledge to observe sportsmanlike rules of conduct in the field; to obey the legally-promulgated rules and regulations covering hunters and hunting wherever they are in force; to hunt wisely, observe the spirit of conservation and, to make that first shot count—that's where the group's name comes in, if you were wondering.

I haven't cited their code verbatim, of course, but that's the gist of it, I think. If I have space I'll print the code here, or pertinent parts of it.

The AFS Kenya hunt was a quite special affair—each hunter was permitted to take lion, leopard, buffalo and elephant, plus the usual plains game. As I've said, I had a rhino on my license, the only one in camp.

In our camp was a young AFS hunter I'll call Glint. He and Mohamed were soon quite thick. Glint suggested I hunt a rhino first—I'd turned down his repeated bid to buy the ticket from me—so that he'd be able to get going after a lion.

The morning of the first full day of hunting Mohamed told us that a Masai had visited camp the night before, reporting that a lion had taken a cow off. We drove around the country for a couple of hours, trying to find the cow, said Mohamed, but we saw no trace of her. Then Mohamed had Glint shoot a wildebeest for bait, which he and Glint alone dragged somewhere—the rest of us weren't invited to attend! Thus began Glint's lion hunting—each morning, for about 10 days, he and Mohamed were up about 4, going off to find a lion. Unhappily, no lion was seen or taken.

I'm tempted to tell here in detail about the several violations of Kenya game rules I saw or heard about—the baiting I've mentioned for lions and the killing of animals for bait, both forbidden in Kenya; the shooting of several impala by one man, his hopes high that the last would be a better one; the unwise and bad shooting, from the safari car, into a biggish herd of Grant's gazelles, the result a dead female, and one that didn't go onto his ticket. Only one impala went on that list, of course. There was also much shooting from the vehicle, aided and, in fact, ordered by Mohamed in several instances. All illegal, of course.

I'm not a foe of baiting where it's allowed, as it is, perhaps oddly, in Kenya for leopards. I know that it will be hard to get a shot at a lion unless he is baited, and I've baited for lion and leopard in other African countries where it was permitted.

I'm not setting myself up as a paragon of the virtues, but I do believe that all of us should gladly obey the rules of hunting, wherever we are. We already have enough thoughtless, scofflaw hunters among us, tainting us all. We can't afford that.

Rhino

Two Masai had located a small band of rhinos, 7 of them. We—Mohamed, his trackers and I—had reached an area of trees, thick brush and thornbush about 8 in the morning, meeting the Masai there. The rhinos, we were told, had moved off. The brush—not grass—was about 5 feet high on average, and the Masai hadn't, in fact, seen the rhinos. Mohamed, talking to them in pidgen Masai and Swahili, learned that one or two were bulls, probably, so off we went.

That was a long, hard day—we walked for miles up and down one hill after another, never coming close

Pat Snook's Cape buffalo, shot with the 458 Winchester, has a good spread—the horns measure about 43 inches.

Pat Snook shot this impala late in the day, using my Ruger 7x57 and Nosler-bulleted handloads. One of our professional hunters (left) is Pakistani Mohamed Nawaz.

This friendly boy, a Masai herdsman, came to our safari car one morning. The beer can he's holding will go in his other ear!

Our other professional hunter was Mike Khan—the good guy!

The Masai men are almost always warm and friendly. Some of their women are not. This tall girl, aloof and unsmiling, was not amused.

Downing old M'bogo calls for a celebration—the camp crew chair Pat Snook.

enough to the group for a shot, nor ever seeing any of them. The Masai said they were moving along at a fair rate, but we had to proceed cautiously, of course. I wondered then, as I did later, just how I was going to shoot—the thick, high brush gave near-perfect concealment for the rhinos. We quit at or near darkness, making our way back to the safari car for the long haul to camp.

Next day, up earlier because our meeting with the Masai would be farther away, we left camp before first light. The Masai, we were glad to learn, had not lost the rhinos. One man had remained with the bunch, trailing after them and waiting for us to catch up. This second day was much like the first, but worse because our walking started earlier! Late in the afternoon we came up to the beasts, though we had yet to see one. At this point the terrain was a little more favorable, too. The brush was still thick and high, as it had been all along, but we were able to get together on a small rise, letting us see better and maybe, be in a better spot for shooting.

There were six of us now—Mohamed, his three trackers, one Masai (the other had left) and I. Before us lay an open patch of brush, perhaps a hundred yards to the trees on its far border. Behind us, as we huddled together whispering, were a few slender trees. The Masai had climbed one of these, but he'd been able to get only a few feet above us. He was pointing to places in the brush where he could see movement. Standing on tiptoe I could see some motion, too, but how would I be able to shoot under these conditions, I asked myself again.

Suddenly the brush all but exploded, the sound of heavy hoofbeats and snorting loud and close. Mohamed and I sprang away from the trees, trying to find shooting room, his 475 No.2 Jeffrey double at the ready, as was my own rifle, a 458 Winchester 70 with a Weaver 1.5-4x scope. The Masai tried to climb higher—and did—and the trackers ran off a few yards and stopped. It had not been a charge, however—the trackers learned in a moment that two of the rhinos had left the others. Those two had probably smelled us, but the remaining 5 had not spooked.

An hour later, still on their trail, Mohamed and I stood on either side of a big tree, again on a small knoll. The Masai had climbed the tree, this time getting about 6 feet or so over our heads. Before us was a small clearing, the high brush beginning about 15 yards away. In the brush, as before, were two or three rhinos. Standing on this slight rise we could see the brush tops move here and there, our eyes directed by the Masai's gestures.

Once more we were startled into action. The Masai grunted hoarsely to catch our attention and, as we looked up at him, he pointed directly behind him! Standing there, broadside to us, stood a rhino bull, some 20 yards away, only his upper body and head visible above the brush. Mohamed and I whirled about, raised our rifles and shot at the same instant. The rhino ran off, disappearing, but after a 20-minute or so wait, while we smoked and talked, we followed his trail. We found him about 75 yards off, quite dead.

Our dual shots had entered the lung-heart area, Mohamed's bullet some 6 inches from mine, both on about the same level. I tried to have the bullets found, but though neither had exited they weren't located. But it was getting late and we had a long walk back to the Toyota.

I'd asked Mohamed not to shoot, but he insisted he had to. He cited a Kenyan law that requires the pro hunter to fire with the client on dangerous game, and he pointed out that the conditions under which we'd killed the rhino were unusually difficult and dangerous. Mike Khan told me later that Mohamed's chief tracker and gunbearer had protested to Mohamed that I shouldn't have been taken into such country for rhino!

My rhino's front horn measured about 19 inches. I heard later that three other rhinos were got, onc of them said to run some 24 inches. I was lucky, and when my shot came I'd have gladly settled for one with a shorter horn—a cow or a calf could have appeared in that small opening.

France and Italy

After the hunting in Kenya was over, the African First Shotters group left Nairobi for Amsterdam, the last Continental stop before flying to New York. I left the party at that Dutch city, for I'd made plans to join Raymond Caranta, our European editor, for a visit to the Laporte operation at Antibes and from there to Brescia, where I had appointments with several gunmakers.

I've told about seeing the Laporte plant and their various claybird machines at another place in this edition, so I'll only add here that the factory as we saw it in late August was in some disarray! Because of a big increase in sales, more room was needed—we saw walls being torn down, concrete being poured to add more floor space, yet production went right on, too.

The drive to Brescia was through lovely country—rolling, forested hills, the day bright and clear. Arriving there in the early evening, we were met by Renato Gamba and guided to our hotel—and "guided" is the right word. The center of the ancient town is a maze of winding, curving streets, many of them hardly wide enough for a car. To make it worse, many streets are marked "One Way," with a lot of lost motion entailed in getting around.

For Renato Gamba—who was to be our kind and generous host for the next three days—finding his way was no problem at all. He was born in the area.

Still, I shuddered now and then as Signore Gamba tooled his BMW 3.0—a relatively big car—at a really rapid rate through those narrow byways. I thought he was going to scrape the walls on several occasions, but he didn't.

Our stay in Brescia was greatly enjoyed and rewarding. Renato—we were soon on a first-name basis—took us all over, including drives into the countryside, a visit to the famed Lake Garda and the resort area around it, and stops for lunches at places that must have rated three stars or better. Between times, of course, we visited gunmakers' shops and factories. Renato was untiring in his efforts on our behalf.

Renato Gamba's new place was our first such call. Formerly a member of the Fratelli Gamba firm, Renato had left his brothers to go on his own. Though his chief line consists of first quality side-by-side double guns, naturally, Gamba also makes a single barrel and over-under shotguns, and a recent starter is a combination rifle-shotgun in superposed-barrel form. This last I was particularly taken with—I'm fond of the type, and I'm trying to talk myself into buying one.

Gamba's Ambassador double guns are beautiful examples of the gunmakers art—made in several grades, these sidelock guns come with stock dimensions and borings to the customer's order, and matched pairs are also available. The Ambassador Extra, top gun of the line, is handsomely engraved and it's stocked in fancy-figure burl or briar walnuts. See our photo of this one.

Renato Gamba also offers—in cooperation with Aldo Uberti—of whom more later—a very full line of replica firearms. These embrace everything, literally—lever action 1866 and 1873 Winchester copies; cap and ball revolvers in a dozen models, including cased sets; Kentucky-styled pistols and rifles; single action cartridge revolvers, and a mixed bag of others—Remington and Sharps derringers, Remington rolling-block pistols, et al.

Renato and I got our heads together on a replica rifle that I've felt should have been made long since. This cartridge rifle—which should be ready in a year or so—will surely have, in my opinion, great appeal. I cannot, regretfully, say anymore at the moment.

I've mentioned Aldo Uberti. This gentleman has recently built one of the most modern and spacious gun factories in Italy—or anywhere else, for that matter. Caranta and I well-spent several interesting hours at this new plant, watching dozens of operations on Uberti's very full line of replica firearms—the types I've listed above, and which numerous models are, in good part, the full line imported by Val Forgett of Navy Arms and Service Armament. The 1875 Remington Single Action revolver is one of Uberti's products, a handgun I've always liked—I have two originals in my collection, one the 1875 form, the other the 1890 version.

I asked Signore Uberti to send one of these to me, via Navy Arms to avoid shipping/license problems, but months went by and no Remington 1875. Then, really unexpectedly, at the second running of the Outstanding Handgunner of the Year ceremonies—at which I again had the pleasure being master of ceremonies—Val Forgett gave me the long-delayed 1875 revolver. I made no complaint about the time lag, though, not after I'd seen the gun! Signore Uberti had prepared a presentation-marked piece, fully and beautifully engraved, with an inscription to me cut into the backstrap. This highly attractive 1875 is pictured nearby and, need it be said, I'm delighted to have it.

Another charming gentleman we met in Brescia was Mario Abbiatico, an old friend of Renato's and the owner-manager-guiding genius of Armi Famars—an interesting and unusual guy, operating a decidedly different gunmaking shop and producing—if ever so slowly—truly magnificent shotguns that, I believe, have no close parallels anywhere.

I wrote about Armi Famars in our 28th edition (pp. 76, 77), commenting particularly on their outside hammer double guns, but also noting that they make as well a select line of conventional double guns. At the time of that writing I hadn't seen any of these shotguns in the flesh. I'd looked over a number of photographs, of course, but even so I wasn't prepared for what I saw in Brescia—the workmanship on Armi Famars guns is superb in every area of construction—fitting of

A new model in the Renato Gamba Armi line is this single-barreled rifle in break-open form, the Mustang. Made in true sidelock design, it is styled about like its German *Kipplaut* counterpart, even to the scope mounting and the double set triggers • The Mustang's action bottom and guard continue the excellent engraving theme found on the sides.

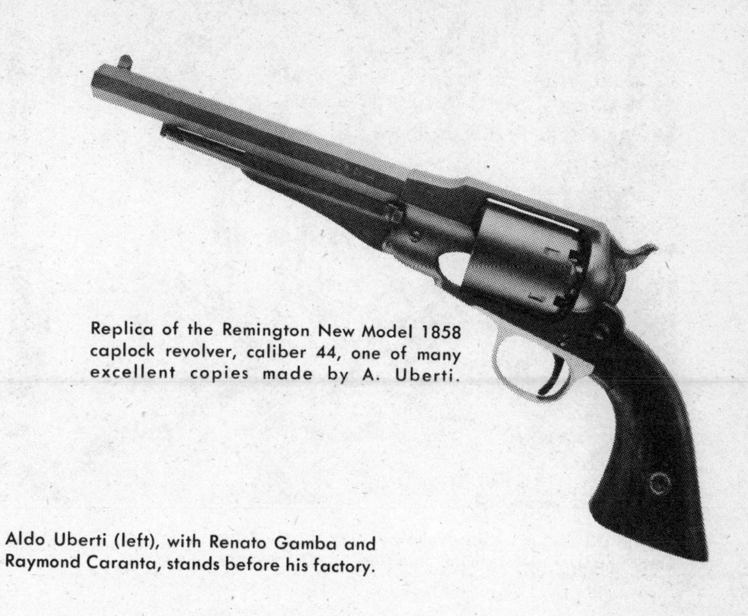

Replica of the Remington New Model 1858 caplock revolver, caliber 44, one of many excellent copies made by A. Uberti.

Aldo Uberti (left), with Renato Gamba and Raymond Caranta, stands before his factory.

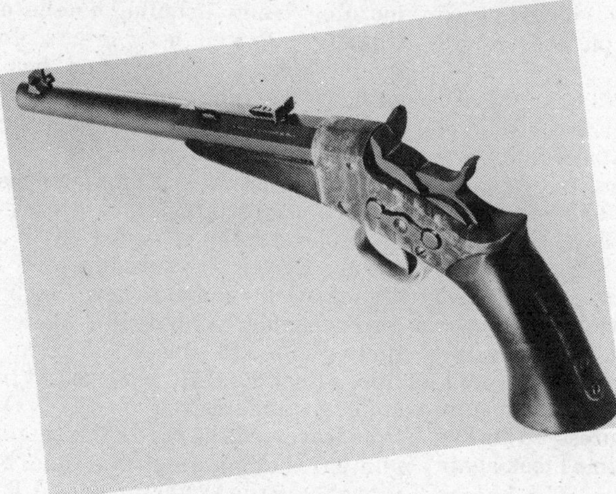

This Remington rolling block pistol is one of many replicas made by Alberto Uberti.

Aldo Uberti's recently built factory is spacious and well lighted—a modern arms plant in every way.

This is the presentation engraved and inscribed replica of an 1875 Remington revolver made for John Amber.

Renato Gamba, in his Brescian showroom, demonstrates one of his over-unders to our man from Aix-en-Provence.

wood to metal, brilliant polishing and frictionless joining of metal parts, flawless tuning and timing of triggers, sears and ejectors. Nothing, apparently, escapes Mario's supercritical eye. As one might well expect—and in keeping with a superb mechanical treatment—these Armi Famars doubles handle and point to perfection. The gun's weight is felt to be well within the hands, and their straight-stock, gracefully-flowing lines rival the best London guns.

I don't know just how I'll pay the $2,000 or so price, but I was so impressed by the sheer magnificence of the Castore 270—Armi Famar's best quality outside hammer gun—that I ordered one, stocked to my dimensions and with (I do hope) a really nice piece of walnut. I told Mario it had better be, otherwise it wouldn't make a good photograph! Well have to wait until next year for the picture, though—the gun isn't ready.

Then, a few weeks ago, Mario Abbiatico sent me a sheaf of photographs showing his Model 700 shotgun given extra special treatment. I haven't had the gun to handle, but as the illustrations show, the intricate wealth of deep relief chiseling almost defies description. This breathtaking artistry is, of course, highly reminiscent of mid-17th century Brescian gunmaking at its finest. The gun is profuse with grotesque masques and other figures—so far I've counted 34, but everytime I look again I seem to find another. The human figures are modeled after two (of four) statues in Florence by Michelangelo—the young woman representing dawn, the old man the end of the day. The bottom of the action shows two delicately carved angels playing trumpets, below them a pair of masques in profile.

Too rich, perhaps in more ways than one for some tastes—Mario mentioned no cost—but all in all, a superb example of the engraver's art, a tour de force in steel.

Caranta and I made the long haul to his home in Aix-en-Provence in good time, driving the Autostrade and the Routes National generally, and passing through the French Alps—an enjoyable ride. Besides being an avid shooter and collector of modern handguns, Raymond is also a Dixieland jazz fan of long standing—as am I. He has hundreds of records—originals and reproductions—so he and I stayed up until the early morning hours listening to the old times greats and near greats. Too, for a Frenchman, Raymond has a good cellar, one including Scotch and gin—I showed his wife how to make a dry Martini.

Among Caranta's accumulated mail was, for me certainly, a big surprise. A 4-color brochure issued by Winchester-Europe—a subsidiary W-W organization—showed a new Winchester over-under double rifle! Made in limited numbers—maybe 25 a year—this caliber 9.3x74R is offered in two states—standard and de luxe. Our front cover shows the better-quality gun, price unknown at this time, but probably in the $2500 range. J.T.A.

This is the Ambassador Extra Lusso by Renato Gamba Armi, a Holland & Holland type detachable sidelock double that's fully engraved—it is beautifully built and balanced.

Armi Famars and Mario Abbiatico

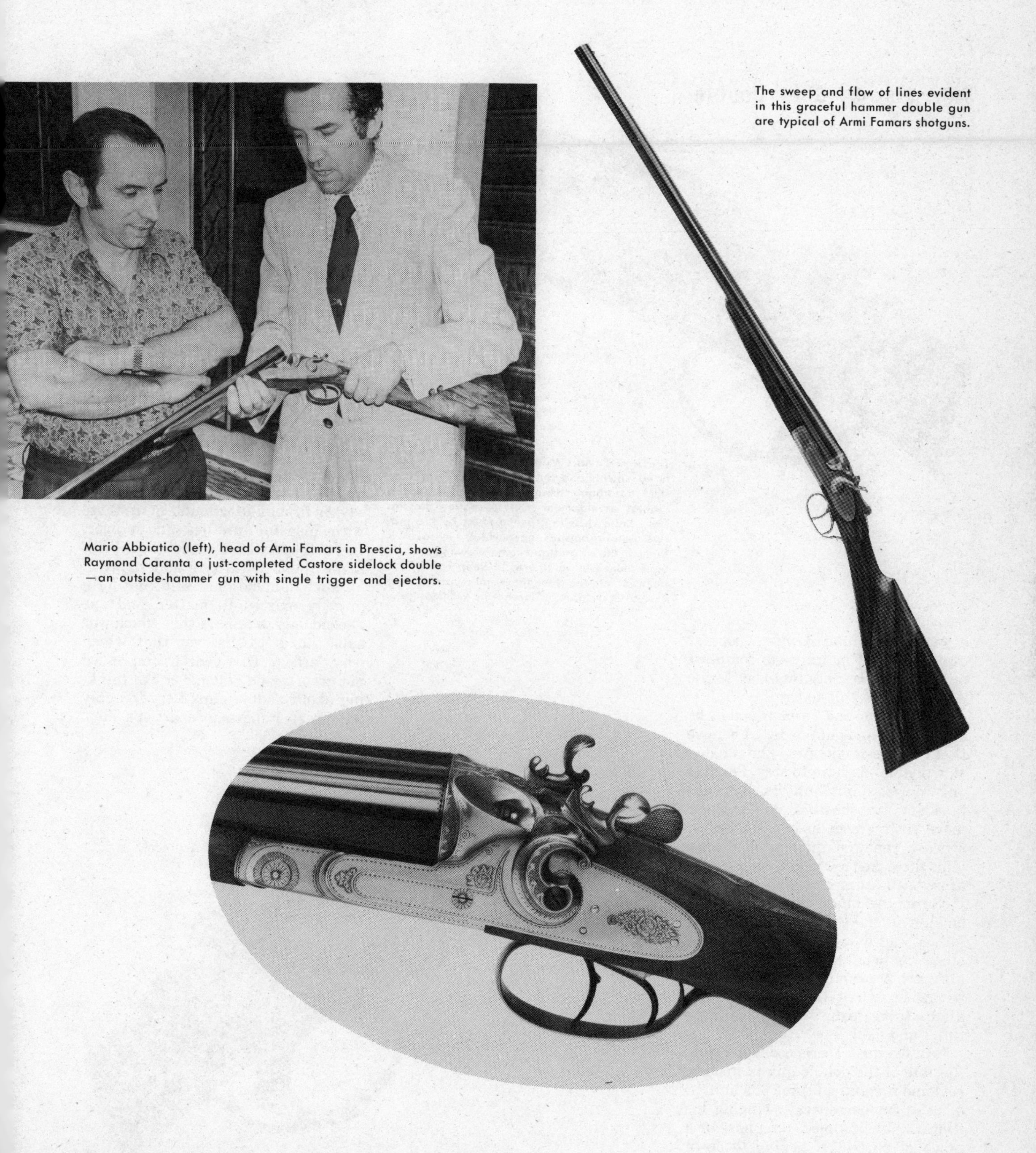

Mario Abbiatico (left), head of Armi Famars in Brescia, shows Raymond Caranta a just-completed Castore sidelock double —an outside-hammer gun with single trigger and ejectors.

The sweep and flow of lines evident in this graceful hammer double gun are typical of Armi Famars shotguns.

Another Armi Famars hammer double, the engraving done with restraint. Note the boldly-chiseled hammer tops and the treatment given the fences.

The Side-by-Side Double

The Armi Famars Model 700 double gun (pictured on this and the next page) illustrates a style of baroque carving in steel that reached its highest development in 17th century Brescia. The ornate chiseling, exemplified by the profuse use of grotesque, gargoyle-like masques, is found in this magnificent Famars fowling piece—three dozen or so figures in deep relief have been cut into the steel, the major creations modeled after a statue in Florence by Michelangelo.

Asked by *Diana Armi*—a popular gun magazine in Italy—to comment on the trends in shotguns today, Mario Abbiatico had this to say:

"In spite of the inroads made by over-unders and autoloaders, I believe that the classic shotgun—the side-by-side double—is here to stay. Perhaps only purist quail hunters, live bird fans and trapshooters, will buy the more costly models, but I seem to sense a renewed interest in double guns these past few years, even among those with lesser income.

"Sure, the other types shoot well enough (I make over-unders myself, in fact), but to me they're illegitimate offspring, to put it politely. Now that's a highly personal opinion, of course, but when we Italians feel strongly about something, we say what we think and feel!

"My feelings, I suppose, stem from the role of the double gun in history, real and romantic. I think of a hunter, afoot or on horseback, swinging his flintlock fowling piece on a hare or a brace of partridge, hoping to down something for the pot. It's different today. Italy on opening day looks like a vast army, well armed, has invaded the country!

"In my opinion the big differences favoring the double gun over other types are in the handling, the mounting of the gun, the smoother and softer feel, as it were. Other guns, to me at least, seem clumsy and artificial. I'm prejudiced, I daresay—my point of view has developed from long association with double guns, both in my work and afield, but, as I've said, I see a shifting in preference nowadays to the double. I hope that's true!

"I've been commenting here, may I say, on first quality double guns, those with pleasing profiles and proportions, those whose esthetic qualities make them distinctive and striking.

"Michelangelo once said that form already existed in matter, and one needed only to remove that which was superfluous to discover that which was perfect. This concept impressed me greatly and, whenever I'm thinking about double guns I try to apply the great Renaissance artist's idea.

A shorebird scene, delicately cut, on a regular Armi Famars side-by-side double, plus scroll work and other design elements.

"Now imagine a fine gun in front of you, held suspended in air by invisible hands and seen from the side—its finely figured stock inclined slightly below the line of the barrels.

"Note the elegant line of the straight English stock, the action and forearm blending and flowing gracefully into the barrels.

"The ideal is reached when no part of the gun interrupts this line; the eye is never disturbed by any detail and the profile in its entirety is beautiful to behold.

"I realize that for some I've fallen into poetic description, but when one sees a great painting, a beautiful woman or a gorgeous sunset, why can't something of the same feeling be experienced when viewing the art and beauty present in a fine double gun?

"I'm thinking of the emotion felt when we open a fine leather gun case and find inside a beautiful matched pair of double guns. Those who understand will know what I mean; those who don't, well...

At left and above—the top tang and bottom of the double gun shown on the preceding page, with more grotesque masques carved into steel.

A more conventional Armi Famars side-by-side double gun—apart from the lion-motif top snap lever—made in the Holland & Holland form, the lockplates quickly detachable.

"So far we've observed the side-by-side gun from a distance. Looking closer we see such important elements as the proportion and curve of the trigger guard, trigger and top lever; the curves and countercurves of the action, the profiles of the forearm and stock and how they're fitted to the metal to make a single perfect union.

"We see also the purity of certain lines along the sides of the action, the perfect inletting of the sideplates into the wood, and the exquisite impact of an old silver finish or the various shades of color hardening, called in Italy *tartarugata*.

"At this point I'd like to mention my special preference for the outside hammer gun, always a side-by-side to be sure, but with a special personality all its own. This construction offers the gunmaker particularly broad scope for his interpretive imagination.

"Last, but just as important as other considerations, are the finishing touches accorded the gun—engraving and the selection of attractively figured walnut wood for the stock. This writer has a weakness for both.

"Please understand that expensive or elaborate engraving is not needed for a satisfying effect. The important thing is that the engraving, be it a large amount or small, must be done in good taste and appropriate for the space available. The engraving, of course, shouldn't smother the gun; rather it should let the gun express a balanced personality. For example, fine border engraving coupled with tiny rose scroll gives a pleasing effect when contrasted with the unadorned metal polished to a mirror finish.

"Wood is extremely important; a beautifully-figured piece of walnut with a wide range of tone values—*chiaroscuro*, if you will—is like...well, a fine quality Parmesan cheese sprinkled over pasta!

"Maybe I've been talking about that "perfect" side-by-side—the one that exists only in my mind, or perhaps the next one to be built. It will, naturally, be up to us gunmakers to build it and it must be soon. Best quality work is becoming more difficult to obtain as each day passes. There are fewer gifted hands nowadays, hands that have been burned in the fever for production—and the waste that results from such hurry."

The Famars sidelocks shown here, beautifully engraved, are from a double gun being made for an American customer. The set will comprise 4 such guns—in different gauges—each one depicting an important event in the War of 1776. The plate at top is titled "The Death of Gen. Mercer," the other reads, "The Battle of Bunker's Hill." Both derive from paintings of the same name ● The underside of an Armi Famars double gun, magnificently engraved in a blending of several schools of design. The figure of Diana, bow in hand and her dog alongside, is like a painting in steel.

All Laporte trap equipment is so rugged as to be, perhaps, overstrong. Is that bad? This is the Model 75, seen here with optional tripod and its seat. The semi-circular unit (arrow) permits instant choice of various angles—lateral and vertical—that can be repeated accurately. A series of irregular cuts control and define the angles and target area.

This latest version (below) of the Laporte Multitrap—the 2000-TR-10—uses 4 motors for highest versatility, with independently controllable vertical and lateral angling.

The 2-speed, spring steel Laporte handtrap.

Laporte Traps

I described and pictured some of these excellent French-made machines at some length in our 28th edition (pp.88-89), but though I'd seen a fair sampling of their numerous models, I hadn't watched the big multi-bird types in operation. I'm referring here to the Laporte Multitrap 2000—an auto-angling, highly versatile tool that holds up to 400 clay targets—and to their Skeet trap, its capacity a staggering 1000 birds!

In September of last year Raymond Caranta (our European editor) and I visited the Laporte works at Antibe, and saw the big machines in operation. This was no special demonstration for our benefit, either, for each of their big traps is fully tested before leaving the factory. I was surprised to see scores of clay targets being thrown as the final inspection and adjustments were made.

If I sounded impressed in my comments last year with the heavy-duty, rugged materials used by Laporte, I'm just as enthusiastic over the performance aspects I saw at Antibe. There were few "no birds" indeed as we watched, but when one did occur the Multitrap 2000 went right on functioning with no hesitation.

The low incidence of broken clays is more surprising because their M2000 machine was throwing birds in the European mode—a lot faster and farther than our targets are tossed—when we saw the testing. The trap's mainspring, by the way, is adjustable almost instantly; by pushing a toggle switch to alter spring tension so varying target velocities can be attained. Would you believe this—because clay birds can be thrown from the M2000 at a one-a-second rate, picture some half-dozen birds in the air at one time; now the operator flicks a switch and the next target out *passes* the last one or two birds! True—I saw it demonstrated, though I can still hardly believe it.

At the NSGA show this year (1974) the Laporte trap equipment was again on view, including a Multitrap 2000. That machine was left in the U.S. in my charge, and you can see it in operation at the Remington Gun Club, Prospect Dr., Lordship-Stratford, CT.

The Laporte Model 75—pictured here with me in the saddle—is seen in the manual mode form. The same machine is available with battery-operated safety controls, though it still requires hand loading and cocking of the throwing arm.

It could be charged that these various Laporte traps are over-engineered, that they're needlessly strong and sturdy. But isn't that a "fault" in the right direction? I think so—take a close look at some other traps and note the differences. J.T.A

Dynamit Nobel (RWS)

Well known for its excellent line of RWS ammunition, the firm also has a line of shotguns, rifles and revolvers. Only the over-under shotgun will be available in the U.S. this year. Labeled the Olympia '72, this O-U lists for $1058 and offers a removable trigger mechanism similar to that on the Mauser 620 or Perazzi over-under and interchangeable stocks. Different trigger mechanisms will be available, as will a choice of barrel lengths and chokes.

RWS will be offering a new line of plastic practice cartridges in several calibers—9mm Luger, 223, 30-06, 308 and 50. These same 5 calibers are also available as blank cartridges.

Because of their sharply-reduced danger areas, these plastic cartridges can be used safely at quite short ranges. Yet because of their very high velocity and careful assembly, flat shooting and good accuracy are maintained.

Ordinarily fired via single shot loading in auto pistols or shoulder arms, special devices are obtainable from RWS to permit repeat firing from a magazine.

Prices start at about $17 per 100 (for the 223 caliber) to some $30 per 100 for 30-06. L.S.S.

New RWS Booklets

The sample ballistic tables illustrated nearby were extracted from the latest issue (1974) of *Ballistic Data*. This RWS publication—as can be seen—offers much interesting information to the hunter-rifleman and handgunner, all in English. The only fact not supplied—as I read over these tables—is the name of the powder used, but that's something most factories don't supply. On the other hand, maximum chamber pressure is shown, which figure is not furnished by U.S. ammo makers.

Ballistic Data (9¼" long by 6³⁄₁₆") runs to 60 pages, covers included, and presents data like that reprinted here on some 22 centerfire cartridges (with as many as 5 different bullets and their ballistics given separate treatment), like data on standard and magnum rimfire cartridges, plus pertinent performance data on centerfire handgun cartridges—from the 25 Auto to the 45 ACP. Most popular U.S. rifle cartridges are covered.

The other new RWS booklet for 1974 is smaller, a pocketable edition of *Useful Hints for Hunters and Shooters*. Only 3¾"x5½", this 60-page publication is also printed in English, and it offers, in compact form, just what the title promises. As in the larger booklet described above, *Useful Hints* . . . discusses the various RWS bullets, comments on maximum range, carries a table for easily finding kinetic energy, etc. In addition, condensed ballistic tables covering the full range of RWS cartridges and bullets is shown.

Either or both of these excellent reference works are yours for the asking—just write to Dynamit Nobel (RWS) at 105 Stone Hurst Court, Northvale, NJ 07647. J.T.A.

① .222 Rem. VM ② .222 Rem. TM				Ballistic Data				Trajectory Inches above (+) or below (–) Line of Sight					
				Distance yds.	Velocity ft./sec.	Energy ft. lbs.	Time of flight sec.	Most recom. Distance 195 yds.	Scope sighted in at 100 yds.	150 yds.	200 yds.	300 yds.	Open Sight at 100 yds.
① ②		Index No.	① 219 ② 220	Muzzle	3180	1120	0						
		Barrel-length in.	23.5	**50**	2890	925	.049	+ 0.5	– 0.4	– 0.1	+ 0.5	+ 2.0	+ 0.2
		Most recommended Distance yds.	195	**100**	2620	760	.104	+ 1.6	⊕	+ 0.7	+ 1.7	+ 4.7	⊕
		V 10 ft./sec.	3120	**150**	2370	625	.164	+ 1.5	– 1.0	⊕	+ 1.6	+ 6.1	– 1.6
Bullet-weight grains	50	Powder-weight grains	23	**200**	2130	505	.229	– 0.2	– 3.5	– 2.1	⊕	+ 6.0	– 4.7
Bullet-length in.	0.65	Max. Chamber Pressure psi	45 500	**300**	1720	330	.380	– 9.3	– 14.2	– 12.1	– 9.0	⊕	– 16.6

x For barrels only of 5.50 mm (approx. .217 in.) and groove-diameter of 5.64 mm (approx. .222 in.). This cartridge cannot be recommended for use in subcaliber barrels.

.375 H & H Magnum KS				Ballistic Data				Trajectory Inches above (+) or below (–) Line of Sight					
				Distance yds.	Velocity ft./sec.	Energy ft./lbs.	Time of flight sec.	Most recommended Distance 170 yds.	Scope sighted in at 100 yds.	150 yds.	200 yds.	300 yds.	Open Sight at 100 yds.
		Index No.	305	Muzzle	2590	4465	0						
		Barrel-length in.	25.5	**50**	2470	4060	.059	+ 0.7	– 0.2	+ 0.3	+ 1.0	+ 2.6	+ 0.4
		Most recommended Distance yds.	170	**100**	2360	3710	.121	+ 1.6	⊕	+ 1.1	+ 2.4	+ 5.6	⊕
		V 10 ft./sec.	2560	**150**	2260	3400	.187	+ 0.8	– 1.6	⊕	+ 2.0	+ 6.7	– 2.2
Bullet-weight grains	300	Powder-weight grains	72	**200**	2160	3105	.255	– 1.6	– 4.9	– 2.7	⊕	+ 6.2	– 6.1
Bullet-length in.	1.35	Max. Chamber Pressure psi	54 100	**300**	1980	2610	.400	– 11.7	– 16.7	– 13.5	– 9.4	⊕	– 19.1

The material above, reduced to 7 inches long, shows the wealth of shooting information offered in the freely-offered RWS 60-page booklet, *Ballistic Data*.

Testfire Report

Short reviews and evaluations on four sporting arms—the Browning 78, High Standard Supermatic Shadow, Savage 24V-A, Squires Bingham M15 and tests of loads from Ballistek, a custom ammunition maker.

by LARRY S. STERETT

Browning 78

Back in 1878 John M. Browning invented an underlever-operated single shot rifle, one that later became the Winchester Model 1885 Winchester or "High Wall," as it was soon called to distinguish it from its later companion action, the "Low Wall." Discontinued around 1920, the High Wall had been made in several frame types and in calibers from 22 rimfire to the 50-caliber Eley centerfire, and even as a 20 gauge shotgun. Barrel shapes and lengths were many and varied.

As Winchester's first single shot rifle and called the Model 1879 for many years, the High Wall reigned for well over 3 decades. Then in 1973 the High Wall reappeared as the Browning 78—a fitting tribute to John M. Unlike the original, or the Winchester version, the new 78 is available only with a 26" barrel, and chambered for a choice of 4 cartridges—22-250, 6mm, 25-06 and the time-tested 30-06.

Made in Japan to Browning's specifications, the 78 is fairly close to the original but constructed of modern materials and via modern technology. The metal parts are highly polished, with a deep blue on all parts but the breechblock and trigger. The tapered barrel, recessed at the muzzle, is not drilled or tapped for iron sights, but scope mount bases and rings come with each rifle—the front base mounts on the barrel, the rear base mounts on the receiver ring. The barrel on the 25-06 test rifle is round, but an octagon version is also available in the same calibers. A heavier barrel, tapped for target scope blocks, was listed earlier, but has not been seen so far.

Lowering the finger lever pulls the breechblock down and ejects the fired case. (A screw-slotted deflector at the top rear of the receiver can be turned to throw cases right or left, or to stop the cases entirely so they can be picked from the action with the fingers to save for reloading.) Returning the lever to the closed position raises the breechblock and cocks the exposed hammer. (The serrated, non-slip hammer can also be cocked with the action closed, and it has a half-cock position for safety.) The firing pin is not the inertia type and, if the rifle is loaded, the only safe way to carry it is with the hammer lowered to the half-cock position.

This is the Browning single shot rifle, caliber 25-06, that author Sterett is loading.

The .35" wide trigger is grooved for positive finger control. It has a double trigger pull, or slack before the final pull. Let-off is adjustable, according to the factory, between 3 and 4½ pounds, but on the test rifle it was good and crisp at 2½ pounds.

The wood on this sample is a beautiful piece of well-figured walnut, finished to a high gloss. The pistol grip cap carries a silver-colored medallion suitable for engraving. The comb, a well-shaped Monte Carlo with cheekpiece, is wide and comfortable, and fluted on both sides. A Pachmayr presentation solid rubber recoil pad with white spacer is standard, and the buttstock and fore-end are fitted with Pachmayr recessed QD swivel studs. The rounded fore-end shows a semi-schnabel, and it's mounted onto a special hanger, so it doesn't attach directly to the barrel. This system permits the barrel to float free, making undue fore-end pressure on the barrel an impossibility. The grip sides and the fore-end are hand checkered 20 lines to the inch, with a 2-line border. Quality of the checkering is good, with only a few runouts and flat diamonds. Wood to metal fit is excellent, as should be expected on a rifle which now lists at $264.50.

Furnished to us with a Browning 5x scope, the 78 weighs 9½ lbs., and is only 42″ over-all. To check accuracy and functioning the M78 was fired at 100 yards from the bench. Three-shot groups were fired, using Browning, Remington and Winchester factory loads, with bullet weights from 87- to 120 grains. Every rifle is a law unto itself, and this Browning 78 was no different. It preferred the Winchester Super Speed load with the 120-gr. PEP bullet. The smallest group measured 19/32″ center-to-center. The Remington 87-gr. hollow point Power-Lokt load and the Super Speed 90-gr. PEP load gave groups at the 1⅛″ mark. Surprisingly the Browning 87-gr. SPS load wouldn't shoot under two inches, and most groups were just over 3 inches. It just proves once again the need to try several different loads before condemning a rifle for inaccuracy, or before settling on a final load for a particular rifle. In any event the Browning 78 can shoot. Loading is easy, and the fired cases are ejected without hesitation, making a second rapid shot possible if needed. With specially tailored handloads, the 78 might even be a ½-MOA rifle or better. As it is, less than 1 MOA is well above average.

High Standard Supermatic Shadow

High Standard has a new autoloading shotgun, and it's a beauty. Made in Japan by the manufacturers of the excellent over-under Shadow shotguns, the new autoloader is tabbed the Supermatic Shadow. If, at first glance you think you may have seen this shotgun somewhere before, you could be correct. With some facial changes, this shotgun has been on the market for a couple of years as the Weatherby Centurion.

The action is of aluminum alloy, the sides finished a dull matte black, the top and bottom a high gloss black. The streamlined alloy trigger guard is also finished a glossy black, while the octagonal bolt, carrier, bolt handle and bolt release button are chromed, with a high polish. The takedown knob at the tip of the fore-end is blued, as are other metal parts excepting the gold-plated trigger.

The Shadow is gas-operated, with a self-compensating system that cleans itself with each shot by preventing carbon buildup. Twin action bars make the operation smooth and reliable. Internally, this latest Shadow has a lot of stampings, including the follower and many of the parts on the trigger assembly, along with spring clips, and other assorted mass-production devices.

The stock and fore-end are of select American walnut, the fore-end having finger panels along the top edge, and a slant-back rear portion that first appeared on the Remington 1100. The bottom of the fore-end is covered with good hand checkering of 22 lines per inch, without borders. The pistol grip has a smaller amount of borderless checkering, along the sides, that runs 20 lines per inch.

The comb is wide, fluted on both sides, and the pistol grip has a rosewood cap with a white spacer and an elongated white diamond inlay. The buttplate, black plastic with a white spacer, doesn't really blend well with the grip cap—a brown recoil pad would have been a better choice. Stock dimensions are pull, 14″ comb and heel 1⅜″ and 2″.

Takedown is simple—unscrew the knurled knob at the front of the fore-end, slip the latter off, retract the bolt and pull the barrel off the magazine tube. (When the bolt is forward, it locks into the barrel extension.) The trigger guard assembly can be removed by pushing out the two receiver pins holding it in place.

The Shadow has some distinguishing features, foremost its aluminum "airflow ventilated rib." This grooved-top rib, .514″ wide, carries a .123″ muzzle bead and a .065″ center bead, both brass. Like the rib, the receiver top is grooved at an angle toward the sides to prevent reflections. The sides of the rib have two grooves—full length—to radiate barrel heat. The free-floating rib is anchored to a solid section of barrel rib near the breech with a single Phillips-type screw. The 28″ barrel on the test gun is choked modified; 26″, 28″ and 30″ barrels are available in 12 gauge, with a variety of chokes, and in 26″ and 28″ in 20 gauge. The 12s are chambered for standard 2¾″ shells, the 20 gauge for 3″ cases, but there's a 12-gauge version with a 30″ full choke barrel chambered for 3″ shells. Over-all length of the Shadow with 28″ barrel is 48″. Price is $264, either gauge.

High Standard's Supermatic Shadow 12-gauge autoloader has an "airflow ventilated rib."

The Supermatic Shadow, first shot during 3 separate trap sessions, will really smoke those clays—if the shooter is on 'em. During these trials some 300 rounds (not many for a trap gun) were put down the tube, and there were no difficulties with feeding or functioning. Even the push-through safety, at the rear of the guard, proved reliable. Next, the Shadow was patterned, contrary to the usual sequence. Five rounds each of 4 different brands of shotshells were patterned at 40 yards. The average percentage of shot in the 30″ circle for the Smith & Wesson (3¾/1¼/6) field load was 53.7, or slightly below what was expected of a modified choke. Switching to the Winchester Super-Speed Mark 5 HD Magnum load—1½ ounces of 2s—jumped the average to 82.9%—darn good. Two trap loads—Federal's Champion II and Remington's RXP—averaged 62.9% and 67.7% respectively, or slightly better than modified and approaching the full choke percentage.

The new High Standard Supermatic Shadow can shoot. It looks good, weighs 7⅝ pounds empty, handles well, and is a definite asset to the High Standard line of shotguns.

Savage 24V-A

The Savage Model 24V-A combination Gun with 30-30 rifle barrel over 20 gauge barrel chambered for 3" shells.

Having been on the market for a couple of years, and with the basic Model 24 offered for some 20 years, the Savage Model 24V-A is not an unproven design. Only the caliber combination is different—30-30 and 20 gauge. When the 24-V was introduced with a 222 Remington barrel over a 20-gauge tube, it was intended for turkey and varmint hunters. The 24V-A is for larger game—deer, where rifle and shotgun are permitted—and general use by ranchers, farmers, trappers, et al. Such combination guns, common in Europe, are ideal in certain hunting situations, but they have never been extensively used in the U.S.

Unlike the basic Model 24, the 24V-A uses a different breech design for holding the barrels together. They are locked together only at the breech, and they're held in line near the muzzle by a barrel with a flat-top .072 post front sight atop. They are not attached elsewhere, and there are no side ribs, so air is free to circulate around them.

The 30-30 barrel is above, and atop it is a short rib carrying a dovetailed folding rear sight. This rib is also tapped for attaching a scope mount base. The barrels are 24" long, over-all length 41⅝". The 3-inch chambered 20-gauge barrel is unmarked as to choke.

The 24V-A opens via a conventional top lever, pushed in either direction—right or left. A single cam-assisted extractor lifts the cases about ¼" for removal. A visible hammer has a selector lever to position the hammer nose—to the rear for firing the rifle barrel or forward for shooting the shotgun barrel. The thumb portion of the selector lever on the 24V-A is smaller than on previous M24 combos, and a little difficult to move forward; it could easily be returned to the former larger shape without any alteration.

The fore-end on the 24V-A is a tapered semi-beavertail with impressed checkering that is decorative only. The buttstock, also of walnut, has the same type of checkering and a black plastic buttplate and pistol grip cap with the inevitable white spacers. A forward-sloping Monte Carlo comb is correct height for iron sight use, but at least an inch too low for scopes. However, a Lodewick Mark II neoprene cheekpiece helped a lot in placing the eye in line with the scope.

Closeup of the 24V-A breech showing the single extractor for the two barrels.

The 24V-A takes down easily—pull down on the fore-end and remove it, then push the top lever over to drop the barrel and lift it off. With scope mounted take-down length is under 28", or less than 25" without the scope.

The 24V-A, without scope, weighs 7¼ lbs. A 4x scope in Savage mounts raised the weight to an even 8 lbs.

What accuracy levels and pattern performance could I expect from the 24V-A? Three-shot groups were fired at 100 yards from the bench, only factory loads were used, the brands including Dominion, Federal, Frontier, Herter's, Gevelot and Winchester Super-Speed. Over 90% of the groups ran between 2-3 inches center-to-center, which is pretty standard hunting accuracy for the distance. The smallest group measured 1 23/32", obtained with the Winchester SS 150-gr. hollow point load.

The shotgun barrel (no choke indicated) was something else! I'd hoped for a modified choke, but it shot more like an improved cylinder. I fired 5 shots for an average at 40 yards, making my percentage count in the 30" circle. The Browning 45 Power load (1¼/4s) averaged 58.6%, the Western Super-X Mark 5 load (1 3/16/Lubaloy 4s) patterned 56.9%. An Alcan Gamemax load (2½/1/7½) averaged 44.6%, the S&W Field load (2½/1/6) averaged only 39.6% The latter two were 2¾" loads, the others 3". The 24V-A 20-gauge barrel is definitely not a modified choke model.

A major problem developed during both patterning and field tests. The extractor slipped past the rim of the fired shotshell every time! I had to drop a small lead weight down the muzzle to free the case. Nothing like this happened with the rifle barrel, which uses the same extractor, but a fast second shot with to 20 ga. barrel is impossible with this particular gun.

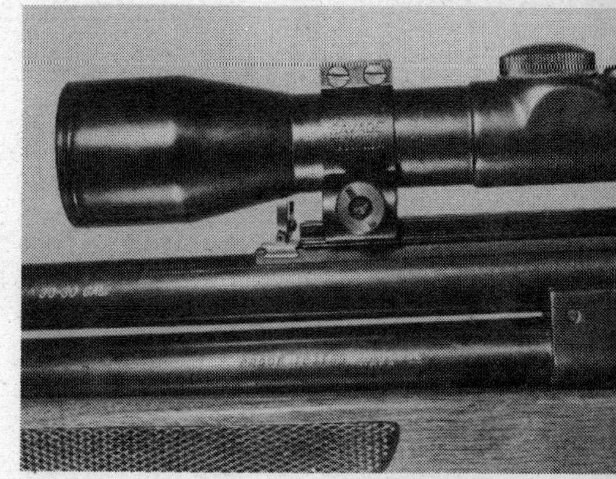

The rib on the rifle barrel provides room for the folding rear sight and the scope mount base.

Squires Bingham Model 15

Priced at $99.95, the Model 15 is this writer's favorite of the Philippine imports—chambered for the 22 rimfire magnum cartridge, it just plain looks and feels good. The well-crowned 24" barrel measures .695" in diameter at the muzzle, and has an open rear sight and a hooded ramp front with an .060" blade. The barrel, the bolt handle and bolt rear, plus the magazine, show a well-polished blue finish. The receiver has a non-glare satin-type blue finish, while the alloy trigger guard is black. The action, a conventional turn bolt, shows some improvements. The rear of the bolt is completely enclosed, which should be adequate protection against escaping gases in the event of a ruptured case. The bolt handle knob is hollow, and cocking is on the upstroke. The receiver is grooved for tipoff scope mounts, with additional smaller grooves between to break up light reflections. A further improvement is the alloy housing which encloses the

Larry Sterett shooting the S-B Model 15, a man-sized rifle in 22 WRM caliber, the scope a Weaver V-22.

trigger mechanism and magazine. When the barreled action is removed from the stock, the entire mechanism goes with it. The 5-round magazine fits into the alloy housing directly ahead of the trigger guard. The magazine release is at the front of the guard.

The 22 magnum cartridge is not a plinking cartridge, but a varmint cartridge and, as such, this writer prefers a rifle of some weight. The M-15 weighs 6⅞ lbs. empty, of which 4½ lbs. is the barreled action. Topped with a Weaver V-22 scope and loaded, the rifle tips the scales at 7 pounds 9 ounces. It measures 41¾″ over-all, and the pull length is 14″.

Using CCI Maxi-Mag cartridges—FMJ and HP—the M-15 got its first firing at 25 yards, from the bench. 5-shot groups were fired to check feeding from the magazine and accuracy. The best groups measured 25/32″, using the FMJ loads, and just over 1″ for the hollow point load. Groups at 100 yards shot into 2-3 inches for 3 shots—a bit large for a varmint rifle.

Checking the bedding, the barrel was found to bear at the fore-end tip and about midway back. There wasn't time to free float the barrel to see if this would improve accuracy, but perhaps removing some wood at the midway point would shrink the groups.

The Model 15 stock is of Pulong Dalaga wood. Each stock varies in color and figure from light blonde to walnut, with dark streaks. The fore-end, round in shape, gives a comfortable grip. It and the pistol grip have more than the usual amount of checkering. The checkering runs 20 lines per inch with a 2-line border, the fore-end checkering wrapping completely around. The diamonds, slightly flat on top, are still better than on some more expensive rifles. A few minutes with a checkering tool would quickly sharpen them. The comb is wide, fluted on each side and flattened at the nose. The butt has a slight Monte Carlo comb with an European-style cheekpiece. Fore-end and pistol grip have what appears to be a cocoawood tip and cap, with white spacers, as does the black plastic buttplate. (A dark brown buttplate would be a better match for the fore-end tip and grip cap.) The stock finish is excellent, the pores sealed and the polishing done without scratches. L.S.S.

An unusual aspect of the S-B M15 rifle appears on take-down—the trigger system and magazine remain with the action and barrel.

Ballistek

Every shooter at one time or another needs ammunition for some rifle or handgun in a caliber not readily available. Custom reloaders have attempted to remedy this situation, but few firms manufacture or load as extensive a line of cartridges as Ballistek (Box 459, Laconia, NH 03246). They list 114 rifle and 30 handgun cartridges. Only virgin factory brass is used, along with the best available jacketed and cast lead bullets, plus the correct primer and powder combination.

Rifle calibers range from the 17 Remington through the 50-70 Gov't., including such cartridges as the 17 Ackley Bee, 220 Swift, 22 Savage High Power, 6mm Lee Navy, 256 Newton, 7x5x55mm Swiss, 35 Whelen and the 460 Weatherby Magnum. Handgun calibers include the 22 Remington Jet, 30 Mauser, 30 Herrett, 8mm Nambu, 9mm Magnum, 357x44 Bain & Davis, and the 454 Casull Magnum. I obtained some 256 Newton cartridges, these, formed from new W-W 30-06 brass and loaded with 140-gr. HPBT bullets, chambered perfectly in an original Newton rifle—and they shot well. At 100 yards from the bench I got 3-shot groups of about 1 MOA, using open sights; with a scope these loads would probably shoot well under an inch.

Three other Ballistek cartridges were tested—222, 308 and 45-70. The 222 held 52-gr. HP bullets in new Remington brass. The 308 was in Remington cases with 165-gr. HPBT bullets. The 45-70 loads were in new W-W brass with 400-gr. FP and 300-gr. HP bullets. The 222s, fired in a H&R 322 topped with a Weaver V-8 scope, averaged ⅜-inch. The 308 loads, fired in a Herter U9 with 5x scope, went into ⅝″ on average. A Navy Arms 45-70 Siamese Mauser with open sights shot into 3 1/16″. (None of these rifles are considered target rifles, but all have proven accurate with regular factory loads.) In the 45-70 the 400-gr. load produced smaller groups than did the 300-gr. rounds, with the smallest group under 2½″. The 45 Colt load with a 250-gr. JHP bullet fired in a new Navy Arms M1875 replica Remington revolver, gave a 5-shot bench rest group at 25 yards that measured 1 9/16″—not bad for a handgun, even with the wrists supported on a sandbag.

Ballistek will reload your fired hulls also if you wish, provided the brass is in good condition. Possibly "remanufactured" cartridges would be a better description, since the process includes case inspection, full length resizing, trimming and neck reaming if necessary. Your choice of bullets, of course, plus a final inspection. Prices? That depends on the cartridge, bullet type, and the load desired. Prices of new cartridges are competitive with regular factory ammunition, and even obsolete and wildcat cartridges are reasonable. Special "match ammunition" is also available, as are such premium bullets as Nosler or Bitterroot. ●

New H&K Model 300 autoloading rifle, cal. 22 Winchester Magnum Rimfire.

New Guns From The Old Continent

Brief notes on the rifles, shotguns and handguns that made news during the past year.

by RAYMOND CARANTA
European Editor

VARIOUS NEW guns have been announced this year (1974) by European manufacturers, in spite of economic instability prevailing everywhere—the floating currencies, the rise everywhere of energy costs (affecting prices in every country), the social troubles prevalent in many nations of the Old Continent and . . . why go on?

Rifles

J. G. Anschutz

The famous J. G. Anschutz company of Ulm, West Germany, has brought out two new sporting rifles chambered for the 22 Hornet, which is still popular in Europe—the Models 1432 E St (DJV) and 1433 St Luxus; a third Anschutz, the 1533 St Luxus, is chambered in 222 Remington. The Anschutz 1432 E St. (DJV) is directly derived from the 1432 E (DJV), a 22 rimfire rifle dating back several years. The new rifle is fitted with a ventilated recoil pad, double-set triggers and a new fore-end. No sights are provided, the rifle being intended only for use with a scope.

The 1433 and 1533 St Luxus models are identical, except for chambering. These are stocked in the usual German style, with a Monte Carlo cheekpiece, and a long fore-end a la Mannlicher.

Both are deluxe with engraved receivers and trigger-guards. Double-set triggers, folding - leaf sights, ventilated rubber recoil pads and modified Monte Carlo stock are standard. Their magazines are detachable, these holding 5 rounds in 22 Hornet and 3 in 222 Remington. Barrels are 20 inches long, total length is 39 inches, and empty weight 6.6 pounds.

Some of the Anschutz rifles are brought to the United States by the Savage Arms Corporation.

Mauser's Model 66 SP, the 66-actioned rifle in target form.

Heckler & Koch

Located at Oberndorf/Neckar, West Germany, H&K is one of the world's leading manufacturers of military small arms.

This year H&K has introduced a self-loading rifle chambered in 22 Magnum Rimfire, the Model 300. As with all H&K products, the new rifle is made using ultra-modern manufacturing processes.

I test fired this new rifle for a French arms magazine and found it completely reliable, with Winchester ammunition, and astonishingly accurate up to 100 yards. The workmanship of our test specimen was excellent internally and externally, despite the fact that the action was made entirely of stampings, castings and plastic materials. The stock was very nicely done also.

Mauser

The old Mauser company, located like H&K at Oberndorf/Neckar, has introduced a new model, the 66 SP

New Sako Finnscout, a bolt action target rifle, caliber 22 LR and 22 WMR.

SIG Neuhausen Model 542 military rifle, made in 5.56mm (223) caliber.

Closeup of Mannlicher-Schönauer M-72 hunting rifle, here with single trigger. Double set triggers are available.

Mannlicher-Schönauer M-72 sporting rifle, made in a wide range of calibers and with full or half stocks.

Carl Walther "KK Match" rifle, cal. 22 LR.

Carl Walther "U.I.T. Moving Target" rifle, cal. 22 LR.

New M-S Model SSG rifle, here in Special or Sniper form, cal. 308.

sniper rifle, the design based on their original 66 bolt action.

The new rifle, chambered for the 308 Winchester cartridge, is offered with a special target stock and a muzzle brake. It can be fitted with a scope or special military sights. Weight without scope is 12 pounds, the scope adding 25 ounces.

Mauser has moved into the ammo field, too, at least in a small way. They've developed a new standard velocity (within the 990 fps muzzle velocity range), high-precision 22 Long Rifle round bearing their trade mark.

Sako

This well-known Finnish company now offers the Finnscout Model P72, a bolt action repeating rifle chambered in 22 Long Rifle and 22 WMR. Magazine capacity is 5 rounds in 22 LR and 4 in the 22 Magnum. The barrels have 12 lands/grooves and the striker travel is very short (.23-inch).

Three variations on the basic action are available—the light Junior Sporter, a Heavy Barrel version and the Running Boar/Biathlon target types.

J. P. Sauer & Son

The Colt-Sauer bolt action rifle is now available in Europe in 22-250, 243 Winchester and 308 Winchester (all in the new short action rifle) and in 458 Winchester as the Grand African model.

SIG

This well-known Swiss armsmaker of Neuhausen (Rheinfalls), has just introduced two new gas-operated light military rifles, one in 5.56mm (223) called the SG 540, and the other in 7.62mm NATO (308 Win), labeled the SG 542. Full automatic fire is possible with both models, the cyclic rate varying from 650 to 800 rpm, and burst-control devices (adjusted for 3 rounds) are available. These rifles can be fitted with a bipod, bayonet, grenade launching attachment, scope sights and a folding stock.

Rumors are that several governments are interested in these new models.

Steyr-Daimler-Puch

The Mannlicher-Schonauer M72 sporting rifles are now in full production at Steyr (Austria). These famous luxury rifles, made with single or double set triggers and rotary magazines, rate among the most modern in the world—and among the best liked as well.

Besides these beautiful hunting rifles, Steyr-Daimler-Puch is also offering a special sniping version based on the M72 action. This rifle is chambered in 7.62mm NATO (308 Win.). Synthetic or conventional wooden stocks are available.

Using this Model SSG rifle, the Austrian army team set a world record in 1970 during the Buenos Aires championship matches. Another version, especially designed for 300-meter international target shooting, wears the SSG-Match designation.

Voere

The Kufstein (Austria) factory of the Voere company, specializing in rifles and shotguns, announced in late 1973 a new streamlined self-loading rifle, the Model 2117, caliber 22 Long Rifle. This new rifle, which can be disassembled rapidly for complete cleaning, features a very simple blowback action.

Our sample was well made and very accurate at 50 yards for its class. Functioning was excellent with several brands of European and American ammunition. 5- and 15-round detachable box magazines are standard.

Voere followed up with, early in

out-cylinder revolvers (Models SR3/6″ barrel, VR4/4″ barrel and TR6/2″ barrel on a light-alloy frame) all with coil-spring lock work. Sauer also makes a line of "Single Action Army" type revolvers, once distributed in the U.S. by Hawes in Los Angeles, California.

Recently the Sauer firm joined forces with the Swiss company, SIG, in the production of a pair of ultra-modern design automatic pistols, the SIG/Sauer models P230 and P220.

Because these new SIG/Sauer 220 and 230 pistols are covered extensively elsewhere in this 29th edition—see the story by Jay B. Wood—I won't take up space with them here except for comments on their calibers.

The P230 won't be available until the end of 1974, in 22 LR, 32 ACP and 380 ACP calibers. In addition, some time in 1975, a P230 pistol will be marketed in a new round, the "9mm Police."

This new cartridge, based on the 380 ACP case, I understand, will be similar in performance to the Soviet 9mm Makarov. Though gas pressure is kept sufficiently low to be safe in a comparatively light blow-back action, its muzzle energy has been raised to about 230 foot pounds against 160 for the standard 380. The announced muzzle velocity is given as 1050 fps from the P230 pistol versus 985 for the same gun chambered in 380 ACP.

If the new "9mm Police" cartridge is truly usable in existing 380 auto pistols, then it is going to have a great future in European police circircles, if not elsewhere.

SIG-Hammerli P240

For this new model, which is specifically intended for target shooting under I.S.U. "center-fire pistol" regulations, the well-proven—but expensive—SIG P210 pistol action has been used.

The P210 action, made of the finest steels available, is noted for its outstanding endurance, reliability under target range conditions, and absence of slide and barrel play—all prime requisites of the perfect target pistol.

The new pistol will be chambered only for the 38 Special Wadcutter cartridge, the most popular caliber used for this class of shooting. The trigger pull is fully adjustable, and the workmanship is up to the best SIG-Hammerli standards.

Walther G.S.P. target pistol, caliber 32 S&W Wadcutter, meant for ISU matches.

Latest version of Walther's competition air pistol, the L.P.3, lies lower in the hand.

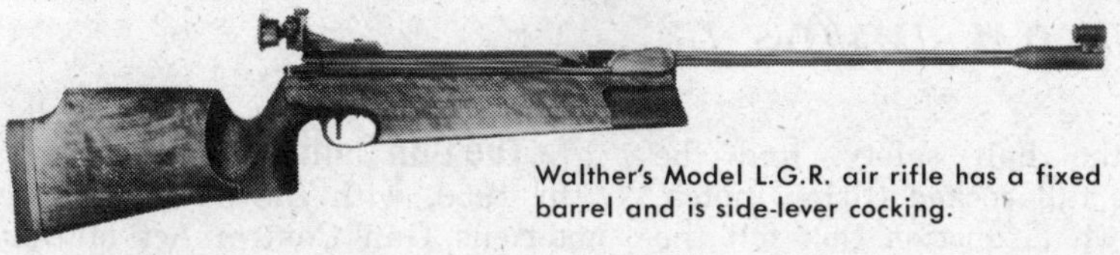

Walther's Model L.G.R. air rifle has a fixed barrel and is side-lever cocking.

A blow-back 22 Long Rifle conversion unit will be available for practice and for shooting the I.S.U. "Standard Pistol" matches using the same receiver. Trigger pull will then be adjusted to 1000 grams (35½ oz.), the minimum allowed by the rules. The P240 should be available by late 1974.

UMA

UMA Jagd und Sportwaffen Fabrik (Munich, West Germany) has introduced a 4-shot Sharps Derringer replica that is usable only with 22 blank cartridges.

Unique

This French company will offer sometime this year (1974) a new Olympic rapid-fire pistol, chambered in 22 Short, for top level competition under I.S.U. regulations.

The "new" pistol is a variation of their well-known D.E.S. Model 69, which is chambered for 22 LR ammo, in accordance with applicable "Standard Pistol" requirements.

Carl Walther

The most important news from Walther is the launching of their G.S.P. target pistol, chambered in 32 S&W Long Wadcutter for I.S.U. "Center-Fire Pistol" competition.

This use of such low-powered ammunition in a heavy automatic pistol reduces recoil to the very minimum and, as all bullet holes are scored on bullet centers, the 32 S&W Long shooter has a distinct advantage over his competitors using 38 Special pistols.

It seems to be the rule now, among the best European makers of target pistols, to furnish a 22 Long Rifle conversion kit, intended for shooting the "Standard Pistol" event with the same basic gun. Trigger pull is then adjusted to 1000 grams or the trigger unit is changed.

If the shooter also uses a Walther O.S.P. chambered in 22 Short, for Olympic rapid-fire shooting, he can finish the complete course with the same basic action.

Air Guns

This year, only three European firms have new air guns.

B.S.A.

Birmingham Small Arms (England), has just released a low-priced conventional single shot spring-air pistol, the Scorpion. No sample was available for testing at press time.

El Gamo

Located in Spain, near Barcelona, this relatively new company will introduce this year another low-priced single-shot air rifle, the "Center." The "Center" has a fixed, non-breaking barrel, an adjustable trigger and a micrometer rear sight, but no sample was available in France for my examination and trial. The new air rifle's weight is reported to be 2⅞ pounds, its barrel length 17.2″ and the sight radius 24 inches.

Carl Walther

Carl Walther last year (1973) improved their L.P.2 Match recoil-less air pistol in various aspects. The new L.P.3 pistol lies low in the hand, and it's about as sophisticated an air gun as you're likely to see. It is meant for top competition under the I.S.U. "10 meter Pistol" regulations.

In the same year the famous Ulm factory revealed a new competition recoil-less air rifle, the L.G.R., made with a fixed barrel and a side-cocking lever, a la Anschutz and Feinwerkbau. I shot this new air rifle extensively, and I found it to be absolutely vibration free and truly without any recoil. In my opinion this new rifle is among the best in the world for 10-meter target shooting at the highest international level. ●

Single Action Revolvers and the safety revolution.

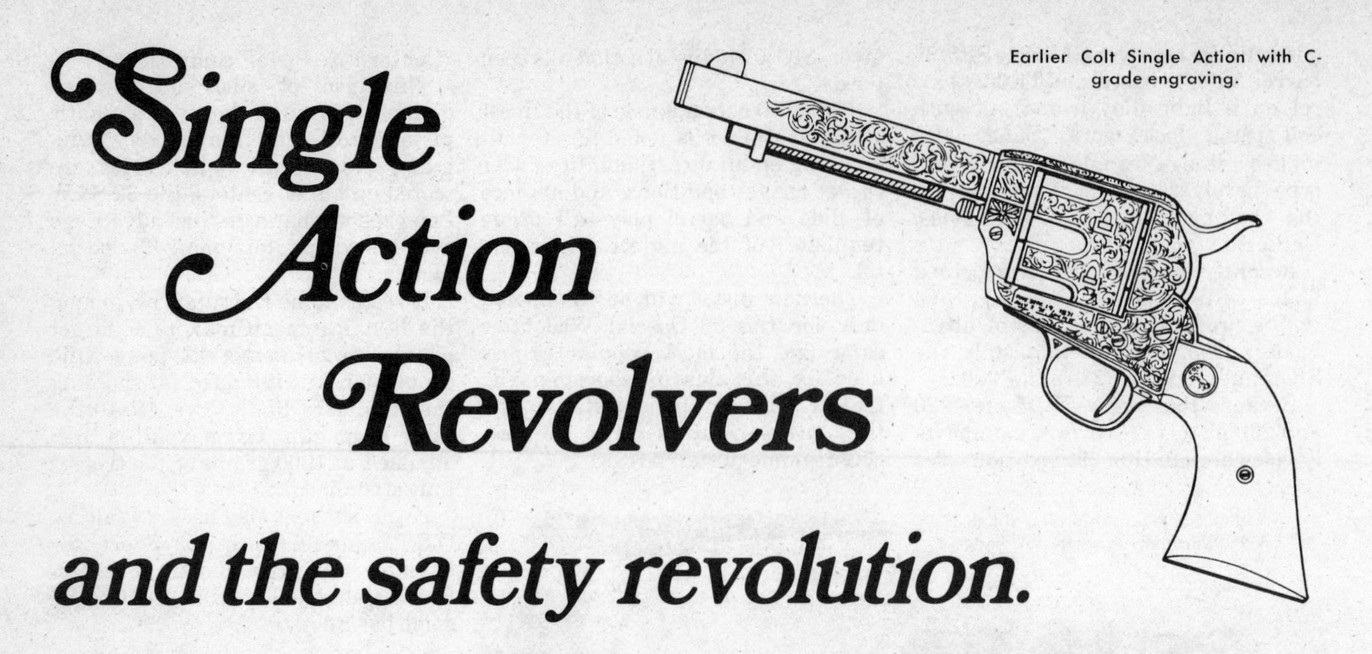

Earlier Colt Single Action with C-grade engraving.

Despite the iniquities and inequities of firearms legislation generally, the Gun Control Act of 1968 brought about one great good—real safety is now built into several Single Action makes and models.

by DONALD M. SIMMONS, JR.

ONE OF THE fallacies of our era is that you can legislate safety. From this one tenet of Big Brotherism have sprung the Ralph Naders of our world. A second error of the safety syndrome is that a politician is the best person to be entrusted with the engineer-oriented question of what is or is not safe.

The Colt Single Action Army

In 1873 Colt introduced the famous Single Action Army revolver. This long popular handgun was made from that date until 1940. Because of an unpredicted demand for this antiquated handgun, Colt resumed manufacture in 1955. By the time Colt had decided that there was a new market for their venerable Model P (as the Single Action was factory-designated), there was a number of other companies already making copies of the Single Action. In all truth, the basic design of the Colt was just a spin-off from their highly successful cap and ball Civil War revolvers. True, the Single Action Colt's frame was given a bridge over the cylinder, which greatly increased its strength. However, the overweight hammer of the earlier cap and ball was retained, to which was added a new quarter safety notch, making this hammer have three distinct notches. The first was the new quarter safety, the second the half safety, and the third the full cocked (firing) notch. Exactly what function Colt felt the quarter notch served is still a moot point. We will delve in depth later on these apparently innocent little cuts in steel.

The Gun Control Act 1968

In 1968, with the advent of the notorious Gun Control Act of that year, the old scarred Single Action was headed for a confrontation with the bright-eyed planners of our era. In 1971 the Department of the Treas-

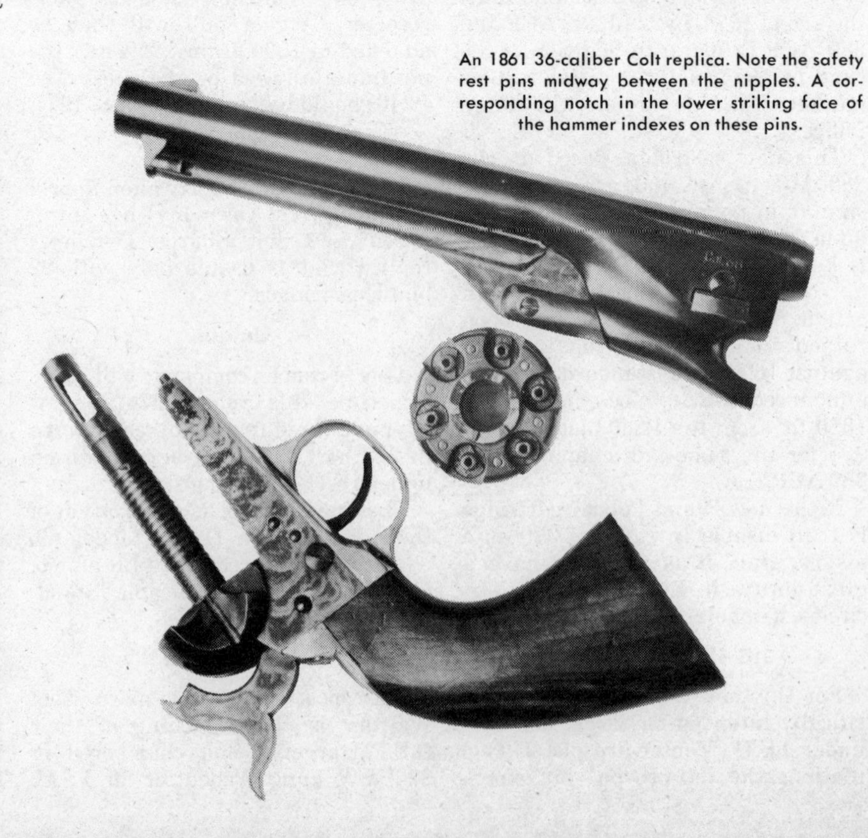

An 1861 36-caliber Colt replica. Note the safety rest pins midway between the nipples. A corresponding notch in the lower striking face of the hammer indexes on these pins.

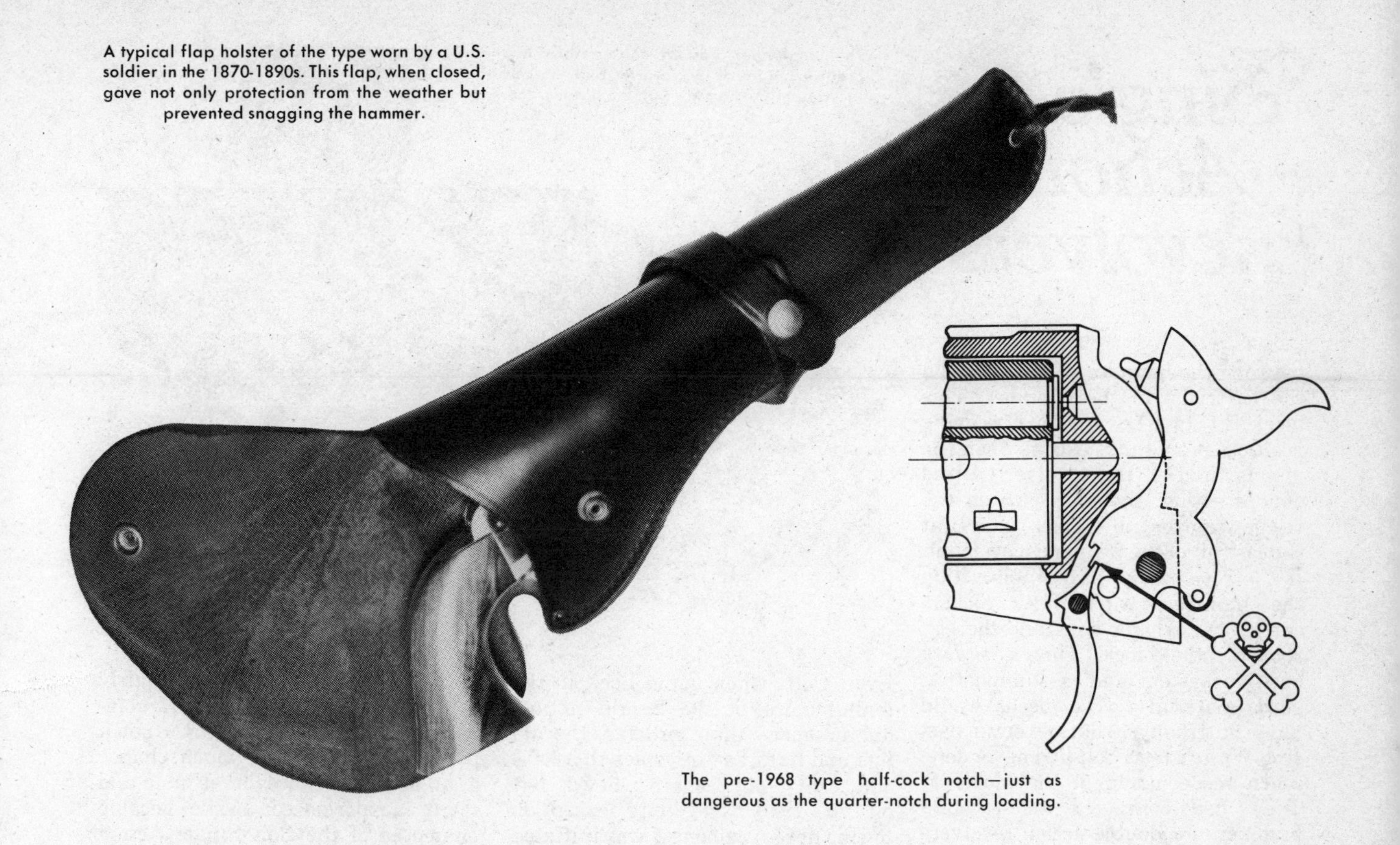

A typical flap holster of the type worn by a U.S. soldier in the 1870-1890s. This flap, when closed, gave not only protection from the weather but prevented snagging the hammer.

The pre-1968 type half-cock notch—just as dangerous as the quarter-notch during loading.

ury, enforcers of the new Firearms Act, contracted with an experienced civilian laboratory, H. P. White & Co., to establish whether a reasonable standard of safety could be found for handguns and, if so, could they design a series of tests to insure this safety. One of the tentative tests that H. P. White came up with was the hammer drop test for exposed hammer revolvers and non-magazine fed pistols. The test which the laboratory devised was tough. The sample gun, held vertically, was set on safety and a weight equal to the weight of the unloaded sample was dropped 36 inches onto the hammer spur. The handgun passed if it could withstand 5 such drops without discharging the under-the-hammer cartridge.

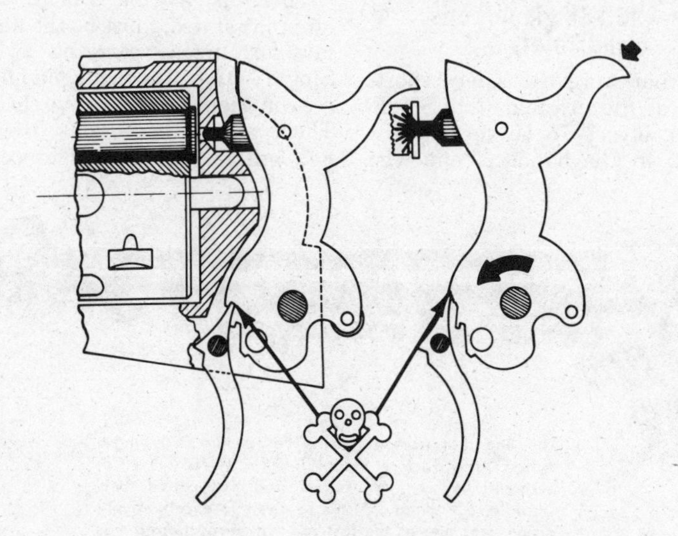

The pre-1968 type quarter-cock notch, showing the potential danger arising from a shearing of sear or notch.

One section of the 1968 Gun Control Act also gave the Treasury Department the right to say what guns could be imported into the United States. The Alcohol, Tobacco and Firearms division of Treasury was made the watchdog of what could be imported. This division, faced with a task for which it had little training and less knowledge, had to quickly establish guide lines for firearms importation. The ATFB came up with a point merit system by which any handgun could be judged acceptable or not acceptable. This Form 4590, "Factoring Criteria for Weapons" had, as its last requirement for revolvers the borrowed H. P. White hammer drop test mentioned above.

The enforcement of this well-meaning drop test rang the death knell for the many foreign-made copies of the Colt Single Action which had flooded the market.

Double Actions vs Single Actions

Modern double action revolvers have a steel positive block placed

Single Action Revolvers

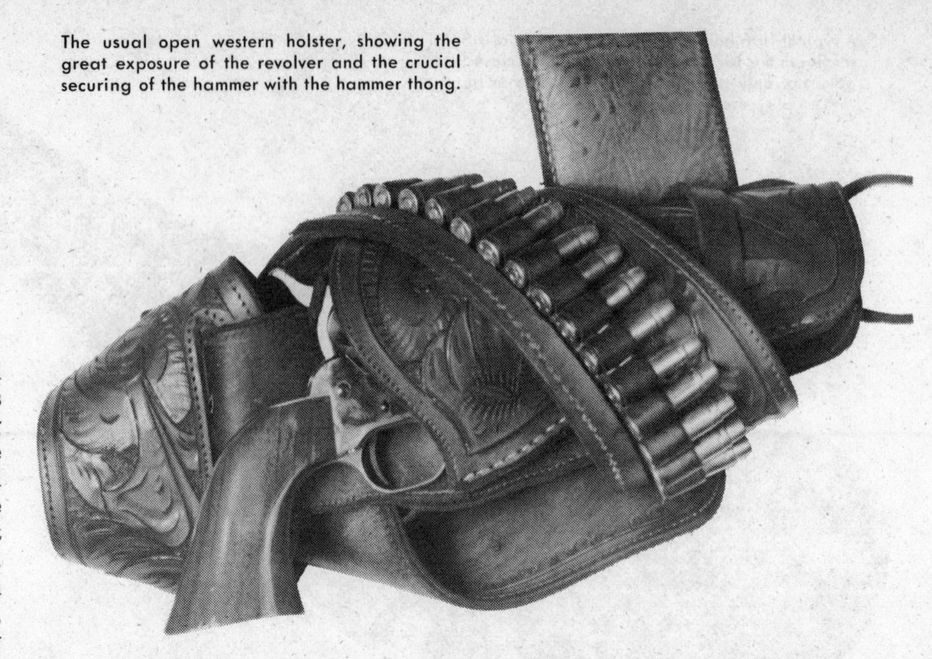

The usual open western holster, showing the great exposure of the revolver and the crucial securing of the hammer with the hammer thong.

between the hammer's firing pin and the cartridge in the chamber. This block is in the hammer-securing position at all times except when the gun is fired. If the revolver is fired double action, the long pull on the trigger moves the block away at the last bit of the trigger's movement. If the revolver is fired single action the hammer, when fully cocked, carries the trigger back and thereby removes the block. This is a very positive system and, assuming that good materials were used, would have no trouble whatsoever in passing White's test. Colt had never done much modernizing of the Model P. They had conceived safe-rebound hammers for double action revolvers in the last decade of the 19th century but, by that time, the Single Action wasn't selling in any exciting quantity. In fact, after 1907, no more than 5000 a year were sold; worse, from Colt's point of view, after the crash of 1929, no more than 1000 a year were sold. One can easily see from this sagging sales curve that Colt would have been loath to put money into any renovation program for this old revolver. When the post-World War II craze for the Single Action hit, all the copies were made as close to the Colt Single Action as possible because that's what nostalgic American shooters were buying. Even Colt, when going back to the manufacture of the Single Action, did no more than pull out the old jigs and fixtures—or copies thereof—and start out where they'd left off in 1940. The only exception to this design sameness was initiated by the then small firm of Sturm, Ruger & Co., whose single action copy was a well-designed updating of the archaic Colt. Ruger replaced all the fragile Colt flat and leaf springs with modern coil springs but, probably because of what was in demand, Ruger didn't revise the beloved "Tic-Tac-Toe" three-notch hammer.

Pre-1968 Single Actions and Safety

Just what were the safety shortcomings of the original Colt Single Action revolver? To be very honest the Colt, in the hands of one who understood its foibles, was a fairly safe arm. If one overlooked a completely redundant quarter-notch position, there wasn't much chance of an accident. However, as more and more inexperienced people became enamored of the Colt Single Action type revolver, the chances for an accident greatly increased. There are 4 dangerous situations that can arise when using any Single Action revolver, be it a Colt or any of its pre-1968 imitators. These are: carrying, loading, dropping a loaded gun and phantom notches.

Carrying Danger

There is a rule which, though often misstated, must be the absolute law for anyone carrying a loaded Single Action. The firing pin must *not* rest on the primer of a live cartridge. There are no exceptions, there are no mitigating circumstances for

The one that started it all. The famous Colt Single Action Army factory Model P. This 44-40 (44 WCF) example has a 7½" barrel and was called their "Frontier Six Shooter." This revolver, in excellent condition, was one of the last pre-war production. It was made in 1939.
(From the collection of the late H. Milton Every.)

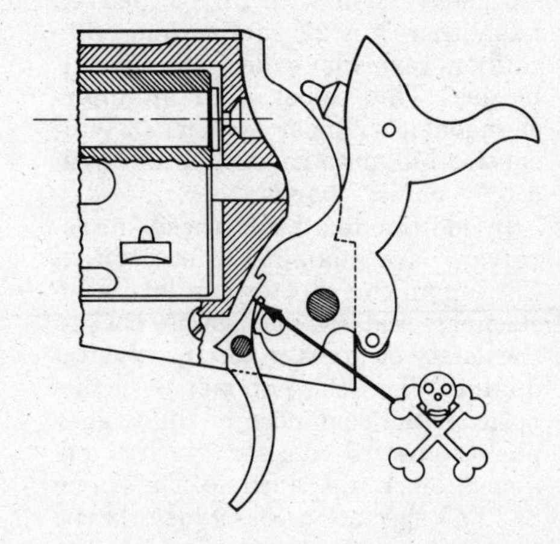

The phantom notch which, though shown here on the half-cock notch, can happen on the quarter-cock notch as well.

relaxing this rule. *NEVER, never,* at no time! However, there are two carrying ways that avoided this mandated carrying law. The one usually parroted is to load only 5 rounds into the cylinder, leaving the 6th chamber empty, and allow the hammer to rest on this empty chamber. This works, but it means that the owner, who bought a 6-shot revolver, then has one that only carries 5 rounds. The more rational way of safely carrying a Single Action revolver is to load all 6 chambers and then lower the hammer to the mid-position between two adjacent cartridge rims. This is not one of my original ideas—in all honesty this technique for a long life goes back to the American Civil War and its cap and ball revolvers. Both Colt and Remington devised methods for a positive between-chambers rest. This method of carrying is not advised for rimfire cartridge revolvers, since the firing pin could be resting too close to the rim for safety, which contains the priming in this type of cartridge. Notice that you don't carry these revolvers with the hammer cocked into any notch—*not* the quarter-notch, *not* the half-notch and, of course, *not* the full-cock notch. The hammer is forward, at rest.

Now let's turn to the holster in which the Single Action is to be carried. One of the things that led to the new popularity of the old Single Action revolver was the post-WW II craze for quick draw shooting. With this madness arose, naturally, a demand for the most open and fastest holster rig. The original Colt Single Actions, when carried by the U.S. Army in the 1870-1890s, were held in deep, flap-top holsters. These, by their very makeup, protected the revolver from the weather while also securing it during a brisk gallop. One ancillary benefit of the flap holster was that the hammer at rest was unable to be brushed by any object which could accidentally cock it and, worse, allow it to fall forward by a sear failure. This type of accident may be the justification of the quarter-notch. In modern open holsters a tight-fitting loop for securing the hammer can also serve this function of keeping the hammer down. Use this loop when carrying a loaded Single Action.

If the hammer is cammed back by some object the quarter notch, if it holds, can stop the hammer from striking the live primer.

Loading Danger

In loading all pre-1968 Single action revolvers it is first necessary to place the hammer at the half-cock position. With the hammer so-positioned, the cylinder is free to turn and, by opening the gate, the handgun can be loaded. The danger in this position doesn't come until the 6th or last round is being loaded. At this moment the hammer is in line with the primer of the first-loaded cartridge and, should the hammer slip from notch, there could be a very bad accident. I've seen idiots loading one of these old revolvers with a half-cock notch so worn by fanning and other abuses that the thumb had to hold back the hammer. Needless to say, such a shooter has a very low life expectancy but, much more important, so do his shooting friends.

Dropping Danger

Anytime *any* firearm is dropped there is always danger of an accidental discharge. With a loaded pre-1968 Single Action, if the hammer is back in any notch and there is a live round in the chamber, it is dangerous. If these conditions exist and the hammer hits the ground first there is a good chance of the revolver firing. On the other hand, if the gun was being carried with the hammer down in the accepted position—between the chambers or on an empty chamber—there is no possibility of a dropping discharge. If the revolver was being loaded when dropped there will be no trouble if only 5 chambers were loaded. Lastly, if the revolver falls with the hammer at full cock (just before firing) there is every chance that the Single Action will jarfire in a completely uncontrolled direction. The only way to avoid the last type of accidental discharge is to treat any firearm with the respect due it. No quick drawing with live ammunition, no fancy spinning or fanning. Leave these examples of exhibitionism to Hollywood or use an empty gun, in front of your bathroom mirror. (You'll see a fool.)

Phantom Notches

Of all the dangers inherent in having intermediate hammer notches, probably the least understood is the phenomenon of the phantom notch. A safety notch is an undercut into which the sear nose of the trigger drops. The sequence of movements is such that, as the nose of the sear drops into the notch, the hammer drops slightly forward, locking the sear under the notch's lip. This means the lip of the notch, as a strength requirement, must have some thickness. It is on this thick edge of the notch that it is possible—under certain conditions—to

One of the only really (pre-1968) fully safe copies of the old Colt Single Action, A Daisy BB magazine-repeater.

Single Action Revolvers

mistakenly feel a safety notch. When the sear nose is on this lip the revolver is in a condition where a touch of the trigger will drop the hammer. These phantom notches will never be a factor if the finger is taken *off* the trigger except when actually firing the arm. Also, try not to come from the full-cock notch to any other notches; in other words, always pull the hammer backward only, with the trigger completely finger free, then let the sear nose of the trigger drop into the notch desired. Since we have already found the quarter-notch redundant and dangerously useless, the only phantom notch that could be possibly entered would appear to be the half-cock for loading. Yet, since by design, the half-cock notch only releases the cylinder when the hammer is pulled back, *not let down,* there is virtually no danger of accidentally landing on the phantom edge of this notch.

The Single Action After 1968

In the years following the 1968 Gun Act all imported hammered revolvers that failed the hammer drop test have been barred from these shores. This means that the flood of Colt Single Action copies from overseas was completely stopped as of the effective date of the Act. Most overseas export manufacturers quit without an attempt to redesign and thereby beat the 1968 law. As I say, *most,* but fortunately not all, for three foreign firms (each in a different country) came up with an answer to making the Single Action safe. Further, even with no legal or economic requirement, one progressive domestic manufacturer redesigned his Single Actions to incorporate a hammer drop-proof safety, along with some fringe benefits. Let's now take a look at how each of these firms solved the problem, one which goes back to the earliest Colt Paterson cap and ball revolver.

The Cattleman Line

In Northern Italy, in the foothills of the Alps, is the town of Gardone Val Trompia. In this Tyrolean spa area is the arms firm of Aldo Uberti and Company. The Uberti Company logo is the business end of a gun barrel with a "U" in it. The Uberti line of "Cattleman" Single Action revolvers is distributed by LA Distributors Inc. of New York City. From my experience with them they are well-made and well-finished revolvers. These Cattleman revolvers have, besides the normal single action features, a one-piece wood grip and a trigger guard and backstrap of polished cast brass.

The basic Cattleman comes in three calibers: 357 Magnum, 44 Magnum and 45 Colt. The 357 and 45 Colt are offered in three regular barrel lengths: 4¾″, 5½″ and 7½″. The 44 Magnum comes only with 6″ and 7½″ barrels. An adjustable-sight version called the "Buckhorn" comes in the same barrel lengths as the fixed-sight models except that no 4¾″ barrel is offered. The Buckhorn can also be had in a legal stocked version with an 18″ barrel. Last, there's a 22 rimfire long rifle caliber revolver called the "Trailblazer." This comes with an interchangeable cylinder for the 22 Winchester Magnum cartridge, and with a 5½″ or 6½″ barrel.

In addition to all this, these fine revolvers have a hammer safety. With a Cattleman the shooter can load all 6 chambers and pull the hammer back to the safety or quarter-notch without a qualm! When the hammer is in this position the sear nose of the trigger pushes upward on a rod which pivots a steel block in the frame. The frame has a special recess, just below the firing-pin hole, into which the block fits when the gun is in a non-firing unlocked position. This

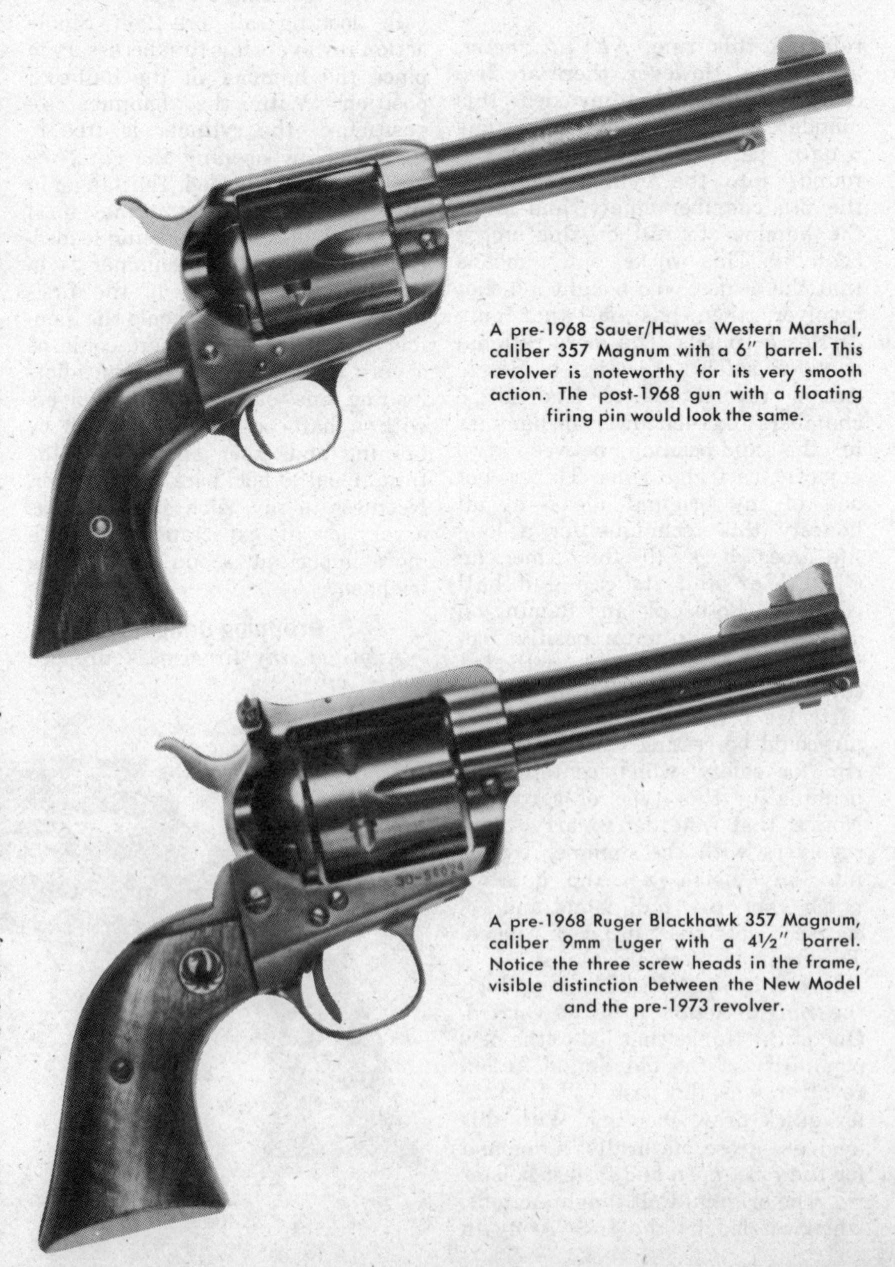

A pre-1968 Sauer/Hawes Western Marshal, caliber 357 Magnum with a 6″ barrel. This revolver is noteworthy for its very smooth action. The post-1968 gun with a floating firing pin would look the same.

A pre-1968 Ruger Blackhawk 357 Magnum, caliber 9mm Luger with a 4½″ barrel. Notice the three screw heads in the frame, visible distinction between the New Model and the pre-1973 revolver.

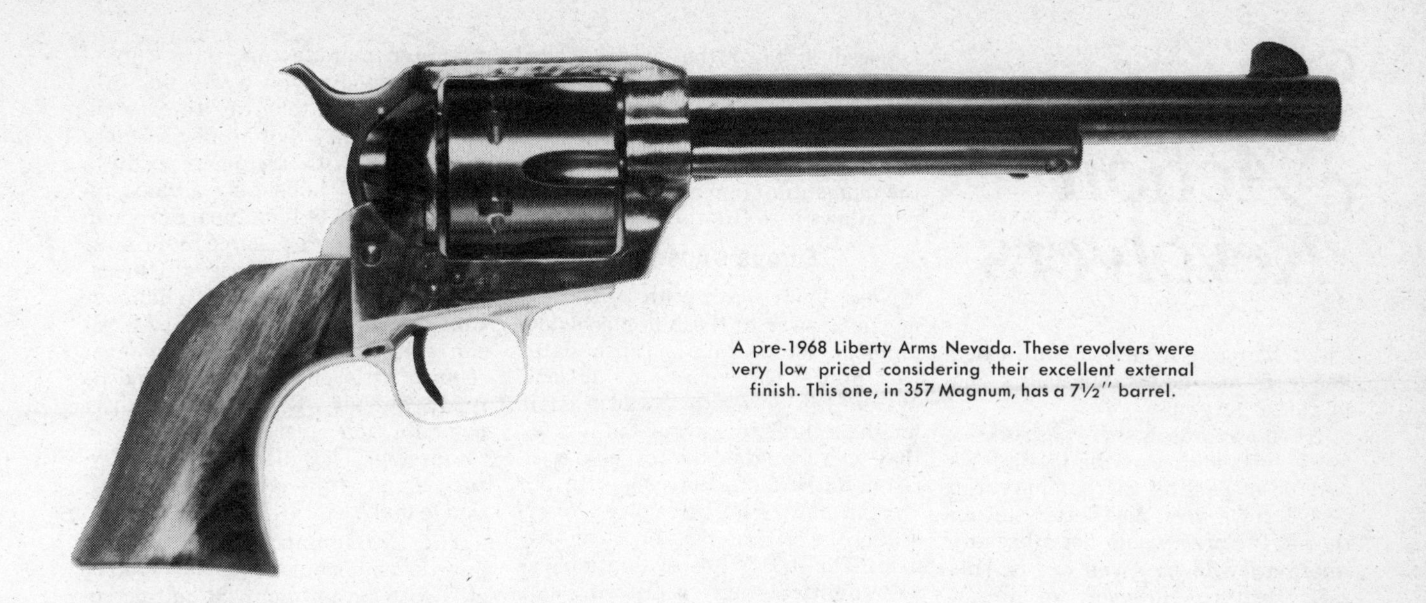

A pre-1968 Liberty Arms Nevada. These revolvers were very low priced considering their excellent external finish. This one, in 357 Magnum, has a 7½" barrel.

means that, were you to drop a Cattleman Single Action carried at quarter-cock, it could land on its hammer safely—a piece of solid steel would fully block any movement of the firing pin toward the loaded cartridge. The fact that such an unlucky drop will usually strip the safety notch off the hammer in no way negates the reliability of this type of safety. Externally this safety device has in no way changed the aesthetic values—if that's the word—set up by Colt so many years ago. At this point, let's give Uberti a merit star for a job well done in solving a century old problem.

The Virginian Line

The firm of Hammerli has long been associated with quality target firearms. The Hammerli plant is located in Lenzburg, Switzerland, in the northern section of this little country. Recently Hammerli has been selling a copy of the old Colt Single Action through the firm of Interarms in Alexandria, Va. When one says "Swiss" and "firearms" one gets a picture of first class precision made guns. The Hammerli "Virginian" Single Action does nothing to tarnish this well-earned reputation. The Virginian is offered in the normal three barrel lengths—4¾", 5½" and 7½", and in 357 Magnum and 45 Colt calibers. This excellent revolver, besides its wonderful finish and chrome-plated backstrap and trigger guard, also exhibits a hammer safety. The Hammerli approach to a hammer safety is nothing like the Uberti's. (It is these differences that make firearms such an interesting field of study for the student and engineer. There is little laudable about copying somebody else's answer to a difficult problem; the excitement is for two—or in our case four—firms to come up with entirely different answers to the same problems.)

The designers at Hammerli saw that if the cylinder pin could be pushed back and locked against the forward part of the hammer it could block any possible *forward movement* of that hammer. The ingenious Swiss found that in no way could they lock the cylinder pin so as to block the hammer in the quarter-cock position. On the other hand the half-cock or loading position left the hammer far enough to the rear to allow the cylinder pin to have a second groove and thereby lock the half-cock position in a very positive manner. To activate the safety on the Hammerli Single Action you half-cock the hammer and push the cylinder-pin catch to the open position; then you push the cylinder pin to the rear until the released cylinder latch locks it into place via the second circumferential groove. This position now assures that the hammer, held at half-cock, is securely locked. To release the cylinder pin safely, the shooter depresses the cylinder-pin latch with his left thumb as he carefully lowers the hammer with his right hand thumb. Alternatively, the cylinder-pin latch can be depressed and the pin pulled forward to the unlocked notch. This method avoids any controlled lowering of the hammer, but it is awkward and it involves some juggling of the gun with both hands held too far forward on the revolver's frame. There is no doubt that the Hammerli solution is simple to the degree that one is tempted to say "Why didn't I think of that?" The extra long, two-grooved cylinder pin is apparently going to be offered—with the latch assembly—as a safety package to all owners of Colt Single Actions and other similar pre-1968 revolvers. Hats off to the Hammerli Virginian, an amazingly simple answer to a seemingly complicated problem.

The Marshal Line

The firm of J. P. Sauer has long been associated with the most progressive firearms design. It was Sauer that designed the 38 (H), the super modern double action automatic pistol just prior to World War II. With this background, it is understandable that when turned loose on the Colt Single Action, one could expect to see some startling innovations. J. P. Sauer & Sohn of Eckernförde, West Germany, makes the Hawes line of Single Action revolvers. The Sauer plant is just at the border of West Germany. These Sauer/Hawes guns are very well made and have the lightest action of any of the big caliber revolvers examined for this article.

The basic Hawes/Sauer line of Single Action "Marshal" revolvers consists of: Three types of 22s, each with a 5½" barrel—one in 22 Long Rifle, one in 22 Magnum and a third in both calibers via 2 cylinders. All of the heavy-caliber Marshals have 6" barrels—these are in 357 Magnum, 44 Magnum and 45 Colt. Each of these can be had with an extra cylinder giving, respectively, 357 Magnum/9mm Luger, 44 Magnum/44-40 (44 WCF) and 45 Colt/45 ACP. I recommend the combos as a good investment at $20 or so more. Any of the above can be had with nickel finish or with brass backstrap and trigger guard. Also a case-hardened frame has been added as an option to replace the normal blue. The top of the line is the

Single Action Revolvers

Chief Marshal, which has an extra heavy frame, adjustable sights and larger target grips.

When I approached Hawes seeking more information about Sauer's method of passing the hammer drop test, I got a very nice letter stating that J. P. Sauer would not allow any information to be given out on this safety feature. However, we are not completely in the dark; the Sauer secret is the same one used many years before by our gun design genius, John M. Browning—the floating or inertial firing pin! In this time honored system, the spring-loaded firing pin is so short that when the hammer is resting on it, it will not reach the primer. Yet when the pin is struck by the hammer during firing, the momentum imparted to the firing pin allows it to fire the primer.

Europe's Answer

Now, before going on to the domestic answer to the hammer safety problem, let us take a consolidated look at the three foreign solutions. Maybe I'm going to sound a little tough on three fine firms, but it is not they who should be the target of criticism. Rather, it's the people in our government who have been overseeing the criteria for importing firearms. The H. P. White evaluation was self admittedly only a faltering step to try to establish what is safe in firearms. Yet this preliminary testing procedure was plucked from the White report as though it was the "voice from the mountain." Thus, if you were a foreign manufacturer of a copy of Colt Model Ps, you were suddenly faced with conforming to criteria which certainly didn't offer a safety panacea or with trying to peddle a whole line of hopelessly archaic revolvers to an enlightened European market. The more feasible first course was taken by the Messrs. Uberti, Hammerli and Sauer—find a hammer safety that would pass the fool American safety test. This solution must require little or no redesign and be ready quickly. Revolvers currently in production must be convertible to this system. They all did it. Ironically, each found a different hammer position to make safe.

The Cattleman drop-proofs the quarter-notch, but leaves the revolver still with an unimproved half-notch. This means that should a Cattleman Single Action be dropped during the latter stages of loading it could fire from half-cock.

The Virginian takes the half-cock position and locks it up but they still leave the now non-functional quarter-notch on the hammer. I strongly suggest that Hammerli remove the quarter-notch and that they add a collar to the cylinder pin to keep it from going too deeply through the frame. I found that if the cylinder-pin safety were activated when the hammer is at full cock, the pin can be pushed beyond its safety locking groove. When the shooter now wants to take the safety off, he must force the cylinder pin back with the hammer and, if he should lose control of the hammer, it could fire the gun. A simple, larger-diameter collar could keep this potentially dangerous condition from happening. The Hawes has just such a collar to keep the cylinder pin located in the frame with a minimum of hunting for the locking groove. Adopting these minor changes, the Virginian will have accomplished both carry and load safety even against the deadly "phantom notch." The only final disadvantage to the Swiss system is that it requires a knowledge of this particular arm to know how to activate the safety. This should be covered by lucid and simple instruction data—these were not present with my sample.

The Sauer inertial-pin answer protects the revolver in the uncocked-hammer position. This makes a dandy way-to-carry firearm, but overlooks the loading dangers as well as the fact that some owners may decide to carry this gun in the quarter-notch position, thereby negating the positive safety with sensitive primers. The Sauer/Hawes also takes no

A post-1968 Cattleman, equipped with a positive hammer safety in the quarter-cock position. Sample is in 357 Magnum with a 4¾" barrel.

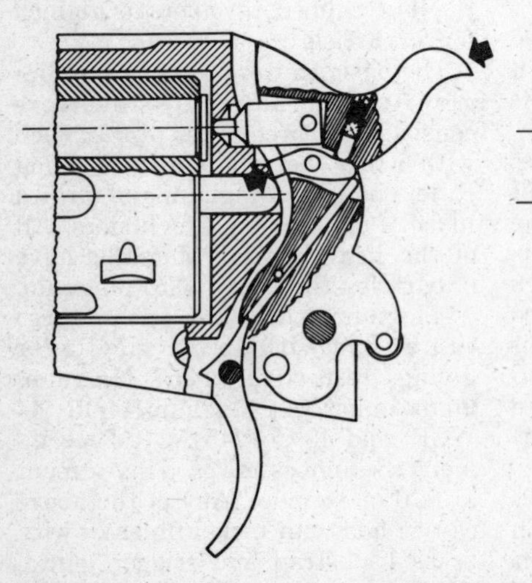

The Cattleman is shown here in the safe quarter-cock notch. This is the Cattleman carrying position.

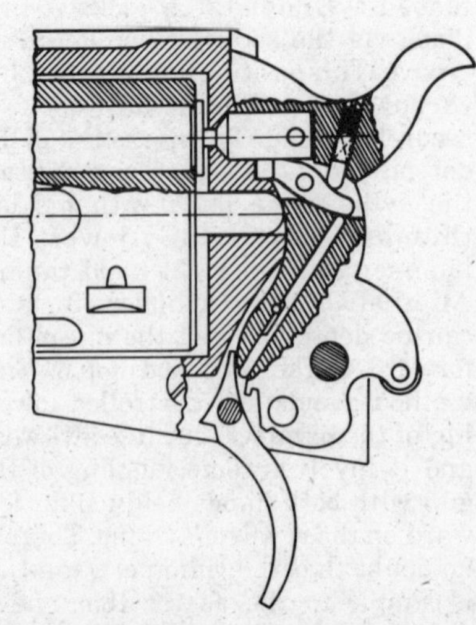

The Cattleman shown as it fires, with the safety block up in its recess in the frame.

precaution against the "phantom notches."

Ruger's Answer

Let us now turn to one domestic manufacturer's answer to the Colt Single Action's perennial safety problem. Bill Ruger of Sturm, Ruger & Co. has come up with a beauty. The Ruger New Model line is as follows: All New Model Super Single-Six 22s come in 22 Long Rifle, with an extra cylinder for the 22 WMR (Winchester Magnum Rimfire). These 22s have 4⅝", 5½", 6½" and 9½" barrels. The Blackhawk series of high powered Single Action revolvers come in calibers 30 Carbine, 357 Magnum, 41 Magnum and 45 Colt, plus a Super Blackhawk in 44 Magnum. The 357 and 45 Colt can also be had with an additional cylinder for 9mm Luger or 45 ACP respectively—a very desirable adjunct, to my mind, and not found in all of the Ruger's overseas cousins. Barrels are 4⅝" and 6½" in 357 and 41 Magnums. The 30 Carbine and the 44 Magnum are logically only offered with a 7½" barrel. The 45 Colt may be had with a 4⅝" or 7½" barrel. All of the Rugers have adjustable target sights as standard equipment, and a big plus is that all of the original Colt's fragile leaf springs have been replaced by music wire springs.

The Ruger, like the Sauer/Hawes, has always been made with the firing pin mounted in the frame, so the first move to make this revolver safe was to relieve the front or breast of the hammer so that it will not reach the firing pin. The Ruger then, in order to fire, needs an additional piece of metal inserted between the falling hammer and the firing pin. This key-like piece is called a transfer bar; it is only in its firing position when the trigger, to which it is mounted, is in its *rearmost* shooting position. We now have a Single Action which has the ability to have its hammer rest safely on a loaded chamber because, with the hammer forward, the trigger is also forward and the transfer bar has dropped away from its firing position. OK, so it's safe to carry but what about loading and "phantom notches" and all those other bugaboos? Ruger took out the quarter-notch as no longer needed, and he also removed the half-cock notch! How do you load? Simple—open the loading gate with the hammer down; the open gate depresses the cylinder lock, allowing the cylinder to spin for loading as do other Single Actions in their half-cock position. Ergo—no intermediate notches are needed anymore and we have what might be described as a

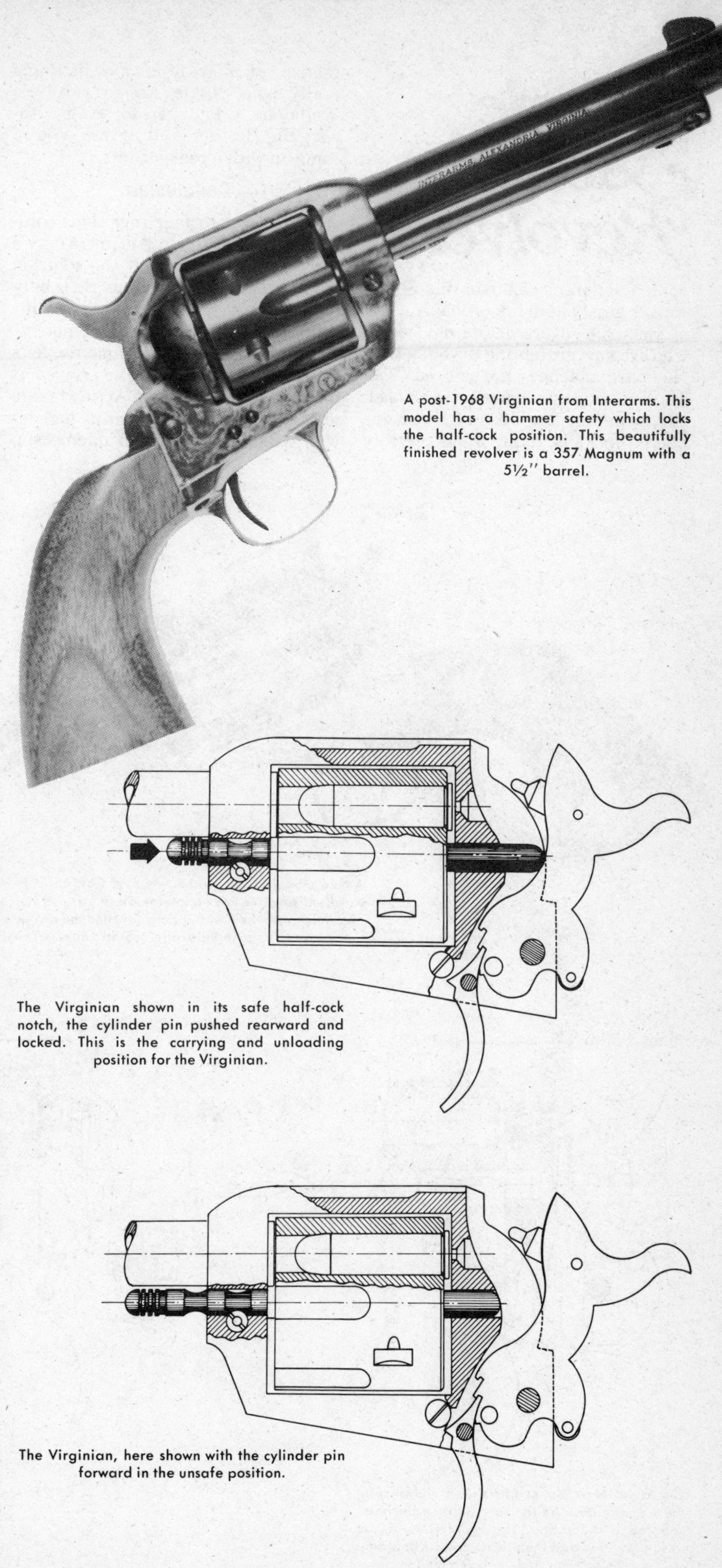

A post-1968 Virginian from Interarms. This model has a hammer safety which locks the half-cock position. This beautifully finished revolver is a 357 Magnum with a 5½" barrel.

The Virginian shown in its safe half-cock notch, the cylinder pin pushed rearward and locked. This is the carrying and unloading position for the Virginian.

The Virginian, here shown with the cylinder pin forward in the unsafe position.

double action mechanism in a Single Action gun. There are probably a few of you true lovers of the old Colt P who are now grumbling to yourselves. No extra notches—no beloved "Tic-Tac-Toe" noises when you crank back the hammer. The loss of these euphonic clicks is, to my mind, entirely compensated for by our now having a really safe Single Action revolver. Well done, Bill Ruger, for even without "Big Brother" telling you, you've come up with a real goodie!

Conclusion

Hail, then, to four ingenious solutions to the Single Action Army's safety problems, even if the solution in the case of the three imports is only partial, and was legislated rather than volunteered. Whatever motivation led to these improvements, let's be thankful that they have arrived at last and that the Single Action is safe at last. In the entire firearms legislative tempest, we find in microcosm, the entire Big Brother socialistic fallacy. Can politicos and bureaucrats be omniscient on the subject of firearms safety? The answer is a demonstrable NO! Nevertheless, the implementation of some control over the Single Action Army safety has been an accidental bonus from Washington. It now becomes very important that all users of Single Action revolvers be completely familiar with the safety method of their own guns. Even more important, just because some borrower of your Single Action says he understands this type of arm—don't believe him! Show him where the safety is and how it works. Keep shooting safe and maybe we can keep shooting. ●

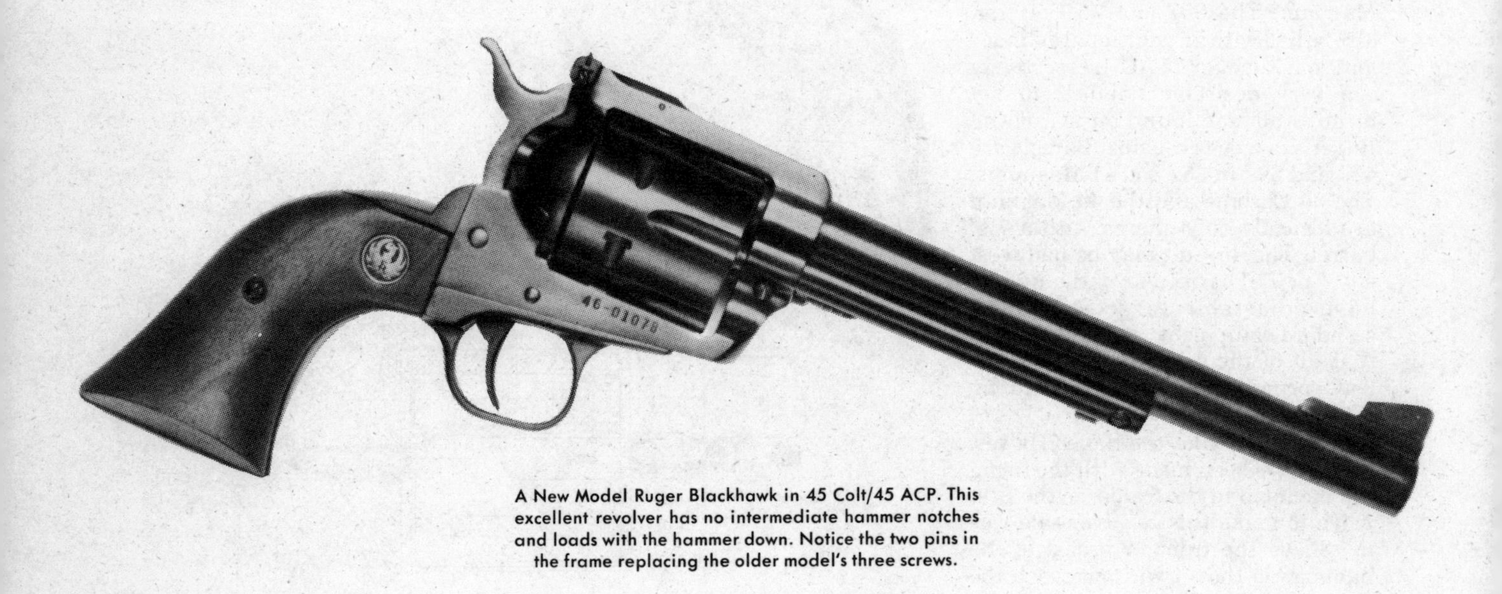

A New Model Ruger Blackhawk in 45 Colt/45 ACP. This excellent revolver has no intermediate hammer notches and loads with the hammer down. Notice the two pins in the frame replacing the older model's three screws.

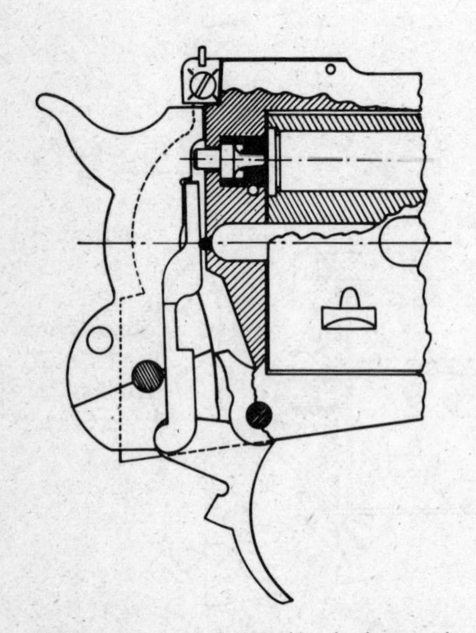

The Ruger New Model Blackhawk, shown with the hammer down in the safe position for both carrying and loading. The transfer bar is in its low position and there is no contact between the hammer and the firing pin.

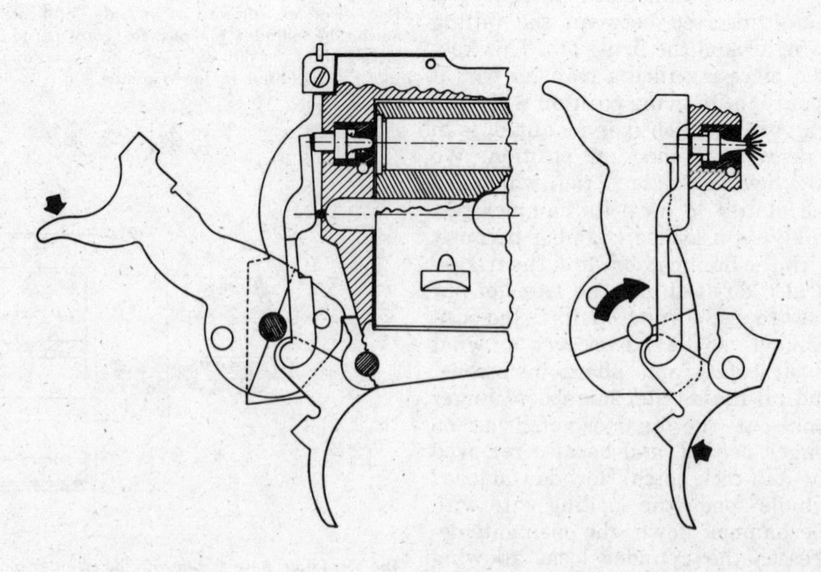

The Ruger New Model Blackhawk shown (left) just before firing—notice the transfer bar is high and the trigger is back. Shown (right) at the moment of firing, it can be seen that the transfer bar acts as an extended hammer face.

A History of Proof Marks

Gun Proof in Germany

This new "History of Proof Marks," begun in our 22nd edition, has been deeply researched by the author. Imperial and modern Germany—East and West—are thoroughly covered in this 8th installment.

by Lee Kennett

Imperial Germany

THOUGH GERMANY has long had an excellent reputation for its firearms, its national proof system is of recent date. The reason is quite simple: Germany did not come into existence as a nation until 1871. Before that time, proof was administered by makers or local proofhouses; Prussia, one of the 30-odd German states, established an official proofhouse, by a royal decree of 30 April 1867, at Solingen, a city famous for its sword blades. The testing, done by Prussian government officials, consisted of a single black powder barrel proof. The proofmark (no. 1) consisted of an eagle and the letters SP (*Solingen Probiranstalt* or Solingen Proof House). Proof was conducted there from 1867 until 1878, when the proofhouse was closed. It is possible that official and semi-official proof installations existed at the same time in others of the German states, but no records of them seem to have survived.[1]

The Proof Law of 1891

By the 1880s Germany had become unified and was well on the way to becoming industrialized as well. The arms industry, concentrated in Suhl, Zella-Mehlis, Oberndorf, Sömmerda, and other towns, was developing rapidly. In 1889 the value of commercial arms exported exceeded two million marks. But the establishment of compulsory official proof in other European countries threatened to curtail German arms exports unless she followed suit. The impetus for national proof seems to have come from the gunmakers themselves, and in 1886 the German government began to study the question. A legislative draft, prepared by a panel of experts, was submitted to the Reichstag late in 1890. The text, which borrowed heavily from the British, Belgian, French (and pending) Austrian legislation, was voted into law on May 19, 1891. The *Ausfuhrungsbestimmungen*, or implementing regulations, appeared on June 22, 1892, and the new system went into effect on April 1, 1893. Proofhouses opened in Suhl, Zella-Mehlis, Frankfurt am Oder, and Oberndorf am Neckar—site of the vast Mauser works.

The 1891 law provided for compulsory proof of all commercial firearms, with a few exceptions: antiques, arms whose chief quality was artistic or scientific, government arms, and those imported from countries whose proofmarks were recognized.

Proof of all types of arms was to be administered with the official black powder then in use by the German Army, known as *Neues Gewehr-Pulver Modell 71 (NGPm/71). Proof of the various types of arms was as follows:*

Revolvers: these were given a definitive proof; service or standard cases and bullets were used, but with as large a powder charge as the cylinder length would permit, one shot being fired from each chamber. The mark designating this proof was the Imperial crown (no. 2). In addition, inspection after proof was indicated by the same crown over the letter U, signifying *Untersuchung* or inspection (no. 3).

Pocket Pistols, Saloon and Flobert type arms: these were proved with 1½ times the service powder charge and the service bullets. Marks affixed were the same as those for revolvers (nos. 2 and 3).

Shotguns: these required provisional and definitive proof, whether muzzle-loading or breech-loading. Barrels submitted to provisional proof had to be in an advanced state of completion; barrels for multi-barreled guns had to be ready for joining, and could also be submitted already joined. Touch holes in false breeches were not to be more than 1.6mm in diameter. Lead shot, 2.5mm in diameter (no. 7), was prescribed for all barrels. A wad was placed over the powder and another over the shot. These were of felt, to exact caliber, and their thickness was not to exceed their diameter. The proofmark for this proof was the Imperial eagle (no. 4).

Definitive proof was given to finished arms, which could be submitted in the white. Shot and wads used were the same, but guns with a rifled choke were proved with a conical-nosed lead slug weighing 1½ times the service shot charge, and 0.2mm smaller in diameter than the unchoked portion of the bore. The mark for definitive proof was the same Imperial eagle used for provisional proof, but with the addition of the inspection mark (no. 5). Bore diameter was measured at the muzzle for cylinder bore guns or at 22cm from the breech for choke bores, the figures stamped next to the definitive proofmark. Nominal bore diameter was not designated in millimeters, but according to the English system, that is 12, 12/1, etc. Cartridge (gauge) size was indicated by the correct number enclosed in a circle (no. 6).

Powder charges were provided in two tables, one for muzzleloaders, and one for breechloaders (Tables I and II). In each case, these give not only provisional and definitive proof charges, but service charges as well, all using the NGPm/71 powder. Charges for provisional proof of breechloaders were triple the service powder charge and double the service shot charge. Definitive proof loads for the same type of arms were twice the normal powder charge and 1⅓ times the standard shot charge.

Shotguns were stamped on the barrels with the Imperial crown over the letter S, signifying *Schrot* or shot (no. 7). Smoothbores with choke were to be so declared by the maker, and were stamped with a supplementary mark, the Imperial crown over the letter W for *Würgebohrung* or choke bore (no. 8). Barrels incorporating rifled choke were stamped with the Imperial crown over the interlaced letters W and S (no. 9). Guns chambered for the 70mm or 2¾ inch case were stamped "70," but those of 65mm length carried no indication.

Rifles: submitted to both provisional and definitive proof in conditions similar to those for shotguns. Proof and service charges were given in the proof table (Table III), lead bullets being used in both proofs. Rifles bore the same provisional and definitive proofmarks as shotguns, but also an additional mark, the Imperial crown over the letter G, signifying *Geschoss*, or bullet (no. 10). One of the most curious features of rifle proof was the caliber designation stamped on the arm. This was not done in millimeters, but in gauge. Thus a 7.62mm rifle was stamped 172.28, indicating 172.28 lead balls to the pound—obviously a confusing designation.[2]

One type of rifle was accorded a separate status. This was the express rifle, for which heavier proof charges were provided (Table IV). Such rifles carried, in addition to the ordinary stamp for rifled arms, the Imperial crown over the letter E (no. 11).

To facilitate the coming into effect of the 1891 legislation, it was provided that all arms already in process of manufacture or in dealer's stocks would be given a special mark, the Imperial crown over a V (no. 12). This was not a true proofmark, being affixed automatically to all arms presented to local police authorities. (It is not uncommon to find this mark and regular proofmarks as well, though the latter were not required). The law did not say if arms in private possession required this stamping, and it is doubtful if many such were submitted.

On request, completed shotguns without choke and rifles could undergo a single definitive proof, although with the stronger charges of provisional proof. This was undoubtedly designed for imported arms whose proofmarks were not recognized. It was designated by a special mark (no. 13).

The law sought to cover proof not otherwise provided for. For example, the proof tables give no proof or service loads for rifles of less than 7.62mm. In such cases the makers were required to submit service loads and the proof authorities devised proof loads accordingly. In this case the service charge was stamped on the barrel near the breech, so as to be clearly visible. Thus the stamp $\frac{\text{4.4gr. NGPm/71}}{\text{25 g. Blei}}$ meant that the service load was 4.4 grams of NGP m/71 powder and a 25-g. lead bullet.

So far, all proof discussed has been in terms of the NGP m/71 powder. The law provided, however, that on request a supplementary proof with another type of powder could be administered. Once again the maker specified the service charge and the proof authorities "devised" proof loads, using the same proportions as used with ordinary proof powder. Thus a shotgun using a service load of 1.6 grams of Walsrode semi-smokeless powder and 30 grams of shot, would undergo a supplementary definitive proof with 3.2 grams of the same powder and 40 grams of shot. Here again, the service load was stamped on the barrel (no. 15).

A final feature of the law was a provision requiring reproof of altered or modified arms. For this proof a special mark was assigned (no. 16).

Students of German proofmarks of the era will note that the visual inspection or view mark (no. 3) is always in evidence. This represented, in fact, a very meticulous inspection of the entire arm, involving not only solidity and safety of the barrel and breech, but also the measurement of touch holes where used, checking for firing pin protrusion, unreliable trigger systems, faulty extraction, etc.

The German government negotiated proof reciprocity with Great Britain in 1893, with France in 1904. The negotiations with other countries led to some difficulties. In 1893 the Austro-Hungarian government proposed mutual recognition, but the German government maintained that Austro-Hungarian proof was too weak, and the Austrians withdrew their proposal. Agreement was reached in 1910, but on condition that Austria-Hungary henceforth refuse to recognize Belgian proofmarks, which she had done for some 13 years![3] German negotations with Belgium were also not without difficulties; Belgium too was obliged to alter her proof procedures, and to use a large-grain black powder similar to the German one, in order to obtain recognition of her marks in 1893.

It is debatable whether German proof was more rigorous than that in use in other countries.[4] When tested in 1911 at Liège, the German provisional proof in 12 and 16 gauge yielded about 14,700 psi; definitive proofs for the same gauges giving about 9,500 psi. While these were adequate pressures—assuming accurate measurement—they were not significantly higher than proof pressures of other countries. In other respects, the German law was defective. As Otto Maretsch wrote in 1909, it was "out of date even before it was published."[5] The preparation of the text seems to have been very hasty, perhaps to put Germany on an equal footing with Austria-Hungary, whose text appeared almost simultaneously (nearly half the arms exported from Germany in this period were sold in the Austro-Hungarian Empire). It also seems likely that the foreign legislation consulted was rather dated. Thus it is that the law provided no nitro proof, special or not, though these powders were already in wide use. The law did permit a supplementary proof with other powders, but required that powder charges for proof be in the same proportion as for the ordinary proof powder, i.e., triple the normal charge for provisional proof and double for definitive proof. This, of course, was an impossible requirement with some of the violent smokeless powders first developed in Germany; no gun could withstand the pressures generated by such proof charges. Some makers submitted guns for proof with the less powerful English Schultze powder; others submitted guns for proof with the German smokeless powders, but stipulating service charges lower than really used, so as to have supportable proof charges.

The problem of smokeless proof was posed in a dramatic way by the Model 1888 Mauser and its commercial derivatives. In this particular case a solution was sought in the decree of 23 July 1893. This provided that such rifles be proved with a government smokeless powder known as the "4,000 atmosphere powder;" proof pressure was 4,000 metric atmospheres or 58,000 psi. Such barrels were stamped with the *proof* load in this powder and the type of projectile used: thus $\frac{\text{2.67 g. GBP}}{\text{St. M.G.}}$, signifying 2.67 grams of smokeless *Gewehr Blattchen* (Rifle Flake) *Powder* and *Stahl Mantel Geschoss,* for a steel-jacketed bullet. More important, a nitro proofmark was stamped, this composed of two Imperial crowns, the second surmounting the letter N (no. 18).

A single crowned N mark (no. 19) was soon applied to shotguns undergoing smokeless proof; when the practice started in connection with smoothbores is unknown, but the mark was in use by 1908; it was used in conjunction with a mark designating the service load in the appropriate smokeless powder (no. 15).

The proof system still left much to be desired in the case of smokeless powder. Thus a new set of rules for smokeless proof was adopted in September, 1911, at Zella-Mehlis, and a few months later by the other proofhouses. Smokeless proof of shotguns was now done with a single smokeless proof powder, so as to obtain proof pressures of 12,800 psi. Nitro proof was signified by mark no. 19, or by the word "Nitro", or both.

The model 1888 Mauser of 8mm was still proved at 58,800 psi. Other rifles were smokeless proved with a quantity of powder to fill the case within 4mm of the base of the service bullet. Smokeless proof was designated by mark no. 19. The new rules also introduced caliber designation in millimeters. The old practice of stamping the proof charge on rifles had given rise to considerable misunderstanding. The proof powder, an exceptionally strong one, was not available commercially. German sportsmen, whose guns were stamped with a proof load of 2.7 grams of powder, were obviously hesitant to use commercial cartridges containing three grams of what actually was a much weaker sporting powder. To end this misunderstanding, all references to powder charges were abolished. Rifles were now marked with caliber, case length, and type and weight of service bullet. Thus $\frac{\text{8 mm}}{57}$ designated the German military service cartridge. The letters $\frac{\text{St. M.G.}}{\text{14.7g.}}$ meant *Stahl Mantel Geschoss* (steel-jacketed bullet) weighing 14.7 grams. Other bullet types were: K.M.G., *Kupfer Mantel Geschoss* or copper-jacket bullet, and Bl.G for *Blei Geschoss,* a lead bullet.

From 1912 to 1939 proof remained essentially the same. Germany's ratification of the Brussels Convention in 1927 undoubtedly required some minor changes in proof so as to bring it into line with international norms. Some German proofhouses adopted the habit of affixing special marks to identify the proofhouse, thus Zella-Mehlis used the interlaced letter Z and M and Suhl simply stamped its name. Guns of this period often bear the proof date as well: thus 8.13 would signify proof in August, 1913. Proof numbers were also sometimes stamped; 572, for example, would indicated the five hundred seventy-second gun proved that year. All of these practices seem to have been left up to the individual proofhouses, whose customs varied.

Footnotes

[1]Occasionally Damascus barrels are seen bearing a mark composed of crossed pistols and the word "Saxony"; though this would indicate an official proofhouse, there is no mention of it in Saxon legal collections.

[2]The proof law did not provide tables for shotguns and rifles as such, but for arms designed to fire shot and those made for solid projectiles. While this amounts to essentially the same thing, it does not preclude the possibility of a smoothbore being proved by table III and bearing the crowned G, if indeed it was actually designed to fire bullets. This was the case for some of the massive smoothbore doubles built for big game hunting in this period.

[3]This measure brought a very vigorous protest from Liège. See "La reconnaissance des poincons des bancs d'épreuves étrangers en Autriche-Hongrie", *Armurerie liegeoise,* January, 1910, pp. 1285-1287.

[4]A comparison of German proof charges with those in use elsewhere shows that while powder charges were not too different, the German proof used a far greater weight of shot. When it was introduced at Suhl there were a great many complaints over the large number of barrels that burst or bulged at proof. "Allemagne", *Bulletin du musee d'armes de Liège,* July-September 1893, p. 57. On the other hand, Jules Polain in his *Des bancs d'epreuves,* p. 3, says that German charges were not stronger than Belgian ones, for much of the large-grain German powder was blown from the barrel unignited.

[5]Otto Maretsch, "Les établissements d'épreuve et d'essais des armes á feu", *Armurerie liegeoise,* November, 1909, p. 1259.

The Law of 1939

The law of 1891 with its various amendments provided fairly satisfactory proof. But gunmakers continued to agitate for a new and comprehensive proof law. The project was taken up in governmental circles several times after World War I, but in the unsettled conditions of the 1920s none of these projects was translated into legislation. It was not until 1937 that the government began work on the draft that was to replace the 1891 legislation. The new law was approved on June 7, 1939, and its implementing regulations were issued on July 8, 1939. The new system went into effect on April 1, 1940.

The 1939 system reaffirmed obligatory proof for commercial firearms, including cattle-killing devices and signal guns. Proof was extended to "essential parts" of guns as well, thus extra or replacement barrels fell within the scope of the law, as did barrel inserts. Excluded from proof were guns with recognized foreign proofmarks (Great Britain and other signatories of the Brussels Convention), those proved under the 1891 legislation, and military arms. Also excluded were guns for firing blanks, those used in scientific work, collectors' items (usually pre-1870), and *Zimmerstutzen*, sub-caliber arms designed for indoor target practice. In general, shotguns and multi-barreled arms underwent provisional and definitive proof; all other types received definitive proof only.

Shotguns: Barrels were to be submitted to provisional proof in advanced state of completion as in the 1891 system (no. 23). This proof was made with a special black powder of fixed composition. This propellant in a specified loading had to produce at least 10,000 psi on the first crusher of the international gauge. Proof charges were fixed in a table (Table V). Definitive proof, administered to the gun in the white or completely finished, required one shot with black powder and two with smokeless (no. 24). The black powder load (Table VI), was designed to test the barrel well forward of the chamber. Thus it was required that this load generate 9,100 psi on the *second* crusher of the international pressure gun, located 16.2 centimeters from the breech. The two smokeless loads had to generate 12,000 psi breech pressure in 16 gauge and larger, and 12,800 psi in the smaller gauges. For shotguns chambered for cartridges longer than 70mm (2¾ inches), the proof pressure was raised by 1,470 psi for each 5mm of extra chamber length.

Rifles: Barrels underwent black powder provisional proof (Table VII) only if they were destined for multi-barreled guns (no. 23). All other rifles (and automatic pistols) underwent definitive smokeless proof, consisting of two shots at 30% excess pressure over the strongest commercial loads (no. 24).

All other types of guns underwent definitive proof with nitro or black powder at 30% excess pressure. Any gun for which smokeless powder loads were available had to be proved with smokeless. Flobert guns and special types of arms which fired no normal projectile (cattle killers, signal guns) were stamped with mark no. 25. Other types bore mark no. 26 if proved with black powder or mark no. 24 if proved with smokeless.

Inspection constituted a very important part of proof; there was inspection before proof *(Vorprufung)* and after proof *(Nachprufung)*. This involved not only a quality and safety check of the arm, but also verification of caliber and markings affixed by the manufacturer. All guns had bore and chamber dimensions measured, and these had to conform to standard dimensions. Shotguns were required to bear marks indicating gauge and chamber length. Other arms were to be clearly marked as to caliber as customarily designated, e.g., 6.5x54 MS, 300 H&H, etc. Arms had to be marked and proved for the largest cartridge they would chamber, thus eliminating the danger of guns designed for freak, pygmy loadings. Flobert arms had to bear the word "Flobert."

Manufacturers also had to affix factory numbers and a distinctive trademark or other identifying mark. Importers of foreign guns were to identify themselves similarly. The proofhouse stamped on long arms the month and year of proof (e.g., 8.40, August, 1940). All centerfire shoulder arms were also required to bear on the barrels the DIN designation. This was a symbol indicating steel hardness, as specified by the German Bureau of Measurements and Standards. Essential parts of firearms were given the same inspection and proof as arms themselves. Replacement parts which could not be mounted without the use of special tools received the E stamp, indicating *Ersatz*—substitute. Guns containing such parts were subject to reproof. Repaired arms or those having such replacement parts received at reproof a special proof mark (no. 27). In addition, the concern making the repairs was required to stamp its identifying mark on the gun, preceded by the letter A signifying *Ausbesserung,* repair or alteration.

Firearms not ordinarily subject to obligatory reproof might be voluntarily submitted by owners. If a firing proof were made, mark no. 28, signifying *Freiwilliger Beschuss* or voluntary proof was applied. If the arm was submitted merely to have caliber or chamber dimensions verified, it was fired with the service load and stamped with mark no. 25.

The 1939 law, coupled with the *Waffengesetz* or Gun Law of 1938, concerning possession and use of firearms, enabled the German government to regulate arms to a very high degree. To begin with, the government fixed cartridge and chamber dimensions in the various calibers, and required conformity for submission to proof. Under this rule, for example, rifles with break-open actions could not be built for the 8mm rimless German service cartridge, but only for its rimmed equivalent. Certain types of alterations and repairs—welding of cracks in barrel walls, for example—rendered firearms illegal. They could not be fired, and were subject to confiscation when submitted to proof.

More interesting still are the retroactive features of the law; thus while proofmarks of certain foreign proofhouses were recognized in general, any shotgun proved abroad for black powder only had to be reproved. Proof under the law of 1891 was validated only in part. Proof under the 1891 rules was valid only for: a) arms which had undergone smokeless proof b) arms proved for black powder, for which black powder proof only was required under the 1939 rules and c) handguns and rimfire shoulder arms proved only for black powder.

The inference is clear that centerfire rifles and shotguns not nitro proved before 1939 could not be legally used until reproved. Theoretically, this restriction by extension applied to all antiques, and made the users therefore subject to the six months' imprisonment and fines fixed by the penal provisions of the law. Even more rigorous was the provision that the Reichsminister of Economics, in accord with the Reichsminister of the Interior might decree that any gun whose proof occurred before a date to be specified, had to be proved again.

There seems little doubt that the intention here was to proceed with an obligatory reproof of all old arms in the country that were used by hunters or sportsmen. This was an undertaking that would have taxed the resources of even Hitler's government, and in fact, this rule has never been put into effect. In practice it is possible only to check such arms when a new owner seeks a permit for them or when they are sent to the proofhouse after alteration. As a general rule the proofhouses did not hesitate to nitro-prove such guns that came into their hands.

The proof establishments under the law of 1939 were divided into two classes. *Beschussamter*, or proofhouses proper, and *Beschussnebenstellen*, or auxiliary proof installations. Three main proofhouses were designated, each of which was accorded a specific house mark, to be applied to guns it proved. These were Oberndorf am Neckar (no. 29), Suhl (no. 30) and Zella-Mehlis (no. 31). Two auxiliary houses were sanctioned, one at Berlin, and the other at Frankfurt am Oder; both of these were administratively dependent on the proofhouse at Suhl. The house marks or *Ortzeichen* were used not only as identifying marks, but were also the marks affixed to guns rejected at proof and returned to the makers for reworking.

A final aspect of the 1939 legislation concerned the elaborate proof regulations for commercial ammunition. We have already seen that one of the goals of the 1939 rules was the standardization of firearms—certainly a laudable feature. The same principle was applied to ammunition. Manufacturers were to observe cartridge dimensions specified by the government. At the same time maximum permissible service pressures were to be established for each type of cartridge. These were not to be exceeded by manufacturers. The legislation did permit in certain instances the loading of excess pressure cartridges; these are specified as rifle cartridges which exceed maximum permissible pressures as specified by the government, and shotgun shells whose pressure is 75% or more of definitive smokeless proof pressure. Such cartridges and shells were to have a special serrated rim, easily identifiable by touch; moreover they could only be sold in sealed packages bearing the notice: *Achtung! In normalgepruften Waffen nicht verwendbar!* Attention! Not to be used in arms having undergone ordinary proof! (These regulations did not apply to excess pressure ammunition destined for export). Shotshells were to bear caliber and length designations and the manufacturer's mark. Similarly, rifle cartridges were to be sold only in sealed packages bearing complete caliber designation and the maker's identity.

These controls over ammunition were far more rigorous than those of other countries. Their application presented several problems, notably how to effect control and proof. Proof authorities obviously could not check each cartridge for dimensions, much less test its pressure. The only logical procedure would be to have manufacturers themselves take care of such matters, the proof authorities simply approving these quality control measures and conducting spot checks. Also there is the problem of imported ammunition and, even more difficult to resolve, the regulation of reloading. The result of this situation has been that although the law of 1939 is still the basis of proof in West Germany, the regulations regarding proof of ammunition have not been put into effect as of this writing.

The German Federal Republic (West Germany)

BY THE TIME the Proof Law of 1939 went into effect Germany was already at war, with the inevitable result that production of commercial firearms was severely restricted. At the end of the war the occupying powers took a dim view, for some years, of German arms production in general. When commercial gun production resumed in significant quantities in the 1950s the new West German government was faced with the problem of proof once again. It was quickly found that the 1939 law, whatever the political views of the regime which drew it up, was still completely serviceable. So the law was revalidated and remains the basis of proof today in the German Federal Republic. The only major change in proof was the introduction of a new eagle to replace the earlier *Reichsadler*, whose association with the Nazi regime was too obvious to be retained. (See marks 1-6).

The first proofhouse was opened at Ulm in 1951, or to be more exact the former proofhouse at Oberndorf was transferred there. The Ulm proofhouse continues to use as its house mark the stag horn symbol of Oberndorf (no. 7). Other proofhouses were soon established: Eckernförde, near Kiel, in 1952, whose house mark is an oak leaf (no. 8); Berlin (1953) uses its symbolic bear (no. 9); Hanover (1953) uses a rampant horse (no. 10); Munich (1953) and Cologne (1955) use distinctive shields (nos. 11 and 12).

Table I (Law of 1891)
Proof of Muzzle Loaders Designed to Fire Shot

Gauge	Bore Diameter (mm)	First Proof Powder (grams)	First Proof Bullet (grams)	Second Proof Powder (grams)	Second Proof Bullet (grams)	Service Load Powder (grams)	Service Load Bullet (grams)
4	26.72	53.1	198.4	35.4	132.3	17.7	99.2
5	24.79	41.4	157.8	27.6	105.2	13.8	78.9
6	23.34	34.8	132.8	23.2	88.5	11.6	66.4
7	22.17	30.0	115.2	20.0	76.8	10.0	57.6
8	21.21	26.25	102.8	17.5	68.5	8.75	51.4
9	20.40	23.7	94.0	15.8	62.7	7.9	47.0
10	19.68	21.3	85.0	14.2	56.7	7.1	42.5
11	19.07	18.6	74.4	12.4	49.6	6.2	37.2
12	18.52	17.4	71.0	11.6	47.3	5.8	35.5
13	18.03	17.4	71.0	11.6	47.3	5.8	35.5
14	17.60	15.9	63.8	10.6	42.5	5.3	31.9
15	17.20	15.9	63.8	10.6	42.5	5.3	31.9
16	16.81	14.7	56.6	9.8	37.7	4.9	28.3
17	16.48	14.7	56.6	9.8	37.7	4.9	28.3
18	16.18	14.7	56.6	9.8	37.7	4.9	28.3
19	15.90	13.2	49.6	8.8	33.1	4.4	24.8
20	15.62	13.2	49.6	8.8	33.1	4.4	24.8
21	15.37	13.2	49.6	8.8	33.1	4.4	24.8
22	15.14	10.8	42.5	7.2	28.33	3.6	21.25
23	14.91	10.8	42.5	7.2	28.33	3.6	21.25
24	14.71	10.8	42.5	7.2	28.33	3.6	21.25
25	14.50	10.8	42.5	7.2	28.33	3.6	21.25
26	14.30	10.8	42.5	7.2	28.33	3.6	21.25
27	14.12	10.8	42.5	7.2	28.33	3.6	21.25
28	13.97	10.8	42.5	7.2	28.33	3.6	21.25
29	13.79	10.8	42.5	7.2	28.33	3.6	21.25
30	13.64	10.8	42.5	7.2	28.33	3.6	21.25
31	13.49	8.0	31.8	5.3	21.2	2.66	15.9
32	13.36	8.0	31.8	5.3	21.2	2.66	15.9
33	13.21	8.0	31.8	5.3	21.2	2.66	15.9
34	13.08	8.0	31.8	5.3	21.2	2.66	15.9
35	12.95	8.0	31.8	5.3	21.2	2.66	15.9
36	12.85	8.0	31.8	5.3	21.2	2.66	15.9
37	12.72	8.0	31.8	5.3	21.2	2.66	15.9
38	12.62	8.0	31.8	5.3	21.2	2.66	15.9
39	12.5	8.0	31.8	5.3	21.2	2.66	15.9
40	12.39	8.0	31.8	5.3	21.2	2.66	15.9
41	12.29	5.25	21.2	3.5	14.1	1.75	10.6
42	12.19	5.25	21.2	3.5	14.1	1.75	10.6
43	12.09	5.25	21.2	3.5	14.1	1.75	10.6
44	12.01	5.25	21.2	3.5	14.1	1.75	10.6
45	11.91	5.25	21.2	3.5	14.1	1.75	10.6
46	11.84	5.25	21.2	3.5	14.1	1.75	10.6
47	11.76	5.25	21.2	3.5	14.1	1.75	10.6
48	11.66	5.25	21.2	3.5	14.1	1.75	10.6
49	11.58	5.25	21.2	3.5	14.1	1.75	10.6
50	11.51	5.25	21.2	3.5	14.1	1.75	10.6

German Democratic Republic (East Germany)

Here commercial arms production seems to have resumed shortly after the end of WW II hostilities, with commercial proof reinstituted before the end of 1945. As in the case of West Germany, the validity of the 1939 law was confirmed and remains the basis of proof today in the German Democratic Republic.

Here again, the only important modification of the law was in the proofmarks themselves. Since proof was now concentrated in the Suhl house, the house mark of this establishment, the "sole and pick," became the basic proofmark element, with the addition of the letter M for provisional proof (no. 1), SP for definitive black powder proof (no. 2), and N for smokeless proof (no. 3). The Suhl proof house was designated by a special mark (no. 4).

The government was anxious to develop the arms industry, particularly in terms of export. Thus manufacture of quality arms bearing the prestigious names of Merkel and Simson began again. It was found that the new Suhl proofmarks were unknown to foreign purchasers, and that this

Table II (Law of 1891)
Proof of Breech Loaders Designed to Fire Shot

Gauge	Bore Diameter (mm)	First Proof Powder (grams)	First Proof Shot (grams)	Second Proof Powder (grams)	Second Proof Shot (grams)	Service Load Powder (grams)	Service Load Shot (grams)
4	26.72	47.7	170.0	31.8	113.3	15.9	85.0
5/2	26.06	47.7	170.0	31.8	113.3	15.9	85.0
5/1	25.42	47.7	170.0	31.8	113.3	15.9	85.0
5	24.79	47.7	170.0	31.8	113.3	15.9	85.0
6/2	23.62	47.7	170.0	31.8	113.3	15.9	85.0
6/1	23.82	47.7	170.0	31.8	113.3	15.9	85.0
6	23.34	47.7	170.0	31.8	113.3	15.9	85.0
7/2	22.94	47.7	170.0	31.8	113.3	15.9	85.0
7/1	22.85	31.8	113.4	21.2	75.6	10.6	56.7
7	22.17	31.8	113.4	21.2	75.6	10.6	56.7
8/2	21.84	31.8	113.4	21.2	75.6	10.6	56.7
8/1	21.51	31.8	113.4	21.2	75.6	10.6	56.7
8	21.21	31.8	113.4	21.2	75.6	10.6	56.7
9/2	20.93	31.8	113.4	21.2	75.6	10.6	56.7
9/1	20.65	31.8	113.4	21.2	75.6	10.6	56.7
9	20.40	31.8	113.4	21.2	75.6	10.6	56.7
10/2	20.14	21.3	85.0	14.2	56.7	7.1	42.5
10/1	19.91	21.3	85.0	14.2	56.7	7.1	42.5
10	19.68	21.3	85.0	14.2	56.7	7.1	42.5
11/1	19.38	21.3	85.0	14.2	56.7	7.1	42.5
11	19.07	21.3	85.0	14.2	56.7	7.1	42.5
12/1	18.80	17.4	71.0	11.6	47.3	5.8	35.5
12	18.52	17.4	71.0	11.6	47.3	5.8	35.5
13/1	18.26	17.4	71.0	11.6	47.3	5.8	35.5
13	18.03	17.4	71.0	11.6	47.3	5.8	35.5
14/1	17.80	15.9	63.8	10.6	42.5	5.3	31.9
14	17.60	15.9	63.8	10.6	42.5	5.3	31.9
15/1	17.40	15.9	63.8	10.6	42.5	5.3	31.9
15	17.20	15.9	63.8	10.6	42.5	5.3	31.9
16/1	16.99	14.7	56.6	9.8	37.7	4.9	28.3
16	16.81	14.7	56.6	9.8	37.7	4.9	28.3
17/1	16.64	14.7	56.6	9.8	37.7	4.9	28.3
17	16.48	14.7	56.6	9.8	37.7	4.9	28.3
18	16.18	14.7	56.6	9.8	37.7	4.9	28.3
19	15.90	13.2	49.6	8.8	33.1	4.4	24.8
20	15.62	13.2	49.6	8.8	33.1	4.4	24.8
21	15.37	13.2	49.6	8.8	33.1	4.4	24.8
22	15.14	13.2	49.6	8.8	33.1	4.4	24.8
23	14.91	10.8	42.5	7.2	28.3	3.6	21.25
24	14.71	10.8	42.5	7.2	28.3	3.6	21.25
25	14.50	10.8	42.5	7.2	28.3	3.6	21.25
26	14.30	10.8	42.5	7.2	28.3	3.6	21.25
27	14.12	10.8	42.5	7.2	28.3	3.6	21.25
28	13.97	10.8	42.5	7.2	28.3	3.6	21.25
29	13.79	10.8	42.5	7.2	28.3	3.6	21.25
30	13.64	8.1	28.4	5.4	18.9	2.7	14.2
31	13.49	8.1	28.4	5.4	18.9	2.7	14.2
32	13.36	8.1	28.4	5.4	18.9	2.7	14.2

could have an adverse effect on the export market. Therefore, in 1950 the government abandoned the post-war marks, and replaced them by the old—but well known—proofmarks of the pre-1939 era. Thus proof is presently administered under the 1939 rules but designated with the 1891 marks (nos. 5-12). The possibility of confusing a pre-1939 gun with one of the post-war East German manufacture is not likely, however, for one who examines the marks carefully. First of all the Suhl house mark adopted in 1939 is now used as such. Secondly, the month and year of proof of all arms are clearly stamped (no. 13). Finally, the Imperial eagle mark has been stylized and simplified.

It will be remembered that a rigorous inspection of all arms—a sort of quality control—has traditionally been a part of German proof procedures. The Suhl proofhouse has followed this tendency to its logical conclusion, instituting a *separate* quality control with appropriate marks. This is a unique development in proof.

This procedure is facilitated by the fact that the proofhouse is now an organization of the *Deutsches Amt fur Messwesen und Warenprufung* (German Bureau for Weights and Measures and Testing of Materials). This agency conducts quality control

Table III (Law of 1891)

Proof of Guns Designed to Fire Solid Projectiles

Gauge	Bore Diameter (mm)	First Proof		Second Proof		Service Load	
		Powder (grams)	Shot (grams)	Powder (grams)	Shot (grams)	Powder (grams)	Shot (grams)
1	42.39	221.4	984.1	147.6	984.1	73.8	738.1
	38.10	159.9	711.3	106.6	711.3	53.3	533.5
2	33.65	109.8	487.7	73.2	487.7	36.6	365.8
	31.75	92.1	408.3	61.4	408.3	30.7	306.2
3	29.39	72.6	322.7	48.4	322.7	24.2	242.0
4	26.72	54.3	241.2	36.2	241.2	18.1	180.9
	25.40	46.5	206.5	31.0	206.5	15.5	154.9
5	24.79	43.2	191.7	28.8	191.7	14.4	143.8
6	23.34	36.0	159.5	24.0	159.5	12.0	119.6
	22.86	33.6	149.6	22.4	149.6	11.2	112.2
7	22.17	30.6	136.3	20.4	136.3	10.2	102.2
	21.59	28.2	125.5	18.8	125.5	9.4	94.1
8	21.21	26.7	118.8	17.8	118.8	8.9	89.1
9	20.40	23.7	105.5	15.8	105.5	7.9	79.1
	20.32	23.4	104.1	15.6	104.1	7.8	78.1
10	19.68	21.3	94.4	14.2	94.4	7.1	70.8
	19.56	20.7	92.7	13.8	92.7	6.9	69.5
	19.30	20.1	89.1	13.4	89.1	6.7	66.8
11	19.07	19.5	86.0	13.0	86.0	6.5	64.5
	19.05	19.5	85.7	13.0	85.7	6.5	64.3
	18.80	18.6	82.3	12.4	82.3	6.2	61.7
	18.54	18.3	78.9	12.2	78.9	6.1	59.2
12	18.52	18.3	78.7	12.2	78.7	6.1	59.0
	18.29	17.4	75.9	11.6	75.9	5.8	56.9
13	18.03	16.8	72.8	11.2	72.8	5.6	54.6
	17.78	16.5	69.9	11.0	69.9	5.5	52.4
14	17.60	16.5	67.9	11.0	67.9	5.5	50.9
	17.53	16.5	66.9	11.0	66.9	5.5	50.2
	17.27	16.5	64.3	11.0	64.3	5.5	48.2
15	17.20	16.5	63.5	11.0	63.5	5.5	47.6
	17.02	16.5	61.7	11.0	61.7	5.5	46.3
16	16.81	16.5	59.7	11.0	59.7	5.5	44.8
	16.76	16.5	59.3	11.0	59.3	5.5	44.5
	16.51	16.5	57.1	11.0	57.1	5.5	42.8
17	16.48	16.5	56.8	11.0	56.8	5.5	42.6
	16.26	16.5	54.9	11.0	54.9	5.5	41.2
18	16.18	16.5	54.3	11.0	54.3	5.5	40.7
	16.00	16.5	53.1	11.0	53.1	5.5	39.8
19	15.90	16.5	52.3	11.0	52.3	5.5	39.2
	15.75	16.5	51.3	11.0	51.3	5.5	38.5
20	15.62	16.5	50.4	11.0	50.4	5.5	37.8
	15.49	16.5	49.7	11.0	49.7	5.5	37.3
21	15.37	16.5	49.1	11.0	49.1	5.5	36.8
	15.24	16.5	48.5	11.0	48.5	5.5	36.4
22	15.14	16.5	48.0	11.0	48.0	5.5	36.0
	14.99	16.5	47.3	11.0	47.3	5.5	35.5
23	14.91	16.5	47.0	11.0	47.0	5.5	35.25
	14.73	16.5	46.4	11.0	46.4	5.5	34.8
24	14.71	16.5	46.4	11.0	46.4	5.5	34.8
	14.66	16.5	46.3	11.0	46.3	5.5	34.7
25	14.50	16.5	46.3	11.0	46.3	5.5	34.7
	14.48	16.5	46.3	11.0	46.3	5.5	34.7
26	14.30	16.5	46.3	11.0	46.3	5.5	34.7
	14.22	16.5	46.3	11.0	46.3	5.5	34.7
27	14.12	16.5	46.3	11.0	46.3	5.5	34.7
28	13.97	16.5	46.3	11.0	46.3	5.5	34.7
29	13.79	16.5	46.3	11.0	46.3	5.5	34.7
	13.72	16.5	46.3	11.0	46.3	5.5	34.7
30	13.64	16.5	46.3	11.0	46.3	5.5	34.7
31	13.49	16.5	46.3	11.0	46.3	5.5	34.7
	13.46	16.5	46.3	11.0	46.3	5.5	34.7

programs in all aspects of industry.

The system has been applied to firearms since 1950, and works as follows: Each arms factory submits its various models, which the Suhl authorities examine thoroughly for design, function, tolerances, and general quality. The model is then graded, according to quality, and an appropriate quality mark stamped on each gun of the series. The quality designation is generally valid for a year. Moreover continuing checks are made, and any modification

Table III (Law of 1891) cont'd

Gauge	Bore Diameter (mm)	First Proof Powder (grams)	First Proof Shot (grams)	Second Proof Powder (grams)	Second Proof Shot (grams)	Service Load Powder (grams)	Service Load Shot (grams)
32	13.36	16.5	46.3	11.0	46.3	5.5	34.7
33	13.21	16.5	46.3	11.0	46.3	5.5	34.7
34	13.08	16.5	46.3	11.0	46.3	5.5	34.7
35	12.95	16.5	46.3	11.0	46.3	5.5	34.7
36	12.85	16.5	46.3	11.0	46.3	5.5	34.7
37	12.72	16.5	46.3	11.0	46.3	5.5	34.7
	12.70	16.5	46.3	11.0	46.3	5.5	34.7
38	12.62	16.5	46.3	11.0	46.3	5.5	34.7
39	12.50	16.5	46.3	11.0	46.3	5.5	34.7
	12.45	16.5	46.3	11.0	46.3	5.5	34.7
40	12.39	16.5	46.3	11.0	46.3	5.5	34.7
41	12.29	16.5	46.3	11.0	46.3	5.5	34.7
42	12.19	16.5	46.3	11.0	46.3	5.5	34.7
43	12.09	16.5	46.3	11.0	46.3	5.5	34.7
44	12.01	16.5	46.3	11.0	46.3	5.5	34.7
	11.94	16.5	46.3	11.0	46.3	5.5	34.7
45	11.91	16.5	46.3	11.0	46.3	5.5	34.7
46	11.84	16.5	46.3	11.0	46.3	5.5	34.7
47	11.76	16.5	46.3	11.0	46.3	5.5	34.7
	11.68	16.5	46.3	11.0	46.3	5.5	34.7
48	11.66	16.5	46.3	11.0	46.3	5.5	34.7
49	11.58	16.5	46.3	11.0	46.3	5.5	34.7
50	11.51	16.5	46.3	11.0	46.3	5.5	34.7
	11.45	16.5	46.3	11.0	46.3	5.5	34.7
51.05	11.43	16.5	46.3	11.0	46.3	5.5	34.7
54.61	11.18	16.5	43.6	11.0	43.6	5.5	32.7
58.50	10.92	16.5	40.9	11.0	40.9	5.5	30.7
62.78	10.67	16.5	38.1	11.0	38.1	5.5	28.6
67.49	10.41	16.5	35.5	11.0	35.5	5.5	26.6
72.68	10.16	16.5	32.8	11.0	32.8	5.5	24.6
78.41	9.91	10.8	31.2	7.2	31.2	3.6	23.4
84.77	9.65	10.2	29.5	6.8	29.5	3.4	22.1
91.83	9.40	9.3	27.9	6.2	27.9	3.1	20.9
99.70	9.14	8.7	26.1	5.8	26.1	2.9	19.6
108.49	8.89	8.1	24.4	5.4	24.4	2.7	18.3
118.35	8.64	7.5	22.9	5.0	22.9	2.5	17.2
129.43	8.38	6.9	21.2	4.6	21.2	2.3	15.9
141.95	8.13	6.3	19.5	4.2	19.5	2.1	14.6
156.14	7.87	5.7	17.7	3.8	17.7	1.9	13.3
172.28	7.62	5.4	16.1	3.6	16.1	1.8	12.1

in the model or change in quality results in a withdrawal of the assigned quality mark and reevaluation. The quality marks are prominently stamped. In the case of doubles, they are usually applied to the lug.

Three separate quality stamps are now in use: Excellent quality is designated by a Q and a numeral 1 (no. 14). Good quality is designated by the numeral 1 inside the triangle (no. 15). Serviceable quality is designated by the numeral 2 in an inverted triangle (no. 16).

Previously, a fourth quality mark was used, whose main element was an S for *Sonderklasse* or special class. It was ranked between excellent and good quality. This mark (no. 17) was dropped in 1961.

As a final note, the same quality control and quality marks are applied to sporting ammunition. Ammunition is checked for maximum pressure (which must not exceed certain limits); velocity and other aspects of projectile behavior are likewise tested, as is over-all quality and uniformity. Thus a serious effort has been made to implement the provisions of the 1939 law regarding proof of ammunition. ●

Bibliography

The text of the 1891 legislation and proof rules, as well as copious commentary and comparison with other proof systems, may be found in Georg Koch, *Gesetz betreffend die Prufung der Läufe und Verschlüsse der Handfeuerwaffen vom 19. Mai 1891,* Berlin, 1892. For the everyday operation of the 1891 system the best sources are Otto Maretsch, "Der staatliche Beschuss der Handfeuerwaffen," *Schuss und Waffe,* 15 August 1908, pp. 525-527; and the anonymous article "Règlement de service du banc d'épreuves de Suhl," *Armurerie liegeoise,* January, 1910, pp. 1288-1289; February, 1910, pp. 1302-1304. The most thorough account of the 1939 system and its application in West Germany is that of Dr. Georg Seitz, "Überblick über die Entwicklung, Organisation und Aufgabe des Beschusswesens," *Explosivstoffe,* no. 4 (April, 1960), pp. 71-78; no. 5 (May, 1960) pp. 89-98. For supplementary information supplied by letter, the author wishes to thank Drs. Georg Seitz and Karl F. Zobel of the Physikalisch-Technische Bundesanstalt, Brunswick, West Germany, and Herr Bornmüller, Director of the Suhl proofhouse.

Table IV (Law of 1891)
Proof of Express Rifles

Gauge	Bore Diameter (mm)	Bore Diameter (inches)	First Proof Powder (grams)	First Proof Ball (grams)	Second Proof Powder (grams)	Second Proof Ball (grams)	Service Load Powder (grams)	Service Load Ball (grams)
24	14.66	.577	32.1	51.9	21.4	51.9	10.7	38.9
37	12.70	.500	29.1	38.0	19.4	38.0	9.7	28.5
51.05	11.43	.450	23.4	37.2	15.6	37.2	7.8	27.9
72.68	10.16	.400	16.5	19.1	11.0	19.1	5.5	14.3
99.7	9.14	.360	9.75	11.2	6.5	11.2	3.25	8.4

Table V
Black Powder Provisional Proof of Shotgun Barrels (Law of 1939)

Bore Diameter (mm)	Proof Load (grams) Powder	Shot	Bore Diameter (mm)	Proof Load (grams) Powder	Shot
up to 12.5	9.5	25	up to 17.9	15	63
up to 13.5	10.3	30	up to 18.9	17	73
up to 14.45	11.1	35	up to 19.9	21	85
up to 15.4	12.1	43	up to 21.5	32	113
up to 16.3	12.9	50	over 21.5	47	170
up to 17.0	13.8	55			

Table VI
Black Powder Definitive Proof of Shotguns (Law of 1939)

Gauge	Bore Diameter (mm)	Chamber Length (mm)	Proof Load (grams) Powder	Shot
4	23.4 to 23.8	82.5	32	113
8	20.8 to 21.2	83.5	21.2	75
10	19.3 to 19.7	70	14.2	58
		75	15.7	60
12	18.2 to 18.6	65	11.6	47
		70	12.2	51
16	16.8 to 17.2	65	9.8	38
		70	10.3	41
20	15.7 to 16.1	65	8.8	33
		70	9.3	36
24	14.6 to 15.0	63.5	7.2	28
		70	7.6	31
28	13.7 to 14.1	63.5	6.9	24
32	12.6 to 13.0	63.5	5.4	19

Table VII (Law of 1939)
Black Powder Provisional Proof of Rifled Barrels
(Destined for Multi-Barreled Guns)

Bore Diameter (mm)	Proof Load (grams) Powder	Ball	Bore Diameter (mm)	Proof Load (grams) Powder	Ball
4	1.5	4.5	10	9.42	28.3
4.5	1.9	5.7	10.5	10.39	31.2
5	2.35	7.0	11	11.4	34.2
5.5	2.84	8.5	11.5	12.48	37.5
6	3.38	10.2	12	13.56	40.7
6.5	4.0	12.0	12.5	14.76	44.3
7	4.62	13.9	13	15.96	47.9
7.5	5.3	15.9	13.5	17.16	51.5
8	6.0	18.0	14	18.5	55.4
8.5	6.8	20.4	14.5	19.8	59.4
9	7.63	22.9	15	21.2	63.7
9.5	8.5	22.5			

German Proof Marks

In this table the mark numbers at left are those assigned by the author, and keyed by him to the text for reference. The 2nd column shows the true form of the proof mark and gives the period of its use. The last column tells of the marks' significance.

Germany to 1945

No.	Mark	Significance
1	 SP 1867-1878	Barrel proof administered by the Prussian proofhouse at Solingen.

System of 1891

No.	Mark	Significance
2	 1891-1939	Single definitive proof of revolvers, pocket pistols, and Flobert arms.
3	U 1891-1939	Supplementary mark signifying inspection or view after proof.
4	 1891-1939	Provisional proof of barrels of shoulder arms.
5	 U 1891-1939	Definitive proof of above.
6	(12) 1891-1939	Supplementary mark indicating gauge designation of shotguns.
7	S 1891-1939	Supplementary mark designating shotgun barrels.
8	W 1891-1939	Supplementary mark indicating barrels with choke.
9	 SW 1891-1939	Supplementary mark for barrels with rifled choke.
10	G 1891-1939	Supplementary mark for barrels firing solid projectiles.
11	E 1891-1939	Supplementary mark applied to express rifles.
12	V 1891-c.1894	Marks applied to arms in course of manufacture or in dealers' stocks when the 1891 law came into effect, without proof.
13	B 1891-1939	Mark indicating a single definitive proof, made with provisional proof charge. Chiefly applied to imported arms.
14	**4.4 g NGP m/71** **25g Bl.** 1891-1939	Supplementary mark indicating service load for a gun of caliber not provided for in proof tables (here, 4.4 grams of NGP m/71 powder and 25 of lead).
15	**2.2g Sch. P.** **32g Bl.** **2.7g Tr. Fl. P.** **32g Bl.** 1891-c.1913	Two examples of early nitro proof marks, indicating service loads in the powders used for proof. Here Schultze and Troisdorfer Flinten (shotgun) powder.
16	R	Mark designating reproof of repaired or altered arms.
17	**2.67g G.B.P.** **St.M.G.** 1893-1913	Mark designating proof load for smokeless proof of rifles. Here, 2.67 grams of Gewehrblattchen powder and Stahlmantelgeschoss, steel jacketed bullet.
18	 N 1893-1939	Mark designation nitro proof rifles. At first used in conjunction with mark no. 17.
19	N c.1908-1939	Mark for nitro proof of shotguns.

No.	Mark	Description
20	Nitro 1912-1939	Mark for nitro proof of shotguns. Often found in conjunction with mark no.4.
21	8mm 9.3mm 57 82 1912-1939	Supplementary marks for caliber designation of rifles.
22	K.M.G. 14.7 g 1912-1939	Supplementary mark designating service projectile for rifles. Here, Kupfermantelgeschoss, copper jacketed bullet, of 14.7 grams.

System of 1939

No.	Mark	Description
23	M 1939-1945	Provisional proof for barrels of all shotguns and rifle barrels destined for multi-barreled arms.
24	N 1939-1945	Smokeless definitive proof of arms of all types.
25	1939-1945	Definitive proof of Flobert guns and explosive devices.
26	SP 1939-1945	Mark for black powder definitive proof (reserved for arms firing black powder commercial cartridges only).
27	J 1939-1945	Designates reproof of repaired or altered arms.
28	FB 1939-1945	Mark designating voluntary proof of arms not normally falling within the scope of obligatory proof.
29	1939-1945	House mark of the Oberndorf proofhouse.
30	1939-1945	House mark of the Suhl proofhouse.
31	1939-1945	House mark of the Zella-Mehlis proofhouse.

New 1973 West German Proof Marks

(See following page)

In 1973 new regulations appeared which contain several changes in proof procedures, changes which represent a more modern approach generally in European proof houses: increasing use of smokeless powder charges, the use of proof as one step in a general quality-control system, and the decline of provisional proof (which has essentially been of benefit to manufacturers, enabling them to find bad barrels at an early stage in manufacture). Arms now submitted to proof in West Germany undergo a series of tests and evaluations which extend even to the grips of handguns. All arms submitted must bear clear manufacturer's markings and an appropriate serial number. Several changes have been made in the proof marks as a result of these new concepts. Mark No. 1 has been dropped, reflecting the lessened need for provisional proof of barrels as steels have improved. Mark No. 2 has been retained, but the meaning has changed. It now signifies "normal" proof, rather than nitro proof. Cartridges used for this proof generate 30% excess pressure. Three new proof marks have been adopted—see table. *Bundesadler* or eagle surmounting the letter V (mark no. 13) represents "strengthened" (*verstärkter*) proof, which is a definitive nitro proof with pressures 50% over standard operating pressures (used mainly on shotguns designed for 3-inch magnum loads). A second new mark is the eagle surmounting the letter L (mark 14), this one to be used on arms which do not fire normal fixed charges, but instead get their propulsive force from the ignition of flammable liquids and gases. Finally, proof of pressure guns themselves and other firing devices is now compulsory, with a new mark (15) replacing mark 4.

German Federal Republic (West Germany)

Proof system since 1945 (for details see under German law of 1939)

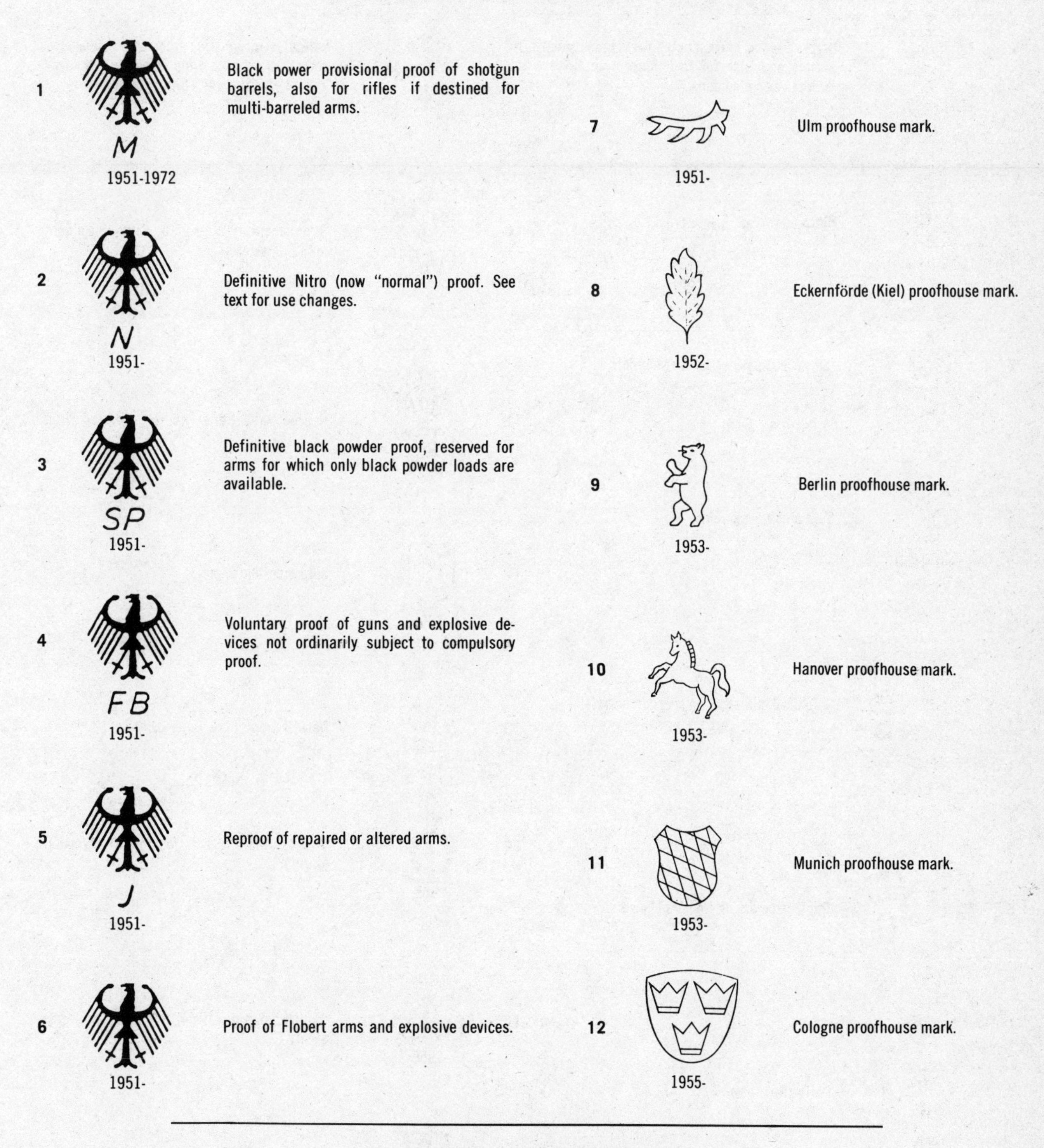

No.	Mark	Description
1	M 1951-1972	Black power provisional proof of shotgun barrels, also for rifles if destined for multi-barreled arms.
2	N 1951-	Definitive Nitro (now "normal") proof. See text for use changes.
3	SP 1951-	Definitive black powder proof, reserved for arms for which only black powder loads are available.
4	FB 1951-	Voluntary proof of guns and explosive devices not ordinarily subject to compulsory proof.
5	J 1951-	Reproof of repaired or altered arms.
6	1951-	Proof of Flobert arms and explosive devices.
7	1951-	Ulm proofhouse mark.
8	1952-	Eckernförde (Kiel) proofhouse mark.
9	1953-	Berlin proofhouse mark.
10	1953-	Hanover proofhouse mark.
11	1953-	Munich proofhouse mark.
12	1955-	Cologne proofhouse mark.

New 1973 West German Proof Marks
(Adopted 1973 – See text)

13 

14  

15 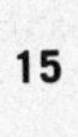 

German Democratic Republic (East Germany)

For details see preceding "German Democratic Republic (East Germany)"

No.	Mark	Period	Description
1	M	1945-1950	Black powder provisional proof of shotgun barrels and also for rifle barrels destined for multi-barreled guns.
2	SP	1945-1950	Black powder definitive proof.
3	N	1945-1950	Smokeless powder definitive proof.
4	15 DR L	1945-1950	Suhl proofhouse mark.
5	S	1950-	Replaced mark no.1 on shotgun barrels.
6	G	1950-	Replaced mark no.1 on rifle barrels.
7		1950-	Definitive proof.
8	U	1950-	Designates inspection after definitive proof (always found in conjunction with mark no.7).
9	N	1950-	Indicates definitive proof with smokeless powder, used as a supplement to mark no.7. In shotguns the word "Nitro" is added.
10	W	1950-	Supplementary mark indicating choke bored shotgun barrels.
11	R	1950-	Reproof of altered and/or repaired arms.
12		1950-	Suhl proofhouse mark.
13	660	1945-	Date of proof; here, June, 1960.
14	1 DDR	1950-	Quality stamp affixed to arms of "excellent quality."
15	1	1950-	Quality stamp affixed to arms of "good quality."
16	2	1950-	Quality stamp affixed to arms of "serviceable quality."
17	S	1950-1961	Quality stamp affixed to arms of "special quality."

Swedish Sjogren automatic shotgun proved under German rules of 1891.

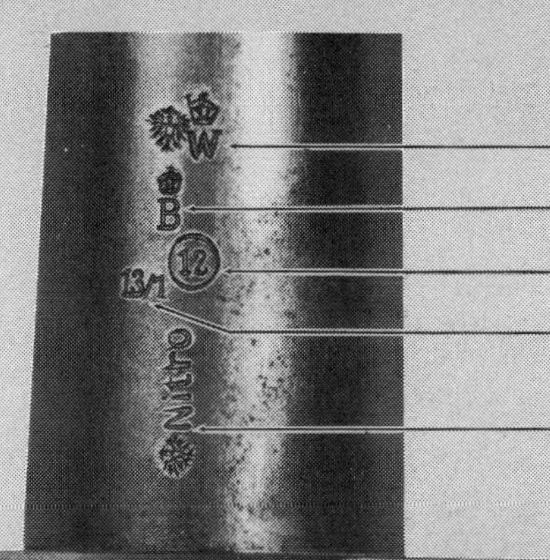

Crowned W—indicates choked barrel.

Mark indicating single definitive proof, but with provisional proof charge.

Nominal gauge.

13/1—bore diameter (18.26mm).

Nitro proof.

Note: The crowned U mark of inspection has been omitted here, though the law of 1891 calls for it's use.

Shotgun proved at Suhl in 1963.

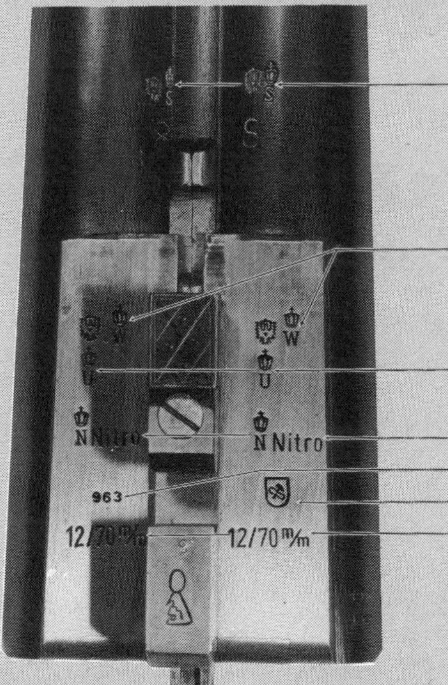

Eagle and crowned S—provisional proof of shotgun.

Crowned W—choke bore barrel.

Eagle and crowned U—definitive proof and inspection.

Indicates definitive proof with smokeless powder.

Date of proof (Sept., 1963).

Suhl house mark.

12/70mm—gauge and chamber length.

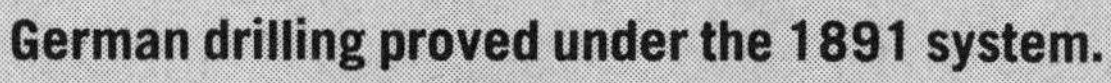

German drilling proved under the 1891 system.

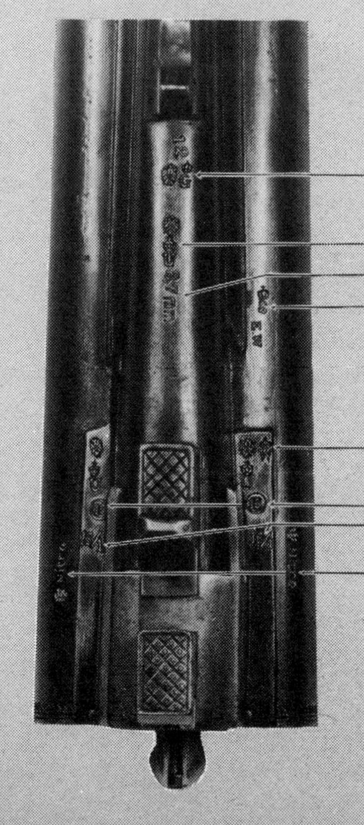

Crowned G—supplementary mark for barrel designed for solid projectile.

Eagle and crowned U—definitive proof.

8.7mm—caliber of rifle barrel.

Crowned S—supplementary mark indicating shot barrel designed for shot.

Crowned W—shows left barrel choked.

16—nominal gauge.

16/1—bore diameter (16.99mm).

Nitro—for smokeless proof.

JOHN KUDLAS

JOHN E. WARREN

Art of the

A display of engraving in fine-line etching. The ad- here will be found in our

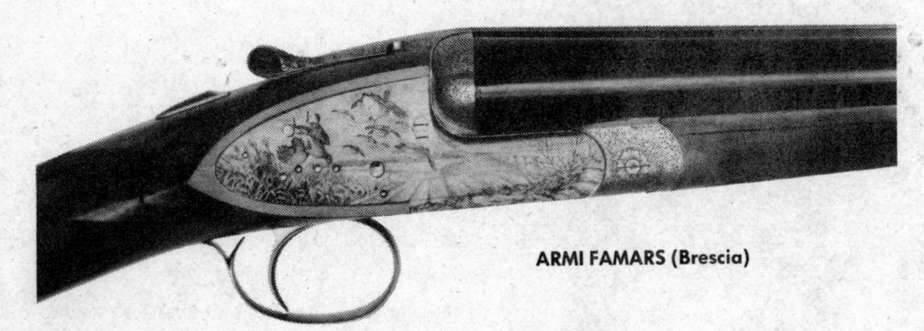

ARMI FAMARS (Brescia)

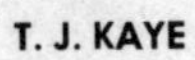

T. J. KAYE

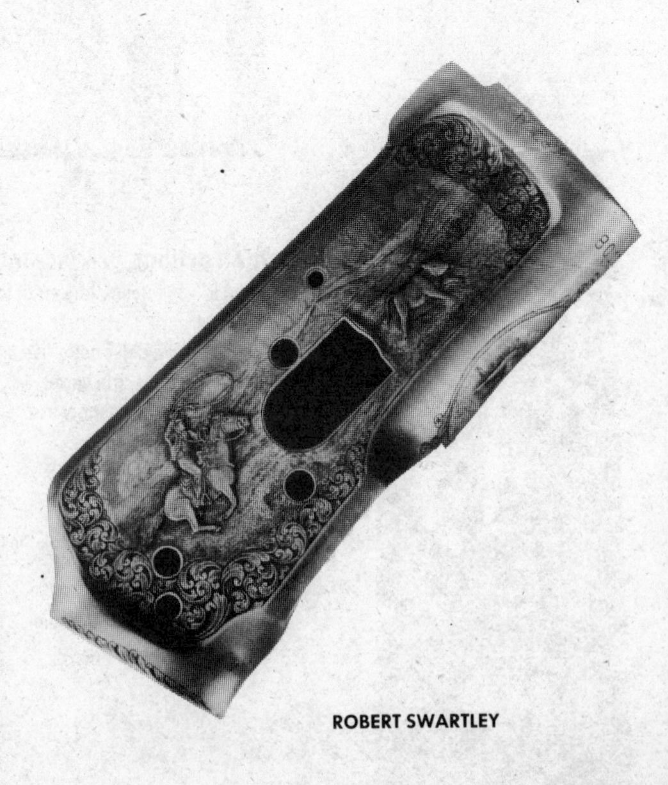

ROBERT SWARTLEY

JOHN E. WARREN

JOHN KUDLAS

Engraver

steel—as well as samples of
dresses of the artists named
Directory of the Arms Trade.

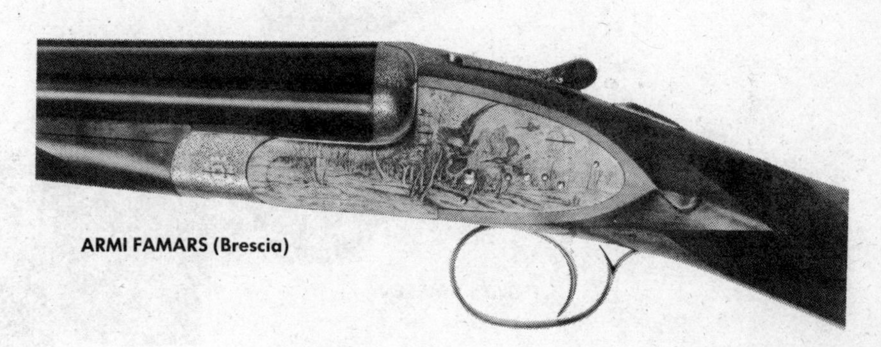

ARMI FAMARS (Brescia)

T. J. KAYE

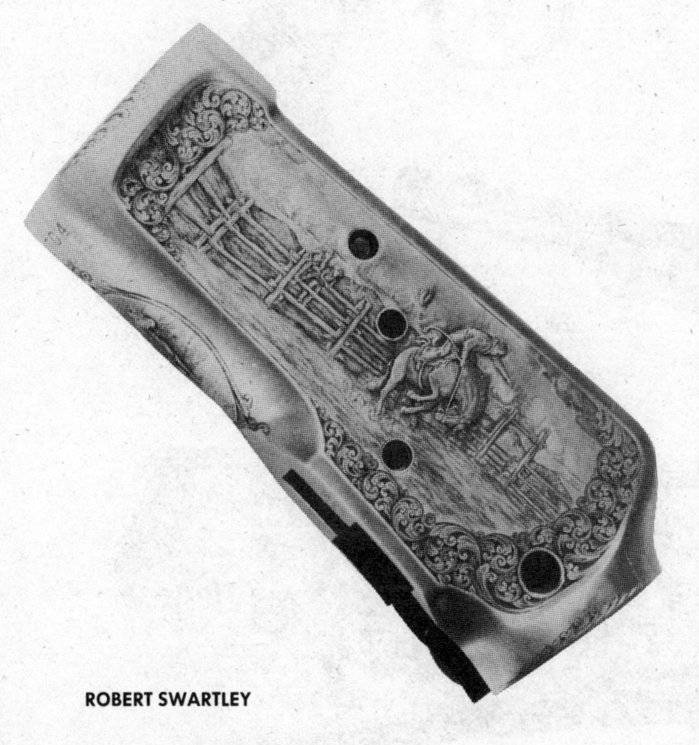

ROBERT SWARTLEY

HOWARD V. GRANT

KEN HURST

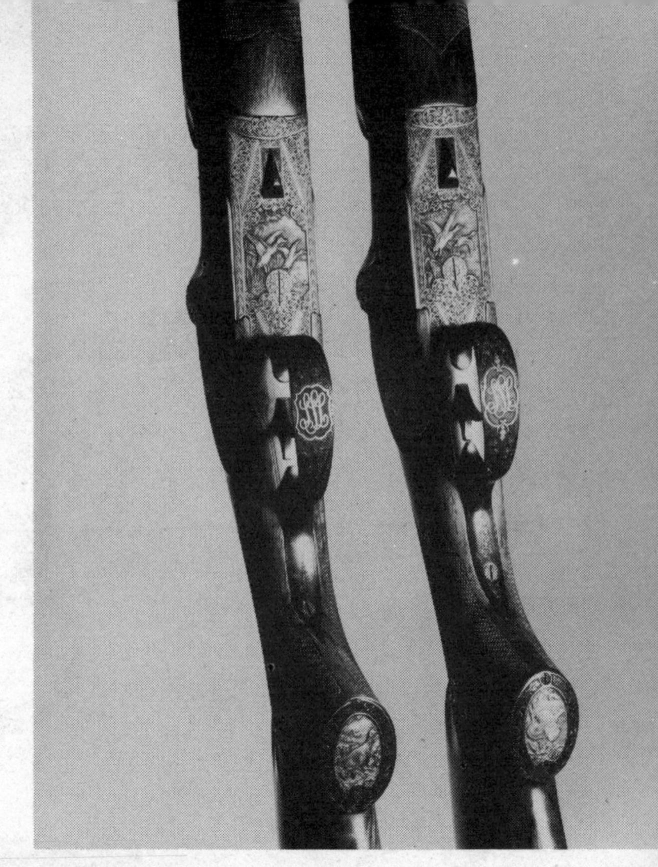

ALBIN OBILTSCHNIG

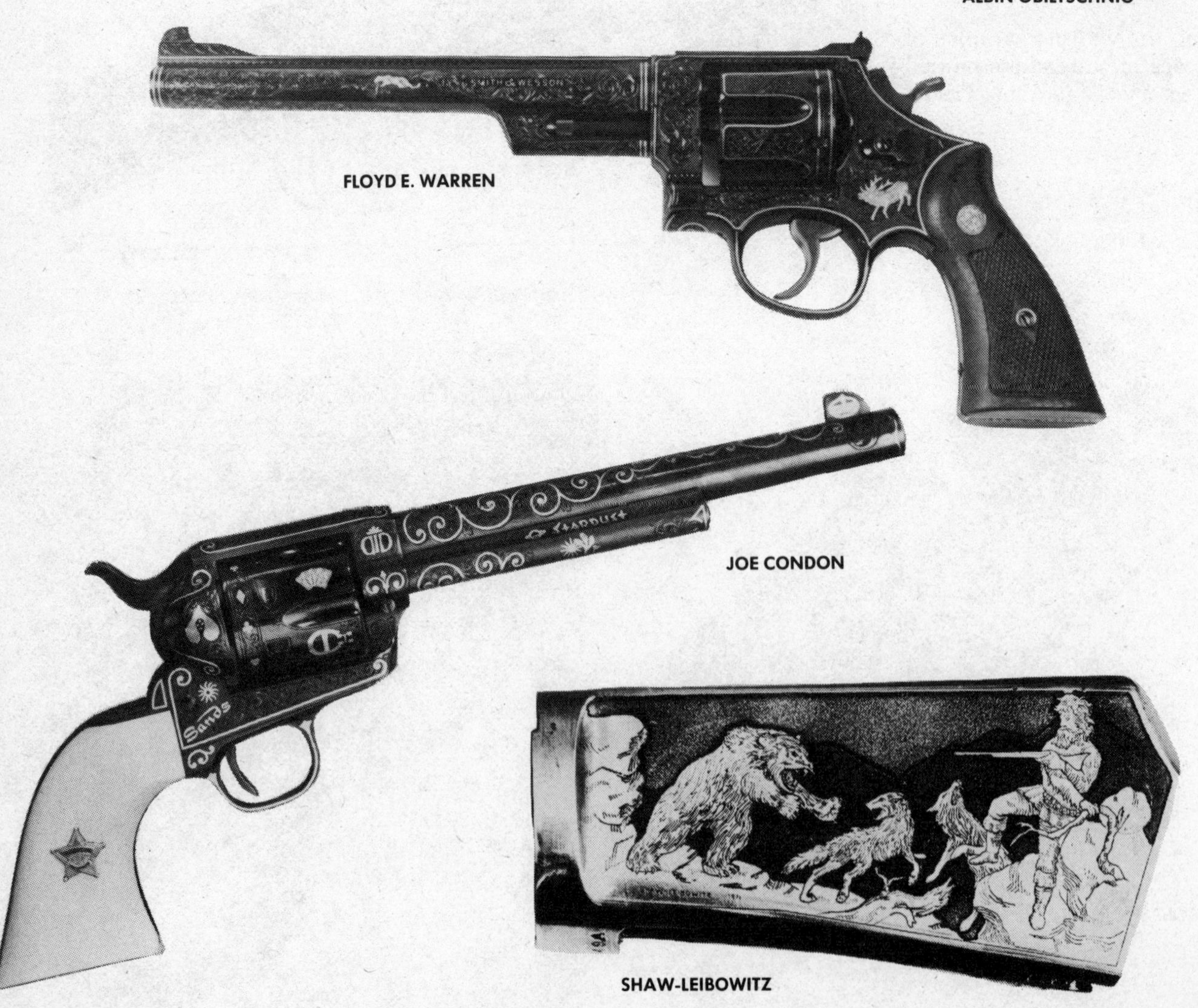

FLOYD E. WARREN

JOE CONDON

SHAW-LEIBOWITZ

KEN HURST

T. J. KAYE

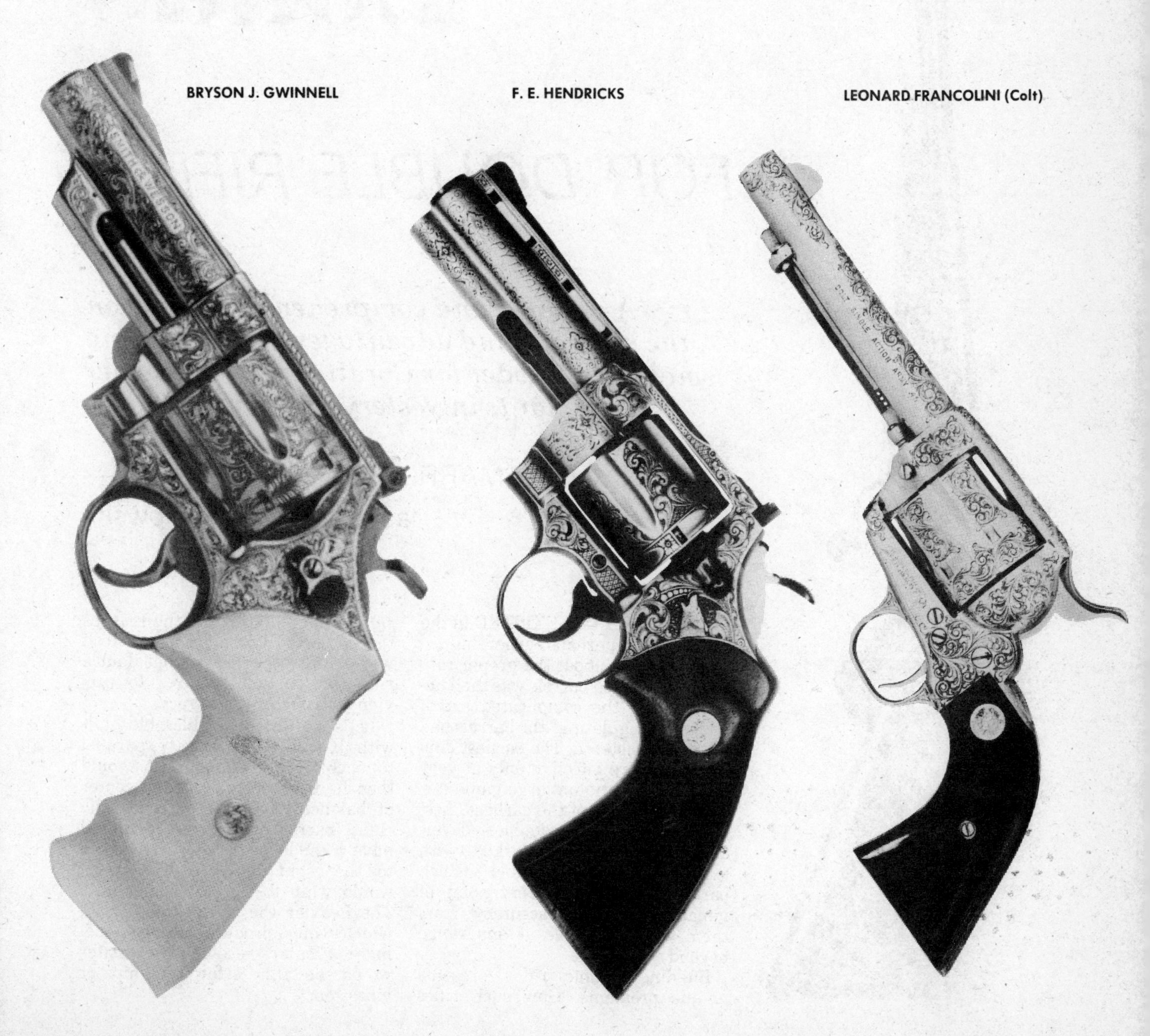

BRYSON J. GWINNELL **F. E. HENDRICKS** **LEONARD FRANCOLINI (Colt)**

Smokeless Loads

FOR DOUBLE RIFLES

A detailed and comprehensive report on the methods and advantages of substituting smokeless powder for Cordite or black powder propellants in yesteryear's bigbore rifles.

by RAY MARRIAGE and DICK VOGT—
as told to Bert Popowski.

DOUBLE RIFLES EXISTED in the 18th century, perhaps earlier, but exact knowledge about the proper rate of twist for rifled barrels was then unknown, and the complicated art of properly "regulating" the barrels had yet to be mastered. The earliest double rifles were effective only at very short ranges and on large game targets. Even some of the earliest "best quality" percussion doubles—several of which we've worked with extensively—gave trouble. Each barrel shot to a different point of impact, thus good accuracy from them was impossible at any range beyond 40 yards.

Building double rifles presents unique problems. How such rifles *should not* be built, and the reasons therefore, is probably as good a way as any to indicate what double rifle construction requires to provide satisfactory accuracy.

Let's imagine a double rifle built with barrel bores exactly parallel to each other. The barrels would then lie to either side of the center of balance of the rifle. When the right barrel was fired it would have a tendency to whip somewhat to the right and the left barrel would whip to the left when fired. The heavier the charge-bullet load, which would produce a correspondingly greater recoil, the greater would be this sidewise whip or vibration.

In short, as each barrel was fired, it would tend to rebound away from the inert mass of the unfired barrel. This effect would be somewhat similar to resting a rifle barrel directly against a vertical support, such as a tree trunk for instance, or some other obstacle to its natural vibration. Even when simply shouldered and held in the hands in the offhand position the net result would be widely separated points-of-impact of bullets from the two parallel barrels. The shooter of such an improperly built rifle would have to know where each barrel hit and compensate by holding off accordingly from true line-of-sight.

A secondary effect has to do with the velocity of the projectiles. The slower its velocity the longer the projectile would remain in the barrel and the more it would be thrown to right or left, ordinarily, depending on which barrel was first fired.

This problem can be solved only by spacing the barrel axes farther apart at the breech than at the muzzle, so they have a definite convergence from rear to front. As noted above, the greater the amount of recoil and the lower the velocity of the bullets the greater will be the amount of convergence required to compensate for this sidewise whip or vibration. Thus an 8-bore rifle will always be found to have considerably more convergence than a more modern caliber, such as a 303 or a 240. However, even in a rifle of small caliber, light recoil and high velocity, some convergence of the barrels is required. Such inaccuracy could cost a hunter his life were he after big, tough and dangerous game.

Experienced doubles gunmakers doubtless learn to make an educated guess as to the amount of convergence required when building a given rifle. But the final adjustment can only be done by the "try" man, who continues to test-fire the rifle, adjusting the regulating wedges and resoldering the barrels together until the accuracy qualities of the rifle are acceptable. Such work requires considerable time and skilled experience, which explains why double rifles are vastly more costly than any other type of firearms. Additionally, while these rifles are not usually intended for use with high-intensity cartridges, they all do operate at higher pressures than other double-barreled firearms—such as ordinary shotguns, for example. Consequently, very careful fitting of all parts is absolutely essential.

Such care in manufacture explains why double rifles made by the better gunsmiths of 70 to 80 years ago are usually found to be sound and tight, even after extensive hard use. Some of these older rifles have been reproofed for modern Cordite loads. This practice is not desirable in that it merely gives the shooter reasonable assurance that modern loads will not destroy his gun. Further, guns which were originally regulated for bullets of specific weight, driven by specified charges of black powder, would print properly with modern factory ammunition only by the sheerest accident or unless used with those factory loads designated "Nitro for Black Powder" arms. However, continued use of such heavier modern loads, even if they did group well, might eventually crack the rifle frames.

Fact and Fiction About Double Rifles

Much misinformation has been passed on as gospel fact about the large English double rifles. Repetition, by word of mouth and also in print, has given these comments the aura of "basic facts." Some years ago the bar-stool set magnified the recoil of these rifles to truly heroic proportions. Men who had never fired anything more potent than a 270 or a 30-06 became "instant experts" in describing the massive, even crippling recoil of such doubles as the 470 Nitro or anything similar. Broken shoulders or collar bones, said these oracles, were frequently suffered. Such reports, of course, are pure hog-wash.

The fact is that rifles as potent as the 458 Winchester, which corresponds to the English 450x3¼-inch Nitro Express, can be fired from bench rest without undue discomfort

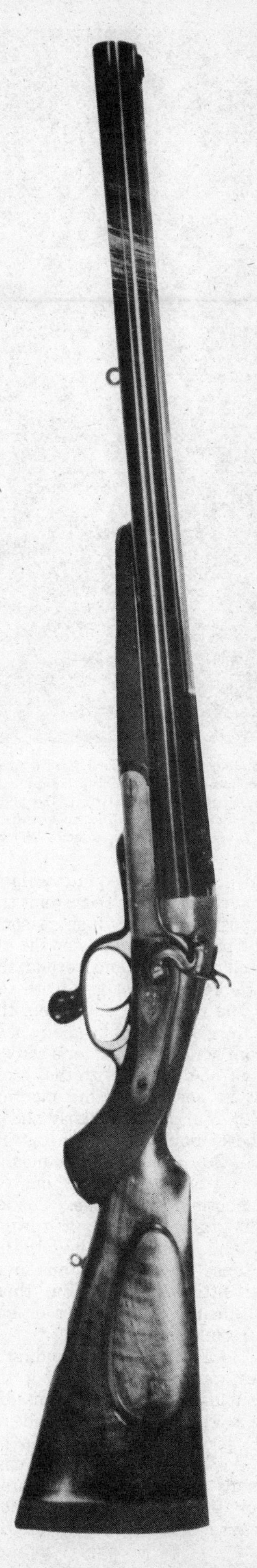

British loading tools—at upper left an 8-gauge brass-case Paradox cartridge, with various bullets below. The tool at the center is a 12-bore re- and decapper, to its right a crimper and a bullet sizer. The pliers-like tool puts circular indents into 8-bore Paradox brass cases. The mould casts the 8-gauge hollow-point bullets seen near the mould.

—given a rifle of adequate weight. Neither should be fired from the prone position for obvious reasons; first, the butt rests directly on the unprotected collarbone and, second, the shooter's body cannot give with the recoil. The really big ones, from the 577 on up, can be fired from any position from which the shooter's body is entirely free to move with the recoil.

(Just in passing let me mention that Ray Marriage regularly shoots an 8-bore double from a sitting position. Ray weighs 120 pounds as he steps from the shower but enjoys shooting this rifle. Loaded with 20 grains of 4759, 350 grains of FG and a 1,330-gr. bullet, this powerhouse always rolls him over from a sitting position. But there is no bruising, no fractures or any other recoil damage.)

For the average man, standing is the best position for shooting the big doubles. It's quite permissible to use a rest, such as the side of a tree, providing one hand is between the rifle and the object used to steady the gun. Direct contact between the rifle and the support will cause interference with the recoil cycle and will usually alter the point of bullet impact. Standing, while resting the fore-end over a bedroll on the hood of a car is a good steady position when testing a rifle or ammunition for accuracy —but again, rest the fore-end in the palm. However, adequate protection must be given to the hood of the vehicle. The first shot fired from an 8-bore in that position, Ray told me, scorched the paint so badly that a repaint job was needed. So much for recoil. The best way to tolerate it is by learning to roll with it.

Load Development

Another misleading belief deals with the supposed inflexibility of the doubles in regard to the ammunition which can be successfully used in them. Each rifle, it's true, was built to shoot properly with a given load and many of the better doubles are clearly marked to indicate that load. In such cases the assembling of suitable loads is greatly simplified.

It is only when a rifle is not marked with its intended ammo requirements that the shooter is faced with a problem. A 450, for example, might have been originally regulated for a given charge of powder and a bullet ranging from lighter than 300 grains up to one heavier than 500 grains. Considerable experimenting might then be required before an accurate load for that particular double was found.

However, the search for a suitable load need not be all guesstimation. A very valuable reference book is *Cartridges of the World*, authored by Frank C. Barnes and edited by John T. Amber. This cites the original loadings offered by the English manufacturers so the handloader can start by duplicating the blackpowder loads or testing equivalent loadings of suitable smokeless powders. The main thing is to start with a load which may be assumed to be safe to fire and then alter such loadings as indicated hereinafter to make the rifle group its shots properly from both barrels.

If the bullet chosen is much too light or too heavy it may not be possible to develop a load which groups properly with it. For instance, the first experimental load may print to the right of the point of aim from the right barrel, and to the left with the left barrel. In nearly all cases the cure for this is to increase the powder charge, assuming that this can be done without producing excessive chamber pressures. This increased powder charge will slightly increase the recoil and thus increase the amount of sidewise whip and might be assumed to make the barrels shoot even more to right and left than with the original lighter load. However, the increase in velocity and thus the decrease in the time the bullet remains in the bore, will nearly always more than offset the effect of increased recoil whip.

On the other hand, if the barrels crossfire—the left delivering to the right of the point of aim and the right to the left of that point—it will nearly always be found that the powder charges should be reduced, thereby leaving the bullet within the bore for a longer period of time while it is exposed to a corrective sidewise whip. Conversely, if the powder charge is left constant and the bullet weight is changed, substitution of a lighter bullet will result in higher velocity. This will have the same effect as increasing the powder charge. Because of different weights of rifles and other individual peculiarities, it is conceivable that reverse effects could be encountered. To date, however, this situation has not been found by Marriage in working with any of many test rifles.

Using the above technique it is occasionally possible to develop reduced loads which will shoot very accurately from some big-bore doubles Since shooting about 20 full-power loads is about all any big-bore devotee wants to handle during any given day, such reduced loads provide considerably more shooting. Such practice is invaluable in prepping for a foreign big game safari or simply for the plain pleasure of handloading for and shooting a handsome and accurate specimen of double rifle craftsmanship. Admittedly, too, there's a certain amount of pride and prestige involved in being able to hand a visitor such a rifle and invite him to try a few shots. Reduced loads permit him to enjoy this without suffering the rather impressive recoil of fullpower loads.

Marriage who formerly operated Montana Custom Handloads,* made a project of developing reduced loads for the 577/3-inch Nitro Express. He found that three different rifles of this caliber shot very well with 588-gr. cast bullets ahead of from 56 to 62 grains of 2400 powder—the exact charge for top accuracy depending on the individual rifles. Inasmuch as 577 factory bullets cost 30¢ apiece the saving on such cast bullets for extensive test shooting was significant. These reduced loads had a muzzle velocity of about 1730 feet per second compared to around 1950 fps for full-power loads—and were just as accurate as any full-power factory loads.

Handloading of such English cartridges offers another valuable advantage which should not be overlooked. American powders are much cooler burning than English Cordite and their proper use may be expected to substantially prolong barrel life. One look through the bores of a double which has been extensively and exclusively used with Cordite loads by a professional hunter is often abundant reason for the wise handloader to eschew Cordite forever. Finally, since Cordite is not available for reloading, this automatically forces the use of less erosive American smokeless powders.

*Ray Marriage was forced out of business by the Gun Control Act of 1968, as were others who had been furnishing cartridges and components by mail.

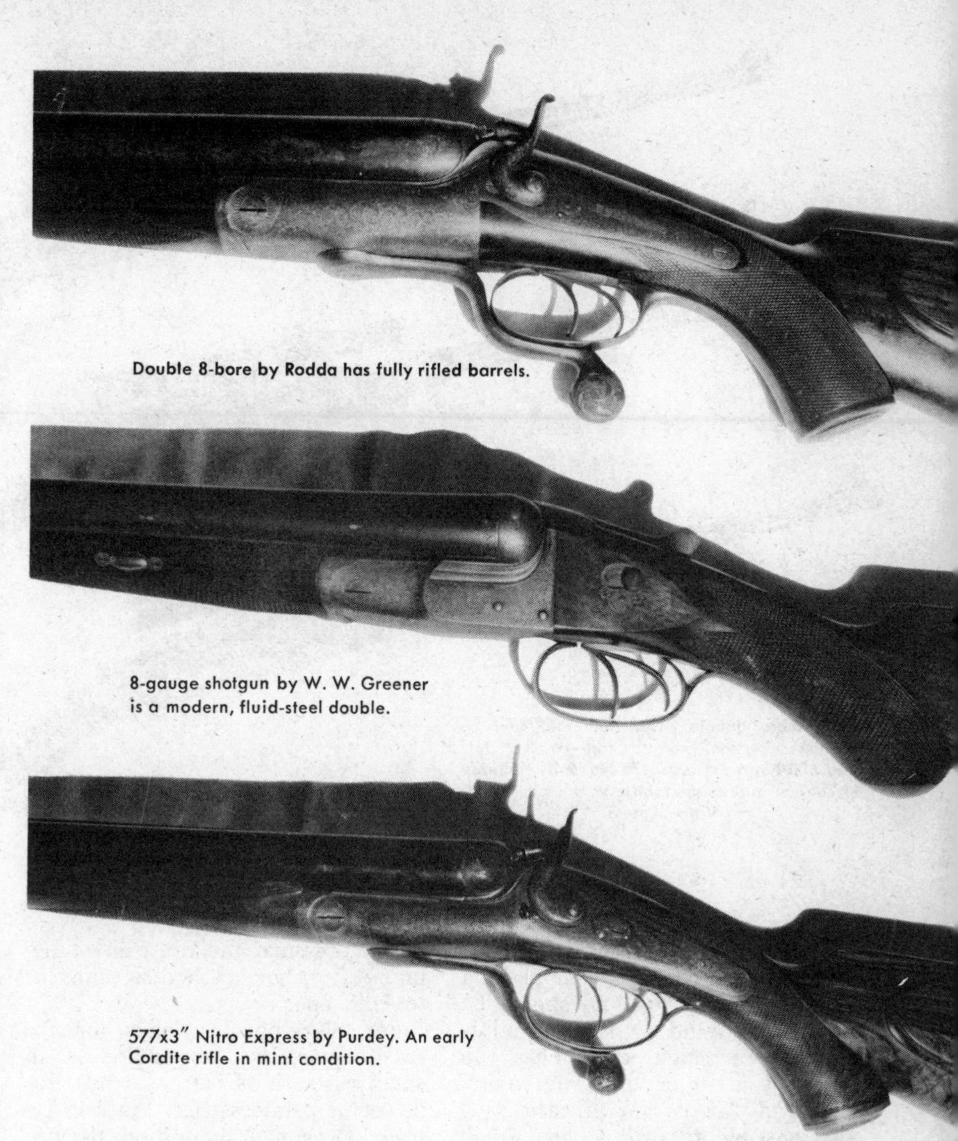

Double 8-bore by Rodda has fully rifled barrels.

8-gauge shotgun by W. W. Greener is a modern, fluid-steel double.

577x3″ Nitro Express by Purdey. An early Cordite rifle in mint condition.

Tools and Components

Gathering specific information on the components, tools and services for handloading for double rifles is often frustrating. Therefore, hereafter, the names of various firms will be mentioned in connection with certain products which might be difficult to locate. Other firms may offer equivalent services or products, but those subsequently named are known to be reliable and their full addresses are listed at the conclusion of this article.

For factory-loaded ammunition for any currently existing caliber write to Oregon Ammunition Service. This firm also stocks empty unprimed cartridge cases, bullets and Berdan primers. From this large stock it is often possible to select and alter an available cartridge case to work just fine for an obsolete caliber. RCBS offers suitable loading dies and shell holders. RCBS has dies for many foreign calibers and will make every effort to help with any specific reloading problems. Lyman offers a fantastic range of bullet moulds. If they don't have a mould suitable for your purpose they'll make a special custom mould for $100. A bit expensive, but it isn't too much to pay for a lifetime of shooting pleasure.

The most potent Berdan caps available are Kynoch primers, available from Oregon Ammunition Service. Their use is indicated where it is necessary to ignite a very large charge of powder, such as 140 grains of 4831 in the 577/3-inch Nitro Express. The seating of Berdan primers is accomplished exactly as with our conventional Boxer primers. It is most easily done by the use of the RCBS Precision Priming Device. The extraction of fired Berdan primers is more complicated but should not be regarded as serious since it simply adds one additional step to conventional loading procedures.

If possible, a European three-legged re- and decapper should be obtained but they are often difficult to find. A simple Berdan decapper

Three more double rifles from the Maynard Buehler collection. From the top—W. & J. Jeffery 600 Nitro Express; 475 No. 2 by Halliday of London and another Jeffery, this one a 400 Nitro Express.

is manufactured in the United States by Lachmiller Engineering Co. The lip of this tool should be carefully ground to fit the radius of the cartridge case head on which it is to be used, but many are used "as is." With care it is also possible to drill a very small hole through the fired primer, toward the edge, after which the primer may be removed with a suitable pick or awl. Whichever method is used, the beginner should have little trouble after a bit of practice, during which he may damage a few primer pockets or anvils in getting this experience!

The hydraulic method of removing Berdan primers should be avoided completely. This is done by filling the case with water, then a slip-fit plug is inserted into the mouth of the case and given a sharp rap to drive the fired primer from its pocket by hydraulic pressure. There are several serious disadvantages to this method. A plug which properly fits a case fired in one chamber will not necessarily fit a case from the rifle's other chamber. It is sometimes desirable to deprime a case which has been resized but not fired and here a plug of still another size would have to be used. This hydraulic method is messy, subjects the walls of the cartridge case to heavy pressure and can cause bulging. Any other method is superior to this one.

For black-powder loads, or for small quantities of smokeless in small cases, it is better to use less powerful primers than the *hot* Kynoch. Oregon Ammunition Service offers RWS 1786 Berdan shotshell primers which are fine for rifle cartridges and Godfrey Reloading Supply sells RWS 1784 rifle primers, which also work well. Although the hard tough brass of Kynoch primers makes them more difficult to seat and extract—compared to RWS primers—this should not be the sole factor in deciding which primer is best for specific purposes in double rifle loads.

Over-powder wads should be used in all except bottleneck cases. Any competent machinist can make a custom wad-cutter at small cost to cut wads from cork-gasket material, and plumber's supply houses often have a variety of gasket cutters. It is just as cheap and far more convenient to use either .135- or .200-inch card wads made for use in shotshells. The Alcan Company manufactures 32-gauge wads which are perfect for use in caliber 500 cases and their 24-gauge wads are ideal for the 577. They save punching out your own wads one at a time.

It is almost impossible to seat properly fitted wads in bottleneck cases, except with full-case black powder loads, though you can try attaching card, greased fiber or other wads to the base of the bullet with grease or a mild adhesive. But it occasionally works very well to fill the over-powder space in them with a pinch of Nylon or Dacron fiber. Such fiber filler material, plus an excellent bullet lubricant, is available from Javelina Products, Inc.

In black-powder loads the over-powder wads offer some protection to the bases of bullets, similar to that provided by metallic gas-checks. To a degree these also act as bore conditioners, wiping out the residue of each shot. In smokeless loads the over-powder wad holds the powder in a uniform position within the cases, thus promoting more uniform ignition. When the load is fired this wad is often fragmented, leaving the muzzle in small pieces. For this reason it is also wise to seat a similar wad at the base of the bullet, to act as gas-check and bore conditioner. When using cast bullets an added refinement is to pour a very thin layer of melted bullet lubricant over this uppermost wad.

Clean burning loads are essential in double rifles, for a single particle of unburned powder, lodged under the extractor or in a couple of other places, may put the rifle out of commission until it is located and removed. If a load isn't burning cleanly more and tighter wadding is generally indicated. Other solutions may require heavier bullets or a faster burning powder. Usually the larger calibers are the ones found to be most difficult to match with suitable loads.

In the 12-bore rifle, using Alcan brass cases with all excess space in the case filled with 10-gauge wads, it was found that 3031 powder burned cleanly only when used with bullets heavier than 800 grains. For bullets weighing under 800 grains it was found necessary to use faster powders. A charge of 90 grains of 3031 was tried with 900-grain bullets but this load did not print properly and was used only as a proof load.

It should be here noted that *experimenting with large calibers, heavy bullets and fast powders is a highly dangerous pastime!* The development of good smokeless loads for the 12-bore proved to be so time-consuming, and presented so many problems, that the idea of working up similar loads for the 10- and 8-bores was abandoned. Some risk of damage to the rifles and injury to the shooter would have been involved. One cannot, nowadays, merely go to the nearest hardware store and buy a new set of 8-bore rifle barrels!

Cast vs. Jacketed Bullets

In casting bullets it should be remembered that changing the alloy of the bullet metal will not only change the hardness but will also change the weight of the finished bullets. In large bullets this change in weight can easily become significant. For instance, when using Lyman mould 585213-S to cast .585-inch bullets they were found to vary from 585- to 605-grains, depending on the type of alloy used. This bullet is a most useful one since it can be used in both black-powder and smokeless powder rifles. To lubricate this bullet it is best to purchase a .580-inch size-and-lube die—the largest die of this kind supplied by Lyman—and hone out the upper portion of the die so that the .585-inch bullet is lubricated but not sized.

Some writers claim that jacketed bullets will cause rapid and noticeable barrel wear in older rifles, whose barrel steel is softer than that which is now used. As a result only cast bullets were used in barrels known to be made of mild steel. Extensive correspondence with two major bullet-making firms indicates considerable doubt about such barrel wear and that further research is needed in this field. Both manufacturers have conducted reasonably extensive tests and have concluded that jacketed bullets do not cause abnormal barrel wear *unless steel-jacketed bullets are used. They believe that gas-cutting is the basic cause of all barrel wear.* Thus if jacketed bullets are large enough to completely fill the barrel grooves, are given sufficient velocity to slightly upset the bases, and if slightly over-sized gas-sealing wads are used, then perhaps the use of jacketed bullets is not nearly as harmful as has been previously believed.

Reloaders curious about the muzzle velocities of their handloads can get excellent chronographs from Oehler Research, Avtron, B-Square, and others. See our Directory of the Arms Trade pages at the back of this book.

Repairs or alterations of double rifles are occasionally required. The sleeving or reboring of doubles should be avoided whenever possible. As of mid-1971, Westley Richards was still rebarreling doubles from $600-$800 with six-months delivery, which will amply take care of most such jobs. Rechambering to an available case while leaving the barrels as they are does not usually affect a rifle's shooting characteristics. Snapp's Gun Shop does such rechambering, including lengthening the 2¾-inch chambers of 577 rifles to 3-inch capacity. Another highly desirable conversion offered by this shop is rechambering 8-bore shotguns or rifles to accept industrial paper and plastic cases. These cases are inexpensive, readily available and the alteration is so slight that all other types of 8-gauge cases can still be used. Fine gunsmithing of double rifles is done by Iver Henriksen and by Purcell's Gun Shop. The latter firm can also re-regulate double rifles if such adjustment is needed.

All loads shown in our Table have been fired in double rifles by R. C. Vogt, Ray Marriage or both. Mr. Vogt has extensive notes, compiled over many years, on load and rifle performance. He was enormously helpful in loaning rifles for testing, test-firing experimental loads and supplying data and comments thereon.

Nearly all of the loads listed were chronographed, except in the few cases where they were found to print the same as with factory ammunition. All of them gave good accuracy in the rifles in which they

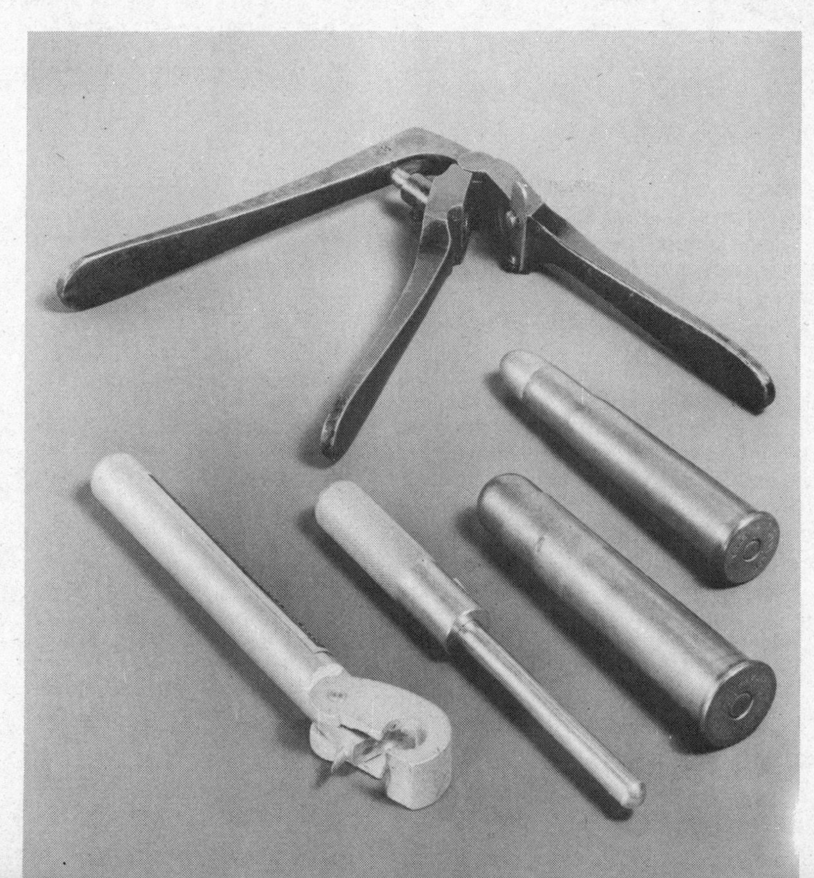

At top is the once-common, and usually German-made, 3-legged tool for de- and recapping Berdan primers. Below is the type of Berdan primer decapper marketed by Lachmiller Engineering, these offered ordinarily only for 8mm Mauser cases and similar case-head sizes. The cartridges seen are a 577-500 (above) and the 600x3" Express.

Five big bore rifles from the collection of Maynard P. Buehler, scope mount maker of Orinda, California. From the top—a 4-bore double by R. Hughes & Son, London. Next, a double-barreled 4-bore by Holland and Holland, London. Third down, an 8-gauge single by Manton, London. Fourth, a W. W. Greener 8-bore double and, last, a 600 Nitro Express 3-inch from W. J. Jeffery.

were tested, but for best accuracy in other rifles, slight variations of these loads should be tried. While these suggested loads were definitely safe to fire *in the test rifles,* that does not positively establish they would be equally safe to use in *all* rifles.

All of the test rifles were in excellent condition and none had Damascus barrels. However, quite a few double rifles were built with twist barrels and most of these are upwards of 80 years old. If the owners of such elderly rifles insist on using them the ammunition should be restricted to black powder loads—and even then they're not really safe.

Nitro Load Table

1. 6.5x53R (256 Mannlicher). 36/4064/160-gr. jacketed bullet, muzzle velocity (MV) 2350, muzzle energy (ME) 1960.

2. 333 Flanged Nitro Express. 64/4064/300-gr. bullet, MV 2150, ME 3090.

3. 400/350 Nitro Express. 45/3031/310-gr. bullet, MV 2000, ME 2752.

4. 400/360 Nitro Express. 50/3031/286-gr. Norma 9.3 bullet, MV 2132.

5. 360 Nitro Express. 30/Hi-Vel 2/300-gr. bullet.

6. 360 #2 Nitro Express. 58/4064/300-gr. bullet.

7. 9.3x74R. 57/4064/286-gr. bullet, MV 2360.

8. 375 Flanged Nitro Express. 42/3031/270-gr. bullet, MV 1975, ME 2340.

9. 450/400/3¼ Nitro Express. 62/4064/400-gr. bullet, MV 2150, ME 4110.

10. 450 3¼ Nitro Express. 71/3031, one wad, case filled with Wheatina, 500-gr. bullet, MV 1930.

11. 450/3¼ Nitro for Black. 53/3031/300-gr. Hornady S.J. bullet. One wad, case filled with Wheatina.

12. 450/3¼ Nitro for Black. 55/Hi-Vel 2/300-gr. Hornady S.J. bullet. One wad, case filled with Wheatina.

13.* 450/3¼ Nitro for Black. 35/4759/350-gr. cast bullet, MV 1550.

14.* 450/3¼ Nitro for Black. 35/4759/400-gr. cast bullet, MV 1500.

15. 500/450 #1 Nitro for Black. 43/3031, one wad, case full of Wheatina, 300-gr. bullet.

16. 500/3 Nitro for Black. 36/3031/blended in case with 6 grains 700-X shotshell powder. One OP wad, another wad at base of bullet; Lyman #509133, 428-gr. cast hollow-point bullet, MV 1600.

17. 500/3 Nitro for Black. 58/3031/with one wad, fill case with Wheatina, 440-gr. bullet.

18. 500/3 Nitro Express. 84/3031/one wad, fill case with Wheatina, 570-gr. bullet.

19.† 577/500 #2 Nitro for Black. 56/3031/one wad, fill case with Wheatina, 440-gr. bullet.

20. 577/3 Nitro Express. 105/3031/one wad, 750-gr. factory bullet, MV 1962.

21. 577/3 Nitro Express. 140/4831/

one wad, 750-gr. factory bullet, MV 1950.

22.** 577/3 Nitro Express. 59/2400/ one OP wad, another at bullet base with a thin layer of melted bullet lube atop; Lyman bullet #585213-S, solid-base version weighing 588 grains when cast from type metal, MV 1735.

23. 577/3 Nitro for Black. 75 to 78/ 3031/one OP wad, case filled with Wheatina, 580-gr. cast bullet.

24. 577/3 Nitro for Black. 35/4759 blended in the case with 37 grains 4895. One OP wad, another .220" thick at bullet base with thin layer of melted bullet lube atop. Lyman bullet #585213-S, cast from medium alloy, weight 600 grains, MV 1690.

25. 12-bore Westley Richards Explora. 37/4756/74-gr. bullet.

26. 12-bore Rigby Paradox. 26/Unique/ two .135" card wads, two ⅜" felt wads, .735" 580-gr. round ball in paper or plastic cases, MV 1250.

27. 12-bore Turner full double rifle. 90/ 3031/Alcan 2¾" brass cases, case full of 10-gauge wads, 860-gr. cast bullet, MV 1200.

*Loads 13 and 14 may have powder charge safely increased to 39 grains in quest for most accurate load.

†Some shooters may prefer to use Nylon or Dacron filler. In some cases this will be as satisfactory as Wheatina or other cereal filler. Also be reminded that 32-gauge shotshell wads are perfect for use in all 50-cal. rifles, 24-gauge wads in 577 rifles.

**Developed as a reduced load for Cordite rifles. Testing in several rifles showed that best accuracy and proper grouping required 56 to 62 grains of 2400. In several rifles tested this load was more accurate than the full-power Cordite loads.

The following firms offer reloading components, equipment, custom loads or gunsmithing for double rifles:

Custom gunsmithing

Iver Henriksen, 1211 S. Second St., Missoula, Mont. 59801

Purcell's Gun Shop, 915 Main St., Boise, Idaho 83702

Bullet moulds, reloading tools, lubes, etc.

Lyman Gun Sight Corp., Middlefield, Conn. 06455

RCBS, Inc., P.O. Box 1919, Oroville, Calif. 95965

Ohaus, 29 Hanover Rd., Florham Park, N.J. 07932

Javelina Products, Box 337, San Bernardino, Calif. 92402

Rechambering

Snapp's Gunshop, 6911 E. Washington Rd., Clare, Mich. 48617

Alcan wads, RWS Berdan primers, etc.

Godfrey Reloading Supply, R.R. 1, Box 688, Brighton, Ill. 62012

Components, English and other foreign factory ammo.

Oregon Ammunition Service, P.O. Box 19341, Portland, Ore. 97219

James Tillinghast, Box 568, Marlow, N.H. 03456

Berdan decapping tools

Lachmiller Co., Box 97, Parkesburg, Pa. 19365

Reboring or rebarreling of double rifles

Westley Richards & Co., Ltd., Grange Road, Bournbrook, Birmingham 29, England

For reliable information and enjoyable reading these books are highly recommended:

Cartridges of the World by F. C. Barnes, edited by J. T. Amber.

African Rifles and Cartridges by John Taylor.

The Gun and Its Development by W. W. Greener.

Cartridge Conversions by George C. Nonte.

English Guns and Rifles by J. N. George.

Finally, if an early Kynoch catalog can be located, especially one printed between World Wars I and II, prior to the discontinuation of so many cartridges, this will prove to be a highly valuable reference. These catalogs list the powder charges used, the weights of bullets and their style, the velocities and energies for various ranges and the breech pressures generated by all loadings listed. Unfortunately these catalogs are scarce and quite difficult to find. ●

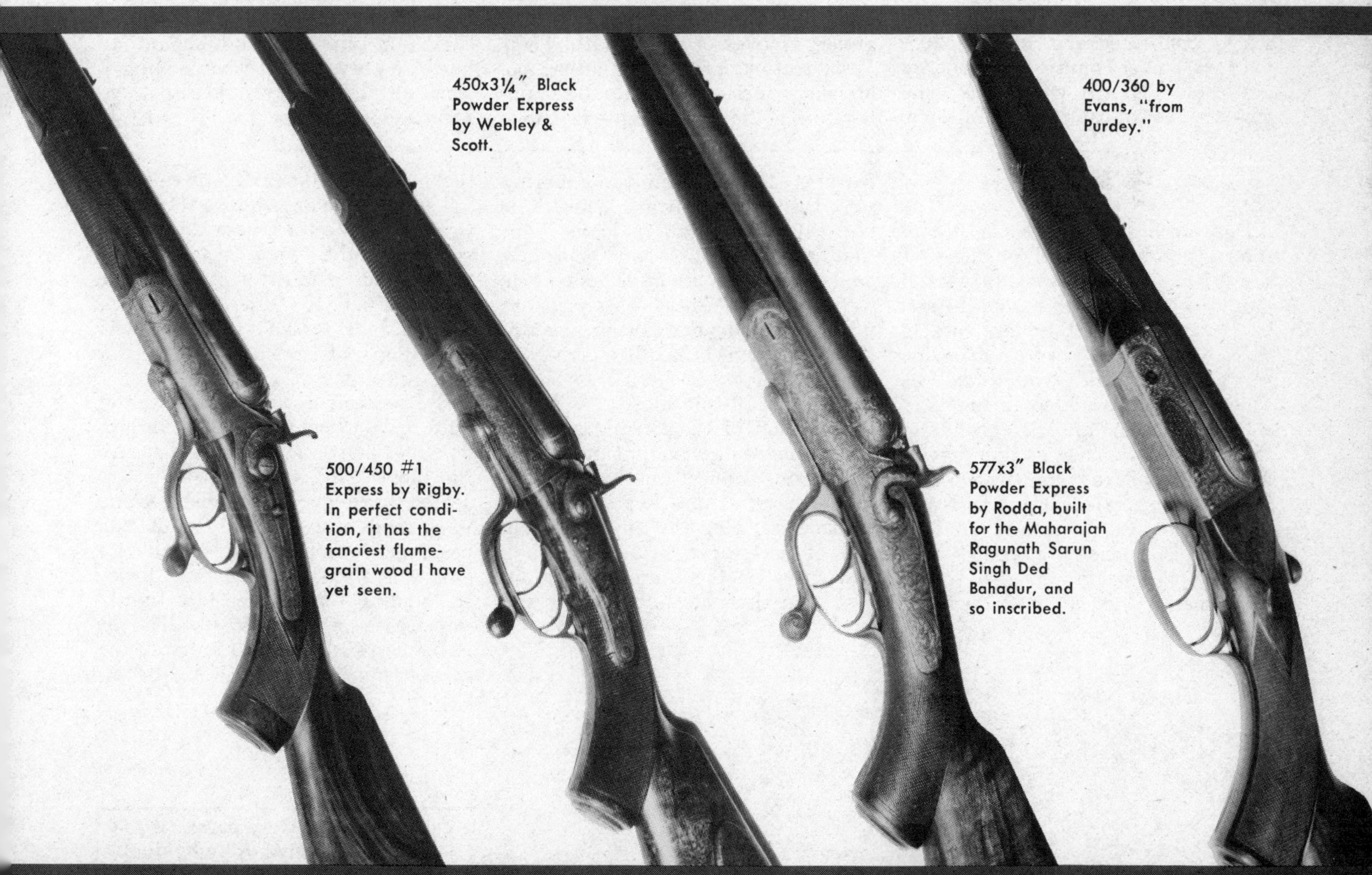

450x3¼" Black Powder Express by Webley & Scott.

400/360 by Evans, "from Purdey."

500/450 #1 Express by Rigby. In perfect condition, it has the fanciest flame-grain wood I have yet seen.

577x3" Black Powder Express by Rodda, built for the Maharajah Ragunath Sarun Singh Ded Bahadur, and so inscribed.

HANDLOADING

Handloading continues to grow and grow—so much so that some products are hard to find. Here's a review of the what's new, stuff that should be readily available.

by John T. Amber

New Speer Manual

Speer's latest Reloading Manual, Number 9, promises to be a topnotch data source; recent developments in the manufacture of popular smokeless powders lets Speer offer the latest, most correct load information.

The new Number 9 carries the greatest number and variety of handgun loads of any reloading handbook.

Many professional photographs and other illustrations reveal handloading details and procedures with exceptional clarity. All cartridge drawings have been revised, these now showing English and metric dimensions, and new tables furnish detailed metric and English equivalents.

The ballistic data have been retested, confirmed and updated. 200-yard hold-over figures and energy are shown for all rifle loads. The glossary contains new definitions, supplemented by detailed illustrations.

Number 9's deluxe hard binding carries a 4-color illustrated cover, plastic coated and soil-proofed for long service. The new book, researched and compiled by dedicated technicians, provides accurate, current, factual reloading information, and it's priced at $5.50 postpaid or from your dealer. J.T.A.

Lee Precision, Inc.

Lee has various new things for 1974, among other new products for the handloader. In the handgun section, Lee has several new designs, intended for the shooter of blackpowder guns. These moulds cast round-nosed bullets, flat based, and each with two grease grooves of good width. Their lower sections are a bit smaller, too, allowing for easy entry into the chambers, with the wider-diameter bands seating tightly to confine the burning gases—which should obviate crossfiring, a good safety factor.

These new Lee moulds are offered in 4 sizes—.456-inch in 22 grains for the Ruger Old Army, in .450-inch at 200 grains, a .380-inch weighing 135 grains and, last, one of .375-inch of 130 grains.

There's been no chance to try any of these new Lee Moulds, but the design and dimensioning should do much to prevent excessive leading—if not all—and they should also prove accurate performers. J.T.A.

B-Square

Dan Bechtel had a booth full of interesting and useful products at the NRA meeting in Atlanta—too many to be described in detail here, but there's a new B-Square catalog ready now that covers his wide range of gunsmith's tools as well as shooter items. Included in the 1974 B-Square catalog are barrel bending/removal presses, a new swaging device for putting chokes in damaged or cut-off shotgun barrels, various drill- and tap jigs, etc.

What isn't shown is Dan's new Model 75 chronograph, an unusual instrument loaded with special features. There's a built-in charging unit that works always when it is plugged in, with an indicator light that gradually dims and goes out as the new-style *wet batteries* become fully charged. These batteries are fully enclosed, and never require water in service. A full charge will let the instrument operate for hours, away from 110-volt lines.

Operation of the B-Square Model 75 chronograph is simple and easy—switch on, connect the twin cables to your screens (any type, including electronics), plug the single lead in and, if the stop light is *out,* shoot. Now read off the illuminated numbers, add them up and refer to the tables furnished to find your velocity.

There are no switches to rotate, no wasted shots either, because the red warning light—when lit—lets you know about a faulty stop screen or disconnection. If all the lights go on, then the start screen is a dud. $149.95 including batteries, and there's a year guarantee.

By the time you read this Bechtel may have a few other things in production. One is a gauge to measure the depth to which primers are seated—obviously a bench-rester's item—and cost will be about $33 postpaid. Another, essentially a gunsmith's tool, is a clamping device for holding screwdriver bits tightly into frozen or rusted screws. The bit is then wrench-turned to remove the screw. This will cost about $20. J.T.A.

Latest B-Square Model 75 chronograph has built-in charger.

Consult our Directory pages for the location of firms or individuals mentioned.

Ferguson Tools

Each time I see a new product from The Fergusons I'm surprised and impressed; I don't think it's an exaggeration to say I'm amazed. In an era that is notorious, generally, for cheap plastic gadgetry, for slap-dash quality in assembly and fitting, it is refreshing to open a box and find clear evidence that all is not lost! The Fergusons seem incapable of making anything that isn't of first class craftsmanship—their wide variety of tools for the serious rifleman, benchresters in particular, show a skillful, precision machining and finishing that surpasses any comparable products, with one exception—the tools for the handloader that L.E. Wilson makes. Both firms offer simply superb products, their quality obvious at a glance. Their cost—surprisingly perhaps for 1974—is remarkably attractive. In all truth, I don't see how such quality can be offered at the prices asked.

The new Ferguson item shown nearby is their tool for shaving cartridge cases necks—on the outside—to obtain a uniform wall thickness. Many shooters contend that cases so turned exhibit a like uniform bullet tension, aiding accuracy. Logical, certainly, if it is agreed that uniformity in all aspects of cartridge preparation is desirable—which theory few argue with. In any case, the practice can do no harm, and it seems to be growing if the several other tools made for the job indicate acceptance of the idea.

The Ferguson neck turner differs from others offered in this respect—before neck turning each case is resized, using the neck-turning arbor (arrow). The arbor is first removed from the turner body, then inserted into the ⅞-14 thread short die (right), held therein by the 10-32 machine screw supplied. With this short die held in the loading press, each case is pushed onto the arbor, this treatment insuring that all cases have a uniform inside diameter. The arbor-resized neck, then, is pushed onto the re-installed arbor and, at the same time, rotated against the hardened steel cutter. The cutter is adjustable, of course, for depth of cut. In practice only a light shaving is taken off the case, just enough to insure uniform wall thickness.

Ferguson says this new tool will turn necks to within 0.0001-inch (one-ten thousandths), which is a damn small amount. It didn't do quite that well in my hands, probably because of my ham-handedness! I got a trifle more than his figure, as an average, in turning ten 308 cases—0.00012 to 0.00013—but that's still a highly uniform wall dimension compared to the neck variations I started with. On some cases I shaved off as much as 0.001″-0.0015″.

The Ferguson neck turning tool, complete for any one caliber, is $29.50. Extra arbors are $3.50, extra case holders are $2—these two items are all you need to convert to another caliber.

Other fine Ferguson products are pictured here—the Versa-Press, a dual adjustable arbor-type press particularly suited to seating bullets via straight-line seaters, and for the use of knockout type neck dies. The larger view shows the Ferguson return-to-battery type machine rest, intended for the experimental class of competition. The entire outfit, save for the re-worked Hart front rest, is Ferguson made. J.T.A.

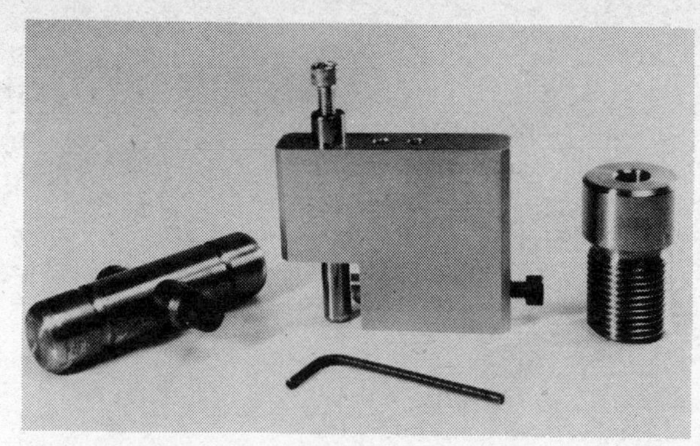

The Fergusons offer this excellently made case-neck turner, capable of achieving .0001″-inch neck wall uniformity.

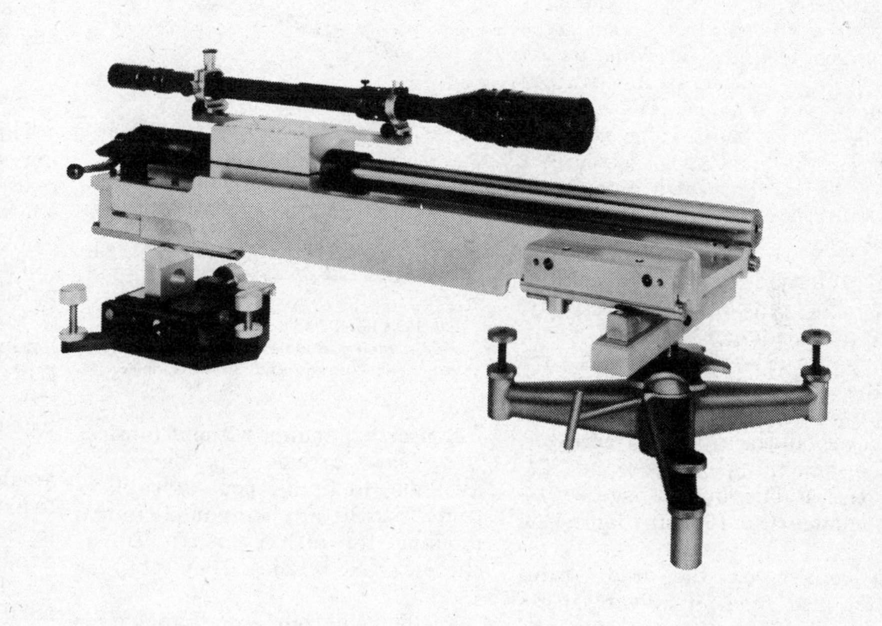

Above—The Ferguson's return-to-battery machine rest. Right below—their Versa-Press, a dual-adjustable arbor type.

Hornady Handbook II

The Hornady Manufacturing Company of Grand Island, Nebraska, has just published (1973) a 2nd edition of their *Hornady Handbook of Cartridge Reloading,* now up to 512 pages, and issued in a sturdy hard cover. This new manual, some 40% bigger than the 1st edition, covers some 100 rifle and handgun cartridges. It is, of course, limited to loading data using Hornady bullets. In addition to load listings, it contains excellent trajectory charts, fine scale drawings of each cartridge discussed, and excellent descriptive data on them. It has some good basic instruction pages and much technical explanation on trajectories, et cetera. It describes powders only in a general way, according to type. While it has no burnloads for the 250 Savage tested in a Model 99 Savage, which is the most common rifle chambered for that cartridge.

Joyce Hornady called to tell me that a few errors can be found, regrettably, in his new loading manual.

On pages 481-483 the range figures for the .358" bullet of 200 grains are shown in 100-yard increments, whereas they should be in 50-yard increases.

The same thing applies to the .321" flat-base 170-gr. bullet (page 470)—just change the 100-yard figures to 50.

In both cases, the drop figures should also read in 50-yard increments. The trajectory, velocity and energy figures are all correct once the foregoing changes have been made. J.T.A.

New Pacific Carbide Neck Expander

Reloaders can improve their Pacific or RCBS metallic reloading dies with an extremely precise case neck expander.

The neck expander unit, made of tungsten carbide, is so tough that Pacific guarantees it for life against any dimensional wear. Pacific says the unit provides effortless, chatter-

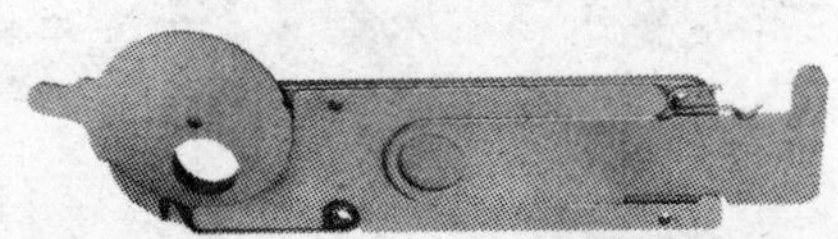

Top, 1974 Pacific Reloading Tools catalog; middle, their carbide-plug neck expander; last, a new powder-shot shut off device.

free neck expanding without lubrication. These carbide expander units, available to fit all popular calibers from 22 to 30, are being made in two models—for either Pacific Durachrome or RCBS dies. They retail for $7.20.

Pacific is, of course, well known for its complete line of tools, accessories and components for shotshell and metallic reloading. Want more dope? Write to Pacific Tool Co., Box 2048, Grand Island, NB 68801.

Pacific's New Universal Wad

Versalite—an improved universal wad design—can simplify shotshell reloading. Introduced in mid-1974 by Pacific Tool Company, the new Versalite plastic wad allows the reloader to prepare his choice of field or target loads without having to change wads or cases. A compressible center section adjusts to the correct wad column length, allowing the Versalite to replace numerous standard wads.

Designed to fit all popular 12 gauge cases, the Versalite gives excellent gas sealing and shot protection for uniform patterns. Its special center section helps recoil—it's a soft-shooting wad with hard-hitting performance, Pacific says.

For extra convenience the Versalite's shot cup is slightly flared to slip easily over the wad seating punch.

The new Versalite wad should be available in your area now, but for complete information write: Pacific Tool Co., P.O. Box 2048, Grand Island, NB 68801. Versalite wads are $3 per bag of 250, $11.50 per 1000.

New Pacific Catalog

The 1974 Pacific catalog of reloading equipment and accessories is now ready. Well-illustrated, its 38 pages show a broad line of tools for rifle, shotgun and handgun reloaders—metallic cartridge and shotshell presses, powder scales and measures, dies, trimmers, wads, everything for reloading. Two tables—one for rifle cartridges, one for handgun—list die sizes and types for 100 different cartridge calibers.

Exploded views of equipment are an aid to assembly, as well as a guide to parts prices, and there's a shotshell load table, too. Want the catalog? Send 25c for handling to Pacific Tool Co., P.O. Box 2048, Grand Island, NB 68801.

A new shot/powder shutoff attachment for Hornady/Pacific's DL-336 shotshell press offers new ease and convenience to the shooter who "rolls his own."

Standard equipment on all new DL-366 reloaders, the device is available as a quick, add-on accessory to older models. It permits the closing off of powder and/or shot when removing hoppers, changing bushings, or re-indexing. This effective unit will eliminate messy cleanups from shot falling onto the plate, or both shot and powder scattering all over the bench. Cost, $19.90. J.T.A.

Ponsness-Warren Shotshell Loaders

I'm sure that most, if not all, owners of P-W shotshell reloading presses will be sent copies of the new P-W instruction manuals. Professionally prepared and fully illustrated, there's a P-W "Owner's Manual" for each of the 3 P-W machines—the Size-O-Matic 800B, the Mult-O-Matic 600, and the Du-O-Matic 375.

Assembly, operation and adjustment are thoroughly covered in each, and there are tips on troubleshooting, common-sense reloading, exploded drawings, complete parts lists (with current prices) and a table of powder and shot bushings.

If you're the owner of a Ponsness-Warren loading machine and did not get the appropriate "Owner's Manual," write to the company at P.O. Box 8, Rathdrum, ID 83858. J.T.A.

News from RCBS

Fred Huntington has several new products in store for the reloader at this point in time, to borrow a hackneyed phrase—and a few more in the works, my West Coast spy has leaked to me, to steal another one.

Nothing big this time—what could the Orovillains do to improve on the compound-leverage RCBS loading press?

Rotary Case Trimmer

As always, in reloading ammunition, uniformity in all operations is the key to high—or higher—accuracy. That applies to cases, of course, but there's also a danger factor in chambering over-long cases—case mouths can wedge into the throat, impeding free release of the bullet, raising pressures. The clear remedy is to check case length with some frequency, say every two or three loadings, using a vernier caliper, a micrometer or a case gauge against a table of maximum case lengths.

Why do cases need trimming? With repeated firings case necks grow longer, some calibers more so than others, and the elongation rate is generally higher when stiff loads are used. In the same conditions, while we're at it, case walls can thicken, too. When this occurs, neck reaming or outside neck turning is called for, particularly if the chamber neck is on the tight side. Necks need room to expand on firing or pressures can jump.

A few cases can be hand trimmed; a flat mill file works well enough, but it's a tedious chore at best. If you have as few as 10 or 20 cases to process, it's more than tiresome. In this instance a machine trimmer is the answer, and the new RCBS Rotary Case Trimmer is a good one indeed.

Well designed and cleanly executed, this tool performs as handsomely as it looks. All metal throughout—no plastics—the cutter blades are of hardened mill-type steel for long life. Cases are held in spring collets, a short turn of the T-handle quickly locking the case head. Four collets are available, these in rifle calibers from the 17 Remington to the 45-70 and 458 Winchester Magnum, and handgun rounds from the 22 Remington Jet to the 45 Colt. There's even a fifth one for the 11mm Mauser and the 50-70 U.S.! Pilots are made in 20 diametral sizes, these ranging from 17 to 50 caliber, so that any cases can be trimmed.

An unusually clear and graphic instruction leaflet is furnished with the RCBS Case Trimmer, including a Reference Table that lists rifle and handgun calibers, the collet number and pilot needed for all of them—121 in all—plus maximum case length and working trim length.

I've used this RCBS Rotary Case Trimmer for several weeks now, and it's performed perfectly—the collets hold the cases firmly, the mouth cutting is smoothly done, and the shaved cases are held to an excellent over-all uniform length. Which is where we came in.

Prices? Complete for 30-cal., $24.95, though I suppose any other pilot-collet combination can be ordered. Pilots are $1 each, the collets $3.25. Component parts are available, too, these listed and pinpointed on an exploded view, all part of the instruction brochure.

Tungsten Carbide Dies

Have you used dies with TC (Tungsten Carbide) inserts? If you haven't, you've got a pleasant surprise coming when and if you try one. Tungsten carbide is an extremely hard substance, second in hardness to a diamond, I believe, and the use of it in full length sizing dies—it's employed mainly in dies for handguns—offers remarkable and valuable advantages.

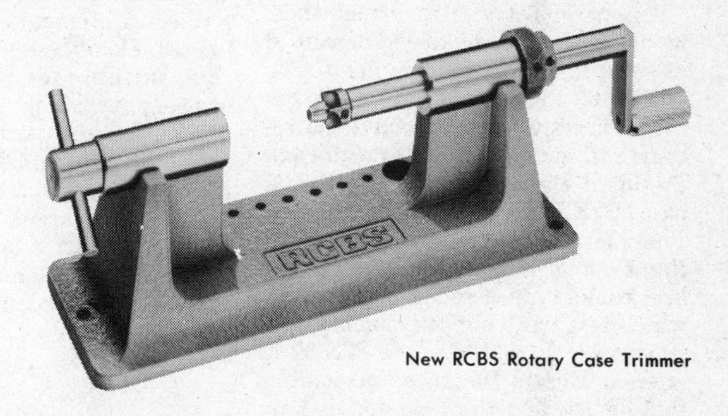

New RCBS Rotary Case Trimmer

Reloading handgunners often load in quantity—perhaps several hundred cases are handled at one sitting. Cleaning cases in large numbers is a time consuming job and a tedious one. But it's also a necessary one, for grit and dirt on uncleaned cases can raise hell with dies and cases—it can scar and scratch both. If the die interior walls are scarred, so will be the rest of your cases passing through that die. Sure, sometimes the injured die can be repolished, but that's going to cost something, if feasible. Prevention, of course, is the better way.

What's all this to do with TC dies? Everything. Because of its inherent non-porosity—coupled with its great hardness—tungsten carbide isn't fazed in the slightest by dirty cases. Clean or grimy, they're all the same to TC dies—the crud is pushed ahead of the TC insert, not driven into die or case. The cases leave a TC die beautifully smooth and polished, not scratched.

Perhaps equally important, cases intended for TC die sizing need *not* be lubricated—another bothersome chore that takes time and trouble. Too, even without the lubing, the physical effort expended in sizing several hundred cases is considerably reduced when TC dies are used.

A third and last feature of RCBS TC dies is their form—these dies are tapered, which means that no longer will belts or shoulders be found on sized cases. That was a fault of some earlier TC dies—not only were such

cases unsightly, but the often-sharp edges of the induced belts formed potential stress areas, weakening the brass.

RCBS now has 5 new TC dies, any of which can be ordered singly (die alone) or as a component of 3-die or 4-die sets. TC dies from RCBS in 30 Carbine are $33; in 45 Colt Auto, $19.50; in 38 Colt Super Auto and 380 Auto, $21 each, and $27 for the TC die in 9mm Luger. Three-die sets, including a TC sizer, run from $30 to $37.50, with 4-die sets $36-$43.50.

Handy Helpers

The other RCBS handloader's helps are less expensive, but quite useful. A primer pocket brush, made with stainless steel bristles, comes in small and large primer-pocket size, with or without a non-rolling plastic handle. $5 complete (both size brushes and handle) or either size, with handle, at $3. Spare brushes are $2.40 each. I tried these brushes, but it seemed to me the wire bristles are too thin and limber. The wires on the perimeter splay out, making smooth entry of the brush into the primer pocket a touch difficult. Thicker bristles would help.

Two straight-leg hex (Allen) set-screw wrenches, each with hexagonal plastic handles, are sized to fit all popular RCBS products—5/64" and 3/32". These handy tools are $1.20 each, both for $2.25.

The new *RCBS Reloading Guide,* a step-by-step booklet on how to reload, is covered in more detail in Robert K. Sherwood's article on handloading literature in our forthcoming 7th ed. *Handloader's Digest.* The Guide, cost $2, is an excellent small manual.

We've just had word from Fred Huntington about several changes/improvements made in the RCBS J.R. 2 and Rock Chucker loading presses.

1. The primer arm housing is now raised to deflect spent primers away from the primer arm groove.

2. The top of the ram housing has been sloped to let spent primers fall away from the shell holder and into the primer catcher.

3. The press handle shoulder and the threads have been enlarged for greater strength in heavy-duty reloading.

4. The toggle has been strengthened, too, on the J.R. 2 press. This has always been the case with the Rock Chucker.

RCBS prices have gone up a little, roughly $3 for the various press packages, and less than 10% for other products. J.T.A.

Telepacific Chronographs

The basic Telepacific system, their Model TPS-02-E, has been described at some length in our 27th and 28th editions. Essentially this system reads directly in foot seconds (no recourse to conversion tables required), the input signals transmitted from a pair of TS-E Electroscreen Detectors. These latter units react to the bullet's flight using ambient light alone—no breakable type screens are needed, which is a truly big convenience and time saver. In addition, the TPS-02-E offers a Muzzle Distance Corrector—this device lets the operator dial in the ballistic coefficient of the bullet he's shooting, thus letting the chronograph indicate true muzzle velocity rather than instrumental velocity. The value of this feature is moot, perhaps, but it does avoid tedious computations, and so far no one else offers it!

This compact instrument, dry-cell battery powered for quick use anywhere, has a time base of 1 megacycle (1 million Hz), and screen spacing is only 4 feet—an easily managed distance and convenient to set up.

A recent change in the TPS-02-E reduces battery consumption by 50%, though this alteration required altering the minimum MV reading from 500 to 600 fps—a negligible loss, but in any case remediable by changing the screen separation to 2 feet or one foot.

Most unusual, the times being what they are, Telepacific has maintained the $270 price of the TPS-02-E system since mid-1972! Or $20 can be saved if the Muzzle Distance Corrector isn't wanted.

For 1974 there's the TPS-02A-E system, identical with the above-described equipment, but with an extended velocity range—90 to 5,000 fps, thus suitable for BB and air guns, archery, etc. This system sells for $305. Also new is the availability of the Electroscreen Detectors (code TS-EK) for use with competitive chronographs using break-wire (or similar) screens via an adapter. Cost $105.

Where the need may exist (archery, shotshell recording and the like) Wide Angle Electroscreens are offered. If these replace the TS-E Electroscreens in the TPS-02-E system (or other variations thereof), their added cost is $15; as *additional* units they're $80 a pair.

Telepacific makes first class, professional quality products, and I recommend them highly, as well as their after-sale service policies. I've used one or another Telepacific chronograph for several years now, and with every satisfaction. J.T.A.

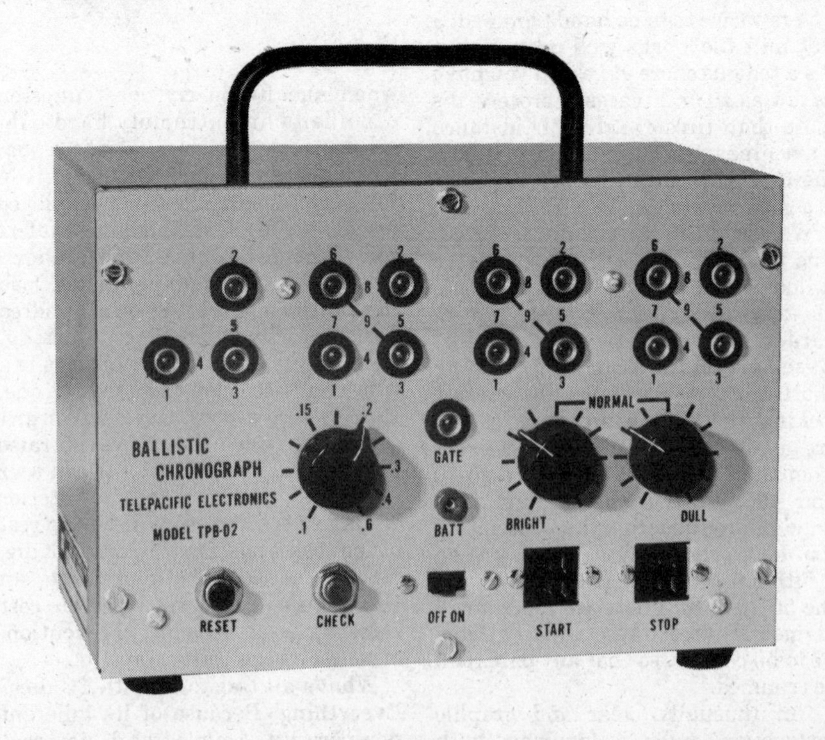

Bitterroot Bullet Company

Bill Steigers, head man of this outfit, and the designer of the justly-famed BBC (Bitterroot Bonded Core) bullets, has a new and informative brochure that big game hunters everywhere will want to see. Among the illustrations are some dozen bullets recovered from various game species—deer, elk, bear, moose, African Cape buffalo and Derby eland. All of them show the usual high weight-retention we've come to expect from BBC bullets, like 97% in some instances!

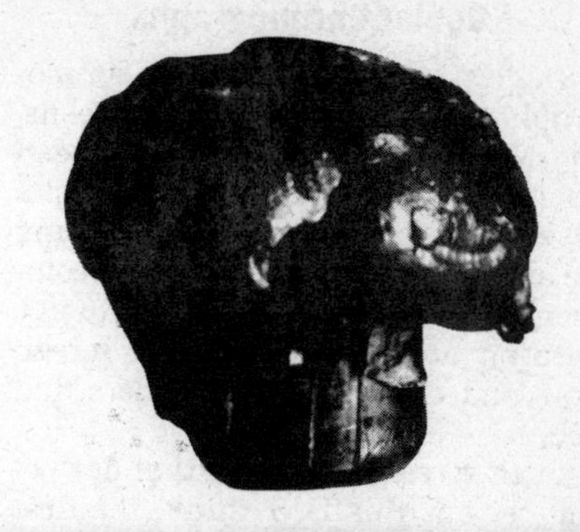

We're showing two of these great BBC bullets—both produced one-shot kills. The 150-gr. bullet at left, fired at a mule deer from 150 yards, the rifle a 270 Winchester, kept 96% of its original weight; the other, a 250-gr. bullet used in a 358 Norma Magnum, killed an elk at 40-odd yards, the recovered bullet weighing 237 grains for 94%. That's *good* performance.

The new BBC brochure describes and pictures all of the 17 bullets Steigers makes—calibers included are 270, 7mm, 30, 338 and 375. Three bullet weights are offered in each size except 270, which has two. Prices range from $6 to $9 for 20 bullets, exact cost depending on caliber and weight. Five-bullet packets are also available, these priced at $1.75 to $2.50 each. Pretty expensive, huh? Sure, compared to bullets of conventional design and construction, but try thinking about these expensive-to-make and ultra-lethal bullets this way—their total cost on a hunting trip, even if they were twice the price, would be a negligible amount against what that hunt took from your pocket in transportation, licenses, outfitter fees, and such like.

This attractive brochure has been a bit costly for Steigers—paper and printing are mighty expensive these days—so if you want one, you'll have to send BBC a No. 10 or larger 10c stamped envelope, or two-bits (25c) in coin. Don't forget to put your name and address on the big envelope. Bitterroot Bullet Co. is at P.O. Box 412, Lewiston, Idaho 83501. J.T.A.

Shooters Accessory Supply

Ted Smith, owner-operator of SAS for these many years, was the first to make and furnish a device for trickling a few granules of powder onto a scale pan. He called that useful gadget the "Little Dripper," and I have a hunch he sold a hell of a lot of them. They filled a need, they worked well, and they were inexpensive.

In recent years other powder tricklers appeared, some of them reasonably designed, others of little account. None improved on Ted's original design, but *he's* now done just that, in my opinion.

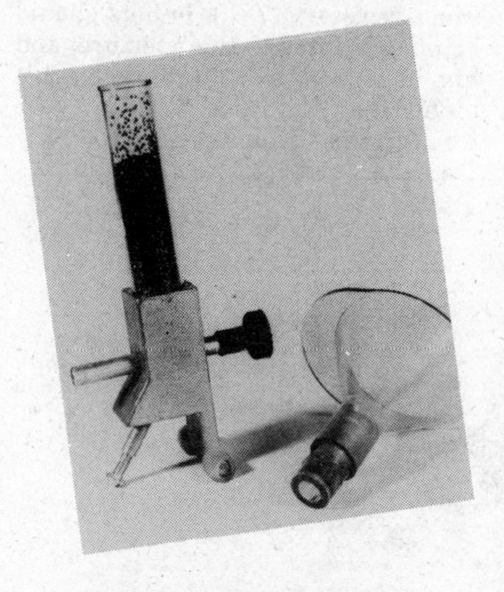

The device pictured here offers two improvements—the major one is the plastic vial, one or more of which can be ordered—that holds the powder. These are removable and, with the furnished cap installed, can be set aside with their small powder load intact—that's handier than dumping the powder back into its canister, and it's a time saver as well. Each carries a small label. The other betterment is the angled screw you see, adjusting which lets the slope of the discharge tube meet your desires for a fast or slow release of powder granules. Some powders, of course, flow faster than others. Again, the device works well.

Price of the new SAS 3-legged bigger dripper is $2.75, including 2 vials. Extra vials are 5 for $1, and I suggest you get several. J.T.A.

22 Long Rifle Shotshells

As many of you must have noticed, the makers of 22 LR shotshells furnish no information on velocity and energy about them. A small matter, no doubt, but a while back I decided to find out just what the MV and ME figures might be. Handgunners use these not infrequently, as snake loads.

I broke down 5 cartridges to see how much powder and shot these small cases contained. The average powder charge for the 5 was 2.0 grains of a grey-green substance, platelets roughly circular in form. The No. 12 shot averaged 26.2 grains per round, separated from the propellant by a single card wad, its weight 0.30-grain average.

These loads were Remington's 22 shotshells. To check muzzle velocity I fired 20 rounds through the chronograph, all from a 6½" barreled Ruger Single Six. Because I felt the velocity would drop rapidly, I did not use an instrument with the usual 10-foot screen separation. I set up the Telepacific TPB-02-E instrument for the job, placing the screens the 4 feet apart specified for them. This chronograph is unusual in using electronic screens that operate *without* artificial light output—set up outdoors daylight works the system, sunny light or dull. Indoor operation is feasible, however, with electric lamps. A 4-foot screen separation is Telepacific's standard screen distance, their crystal-controlled circuitry operating at 1,000,000 Hz or cycles.

The 20 shots averaged 1008 fps; the highest reading was 1041, the lowest 992. The computed energy comes to about 59 foot pounds. I fired these rounds with the gun's muzzle one foot from the first screen, thus my instrumental velocity was at three feet; however, because the TPB-02-E is unique in having a ballistic coefficient adjustability—which was set as low as possible—the average velocity figure mentioned may be viewed as pretty close to true muzzle velocity. A mere two grains of powder gets pretty good results, huh? J.T.A.

Oehler Chronographs

Dr. Ken Oehler's Model 11 chronograph and his latest bullet screens, the Model 61 Skyscreens, have been letting me do a lot more shooting in a given time span. Instead of jumping up after every shot to change the common paper or plastic screens, to say nothing about finding a dud screen now and again, I just sit there and shoot.

Such screens aren't all that new, of course, but this is, I think, the first time such relatively effortless chronographing has been offered at low cost.

The Oehler Skyscreens, self-contained and 9-volt dry battery powered, are small packages—6¼" long by 2" thick, and 4½" wide. I mounted my sample pair on a 6-foot 2x4, which was handy and offers good rigidity, placing the Skyscreen 5 feet on centers.

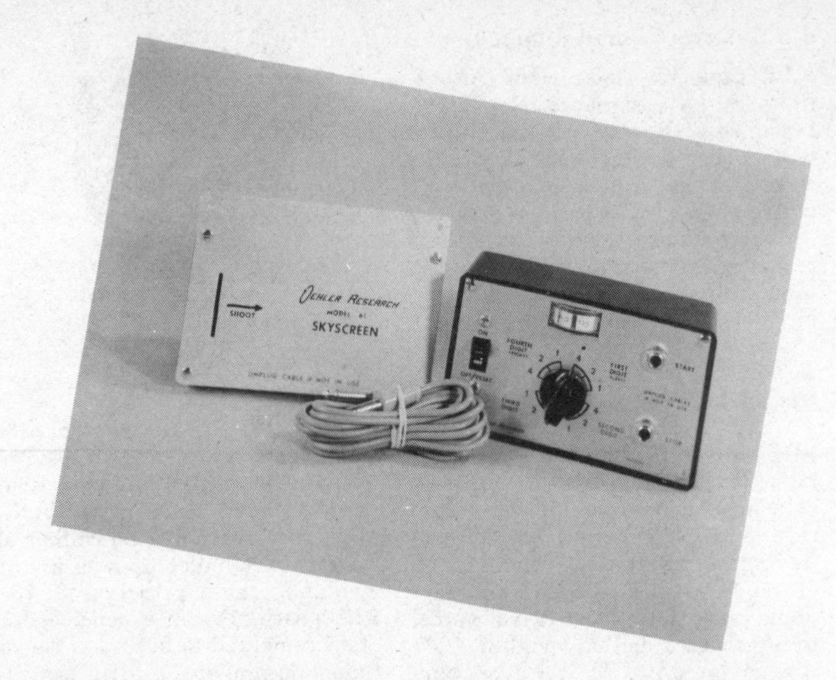

As the bullet passes over the small slots in succession, light from the sky casts a shadow onto the photo-eye cell in each unit—and there's your reading. The Model 11 instrument, not much larger than the screens, stores the reading until a switch is rotated and the figures read off—1 to 4—via a yes-no needle. The 3-figure total is then referred to a table, and the velocity found in foot seconds.

The sensitive area above the light slot is keystoned in shape, about 2" wide at the bottom and flaring to about 8" at a 10" height. Bullets passing outside of this imaginary frame won't register; 17-cal. bullets should be placed closer to the aperture, and big bullets can be detected a bit higher than 10 inches.

A further advantage of these Skyscreens is that shooting for groups can be easily done with the same string of shots—a time and money saver!

At $175 for the complete package, I consider this an excellent buy in a chronograph. Moreover, deduct the cost of standard screens, some 15c or so per pair per shot, and the Oehler outfit is an even better bargain. J.T.A.

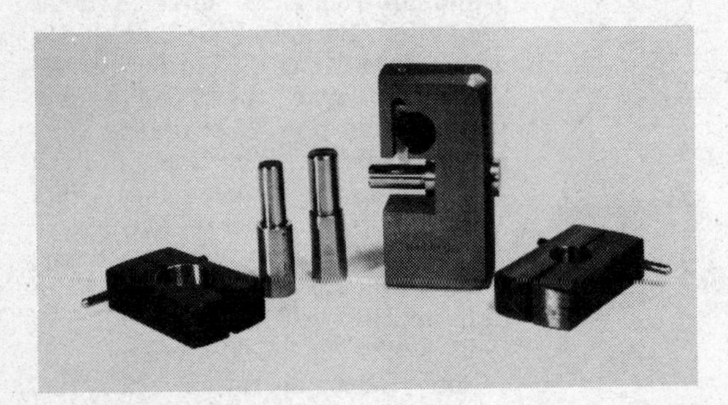

Paul Marquart's case-neck turning tool, highly compact and efficient.

Marquart Precision Case Neck Turning Tool

Paul Marquart's very compact device for taking a shaving cut on metallic cartridge case necks is operated a bit differently than other like-purpose tools available today. Its dimensions are ½"x1"x2", approx.

To get started, retract the retaining screw in the case holder so the two halves will open, then suspend the case holder by its protruding pins over the end of a bench vise. Now insert the case into the holder and tighten the vise jaws just enough to hold the case over the solid head section. Now, having lightly lubricated the arbor or pilot, push the cutter onto the arbor, rotating the cutter *always* to the right or clockwise. The arbor can be adjusted in the frame to control the depth of the cut, the arbor shoulder acting as a stop. Having completed the cut, keep turning the cutter clockwise and pull the cutter of the case neck. The hardened cutter bit is fully adjustable for depth of cut, a full turn of its screw advancing the cutter .025".

This is a well-made, truly precision tool, and it will turn case necks uniform to within .0001" if the work is carefully done. I held ten 222 necks to just that tolerance.

Price of the complete tool, one arbor and one case holder included, is $25. Extra arbors are $3, extra case holder $4. J.T.A.

Vickerman Bullet Seaters

Vickerman's straight-line bullet seaters—made for virtually all calibers, and with a single caliber size handling a fair range of different cartridge designations—were discontinued for a time because of cost problems.

Now these well-made and useful tools, threaded ⅞-14 for use in standard loading presses, are back in production. Prices are higher, of course, but unavoidably so, W.S. Vickerman wrote recently.

Complete seaters are $22.50; punch and guide sets for converting to another basic caliber, are $11.50. Shellholder extensions—needed for 17, 22, 6mm and 25 calibers when using the shorter cartridge cases—are $1.50 each. These same extensions will be furnished at no added cost when any of the four calibers just listed are ordered.

Customer service by Vickerman wasn't all that it should have been for some months—as several readers told us—but that should now be a thing of the past. J.T.A.

The Hunter

A man for all seasons

AUTUMN IS the time of the hunter. With the coming of fall weather, some 20 million Americans make ready to act out a part of the national heritage going back to Daniel Boone and beyond.

But things have changed since the days when Squire Boone "cilt a bar" and recorded his feat on a tree. No longer is hunting a matter of survival or commercial enterprise. Agricultural technology and refrigeration have taken care of the first need for most of us; the tragedy of market hunting was ended in 1918 after sportsmen and conservationists rose in opposition to the annihilation of wildlife for profit.

The modern hunter may go afield for any number of reasons but, regardless of individual motivation, most sportsmen are more concerned with the future of wildlife than the present contents of their game bags. In fact, the National Shooting Sports Foundation has compiled statistical evidence that hunters have done more to support the cause of practical conservation than *any other group* in the country. Here are some interesting facts about these space age nimrods and the game they pursue:

- Through a self-imposed tax on sporting arms and ammunition, hunters and shooters have, in the last 30 years, provided nearly half a billion dollars for wildlife management. These taxes continue to add over $40 million annually to conservation funding.
- Through the purchase of hunting licenses and permits, today's hunters provide more than $105 million a year to support the 50 state fish and game departments.
- Of the 914 species of mammals in North America, only 35 are hunted in the United States. None of these is, in any real sense, endangered.
- Of the 796 species of birds in America, only 74 are hunted. All, though, benefit from sportsman-financed programs.
- One in every five men in the United States is a hunter.
- Hunters contribute over $2 billion annually to the nation's economy.
- Thanks to sportsman-supported management programs: **In 1900**, only 500,000 deer existed in the United States. Today, after 70 years of wildlife management, there are 30 times as many–15,000,000. **There** are about 5 times as many elk in the nation today as there were 60 years ago, about 7 times as many antelope. **Turkeys** numbered less than 100,000 as recently as 1952; they now total well over 1,000,000.
- Almost 500,000 men over the age of 65 are active hunters.
- Over 1,000,000 American youngsters between 9 and 11 enjoy the sport of hunting.
- Through the purchase of Federal Duck Stamps, hunters annually contribute almost $7,000,000 for waterfowl conservation. Since the enactment of this program in 1934, Federal Duck Stamps have raised over $129 million.
- The colorful ringneck pheasant, of which there are countless millions today, did not even exist here 100 years ago. The immigrant ringneck was introduced by sportsmen in 1882. The thriving Hungarian partridge and the chukar were also sportsmen-introduced.
- Pennsylvania leads the nation in the number of hunters–1,122,399 in 1972. Dollars from such hunters have purchased for the state over one million acres of game land, areas open not only to hunters but to birdwatchers, hikers, Boy Scouts and nature lovers as well.
- Hunters spend an estimated $100 million each year developing wildlife habitat on privately owned lands. None of the 101 animals on the official Endangered Species List are hunted, according to the Office of Endangered Species, U.S. Department of the Interior.
- Sportsmen were active in founding of the nation's wildlife refuge system, which now includes over 440 separate management areas with a total of over 31,000,000 acres.
- Sportsmen were behind the organization and development of nearly all major conservation groups. Sportsmen continue to back the National Wildlife Federation, Izaak Walton League and many others.
- In the past 50 years hunters alone have contributed over $2.3 *billion* for conservation and wildlife management.

As shown by this mountain of multi-digit numbers, hunting for sport is still very much a part of the American scene. While many people never go beyond rhetoric in their environmental concerns, hunters are vitally involved in supporting and financing practical conservation programs all over the nation. Autumn may be the time of the hunt, but when it comes to preserving our natural heritage, the hunter is a man for all seasons. ●

HIGH COUNTRY CHUCKING

High country indeed—the author, going afoot in the mountain meadows and rock falls above timberline, finds his most rewarding shooting. A load table covering several calibers is included.

by DAN L. FLORES

THE VIEW FROM the high, windswept pass was something you might expect to see on a scenic postcard. Lofty mountain peaks, partially draped with snow, rose to vast heights as far as the eye could see. Lush, green alpine meadows, dotted with rock outcroppings and laced with blue glacial lakes, sloped to meet jagged canyon walls. There were no trees at this elevation. We were far above timberline.

"Are there chucks up this high?" my wife asked me, somewhat dubiously. She was panting from the climb. "I don't see how they could breathe up here."

"They're up here all right, Susie," I said. "Scads of 'em." I was about to elaborate when she interrupted me.

"Look, there's one!" she said, pointing. "He's on that flat rock, right over there." For the moment she had forgotten that she was out of breath.

'Right over there,' I should explain, proved to be about 200 yards across a rockslide (it looked closer in the rarified air) and the critter she'd spotted was indeed a rockchuck. It was a good one, too, idly passing the time stretched out serenely on a big boulder, totally absorbed in contemplating the assorted charms of various lady chucks, or whatever it is that high country chucks do under such circumstances. The brightly colored marmot was, needless to say, completely unaware of our presence.

Somewhat chagrined at not having spotted the chuck myself, I put the binoculars aside, slid a cartridge into the 25-06, and stretched out prone in the grass. There was nothing particularly difficult about the shot. I simply held the crosshairs on the left side of the chuck to allow for a rather stiff mountain breeze, and squeezed the trigger. The report of the rifle was followed by a *thunk* as the deadly 100-gr. bullet slammed home, and the chuck flew into the air, seemingly determined to go into orbit.

Susie turned to me and made a face. "I was watching through the binoculars. It looked like a bomb hit him."

She said something else, but I wasn't paying attention. Having already spotted several more chucks on the steep mountain slope, I was trying to decide which one offered the most challenging target.

The month was August, and my wife and I were hunting rockchucks, or yellow-bellied marmots as they are often called, in the high, tundra-like country of Beartooth Pass, up near the Wyoming-Montana border. We weren't nailing any vast number of these wary pests, but we were having a fine shoot—a real refresher course in long range, cross canyon shooting—and seeing some fantastic country as well.

I've been something of a nut about rockchucks and rockchuck hunting for as long as I can remember. Long before I shot my first rockchuck (for I grew up in the Southwest, hundreds of miles from the nearest chucks) I had decided that hunting the high country marmots was bound to be the epitome in challenging, precision shooting. After that first rockchuck hunt, several years ago in Colorado, I was firmly and decidedly hooked.

One of Three Species

The rockchuck (sometimes called yellow-footed instead of yellow-bellied marmot) is a fascinating little creature. He is one of three distinct subspecies of chucks in North America, the other two being the eastern woodchuck and the large hoary marmot of the northwestern U.S. and Canada. In physical configuration rockchucks don't differ a great deal from woodchucks, the primary differences being in coloration. Many old rockchucks are brightly marked with orange and black. Some hunters say they're smaller than woodchucks, others insist they are larger. Although I've never weighed a mature rockchuck, the general impression I get is that they run a bit smaller than the largest woodchucks. Unless I have been deceived, they also seem to be somewhat more wary.

Considered as a body, the various species of chucks make up the number one varmint hunting targets in the United States. The sport of shooting unprotected animals like woodchucks and rockchucks began in the first decades of the 20th century, when sportsmen realized that such shooting was excellent practice for big game hunting. From this humble origin, chuck hunting has mushroomed into one of the top shooting sports in America. With no closed seasons and no bag limits, it's no wonder that more powder is burned in this sport than most other shooting sports combined. Scores of chuck hunting clubs and associations have been organized in the East and the West, and a whole army of hunters devote their time and money to this off-season varminting. Much of the progress in high velocity cartridges, telescopic sights, and improved bullets and rifle accuracy can be directly or indirectly attributed to the popularization of chuck shooting. Cartridges have been named after the stocky pests, and one major loading tool company even uses the marmot as its trademark! No hunting sport can claim more avid followers.

The species under discussion, *Marmota flaviventris* to be biologically precise, inhabits some of the most beautiful and spectacular country in America. Its range extends from northern New Mexico on the south to the Canadian Rockies on the north. Only Arizona, among the western mountain states, is not home to the rockchuck. All the other mountain states have them in varying numbers, with the greatest concentrations being found in the more northerly regions. Wyoming, Montana, and Idaho probably have the greatest number of chucks, but in isolated spots all over the West they often become exceedingly abundant.

Despite this fact, chucks can be difficult to locate, particularly for the out-of-stater who is unfamiliar with the country, and even for residents who may be unfamiliar with the habits of rockchucks. The most likely chuck terrain is where rockslides and lava outcroppings meet meadows or grassy areas. Rockchucks are never found far from an available source of food. I may be going against the prevailing notions, but in my experience chucks are also found in much greater numbers *above* timberline, in the windswept, tundra-like terrain of the high elevations. I've never had much success in locating large colonies below the tree line, whereas in many of the high mountain passes I have seen them in concentrations that virtually stagger the imagination.

Finding Rockchucks

I have a foolproof method for locating rockchucks, even in areas which I've never hunted. It is remarkably simple, and has never failed me yet.

Rockchucks are found in the greatest numbers high above timberline. Here, glassing for more targets at 10,000 feet, I've spotted a youngster.

Susie got these two chucks, one a rockchuck and one a hoary marmot, on Beartooth Pass, up on the Wyoming-Montana border. This is the type of high altitude, rugged country that big chucks thrive in.

This heavy-barreled 22-250 with its 15x scope makes a fine varminter—but it is a bit heavy.

It operates on the sole principle that rockchucks prefer the high elevations and will be found in greatest numbers above 9,000 feet. For locating such areas, I secure a topographical map (a road map will do in some areas) of National Forest lands and circle every peak or pass I can find that is above 9,000 feet and is within a couple of miles of a navigable road. Then I simply drive out, park the car, and begin walking and glassing rockslides and outcroppings where chucks like to sun. I *start* glassing at timberline and work up from there. It's not unusual to find three times as many chucks at 12,000 or 13,000 feet as at 9,000. The important thing to remember, always, is to get up high, as high as you can go.

Note also that I do my hunting on foot. Sure, I know that many if not most rockchuck hunters hunt from 4WD vehicles and either shoot the animals out of the car or over the hood. I am also ready to concede that such hunters probably see and shoot more chucks than I do, which is all right with me. I long ago lost any desire to simply shoot as many chucks as possible, and instead came to measure the success of a hunt by the "total experience." Included in this total experience, for me at least, is the pleasure I derive from just walking across those high, alpine meadows, stalking on my belly through the mountain clover (it smells lovely), and spending quiet and peaceful hours glassing unspoiled country. If I don't shoot up three or four boxes of cartridges an afternoon I'm not disappointed, for I've seen and done things the car hunters never experience.

Perhaps I should mention, in this connection, that in many wilderness areas (some of the National Forests, for example), off-road travel by any motorized vehicle is strictly prohibited. I like that. It means that if a hunter wants to shoot rockchucks then he damn near has to get out and *hunt* them.

Techniques of Hunting

Hunting rockchucks is amazingly like big game hunting. All those techniques which work well on other mountain game, such as sheep, goats, and high country mule deer, also work well on rockchucks. This, plus the fact that the habitat is much the same, is why rockchuck hunting has always been recognized as an excellent tune-up stint for going after larger game. If you can stalk and then hit rockchucks at 250 or 300 yards, you'll encounter no problems with a ram.

Rockchuck shooting is usually long-range work, especially in areas where the chucks have had prior experience with riflemen. Young chucks, and those which have never seen a high velocity bullet shatter rock with a near miss, are apt to be a mite trusting, but older and more experienced marmots often become fantastically wary. Most rockchuck hunters take pride in their ability to hit these small targets at great distances, and shun any shots at less than 200 yards. Such precision shooting demands the very best in the way of equipment and shooter ability.

Serious rockchuck hunters use only centerfire calibers, beginning with the 22 Hornet and going on from there. In the past few years the 17 caliber has made some inroads, but since the Hornet was introduced in 1930, the two-two has been *the* varmint caliber. I've used most all of them, including the three most popular—the 222, the 22-250 and the 220 Swift—and I'm ready to admit that this trio has certain advantages. Some of the longest hits I've made on rockchucks were from a heavy-barreled M70 in 22-250 with a 10x scope. Similarly, for pleasant shooting and fine performance out to about 250 yards, I've never found anything to beat my old Remington M722 in 222 caliber.

But the virtues of the centerfire 22s (and they are many) often lose some of their luster when the little cartridges are used out of their intended environment. That superb accuracy that makes a 220 Swift such a death ray on southern crows has a tendency to go to pot in the windy western mountains. The low noise level and nearly negative ricochet properties which make a 222 so desirable for shooting woodchucks in the populated areas of the East are wasted on the wide open spaces commonly encountered in high country chucking. The 22 centerfires, for all their attributes, are simply not ideal for western rockchucks.

The Bigger Calibers

Experienced chuck hunters tend to lean toward the heavier calibers for rockchucks. For one thing, many

I shoot the 270 uphill at a distant marmot. Uphill-downhill shooting is tricky, requires holding low in either event if angles are steep.

A steady position is a must. I shoot the 243 from prone.

hunters enjoy using their big game rifles on varmints, and hunting chucks exactly as if they were sheep or mule deer. Then, too, from the practical standpoint the larger calibers are more efficient on high altitude chucks because, with proper bullets, they are much more effective wind buckers than the 22 centerfires.

This advantage may need some explanation, and rather than listing a table of wind angles and velocities, with bullet drift compared in inches, let's reduce the whole thing to a practical field comparison. Look at it this way: the shooter who uses a 243 or a 25-06, loaded with bullets having a ballistic co-efficient of .320 or over (which means a spitzer or hollow point of at least 90 grains in 6mm; 100 grains in 25 caliber) can nearly *double* the range over the hot 22s; he can score a hit by holding on the *windy* side of a chuck, and this under most any conditions of wind and/or range. Anyone who has done much long range shooting knows how strong the tendency is to keep the crosshairs on fur, so this adds up to a terrific advantage for the larger varmint calibers.

As an example of how this works, a couple of years ago I spent several hours one morning shooting chucks with a 22-250 and a 243, comparing the effectiveness of these two fine varmint cartridges on high country marmots. This took place up on Colorado's Loveland Pass at an elevation of about 12,000 feet. I'll admit that the wind was not blowing that badly, as far as mountain breezes go.

At any rate, I was using 53-gr. hollow points in the 22 Varminter, and was able to score pretty consistent hits on chucks 150 or so yards away by holding on the left edge of their bodies to allow for wind drift. Past that range, however, at distances at which most chucks are shot, I was having to guess at windage hold-off. I wound up missing more than I hit. The 243 was loaded with 90-gr. spitzers and, although it is not as accurate a rifle as the 22-250, I was able to kill chucks quite neatly out to about 275 yards with that edge-of-the-body hold. I came away from that hunt pretty firmly convinced of the 243's superiority for this kind of shooting.

On really windy days I've found that even heavier bullets are not a bad idea. The 100-gr. spitzers in 6mm buck the wind with even more authority than the 85- and 90-gr. bullets, and the same holds true of 120-gr. bullets versus 100-gr. slugs in 25 caliber. The 130-gr. bullets in the 270 seem to give more consistent hits at long range than those of 110 grains under windy conditions. These heavy game bullets should not be used in settled country, where they are apt to ricochet wildly, but for cross-canyon, wilderness chuck hunting they are tough to beat.

Favored Calibers

My favorite rockchuck rifle? I can make no bones about this—it has to be the 270. My current rifle in this

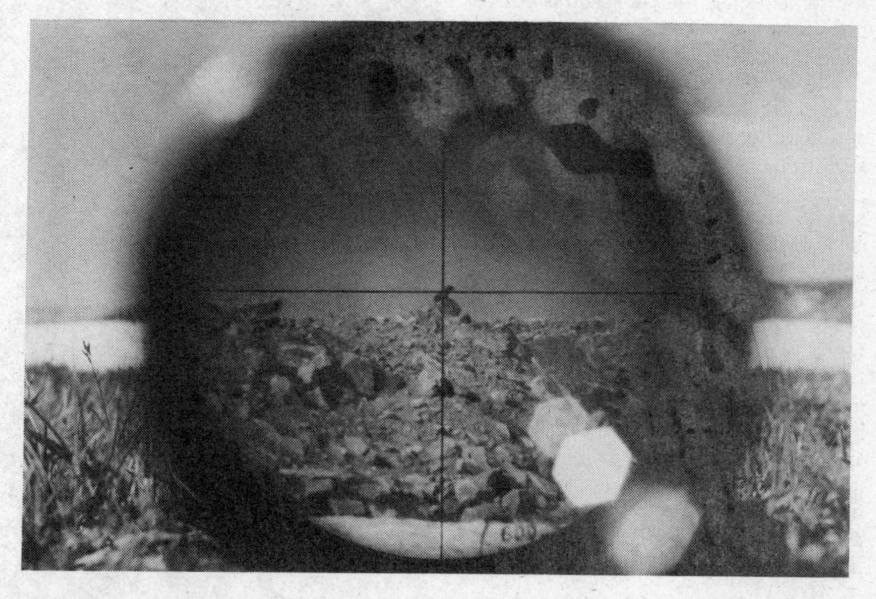

This is what the hunter sees. Scope is a 9x, range about 250 yards. This kind of shooting will develop your skill to the utmost!

chambering is a standard weight pre-1964 Winchester model 70. Shooting 110- or 130-gr. spitzers, and using a good 10x scope, this rifle has given more dependable long range performance on rockchucks than any other sporter-weight varmint piece I've owned. I don't mean to imply that I *never* miss with this rifle, but under favorable conditions, and with a good rest, a chuck at 400 yards is in a reasonable degree of jeopardy.

In close second place, so close, in fact, that I have almost no preference, is the 25-06. I now have two rifles in this caliber—one a Remington M700 BDL, the other a special, heavyweight job on an M70 action. The latter rifle is used mostly on prairie dogs and crows, as it is far too heavy to lug around in the mountains. For car hunters this rig would be pure poison on long range chucks, but for my kind of chuck hunting the sporter weight Remington is the thing.

There is really only one disadvantage in shooting these spitzer-weight larger-bore rifles at chucks, and that is *recoil!* It is hard for people who don't do a lot of shooting to realize that the recoil of a 270 or a 25-06 actually causes many shooters to close their eyes and yank the trigger, but nevertheless this does happen. The only cure is plenty of practice with live ammunition—practice which can be obtained shooting chucks, not on a deer or pronghorn hunt, when it's too late.

For the experienced hunter who doesn't flinch, but who is honestly bothered by the recoil of something like a 270, the logical step is to go to one of the 6mms, either the 243 or the 6mm/244. These calibers are superb for rockchucks, and yet recoil is noticeably less than it is from a 25-06 or a 270 of the same weight. My wife, who is 5′4″ and weighs 114 lbs., does not like to shoot my 25-06, but she does remarkably well with a M70 Featherweight in 243.

It goes without saying that a good scope of high magnification and crystal-clear definition is required for this type of long range shooting. Anything under 6x is too little, and anything over 12x is probably too much for the prone or sitting positions. I like the variables, and the ones that go up to 10x or 12x can double as binoculars. A rangefinder reticle which operates on the 18-inch principle is not a bad idea, as a large chuck, when standing erect, approaches that height. Such an outfit vastly simplifies the problem of range estimation.

High and Low

Another difficulty met in high

High Country Rockchuck Loads

The Author's Favorites*

22-250

Bullet	Powder/grs.	Primer	Case	MV	Rifle
53 H. HP	3031/33	CCI 250	R-P	3,700	Win. 70 Var.
63 S.	4064/34.5	CCI 250	R-P	3,500	Cust. Mauser

243

Bullet	Powder/grs.	Primer	Case	MV	Rifle
85 S.	4831/49	CCI 250	R-P	3,200	Win. 70 Fwt.
87 H.	4350/44	Rem. 9½	R-P	3,325	Rem. 700 Var.
95 N.	N-205/48**	CCI 250	R-P	N.A.	Win. 70 Fwt.
100 S.	4831/47	CCI 250	R-P	2,980	Win. 70 Fwt.

25-06

Bullet	Powder/grs.	Primer	Case	MV	Rifle
87 S.	4064/48	Rem. 9½M	W-W	3,425	Cust. 70 HB
90 S. HPBT	4350/56	CCI 250	W-W	3,400	Rem. 700 BDL
100 H.	4831/58	CCI 250	R-P	3,275	Rem. 700 BDL
100 S.	N-205/58	Rem. 9½M	W-W	3,400	Cust. 70 HB
100 Sp. HP	4064/46	CCI 250	R-P	3,200	Cust. 70 HB
117 S.	N-205/54	Rem. 9½M	W-W	3,225	Rem. 700 BDL

270

Bullet	Powder/grs.	Primer	Case	MV	Rifle
110 S.	4064/51.5	CCI 250	R-P	3,360	New 70
130 S. BT	4831/62	CCI 250	W-W	3,175	New 70
130 S.	4350/55	CCI 250	R-P	3,150	Pre-'64 70

*Several of the above loads are maximum charges and should be approached cautiously and from below. Neither the author nor the publisher can assume any responsibility for persons using or duplicating this loading data.
**N-205 exhibits an unusual amount of variation from lot to lot. These loads were with lot #051216. With another lot these loads might be prohibitive. Accuracy of the N-205 loads listed is excellent, however.
Key: H. for Hornady, S. for Sierra. N. for Nosler. Sp. for Speer.

Good rockchuck cartridges include, from left—224 Weatherby, 225 Winchester, 22-250 Remington (all a bit wind sensitive); 243 Winchester, 6mm Remington, 25-06 (all nearly perfect for rockchuck sniping). Not shown is the author's personal favorite, the 270.

Handloading Notes

BOTH of the loads mentioned for the 22/250 apparently develop mild pressures, as cases have been loaded up to 30 times and primer pockets are still tight. However, my custom-built Mauser has a long throat and will handle heavier charges than rifles with normal throating. The 63-gr. Sierra load may well turn up excessive pressures in a rifle with a shorter throat, so don't use this one without dropping down first. As for accuracy, the 53-gr. Hornady HP/33 grains of 3031 load is the most accurate combination I've ever cooked up in a 22-250. 100-yard 5-shot groups in the heavy-barreled M70 average ⅝-inch. In the Mauser, the heavier 63-gr. bullet averages about ¾-inch for 5 shot strings at 100 yards.

The only load listed for the 243 which shows signs of being hot, at least in my rifles, is 48/N-205 with the 95-gr. Nosler. This one should be approached cautiously, and from below. Accuracy is excellent—the first 5-shot group I fired with it clustered into ¾-inch, with 4 shots in a ragged ⅜-inch hole! Although both of the listed loads with 4831 (Hodgdon's, not the new DuPont IMR-4831, which I haven't yet had an opportunity to test) exceed the manual-recommended maximums by a grain or two, pressures in my Model 70 Featherweight seem very mild, and both of these loads are exceptionally accurate, with groups averaging around one inch at 100 yards. Once again, however, these loads should not be duplicated in other rifles without working up to them. The 4350 load is well on its way to becoming one of the classic loads for the 243. Pressures are moderate, and in the heavy barreled Remington M700 groups run under ¾-inch more often than not.

A number of the loads listed for the 25-06 are at or near maximum, and may produce excessive pressures in other rifles. Both of the loads with 100-gr. bullets develop near maximum pressures in my two rifles. A switch in lot number with N-205, or changing from Winchester cases to the thicker Remington cases, could result in loosened primer pockets after only three or four loadings. Speer's manual records much heavier charges with N-205 and the 100 gr. bullet, but I understand that their test rifle has a very long throat. 58 grains of N-205 is absolute tops in my rifles; this loads produces groups of ⅝-inch in the heavy barreled M70, and blows rockchucks apart as if by lightning. The heavy M70 does even better with the 87-gr. Sierra/48. 4064 combination, with 100- and 200-yard groups beating ½ MOA when everything is perking right. Recoil is mild, and pressures seem moderate, as some of the cases have been loaded over 20 times. In the 25-06 Remington M700 the 90-gr. Sierra HPBT load punches out 5-shot clusters of from ⅞- to 1¼ inches, with flat trajectory and good bullet blowup. For really windy-day shooting, the 117-gr. Sierra and 54 grains of N-205 in the same rifle is tough to beat, however. Groups run around 1¼- to 1½ inches, and pressures appear to be moderate. Recoil is right up there, but nothing to worry about.

None of the 270 loads I've listed has shown signs of excessive pressures in my rifles, though the 62-gr. charge of H-4831 has proved a bit much in other rifles I've checked. The two loads with the 130-gr. Sierra shoot into 1¼ inches for 5 shots at 100 yards. For 400-450 yard cross-canyon chuck shooting they are superb. The 110-gr. Sierra pushed by 51.5/4064 delivers groups of less than an inch, and often as small as ¾-inch, in the new Model 70. It is accurate, but less relaible under windy conditions than the 130-gr. bullet.

Dan Flores

---

country chuck hunting is the uphill-downhill shooting problem. For those who have had no previous experience with this, it can cause some apparently inexplicable misses. A chuck can be 400 or 500 yards from the muzzle, and yet require *no* holdover at all! This phenomenon results from what is called "horizontal trajectory." Regardless of the angle of the shot, whether it be uphill or down, the bullet will respond to gravity (and hence, drop) only over the horizontal distance. Thus, if our chuck is in a canyon 350 yards below us, at a nearly perpendicular angle, he may well be only 100 *horizontal* yards away, and the shooter would actually have to hold *low* to score a hit. Likewise, if the chuck were 350 yards *above* us, the hold would be the same.

Only occasionally, of course, are such extreme angles encountered even in high country chucking, but even less frequently will the shooter fire across level meadows. The tip to remember is to hold a bit low on both uphill and downhill shots of any *substantial* angle, else you'll be shooting over lots of chucks.

Spotting chucks at long distances, even in the clear air of the West, demands a high quality pair of binoculars. Except for his rifle, no other bit of gear is so important to the rockchuck hunter. The common 7x35 field glasses are barely adequate; much more effective are those of 8x or even 10 power. Often these high-powered glasses will have to be steadied over a rolled up jacket on a boulder, but they are worth their weight in gold on overcast days when it is difficult to distinguish chuck from rock, or in spotting den sites at 300 or 400 yards.

In passing, there's one other thing I'll mention. I don't know what kind of chord this is going to strike with some chuck hunters, but many shooters I know do not hesitate to eat the rockchucks they kill. After the self-imposed closed season during spring, when most of the females are gravid, the young chucks are much sought after as tender and juicy fryers. Even the older ones, if dressed out immediately, make very good eating. I have tried them. They're not bad.

The most important advice I can offer, however, is to urge shooters to try this high country marmot hunting. If you don't live in rockchuck country, devote some of your summer vacation time to going after these abundant animals. In my admittedly biased opinion, few hunting sports on earth can match the exhilaration and downright fun of glassing the high mountain passes, crawling on your belly across a grassy meadow at 12,000 feet, and then picking off a grizzled old chuck a quarter-mile away. Give it a whirl. My guess is you won't be disappointed. ●

Pachmayr's Signature System

a radical technique for accurizing the 45 auto.

MENTION accurized 45 Colt automatics to Frank Pachmayr, and he'll drag out of the files numerous complimentary letters from distinguished pistol shooters going back to the 1930s. That is how long he's been in the accurizing business, and that's the amount of time he's spent studying the problems inherent in extracting the maximum mechanical and practicable accuracy from the ugly, slab-sided, much-maligned—and much-loved—Colt Government Model 45 pistol.

In the beginning, Frank used the same methods employed by contemporary pistolsmiths—closely-fitted barrel-to-bushing-to-slide, long barrel links and built up tangs, slide lapped to receiver, and all manner of meticulous fitting and polishing which did not change or add to the basic gun, but which reduced all its tolerances to the absolute minimum compatible with reasonably reliable functioning under match conditions.

That sort of toolroom-class work certainly increased the accuracy of the old pistol, and produced over the years some phenomenal National Match Course scores in competition. If you question the improvement obtained thereby, check back and compare National Championship 45 Match scores of the 1930s with championship scores of some 20 years later, in the 1950s.

In any event, while other 'smiths continued to develop the traditional 45 accurizing methods to the nth degree, Frank began looking afield to correct what he considered design deficiencies within that 60-year-old gun which limited its practical accuracy potential. Today, many patents and a decade later, he has more or less perfected what is called the Pachmayr "Signature" maximum-accuracy conversion of the M1911 45 auto.

Both ye olde GUN DIGEST editor, John T. Amber, and I have been shooting a total of four examples of this Signature conversion for several months. John's gun and one of mine are standard-length Government Model pistols, while my second gun is a long-slide conversion with 6-inch barrel, originally built up by Jim Clark. All have the full Signature treatment, there being no difference in its application to guns with different lengths of barrels and slides.

The fourth 45 is a short-barreled (3.9") combat version, this one given the full Signature treatment also.

Four Basic Points

There are four main components to the Signature system. First, at least chronologically, because it was developed and employed several years ago, is the Pachmayr "Wide Link." This is a special barrel link about three times the thickness of the relatively fragile Colt item it replaces. To provide a seat for it, the link recess in the frame above the trigger guard must be milled wider and accurately aligned with a broad flat forming its bottom. Then, the wide link is carefully fitted to a new, oversize, hardened, slide-stop pin for which the hole in the frame has been reamed for a precise fit. This eliminates the inordinate amount of sloppiness found in the original link system. Further, the lower portion of the link forms a broad foot which comes to bear on the bottom of the slot in the frame when the slide and barrel move into battery. This foot positively positions the barrel vertically as the gun locks up—and is virtually wear-proof inasmuch as the final positioning of the barrel is not dependent on friction and sliding surfaces as it is in some other accurizing systems. Properly fitted—and, of course, this is done by Pachmayr—the wide link adds greatly to the stability of the rear of the barrel and provides more consistent shot-to-shot positioning.

In order to fit the wide link properly, the bottom of the barrel lug (the curved extension which normally comes to rest on the slide-stop pin) is machined off parallel to the bore centerline to match a corresponding shoulder on either side of the link. Thus, when the link rotates forward and its foot contacts the inside of the frame, these shoulders also make contact and add to the vertical rigidity of the barrel. The wide link is also closely fitted between the sides of its new recess in the frame, and is equally closely fitted to the barrel lug, to insure maximum lateral rigidity of the barrel. In short, there is none of that side-to-side and up-down play to be found in guns fitted with the conventional link. This system adds positive mechanical stops to barrel movement, stops which are of substantial area to reduce wear and to increase service life in terms of the number of rounds that may be fired.

Additionally, the rearward protrusion from the recoil spring guide flange is slotted vertically to fit very closely over the front surface of the wide link to a depth of about 5/64-inch. This aids in positioning the recoil spring guide, and is also necessary to provide proper clearance for the more massive link. In addition, as a side benefit, it keeps the guide and recoil spring in position if one chooses to remove the slide/barrel/nose-piece assembly from the frame as a unit. If this is attempted with the standard Government Model or with most other accurized versions, the spring and guide jump violently out of place as soon as the slide clears the receiver—not so with the Signature accurizing system.

A complete report on a unique and patented accuracy treatment—how it works and why, plus performance figures for four 45 auto pistols.

by GEORGE C. NONTE, JR.

Muzzle Support System

Next in line we have what I choose to call the "muzzle support system," which is comprised of what Pachmayr calls the slide *nose piece* and *spherical barrel bushing*. This device replaces the conventional barrel bushing and recoil spring plunger; it requires opening up and truing the inside of the slide muzzle and threading the original seat of the spring plunger. The nose piece is then a slip fit in the barrel portion of the slide muzzle and is secured there by a large-diameter, hollow, threaded plug turned into the spring tunnel in the slide beneath. When this screw is turned up properly, the complete nose-piece assembly is locked immoveably in the slide.

Inside the nose piece and surrounding the barrel muzzle is a unique form of bushing known as a "Messerschmidt bushing" and also described as a spherical bushing. It is best likened to a ball and socket joint, with the bushing being the ball with the barrel passing through it, and the socket being formed in the nose piece.

With this design the spherical bushing proper is fitted very closely

All three of these 45 Colt autos have been given the Pachmayr Signature accurizing treatment. Top—standard length barreled gun; middle, fixed-sight 3.9" barreled pistol has modified Signature system; below, originally a Jim Clark accurized long slide model. The short barreled gun and the long slide gun carry Pachmayr's new Signature wraparound grips.

to the barrel and moves with the barrel as it tips for unlocking and locking. In all other forms of barrel bushing adapted to this 45 Colt, sufficient clearance must exist between barrel and bushing to allow the barrel to move angularly, independent of the bushing. This spherical bushing design eliminates that requirement for there is no angular displacement between barrel and bushing when the barrel tips—the closely-fitted bushing simply moves with the barrel, rotating in its precisely-fitted spherical seat in the nose piece or socket.

Pachmayr's design, then, provides for more consistent shot-to-shot barrel positioning, and far less clearance of moving parts, than is achieved by any existing system in which the barrel is displaced angularly *independent* of the bushing.

Installation of the barrel support system increases over-all length of the gun about .475-inch in the standard configuration; the pistol has a rather bell-mouthed appearance by virtue of the .600-inch cup extending beyond the muzzle.

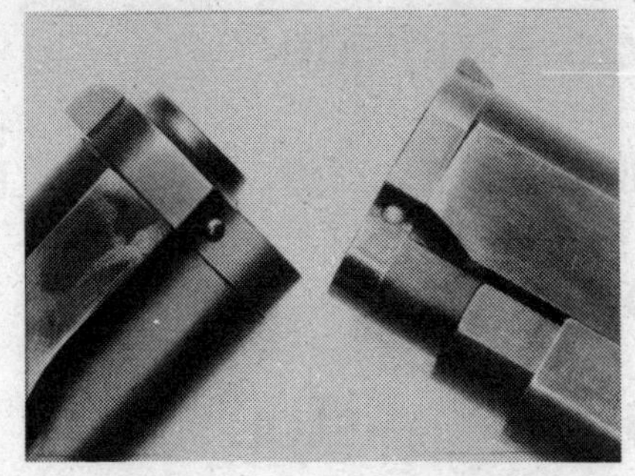

Left is standard nose piece, at right is shortened variation for sawed-off combat gun. Note integral front sights.

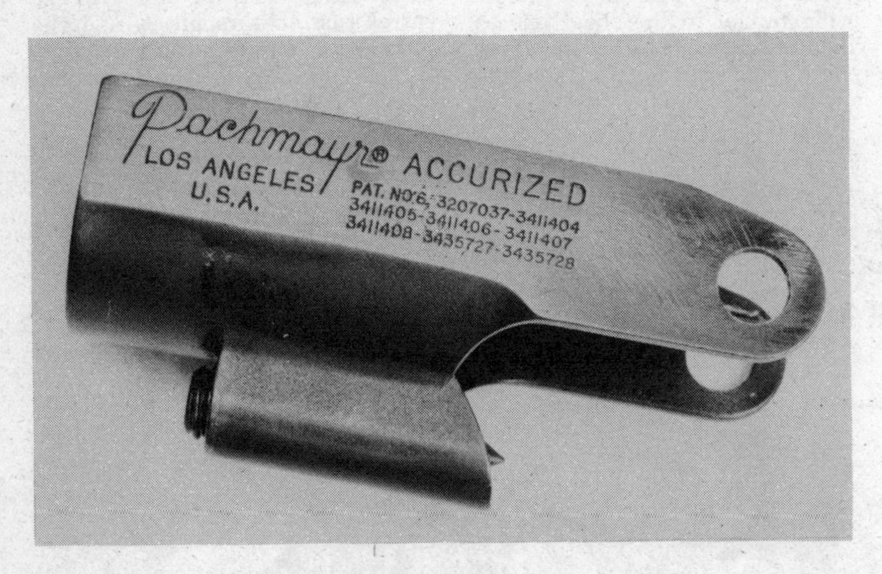

Note 8 patents granted to Frank Pachmayr on his new accurizing system. This is the slide tightener, beveled on its upper edges to form a V-block system with the slide. Slide tightener pivots on slide stop pin, upward pressure regulated by pointed screw, visible in underlug.

The nose piece proper is made with an integral new front sight; to employ this sight and the greater sight radius it produces the original front sight is removed. If one objects to this additional length, it can be pared down to about ¼-inch by trimming the nose piece back, which doesn't affect the accuracy-producing capabilities of the assembly.

The Slide Tightener

The third component of the Pachmayr Signature system is a cradle-like device called the slide tightener. It is a pivoted, U-shaped steel yoke which wraps around the underside of the frame forward of the trigger guard, and rotates upon the elongated slide-stop pin which holds it in place. Because of interference of the unit on the left side, a new offset slide stop is supplied; this is pivoted separately on the pin, making a two-part unit as opposed to the one-piece unit of the original Government Model pistol. Aside from that, the slide stop functions in the normal fashion. The new and longer slide-stop pin or "link pin," as Pachmayr calls it, is secured by a flanged head on its left end, and a small snap-ring on its right end.

Pivoting about the link pin, the slide tightener is designed to place upward pressure on the underside of the slide rails forward of the barrel breech. In order to do this, a lug on its underside contains a spring-loaded plunger which seats in a small detent machined in the front of the trigger guard. This plunger and its spring are pre-loaded by a socket-head screw entering the lug from the front. Thus, the tightener is forced up against the slide with a force determined by the compression of the spring, pivoting about the link pin. An earlier variation of the slide tightener used a solid, non-spring adjustment screw to control this upward pressure, but its rigidity made it more sensitive to variations than the spring-loaded design now used.

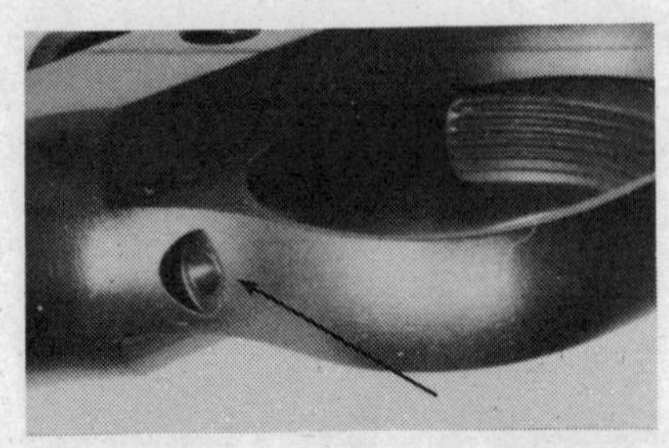

Small dimple is machined into front of trigger guard (arrow) to accept plunger of Signature slide tightener.

The upper outer edges of the tightener are beveled at about 45 degrees inward. A corresponding bevel is ground on the outer edges of the slide rails, thus the V-block principle centers the slide in the yoke of the tightener, and the tightener is centered on the frame by its own snug fit thereon. Consequently, so long as adequate upward pressure is maintained on the slide by the tightener, it is centered on the frame.

Simultaneously, upward pressure by the tightener forces the slide upward into solid contact with the guide ribs on the frame; this eliminates the excess vertical play so commonly found in the 45 pistol.

In short, rather than depending upon very precise hand-fitting, peening, lapping, etc., to remove play between the slide and the frame, the original clearances essential for positive functioning are retained, but the tightener and V-block principle are used to take those clearances out as the slide and barrel move into battery; this insures optimum uniformity of

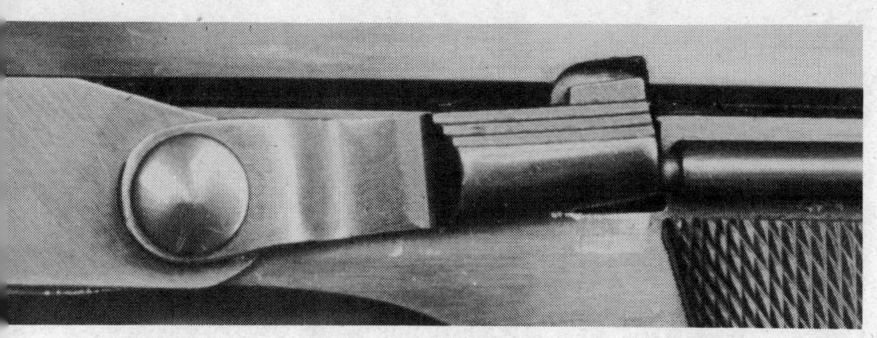

New slide stop is offset, rising at front to clear thickness of slide tightener wall.

barrel/slide/frame relationship at the instant of firing, and until the bullet has *left the muzzle*.

A slight taper exists between slide and tightener so that, as the slide and barrel begin to move rearward in recoil (after the bullet has left the muzzle and thereby not affecting its flight), clearance opens up between frame and slide to insure free movement of recoiling parts and the subsequent functional reliability that this clearance provides.

Zero Headspace Device

The fourth element in the Signature accurizing system corrects a condition long known to exist, but one which has been generally ignored in the search for maximum accuracy insofar as altering the gun proper is concerned. Pachmayr calls it his "Zero-Headspace" modification. It consists of a hemispherical-nosed, spring-loaded plunger seated in a longitudinal hole drilled in the slide breech face about ⅛-inch above the firing-pin hole.

The function of this plunger is to force every cartridge firmly against the headspacing shoulder in the chamber as the slide goes into battery. This insures that the primer of every cartridge will receive the full force of the firing pin impact and will thereby be ignited with maximum uniformity. This eliminates any forward movement of the cartridge upon firing-pin impact, which would otherwise provide some degree of *cushioning* of the firing-pin blow. Though the value of this system has been questioned by a number of people with whom I've discussed it, Pachmayr's tests do indicate a higher degree of velocity consistency than when the plunger is not present. It is commonly known that variations in firing-pin impact will produce variations in primer flame; this produces subsequent variations in ignition rate of the propelling charge which, in turn, produces further variations in velocity. It is also common knowledge that 45 ACP cartridge cases do vary in length—as a matter of manufacturing necessity. Thus a chamber deep enough to accept maximum-length cartridge cases will permit shorter cases to move forward under firing-pin impact.

Though it is an admittedly extreme example, I have seen 45 ACP *Match* ammunition with case lengths varying as much as .030-inch, not only within the same ammunition lot, but within the same box. This Pachmayr zero-headspace plunger automatically corrects for any such case-length (headspace) variations and produces more uniform ignition.

Pachmayr zero-headspace modification consists of spring-loaded plunger let into slide breech face (arrow) above firing-pin hole.

Those are the main mechanical features of the Pachmayr Signature accurizing system. Of course, the factory installation of this system—and in view of the necessary jigs and fixtures and special machining required, it can only be installed at the Pachmayr plant—includes a superb trigger job, a proper screw-adjustable trigger stop, checkering of the front and back straps, and installation of whichever target sights the customer chooses. Other refinements added are additional tightening and alignment of the barrel breech in the slide by conventional methods, feedramp and chamber modifications essential to reliable functioning with semi-wadcutter target loads, and a general tuneup of the gun and magazines to insure maximum functional reliability.

Pachmayr Signature Grips

Pachmayr has also introduced a new type of grip for the 45 auto which bids fair to become a standard against which others may be judged. Those experienced with the old Mershon revolver grips will be familiar with the material involved. It is a medium-soft rubber compound with a "tacky," clinging feel and a resilient consistency which make for a more secure and non-shifting hold than any grip material I have encountered.

Also designated by the "Signature" trademark, this is a wraparound grip moulded in one piece, containing rudimentary thumb rest swells on both sides, and almost completely covered with very fine moulded-in checkering. The right and left grip panels are formed around steel insert plates which produce the essential rigidity required. These panels are perforated to fit over the grip screw bushings in the frame and position the entire unit properly. The two panels are connected by an integral

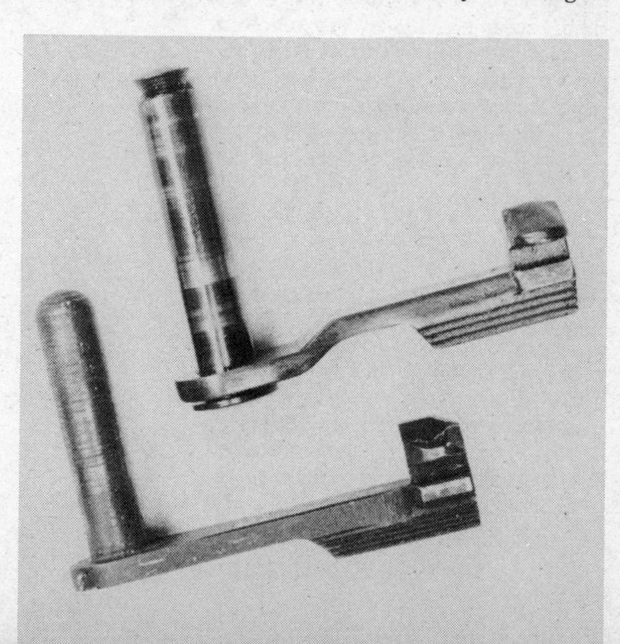

Above—separate replacement slide-stop pin (link pin) is retained by snap ring on right side. Note dogleg to clear slide tightener wall. Standard slide-stop is seen below.

Left, new Pachmayr ring bushing (here removed) has spherically-radiussed outside profile; for convenience it is called a "spherical bushing."

thin section which wraps around the front strap and is dimensioned so that it must be placed under substantial tension to fit the panels in place. It, too, is covered with moulded-in checkering of slightly larger diamonds, and a forward-thrusting lip at the bottom for additional support of the little finger of the shooting hand.

Signature Gun Takedown

Fully converted to the Pachmayr Signature system, the 45 auto requires somewhat different disassembly procedures. Two different methods may be used: First, with slide forward in battery, use a flattened dime or properly-fitting screwdriver to carefully turn out the nose piece retaining screw beneath the muzzle. As this screw is backed out, it pulls the nose piece with it—and it is also under load from the recoil spring; thus the last few turns should be taken carefully to avoid having it hurled across the room by the spring; then the snap ring is removed from the right end of the link pin, and the pin is started out to the left; after which the barrel muzzle is centered in the slide with the fingers, and the slide is drawn back until the new dismount notch (directly behind the slide stop notch) is aligned with the slide stop lug, and the stop and link pin may be drawn out to the left; the slide and barrel are then drawn off the frame to the front, the recoil spring and guide lifted out, and the barrel removed through the front of the slide.

A second method is the one I prefer because of its simplicity: remove the snap ring from the end of the link pin and press the link pin as far to the left as possible with the finger; draw the slide back until the dismount notch aligns with the slide stop, and pull the slide stop left to the limits of the link pin to clear it from the slide; ease the slide forward, then pull on the slide stop to extract the link pin; move the slide forward off the frame, invert, and lift out the recoil spring and guide carefully; now, turn out the nose piece retaining screw and remove the entire nose piece assembly; remove the barrel through the front of the slide.

In either instance, as soon as the link pin has been withdrawn completely, the slide tightener should be removed downward and forward from the frame.

The spherical barrel bushing remains in the nose piece, but it may be removed for cleaning and lubrication. Simply hold the nose piece, reach

Center, spherical bushing has now been inserted into nose piece and partially rotated.

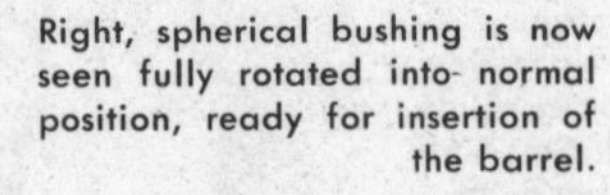

Right, spherical bushing is now seen fully rotated into normal position, ready for insertion of the barrel.

inside with the little finger, and rotate the spherical bushing 90 degrees until it is aligned with the two rectangular notches that may be seen on opposite sides of its opening in the rear of the nose piece. With the bushing so aligned, it may be pulled easily out to the rear. *Caution*—under no conditions should any abrasive material of any sort be used to clean the bushing, its seat in the nose piece, or the entire length of the barrel over which it rides. To do so will spoil the very smooth finish supplied by Pachmayr, and might also remove sufficient metal to increase clearances to the point that accuracy would deteriorate. Simply wiping these areas with a solvent-moistened cloth and then relubricating them is sufficient for normal service. I prefer a sparing application of MO_2 (molybdenumdisulphide) grease for lubrication on these areas, as well as the mating area of slide, frame, and tightener. Other shooters have their own favorites which will probably work just as well.

Pachmayr's Unique Approach

By taking this unique approach to redesigning certain portions of the gun to remove critical clearances, Pachmayr has taken much of the mumbo-jumbo out of accurizing the 45 ACP. The ultimate in accuracy is no longer dependent (with this system) upon components being so closely fitted that acceptable functional reliability can be obtained only under ideal conditions. Also, where previous accurizing methods require a complete rebuild after significant wear develops, simple replacement of parts will restore Signature unit accuracy, even if very badly worn. Simply installing a new properly-sized spherical bushing will eliminate barrel-muzzle play, and the spring-loaded slide tightener *automatically* compensates for wear on all three involved surfaces (slide, frame, and tightener).

In short, though this may be the most sophisticated and mechanically complicated system that has yet been applied to obtain maximum accuracy from the venerable Colt Government Model pistol, it would appear to be the most practical. On the other hand, where a simple slide-tightening job and installation of a tighter barrel bushing can be performed by the average pistolsmith for a nominal charge ($50 to $75) rather than going to a full-house conversion, there are no half-way measures with the Signature system. It is all or nothing, and the cost—around $250—might be a bit steep for the pistolero who would prefer to upgrade his gun one step at a time at a lesser investment. However, he'd probably be better off in the end to go ahead and visit his banker and make arrangements to have the complete Signature system installed.

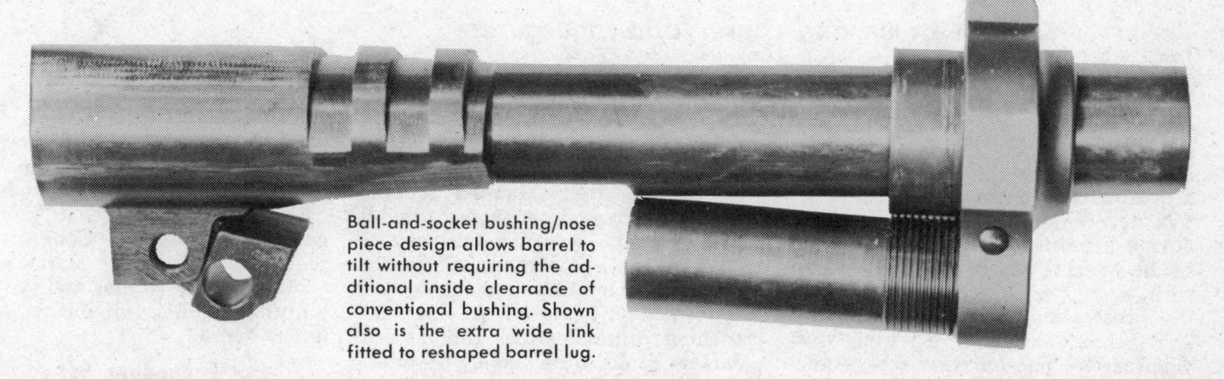

Ball-and-socket bushing/nose piece design allows barrel to tilt without requiring the additional inside clearance of conventional bushing. Shown also is the extra wide link fitted to reshaped barrel lug.

Signature 45 Performance

As far as performance is concerned, we believe the four guns we've been shooting justify Frank Pachmayr's claims. The long-slide gun was taken on a handgun hunting trip out west last fall, and when used with Super Vel 190-gr. JHP high-performance ammunition, it produced consistent one-shot kills on small varmints at 50 to 80 yards. All manner of *small* targets of opportunity (pebbles, pine cones, etc.) were hit consistently at 50 to 60 yards, indicating a group capability on the order of 1½ inches at those ranges, using service-type ammunition under field conditions. That gun was finished just in time for that trip, and since then we have not had an opportunity to lock it into the machine rest and determine precisely what it will do under ideal conditions with purely target ammunition. At the other end of the scale, the shortened gun (3.9″ barrel) with the full-house Signature treatment has produced machine-rest groups with factory target loads on the order of ¾-inch at 25 meters.

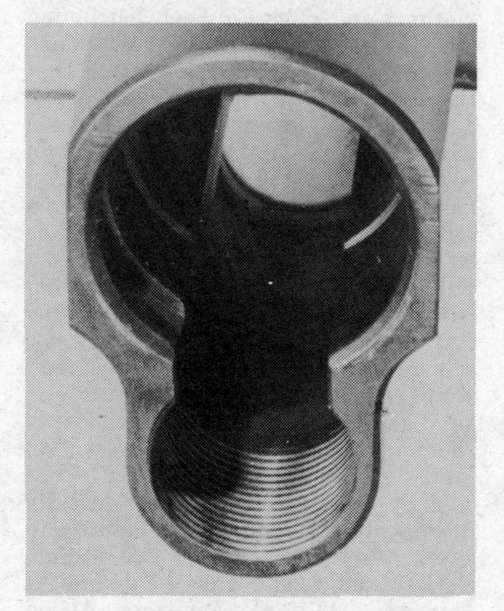

Upper part of slide muzzle is counterbored and reamed to close fit on nose piece; lower portion is threaded.

My standard-length gun, and Amber's of the same ilk, both with full Signature treatment, appear to be doing just about the same, though they haven't been shot as much as the other two. Functionally, none of the four guns have indicated any problems whatever under normal conditions. In the course of several hundred rounds through the guns collectively, the only malfunctions seen were failures to eject with my standard-length gun when locked into the machine rest. This took the form of case rims hanging up in the barrel-tang notch in the slide, thus "stove-piping," but this did not and does not occur when the gun is fired from the hand. I suspect a bit of judicious trimming of the ejector would cure this propensity, but since one doesn't normally use a gun in a machine rest, I haven't seen any need to take any corrective action.

All in all, we think Pachmayr's Signature accurizing system is the most refreshing and intelligent approach that has yet been taken to the problem of achieving maximum accuracy for the fine old Colt U.S. Service auto. ●

HUNTING ON INDIAN RESERVATIONS

by BERT POPOWSKI

Time was—less than a hundred years ago—when Indians and palefaces hunted each other. Today, on many reservations, red men and white join forces in pursuit of game and conservation measures.

FOR HUNDREDS of years the American Indian has been hailed as a peerless stalker and hunter—but he was never much of a conservationist during primitive times. He took meat as he needed it, often the females with youngsters beside them during the procreation seasons. If game became thinned out in a given area whole tribes packed their tepees and moved into better hunting country. Many ferocious inter-tribal battles were fought over choice hunting grounds, especially in those areas where big game—antelope, deer, elk and buffalo — migrated through in season. Indians literally fought for their subsistence lives in protecting choice game areas against invasion by hostile tribes. In fact the basic reason behind Indian hostility toward invading whites stemmed from the despoliation of choice hunting lands.

Many autumn Indian camps were established on traditional game areas for weeks of socializing — dancing, hunting, feasting and "making meat"; that is, they ate hugely of fresh meat and at the same time scraped hides for clothing and tepee leather, tanned hair-on robes for bedding and dried meat into stick-hard jerky to see them through the lean winter months. Some of them combined dried fruits and berries and dried jerky, all pounded to a powder, to make a highly concentrated food known as pemmican. This was thoroughly mixed with bone marrow or melted tallow and tamped into hide containers for easy handling and storage. Those fall hunting camps were a time of harvest in preparation for months when fresh meat would be hard to come by. Skilled hunters who could keep several families fed and clothed were held in high regard and ranked right up there with honored chiefs and medicine men.

When U.S. troops herded Indians onto featureless reservations, usually barren of game, this nomadic way of life came to a standstill. Shorn of their autumn hunts because game had been wastefully butchered by encroaching whites, neither Indians nor palefaces could subsist solely by hunting. This was especially tough on the Indians, who had to reverse their economy by living off paleface foods and in squalid fixed residences. What little game remained on the reservations was quickly killed off in a year-round search for traditional protein foods. The rest of their survival rations came from periodic issues of clothing and domestic beef distributed by frequently-crooked Indian agents.

Game protection didn't exist in that transitional 19th century era. Whites adopted the Indian custom of killing game whenever they wanted wild meat and could find it. Later, when each state set game laws and hired a handful of game wardens, they couldn't begin to control out-of-season hunting. Layman reasoning was that game belonged to whoever could find it and bag it. Reservation Indians, now wards of the federal government, were permitted to take game at any time and whites felt they should have the same privilege on non-reservation lands.

That kind of thinking gradually disappeared when such famous conservationists as Ernest Thompson Seton, George B. Grinnell, William T. Hornady, Gifford Pinchot, Alfred Leupold, Edward Nelson and even Theodore Roosevelt inveighed against such practices, and acted as well. They awoke the conscience of American sportsmen and legislators, state game departments were formed to assist at state levels, and game everywhere began a slow but sure comeback. But the U.S. Congress didn't see fit to change the status of game on Indian reservations and year-round hunting by their inhabiants was left unchecked.

Seasons Set

However, there are now reservations where Tribal Councils, backed by Indian police and rangers, promote game conservation. In some cases they follow the lead of state game departments as to seasons but reserve the right to keep most game for Indian tenants. In others white hunters must have regular hunting licenses and pay additional fees for the right to hunt on Indian lands. Some reservations also provide guides who will direct hunting parties to the best game areas.

In South Dakota reservation hunting by Indians is still on an all-year basis. However, the Oglala Sioux tribe of the Pine Ridge Reservation is trying to get a closed season from April 1 through the end of August in order to increase the deer population. The game department is very interested in such a move on all reservations within South Dakota, and has offered to stock antelope on them if the various Tribal Councils will confine open hunting to short seasons so these animals will have a chance to increase to significant populations.

During the 1967 deer hunting season I applied for license in Shannon County, which is a tiny fraction of the huge Pine Ridge Reservation. Only 20 permits were offered for this county simply because there is some

I downed my buck in a deep draw, behind and to the right of where the boys are now. This is rough country, the slopes steep, and getting a big muley out is hard work.

My hunting partners take a breather as they near the table top with my muley buck.

deeded land within the county which is owned by whites. My elder son, John, now Chief of Game Management for South Dakota, had tipped me off to the abundance of deer he had seen in that area while flying over it. He and his hunting party had planned on applying for muley licenses there. But when only 20 permits were available they felt their chances of drawing 5 of them were very slim. Meanwhile I had applied there and got my permit but was then left without any hunting partners. It looked as if I'd have to hunt solo in some rough country, a prospect that wasn't very appealing.

A little judicious mail and phone shopping uncovered Jack Kirk, Director of the Oglala Sioux Ranger Corps. He directed me to Johnny Swallow, Jr., who lives near the wee Indian village of Red Shirt. He also said that Ranger Sammy Cook from Pine Ridge would be available for guiding and transportation into that rugged hunting area. All I had to do was set up a meeting with these two Sioux Rangers and Jack assured me they'd show me game.

So far so good, but I still had to find a spot to camp, sleep and eat within easy reach of Red Shirt. Indian reservations are not noted for a plethora of motels where visitors can put up. Nor, for that matter, are paleface motels plentiful adjacent to reservations. I had visions of sleeping in my station wagon and eating sandwiches for breakfast, lunch and dinner, washed down with spring water. For an elderly gent who needs creature comforts it wasn't an entrancing prospect. However, a letter to Larry Walker elicited an offer to put me up and feed me during the duration of my hunt. It so happened that Larry's father-in-law, Don Kaiser, knew many of the Indians at Red Shirt and his wife Edna had taught at the community school there. I was plain shot with good luck.

My Rifles and Loads

The lure of a hunt in wild country was so strong that I got there a day early. Hoping for prairie dogs I took along a Remington BDL 700 in 22-250 fitted with a Redfield 2-7x variable on Redfield mounts. For ammo I had some factory 55-gr. fodder in both hollow- and soft-points. Additionally, I had loaded up a couple of boxes each of 60-gr. Hornady spire points ahead of 33 grains of 4064, 55-gr. Nosler Zipedos with 36 grains of 4895 and 50-gr. Speer hollow points loaded with 40 grains of 4350. These handloads were all in necked-down 250 Savage brass and primed with Winchester 120s. The 50- and 55-gr. loads were for accuracy tests and for prairie dogs, but I thought I might use the Hornady loads on deer if opportunity offered. This would depend chiefly on wind velocity since even the heaviest of ultra-velocity 22 centerfire bullets are very susceptible to wind drift at long ranges.

However, under the normally windy conditions of this piece of western real estate, I planned to use my 300 Weatherby magnum loaded with 300 H&H handloads in new Norma brass. Using 180-gr. bullets—Speer spitzers, Hornady spire points, Winchester Silvertips and others — even maximum H&H loadings produce near 3,000 foot seconds at the muzzle, moderate recoil and excellent wind-bucking qualities. Best of all, they maintain velocity and provide excellent accuracy over long ranges, yet aren't overly destructive of meat at any range. These are all faults of light ultra-velocity bullets in the 22 varmint calibers. These H&H handloads fire-form in the Weatherby chamber, the brass is then reused for suitable Weatherby reloads of increased velocity and power.

Because of their large case capacity the best powders for such 300 H&H and Weatherby handloads are the slow-burning propellants—4831, 4350 and others. However, my pet loads for the H&H cases range between 57 and 59 grains of 4064 behind any of the 180-gr. bullets mentioned, some 67 to 68 grains of the same powder after these cases have been fire-formed to fit Weatherby chambering. Even when used interchangeably these loads group only a trifle over an inch apart at 300 yards, which is far closer than the average hunter can hold on game in the field. I've used both for some 15 years.

While Larry and his brother-in-law, Herb Kaiser, tended to the ranch chores, Don Kaiser and I drove to the village of Red Shirt and looked up Johnny Swallow and Stanley Cook. Within 15 minutes we had set a time and place for an opening day morning meeting. Johnny told us he had popped a forkhorn muley a few days earlier, after stalking it to within 22 rimfire range and killing it with a brain shot. Stanley still needed a deer and carried a Winchester 243 that suited him very well. As a former coyote and bobcat hunter and trapper he liked the performance of that caliber and I was anxious to see him use it on a sizable buck. As things developed, I wasn't to see that.

Bone Hunters

Very few Indians are "bone hunters" of big-racked heads. They seldom hunt for trophies. Most of them regard game strictly from its food potential and take it with shots which will result in minimal damage to eating meat and slight expenditure of ammunition. They just don't care for trophy racks and frequently discard the antlers on the spot where the game is taken. On their reservations they don't have to prove an animal is male or female. That's a strictly paleface requirement, needed when game is in short supply and the females are needed to boost procreation potential.

From our first meeting I was thoroughly impressed by my two Ranger guides. Both were neatly dressed in suitable outdoor clothing and presented a very businesslike appearance for the job ahead. With typical Indian reserve they proferred a minimum of information, but they gave it freely whenever I asked for it—sometimes very freely.

I had several reasons for wanting to hunt this Shannon County portion of the Pine Ridge reservation: First, because John's report indicated it held a good many buck deer; second, because its rugged country was part of historic Indian hunting grounds and was too rough to be readily invaded by motorized equipment; third, it was in the vicinity of the famous Stronghold Table where the Sioux had baffled pursuing U.S. troops until they were overtaken and slaughtered on the gentler slopes of Wounded Knee, many miles to the southwest.

Many of today's place names of this weatherworn country reflect occupancy by noted Indian families or happenings during Indian times. Charley Red Shirt lives in the village

They're bringing my buck out of a 45° hole in the badlands of the Pine Ridge Indian reservation in Shannon Co., South Dakota.

bearing an ancestral family name dating back to the 1870s, the days of Sitting Bull and Crazy Horse. Vast Cuney Table, a high, gently-rolling plateau of virgin grasslands also named for an Indian family, originally served as a buffalo pasture and also fattened herds of Indian ponies. Now, aside from muley deer and rare antelope, large parts of this country serve as pasturage for domestic beef, on leases granted by the Sioux Tribal Council. There are many lesser forms of prairie wildlife; coyotes, bobcats, two kinds of prairie grouse — sharptails and pinnated or prairie chickens — jackrabbits, prairie dogs and many smaller birds and rodents. But it is no longer the game paradise it was during primitive and pioneer days, when a hunter could bag fresh meat during any hour of the day.

As the zero hour neared Larry and Herb Kaiser, both eager rock and fossil hounds, wanted to go along to look over the badlands country where I would hunt. With that much manpower in two vehicles I was surely the best attended paleface who had ever gone after deer on the Pine Ridge Reservation, at least in recent years. As it turned out I needed all of that help before the hunt was over.

Before daybreak Stanley and Johnny led off on trails which would have broken a snake's back. As daylight came on we peered into a good many grassy and brushy draws. One of them contained three deer; doe, fawn and a burly three-point buck who immediately stuck his rack into a thick juniper tree and thought himself completely hidden. He stayed there for five minutes while, from 60 yard away, we glassed him with binoculars and scope. He was a grand meat animal but short on the substantial antlers I needed for picture purposes.

For some odd reason both Rangers missed seeing him and, when we caught up with them a half-mile farther on, Stanley immediately turned back to investigate. That herd, though, had dropped off the high rim and headed for the cover of Battle creek, one boundary of our legal hunting area. Stanley took some good-natured chaffing about that oversight but he had a ready answer: "I was wrestling with my 14-month-old warrior last night and he is tougher than I thought," he proudly exclaimed, pointing to his badly cracked eyeglasses. "When I whiskered him on his fat belly he tomahawked me with both fists."

Thus far we had climbed atop a fairly level table and had been prospecting its rugged edges. Then Stanley led off through a series of badland slopes and dry washes. It was truck-wrenching travel and we had scant chance to peek into the deep pockets in which muleys love to hide by daylight. Then, when spooked, they usually go up over the nearest ridges and dive into the rugged country beyond. Once in full flight they employ distance instead of the stealth which whitetails exhibit. Thus muleys range much more widely and openly than their less hefty cousins, and generally offer longer shots. You can hunt a sneaky whitetail buck all day on a square mile of land and rarely glimpse him. When a muley takes it on the lam he may line out for miles, often in full sight of hunters, and literally leave the country.

Stanley finally got us atop Plenty Stars table—also named for a noted Indian family—and clear across to its far edge. When we gathered to plan on how best to hunt that dropoff two fine muley bucks crossed the flat scarcely 60 yards ahead of our trucks. By the time we grabbed our rifles they were already tipping off the edge. When we got to that rim they were dodging through concealing junipers and angling across the wrinkles of a steep slope.

They finally came out about 150 yards away, slowing now and picking their escape route—mostly on a beeline. At that range I'd sooner get one aimed shot than a half-dozen of the snap variety. So I perched on the rim,

Up to the top at last after a long, tough haul.

wrapped into my Latigo sling, and waited. Forty yards to my left Stan was also ready. Ahead was a barren slope of upward slanting badlands. When those bucks hit that they'd slow greatly and might even stop for that major muley failing, a last look back.

One buck did exactly that. He slowed to a trot, then a walk and, as my scope settled on him, he stopped. My bullet was instantly on its way. Stanley's rifle cracked at the same moment. The buck staggered a step or two, turned back and fell; then struggled as he slid down the steep slope toward us. There he collapsed and was still.

Downed in a Draw

I estimated the range at just under 200 yards and angle of fire at almost 45 downhill degrees. Stanley, Larry and Herb all plunged off the rim but I yelled at Johnny that I had a coil of nylon dragging cord. Did he want it? He nodded and took it along. Meanwhile I unlimbered cameras and started burning film.

It took all four of those young men—two on the antlers and two on the drag rope tied to a handhold of juniper branch—to bring that buck up to the table from which we had shot it. At no spot did they drag him more than 20 yards before stopping to blow. He had been hit by both bullets. One broke his back and the other had hit the front of his lower jaw. We had no positive way of telling which bullet had done which damage, but I believe mine hit the back and Stan's broke the jaw. I hadn't hit where I had wanted to since that downward angle of fire had produced a higher-than-normal hit.

We left the buck to cool in the rising wind and scouted the rest of the rim of that huge table. But if there were other deer hidden among the scattered junipers we didn't find them. Enroute back to pick up our game we flushed a score of sharp-tailed grouse out of knee-high grass. Although I had a shotgun along neither Stanley nor Johnny seemed interested in such small-fry game. Hidden in the grass were the den mounds of a former prairie dog village, probably one poisoned into extinction so livestock could eat the forage saved. We careened over those weathering mounds on our way back to the twisty trail which had brought us atop Plenty Stars Table. With black clouds building in the west we had to get out of that gumbo country before the thin rain became a downpour which could strand us at any one of a dozen dry washes. It's no country in which to ride out a storm.

I had included a 5-gallon can of gasoline in my gear. When Stan reported he'd have to head for a cow camp to refuel we poured that in. Minutes later, when we pulled up at a gate leading to gravel, Red Shirt and home, their truck was missing. Then we saw it running up the bottom of a long draw leading back into hunting country. Stanley still needed a deer and he'd wasted no time in going right after it.

Pine Ridge is only one of several Indian reservations in South Dakota where whites may hunt with tribal permission. It used to be called White Clay because of the chalky color of its gumbo soil, which also helped name its main stream, now known as White River. The other reservations within the state are the Rosebud, Lower Brule, Crow Creek, Cheyenne, and the Standing Rock reservation which straddles the common border of the two Dakotas. These are all lightly populated and when the various Tribal Councils adopt game-protecting regulations to maintain closed seasons from April 1 to September 1—a move which is now under consideration—they'll produce superior deer and small game hunting. The present population of mule deer, as only one instance, is now only two per square mile and a five-fold increase is possible.

On a national basis there are some 50,000,000 acres of reservation lands in 25 states, occupied by more than 263 known tribes. In the East only North Carolina, Florida and Mississippi still have existing reservations, but beginning with Michigan, Wisconsin and Minnesota, there are reservations in every state out to the Pacific Coast. Additionally, other reservations range from Alaska down both flanks of the Rocky Mountains clear

Prairie muleys are invariably big-bodied animals and usually require flat-shooting rifles.

Hatrack trophies like this muley buck are burly-bodied, at least 5 years old.

down to Arizona and New Mexico. A complete map of these has been prepared by the Bureau of Indian Affairs and is available from the Government Printing Office, Washington, D.C. 20402 at a cost of 30 cents. Included is an annual Calendar of Events on these reservations which list tribal dances, religious celebrations and other tribal gatherings. These aren't necessarily scheduled by the clock; they may depend on the growth of plants, phases of the moon or the whims of tribal medicine men. Such gatherings carry on century-old traditions and should be viewed in that context. Whites are welcome, and need only remember they are guests on Indian lands and behave acordingly. But, whether hunting or spectating, a visit to any Indian reservation can provide a better knowledge and appreciation of these fine people.

Muleys like this hide in the sharp dips of the table in South Dakota's Badlands area.

Rifles and Cartridges

Rifles suitable for reservation deer, where muleys predominate, don't follow the rules for suitable whitetail rifles. It isn't that muleys are significantly harder to kill than whitetails —it's because they rarely pop up at short range, especially if the hunter is after the older and more sagacious trophy bucks. The few times I've seen big-racked bucks at point-blank range was when they were fleeing from other hunters and came past by happenstance. They usually bed where they can see approaching hunters, or the lesser deer that have been flushed, and quit the country on generally beeline courses. Shots at muleys are often quite open, and average fully 100 yards longer than at whitetails; 150-yard shots are common and 300-yard pokes not unusual.

During the years when the 270 was reaching its peak of popularity it was highly esteemed for plains hunting, both on antelope and muleys. It set a standard that's been adopted by many of today's hunters in choosing rifles for the game riches of such open country. Any hunter with an accurate 270 and the skill to use it efficiently is ideally equipped—he's got one of the world's truly great long-range flat-shooting calibers. Range on the rolling plains is often tough to figure so the flat trajectory of 130-gr. commercial loads and 150-gr. bullets in proven handloads simplify that chore for 270 users.

A general rule of thumb is that any rifle churning out its bullets at from 2800 to 3000 foot seconds or more should make a dandy muley rifle. To that should be added a bullet weight of at least 100 grains so that it will maintain accuracy in strong winds and retain considerable velocity — and energy — out to at least 300 yards. Out to that distance bullets of 100-130 grains or so will do well, assuming calibers from 6mm to 7mm, but for longer ranges and in wind I'd set the minimum at 10 to 30 grains heavier, depending on caliber. Too light a bullet invites excessive wind drift.

The light and handy 6.5mm Remington Magnum falls into this classification, and I look for it to become highly popular for plains game and varmints. For muleys I would advise nothing lighter than the equivalent of the factory 120-gr. bullets and 140-gr. handloads would be better. Muleys have significantly heavier bones on which to carry their king-sized carcasses and require more penetrating power than is regularly provided by some otherwise excellent varmint cartridges. Among these are the 80-gr. bullets for the Winchester 243 and Remington 6mm, 55-gr. loads in the 222 Remington, standard and magnum, and 55- and 60-gr. bullets in the 22-250. I have seen all of these do good work on plains game, when in good hands at moderate ranges, but they lose velocity and energy so rapidly they shouldn't be used on long shots.

To bolster that advice the last three outstanding mule bucks I've seen taken were shot like this: a 300-yard kill with 130-gr. handloads in a 270 Model 70; a 300 Weatherby Magnum using 180-gr. Hornady Spire-Point handloads, and a magnificent 425-yard kill with 150-gr. commercial ammo in a super-accurate 308 Winchester. To me those three kills were a perfect example of what three different hunters can do when they mate rifles of suitable caliber with bullets of proper weight for the ranges at which trophy muleys offer shots.

The first buck of this trio went a mere 25 yards after being raked through the lungs with the 270 bullet. The Weatherby kill was a spine shot which dropped that buck right where he stood. The 308 bullet cut the main veins and arteries so cleanly that we found the heart lying loose in the chest cavity. The resulting enormous hemorrhage allowed him to stagger no more than 15 feet before collapse. All of these shots were on standing targets when the bucks paused for what proved to be their last look toward capable hunter-marksmen. ●

A fine eating animal, this 3-pointer didn't hold much appeal for a trophy hunter.

TORTURE TEST!

by GENE WEST

Smith & Wesson's new stainless steel Combat Magnum passed the author's rigorous tests—water and mud, salt baths, freezing and heating—without a murmur of any alteration in performance, appearance or reliability.

The new S&W 357 Combat Magnum, grips and sideplate removed. The metal is all stainless steel except for the mainspring.

S&W Model 66 stainless steel Combat Magnum.

THE S&W 357 Combat Magnum, despite its light weight (35 oz. with a 4" barrel) has shown itself fully reliable and versatile. It handled without trouble every ammo from light 38 wadcutters to the heaviest 357 loads. The 4" barreled Combat Magnum, at 35 oz., is only one ounce heavier than the Combat Masterpiece, and much lighter compared to the 42 oz. (approx.) of the S&W M27 and M28 models, both in 357 Magnum. It proved to be a top choice among those who tote a sixgun all day. With its adjustable sights, fine trigger pull – both DA and SA – small size and heft, as well as its ability to digest all rounds from light 38 Special target wadcutters to the heaviest of 357 loads, it was a natural for hunter, lawman, cowboy, plinker or anyone else having the desire or need for a good – and eminently portable – 357 sixgun.

Now S&W has made it even better, more versatile. Except for the mainspring and grips, it's made now in all stainless steel, dubbed the Model 66. All remains the same, except the price, now up to $157.45.

I ordered one, and it looked good. Not at all bright and shiny, it resembled instead dull, polished aluminum. This S&W won't reflect light as would a chromed or nickel-plated gun. The oversized grips were well figured, with dark stripes. Good though it looked, however, it still had to prove a good shooter, and it had to be rust and corrosion resistant.

I removed the grips and sideplate to verify that the internal working parts were also stainless steel, which they are, springs aside. I had on hand Remington's new SJHP 125-gr. 357 ammo (Index 7235) and their 38 Special (Index 4038), with 158-gr. lead semi-wadcutter bullet.

As expected, the gun performed well. The trigger pull, though a bit stiff on double action, was light, smooth and crisp on single action. With the hot 125-gr. HP loads, it performed well on small game and varmints to 50-75 yards. Firing fast, double action, it performed well at 30 feet, and with the 158-gr. 38 Special rounds, I could usually keep a cylinderful in a 10" circle, pulling the trigger as fast as I could. OK, performance seemed fine, so now came the brutal and crucial part of my testing.

Tough tests of the Combat Magnum included alternate coating with salt and wetting for 48 hours, cartridges as well.

New stainless steel Smith & Wesson 357 was held frozen in ice block for two days, along with six fresh factory cartridges.

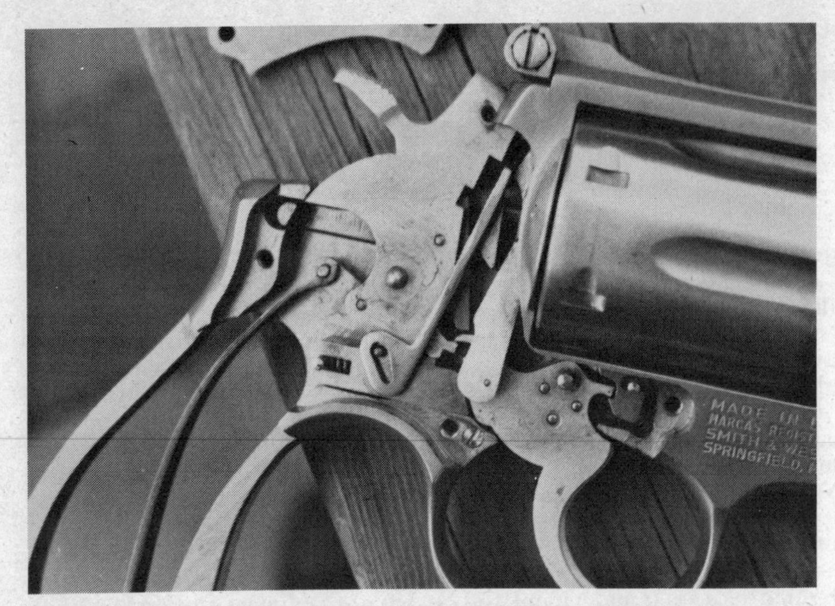

Interior of tortured S&W revolver after final tests, dried but not otherwise touched. Only evidence of prolonged immersion was slight staining of some parts. This was easily removed by steel wool and oil, bringing gun back to as-new condition.

Rough, Tough Test

With a cylinder full of the 125-gr. ammo, I removed the grips and placed the gun in a shallow depression in the ground, a wet and muddy spot. I turned the sprinkler on and left it on. The gun was not prepared for this test in any way. Its condition at the time would have equaled that of any gun used in the field or lost for a period of time. The gun lay in the mud on the bottom of the depression, its top partially submerged in water. The trees nearby kept it alternately in shade and sun. After two days of this, the water was turned off, the gun allowed to dry out on its own. Next, for two days, I alternately doused it with water and sprinkled it with salt, making sure that the salt got into the ejector rod housing, bolt stops in the cylinder, and any place else where it would remain. After two days of this, it was hosed off well, placed in a pan of water, still fully loaded, and then put in the freezer. Frozen solid into the cake of ice that resulted, it remained in the freezer for another couple of days. Then, after letting the ice melt, it soaked in a pan of water for two more days. It was hot, temperatures well into the 90's, so it had been well exposed to heat as well as to freezing. Finally it was removed from water, placed on a table in the sun, and allowed to dry.

The gun was unloaded, wiped off, and taken apart. The very base of the spring showed a slight spot of rust, as did the knurling of the tip of the ejector rod, and the underside of the hammer. A brief session with steel wool and a bit of oil, however, removed all traces of rust. The gun was then well cleaned, lightly oiled and the grips reinstalled. It looked as good as new. It was every bit as tight and smooth as before, and appeared to be none the worse for its torture test. The bore—not a sign of any change!

Again I headed out to fire it, the chamber holding those same 6 rounds of Remington ammo that had gone through all the tests. All fired perfectly, and the gun performed as well as it had before. Neither gun nor ammo gave any indication that they'd suffered a grueling torture test of water, mud and salt, of freezing and hot temperatures. Certainly this should be proof that these S&W stainless steel guns are ideal for use in damp, humid climates, be they Arctic or tropical or anywhere else. •

Here is the re-assembled S&W Combat Magnum, including the 6 Remington factory loads that also went through all tests. Post-test shooting, using the 6 test cartridges plus others, saw functioning, performance and appearance entirely unimpaired.

Scopes and Mounts

Here's a detailed report—with current prices for most products—on what's been developed in scopes, mounts and related accessories over the past year.

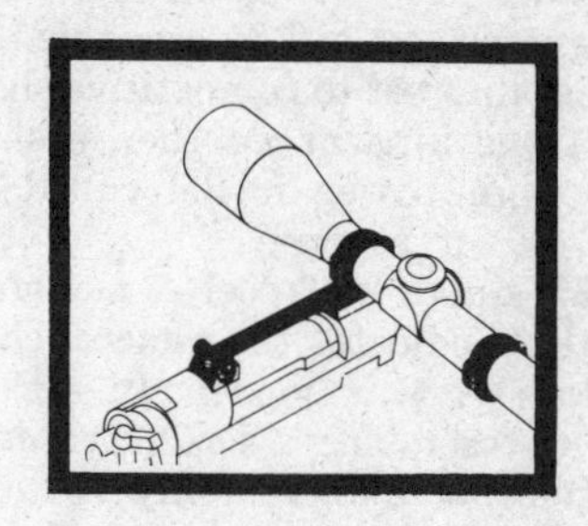

Leupold's STD Standard Mounts mount easily, interchange with Redfield JR and SR components.

by BOB BELL

Leupold & Stevens, Inc. have come up with a raft of new items this year, and that can't be anything but good news for hunters—and bench shooters—who have found this Oregon company top contenders in producing superb quality scopes. There are 4 brand new hunting models, including a 1-4x variable in the popular Vari-X II series and 3 scopes, all variables, in a new series named the Vari-X III Gold Medallion. Then, for the benchresters, there is a short, light 24x designed for solid mounting on the rifle action only.

The Vari-X II 1-4x rounds out that line of big game scopes by providing a model specifically slanted toward big game hunting at what might be called normal ranges—anything from slingshot distance to perhaps an occasional 400-yard shot when you wander out of the woods and see an elk on the opposite hillside. Scopes in this category aren't intended to be part-time varmint glasses, and they're probably not the top choice for the pronghorn specialist; they're just great outfits for the majority of big game hunters, the guys who go after whitetail and mule deer, elk and bear, moose caribou, etc., as well as for those who must use a scope on dangerous game.

This Vari-X II is about 9½" long, weighs that many ounces, has an actual magnification of about 1½-4x, fields of 70½-28½ feet, and can be had with any Leupold reticle—Duplex, Post with Duplex, CPC (tapered crosshair), crosshair, or center dot ($10 extra) installed on the CPC. Price, $94.50.

The Vari-X III line is made up of a 1½-5x, 2½-8x, and 3½-10x glasses. The fields, respectively, are 64-23 feet, 36-12½, and 29½-10½. Eye relief is about 3½" minimum (more at bottom powers), which permits mounting on any Magnum without having to worry about getting walloped in the eyebrow, assuming the scope is mounted far enough forward to take advantage of the full eye relief.

According to Leupold, this series of glasses features a new "anastigmat" power changing system, similar to that used in high-grade cameras, with more sophisticated optical and mechanical systems than were used previously in variable power scopes. There's no way an old deer hunter can verify this—it would probably take a lab full of equipment and more knowhow than I've got—but the Leupold people describe it thusly: "The heart of the Vari-X III is a sophisticated combination of a field lens and 3 erector lenses in a new erecting system ... moving the external power-selector ring causes a precise change in the relative positions of these 4 lenses *and* also changes each of their relations to the other 7 lenses in the total 11-lens optical system ..."

The Vari-X III's are supplied with Duplex reticle only—understandable, since over 80% of Leupold's customers specify this design. Prices are: 1½-5x, $119.50; 2½-8x, $129.50; 3½-10x, $139.50.

The new high power scope is part of the familiar M8 Golden Ring straight power line, designated the M8-24x AO (for Adjustable Objective, as on the 7½, 10 and 12 powers, and 3-9x and the new 3½-10x). This model already has found favor with a number of topnotch benchrest competitors, for its design gets all scope weight off the barrel and its internal adjustments permit the solid mounting which eliminates some causes of error when groups are measured in thousandths of an inch.

The M8-24x is 15¼" long, weighs 15½ oz., has a 4½' field, 3½" eye relief, a clear objective lens diameter of 1.58", and ¼-minute click adjustments. Maximum adjustment in either windage or elevation is 60 inches at 100 yards. Either crosshair (0.03") or center dot (⅛ or ¼ MOA) reticle is available. A 2¼" screw-on sunshade is provided. Price, $169.50.

Leupold still markets the excellent straight power M8 hunting scopes in 3x, 4x and 6x, the varmint jobs in 7½x, 10x and 12x, and the Vari-X II's in 2-7x and a pair of 3-9's, of course, as well as rugged STD mounts ($27.50) for many popular rifles with rings in three heights, and the W94 Detacho mount ($22) which adapts the long eye relief M8 2x scope to the M94 Winchester carbine.

Bob Bell (left) with his Remington 25-06, the scope a Lyman 10x. The Bill Anderson rifle rest (551 Fletcher Rd., Wayne, PA 19087) has a metal triangle at the bottom which, pushed into the ground, gives excellent stability • Leupold's new Vari-X II scope, here in 1-4x type, mounted on Remington's Custom Grade 700 in 375 H & H.

Redfield has announced 4 new scopes for 1974—2½x, 4x and 10x in straight power, a 3-9x variable and, of most interest to competitive shooters of one kind or another, a short, light high power model called the RM 6400 target scope.

"RM" stands for "receiver mounted," and that indicates the general classification of this model. In appearance it resembles a scrunched down Redfield 3200, for it's only 17" long, is built on a 1" tube, has enlarged objective and ocular lenses, internal adjustments, and weighs a mere 18 oz. The short length and light weight put it in the same category as Lyman's LWBR and Unertl's BV-20, both 20x models, and it has the same obvious advantage—providing target scope magnification without putting any weight on the rifle barrel.

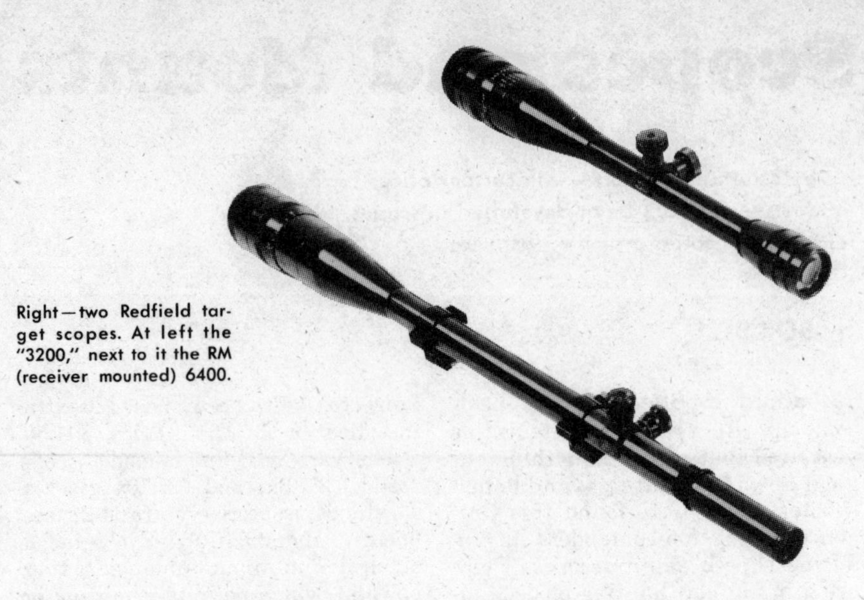

Right—two Redfield target scopes. At left the "3200," next to it the RM (receiver mounted) 6400.

The RM 6400 will be offered in 3 powers (16x, 20x and 24x), and should be available by the time this article appears. All magnifications have the same size lenses—1.5" clear aperture of objective and an enlarged ocular, which gives a field of view approximately 25% larger than the same powers in the 3200; specifically: 6.5 feet at 100 yards in the 16x, 5.1 in 20x, and 4.7 in 24x. Eye relief is 3" with all powers, also slightly greater than that of the 3200—an advantage on solidly mounted scopes used for high power rifles.

The RM 6400's internal click adjustments are rated at ¼ MOA (accurate to ±1/32 MOA), with a maximum adjustment of 60 MOA for both windage and elevation. This is plenty for short to midrange target shooting—up to 500 or 600 yards, say, with the cartridges typically chosen for such shooting—but may not be fully adequate for 1000-yard shooting with conventional scope blocks. Other height blocks are available, which make it easy to get centered at 1000 yards and still have a reasonable amount of adjustment left. However, installing a mount block specifically for this long range shooting makes it difficult to use the same rig at the shorter distances. In effect, you end up with a specialized rifle/scope combination, well suited for either short/medium or ultra long range shooting, but not really satisfactory for both. This is one of the problems resulting from the internal adjustment design—which admittedly has several advantages over the older external mounts. It's a pay-your-money, take-your-choice thing, but it makes sense for the prospective buyer to consider all the angles.

As for the disadvantages of internal adjustments, we should mention that they make it comparatively hard to switch the scope from one rifle to another. With the blocks solidly mounted on the gun, and the rings just as solid on the scope, both have to be *exactly* the same distance apart for proper alignment and fit. In practice, it is rare to find blocks installed to such exact measurements. With external mounts, there is no problem, for they're movable on the tube. However, moving the rings on the 3200 or this new 6400 requires a good screwdriver and considerable time. For the shooter who rarely switches his scope from one rifle to another this is no problem, but countless target riflemen use the same glass on several guns, so this can be a real chore.

Three mounting systems are offered for the RM 6400:

(1) Standard target rings and bases such as have been available on the 3200 since its inception, 5.5 oz; a big bore base set is available for the Remington 40X, M700 short or long action, and the M70 Winchester Target, price $6.40 for the base, $14.40 for rings. A small bore base set, at $7, is offered for the Anschutz 1400 series, the Remington 40X and Winchester's M52.

(2) JR/SR machined steel rings and mounts, at 7 oz. and 6 oz., allow mounting the RM 6400 scope on almost any rifle.

(3) FR rings and mounts, of machined aluminum, also are available for many rifles and their light weight, 3.5 oz., makes them popular for bench shooting in classes where weight is unusually important. In these mounts, the RM 6400 sighting system weighs only 21.5 oz.

Reticles in the 6400 are fine crosshair, medium crosshair, and a center dot of ⅛ or ¼ MOA.

RM 6400 price, $225.

Hunting scopes of 2½x are about the oldest type in America, yet Redfield now offers a new "traditional" model (round eyepiece) in this power. It has a 43' field, 1" tube, 3½" eye relief, weighs 8.5 oz, and has internal graduations valued at 1.5 inches at 100 yards. $54.30.

Another new traditional model is the 10x, which sells for $105. In appearance and weight a twin of the older 12x, it also has Redfield's unique third turret adjustment for parallax and focus, with quick detachable target style knobs at no extra cost.

The new 3-9x is conventional in looks, has the 4-Plex reticle that serves so well under the vast majority of hunting conditions, and sells for $99.60.

Redfield's new 4x LP gets its monicker from its Low-Profile lens design. It has the now-familiar Widefield design on both objective and eyepiece ends, thus gives a somewhat lower silhouette than a round lens objective. With an actual magnification rating of 3.6x, this LP model has a 37.5' field, which is big enough for even fast moving game at close range, if the shooter has made a reasonable effort to familiarize himself with his outfit. Reticle in this model is also the 4-Plex. Price, about $90.00.

Also new from Redfield this year are highly streamlined 2-piece bases for the Colt Sauer rifle; they accept regular Redfield scope rings, sell for $18 per pair. Other items are Supreme lens covers, $6.90 per set, to fit either traditional or Widefield scopes. These have hinged, spring-loaded covers that flip open when a lever is thumbed. A new high-impact styrene carrying case for the Redfield 15-45x or 15-60x spotting scope, with room for a tripod or bipod, is $44.

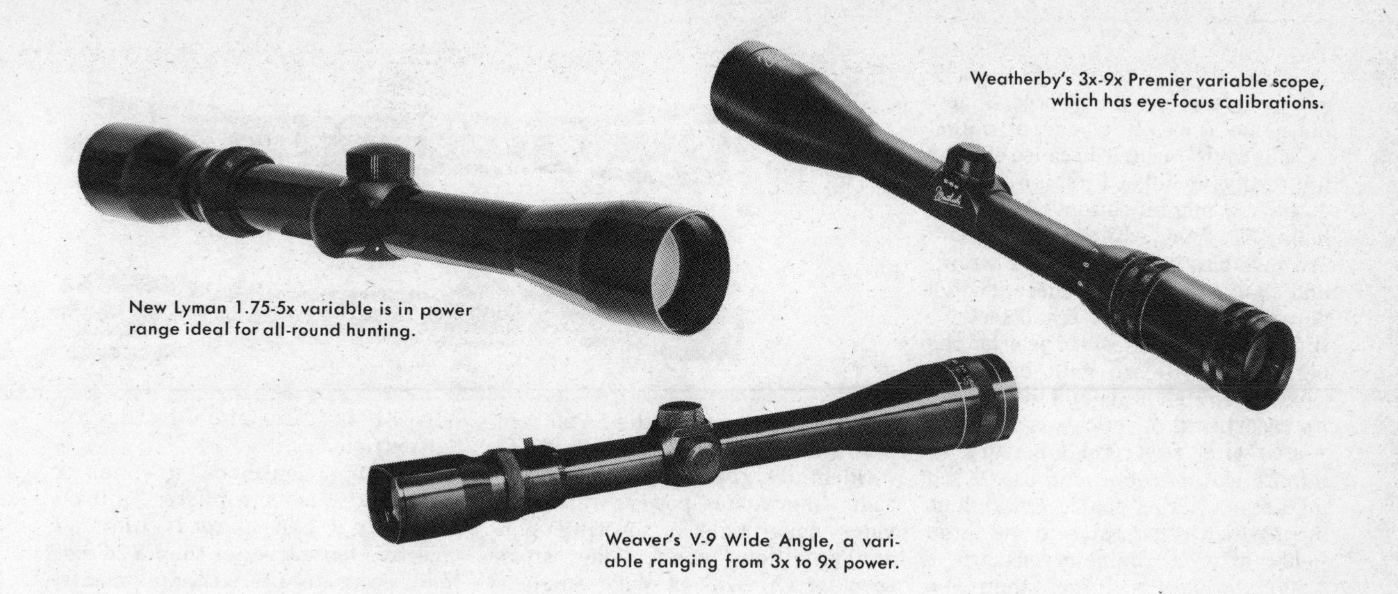
Weatherby's 3x-9x Premier variable scope, which has eye-focus calibrations.

New Lyman 1.75-5x variable is in power range ideal for all-round hunting.

Weaver's V-9 Wide Angle, a variable ranging from 3x to 9x power.

Lyman extends their scope line with a pair of new glasses this year. Interestingly, in view of the fact that for many years they resisted the swing to variables, they have added a 1.75-5x model this year (their fine 3-9x was described in last year's Scope Review), as well as a straight power unit called the 6x-P.

As with all Lyman hunting glasses, this new pair has 1-inch tubes with internal adjustments. The 6x-P derive its name from its adjustable objective lens unit, which eliminates all parallax from 50 yards to infinity. This design has been available on the 8x and 10x models for years; its addition here (the standard 6x hunting model lacks this feature) makes this scope a fine choice for use on hunter style bench matches. The 6x-P is 14" long, weighs 14 oz., has half-inch clicks, a 20-foot field and 3¼" eye relief. Price, $89.50.

The 1.75-5x should make a fine choice for all kinds of big game hunting. At bottom power the field is a full 47 feet, dropping to 18 feet at 5x; eye relief is 3", length 12¼" and weight 12¼ oz. Internal clicks are ¼-inch. Price, $99.50.

Weatherby has for years offered two scope lines—the older Imperial models in 2¾x, 4x, 6x, and 2-7x and 2¾-10x variables, and the Premiers in 2¾x, 4x and 3-9x. New this year in the Premier line are a pair of Wide Angle scopes, a 4x and a 3-9x. These have an increased horizontal field, measuring almost 36′ in the straight 4 power and 43½-14½ in the variable.

All Premiers have non-magnifying, constantly centered reticles, ¼-minute click adjustments, binocular type focusing and neoprene-padded eyepieces. Besides the familiar crosshair and post reticles, available in all models, the round-view scopes can be had with an open dot, which doesn't obscure any significant portion of the target. A Lumi-Plex reticle is offered in both standard and Wide Angle scopes. This is the comparatively new 4-posts-with-crosswires type, but in these Weatherby scopes the reticle reportedly brightens as daylight fails and you're aiming against a dark background. The advantages are obvious, for the best hunting opportunities often come in late afternoon.

W. R. Weaver Co. has taken a breather this year—as might be expected after their introduction of a number of new scopes described in GD28. Currently Weaver offers 8 of the long-popular K models, ranging from 1½x to 12x, 3 Wider-View Ks, 4 round-view variables and 3 of the Wider-Views—all the above being big game scopes suitable for mounting on anything you'd shoot from the shoulder, prices going from $29.95 to $94.95, with another $7.50 for a dot reticle—plus 3 glasses for rimfires.

Then there is the Qwik-Point, now made in 4 versions, for big game rifles, for 22s, for shotguns, and for the Remington 1100 and 870 smoothbores, as well as other Remington arms (but not the 20-gauge lightweight). This unit provides a blaze-orange dot as an aiming point seen in the same focal plane as the target. It can be zeroed in so you know precisely where your pattern is going, or on a rifle provides a conspicious aiming point even in the dark, dense cover. $39.95.

In the mount line, Weaver has come up with a detachable long side mount, intended for use on such rifles as the M94, which require side attachment. It has split rings for 1-inch scopes, and its greater-than-normal length lets it accept a wider variety of glasses than usual. $11.95.

I'm still highly attached to my Weaver V4.5 scope, which has been riding on the top deck of a little 284 Mauser for some years now. It came through again during the past Pennsylvania deer season, when a small buck stuck his neck out of some thick stuff at about 90 yards. I slid the dot onto the middle it it, squeezed the trigger, and the 139-gr. Hornady squirted out by 50/4895 put a baseball-size hole through my aiming point. We ate the last of his chops an hour before I typed these lines—and gosh, it seems like a long time till next season! But I want to say again, as I have many times in the past—one of these little variables is just about perfect as a big game scope. At top power you can aim at a deer or anything larger at any range the average hunter should be shooting, and at bottom power the field is more than enough for fast work in the brush. In addition, a little scope like this looks like it belongs on a hunting rifle...as it does.

Swift currently offers 5 big game scopes—the 4x Aerolite, Stag and Buck models. The latter is unusual because its adjustments are located *beneath* a ring at the rear of the tube rather than inside a turret. There are also the 2½-8x Aerolite and the 3-9x Yukon. Prices range from $29.95 to $55. Weaver-type mounts are $4. For rimfire riflemen they have the 4x Gopher, $9.95 with tip-off mount.

Browning has announced 3 new big game scopes this year, all called "Wide Angle" models because of their unusually big fields. First is a straight 4x (actual magnification 3.6x), which has a 37′ field, while the other two are variables in 2-7x (2.5-6.6x actual) and 3-9x (3.3-8.5x). These switch powers have fields of 50-20 feet for the smaller model, 39-15 feet for the bigger one. All are built on 1-inch tubes, eye relief is about 3 inches, and an assortment of reticles is available —crosswire, post and crosswire, 3-minute dot or dual purpose. Each features a large ocular (rear) lens unit, which contributes to the large fields; external diameter on each is 1.595″, which is larger than the 1.520″ objective of the 4x and 2-7x, slightly smaller than the 1.720″ objective of the 3-9x. These objectives, incidentally, give exit pupils of better than 4mm at top power, which provides enough light for shooting under any conditions where game can be seen at all. The 4x Wide Angle is $74.95, the 2-7x is $99.95, and the 3-9x, $104.95. Center dot reticles are $10 extra in each.

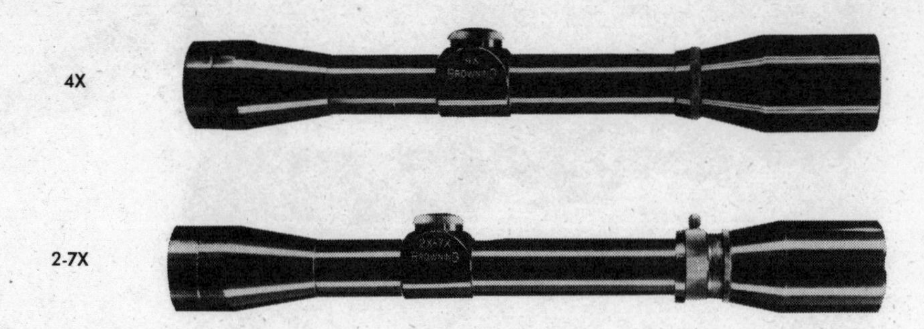

Browning continues to offer a high grade 4x for rimfires. Built on a ¾″ tube, it has enlarged ocular and objective lenses, better than a 24-foot field, accurate internal adjustments, and it weighs only 6 oz. Price, $31.95.

Bushnell is standing pat on their top-of-the-line Scopechief IV scopes this year, with 3 fixed powers and 3 variables blanketing the field for all hunting uses. They also continue to offer the Scopechief V Lite-Site models in 4x, 1½-4x and 3-9x—so called because a built-in switch-operated lighting system creates a center dot of light for use under the worst conditions of visibility. It's a weird experience to use one of these, but they certainly are efficient; you can aim with precision at an animal in twilight so dim that its body is simply a dark indistinct mass.

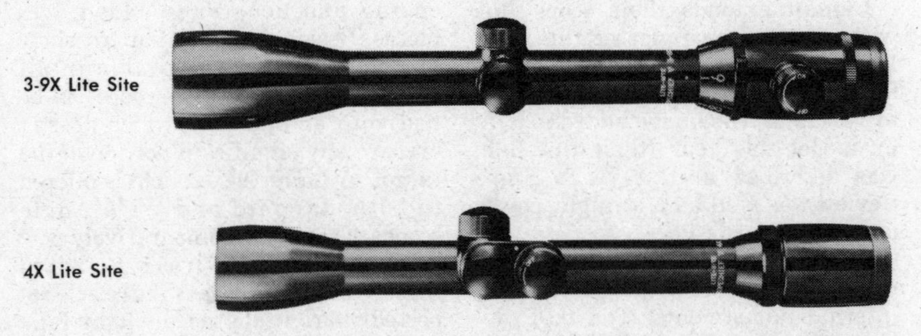

A pair of new items is offered in the Banner line, a 4x "general purpose wide angle" and a 3-9x "all purpose variable wide angle." The 4x has a 40mm objective and a 35½-foot field, sells for $69.95. The variable's field also is significantly larger than many similar-power scopes. It sells for $89.95

All Scopechief IV and V models and all Banners except the new Wide Angles now have soft neoprene eye guards to reduce the chance of cut eyebrows. Since all Bushnell big game scopes have 3 or more inches of eye relief, this should be no big problem; still, it's probably a good idea for those hunters who don't fully consider the question of properly positioning the scope. One too far to the rear can really surprise you... especially if mounted on a 338 or 375!

Another new Bushnell glass is the Sportview 22, a 4x for rimfires. It's built on a ¾″ tube, has internal adjustments, sells for $14.95.

A couple of Marlins—the carbine is their Model 1894, the scope Marlin's Model 425.

Marlin Firearms Co. still offers two big game scopes of conventional design—a 4x and a 3-9x, a 1½x long eye relief model and a couple of rimfire scopes under their own name, plus a straight 4x for high-powered rifles and one for 22s under the Glenfield label.

Marlin big game scopes can be had with the 1-MR range-finding reticle, heavy crosswires (1 MOA) plus pointed posts at 3, 6 and 9 o'clock. Distance between opposing points of the horizontal posts is 30″ at 100 yards; the bottom post comes within 3″ of the horizontal wire at the same distance. Knowing these measurements and the approximate size of the game hunted makes it possible to get a good idea of the range.

Del-Sports, Inc., tells me that they are no longer offering European-made made scopes, binoculars, etc. They formerly imported the Kahles and Habicht lines, but prices have risen so high they have quit.

Kuharsky Bros. have discontinued making the custom line of Bausch & Lomb type mounts, following B&L's decision to abandon their custom "A" line of scopes and to turn all Trophy "B" scope and mount sales over to Bushnell. Orders will be filled if items are in stock, but no further production is planned. All related equipment has been bought by Modern Industries, 613 West 11th St., Erie, Pa., which will continue to supply the Kuharsky Weaver-type clamp ring assembly for Weaver bases.

Pachmayr has redesigned their Lo-Swing top mount so that the scope can be mounted farther forward than formerly. This of course permits moving the glass ahead—and it's a pious idea to take advantage of all possible eye relief when shooting the heavy-recoiling Magnums so popular these days. Other changes in this mount are minor—after being on the market as many years as it has, there are no real bugs—but they show that Pachmayr works to improve a good product. First, re-tooling has made it possible to get even closer tolerances of mating surfaces, which doubtless helps maintain accuracy; second, appearance has been upgraded a bit via changes in the finishing and tumbling procedures before anodizing; and the hold-down spring has been redesigned to give a more secure locking setup.

For the benefit of new shooters the Lo-Swing mount lets the scope be rotated out of the way so iron sights can be used in case of extremely bad weather, damage or whatever. It has windage and elevation adjustments so that the scope's internal adjustments need be used, at most, only for final precise zeroing, thus keeping the reticle in the best optical location. The Lo-Swing, made to fit most popular rifles—and some that few people know much about!—sells for $25 in the top mount version, $20 for the side mount.

Realist, Inc. no longer offers rifle scopes. The Auto/Range Camputer scopes described in previous editions are now handled exclusively by James Leatherwood of Leatherwood Bros., Box 111, Stephenville, Texas 76401.

W.H. Siebert keeps busier than the proverbial cat on a hot tin roof, converting such short, medium-power varmint scopes as the Lyman and Leupold 10x and 12x models to action-mounted high-power jobs for bench shooting. During 1973, he tells me, new NBRSA world records were set in 3 varmint classes using Siebert-converted Leupolds and Lymans, and nine of the Top Twenty competitors as the NBRSA Varmint Nationals used his conversions for at least one category of the 3-gun aggregate. One 5-shot 100-yard light varmint group by Mac McMillan, using a Leupold/Siebert 24x, went .009", according to Siebert's letter (apparently the same group which *Rifle Magazine,* March-April 1974, reported as range-measured at .000). At any rate, it's hard to get much smaller, even if only one shot is fired!

Siebert's success in boosting varmint glasses to target scope powers undoubtedly has been influential in convincing the big manufacturers to produce their own such scopes—or scopes of this general size and magnification, we should say. More recently, Bill has been working with Leupold on their new target scope of this type. The prototype 24x Leupold was used by about 20 top benchrest shooters during 1973, with excellent results.

Anyone who wants his own Perma Center Lyman, Leupold or Weaver converted to 15x-24x (exact top power varies with make and model) can have it done by Siebert for $30.

For guys wanting to go the other way, Siebert reduces the 12x Redfield to 5x or 6x to give XP-100 shooters almost a foot of eye relief for handgun hunting.

Southern Precision Instrument Co. offers an extensive line of scopes, including several for 22s and big game models in 2½x, 4x, 6x, 1½-5x and 3-9x variables. Most are available with 32mm or 40mm objectives, the larger size, of course, giving more light at the higher magnifications at the expense of more bulk. The 1½-5x has a 40mm objective, which will give an 8mm exit pupil at top power—bigger than most scopes supply at that setting. This makes for fast aiming, which can be important in woods hunting.

SPI also supplies three spotting scopes—the M552, a wide angle 20x with 80mm objective, roof prism construction and 45° eyepiece; the M549, which has a 60mm objective and 15, 20, 30, 40 and 60 power eyepieces; and the M551, which has a turrent head eyepiece with powers from 15 to 60x, and an 80mm objective.

Thompson/Center Arms has discontinued the Puma scope, which was offered, for some years, for use on the single shot T/C Contender pistols. Another pistol scope has been in the works for some time, and it should be ready for delivery by the time you read this. With the Contender chambered for such hotshot cartridges as the Hornet, Jet, Fireball, Bee, and even bigger loads, the value of a good scope on this pistol is obvious. It can really make varmint shooting interesting.

Carl Zeiss, Inc., is importing rifle scopes on a special order basis only, at this time, according to marketing manager Sidney M. Bernstein.

Mounts and Accessories

Buehler, Inc., has 5 basic styles of mount bases; one or another will permit attaching almost any scope to almost any rifle, and at the same time give the user the best position for proper eye relief. This might seem a simple chore, but actually it isn't, as scopes of different powers have somewhat different eye reliefs, the position of the turrents on internally adjusted scopes is different on many models, and the power selector ring on variables cause problems at times, as does the length of the enlarged objective lens housing on certain models. Despite all these problems, though, a Buehler mount can provide proper positioning. In addition, it's a strong unit, one that will take the recoil of anything that can be fired from the shoulder—including, for instance, the 600 Nitro Express, as Maynard Buehler proved many years ago. I mentioned that on the off chance you're perturbed by ponderous pachyderms out your way.

The Buehler mount, a low bridge type, is machined steel throughout, weighs about 4½ oz. total. The rings are lined with an oil-resistant synthetic rubber, less than .001" thick, which both protects the scope's finish and gives a positive grip.

New this year are 2-piece bases to fit the Colt Sauer rifle, Code CS, and to fit the HVA-Carl Gustaf rifle, formerly the Husqvarna. Code H-2 for this one.

Conetrol, a super-sleek scope saddle from Seguin, Texas, has an awful lot besides look going for it. It's strong, made for most guns, and—an interesting fact, seems to me—has 4 screw holes in the bridge base, so you can snug it down into all the holes the factory taps in the receiver ring and bridge. I've wondered for years why so many mount makers ignored that one hole in the bridge, especially since the 6-48 screws used to anchor most bases aren't the strongest, most durable fastening I've ever seen. At any rate, Conetrol uses all 4 holes, I'm very glad to see.

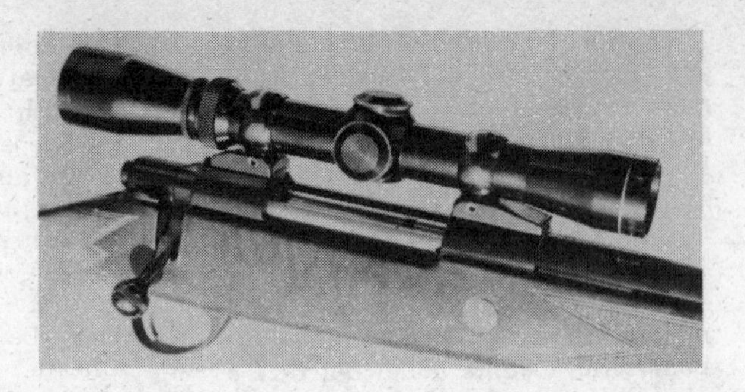

Conetrol's short-ring-spacing Custom base and rings on an L-61R Sako rifle. The scope is a Leupold 2-7x.

Users of Sako rifles with integral dovetail bases will be interested to know that Conetrol offers an option of short ring spacing models for the long actions. With, these, the front mount ring is located over the rear of the receiver ring—at the *rear* of the front base segment rather than the front. This arrangement simplifies mounting scopes having a limited length between the enlarged portions of the tube, such as attaching a variable power Leupold to the L 61R Sako. These Short Ring Spacing mounts also give more latitude in positioning a scope for proper eye relief.

Conetrol mounts are available with bridge or two-piece bases, with solid or split rings, in three grades at $22.85, $27.85 and $34.85.

J. B. Holden's Ironsighter mount, which raises the scope high enough to permit aiming with the factory sights through large oval holes, is now made, in modified version, for the M94 Winchester. This S-94 is a side mount which uses the factory drilled holes in the left side of the action (for M94s made after 1946 bearing serial numbers 1,400,000 and higher; lower numbered 94s require tapping two 6-48 holes). This mount, made without the oval holes, simply offsets the scope (any 1" tube can be accommodated) to the left, which permits case ejection and iron sight use. $14.95. As announced previously, the Ironsighter is also made for the M94 to position a long eye relief scope centrally over the bore and ahead of the action. $19.95.

Marble Arms Corp. has added a new side mount for two Winchester lever actions, the M64 and M94, and that's the name of the mount—the 64-94. As with Holden's Ironsighter, the 64-94 fastens to the left side of the action and is offset to permit top ejection; this makes the iron sights usable, of course. Available for 1-inch scope tubes, this mount is made of lightweight alloy, it comes in black or gold colors. Price, about $15. Marble also supplies the Game Getter mount for most rifles, which permits use of the iron sights through a tunnel beneath the rings, and 4 big game scopes—a 2½x and 4x at $39.50, and two 3-9x variables at $69.50. Tubes of these scopes are machined from a solid bar of duralumin, which eliminates the joints found in many scopes where enlarged objective units and turret are attached.

Numrich Arms manufactures a scope mount that attaches 1-inch tube models directly over the bore of the original GI 30-cal. carbine or commercially manufactured versions such as the Plainfield, Universal or Erma M22 rimfire. All steel. $9.20 delivered.

Ranging, Inc. makes a highly useful item for hunters interested in knowing the distance to a target with a high degree of accuracy. This is the Rangematic Mark V, a split-image rangefinder calibrated to 1000 yards. It has a 6x eyepiece, is 10½" long and weighs 22 oz., sells for $42.95 plus $7.95 for a carrying case/holster.

S&K Mfg. Co., maker of the popular Insta-Mount for many military rifles, plus conventional ring mounts for commercial models, has added a new I-M design this year. It fits the 94 and 64 Winchester (a big year for scoping these models, it seems). The base, of machined aircraft alloy, consists of two pieces, an adaptor plate to fit factory-drilled holes in the left side of the action, and a mounting plate which bolts to the adaptor and accepts S&K steel rings. Base unit, $10.20, rings $10.20 satin finish, $12.20 high gloss.

Supreme Lens Covers (formerly Vissing) are now available from Butler Creek Corp., PO Box GG, Jackson Hole, Wyo. 83001, at $7.50 per set. Made for practically every scope model, including the Redfield Widefields, these units slip on each end of the scope, the hinged lens cover flipping out of the way when a release button is thumbed. I've used these on several scopes for years, and I can tell you they work...and at times they're invaluable. When the weather is nice, you simply hunt with them open; when miserable, you're grateful you can close 'em.

Holden's Iron Sighter

Ranging's Mark V Rangematic

S&K mount for 94/64 Winchester

Supreme Lens Covers

Anderson Storm King shoot-through lens covers.

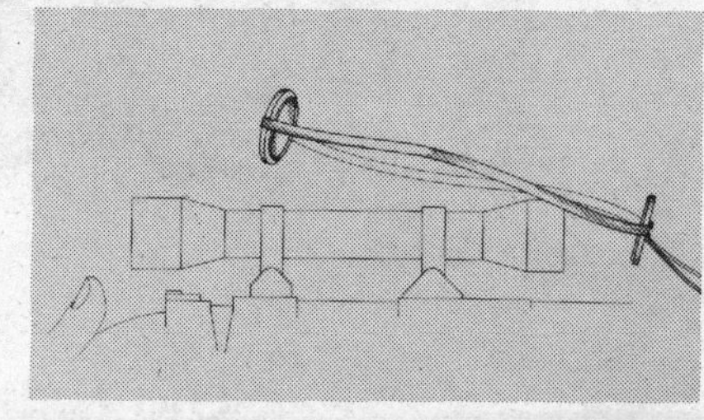

Anderson Storm Queen lens covers.

Herter 2x long-eye relief 94 Winchester scope.

American Import Co. tells me their scope/mount line remains the same as last year.

Anderson & Co., maker of the well known Storm King and Storm Queen lens covers, the former a hinged design with see-through lenses for fast shooting, the latter a flip-off type, has had to increase prices a bit—to $3.95 for the Kings, $3.45 for the Queens—but that's still cheap insurance on a wet or snowy day when the success of a trip can depend on your ability to aim with your scope. Hunting days rarely seem to coincide with nice weather, so lens covers like these should receive consideration. A yellow lens is available for the ocular unit at $2.50; it's useful when things are hazy.

Anderson also offers Buffer Rings, designed to keep your eyebrow from being bumped—and which protect the scope from damage, too—at $1 each, or if ordered with his Model 3 Storm Queens, cost is $4.45.

Herter's, Inc., offers a line of hunting scopes to meet all normal needs. Called the Hudson Bay models, they come in 2¾x and 4x fixed powers, 1½-4½x, 3-9x and 4-12x variables, a long eye relief 2x for the M94 Winchester, and an interesting 4x rimfire model built on a one-inch tube with enlarged objective and ocular lenses. There's also a 1½x for handguns and a unit power model for smoothbores.

Walter H. Lodewick (2816 N. E. Halsey St., Portland, OR 97232) supplies two items useful to scope hunters. One is the Mark II Cheekpiece, made of walnut-colored neoprene. Made in right- or lefthand versions, it cements to the stock of low-comb rifles, thus raising the hunter's eye to align with the scope. $4.50.

Second item is the Mark II Safety, a hardened steel unit with nylon friction piece to eliminate rattles. Variations are available to replace the military safeties on the M98 and M95 Mausers and the '03 Springfield. $5.65.

Tasco continues to offer a very extensive line of scopes—26 big game models if I count correctly, a handful of rimfire jobs, a pistolscope, a big variable power target scope, plus assorted related items—a collimator and a Scope Guide (for bore sighting), 5 spotting scope models, Weaver-type mount rings, bridge and side mount bases, target scope blocks, etc. They also have many binocular models, including a selection of roof prism designs in several magnifications and objective lens sizes.

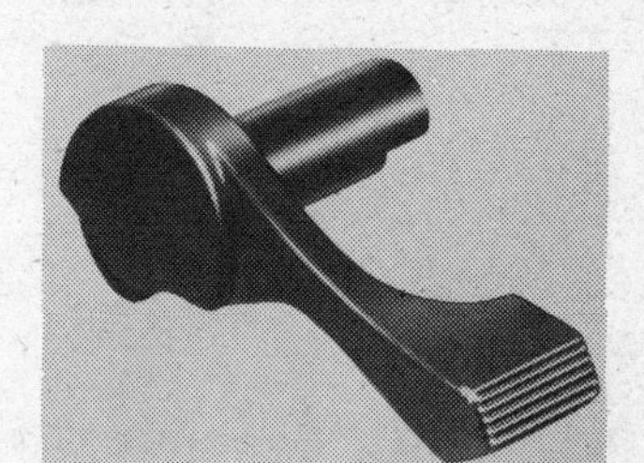

Lodewick Mark II safety for 95/98 Mausers, '03 Springfields.

Williams GunSight Co. has for several years been marketing two lines of scopes, in addition to their very popular mounts. Their Guide-Line comes in 4 models—a straight 4x and 3 variables, 1½-4½x, 2-6x, and 3-9x, as it's the Williams' feeling that power changes should be multiples of the bottom magnification for best optical results. These are fine scopes, at prices from $88.50 to $130.

Tasco 3-9x Omni-View Zoom Scope.

The medium-price Williams line, called the Twilight, is made in 2½x, 4x, 2-6x and 3-9x, at prices from $40 to $75; the Wide Guide 4x is still offered at $88.50.

Besides the Quick Convertible bridge and side mounts, long known for their sturdiness and low position, Williams has the Sight-Thru mount, which lifts the scope high enough to permit iron sight aiming through the tunneled risers. I can't say I've ever been intrigued with this approach—I like scopes as close to the gun as possible—but apparently it appeals to a lot of hunters, as more and more of these are seen each season. I guess things move in circles, for a lot of shooters favored this idea back in the '30s. If you like it now, have at it. The workmanship and materials on this Williams job, as on all their equipment, is top notch.

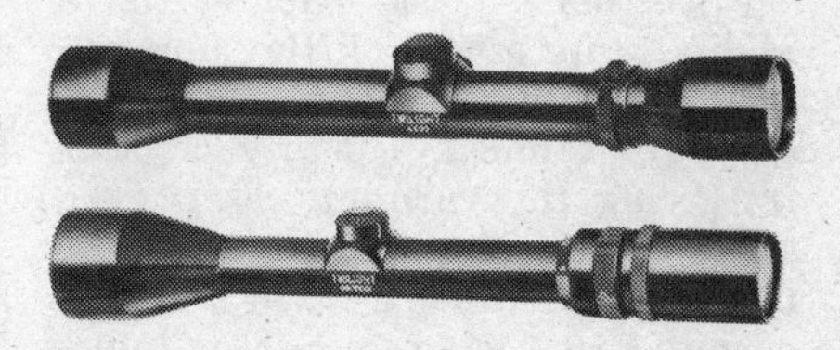

Williams 4x (top) and 3-9x Twilight scopes.

Williams 94 Winchester mount.

22 HORNET

by ROY F. DUNLAP

Our first high velocity 22 in regular production, this little centerfire cartridge was the small wonder of its long ago day. Townsend Whelen said of it "...the Hornet rifle and its cartridge give us the most super accuracy that we riflemen have ever known.

TO THE NOW generation of varmint and group shooters interested in 22 centerfires, the 22 Hornet is a quaint little old-timer, the one that old Uncle Ed talks about having when he was a boy. Hell, it's hardly considered a real cartridge today. Nobody even makes rifles for it any more, at least not in the U.S. of A. Hornet ammunition is still being made, though, so some people must be shooting 'em. Know something? The cartridge companies made Hornet ammunition *before* any of the arms firms started making rifles for it in the first place!

Nevertheless, the Hornet is a highly interesting little number, and all 22 handloaders and shooters owe it much. Up to 175 yards it'll bring the varmints down even today—when the critters must be tougher than they used to be, since people keep using bigger and bigger rifles. Seriously, before even starting Hornet-talk it is necessary to light up a very considerable background—the period from 1929 to 1940. Those were the "depression years," when nobody had much money, but everyone had time. Time to think, write letters, read, to work on guns, experiment with reloading, time to shoot. Out of those years came almost every development in rifles and ammunition we now have available. (While reading up to refresh my memory, I saw an ad offering a 25-06 rifle—in the January, 1937 issue of the *American Rifleman*).

The first report on the 22 Hornet (which was not at this time called the Hornet) was by Captain Wotkyns in the *American Rifleman* for June 1930, page 8. His rifle was a BSA-Martini action, the barrel a Springfield Model 1922, the stocking having been done by Griffin & Howe in varmint style. The bullets he used were the Niedner of 44.5 grains and of .233″ diameter, these being soft points, and the Velo Dog of .225″ diameter, and of 45-gr. weight. 1204 powder was then used, and Wotkyns reported that 12 grains of it was maximum in his rifle, which had the tight-necked chamber typical of custom rifles of that period.

In the July 1930 issue of the *American Rifleman* Griffin & Hobbs (not Howe) carried an advertisement on page 48 for the just-developed 22 Express. Harry L. Hobbs had just become an officer of the company, said the ad, hence the new name. It became Griffin & Howe again via another advertisement in the *American Rifleman* on October 1930, page 49! Incidentally, in the same issue the new Pacific C-Tool was reported on by J. R. Mattern. This is apparently the first incidence of the offering of that Pacific tool, now a quite famous reloading press.

Then, in the January 1931 issue of the *American Rifleman* Townsend Whelen recounts the history of the 22 Hornet in an article called "New Dope on Wotkyns Cartridge," Whelen commenting on the article by G. L. Wotkyns, and that Wotkyns had told him, Mr. G.A. Woody and A. L. Woodworth (all of Springfield Armory) about his (Wotkyns') 22 Hornet several months before the Wotkyns article appeared. Using a new Woody-made bullet of .2233″ diameter and of 45 grains, these bullets made by using 22 Short cases before the cases were headed, and the Woody bullets being of a medium sharp point, a muzzle velocity of 2400 foot seconds was obtained. The load was 11 grains of 1204 (no more, no less, Whelen cautioned). In that same article Whelen notes that Winchester now has the 22 Winchester Hornet cartridges on the market, their muzzle velocity being 2350 foot seconds, and he adds "The fact that Winchester has brought out this cartridge before any rifle had been regularly produced (for it) shows their confidence in its future."

The first advertisement, by Griffin & Howe, for the new 22 Hornet as such was carried in the *American Rifleman*, for February 1931, page 47, and in the ad is pictured the new cartridge, presumably the Winchester factory loading. In the March 1931 issue of the *American Rifleman*, another Griffin & Howe ad calls the new cartridge the "22 Hornet Winchester."

Then, in the May 1931 issue of the *American Rifleman*, Sedgley had an ad for the Springfield Hornet, the price $75.

From left—factory 22 Hornet, Kilbourn Hornet, factory 218 Bee and Mashburn Bee.

In the September 1931 *American Rifleman*, page 13, Townsend Whelen has an article called "The Standardization of the .22 Hornet Cartridges and rifles." In his first paragraph he said, "... at their best the (22) Hornet rifle and its cartridge give us the most superb accuracy that we riflemen have ever known." Whelen mentions in the article the conversations he and Capt. Woody had with Winchester's engineers on the standardization of the 22 Hornet, and that because of the many handmade 22 Hornet rifles already in use, most of them with barrels of 22 rimfire dimensions internally, that it was decided to use a bullet in the 22 Hornet with a maximum groove dimension of .2235", but that Winchester would try to hold maximum groove dimension to .223". This bullet was intended for use in barrels of .217" bore and .222" groove, these maximum dimensions. In practice, Whelen noted, barrels would "seldom be found which measure under .2225-inch groove diameter."

A contemporary publication, some years ago, reported that the initial velocity of the first 22 Hornet factory loaded cartridges was 2600 foot seconds at the muzzle, but this was in error.

Until some time in 1932, the primers in the Hornet cartridge (as in other cartridges as well) were of the mercuric type, though non-corrosive. The use of these mercuric primers lead to brittle cases after firing, as is well known today, and this brittleness made for short case life. This short case life was aggravated as well by the quite thin side walls of the original Hornet cases. Even after the advent of the non-mercuric, non-corrosive primers (some time in 1932 for many cartridges, including the Hornet), case life was relatively short. Perhaps 6 to 10 firings could be managed, and this aspect of handloading the Hornet may also have discouraged a number of users.

Way back then many riflemen not only didn't have much to work with, they didn't know what they really wanted or needed! But a lot of them thought that between the 22 Long Rifle and the 250/3000 Savage there ought to be something better than the 25-20 to play with. In the 22 centerfire field there were two long-time cartridges, the 22 Savage Hi-Power, nicknamed the "Imp," and the 22 Winchester Center Fire, a little black powder cartridge. The Savage entry used a 70-gr. .227" diameter tough-jacketed bullet "designed for big-game," in the lever-action M99 rifle, with a 10" twist. It wasn't popular for either paper or woodchucks, a folding rule sometimes being needed to measure groups. The little W.C.F. pushed a 45-gr. lead bullet at 1500 feet per second, making it less potent than the current 22 Rimfire Magnum. Ad Niedner and other top custom gunsmiths, true, made 22 centerfire wildcats in the early 1920s, nearly all on such single-shot actions as the Winchester and Farquharson. They used reshaped 22 Savage, 25-35 and even 30-40 Krag cases, and made jacketed bullets for their customers, these being expensive special jobs, beyond the average gunsmith and beyond the wallet-capacity of his customers. Such rifles were excellent. In spite of powders made for larger bores, erosive and corrosive primers and bullets jacketed in fired 22 Short cases, in the war years, they shot. I saw many test groups on the walls of the old Niedner shop in Dowagiac, Michigan, that few modern bench-rest shooters would not approve. Not many of us, however, could afford the equipment.

The 22 W.C.F.

The little 22 Winchester center-fire caliber was being ignored, though its potential had long been known to a few adherents. Reuben Hargrove of Massachusetts made cast bullets of linotype metal and got up to 2000—in 1894! Over in Europe, by 1910 the Germans had made 22 WCF ammo with jacketed bullets, loaded to over 2000 fps. They named their version of the 22 WCF the 5.6mm Vierling, its official listing being the 5.6 x 35mmR.

In the U.S. nothing happened until the depression hit. A group of Army Ordnance men – Al Woodworth, Captains Woody and Wotkyns, Major Whelen—evidently having some time on their hands, reworked a 22 M1 Springfield to take the 22 W.C.F., made their own jacketed bullets, and loaded to 2400 fps. Results were startling on varmint and target. They called it the Hornet, publicized it as much as possible, making strong and successful efforts to divorce it from the 22 W.C.F. so that possessors of old and infirm black powder rifles would not try to use "Hornet" loads. The cases were and are, of course, interchangeable, in fact identical outwardly, saving for the headstamp and a ring-cannelure around the Hornet case made for instant identification when Hornet ammo became a factory product.

Publicity, though limited as it was at the time, resulted in literally hundreds of gunsmiths making reamers, chambering rifles and pushing the cartridge. The late R. B. Sisk jumped into the bullet-making, along with others who later faded away, and reasonably good jacketed bullets became available. Pressure (and very hard times) caused Winchester to bring out factory ammunition in 1932, and ultimately to begin developement of factory Hornet rifles. Incidentally,

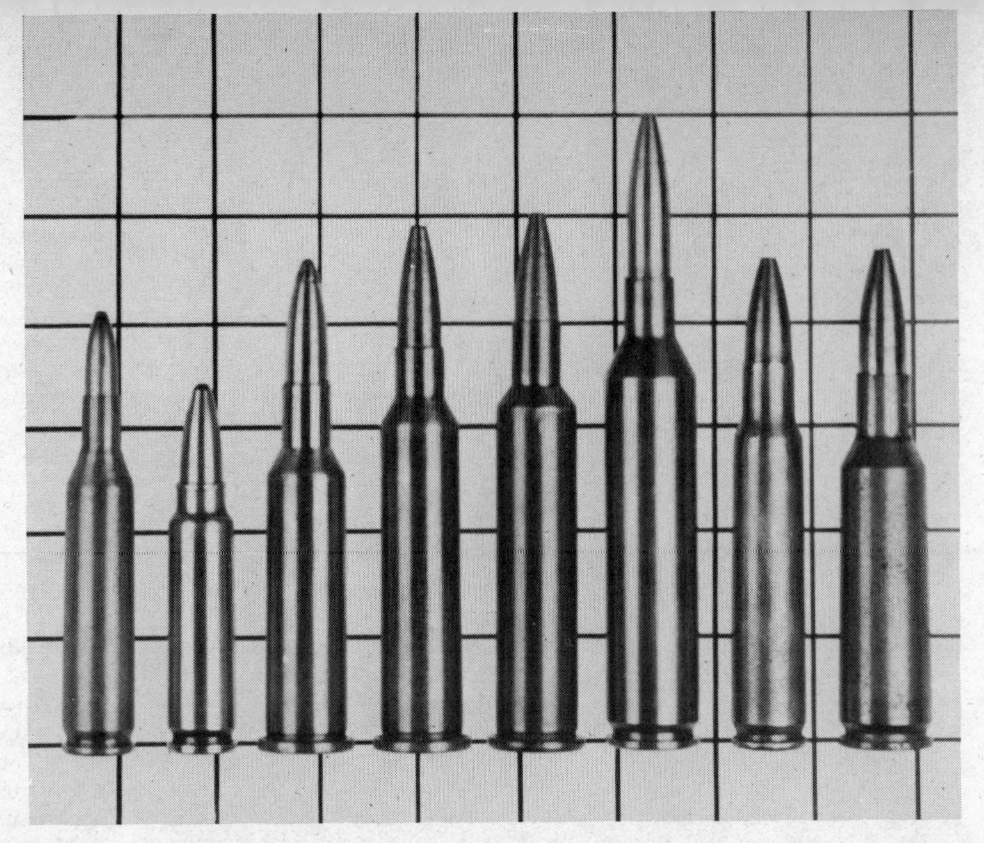

Some 22 calibers, old and new. From left—17-222, MMJ 5.7, 219 Don. Wasp, 219 Imp. Zipper, 22-30/30, 224 Clark, 6mm Don. Intl. and the 6mm-47.

the name "Hornet" wasn't too new, either, having been copyrighted in 1912, along with the name "Wasp," in Ireland, of all places.

First Factory Rifles

By 1934 rifles were coming over the counter. Winchester chambered their new Model 54 for the Hornet, then Savage decided their 23D model would make a nice Hornet sporter and, in the style of their M19 22 target rifle, a 19-H would be a fine little varmint rifle. Stevens, then still a separate company, soon announced a single shot on their revamped Walnut Hill action. (The Hornet proved a little too much for it, and much shooting soon developed much headspace!). Factory arms with standardized chambers and factory ammunition of fixed dimensions made the Hornet a solid citizen. Fecker brought out "varmint" scopes, W. R. Weaver proved hunting type scopes could be made at prices people could pay, and about a hundred thousand varmint hunters were born, all anxious to handload.

Factory bullets cost 70c a hundred, list price. Lead could always be scrounged for free, and a lot of lead went out of Hornet barrels in those years, since hard-alloy gas-checked bullets would stand velocities to 2000 fps. All shapes of lead bullets were tried, of course, but perhaps the most widely-used was a round-nosed type designed by Guy Loverin, for which Ideal made moulds. Mr. Loverin simply copied the general shape of the 22 Long Rifle match bullet of the day, putting three lubricant grooves and a gas-check on it—weight, 43 grains. Accurate at velocities from 1000 to 1600 fps, excellent for squirrels and groups. Sisk made bullets of every type and weight desired, even a "revolver" bullet, for handgunners were having arms made to take the Hornet cartridge! The previously-mentioned Captain Wotkyns teamed with a Mr. Morse to design and make a bullet, the 8-S (8-caliber spire point)—this first deliberately-designed-for-accuracy smallbore bullet proved so good that group shooting became an end in itself. The present-day bench rest game was really born with this bullet. All previous bullets, including the often-as-accurate Sisk line had been originated primarily for effective use in vermin shooting.

Hornet handloaders were nearly always quite successful or quite unsuccessful. The very small capacity of the case magnified errors caused by minute variations in powder charges, bullets, primers, even the temperatures at times of shooting. So, if a man didn't carefully clean cases and weigh out powder and bullets he really couldn't accomplish much in the group field. While the new factory cartridges cases were pretty sturdy at the back end, the walls tapered to as little as .006" thickness at necks. Repeated firing and sizing thinned then even further, changing the effect of expanding plugs, etc., so that it was necessary to select and segregate cases for accurate loads. (Just in the past year, long after all factories ceased manufacture of Hornet rifles, have the ammunition makers made the necks heavier.)

Early Troubles

Every once in a while in the old days a batch of cases with soft heads would turn up and, loaded hot, heads would expand and primers blow out. This happened with the best cases occasionally, especially when overloads were used, since there is only about 1/16" of brass wrapped around the primer pocket, not enough to offer much support. The Hornet developes pressures in the 40,000 lb. class, along with such cartridges as the 30-30, 303 British, et al. With the pressure held in a much smaller boiler-room, everything concerned has to be in pretty good shape!

What made early Hornet reloading extra interesting were the rifle barrels used and the bullets made. Remember, there was little literature widely available. Just about all the arms and ammunition writers in the country could be counted on your fingers, without including thumbs—the only gun magazine was the *American Rifleman,* published by the National Rifle Association for its members, who were not very numerous in those days. After all, it cost $3 a year! So, perhaps as high as 90% of the interested riflemen had no acess to real information on developments made by individuals in various parts of the country, as they were made. Consequently many men made the same mistakes. We were all pretty unsophisticated then compared to the present-day riflemen,

Several old wildcats. From left—22 Ackley, Imp. Zipper, 22 G&H Imp. Magnum, 22 Niedner, rimless and rimmed; 240 Super Varminter, 230 Thunderbolt and 22 Davis Sniper. *Dick Simmons photo.*

who have a wealth of published data flowing toward them constantly.

The original Hornet rifle, that rechambered 1922 22 Long Rifle Springfield, shot well and held up for barrel life with the bullets made for it—and probably 95% of the early custom Hornets were made using barrels dimensioned for the 22 rimfire cartridge. When of tough alloy—nickel or ordnance steel, as in the Springfield 22s, they did well, but those of the soft steel made expressly for rimfire lead bullet barrels lasted quick. I shot one out myself in 1934 with seven boxes of factory ammo. However, the 22 Winchester Center Fire rifle had really a larger bore—.220″ as opposed to the .217″ of the 22 Long Rifle barrels. (Used also for the 22 Winchester Rim Fire, generally called the "22 Special," which has lately been modernized as the 22 Rim Fire Magnum). Thus when the factories began making Hornet rifles they often copied exactly the original 22 Winchester Center Fire chamber and rifling specifications. The bullets, too, were made to suit: .223″ to .2235″ diameters, and these sizes were followed by the independent bulletmakers. Hence, the Hornet might have a barrel to fit factory bullets or it might not. Bullet jackets were thin though, and the bullets *could* be used in rimfire type barrels, but the loads had to be worked up carefully. Pretty soon the big 22 centerfires, the wildcat 22/250 and the 220 Swift appeared, but their barrels were made even larger in bore and groove dimensions, for .224″ bullets, no less. Now 22 bullet and barrel makers had to produce four sizes, including the larger-yet 22 Savage, whose width across the grooves was .228″. Hornet loaders suddenly had a lot of bullets to choose from, a lot of experimenting to do, and a lot of trouble to get into! R. B. Sisk was their best friend, making a good selection of bullets especially for the Hornet, diameters from .222″, and light types from 35 to 45 grains. He even printed safe loads on the boxes.

Shooters experimented with all sorts of powders, even screening shotgun powders for effective light loads. There was a good selection of

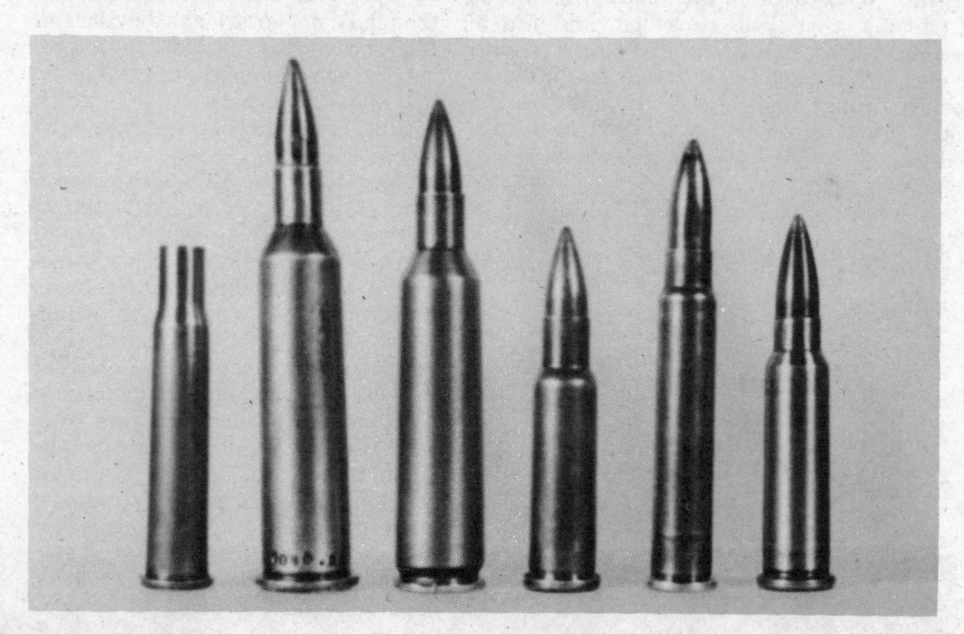

Five old configurations and one that's new-old. From left, the bottlenecked Maximum 2R Lovell, the 22-4500 Donaldson Krag, the 22 Varminter, still going strong as the 22-250 Remington; the 218 Bee and 22 Lovell, both Ackley Improved versions and, last, the Mashburn Improved 218 Bee. *Dick Simmons photo.*

22 HORNET
Maximum Cartridge Dimensions

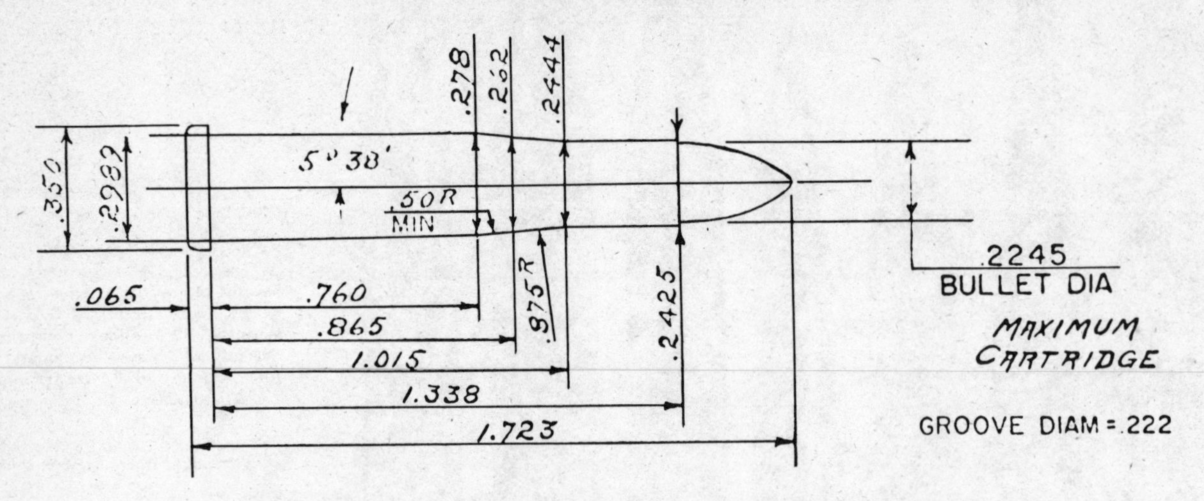

The drawing reproduced here is a photo copy of a Sporting Arms & Ammunition Institute drawing (No. 1467, formerly No. 1465) approved as late as October 1, 1969. Bullet diameter was revised, per one J.W., as of 8-31-56, to .2245″ from .2235″, yet the groove diameter, as can be seen at lower right, is .222″.

powders made at the time, better than today, really, and Hercules 2400 was well-suited to the little Hornet. DuPont came out with 4227 just for small rifle cases, and that made the day. Small rifle primers varied somewhat from lot to lot and between makers, Remington, Winchester, Peters and Western all being individual firms at the start of the Hornet era.

The Kilbourn Hornet

Naturally, as always, there were the unsatisfied: "So the Hornet's good, but why can't it be better?" Lyle Kilbourn had an idea—the Hornet case had a nice rim, therefore the case couldn't go anywhere back; if the chamber were to be enlarged, cases should expand to fit it. So he enlarged the chamber to a bottle-neck form, .288″ diameter at the 35-degree shoulder. Shoot a factory cartridge, take out a bottle-neck K-Hornet case, which could be loaded to higher velocity with no increase in pressure. For $4 or so your Hornet could have a couple hundred feet more velocity. From this beginning came all the blown-out "improved" case changes and the innumerable wildcat cartridges of the past and the present, the sharp-shouldered straight factory cases of today. Before Mr. Kilbourn's idea people had necked down cases, reformed shoulders and shortened them, but nobody had expanded cases to increase capacity, change design and powder-burning characteristics.

A good Hornet barrel would last many thousands of rounds, ammunition cost little to make, even factory ammo was not too high—$1.35 a box of 50 in the middle '30s. It was a nice little cartridge, and fun to shoot, but its limited range on varmints and the shooter's urge for more range and velocity brought on the developement of all the 22 centerfires that followed. Its last stand was in the federal survival arms of a decade past; the defense and game-getting capacities were there, and the small size of the cartridge allowed a fair supply of ammo to be carried.

I hate to see the Hornet disappear completely, and maybe it won't—which is probably wishful thinking. Still, in much of the nation population expansion—housing—is limiting small-game and varmint field shooting. The crack of a Hornet doesn't compare with the blast of a 22/250, a 220 Swift or a 6mm, and the long ranges, sadly, must get shorter. The little Hornet may be tolerated by people in areas who'd look askance at the super-whoopers. It can be useful, even, though I'd not go as far as the Alaskan Indian who, years ago, sent me a shot-out Hornet for rebarreling; he listed his old 70 Hornet's record, which began, "Six large polar bears; over 50 moose, 800 seals ..."

Now—early in 1974—we've been assured that Ruger will offer the 22 Hornet chambering in the No. 3 version of his single shot rifle. The Czechoslovakian BRNO-made Model 465—a small bolt action rifle in miniature '98 Mauser form—has been offered for years in 22 Hornet caliber, but not, unfortunately to U.S. citizens. Rifled firearms from Iron Curtain countries may not be imported into the U.S. Canada, though, makes no such restrictions; there the whole BRNO line is available.

I have a 19-H Savage in perfect condition and I'm going to keep it! ●

22 Hornet Load Data and Factory Ballistics

Bullet (grs.)	Powder/grs.	MV	ME	
40	2400 10	2765	679	
40	4227 12	2940	768	Max.
45	2400 9	2500	725	
45	4227 11	2680	718	Dup. fact. ball.
50	2400 9	2378	629	
50	4227 11	2575	736	
55	4227 11	2390	697	
55	4198 12	2400	703	
45	FL	2690	720	200 yd. MRT=4.3″

For light loads use 43 or 45 gr. gas check bullets and 9 grs. of 2400 for 2340 fps.

Notes on Knives

The Bowen Knife Company's 1974 full-color catalog is now ready. Included are Bowen's exclusive patented belt knives—an unusual series of survival and hunting types—plus a big selection of all-stainless-steel pocket knives with genuine rosewood handles.

Every knife enthusiast, whatever his special interest, will find something to whet his appetite in this new catalog. It's one of the biggest half-buck's worth of knife education offered today, and all items are American made products. J.T.A.

Dan-D Custom Knives. Dan Dennehy's catalog is an excellent one, to be sure. In its pages (48 in the 7th ed.) you'll learn a lot about Dan's blades and a lot about Dan himself. Highly recommended, and his 8th ed. catalog should be ready soon.

The Dan-D Knife at top in our photo is his No. 4 Pro Scout—4¾″ slightly upswept blade. The other, a favorite of navy frogmen, is the Hoss—its full tang blade 6½″x¼″ of stainless steel.

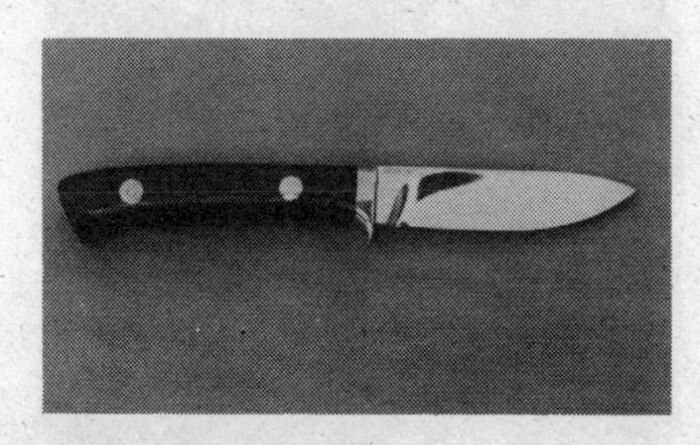

Herron's full-tang skinner

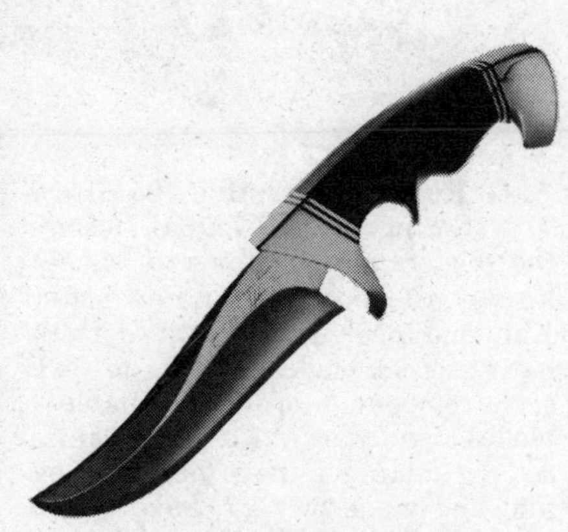

Davis' Barren Ground Caribou

Davis Custom Knives has an unusual and attractive 8-page, single sheet foldout, done in full color and laid out in a highly distinctive style. Rod Chappel's numerous designs are clearly shown and clearly described. A separate sheet shows current prices and an order form is included. Pictured is the Davis "Barren Ground Caribou," its stainless steel blade 6″ by 2″, the handle of Micarta. It is Chappel's favorite hunting knife.

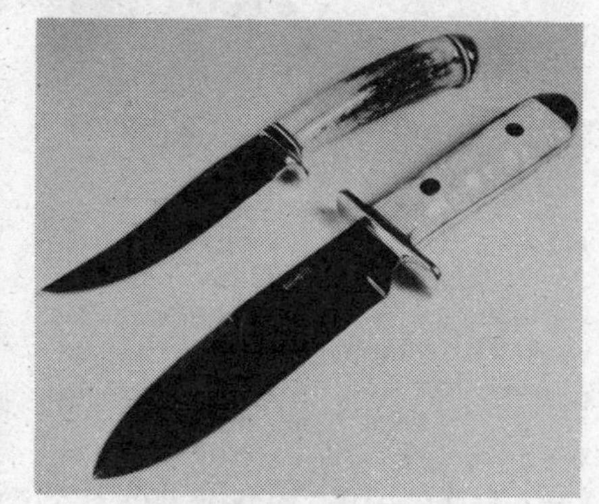

Dan-D's No. 4 Pro Scout

George H. Herron (920 Murrah Ave., Aiken, SC 29801). Not a catalog, really, but a big full-color postcard that pictures an even dozen of Herron's interesting knives. A detailed descriptive brochure is mailed with the card, identifying the knives, and all prices are listed. The clearly designed functional knife illustrated is his No. 7, a dropped-point, full tang skinner with 4½″ blade, cost $60.

Chubby Hueske's blades

Chubby Hueske (4808 Tamarisk, Bellaire, TX 77401) has a new catalog ($1) that shows the many styles he makes. He also tells how he makes blades (full tang and narrow) and why. His guarantee reads: "Your satisfaction for your lifetime." The knives shown are Hueske's D-2 steel Pro Hunter (3½″-5″) with Sambar stag handle, $70, and his 3″ blade Backpacker, also of D-2 steel, at $50. J.T.A.

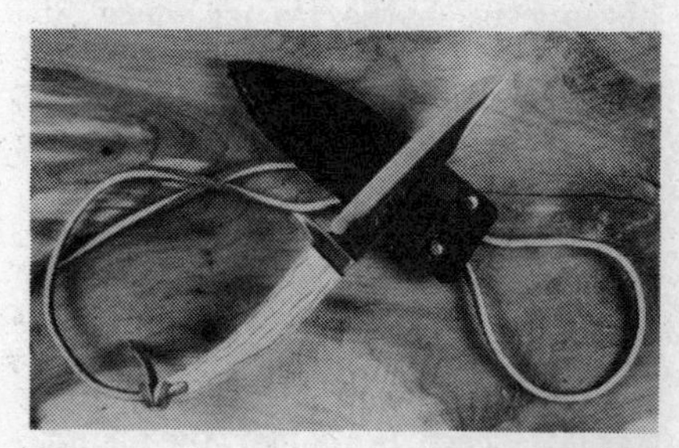

Kirk's patch knife

Knives by Kirk (800 N. Olive, Fayetteville, AR 72701). Jon Kirk makes a fairly small range of hunting knives, plus a Bowie and the patch knife pictured. He'll make knives to order. Kirk hot forges and shapes his blades in the age-old way—handles can be a variety of woods or stag horn. His prices run from about $30 to $110 (for the Bowie). The 3-inch bladed patch knife, with sheath and thong-lanyard is $30, and it could serve well as a small game or boat knife.

Harvey McBurnette (Rt. 4—Box 337, Piedmont, AL 36272) has a new catalog (50c), which describes the full tang treatment used in his knifemaking. The knife pictured is his Model J—5¾-inch blade, stag handle, cost $80. Walnut, Micarta, stag, etc., are available, and his chrome-steel knives are all hardened to about Rockwell C-59. Stainless (440-C) can be furnished, about C-57 hard, at $5 over regular prices.

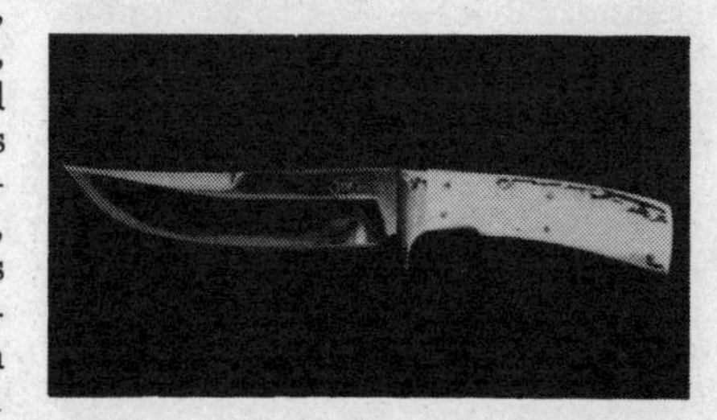

McBurnette's Model J knife

Heinrich H. Frank (#1 Mountain Meadow, Whitefish, MT 59937) made the beautiful folding knives pictured here, and he also did the excellent engraving—which he's now doing on firearms, too, though to a limited degree. The 3½-inch bladed skinner (top) is elaborately cut, showing a turkey hunting scene. The other side continues the theme. The handles are of elk antler tops. The 4-inch caper, which Frank terms his semi-plain model, has moose handles. Superb work, this.

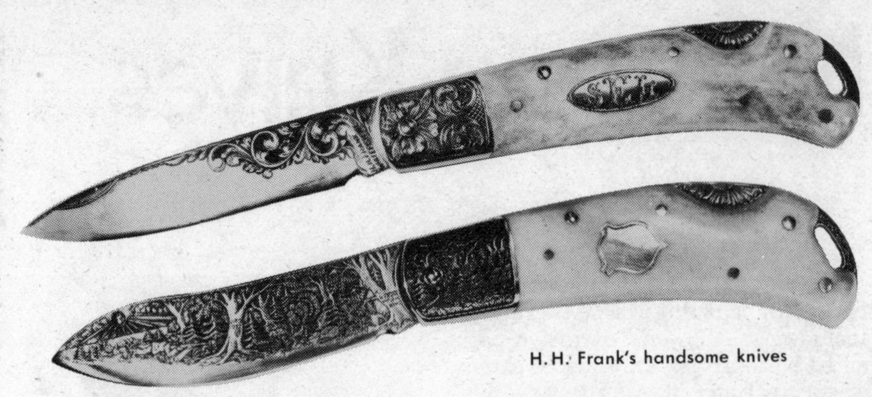

H. H. Frank's handsome knives

William F. Moran, Jr. (Rt. 5, Frederick, MD 21701) hardly needs an introduction! His knives—made in many types and styles, but all of equally high quality—are *entirely handmade,* by Moran himself, and so are his superb sheaths. He has a new catalog ready—this tells in detail about the methods he uses, the long hours put into every Moran knife, and his prices—from $26 for a woman's poniard to $600 for a Cinquedea renaissance dagger. Moran is some *4 years behind* on delivery! He takes no deposits.

The knives shown here are extra-specials—each is a folder, the mountings, German silver and ivory, handsomely fluted. The center knife has a curly maple handle with silver wire inlaid. Prices by quotation.

A. G. Russell-Morseth (1705 Hiway 71 N, Springdale, AR 72764). Besides the big range of Morseth sheath knives offered, you can now order Knifemaking Kits, all with Morseth hand-ground blades, at $27 to $38, or the components are also available—blades alone start at $18. Russell also sells 3 folding knives (designed by him and made by Ogg, Lake or LeBlanc) at $60 to $150. Morseth knives have been made for 40 years, and they're guaranteed against defects for the life of the original owner.

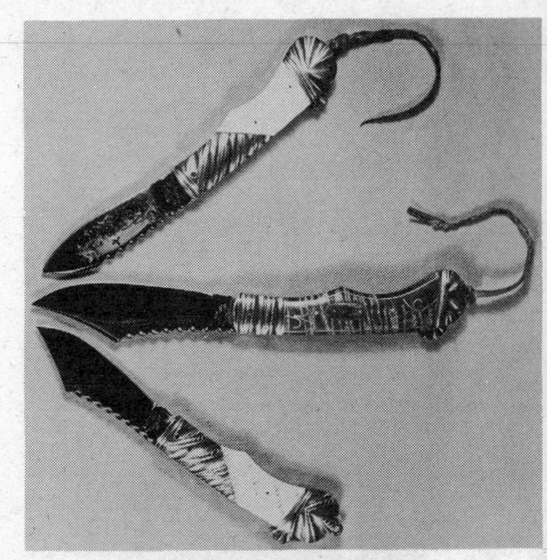

W. F. Moran's special deluxe folders

Shaw-Leibowitz (Rt. 1—Box 421, New Cumberland, WV 26047) are specialists in etching scenes of all kinds on knives, firearms, etc. The Eskimo-type skinner pictured—the knife one of Bill Imel's—is only one of many designs offered. Too, S-L will work from designs or scenes furnished to them. Gold—red, green or yellow—and silver plating can also be done, colored enamels inlaid and scrimshawing or paintings, executed as desired. First class craftsmanship, and fully detailed in the S-L catalog.

Above—Shaw-Leibowitz' skinner

Sonneville Knives (1050 Chalet Dr., W., Mobile, AL 36608) offers a good variety of blades—all sheath types—including Bowies, carvers and diver's knives, and a ring-guard non-slip skinner. Prices—$54 to $135 generally, though his grand Royal Oak Bowie is $550-$650, the latter in stainless steel.

The knife at left in the photo is a new one—the semi-flexible blade is 6¼" long, the handle of Micarta, cost $58. Next is a scale-back fishing knife. Last is the Badger, a utility skinner, made with 4" or 5" blade. Send 50c for Sonneville's literature.

Robert G. Ogg (Rt. 1—Box 230, Paris, AR 72855) has a new folder, with current prices given, but a photo was not sent, I'm sorry to say. Ogg has expanded his folding-knife line—all sturdy, all reasonably priced—$50 to $58, extra for stag or ivory handles, etc. Ogg's delivery time is now running to 16 months. Good stuff.

Sparks Handmade Knives (Box 32, Dingle, ID 83233) offer sheath and folding knives in good variety, but Bernard Sparks rather specializes in folders. This interesting folder—a new design by Sparks—is the smallest of its kind so far at 4¾" fully open. It has a walrus ivory handle and brass bolster, cost $65. Write for the latest Sparks catalog.

Three blades by Sonneville

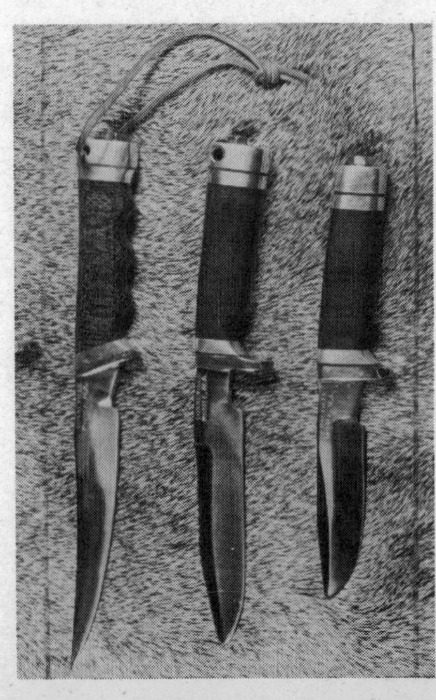

Sid Bell-Bill Mains Knives

This trio of handsome knives was sent to me for examination and photography by Bill Mains (Mains Custom Knives, 2895 Seneca St., Buffalo, NY 14224). Sid Bell, famed today for his silver and gold shooters' jewelry—tie tacks, bolos and such like—has designed some new knives for Mains, and two of Sid's designs are pictured here.

At left is a Sid Bell skinner with Sambar stag handle, the polished brass cap carved in baroque style. The blade, tastefully engraved both sides by Mains, in 3½ inches long. As seen, about $156.

The middle knife—made of Mains Super Tough Steel, as are all of his blades—has an impregnated rosewood-grain handle in the deerfoot curve. Fittings are of polished brass, and the cost is $85.

The knife at right is about identical to the one at left, aside from the finger grooves and engraving. Cost is $90.

These new knives show excellent craftmanship—wood to metal fit is top notch, and their sturdy, solid construction assures a long lifetime of heavy duty use.

Of the 3, I'd prefer the middle blade because of its handle form and fit, the circumference of which is a bit less than the two stag-handled blades. The others would, of course, be suited to a bigger mitt. J.T.A.

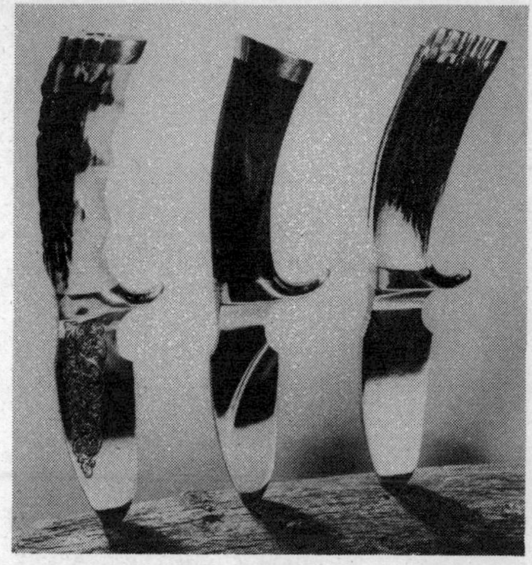

Sid Bell-Bill Mains knives are made of Mains super tough steel.

Jimmy Lile Interframe Knives

The "Arkansas Knifesmith" has come up with an entirely new concept in knifemaking—Lile calls this the Interframe Knife. Made entirely from one piece of D-2 or 440C steel, Lile had originally intended to offer it in only 7 shapes, all of these original Lile designs—the Models 1, 7, 8, Utility, Boot, and scaled down versions of his Confederate Bowie and Arkansas Toothpick. Though this group of 7 pieces will still comprise the collector's set of original Interframes, he has now decided to offer the same unique design in any model for which it is adaptable.

The guard and handle frame of this new design are formed during the removal of excess material from the blade. This construction results in a very lightweight knife, the whole an integrated and highly functional concept. In addition, the inlaid handle material is well protected—especially important when ivory is used. Because the ivory—or whatever—is surrounded so tightly by the frame it can hardly crack but, even if it does it can't go anywhere because of the concealed pins which hold it in place.

The Interframe knife lends itself nicely to decoration—there's ample area for angraving and, if ivory is chosen for the inlay, it can be tastefully scrimshawed by Jim Laymon, who recently moved to Russellville to practice this art exclusively for Lile. Now, with the Interframe line and Laymon's scrimshaw, Jimmy says the collector's imagination is his only limitation.

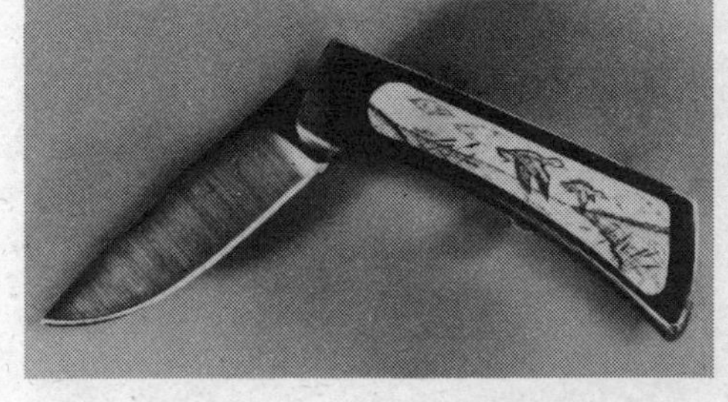

These Interframe knives, graceful yet highly functional, are not inexpensive at $175 for the wood-inlaid version—plus another $50 if ivory is wanted—but I don't consider them over-priced, not in today's market. Scrimshaw work will be quoted on request, your design or theirs.

Other products are offered, too—belt buckles, bolo ties, cufflinks, brooches, and the like, and in gold or silver.

A new and colorful brochure is ready—send $1 to Jimmy Lile Handmade knives, Route 1, Russelville, AR 72801. J.T.A.

T.M. Dowell Knives

The 1974 TMD Catalog has just arrived, and it is easily one of the best of its kind. In his introduction, and in his comments on knife blade steel, Dowell tells it like it is—or certainly as he sees the custom knife field. His frankness is refreshing and disarming. His several types of knife construction are illustrated and described fully—full- and narrow tang styles, integral-hilt designs and his ultimate form—and most expensive, for good reasons—integral hilt *and* cap treatments. These last are, to my eye and, I'd guess, to yours, knives at their handsomest. Also shown are Dowell's axe, kitchen knives and a couple of folders.

The TMD knife illustrated is his full tang style, here with a wide bolster in nickel silver—the stag grips are wedged beneath the bolster. Cost, about $135. Dowell's prices run to $250.

Knife fancier or not, the new Dowell catalog is worth the $1 it costs to get one. Write to TMD at 139 N.W. St. Helens Place, Bend, OR 97701. J.T.A.

T.M. Dowell knife at left

Norman H. Schiffman

The pair of Schiffman knives shown here—excellent quality materials, and made with careful precision—are his combat type (at left with cocobolo handle) and survival style, with horn handle. Schiffman knives are among the best, and his custom rifle work comes under the same high classification. See our Custom Guns pages, further on in this issue, for a very well turned out bolt action sporter. J.T.A.

N.H. Schiffman knives, right

Short Barrels for Grouse

Fast, short-barreled shotguns for brush busting grouse and the like aren't all that new, but straight-cylinder, no-choke barrels? That's right – and with today's loads they do a great job.

by NICK SISLEY

I CAN STILL remember the last grouse of the season coming to bag. It went down with not only a puff of feathers, but also a puff of powdery snow. There was a snow-covered evergreen between me and the flushing bird, and the shot pattern had centered on much of that snow, in addition to ole ruff. That ending of the 1969 grouse season marked the best year I had ever had in the percentage of grouse bagged per shot fired. I attribute the new success to a short barreled shotgun.

Some firearms manufacturers have been making a concentrated effort at putting out lightweight smoothbores for field use on such species as quail, grouse and woodcock. Other manufacturers have "stuck by their guns," and maintained that a shotgun must have a certain amount of weight to retain the needed handling qualities necessary for an arm that is pointed and not aimed. Speaking from my experience, I lean toward the lightweight theories. More about that later.

With few exceptions, the shotgun industry sticks with three standard barrel lengths—26, 28 and 30 inches. (The federal minimum shotgun barrel length is 18 inches. Some states have laws prohibiting shotgun barrels shorter than 24, 22, or 20 inches. Check your own state laws before acting.) Usually a prospective buyer can purchase an improved cylinder of modified choke in 26" barrels, or a modified or full choke in 28" or 30" barrels. There are several exceptions, but from most manufacturers, these are the choices.

Only one or two firms offer a shorter barrel. A 24", even a 22" barrel, does not lose any degree of handling quality. In fact, for snap shooting—which one always encounters when hunting quail, grouse or woodcock—the short-barreled guns excel. We keep several rifles for different types of hunting conditions; why not keep different types of shotguns to hunt varying prey under different conditions?

There may be some who are quick to say that familiarity is more important when handling a shotgun on fast-moving game. Game fired at with a centerfire rifle is not always moving. The shooter can sometimes take his time. Thus, using several different rifles is possible. If a rifleman is not extremely familiar with his firearm, it is going to cost him many trophies over the course of a lifetime. Still, continual use of the same arm does have its points. Barring other factors, a hunter will bag more game with a shotgun that is thoroughly familiar.

Here's the one-hand carry I use when plowing through exceptionally thick cover. With a shotgun of normal weight, this is not possible. It's easy with a short-barreled gun of 5 pounds, so I'm ready to swing into action at a moment's notice.

A shooter can buy one shotgun with two or more barrels from most manufacturers. In the case of pumps and autos, he can buy another barrel from the factory at a reasonable price—far less than the cost of an additional shotgun. The same stock will naturally be used, so only the difference in barrel length will make the arm handle differently. Additional barrels can also be purchased for side-by-side and over-and-under doubles from some manufacturers.

Shotguns for Grouse

A decade ago I became interested in shotguns especially suited to grouse hunting. Since then I have used four different shotguns extensively on my woodlot ventures for grouse. I chose them because they seemed well suited to this game bird. From 1961 to '63, I used a 16-gauge Model 37 Ithaca Featherweight. Barrel length was 25 inches, and it was fitted with a Poly-Choke. I used the cylinder bore setting for grouse. Weight was about 6¾ pounds. Results were good, and this was a top choice for grouse hunting. I had an offer, however, that I couldn't turn down, so I sold that particular shotgun. I also felt the added muzzle weight of a choking device could be detrimental when extra fast. handling was required.

In 1964 and '65, I used a 12-gauge Parker side-by-side double. It is bored improved cylinder and full choke, the barrels 28" long. Weight is about 7¾ pounds. It's a fine gun, and I still have it, but I don't use it for grouse hunting anymore. For me, it is too heavy, and the barrels are too long. In 1966, I went to a 20-gauge Richland Model 707 side-by-side double with 26" barrels bored improved

Here is the shotgun carry I use *continually* while in the grouse woods. Being ready for every flush not only increases the chance of getting off a shot, it also permits the shooter to get on target more quickly.

and modified. It weighs 6¼ pounds. It served my needs well, and my shooting average on grouse improved.

Midway in the 1967 season, I bought a 20-gauge Franchi Automatic. It was fitted with a 26″ barrel bored improved cylinder. I tried it several times during that season and again early in the 1968 season. Recorded results at grouse shooting were comparable to shooting with the Richland 707. I preferred the latter because of the choice of two chokes, and because it handled a bit better.

The receiver of an automatic or pump shotgun encases the loading mechanism. It takes up three to four inches which adds to the total length of the arm. A double does not have a receiver. That's why you have heard so many times that a double has superior handling qualities.

However, the Franchi had a lightness that I thought was beneficial. It weighed only 5 pounds and 2 ounces. Recoil was noticeable when firing at clay targets, but was not felt during the excitement of a game bird flush. I felt that if I could shorten this gun, it would match or better the handling qualities of the Richland I liked, and it would be much lighter.

I talked with a firearms editor friend. He too was of the opinion that a shorter barrel would improve handling qualities, although he advised against removing a portion of the barrel because doing so would reduce the gun's value. However, I was determined to experiment.

A gunsmith cut off 3″ from the barrel and replaced the front sight. Cost was minimal. With a 1-ounce load in the chamber and one in the magazine, the gun still weighs only 5 pounds, 2 ounces. Empty, it weighs a hair less than 5 pounds. I think the handling qualities are much better than they were before.

Grouse and woodcock are hunted and found in the thickest cover imaginable. Anyone who has spent a few hours hunting these great game birds is familiar with how they can bust out at the most inopportune times. Accordingly, a fast swing often catches the gun barrel against intervening brush. The shorter the barrel, the less likely this will happen.

Further, a shorter barrel cuts down on muzzle weight, and this aids in the fast swings so necessary in this sport. In waterfowl, dove, pheasant, crow and other shotgunning, a long barrel is more beneficial. When the quarry is seen for at least a brief period of time, it is proper shotgun practice to blot out the target and pull the trigger after swinging some distance ahead. The longer barrel helps keep the gun swinging for proper follow through.

This type of shooting is recommended in grouse hunting, but the gun is often fired the instant it touches the shoulder. At times the bird is passing out of sight when the trigger is pulled. Follow through of the swing is still necessary, but it is imperative that the shooter learn to do this himself. He can't depend on the gun to do it for him.

The short barrel and light weight also help in another area to bag these birds. The gun must be carried in a ready manner if you expect to get shots off regularly. The carry I use *continually* in the grouse woods is illustrated. Carrying a heavy gun all day in the manner shown is impossible, at least for me. With my short, light Franchi, however, it's easy. Also, when bulling through thick stuff, with the gun in this position, the longer the barrel, the more it will tend to hang up on branches. Mine seldom does. In an especially thick spot, I carry it with my right hand in the normal position around the pistol grip. I let go with the left hand. With a heavier gun, this also is not possible. The light gun can be pushed straight ahead through any exceptionally thick stuff. It's ready to swing into action at a moment's notice. Keep in mind that the shorter barrel shifts the center of gravity back toward the pistol grip. This makes the gun much easier to carry with this one-hand method.

Naturally, I don't use this one-hand carry often, only when pushing through the thickest cover. I do use it, however, and there is a grouse or two each year bouncing against the seat of my pants, rather than flying off without a shot being fired.

When I made the switch to the short barreled and lightweight Franchi for the 1969 season, I was rewarded by almost *doubling* my average on grouse hits. That is a tremendous improvement. I had used the Franchi with the 26″ barrel for periods in two previous years, and results were similar to the Richland. It was not until 3″ were cut off the barrel that I saw such a dramatic change in my shooting results. The decrease in muzzle weight, I believe, had almost as much to do with this new success as the decrease in barrel length.

Open Boring

In addition, I changed chokes. Here lies another part of the answer to improved success. Cutting 3″ off the barrel left me with a cylinder bore. The Franchi had been bored improved cylinder. I patterned the gun with Winchester Mark V 1-ounce loads of 7½ shot. Results showed a 10-shot average with 32% of the pellets hitting within a 30″ circle at 40 yards. Patterns were even, with no signs of wide "gaps." Tests were also made at 80 yards. Pellets were not counted here. The test was to further determine if blown patterns resulted from a boring of true cylinder, and to see if a killing pattern resulted at that range. Pellet holes *were* dense enough to assure clean kills on grouse. These cylinder bore patterns were as even as any modified or full pattern I had ever seen. Modern shotshells with star crimps and plastic shot protectors help produce these even patterns in a barrel actually bored *true* cylinder. Before the advent of these modern loads blown patterns were the rule, rather than the exception, in this open boring.

I also started checking results on shots fired at grouse. I've just started this, so I don't have enough data for unquestioned results. I pace off the distance to where the grouse was when I shot the first time—whether the bird was hit or not. Preliminary tests show the average to be well under 30 yards. My pattern tests at that distance have already convinced me that clean kills are certain if I do my job in accurately pointing the gun.

Perhaps in the near future, some of the firearms manufacturers will start marketing more shotguns that are lighter in weight and have shorter barrels. For the specialized hunting of grouse, woodcock and quail such guns would be ideal. Compared to rifles, shotgun versatility lags far behind. Centerfire rifles are now produced in such a wide variety of calibers, actions, weights and lengths that one or more of them is fully suitable for every imaginable situation.

In comparison with rifles we have been very conserative and stodgy with smoothbores. Wholly new ideas could make shotguns more suitable for a wider range of hunting situations. True, the different calibers possible with rifles contributes greatly to the variety of situations in which they can be used, but the different actions, weights and lengths also contribute to doing more things better with these rifles. We shouldn't sit back and feel assured that the ultimate shotgun is now available. It isn't. There are too many varied shotgun needs, and we don't have enough of a variety in smoothbores to supply them all.

Summary

I'm satisfied that I now have a better grouse gun. I bought the lightest available and shortened it. The gun also fits me well. I'm not through experimenting, by any means. Because of a shorter barrel length, the consequent lighter muzzle weight, cylinder boring, and the gun's light initial weight, I have almost doubled my former grouse bag. There are, however, many more ways to improve on this shotgun. One would be a side-by-side or over-and-under of comparable weight and barrel length. This gun would save the 3" to 4" taken up by my auto's receiver. Over-all length would be much shorter. In addition, the shooter would have the advantage of two chokes available. Ah, but would the manufacturer make it available with one choke (or rather without choke) of cylinder bore? Would it also be available with other sets of barrels for use in different types of hunting? Finally, how about a choice of gauges and different standards of craftsmanship so shooters could have a greater variety to choose from?

A little more research, experimenting and ingenuity may bring an even greater feeling of accomplishment when the last bird of the season is bagged next year! •

Three of the four grouse guns I've used extensively over the last decade. Left to right—20-gauge Richland 707, its 26" barrels bored improved and modified; my current favorite, a Franchi 20-gauge auto with 23" barrel bored "cylinder;" last, a 12-gauge Parker 12 with 28" barrels bored improved and full.

The Handgun Scene

Many pistols and revolvers are still hard to find, so it's a sellers' market—some models are bringing premium prices. Quality of construction, too, remains a problem.

by GEORGE C. NONTE and the editors

I CAN'T RECALL a time in the past when interest in handguns ever even approached what we see today. Every factory, large and small alike, is striving to turn out more guns than ever before. Production capacity is continuously being increased by various methods, yet nearly every really *good* make and model is in short supply at the consumer level. Certain special interest guns—of which the Smith & Wesson M29/44 Magnum and M59/9mm auto are excellent examples—are bringing more than twice their established retail price on the open market. Believe it or not, some dealers have listed the long-barreled M29 at $450 each! Robbery without a gun! Or is it?

This isn't to say there aren't lots of new handguns around—there are, but they turn over rapidly, and even the ubiquitous 4-inch, fixed-sight 38 Special revolvers don't dwell long in dealers' shelves. One local dealer I know well tells me he orders regularly from a round dozen wholesalers, so he gets a lot of guns, but never enough; his shelves remain thinly populated.

One of the biggest factors effecting availability of handguns is the long strike (April to August) at Colt's last year. For a major supplier to be out of production nearly 5 months is certain to greatly increase demand on the relatively few other makers. Another significant factor is greatly increased law-enforcement buying. Not only are the numbers of officers increasing rapidly, but each new man or woman usually requires at least two guns, and many obtain three or more by issue and purchase. In addition to that, many departments are replacing older handguns at a rapid rate. A prime example of this is that virtually all of the many thousands of S&W M59 autos produced in the past year have gone to fill outstanding law-enforcement orders. Even at that, there is a backlog of several months production. Similar situations exist for numerous other makes and models.

All told, over 2,500,000 *new* handguns were sold in this country during 1973—without even coming close to filling all the orders.

One obvious result of demand exceeding supply are the high "black market" prices demanded for many models. Another reason, even more important to professional gun users, is the general deterioration of quality I've mentioned before in these pages.

The most common new-gun complaints are failures of autos to feed (even with standard metal-cased cartridges), and horribly rough functioning in revolvers. Next in line would probably be hard extraction in revolvers. All of these 'plaints are due—in my considered opinion—to too hurried assembly without those few final touches of hand work essential to the smooth operation of first-class guns. Though we are told that all guns are test-fired before shipment, it's awfully hard to believe when new guns, fresh out of the box, fail to function well even for the first loading.

But it isn't all bad news—far from it. Manufacturers are getting so much heat we are certain that quality will improve soon.

More interesting, anyway, are the new developments nearing completion and availablilty. We know of at least one intriguing new autoloader cartridge well along toward production—and its performance will exceed anything currently available in a service-type gun.

Ever since the Walther TPH was eliminated by GCA '68, pistoleros have drooled over the Budischowsky TP-70 DA pocket auto. None was available until now—but in April I visited the Norarmco plant where it is made, and I saw guns coming off the line. By now several hundred per month should be filtering into the marketplace. The same is true of the Indian Arms stainless-steel copy of the Walther PPK.

Some other guns we expected to see by now have failed to appear, and we simply cannot predict with any certainty they'll be available soon. Among them are the American Firearms stainless 380 auto, and the Sterling Arms DA 380 auto. Others that have had lots of publicity as prototypes are no nearer production now than they were this time last year.

One particular gun that generated much interest was the Spanish/American Colt Pony, a locked-breech 380 autoloader. Announced and shown by Colt early in 1973, it appears to be a dead issue now. When Colt authorities were queried recently about the Pony, they answered "Don't look for it." I take that to mean there won't be any 380 Pony in the foreseeable future.

On the bright side, Charter Arms did get its 44 Special Bulldog 5-shooter off the mark, and they're now shipping them out in quantity. It's a fine little gun for its intended purpose.

The Spanish Star auto in 45 ACP—a 23-ounce light pistol, and correspondingly small sized—has been announced.

High Standard has a couple of new replica black powder caplock revolvers, and Colt has announced two commemorative single action sixshooters.

As for trends and predictions, look for more slow-moving models to be discontinued. The small 32 revolvers are on the way out, and the days of the 41 Magnum are numbered. We'll see fewer new models in the future than the past, at least until that happy day when backlogs are wiped out and it is practicable to devote production capacity to them.

We will see more double-action autos, and more small guns chambered for more potent cartridges. There will be more stainless-steel handguns; several Ruger SS models may be on sale as you read this. Colt is the only one of the Big Three handgun makers without a stainless model now. You can expect more potent small-size revolvers, and S&W is sure eventually to counter Colt's improved Cobra and Detective Special with a small-frame 6-shot 38 Special.

Keep your eyes peeled. You'll see some mighty interesting things on the handgun scene before too long. ●

Outstanding American Handgunner

Colonel Charles Askins, world-famed champion pistol marksman, won this 1974 top handgunning award—and the big bronze trophy that goes with it—at ceremonies held early this year.

by JOHN T. AMBER

The first of the annual Outstanding American Handgunner Awards was presented in 1973, and I had the good fortune to participate in that worthy event. The 1974 second such ceremonies were held at the McCormick Inn in Chicago March 9, the day before the NSGA show opened. It was, of course, a bit smoother, what with some experience behind us all, and things went off well, if I may say so—I presided at the 1974 affair also.

Speculation was rife beforehand as to who the '74 winner might be. During the pre-presentation cocktail party it appeared to be a tossup between some three of the Top Ten contenders. Everybody except the Selection Committee and Lee Jurras and Ernie Wallien of Super Vel had to sweat it out, though, for this year the committee selection remained secret until the last moment.

The winner was, as the nearby photo shows, an old and valued friend—Col. Charles Askins, late of the U. S. Army, and widely known throughout the world to members of the shooting fraternity.

National Pistol Champion in the late 1930s as a U. S. Border Patrol officer, Askins has burned powder all his life; first at his father's (Maj. Charles Askins) knee, then in the U. S. Forest Service, the Border Patrol and the U. S. Army through a couple of wars and other shooting actions. More important to the winning of this award were Askins' continuous efforts to promote handgunning, to improve guns and equipment, and to likewise improve the shooting breed. A prolific—if sometimes controversial—writer, Askins has authored 8 books and hundreds of articles, several of the latter appearing in this book. He has related his experiences and given his informed views freely, with the hope that shooting in general and handgunning in particular would grow.

Askins is a living example that guns do not of themselves corrupt or commit crimes. For over 20 years he used his guns daily to support the laws of the land, and to survive personally—yet during that same period he employed those same guns as recreational and skill-developing tools. Askins credits much of his own development as a man, as a human being, to shooting as an avocation.

Askins was voted the winner as a member of the Top Ten—ten handgunners chosen from all walks of life. All are known for their accomplishments in the handgunning field (which are not limited to shooting expertise alone) and you'll recognize most if not all of them.

Joe Benner, late U. S. Army, many times National Pistol Champion and former coach of the West Point Pistol Team.

Bill Blankenship, late U. S. Army, Olympic Gold Medal winner and several-times National Pistol Champion.

Jeff Cooper, combat pistolcraft specialist and instructor on an international scale, arms consultant, author and editor.

Steve Herrett, handgun hunter par excellence, founder of Herrett's Stocks, and an avid promoter of handgunning.

J. D. Jones, handgun enthusiast, ammunition experimenter, author and perennial hunter of big game with handguns.

Bill Jordan, retired U. S. Border Patrol officer, author, competitive and exhibition shooter, and NRA representative.

Thell Reed, exhibition shooter, fast-draw world record holder, and actor.

Wm. B. Ruger, founder of Sturm, Ruger & Co., firearms inventor and developer of the Ruger handgun line, and responsible for the renaissance of the single action revolver.

Skeeter Skelton, author, handgun buff and hunter, late U. S. Enforcement Officer, and former competitive shooter.

These men have contributed much to handgunning, and it is significant that several of them have since been selected for the 1975 Top Ten.

These annual awards aren't solely a Super Vel promotion—though Lee Jurras and Ernie Wallien should get due credit for initiating and furthering the project. The Super Vel role was low-keyed from the beginning, and numerous other shooting industry members have participated in various ways. Among these are Garcia, Charter Arms, High Standard, Sturm-Ruger, Wesson Arms, Interarms, Navy Arms, Browning, Thompson/Center, Custom Gun Shop, TDE, Inc. (Auto-Mag), and Security Arms.

Industry participation was increased over last year and, from the general attitude displayed, there will be more and more industry involvement in the future.

A number of well-known, public figures also participated, including ex-Sheriff Buford (Walking Tall) Pusser, the guest speaker, and Don Mitchell (High Standard), industry spokesman. Significantly, not one of the several Illinois political figures invited made an appearance. Apparently none was willing to associate himself, however briefly, with handgunning in any way. Well, considering the fanatical opposition of Mayor Daley and other influential politicians to private ownership of any firearms at all, that's understandable.

All things considered, it was a good show, for which Jurras and Wallien deserve much credit. This is an important new vehicle for handgunning promotion, and I fervently hope it continues to grow. The 1975 program will be held in Houston, Texas, in conjunction with the NSGA convention—and I'll bet the Texas politicos don't boycott it.

New Compact 45 Auto

Making the old GI 45 auto a more compact weapon has been a continuous project since 1911, when it was introduced. The result has been such real nice pieces as the Swensen Bob-Cat and some butchered up dogs.

Well, at last someone has gone and designed a pocket-sized double action 45 auto. His name is Frank Thomas Jr. and the pistols should be in production this fall by Alexander James Arms, a division of N&N Mini-Craft Corp., of Covina, California.

As the photo shows, the new pistol looks nothing like the Colt 45. It has a stationary 3½" barrel, overall length is 6⅜", and it's 4⅝" high by 1" thick. It weighs 33½ ounces. Made entirely of steel, the compact Thomas Pistol holds 7 rounds plus one in the chamber, and uses a shortened Colt 45 magazine. Hard chrome finished, the pistol has wood grips.

The usual lockup mechanism is actuated by hand pressure, via a lever in the back strap, similar to a grip safety. A simple bar blocks the slide until the right amount of pressure is applied; then the bar lowers, allowing the gun to fire and function. Recoil is no worse than the Government 45 offers, so it can be handled quite easily.

As noted, the Thomas 45 is a double action handgun, and it is that only. There are only 3 major moving parts—trigger, transfer bar and firing pin. Pulling the trigger about ¾ of the way back releases the firing pin, firing the cartridge. Trigger pull weight, about 5 pounds, is smooth. The slide locks open after the last round is fired. The magazine disconnector can be readily removed if desired.

It's an impressive looking gun and, though not yet fixed, it will sell for about $200.00. *Walter L. Rickell.*

This is how the Cresap L-Tronic Night Sights appear in dim or dark conditions.

L-Tronic Night Sight

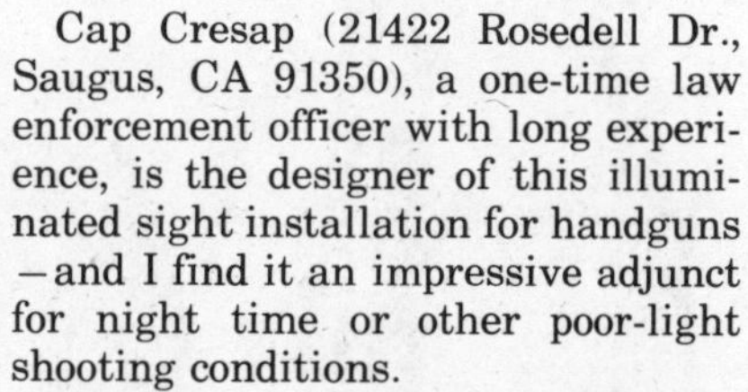

Cap Cresap (21422 Rosedell Dr., Saugus, CA 91350), a one-time law enforcement officer with long experience, is the designer of this illuminated sight installation for handguns—and I find it an impressive adjunct for night time or other poor-light shooting conditions.

Shock proof (the system withstands 44 Magnum forces) and non-radioactive, the front and rear sights as installed by Cresap are Nicad battery operated by means of a second-finger pressure plate set into the left grip—for right-hand shooters.

The installation I saw was well done—wires were concealed, the battery lies between the grips, and a casual examination shows only an ordinary revolver. Grab the gun and raise it to shooting stance, though, and as soon as the small wood disc is touched there's a big difference—in dim or dark conditions the front and rear sights appear red, and a good sight line-up is readily achieved, no matter how black the night.

The device has been tested and approved by the Los Angeles Police Dept., and everyone I've demonstrated it for seems to like it.

So far the L-Tronic Night Sight is made only for revolvers with sight ramps, but Cresap says that other types of guns—including shotguns—will soon be done as well.

Cost of the installation is $53, including a battery charger, and the gun is perfectly usable if the sights malfunction for any reason.

Cap Cresap will gladly supply complete details, shipping instructions, etc. J.T.A.

No-Sho Gun Mounts

The No-Sho "holster" was described and illustrated in our 28th edition, page 212—in brief for now, these Corfam-covered stainless steel handgun belt carriers are ultralight (at a few ounces or so) and they're made in such open, coverless fashion that truly fast draw is easily possible with them. No-Sho gun mounts are fully described in a free folder—they sell for $19.95 retail. Write to the company at 10727 Glenfield Ct., Houston, TX 77035.

Now, though, let me tell about the Custom Made Combat Grip shown nearby on a S&W Chiefs' Special. These can be had for just about any revolver or auto pistol, and each grip set is made to fit the customer's hand.

Woods used are rosewood, ebony, zebra, teak and cocobola, selected for figure, color and freedom from imperfections. Depending on the wood selected, grip size and labor, these Combat Grips by No-Sho run from $39.95 to $59.95 for revolvers. Most auto pistol grips cost about $26.

Our photo fails to reveal the rich color in this rosewood Combat Grip, but I can tell you it's a comfortable, handfilling handle, and one that absorbs recoil to a good degree. J.T.A.

New Swiss Target Pistol

The latest in centerfire target pistols is the SIG-Hämmerli Model P240, an autoloader chambered primarily for 38 Special ammunition in wadcutter form. A conversion unit, caliber 22 Long Rifle, is also offered.

The new P240 weighs just over 41 ounces with a 5-shot clip (slightly more with the 10-shot 22LR magazine), has a 6" barrel and fully adjustable micro-click rear sight, its square notch ⅛" wide.

The new gun is a semi-automatic—an autoloader, more correctly—its action a locked, recoil-operated design.

The 2-stage trigger is adjustable, and has a trigger stop. There is a positive safety, and take-down is said to be simple.

The thumb-rest grips shown in our photograph are for a right-handed shooter, and unfinished grips (pre-inletted) are offered as well. Whether thumb rest grips are available for southpaws is not known.

Gil Hebard Guns (Box 1, Knoxville, IL 61448) is the new and exclusive importer for Hämmerli pistol models 120, 150, 208 and 230, as well as for the SIG-Hämmerli P240 described here. Prices are not fixed at this time, but one thing is certain—they won't be cheap. J.T.A.

Speer, Inc.

Speer has a couple of new lead bullets, both flat-base semi-wadcutters, that will appeal, I'm sure, to big caliber handloading handgunners. One, meant for 44 Special/Magnum loading, weighs 240 grains, measures .430-inch, and is made with grease and crimp grooves. The second one, somewhat similar to the other, is a .452-inch bullet of 250 grains, intended for 45 Colt/45 Auto Rim use.

Both bullets are lubricated all over with Film-Cote, a new treatment that Speer says will do away with leading—well, nearly so. I know—as soon as this is published some guy is sure to write and tell us—or Speer—that he leaded the hell out of his barrel with one of these bullets! J.T.A.

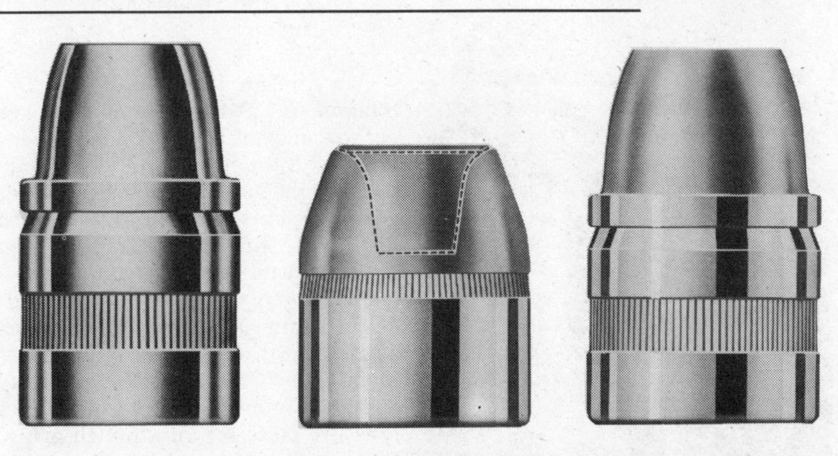

From left—Speer's new 240-gr. 44-cal. semi-wadcutter; 200-gr. 45-cal. hollow point, and their 250-gr. SWC, also in 45 caliber. All are covered with a new lube called Film-Cote, said to virtually eliminate leading.

Thompson/Center

In addition to the recently-introduced Seneca caplock rifle—a lightweight hunting rifle at 6 lbs. or so, which is reviewed elsewhere in this 29th edition—T/C has greatly improved the Contender barrel for their 357 and 44 Hotshot shot cartridges. The new barrel, chambered for the 357 or 44 Magnum cartridge, and straight-rifled, is a trimmer, neater job by virtue of its redesigned form. This choked sleeve or tube now threads *inside* the main barrel, thus reducing the whole to the same diameter or nearly so and, as well, permitting a lower front sight at the end of the rifled barrel proper. As before, of course, with the Hotshot choke tube removed, the Contender becomes a 357 or 44 Magnum pistol. J.T.A.

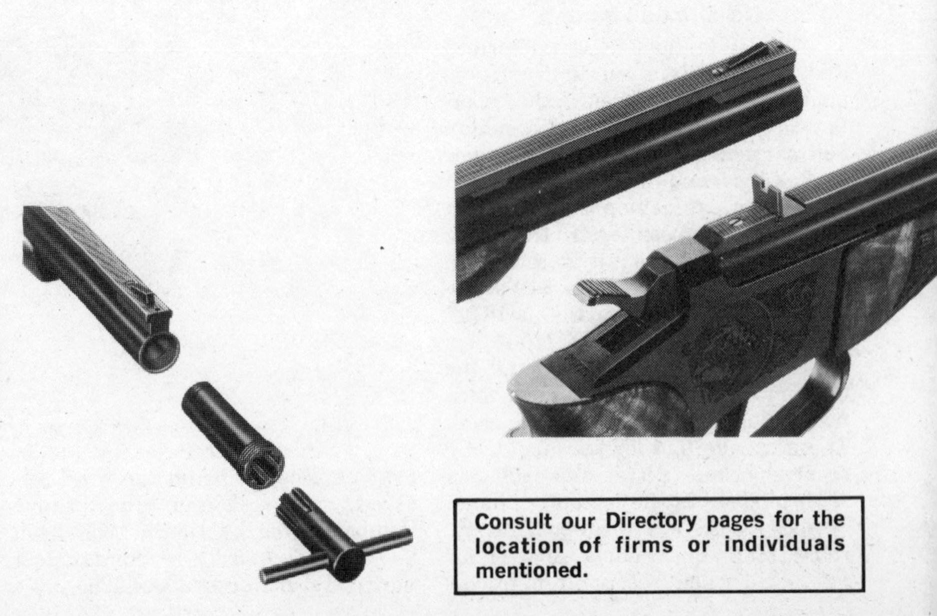

Consult our Directory pages for the location of firms or individuals mentioned.

Mag-Na-Port

It's still a little hard to believe, but it's true—send a handgun, rifle or shotgun (single barrel or over-under; no side-by-sides yet) to Mag-Na-Port and, only a few days or so later, the arm is returned, the operation completed. The slots or ports are readily seen if you look closely, but there is no indication of how the job was done—all edges are clean and crisp, no roughness or file marks whatsoever. This even applies to nickeled guns, in which some flaking or fraying of the plating might be expected, perhaps. Not so—clean as a whistle.

How is it done? By EDM, which stands for "electro-discharge machining," a modern metal-cutting technique that would take more space than I've got to describe in detail. Briefly, a carefully controlled electrical flow eats or etches away the pre-determined shape of the parts, with outer and inner surfaces completely free of burrs.

What does Mag-Na-Port do for the gun and its user? Its essential job is recoil reduction, and studies have shown that felt-recoil is reduced by as much as 15% with high-energy handgun loads—as in the magnums—but less so with lighter loads. But the latter don't really *need* reduction, do they?

The Mag-Na-Ports slots are cut to vent the burning powder gases upward at about a 45° angle, thus the barrel is held down for faster subsequent-shot recovery, and the twisting or torque effect on the shooter's hand is reduced.

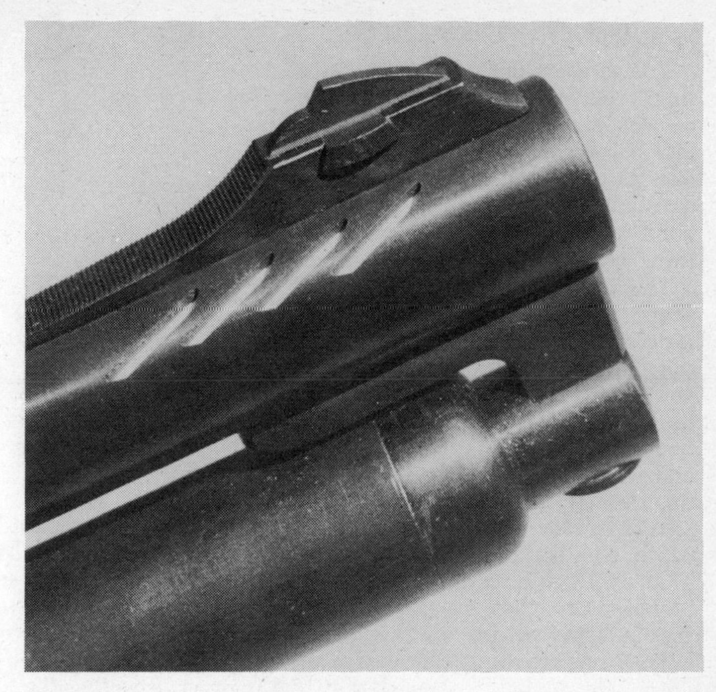

This is how the Mag-Na-Port cuts look on a rifle. Four like cuts appear on the other side, of course.

Because Mag-Na-Porting is relatively new as applied to shotguns, I elected to send Larry Kelley a rifled slug barrel I use in a Winchester M1200 pump gun. I wanted to see how much the heavier recoil of 12-gauge slug loads might be reduced. I wasn't disappointed—I didn't have any figures on just how much shoulder punch is lessened, but the *total* effect is considerably softened. I say "total" because I'm sure that the reduced muzzle jump contributed much to the whole recoil-sensation lessening. I know this much—that slug gun is more of a pleasure to shoot than it used to be—and I'm not ordinarily recoil sensitive.

Now, because their Mag-Na-Porting work has brought so many handguns into their shop, with many requests for pistolsmithing at the same time—Kelley and his partners are accepting such work, on handguns chiefly, but some rifle and shotguns jobs are handled, too.

Full information is available on all work. Write to Mag-Na-Port at 16746—14 Mile Rd., Fraser, MI 48026.

J.T.A.

Numrich Luger Barrels

At a mere $13.55, here's a ready means of upgrading that war souvenir, though it will also cost you something more to have the old barrel pulled and the new 4½" Numrich barrel—caliber 9mm—installed.

The photo shows what appears to be a well-machined, properly sighted barrel, crisply and sharply made, but we haven't seen one.

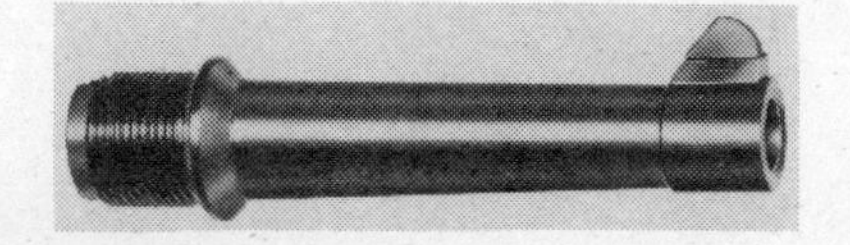

Ransom Rests

The Ransom Master Series handgun rest was briefly described last year (28th ed. page 210). This is an excellently made tool, highly useful if you want to know just how well *your* handgun is shooting—or your handloads. Grip inserts are available for many handgun, foreign or domestic, and the cost of the Master Series rest in 1974 is $112.50, including one set of inserts.

New for this year is an accessory unit for the Master Series rest—and a useful item it should be. This is a Windage Base, and it's intended to do just what the name implies. The price will be under $40, and it will fit the earlier-type Ransom rests as well.

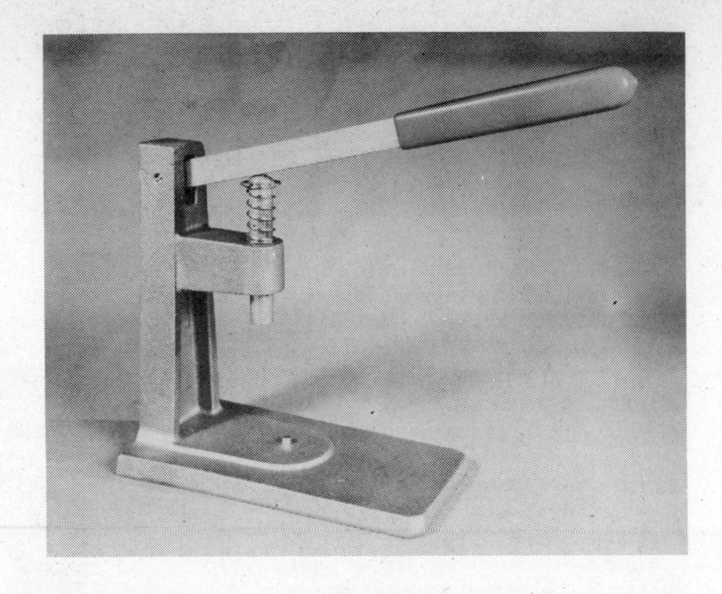

Caplock Revolver Loader

You've seen 'em behind the firing line at black powder matches, their caplock sixshooters cradled more or less awkwardly in their left hand and arm as they struggle to load powder and ball into the chambers. A third hand to grab and lower that loading lever would be pretty handy.

The useful tool shown here just about answers that plea—all that's needed is to remove the cylinder from the gun, charge the chambers with powder and place the cylinder—on the built-in pivot pin—then seat the balls by pulling down on the lever. The fuss and excess effort disappears and, more importantly for good shooting, each ball is seated to the same uniform depth. The bottom end of the ram is grooved all around at 1/16″ intervals—choose one that suits your operation and stay with it.

The rams are nicely concaved to approximate 44 ball size, and they're also center-relieved to take the sprue projection. Construction is all metal—aluminum and steel. Weight is less than 1¾ lbs., and the base dimensions—6″x3¼″—offer good stability.

The Standard Model (pictured) loads 44 caliber original and replica Remingtons, as well as the New Army Ruger caplock. These 44s are in stock, but 36 and 31 caliber tools (or spare rams) can be furnished without extra cost if ordered with the tool, or bought at $2.50 as extras. The tool complete is $17.95, postpaid in the U.S., and I think it's good value. J.C. Hoelle, 2231 Charlotte Ave., Ft. Wayne, IN 46805 is the maker. J.T.A.

Interarms P-08 Parabellum

This year the Mauser-made Luger of 1929 Swiss-type that Interarms has offered for some years will have a near-twin.

The P-08 Parabellum autoloader differs from the Swiss model in various ways—the new-production pistol has the curved lower front strap, the traditional old trigger, take-down lever and a *GELADEN*-marked extractor/loaded indicator. The new P-08 will also show an American Eagle engraved atop the receiver and, as the photo shows, a grip safety.

The caliber first available is 9mm Parabellum (Luger), with 7.65 barrels coming along later, 4″ or 6″ lengths. The P-08—mechanically quite like the Swiss-type version—lists at $350. J.T.A.

J-R Grips

The unusual and functional grips pictured here, supplied in genuine rosewood, are made exclusively for the S&W Chiefs Special (round butt) and the new-Model Colt Detective Special, Cobra or Agent.

This is a good hand-filling grip—the finger grooves fit my hand well, without any cramping of the little finger and, as can be seen, the grips are shaped as well to offer support to the second finger.

Perhaps the most important aspect, though, is their high coverage of the frame, giving a full hammer-shroud effect, and thus avoiding possible snagging of the hammer on clothing or whatever. The hammer, note, can readily be cocked when desired. Recoil, naturally, will be reduced by such grips, and with full loads particularly.

These J.R. grips are $24 a pair (plus $1 for postage and handling. The high quality quick-draw holster seen—made by Bianchi—is spring-loaded, comes in black or brown, left- or right hand, cost $11.95. J.T.A.

New Bulldog Holster

A new belt holster, designed specifically for the Charter Arms Bulldog 44 Specials has been introduced. Hand made of lightweight, top grade saddle leather, molded for a snug fit, it is nylon stitched and reinforced for durability. A rich cordovan color, the high-riding holster has a front snap for both security and accessibility. A quick thumb motion unsnaps the retaining strap for a natural fast draw.

Want a pocket-size folder describing the full line of handguns offered by Charter Arms?

This handsomely done booklet is printed in full color; illustrations and brief descriptions are offered on the Bulldog 44 Spl., Undercover 38 Spl., Undercoverette 32 and the Pathfinder 22. Also included is information on matching holsters, optional Bulldog grips, other accessories and engraving.

For free copies, write: Pocket Folder, Charter Arms Corp., 265 Asylum St., Bridgeport, CT 06610.

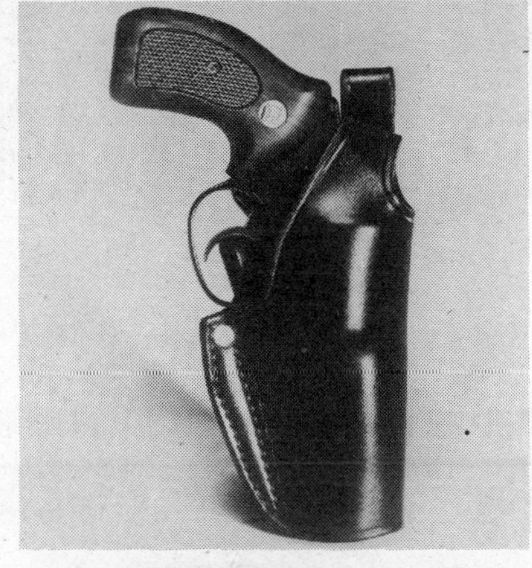

Arizona Ranger Colt

An Arizona Ranger commemorative handgun, the latest in a series of Colt guns issued to honor important people and events in American history, was presented by Colt Firearms earlier this year to Senator Barry Goldwater at his home in Scottsdale, Arizona. Production of these will be only 3,000.

The revolver, a single-action "Peacemaker 22," salutes the famed Arizona Rangers. Formed in 1901 and disbanded 7 years later, they set an enviable record for crime fighting that helped pave Arizona's road to statehood. A favorite arm of the Rangers was the Colt Single Action Army revolver.

The Arizona commemorative has a royal blue 5½" barrel, the back strap and trigger guard are nickel-plated, as are the hammer and trigger, and its stocks are of rosewood with nickeled Colt medallions. The presentation case, made of oiled walnut, has an Arizona Ranger badge permanently affixed to its inside bottom.

Garcia's New 45 Auto

Pete Dickey, head of Firearms International, a Garcia division, showed me a new and highly compact auto-loading pistol at the Atlanta (Ga.) NRA meeting, but then swore me to secrecy! The gun was a prototype, couldn't be reported on, etc.

Now, though, it can be told—I've just had a letter from Pete, giving me *approximate* specs and an OK to tell our readers about the new 45. Here's the dope, but be warned that their newest Star-made pistol won't be available until the end of the year, if that early.

As these figures show, the 45 Star is quite close to the same maker's Starlight autoloaders in dimensions and weight, which makes the new pistol a small, light handgun, especially for one in that caliber. The specimen I handled in Atlanta was certainly ultra light, but it fitted my hand well—apart from an inevitable bit of shortness in the grip—and it appeared to be very nicely put together. The barrel length (not given to us) is about 4 inches.

Caliber: 45 ACP
Weight: 22-24 oz. **Length:** 7 1/16". **Height:** 4 5/8".
Frame: Forged duraluminum, all other parts steel.
Mag. capacity: Six.
Safeties: Standard Star thumb safety, blocking hammer, plus disconnector and half-cock notch.
Firing pin: True inertia type.
Grips: Checkered walnut.
Sights: Low profile, fully click-adjustable rear (W&E), following normal slide contour.
Price: Probably $175, retail.

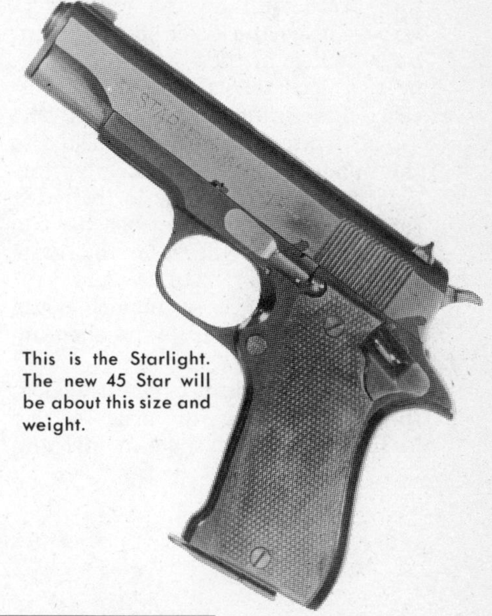

This is the Starlight. The new 45 Star will be about this size and weight.

High Standard

Rumors were rife at the N.S.G.A. show that Don Mitchell, president of High Standard, was on the verge of buying an interest in the company now making Auto Mag pistols (357 and 44 AMP), perhaps even acquiring the whole shebang, setting up a new and bigger plant, etc.

Nor did the rumors stop there—it was also hinted about that the same Don Mitchell was going to obtain distribution of a new Jerry Haskins-designed rifle. Haskins was displaying at the N.S.G.A. show an ultra-fancy, fully engraved bolt action rifle that was priced at about $3500! High Standard would, it was said, market a standard form of the new-action Haskins rifle.

What's the situation now? Nobody seems to know, or at least doesn't want to say.

High Standard does, however, have two new handguns, both near-replicas of Civil War revolvers, these the first in a series they call "Arms of the Confederacy." One of these copies the Leech & Rigdon, the other the Griswold & Gunnison, both famed in their own original day, and both produced in imitation then of the caplock Navy Colt, caliber 36. J.T.A.

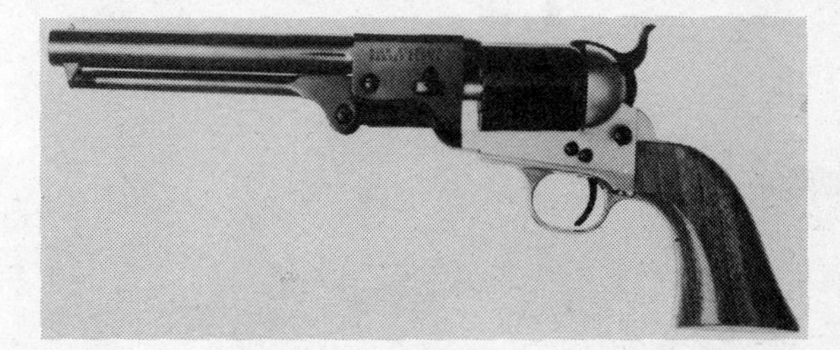

SHOOTING at 1000 YARDS

That's a hell of a long way to shoot a rifle—and it's not much easier to score well than it was a hundred years ago! Despite great advances in the making of barrels and bullets, the over-all group averages aren't all that much smaller than they were at Creedmoor. The top shooters? They do a lot better.

BY BOB BELL

IF YOUR EYESIGHT is good and the weather is better, you might not need optical aid to see that 12-inch bullseye 'way out there on the mountain. That bull on the military A target forms the basic aiming point for riflemen in these matches. However, a good target scope is a necessity for defining and aiming at the 4-inch white square thumbtacked to the middle. The reason such big targets are so hard to see is their distance from the shooting benches—to be precise, 1022 yards, for the range was deliberately fixed by survey at this odd distance so no one could accuse these competitors of shooting a "short 1000."

Now, 1000 yards—honest-to-God, three-feet-to-the-yard yards—is one helluva distance to shoot at anything with a rifle. It's well over half a mile, and the first time a garden-variety deer shooter or self-deluding antelope hunter gazes downrange toward those distant specks of black (which happen to approximate the vital area of a pronghorn or whitetail) his long-bragged-on tales of 700- or 800-yard kills—on running game!—suddenly begin sliding toward more realistic estimates, perhaps parelleling the sinking feeling in his stomach.

Yet all summer long, at roughly two-week intervals, some 100 shooters pile ponderous bench rifles, boxes of precisely handloaded ammo and assorted scopes, sandbags, etc., into their cars and make the trek to a mountaintop, leased from Irvin E. Plants, about 24 miles northeast of Williamsport, Pa.—the site of the Original Pennsylvania 1000-Yard Benchrest Club, Inc. Some of them drive hundreds of miles to compete. Most are from Pennsylvania, of course, but others come from the surrounding states and others not so near. Occasionally some gifted rifleman, unable to go on not knowing how his skill stacks up against these top rifles, makes the long trip from perhaps the other side of the continent, doubtless driven by the same urge that sent gunslingers of our frontier days toward Abilene, Dodge or Tombstone—wherever the current No. One Gun hung out.

During the actual 1000-yd. match competition, coaching is not allowed and shots are not spotted. When conditions change—as they often do during the 10-minute period—the shooter must dope them as best he can and make his own allowances.

Results aren't as final here. A second-place finisher can come back next match and maybe take all the marbles. In fact, there are two first-place winners in every shootout here, for there are in effect two objectives in each—smallest group and highest score—and one shooter cannot win both in a given match. That is, if the smallest group happens to be so well centered that it also scores the highest, that shooter wins for group (in earlier years he took top score), but the next-highest score wins that category.

A day's competition is called a "shoot," and each relay of 10 shooters (the range currently has 10 covered benches) is termed a "match." The riflemen turning in the smallest group and highest score in each match compete in a shootoff at the end of the day to determine the day's two over-all winners.

Simple Rules

Basic rules are simple. Before each match there's a 6-minute period during which an unlimited number of shots may be fired. Each shot is spotted as it's fired with a military-type disc that's visible through the scope, and coaching is permitted. The objectives at this time are to get zeroed and do some doping of wind and mirage.

A match consists of 10 shots fired for record during a 10-minute period. No sighters are permitted and shots are not spotted. If conditions change—as they usually do, for there are two small valleys between the benches and the butts, and sometimes the wind is blowing in opposite directions in each—it's up to the shooter to make corrections based on his own experience and ability. This often leads to a beautiful 9-shot group.

Pit personnel (everyone takes turns pulling targets) make a small replica of each target on which they locate and number every shot as it's fired. This is taped to the real target, which is rough scored and signed by the pit men, and returned to the rear for official scoring. Targets are given to the shooters, along with the replica which shows him how his group formed. Integrated with notes he makes during firing, this helps him build up a backlog of data during a summer. This keeping track of range conditions, "holds," etc., can be vitally important.

Long-range riflemen Bill Theis and Dave Troxell, of Williamsport, and George Reeder, of Cogan Station, Pa., organized the club in 1967, and it was incorporated in August of 1968. It seemed a logical extension of the bench shooting game which has fascinated so many dedicated shooters since the end of World War II. If little round holes in targets at 100 and 200 yards were interesting, they should be even more so at 5 or 10 times those distances, right? Too, the long range would not only permit, but even make almost necessary, the Magnum cartridges which intrigue many shooters nowadays—those oversize powder-gobblers so out of place at the short distances.

The concept gained an immediate following. In the first year of competition attendance averaged over 50 riflemen per shoot, with a total of 121 different entrants. Almost twice that number of shooters is average now (see Table I), and 173 different shooters competed in 1973. It should be mentioned right now that a significant percentage of these "riflemen" are women. There's nothing at all uncommon about somebody's wife or daughter using Pop's big gun (or maybe her own) during the day, and typical female scores fit right into the males' avergaes. In fact, the smallest group fired in competition to date is the 7.687-incher turned in by Mary Louise DeVito in 1970 with her 7mm-300 Weatherby.

The 1000-yd. firing line in 1973.

Rifles and Barrels

There are few restrictions on equipment. Each rifle must be mechanically safe and no return-to-battery machine-rest type rigs are allowed. The rifle must be rested on sandbags front and rear. Otherwise, the sky's the limit, but the truth is, most rifles are conventional in appearance to anyone used to bull barrels, thumbhole laminated stocks and target scopes. Turnbolt actions are the only logical choice for the Magnum cartridges used by most, and all common models are seen. Remington M700s and 40Xs, Winchester 70s and FN Mausers are the most numerous among commercial actions. Military Mausers and Springfields are chosen by many, the crude but strong M38 Japanese Arisaka by a few, and the big beautifully built custom actions of Howard Wolfe, Bob Hart and Ed Shilen by others. Most actions are used as single shots, the lack of a magazine well permitting a more rigid stock, and many are sleeved, which stiffens the action and gets the scope bases off the barrel.

Barrels by such top custom makers as Hart, Douglas and Shilen are used by the majority, though some have found commercial outfits, particularly from the Remington custom shop, deliver equivalent accuracy. Whereas many 200-yard benchresters have gone to short barrels for various reasons, longer ones—28 to 30 inches usually—are favored here, as they give more velocity from the slow-burning powders needed in Magnum cases, and cut down muzzle blast. Full diameters are common, the weight helping to reduce recoil and making precise holding easier.

Stocks tend to be king-size, laminated to reduce warping, flat-bottomed for easier control, with a thumbhole to allow straight-back trigger movement. Glass or metal bedding is used around the action and the first few inches of the barrel. Occasionally barrels are glassed full length. Various bedding techniques have been tried in addition to "normal" glassing, especially by Mechanicsburg, Pa., rifle-builder Al Wardrop, a longtime contender in these shoots and for several decades a competitor in conventional rifle matches.

Wardrop's Methods

Wardrop sleeves most of the rifles he builds, and has several ways of doing it. His sleeves are seamless steel tubing having .250" wall thickness with an inside diameter about ¼" greater than the barrel diameter; this gives ⅛" clearance all around the barrel. By one method, a 9" length of sleeve is centered over the barrel with the sleeve's rear end near the front of the receiver ring. The inside of the sleeve and the portion of barrel it encloses are slighly roughened. The space between the barrel and sleeve is then filled with glass. The outside of the sleeve is also glassed and screwed into the stock, but the receiver and the unsleeved section of the barrel float completely—no guard screws are used in the action. The rear face of the sleeve, trued up earlier, acts as a recoil shoulder. This face has three or four times the area of a conventional recoil shoulder. Some riflemen might feel concern that the sleeve will let go under recoil, but this has never happened to Wardrop's knowledge. Once, when he wanted to remove a sleeve, he tried heating, twisting, etc., with no noticeable effect, and ended up turning it off on the lathe. In some versions, a slightly longer sleeve also encloses the receiver ring.

This is Al Wardrop, Mechanicsburg, Pa., gunsmith who has built many of the rifles used in the 1000-yd. matches, and is himself a top competitor. Al has done a lot of experimenting with bedding techniques (described in text). Rifle seen is typical of the type used—laminated stock, broad flat fore-end, heavy barrel, target scope.

A different operation encloses the entire action, the sleeve being epoxied to the receiver and extending forward over some 6 inches of the barrel. Sometimes the sleeve clears the barrel completely, but Al prefers to pour glass to give about a half-inch collar around the barrel at the front of the sleeve. In his testing, this has always given better accuracy than a fully floating barrel. Some gunsmiths who sleeve actions completely enclose them, making it necessary to remove the bolt to extract a case and insert a cartridge, but Wardrop prefers to cut a loading port into the sleeve, perhaps sacrificing a little stiffness but making it easier to remove a case that's suffered a head separation. With the sleeved action, he usually installs several ¼" allen screws through the sleeve and into the action, to increase the safety factor if by some chance the glass should let go during firing. Again, the rear face of the sleeve acts as the recoil shoulder, though in some cases he has added another one by soldering a ¼"-thick piece of metal, about one-third the circumference of the sleeve, to the bottom of the sleeve.

Table 1
Average Number of Competitors per Shoot

Year		Competitors
1969	–	83
1970	–	81
1971	–	91
1972	–	94
1973	–	90

High—121 at Shoot 6, Aug. 13, 1972

In all cases described above, the sleeves are glassed into the stocks and held by three or four ¼ x 28 allen head cap screws. To allow these to be pulled up firmly, Al makes 1-¼"-diameter, ½"-thick washers, and counter-sinks and epoxies them into the wood, to secure the screw heads.

A newer bedding system Wardrop has been trying consists of two steel blocks each measuring about 2" on a side. These are drilled and contoured to fit the barrel, split into halves, and installed on the barrel on 7¼" centers (which permits scope block mounting on top). Four ¼ x 28 allen head cap screws bind the halves together. The bottom halves are glassed into the stock, while everything else floats.

Some of these systems seem unconventional, but Wardrop-built rifles have been among the winners for years.

Target scopes are used almost universally in these matches, to take advantage of their comparatively precise adjustments (a quarter-minute click gives a 2½" change at 1000 yards!) and good optics. Medium magnifications, 15x to 20x, are generally preferred, as they give less mirage trouble than the 24x to 30x models popular with the short range bench shooters. As weight is no worry, the 2" Unertl is a favorite of many, with others choosing the solidly mounted 3200 Redfield or the older Lyman Super Targetspot. A few old 6-24x Bausch & Lombs are seen (usually with Unertl type mounts), the variable power making it easy to choose a magnification to suit conditions.

Choice of Calibers

In the early days of the club, the most popular cartridge was the 6.5 WWH (Weatherby-Wright-Hoyer) Magnum (Table 2), an impressive design made by necking the 300 Weatherby case down to 6.5mm. Col. Paul Wright, a skilled long-range rifleman, fathered this creation, with the mechanical work being done by the late Al Hoyer. This Mifflintown, Pa., gunsmith, a big, quiet, kindly man, was long recognized as a leader in the extreme-range shooting game, both from the bench and in the field. It's one of the tragedies of the shooting world that he didn't take time to assemble and publish the countless facts he learned through his decades of shooting.

The 6.5 WWH seemed to be the

Calibers Winning Over-all Match or Shootoff, 1969-1973

	1969	1970	1971	1972	1973
6.5-300 WWH	5	4	2	2	0
7mm Wby. Mag.	1	0	1	0	0
7mm Rem. Mag.	0	0	0	0	1
7mm-300 Mag.	0	1	2	2	6
308 Norma Mag.	2	4	2	2	1
30-338 Mag.	0	0	0	1	0
300 Win. Mag.	2	0	2	3	2
300 Wby. Mag.	0	0	1	0	0
30-378 Mag.	0	1	0	0	0

ultimate in long-range efficiency. It won many matches, made many excellent groups. Yet after being the overwhelming choice to start with (330 matches were shot with it in 1969), it steadily dropped in favor until it was used in only 107 matches in 1973 (Table 3). By comparison, the 300 Winchester Magnum rose from 120 matches to 218 in the same period; the somewhat smaller 308 Norma Magnum held its own at around the 125 mark most of this time, and the wildcat 7mm-300, the 300 Weatherby case necked down to 284-cal., skyrocketed from a mere 17 matches in 1969 to 199 in 1973. The smaller 7mm Remington Magnum also gained a fine following after a slow start.

Different factors might be involved in the rating changes among these cartridges (many cartridges, from 6mm up through such monsters as the 30-378, are regularly shot in these 1000-yard competitions, but the 5 just named are the leaders), but the most important seems to be bullets... and perhaps an intangible known as shooter gossip.

Top-quality, properly bedded barrels and near perfect bullets are absolute necessities for all benchrest shooting. Since barrels of similar quality are available in all calibers and there is little bedding variation, at least within a given string of shots, bullet quality inherits by default most of the blame, or credit, for groups. The 6.5, for some reason, did not seem to have consistently good bullets. An inordinate amount of flyers appeared in groups fired with this caliber, many shooters said. Pit workers reported watching 8 or 9 bullets snap into a volleyball-size group, with the other shot or two wandering far out. They felt this occured too often, when compared with the 30-calibers being fired in the same match, say, to be blamed on wind or shooter error, and concluded that poor projectiles were to blame. The theory gained reinforcement when occasional shooters got supplies of "better" bullets and turned in fine groups with them. Since such bullets couldn't regularly be found, many shooters gave up on the 6.5 and turned largely to the big 30 calibers. The success of Paul Kempfer, who won the 1968 aggregate with a 12.8" average using a 308 Norma, probably had some influence on their thinking, as did the ready availability of the excellent Sierra Matchking bullets. These bullets had made the various 30-cal. Magnums hot contenders from the first, and over the long haul they gained followers as the 6.5-300 lost them.

Mary Louise DeVito with her 7mm-300. She currently holds the record for the smallest 10-shot group ever fired at the 1000-yd. range—7.687".

The Surging 7mms

Another factor was the surging 7mms, particularly the 7mm-300. This load started slowly (Table 2), then almost tripled its popularity between the end of the 1970 matches and the following season. The reasons are obvious. First, Sierra had marketed the highly efficient 168-gr. spitzer boat-tail in 7mm, and on October 11, 1970, Mary Louise De Vito put 10 of these Matchkings, kicked out by 87 grains of H570, into a 7.687" group, for a record not equaled to date, though Boydell Theis came within .188" of it in 1971, with a 7.875" group shot with a 300 Weatherby. Mrs. DeVito's effort followed by a few months a Wimbledon Cup record fired in the National Matches by Tom Treinen, who used the same bullet in a custom 7mm Remington Magnum for his win. Treinen went clean for the 20 shots of his match, putting them all into the 20-inch V-ring of the 1000-yard target, then drilled in 12 more to break a record which had been set in 1939. With examples like these, the Big 7s had to gain followers, and the trend was reinforced in 1971 when Mary Louise's husband, Guido DeVito, took the year's aggregate with a 13.5" average using the 7mm-300.

Not all shooters gave up on the 6.5-300, and more than a few were convinced that the specific cartridge had little to do with winning, reasoning that most of the top choices, regardless of caliber, used bullets of similar ballistic coefficients at similar velocities, thus should deliver similar results if the shooters did their part. They pointed out that the 6.5/140-gr., the 7mm/168-gr., and the 30/190-gr. Sierra spitzer boattails had ballistic coefficients (BCs) closer than kissin' cousins (.54-.62). All other things being equal, it seemed logical to assume that the 6.5-300 would have a little edge because it delivered higher velocity.

Looking for more of that edge based on velocity, Tom Drummond, Sr., of Williamsport, developed two series of long range cartridges. Those of most interest to the 1000-yard shooters are based on the Weatherby 300 and 378 cases. Each design

1969 Group Winners

Shoot	Name	Rifle	Group
1	Lawrence Wog	6.5-300 WWH	13.8
2	Richard Kepp	6.5-300 WWH	12.6
3	Lance Heller	7mm Wby. Magnum	9.2
4*	Walter Bryan	308 Norma Magnum	9.7
5	Art Mackey	6.5-300 WWH	11.7
6	Lee Hocker	300 Win. Magnum	8.4
7	Ray Rink	6.5-300 WWH	10.9
8	Ritchie Moorhead	300 Win. Magnum	11.1
9	Ted Mackey	6.5-300 WWH	9.6
10	Jerry Stocum	308 Norma Magnum	12.3

*Cliff Hocker shot a 9.1 group in this match, but also shot the top score—a possible 50—and under regulations then prevailing took top score rather than best group. An individual shooter is not awarded top place for both group and score in a given match.

1970 Group Winners

Shoot	Name	Rifle	Group
1	Richard Beaver	308 Norma Magnum	12.9
2	Guy Mitchell	6.5-300 WWH	12.4
3	Bob Tillinghast	308 Norma Magnum	13.4
4	Bob Longley	6.5-300 WWH	12.3
5	Earl Chronister	308 Norma Magnum	9.98
6	Frank Weber	6.5-300 WWH	10.2
7	Earl Chronister	308 Norma Magnum	9.1
8	Frank Weber	6.5-300 WWH	8.5
9	Mary Louise DeVito	7mm-300 Magnum	7.687
10	Howard Wolfe	30-378 Magnum	8.75

1971 Shootoff Winners*

Shoot	Name	Rifle	Group
1	Tom Drummond, Sr.	6.5-300	17.8
2	Joe Reitz	6.5-300	11.1
3	Guido DeVito	7mm-300 Magnum	16.3
4	Boydell Theis	300 Wby. Magnum	8.7
5	Bob Bitner	308 Norma Magnum	12.1
6	Guido DeVito	7mm-300 Magnum	12.0
7	Nick Leach	300 Win. Magnum	10.4
8	George Miller	308 Norma	12.4
9	Leonard Heller	7mm Wby. Magnum	12.7
10	Craig Steinmetz	300 Win. Magnum	17.8

*Beginning in 1971, a shootoff match was held at the end of each day, competitors being the group and score winners of the 10 matches held earlier, rather than the two men having the top score and best group out of the entire day's shooting being over-all winners, as had been done in earlier years.

1972 Shootoff Winners

Shoot	Name	Rifle	Group
1	Tony Mariano	30-378 Magnum	29.0
2	Guy Mitchell	6.5-300 WWH	13.75
3	Ken Madeira	6.5-300 WWH	12.5
4	Bill Jodun	7mm-300 Magnum	21.6
5	Clair Peters	308 Norma Magnum	13.6
6	Clair Peters	308 Norma Magnum	13.6
7	Cliff Hocker	308 Norma Magnum	19.25
8	George Reeder	300 Win. Magnum	19.0
9	(Not shot—fog)	—	—
10	Ritchie Moorhead	300 Win. Magnum	10.5

1973 Shootoff Winners

Shoot	Name	Rifle	Group
1	Eileen Baskin*	7mm-300 Magnum	11.6
2	Bob Bitner	308 Norma Magnum	12.6
3	Pete Romani	7mm-300 Magnum	11.9
4	Chet Leach	300 Win. Magnum	11.1
5	George Stephanis	7mm Rem. Magnum	8.9
6	Les Wilcox	300 Win. Magnum	11.6
7	Pete Romani	7mm-300 Magnum	19.4
8	Bill Hagerman	7mm-300 Magnum	11.9
9	Les Wilcox	7mm-300 Magnum	16.7
10	Clarence Palmer	7mm-300 Magnum	14.6

*Eileen Baskin, in this match, was the first woman to win a shootoff.

features a 60-degree shoulder, intended to give maximum powder capacity, with three calibers on each case, the 6.5mm, 7mm and 30. (For long range hunting and bench shooting at less than 1000 yards, Drummond offers 257, 264, 270, 7mm and 30-cal. cartridges, all with a 60-degree shoulder, based on the 270 Weatherby Magnum case, and for extreme-range varmint shooters 60-degree shouldered 22 and 6mm cartridges based on 240 Weatherby brass.) Drummond sells heavy bench guns and heavy sporters, all chambered by Harry Keiser and featuring stainless steel Douglas barrels. Supreme FN Mauser single shot actions are used for the bench jobs, Sako Finnbear Magnum actions for the hunting models. Actions are glass bedded, the barrels floated.

Long Range Chronographing

The Drummonds—Tom Sr. and Jr.—have done a great deal of test shooting with these loads, including chronographing for instrumental velocities and, of great interest, chronographing of remaining velocity at 1000 yards. (See table.) Avtron models K233 and T973 were used for this, with special screens for the 1000-yard shooting. These screens, 7½ x 14 inches, are custom made of plastic with metallic ink as a conductor. A 5-foot spacing was used for the 1000-yard testing, with a minimum of 3 shots (usually 5) for average. At this range, it normally was necessary to fire far more shots than that to get the requisite hits, but it was less expensive to shoot up the ammo than to pay for larger screens.

Drummond told me he thought that the comparatively new 162-gr. Hornady boat-tail HP 7mm bullet, with an advertised ballistic coefficient of .725, was the greatest long range projectile he had found, the first bullet he felt was superior to the 6.5mm. However, many longtime Big 7 shooters, including the DeVitos, stick with the 168-gr. Sierra Matchking, which has a BC of .628.*

The Drummond cartridges came into common use during the 1971 season, and a number of fine groups have been made with them since. However, they have not, at this

*In recent test firing with a Remington 40X 7mm Rem. Magnum, 27½" barrel, Drummond got the following results: Hornady 162-gr., 68½/N205, Fed. 215—muzzle velocity 3245 fps, remaining velocity at 1000 yds. 1852, loss 1393; Sierra 168-gr., 67½/N205, Fed. 215—MV 3180 fps, remaining velocity at 1000 yds. 1760, loss 1420. Since the Sierra bullet lost only 27 fs more than the Hornady over 1000 yards, I'm dubious whether the ballistic coefficients actually are as different as indicated. B.B.

writing, proved more accurate than smaller, more-conventional Magnums. Their higher velocity should be a benefit, but possibly their speed requires bullets even more perfect than those now available. One thing is certain: even this group of shooters, to whom the roar of a Magnum is routine, notices when one of these big Drummonds blasts off.

Rifle nut Cliff Hocker, of Camp Hill, Pa. who has long believed that any cartridge in this general class of Magnums can do the job, proved this to his own satisfaction by taking the 1972 aggregate with a 15.4″ average compiled with 4 or 5 different rifles—6.5-300, a couple of Big 7s and several

Each shooter takes his turn pulling and marking targets in the pits. A 4″ white square is thumbtacked to the center of the black bull to provide a better aiming point for the scope—on those shots where the shooter actually aims at the bull. Sometimes he might be holding several feet off.

1969 Score Winners

Shoot	Name	Rifle	Score
1	Leonard Heller	7mm Wby.	45
2	Mike Grove	6.5-300	46
3	Craig Wilkin	6.5-300	47
4	Cliff Hocker	300 Win.	50
5	Ted Mackey	6.5-300	48
6	Trudy Miller	300 Win.	48
7	Larry Wog	6.5-300	47
8	Ted Mackey	6.5-300	48
9	Tony Hopkins	308 Norma	48
10	Jon Smeigh	300 Win.	47

1970 Score Winners

Shoot	Name	Rifle	Score
1	Gene Plants	6.5-300	44
2	Jon Smeigh	300 Win.	47
3	Lance Heller	7mm Wby.	47
4	Al Wardrop	300 Win.	46
5	Bill Theis	300 Win.	48
6	Earl Chronister	308 Norma	46
7	Mary Louise DeVito	7mm-300	46
8	Earl Chronister	308 Norma	48
9	Joe Reitz	6.5-300	48
10	Bob Brown	6.5-300	48

1971 Score Shootoff Winners

Shoot	Name	Rifle	Score
1	John Smith	30-378	38
2	Tom Drummond, Sr.	30-378	43
3	Clyde Bonnell	308 Norma	39
4	George Horton	7mm Rem.	46
5	Lois Kertesz	7mm-300	41
6	Bill Miller	300 Win.	47
7	Willard Nelson	30-338	43
8	Trudy Miller	300 Win.	42
9	Tony Mariano	30-338	40
10	Joe Reitz	6.5-378	44

1972 Score Shootoff Winners

Shoot	Name	Rifle	Score
1	Bill Miller	300 Win.	35
2	Don Bower	7mm-300	46
3	Joe Reitz	6.5-378	43
4	Frank Popp, Sr.	6.5-300	40
5	Ken Madeira	6.5-300 Imp.	45
6	Lee Aunkst	300 Win.	43
7	Arlan Laity	6.5-300	3*
8	Ken Reeder	7mm-300	46
9	(No contest---fog)		
10	Cleon Bradley	7mm Rem.	46

*It was windy!

1973 Score Shootoff Winners*

Shoot	Name	Rifle	Score
1	Gene Stephanis	7mm Rem.	75
2	Judy Smith	308 Norma	88
3	Clair Peters	308 Norma	91
4	Eileen Baskin	7mm-300	84
5	Dot Kerstetter	6.5-300	86
6	Joe Doebler	264 Win.	86
7	Sue Dewalt	300 Win.	88
8	Dave Jarrell	7mm Rem.	85
9	Ray Guinther	7mm-300	75
10	Bill Theis	264 Win.	79

*Beginning in 1973 a possible was 100 rather than 50, through an unavoidable change in targets. The black center of the new target measured 13 inches instead of 12, with a 7-inch 10 ring.

30s. He occasionally won a match with one rifle and then fired a different one in the day's shootoff.

Cartridges Compared

The similarity of results is best illustrated in Table 3, where all cartridges used during the 5-year period of 1969 through 1973 are listed.
(Complete data on earlier matches could not be obtained, so this survey was limited to these 5 years.) Every group fired by each cartridge in the regular shoots of these years is shown in this table, with a yearly average for each. (Groups which did not have 10 shots on the paper are listed, but of course don't figure in the averages.) Perhaps the most interesting conclusion to be drawn is that, as Hocker claims, there is little to choose among them, if we eliminate the few obvious non-contenders, such as the 22-250. Aggregate average group size is about 25 inches, or 2½ MOA. This is considerably larger than the winning aggregate for each year—or even the Top 20 aggregate—but it should be pointed out that the Club's aggregates are figured on 6 shoots per year, with competitors who fire more than that being permitted to discard their worst scores—up to 4, in the case of those who compete in all 10 shoots. This is a fair regulation so far as the shooters are concerned, as it benefits these who make the effort to take part in all matches, but we included all groups in the averages in order to better reflect the total picture of what is being done by this group at this time.

Aggregate Winners and Data

1968	Paul Kempfer	308 Norma Magnum	12.810
1969	Richard Kepp	6.5-300 WWH Magnum	13.880
1970	Earl Chronister	308 Norma Magnum	11.369
1971	Guido DeVito	7mm-300 Magnum	13.531
1972	Cliff Hocker	7mm-300 Magnum	15.417
1973	Chet Leach	300 Winchester Magnum	13.479

This aggregate is based on the best 6 matches out of a possible ten.

Some cartridges might appear to be well under the general 2½ MOA level—for instance, if we consider the average group size only, the 7x61 Sharpe & Hart came up with 13". However, this was used only in one match, so that doesn't prove anything. As more groups are fired, the tendency is to enlarge the average, for one wild shot can foul up everything, while it takes a lot of good 10-shotters to decrease an average significantly.

That being the case, the performances of such Big 30s as the 308 Norma, its near-twin, the 30-338, and the 300 Winchester; the Big 7s like the Remington Magnum and the 7mm-300, are outstanding. They keep plugging along, even with many different shooters using them in a helluva lot of matches. Looking back a bit, an even more impressive record was compiled by the now-somewhat maligned 6.5-300. In 1969, when this load was used for 279 groups, each of what registered 10 shots on the paper, its average was 22.6"—better than any of the Big 30s above, despite the fact they were used for fewer matches. It continued to hold an edge the following year, but dropped off slightly since then, though it's still very close. Such averages make one wonder if those 6.5's fliers that some shooters talked about so much a few years back, actually occurred any more often with that caliber than with others, or if they simply wanted to believe that...

Handloading

Handloading for 1000-yard matches is mechanically the same as for the 100-yard shoots, the most noticeable difference being how quickly a powder hopper empties when it's dumping 105-gr. charges instead of 20-gr. ones. Basically, you simply resize, decap, and reprime a case, drop a powder charge and seat a bullet. Some 1000-yarders go to most of the extremes practiced by the short-range experts—segregating cases by make, volume, flash-hole diameter, times fired, etc., trimming to a given length, perhaps weighing powder charges, spinning bullets and seating them in some pre-

Many competitors arrive with campers and vans to spend the weekend. This is a behind-the-line shot. The spotting scopes cannot pick up bullet holes at this 1000-yd. range, but conditions can be studied—mirage, wind, etc.

cise relationship to the bore throat, and so on. Few if any make their own bullets or use handmade ones; apparently in the larger calibers used here, large quantity custom makers such as Sierra and Hornady offer acceptable projectiles.

Many competitors are more casual about their loading. They pay attention to ordinary details and safety, but usually load bullets straight from the box, measure powder charges (as most short-range benchresters also do), etc. They argue, perhaps correctly, that any improvements accruing from such minutiae are so small they simply get lost in the winds that sweep that long, long range. In general, this argument prevails, for the less picky loaders seem to do as well as their more persnickety brothers...yet when a given group comes within a fraction of an inch of taking a shoot or a fifth of an inch of breaking a record, it would be surprising if that also-ran rifleman didn't give at least a fleeting thought to his loading techniques, perhaps wondering if attention to some minor detail might have made him Number 1.

Table 2
Number of Times 5 Most Popular Cartridges Were Used in 1969-1973 Shoots

Cartridge	1969		1970		1971		1972		1973	
6.5-300 WWH Mag.	279	(51)	186	(48)	149	(24)	106	(21)	91	(16)
7mm Rem. Mag.	23	(9)	23	(2)	63	(14)	54	(17)	76	(11)
7mm-300 Mag.	17	(--)	21	(3)	81	(8)	113	(9)	175	(24)
308 Norma Mag.	112	(24)	133	(20)	114	(29)	97	(26)	102	(17)
300 Win. Mag.	97	(23)	173	(31)	173	(25)	183	(34)	193	(25)

Note: Numbers in parentheses are groups which didn't have 10 shots on target.

Getting ready to score a target. Only official scorers are allowed inside scoring area during this operation.

Ranges Compared

Shooters who have never fired a rifle at 1000 yards may or may not be impressed with the 2-foot groups we've been talking about. They sound awfully big when you're used to seeing nickel-size clusters from ordinary varmint rifles. But 1000 yards is an awful lot farther than 100 yards, which is where most chuck shooters do their load testing. Mathematically, it's just 10 times as far, but unless you're shooting in a vacuum problems don't increase in simple proportion with the range, but at some accelerating ratio as the distance increases. There's a psychological aspect to this long-range shooting, too. Gazing way down there into the hazy distance where those tiny black bulls stand defiantly, the distance simply *seems* like more than 10 times as far as the old familiar 100-yard butt. Even the 2-foot circle needed to enclose a more or less average group doesn't look very big at all when viewed from well over a half-mile away.

It's inevitable that some will try to compare this 1000-yard shooting with the shorter range bench stuff. This can't be done directly, as identical matches aren't shot in both. In a general sense, it's obvious that the 100/200-yard shooters turn in tighter groups. Quarter-minute groups are common here, while even full MOA groups are still rare at 1000, and those in the ¾-minute category are records. Still, the 1000-yarders have no reason to feel like second-raters. It's possible for a 100-yard bench shooter to turn in a ¾-minute group from an outfit that has almost no measurable recoil, and even worse groups are fairly common.

Recoil is a factor of some importance in the Magnums. In rifles weighing 20 to 40 pounds it's nothing to be afraid of it in a physical sense, but there's no doubt that a 190-gr. 30-cal. bullet propelled by 109 grains of H570, will be more difficult to control, shot after shot, than a 22-cal. 52-gr. squirted downrange by 20 gr. of 4198.

Wind and Mirage

The big problem with this 1000-yard shooting, through, are the same ones which give the short-rangers fits—wind and mirage. It takes a genuine expert to dope these factors closely at 100 yards; at 10 times that distance it's doubtful if anyone can really do a topnotch job. Some obviously are better at it than others, for

Calibers and Groups 1969-1970

Caliber	1969 1st	1969 2nd	1970 1st	1970 2nd
6.5-300 WWH	5	5	4	2
7mm Wby.	1	0	0	0
7mm-300	0	0	1	1
308 Norma	2	2	4	3
300 Win.	2	2	0	4
300 Super	0	1	0	0
30-378	0	0	1	0

In 1969-70, there were no shootoffs to determine the overall group and score winners of the day. Each competitor fired one 10-shot group which was judged against all others for size and score. This table shows the times in those two years that the calibers listed turned in the first- and second-place groups. No other calibers placed in those positions.

Cartridges Compared

Beginning in 1971, each relay of ten shooters was termed a match, and the winners of these matches fired in a shootoff at the end of the day to determine the over-all winners (group and score) of the shoot. To give some idea of how the various cartridges compared with each other, this table shows the total number of times each won an individual match in the 1971-72-73 competitions. Shootoff winners are shown in other tables.

Cartridge	Match Wins	Cartridge	Match Wins
25-06	2	7mm-378 Dr.	1
264 Win. Mag.	10	308 Win.	1
6.5-257 Wby.	1	30-338	9
6.5-270 Wby.	1	308 Norma	43
6.5-300 WWH	42	300 Win. Mag.	77
6.5-300 Imp.	2	300 Wby. Mag.	9
6.5-300 Dr.	4	300 Dr.	1
284 Win.	1	300 Super	3
7mm Wby. Mag.	2	30-378	12
7mm Rem. Mag.	21	30-378 Dr.	1
7mm-300	56	Not specified	2
7mm-300 Dr.	6		

firing of 30-06 ammo for the National Matches in the years 1919 to 1930, and for Palma Match ammo in about the same period. The former gave a mean radius averaging some 7 inches, for a group diameter of approximately 22 inches, while the Palma Match ammo went about 5½ inches mean radius, or about 18 inches group diameter.

An article in the July 1967 *American Rifleman* indicates testing of National Match ammo at 600 yards in the 1957-61 period averaged about 3 inches mean radius, and 2-plus during 1962-66.

This is not greatly different than the results achieved by the Original Benchrest Club shooters, though the ammo testing covered more groups, acceptance being based on 27 consecu-

their names keep cropping up among the Top 20 riflemen, shoot after shoot, year after year. But even they have not reached the level of consistency that the best 100/200-yard shooters show. It's unlikely that they will, at least in the foreseeable future, for nobody has the time it would take to spend on the 1000-yard range, firing under all conditions, studying every sign of change between the bench and the butts, constantly tuning rifles, adjusting loads...replacing barrels. It's easy to find a 100-yard range to practice on, but not so a 1000-yarder. Yet, until something like this takes place, it's hard to believe that anyone will start to shoot 2½-inch groups at that distance, to equal the quarter-minute level of the short-range groups.

The results of other long-range shooting reinforce these views. *Hatcher's Notebook* gives data on test

Mary Louise DeVito updating scoreboard. Results are posted immediately after final scoring, which is done as targets are brought back.

Typical Loads Used for 1000-Yard Matches

Cartridge	Bullet	Load	Primer
25-06	117 gr. Sierra	53/4831	CCI Mag.
264 Win. Mag.	140 gr. Sierra MK	64/4831	Fed. 215
6.5-300 WWH	139 gr. Norma	82/H870	Fed. 215
6.5-300 Drummond	139 gr. Norma	86/H870	Fed. 215
6.5-378 Drummond	139 gr. Norma	98/H570	Fed. 215
	140 gr. Sierra MK	95/H570	Fed. 215
7mm Rem. Mag.	162 gr. Hornady	69/4831	Rem. 9½M
7mm-300	162 gr. Hornady	87/H570	Rem. 9½M
	168 gr. Sierra MK	85/H570	Rem. 9½M
7mm-300 Drummond	162 gr. Hornady	90/H570	Fed. 215
	168 gr. Sierra MK	83/H570	Fed. 215
7mm-378 Drummond	162 gr. Hornady	104/H570	Fed. 215
	168 gr. Sierra MK	101/H570	Fed. 215
308 Norma	190 gr. Sierra	75/4831	Fed. 215
	190 gr. Sierra	73/4831	Rem. 9½M
300 Win. Mag.	190 gr. Sierra MK	69/4350	Win. 120
	190 gr. Sierra MK	70/4350	Win. 120
	190 gr. Sierra MK	75/4831	Fed. 215
	190 gr. Sierra MK	78/4831	Rem. 9½M
300 Drummond	168 gr. Sierra MK	82/4831	Fed. 215
30-378 Mag.	190 gr. Sierra MK	105/H570	Rem. 9½M
30-378 Drummond	168 gr. Sierra MK	112/H570	Fed. 215
	190 gr. Sierra MK	108/H570	Fed. 215

tive 10-shot groups divided among 3 test barrels. That being the case, it might be argued that no progress has been made in over a half-century, since in 1919, using a 30-06 with 150-gr. flat base bullet and 46.5 gr. Pyro 1406, a mean radius of 9.65 inches was recorded, and many of today's bench shooters don't surpass that regularly. However, this conclusion is not necessarily correct. Conditions under which the firing takes place must be considered. The government ammunition testing was by machine rest under weather conditions we can assume were decent if not necessarily perfect. Furthermore, since the machine rest eliminates the necessity for recovering from recoil, moving the gun back into position, and aiming, shots can be fired at an extremely fast rate. The 10 rounds of a given

Table 3

Caliber	1969 Groups Shot*	1969 Average Spread (ins.)	1970 Groups Shot*	1970 Average Spread (ins.)	1971 Groups Shot*	1971 Average Spread (ins.)	1972 Groups Shot*	1972 Average Spread (ins.)	1973 Groups Shot*	1973 Average Spread (ins.)
22-250	1 —	32.5	— —	—	— —	—	— —	—	— —	—
6mm	— (1)	—	— (1)	—	— —	—	— —	—	— —	—
257	7	22.4	1 —	46.2	— —	—	— —	—	— —	—
25-06	14 (8)	24.7	5 (3)	21.7	20 (2)	25.3	4 (9)	30.1	11 (5)	22.1
25-06 Imp.	— (1)	—	— —	—	— —	—	— —	—	— —	—
6.5-06	— —	—	2 (2)	31.7	2 —	26.3	— —	—	— —	—
6.5 Rem. Magnum	— (1)	—	— (2)	—	6 —	29.2	— —	—	— —	—
6.5-257 Wby. Magnum	— —	—	— —	—	— —	—	— —	—	8 —	19.6
6.5-270 Wby. Dr. Magnum	— —	—	— —	—	— (1)	—	— —	—	4 —	17.4
264 Win. Magnum	34 (12)	26.9	2 (3)	33.5	19 (6)	26.3	15 (7)	19.0	20 (2)	19.6
6.5-300 Win. Magnum	— —	—	— —	—	— (2)	—	— —	—	— —	—
6.5-300 Imp.	— —	—	— —	—	— —	—	16 (2)	20.4	— —	—
6.5-300 WWH	279 (51)	22.6	186 (48)	21.6	149 (24)	25.5	106 (21)	24.1	91 (16)	24.2
6.5-300 Drummond	— —	—	— —	—	11 (3)	26.9	16 (2)	24.5	6 (4)	19.7
6.5-378 Magnum	— —	—	— —	—	— —	—	7 —	24.2	1 —	26.3
6.5-378 Drummond	— —	—	— —	—	2 —	21.9	4 (2)	24.4	— —	—
270 Win.	1 (1)	29.1	3 (1)	17.0	— —	—	— —	—	— —	—
270 Wby. Magnum	— (3)	—	— —	—	— —	—	— —	—	— —	—
284 Win.	— —	—	— —	—	— —	—	— —	—	1 —	17.6
7x61 S & H Magnum	— —	—	— —	—	— —	—	1 —	13.0	— —	—
7x67 Wardrop	— —	—	— —	—	— —	—	2 —	28.1	— —	—
7mm Wby. Magnum	12 (5)	21.9	5 (2)	34.1	7 (4)	23.0	3 (3)	28.7	8 —	22.9
7mm Rem. Magnum	23 (9)	26.5	23 (2)	23.3	63 (14)	21.1	54 (17)	25.8	76 (11)	20.4
7mm-300 Magnum	17 —	24.9	21 (3)	19.8	81 (8)	23.7	113 (9)	23.7	175 (24)	21.1
7mm-300 Imp. Magnum	— —	—	— —	—	— —	—	— —	—	1 —	23.7
7mm-300 Drummond	— —	—	— —	—	5 (1)	27.3	15 (3)	23.5	16 (3)	20.8
7mm-378 Magnum	— —	—	— —	—	— —	—	15 —	22.8	— —	—
7mm-378 Drummond	— —	—	— —	—	5 (1)	26.4	16 (3)	21.7	— —	—
308 Win.	— (2)	—	— —	—	4 (1)	23.5	— —	—	— —	—
30-284	5 (2)	22.3	— —	—	— —	—	— —	—	— —	—
30-350	— —	—	— —	—	— —	—	1 (2)	38.6	— —	—
30-06	5 (3)	30.2	— —	—	3 (4)	26.4	1 (1)	39.1	2 (2)	34.9
30-06 Imp.	— —	—	2 (3)	28.5	— —	—	— —	—	— —	—
300 H & H Magnum	1 —	46.9	4 —	35.1	— —	—	— —	—	— —	—
30-338 Magnum	3 (2)	23.8	28 (1)	19.9	32 (9)	24.9	29 (8)	21.0	18 (5)	22.7
308 Norma	112 (24)	23.5	133 (20)	22.1	114 (29)	23.4	97 (26)	23.5	102 (17)	24.2
30 Belted Newton	4 —	27.7	— —	—	— —	—	— —	—	— —	—
300 Win. Magnum	97 (23)	24.5	173 (31)	22.6	173 (25)	23.9	183 (34)	23.8	193 (25)	24.5
30-375 Magnum	— —	—	— —	—	— —	—	— (1)	—	— —	—
300 Wby. Magnum	13 (2)	27.1	30 (6)	18.6	33 (3)	21.9	14 (4)	27.7	4 (4)	23.0
300 Ackley Magnum	15 (4)	29.0	12 (2)	26.1	— —	—	— (1)	—	6 (2)	26.1
300 Super Magnum	7 —	22.6	9 (2)	23.8	8 (1)	22.5	6 —	23.2	3 (1)	17.4
300 Drummond	— —	—	— —	—	4 (2)	19.1	2 (1)	27.6	— —	—
30-378 Magnum	19 (3)	20.0	26 (4)	19.3	55 (1)	22.4	39 (7)	23.9	14 (4)	20.9
30-378 Drummond	— —	—	— —	—	4 —	18.8	5 (1)	24.1	4 —	27.7
Not Specified	— —	—	— —	—	19 —	—	3 —	—	8 —	—

*Numbers in parentheses are groups which didn't have 10 shots on target.

This table is based on five years' shooting as reported in official bulletins. There is some inevitable error, as shooters are not always precise or complete in their caliber listings, sometimes listing only 6.5-300 instead of 6.5-300 Drummond, for instance; however, it is believed this table is accurate enough to give a good over-all picture of results during this period.

group often were fired in 5 to 8 seconds, according to Col. E. H. Harrison of the NRA technical staff, who was directly involved in the testing in the 1960s. This had the great advantage of getting all shots off under essentially the same conditions of wind.

By comparison, these 1000-yard benchrest competitors do all their shooting in a normal manner, and they do it under whatever conditions happen to be prevailing when they're called to the line. It might be so hazy, or raining so hard, that the targets are barely visible; the wind might be of gale proportions; it might even be snowing, for a winter match is scheduled at this writing. Regardless, when the command to commence firing is given, they commence.

The proof that they don't do very badly is shown by an accident of a few years back. Apparently intrigued by the reports trickling out of those north-Pennsylvania hills, some shooters who earn their daily bread in the technical shops of one of the country's great gun building companies, arrived on the scene, weighted down with all the goodies at their command. It was their intention, obvious if unstated, to show the local hillbillies just how 10 bullets should be neatly placed in those far-off bullseyes. Alas'n'alack, things somehow didn't turn out as expected. At the end of that day's shoot those newly-educated New Englanders—expert riflemen all, truly—packed their gear like the Arabs, and silently stole away.

Well... who ever said it was supposed to be *easy* to put 10 shots in a grapefruit size group at 1000? A *challenge?* It's all of that. So why not get your gear together, head up back of Williamsport, ask for Irv Plants' place—or just listen for the shooting—and sign up. Who knows—maybe the barrel and 10 bullets which are going to give that first 2½-inch, 1000-yard group are yours. ●

Custom

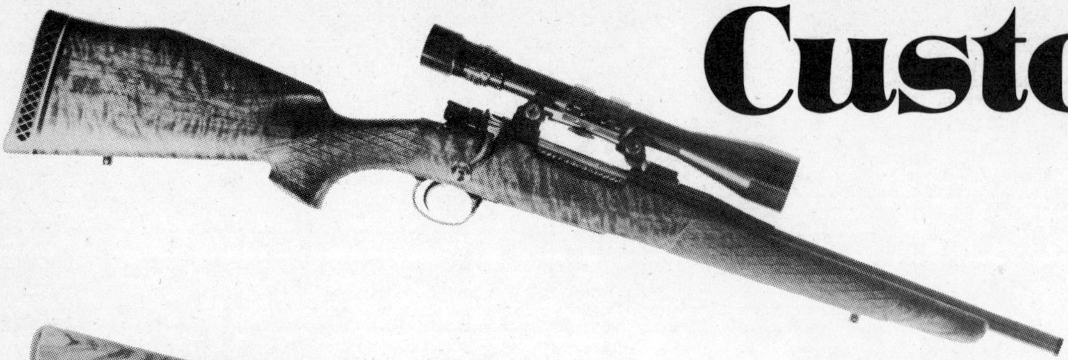

SMITTY'S GUN SHOP
A 98 Mauser, caliber 270, stocked in fiddleback English walnut, the fore-end tip and grip cap of burl walnut. The checkering is in skipline style.

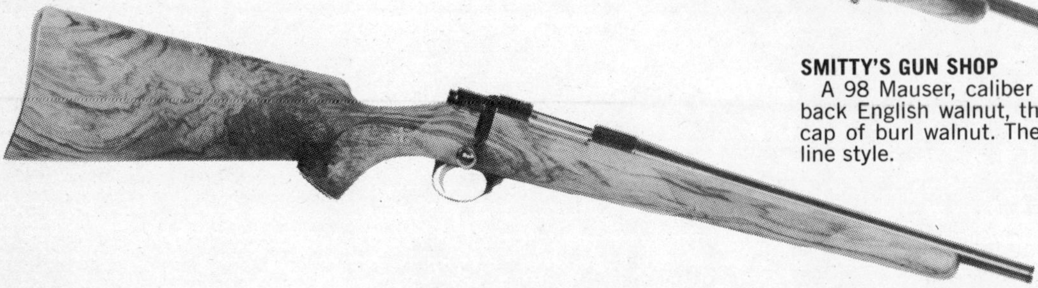

HUBERT J. HECHT
Simple, elegant stocking, the wood an ultra-fancy piece of California-English walnut. The rifle is a Sako in 222 Magnum, the safety lowered to be unobtrusive.

NORMAN H. SCHIFFMAN
A handsome and classic-styled rifle, the action an FN 400, the Douglas barrel in 7mm Rem. Mag. caliber. The wood is fine French walnut, checkered 22 LPI.

WALTER S. ABE
Classic-style stocking in French walnut of a Winchester 70 action and barrel, cal. 30-06. An unusual and attractive checkering pattern.

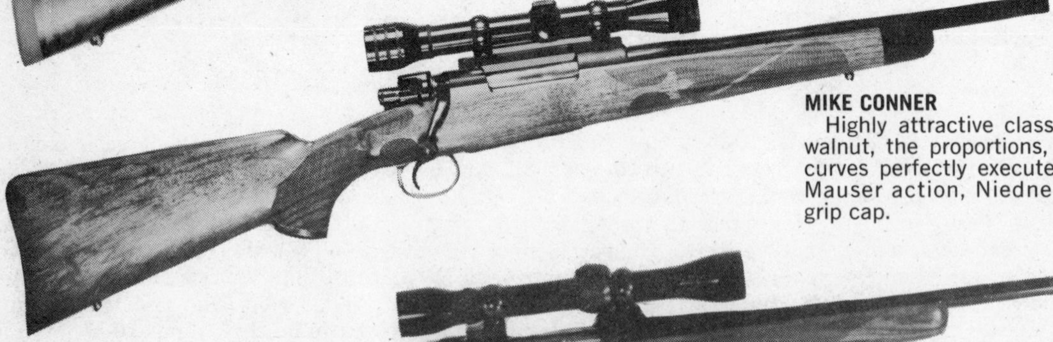

MIKE CONNER
Highly attractive classic stocking in French walnut, the proportions, profile, the lines and curves perfectly executed. Douglas barrel, 98 Mauser action, Niedner-type buttplate and grip cap.

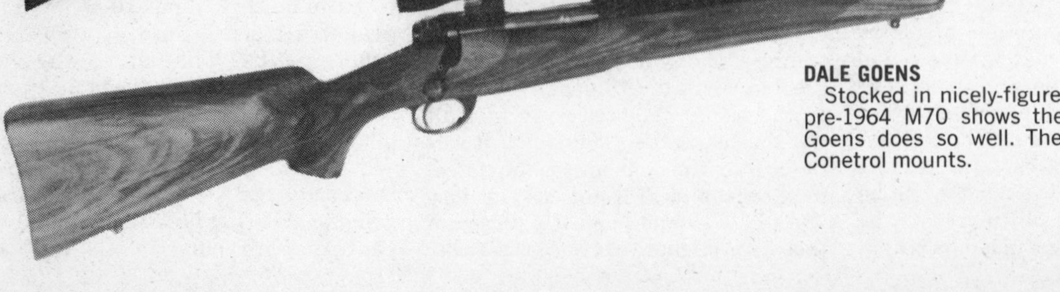

DALE GOENS
Stocked in nicely-figured French walnut, this pre-1964 M70 shows the classic styling that Goens does so well. The Weaver scope is in Conetrol mounts.

Guns

SMITTY'S GUN SHOP
A 98 Mauser, caliber 270, stocked in fiddleback English walnut, the fore-end tip and grip cap of burl walnut. The checkering is in skipline style.

HUBERT J. HECHT
Simple, elegant stocking, the wood an ultrafancy piece of California-English walnut. The rifle is a Sako in 222 Magnum, the safety lowered to be unobtrusive.

NORMAN H. SCHIFFMAN
A handsome and classic-styled rifle, the action an FN 400, the Douglas barrel in 7mm Rem. Mag. caliber. The wood is fine French walnut, checkered 22 LPI.

Consult our Directory pages for the location of firms or individuals mentioned.

WALTER S. ABE
Classic-style stocking in French walnut of a Winchester 70 action and barrel, cal. 30-06. An unusual and attractive checkering pattern.

EARL MILLIRON
Milliron calls this handsome stock form "modern classic." Note cheekpiece and comb nose treatment. The action is a 98 Mauser, has been worked over by Tom Burgess.

DALE GOENS
Stocked in nicely-figured French walnut, this pre-1964 M70 shows the classic styling that Goens does so well. The Weaver scope is in Conetrol mounts.

TRINKO'S GUN SERVICE
Mauser actioned 270, McGowan barrel, stocked in American walnut. Timney trigger, Buehler safety.

R. E. ANDERSON
7mm Rem. Mag. on a Sako action, custom built in the classic style. Bastogne walnut, multi-point checkering, Leupold 4x in Conetrol mounts. Screws and fittings checkered or engraved, parallel aligned.

HAL HARTLEY
A Hawken-type caplock rifle, the 53-cal. octagon barrel by Bill Large 33″ long and ⅞″ at the muzzle. HH did the bear scene on the patchbox.

HOLLIS GUN SHOP
Springfield '03 with 25-06 Douglas barrel, stocked in Circassian walnut, carved-border checkering, ebony trim.

ROBERT M. WINTER
Classic stocking in fancy American walnut of a Shilen-barreled Mauser, cal. 22-250. Double set triggers.

KESS ARMS
Mauser 98, 7mm Mag. Douglas barrel, striking French walnut, carved and checkered in Mannlicher style.

EARL MILLIRON
Pre-1964 Winchester 70, simple, elegant. Metal work—guard release, bolt knob, scope bases—by Tom Burgess.

CHARLES DEVETO
Classic treatment of 375 H&H rifle, made on a pre-1964 M70 action. The wood is French walnut, but fairly straight grained for higher strength.

CARL ROTH, JR.
This M12 Winchester has a release trigger, the Monte Carlo trap stock in fancy Circassion walnut. The 22 line multi-point checkering runs full length of the fore-end.

TALMAGE ENTERPRISES
Something different! A Savage 219 in 22 Hornet, stocked in presentation-grade Claro walnut, the grip cap and fore-end tip in burl maple. Receiver is engine turned.

TALMAGE ENTERPRISES
The FN Mauser action and 24" Douglas Premium barrel are stocked in full fancy grade Mesquite, grip cap and tip of rosewood. Note high Monte Carlo.

RUSSELL R. ZEERYP
A Remington 18"-barreled action stocked in maple, with steel barrel band and fore-end cap. The scope is in See-Thru mounts for brush use.

SWANSON CUSTOM GUNS
Simple classic styling in the rarely-seen straight grip style. Clean and racy looking. The multi-point checkering pattern is well handled.

C. D. MILLER
This is the DeHaas-Miller single-shot rifle, the stock and all metal work by Miller Arms. A classic treatment, the whole attractively done.

EDW. O. HEFTI
Mauser '98 in 35 Whelen, stocked in Flaig's Circassian walnut, the extensive checkering multi-pointed.

CHARLES DEVETO
Ultra fancy, marble-cake French walnut was used to stock this D.H.E. grade Parker double, checkered 24 LPI, with 28 line recessed panels.

TRINKO'S GUN SERVICE
Mauser-actioned 270, McGowan barrel, stocked in American walnut. Timney trigger, Buehler safety.

CLAYTON NELSON
A Champlin action with 25-06 full octagon barrel, the handsome stock in best classic fashion. The bolt knob is checkered, as are the steel buttplate and grip cap.

CLOWARDS
A Sako L461 action, 222 Rem., Douglas #1 barrel. Stocked in French walnut with 25 LPI checkering. Rifle weighs 6¾ lbs.

M. VAN EPPS
This small rifle, a 99 Savage, was stocked in top quality tigertail maple for a woman. Epps operates Breckheimers Gun Supply of Parish, N.Y.

CHAMPLIN FIREARMS, INC.
An excellent example of the classically simple rifles made in Enid, Oklahoma, the action a Champlin, of course. Mike Desbian works the metal, Maurice Ottmar carves the wood.

KLAUS HIPTMAYER
A full restoration of the broken original stock form, including the intricately carved horn trigger guard, was carried out in Circassion walnut.

TALMAGE ENTERPRISES
Little rifle, big scope. A 310 Martini SS action rebarreled to 17 Ackley Bee. The wood is best grade screw-bean Mesquite, with rosewood tip and cap.

SWANSON CUSTOM GUNS
A Sako-actioned bolt rifle, the graceful and well-shaped stock in a full fancy piece of French walnut, the checkering a fleur de lis pattern.

CHARLES DEVETO
Full fancy feather-grain American walnut stocks this Westley Richards 16-gauge double gun, the dimensions and detailing close to the original English stock.

TALMAGE ENTERPRISES
The FN Mauser action and 24" Douglas Premium barrel are stocked in full fancy grade Mesquite, grip cap and tip of rosewood. Note high Monte Carlo.

The All-Round Rifle — pursuit of a myth?

The hunter must be a rifleman in Montana's high plains country. The trees in the foreground are a good 300 yards away from my camera. Country like this, found all over the West, was responsible for the early great reputation of the 270 Winchester.

Maybe yes, maybe no — it all depends, as it always has, on the game to be hunted, the rifleman's ability to shoot well and true, whether he can take recoil and . . . well, here we go again, probably settling nothing.

by CLIFF DEMPSTER

THERE WAS A TIME, a while back, when great grandpa did all his hunting with one rifle. Whitetails, antelope, elk, black bear—they all fell to his trusty smoke-pole, and grandpa took the thing out after rabbits and squirrels after the chores were done. This rifle was 36 to 44 caliber, took a round ball and a generous handful of black powder which pushed the bullet along at some 1500 to 2000 fps, with muzzle energy maybe 1000 ft. lbs. These old rifles were often surprisingly accurate, and the men who used them made every shot count. Then came civilization, smokeless powder, air and water pollution and subdivisions. The game got wilder, became gun and man shy. Repeaters came into vogue, and shooters got sloppy. With smokeless powder, we started to develop specialized cartridges, and we've been looking for an all-round rifle ever since. There is no point in bewailing this state of affairs; many of our modern cartridges and rifles perform beautifully on many types of game, and I'm sure that the old-timers would have given their eyeteeth to have had them. So, what *have* we got for an up-to-date all-round rifle? If any?

I have to agree with John Taylor in that you can laugh this question out of existence unless you define your terms. The accurate 458 is ridiculous for groundhogs, and as much as I like it, I'm not about to take my 225 lion hunting. If you're going to Africa or Asia for dangerous game hunting, then you've got the dough for your big rifle, or you can rent one if you like. If, on the other hand, you're married, or broke—the terms are not mutually exclusive—and you like to hunt, this question has profound relevance for you. Another point is that future legislative hysteria may make it damned expensive to own many rifles. By all-round rifle, I mean a rifle for use in American game hunting, North or South, with maybe Australia or New Zealand thrown in, which meets some minimum requirements for accuracy and power.

Now, lacking the dough (or for other reasons) to keep a huge selection of rifles, how do we go about getting one that will fit most hunting? For a mini-battery, let's start by defining our hunting situations. Basically, aside from tin-can plinking and pest-destruction of the 22 rimfire variety, there are five general hunting situations that most of us can expect to encounter: 1) Small and large varmint hunting (small targets at long ranges); 2) Bush or woods deer and black bear hunting (medium targets at short ranges); 3) Plains and mountain deer, antelope and sheep hunting (medium targets at short to long range); 4) Large deer (elk, moose, caribou), often at long ranges; and 5) Dangerous big game, the greater bears and Russian boar (usually taken at short and medium ranges.) Since most of us can't stalk like Dan'l Boone, mediocre accuracy is acceptable only for short-range woods hunting, which is where the lever-action carbine performs well. Speaking of accuracy, your rifle may shoot 100-yd. 1" groups off a rest, but the excitement and fatigue of hunting will open this to 3"—still off a rest! This means a 9" group at 300 yards, and that's as big as the vital area on many animals. Also, at over 300 yards even many magnums are in the 30-30 class for energy. Bear this in mind the next time you hear about 400- or 500-yd. kills!

We just don't buy guns on approval—at least most of us can't. This means that we have to depend on some informational source for selecting our rifles and choosing the cartridge that we want them chambered for. Field reports are one good source. If Page, Askins, or O'Connor say that a 395 Wifflepoof Magnum is death on grizzlies, you can be sure that if you hit him well you'll be using his hide for a rug rather than vice versa. The most important element in killing power and bullet performance is proper bullet placement. It is the responsibility of every sportsman to shoot only if he has a reasonable chance of connecting. But what should you shoot with?

Bullet Performance

Four factors combine to determine the effectiveness of a bullet when it hits something. *Proper bullet construction* is vital; for example, many deer hunters wonder why their 30-06's aren't putting deer down as well as a smaller rifle. The reason, often enough, is that they use the heavily built 180-gr. bullets that are fine for moose but can't possibly expand properly on a deer which isn't nearly so massive. Match your bullet to the game; the major ammunition companies and the custom bullet makers will be happy to tell you just what bullet you should use on what type of game. After bullet construction, we need to consider *bullet shape*, because that determines how fast the bullet will be traveling at the target, and how flat its trajectory will be. Incidentally, while a blunt bullet may penetrate better on elephant and similar game, there is no evidence to suggest that it will out-perform the familiar spitzer on most game, nor is the spitzer necessarily any more susceptible to brush deflection. Both of these latter qualities are determined by the bullet's weight in relation to its diameter. The numerical expression of this ratio is called *sectional density (sd)*, and equals the weight of the bullet in grains divided by the square of the groove diameter (.308, for example, for 30 caliber rifles) times 7000. A bullet with high SD is long and slender (at least in the medium calibers) while a bullet with low SD is short and fat. Just as you can drive a nail through wood far more easily than you can a ball bearing of equal weight, so a bullet with high SD will penetrate far better than one with low SD. It is this fact that explains the wonderful reputation of the 6.5mm Mannlicher, although its muzzle energy is about the same as the 30-30. *Velocity* is the final major factor in bullet performance. (There's an Army demonstration where they shoot into two 10-pound sauerkraut cans that are standing side by side, one shot with the M-14 (308 Winchester) 150-gr. bullet at 2800 fps. the other with the M-16 (223 Remington) 55-gr. bullet at 3300 fps. The 308 puts a good sized hole in its can, but the 223 bullet, with only half the energy of the 308, literally explodes its can. The same performance holds true in animal tissue, provided the bullet holds together long enough to get into a vital cavity.) The force of a shock wave in a fluid (which includes the organs in the chest cavity) is proportional to the cube of its velocity, and this is why high velocity works so well with chest shots if the bullet holds together on its way

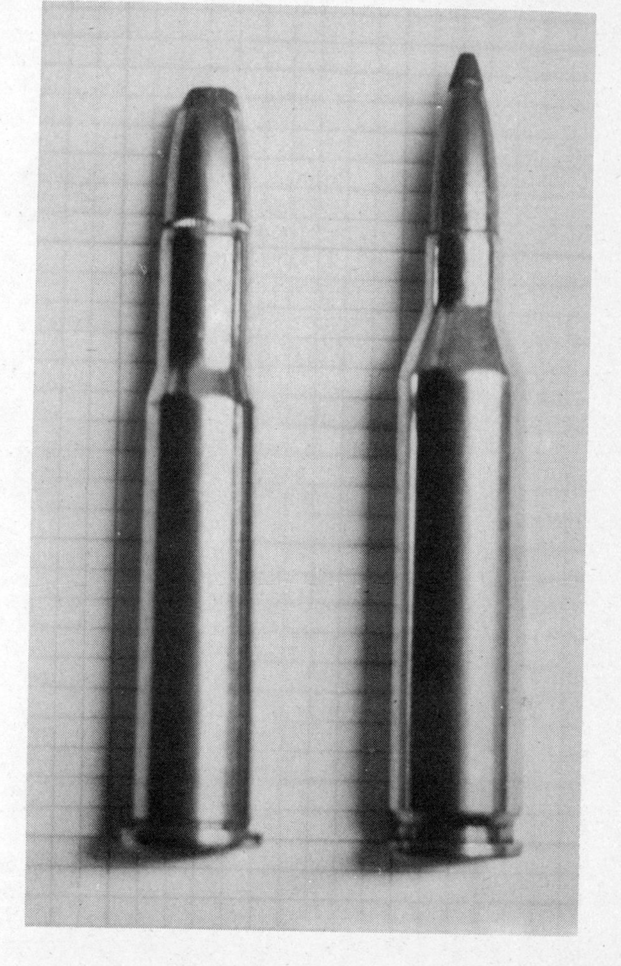

The fallacy of muzzle energy: A 170-gr. 30-30 load and a 100-gr. 243 Winchester have about the same muzzle energy (so do the 44 Magnum and the 6.5mm Mannlicher) but what a difference down range! The higher velocity and better ballistic coefficient of the 243 give it at least another 100 yards of effective range over the 30-30.

through the rib cage. For additional evidence, when a gut shot with high velocity has produced results, it has almost invariably been the case that the animal had just eaten and the intestines were full and distended—providing the fluid mass to transmit the energy to vital organs.

The three major schools of thought on killing power revolve around various combinations of these bullet performance factors. The first school originated with black powder, and we'll call it the *momentum* school. Since there is a limit of about 2000 fps on the velocity that can be produced with black powder, the only way left of increasing the performance of such rifles is to increase the weight of the bullet. The modern equivalent of this school may be found in the handgun hunter, since there is a limit on velocity in a pistol, and the user of rifled slugs. At close ranges, say less than 50 yards or so, modern rifled slugs will out-do a 30-30, and will stay in a 5-6 inch circle, fine for deer or black bear. The Ballistic Research Laboratories (BRI) 50-caliber Sabot slug, the European Balle Blondeau and Brenneke slugs (Stoeger) are substantial improvements; all three closely equaling the 30-06 at short ranges. Before you get too enthused, though, consider this: advocates of this school claim that use of these big bullets leaves a good blood trail for tracking purposes. This is a nice way of saying that they'll kill the animal, hit right, but he may travel some! The second school, which we'll call the *classical*, is distinguished by a preference for bullets of high SD, such as the 160 gr. 6.5 Mannlicher and 175-gr. 7mm Mauser bullets, at modest velocities. Because of the modest muzzle velocities involved, 2100-2400 fps, trajectories are pretty high, creating problems for the plains shooter or mountaineer. The classical school has an important lesson for us in that a good shot, careful about bullet placement, and using a bullet with high SD, can get by with a rifle that most of us would consider a pipsqueak. Proper placement of bullets with high SD can make up for a lot of other deficiencies in a cartridge. Last, the *high-velocity* school, exemplified by the Weatherby Magnums. We've already mentioned the destructive effects of high velocity on tissue, and the importance of proper bullet construction (most custom bullet makers have solved this problem) so that the bullet won't fly to pieces on the skin of the animal. Most high velocity cartridges of the magnum genre tend to be substantially over-bore with all but the slowest burning powders—also, you sure pour a lot in for what comes back out! A more conservative view-point suggests that the use of high-velocity is best reserved for varmints and thin-skinned non-dangerous game, while some dangerous game (elephant, buffalo) might be more surely pursued with bullets of high SD. Some cartridges combine the best of both of these two schools: the 30-06 is an excellent example, with its 125-gr. load for varmints and long-range shooting, and the 200-gr. bullet with its high sectional density for fairly big game.

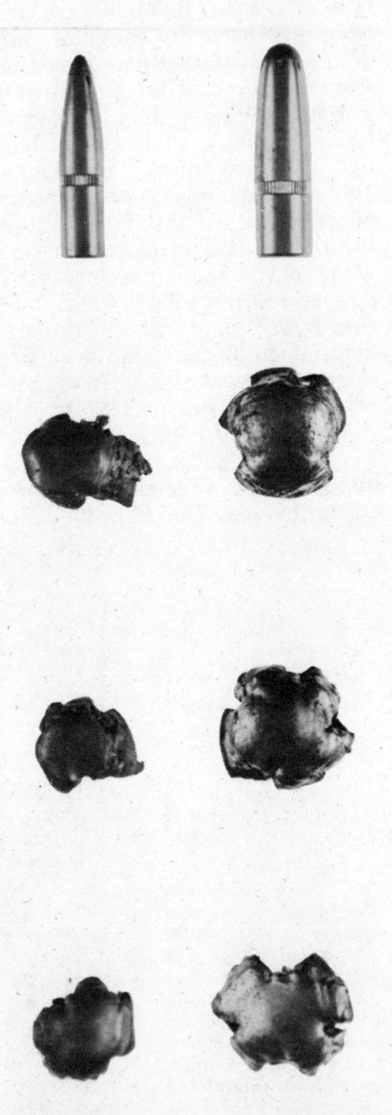

Expansion of Winchester Power Point bullets. 100-gr. 243 (left) and 180-gr. 308, fired at 50, 100 and 300 yards, top to bottom.

Since any all-round rifle is a compromise, we need now to list the elements that will have to be present. For varmints, we need high velocity and a flat trajectory, with the 222 Remington representing a minimum in both departments. For long range deer and antelope, we need a bit more energy (SAAMI recommends that any deer rounds have a minimum energy level at 100 yards of 945 fp) and the 243 probably represents this level. The first element in our compromise, obviously, has thus become that our cartridge be available with a factory or handloaded round having a velocity in excess of 3000 fps and a mid-range trajectory at 300 yards of 5" or less (3" or less at 200). Our second element is the availability of a bullet with a remaining energy of over 1400 ft. lbs. at 300 yds. for larger game. Finally, for dangerous or really large game, we need a bullet with high sectional density—preferably at least .300 which is the SD of the 200-gr. 308 bullet. In many cases the handloader has a real advantage. For example, the heaviest American loading for the 270 is the 150-gr. bullet, which has an SD of .281. Handloaded, the 160-gr. Nosler (SD .300) or 170-gr. Speer (SD .317) bullets are far better choices for really big game.

Choice of Caliber

In considering various possible calibers for all-round rifles, we can start by eliminating some calibers. Above 30 caliber, there are few good varmint bullets available—some for the 8mm rounds, none for the 338, and only short-jacketed pistol bullets, which have very poor ballistic qualities, for the 35s. The very small bores suffer also, in the opposite direction. The 17-caliber wildcats and the 17 Remington make beautiful, accurate, light rifles, with little recoil and less noisy reports. These ultra-small bores, which fire 25-gr. bullets at speeds up to 4200 fps, have had special fouling problems, and the bullets so far made have very thin jackets—they're explosive on varmints but very poor for penetration. Heavier bullets or jackets would defeat the whole purpose of the little wildcats. The 22 rimfires (and the 5mm Remington Magnum) generally lack power for all but small game; the 22 Magnum Winchester hollow-points and all factory-loaded 22 centerfire bullets blow up too badly.

When we reach the 243 or 6mm cartridges, we start to pick up some candidates for an all-round rifle and cartridge. Probably 90% of all hunting done with a rifle on the American continents is for varmints or various brands of deer and antelope. For these animals, a 6mm is plenty with anything like decent bullet placement. In Ken Waters' review of "American Bulleted Cartridges" in the GUN DIGEST, he calls the 243 Winchester "excellent for the one-gun hunter of game not larger than deer," which applies as well to the 6mm/244 Remington and the 240 Weatherby. The 243 can be reloaded from cheap 308 GI brass necked down, though the 6mm has slightly more powder capacity and better shape for ignition and burning. Both suffer from the handloader's standpoint because their short necks discourage the use of long bullets. The 243 Winchester is more widely distributed and loaded.

Good long range cartridges for most North American game. From left—270 and 280, plus three magnums, the 264, 7mm Remington and 300 Winchester. Magnums shoot flatter, are more powerful, but they kick more, too. If recoil bothers you, stick to the standard loads—if you don't hit 'em you won't kill 'em.

Initial tests of the 240 Weatherby Magnum suggested that it might not have the accuracy of the smaller 6mm rounds, at least not in full-power loads. As the cartridge was tested in the excellent Weatherby Mark V action, one can only speculate about possible problems with either bullets or powder. In addition, the 240 is over-bore except with very slow-burning powders (like all Weatherby rounds), and the resultant barrel life, throat erosion problems, and price of a Weatherby should be taken into account. Finally, while the initial velocity and energy of the Weatherby round is high, the trajectory is not a great deal flatter than the other 6mms, and at longer ranges differences in velocity tend to dissipate as well. If you are contemplating a 6mm, you also need to check your state game laws to make sure your rifle will be legal for any game you can reasonably expect to hunt.

The 250 Savage (reborn again this year in the Savage 99-A) lives because of its light recoil and the fact that it's a lot more effective on medium-long range deer than the 30-30. The 257 Weatherby and the 25-06 are really quite close to each other in performance. The 257 WM was the cartridge upon which most recent claims about high velocity have been founded, and it has taken a lot of really big game in the hands of accomplished riflemen. Of U.S. made rifles, only the expensive Mark Vs are chambered for it, and it uses expensive belted brass. The most recent big news, of course, was the Remington chambering in 1970 of the 25-06. Factory ammunition has given outstanding accuracy, and for tight budgets the supply of good 30-06 GI brass seems nearly inexhaustible. The 25-06 is a superlative long-range varmint cartridge, though a bit loud, with the 87-gr. Remington or new 90-gr. Winchester factory loads, but what will it do on bigger game? The *NRA* recommends that use of the 25-06 be limited to deer-sized animals. This is very likely not the case. For example, the 120-gr. factory load pretty well approximates the 130-gr. 270 load, with which Jack O'Connor has taken 12 moose and Hosea Sarber used as a backup rifle for clients on Kodiak bear. Here in Montana scads of big elk are done in every year with the 25-06, and according to the Speer people the 120-gr. 25-06 combination will handle all but the biggest game on the American continent. Recoil with the 25-06 is still very light, not noticeably more than a lightweight 30-30 carbine or a 300 Savage. For the careful hunter who is a good shot and who won't be hunting Kodiak bear or possibly moose, the 25-06 should be eminently satisfactory.

Even in the high mountains, close on the Continental Divide, Montana has trees! This thickly wooded area is good bear and winter elk country.

For a long time, the world-wide hunter might have been strongly tempted to glance at the 6.5mm rifle, particularly if it had the magic word Mannlicher on it. With careful shooting, at reasonable

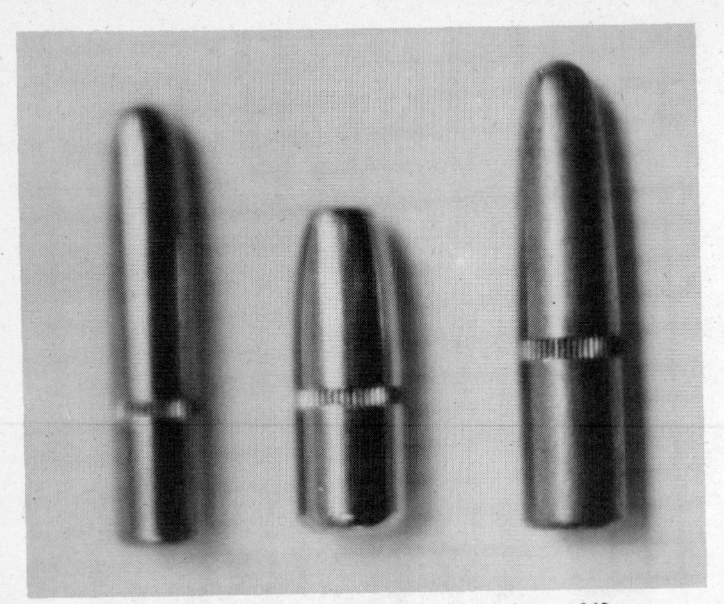

Sectional density illustrated: On the left is the famous 160-gr. 6.5mm Mannlicher bullet, one that has accounted for much big and dangerous game. In the center, weighing slightly more, is the 170-gr. 30-30 flat-nose bullet, at best a deer and black bear number. How short and stubby it looks compared to the long, slender 6.5mm bullet. For comparison, the 220-gr. 30-06 bullet, which has the same SD as the 6.5mm Mannlicher bullet shown, is on the right.

ranges, the old 6.5 Mannlicher will still do the job quite easily on deer and elk. Its weakness is the lack of a reasonable varmint load. The 6.5 Remington will do nothing that the 25-06 or the 270 Winchester cannot do far better except feed through a short bolt action. If you are attracted to short bolt-action carbines, the 6.5 Remington does offer a 120-gr. load for deer and maybe elk, and a 100-gr. varmint load. You will have difficulty in handloading 140-gr. bullets, and the 160-gr. bullet which gave the 6.5 its original great reputation just is not feasible for most 6.5 Remington rifles, with the possible exception of the Model 700. The 264 Winchester is rapidly headed towards extinction, and you can't help but feel a little sad about this. It has a tremendous varmint load, but this load has a relatively tremendous recoil, and uses up a lot of powder which creates fairly severe barrel life problems. The 140-gr. 264 load will certainly handle deer, elk, and moose, and it *can* be loaded with the 160-gr. big-game bullet to handle even Kodiak bear, in the hands of a cool shooter properly backed up. Although brass is expensive, barrel life relatively short, and powder consumption high, there are certainly much worse choices.

The 270 Winchester is certainly one of the best candidates for an all-round rifle. If Speer ammunition is ever issued with the 170-gr. 270 bullet at 2800 fps or so, the 270 even in factory loads will be in good shape to challenge all comers. Originally introduced in 1925 with the 130-gr. bullet, and formed by necking down '06 brass, the 270 has killed big game all over the world. Factory domestic rounds range from 100- to 150-grs., with a 160-gr. round (Canadian Dominion) at 2800 fps. doing well on big game in the Far North. The handloader is really in excellent shape, with bullet weights running from 90- to 180-grs. (this last, a Barnes bullet now made by Colorado Custom Bullets, has a good reputation for accuracy ahead of 55 grains of 4831.) Nosler offers an excellent

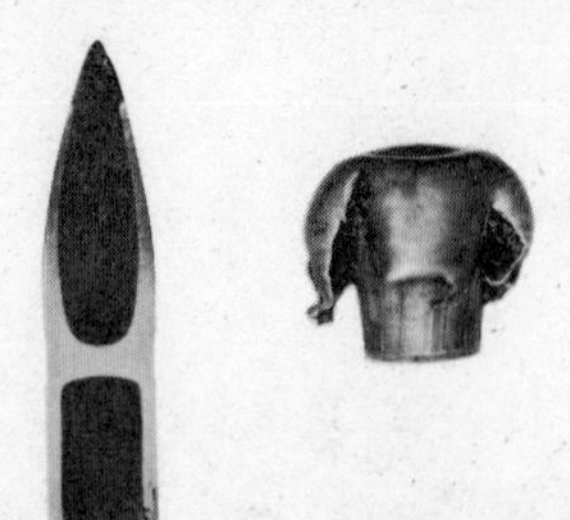

It's Nosler bullet design that makes for their superb expansion in game. That partition makes the difference—lets the forepart open up yet holds the base section together for deep penetration.

heavy big game bullet, the 160-gr. pointed partition bullet which can be driven at 2900 fps for 3015 fp—more than any '06 factory load. The selling points of the 270 Winchester are flatness of trajectory, high velocity, excellent killing power, accuracy, ease of reloading, and availability of good, heavy bullets. This old standard shoots nearly as flatly as the vaunted 7mm Magnums with 15% less powder, and certainly deserves long and serious consideration by any shooter, and especially by the handloader.

Recent developments suggest that the battleworn 7mm Mauser (7x57) may be about to receive a new lease on life. For a long time, the only American load available was the standard 175-gr. roundnose, excellent for large game and brush and woods hunting, but limited for longer range deer hunting. Norma introduced 110- and 150-gr. loads for more flexibility, and Federal recently announced a 139-gr. load at 2710 fps. Speer-DWM has added a 103-gr. varmint load (3300 fps), and a well-built 162-gr. (2785 fps) to go with a 145-gr. (2750 fps) bullet. These new rounds give factory varmint loads, longer range deer loads, and, with the 162-gr. and 175 numbers, good big game loads. For the handloader, there is a good variety of 7mm bullets to work with, starting with Norma 110-gr. and Speer 115-gr. bullets, on up to 175-gr. bullets. The 7mm Mauser furnished much of the impetus for the development of the 270 Winchester, and it is especially encouraging that the ultra-modern Ruger Number One single shot rifle is now available in 7mm—the old warrior is still kicking despite the fact that it is ballistically overshadowed by the 7x64mm, 284, 280, 270, and 7mm Remington Magnum rounds.

The 280 Remington and 284 Winchester, offering about the same bullets and like ballistics, will be discussed together. However, a heavier load, the 165-gr. at 2820, is offered for the Remington rounds. Both cartridges were developed for special problems; the lower pressure 280 for autoloading-rifle functioning, the 284 to provide a short round with 270 ballistics for short bolt- and lever actions. Both have the same potential as the 270, yet unless you want a short bolt- or lever-action rifle, why settle for the imitation? The 284 also has the usual short neck of modern cartridges, which cramps your style when trying to seat a 175-gr. bullet down far enough to work through the action.

Then there are the various 7mm magnums, more or less the brain children of the late, great Phil Sharpe. The sexy Sevens feature large bangs, much powder and, unless used with very slow powders, quite over-bore. We will use the 7mm Remington as representative of the group since it is a very good round, with better published ballistics than the 270. A note of caution: the published figures derive via 26″ barrels, yet barring the Ruger No. 1, the 7mm R.M. is issued only in 22″ and 24″ barrels. Actually, with 125- and 150-gr. loads, there is little difference between the big 7mm and the 270 when these shorter barrels are taken into account. The real advantage of the 7mm R.M. lies in the excellent R-P 175-gr. pointed bullet, which is superb over long ranges, has high sectional density and terrific effects on game. While the 125-gr. bullet will work on varmints, it's a bit much. This is the handicap for the 7mm R.M.—no true varmint factory loads. Speer's good 115-gr. hollow-point puts the handloader in business. The choice between the 7mm Magnum and the 270 Winchester boils down to this: both do well on varmints and game, yet you have to handload the 7mm for best varmint work and, for best big-game results with the 270, you would want to consider the Dominion 160-gr. load, or perhaps handload. Then, too, 7mm R.M. brass costs more (you can resize 270 from 30-06 GI brass) and it uses more powder. The non-handloader with any interest at all in varmints should stick to the 270.

Finally we come to the 30-caliber cartridges which represent the upper end of our all-round rifles. We'll consider first the 30-06 (and the 308, though not quite so powerful, and limited to a maximum bullet weight of 200 grains). No other cartridge in the world has had so much money spent on its technical development, though the 22 Long Rifle may come close. The result is a variety of factory rounds, a bit too potent for varmints—which handloading can fix—and suitable for most of the world's game. The 220-gr. '06 bullet (SD .330) and the new Speer-DWM 180 gr. will do the job on just about anything. Also for the '06, Speer's 165-gr. bullet at 2840 fps shoots flatter than the 180-gr. load at 2700, and has more energy all the way through than any other load except the DWM 180-gr. number. It is the handloader, though, who gets the maximum use from the '06. There are 120-, 125-, and 130-gr. varmint loads, 165- and 180-gr. game loads, and for really big game, 220- and even 250-gr. bullets. A man who loads the 130-gr. Hornady bullet to 3300, and 165-gr. Speer bullet to 2900, and the 220-gr. Hornady to 2600 (these are all near-maximum loads) could do well no matter what he wanted to shoot. The '06 isn't quite as flat as the 270, nor does it have good factory varmint loads, but it'll do!

Going up the scale, the various 30 caliber Magnums tend more to use extra powder than to add much to the '06 killing power, and do not have factory varmint loads. Recoil is greater and ammunition expensive. The 300 Weatherby deserves some special mention, albeit it heads the list in recoil and expense. If there is such a thing as a world-wide cartridge, provided you are willing to accept its recoil and handload for varmints, this has got to be it. While not legal for large game in parts of Africa, Elgin Gates and others have amply proved its reliability in stopping the biggest and most dangerous game in the world.

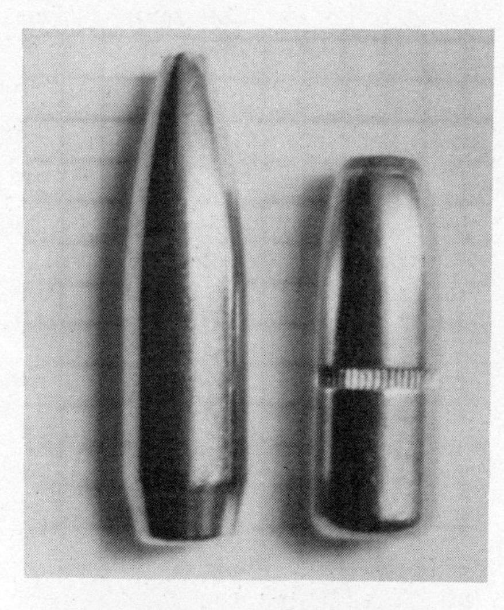

Ballistic coefficient: Both bullets here, a 170-gr. flat nose and a 168-gr. pointed boat-tail, both 30 caliber, have the same sectional density, bu the long, gradually tapered curves of the 168-gr. bullet give it a much higher ballistic coefficient.

A Summary

Well, there is a big list to choose from, but we can boil it all down pretty well. If you're never (a long time) going to hunt anything bigger than deer or antelope, the 243 Winchester is a good choice, and its light recoil will make it fun for the rest of the family to shoot. The 6mm Remington might be a better choice if you are not going to handload because of the slightly greater variety of bullets available. Going up the scale, if you might expect to include an elk sometime and can shoot well, a 25-06 could be a good choice. Recoil is light, and though you might dream about Kodiak bear or moose, you can always deal with that problem in the fortunate event that it arises. If you are going to wish to keep your hand in on varmints, but can expect to have a chance to hunt from the Arctic Circle to Tierra del Fuego, the 270 Winchester is an outstanding choice, especially for the handloader.

The various 7mms? The 7x57mm, the 280 (7x64mm) and 284 will do anything the 270 will, especially if handloaded, and a couple of them —the 7x57mm and the 7x64mm—can be had with heavy bullets for the bigger stuff. Both have a fine worldwide history of success, notably in Africa.

For the non-varmint shooter who doesn't reload, the 30-06 is a good second choice, being perhaps better than the 270 for really large game (although the debate might be somewhat academic.) The 7mm Remington Magnum has a lot of power, but if you can handle the power and reload for varmints, it isn't a bad choice. Certainly its tremendous popularity must indicate something! If you're going farther afield, you'd better read John Taylor or Elmer Keith, and act accordingly, which means like a 338 or 375 H&H! ●

Bibliography

Keith, Elmer, *Guns and Ammo for Hunting Big Game.* Los Angeles; 1967.

Taylor, John, *African Rifles and Cartridges.* Harrisburg, Pa. 1948.

Truesdell, S. R., *The Rifle.* Harrisburg, Pa., 1947*.

White, Stewart Edward, *The Land of Footprints.* New York, 1913*.

——————, *Lions in the Path.* New York, 1925*.

Hatcher, Julian S., *Hatcher's Notebook.* 3rd ed. Harrisburg, Pa., 1962.

Waters, Ken, "Ye compleat exterior ballistics," GUN DIGEST, 25th ed., Northfield, Ill.

O'Connor, Jack, "The place to shoot", *Outdoor Life,* Jan. 1971.

——————, *Complete Book of Rifles and Shotguns.* 2nd ed., New York, 1965. See ch. 23, pp. 328-336.

Any GUN DIGEST, Chicago or Northfield, Ill.

*Out of print

Shooter's Showcase

Recommended Reading

Scrimshaw and Scrimshanders, by E. Norman Flayderman, is a whale of a good book (I couldn't resist that) on the art of scrimshaw and those who practiced it, mainly sailormen. This big volume (293 pages plus a bibliography, chapter notes and an index) contains 450 illustrations, the photography crisp and clear. Published by the author at New Milford, CT, 1972. $19.95

Small Arms of the Sea Services, by Robert H. Rankin (Col. USMC, ret.), is an important, major contribution to naval arms history. It covers the firearms and edged weapons of the U.S. Navy, Coast Guard and Marines, from the Revolution to 1972. The author's highly interesting and factual 215-page text is accompanied by some 350 excellent photographs. Published by N. Flayderman & Co., Inc., New Milford, CT, 1972. $14.50.

Firearms Control, by Colin Greenwood. The author, a Chief Inspector of Police in England, spent several months at Cambridge University's Institute of Criminology in researching this most important book. In it he traces the course of firearms controls in England and Wales from their onset in 1920 to the present. He found the control acts ineffectually written, generally, yet he notes that "...fifty years of very strict controls on pistols have left a vast pool of illegal weapons." On page 243 he wrote: "...one is forced to the rather startling conclusion that the use of firearms in crime was very much less when there was no controls of any sort and when anyone, convicted criminal or lunatic, could buy any style of firearm without restriction."

I urge you to buy or borrow this book, read it carefully, and use its surprising content in whatever way you can to inform and educate our opposition.

Published by Routledge & Kegan Paul, London, 1972. 255 pages plus appendix, references and an index. $11.50.

The Art of Engraving

The publisher of this new book is Bob Brownell (Brownells Inc., Rte. 2, Box 1, Montezuma, IA 50171), and it is only natural that he should describe author James B. Meek's efforts in glowing terms, exhausting the superlatives, ringing all the changes of laudatory encomiums. Listen to Bob: "...for the first time ever, a complete, authoritative, imaginative and detailed introduction—and training help—in the art of gun engraving."

What do I think? I couldn't agree more. This is truly a unique book, beautifully compiled, edited, and bound, full of top quality illustrations—almost 1400 photographs, drawings, layouts and designs, among them numerous instances of great engravers' works, their different styles, and so on. Hardbound in cloth, the special paper used amplifies the illustrations, many in color. Designed to lie flat on the bench, this 8½"x11" book should be in the library of anyone having the slightest interest in gun engraving.

There's a 600-entry cross-referenced index, a list of reference books and a directory of suppliers to the field. This is *the* book for the beginner, for the engraver who wants to better his work and sharpen his skills, and for even the masters. Why did I say "even?" It's the masters who remain insatiably curious, always seeking to learn. Arnold Griebel, when he was past 70, spent a couple of years at Chicago's Art Institute, studying anatomy! *The Art of Engraving* is $19.95, and a bargain at the price. J.T.A.

Replica Gun Books

Facsimiles of old firearms and ammo catalogs has grown greatly in recent years, and the Personal Firearms Record Book Co. (Box 201, Park Ridge, IL 60068) now has a raft of titles available. Their latest brochure, yours for a stamp, describes some 40 catalogs, including old Colt, S&W, Maynard, Remington, Stevens, Winchester, you name 'em. Prices are reasonable—from $1 to $3 for most, with a few big ones at up to $7.50.

New Walther Book

James L. Rankin, assisted by Gary Green, has authored and produced an excellent new hard-cover work, *Walther Models PP and PPK 1929-1945.* Shown in its 142 pages (8½"x 11",) are 91 illustrations—87 are big-scale photographs, most by far fine quality, and 4 pages of drawings.

An ample and highly detailed text fully complements the profuse photography. Though an index is not included, and there are several misspellings of German words here and there, these are minor matters that in no way affect the basic worth of this big contribution to collectors of the Walther models covered. Highly recommended.

Copies are available by mail from James L. Rankin, 3615 Anderson Road, Coral Gables, FL 33134, at $11.95 plus 50¢ postage. J.T.A.

Films on the Outdoors

That's the title of the latest revised and updated booklet listing outstanding 16mm sound films—mostly in full color—produced by members of the National Shooting Sports Foundation (NSSF).

Dozens of titles are listed, many of them loaned free, and the subjects covered show a broad range—hunting, gun safety, reloading, Skeet and trap shooting, wildlife and conservation.

See your sports shop first for a copy, or send a 10c stamped large envelope to the NSSF, 1075 Post Road, Riverside, CT 06878. J.T.A.

New Bishop Catalog

Bishop's latest catalog, with over 200 illustrations of the standard and custom gunstocks they make, from log to finish, is ready for mailing. Many views are in full color, and there's detailed information about gunstocks and how to order them.

The new Bishop catalog will be sent on receipt of $1.00, which applies toward the first order from the book. Want more information? Write E.C. Bishop & Son. Inc., P.O. Box 7, Warsaw, MO 65355. J.T.A.

Woodcraft Supply Corp.

If you're interested in woodworking the latest 8½x11 WSC catalog (50c postpaid) has to be a must. Its 48 pages, many in full color, show the finest in tools of all kinds. Many of the quality products pictured and described are exclusive with WSC. Where else can you find "brass" finger planes? J.T.A.

CVA Rifle Kit

Do-it-yourself gun kits are nothing new to the black powder crowd. Quite a few companies offer kits to build anything from colonial pistols, flint and percussion rifles and derringers to Zouave rifles, but Connecticut Valley Arms now offers something different—a kit to build a Mauser-action hunting rifle.

The heart of the rifle is the well-known Santa Barbara Mauser-type barreled action, already fitted and headspaced. Furnished in the white, it needs only final polishing and bluing to complete. Or, it can be left in the white—it's up to the individual. The hammer-forged barrel, though not of match quality, should be amply accurate for the average hunter's needs. The action is tapped for scope mounting, leaving one less critical operation to be completed by the home gunsmith.

Also included in the kit are a fully adjustable trigger with side safety, steel trigger guard and hinged quick-release floorplate and a ventilated recoil pad.

The stock is European walnut, fully contoured and 90% inletted, requiring only final fitting, finishing and, if desired, checkering. Surprisingly, a checkering tool is included, with full instructions on its use.

The rifle is offered in a fairly wide array of calibers—243, 270, 7x57, 308, 30-06, 7mm Rem. Mag. and 300 Win. Mag. Magazine capacity is 5 rounds for standard calibers, 3 in magnums.

Barrels are 24" long, over-all length is about 44" and the weight is 7-7½ pounds.

At $139.95 this kit isn't cheap, but may give hours of pleasure as you put it together to suit your tastes. Buying all the pieces separately would cost more, certainly, but on the other hand, you could buy a new Ruger 77 for only some $30 more! CVA is also doing the collecting fraternity a favor by saving uncommon or even rare rifles the agony of "sporterizing." The supply of military guns has been drying up since the 1968 importation laws went into effect, and collectors need all the original guns they can get. We've seen far too many fine guns ruined by shortening stocks, checkering, rebluing and whatnot.

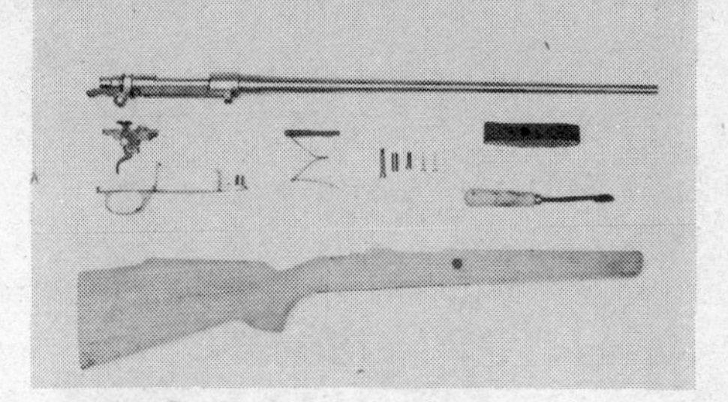

To introduce their new kit CVA is holding a contest to find the best completed rifle. The winner will receive a free trophy Ibex hunt at the YO Ranch in Texas. Second through 5th place prizes are various black powder guns from the CVA line. Rifles will be judged on the basis of stock design, fit, finish and attention to detail. All operations, except bluing, but not including polishing, must be done by the contestant. Five finalists will have their dealers send the rifles to CVA (CVA covers shipping and insurance costs) for final judging. The contest is open to amateurs only. Anyone deriving more than 20% of his income from gunsmithing will not be considered eligible.

More information? Write to Connecticut Valley Arms, Inc. Saybrook Road, Haddam, CT 06483. H.A.M.

GVA/Rif-L-Vise

GVA Enterprises is marketing a novel and useful tool called Rif-L-Vise. The device is a padded fixture to hold long guns for a variety of operations and can be used easily and efficiently by the tinkerer or professional gunsmith.

The test sample, ruggedly constructed of first grade lumber without knots or holes, is stained a light color and finished with a plastic material impervious to most solvents. All corners have been shaped and smoothed to prevent slivers or abrasions when working around it. Carpeting covers the fore-end block, grip block, rear stock block and clamping block—all parts that will come in contact with the gun once it is mounted. Base of the Rif-L-Vise measures 28"x5½"x1½", the fore-end block is 9"x5½"x1½" and has a deep V-notch that will accomodate most guns.

Rif-L-Vise is a high-quality, rugged tool that should prove handy to both the master gunsmith and the "kitchen table mechanic" alike. It provides a "third hand" to hold the work during disassembly and assembly operations with a minimum of obstructions and with little danger of damaging the gun. Because of the necessary bulk of the design and construction the

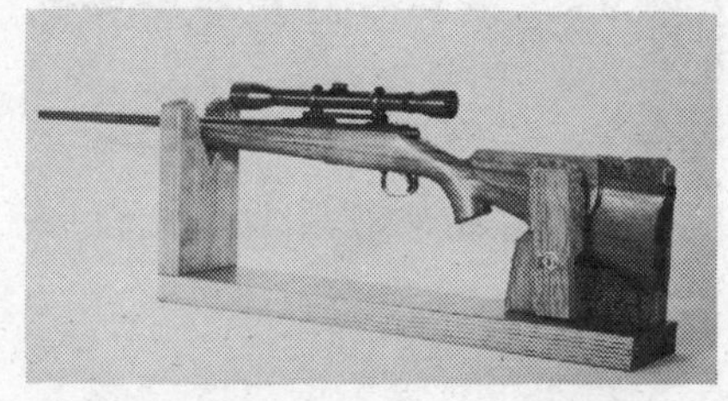

vise may present storage problems to the apartment or small home dweller, but the tool does perform its designed task well. It is available from GVA Enterprises, P.O. Box 725, Garland, TX 75040 for $19.95. H.A.M.

NH Shooting Stand

Looking for a portable shooting rest to take into the field? NH Industries is manufacturing and distributing a monopod design that we have been testing with good results. This one is simple, yet rugged enough to give many years of hard use.

The rest is comprised of a ⅝" rod, handle, slide with thumbscrew and rest arm.

The handle is made of 1"x3½" aluminum alloy with rounded ends, giving ample gripping area for pushing the stand into the ground. The heart of the stand is the ⅝-inch round rod 36 inches long, pointed and fluted at the end for easy insertion. The handle is threaded to the vertical rod, not pinned or sweated-on. The rest arm is ⅜-inch round aluminum, cold forged to shape and cold pressure-welded in the slide. Foam rubber covers the moveable arm to prevent marring of rifle stocks and to provide a cushioned rest for the hand.

This is an excellent shooting accessory and while crossed sticks are cheaper, they don't offer the durability and sturdiness of the NH product. The stand is available for $13.95 postpaid from NH Industries, James Drive, R.D. 1, Denver, PA 17517 H.A.M.

Remington Belt and Buckle

Remington Arms Co. has an attractive offer for the well-dressed shooter. It is a combination leather belt and strikingly good looking trophy belt buckle. The belt is 1¾" wide, attractively saddle-stitched, dark brown in color. It has a triple snap, folding loop at the end to accomodate any buckle made for 1¾" belts. Four sizes are available: small (30-32), medium (34-36), medium large (38-40) and large (42-44).

The buckle is a handsome combination of current design and popular 19th century styling favored by collectors and shooters alike. It has a hand brushed, antique brass finish and is 3¼"x2⅛" in size. Dominant feature on the buckle is a large English setter on point, sculpted in bas relief with a tastefully lettered Remington logo on top and a Remington Model 1100 shotgun across the bottom.

To get this belt and buckle set, just send the tops from two boxes of Remington ammunition (shotshell or metallics) with a check or money order for $5 to Remington Arms Co., Inc., P.O. Box 9500, Bridgeport, CT 06602. Be sure to specify the size you want.

H.A.M.

Lou Imperato Buys Iver Johnson

Lou Imperator, now the President and owner of Iver Johnson Arms & Cycle Works, was the founder of L.A. Distributors, once one of the largest importers and distributors of handguns in the U.S.

Imperato has already added new products to the Iver Johnson line; the Cattleman single-action revolvers and a new over-under shotgun, and they're also tooling-up for a new double-barrel shotgun. We feel that we can look to a bright future for both Lou and Iver Johnson Arms & Cycle Works.

J.T.A.

New Hornady Bullet Board

Ninety-two rifle, jacketed pistol and lead bullets are shown on Hornady's latest Bullet Board. Designed for reloaders as a ready reference to the Hornady bullet types and calibers, it shows 10 more bullets than ever before, including Hornady's latest match rifle bullets with the new rebated boat-tail design.

The board, note, displays real bullets, from 17 to 45 caliber, these set off by a wide, handsome frame depicting hand-carved scenes of hunting and wildlife. The bullets, permanently bonded to the board, are tarnish-proofed to preserve their bright appearance indefinitely.

Considered collector's items by reloaders and others, the new Bullet Board costs $25, and your dealer should have them. Let's see – allowing $5 for the frame, that's about 20¢ a bullet.

J.T.A.

New Predator Call

Johnny Stewart has a new – and patented – call for bringing in predatory animals and birds. The patented aspect lies in a pitch/tone control that offers a wide range of sounds. Soft, high-pitch squeaks, mid-range tones and the loudest of long-range calls are produced by pressure from the lips or teeth against a soft "button" above the vibrating reed or "voice."

The new call eliminates any need for movement – the hands are free to operate the gun or camera. However, the pitch can be also controlled by pressures applied to the button by the index finger instead of the lips or teeth. A tool is included for insertion or removal of the "voice."

Stewart considers this new call the finest mouth-blown predator call ever made. For more information write to Johnny Stewart Game Calls, Inc., Box 7594, Waco, TX 76710.

J.T.A.

B & M Shooting Rest

This is the lightweight and versatile rifle rest introduced by Belding & Mull – makers of loading tools and shooters' supplies. Single-post and bipod rests have a place, but nothing equals a tripod for stability. About $25.

Numrich 44/40 Gun Blue

Used daily by many large gunmakers, Numrich Arms 44/40 Gun Blue is a best seller in its field. Not a paste, 44/40 is an easy-to-apply liquid – just wipe it on and wipe it off. It all takes only seconds.

The resulting deep, blue-black finish will beautify any gun, and you'll have a long-lasting protective coating. Cost – $2.79 for a 2-ounce bottle (add 60¢ for postage and handling).

Hat Saver

A useful device, this Hat-Saver, especially in such vehicles as pickups, FWDs and such, where space up front is often scarce. The chromed wire hat holder, attached to a spring-loaded bracket, is quickly mounted centrally above the windshield, usually by clamping it behind the screw that holds the sun visor clamp. Pull the Hat Saver down, put your hat inside the wire loop, let go and all snaps upward against the roof – out of the way but readily accessible.

Send $3.95 to Hat Saver Co., Box 307, Rosenberg, TX 77471.

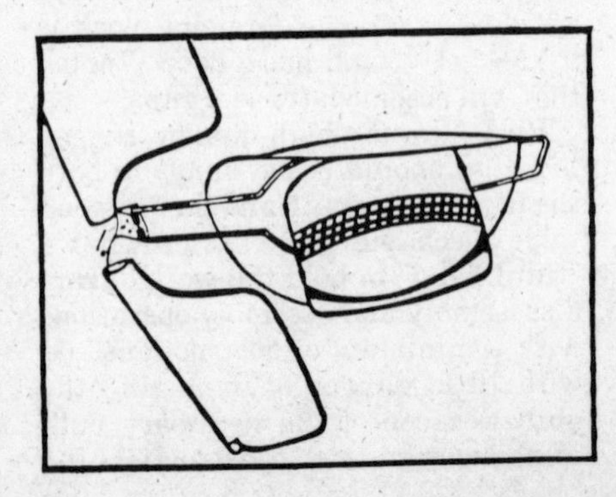

AMERICAN BULLETED CARTRIDGES

A detailed and comprehensive report on recently developed and introduced metallic cartridges and components—including a few potent wildcats.

by KENNETH L. WATERS

LATEST DEVELOPEMENTS IN METALLIC CARTRIDGES

Undistinguished by startling announcements, the past year has nevertheless witnessed a number of worthwhile developments, particularly evident in the various components supplied to the burgeoning handloaders' market. New bullets, powders and primers induce continuing experimentation of the sort that has historically proven beneficial to improved accuracy and—sometimes at least—enhanced game stopping ability. Claims for the latter quality, of course, require more prolonged testing to verify than does the question of accuracy.

Especially noticeable this year has been a renewed interest in the use of cast bullets. In my opinion not all of this ground-swell can be attributed to the spiraling costs of jacketed bullets. The typical reloader these days is probably more inquisitive concerning ballistics, both internal and external, than formerly, more demanding of factual information, and, perhaps, more inclined to try things for himself. Industry appears to be bending an ear to his requests.

Winchester - Western

First, correction of an error in last year's ABC section, in which it was stated that Winchester had resumed production of 220 Swift cartridges and components. This wasn't wholly correct. New W-W 220 Swift *cases* are being produced for reloaders, but not loaded Swift cartridges. Norma, however, can furnish 220 Swift loaded ammo.

No new cartridges from the Big Red W this year, but we'll have the makings of many a fine handload, with a so far un-named new slow-burning ball powder to replace the discontinued 780-BR for use in large capacity rifle cartridges. This powder rounds out the revised line of Winchester-Western Ball powders introduced in 1973, plus 7 new primers and a spate of new match-grade rifle bullets.

Manufactured to closer tolerances for increased uniformity of ignition, the new primer line includes a standard Large Rifle cap to replace the famous 120, a Magnum Large Rifle primer (a first for Winchester) to be used with ball and slow-burning "stick" powders, a Small Rifle primer designed for suitability with high-pressure as well as lower intensity loads in the smaller cases, two pair of pistol primers—Large (.210") Standard and Magnum and Small (.175") Standard and Magnum.

It's a fair assumption that these new primers are keyed to the improved line of W-W ball powders, in which event it is interesting that there will *not* be a Magnum Small primer. Probable release date for the new primers is said to be about February, 1975, with the first production run scheduled for September, 1974.

Earliest of the new bullets to appear are expected to be in calibers 22 (.224"), 6mm (.243") and 30 (.308"). Further details were lacking at the time of this writing.

Apparently discontinued this year, since they are missing from the 1974 W-W arms and ammunition catalog, are the 22 Winchester Automatic rimfire cartridge and the 30 Carbine loading with FMC bullet.

Remington-Peters

No. 1 item in the R-P ammo line for 1974 is their new loading for the 45 ACP—a high velocity round with 185-gr. JHP bullet said to develop 950fps MV from a 5" test barrel, with 370 f.p. of muzzle energy. At 50-yards, velocity is still 900fps, giving a mid-range trajectory of only 1.3"; at 100 yards the comparable figures are 860 fps and 5.3"—not bad for the old war horse!

This new R-P loading will probably find favor with those handgunners wanting to use the Government Model Colt for hunting. Whether a striking velocity averaging 900 fps will let the hollow-point bullet expand reliably on suitable size game remains to be seen. We haven't been able to run trials with the new load, but one thing's certain—it's almost sure to be better than the slow-moving 230-gr. FMJ standard bullet of the 45 Auto.

Two good 38 Special High Velocity loads—125- and 158-

gr. "Semi-Jacketed HP" with muzzle velocities of 1370- and 1150 fps respectively—were omitted from the 1974 Remington arms and ammo catalog. Ted McCawley, Remington's PRO, had the answer. The 125-gr. HP load, mistakenly left out of the catalog, *is* being produced. The 158-gr. HP has been dropped, I learned, because they couldn't get adequate performance. A commendable action, I'd say.

Sad to relate, Remington didn't adopt a single one of my suggestions, advanced last year, as to how existing components could be paired in additional combinations to produce a more varied and useful factory cartridge line-up; I felt and hoped that such a step(s) would increase the popularity of some of the better old cartridges. Had those suggestions entailed the expense of producing new components, this lack of action would be readily understandable. Less obvious are the reasons for not combining a standard production bullet, the 25-cal. 100-gr. PSP for example, with a regularly produced case such as the 257 Roberts, to provide an improved factory loading. If it's mystifying to you why this isn't done, it's even more so to me.

Federal

New centerfire metallic cartridges from Federal for 1974 include two 25-06 rifle loadings and 3 handgun cartridges—one each for the 9mm Luger, 38 Special and 357 Magnum.

The new 25-06 loads are: a 90-gr. HP with 3500fps MV and 2450 f.p. ME, plus a 117-gr. Hi-Shok SP with 3130fps MV and 2500 f.p. ME, all figures from a 26" barrel. Mid-range trajectories over 300 yards are listed at only 4.7" and 5.5" respectively—flat shooting loads indeed! Federal recommends the 90-gr. loading for varmints, the 117-gr. for medium game.

Ballistics for the new Federal handgun rounds are shown nearby.

Cartridge	Bullet (grs)	MV (fps)	ME (f.p.)	MRT @ 50 yds.	Bbl.
9mm Auto	115 gr JHP	1160	345	0.9"	4"
38 Special HV	125 gr JHP	1370	520	0.7"	6"
357 Magnum HV	125 gr JHP	1675	780	0.5"	8⅜"

These should make terrific handgun hunting loads.

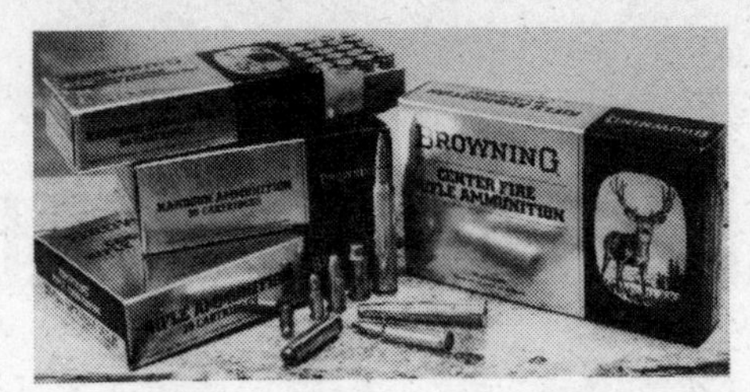

Browning

As everyone must know by now, Browning is deeply involved in marketing factory-produced metallic ammunition. In my tests it proved to be a quality line, both as to component materials and resultant accuracy.

Their newest listing (mid-1974), shows the addition of a 22 Rimfire Magnum loading with a jacketed HP bullet, a move which would seem to reflect the increasing popularity of that cartridge.

Two Browning centerfires may have been dropped—unless this too is a listing mistake! Absent from the price list is the 30 Carbine round, though still appearing in the catalog ammunition table. Vanished from *both* references is the 9mm Luger HV loading with 100-gr. JHP bullet.

Super Vel

Here's one of the hottest items this year (the pun's intended)! In December of 1973 Lee Jurras announced his intentions to produce 44 Auto Mag cartridges, along with the still newer 357 Auto Mag rounds, this last the 44 AMP case necked down to take .357" bullets. Then in February, 1974, came further word that empty cases as well as factory ammo for the 357 AMP "should be available within the next 90 days"—in other words, before you read this.

Lee added that they were still working to develop what they consider to be a suitable 44 AMP factory loading, expected to materialize sometime soon after the 357 AMP.

Plans for the 357 AMP tentatively call for a 158-gr. JSP Super Vel bullet at around 1657 fps, and a 137-gr. JSP at about 1950fps from the standard 6½" barrel. Velocities from the special 8½" unribbed barrel will, of course, be higher—perhaps 2075fps with the 137-gr. load. This will make the 357 AMP just about the flattest-shooting pistol yet if one doesn't include those single shot arms chambered for small rifle cartridges.

From a number of years experience testing Super Vel ammo, I've come to have a great deal of respect for and faith in Lee Jurras' products, most recent of which has been his 190-gr. JHP load for the 45 ACP. Any time you can revitalize the old auto the way that load does and still get target accuracy—my 45 delivering 5-shot groups as small as 1¾" at 50 feet—even a working handloader is impressed!

Omark - CCI

The "Good Ol' Boys" (as they're now calling themselves) have come through with two important items this year.

The first is a pair of loadings for the 22 Winchester Rimfire Magnum—one with a fully copper-coated bullet, the other a hollow-point—loaded into a case constructed with extra thick walls in the critical base area, for additional strength. Called the 22 Maxi-Mag by CCI, muzzle velocity of these new rounds is given as 2025fps from a 24" barrel and 1565 from a 6½" revolver barrel. Remaining velocities from the rifle are 1688 fps at 50 yards, 1407 at 100 and 1186 at 150 long steps. A welcome addition indeed for rimfire shooters and non-reloading short range varminters with humane killing power far beyond any 22 Long Rifle cartridge.

Second in order, but maybe more important, are CCI's new Bench Rest primers, production of which began in January, 1974. Available in two sizes—Small Rifle (numbered BR-4) and Large Rifle (numbered BR-2)— these caps represent an all-out effort to perfect primer performance for maximum accuracy.

Of the same size as CCI's standard No. 5. 400 and 200 primers they can, of course, be seated in cases in the same manner. The difference lies in the special care exercised in their fabrication, assembly and inspection. Already they've turned in some pretty fantastic accuracy results, and indications are there'll be much more to come as they receive more widespread use. Their higher cost ($11.95 per thousand in mid-1974) can be nominal for accuracy-conscious match and varmint shooting riflemen.

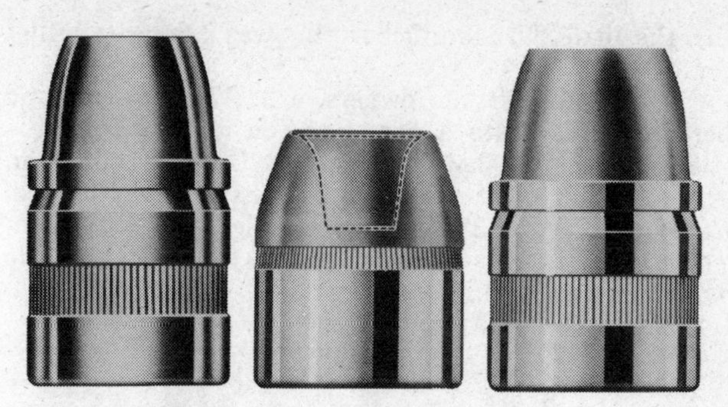

Speer's 1974 handgun bullets. From left—44-cal. 240-gr. semi-wadcutter; 45-cal. 200-gr. hollow point and, last, 45-cal. 250-gr. semi-wadcutter.

Speer

The Speer product line for 1974, as usual, offers shooters a number of new goodies. For precision-minded bench-resters and varminters there is an ultra-accurate .224″ bullet weighing 52 grains, called the Gold Match. A hollow-point, and soft-swaged under the utmost quality

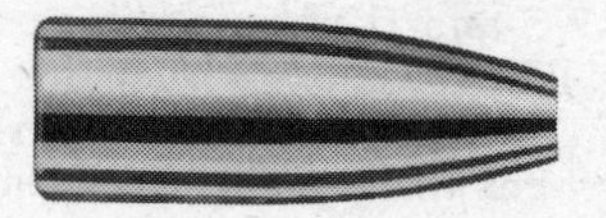

Speer's 22-cal. 52-gr. Gold Match bullet, designed for top competition shooting.

control, they are said to be (we haven't tested them yet) capable of ⅓-MOA groups. Too, their thin jackets should insure rapid expansion, eliminating ricochets.

My turkey hunting friends, along with riflemen who pursue small fur-bearing animals, will be glad to learn of Speer's new full-metal-jacketed bullets—a 55-gr. in 22-caliber (.224″) and a 90-gr. in 6mm (.243″)—both spit-

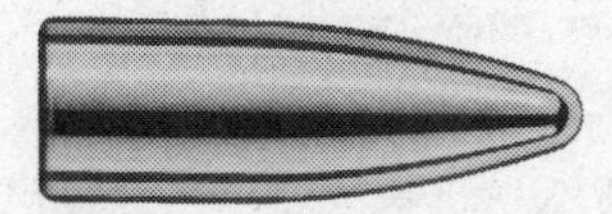

Speer's 22-cal. 55-gr. full metal jacket should make good turkey load.

zers. Capable of taking game up to the size of foxes and coyotes with properly placed hits, they can eaily be loaded ed to lower velocities for shooting small game without excessive destruction of meat or skin.

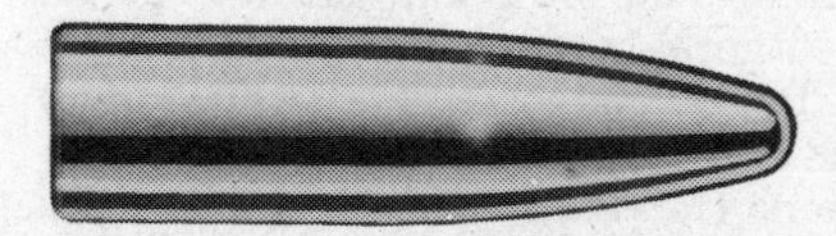

Speer's 6mm 90-gr. full metal jacket bullet, meant for minimal damage to meat and hide.

Handgunners, too, have been thought of—there's a 125-gr. 9mm round-nose lead bullet that will feed reliable through autoloading pistols, a 240-gr. lead .430″ semi-wadcutter for 44 Specials and Magnums, and a 452″ lead SWC weighing 250 grains for the 45s. Carrying a special lubricant called "Film-Cote" to prevent bore leading at low-to-medium velocities, these bullets are intended to give match accuracy at economy prices.

Another handgun bullet, the Speer 45-cal. 200-gr. jacketed, has been redesigned from its round nose, soft point form to a hollow-point type with wide and deep nose cavity, meant to give maximum expansion even at moderate velocities. Lead nose exposure has also been eliminated to prevent malfunctions in feeding from autoloader magazines. Having had some less-than-satisfactory experiences with similarly-designed bullets (of other makes) in autoloading pistols, I'll reserve judgment on this one until I've had a chance to try them.

Since writing last year's report I've been testing Speer's Mag-Tip rifle bullets in 7mm caliber. The idea here was to produce a big-game hunting bullet which would be the best possible compromise between a round nose and spitzer shapes. If it could be given the ballistic superiority of a spitzer, with flat trajectory and a high percentage of retained energy at long range, coupled with a round-nose's reliable expansion characteristics at varying striking velocities, as well as resistance to deformation in the magazine, it would embody the best of both worlds.

Naturally, the result is a compromise. I doubt that they are the full equal of both conventional types in *all* respects, but that is to be expected, and they do seem to have gone a long way in that direction, proving nicely accurate in the bargain. Currently, Mag-Tips are available in 7mm (160- and 175-gr.) and 30 calibers (150- and 180-gr.).

Finally, attention should be called to a pair of Speer bullets of somewhat unusual diameters which can well turn out to be lifesavers to those shooters having rifles in these calibers. I refer to the 9.3mm (.366″) 250-gr. soft point (this writer has been using these in a 9.3X62mm Mauser and a 360 No. 2 Greener double rifle) and the .228″ 70-gr. semi-spitzer adapted to such rifles as the 22 Savage High Power and the 228 Ackley. Understandably, they won't sell like the more common calibers, but where needed they're bound to be appreciated. Speer deserves a vote of thanks.

Hornady

Forward-looking Joyce Hornady has been busy (as usual), not only expanding his line of first-class bullets, but improving them, as witness his 3 great boat-tail match bullets: a 7mm 162-gr. HP, a 30-cal. 168-gr. HP, and another 30-cal. HP, this one a heavier 190-gr. for long range shooting a la Wimbledon, Leech, etc.

These comparatively new bullets, though amply tested and proven in tough competition, have now been modified slightly by giving them a rather sharp and precisely formed shoulder at the juncture of bullet body and tapered boat-tail base, giving them a rebated and radiused profile. Hornady says this new form gives improved concentricity between body and boat-tail, and that the uniformly-shaped heel prevents uneven gas escape, thereby assuring evenly distributed gas pressure against the bullet bases as they leave the muzzle. Great expectations are entertained for this trio.

Although I have yet to learn why, Hornady has discontinued the useful 129-gr. round-nose 6.5mm bullet. For use in taking deer-size game in brush or woods hunting with the little 6.5 Mannlicher, this was a favorite bullet of mine.

A final note. All you owners of 33 Winchesters (and there must be quite a passel of you judging from the letters I receive), should know that Hornady offers an excellent 200-gr. flat-nose SP which is a near-duplicate of the original factory 33 Winchester bullet, even to the cannelure location. This bullet eliminates the major obstacle to handloading for that fine old rifle.

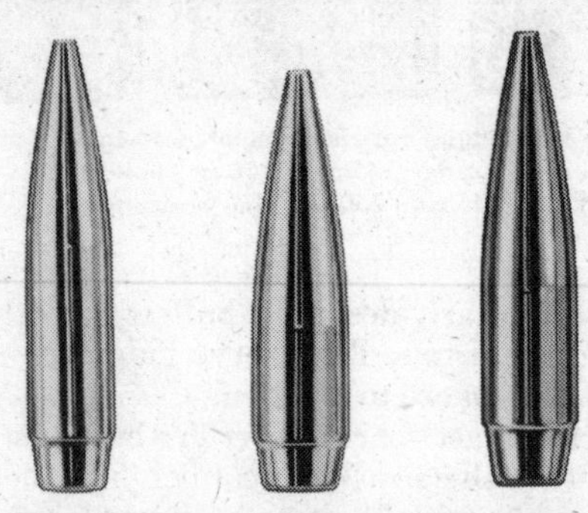

Horandy's newly designed Match bullets with rebated boat-tail. From left—162-gr. 7mm; 168-gr. 30-cal. and 190-gr. 30-cal.

Sierra

Latest arrival from Sierra is a 30-cal. 165-gr. spitzer SP, which should be just the ticket for handloaders of the 300 Savage, 308 Winchester and 30-06, as well as the various 30-cal. magnums. It is by now pretty common knowledge that 165 grains is considered the optimum weight ballistically in this bore size, and that is particularly true of cartridges with the case capacity of 30-06 or 308.

In my 30-cal. rifles Sierra's earlier 165-gr., a hollow-point boat-tail, was a fine performer, delivering splendid accuracy along with high retained velocity, but I frankly expect the new spitzer SP to be a superior hunting bullet, combining the best features of both 150- and 180-gr. spitzers.

Quite as important is a trio of Sierra bullets received too late for reporting in last year's ABC. These are the 338-cal. 250-gr. spitzer boat-tail, a 35-cal. 200-gr. round nose, and a 300-gr. flat nose SP for the 45-70.

These 3 bullets, representing Sierra's entry into the big-caliber field, have made impressive showings, and they fill a great need of reloaders in these bore sizes. Made to Sierra's demanding standards of exactness, these are hunting bullets emphasizing controlled expansion and weight retention for enhanced game field performance. We hope that one day Sierra will add a 375-cal. spitzer and a second, heavier 35-cal. to their impressive bullet line.

Paul Jaeger

Yes, I know this report is supposed to be concerned with *American* bulleted cartridges (hence ABC), but I've previously stretched things a bit to include Americanized products—those imports marketed for, sold to and used by American shooters.

With many Americans owning numerous firearms of foreign make, many for which no ammunition is produced domestically, I'm going to include potential sources of supply. This problem has assumed particular importance with the disappearance of the formerly great DWM concern.

Paul Jaeger, Inc. (Box 67, Jenkintown, PA 19046), is one such source of RWS centerfire rifle cartridges and Geco handgun ammunition. A brochure just received (mid-1974) from RWS shows 71 different rifle loadings in 23 calibers, plus 4 handgun calibers. Some, such as the 7x57, 8x57 and 375 H&H Magnum are familiar numbers, but many others, ranging from the 5.6x50 Magnum to the 9.3x74R, are German calibers. Included is the 5.6x52R, which is none other than the American (discontinued) 22 Savage High Power. The 375 H&H is a new loading for RWS.

Latest word is that RWS and DWM are now one company, but availability of RWS products here may be a bit uncertain. Shortages of critical materials is as great in Europe as it is here, perhaps more so. To riflemen especially this will be a cause for regret; let's hope it doesn't last long.

The Bullet Boys

Under the expert guidance of George Huebner, a new organization calling itself "The Bullet Boys" was formed early in 1973 at Jaffrey, New Hampshire. Specializing in the custom casting of bullets of all types for obsolete as well as modern arms, the BBs claim to offer "The world's largest, most comprehensive line of cast bullets," with "over 500 different designs in stock."

From what I can gather, they appear to have assembled a very large number of Lyman and other moulds, so they're prepared to cast bullets for just about any caliber you care to name, sizing and lubricating them to suit each individual bore size inscfar as possible. Materials used include virgin lead with tin and antimony as hardening agents, offered in a choice of three alloys. Sample bullets can be ordered with their "price refunded on orders of 100 or more."

To give you some idea as to the scope of their listings, there are tiny 25-gr. bullets for the 17 calibers and 550-gr. slugs for the 460 Weatherby amongst the moderns. Old U.S. rifle calibers extend from the 22-15-60 Stevens to the 50-140 Sharps and 58 Berdan carbine, with just about everything in between. Handgun bullets are available from the 22 Rem-Jet to the 50 Remington Navy, and there's an equally complete listing for British and European sporting cartridges, as well as most military rifle calibers, modern and obsolete.

I've found my test samples of these bullets to be of professional quality. This is a good way to get that 11mm Spanish Rolling Block, Winchester 50-110 Express or what-have-you shooting again. They also operate an ammunition reloading service, custom loading with either smokeless or black powder. An excellent catalog is available.

Elk Mountain Shooters Supply

This Pasco, Washington, firm offers an unusual service to shooters; in particular, to shooters of the various 6mm rifles.

Their very special hunting bullet is called the "Alaskan 155," a 6mm (.243") bullet that weighs *156 grains!* It has a two-piece core, the forward part made the same as a typical SP bullet, but with a non-deformable tungsten alloy rear core weighing 65-grains, intended to remain intact and continue to penetrate if the nose section should shatter on contact with bone.

Ordinarily a 6mm bullet of this weight would be too long to stabilize with normal rifling twists, but since the tungsten alloy used in the base section has a specific gravity about twice that of lead, these Alaskan bullets have proven stable in the writer's 6mm Remington, 243 Winchester and 240 Weatherby rifles.

The originator's basic premise is best set forth in his own words: "With this type of construction it is unnecessary to sacrifice the rapid expansion useful when hunting smaller game to gain the penetration necessary when hunting larger species." Loading data provided for this bullet in 243 and 6mm calibers indicates that velocities of 2130 fps to as high as 2850 are possible, but includes a warning that they must be seated deeply in cases (to an over-all cartridge length of 2½" in the 243 and 2⅝" in the 6mm Remington) in order to obtain a freebore effect necessary to allow for the higher inertia of these heavy bullets, and to prevent the development of excessively high pressures.

They're expensive, but might well be the answer for those hunters who insist upon using 6mms for the larger big game. Too, if a single bullet can spell the difference between success and failure of a costly hunt, then it becomes cheap at any price within reason.

A New Big Game Cartridge?

Although I'd been thinking for some years about the desirability of a new 40-cal. cartridge for big game, I hadn't done anything about it, so when I heard that Bob Chatfield-Taylor had designed a new wildcat, calling it the 416 Taylor, I promptly called him. Rumors were flying about that one of the big arms and ammunition companies was thinking of adopting the cartridge and I wanted to get in on the ground floor.

While not exactly what I'd had in mind, his cartridge seemed reasonably close. Bob had taken the 458 Winchester Magnum case and necked it down to hold .416" bullets with an eye to duplicating the ballistics for the far-larger cased 416 Rigby in the smaller-capacity U.S. case. What's more, he'd succeeded in doing it, attaining 2400 fps with 400-gr. bullets out of a 22" barrel.

John Taylor, the late renowned African hunter, had maintained there was no finer cartridge for use in bolt action rifles on dangerous game than the 416 Rigby. And here Bob Chatfield-Taylor had developed its full equivalent with the important advantages of using a standard American-made case taking our Boxer-type primers and sufficiently compact to be accommodated by standard length actions.

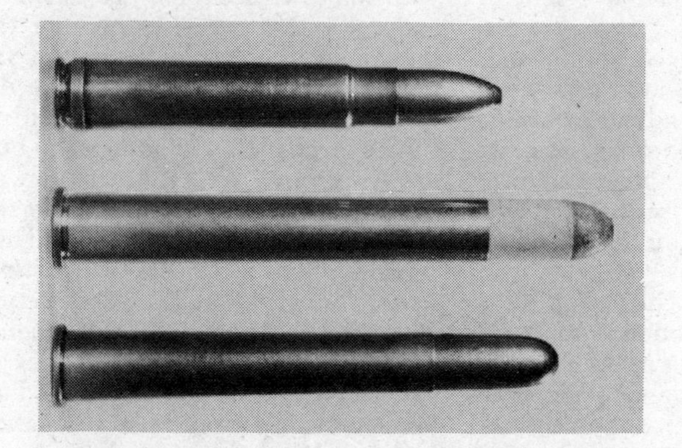

From the top—Bob Chatfield-Taylor's 416 Belted Magnum, the new RCBS 45 Basic case (3.15" long) with an old 400-gr. Sharps bullet seated, and John Amber's 416 Creedmoor, made on the earlier Nonte 2¾" basic case.

Bob has further pointed out that, because of its higher velocity, the 416 Taylor is flatter shooting than a 458, extending its range somewhat, while delivering less recoil to the shooter. To me there's little doubt but what he has produced a most excellent cartridge for African hunting.

My own plans for a Big 40, however, had evolved around the concept of a potent stopper for Alaskan game rather than African hunting, dating back to Elmer Keith's early work with the 400 Whelen. Now, with Chatfield-Taylor's 416 a reality, I reasoned that all that was needed was to change bullets—switch from his 400-gr. prescription to a 300-gr. Properly constructed bullets of that weight should be plenty adequate, even for Kodiak bears, in addition to which velocities would be still higher, trajectories even flatter and recoil reduced considerably.

With those thoughts in mind, I prevailed upon Bob to allow me the use of his reamers, with which Buzz Huntington of RCBS could make me a set of their incomparable forming and loading dies. Bob graciously agreed, as did Buzz, and the dies promptly arrived. CCB likewise sent me some 416 bullets, 300-gr. semi-spitzers and 400-gr. round nose style.

All that remained was to have a rifle built for the 416 Taylor, not exactly a lightweight chore in itself. But fortune smiled once again when, in a talk with Steve Vogel of the Ruger organization, he offered the loan of a Model 77 Ruger which had been made up experimentally for the Taylor cartridge. Needless to say I accepted—like immediately!

The Ruger has a 24" barrel. Because of that, but also as a result of using a different powder (4320 in place of the 3031 Chatfield-Taylor had used), velocity with the 400-gr. bullets was boosted to 2447 fps.

Just as I had hoped, though, working with the 300-gr. semi-spitzer proved to be a whole new ball game. Even with the heaviest loads behind these bullets, recoil is so noticeably less that it more nearly resembles a 375 Magnum than a 458. Velocities of 2569 fps with 4064, 2680 with 3031, and a peak of 2711 with 4320 were chronographed, and when these figures are compared to the 300-gr. 375 Magnum's M.V. rating of 2550 fps, not to mention the difference in bullet diameter, it becomes obvious that the 416 Taylor is quite as capable of distinguishing itself in North America as it is in Africa.

Our Ruger 77 test rifle has stood up and functioned perfectly under the battering of several hundred potent 416 rounds, averaging between 1½" and 3" spreads for 5-shot groups from bench-rest at 100 yards. A fine consistent performance for any rifle with loads of this intensity and recoil.

Now if only Ruger could be persuaded to offer this rifle as a standard chambering, perhaps one of the big ammunition makers would see fit to adopt the cartridge as a factory standard. With its greater flexibility, the 416 Taylor could be expected to equal and very possibly exceed the popularity of the 458 Magnum.

Other Big 40s

Working independently, Bob Hagel has produced his 416-338, a cartridge varying only in dimensional details from the 416 Taylor, while using the same 300- and 400-gr. .416" Colorado Custom bullets. Despite its name, Bob reports actually using 458 Winchester cases necked down rather than 338 cases necked up, thus the basic case is also the same as that used by Chatfield-Taylor.

Ballistics, too, are quite similar, as one would expect from so many like components. For instance, Bob Hagel lists 68 grains of 3031 with the 400-gr. CCB bullet as

giving 2319 fps at the muzzle. The same identical load, except for primers, chronographed an average 2400 fps in my 416 Taylor-Ruger.

Apparently Hagel's barrel requires—and can use—somewhat heavier powder charges than mine, since he was able to go as high as 74/4320 with 400-gr. bullets while recording 2373 fps MV, whereas my cases started shedding primers at 73/4320, with readings averaging 2469 fps. Both rifles have 24" barrels.

Similarly, with the lighter 300-gr. semi-spitzers and 73/3031, Hagel's rifle developed 2646 fps compared to 2680 from our Ruger with 72/3031. However, these are only the sort of differences one might expect between any two rifles of the same caliber, and do not signify any superiority due to design.

A far more significant variance is to be seen in our differing findings concerning the use of 300-gr. bullets in this caliber, Hagel reporting some dissatisfaction with accuracy of the lighter slugs and concluding that they are less desirable than the 400-gr. for use on really big game species (which are seldom shot at long range anyway).

On the other hand, I've had excellent accuracy with 300-gr. bullets and selected loads in the 416 so long as all bullets were of uniform diameter, many 5-shot groups at 100 yards running only 1⅛" to 1⅞". Furthermore, it's my feeling that 300 grains is ample bullet weight for even the largest North American game animals, and I'd rather have the extra 250 fps velocity and the lighter recoil. In the final analysis, it's all a matter of what is being hunted. With Africa in mind, I'd have to go along with the 400-gr. bullets.

While on the subject of Big 40s, let's not forget Editor John Amber's contribution of a couple of years ago. Obviously with single shot rifles in mind, John dubbed his cartridge the "416 A.C." (for Amber Creedmoor—what else?), and chose the Nonte "Basic 45" case—a long straight rimmed shell with 45-70 rim and body diameters, but 2¾" long for greater powder capacity.

Necking these cases to hold the same 400-gr. .416" CCB (formerly Barnes) bullets with what John described as "not a bottleneck, just a taper that straightens out," he Hobaugh-barreled one of the large Farquharson actions, the stock a handsome job by Clayton Nelson of Enid, Oklahoma. From its 26" medium-weight barrel he tells me he's been getting about 2300-2350 fps, placing that cartridge in the same company as the 416 Taylor and 416-338 Hagel ballistically. Amber developed the 416 AC in 1972, and it's described and pictured in GD 27, pp. 54-55.

RCBS

For those shooters desiring to follow the Amber route and build a big 40-, 44- or 45-caliber rifle on one of the single-shot actions requiring a rimmed shell, RCBS has just announced availability of their new RCBS 45 Basic Case. Like the former Nonte Basic 45, this one has the same rim and body diameters of a 45-70 case, but with a length of 3.17" so that it may be used as-is for the 45-120-3¼" Sharps, or cut off to length for any of twenty-some other calibers ranging from the 33 Winchester to the 45-90 WCF and various long-case Sharps.

This is a drawn-brass case (as it must be to permit reforming to other calibers), and our solid head sample exhibits careful workmanship. Their price is not known so far, but I fully intend having a single shot rifle built or rebarreled in 45-120 Sharps caliber, and I'm reasonably certain I won't be alone in doing so.

Why the Buffalo Disappeared

Technically, his correct name is the American Bison. But the eulogies of history have immortalized him as the buffalo, and it seems likely this will remain his most common name.

An immigrant from the Asian continent, the buffalo was already here 200,000 years ago. Although primarily a grasslands animal of the great plains that stretched from Mexico into Canada, he ranged laterally from nearly coast to coast at one time. It was to the Plains Indian, however, that the presence of the shaggy king of the prairie was both unique and critical. He was not only their chief source of sustenance, but the cornerstone of their very survival.

Buffalo meat provided the Indians with food. Buffalo robes kept them warm in winter. The tanned hides made moccasins, clothing, teepees, even small boats. Rawhide from the buffalo was the Indians' rope. Horns, bones and hooves as well were put to a myriad of uses. If the buffalo did not need the Indian, these original and truly native Americans had surely come to need the buffalo.

In their estimated numbers of up to 60 million, the buffalo supply seemingly was inexhaustible. No doubt it would have been, except for one factor—the great westward movement of settlers.

As the settlers arrived, an unavoidable confrontation on land use began between a relatively advanced agrarian society on one side and a basically primitive nomadic society on the other. The ultimate result was inevitable. Both the Indians and the buffalo were doomed.

It is often said that the buffalo were *hunted* to near extinction. This is not so in the true sense of sport hunting. Rather, they were simply eliminated for a number of immediate reasons. They were slaughtered as a part of the white man's attempt to conquer the Indians, to clear them off land that was to be plowed, to feed hordes of railroad workers or just keep them off the tracks, and finally, to fatten the wallets of commercial hide entrepreneurs.

But, in the last analysis, the buffalo was the victim of a fundamental problem that confronted the settlers of the West. In the tillable plains areas, roaming hordes were incompatible with the sown sections of corn, wheat and oats that were to become the bread basket of a growing nation. On the range and farther west, the decision of those in the burgeoning towns and cities who would buy rather than raise their food was equally definitive. They preferred beef steaks to buffalo steaks. Thus these animals came close to extinction as much because of destruction of their habitat as well as from being over hunted.

Fortunately for posterity, the buffalo was saved from total extinction in time. His numbers today on protected refuges are such that annual harvests are now not only possible but necessary.

Dick Dietz

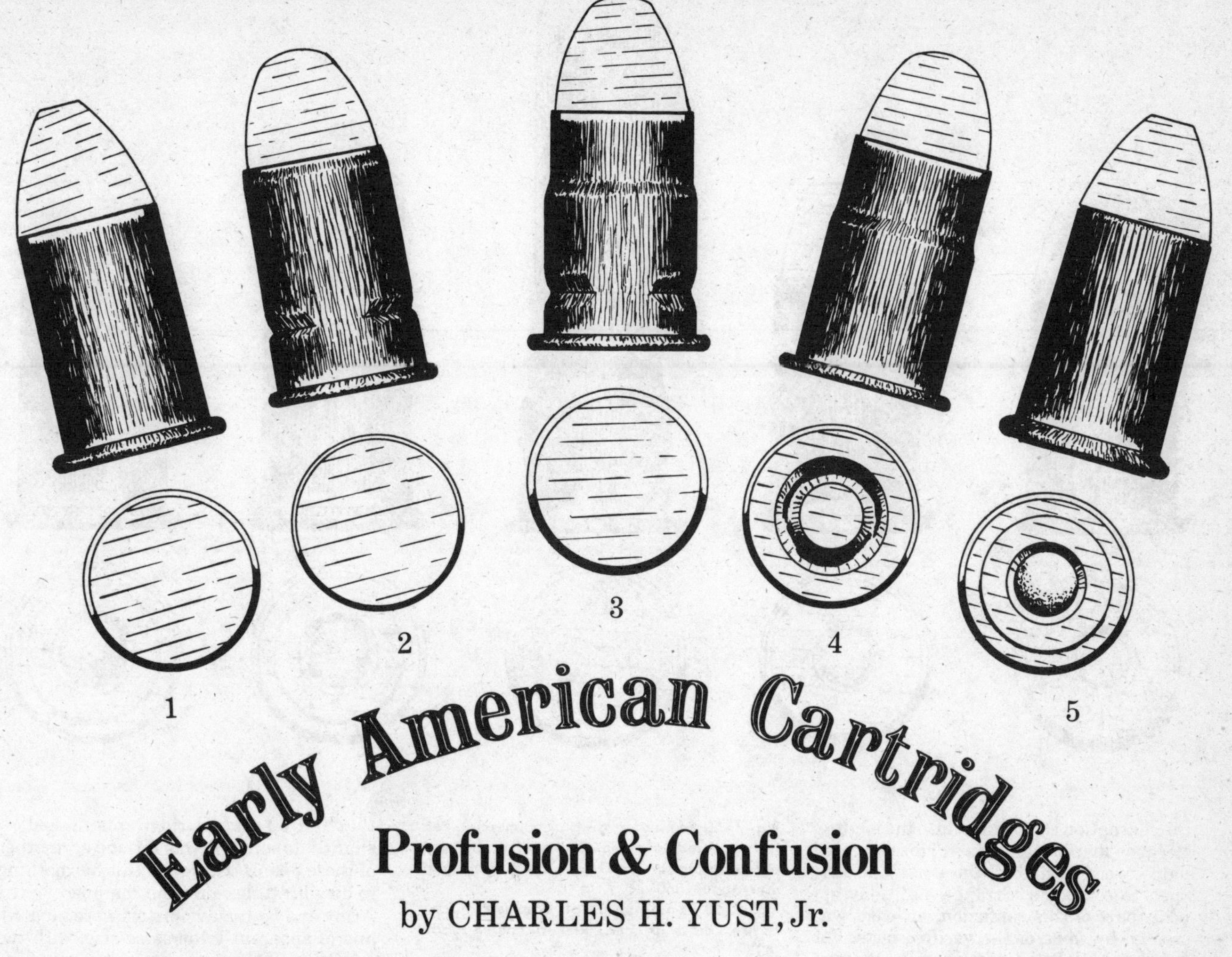

Early American Cartridges

Profusion & Confusion

by CHARLES H. YUST, Jr.

These early groups, originally military rounds, have bothered collectors for years — 50 Remington Pistol, 50 Carbine and 58 Carbine/Musket. An acknowledged authority ends the mystery.

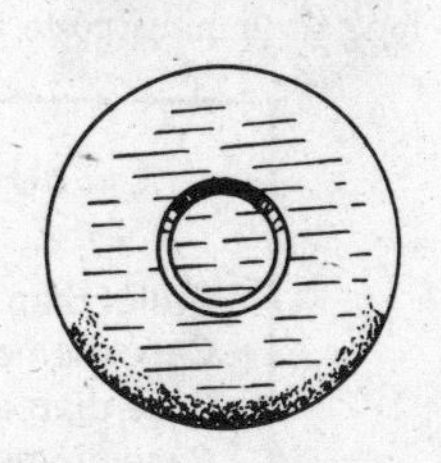

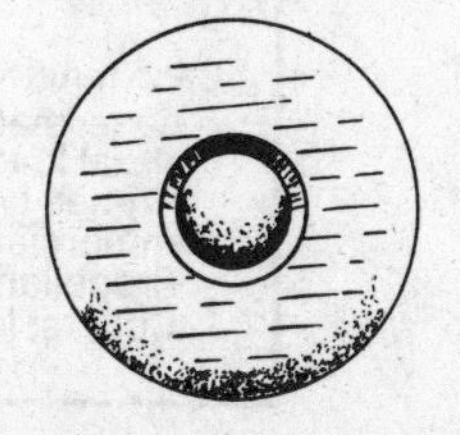

IT IS HARD to understand – or explain – just how the present confusion began. There was no direct starting point, really, but rather a gradual growth which developed in comparatively recent times with the advent of more wide-spread collecting of cartridges. This growing interest resulted in a flurry of new research.

There was, I'm sure, no confusion in the days when these cartridges were standard small arms service ammunition. Those who made the decision to adopt them, their manufacturers and any who used them, no doubt, knew exactly what they were.

Unfortunately, much of that information was merely common knowledge at the time, never a matter of the printed record, as far as I can learn. Much of what was documented has become lost; only fragments have been uncovered by the probings of present day researchers.

With all this activity, many popular

Fig. 1. 50 Remington pistol. Navy, rimfire. Rim diameter about .643″.

Fig. 2. 50 Remington pistol. Navy, centerfire. Benet cup, inside primer. Rim diameter about .643″.

Fig. 3. 50 Remington pistol. Army, centerfire. Martin bar anvil, inside primer. Rim diameter about .665″.

Fig. 4. 50 Remington pistol. Army, centerfire. Martin folded head, inside primer. Rim diameter about .665″. This same cartridge also exists with a tapered case.

Fig. 5. 50 Remington pistol. Commercial, centerfire. 3-hole Berdan brass primer. Rim diameter about .650″.

Fig. 6. 50 Remington pistol. Commercial, centerfire. F.A.C. Hobbs patent of Sept. 14, 1869, made by Union Metallic Cartridge Co. Rim diameter (upper) about .630″. Lower head design has rounded primer. Rim diameter about .640″. Primers are copper.

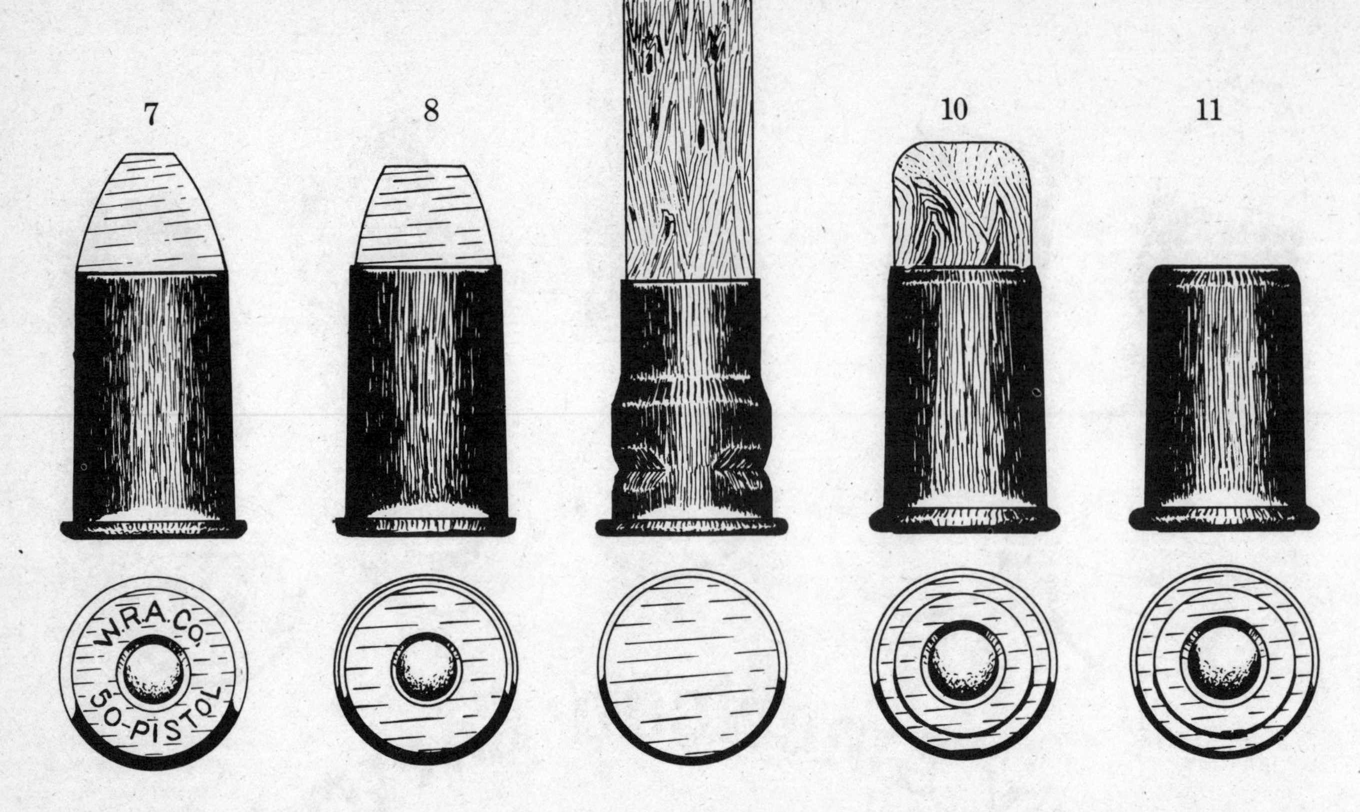

misconceptions have crept into the picture. Because mere fragments—of disconnected data—were available, the door was wide open to confusion. Strange as it may appear, part of this confusion, at least, was created by some of the verified facts. For example, a labeled package of cartridges would turn up, giving the cartridge a name. Now, what happens when several package labels show a *different* name for the same cartridge? Again, someone might locate an arms manual which included an illustration of the cartridge to be used with it, yet the weapon's name doesn't match the name on the newly-located cartridge package label.

This would not be so bad if, for instance, the same researcher had all of these items together; by comparing them a rather clear picture would gradually take shape. Unfortunately, not long ago, this was not the case, thus resulting in the "popular misconceptions" which are still hard to erase, even with the much larger store of factual data now out in the open.

Using this material, I've set down the details that follow; with it, you should be able to identify the individual rounds of these three cartridge groups.

50-cal. Remington Army and Navy pistols

The confusion in this case lies in determining the differences between the Navy cartridges and those used in the Army pistols.

The U.S. Navy adopted a single shot Remington pistol in 1866, chambered for a 50-cal. rimfire cartridge (fig. 1). In 1867 the Navy replaced this pistol with one firing a centerfire round.

The U.S. Army then became interested

Fig. 7. 50 Remington pistol. Commercial, centerfire. Winchester No. 2 copper primer patented by Stetson on Oct. 1, 1878. Rim diameter about .660".
Fig. 8. 50 Remington pistol. Commercial, centerfire. Brass primer. Rim diameter about .638".
Fig. 9. 50 Remington pistol. Army, rimfire. Shot-loaded round made and sold by W. Stokes Kirk of Philadelphia, Pa. Case of fig. 3 was used.
Fig. 10. 50 Remington pistol. Commercial, centerfire. Shot-loaded. Same case as fig. 5. Rim diameter about .645".
Fig. 11. 50 Remington pistol. Commercial, centerfire. Blank. Same case as fig. 5. Rim diameter about .648".

in this last version of the Navy pistol. After changes were made in the Navy design (recommended by an Ordnance Board known as the "St. Louis Commission") the Army brought out their Model 1871 pistol, again a single shot Remington rolling block.

For a long time many collectors thought that if a 50-cal. cartridge was necked, or slightly tapered, it was for one or another of these pistols. However, this has nothing to do with it, because the chambers in the Army and both Navy pistols were tapered, and of apparently the same size, with the exception of the *counterbore* to receive the case rim.

There's the key to the riddle. Counterbore diameter of the Navy weapons ran between .658" and .664", of the Army model .692" and .693".

Here is the breakdown for the cartridges. Any round with a rim diameter that will fit into the .658" to .664" counterbore diameter may be used in all of the weapons, Army or Navy models. It probably is safe to say that any of this ammunition, which was of government manufacture, was intended for use primarily in the Navy pistols. This, of course, includes the rimfire cartridges.

Any round with a rim diameter in the .692" to .693" counterbore-diameter

50-cal. Army and Navy Pistol Cartridges

Dimensional Data in inches

Bullet diameter	.510 to .535
Case diameter at neck	.527 to .542
Case diameter above rim	.562 to .568
Case diameter at rim	Navy .635 to .651
	Army .663 to .666
Case length	.861 to .896

Case material: copper for government make, brass for commercial loads.
Primer types: centerfire government rounds had inside type, commercial cartridges had Boxer or 3-hole Berdan patterns.
Propellant: black powder.
Bullets: lead, of about 300 grains.

bracket is obviously for use only in the Army pistol, and won't fit Navy weapons.

It is doubtful if the government made any of these cartridges much beyond the early 1870's. However, they were produced commercially up to about 1920 by several U.S. manufacturers, these with a rim diameter which permitted use in either Army or Navy pistols.

The long life of this commercial round was due to the fact that these pistols were quite popular, for some reason or other, with shooters long after the military had discarded them.

Another factor, which abetted the confusion, is the difficulty in finding these pistols in their original form, a large number of them having been altered—or butchered—by their subsequent owners.

There were also blank and shot cartridges. One shot cartridge worthy of mention (fig. 9) was not an official government round. They were made by using the government necked case of fig. 3, with a wooden shot container substituted for the regular bullet. The W. Stokes Kirk Co. of Philadelphia, Penn., made and sold these cartridges.

Fig. 12. 50 Remington pistol. Commercial, centerfire. Blank. Same case as fig. 7. Rim diameter about .653".
Fig. 13. 50 Govt. carbine. Centerfire, copper case, length 1-9/64". Martin folded head, inside primer.
Fig. 14. 50 Govt. carbine. Centerfire, copper case, length 1-9/32". Martin bar anvil, inside primer.
Fig. 15. 50 Govt. carbine. Centerfire, copper case, length 1-3/8". Benet cup, inside primer.
Fig. 16. 50 Govt. carbine. Brass case, length 1-11/32".
Fig. 17. 50 Govt. carbine. Brass case, length 1-11/32", solid head. Berdan primer.
Fig. 18. 50 Govt. carbine. Brass case, length 1-5/16." Made by E. Remington & Son. 375-gr. bullet. Boxer centerfire, .210" primer.

50-cal. Carbine Cartridges

The next series to attempt to untangle is also of caliber 50. Commonly known as 50 Government Carbine, it is also called the 50 Springfield Pistol M1869; 50 Cadet; 50 Springfield and Remington Cadet.

These rounds, intended for use in the Sharps and Remington carbines, should not be confused with the 50/55/450 carbine cartridge of 1872, which used the 50-70-1¾" case, but with a 55-gr. powder charge.

They were also for use in early cadet rifles made for the Cadet Corp, U.S. Military Academy at West Point, New York.

In addition, this is the cartridge which was to be used in the experimental Springfield Pistol Model of 1869, which had the identical Allin breech-loading system of the converted rifles.

In spite of variations in case length, for all intents and purposes they are all the same cartridge.

The only doubtful one is shown in fig. 13, which has a case length of 1.136". It came in a wooden box, without a label, which held 18 rounds. Someone had printed in ink on the outside of the box, ".50 Cadet

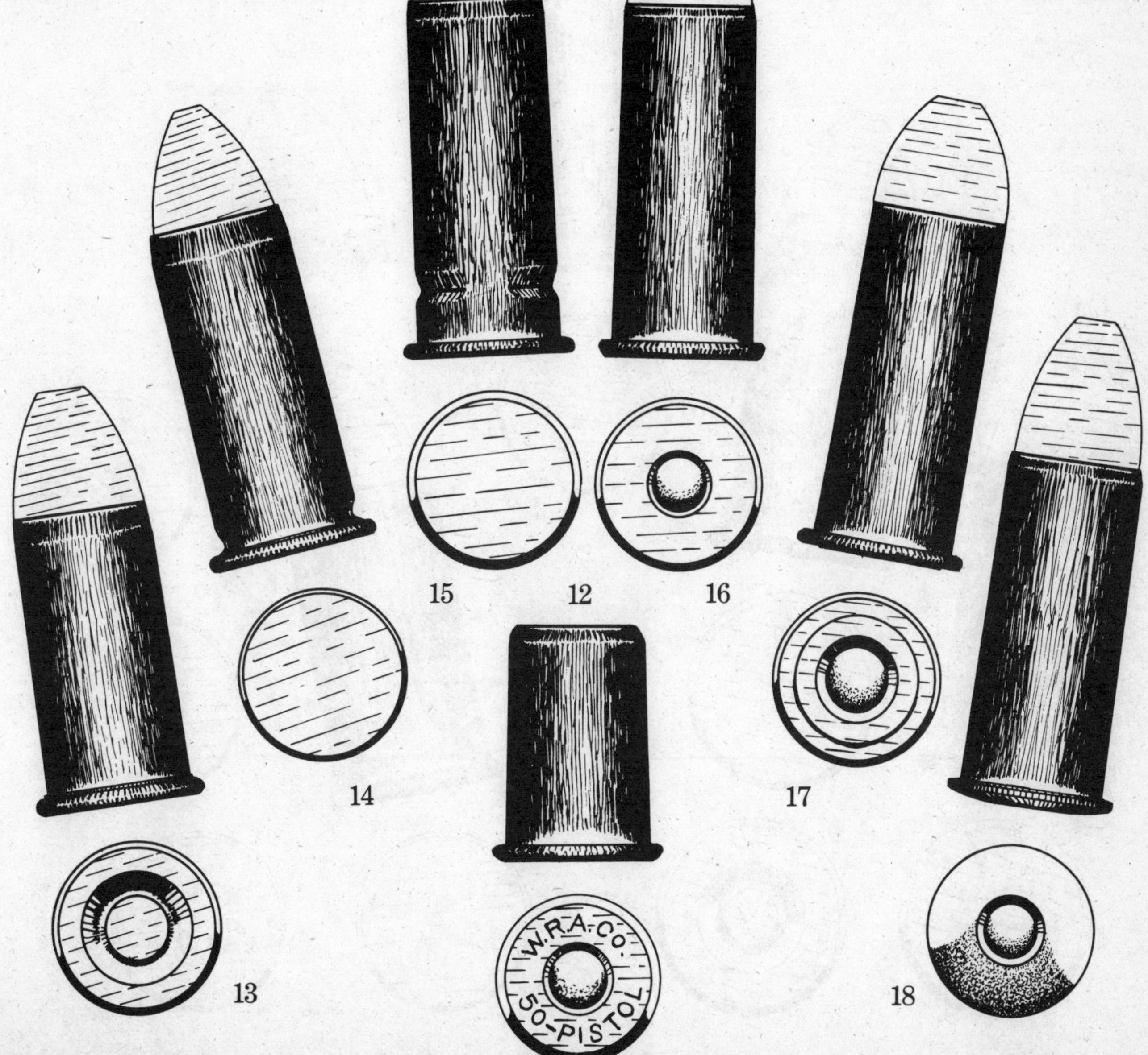

Musket." However, the diameters would permit it to chamber in any of these arms.

The cartridge in fig. 15 came in a carton labeled, "20 Centre-Primed, Metallic Cartridges, Cal: .50. Charge, 45 Grains Musket Powder. Weight of Bullet, 385 Grains. Frankford Arsenal, 1869."

The cartridge in fig. 16 was also found headstamped, "W.R.A. Co. .50 CARB."

The cartridge in fig. 18 has a rounded head.

The primers in figs. 16, 17 and 18 are brass.

Of course, not all of the variations of this cartridge which exist are presented here; there were also blank and shot types, as well as other variations of ball. However, this will prove sufficient to act as a guide for those interested in this cartridge group.

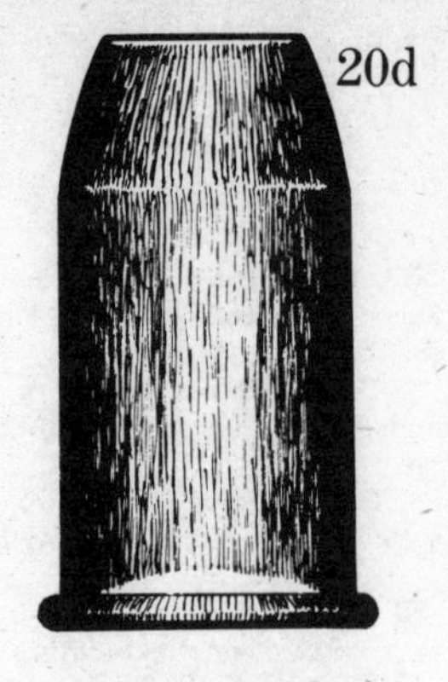

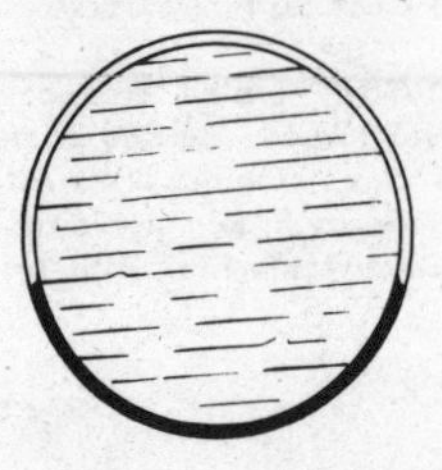

Fig. 19. 58 Springfield. 19a-rimfire; 19b-centerfire. Copper cases.
Fig. 20; a, b, c and d. 58 Miller. All are copper-cased rimfires.

58-cal. Cartridges

This third group consists of a variety of caliber 58 cartridges. Most of these were for use in the several types of actions tried out in the conversion of the muzzle-loading rifles to breech-loaders.

Fig. 19 illustrates the rimfire and centerfire cartridges used in the converted Springfield rifles which, mainly, were fitted with the Allin receiver alteration. These 58 Springfield musket cartridges were of government manufacture. The two centerfire rounds depicted (right) appear identical except for the head. The upper round has the Benet cup, inside primer. The lower cartridge has the Martin folded head, inside primer. Case length is 1-3/16"; rim diameter about .760". Head diameter (above rim) about .653". Case diameter at mouth about .625", just below rolled-in section which crimps bullet.

We now come to one of the confusing points. The 58 Miller rimfire (fig. 20) is often confused with the 58 Springfield musket round. At a glance they do look alike and, unless both are on hand to actually compare, it is very hard to distinguish one from the other. Even then it takes a

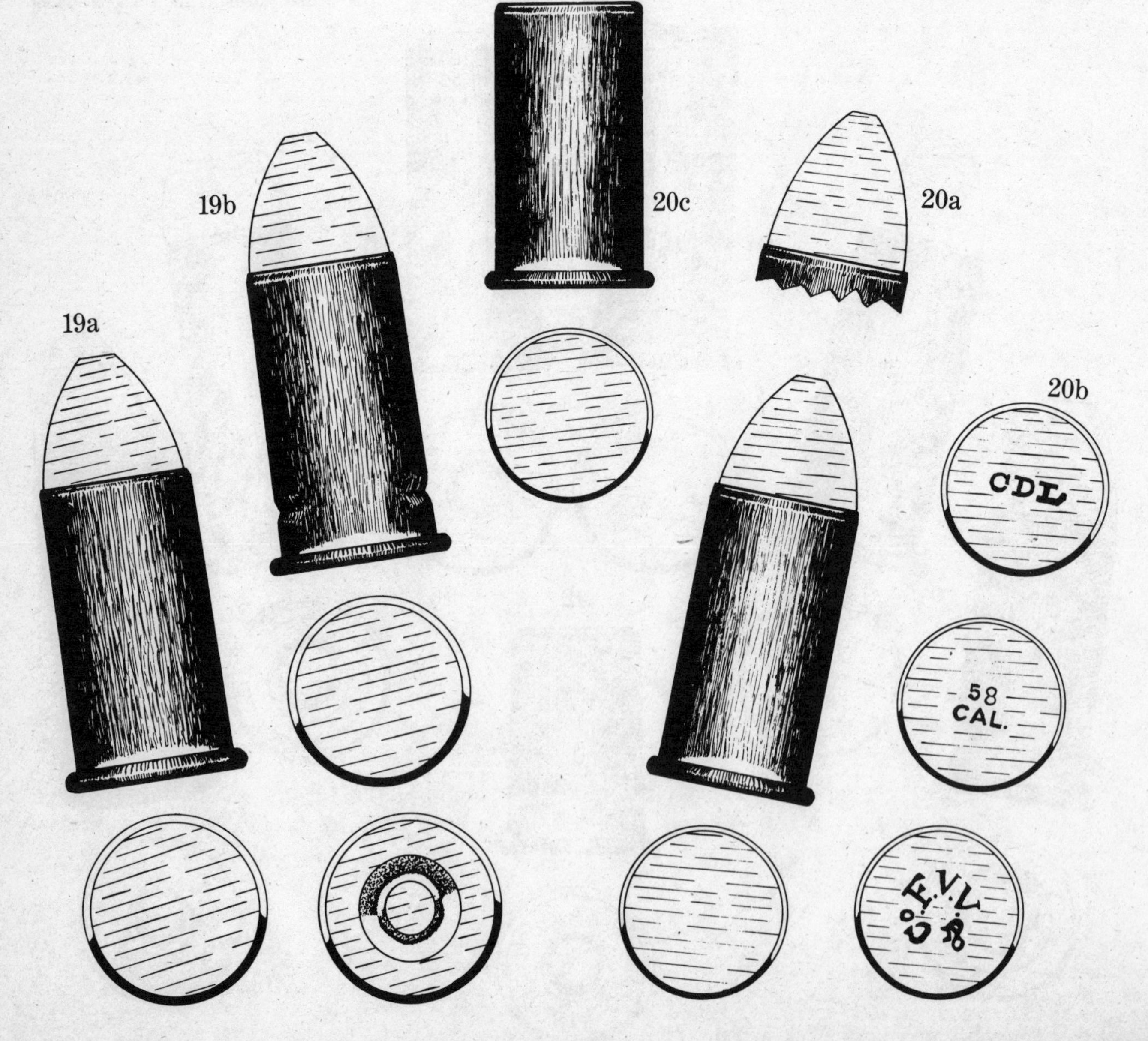

close look, and both have the same case length.

The key is to use a micrometer on the rim and body diameters of these 58 Miller rounds. The former is about .705″, head diameter (just above rim) is about .630″. Case diameter, just below rolled-in section crimping bullet at mouth, is approximately .615″.

The 58 Miller was another experimental system of altering the muzzle-loading rifles to breechloaders.

Fig. 20 illustrates two loadings of ball and two patterns of blank, as well as three headstamp patterns found with the shorter bullet. Many of you will probably recognize them. "CDL" is for C.D. Leet, while "FVVCo" is for Fitch, Van Vechten & Co. The "58 CAL" may have been made by anyone, even the government; this one aggravated the confusion for many thought it was the 58 Springfield cartridge.

Fig. 21 shows two varieties of the caliber 58 Carbine, the "Berdan" cartridge named after Colonel Hiram Berdan; these were for use in the altered carbines produced by Colt's Patent Firearms Co. under Berdan's Patent of March 30, 1869.

Case length is 1-3/32″; rim diameter .730″ to .740″; head diameter (above rim) .640″; case diameter at mouth .625″; bullet weight is 530 grains. Primer is Berdan type.

Fig. 22 is the caliber 58 Berdan musket cartridge for the Colt-Berdan musket, altered from muzzleloader under Berdan's Patent No. 88,436 of March 30, 1869. It is the companion to the 58 Carbine cartridge above.

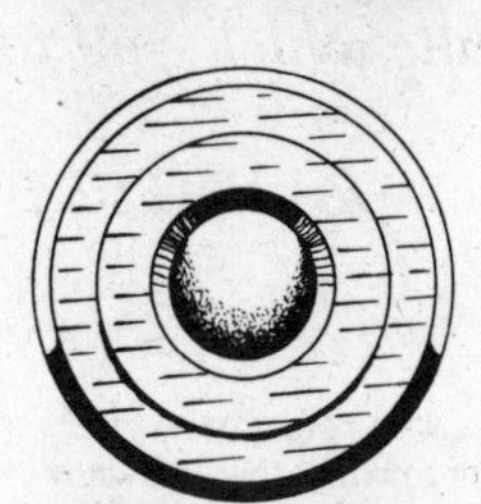

This round was also known as: 58 Berdan N.M. (New Model); 58 Transformed Musket and 58 Calibre N.M.

Bullet weights ran from approximately 530 grains to 570 grains. Case length is 1-21/32″; rim diameter about .730″; head diameter (above rim) about .640″; case diameter at mouth about .615″. Berdan primer.

The last cartridge in this series is fig. 23, known as the caliber 58 Roberts, and used in Roberts' alteration of muzzle-loading rifles under his patent of June 11, 1867. Bullet weight is 620 grains; case length is 1-11/32″; rim diameter is about .745″; head diameter (above rim) is about .655″; case diameter at mouth is about .605″. Berdan primer.

Many collectors in the past felt uncertain about these 58 cartridges; there was a possibility, it was said, that any of these types might be a variation of the other, perhaps through manufacturers' differences. This is not true—the data presented here is factual and verified. ●

Fig. 21. 58 carbine. Cartridge on left (21a) made by Winchester Repeating Arms Co., cartridge on right (21b) made by UMC. Both have brass cases and primers, centerfire.
Fig. 22. 58 Transformed musket. 22a—two sizes of bullets shown. Blank cartridge (22b). Both have brass cases and primers.
Fig. 23. 58 Roberts. Cartridge on left (23a) made by UMC, blank cartridge (23b) on right. Both have brass cases and primers.

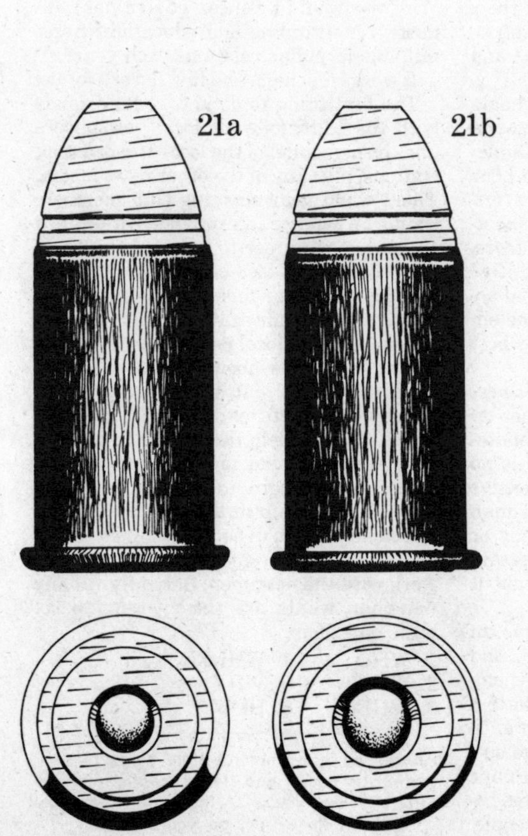

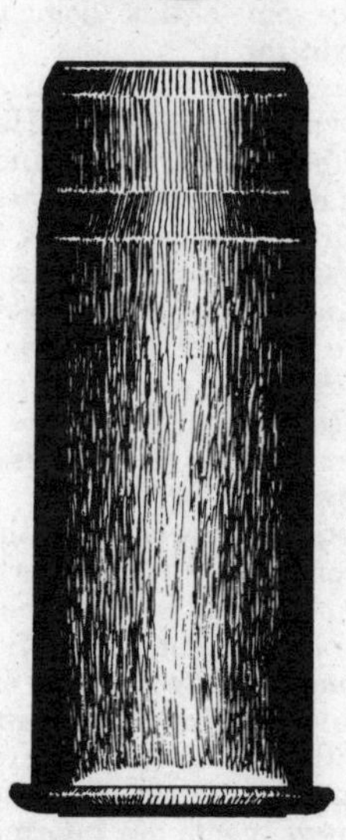

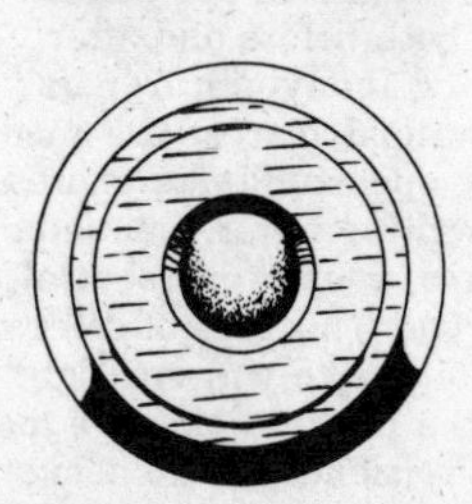

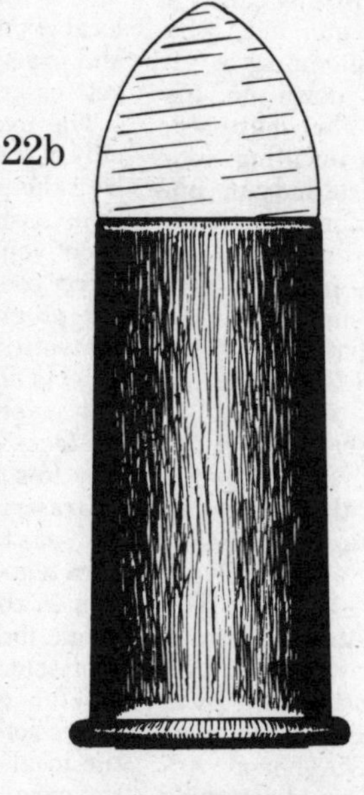

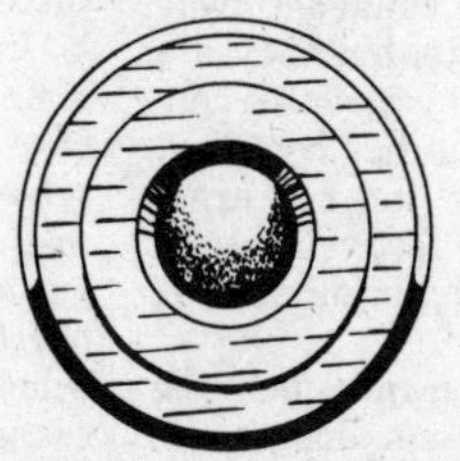

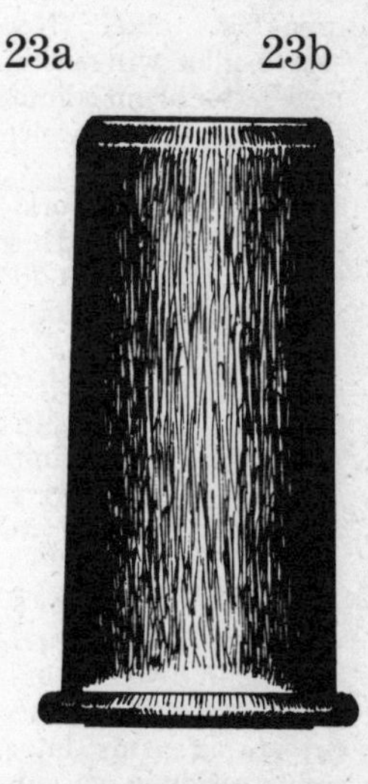

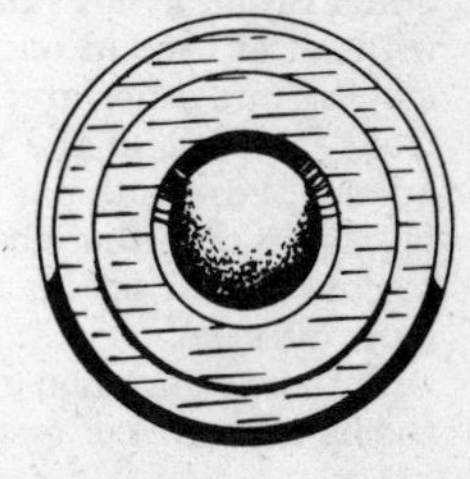

Doing Good and Getting Credit For It

Public relations is an important facet of American life. Right now it is badly needed by gun owners, particularly at the local level, as clubs and individuals need to become active in local public relations efforts. It is one of the few positive ways we have of getting the truth of our message across to a public which—all too often—hears only the other side.

by J. DAVID TRUBY

I'M SICK AND TIRED of being called a criminal, mad killer and gun nut," the man sputtered angrily, slamming a vicious, anti-gun editorial down on his breakfast table. "Now," he muttered, "some idiot will write an insulting, red-neck letter about communists and gun control . . . and bingo, we've got more anti-gun people!"

On his way to work, the man began to wonder what he and his friends at the local shooting club might do to better the situation. His answer should be *local public relations.*

"Doing good and getting credit for it," is the way our hero's gun club defined public relations. It's a definition that more gun owners had better start using in the face of influential people trying to outlaw private gun ownership.

Milton Eisenhower's National Commission on the Causes and Prevention of Violence is in favor of confiscating all private handguns at $20 apiece, then moving to all private firearms later. The Nixon Administration is not sure it could get away with all of that in one bite, but they are looking into other areas of restrictive control. The logic of the issue has been lost among the emotional pro and con arguments, so that the most effective rhetoric to date is that of the anti-gun forces, i.e., guns must go!

With so many non-gun owners pushing the bandwagons of restriction along, *right now* is the time for gun owners and their local clubs to rally to our own bandwagon, and practice some of this "doing good and getting credit for it!"

The average non-shooter citizen hears only of the violence of firearms. He remembers the publicity of the King and Kennedy assassinations. This citizen doesn't hear about youth education programs, firearms' safety courses, hunter training, safe shooting programs, game feeding volunteers, competitive shooting, and other positive aspects of the legal, moral and ethical activities of sportsmen. That's the problem we face—and public relations is the best way to solve it.

Grassroots public relations is the easiest and most effective way for sportsmen to earn a good name and a favorable reputation in the local community. There is no magic formula or any need for expensive professional consultants. Each sportsman or club with some worthwhile event or service of public interest should be certain the local news media are informed about the event, both before and after.

Unhappily, many gun owners have an almost paranoid fear of the media, and take every opportunity to express themselves by writing bitter, emotional letters to the editor, usually in rebuttal to anti-gun editorials. This type of defensive outburst is no way to win our fight. Public relations is a positive, effective means because it wins friends and influences people. Why else would business, government, industry, institutions and education invest millions in public relations each year?

It works for them, and it will work for us!

The first thing to do is to make friends with the editor of your local newspapers and the personnel of the local broadcasting stations, plus any of the other news media. Then, when your shooting club members conduct a safety clinic, provide winter feed for game, volunteer to help fight a forest fire, search for lost children, sponsor a shoot or picnic, or furnish a speaker for a local civic club, for example, be absolutely certain that the local papers, the radio and TV stations know about it. Give them the facts before the event, and be sure they get the story and pictures during and after the event. Offer to help them. This is such an easy and sure road to better public relations that it ought to be used by every sportsmen's group in the country.

You don't have to be a journalism school genius to write a good news story or to work with the newsmen. Basically, all any newsman wants are the answers to six basic questions:

1. WHO
2. WHAT
3. WHEN
4. WHERE
5. WHY
6. HOW

Above: An easy, natural style helps in presenting an honest and sincere public relations effort. When you're being interviewed on radio or TV, be yourself!

If your news write-up answers these questions, you'll be getting news out to the public—provided you're always open and honest with the newsmen with whom you'll be working. For the most part, they're honest, friendly, reasonable guys—if you level with them.

When you're getting news ready, don't forget to have photos. Be sure someone who can handle a camera is around when you're doing something newsworthy—even if you have to hire a local shutter bug. Local pictures—good pictures—are a sure route to an editor's heart.

OK, you've got the basic idea—newsmen want stories and pictures about local people and what they're doing in local situations. If you're honest with yourself and with newsmen about what is genuinely news—not just blatantly free publicity—you'll have many opportunities to tell the public our side of the firearms story.

In addition to those basics, here are a few specific tips to make you a top-notch public relations man not only for your local gun club, but for all gun owners. Take a look, too, at the sample news release with this article.

1. Be sure the item you're reporting is really newsworthy, so other people will find it interesting, too. Don't try to invent publicity stunts, just stick to the facts. Remember, local names and pictures—human interest—are the backbone of local news.

2. Try to summarize your story in simple, direct terms using the first paragraph as the over-all summary. This is the style newsmen use.

3. Write the story in factual, informational terms, using as few "puffy" words as possible. Stick to answering those 6 basic questions covered earlier.

4. Type your story, double-spaced, on one side only of a standard sheet of 8½ x 11 paper. Don't use onion skin paper, lined paper, or that crinkly bond stuff either. Be sure to leave lots of room at top, sides and bottom for the editor's markups.

5. Put your name, address and telephone number at the top of the page, so a newsman can reach you if he needs more information. Under that, put in a brief title of the article, explaining in one line what the story's about.

6. When reporting names, remember people have first names and last names—use them both the first time you mention someone, then switch to the last name alone for mentions afterwards. Use titles or other identification if appropriate.

7. Before you get prints of pictures for your story, be sure of the newspaper or television station's mechanical requirements for size.

8. Write captions for your pictures, telling exactly what is happening. Identify all people fully, even if this duplicates some of what you've written in the story. Often a newspaper won't have room for both a story and the picture, so each must be able to stand alone on its own news and informational merits.

9. Feel free to ask the local newsmen for advice and help on your public relations effort. If you're open and honest with them, they'll be glad to help you, because you're helping them to report local news.

FOR MORE INFORMATION:
Call Rick G. Croup, 463-6975

FOR IMMEDIATE RELEASE

"SAFETY CLASS"

The Derksburg Sportsmen's Club — WHO
held its semi-annual "Safe Shooter Clinic" — WHAT
for 35 boys and girls from local high schools
WHEN — this past weekend. This is the 8th year the
Club has sponsored these clinics which teach — WHY
safe shooting habits to youngsters.

William Gote, an instructor in the Clifford High School, was the chief safety instructor for the program, assisted by Mandel Jackson of the State Game Commission; J. Alex Cobb, district Game Warden; and Maslow Frean, firearms safety instructor for the local Club. The Clinic was an all-day affair, in which the following
classes, demonstrations, lectures and — HOW
tests were conducted:

(List the activities here)

Held at the Club's safety-rated range, — WHERE
the Clinic...

(add more details; finish with the names of local youngsters involved.)

10. Be sure to use all available news media in your local area—newspapers, radio, television, magazines, news letters, company publications, school papers, etc. Each one is important because it reaches many people who ought to read our side of the firearms story. Overlapping coverage is helpful and is in no way harmful to our cause.

11. Have several club members available as speakers for local organizations needing guest speakers for meetings, etc. Be sure, however, to work for lots of news coverage, before and after, the speaker's appearance! If you don't belong to an organized gun club, you can speak to civic groups. Don't be modest about personal publicity—it all helps the cause.

Those 11 tips supplement our basic, grassroots public relations program. Apply them to a local effort. It works. Witness the successful efforts of organized sportsmen in Connecticut and Maryland in the 1970 elections. Both Dodd and Tydings went down to defeat. Much of their work was positive public relations—acquainting the public with the many good things that shooters and shooting accomplish, things they didn't know about before. These groups provided a logical, reasoned, and non-frantic opposition to restrictive legislation—and legislators. Their public relations efforts, handled entirely by volunteer members, were highly successful.

"Their work showed some of my colleagues that all firearms' people aren't a bunch of rednecked kooks and minutemen," one Congressman told me.

"This effort was sophisticated, and what they said made sense . . . quite a change from some of the letters I get from gun people" was the published judgment of one journalist.

Public relations is an important facet of American life. Right now it is badly needed by gun owners, particularly at the local level, as clubs and individuals need to become active in local public relations efforts. It is one of the few positive ways we have of getting the truth of our message across to a public which—all too often—hears only the other side.

"DO GOOD," to be sure, but, remember to "GET CREDIT FOR IT!"

That is public relations in action . . . which is what we need right now . . . ACTION!

See you in the newspapers . . . . . •

CENTER RIFLE CARTRIDGES — BALLISTICS AND PRICES

Winchester-Western, Remington-Peters, Federal and Speer-DWM

Most of these centerfire loads are available from Winchester-Western and Remington-Peters. Loads available from only one source are marked by a letter, thus: Winchester (a); Western (b); Remington (c); Peters (d); Speer-DWM (f). Those fewer cartridges also available from Federal are marked (e). Contrary to previous practice, W-W and R-P prices are not necessarily uniform, hence prices are approximate.

Cartridge	Bullet Wt. Grs.	Bullet Type	Velocity (fps) Muzzle	Velocity (fps) 100 yds.	Velocity (fps) 200 yds.	Velocity (fps) 300 yds.	Energy (ft. lbs.) Muzzle	Energy (ft. lbs.) 100 yds.	Energy (ft. lbs.) 200 yds.	Energy (ft. lbs.) 300 yds.	Mid-Range Trajectory 100 yds.	Mid-Range Trajectory 200 yds.	Mid-Range Trajectory 300 yds.	Price for 20*
17 Remington	25	HP, PL	4020	3290	2630	2060	900	600	380	230	Not Available			$ 5.25
218 Bee*	46	HP	2860	2160	1610	1200	835	475	265	145	0.7	3.8	11.5	11.75
22 Hornet*	45	SP	2690	2030	1510	1150	720	410	230	130	0.8	4.3	13.0	10.25
22 Hornet* (c, d)	45	HP	2690	2030	1510	1150	720	410	230	130	0.8	4.3	13.0	9.85
22 Hornet*	46	HP	2690	2030	1510	1150	740	420	235	135	0.8	4.3	13.0	9.85
222 Remington (a, e)	50	PSP, MC, PL†	3200	2660	2170	1750	1140	785	520	340	0.5	2.5	7.0	4.50
222 Remington Magnum (c, d)	55	SP, PL†	3300	2800	2340	1930	1330	955	670	455	0.5	2.3	6.1	4.90
222 Remington Magnum (c, d)	55	HP, PL	3300	2830	2400	2010	1330	975	700	490	Not Available			5.25
223 Remington (a, c, d, e)	55	SP, PL†, PSP	3300	2800	2340	1930	1330	955	670	455	0.5	2.1	5.4	4.90
22-250 Remington	55	PSP	3810	3270	2770	2320	1770	1300	935	655	0.3	1.6	4.4	5.25
22-250 Remington (c, d)	55	HP, PL	3810	3330	2890	2490	1770	1360	1020	760	Not Available			5.25
225 Winchester (a, b)	55	PSP	3650	3140	2680	2270	1630	1200	875	630	0.4	1.8	4.8	5.05
243 Winchester (e)	80	PSP, PL†	3500	3080	2720	2410	2180	1690	1320	1030	0.4	1.8	4.7	6.25
243 Winchester (c, d)	80	HP, PL	3450	3050	2675	2330	2115	1650	1270	965	Not Available			6.65
243 Winchester (e)	100	PP, CL, PSP	3070	2790	2540	2320	2090	1730	1430	1190	0.5	2.2	5.5	6.25
6mm Remington (a, c, d)	80	PSP, HP, PL†	3450	3130	2750	2400	2220	1740	1340	1018	0.4	1.8	4.7	6.25
6mm Remington (a, c, d)	100	PCL, PSP	3190	2920	2660	2420	2260	1890	1570	1300	0.5	2.1	5.1	6.25
244 Remington (c, d)	90	PSP	3200	2850	2530	2230	2050	1630	1280	995	0.5	2.1	5.5	5.70
25-06 Remington (c, d)	87	HP	3500	3070	2680	2310	2370	1820	1390	1030	Not Available			6.80
25-06 Remington (c, d)	120	PSP, CL	3120	2850	2600	2360	2590	2160	1800	1480	Not Available			6.80
25-20 Winchester*	86	L, Lu	1460	1180	1030	940	405	265	200	170	2.6	12.5	32.0	9.05
25-20 Winchester*	86	SP	1460	1180	1030	940	405	265	200	170	2.6	12.5	32.0	10.10
25-35 Winchester	117	SP, CL	2300	1910	1600	1340	1370	945	665	465	1.0	4.6	12.5	6.35
250 Savage (a, b)	87	PSP, SP	3030	2660	2330	2060	1770	1370	1050	820	0.6	2.5	6.4	5.85
250 Savage	100	ST, CL, PSP	2820	2460	2140	1870	1760	1340	1020	775	0.6	2.9	7.4	5.85
256 Winchester Magnum* (b)	60	OPE	2800	2070	1570	1220	1040	570	330	200	0.8	4.0	12.0	10.80
257 Roberts (a, b)	87	PSP	3200	2840	2500	2190	1980	1560	1210	925	0.5	2.2	5.7	6.40
257 Roberts (a, b)	100	ST, CL	2900	2540	2210	1920	1870	1430	1080	820	0.6	2.7	7.0	6.40
257 Roberts	117	PP, CL	2650	2280	1950	1690	1820	1350	985	740	0.7	3.4	8.8	6.40
6.5 Remington Magnum (c)	100	PSPCL	3450	3070	2690	2320	2640	2090	1610	1190	Not Available			8.40
6.5mm Remington Magnum (c)	120	PSPCL	3030	2750	2480	2230	2450	2010	1640	1330	0.5	2.3	5.7	8.40
264 Winchester Magnum	100	PSP, CL	3700	3260	2880	2550	3040	2360	1840	1440	0.4	1.6	4.2	8.40
264 Winchester Magnum	140	PP, CL	3200	2490	2700	2480	3180	2690	2270	1910	0.5	2.0	4.9	8.40
270 Winchester	100	PSP	3480	3070	2690	2340	2690	2090	1600	1215	0.4	1.8	4.8	6.80
270 Winchester (e)	130	PP, PSP	3140	2880	2630	2400	2850	2390	2000	1660	0.5	2.1	5.3	6.50
270 Winchester	130	ST, CL, BP, PP	3140	2850	2580	2320	2840	2340	1920	1550	0.5	2.1	5.3	6.80
270 Winchester (c, d)	150	CL	2800	2440	2140	1870	2610	1980	1520	1160	0.6	2.9	7.6	6.80
270 Winchester (a, b, e)	150	PP	2900	2620	2380	2160	2800	2290	1890	1550	0.6	2.5	6.3	6.80
280 Remington (c, d)	150	PCL	2900	2670	2450	2220	2800	2370	2000	1640	0.6	2.5	6.1	6.80
280 Remington (c, d)	165	CL	2820	2510	2220	1970	2910	2310	1810	1420	0.6	2.8	7.2	6.80
284 Winchester (a, b)	125	PP	3200	2880	2590	2310	2840	2300	1860	1480	0.5	2.1	5.3	6.80
284 Winchester (a, b)	150	PP	2900	2630	2380	2160	2800	2300	1890	1550	0.6	2.5	6.3	6.80
7mm Mauser (e)	139	SP	2710	2440	2190	1960	2280	1850	1490	1190	0.7	3.0	7.8	6.80
7mm Mauser (e)	175	SP	2490	2170	1900	1680	2410	1830	1400	1100	0.8	3.7	9.5	6.80
7mm Remington Magnum	125	CL	3430	3080	2750	2450	3260	2630	2100	1660	0.6	1.8	4.7	8.40
7mm Remington Magnum (e)	150	PP, CL	3260	2970	2700	2450	3540	2940	2430	1990	0.4	2.0	4.9	8.40
7mm Remington Magnum (e)	175	PP	3070	2720	2400	2120	3660	2870	2240	1750	0.5	2.4	6.1	8.40
7mm Remington Magnum (c, d)	175	PCL	3070	2860	2660	2460	3660	3170	2740	2350	0.5	2.1	5.2	8.40
30 Carbine* (e)	110	HSP, SP	1980	1540	1230	1040	950	575	370	260	1.4	7.5	21.7	10.70
30-30 Winchester (c, d)	150	CL	2410	1960	1620	1360	1930	1280	875	616	0.9	4.5	12.5	5.30
30-30 Winchester (e)	150	HP	2410	2020	1700	1430	1930	1360	960	680	0.9	4.2	11.0	5.30
30-30 Winchester (a, b)	150	PP, ST, OPE	2410	2020	1700	1430	1930	1360	960	680	0.9	4.2	11.0	5.30
30-30 Winchester (e)	170	PP, HP, CL, ST, MC	2220	1890	1630	1410	1860	1350	1000	750	1.2	4.6	12.5	5.30
30 Remington	170	ST, CL	2120	1820	1560	1350	1700	1250	920	690	1.1	5.3	14.0	6.35
30-06 Springfield (a, b)	110	PSP	3370	2830	2350	1920	2770	1960	1350	900	0.5	2.2	6.0	6.80
30-06 Springfield	125	PSP	3200	2810	2480	2200	2840	2190	1710	1340	0.5	2.2	5.6	6.80
30-06 Springfield (c, d)	150	BP	2970	2710	2470	2240	2930	2440	2030	1670	0.5	2.4	6.0	6.80
30-06 Springfield (e)	150	PP	2970	2620	2300	2010	2930	2280	1760	1340	0.6	2.5	6.5	6.80
30-06 Springfield	150	ST, PCL, PSP	2970	2670	2400	2130	2930	2370	1920	1510	0.6	2.4	6.1	6.80
30-06 Springfield	180	PP, CL, PSP	2700	2330	2010	1740	2910	2170	1610	1210	0.7	3.1	8.3	6.80
30-06 Springfield (e)	180	ST, BP, PCL	2700	2470	2250	2040	2910	2440	2020	1660	0.7	2.9	7.0	6.80
30-06 Springfield	220	PP, CL	2410	2120	1870	1670	2830	2190	1710	1360	0.8	3.9	9.8	6.80
30-06 Springfield (a, b)	220	ST	2410	2180	1980	1790	2830	2320	1910	1560	0.8	3.7	9.2	6.80
30-40 Krag	180	PP, CL	2470	2120	1830	1590	2440	1790	1340	1010	0.8	3.8	9.9	6.90
30-40 Krag	180	ST, PCL	2470	2250	2040	1850	2440	2020	1660	1370	0.8	3.5	8.5	6.90
30-40 Krag (a, b)	220	ST	2200	1990	1800	1630	2360	1930	1580	1300	1.0	4.4	11.0	6.90
300 Winchester Magnum (a, c, e)	150	PP, PCL	3400	3050	2730	2430	3850	3100	2480	1970	0.4	1.9	4.8	8.70
300 Winchester Magnum (a, c, e)	180	PP, PCL	3070	2850	2640	2440	3770	3250	2790	2380	0.5	2.1	5.3	8.70
300 Winchester Mag (a, b)	220	ST	2720	2490	2270	2060	3620	3030	2520	2070	0.6	2.9	6.9	8.70
300 H&H Magnum (a, b)	150	ST	3190	2870	2580	2300	3390	2740	2220	1760	0.5	2.1	5.2	9.35
300 H&H Magnum	180	ST, PCL	2920	2670	2440	2220	3400	2850	2380	1970	0.6	2.4	5.8	8.70
300 H&H Magnum (a, b)	220	ST, CL	2620	2370	2150	1940	3350	2740	2260	1840	0.7	3.1	7.7	8.70
300 Savage (e)	150	PP	2670	2350	2060	1800	2370	1840	1410	1080	0.7	3.2	8.0	6.20
300 Savage	150	ST, PCL	2670	2390	2130	1890	2370	1900	1510	1190	0.7	3.0	7.6	6.60
300 Savage (c, d)	150	CL	2670	2270	1930	1660	2370	1710	1240	916	0.7	3.3	9.3	6.60
300 Savage (e)	180	PP, CL	2370	2040	1760	1520	2240	1660	1240	920	0.9	4.1	10.5	6.35
300 Savage	180	ST, PCL	2370	2160	1960	1770	2240	1860	1530	1250	0.9	3.7	9.2	6.60
303 Savage (c, d)	180	CL	2140	1810	1550	1340	1830	1310	960	715	1.1	5.4	14.0	7.00
303 Savage (a, b)	190	ST	1980	1680	1440	1250	1650	1190	875	660	1.3	6.2	15.5	6.75
303 British (e)	180	PP, CL	2540	2300	2090	1900	2580	2120	1750	1440	0.7	3.3	8.2	6.85
303 British (c, d)	215	SP	2180	1900	1660	1460	2270	1720	1310	1020	1.1	4.9	12.5	6.60
308 Winchester (a, b)	110	PSP	3340	2810	2340	1920	2730	1930	1340	900	0.5	2.2	6.0	6.80
308 Winchester (a, b)	125	PSP	3100	2740	2430	2160	2670	2080	1640	1300	0.5	2.3	5.9	6.80
308 Winchester (e)	150	PP	2860	2520	2210	1930	2730	2120	1630	1240	0.6	2.7	7.0	6.55
308 Winchester	150	ST, PCL	2860	2570	2300	2050	2730	2200	1760	1400	0.6	2.6	6.5	6.80
308 Winchester (e)	180	PP, CL	2610	2250	1940	1680	2720	2020	1500	1130	0.7	3.4	8.9	6.55
308 Winchester	180	ST, PCL	2610	2390	2170	1970	2720	2280	1870	1540	0.8	3.1	7.4	6.80
308 Winchester (a, b)	200	ST	2450	2210	1980	1770	2670	2170	1750	1400	0.8	3.6	9.0	6.80
32 Winchester Special (c, d, e)	170	HP, CL	2280	1920	1630	1410	1960	1390	1000	750	1.0	4.8	12.5	5.45
32 Winchester Special	170	PP, ST	2280	1870	1560	1330	1960	1320	920	665	1.0	4.8	13.0	5.30
32 Remington (c, d)	170	CL	2120	1800	1540	1340	1700	1220	895	680	1.0	4.9	13.0	6.60
32 Remington (a, b)	170	ST	2120	1760	1460	1220	1700	1170	805	560	1.1	5.3	14.5	6.60
32-20 Winchester*	100	SP	1290	1060	940	840	370	250	195	155	3.3	15.5	38.0	9.65
32-20 Winchester*	100	SP, L, Lu	1290	1060	940	840	370	250	195	155	3.3	15.5	38.0	7.75
8mm Mauser (e)	170	PP, CL	2570	2140	1790	1520	2490	1730	1210	870	0.8	3.9	10.5	6.80

CENTERFIRE RIFLE CARTRIDGES — BALLISTICS AND PRICES (continued)

Cartridge	Bullet Wt. Grs.	Bullet Type	Velocity (fps) Muzzle	Velocity 100 yds.	Velocity 200 yds.	Velocity 300 yds.	Energy (ft. lbs.) Muzzle	Energy 100 yds.	Energy 200 yds.	Energy 300 yds.	Mid-Range Trajectory 100 yds.	Mid-Range Trajectory 200 yds.	Mid-Range Trajectory 300 yds.	Price for 20*
338 Winchester Magnum (a, b)	200	PP	3000	2690	2410	2170	4000	3210	2580	2090	0.5	2.4	6.0	$9.10
338 Winchester Magnum (a, b)	250	ST	2700	2430	2180	1940	4050	3280	2640	2090	0.7	3.0	7.4	9.10
338 Winchester Magnum (a, b)	300	PP	2450	2160	1910	1690	4000	3110	2430	1900	0.8	3.7	9.5	9.10
348 Winchester (a)	200	ST	2530	2220	1940	1680	2840	2190	765	509	0.4	1.7	4.7	9.50
348 Winchester (c, d)	200	CL	2530	2140	1820	1570	2840	2030	1470	1090	0.8	3.8	10.0	9.50
35 Remington (c, d)	150	CL	2400	1960	1580	1280	1920	1280	835	545	0.9	4.6	13.0	6.15
35 Remington (e)	200	PP, ST, CL	2100	1710	1390	1160	1950	1300	860	605	1.2	6.0	16.5	6.15
350 Remington Magnum (c, d)	200	PCL	2710	2410	2130	1870	3260	2570	2000	1550	Not Available			8.40
350 Remington Magnum (c, d)	250	PCL	2410	2190	1980	1790	3220	2660	2180	1780	Not Available			8.40
351 Winchester Self-Loading*	180	SP	1850	1560	1310	1140	1370	975	685	520	1.5	7.8	21.5	13.45
358 Winchester (a, b)	200	ST	2530	2210	1910	1640	2840	2160	1610	1190	0.8	3.6	9.4	8.40
358 Winchester (a, b)	250	ST	2250	2010	1780	1570	2810	2230	1760	1370	1.0	4.4	11.0	8.40
375 H&H Magnum	270	PP, SP	2740	2460	2210	1990	4500	3620	2920	2370	0.7	2.9	7.1	10.80
375 H&H Magnum	300	ST	2550	2280	2040	1830	4330	3460	2770	2230	0.7	3.3	8.3	10.80
375 H&H Magnum	300	MC	2550	2180	1860	1590	4330	3160	2300	1680	0.7	3.6	9.3	10.80
38-40 Winchester*	180	SP	1330	1070	960	850	705	455	370	290	3.2	15.0	36.5	11.50
44 Magnum* (c, d)	240	SP	1750	1360	1110	980	1630	985	655	510	1.6	8.4	—	4.85
44 Magnum (b)	240	HSP	1750	1350	1090	950	1630	970	635	480	1.8	9.4	26.0	4.85
444 Marlin (c)	240	SP	2400	1845	1410	1125	3070	1815	1060	675	Not Available			6.85
44-40 Winchester*	200	SP	1310	1050	940	830	760	490	390	305	3.3	15.0	36.5	13.80
45-70 Government	405	SP	1320	1160	1050	990	1570	1210	990	880	2.9	13.0	32.5	8.40
458 Winchester Magnum	500	MC	2130	1910	1700	1520	5040	4050	3210	2570	1.1	4.8	12.0	20.10
458 Winchester Magnum	510	SP	2130	1840	1600	1400	5140	3830	2900	2220	1.1	5.1	13.5	13.20

* Price for 50 HP—Hollow Point SP—Soft Point PSP—Pointed Soft Point PP—Power Point L—Lead Lu—Lubaloy ST—Silvertip HSP—Hollow Soft Point MC—Metal Case BT—Boat Tail MAT—Match BP—Bronze Point CL—Core Lokt PCL—Pointed Core Lokt OPE—Open Point Expanding †PL—Power-Lokt (slightly higher price) (1) Not safe in handguns or Win. M73.

WEATHERBY MAGNUM CARTRIDGES — BALLISTICS AND PRICES

Cartridge	Bullet Wt. Grs.	Bullet Type	Velocity (fps) Muzzle	Velocity 100 yds.	Velocity 200 yds.	Velocity 300 yds.	Energy (ft. lbs.) Muzzle	Energy 100 yds.	Energy 200 yds.	Energy 300 yds.	Mid-Range Trajectory 100 yds.	Mid-Range Trajectory 200 yds.	Mid-Range Trajectory 300 yds.	Price for 20
224 Weatherby Varmintmaster	50	PE	3750	3160	2625	2140	1562	1109	1670	1250	0.7	3.6	9.0	$6.95
224 Weatherby Varmintmaster	55	PE	3650	3150	2685	2270	1627	1212	881	629	0.4	1.7	4.5	6.95
240 Weatherby	70	PE	3850	3395	2975	2585	2304	1788	1376	1038	0.3	1.5	3.9	9.95
240 Weatherby	90	PE	3500	3135	2795	2475	2444	1960	1559	1222	0.4	1.8	4.5	9.95
240 Weatherby	100	PE	3395	3115	2850	2595	2554	2150	1804	1495	0.4	1.8	4.4	9.95
247 Weatherby	87	PE	3825	3290	2835	2450	2828	2087	1553	1160	0.3	1.6	4.4	9.95
247 Weatherby	100	PE	3555	3150	2815	2500	2802	2199	1760	1338	0.4	1.7	4.4	9.95
247 Weatherby	117	SPE	3300	2900	2550	2250	2824	2184	1689	1315	0.4	2.4	6.8	9.95
270 Weatherby	100	PE	3760	3625	2825	2435	3140	2363	1773	1317	0.4	1.6	4.3	9.95
270 Weatherby	130	PE	3375	3050	2750	2480	3283	2685	2183	1776	0.4	1.8	4.5	9.95
270 Weatherby	150	PE	3245	2955	2675	2430	3501	2909	2385	1967	0.5	2.0	5.0	9.95
7mm Weatherby	139	PE	3300	2995	2715	2465	3355	2770	2275	1877	0.4	1.9	4.9	9.95
7mm Weatherby	154	PE	3160	2885	2640	2415	3406	2874	2384	1994	0.5	2.0	5.0	9.95
300 Weatherby	150	PE	3545	3195	2890	2615	4179	3393	2783	2279	0.4	1.5	3.9	10.95
300 Weatherby	180	PE	3245	2960	2705	2475	4201	3501	2925	2448	0.4	1.9	5.2	10.95
300 Weatherby	220	SPE	2905	2610	2385	2150	4123	3329	2757	2257	0.6	2.5	6.7	10.95
340 Weatherby	200	PE	3210	2905	2615	2345	4566	3748	3038	2442	0.5	2.1	5.3	10.95
340 Weatherby	210	Nosler	3165	2910	2665	2435	4660	3948	3312	2766	0.5	2.1	5.0	10.95
340 Weatherby	250	SPE	2850	2580	2325	2090	4510	3695	3000	2425	0.6	2.7	6.7	10.95
378 Weatherby	270	SPE	3180	2850	2600	2315	6051	4871	4053	3210	0.5	2.0	5.2	12.95
378 Weatherby	300	SPE, FMJ	2925	2610	2380	2125	5700	4539	3774	3009	0.6	2.5	6.2	20.95
460 Weatherby	500	RN, FMJ	2700	2330	2005	1730	8095	6025	4465	3320	0.7	3.3	10.0	24.95

Trajectory is given from scope height. Velocities chronographed using 26″ bbls. Available with Nosler bullets; add $2.00 per box.
SPE—Semi-Pointed Expanding RN—Round Nose PE—Pointed Expanding FMJ—Full Metal Jacket

RIMFIRE CARTRIDGES — BALLISTICS AND PRICES

Remington-Peters, Winchester-Western, Federal & Cascade Cartridge, Inc.

All loads available from all manufacturers except as indicated: R-P (a); W-W (b); Fed. (c); CCI (d). All prices are approximate.

CARTRIDGE	BULLET WT. GRS.	BULLET TYPE	VELOCITY FT. PER SEC. MUZZLE	VELOCITY 100 YDS.	ENERGY FT. LBS. MUZZLE	ENERGY 100 YDS.	MID-RANGE TRAJECTORY 100 YDS.	HANDGUN BARREL LENGTH	BALLISTICS M.V. F.P.S.	BALLISTICS M.E. F.P.	PRICE FOR 50
22 Short T22 (a, b)	29	C, L*	1045	810	70	42	5.6	6″	865	48	$ .98
22 Short Hi-Vel.	29	C, L	1125	920	81	54	4.3	6″	1035	69	.98
22 Short HP Hi-Vel. (a, b, c)	27	C, L	1155	920	80	51	4.2	—	—	—	1.07
22 Short (a, b)	29	D	1045	—	70	—	—	—	—	(per 500)	9.00
22 Short (a, b)	15	D	1710	—	97	—	—	—	—	(per 500)	9.00
22 Long Hi-Vel.	29	C, L	1240	965	99	60	3.8	6″	1095	77	1.07
22 Long Rifle T22 (a, b)†-1	40	L*	1145	975	116	84	4.0	6″	950	80	1.12
22 Long Rifle (b)†-2	40	L*	1120	950	111	80	4.2	—	—	—	1.85
22 Long Rifle (b)†-3	40	L*	—	—	—	—	—	6¾″	1060	100	1.85
22 Long Rifle (d)†-4	40	C	1165	980	121	84	4.0	—	—	—	.99
22 Long Rifle Hi-Vel.	40	C, L	1285	1025	147	93	3.4	6″	1125	112	1.23
22 Long Rifle HP Hi-Vel. (b, d)	37	C, L	1315	1020	142	85	3.4	—	—	—	1.24
22 Long Rifle HP Hi-Vel. (a, c)	36	C	1365	1040	149	86	3.4	—	—	—	1.24
22 Long Rifle (b, c)	No.	12 Shot	—	—	—	—	—	—	—	—	2.32
22 WRF [Rem. Spl.] (a, b)	45	C, L	1450	1110	210	123	—	—	—	—	3.19
22 WRF Mag. (b)	40	JHP	2000	1390	355	170	1.6	6½″	1550	213	3.05
22 WRF Mag. (b)	40	MC	2000	1390	355	170	1.6	6½″	1550	213	3.05
22 Win. Auto Inside lub. (a, b)	45	C, L	1055	930	111	86	—	—	—	—	3.27
5mm Rem. RFM (a)	38	PLHP	2100	1605	372	217	Not Available				4.48

†—Target loads of these ballistics available in: (1) Rem. Match; (2) W-W LV EZXS, Super Match Mark III; (3) Super Match Mark IV and EZXS Pistol Match; (4) CCI Mini-Group. C—Copper plated L—Lead (Wax Coated) L*—Lead, lubricated D—Disintegrating MC—Metal Case HP—Hollow Point JHP—Jacket Hollow Point PLHP—Power-Lokt Hollow Point

NORMA C.F. RIFLE CARTRIDGES — BALLISTICS AND PRICES

Norma ammunition loaded to standard velocity and pressure is now available with Nosler bullets in the following loads: 270 Win., 130-, 150-gr.; Super 7x61 (S&H), 160-gr.; 308 Win., 180-gr.; 30-06, 150-, 180-gr., all at slightly higher prices. All ballistic figures are computed from a line of sight one inch above center of bore at muzzle. Write for their latest prices.

Cartridge	Bullet Wt. Grs.	Type	Velocity, feet per sec. V Muzzle	V 100 yds.	V 200 yds.	V 300 yds.	Energy, foot pounds E Muzzle	E 100 yds.	E 200 yds.	E 300 yds.	Max. height of trajectory, inches Tr. 100 yds.	Tr. 200 yds.	Tr. 300 yds.	Price for 20
220 Swift	50	SP	4111	3611	3133	2681	1877	1448	1090	799	.2	.9	3.0	$7.05
222 Remington	50	SP	3200	2660	2170	1750	1137	786	523	340	.0	2.0	6.2	4.60
22-250	50	SP	3800	3300	2810	2350	1600	1209	885	613	Not Available			5.25
	55	SP	3650	3200	2780	2400	1637	1251	944	704	Not Available			5.25
243 Winchester	100	SP	3070	2790	2540	2320	2093	1729	1433	1195	.1	1.8	5.0	6.25
6mm Remington	100	SP	3190	2920	2660	2420	2260	1890	1570	1300	.4	2.1	5.3	6.25
250 Savage	87	SP	3032	2685	2357	2054	1776	1393	1074	815	.0	1.9	5.8	6.00
6.5 Carcano	156	SP	2000	1810	1640	1485	1386	1135	932	764	Not Available			8.50
6.5 Japanese	139	SPBT	2428	2280	2130	1990	1820	1605	1401	1223	.3	2.8	7.7	8.50
	156	SP	2067	1871	1692	1529	1481	1213	992	810	.6	4.4	11.9	8.50
6.5 x 55	139	SPBT	2789	2630	2470	2320	2402	2136	1883	1662	.1	2.0	5.6	8.50
	156	SP	2493	2271	2062	1867	2153	1787	1473	1208	.3	2.9	7.9	8.50
270 Winchester	110	SP	3248	2966	2694	2435	2578	2150	1773	1448	.1	1.4	4.3	6.80
	130	SPBT	3140	2884	2639	2404	2847	2401	2011	1669	.0	1.6	4.7	6.80
	150	SPBT	2802	2616	2436	2262	2616	2280	1977	1705	.1	2.0	5.7	6.80
7.5 x 55 Schmidt Rubin (7.5 Swiss)	180	SP	2650	2450	2260	2060	2792	2350	1990	1665	Not Available			8.70
7 x 57	110	SP	3068	2792	2528	2277	2300	1904	1561	1267	.0	1.6	5.0	6.95
	150	SPBT	2756	2539	2331	2133	2530	2148	1810	1516	.1	2.2	6.2	6.95
7mm Remington Magnum	150	SP	3260	2970	2700	2450	3540	2945	2435	1990	.4	2.0	4.9	8.40
7 x 61 S & H (26 in.)	160	SPBT	3100	2927	2757	2595	3415	3045	2701	2393	.0	1.5	4.3	9.45
30 U.S. Carbine	110	SPRN	1970	1595	1300	1090	948	622	413	290	.8	6.4	19.0	4.40
308 Winchester	130	SPBT	2900	2590	2300	2030	2428	1937	1527	1190	.1	2.1	6.2	6.80
	150	SPBT	2860	2570	2300	2050	2725	2200	1762	1400	.1	2.0	5.9	6.80
	180	SPBT	2610	2400	2210	2020	2725	2303	1952	1631	.2	2.5	6.6	6.80
	180	SP	2610	2400	2210	2020	2725	2303	1952	1631	.7	3.4	8.9	7.50
7.62 Russian	180	PSPBT	2624	2415	2222	2030	2749	2326	1970	1644	.2	2.5	6.6	8.50
308 Norma Magnum	180	DC	3100	2881	2668	2464	3842	3318	2846	2427	.0	1.6	4.6	10.98
30-06	130	PSPBT	3281	2951	2636	2338	3108	2514	2006	1578	.1	1.5	4.6	6.80
	150	PS	2972	2680	2402	2141	2943	2393	1922	1527	.0	1.9	5.7	6.80
	180	PSPBT, SPDC	2700	2494	2296	2109	2914	2487	2107	1778	.1	2.3	6.4	6.80
	180	SPDC	2700	2494	2296	2109	2914	2487	2107	1778	Not Available			7.50
7.65 Argentine	150	SP	2920	2630	2355	2105	2841	2304	1848	1476	.1	2.0	5.8	8.50
303 British	130	SP	2789	2483	2195	1929	2246	1780	1391	1075	.1	2.3	6.7	7.00
	150	SP	2720	2440	2170	1930	2465	1983	1569	1241	.1	2.2	6.5	7.00
	180	SPBT	2540	2340	2147	1965	2579	2189	1843	1544	.2	2.7	7.3	7.00
7.7 Japanese	130	SP	2950	2635	2340	2065	2513	2004	1581	1231	.1	2.0	5.9	8.50
	180	SPBT	2493	2292	2101	1922	2484	2100	1765	1477	.3	2.8	7.7	8.50
8mm Mauser (.323 in.)	123	SP	2888	2515	2170	1857	2277	1728	1286	942	Not Available			7.00
	196	SP	2526	2195	1894	1627	2778	2097	1562	1152	Not Available			7.00
358 Winchester	250	SP	2250	2010	1780	1570	2811	2243	1759	1369	Not Available			8.85
358 Norma Magnum	250	SP	2790	2493	2231	2001	4322	3451	2764	2223	.2	2.4	6.6	11.05

P—Pointed SP—Soft Point HP—Hollow Point FP—Flat Point RN—Round Nose BT—Boat Tail MC—Metal Case DC—Dual Core SPS—Soft Point Semi-Pointed NA—Not announced *Price for 50

CENTERFIRE HANDGUN CARTRIDGES — BALLISTICS AND PRICES

Winchester-Western, Remington-Peters, Norma and Federal

Most loads are available from W-W and R-P. All available Norma loads are listed. Federal cartridges are marked with an asterisk. Other loads supplied by only one source are indicated by a letter, thus: Norma (a); R-P (b); W-W (c). Prices are approximate.

Cartridge	Bullet Gr.	Bullet Style	Muzzle Velocity	Muzzle Energy	Barrel Inches	Price Per 50
22 Jet (b)	40	SP	2100	390	8⅜	$9.65
221 Fireball (b)	50	SP	2650	780	10½	4.45
25 (6.35mm) Auto*	50	MC	810	73	2	6.15
256 Winchester Magnum (c)	60	HP	2350	735	8½	10.10
30 (7.65mm) Luger Auto	93	MC	1220	307	4½	9.75
32 S&W Blank (b, c)	No bullet		—	—	—	4.35
32 S&W Blank, BP (c)	No bullet		—	—	—	4.35
32 Short Colt	80	Lead	745	100	4	5.35
32 Long Colt, IL (c)	82	Lub.	755	104	4	5.60
32 Colt New Police	100	Lead	680	100	4	6.50
32 (7.65mm) Auto*	71	MC	960	145	4	7.00
32 (7.65mm) Auto Pistol (a)	77	MC	900	162	4	6.50
32 S&W	88	Lead	680	90	3	5.35
32 S&W Long	98	Lead	705	115	4	5.60
32-20 Winchester	100	Lead	1030	271	6	7.75
32-20 Winchester	100	SP	1030	271	6	9.20
357 Magnum (b)*	158	SP	1550	845	8⅜	9.20
357 Magnum	158	MP	1410	695	8⅜	9.20
357 Magnum	158	Lead	1410	696	8⅜	7.80
357 Magnum (a)	158	JHP	1450	735	8⅜	9.20
9mm Luger (a)	116	MC	1165	349	4	8.30
9mm Luger Auto*	124	MC	1120	345	4	8.70
38 S&W Blank	No bullet		—	—	—	4.75
38 Smith & Wesson	146	Lead	685	150	4	6.55
38 S&W (a)	146	Lead	730	172	4	6.15
38 Special Blank	No bullet		—	—	—	7.00
38 Special, IL (c)	150	Lub.	1060	375	6	6.75
38 Special, IL (c)	150	MP	1060	375	6	8.20
38 Special	158	Lead	855	256	6	6.60
38 Special	200	Lead	730	236	6	6.90
38 Special	158	MP	855	256	6	8.20
38 Special (b)	125	SJHP	Not available			8.20
38 Special (b)	158	SJHP	Not available			8.20
38 Special WC (b)	148	Lead	770	195	6	6.75
38 Special Match, IL (c)	148	Lead	770	195	6	6.75
38 Special Match, IL (b, c)	158	Lead	855	256	6	6.75
38 Special Hi-Speed*	158	Lead	1090	425	6	7.10
38 Special (a)	158	RN	900	320	6	6.75
38 Short Colt	125	Lead	730	150	6	6.00
38 Short Colt, Greased (c)	130	Lub.	730	155	6	6.00
38 Long Colt	150	Lead	730	175	6	6.60
38 Super Auto (b)	130	MC	1280	475	5	7.40
38 Auto, for Colt 38 Super (c)	130	MC	1280	475	5	7.40
38 Auto	130	MC	1040	312	4½	7.40
380 Auto*	95	MC	955	192	3¾	7.15
38-40 Winchester	180	SP	975	380	5	11.50
41 Remington Magnum (b)	210	Lead	1050	515	8¾	10.15
41 Remington Magnum (b)	210	SP	1500	1050	8¾	11.60
44 S&W Special	246	Lead	755	311	6½	9.00
44 Remington Magnum	240	SP	1470	1150	6½	11.75
44 Remington Magnum	240	Lead	1470	1150	6½	11.75
44-40 Winchester	200	SP	975	420	7½	13.80
45 Colt	250	Lead	860	410	5½	9.05
45 Colt, IL (c)	255	Lub., L	860	410	5½	9.05
45 Auto	230	MC	850	369	5	9.40
45 ACP (a)	230	JHP	850	370	5	9.95
45 Auto WC*	185	MC	775	245	5	9.95
45 Auto MC (a, b)	230	MC	850	369	5	9.95
45 Auto Match (c)	185	MC	775	247	5	9.90
45 Auto Match, IL (c)	210	Lead	710	235	5	9.95
45 Auto Match*	230	MC	850	370	5	9.90
45 Auto Rim (b)	230	Lead	810	335	5½	9.85

IL—Inside Lub. JSP—Jacketed Soft Point WC—Wad Cutter
RN—Round Nose HP—Hollow Point Lub—Lubricated
MC—Metal Case SP—Soft Point MP—Metal Point
LGC—Lead, Gas Check JHP—Jacketed Hollow Point

SUPER VEL HANDGUN CARTRIDGES — BALLISTICS AND PRICES

The cartridges listed below are perhaps the most powerful and destructive of these calibers commercially manufactured. Bullets listed can be had as components — other weights (not loaded by Super Vel) are also available.

Cartridge	Bullet Gr.	Bullet Style	Muzzle Velocity	Muzzle Energy	Barrel Inches	Price Per 50
380 ACP	88	JHP	1065	227	4	$9.50
9mm Luger	90	JHP	1485	441	4	10.50
9mm Luger	112	JSP	1330	439	4	10.50
9mm Luger	125	FMJ	995	274	4	10.50
9mm Luger	125	FMJ	1120	345	4	10.50
38 Special	110	JHP	1370	458	6	9.50
38 Special	110	JSP	1370	458	6	9.50
38 Special	125	JHP	1370	520	6	9.50
38 Special	158	SWC-lead	885	256	6	8.20
38 Special	158	RN-lead	855	256	6	8.20
38 Special	148	HBWC	775	196	6	8.20
357 Magnum	110	JHP	1690	697	6	10.50
357 Magnum	110	JSP	1690	697	6	10.50
357 Magnum	137	JSP	1620	796	6	10.50
357 Magnum	158	JHP	1300	593	6	10.50
357 Magnum	158	JSP	1300	593	6	10.50
45 Auto	190	JHP	1060	473	5	11.95
44 Magnum†	180	JHP	2075	1591	8⅜	6.00
44 Magnum†	180	JSP	2075	1591	8⅜	6.00

JHP—Jacketed Hollow Point SP—Jacketed Soft Point
HBWC—Hollow Base Wad Cutter †Price per 20

SHOTSHELL LOADS AND PRICES

Winchester-Western, Remington-Peters, Federal & Eley

In certain loadings one manufacturer may offer fewer or more shot sizes than another, but in general all makers offer equivalent loadings. Sources are indicated by letters, thus: W-W (a); R-P (b); Fed. (c); Eley (d). Prices are approximate.

GAUGE	Length Shell Ins.	Powder Equiv. Drams	Shot Ozs.	Shot Size	PRICE FOR 25
MAGNUM LOADS					
10 (a[1], b)	3½	5	2	2	$11.05
12 (a, b, c)	3	4½	1⅞	BB, 2, 4	6.15
12 (a[1], b)	3	4¼	1⅝	2, 4, 6	6.15
12 (a)	3	Max	1⅜	2, 4, 6	6.15
12 (a[1], b, c, d)	2¾	4	1½	2, 4, 5, 6	6.15
16 (a, b, c, d)	2¾	3½	1¼	2, 4, 6	5.35
20 (a, b, c)	3	3¼	1¼	4, 6, 7½	5.45
20 (a[1])	3	Max	1 3/16	4	5.45
20 (a[1], b, c, d)	2¾	3	1⅛	2, 4, 6, 7½	4.85
LONG RANGE LOADS					
10 (a, b)	2⅞	4¾	1⅝	4	6.55
12 (a[1], b, c, d)	2¾	3¾	1¼	BB, 2, 4, 5, 6, 7½, 9	4.85
16 (a, b, c, d)	2¾	3¼	1⅛	4, 5, 6, 7½, 9	4.45
20 (a[1], b, c, d)	2¾	2¾	1	4, 5, 6, 7½, 9	4.20
28 (a, b)	2¾	2¼	¾	6, 7½, 9	4.20
28 (c)	2¾	2¼	⅞	4, 6, 7½, 9	4.05
410 (b)	2½	max.	½	4, 6, 7½, 9	3.40
410 (b)	3	max.	11/16	4, 5, 6, 7½, 9	3.95
FIELD LOADS					
12 (a, b, c)	2¾	3¼	1¼	7½, 8	4.30
12 (a, b, c, d)	2¾	3¼	1⅛	4, 5, 6, 7½, 8, 9	4.15
12 (a, b, c, d)	2¾	3	1	4, 5, 6, 8	3.80
16 (a, b, c, d)	2¾	2¾	1⅛	4, 5, 6, 7½, 8, 9	3.80
16 (a, b, c)	2¾	2½	1	6, 8	3.65
20 (a, b, c, d)	2¾	2½	1	4, 5, 6, 7½, 8, 9	3.70
20 (a, b, c)	2¾	2¼	⅞	6, 8	3.40
SCATTER LOADS					
12 (a, b)	2¾	3	1⅛	8	4.35
TARGET LOADS					
12 (a, b, c)	2¾	3	1⅛	7½, 8	4.05
12 (a, b, c)	2¾	2¾	1⅛	7½, 8	4.05
16 (a, b, c)	2¾	2½	1	9	3.85
20 (a, b, c)	2¾	2¼	⅞	9	3.40
28 (a, c)	2¾	2¼	¾	9	4.20
410 (a, b, c, d)	3	Max	¾	9	4.20
410 (a, b, c)	2½	Max	½	9	3.35
SKEET & TRAP					
12 (a, b, c, d)	2¾	3	1⅛	7½, 8, 9	4.05
12 (a, b, c, d)	2¾	2¾	1⅛	7½, 8, 9	4.05
16 (a, b, c, d)	2¾	2½	1	9	3.80
16 (c)	2¾	1⅛	1⅛	8, 9	3.80
20 (a, b, c)	2¾	2¼	⅞	9	3.40
BUCKSHOT					
12 (a, b, c)	3 Mag.	4½	—	00 Buck—15 pellets	8.50
12 (a, b, c)	3 Mag.	4½	—	4 Buck—41 pellets	8.50
12 (b)	2¾ Mag.	4	—	1 Buck—20 pellets	7.35
12 (a, b, c)	2¾ Mag.	4	—	00 Buck—12 pellets	7.35
12 (a, b, c)	2¾	3¾	—	00 Buck— 9 pellets	6.60
12 (a, b, c)	2¾	3¾	—	0 Buck—12 pellets	6.60
12 (a, b, c)	2¾	3¾	—	1 Buck—16 pellets	6.60
12 (a, b, c)	2¾	3¾	—	4 Buck—27 pellets	6.60
16 (a, b, c)	2¾	3	—	1 Buck—12 pellets	6.50
20 (a, b, c)	2¾	2¾	—	3 Buck—20 pellets	6.50
RIFLED SLUGS					
12 (a, b, c, d)	2¾	3¾	1	Slug	7.60
16 (a, b, c)	2¾	3	⅞	Slug	7.25
20 (a, b, c)	2¾	2¾	⅝	Slug	7.00
410 (a, b, c)	2½	Max	⅕	Slug	6.60

W-W 410, 28- and 10-ga. Magnum shells available in paper cases only, as are their scatter and target loads; their skeet and trap loads come in both plastic and paper.

RP shells are all of plastic with Power Piston wads except: 12 ga. scatter loads have Post Wad: all 10 ga., 410-3″ and rifled slug loads have standard wad columns.

Federal magnum, range, buckshot, slug and all 410 loads are made in plastic only. Field loads are available in both paper and plastic.

Eley shotshells are of plastic-coated paper.

[1]—These loads available from W-W with Lubaloy shot at higher price.

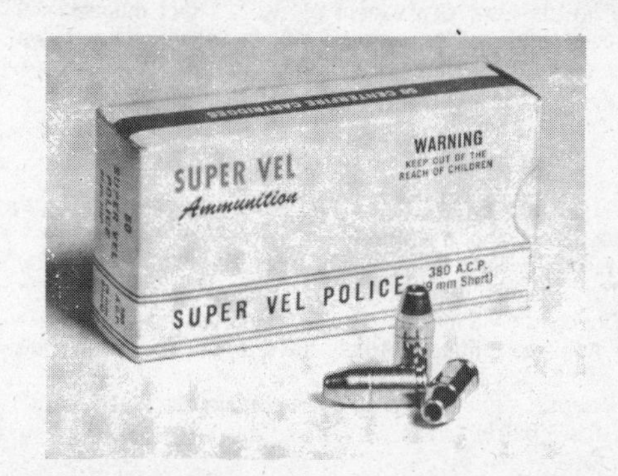

U.S. HANDGUNS — TARGET AUTOLOADERS

BROWNING 22 AUTO CHALLENGER PISTOL
Caliber: 22 LR, 10-shot magazine.
Barrel: 4½" or 6¾".
Length: 8⅞" over-all (4½" bbl.). **Weight:** 35 oz. (4½" bbl.).
Stocks: Simulated walnut (Novadur plastic).
Features: Steel frame, manual stop-open latch (automatic after last shot); gold plated grooved trigger; trigger pull adjustment screw on rear face of frame.
Sights: ⅛" non-glare blade front; frame-mtd. rear, screw adj. for w. & e.
Price: Blue, either bbl. **$134.50**
Price: Renaissance Grade, engraved, chrome plated, 6¾" bbl. ... **$334.50**

BROWNING 22 AUTO MEDALIST PISTOL
Caliber: 22 LR, 10-shot magazine.
Barrel: 6¾", med.-heavy vent. rib.
Length: 11$^{5}/_{16}$" over-all. **Weight:** 46 oz. less weights.
Stocks: Full wrap-around thumbrest of select checkered walnut; matching fore-end. Left hand grips available.
Features: Dry-fire mechanism permits practice without mechanical harm. Fore-end holds variable weights. Trigger adj. for weight of pull and backlash.
Sights: ⅛" undercut removable blade front; rear frame-mtd., has micrometer clicks adj. for w. and e. Sight radius, 9½".
Price: Blued **$224.50**
Price: Renaissance Grade, chrome plated **$444.50**

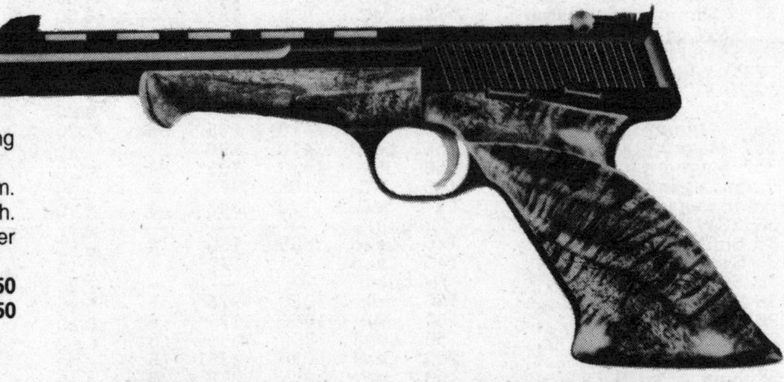

COLT WOODSMAN MATCH TARGET AUTO PISTOL
Caliber: 22 LR, 10-shot magazine.
Barrel: 4½" or 6".
Length: 10½" (4½" bbl.). **Weight:** 39 oz. (6" bbl.), 34½ oz. (4½" bbl.).
Stocks: Walnut with thumbrest; checkered.
Sights: Ramp front with removable undercut blade; ⅛" standard, $^{1}/_{10}$" on special order; Colt-Elliason adjustable rear.
Features: Wide trigger, automatic slide stop.
Price: Colt Blue only **$139.50**

COLT WOODSMAN SPORT AND TARGET MODEL
Caliber: 22 LR, 10-shot magazine.
Barrel: 4" (Sport), 6" (Target).
Length: 9" (4" bbl.). **Weight:** 30 oz. (4" bbl.) 32 oz. (6" bbl.).
Stocks: Walnut with thumbrest; checkered.
Sights: Ramp front, adjustable rear for w. and e.
Features: Wide trigger, automatic slide stop.
Price: Colt Blue only **$117.50**

Colt Targetsman
Same as Woodsman S&T model except: 6" bbl. only; fixed blade front sight, economy adj. rear; without auto. slide stop **$99.50**

COLT GOLD CUP NAT'L MATCH AUTO
Caliber: 38 Spec. Mid-Range, 9-shot magazine.
Barrel: 5", with new design bushing.
Length: 8⅜". **Weight:** 38½ oz.
Stocks: Checkered walnut, gold plated medallion.
Sights: Ramp-style front, Colt-Elliason rear adj. for w. and e.
Features: Arched or flat housing; wide, grooved trigger with adj. stop; ribbed-top slide, hand fitted, with improved ejection port.
Price: Colt Royal Blue **$219.50**

Colt Gold Cup Nat'l Match Mk IV Series 70 Auto
Identical to the Gold Cup except 45 ACP, 7-shot magazine, 6¾" sight radius, fitted with a split-finger, collet-type barrel bushing and reverse-taper barrel to match for improved accuracy.
Price: **$219.50**

HI-STANDARD SUPERMATIC STANDARD CITATION
Caliber: 22 LR, 10-shot magazine.
Barrel: 5½" bull weight.
Length: 10" (5½" bbl.). **Weight:** 42 oz. (5½" bbl.).
Stocks: Checkered walnut with or w/o thumbrest, right or left.
Features: Adjustable trigger pull; over-travel trigger adjustment; double acting safety; rebounding firing pin.
Sights: Undercut ramp front; click adjustable square notch rear.
Price: 5½" bull barrel **$149.95**

HI-STANDARD VICTOR
Caliber: 22 LR, 10-shot magazine.
Barrel: 4½", 5½".
Length: 8¾" (4½" bbl.). **Weight:** 43½ oz. (4½" bbl., vent. rib), 43¾ oz. (solid rib), 46 oz. (5½" bbl., vent. rib), 46¼ oz. (solid rib).
Stocks: Checkered walnut.
Sights: Undercut ramp front, rib mounted click adj. rear.
Features: Vent. rib, interchangeable barrel, 2 - 2¼ lb. trigger pull, blue finish, back and front straps stippled. Also available with aluminum solid rib.
Price: Either bbl. length **$198.00**
Price: Solid rib, either bbl. length **$193.00**

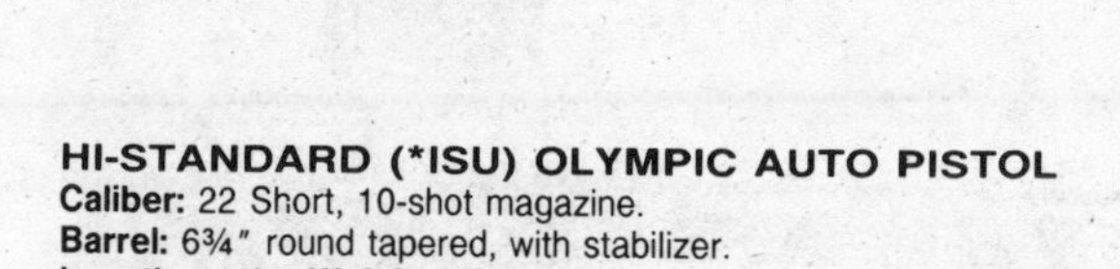

HI-STANDARD (*ISU) OLYMPIC AUTO PISTOL
Caliber: 22 Short, 10-shot magazine.
Barrel: 6¾" round tapered, with stabilizer.
Length: 11¼". **Weight:** 40 oz.
Stocks: Checkered walnut w or w/o thumbrest, right or left.
Sights: Undercut ramp front; click adj., square notch rear.
Features: Integral stabilizer with two removable weights. Trigger adj. for pull and over-travel; Citation grade finish.
Price: Blued **$189.95**
*Complies with all International Shooting Union regulations.
Olympic model with frame-mounted rear sight **$189.95**

HI-STANDARD SUPERMATIC TROPHY MILITARY
Caliber: 22 LR, 10-shot magazine.
Barrel: 5½" heavy, 7¼" fluted.
Length: 9¾ inches (5½" bbl.). **Weight:** 44½ oz.
Stocks: Checkered walnut with or w/o thumbrest, right or left.
Features: Grip duplicates feel of military 45; positive action mag. latch; front- and backstraps stippled. Trigger adj. for pull, over-travel.
Sights: Undercut ramp front; frame mounted rear, click adj.
Price: Either bbl. length **$155.95**

SMITH & WESSON 22 AUTO PISTOL Model 41
Caliber: 22 LR or 22 S, 10-shot clip.
Barrel: 5" or 7⅜", sight radius 9 5/16" (7⅜" bbl.).
Length: 12", incl. detachable muzzle brake, (7⅜" bbl. only).
Weight: 43½ oz. (7⅜" bbl.).
Stocks: Checkered walnut with thumbrest, usable with either hand.
Features: ⅜" wide, grooved trigger with adj. stop; wgts. available to make pistol up to 59 oz.
Sights: Front, ⅛" Patridge undercut; micro click rear adj. for w. and e.
Price: S&W Bright Blue, satin matted bbl., either caliber **$159.50**

SMITH & WESSON 22 MATCH HEAVY BARREL M-41
Caliber: 22 LR, 10-shot clip.
Barrel: 5½" heavy, without muzzle brake. Sight radius, 8".
Length: 9". **Weight:** 44½ oz.
Stocks: Checkered walnut with modified thumbrest, usable with either hand.
Features: ⅜" wide, grooved trigger; adj. trigger stop.
Sights: ⅛" Patridge on ramp base. S&W micro click rear, adj. for w. and e.
Price: S&W Bright Blue, satin matted top area **$159.50**

S & W 22 Auto Heavy Barrel EFS Model 41
Same as Model 41 Heavy Barrel but with extendible ⅛" front sight. Without muzzle brake or weights. Blued **$176.00**

HI-STANDARD S'MATIC CITATION MILITARY
Caliber: 22 LR, 10-shot magazine.
Barrel: 5½" bull, 7¼" fluted.
Length: 9¾" (5½" bbl.). **Weight:** 46 oz.
Stocks: Checkered walnut with or w/o thumbrest, right or left.
Sights: Undercut ramp front; frame mounted rear, click adj.
Features: Same as regular Citation plus military style grip, stippled front- and backstraps, positive magazine latch.
Price: Either bbl. length **$149.95**

RUGER Mark 1 TARGET MODEL AUTO PISTOL
Caliber: 22 LR only, 9-shot magazine.
Barrel: 6⅞" or 5½" bull barrel (6-groove, 14" twist).
Length: 10⅞" (6⅞" bbl.). **Weight:** 42 oz. with 6⅞" bbl.
Stocks: Checkered hard rubber.
Features: Rear sight mounted on receiver, does not move with slide; wide, grooved trigger.
Sights: ⅛" blade front, micro click rear, adjustable for w. and e. Sight radius 9⅜" (with 6⅞" bbl.).
Price: Blued, either barrel length **$71.50**
Price: Checkered walnut panels with left thumbrest **$75.85**

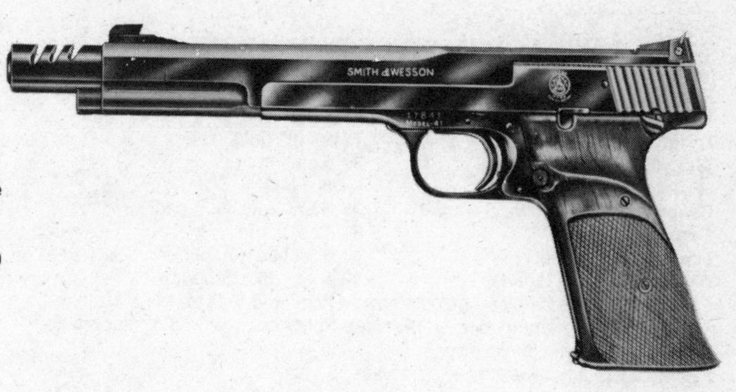

Smith & Wesson Conversion Kit
Converts Models 41 and 46 from 22 Short to 22 LR and vice versa. Consists of barrel, slide, magazine, slide stop and recoil spring.
Price, parts only **$75.00**
Price, factory installed and tested **$85.00**
Price, 5½" heavy bbl. only with sights for M41 or M46 .... **$43.00**

U.S. HANDGUNS—TARGET AUTOLOADERS

SMITH & WESSON 38 MASTER Model 52 AUTO

Caliber: 38 Special (for Mid-range W.C. with flush-seated bullet only). 5-shot magazine.
Barrel: 5″.
Length: 8⅝″. **Weight:** 41 oz. with empty magazine.
Features: Top sighting surfaces matte finished. Locked breech, moving barrel system; checked for 10-ring groups at 50 yards. Coin-adj. sight screws. Dry firing permissible if manual safety on.
Stocks: Checkered walnut.
Sights: ⅛″ Patridge front, S&W micro click rear adj. for w. and e.
Price: S&W Bright Blue **$247.50**

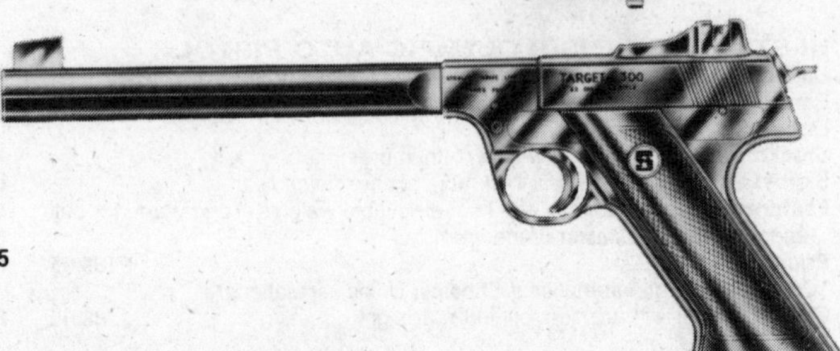

STERLING MODEL 283 TARGET

Caliber: 22 LR, 10-shot magazine.
Barrel: 4½″, 6″, and 8″.
Length: 9″ (4½″ bbl.). **Weight:** 36 oz. (4½″ bbl.).
Stocks: Checkered plastic.
Features: Adjustable trigger and balance weights; sear lock safety.
Sights: ⅛″ blade front; Click adj. square notch rear.
Price: Blued **$109.95**

U.S. HANDGUNS— TARGET REVOLVERS

COLT DIAMONDBACK REVOLVER

Caliber: 22 S, L or LR, or 38 Special, 6 shot.
Barrel: 2½″ or 4″, with ventilated rib.
Length: 9″ (4″ bbl.). **Weight:** 24 oz. (2½″ bbl.), 28½ oz. (4″ bbl.).
Stocks: Checkered walnut, target type, square butt.
Features: Ventilated rib; grooved, crisp trigger; swing-out cylinder; wide hammer spur.
Sights: Ramp front, adj. notch rear.
Price: Colt Blue **$151.00**
Price: Nickel finish (38 Spl. only) **$161.50**

SMITH & WESSON 22 CENTER FIRE MAGNUM M-53

Caliber: Rem. 22 Jet and 22 S, L, LR with inserts. 6 shot.
Barrel: 4″, 6″ or 8⅜″.
Length: 11¼″ (6″ bbl.). **Weight:** 40 oz.
Stocks: Checkered walnut, target.
Features: Grooved tangs and trigger, swing-out cylinder revolver.
Sights: ⅛″ Baughman Quick Draw front, micro click rear, adjustable for w. and e.
Price: Blued, 4″, 6″ **$180.00**
Price: 8⅜″ bbl. **$186.50**
Price: Extra cylinder for 22 RF. (fitted) **$43.00**

SMITH & WESSON MASTERPIECE TARGET MODELS

Model:	K-22 (M17).	K-22 (M48).
Caliber:	22 LR, 6 shot.	22 RF Magnum, 6 shot.
Barrel:	6″, 8⅜″.	4″, 6″ or 8⅜″
Length:	11⅛″ (6″ bbl.).	11⅛″ (6″ bbl.).
Weight:	38½ oz. (6″ bbl.).	39 oz.(6″ bbl.).
Model:	K-32 (M16). (Illus.)	K-38 (M14).
Caliber:	32 S&W Long, 6 shot.	38 S&W Special, 6 shot.
Barrel:	6 inches.	6″, 8⅜″.
Length:	11⅛ inches.	11⅛ inches. (6″ bbl.)
Weight:	38½ oz. (Loaded).	38½ oz. (6″, loaded).

Features: All Masterpiece models have: checkered walnut, Magna stocks; grooved tang and trigger; ⅛″ Patridge front sight, micro. adj. rear sights. Swing out cylinder revolver.
Price: Blued, all calibers M-17 and M-48, 6″ bbl. **$130.00**
Price: 8⅜″ bbl. **$136.50**

SMITH & WESSON 1955 Model 25, 45 TARGET

Caliber: 45 ACP and 45 AR, 6 shot.
Barrel: 6½″ (heavy target type).
Length: 11⅞ inches. **Weight:** 45 oz.
Stocks: Checkered walnut target.
Features: Tangs and trigger grooved; target trigger and hammer standard, checkered target hammer. Swing-out cylinder revolver.
Sights: ⅛″ Patridge front, micro click rear, adjustable for w. and e.
Price: Blued **$175.00**

COLT PYTHON REVOLVER

Caliber: 357 Magnum (handles all 38 Spec.), 6 shot.
Barrel: 2½″, 4″ or 6″, with ventilated rib.
Length: 9¼″ (4″ bbl.). **Weight:** 38 oz. (4″ bbl.).
Stocks: Checkered walnut, target type, square butt.
Features: Ventilated rib; grooved, crisp trigger; swing-out cylinder; target hammer.
Sights: ⅛″ ramp front, adj. notch rear.
Price: Colt Royal Blue ..... **$217.00** Nickeled **$242.00**

Smith & Wesson Accessories

Target hammers with low, broad, deeply-checkered spur, and wide-swaged, grooved target trigger. For all frame sizes, **$5.75** (target hammers not available for small frames). Target stocks: for large-frame guns, **$12.25** to **$14.00**; for med.-frame guns, **$9.50** to **$12.25**; for small-frame guns, **$8.00** to **$11.75**. These prices applicable only when specified on original order. As separately-ordered parts: target hammers and triggers, **$9.25**; stocks, **$10.75-$17.00**.

U.S. HANDGUNS—TARGET REVOLVERS

SMITH & WESSON COMBAT MASTERPIECE

Caliber: 38 Special (M15) or 22 LR (M18), 6 shot.
Barrel: 2″ (M15) 4″ (M18)
Length: 9⅛″ (4″ bbl.). **Weight:** Loaded, 22 36½ oz, 38 30 oz.
Stocks: Checkered walnut, Magna. Grooved tangs and trigger.
Sights: Front, ⅛″ Baugham Quick Draw on ramp, micro click rear, adjustable for w. and e.
Price: Blued, M-15 and M-18 .... **$125.00**
Price: Nickel M-15 .... **$135.00**

U.S. HANDGUNS — SERVICE & SPORT

AUTO MAG AUTO. PISTOL

Caliber: 44 Auto Mag or 357 Auto Mag, 7-shot.
Barrel: 6½″.
Weight: 57 oz. (44), 54 oz. (357). **Length:** 11½″ over-all.
Stocks: Checkered polyurethane.
Sights: Target-type ramp front, fully adj. rear.
Features: Short recoil, rotary bolt system. Made of stainless steel. Conversion unit available to change caliber using same frame. Comes in plastic carrying case with extra magazine, wrenches, lubricant and manual. From High Standard.
Price: 44 AMP or 357 AMP **$298.00**
Price: Conversion unit **$150.00**
Price: Engraved models from **$565.00**

BAUER 25 AUTOMATIC PISTOL

Caliber: 25 ACP, 6-shot.
Barrel: 2⅛″.
Length: 4″. **Weight:** 10 oz.
Stocks: Plastic pearl or checkered walnut.
Sights: Recessed, fixed.
Features: Stainless steel construction, positive manual safety, magazine safety. With padded zipper case.
Price: Satin stainless steel **$79.95**

BROWNING HI-POWER 9mm AUTOMATIC PISTOL

Caliber: 9mm Parabellum (Luger), 13-shot magazine.
Barrel: $4\frac{21}{32}$ inches.
Length: 7¾″ over-all. **Weight:** 32 oz.
Stocks: Walnut, hand checkered.
Sights: Fixed front; rear adj. for w.
Features: External hammer with half-cock safety, thumb and magazine safeties. A blow on the hammer cannot discharge a cartridge; cannot be fired with magazine removed. Fixed rear sight model available.
Price: Fixed sight model **$174.50**
Price: 9mm with rear sight adj. for w. and e. **$184.50**

Browning Renaissance Hi-Power 9mm Auto

Same as Browning Hi-Power 9mm Auto except: fully engraved, chrome plated, polyester pearl grips **$449.50**

BROWNING 380

Caliber: 380 ACP.
Barrel: $4\frac{7}{16}$″.
Length: $7\frac{1}{16}$″. **Weight:** 23 oz.
Stock: Novadur plastic w/thumb rest.
Sights: Front, $\frac{1}{10}$″ fixed blade. Rear, adjustable for w. & e.
Features: Fixed barrel, non-glare rear sight, magazine safety, loaded chamber indicator.
Price: Blue **$119.50**
Price: Renaissance Grade, engraved & chrome plated **$339.50**

BUDISCHOWSKY TP-70 AUTO PISTOL

Caliber: 25 ACP, 6-shot.
Barrel: 2.6″.
Length: 4⅔″. **Weight:** 12⅓ oz.
Stocks: Checkered ABS plastic.
Sights: Fixed. Full length serrated rib.
Features: Double action, exposed hammer, manual and magazine safeties. Slide stop, action hold-open after last shot. All stainless steel construction. Available in 22 LR—late 1974 ($120.00). Norton Armament Corp., manufacturer.
Price: **$110.00**

COLT COMMANDER AUTO PISTOL
Caliber: 45 ACP, 7 shot; 38 Super Auto, 9 shot; 9mm Luger, 9 shot.
Barrel: 4¼".
Length: 8". **Weight:** 27 oz.
Stocks: Sandblasted walnut.
Features: Grooved trigger and hammer spur; arched housing; grip and thumb safeties.
Sights: Fixed, glare-proofed blade front, square notch rear.
Price: Blued **$149.50**

Colt Combat Commander
Same as Commander except steel frame, wood panel grips, weight 36½ oz. (9mm and 38 Super).
Price: Blue or satin nickel **$149.50**

COLT GOV'T MODEL MK IV/SERIES 70
Caliber: 9mm, 38 Super, 45 ACP, 7-shot.
Barrel: 5".
Weight: 40 oz. **Length:** 8⅜" over-all.
Stocks: Sandblasted walnut panels.
Sights: Ramp front, fixed square notch rear.
Features: Grip and thumb safeties, grooved trigger. Accurizor barrel and bushing. Blue finish or nickel in 45 only.
Price: Blue **$149.50**
Price: Nickel **$164.50**

Colt Conversion Unit
Permits the 45 and 38 Super Automatic pistols to use the economical 22 LR cartridge. No tools needed. Adjustable rear sight; 10-shot magazine. Designed to give recoil effect of the larger calibers. Not adaptable to Commander models. Blue finish **$80.50**

COLT HUNTSMAN AUTO PISTOL
Caliber: 22 LR, 10-shot magazine.
Barrel: 4", 6".
Length: 8⅝" (4" bbl.). **Weight:** 29½ oz. (4" bbl.), 31 oz. (6" bbl.).
Stocks: Checkered walnut. Wide trigger.
Sights: Fixed ramp front, square notch rear, non-adjustable.
Price: Colt Blue **$74.95**

CLERKE TARGET AUTOMATIC
Caliber: 22 LR, 380 ACP (9-shots 22, 6-shots 380).
Barrel: 4¼".
Length: 8" over-all. **Weight:** 30 oz.
Stocks: Checkered plastic or simulated rosewood.
Sights: Blade front, fixed rear.
Features: Adj. trigger, target sights available at extra cost, grip safety, blue finish.
Price: 22 LR with standard sights **$42.75**
Price: 22 LR with target sights **$50.00**
Price: 380 ACP with standard sights **$55.00**
Price: 380 ACP with target sights **$62.00**

F.I. MODEL D AUTO PISTOL
Caliber: 380 ACP, 6-shot.
Barrel: 3⅛".
Weight: 20 oz. **Length:** 6⅛" over-all.
Stocks: Checkered walnut.
Sights: Blade front, rear adj. for w.
Features: Loaded chamber indicator, all steel construction. Thumb safety locks hammer. No magazine safety. Lanyard ring. Made by Firearms International Industries. From Garcia/F.I.
Price: Approx. **$137.60**

HIGH STANDARD SPORT-KING AUTO PISTOL
Caliber: 22 LR, 9-shot.
Barrel: 4½" or 6¾".
Weight: 39 oz. (4½" bbl.). **Length:** 9" over-all (4½" bbl.).
Stocks: Black checkered plastic.
Sights: Blade front, fixed rear.
Features: Takedown barrel. Blue or nickel finish.
Price: Either bbl. length, blue finish **$79.95**
Price: Nickel finish **$89.95**

HI-STANDARD MODEL D-100 AND DM-101 DERRINGER
Caliber: 22 S, L or LR: 22 Rimfire Magnum. 2 shot.
Barrel: 3½", over and under, rifled.
Length: 5" over-all. **Weight:** 11 oz.
Stocks: Smooth plastic.
Features: Hammerless, integral safety hammerblock, all steel unit is encased in a black, anodized alloy housing. Recessed chamber. Dual extraction. Top break, double action.
Sights: Fixed, open.
Price: Blued .... **$55.25** Nickel **$67.00**
Price: 22 WMR, Blued .... **$57.50** Nickel **$69.25**

F.I.E. E27 TITAN PISTOL
Caliber: 25, 6-shot magazine
Barrel: 2⁷⁄₁₆".
Length: 4⅝" over-all. **Weight:** 12 oz.
Stocks: Checkered plastic.
Features: Visible hammer; fast simple takedown.
Sights: Fixed.
Price: Blued .... **$40.95** Chromed: **$43.95**

HI-STANDARD SHARPSHOOTER AUTO PISTOL
Caliber: 22 LR, 9-shot magazine.
Barrel: 5½″.
Length: 9″ over-all. **Weight:** 45 oz.
Stocks: Checkered laminated plastic.
Features: Wide, scored trigger; new hammer-sear design. Slide lock, push-button take down.
Sights: Fixed, ramp front, square notch rear adj. for w. & e.
Price: Blued **$109.95**

PLAINFIELD MODEL 71
Caliber: 22 LR (10-shot) and 25 ACP (8-shot).
Barrel: 1″.
Length: 5⅛″ over-all. **Weight:** 25 oz.
Stocks: Checkered walnut.
Sights: Fixed.
Features: Easily converts from 22 cal. to 25 cal. by changing bolt, bbl. and magazine. Stainless steel frame and slide.
Price: With conversion kit. . **$87.00** M71 in 22 cal. only **$66.00**
Price: M71 in 25 cal. only **$66.00**

STERLING MODEL 286 TRAPPER
Caliber: 22 LR, 10-shot magazine.
Barrel: 4½″ or 6″.
Length: 9″ (4½″ bbl.). **Weight:** 36 oz. (4½″ bbl.).
Stocks: Checkered plastic.
Sights: Fixed ramp (6″ bbl.) or blade (4½″ bbl.) front. Square notch rear.
Features: Interchangeable safety (4½″ bbl.).
Price: Blued (M286) 4½″ or 6″ tapered **$89.95**

STERLING MODEL 300
Caliber: 25 ACP, 6-shot.
Barrel: 2½″.
Length: 4½″ over-all. **Weight:** 13 oz.
Stocks: Cycolac, black or white.
Sights: Fixed.
Features: All steel construction.
Price: Blued .... **$49.95** Satin nickel **$54.95**

STERLING MODEL 400 DOUBLE ACTION
Caliber: 380 ACP, 7-shot.
Barrel: 3¾″.
Length: 6½″ over-all. **Weight:** 24 oz.
Stocks: Checkered walnut.
Features: All steel construction. Double action.
Price: Blued .... **$89.95** Satin nickel **$94.95**

STERLING MODEL 402 DOUBLE ACTION
Caliber: 22 LR, 8-shot.
Barrel: 3¾″.
Length: 6½″ over-all. **Weight:** 24 oz.
Stocks: Checkered walnut.
Features: Double action, all steel construction.
Price: Blued .... **$89.95** Satin nickel **$94.95**

STERLING MODEL 302
Caliber: 22 LR, 6-shot.
Barrel: 2½″.
Length: 4½″ over-all. **Weight:** 13 oz.
Stocks: Cycolac, black or white.
Sights: Fixed.
Features: All steel construction.
Price: Blue **$56.95**
Price: Satin nickel **$62.95**

INDIAN ARMS STAINLESS DOUBLE ACTION AUTO
Caliber: 380 ACP, 6-shot magazine.
Barrel: 3¼″.
Weight: 20 oz. **Length:** 6 1/16″.
Stocks: Checkered walnut.
Sights: Fixed blade front, drift-adj. rear.
Features: All stainless steel, natural or blued finish. Double action, stays open after last shot. Optional lock with key to lock safety is integral with slide. From Indian Arms.
Price: With or without safety lock, either finish **$135.00**

Plainfield Model 72
Same as Model 71 except: has 3½″ bbl. and aluminum slide.
Price: Model 72 & conversion kit **$95.95**
Price: 22 cal. only **$75.95**
Price: 25 cal. only **$75.95**

RUGER STANDARD MODEL AUTO PISTOL
Caliber: 22 LR, 9-shot magazine.
Barrel: 4¾″ or 6″.
Length: 8¾″ (4¾″ bbl.). **Weight:** 36 oz. (4¾″ bbl.).
Stocks: Checkered hard rubber.
Sights: Fixed, wide blade front, square notch rear.
Price: Blued **$51.50**
Price: With checkered walnut grips **$55.75**

SMITH & WESSON 9mm MODEL 39 AUTO PISTOL
Caliber: 9mm Luger, 8-shot clip.
Barrel: 4″.
Length: 7 7/16″. **Weight:** 26½ oz., without magazine.
Stocks: Checkered walnut.
Features: Magazine disconnector, positive firing pin lock and hammer-release safety; alloy frame with lanyard loop; locked-breech, short-recoil double action; slide locks open on last shot.
Sights: ⅛″ serrated ramp front, adjustable rear.
Price: Blued .... **$137.50** Nickeled **$152.50**

U.S. HANDGUNS—SERVICE & SPORT

STOEGER LUGER 22 AUTO PISTOL

Caliber: 22 LR, 12-shot (11 in magazine, 1 in chamber).
Barrel: 4½" or 5½".
Weight: 30 oz.
Stocks: Checkered wood, identical to P-08.
Features: Action remains open after last shot and as magazine is removed. Grip and balance identical to P-08.
Price: Either bbl. length **$89.95**

SMITH & WESSON MODEL 59 DOUBLE ACTION

Caliber: 9mm Luger, 14-shot clip.
Barrel: 4".
Length: 7 7/16" over-all. **Weight:** 27½ oz., without clip.
Stocks: Checkered high impact moulded nylon.
Sights: ⅛" serrated ramp front, square notch rear adj. for w.
Features: Double action automatic. Furnished with two magazines. Blue finish.
Price: Blued **$165.00**
Price: Nickel **$180.00**

U.S. HANDGUNS — REVOLVERS SERVICE & SPORT

CHARTER ARMS BULLDOG

Caliber: 44 Special, 5-shot.
Barrel: 3".
Weight: 19 oz.
Stocks: Checkered plastic.
Sights: Patridge type 9/64" front, square notch rear.
Features: Wide trigger and hammer, chrome-moly steel frame, unbreakable firing pin, transfer bar ignition.
Price: **$125.00**

CHARTER ARMS "UNDERCOVER" REVOLVER

Caliber: 38 Special, 5 shot.
Barrel: 2" or 3.
Length: 6¼" (round butt). **Weight:** 16 oz.
Stocks: Smooth walnut.
Sights: Fixed; matted ramp front, ⅛" wide blade.
Features: Wide trigger and hammer spur
Price: Polished Blue ...... **$97.00** Nickel **$108.00**
Price: With checkered, finger-rest Bulldog grips (blue) **$104.00**

Charter Arms Pathfinder

Same as Undercover but in 22 LR caliber, and has 3" bbl. Fitted with adjustable rear sight, ramp front. Weight 18½ oz.
Price: Blued **$107.00**
Price: With checkered, finger-rest Bulldog grips **$114.00**

Charter Arms Undercoverette

Like the Undercover, but a 6-shot 32 S&W Long revolver available with 2" barrel only, and weighing 16½ oz.
Price: Polished blue **$98.00**

COLT DETECTIVE SPECIAL

Caliber: 38 Special, 6-shot.
Barrel: 2".
Length: 6⅝" over-all. **Weight:** 22 oz.
Stocks: Full, checkered walnut, round butt.
Sights: Fixed, ramp front, square notch rear.
Features: Glare-proofed sights, smooth trigger. Nickel finish, hammer shroud available as options.
Price: Blue **$117.50**
Price: Nickel **$128.50**

COLT COBRA REVOLVER

Caliber: 38 Special, 6 shot.
Barrel: 2".
Length: 6⅝" over-all. **Weight:** 16½ oz.
Stocks: Checkered walnut, round butt. Grooved trigger.
Sights: Fixed, glare-proofed ramp front, square notch rear.
Price: Blued .... **$123.00** Nickeled **$139.00**

COLT AGENT REVOLVER

Caliber: 38 Special, 6 shot.
Barrel: 2" (Twist, 1-16).
Length: 6⅝" over-all. **Weight:** 16 oz.
Stocks: Checkered walnut, round butt. Grooved trigger.
Sights: Fixed, glare-proofed ramp front, square notch rear.
Price: Blued .... **$120.50** With a hammer shroud installed .. **$125.50**

COLT OFFICIAL POLICE Mk III REVOLVER

Caliber: 38 Special, 6 shot.
Barrel: 4″.
Weight: 33 oz.
Length: 9⅜″.
Stocks: Checkered walnut, service style.
Sights: Fixed, glare-proofed ramp front, square notch rear.
Price: Blued **$126.00**

Colt Lawman Mk III Revolver

Same as Official Police MK III but with 2″ or 4″ heavy barrel. Weight 35 oz. (4″ bbl.). 357 only.
Price: Blued .... **$128.50** Nickeled **$136.00**

COLT TROOPER MK III REVOLVER

Caliber: 357 Magnum, 6-shot.
Barrel: 4″ 6″.
Length: 9½″ (4″ bbl.). **Weight:** 39 oz. (4″ bbl.), 42 oz, (6″ bbl.).
Stock: Checkered walnut, square butt. Grooved trigger.
Sights: Fixed ramp front with ⅛″ blade, adj. notch rear.
Price: Blued with target hammer and target stocks **$161.50**
Price: Nickeled **$171.50**

ESFAC "LITTLE ACE" DERRINGER

Caliber: 22 Short, single-shot.
Barrel: 2″.
Weight: 2⅞ oz. **Length:** 3⅞″ over-all.
Stocks: High impact black plastic.
Sights: None.
Features: Manganese bronze frame, color case hardened trigger and hammer, blued barrel. Spur trigger. Rifled barrel. From ESFAC.
Price: **$24.95**

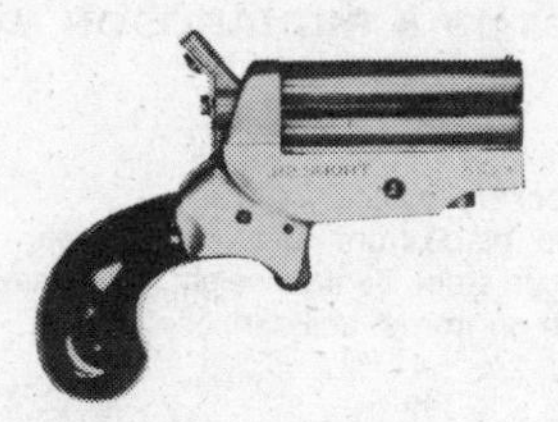

ESFAC "Four Aces" Model 4 Derringer

Same as Model 2 except chambered for 22 LR, over-all length 4″, barrel length 2″, weight 5½ oz. **$49.95**

F.I.E. "38" MODEL F38 REVOLVER

Caliber: 38 Special.
Barrel: 2″ or 4″.
Length: 6¼″ over-all. (2″ bbl.). **Weight:** 27 oz.
Stocks: Plastic Bulldog.
Sights: Fixed.
Features: Swing-out cylinder.
Price: Blued 2″ .... **$59.95** 4″ bbl. **$63.95**

Colt Hammer Shroud

Facilitates quick draw from holster or pocket. Hammer spur projects just enough to allow for cocking for single action firing. Fits only Colt Detective Special, Cobra and Agent revolvers. Factory installed on new guns, **$5,** or as a kit for installation. Blued only **$6.00**
Factory installed on your gun (listed above). Blued only **$7.50**

ESFAC "POCKET PONY" REVOLVER

Caliber: 22 LR, 6-shot.
Barrel: 1¾″.
Weight: 10½ oz. **Length:** 4¾″ over-all.
Stocks: High impact black plastic.
Sights: Fixed.
Features: Single-action revolver. Manganese bronze frame, rifled, blued barrel. Trigger and hammer color case hardened. Non-fluted cylinder. From ESFAC.
Price: **$59.50**

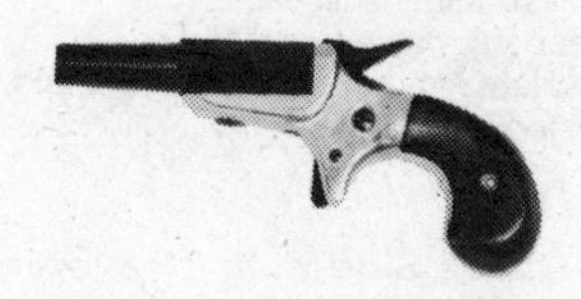

ESFAC "FOUR ACES" MODEL 1 DERRINGER

Caliber: 22 Short, 4-shot.
Barrel: 1 11/16″.
Weight: 5 oz. **Length:** 3⅜″ over-all.
Stocks: High impact black plastic. Round butt.
Sights: Post front.
Features: Spur trigger, barrel selector on hammer. Manganese bronze frame. Rifled, blued steel barrels. From ESFAC.
Price: **$39.95**

ESFAC "Four Aces" Model 2 Derringer

Same as Model 1 except has square butt frame. Spur Trigger, 4-shot. Weight is 5¼ oz. **$43.95**

ESFAC "Four Aces" Model 3 Derringer

Same as Model 4 except chambered for 22 LR cartridge. Over-all length is 3¾″, barrel length is 2″, weight 5¼ oz. **$45.95**

ESFAC "Four Aces" Cased Set

Contains one each of Pocket Pony, Model 1 and Model 4, with matching serial numbers, in fitted mahogany presentation case **$189.95**

F.I.E. DERRINGER

Caliber: 38 Special.
Barrel: 3″.
Weight: 14 oz.
Stocks: White plastic.
Sights: Fixed.
Features: Blue frame, chrome barrels. Spur trigger. Made in U.S.
Price: **$43.95**

HARRINGTON & RICHARDSON Model 925 "Defender"
Caliber: 38 S&W 5 shot.
Barrel: 2½".
Length: 7½" over-all. **Weight:** 22 oz.
Stocks: Smooth walnut, birds-head style, one piece wrap-round.
Sights: Rear with windage adj.
Features: Top-break double action, push pin extractor.
Price: H&R Crown Luster Blue $71.00

HARRINGTON & RICHARDSON Model 926 REVOLVER
Caliber: 22 S, L, or LR, 9-shot, 38 S&W 5-shot.
Barrel: 4". **Weight:** 31 oz.
Stocks: Checkered walnut.
Sights: Fixed front, read adj. for w.
Features: Top-break, double or single action
Price: Blued $76.00

H&R Model 940 Ultra "Side-Kick" REVOLVER
Caliber: 22 S, L or LR, 9 shot.
Barrel: 6" target weight with ventilated rib.
Weight: 33 oz.
Stocks: Checkered walnut with thumbrest.
Sights: Ramp front; rear adjustable for w. and e.
Features: Swing-out, safety rim cylinder; safety lock and key.
Price: H&R Crown-Luster Blue $74.00

H&R Model 939 Ultra "Side-Kick" Revolver
Like the Model 940 but with a flat-sided barrel.
Price: H&R Crown-Luster Blue $76.00

HARRINGTON & RICHARDSON Model 732 Guardsman
Caliber: 32 S&W or 32 S&W Long, 6 shot.
Barrel: 2½" or 4" round barrel.
Weight: 23½ oz. (2½" bbl.), 26 oz. (4" bbl.).
Stocks: Checkered, black Cycolac.
Sights: Blade front; adjustable rear on 4" model.
Features: Swing-out cylinder with auto. extractor return. Pat. safety rim cylinder. Grooved trigger.
Price: Blued .... **$58.00** Nickel (Model 733) 2½" bbl. only **$65.00**

High Standard Long Horn Convertible
Same as the Double-Nine convertible but with a 9½" bbl., fixed sights, blued only, Weight: 40 oz.
Price: 22 LR only $102.00
Price: With dual cyl. $107.00

HARRINGTON & RICHARDSON SPORTSMAN Model 999 REVOLVER
Caliber: 22 S, L or LR, 9 shot.
Barrel: 6" top-break (16" twist), integral vent. rib.
Length: 10½". **Weight:** 30 oz.
Stocks: Checkered walnut, semi-thumbrest.
Sights: Front adjustable for elevation, rear for windage.
Features: Wide hammer spur; rest for second finger.
Price: Blued $82.00

HARRINGTON & RICHARDSON Model 929 "Side-Kick"
Caliber: 22 S, L or LR, 9 shot.
Barrel: 2½", 4" or 6".
Weight: 26 oz. (4" bbl.).
Stocks: Checkered, black Cycolac.
Sights: Blade front; adjustable rear on 4" and 6" models.
Features: Swing-out cylinder with auto. extractor return. Pat. safety rim cylinder. Grooved trigger. Round-grip frame.
Price: Blued, 2½", 4" or 6" bbl. $58.00
Price: Nickel (Model 930), 4" bbl. $65.00

HARRINGTON & RICHARDSON Model 622 REVOLVER
Caliber: 22 S, L or LR, 6 shot.
Barrel: 2½", 4", round bbl.
Weight: 22 oz. (2½" bbl.).
Stocks: Checkered black Cycolac.
Sights: Fixed, blade front, square notch rear.
Features: Solid steel, Bantamweight frame; snap-out safety rim cylinder; non-glare finish on frame; coil springs.
Price: Blued, 2½", 4", bbl. $45.00
Price: Model 632 (32 cal.) $47.00

HARRINGTON & RICHARDSON M-949 FORTY-NINER
Caliber: 22 S, L or LR, 9 shot.
Barrel: 5½" round with ejector rod.
Weight: 31 oz.
Stocks: One-piece smooth walnut frontier style.
Sights: Round blade front, adj. rear.
Features: Contoured loading gate; wide hammer spur; single and double action. Western type ejector-housing.
Price: H&R Crown-Luster Blue $56.00
Price: Nickel (Model 950) $62.00

HIGH STANDARD DOUBLE-NINE CONVERTIBLE
Caliber: 22 S, L or LR, 9-shot (22 WRM with extra cylinder).
Barrel: 5½", dummy ejector rod fitted.
Length: 11" over-all. **Weight:** 32 oz.
Stocks: Smooth walnut, frontier style with medallion
Sights: Fixed blade front, notched rear.
Features: Western styling; rebounding hammer with auto safety block; spring-loaded ejection.
Price: Blued .... **$97.00** Nickeled **$102.00**

HIGH STANDARD HIGH SIERRA DOUBLE ACTION

Caliber: 22 LR and 22 LR/22 Mag., 9-shot.
Barrel: 7″ octagonal.
Weight: 36 oz. **Length:** 12½″ over-all.
Stocks: Smooth walnut.
Sights: Blade front, fixed or adj. rear.
Features: Gold plated backstrap and trigger guard. Comes with walnut presentation case.
Price: Fixed sights, 22 LR cyl. **$129.95**
Price: Fixed sights, dual cyl. **$134.00**
Price: Adj. sights, dual cyl. **$139.95**

HIGH STANDARD SENTINEL MK I AND MK IV REVOLVERS

Caliber: 22 LR (MK I), 22 Mag. (MK IV), 9-shot.
Barrel: 2″, 3″ or 4″.
Weight: 21½ oz. (2″). **Length:** 6⅞″ over-all (2″ bbl.).
Stocks: Smooth walnut.
Sights: Ramp front, fixed or adj. rear.
Features: Blue or nickel finish (add $10 for nickel).
Price: Fixed sights, blue finish, 22 LR **$89.95**
Price: Adj. sights, blue finish, 22 LR **$99.95**
Price: Magnum, 2″ bbl., fixed sights **$96.50**
Price: Magnum, 3″ bbl., adj. sights **$106.50**

HI-STANDARD SENTINEL MKII, MKIII

Caliber: 357 or 38 Spec.
Barrel: 2½″, 4″, 6″.
Weight: 38 oz. (4″ bbl.). **Length:** 9″ over-all (4″ bbl.).
Stocks: Walnut, service type or combat.
Sights: Fixed on MKII. MKIII has fully adj. rear.
Features: Cylinder latch located in front of cylinder. Fast lock time. Blue finish only.
Price: MKII **$92.95**
Price: MKIII **$124.95**

High Standard Durango Revolver

A variation of the High Standard Double-Nine with a brass finished trigger guard and backstrap. 5½″ bbl., 10″ over-all, weight 25 oz. 22 S, L or LR only. Walnut grips.
Price: Blued **$92.00**
Price: Nickel **$97.00**
Price: Blue with adj. sights **$102.00**

IVER JOHNSON MODEL 50A SIDEWINDER REVOLVER

Caliber: 22 S, L, LR, 8 shot.
Barrel: 6″.
Length: 11¼″. **Weight:** 31 oz.
Stocks: Plastic Stag Horn.
Sights: Fixed, blade front.
Features: Wide spur hammer, half-cock safety, scored trigger, Flash Control cylinder, recessed shell head, push rod ejector.
Price: Blued **$51.50**
Price: Model 50-B with dual cyl. (22 LR/22 Mag.) **$53.95**
Price: Model 50-SD, dual cyl., adj. sights **$65.25**

IVER JOHNSON TARGET MODEL 57A REVOLVER

Caliber: 22 S or LR, 8 shot, double action.
Barrel: 4½″, 6″.
Length: 10¾″ (6″ bbl.). **Weight:** 30½ oz. (6″ bbl.).
Stocks: Checkered thumbrest, Tenite.
Sights: Adjustable Patridge type.
Features: Flash Control cylinder, akj. mainspring.
Price: Blued **$51.50**

Iver Johnson Target Model 55A Revolver

Same as Model 57A except without adjustable sights. Price **$47.95**

Iver Johnson Cadet Model 55SA

Same as Model 55 except with 2½″ barrel only, rounded tenite grips; weight 24 oz. Price, blued **$46.50**
Also available in 32 or 38 S&W caliber, 5 shot **$54.75**
Price: 22 Mag. **$46.50**

U.S. HANDGUNS — REVOLVERS SERVICE & SPORT

RUGER SECURITY-SIX Model 117
Caliber: 357 Mag. (also fires 38 Spec.), 6-shot.
Barrel: 2¾", 4" or 6".
Weight: 35 oz. (4" bbl.). **Length:** 9¼" (4" bbl.) over-all.
Stocks: Hand checkered American walnut, semi-target style.
Sights: Patridge-type front on ramp, rear adj. for w. and e.
Features: Music wire coil springs throughout. Hardened steel construction. Integral ejector rod shroud and sighting rib. Can be disassembled using only a coin.
Price: **$107.00**

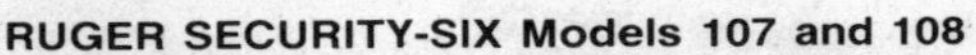

RUGER SECURITY-SIX Models 107 and 108
Caliber: 357 (Model 107), 38 Spec. (Model 108), 6-shot.
Barrel: 2¾" or 4".
Weight: 33½ oz (4" bbl.). **Length:** 9¼" (4 bbl.) over-all.
Stocks: Checkered American walnut, semi-target style.
Sights: Patridge-type front, square notch rear.
Features: Solid frame with barrel, rib and ejector rod housing combined in one unit. All steel construction. Field strips without tools.
Price: Model 107 (357) **$102.00**
Price: Model 108 (38) **$91.00**

RUGER SPEED-SIX Models 207 and 208
Caliber: Model 207—357 Mag. (also fires 38 Spec.); Model 208—38 Spec. only, 6-shot.
Barrel: 2¾".
Weight: 31½ oz. **Length:** 7½" over-all.
Stocks: Round butt design, diamond pattern checkered American walnut.
Sights: Patridge-type front, square-notch rear.
Features: Same basic mechanism as Security-Six. Hammer without spur available on special order. All steel construction. Music wire coil springs used throughout.
Price: Model 207 (357 Mag.) **$102.00**
Price: Model 208 (38 Spec. only) **$91.00**

SMITH & WESSON M&P Model 10 REVOLVER
Caliber: 38 Special, 6 shot.
Barrel: 2", 4", 5" or 6"
Length: 9¼" (4" bbl.). **Weight:** 30½ oz. (4" bbl.).
Stocks: Checkered walnut, Magna. Round or square butt.
Sights: Fixed, ⅛" ramp front, square notch rear.
Price: Blued .... **$102.00** Nickeled **$112.00**
Smith & Wesson 38 M&P Heavy Barrel Model 10
Same as regular M&P except: 4" ribbed bbl. with ⅛" ramp front sight, square rear, square butt, wgt. 34 oz.
Price: Blued .... **$102.00** Nickeled **$112.00**

SMITH & WESSON 38 M&P AIRWEIGHT Model 12
Caliber: 38 Special, 6 shot.
Barrel: 2 or 4 inches.
Length: 6⅞" over-all. **Weight:** 18 oz. (2" bbl.)
Stocks: Checkered walnut, Magna. Round or square butt.
Sights: Fixed, ⅛" serrated ramp front, square notch rear.
Price: Blued .... **$108.00** Nickeled **$123.00**

SMITH & WESSON 357 COMBAT MAGNUM Model 19
Caliber: 357 Magnum and 38 Special, 6 shot.
Barrel: 2½", 4", 6".
Length: 9½" (4" bbl.). **Weight:** 35 oz.
Stocks: Checkered Goncala Alves, target. Grooved tangs and trigger.
Sights: Front, ⅛" Baughman Quick Draw on 2½" or 4" bbl., Patridge on 6" bbl., micro click rear adjustable for w. and e.
Price: S&W Bright Blue or Nickel **$160.00**

SMITH & WESSON 44 MAGNUM Model 29 REVOLVER
Caliber: 44 Magnum, 44 Special or 44 Russian, 6 shot.
Barrel: 4", 6½", 8⅜".
Length: 11⅞" (6½" bbl.). **Weight:** 47 oz. (6½" bbl.), 43 oz. (4" bbl.).
Stocks: Oversize target type, checkered Goncala Alves. Tangs and target trigger grooved, checkered target hammer.
Sights: ⅛" red ramp-front, micro. click rear, adjustable for w. and e.
Price: S&W Bright Blue or Nickel 4", 6½" **$228.00**
Price: 8⅜" bbl. **$234.50**

RUGER STAINLESS SECURITY-SIX Model 717
Caliber: 357 Mag. (also fires 38 Spec.), 6-shot.
Barrel: 2¾", 4" or 6".
Weight: 35 oz. (4 bbl.). **Length:** 9¼" (4" bbl.) over-all.
Stocks: Hand checkered American walnut.
Sights: Patridge-type front, fully adj. rear.
Features: All metal parts except sights made of stainless steel. Sights are black alloy for maximum visibility. Same mechanism and features found in regular Security-Six.
Price: **$132.50**

SMITH & WESSON HIGHWAY PATROLMAN Model 28
Caliber: 357 Magnum and 38 Special, 6 shot.
Barrel: 4", 6".
Length: 11¼" (6" bbl.). **Weight:** 44 oz. (6" bbl.).
Stocks: Checkered walnut, Magna. Grooved tangs and trigger.
Sights: Front, ⅛" Baughman Quick Draw, on plain ramp. micro click rear, adjustable for w. and e.
Price: S&W Satin Blue, sandblasted frame edging and barrel top . **$135.00**
Price: With target stocks **$142.00**

SMITH & WESSON 357 MAGNUM M-27 REVOLVER
Caliber: 357 Magnum and 38 Special, 6 shot.
Barrel: 3½", 5", 6", 8⅜".
Length: 11¼" (6" bbl.). **Weight:** 44 oz. (6" bbl.).
Stocks: Checkered walnut, Magna. Grooved tangs and trigger.
Sights: Any S&W target front, micro click rear, adjustable for w. and e.
Price: S&W Bright Blue or Nickel, 3½", 5", 6" .... **$$190.00**
Price: 8⅜" bbl. **$196.50**

SMITH & WESSON 1953 Model 34, 22/32 KIT GUN
Caliber: 22 LR, 6 shot.
Barrel: 2", 4".
Length: 8" (4" bbl. and round butt). **Weight:** 22½ oz. (4" bbl.).
Stocks: Checkered walnut, round or square butt.
Sights: Front, ⅒" serrated ramp, micro. click rear, adjustable for w. & e.
Price: Blued .... **$117.00** Nickeled **$127.00**

Smith & Wesson Model 51 22/32 Kit Gun
Same as Model 34 except chambered for 22 WRF Magnum; 3½" barrel; weight, 24 oz. Choice of round or square butt.
Price: Blued **$130.00**

Smith & Wesson Kit Gun Airweight (Model 43, not illus.)
Same as M34 except 3½" barrel, square butt; weight 14¼ oz. 22LR.
Price: Blued **$130.00**

SMITH & WESSON 38 CHIEFS SPECIAL & AIRWEIGHT
Caliber: 38 Special, 5 shot.
Barrel: 2", 3".
Length: 6½" (2" bbl. and round butt). **Weight:** 19 oz. (2" bbl.; 14 oz. AIRWEIGHT).
Stocks: Checkered walnut, Magna. Round or square butt.
Sights: Fixed, ⅒" serrated ramp front, square notch rear.
Price: Blued std. M-36 ... **$104.00** Standard weight Nickel ... **$114.00**
Price: Blued AIR'W M-37 . **$108.00** AIRWEIGHT Nickel **$123.00**

SMITH & WESSON 41 MAGNUM Model 57 REVOLVER
Caliber: 41 Magnum, 6 shot.
Barrel: 4", 6" or 8⅜".
Length: 11⅜" (6" bbl.). **Weight:** 48 oz. (6" bbl.).
Stocks: Oversize target type checkered Goncala Alves wood and target hammer. Tang and target trigger grooved.
Sights: ⅛" red ramp front, micro. click rear, adj. for w. and e.
Price: S&W Bright Blue or Nickel 4", 6" **$228.00**
Price: 8⅜" bbl. **$234.50**

SMITH & WESSON 41 M&P Model 58 REVOLVER
Caliber: 41 Magnum, 6 shot.
Barrel: 4".
Length: 9¼" over-all. **Weight:** 41 oz.
Stocks: Checkered walnut, Magna.
Sights: Fixed, ⅛" serrated ramp front, square notch rear.
Price: Blued .... **$125.00** Nickeled **$135.00**

SMITH & WESSON 32 REGULATION POLICE
Caliber: 32 S&W Long (M31), 6 shot.
Barrel: 2", 3", 4".
Length: 8½" (4" bbl.).
Weight: 18¾ oz. (4" bbl.).
Stocks: Checkered walnut, Magna.
Sights: Fixed, ⅒" serrated ramp front, square notch rear.
Price: Blued .... **$102.00** Nickeled **$112.00**

SMITH & WESSON 32 HAND EJECTOR Model 30
Caliber: 32 S&W Long, 6 shot.
Barrel: 2", 3", 4".
Length: 8 inches (4" bbl.). **Weight:** 18 oz. (4" bbl.).
Stocks: Checkered walnut, Magna.
Sights: Fixed, ⅒" serrated ramp front, square notch rear.
Price: Blued .... **$102.00** Nickeled **$112.00**

SMITH & WESSON K-38 MASTERPIECE
Caliber: 38 Spec., 6-shot.
Barrel: 6", 8⅜".
Weight: 38½ oz. (6" bbl.). **Length:** 11⅛" over-all (6" bbl.)
Stock: Checkered walnut, service.
Sights: ⅛" Patridge front, micro click rear adj. for w. and e.
Price: 6" bbl. **$125.00**
Price: 8⅜" bbl. **$131.50**

Smith & Wesson 60 Chiefs Special Stainless
Same as Model 36 except: 2" bbl. and round butt only.
Price: Stainless steel **$135.00**

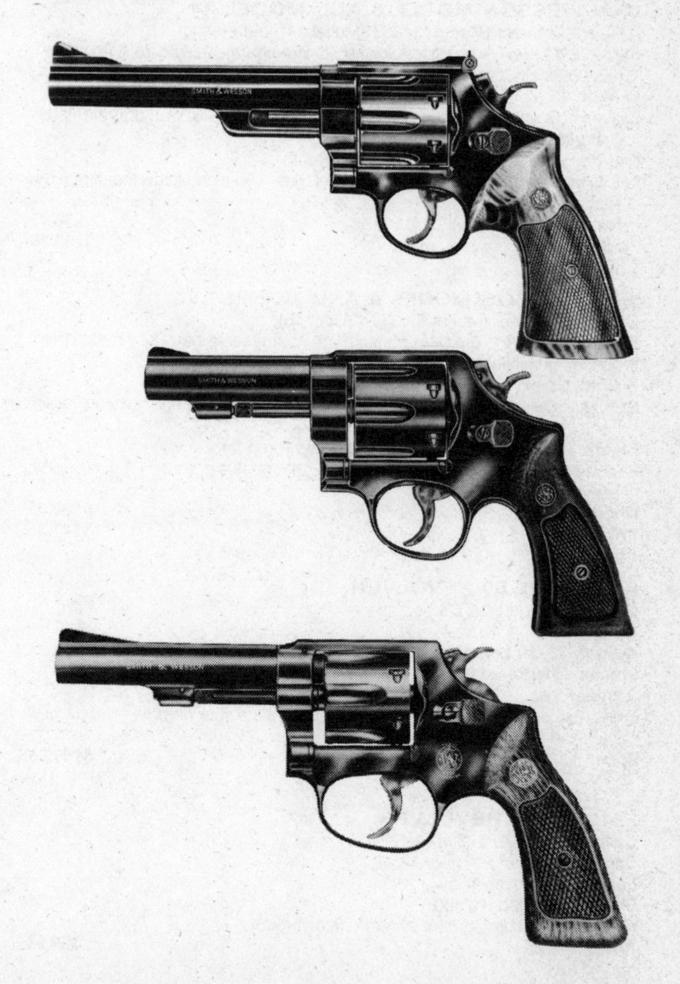

SMITH & WESSON MODEL 64 STAINLESS M&P
Caliber: 38 Special, 6-shot.
Barrel: 4″.
Length: 9½″ over-all. **Weight:** 30½ oz.
Stocks: Checkered walnut, service style.
Sights: Fixed, ⅛″ serrated ramp front, square notch rear.
Features: Satin finished stainless steel, square butt.
Price: **$135.00**

SMITH & WESSON MODEL 67 K-38 STAINLESS COMBAT MASTERPIECE
Caliber: 38 special, 6-shot.
Barrel: 4″.
Length: 9⅛″ over-all. **Weight:** 34 oz. (loaded).
Stocks: Checkered walnut, service style.
Sights: Front, ⅛″ Baughman Quick Draw on ramp, micro click rear adj. for w. and e.
Features: Stainless steel. Square butt frame with grooved tangs, grooved trigger with adj. stop.
Price: **$152.00**

Smith & Wesson Bodyguard Model 38 Revolver
Caliber: 38 Special; 5 shot, double action revolver.
Barrel: 2″.
Length: 6⅜″. **Weight:** 14½ oz.
Features: Alloy frame; integral hammer shroud.
Stocks: Checkered walnut, Magna.
Sights: Fixed 1/10″ serrated ramp front, square notch rear.
Price: Blued .... **$108.00** Nickeled **$123.00**

Smith & Wesson Bodyguard Model 49 Revolver
Same as Model 38 except steel construction. Weight 20½ oz.
Price: Blued .... **$106.00** Nickeled **$116.00**

DAN WESSON MODEL 8 AND MODEL 14
Caliber: 38 Spec. (Model 8); 357 (Model 14), both 6-shot.
Barrel: 2¼″, 3¾″ and 5¾″. "Quickshift" interchangeable barrels. Fixed barrels optionally available.
Weight: 36 oz. (3¾″ bbl.) **Length:** 9″ over-all (3¾″ bbl.)
Stocks: "Quickshift" Powerwood Traditional checkered, walnut grain. Interchangeable with five other styles.
Sights: Fixed rear, ⅛″ serrated ramp front.
Features: Interchangeable barrels, 6 interchangeable grips, few moving parts, easy disassembly.
Price: Satin Blue **$98.95**
Price: Nickel **$109.95**

DAN WESSON MODEL 9 AND MODEL 15
Caliber: 38 Spec. (Model 9); 357 (Model 15), both 6-shot.
Barrel: 2¼″, 3¾″, 5¾″ "Quickshift" interchangeable barrels. Fixed barrels optionally available.
Weight: 36 oz. (3¾″ bbl.) **Length:** 9″ over-all (3¾″ bbl.)
Stocks: "Quickshift" Powerwood oversize target, checkered, walnut grain. Interchangeable with five other styles.
Sights: Rear adj. for w. & e., ⅛″ serrated ramp front.
Features: Interchangeable barrels, 6 interchangeable grips, few moving parts, easy disassembly.
Price: Brite Blue **$130.35**
Price: Nickel **$141.35**

RG MODEL 88 REVOLVER
Caliber: 38 Spec., 357 Mag.
Barrel: 4″.
Weight: 33 oz. **Length:** 9″ over-all.
Stocks: Checkered walnut.
Sights: Fixed.
Features: Swing out cylinder, spring ejector. Wide spur hammer and trigger. Imported by RG Industries.
Price: **$109.95**

RMAC MINI REVOLVER
Caliber: 22 short, 5-shot.
Barrel: 1″.
Length: 3¼″ over-all.
Stocks: Polished walnut.
Features: Finished in hard chrome. Spur trigger.
Price: **$69.95**

SMITH & WESSON MODEL 66 STAINLESS COMBAT MAGNUM
Caliber: 357 Magnum and 38 Special, 6-shot.
Barrel: 4″.
Length: 9½″ over-all. **Weight:** 35 oz.
Stocks: Checkered Goncala Alves target.
Sights: Front, ⅛″ Baughman Quick Draw on plain ramp, micro click rear adj. for w. and e.
Features: Satin finish stainless steel, grooved trigger with adj. stop.
Price: **$185.00**

SMITH & WESSON CENTENNIAL Model 40 & AIRWEIGHT Model 42 REVOLVERS
Caliber: 38 Special, 5 shot.
Barrel: 2″.
Length: 6½″. **Weight:** 19 oz. (Standard weight), 13 oz. (AIRWEIGHT).
Stocks: Smooth walnut, Magna.
Sights: Fixed 1/10″ serrated ramp front, square notch rear.
Price: Blued, standard wgt. **$110.00** Nickeled, standard wgt. ... **$120.00**
Price: Blued AIRWEIGHT . **$114.00** Nickeled, AIRWEIGHT **$129.00**

U.S. HANDGUNS—SINGLE ACTION REVOLVERS

COLT SINGLE ACTION ARMY REVOLVER

Caliber: 357 Magnum or 45 Colt, 6 shot.
Barrel: 4¾", 5½" or 7½".
Length: 10⅞" (5½" bbl.). **Weight:** 37 oz. (5½" bbl.).
Stocks: Black composite rubber with eagle and shield crest.
Sights: Fixed. Grooved top strap, blade front.
Price: Blued and case hardened 4¾", 5½" bbl. **$211.50**
Price: Nickel with walnut stocks **$252.00**
Price: Buntline Spec., cal. 45 only. 12 bbl., wood stocks **$252.00**
Price: With 7½" bbl. **$217.00**

Colt Single Action Army—New Frontier

Same specifications as standard Single Action Army except: flat-top frame; high polished finish, blue and case colored; ramp front sight and target rear adj. for windage and elevation; smooth walnut stocks with silver medallion.
Price: **$252.00**

COLT FRONTIER SIX SHOOTER

Caliber: 44-40
Barrel: 7½"
Stocks: Black hard rubber with Colt insignia.
Sights: Fixed
Features: Accurate copy of the original. Bright nickel finish. 1873 flat top style hammer, original-type cylinder locking screw and ejector-rod head. Comes with presentation case covered with leather.
Price: **$300.00**

COLT PEACEMAKER CENTENNIAL

Caliber: 45
Barrel: 7½".
Stocks: One piece black walnut with inspector's initials.
Sights: Fixed.
Features: Accurate-copy of the original. Blue finish with color hardened frame carrying two line patent dates and "U.S." Original-type cylinder locking screw and ejector-rod head, 1873 flat top style hammer. Comes with oiled walnut presentation case.
Price **$300.000**

COLT PEACEMAKER 22

Caliber: 22 LR/22 Magnum.
Barrel: 4⅜", 6" or 7½" (Buntline).
Length: 9⅝" (11¼" in 6", 12¾" for Buntline). **Weight:** 29½ oz. (31 oz. in 6", 33 oz. for Buntline).
Stocks: Black composite rubber with eagle and shield crest.
Sights: Fixed. Grooved top strap, blade front.
Features: Color case hardened frame, all steel construction, smooth trigger, knurled hammer spur.
Price: Blued, dual cyl. **$85.50**
Price: Buntline, dual cyl. **$91.00**

F.I.E. E15 BUFFALO SCOUT REVOLVER

Caliber: 22 LR, 22 Mag., 6-shot.
Barrel: 4¾.
Length: 10" over-all. **Weight:** 30 oz.
Stocks: Black plastic.
Features: Slide spring ejector.
Sights: Fixed.
Price: Blued **$34.95**
Price: Model E15MB with extra interchangeable 22 WMR Mag. cylinder, blue finish **$42.95**
Price: Chrome, single cyl. **$41.95**
Price: Chrome, dual cyl. **$47.95**

COLT NEW FRONTIER 22

Caliber: 22 LR/22 Magnum.
Barrel: 4⅜", 6" or 7½" (Buntline).
Length: 9⅝", (11¼" w/6" bbl., 12¾" for Buntline). **Weight:** 28 oz. (30½ oz. w/6" bbl., 32 oz. for Buntline).
Stocks: Black composite rubber with eagle and shield crest.
Sights: Ramp front, adjustable rear.
Features: Blue finish, smooth trigger, knurled hammer spur.
Price: Dual cyl. **$96.00**
Price: Buntline Dual cyl. **$101.00**

RMAC CASULL SUPER MAG

Caliber: 454 Casull Super Mag., 44 Casull Super Mag., 41 Casull Super Mag., 357 Casull Super Mag.
Barrel: 7½" standard.
Weight: 3 lbs.
Stocks: Highly polished one-piece.
Sights: Blade front, grooved top strap rear.
Features: Single action only, 4140 steel construction.
Price: 454, 44 and 41 .... **$295.00** 357 Casull Super Mag. ... **$275.00**

U.S. HANDGUNS—SINGLE ACTION REVOLVERS

RUGER NEW MODEL SUPER BLACKHAWK
Caliber: 44 Magnum, 6-shot. Also fires 44 Spec.
Barrel: 7½" (6-groove, 20" twist).
Weight: 48 oz. **Length:** 13⅜" over-all.
Stocks: Genuine American walnut.
Sights: ⅛" ramp front, micro click rear adj. for w. and e.
Features: New Ruger interlocked mechanism, non-fluted cylinder, steel grip and cylinder frame, square back trigger guard, wide serrated trigger and wide spur hammer. Deep Ruger blue.
Price: **$135.00**

RUGER NEW MODEL BLACKHAWK REVOLVER
Caliber: 357 or 41 Mag., 6-shot.
Barrel: 4⅝" or 6½", either caliber.
Weight: 40 oz. (6½" bbl.). **Length:** 12¼" over-all (6½" bbl.).
Stocks: American walnut.
Sights: ⅛" ramp front, micro click rear adj. for w. and e.
Features: New Ruger interlocked mechanism, independent firing pin, hardened chrome-moly steel frame, music wire springs throughout.
Price: Blued **$109.00**
Price: Stainless steel **$140.00**

RUGER NEW MODEL SUPER SINGLE-SIX
Caliber: 22 S, L, LR, 6-shot. 22 WMR in extra cylinder.
Barrel: 4⅝", 5½", 6½" or 9½" (6-groove).
Weight: 32 oz. (6½" bbl.) **Length:** 11⅞" over-all (6½" bbl.).
Stocks: Smooth American walnut.
Sights: Improved patridge front on ramp, fully adj. rear protected by integral frame ribs.
Features: New Ruger "interlocked" mechanism, transfer bar ignition, gate-controlled loading, hardened chrome-moly steel frame, wide trigger, music wire springs throughout, independent firing pin.
Price: 4⅝", 5½", 6½" barrel **$87.50**
Price: 9½" barrel **$95.00**
Price: 4⅝", 5½", 6½" bbl., stainless steel **$125.00**
Price: 9½" bbl., stainless steel **$135.00**

Ruger New Model 357/9mm Blackhawk
Same as the 357 Magnum except furnished with interchangeable cylinders for 9mm Parabellum and 357 Magnum cartridges **$119.00**
9mm cylinder, fitted to your 357 Blackhawk **$16.00**

Ruger New Model 30 Carbine Blackhawk
Specifications similar to 45 Blackhawk. Fluted cylinder, round-back trigger guard. Weight 44 oz., length 13⅛" over-all, 7½" barrel only.
Price: **$109.00**

RUGER NEW MODEL CONVERTIBLE BLACKHAWK
Caliber: 45 Colt or 45 Colt/45 ACP (extra cylinder).
Barrel: 4⅝" or 7½" (6-groove, 16" twist).
Weight: 40 oz. (7½" bbl.). **Length:** 13⅛" (7½" bbl.).
Stocks: Smooth American walnut.
Sights: ⅛" ramp front, micro click rear adj. for w. and e.
Features: Similar to Super Blackhawk, Ruger interlocked mechanism. Convertible furnished with interchangeable cylinder for 45 ACP.
Price: Blued, 45 Colt **$109.00**
Price: Convertible **$119.00**

SMITH & WESSON K-38 S.A. M-14
Caliber: 38 Spec., 6-shot.
Barrel: 6", 8⅜".
Length: 11⅛" over-all (6" bbl.). **Weight:** 38½ oz. (6" bbl.).
Stocks: Checkered walnut, service type.
Sights: ⅛" Patridge front, micro click rear adj. for w. and e.
Features: Same as Model 14 except single action only, target hammer and trigger.
Price: 6" bbl. **$145.00**
Price: 8⅜" bbl. **$151.50**

U.S. HANDGUNS—MISCELLANEOUS

MBA GYROJET PISTOL

Caliber: 12 mm, 6-shot magazine.
Barrel: 8¼″.
Length: 9¾″ over-all. **Weight:** 16 oz.
Stocks: Walnut, smooth.
Sights: Fixed. Post front, square notch rear.
Features: Semi-automatic, fires rocket projectile instead of conventional cartridge.
Price: **$99.00**

MERRILL SPORTSMAN'S SINGLE SHOT

Caliber: 22 S, L, LR, 22WMR, 22WRF, 22 Rem. Jet, 22 Hornet, K-Hornet, 357, 38 Spl., 256 Win. Mag., 45 Colt/410 (3″).
Barrel: 9″ hinged type break-open. Semi-octagon.
Length: 10½″. **Weight:** 54 oz.
Stocks: Smooth walnut with thumb & heel rest.
Sights: Front 125″ blade, square notch rear adj. for w. & e.
Features: .355″ rib on top, grooved for scope mounts, auto. safety, cocking indicator, hammerless.
Price: **$150.00**
Price: Extra bbls. .... **$39.50** Wrist rest attachment **$12.50**

THOMPSON-CENTER ARMS CONTENDER

Caliber: 218 Bee, 221 Rem., 25-35 Win., 30-30 Win., 22 S, L, LR, 22 WMR, 22 Rem. Jet, 22 Hornet, 22 K Hornet, 256 Win., 9mm Parabellum, 38 Super, 357/44 B & D, 38 Spl., 357 Mag., also 222 Rem., 30 M1, 45 ACP, 44 Mag., 5mm Rem., 45 Long Colt.
Barrel: 8¾″, 10″, tapered octagon. Single shot.
Length: 13¼″ (10″ bbl.). **Weight:** 43 oz. (10″ bbl.).
Stocks: Select checkered walnut grip and fore-end, with thumb rest. Right or left hand.
Sights: Under cut blade ramp front, rear adj. for w. & e.
Features: Break open action with auto-safety. Single action only. Interchangeable bbls., both caliber (rim & center fire), and length. Drilled and tapped for scope. Engraved frame.
Price: Blued (rimfire cals.) **$144.00**
Price: Blued (centerfire cals.) **$144.00**
Price: Extra bbls. **$52.00**
Price: 30 cal. Herrett bull bbl. with fore-end, less sights **$57.00**
Price: As above except with sights **$67.00**
Price: Bushnell Phantom scope base **$5.00**
Price: Fitted walnut case **$39.50**

UNIVERSAL ENFORCER MODEL 3000 AUTO CARBINE

Caliber: 30 M1 Carbine, 30-shot magazine.
Barrel: 10¼″ with 12-groove rifling.
Length: 17¾″. **Weight:** 4½ lbs.
Stocks: American walnut with handguard.
Features: Uses surplus 5- or 15-shot magazine. 4½-6 lb. trigger pull.
Sights: Gold bead ramp front. Peep rear adj. for w. and e. 14″ sight radius.
Price: Blue finish **$149.95**
Price: Nickel plated finish **$194.95**
Price: Gold plated finish **$212.95**

REMINGTON MODEL XP-100 Bolt Action Pistol

Caliber: 221 Fireball, single shot.
Barrel: 10½ inches, ventilated rib.
Length: 16¾ inches. **Weight:** 60 oz.
Stocks: Brown nylon one-piece, checkered grip with white spacers.
Features: Fits left or right hand, is shaped to fit fingers and heel of hand. Grooved trigger. Rotating thumb safety, cavity in fore-end permits insertion of up to five 38 cal., 130-gr. metal jacketed bullets to adjust weight and balance. Included is a black vinyl, zippered case.
Sights: Fixed front, rear adj. for w. and e. Tapped for scope mount.
Price: Including case **$119.95**

U.S. CENTERFIRE RIFLES—LEVER ACTION

BROWNING BLR LEVER ACTION RIFLE
Caliber: 243 or 308 Win. 4-shot detachable mag.
Barrel: 20″ round tapered.
Weight: 6 lbs. 15 oz. **Length:** 39¾″ over-all.
Stock: Checkered straight grip and fore-end, oil finished walnut (13¾″x1¾″x2⅜″).
Sights: Square notch adj. rear, gold bead on hooded ramp front.
Features: Wide, grooved trigger; half-cock hammer safety. Receiver tapped for scope mount. Recoil pad installed.
Price: **$199.50**

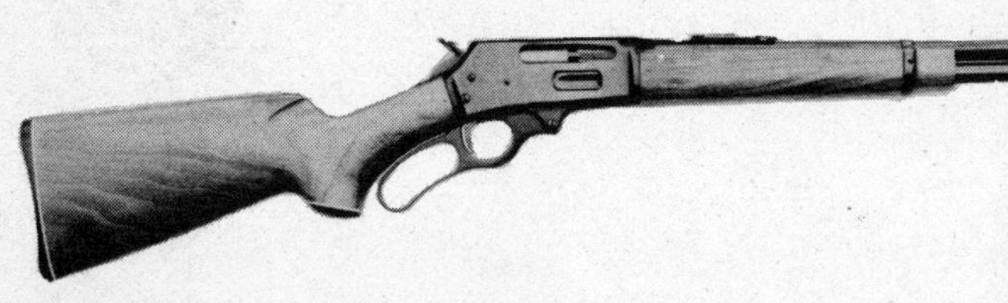

MARLIN 336C LEVER ACTION CARBINE
Caliber: 30-30 or 6-shot tubular magazine
Barrel: 20″ Micro-Groove
Weight: 7 lbs. **Length:** 38½″
Stock: Select American walnut, capped p.g. with white line spacers.
Sights: Wide-Scan ramp front, semi-buckhorn rear adj. for w. & e.
Features: Gold plated trigger, receiver tapped for scope mount, offset hammer spur, top of receiver sand blasted to prevent glare.
Price: **$116.95**

Marlin 336T Lever Action Carbine
Same as the 336C except: straight stock; cal. 30-30 only. Squared finger lever. .... **$116.95.**

Marlin 336A
Same action as the 336C with 24″ round barrel, ½-magazine tube with 5-shot capacity. Blued fore-end cap and sling swivels. Available in 30-30 Win. only **$121.95**

Marlin Glenfield 30A Lever Action Carbine
Same as the Marlin 336C except: checkered walnut finished hardwood p.g. stock, 30-30 only, 6-shot. **$109.95**

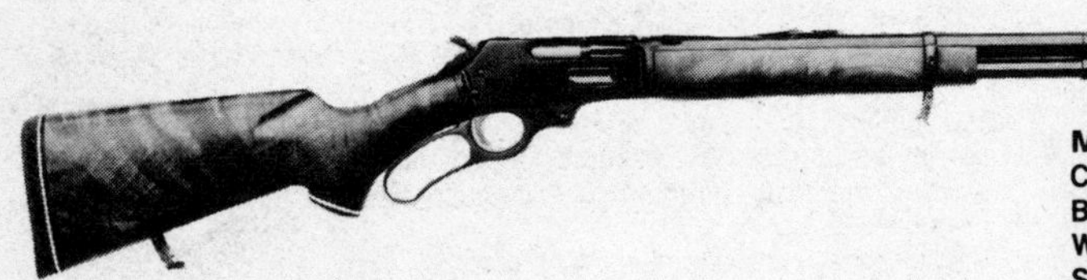

MARLIN 444 LEVER ACTION SPORTER
Caliber: 444 Marlin, 4-shot tubular magazine
Barrel: 22″ Micro-Groove
Weight: 7½ lbs. **Length:** 40½″
Stock: American walnut, capped p.g. with white line spacers, recoil pad.
Sights: Bead front, folding leaf rear adj. for w. & e.
Features: Gold plated trigger, receiver tapped for scope mount, offset hammer spur, leather sling with detachable swivels.
Price: **$145.00**

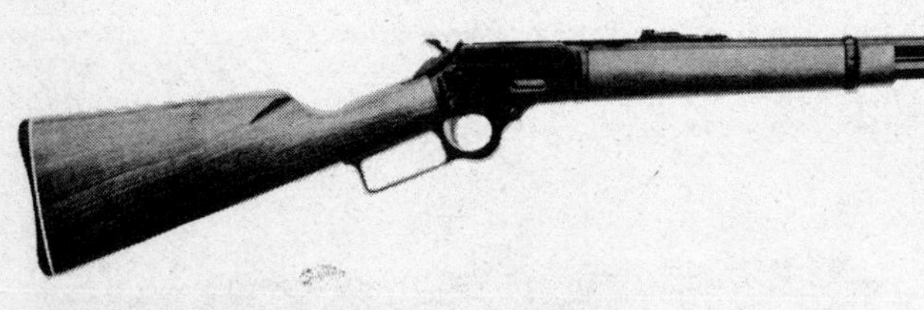

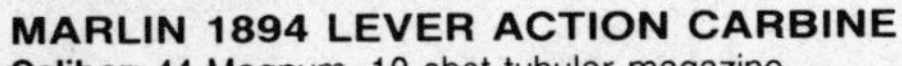

MARLIN 1894 LEVER ACTION CARBINE
Caliber: 44 Magnum, 10 shot tubular magazine
Barrel: 20″ Micro-Groove
Weight: 6 lbs. **Length:** 37½″
Stock: American walnut, straight grip and fore-end.
Sights: Bead ramp front, semi-buckhorn rear adj. for w. & e.
Features: Gold plated trigger, receiver tapped for scope mount, offset hammer spur, solid top receiver sand blasted to prevent glare. Marlin scope extra .... **$31.95.**
Price: **$116.95**

MARLIN 1895 LEVER ACTION RIFLE
Caliber: 45-70, 4-shot tubular magazine.
Barrel: 22″ round.
Weight: 7 lbs. **Length:** 40½″.
Stock: American walnut, straight grip.
Sights: Bead front, semi-buckhorn rear adj. for w. and e.
Features: Solid receiver tapped for scope mounts or receiver sights, offset hammer spur.
Price: **$185.00**

MOSSBERG MODEL 472 LEVER ACTION
Caliber: 30-30, 35 Rem., 6-shot magazine.
Barrel: 20″. 35 Rem.
Weight: 7½ lbs. **Length:** 38½″ over-all.
Stock: Walnut, fluted comb, p.g., rubber buttplate, white line spacers at p.g. cap and butt.
Sights: Ramp front, rear adj. for e.
Features: Trigger moves with lever on opening, hammer-block safety. Solid top receiver with side ejection. Also available with straight grip stock, either cal., same price
Price: **$132.60**
Price: "Brush Gun". 18″ bbl., straight stock, 30-30 only **$132.60**
Price: 472 PRA (24″ bbl., hooded ramp front sight, ½ magazine tube) **$133.30**

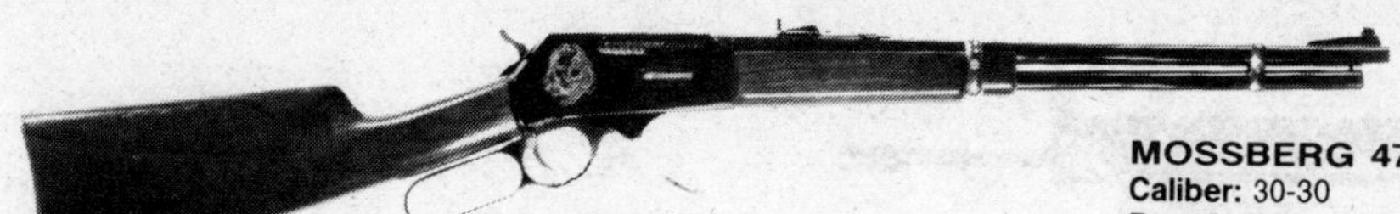

MOSSBERG 472 "ONE IN FIVE THOUSAND" CARBINE

Caliber: 30-30
Barrel: 18″
Stock: Straight grip walnut.
Sights: Ramp front, rear adj. fore.
Features: Collector's series edition. Brass buttplate, brass saddle ring and barrel bands, gold trigger, and scenes etched on both sides of receiver.
Price: **$154.80**

Savage 99A Lever Action Rifle

Same as the 99E except: straight-grip walnut stock with schnabel fore-end, top tang safety. Folding leaf rear sight. Available in 250-3000 (250 Savage) 300 Savage, 243 or 308 Win. **$167.95**

Savage 99C Lever Action Clip Rifle

Similar to M99A except: Detachable staggered clip magazine with push-button ejection. Wgt. about 6¾ lbs., 41¾″ over-all with 22″ bbl. cals. 243, 308 .... **$173.20**

SAVAGE 99E LEVER ACTION RIFLE

Caliber: 300 Savage, 243 or 308 Win., 5-shot rotary magazine.
Barrel: 20″ Chrome-moly steel.
Weight: 7 lbs. **Length:** 39¾″ over-all.
Stock: Walnut finished with checkered p.g. and fore-end (13½x1½x2½).
Sights: Ramp front with step adj. sporting rear. Tapped for scope mounts.
Features: Grooved trigger, slide safety locks trigger and lever.
Price: **$146.95**

Western Field Deluxe Model 72A

Same as Standard Model except: Select walnut stock and fore-end, hand checkered p.g. and fore-end. Gold plated trigger and bbl. band. Gold filled "deer" scenes on receiver sides.
Price: **$136.00**

WESTERN FIELD 72 LEVER ACTION CARBINE

Caliber: 30-30, 6-shot magazine.
Barrel: 18″, 20″.
Weight: 7½ lbs. **Length:** 38½″ over-all.
Stock: Walnut, fluted comb, p.g., rubber buttplate and p.g. cap with white spacers.
Sights: Ramp front, rear adj. for e.
Features: Trigger moves with lever on opening, hammer-block safety. Gold plated trigger. Solid top receiver with side ejection.
Price: Standard Model **$109.00**
Price: 18″ bbl., straight stock, steel buttplate **$98.00**

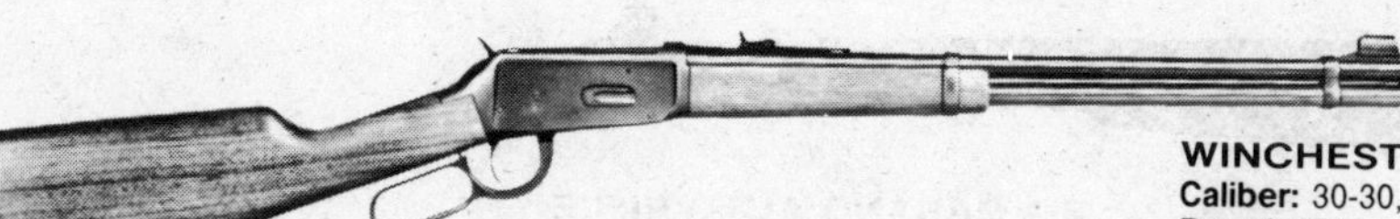

Winchester 94 Antique Carbine

Same as M94 except: color case-hardened and scroll-engraved receiver, brass-plated loading gate and saddle ring. 30-30 only **$125.95**

WINCHESTER 94 LEVER ACTION CARBINE

Caliber: 30-30, (12″ twist), 32 Special (16″ twist) 6-shot tubular mag.
Barrel: 20″
Weight: 6½ lbs. **Length:** 37¾″ over-all
Stock: Walnut straight grip stock and fore-end (13″x1¾″x2½″).
Sights: Bead front sight on ramp with removable cover; open rear. Tapped for receiver sights.
Features: Solid frame, top ejection, half-cock hammer safety.
Price: **$115.95**

U.S. CENTERFIRE RIFLES—AUTOLOADING

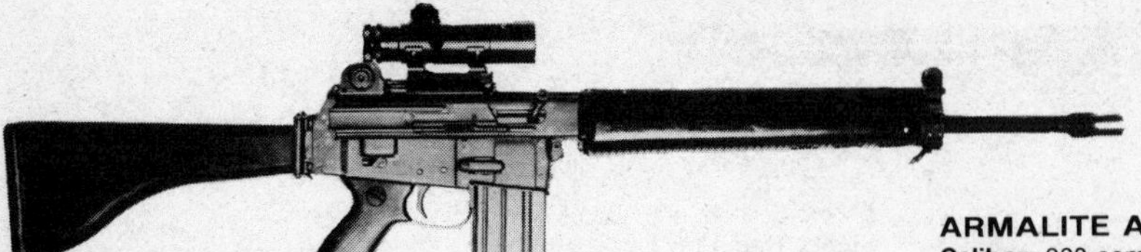

ARMALITE AR-180 SPORTER CARBINE

Caliber: 223 semi-automatic, gas operated carbine.
Barrel: 18¼" (12" twist).
Weight: 6½ lbs. **Length:** 38" over-all
Stock: Nylon folding stock, phenolic fiber-glass heat dissipating fore-end.
Sight: Flip-up "L" type sight adj. for w., post front adj. for e.
Features: Safety lever accessible from both sides. Flash hider slotted to prevent muzzle climb.
Price: **$294.30**
3x (2.75 x 20mm) scope with detachable side-mount. **$88.49**
Extra 5-round magazine **$5.75**

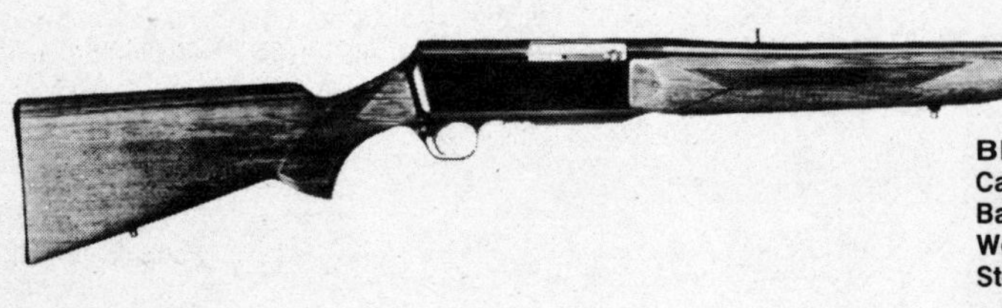

BROWNING HIGH-POWER AUTO RIFLE

Caliber: 243, 270, 30-06, 308.
Barrel: 22" round tapered.
Weight: 7⅜ lbs. **Length:** 43½" over-all.
Stock: French walnut p.g. stock (13⅝"x2"x1⅝") and fore-end, hand checkered.
Sights: Adj. folding-leaf rear, gold bead on hooded ramp front.
Features: Detachable 4-round magazine. Receiver tapped for scope mounts. Trigger pull 4 lbs.
Price: Grade I **$289.50**
Grade II. Same as Grade I except hand-rubbed selected French walnut stock, hand engraved receiver **$314.50**
Other Grades and prices to **$1,200.00**

Browning Magnum Auto Rifle
Same as the standard caliber model, except weighs 8½ lbs., 45¼" over-all 24" bbl., 3-round mag., Cals. 7mm Mag., 300 Win. Mag. and 338 Mag.
Grade I .... **$319.50** Grade II **$344.50**
Other Grades and prices to **$1,200.00**

COLT AR-15 SPORTER

Caliber: 223 Rem.
Barrel: 20".
Weight: 7¼ lbs. **Length:** 38⅜" over-all.
Stock: Reinforced polycarbonate with buttstock stowage compartment.
Sights: Post front, rear adj. for w. and e.
Features: 5-round detachable box magazine recoil pad, flash suppressor, sling swivels.
Price: **$252.00**

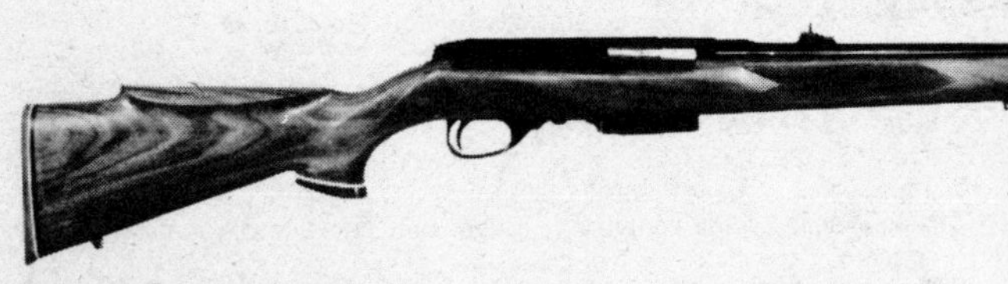

HARRINGTON & RICHARDSON 360 ULTRA AUTO

Caliber: 243, 308 Winchester. 3 round mag.
Barrel: 22" round, tapered.
Weight: 7½ lbs. **Length:** 43½" over-all.
Stock: One-piece American walnut Monte Carlo p.g. stock, roll-over cheekpiece.
Sights: Open adj. rear sight, gold bead ramp front.
Features: Sliding trigger guard safety. Manually operated bolt stop. Receiver tapped for scope mount.
Price: **$199.00**

M-1 TANKER GARAND

Caliber: 30-06, 8-shot clip.
Barrel: 17½".
Weight: 8½ lbs.
Stock: Birch, walnut finish.
Sights: Blade front, peep rear adj. for w. & e.
Features: Gas-operated semi-automatic. Shortened version of M-1 Garand rifle. From National Ordnance.
Price: **$199.95**

M-1 GARAND AUTO RIFLE

Caliber: 30-06, 8-shot clip.
Barrel: 24".
Length: 43½" over-all. **Weight:** 9½ lbs.
Stock: Birch, walnut finish.
Sights: Blade front, peep rear adj. for w. & e.
Features: Semi-automatic, gas operated, completely new manufacture. From National Ordnance.
Price: **$199.95**

U.S. CENTERFIRE RIFLES—AUTOLOADING

NATIONAL ORDNANCE M-1 CARBINE
Caliber: 30 Carbine, 15-shot magazine.
Barrel: 18″.
Weight: 5½ lbs. **Length:** 35½″ over-all.
Stock: Walnut.
Sights: Blade front, rear adj. for w. and e.
Features: Gas operated, cross lock safety, hammerless, military style.
Price: **$89.95**
With scope base mounted **$99.95**
With folding "paratrooper" stock and 30-shot magazine **$109.95**
With scope base mounted **$119.95**

PLAINFIELD MACHINE CO. CARBINE
Caliber: 30 U.S. Carbine or 223 (5.7mm)
Barrel: 18″ six-groove.
Weight: 6 lbs. **Length:** 35½″ over-all.
Stock: Glossy finished hard wood.
Sights: Click adj. open rear, gold bead ramp front.
Features: Gas operated semi-auto carbine. 15-shot detachable magazine.
Price: **$114.00**
Paratrooper. With telescoping wire stock, front vertical hand grip **$135.00**
Plainfielder. With walnut Monte Carlo sporting p.g. stock **$150.00**

PJK M-68 CARBINE
Caliber: 9mm Luger, 30-shot magazine.
Barrel: 16 3/16″.
Weight: 7 lbs. **Length:** 27″.
Stock: Black plastic.
Sights: Blade front, aperature rear.
Features: Straight blowback operation, cross-bolt safety, removeable flash hider. Semi-automatic only.
Price: **$179.00**

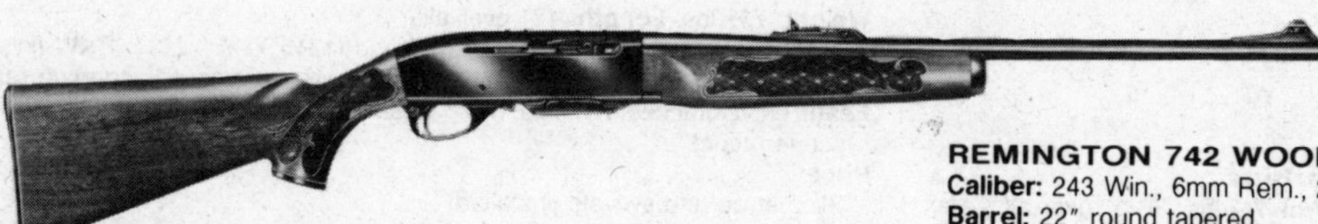

REMINGTON 742 WOODMASTER AUTO RIFLE
Caliber: 243 Win., 6mm Rem., 280 Rem., 308 Win. and 30-06.
Barrel: 22″ round tapered.
Weight: 7½ lbs. **Length:** 42″ over-all
Stock: Walnut (13¼″x1⅝″x2¼″) deluxe checkered p.g. and fore-end.
Sights: Gold bead front sight on ramp; step rear sight with windage adj.
Features: Positive cross-bolt safety. Receiver tapped for scope mount. 4-shot clip mag.
Price: **$189.95**
Extra 4-shot clip magazine **$5.25**
Sling strap and swivels (installed) **$9.10**
Peerless (D) and Premier (F) grades .... **$660.00** and **$1,350.00**
Premier with gold inlays **$2,100.00**

Remington 742 Carbine
Same as M742 except: 18½″ bbl., 38½″ over-all, wgt. 6¾ lbs. Cals: 30-06, 308 Win. **$189.00**

Remington 742 BDL Woodsmaster
Same as 742 except: "stepped" receiver, Monte Carlo with cheekpiece (right or left), whiteline spacers, basket-weave checkering on p.g. and fore-end, black fore-end tip, RKW finish (13 5/16″x1⅝″x1 13/16″x2½″). Cals. 30-06, 308 .... **$209.95**

RUGER MINI-14 223 CARBINE
Caliber: 223 Rem., 5-shot detachable box magazine.
Barrel: 18½″.
Weight: 6½ lbs. **Length:** 37¼″ over-all.
Stock: Walnut, steel reinforced.
Sights: Gold bead front, fully adj. rear.
Features: Fixed piston gas-operated, positive primary extraction. 20-shot magazine available only to police departments. **Factory accepting police orders only for balance of 1974.**
Price: **$200.00**

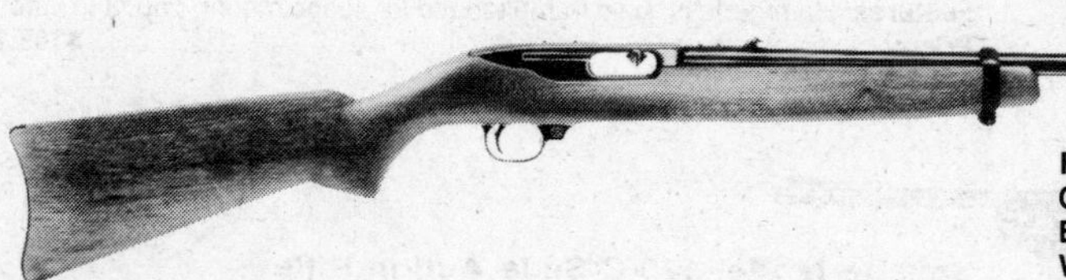

RUGER 44 AUTOLOADING CARBINE
Caliber: 44 Magnum, 4-shot tubular magazine.
Barrel: 18½″ round tapered.
Weight: 5¾ lbs. **Length:** 36¾″ over-all
Stock: One-piece walnut p.g. stock (13⅜″x1⅝″x2¼″)
Sights: 1/16″ front, folding leaf rear sights.
Features: Wide, curved trigger. Sliding cross-bolt safety. Receiver tapped for scope mount, unloading button.
Price: **$119.00**

U.S. CENTERFIRE RIFLES—AUTOLOADING

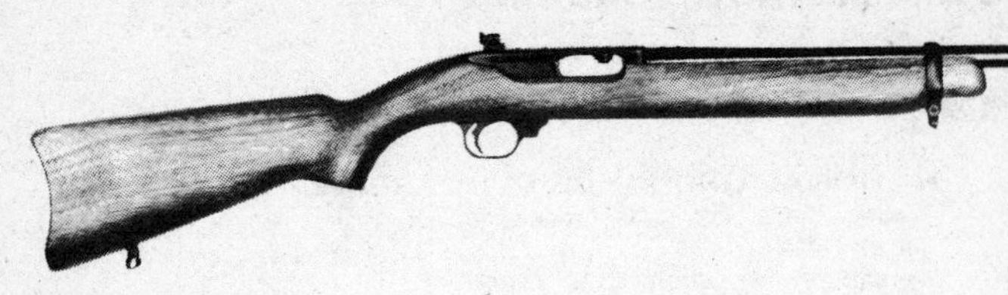

RUGER 44 AUTOLOADING DELUXE CARBINE
Caliber: 44 Magnum, 4-shot tubular magazine.
Barrel: 18½" round tapered.
Weight: 5¾ lbs. **Length:** 36¾" over-all.
Stock: One piece American walnut with sling swivels.
Sights: Gold bead front, Ruger adj. peep rear.
Features: Automatic bolt hold-open after last shot, magazine unloading button. Drilled and tapped for scope mount.
Price: **$122.00**

UNIVERSAL 1003 AUTOLOADING CARBINE
Caliber: 30 M1, 5-shot magazine.
Barrel: 18"
Weight: 5½ lbs: **Length:** 35½" over-all
Stock: Walnut stock inletted for "issue" sling and oiler.
Sights: Blade front aperture rear. With protective wings, adj.
Features: Gas operated, hammerless. Cross lock safety. Receiver tapped for scope mounts.
Price: **$118.95**
Price: Model 1011 nickel plated **$131.95**
Price: Model 1016 gold plated **$194.95**

Universal Model 1002 Carbine
Same as Model 1000 except: Military type with metal handguard. Blue
Price: **$122.95**

U.S. CENTERFIRE RIFLES—SLIDE ACTION

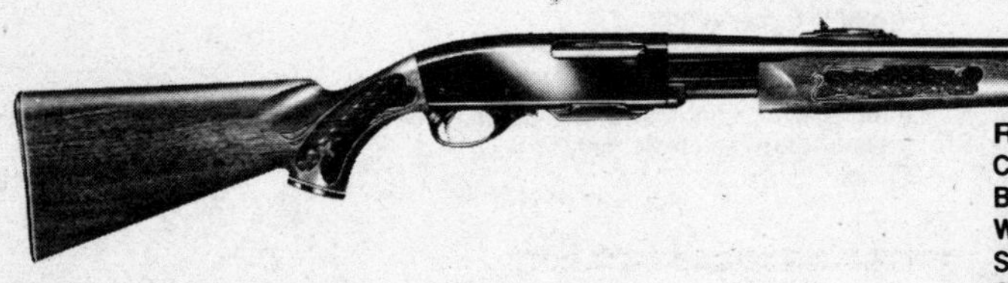

REMINGTON 760 GAMEMASTER SLIDE ACTION
Caliber: 6mm Rem., 243, 270, 308 Win., 30-06.
Barrel: 22" round tapered.
Weight: 7½ lbs. **Length:** 42" over-all.
Stock: Checkered walnut p.g. and fore-end (13¼"x1⅝"x2⅛") RKW finish
Sights: Gold bead front sight on matted ramp, open step adj. sporting rear.
Features: Detachable 4-shot clip. Cross-bolt safety. Receiver tapped for scope mount.
Price: **$164.95**
Sling strap and swivels (installed) **$9.10**
Extra 4-shot clip **4.50**

Remington 760 Gamemaster Carbine
Same as M760 except has 18½" barrel. Wgt. 7¼ lbs., 38½" over-all. Cals: 308 Win. and 30-60 .... **$164.95**

Remington 760 BDL Gamemaster
Same as 760 except: "stepped receiver," Monte Carlo stock with cheekpiece (right or left), whiteline spacer, basket-weave checkering on p.g. and fore-end, black fore-end tip, RKW finish. (13 5/16"x1⅝"x1 13/16"x2½"). Cals. 270, 30-06, 308 .... **$184.95**
Also in Peerless (D) and Premier (F) grades ..... **$595.00** and **$1,350.00**
(F), with gold inlay **$2,100.00**

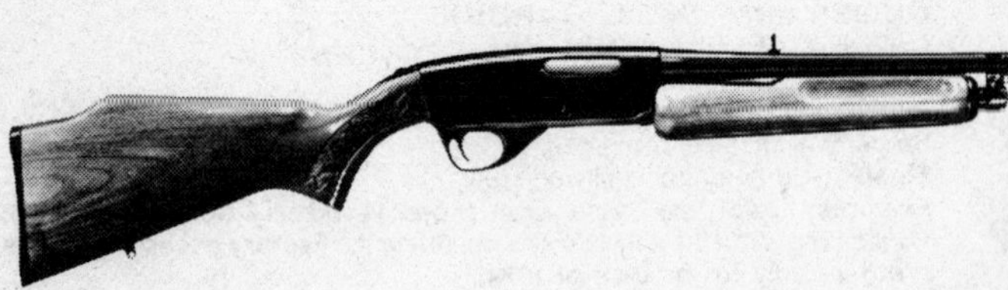

SAVAGE MODEL 170 SLIDE ACTION
Caliber: 30-30 only. 3-shot mag.
Barrel: 22" round tapered.
Weight: 6¾ lbs. **Length:** 41½" over-all.
Stock: Walnut (14"x1½"x2½"), with checkered p.g. Hard rubber buttplate.
Sights: Gold bead ramp front, folding-leaf rear.
Features: Hammerless, solid frame tapped for scope mount. Top tang safety.
Price: **$105.10**

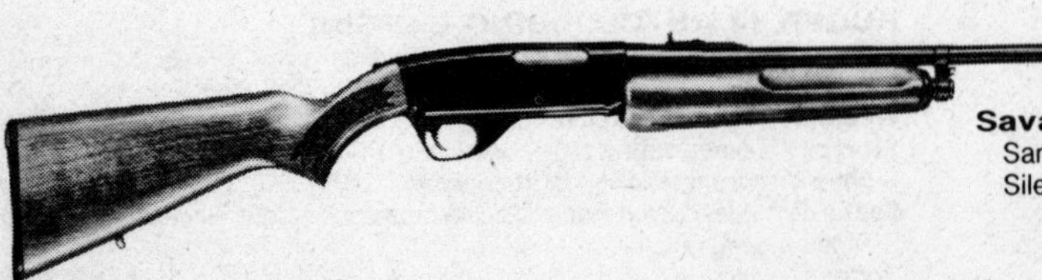

Savage Model 170-C Slide Action Rifle
Same as Model 170 except has 18½" barrel, no Monte Carlo on stock. Silent-Lok feature eliminates slide handle rattle. **$105.10**

U.S. CENTERFIRE RIFLES—BOLT ACTION

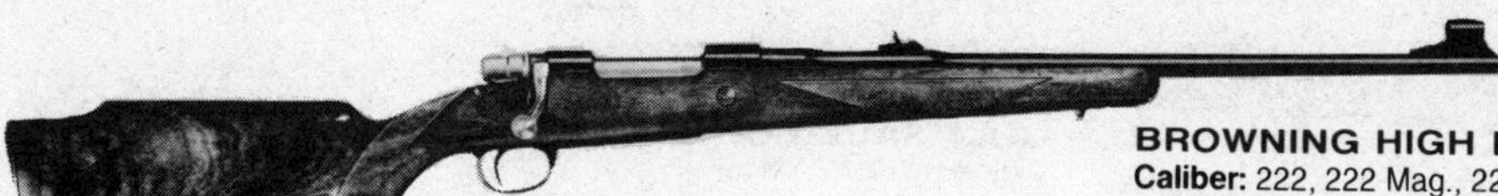

BROWNING HIGH POWER RIFLE

Caliber: 222, 222 Mag., 22-250, 284, 243, 308, 270, 30-06, 7mm Rem. Mag., 300 Win. Mag., 308 Norma, 338 Win. Mag. 375 H&H, 458 Win. Mag.
Barrel: 22" standard, 24" Magnum.
Weight: 6⅛ to 8¼ lbs. **Length:** 43"
Stock: Checkered walnut p.g. with Monte Carlo (13⅝"x1⅝"x2⅜").
Sights: Hooded ramp front, removable adj. folding-leaf rear; except none on 458.
Features: 3-position side safety, hinged floorplate, receiver tapped for scope mount.
Price: Safari Grade .... **$410.00** to **$460.00**
Medallion Grade, except 222 .... **$700.00**
Olympian Grade, except 222 .... **$1,200.00**

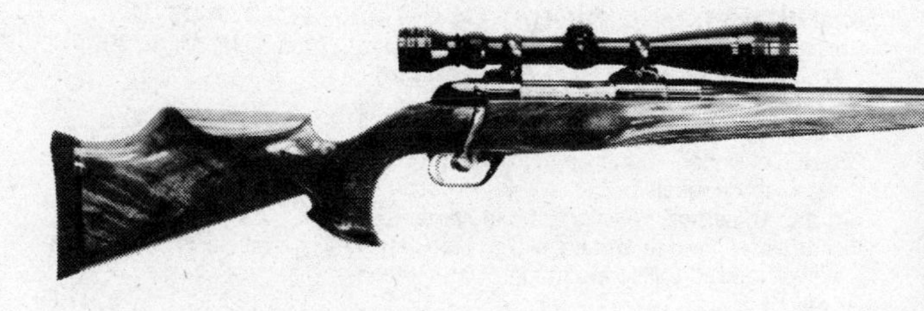

BORTMESS BIG HORN RIFLE

Caliber: All cals. from 22-250 thru 458 Win.
Barrel: 24" or 25" Douglas Premium.
Weight: 7¼ lbs. **Length:** 46" over-all.
Stock: American walnut. Monte Carlo with rollover cheekpiece, half-curl p.g. with rosewood cap, tapering cut fore-end with cap.
Sights: None furnished. Drilled and tapped for scope mounting.
Features: Uses Ranger Arms action. Choice of Nidner steel or Pachmayr rubber recoil pad. High gloss stock finish. From Bortmess Gun Co.
Price: From **$455.00**

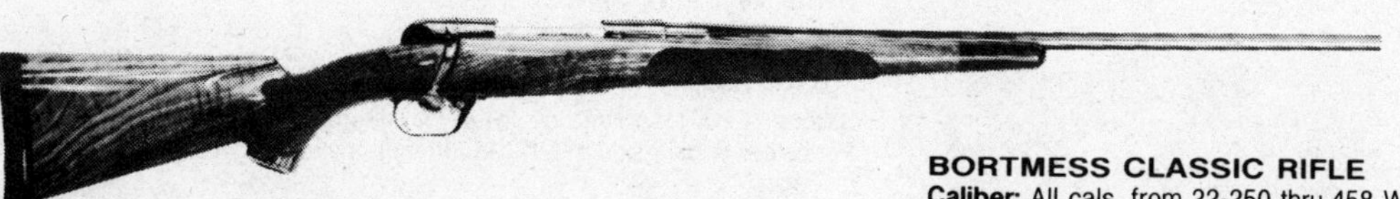

BORTMESS OMEGA RIFLE

Caliber: All cals. from 22-250 thru 358 Norma (no long magnums).
Barrel: 24" and 25" Douglas Premium.
Weight: 7¼ lbs. **Length:** 46" over-all.
Stock: Two-piece American walnut. High gloss finish.
Sights: None furnished. Drilled and tapped for scope mounting.
Features: Built by Omega Arms, distributed by Bortmess Gun Co.
Price: From **$500.00**

BORTMESS CLASSIC RIFLE

Caliber: All cals. from 22-250 thru 458 Win.
Barrel: 24" or 25" Douglas Premium.
Weight: 7¼ lbs. **Length:** 46" over-all.
Stock: American walnut. Length of pull 13¾". Plastic fore-end tip and p.g. cap. Pachmayr solid rubber recoil pad.
Sights: None furnished. Drilled and tapped for scope.
Features: Uses Ranger Arms action. Hand checkered p.g. and fore-end. High gloss stock finish. Exotic stock woods available at extra cost. From Bortmess Gun Co.
Price: From **$455.00**

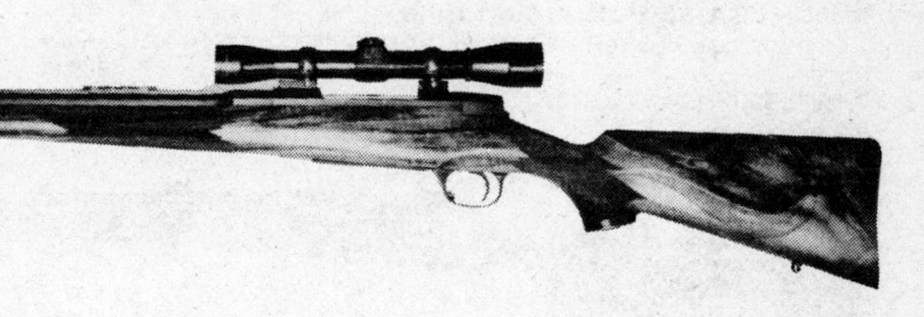

CHAMPLIN RIFLE

Caliber: All std. chamberings, including 458 Win. and 460 Wea. Many wildcats on request.
Barrel: Any length up to 26" for octagon. Choice of round, straight taper octagon, or octagon with integral quarter rib, front sight ramp and sling swivel stud.
Length: 45" over-all. **Weight:** About 8 lbs.
Stock: Hand inletted, shaped and finished. Checkered to customer specs. Select French, Circassin or claro walnut. Steel p.g. cap, trap buttplate or recoil pad.
Sights: Bead on ramp front, 3-leaf folding rear.
Features: Right or left hand Champlin action, tang safety or optional shroud safety, Canjar adj. trigger, hinged floorplate.
Price: From **$1,280.00**

COLT SAUER RIFLE

Caliber: 25-06, 270, 30-06, (std.), 7mm Rem. Mag., 300 Win. Mag. (Magnum).
Barrel: 24", round tapered.
Length: 43¾" over-all. **Weight:** 8 lbs. (std.).
Stock: American walnut, cast-off M.C. design with cheekpiece. Fore-end tip and p.g. cap rosewood with white spacers. Hand checkering.
Sights: None furnished. Specially designed scope mounts for any popular make scope furnished.
Features: Unique barrel/receiver union, non-rotating bolt with cam-actuated locking lugs, tang-type safety locks sear. Detachable 3- and 4-shot magazines.
Price: Standard cals. ..... **$450.00** Magnum cals. **$460.00**

Colt Sauer Short Action Rifle

Same as standard rifle except chambered for 22-250, 243 and 308 Win. 24" bbl., 43" over-all. Weighs 7½ lbs. 3-shot magazine. **$450.00**

COLT SAUER GRAND AFRICAN

Caliber: 458 Win. Mag.
Barrel: 24″, round tapered.
Length: 44½″ over-all. **Weight:** 10½ lbs.
Stock: Solid African bubinga wood, cast-off M.C. with cheekpiece, contrasting rosewood fore-end and p.g. caps with white spacers. Checkered fore-end and p.g.
Sights: Ivory bead hooded ramp front, adj. sliding rear.
Price: **$480.00**

HARRINGTON & RICHARDSON 300 BOLT ACTION

Caliber: 22-250, 243, 270, 308, 30-06 (5-shot), 7mm Rem. Mag., 300 Win. Mag. (3-shot)
Barrel: 22″ round, tapered.
Weight: 7¾ lbs. **Length:** 42½″ over-all.
Stock: American walnut, hand checkered p.g. and fore-end, Monte Carlo, roll-over cheekpiece.
Sights: Adjustable rear, gold bead ramp front.
Features: Hinged floorplate; sliding side safety; sling swivels, recoil pad. Receiver tapped for scope mount. Sako action.
Price: **$237.00**

HARRINGTON & RICHARDSON 301 ULTRA CARBINE

Similar to M300, except: Mannlicher style stock (no roll-over cheek-piece) metal fore-end tip. 18″ bbl., 39″ over all, wgt. 7¼ lbs., not available in 22-250. ...... **$252.00**

HARRINGTON & RICHARDSON 317 ULTRA WILDCAT

Caliber: 17 Rem., 222, 223 or 17/223 (handload) 6-shot magazine.
Barrel: 20″ round, tapered.
Weight: 5¼ lbs. **Length:** 38½″ over-all.
Stock: Walnut, hand polished, hand checkered capped p.g. and fore-end, with Monte Carlo.
Sights: None. Receiver dovetailed for integral scope mounts.
Features: Sliding side safety, adj. trigger. included. Sliding side safety, adj. trigger.
Price: **$262.00**
Model 317P has better wood, basketweave checkering **$474.00**

HARRINGTON & RICHARDSON MODEL 333 RIFLE

Caliber: 30-06 (5-shot), 7mm Rem. Mag. (3-shot).
Barrel: 22″.
Weight: 7¾ lbs. **Length:** 42½″ over-all.
Stock: Walnut finish hardwood.
Sights: None furnished.
Features: Barrel and action made by Sako of Finland. Adjustable trigger. Short throw action. Sliding thumb safety.
Price: **$169.00**

Ithaca LSA-65 Bolt Action Rifle

Same as the LSA-55 except in 25-06, 270 or 30-06 caliber (4-shot clip only).
Price: **$209.95**
Price: LSA-65 Deluxe **$244.95**
Price: 222 cal. **$244.95**

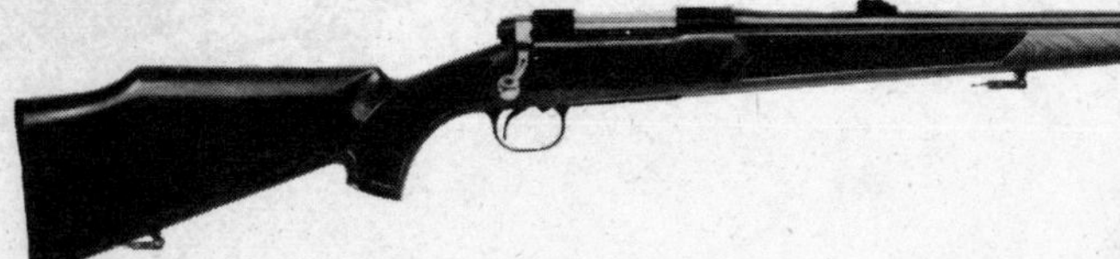

ITHACA LSA-55 BOLT ACTION RIFLE

Caliber: 243, 308, 22-250, 6mm Rem. 270 and 30-06.
Barrel: 23″ round tapered, full-floating.
Weight: About 6½ lbs. **Length:** 41½″ over-all
Stock: Hand checkered walnut, Monte Carlo with built-in swell on p.g.
Sights: Removable rear adj. for w. & e. ramp front.
Features: Detachable 3-shot magazine, adj. trigger, top tang safety. Receiver tapped for scope mounts.
Price: 243, 308, 22-250 & 6mm **$209.95**
Price: 270 & 30-06 ...... **$209.95**
Price: 222 Standard, heavy bbl. **$269.95**
Price: Deluxe Heavy Bbl., 22-250 ...... **$269.95**

Ithaca LSA-55 Deluxe Bolt Action

Same as the std. except rollover cheekpiece, fore-end tip and pistol grip cap of rosewood with white spacers. Scope mount rings supplied. Sling swivels installed.
Price: 243, 308, 22-250 & 6mm **$244.95**
Price: 270 & 30-06 ...... **$244.95**
Price: 222 cal. **$209.95**

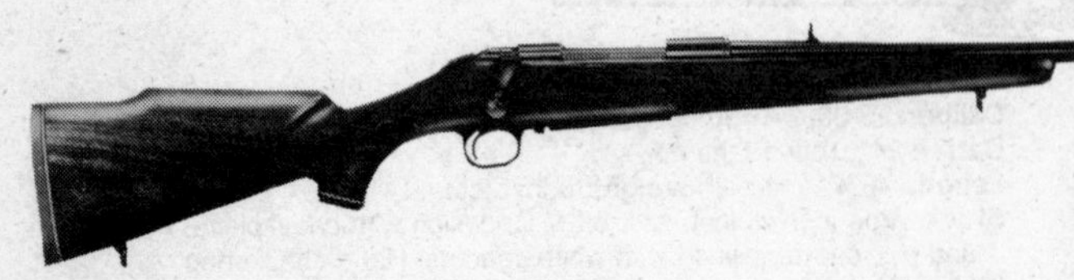

MOSSBERG 810A BOLT ACTION RIFLE

Caliber: 30-06, 270, 4-shot magazine, 338, 3-shot.
Barrel: 22″ AC-KRO-GRUV, straight taper.
Weight: 7½ to 8 lbs. **Length:** 42″ over-all.
Stock: Walnut Monte Carlo with checkered fore-end and capped p.g. recoil pad and sling swivels installed.
Sights: Gold bead on ramp front, folding-leaf rear.
Features: Receiver tapped for metallic sight or scope mounts. Top tang safety. Detachable box magazine.
Price: **$154.30**
Price: With 4x scope as 810 ASM **$181.50**

Mossberg 810B Bolt Action Rifle

Same as 810A except in 7mm Rem. Mag. only, length is 33″ over-all **$170.30**
810 BSM with M 84 4x scope **$195.00**

Mossberg 810C Bolt Action Rifle
Same as 810A except in 270 Win. **$154.30**
With 4x scope as 810 CSM **$181.50**

Mossberg 810D Bolt Action Rifle
Same as 810A except in 338 Win. Mag. **$170.30**
With 4x scope as 810 DSM **$197.90**

MOSSBERG 800 BOLT ACTION RIFLE
Caliber: 22-250, 243 and 308. 4-shot magazine.
Barrel: 22″ AC-KRO-GRUV round tapered.
Weight: 6½ lbs. **Length:** 42″ over-all.
Stock: Walnut, Monte Carlo, checkered p.g. and fore-end.
Sights: Gold bead ramp front, adj. folding-leaf rear.
Features: Top tang safety, hinged floorplate, 1″ sling swivels installed. Receiver tapped for scope mounts.
Price: **$141.75**

Mossberg 800SM Scoped Rifle
Same as M800 except has Mossberg M84 4x scope, but no iron sights. Wgt. 7½ lbs. **$166.85**

Mossberg 800 V/T Varmint Target Rifle
Model 800 with heavy 24″ bbl, target scope bases, no iron sights. Cals. 243 and 22-250 only. 44″ overall, wgt. about 9½ lbs. **$155.55**

OMEGA III BOLT ACTION RIFLE
Caliber: 25-06, 270, 30-06, 7mm. Rem. Mag., 300 Win. Mag., 338 Win. Mag., 358 Norma Mag.
Barrel: 22″ or 24″.
Length: 42″ over-all (24″ bbl.). **Weight:** 7¼ lbs.
Stock: Choice of three styles: Monte Carlo, Cassic or Thumbhole Varminter in either Claro walnut, English walnut or laminated.
Sights: None furnished.
Features: Right or left hand action, octagonal bolt, square locking system with enclosed bolt face gives 50 degree lift. Rotary magazine holds five standard or four belted cartridges, dual safety, fully adj. trigger, interchangeable stock and fore-end. Omega Arms Co.
Price: Left or right-hand version **$397.50**
Extra set of stocks **$97.50**

PEDERSEN 3000 BOLT ACTION RIFLE
Caliber: 270, 30-06, 7mm Rem. Mag., 338 Win. Mag., 3-shot magazine.
Barrel: 22″ (270, 30-06), 24″ (7mm Rem. Mag., 338 Win. Mag.).
Weight: 7 lbs. **Length:** 42″ over-all.
Stocks: Walnut, roll-over cheekpiece, M.C., wrap-around checkering at p.g. and fore-end.
Sights: Drilled and tapped for scope mounts. Iron sight model available.
Features: Adjustable trigger, sling swivels, medium weight barrel, bull barrel on 338. Grades differ in extent of engraving and stock figure. Mossberg M800 action.
Price: Grade I **$800.00**
Price: Grade II **$650.00**
Price: Grade III **$550.00**

RANGER ARMS BOLT ACTION RIFLE
Caliber: All major calibers from 22-250 to 458 Win. Mag.
Barrel: Lengths up to 25½″, & contour desired.
Length: Varies with bbl. lengths. **Weight:** Varies with options.
Stock: Rollover, cheekpiece, thumbhole, Mannlicher. Available in claro walnut, laminated walnut & maple, fiddleback & quilt maple, with hand checkering, rosewood p.g. & fore-end cap. Recoil pad installed.
Sights: None furnished. Drilled and tapped for scope mount.
Features: Push-button safety, adj. trigger. Available in left or right hand models at same price.
Price: .... **$400.00** & up.

Remington 700 BDL Bolt Action Rifle
Same as 700-ADL, including 17 Rem., except: fleur-de-lis checkering; black fore-end tip and p.g. cap, white line spacers. Matted receiver top, quick release floorplate. Hooded ramp front sight. Q.D. swivels and 1″ sling.
Price: **$189.95**
Available also in 6.5 Rem. Mag., 350 Rem. Mag., 7mm Rem. Mag., 264 and 300 Win. Mag., caliber. 44½″ over-all, weight 7½ lbs. **$204.95**
Peerless Grade .... **$595.00** Premier Grade **$1295.00**

REMINGTON 700 ADL BOLT ACTION RIFLE
Caliber: 222, 22-250, 6mm Rem., 243, 25-06, 270, 7mm Rem. Mag., 308 and 30-06.
Barrel: 22″ or 24″ round tapered.
Weight: 7 lbs. **Length:** 41½″ to 43½″
Stock: Walnut, RKW finished p.g. stock with impressed checkering, Monte Carlo (13⅜″x1⅝″x2⅜″).
Sights: Gold bead ramp front; removable, step-adj. rear with windage screw.
Features: Side safety, receiver tapped for scope mounts.
Price: (except 7mm Rem. Mag.) **$164.95**
7mm Rem. Mag. **$179.95**

U.S. CENTERFIRE RIFLES—BOLT ACTION

Remington 700 Safari
Same as the 700 BDL except 375 H&H or 458 Win. Magnum calibers only. Hand checkered, oil finished stock with recoil pad installed. Delivery time is about five months. **$360.00**

Remington 700BDL Left Hand
Same as 700 BDL except: mirror-image left-hand action, stock. 270, 30-06 **$179.95;** 7mm Rem. Mag. **$194.95**

Remington 700 C Custom Rifle
Same as the 700 BDL except choice of 20″, 22″ or 24″ bbl. with or without sights. Jewelled bolt, with or without hinged floor plate. Select American walnut stock is hand checkered, rosewood fore-end & grip cap. Hand lapped barrel. 16 weeks for delivery after placing order **$360.00**
M700 C Custom Magnum **$372.00**
Optional extras: recoil pad **$12.00,** oil finish **$13.75,** left hand cheekpiece **$25.00.**

Remington 700 BDL Varmint
Same as 700 BDL, except: 24″ heavy bbl., 43½″ over-all, wgt. 9 lbs. Cals. 222, 223, 22-250, 6mm Rem., 243 and 25-06. No sights........ **$204.95**

Remington 788 Left Hand Bolt Action
—Same as 788 except cals. 6mm & 308 only and left hand stock and action.
Price: **$109.95**

REMINGTON 788 BOLT ACTION RIFLE
Caliber: 222 (5-shot), 22-250, 6mm Rem., 243, and 308 (4-shot).
Barrel: 22″ round tapered (24″ in 222 and 22-250).
Weight: 7-7½ lbs. **Length:** 41⅝″ over-all.
Stock: Walnut finished hardwood with Monte Carlo and p.g. (13⅝″x1⅞″x2⅝″).
Sights: Blade ramp front, open rear adj. for w. & e.
Features: Detachable box magazine, thumb safety, receiver tapped for scope mounts.
Price: **$104.95**
Sling strap and swivels, installed **$5.40**
Model 788 with Universal Model UE 4x scope, mounts and rings in cals. 6mm Rem., 243 Win., 308 and 22-250 .... **$124.95**

Ruger Model 77 Magnum Round Top
Same as Model 77 except: round top receiver, drilled and tapped for standard scope mounts. Open sights are standard equipment. Calibers 25-06, 270, 30-06, 7mm Rem. Mag., 300 Win. Mag., 338 Win. Mag.
Price: All cals. except 300 and 338 .... **$176.00**
Price: 300 and 338 .... **$186.00**

RUGER 77 BOLT ACTION RIFLE
Caliber: 22-250, 220 Swift, 243, 6mm. 250-3000, (5-shot).
Barrel: 22″ round tapered, 26″ in 220 Swift.
Weight: 6¾ lbs. **Length:** 42″ over-all.
Stock: Hand checkered American walnut (13¾″x1⅝″x2⅛″), p.g. cap, sling swivel studs and recoil pad.
Sights: Optional gold bead ramp front, folding leaf adj. rear, or scope rings.
Features: Integral scope mount bases, diagonal bedding system, hinged floorplate, adj. trigger, tang safety. Scope optional.
Price: With Ruger steel scope rings **$176.00**
Price: With rings and open sights **$190.00**

Ruger Model 77 Magnum Rifle
Similar to Ruger 77 except: magnum-size action. Calibers 25-06, 270, 7x57, 30-06 (5-shot), 7mm Rem. Mag., 300 Win. Mag., 338 Win. Mag., 458 Win. Mag. (3-shot). 270 and 30-06 have 22″ bbl., all others have 24″. Weight and length vary with caliber.
Price: With rings only, 300 Win. Mag. and 338 Win. Mag. **$186.00**
Price: With rings only, all cals. except 458 .... **$176.00**
Price: With rings and sights, 300 and 338 .... **$200.00**
Price: With rings and sights, 458 .... **$253.00**
Price: With rings and sights, other cals. **$190.00**

RUGER MODEL 77 VARMINT
Caliber: 22-250, 220 Swift, 243, 6mm, 25-06.
Barrel: 24″ heavy straight tapered, 26″ in 220 Swift.
Weight: Approx. 9 lbs. **Length:** Approx. 44″ over-all.
Stock: American walnut, similar in style to Magnum Rifle.
Sights: Barrel drilled and tapped for target scope blocks. Integral scope mount bases in receiver.
Features: Ruger diagonal bedding system, Ruger steel 1″ scope rings supplied. Fully adj. trigger. Barreled actions available in any of the standard calibers and barrel lengths.
Price: **$183.00**
Price: Barreled action only all cals. except 300, 338 .... **$137.00**
Price: Bbld. action, 300, 338 .... **$144.00**
Price: Bbld. action, 458 Win. Mag. **$197.00**

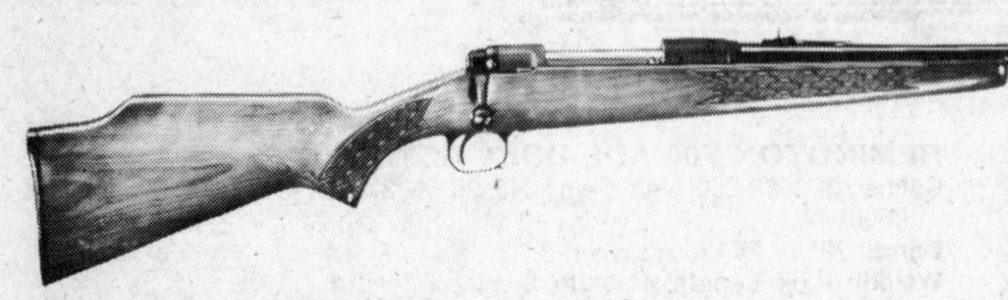

Savage 110C Bolt Action Rifle
Same as the 110D except: Detachable box magazine. Cals. 270 and 30-06 (4-shot). Also in 7mm Rem. (3-shot) at $15 extra.
Price: Right hand std. cals. **$155.55** Left hand (110 CL) std. cals. **$163.30**
Price: Right hand, magnum **$172.20** Left hand, magnum **$176.30**

SAVAGE 110E BOLT ACTION RIFLE
Caliber: 30-06, 4-shot. Also 7mm Rem. Mag., 3-shot.
Barrel: 20″ round tapered (7mm 24″ stainless).
Weight: 6¾ lbs. (7mm-7¾ lbs.) **Length:** 40½″ (20″ bbl.)
Stock: Walnut finished hardwood with Monte Carlo, checkered p.g. and fore-end, hard rubber buttplate.
Sights: Gold bead removable ramp front, step adj. rear.
Features: Top tang safety, receiver, tapped for peep or scope sights. Right or left hand models available.
Price: Std. cals. **$128.15**
Price: Magnum **$143.55**

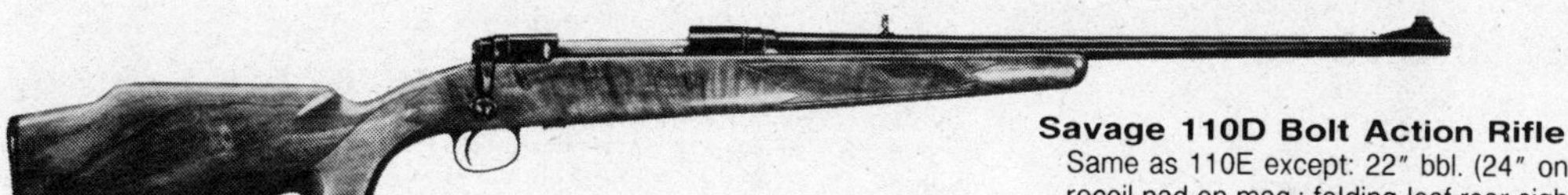

Savage 110D Bolt Action Rifle
Same as 110E except: 22" bbl. (24" on Mag.); walnut stock, cheekpiece; recoil pad on mag.; folding-leaf rear sight; weight 6¾-8 lbs. Cals. 243, 270 and 30-06. Also available in 7mm Rem. at $15 extra.
Price: Right hand std. cals. **$155.55** Left hand std. cals. **$163.30**
Price: Right hand, magnum **$172.20** Left hand, magnum **$176.30**

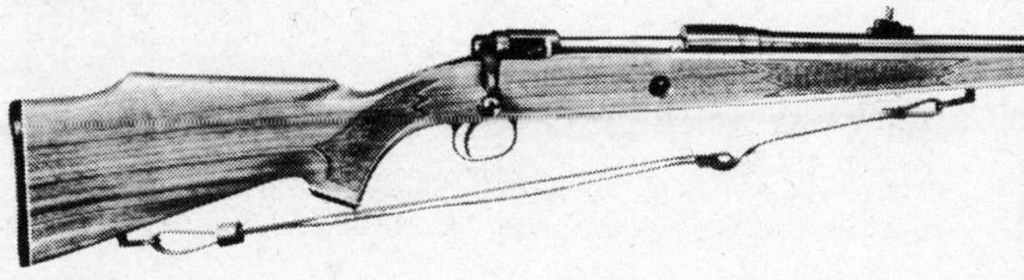

SAVAGE MODEL 111 CHIEFTAIN BOLT ACTION RIFLE
Caliber: 30-06, 270 (5-shot), 7mm Rem. Mag. (4-shot).
Barrel: 22" (standard cals.), 24" (mag. cals.). Free floating.
Weight: 7½ lbs. (std.), 8¼ (mag.) **Length:** 43" over-all.
Stock: Walnut, Monte Carlo, checkered fore-end and p.g., p.g. cap, white spacers.
Sights: Removeable hooded ramp front, open rear adj. for w. and e.
Features: Top tang safety, ejector clip magazine, teardrop design bolt handle. Electro-Cote stock finish. Stainless steel barrel in magnum calibers. Drilled and tapped for scope mounts.
Price: Standard calibers **$184.50**
Price: Magnum calibers **$194.50**

SAVAGE 340 CLIP REPEATER
Caliber: 222 Rem. (4-shot) and 30-30 (3-shot).
Barrel: 24" and 22" respectively.
Weight: About 6½ lbs. **Length:** 40"-42"
Stock: Walnut, Monte Carlo, checkered p.g. and fore-end white line spacers.
Sights: Gold bead ramp front, folding-leaf rear.
Features: Detachable clip magazine, sliding thumb safety, receiver tapped for scope mounts.
Price: **$94.40**

SPRINGFIELD MODEL 1903-A3
Caliber: 30-06, 5-shot magazine.
Barrel: 24".
Length: 43¼" over-all. **Weight:** 8½ lbs.
Stock: Birch, walnut finish.
Sights: Military ramp front, peep rear adj. for w. & e.
Features: Bolt action. All parts, including receiver, are new manufacture. From National Ordnance.
Price: **$79.95**

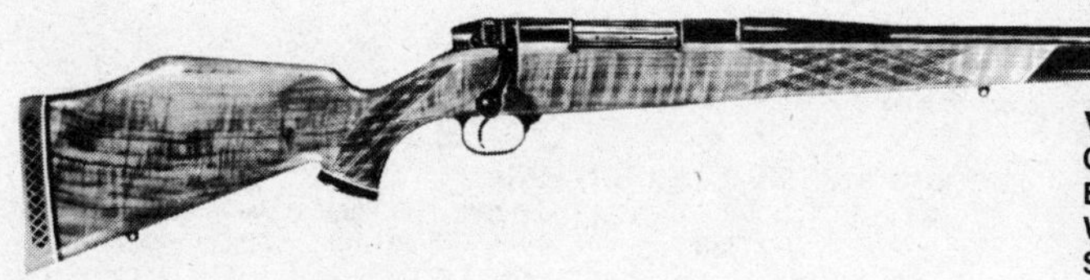

WEATHERBY MARK V BOLT ACTION RIFLE
Caiber: All Weatherby Cals., 22-250 and 30-06.
Barrel: 24" or 26" round tapered.
Weight: 6½-10½ lbs. **Length:** 43¼"-46½"
Stock: Walnut, Monte Carlo with cheekpiece, high luster finish, checkered p.g. and fore-end, recoil pad.
Sights: Optional (extra).
Features: Cocking indicator, adj. trigger, hinged floorplate, thumb safety, quick detachable sling swivels.
Price: Cals. 224 and 22-250, std. bbl. **$369.50**
With 26" semi-target bbl. **$379.50**
Cals. 240, 257, 270, 7mm, 30-06 and 300 (24" bbl.) **$389.50**
With 26" No. 2 contour bbl. **$389.50**
Cal. 340 (26" bbl.) **$399.50**
Cal. 378 (26" bbl.) **$495.00**
Cal. 460 (26" bbl.) **$575.00**

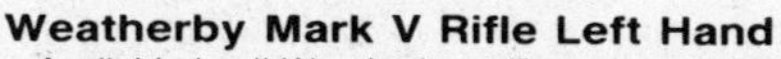

Weatherby Mark V Rifle Left Hand
Available in all Weatherby calibers except 224 and 22-250 (and 26" No. 2 contour 300WM). Complete left handed action; stock with cheekpiece on right side. Prices are $10 higher than right hand models except the 378 and 460WM are unchanged.

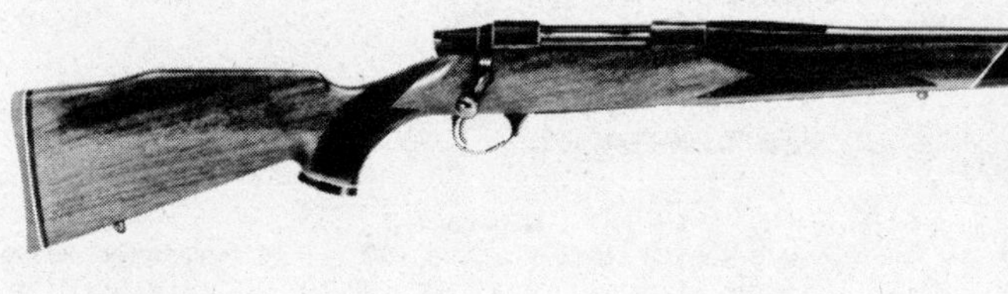

WEATHERBY VANGUARD BOLT ACTION RIFLE
Caliber: 25-06, 243, 270, 30-06 and 308 (5-shot), 7mm Rem. and 300 Win. Mag. (3-shot).
Barrel: 24" hammer forged.
Weight: 7⅞ lbs. **Length:** 44½" over-all.
Stock: American walnut, p.g. cap and fore-end tip, hand inletted and checkered, 13½" pull.
Sights: Optional, available at extra cost.
Features: Side safety, adj. trigger, hinged floorplate, receiver tapped for scope mounts.
Price: **$229.50**

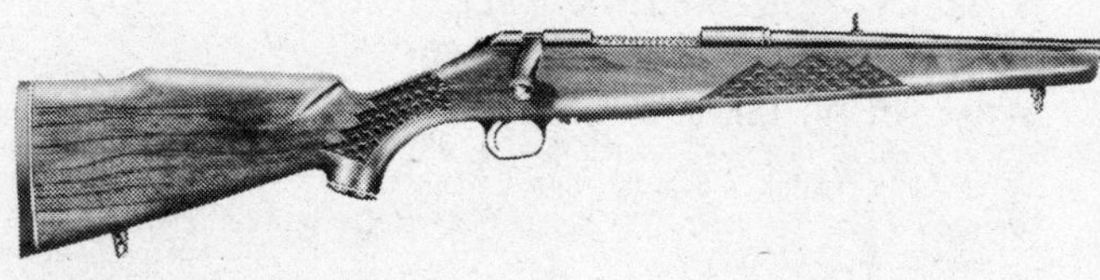

WESTERN FIELD MODEL 732 BOLT ACTION RIFLE
Caliber: 7mm (4-shot), 30-06 (5-shot).
Barrel: 22".
Weight: 8½ lbs. (30-06). **Length:** 43½" over-all.
Stock: Walnut. Monte Carlo cheekpiece, checkered p.g. and fore-end.
Sights: Gold bead front, adj. folding leaf rear.
Features: Adjustable trigger. Rubber recoil pad, p.g. cap. Receiver drilled and tapped for scope mounts. 1" sling swivels. Top receiver safety.
Price: 7mm **$139.00**
Price: 30-06 .... **$150.00**

WESTERN FIELD 780 BOLT ACTION RIFLE

Caliber: 243, 308, 5-shot mag.
Barrel: 22″ round tapered.
Weight: 6½ lbs. **Length:** 43″ over-all.
Stock: Walnut, Monte Carlo, checkered p.g. and fore-end.
Sights: Ramp, gold bead front; rear adj. for e.
Features: Recessed bolt head, top tang safety, hinged magazine floorplate, Receiver tapped for scope mount.
Price: $125.00

Winchester 70A Magnum Rifle

Same as 70A except with black recoil pad and in these cals.: 264, 7mm Rem., 300 Win., 3-round mag. capacity. Wgt. 7¼ lbs. 24″ bbl., 44″ over-all. R. H. twist: 9″ in 264, 9½″ in 7mm Rem. 10″ in 300 Win. **$180.00**

WINCHESTER 70A BOLT ACTION RIFLE

Caliber: 222, 22-250, 243, 25-06, 270, 30-06, 308.
Barrel: 22″ (25-06, has 24″).
Weight: 7⅛ to 7½ lbs. **Length:** 42½″ (22″ bbl.).
Stock: Monte Carlo, checkering at p.g. and fore-end.
Sights: Removeable hooded ramp front, adj. open rear.
Features: Sling swivels installed, three position safety, deep cut checkering.
Price: **$165.00**

Winchester 70 Target Rifle

Same as M70 except: heavy 24″ barrel, contoured aluminum handstop that fits left and right hand shooter, high comb target stock. Tapped for micrometer sights, clip slot in receiver, cals. 308 and 30-06. .... **$295.00**

WINCHESTER 70 STANDARD RIFLE

Caliber: 222, 22-250, 25-06, 243, 270, 308 and 30-06, 5-shot.
Barrel: 22″ swaged, floating. 10″ twist (222 & 22-250 have 14″ twist, 308 is 12″).
Weight: 7½ lbs. **Length:** 42½″ over-all.
Stock: Walnut, Monte Carlo, (13½″x1¾″x1½″x2⅛″) checkered p.g. and fore-end.
Sights: Removable hooded bead ramp front, adj. open rear.
Features: Sling swivels installed, steel p.g. cap, hinged floorplate, receiver tapped for scope mounts.
Price: **$195.00**

Winchester 70 Magnum Rifle

Same as M70 Standard except with recoil pad and in these magnum cals.: 7 Rem., 264, 300, 338 Win., 375 H&H, 3-round mag. capacity. Wgt. 7¾ lbs. (8½ lbs. in 375), 24″ bbl., 44½″ over-all. R.H. twist: 9″ in 264, 9½″ in 7mm, 10″ in 300, 338. .... **$210.00**
Cal. 375 H&H **$285.00**

Winchester 70 African

Same as M70 Standard except: 458 Win. Mag. only, 3-shot. 22″ non-floating heavy bbl. 14″ twist. Stock measures 13½″x1⅜″x1¾″x2⅜″, has ebony fore-end tip and grip cap; wgt. 8½ lbs., recoil pad and special rear sight.
Price: **$375.00**

Winchester 70 Varmint Rifle

Same as M70 Standard except: 222, 22-250, and 243 only, target scope blocks, no sights, 24″ heavy bbl., 14″ twist in 22-250, 10″ twist in 243. 44½″ over-all, 9¾ lbs. Stock measures 13½″x9/16″x15/16″x⅜″ from bore line.
Price: **$210.00**

WINSLOW BOLT ACTION RIFLE

Caliber: All standard cartridges (magnum add $10).
Barrel: 24″ Douglas premium. (Magnums 26″)
Weight: 7-7½ lbs. **Length:** 43″ over-all.
Stock: Hand rubbed black walnut, choice of two styles
Sights: None. Metallics available at extra cost.
Features: Receivers tapped for scope mounts, QD swivels and recoil pad installed. 4-shot blind mag.
Price: Regal Grade **$390.00**
Regent, Regimental, Crown, Emperor and Imperial grades in ascending order of carving, engraving and inlaying, to **$3525.00**
Regal grade Varmint in 17/222 (std or Mag.) or 17/223.
Price: From **$430.00**

BROWNING MODEL '78 SINGLE-SHOT RIFLE
Caliber: 30-06, 25-06, 6mm Rem. 22-250.
Barrel: 26", tapered octagon or medium round.
Length: 42" over-all. **Weight:** Oct. bbl. 7¾ lbs., round.
Stock: Select walnut, hand rubbed finish, hand checkered (13⅝"x1⅛"*x8/32"*). Rubber recoil pad. *Bore measurement.
Sights: None. Furnished with scope mount and rings.
Features: Closely resembles M1885 High Wall rifle. Falling block action with exposed hammer, auto. ejector. Adj. trigger (3½ to 4½ lbs.) Half-cock safety.
Price: **$264.50**

Clerke Deluxe Single-Shot Hi-Wall
Same as standard model except: Adj. trigger, features half-octagon barrel, presentation grade walnut checkered p.g. stock with cheekpiece. Plain trigger. Double set trigger avail. for $35.00 extra. Without slot cut in bbl. for rear sight **$240.00**

CLERKE SINGLE-SHOT HI-WALL RIFLE
Caliber: 222, 223, 22-250, 243, 6mm Rem., 250 Sav., 257 Rob., 25-06, 264 Win., 270, 7mm Rem. Mag., 30-30, 30-06, 300 Win., 375 H&H, 458 Win., 45-70.
Barrel: 26" medium weight.
Stock: Walnut p.g. stock and for-end,white line spacer with black buttplate.
Sights: None furnished. Drilled and tapped.
Features: Std. model: Exposed hammer, curved finger lever, Schnabel fore-end.
Price: **$190.00**

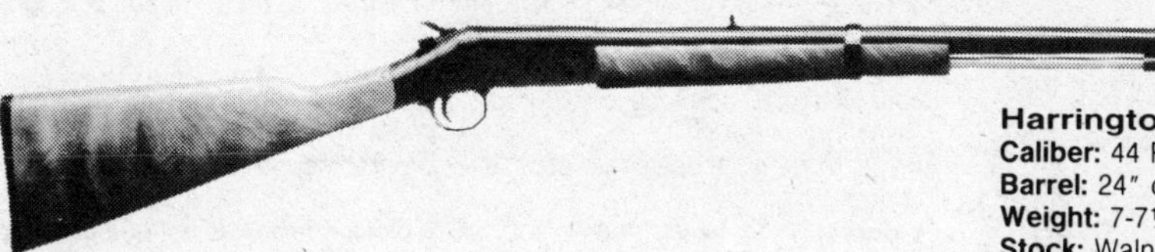

Harrington & Richardson Model 155 "Shikari"
Caliber: 44 Rem. Mag. or 45-70, single-shot.
Barrel: 24" or 28" 45-70, 24" (44 Mag.).
Weight: 7-7½ lbs. **Length:** 39" over-all (24" bbl.).
Stock: Walnut finished hardwood.
Sights: Blade front, adj. folding leaf rear.
Features: Blue-black finish with color case hardened frame. Exposed hammer. Solid brass cleaning rod with hardwood handle included.
Price: Either caliber **$73.00**

HARRINGTON AND RICHARDSON 158 TOPPER RIFLE
Caliber: 30-30 and 22 Hornet.
Barrel: 22" round tapered.
Weight: 5¼ lbs. **Length:** 37½"
Stock: Walnut finished stock and fore-end; recoil pad.
Sights: Lyman folding adj. rear and ramp front sights.
Features: Side lever break-open action with visible hammer. Easy takedown. Converts to 20 ga. Shotgun with accessory bbl. ($20 extra).
Price: 22 Hornet or 30-30 .... **$53.00**
Price: Rifle/shotgun combo **$73.00**

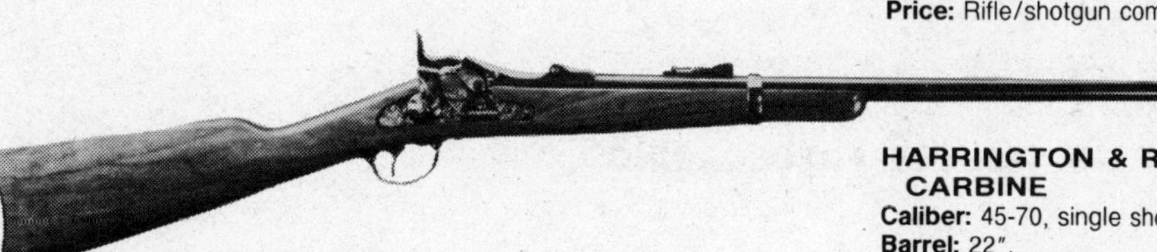

HARRINGTON & RICHARDSON OFFICERS MODEL 1873
Caliber: 45-70, single shot
Barrel: 26" round.
Weight: About 8 lbs. **Length:** 44" over-all
Stock: Oil finished walnut, checkered at wrist and fore-end white metal tipped.
Sights: Blade front, vernier tang rear adj. for w. & e.
Features: Replica of the 1873 Springfield has engraved breech block, side lock and hammer. comes with commemorative plaque.
Price: **$250.00**

HARRINGTON & RICHARDSON CAVALRY MODEL CARBINE
Caliber: 45-70, single shot.
Barrel: 22".
Weight: 7 lbs. **Length:** 41".
Stock: American walnut with saddle ring and bridle.
Sights: Blade front, barrel mounted leaf rear adj. for e.
Features: Replica of the 1871 Springfield Carbine. Blue-black finish.
Price: **$158.00**
Deluxe version shown shown has engraved breech block, side lock & hammer **$211.00**
Springfield Armory Museum silver plated carbine **$1,000.00**

HARRINGTON & RICHARDSON L.B.H. COMMEMORATIVE CARBINE
Caliber: 45-70, single shot.
Barrel: 22".
Weight: 7 lbs., 4 oz. **Length:** 41".
Stock: American walnut with metal grip adapter.
Sights: Blade front, tang mounted aperature rear adj. for w. and e.
Features: Replica of the 1871 Springfield carbine. Engraved breech block, side lock and hammer. Action color case hardened. Each comes with book entitled "In the Valley of the Little Big Horn".
Price: **$211.00**

U.S. CENTERFIRE RIFLES—SINGLE SHOT

HYPER-SINGLE RIFLE

Caliber: All calibers, standard and wildcat.
Barrel: Choice of maker, weight, length (std. twist and contours).
Length: To customer specs. **Weight:** To customer specs.
Stock: To customer specs. AA fancy American black walnut is standard.
Sights: None furnished. Drilled and tapped for scope mounts.
Features: Falling block action. Striker rotates on bronze bearing and is powered by dual coil springs. Trigger adj. for weight, pull and travel. Tang safety. Octagon receiver on special order (same price).
Price: Complete Rifle .... **$850.00** Barreled action **$525.00**
Price: Action only (blank extractor) **$400.00**
Price: Stainless steel barrel (extra) **$60.00**
Price: Fluted or octagon barrel (extra) **$75.00**

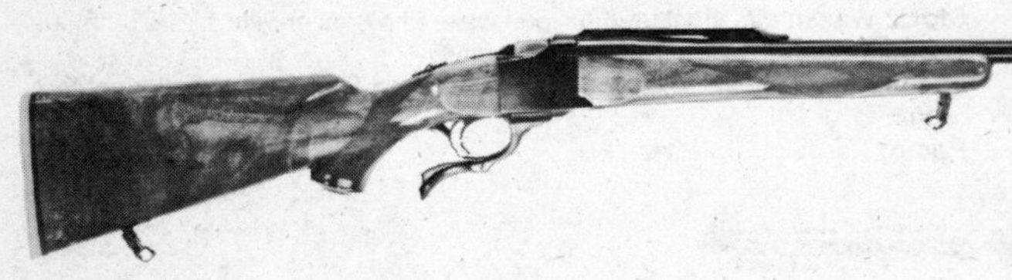

RUGER NUMBER ONE SINGLE SHOT

Caliber: 22-250, 243, 6mm Rem., 25-06, 270, 30-06, 7mm Rem. Mag., 300 Win., 45-70, 458 Win. Mag., 375 H&H Mag.
Barrel: 26″ round tapered with quarter-rib (also 22″ and 24″, depending upon model).
Weight: 8 lbs. **Length:** 42″ over-all.
Stock: Walnut, two-piece, checkered p.g. and fore-end (either semi-beavertail or Henry style).
Sights: None, 1″ scope rings supplied for integral mounts. 3 models have open sights.
Features: Under lever, hammerless falling block design has auto ejector, top tang safety. Standard Rifle 1B illus.
Price: **$265.00**
Available also as Light Sporter, Medium Sporter, Special Varminter or Tropical Rifle **$265.00**

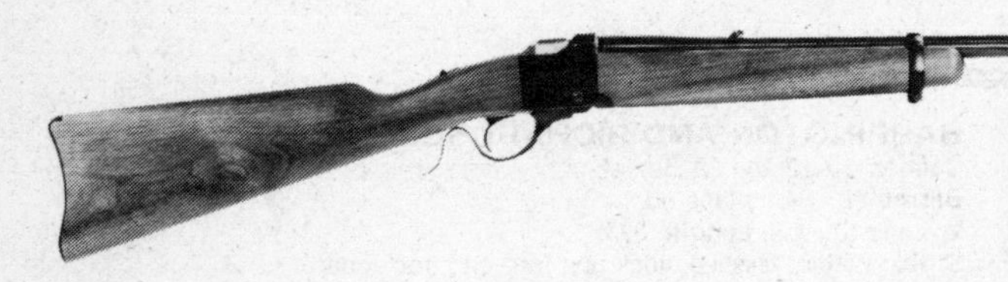

RUGER NO. 3 CARBINE SINGLE SHOT

Caliber: 22 Hornet, 30-40 Krag, 45-70.
Barrel: 22″ round.
Weight: 6 lbs. **Length:** 38½″.
Stock: American walnut, carbine-type.
Sights: Gold bead front, adj. folding leaf rear. 22 Hornet tapped for target scope mounts.
Features: Same action as No. 1 Rifle except different lever. Has auto ejector, top tang safety, adj. trigger.
Price: **$165.00**

U.S. RIMFIRE AUTOLOADING

BROWNING AUTOLOADING RIFLE

Caliber: 22 LR, 11-shot.
Barrel: 19¼ lbs.
Weight: 4¾ lbs. **Length:** 37″ over-all.
Stock: Checkered select walnut (13¾″x1 13/16″x2⅝″) with p.g. and semi-beavertail fore-end.
Sights: Gold bead front, folding leaf rear.
Features: Engraved receiver is grooved for tip-off scope mount; cross-bolt safety; tubular magazine in buttstock; easy take down for carrying or storage.
Price: Grade I .... **$119.50** Grade II .... **$179.50** Grade III **$349.50**
Also available in Grade I, 22 S (16-shot) **$119.50**

CHARTER AR-7 EXPLORER CARBINE

Caliber: 22 LR, 8-shot autoloading.
Barrel: 16″ alloy (steel-lined).
Weight: 2¾ lbs. **Length:** 34½″/16½″ stowed.
Stock: Moulded grey Cycloac, snap-on rubber butt pad.
Features: Take-down design stores bbl. and action in hollow stock. Light enough to float.
Price: **$59.95**

COLT COLTEER AUTOLOADING CARBINE

Caliber: 22LR, 15-shot tubular mag.
Barrel: 19⅜".
Weight: 4¾ lbs. **Length:** 37" over-all
Stock: Straight grip black walnut stock (13¾"x1⅝"x2¼") beavertail fore-end.
Sights: Hooded gold bead front sight with notched rear adj. for w. and e.
Features: Full length magazine tube; Cross-bolt Safety. Receiver grooved for tip-off scope mount.
Price: **$65.50**

Colt Courier Autoloading Rifle

Same as the Colteer except; p.g. stock with tapered fore-end (no fore-end bbl. band).
Price: **$65.50**

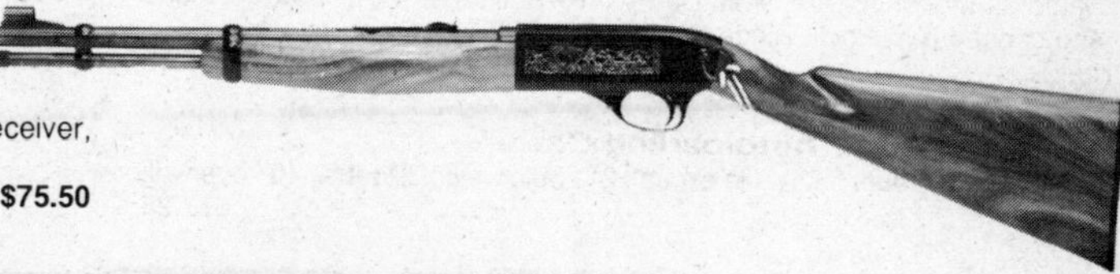

Colt Stagecoach Autoloading Carbine

Similar to Colteer except: 16" bbl., 33⅝" over-all. Scroll engraved receiver, with saddle ring. 22 LR only.
Price: **$75.50**

HIGH STANDARD SPORT KING AUTO RIFLE

Caliber: 22 S (21), L (17), LR (15). Tubular magazine.
Barrel: 22¼".
Weight: 5½ lbs. **Length:** 42¾" over-all.
Stock: Walnut. Monte Carlo cheekpiece, semi-beavertail fore-end.
Sights: Post front, "Rocky Mountain" rear adj. for e.
Features: Right-side thumb safety, side loading magazine. Checkered p.g. with cap. Receiver dove-tailed for scope mounting.
Price: **$74.95**

MARLIN 49DL AUTOLOADING RIFLE

Caliber: 22 LR, 18-shot tubular magazine
Barrel: 22" Micro-Groove
Weight: 5½ lbs. **Length:** 40½"
Stock: American walnut, Monte Carlo capped p.g., checkered fore-end and p.g.,
Sights: Blade ramp front, step rear adj. for w. & e.
Features: Gold plated trigger, bolt hold-open for safety and cleaning, scroll-engraved receiver grooved for tip-off scope mounts.
Price: **$65.95**

MARLIN 99 M1 AUTOLOADING CARBINE

Caliber: 22 LR, 9-shot tubular magazine
Barrel: 18" Micro-Groove
Weight: 4½ lbs. **Length:** 37"
Stock: Monte Carlo American walnut with p.g. and handguard. White buttplate spacer.
Sights: Blade on band type ramp front, removable flat-top mid-sight adj. for w. & e.
Features: Gold plated trigger, bolt hold-open, serrated receiver top is grooved for tip-off scope mount, sling swivels attached.
Price: **$58.95**

Marlin 99C Autoloading Rifle

Same as the Marlin 49DL except: one piece American walnut stock with checkered p.g. and fore-end.
Price: **$58.95**

Marlin 989 M2 Autoloading Carbine

Same as the Marlin 99 M1 carbine except 7-shot detachable clip magazine.
Price: **$58.95**

MARLIN GLENFIELD 60 AUTOLOADER

Caliber: 22 LR, 18-shot tubular mag.
Barrel: 22" round tapered.
Weight: About 5½ lbs. **Length:** 41" Over-all.
Stock: Walnut finished Monte Carlo, checkered p.g. and fore-end.
Sights: Blade ramp front, step adj. rear.
Features: Chrome plated trigger, matted receiver is grooved for tip-off mounts.
Price: **$50.95**

MOSSBERG MODEL 353 RIFLE

Caliber: 22 LR, 7-shot clip.
Barrel: 18" "AC-KRO-GRUV".
Weight: 5 lbs. **Length:** 38" over-all.
Stock: Walnut, checkered at p.g. and fore-end. Black Tenite two-positions.
Sights: Open step adj. U-notch rear, bead front on ramp.
Features: Sling swivels and web strap on left of stock, extension fore-end folds down for steady firing from prone position. Receiver grooved for scope mounting.
Price: **$66.90**

REMINGTON 552A AUTOLOADING RIFLE
Caliber: 22 S (20), L (17) or LR (15) tubular mag.
Barrel: 23″ round tapered.
Weight: about 5¾ lbs. **Length:** 42″ over-all.
Stock: Full-size, walnut with p.g.
Sights: Bead front, step adj. open rear.
Features: Positive cross-bolt safety, receiver grooved for tip-off mount.
Price: $77.95
Price: M552GS (22 Short only) $89.95

Remington Model 552BDL Auto Rifle
Same as Model 552A except: Du Pont RKW finished checkered fore-end and capped p.g. stock. Blade ramp front and fully adj. rear sights.
Price: $87.95

Remington 552C Autoloading Carbine
Same as the Model 552A rifle except: 21″ bbl., weight 5½ lbs., 40″ over-all.
Price: $77.95

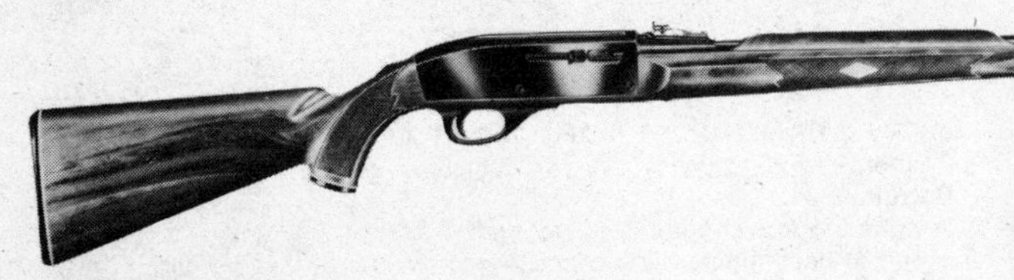

REMINGTON NYLON 66MB AUTO RIFLE
Caliber: 22 LR, 14-shot tubular mag.
Barrel: 19⅝″ round tapered.
Weight: 4 lbs. **Length:** 38½″ over-all.
Stock: Moulded Mohawk Brown Nylon, checkered p.g. and fore-end.
Sights: Blade ramp front, adj. open rear.
Features: Top tang safety, double extractors, receiver grooved for tip-off mounts.
Price: $64.95
Price: Model 66GS (22 Short only) $74.95
Price: With Universal UA 4x scope $69.95

Remington Nylon 66AB Auto Rifle
Same as the Model 66MB except: Apache Black Nylon stock, chrome plated receiver.
Price: $69.95

Remington Mowhawk 10C Auto Rifle
Same as Nylon 66 rifle except: removable 10-shot 22 LR clip magazine.
Price: $54.95
Extra 5-shot clip .... $2.75 Extra 10-shot clip $3.50

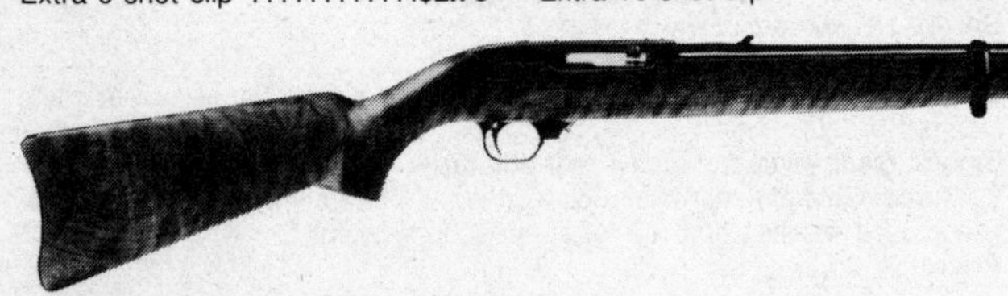

RUGER 10/22 AUTOLOADING CARBINE
Caliber: 22 LR, 10-shot rotary mag.
Barrel: 18½″ round tapered.
Weight: 5 lbs. **Length:** 37″ over-all.
Stock: American walnut with p.g. and bbl. band.
Sights: Gold bead front, fully adj. folding leaf rear.
Features: Detachable rotary magazine fits flush into stock, cross-bolt safety, receiver tapped and grooved for scope blocks or tip-off mount. Scope base adapter furnished with each rifle.
Price: $59.75

Ruger 10/22 Auto Sporter
Same as 10/22 Carbine except: Hand checkered p.g. and fore-end with straight buttplate, no bbl., bands, sling swivels.
Price: $74.50

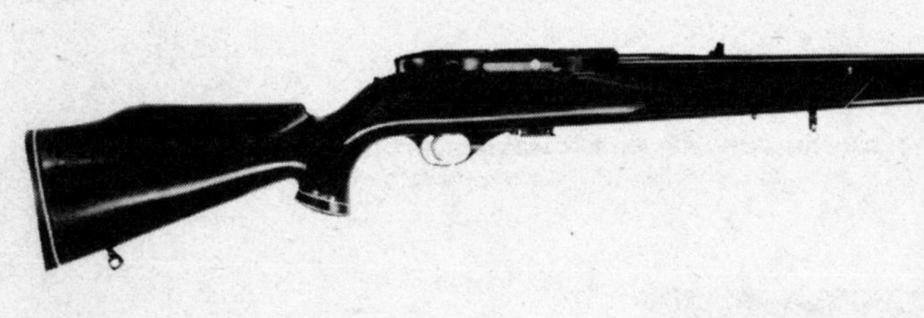

WEATHERBY MARK XXII AUTO RIFLE, CLIP MODEL
Caliber: 22 LR only, 5- or 10-shot clip loaded
Barrel: 24″ round contoured.
Weight: 6 lbs. **Length:** 42¼″ over-all.
Stock: Walnut, Monte Carlo comb and cheekpiece, rosewood p.g. cap and fore-end tip. Skip-line checkering.
Sights: Gold bead ramp front, 3-leaf folding rear.
Features: Thumb operated side safety also acts as single shot selector. Receiver grooved for tip-off scope mount. Single pin release for quick take-down.
Price: $149.50
Extra 5-shot clip .... $3.95 Extra 10-shot clip $4.50

Weatherby Mark XXII Tubular Model
Same as Mark XXII Clip Model except: 15-shot tubular magazine. $149.50

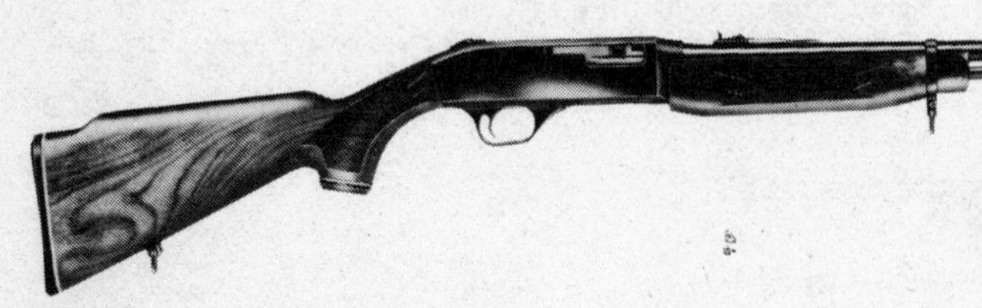

WESTERN FIELD 894 AUTO RIFLE
Caliber: 22 LR, 15-shot tubular mag.
Barrel: 20″ round.
Weight: 6¼ lbs. **Length:** 39″ over-all.
Stock: Walnut, checkered p.g. and fore-end, p.g. cap and butt plate with white line spacers.
Sights: Bead front on ramp, folding leaf rear.
Features: Top side safety, automatic bolt hold open after last shot.
Price: $63.95

WESTERN FIELD 868 AUTO RIFLE
Caliber: 22 LR, 15-shot tubular mag.
Barrel: 20″.
Weight: 6½ lbs. **Length:** 39½″ over-all.
Stock: Walnut finish p.g. and fore-end.
Sights: Ramp front, rear adj. for e.
Features: Sling swivels, plastic butt plate.
Price: $52.95

U.S. RIMFIRE—AUTOLOADING

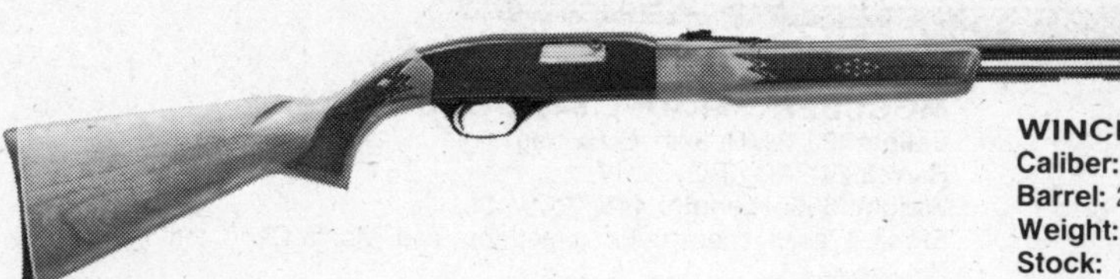

WINCHESTER 290 AUTOLOADING RIFLE
Caliber: 22 L (17) or LR (15), tubular mag.
Barrel: 20½″ round tapered (16″ twist).
Weight: 5 lbs. **Length:** 39″ over-all.
Stock: 2-piece walnut finished hardwood. checkered p.g. and fore-end, (13⅝″x1¾″x2¾″).
Sights: Bead post front, step adj. rear.
Features: Cross-bolt safety, composition buttplate with white line spacer, receiver grooved for tip-off scope mount.
Price: **$72.95**

Winchester 190 Auto Rifle
Same as M290 except: No checkering, pistol grip cap or buttplate spacer.
Price: **$59.95**

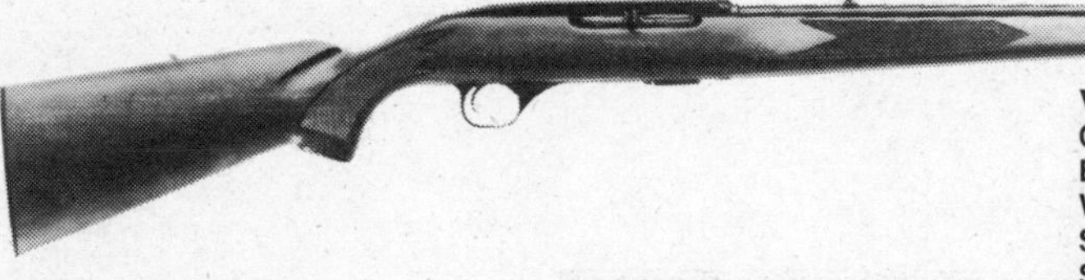

WINCHESTER MODEL 490 AUTO RIFLE
Caliber: 22 LR only, detachable 5-shot clip.
Barrel: 22″.
Weight: 6 lbs. **Length:** 42″ over-all.
Stock: Walnut, checkered p.g. and fore-end, p.g. cap.
Sights: Folding leaf rear, hooded ramp front.
Features: Receiver grooved for scope mounting, hold-open lock, cross bolt safety. Ten-shot clip available at extra cost.
Price: **$94.95**

U.S. RIMFIRE—BOLT ACTION

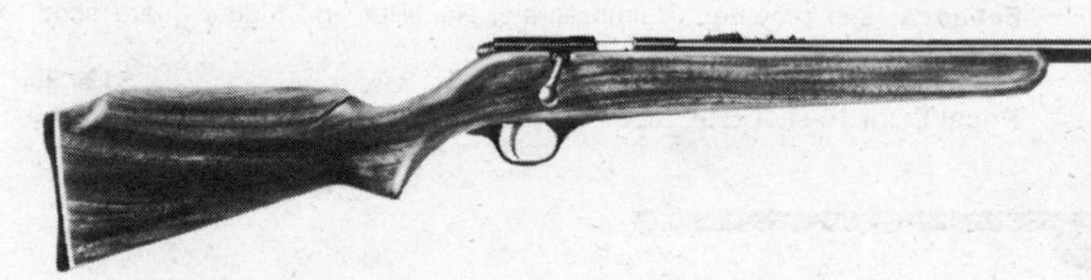

HARRINGTON & RICHARDSON 865 PLAINSMAN RIFLE
Caliber: 22 S, L or LR. 5-shot clip mag.
Barrel: 22″ round tapered.
Weight: 5 lbs. **Length:** 39″ over-all.
Stock: Walnut finished hardwood with Monte Carlo and p.g.
Sights: Blade front, step adj. open rear.
Features: Cocking indicator, sliding side safety, receiver grooved for tip-off scope mounts.
Price: **$51.00**

MARLIN 780 BOLT ACTION RIFLE
Caliber: 22 S, L, or LR; 7-shot clip magazine.
Barrel: 22″ Micro-Groove
Weight: 5½ lbs. **Length:** 41″
Stock: Monte Carlo American walnut with checkered p.g. White line spacer at buttplate.
Sights: "Wide-Scan" ramp front, folding semi-buckhorn rear adj. for w. & e.
Features: Gold plated trigger receiver anti-glare serrated and grooved for tip-off scope mount.
Price: **$54.95**

Marlin 781 Bolt Action Rifle
Same as the Marlin 780 except: tubular magazine holds 25 Shorts, 19 Longs or 17 Long Rifle cartridges. Weight 6 lbs. **$56.95**

Marlin 782 Bolt Action Rifle
Same as the Marlin 780 except: 22 Rimfire Magnum cal. only, weight about 6 lbs. Sling and swivels attached. **$59.95**

Marlin 783 Bolt Action Rifle
Same as Marlin 782 except: Tubular magazine holds 13 rounds of 22 Rimfire Magnum ammunition. **$61.95**

Marlin Glenfield 20 Bolt Action Repeater
Similar to Marlin 780, except: Walnut finished checkered p.g. stock, without Monte Carlo, conventional rifling. **$44.95**

MOSSBERG MODEL 341 RIFLE
Caliber: 22 S, L, LR, 7-shot clip.
Barrel: 24″ "AG-KRO-GRUV"
Weight: 6½ lbs. **Length:** 43½″ over-all.
Stock: Walnut, checkered p.g. and fore-end, Monte Carlo and cheek piece. Buttplate with white line spacer.
Sights: Open, U-notch rear adj. for w. and e.
Features: Sliding side safety, 8 groove rifling, "Magic 3-way" clip adjusts to Short, Long or Long Rifle cartridges.
Price: **$58.70**

MOSSBERG MODEL 340B RIFLE
Caliber: 22 S, L, LR, 7-shot clip.
Barrel: 24″ "AC-KRO-GRUV".
Weight: 6 lbs. **Length:** 43½″ over-all.
Stock: Walnut finish with p.g., Monte Carlo and cheek piece, sling swivels.
Sights: Mossberg S331 receiver peep with ¼-minute adjustments for w. and e. S320 Mossberg hooded ramp front.
Features: Front sight offers choice of post or aperture elements. "Magic 3-Way" clip adjusts for Short, Long or Long Rifle cartridges. Receiver grooved for scope mount.
Price: **$63.50**

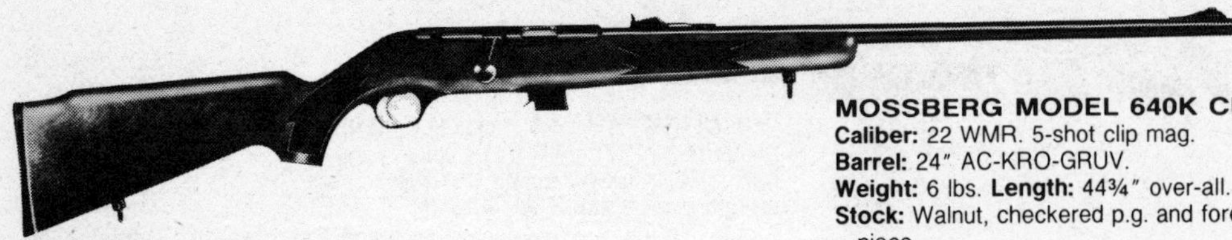

MOSSBERG MODEL 640K CHUCKSTER
Caliber: 22 WMR. 5-shot clip mag.
Barrel: 24″ AC-KRO-GRUV.
Weight: 6 lbs. **Length:** 44¾″ over-all.
Stock: Walnut, checkered p.g. and fore-end, Monte Carlo comb and cheekpiece.
Sights: Ramp front with bead, fully adj. leaf rear.
Features: Grooved trigger, sliding side safety, double extractors, receiver grooved for tip-off scope mounts and tapped for aperture rear sight.
Price: **$67.40**

MOSSBERG MODEL 321K
Caliber: 22 S, L, LR, single shot.
Barrel: 24″.
Length: 43½″ over-all. **Weight:** 6½ lbs.
Stock: Walnut finish, cheekpiece, checkered p.g. and fore-end.
Sights: Ramp front, adj. rear.
Features: Hammerless bolt action with drop-in loading platform and automatic safety, black buttplate. Model 321B has S330 peep sight with ¼-minute click adjustments.
Price: **$51.70**

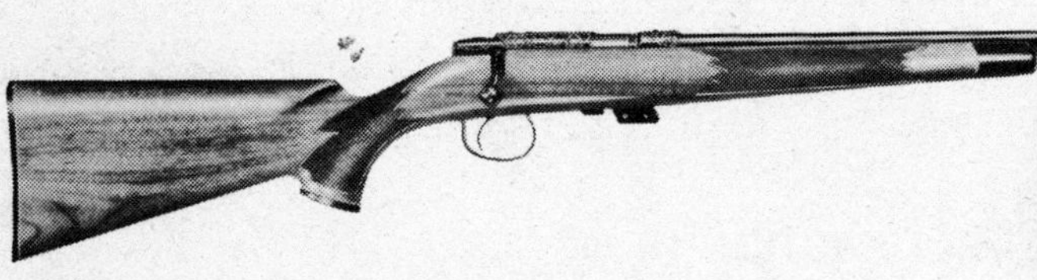

REMINGTON MODEL 541-S
Barrel: 24″
Weight: 5½ lbs. **Length:** 42⅝″.
Stock: Walnut, checkered p.g. and fore end.
Sights: None. Drilled and tapped for scope mounts or receiver sights.
Features: Clip repeater. Thumb safety. Receiver and trigger guard scroll engraved.
Price: **$134.95**
Price: Extra 10-shot clip **$3.50**

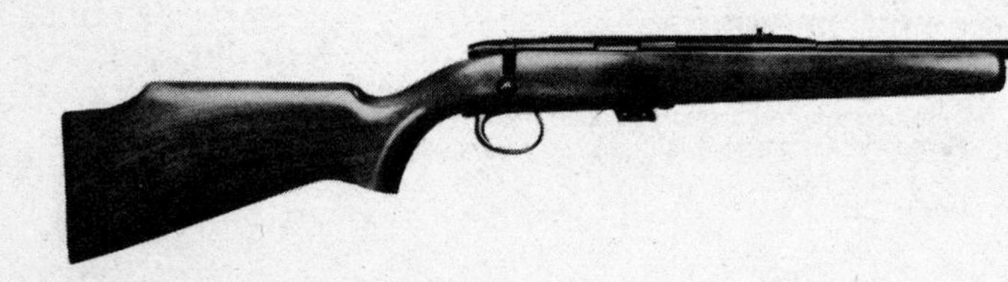

REMINGTON MODEL 581 RIFLE
Caliber: 22 S, L or LR. 5-shot clip mag.
Barrel: 24″ round.
Weight: 4¾ lbs. **Length:** 42⅜″ over-all.
Stock: Walnut finished Monte Carlo with p.g.
Sights: Bead post front, screw adj. open rear.
Features: Sliding side safety, wide trigger, receiver grooved for tip-off scope mounts.
Price: **$57.95**
Price: Left hand action and stock **$62.95**

Remington Model 582 Rifle
Same as M581 except: tubular magazine under bbl. holds 20 S, 15 L or 14 LR cartridges. Wgt. 5½ lbs.
Price: **$64.95**

SAVAGE/ANSCHUTZ 164 BOLT ACTION RIFLE
Caliber: 22 LR. 5-shot clip mag.
Barrel: 24″ round tapered.
Weight: 6 lbs. **Length:** 40¾″ over-all
Stock: Walnut, hand checkered p.g. and fore-end, Monte Carlo comb and cheekpiece, schnabel fore-end.
Sights: Hooded ramp gold bead front, folding-leaf rear.
Features: Fully adj. single stage trigger, sliding side safety, receiver grooved for tip-off mount.
Price: **$146.00**
Price: Model 164M in 22 WRM (4-shot) **$161.00**

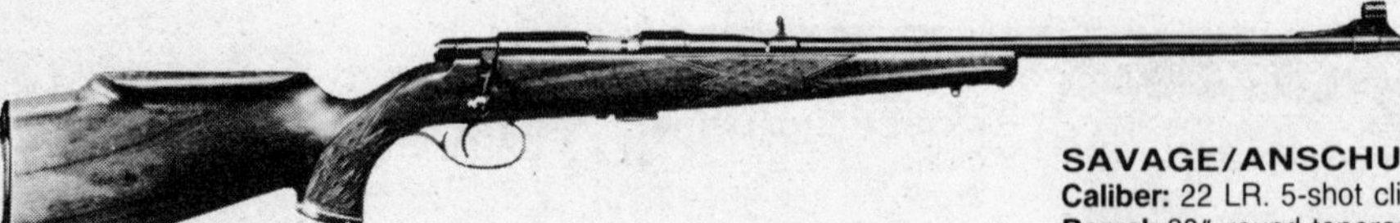

SAVAGE/ANSCHUTZ MODEL 54 SPORTER
Caliber: 22 LR. 5-shot clip mag.
Barrel: 23″ round tapered.
Weight: 6¾ lbs. **Length:** 42″ over-all.
Stock: French walnut, checkered p.g. and fore-end. Monte Carlo roll-over comb, schnabel fore-end tip.
Sights: Hooded ramp gold bead front, folding-leaf rear.
Features: Adj. single stage trigger, wing safety, receiver grooved for tip-off mount, tapped for scope blocks.
Price: **$255.00**
Price: Model 54M (22 WRM) **$270.00**

Savage/Anschutz Model 1432 Sporter
Same as Model 54 except chambered for 22 Hornet, 24″ barrel, 5-shot capacity, over-all length 43⅝″ **$298.50**

SAVAGE/ANSCHUTZ MODEL 184 BOLT ACTION RIFLE
Caliber: 22 LR, 5-shot clip.
Barrel: 21½″.
Weight: 4½ lbs. **Length:** 39½″.
Stock: Walnut, Monte Carlo comb, hand checkered p.g. and fore-end, schnabel fore-end.
Sights: Hooded ramp gold bead front, folding-leaf rear.
Features: Side safety, crisp factory-set trigger, receiver grooved for scope mounting.
Price: **$114.99**

U.S. RIMFIRE—BOLT ACTION

Savage/Stevens Model 34 Rifle
Same as the Model 65-M except: 22 LR, walnut finished hardwood stock, bead post front sight.
Price: **$45.65**

SAVAGE MODEL 65-M RIFLE
Caliber: 22 WRM, 5-shot.
Barrel: 20″ lightweight, free floating.
Weight: 5 lbs. **Length:** 39″ over-all.
Stock: Walnut, Monte Carlo comb. checkered p.g. and fore-end.
Sights: Gold bead ramp front, step adj. open rear.
Features: Sliding side safety, double extractors, receiver grooved for tip-off scope mount.
Price: **$55.65**

WESTERN FIELD 832 BOLT ACTION RIFLE
Caliber: 22 S, L, LR; 7-shot clip.
Barrel: 24″ round tapered.
Length: 43″ over-all. **Weight:** 6½ lbs.
Stock: Walnut p.g. and fore-end, checkered p.g.
Sights: Ramp front, rear adj. for e.
Features: Thumb operated safety, sling swivels.
Price: **$50.00**
Price: Model 822 in 22 WRM **$60.00**

WINCHESTER 320 BOLT ACTION REPEATER
Caliber: 22 S, L, LR, 5-shot clip.
Barrel: 22″ round tapered.
Weight: 5⅝ lbs. **Length:** 39½″ over-all.
Stock: Walnut, Monte Carlo, checkered p.g. and fore-end. 13½″ pull.
Sights: Bead on ramp front, step adj. rear.
Features: Wide serrated trigger, positive safety, matted receiver is tapped for scope and micrometer sights. Sling swivels installed.
Price: **$59.95**
Extra 5-shot clip **$3.15**
Extra 10-shot clip **$3.95**

U.S. RIMFIRE — LEVER ACTION

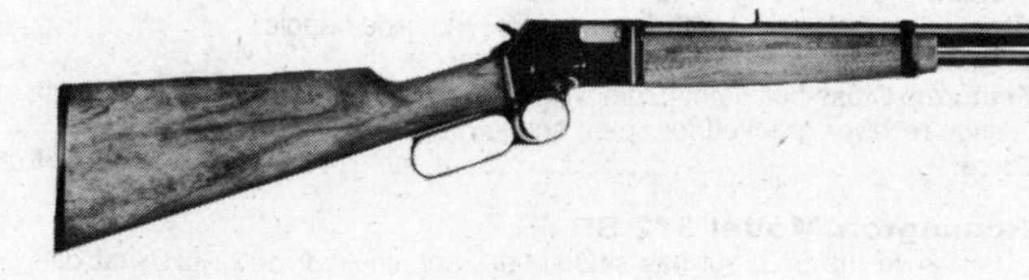

BROWNING BL-22 LEVER ACTION RIFLE
Caliber: 22 S(22), L(17) or LR(15). Tubular mag.
Barrel: 20″ round tapered.
Weight: 5 lbs. **Length:** 36¾″ over-all.
Stock: Walnut, 2-piece straight grip western style.
Sights: Bead post front, folding-leaf rear.
Features: Short throw lever, ½-cock safety, receiver grooved for tip-off scope mounts.
Price: Grade I **$99.50**
Price: Grade II, engraved receiver, checkered grip and fore-end .. **$116.50**

Ithaca Model 72 De Luxe
Same as standard Model 72 except has octagon barrel, engraved silver-finish frame, "semi-fancy" European walnut stock, steel buttplate **$149.95**

ITHACA MODEL 72 SADDLEGUN
Caliber: 22 LR, 15-shot magazine tube.
Barrel: 18½″.
Weight: 5 lbs.
Stock: American walnut.
Sights: Hooded front, step-adj. rear.
Features: Half-cock safety, steel receiver grooved for scope mounts.
Price: **$99.95**

MARLIN GOLDEN 39A LEVER ACTION RIFLE
Caliber: 22 S(26), L(21), LR(19), tubular magazine.
Barrel: 24″ Micro-Groove.
Weight: 6¾ lbs. **Length:** 40″.
Stock: American walnut with white line spacers at p.g. cap and buttplate.
Sights: Bead ramp front with detachable "Wide-Scan" hood, folding rear semi-buckhorn adj. for w. and e.
Features: Take-down action, receiver tapped for scope mount (supplied), gold plated trigger, sling swivels, offset hammer spur. Scope **$19.95** extra.
Price: **$111.95**

U.S. RIMFIRE—LEVER ACTION

MARLIN GOLDEN 39M CARBINE

Caliber: 22 S(21), L(16), LR(15), tubular magazine.
Barrel: 20″ Micro-Groove.
Weight: 6 lbs. **Length:** 36″.
Stock: American walnut, straight grip, white line buttplate spacer.
Sights: "Wide-Scan" bead ramp front with hood, folding rear semi-buckhorn adj. for w. and e.
Features: Receiver tapped for scope mount (supplied) or receiver sight, gold plated trigger, offset hammer spur, sling swivels, take-down action.
Price: **$111.95**

WINCHESTER 9422 LEVER ACTION RIFLE

Caliber: 22 S(21), L(17), LR(15). Tubular mag.
Barrel: 20½″ (16″ twist).
Length: 37⅛″ over-all. **Weight:** 6½ lbs.
Stock: American walnut, 2-piece, straight grip (no p.g.).
Sights: Hooded ramp ront, adj. semi-byckhorn rear.
Features: Side ejection, receiver grooved for scope mounting, takedown action.
Price: **$124.95**

Winchester 9422M Lever Action Rifle
Same as the 9422 except chambered for 22 WMR cartridge, has 11-round mag. capacity **$129.95**

U.S. RIMFIRE — SLIDE ACTION

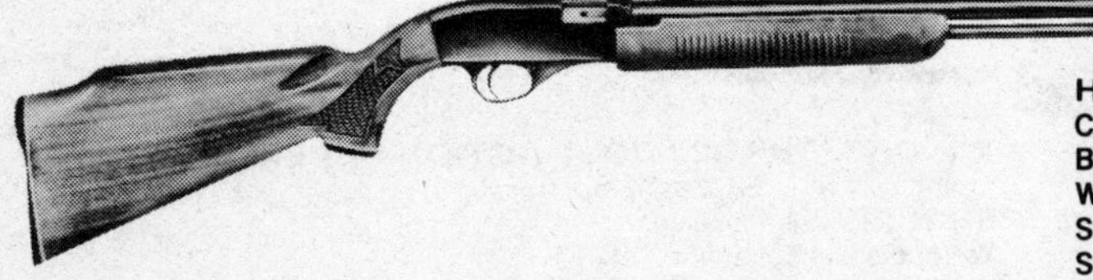

HIGH STANDARD FLITE-KING PUMP RIFLE

Caliber: 22 S (24), L (19), LR (17). Tubular magazine.
Barrel: 24″.
Weight: 5½ lbs. **Length:** 41¾″ over-all.
Stock: Walnut. Monte Carlo cheekpiece, semi-beavertail fore-end.
Sights: Post front, "Rocky Mountain" read adj. for e.
Features: Checkered p.g., grooved slide handle, p.g. cap and buttplate with white line spacers. Side ejection. Receiver grooved for scope mount.
Price: **$79.95**

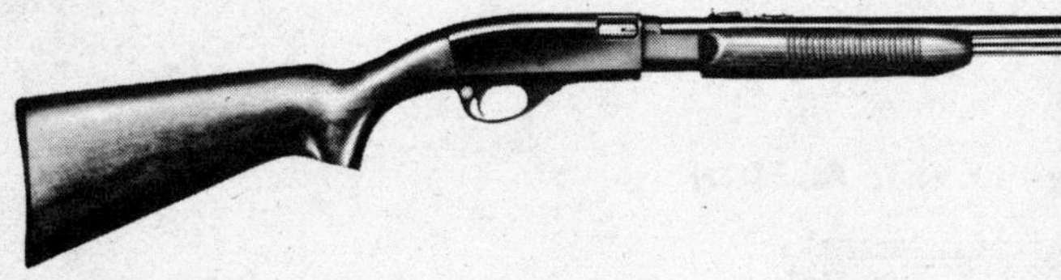

REMINGTON 572 FIELDMASTER PUMP RIFLE

Caliber: 22 S(20), L(17) or LR(14). Tubular mag.
Barrel: 24″ round tapered.
Weight: 5½ lbs. **Length:** 42″ over-all.
Stock: Genuine walnut with p.g. and grooved slide handle.
Sights: Bead post front, step adj. open rear.
Features: Cross-bolt safety, removing inner mag. tube converts rifle to single shot, receiver grooved for tip-off scope mount.
Price: **$79.95**

Remington Model 572 BDL Deluxe
Same as the 572 except: p.g. cap, RKW finish, checkered grip and fore-end, ramp front and fully adj. rear sights.
Price: **$89.95**

Remington Model 572 SB
Similar to the 572, but has smoothbore bbl. choked for 22 LR shot cartridges.
Sling and swivels installed **$7.50**
Price: **$89.95**

U.S. RIMFIRE — SINGLE SHOT

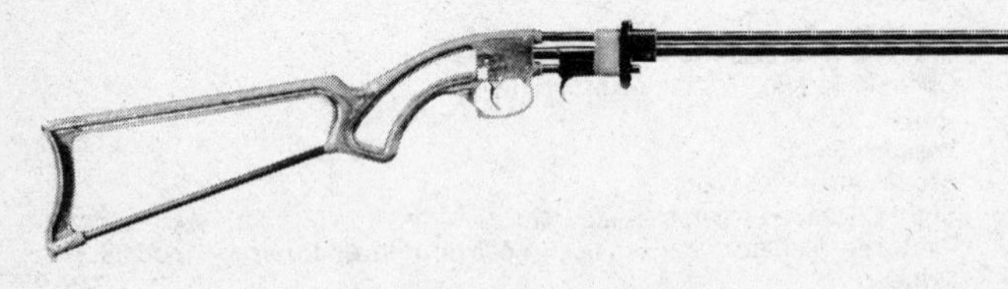

GARCIA BRONCO 22 RIFLE

Caliber: 22 S, L or LR. Single-shot.
Barrel: 16½″ round.
Weight: 3 lbs. **Length:** 32″ over-all.
Stock: Skeletonized crackle finished alloy casting.
Sights: Protected blade front, adj. rear.
Features: Cross-bolt safety, swing-out chamber, ultra lightweight for easy portability, instant takedown.
Price: **$25.00**

HARRINGTON & RICHARDSON MODEL 750 PIONEER

Caliber: 22 S, L or LR. Single-shot.
Barrel: 22″ round tapered.
Weight: 5 lbs. **Length:** 39″ over-all.
Stock: Walnut finished hardwood with Monte Carlo comb and p.g.
Sights: Blade front, step adj. open rear.
Features: Double extractors, feed platform, cocking indicator. sliding side safety, receiver grooved for tip-off scope mount, tapped for aperture sight.
Price: **$39.00**

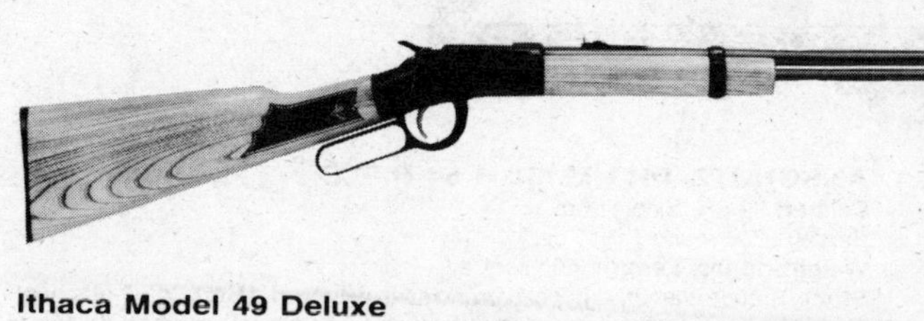

Ithaca Model 49 Deluxe
Same as the M49 except: figured walnut stock, better finish, gold plated trigger and hammer, Sling and swivels installed.
Price: **$49.95**

ITHACA MODEL 49 SADDLEGUN
Caliber: 22 S, L or LR. Single-shot.
Barrel: 18″ round.
Weight: About 5½ lbs. **Length:** 34½″ over-all
Stock: Two-piece walnut, checkered straight grip, fore-end has bbl. band.
Sights: Bead post front, step adj. open rear.
Features: Rebounding hammer safety, Martini-type lever action, rifle can be ordered with shorter (youth) stock at no extra cost.
Price: **$39.95**
Price: Chambered for 22 WRM only **$49.95**

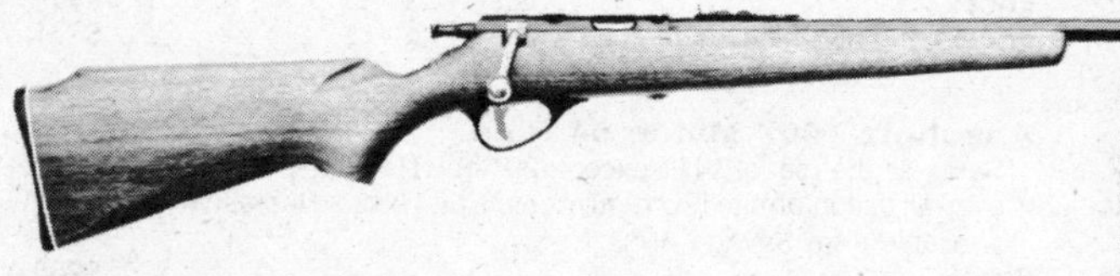

MARLIN 101 SINGLE SHOT RIFLE
Caliber: 22 S, L or LR; Single shot.
Barrel: 22″ Micro-Groove
Weight: 4½ lbs. **Length:** 40″
Stock: Monte Carlo American walnut with p.g. and white line spacer at buttplate.
Sights: Ramp front with "Wide-Scan" hood, folding semi-buckhorn rear adj. for w. & e.
Features: Gold plated trigger, T-shaped cocking knob, non-jamming feed throat, receiver grooved for tip-off scope mount. Manual cocking action. Scope **$17.95** extra.
Price: **$38.95**

REMINGTON MODEL 580 SINGLE SHOT RIFLE
Caliber: 22 S, L or LR. Single-shot.
Barrel: 24″ round tapered.
Weight: 4¾ lbs. **Length:** 42⅜″ over-all.
Stock: Walnut finished hardwood, Monte Carlo comb and p.g., black composition buttplate.
Sights: Bead post front, screw-lock adj. rear.
Features: Single screw take-down, integral loading platform, sliding side safety, receiver grooved for tip-off mount, can be had with 1″ shorter (youth) stock.
Price: **$47.95**
Price: M580 SB (smooth bore) **$52.95**

SAVAGE STEVENS MODEL 73 SINGLE SHOT RIFLE
Caliber: 22 S, L or LR. Single-shot.
Barrel: 20″ round tapered.
Weight: 4¾ lbs. **Length:** 38½″ over-all.
Stock: Walnut finished hardwood.
Sights: Bead post front, step adj. open rear.
Features: Cocks on opening, automatic safety, key locks trigger against unauthorized use, may be had with 12½″ pull stock (youth model) at same cost.
Price: **$32.50**

SAVAGE STEVENS MODEL 72 CRACKSHOT
Caliber: 22 S, L, LR.
Barrel: 22″ octagonal.
Weight: 4½ lbs. **Length:** 37″.
Stock: Walnut, straight grip and fore-end.
Sights: Blade front, step adj. rear.
Features: Deluxe version of Model 74, color case hardened frame.
Price: **$60.40**

WINCHESTER MODEL 310 RIFLE
Caliber: 22 S, L or LR. Single-shot.
Barrel: 22″ round tapered (16″ twist).
Weight: 5⅝ lbs. **Length:** 39½″ over-all.
Stock: Walnut, fluted Monte Carlo comb, checkered p.g. and fore-end (13½″ x 1⅝″ x 2⁷⁄₁₆″).
Sights: Bead post ramp front, step adj. open rear.
Features: Twin extractors, sliding side safety, wide serrated trigger, receiver grooved for tip-off scope mounts tapped for aperture rear sight.
Price: **$53.95**

U.S. TARGET RIFLES—CENTERFIRE AND RIMFIRE

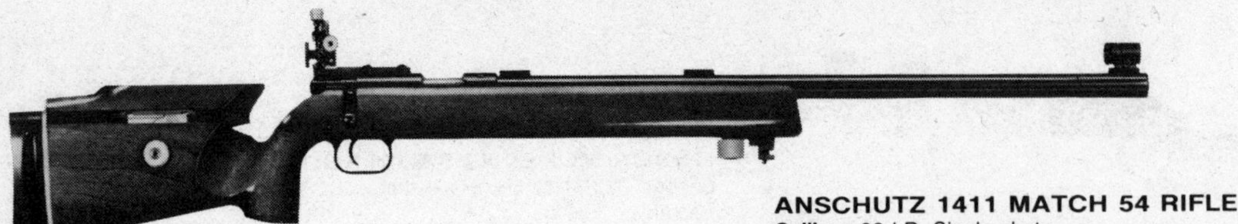

ANSCHUTZ 1411 MATCH 54 RIFLE

Caliber: 22 LR. Single shot.
Barrel: 27½ round (15/16" dia.)
Weight: 11 lbs. **Length:** 46" over-all.
Stock: French walnut, American prone style with Monte Carlo, cast-off cheekpiece, checkered p.g., beavertail fore-end with swivel rail and adj. swivel, adj. rubber buttplate.
Sights: None. Receiver grooved for Anshutz sights (extra). Scope blocks.
Features: Single stage adj. trigger, wing safety, short firing pin travel. Available from Savage Arms.
Price: **$307.75**
Price: Left hand stocked rifle, no sights **$331.75**

Anschutz 1413 Super Match Rifle

Same as the model 1411 except: International type stock with adj. cheekpiece, adj. aluminum hook buttplate, weight 15½ lbs., 50" over-all. Available from Savage Arms.
Price: **$554.75**
Price: Left hand stocked rifle, no sights **$579.75**

Anschutz 1407 Match 54 Rifle

Same as the model 1411 except: 26" bbl. (⅞" dia.), weight 10 lbs., 44½" over-all to conform to ISU requirements and also suitable for NRA matches. Available from Savage Arms.
Price: **$280.00**
Price: Left hand stocked rifle, no sights **$299.25**

SAVAGE/ANSCHUTZ 64 MATCH RIFLE

Caliber: 22 LR only. Single shot.
Barrel: 26" round (11/16" dia.)
Weight: 7¾ lbs. **Length:** 44" over-all.
Stock: Walnut finished hardwood, cheekpiece, checkered p.g., beavertail fore-end, adj. buttplate.
Sights: None (extra). Scope blocks.
Features: Sliding side safety, adj. single stage trigger, receiver grooved for Anschutz sights.
Price: ...... **$129.95** 64L (Left hand) **$141.95**
As above but with Anschutz 6723 Match Sight Set.
Price: Model 64S (Right hand) .... **$162.95** 64SL (Left hand) **$174.95**

MOSSBERG MODEL 144 TARGET RIFLE

Caliber: 22 LR only. 7-shot clip.
Barrel: 26" round (15/16" dia.)
Weight: About 8 lbs. **Length:** 43" over-all.
Stock: Walnut with high thick comb, cheekpiece, p.g., beavertail fore-end, adj. handstop and sling swivels.
Sights: Lyman 17A hooded front with inserts, Mossberg S331 receiver peep with ¼-minute clicks.
Features: Wide grooved trigger adj. for wgt. of pull, thumb safety, receiver grooved for scope mounting.
Price: **$91.20**

REMINGTON 40-XB RANGEMASTER TARGET Centerfire

Caliber: 222 Rem., 222 Rem. Mag., 223 Rem., 22-250, 6mm x 47, 6mm Int., 6mm Rem., 243, 25-06, 6.5mm Rem. Mag., 7mm Rem. Mag., 30-338, 30-7mm Rem. Mag., 300 Win. Mag., 7.62 NATO (308 Win.), 30-06. Single shot.
Barrel: 27¼" round (Stand. dia.-¾", Hvy. dia.-⅞")
Weight: Std.—9¼ lbs., Hvy.—11¼ **Length:** 47"
Stock: American walnut with high comb and beavertail fore-end stop. Rubber non-slip buttplate.
Sights: None. Scope blocks installed.
Features: Adjustable trigger pull. Receiver drilled and tapped for sights.
Price: Standard ss., stainless steel **$279.95**
Price: Repeating model **$299.95**
Price: Extra for 2 oz. trigger **$40.00**

REMINGTON 40-XC NAT'L MATCH COURSE RIFLE

Caliber: 7.62 NATO, 5-shot.
Barrel: 23¼", stainless steel.
Weight: 10 lbs. without sights. **Length:** 42½" over-all.
Stock: Walnut, position-style, with palm swell.
Sights: None furnished.
Features: Designed to meet the needs of competitive shooters firing the national match courses. Position-style stock, top loading clip slot magazine, anti-bind bolt and receiver, bright stainless steel barrel. Meets all I.S.U. Army Rifle specifications. Adjustable buttplate, adjustable trigger.
Price: **$400.00**

U.S. TARGET RIFLES—CENTERFIRE AND RIMFIRE

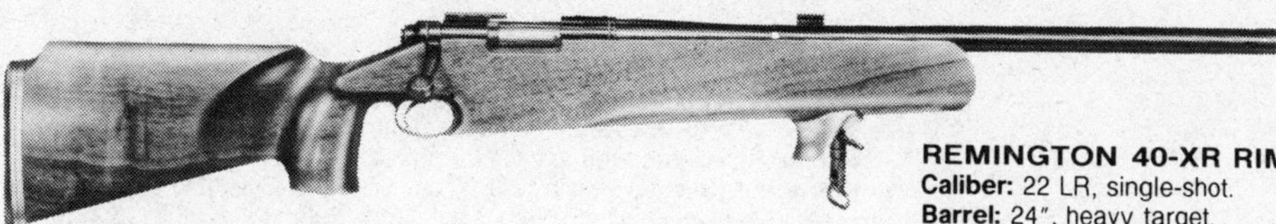

REMINGTON 40-XR RIMFIRE POSITION RIFLE
Caliber: 22 LR, single-shot.
Barrel: 24″, heavy target.
Weight: 10 lbs. **Length:** 43″ over-all.
Stock: Position-style with front swivel block on fore-end guide rail.
Sights: Drilled and tapped. Furnished with scope blocks.
Features: Meets all I.S.U. specifications. Deep fore-end, buttplate vertically adjustable, wide adjustable trigger. Redfield Olympic front and rear sights available with 10 inserts for $47.95.
Price: **$240.00**

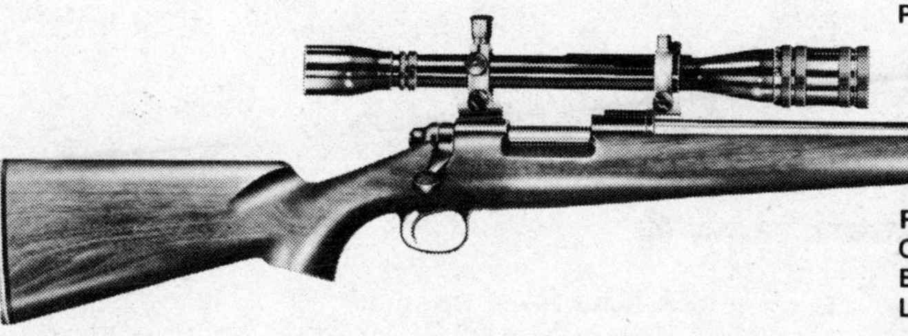

REMINGTON MODEL 40XB-BR
Caliber: 222 Rem., 222 Rem. Mag., 223, 6mm x 47, 7.62 NATO (308 Win.).
Barrel: 20″ (light varmint class), 26″ (heavy varmint class).
Length: 38″ (20″ bbl.), 44″ (26″ bbl.). **Weight:** Light varmint class, 7¼ lbs., Heavy varmint class, 12 lbs.
Stock: Select walnut.
Sights: None. Supplied with scope blocks.
Features: Unblued stainless steel barrel, trigger adj. from 1½ lbs. to 3½ lbs. Special 2 oz. trigger at extra cost. Scope and mounts extra.
Price: **$299.95**

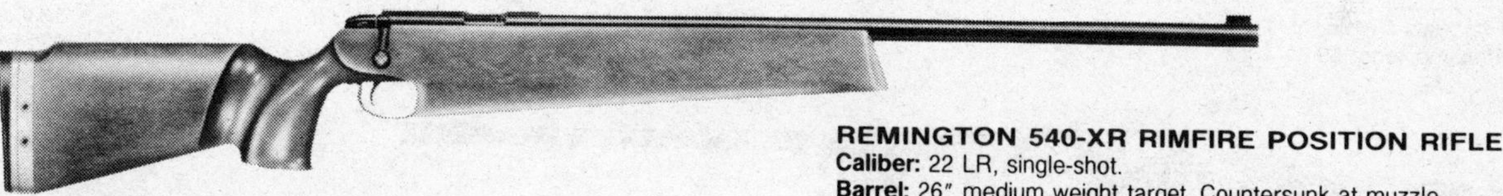

REMINGTON 540-XR RIMFIRE POSITION RIFLE
Caliber: 22 LR, single-shot.
Barrel: 26″ medium weight target. Countersunk at muzzle.
Weight: 8 lbs., 13 oz. **Length:** Adj. from 43½″ to 46¾″.
Stock: Position-style with Monte Carlo, cheekpiece and thumb groove. 5-way adj. buttplate and full length guide rail.
Sights: None furnished. Drilled and tapped for target scope blocks. Fitted with front sight base.
Features: Extra-fast lock time. Specially designed p.g. to eliminate wrist twisting. Adj. match trigger. Match-style sling with adj. swivel block ($6.95) and sight set ($29.95) available.
Price: **$124.95**

Remington 540-XRJR Junior Rimfire Position Rifle
Same as 540-XR except fitted with 1¾″ shorter stock to fit the junior shooter, Over-all length adjustable from 41¾″ to 45″. Length of pull adjustable from 11″ to 14¼″.
Price: **$124.95**

WINCHESTER 52D BOLT ACTION TARGET RIFLE
Caliber: 22 LR only. Single shot.
Barrel: 28″, standard or heavy weight.
Weight: 9¾ lbs. Std. 11 lbs. Hvy. **Length:** 46″
Stock: Marksman stock of choice walnut with full length accessory channel and adj. bedding device and non-slip butt pad.
Sights: None. Barrel tapped for front sight bases.
Features: Adjustable trigger.
Price: **$215.00**

WINCHESTER 52 INTERNATIONAL MATCH RIFLE
Caliber: 22 LR. Single shot.
Barrel: 28″ heavy bbl.
Weight: 13½ lbs. **Length:** 44½″
Stock: Laminated International-style, aluminum fore-end assembly, adj. palm rest.
Sights: Receiver tapped for sights and scope bases; scope blocks are included.
Features: Non-drag trigger. Lead-lapped barrel with Winchester muzzle counterbore.
Price: **$455.00**
With kenyon trigger **$500.00**
With ISU trigger **$500.00**

WINCHESTER 70 INT'L ARMY MATCH RIFLE
Caliber: 308 (7.62mm NATO) 5-shot.
Barrel: 24″ heavy-contour.
Weight: 11 lbs. **Length:** 43¼″ over-all.
Stock: Oil finished walnut, (12″ x 1¼″ x 1¼″) meets ISU requirements.
Sights: None. Receiver tapped for M70 sights (available at extra cost).
Features: Fore-end rail takes most std. accessories, vertically adj. buttplate, externally adj. trigger, glass bedded action.
Price: Match .... **$445.00** Ultra Match **$395.00**

Browning Auto-5 Magnum 12
Same as Std. Auto-5 except: chambered for 3″ magnum shells (also handles 2¾″ magnum and 2¾″ HV loads). 28″ Mod., Full; 30″ and 32″ (Full) bbls. 14″x1⅝″x2½″ stock. Recoil pad. Wgt. 8¾ lbs.
Price: .... **$299.50** With vent. rib. Wgt. 9 lbs. **$317.50**

Browning Auto-5 Magnum 20
Same as Magnum 12 except barrels 28″ Full or Mod., or 26″ Full, Mod. or Imp. Cyl. 7 lbs. **$299.50**
With ventilated rib, 7½ lbs. **$317.50**

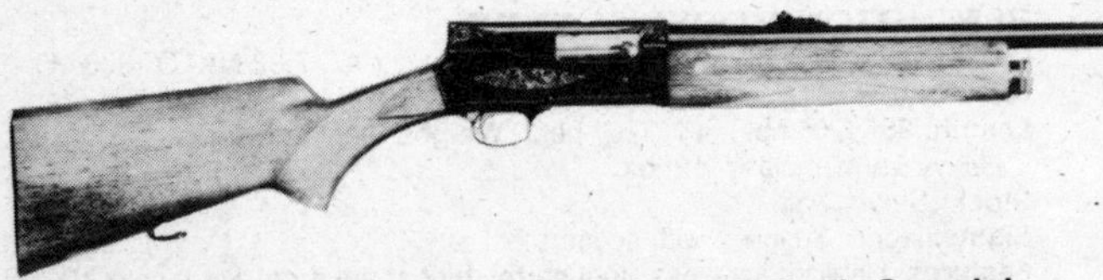

Browning Auto-5 Light 12, 16, 20, or 12 Buck Special
Same as Std. Buck Special except: with gold trigger and of less weight. Wgt. 12 ga., 7 lbs.; 16 ga., 6⅜ lbs.; 20 ga., 6 lbs. 2 oz.; 3″ Mag. 12, 8¼ lbs.
Price: **$326.50**
All Buck Specials are available with carrying sling, detachable swivels and swivel attachments for $9.00 extra.

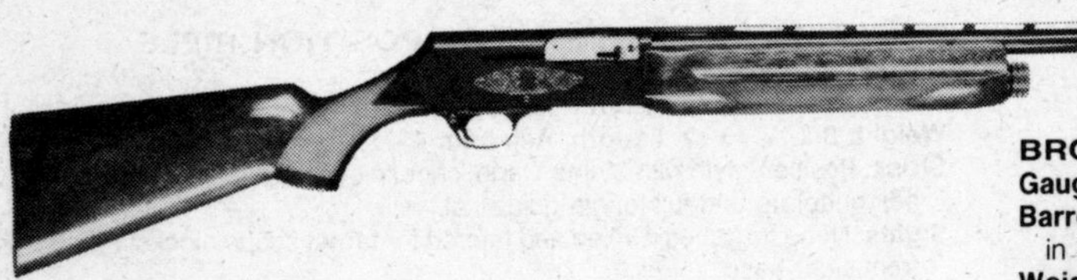

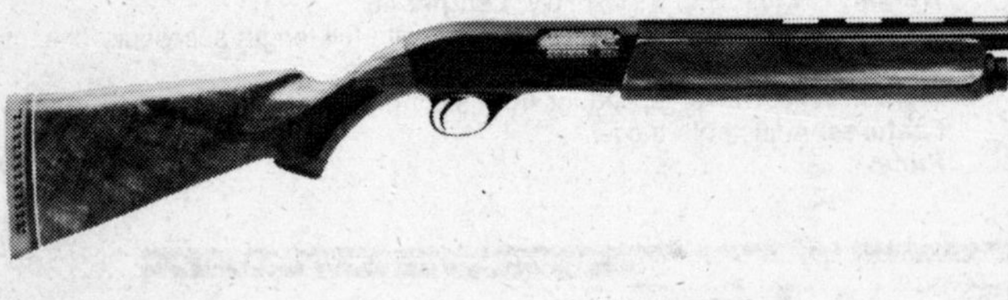

Hi-Standard Supermatic Skeet
Same as Supermatic DeLuxe except: 26″ Skeet choke bbl.; all external parts high polished; internal parts super finished; better grade American walnut stock (no recoil pad) and fore-end with cabinet finish. weight about 7½ lbs. **$209.95**

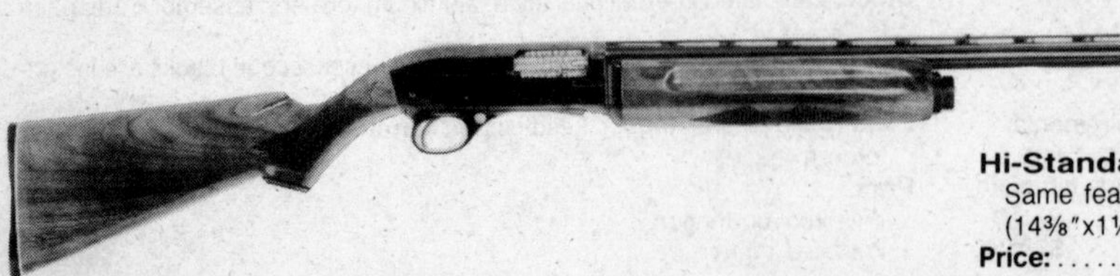

BROWNING AUTO-5 LIGHT 12, 20 and SWEET 16
Gauge: 12, 20, 16 (5-shot; 3-shot plug furnished). 2¾″ chamber.
Action: Recoil operated autoloader; takedown.
Barrel: 26″ (Skeet boring in 12 & 20 ga., Cyl., Imp. Cyl., Mod. in 16 & 20 ga.); 28″ (Skeet in 12 ga., Full in 16 ga., Mod., Full); 30″ (Full in 12 ga.).
Weight: 12 ga. 7¼ lbs., 16 ga. 6¾ lbs., 20 ga. 6⅜ lbs.
Stock: French walnut, hand checkered half-p.g. and fore-end. 14¼″ x 1⅝″ x 2½″.
Features: Receiver hand engraved with scroll designs and border. Double extractors, extra bbls. interchangeable without factory fitting; mag. cut-off; cross-bolt safety.
Price: **$296.50**
Price: Vent. rib **$314.50**

Browning Auto-5 Buck Special
Same as A-5 Light model except: 24″ bbl. choked for slugs, gold bead front sight on contoured ramp, rear sight adj. for w.&e. Wgt. (12 ga.) 7⅝ lbs.
Price: **$317.50**

Browning Auto-5 Light Skeet
Same as Light Standard except: 12 and 20 ga. only, 26″ or 28″ bbl. (Skeet). Wgt. 6¼-7¼ bls. **$296.50**
With vent. rib. Wgt. 6⅜-7½ lbs. **$314.50**

BROWNING B/2000 GAS OPERATED AUTO SHOTGUN
Gauge: 12 ga. only. (5-shot, 4-shot in Magnum).
Barrel: 26″, 28″ or 30″ in 2¾″ Field Models, plain or vent. rib; 28″, 30″ or 32″ in 3″ Magnum models, vent. rib only.
Weight: 7½ lbs. (26″ vent. rib) **Length:** 45⅜″ (26″ bbl.).
Stock: French walnut, hand checkered, full pistol grip, no recoil pad 14¼″x1⅝″x2½″.
Sights: Medium raised bead, German nickel silver.
Features: Internal self-cleaning gas system, soft recoil, speed loading/unloading, extra bbls. interchangeable without factory fitting. No adjustment necessary to gas system for varying loads.
Price: Vent. rib **$289.50**
Price: Plain bbl. **$269.50**
Price: Vent. rib, 3″ Mag. **$289.50**
Price: Buck Special .... **To be announced**
Price: Trap and/or Skeet Models .... **To be announced**

HI-STANDARD SUPERMATIC DELUXE AUTOS
Gauge: 12 ga. (5-shot; 3-shot plug furnished). 20 ga. (3 shots only).
Action: Gas operated autoloader (12 ga. 2¾″, 20 ga. 3″ chambers).
Barrel: 12 gauge, 30″ (Full), 26″ (Imp. Cyl.), 12 and 20 gauge, 28″ (Mod. or Full). Plain Barrel.
Stock: 14″x1½″x2½″. Walnut, checkered p.g. and semi-beavertail fore-end. Recoil pad. 20 ga. guns have longer fore-end with sloped front.
Weight: 7½ lbs. (12 ga.) 47¾″ over-all (12, 28″).
Features: 12 ga. uses all 2¾″ shells, 20 ga. all 2¾″ or 3″ shells, including rifled slugs, manual adjustment, engraved receiver.
Price: Field, plain bbl., no rib **$184.95**
Price: Deluxe vent. rib, checkered stock, w/o adj. choke **$204.95**
Price: Checkered stock, vent.-rib, adj. choke **$204.95**
Price: Duck, 3″ Magnum, 12 ga., 30″ full, recoil pad, with vent. rib bbl. **$204.95**

Hi-Standard Supermatic Trap
Same features as Supermatic Skeet except: 30″ full choke barrel; stock (14⅜″x1½″x1⅞″); recoil pad. Wgt. 8 lbs. 12 ga. only.
Price: .... **$209.95** With Monte Carlo stock ... **$214.95**

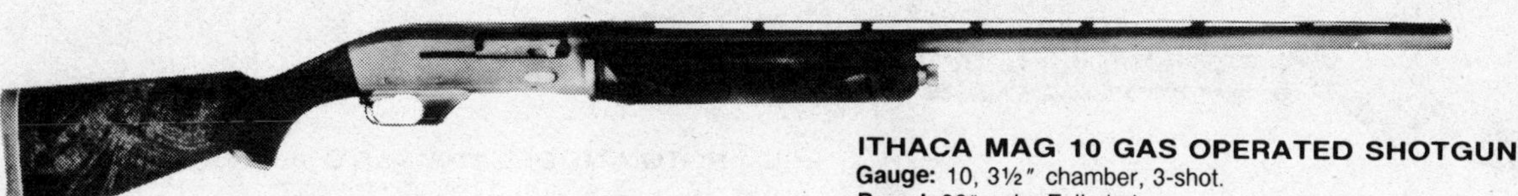

ITHACA MAG 10 GAS OPERATED SHOTGUN

Gauge: 10, 3½″ chamber, 3-shot.
Barrel: 32″ only. Full choke.
Weight: 11¼ lbs.
Stock: American walnut, checkered p.g. and fore-end (14⅛″x2⅜″x1½″), p.g. cap, rubber recoil pad.
Sights: White Bradley.
Features: Counterecoil gas system. Piston, cylinder, bolt, charging lever, action release and carrier made of stainless steel. ⅜″ vent. rib. Reversible cross-bolt safety. Low recoil force.
Price: **$424.95**

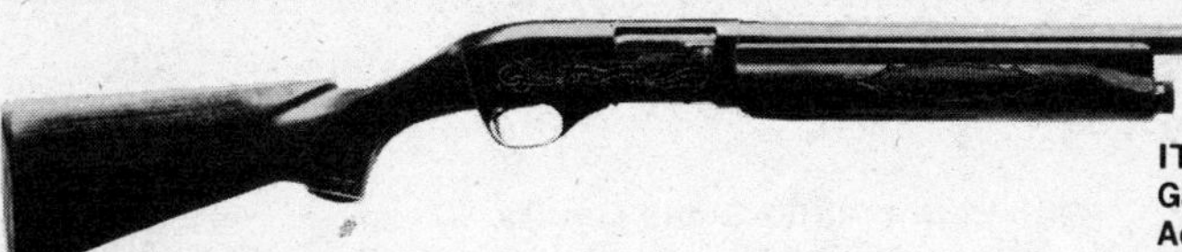

ITHACA MODEL 51 FEATHERLIGHT AUTOMATIC

Gauge: 12 ga. 2¾″ chamber.
Action: Gas-operated, rotary bolt has three locking lugs. Takedown. Self-compensating for high or low base loads.
Barrel: Roto-Forged, 30″ (Full), 28″ (Full, Mod., or Skeet), 26″ (Imp. Cyl. or Skeet). Extra barrels available. Raybar front sight. Vent. rib $25.00 extra.
Stock: 14″x1⅝″x2½″. Hand checkered walnut, white spacers on p.g. and under recoil pad.
Weight: About 7½ lbs.
Features: Hand fitted, engraved receiver, 3 shot capacity, safety is reversible for left hand shooter.
Price: Standard **$194.95**

Ithaca Model 51 Magnum

Same as Standard Model 51 except has 3″ chambers.
Price: Magnum Standard **$214.95**
Price: Magnum vent. rib **$239.95**

Ithaca Model 51 Featherlight Automatic Trap

Same gun as Model 51 with vent. rib, trap recoil pad, stock dimensions are 14¼″x1½″x1⅞″.
Price: .... **$249.95** With Monte Carlo stock ... **$259.95**

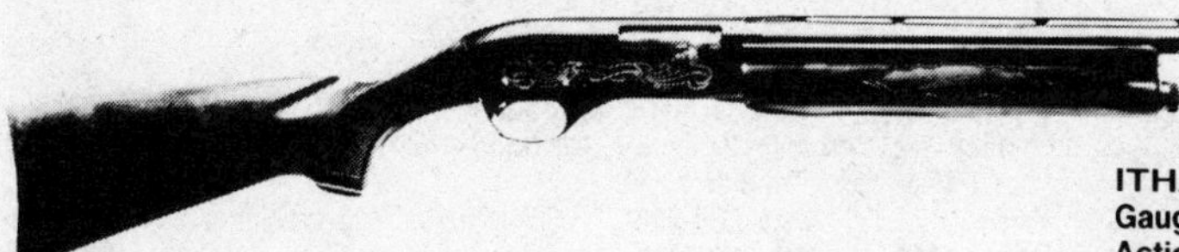

ITHACA MODEL 51 20 GAUGE

Gauge: 20 only, 2¾″ or 3″ chamber.
Action: Gas-operated rotary bolt.
Barrel: Standard Grade, 26″ (Imp. Cyl.), 28″ (Full, Mod.), Target Grade, 26″ (Skeet).
Weight: 7½ to 8½ lbs.
Stock: 14″x1½″x2¼″, American walnut.
Sights: Raybar front sight.
Features: Quick take-down, reversible safety, interchangeable barrels. Easily field stripped without tools.
Price: Standard model **$194.95**
Price: Standard model with vent. rib **$219.95**
Price: Standard magnum **$214.95**
Price: Vent. magnum **$239.95**
Price: Standard Skeet **$219.95**
Price: Deluxe Skeet **$254.95**

Ithaca Model 51 Featherlight Automatic Skeet

Same gun as Model 51 with vent. rib, skeet recoil pad, stock dimensions are 14″x1⅝″x2½″.
Price: .... **$219.95** Deluxe Skeet **$254.95**

Ithaca Model 51 Featherlight Deluxe Skeet

Same gun as Model 51 Skeet with fancy American walnut stock, 28″ or 29″ (Skeet) barrel.
Price: **$254.95**

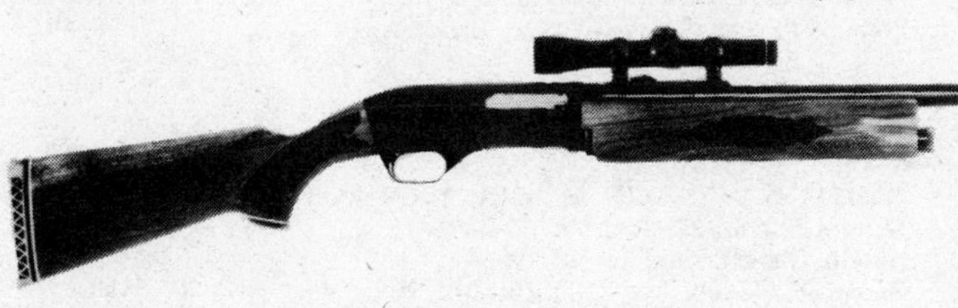

ITHACA MODEL 51 DEERSLAYER

Gauge: 12 or 20 ga., 2¾″ chamber.
Action: Gas-operated, semi-automatic.
Barrel: 24″, special bore.
Weight: 7½ lbs. (12 ga.), 7¼ lbs. (20 ga.).
Stocks: 14″x1½″x2¼″, American walnut. Checkered p.g. and fore-end.
Sights: Raybar front, open rear adj. for w. and e.
Features: Sight base grooved for scope mounts. Easy takedown, reversible safety.
Price: **$214.95**

Ithaca Model 51 Featherlight Deluxe Trap

Same gun as Model 51 Trap with fancy American walnut stock, 30″ (Full or Imp. Cyl.) or 28″ (Full or Imp. Mod.) barrel.
Price: .... **$274.95** With Monte Carlo stock ... **$284.95**

ITHACA MODEL XL 900

Gauge: 12 (2¾″), 20 (2¾″, 3″ chamber); 5 shot capacity.
Action: Gas-operated autoloader.
Barrel: 12 ga., Field Grade - 30″ (Full), 28″ (Full or Mod.), 26″ (Imp. Cyl.); 20 ga., 28″ (Full or Mod.,) 26″ (Imp. Cyl,), Trap - 30″ (Full or Imp. Mod.), Skeet - 26″ (Skeet).
Weight: 6¾ lbs. **Length:** 48″ overall.
Stock: 1½″x2½″x14″ (Field Grade). Walnut finish.
Sights: Ventilated rib with Raybar front sight on field grades; Bradley-type on target grades.
Features: Self-compensating gas system, reversible safety, action release button.
Price: Ventilated rib ...... **$214.95** Trap grade (12 ga. only) .. **$229.95**
Price: Skeet grade .... **$229.95** Slug gun **$204.95**
Price: Trap Monte Carlo **$239.95**

ITHACA MODEL XL 300

Gauge: 12 (2¾″), 20 (2¾″ or 3″ chamber).
Action: Gas-operated autoloader.
Barrel: 12 ga. Field Grade - 30″ (Full), 28″ (Full or Mod.), 26″ (Imp. Cyl.). 20 ga. Field Grade - 28″ (Full or Mod.) 26″ (Imp. Cyl.). Trap Grade - 30″ (Full or Mod.); Skeet-26″ (Skeet).
Weight: 7½ lbs. **Length:** 48″ over-all.
Stock: 1½″x2½″x14″ (Field Grade). Walnut.
Sights: Raybar front sight on ventilated rib.
Features: Self-compensating gas system, reversible safety.
Price: Standard .... **$189.95** Ventilated rib **$204.95**

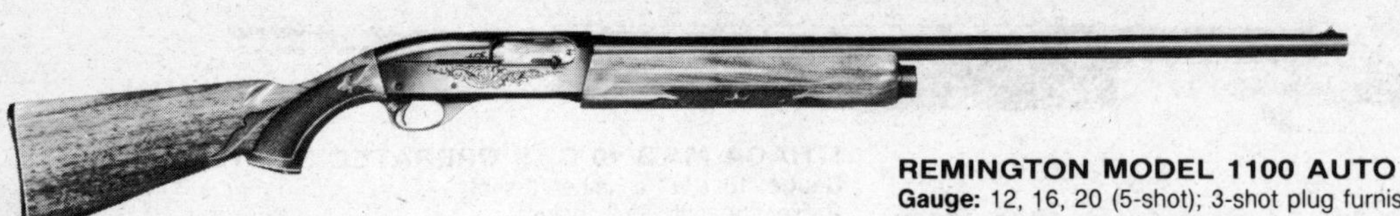

REMINGTON MODEL 1100 AUTO
Gauge: 12, 16, 20 (5-shot); 3-shot plug furnished.
Action: Gas-operated autoloader.
Barrel: 26″ (Imp. Cyl.), 28″ (Mod., Full), 30″ Full in 12 ga. only.
Stock: 14″x1½″x2½″ American Walnut, checkered p.g. and fore-end.
Weight: 12 ga. 7½ lbs., 16 ga. 7⅜ lbs., 20 ga. 7¼ lbs.; 48″ over-all (28″ bbl.).
Features: Quickly interchangeable barrels within gauge. Matted receiver top with scroll work on both sides of receiver. Crossbolt safety.
Price: .... **$194.95** With vent. rib **$219.95**
Price: Left hand model with vent. rib **$224.95**

Remington 1100 Magnum
Same as 1100 except: chambered for 3″ magnum loads. Available in 12 ga. (30″) or 20 ga. (28″) Mod. or Full, 14″x1½″x2½″ stock with recoil pad, Wgt. 7¾ lbs. **$214.95**
Price: With vent. rib **$239.95**
Price: Left hand model with vent. rib **$244.95**

Remington 1100 Small Gauge
Same as 1100 except: 28 ga. 2¾″ (5-shot) or 410, 3″ (except Skeet, 2½″ 4-shot). 45½″ over-all. Available in 25″ bbl. (Full, Mod., or Imp. Cyl.) only.
Price: Plain bbl. .... **$204.95** With vent. rib **$229.95**

Remington 1100 Deer Gun
Same as 1100 except: 12 ga. only, 22″ bbl. (Imp. Cyl.), rifle sights adjustable for w. and e.; recoil pad with white spacer. Weight 7¼ lbs. **$214.95**

Remington 1100 SA Skeet
Same as the 1100 except: 26″ bbl., special skeet boring, vent. rib, ivory bead front and metal bead middle sights. 14″x1½″x2½″ stock. 20 and 12 ga. Wgt. 7½ lbs.
Price: **$229.95**
Price: 1100 SB (better grade walnut) **$254.95**
For Cutts Comp add **$25.00**
Left hand model with vent. rib **$234.95**
28 & 410 ga., 25″ bbl. **$239.95**

Remington 1100D Tournament Auto
Same as 1100 Standard except: vent. rib, better wood, more extensive engraving **$660.00**

Remington 1100F Premier Auto
Same as 1100D except: select wood, better engraving **$1,350.00**
With gold inlay **$2,100.00**

Remington 1100 TB Trap
Same as the 1100 except: better grade wood, recoil pad. 14⅜″x1⅜″x1¾″ stock. Wgt. 8¼ lbs. 12 ga. only. 30″ (Mod., Full) vent. rib bbl. Ivory bead front and white metal middle sight.
Price: .... **$264.95** With Monte Carlo stock **$274.95**
Price: 1100TB Trap, left hand **$269.95**
Price: With Monte Carlo stock **$279.95**
Remington 1100 Extra bbls.: Plain **$49.95** (20, 28 & 410, **$52.95**). Vent. rib **$74.95** (20, 28 & 410, **$77.95**). Vent. rib Skeet **$79.95.** Vent. rib Trap **$79.95** Deer bbl. **$60.95,** Skeet, with cutts comp. **$104.95.** Available in the same gauges and chokes as shown on guns.

Remington 1100 20 ga. Lightweight
Basically the same design as Model 1100, but with special weight-saving features that retain strength and dependability of the standard Model 1100.
Barrel: 28″ (Full, Mod.), 26″ (Imp. Cyl.).
Weight: 6½ lbs.
Price: .... **$204.95** With vent. rib **$229.95**
Price: 20 ga. Lightweight magnum (28″ Full) **$224.95**
Price: With vent. rib **$249.95**

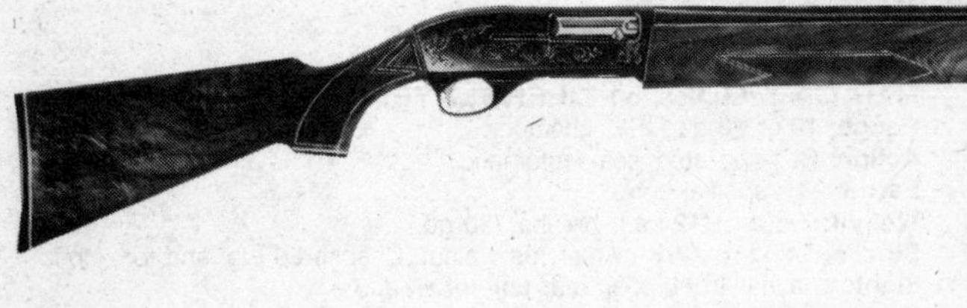

SMITH & WESSON MODEL 1000 AUTO
Gauge: 12 only, 2¾″ chamber, 4-shot.
Action: Gas-operated autoloader.
Barrel: 26″ (Skeet, Imp. Cyl.), 28″ (Imp. Mod., Mod., Full), 30″ (Full).
Length: 48″ over-all (28″ bbl.). **Weight:** 7½ lbs. (28″ bbl.).
Stock: 14″x1½″x2⅜″, American walnut.
Features: Interchangeable crossbolt safety, vent. rib with front and middle beads, engraved alloy receiver, pressure compensator and floating piston for light recoil.
Price: **$229.95**
Price: Extra barrels (as listed above) **$84.95**

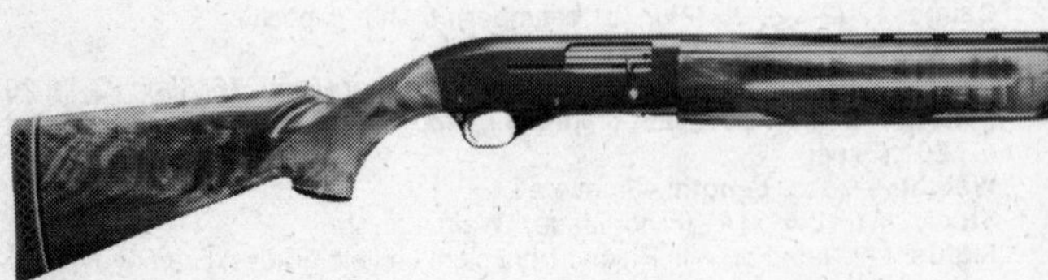

WEATHERBY CENTURION AUTO
Gauge: 12 only, 2¾″ chamber.
Action: Gas operated autoloader with "Floating Piston."
Barrel: 26″ (Mod., Imp. Cyl, Skeet), 28″ (Full, Mod.), 30″ (Full), Vent. Rib.
Weight: About 7½ lbs. **Length:** 48¼ (28″).
Stock: Walnut, hand checkered p.g. and fore-end, rubber recoil pad with white line spacer.
Features: Cross bolt safety, fluted bolt, gold plated trigger. Extra interchangeable bbls. **$89.95**
Price: Field or Skeet grade **$269.50** Trap grade **$299.50**

U.S. SHOTGUNS—AUTOLOADING

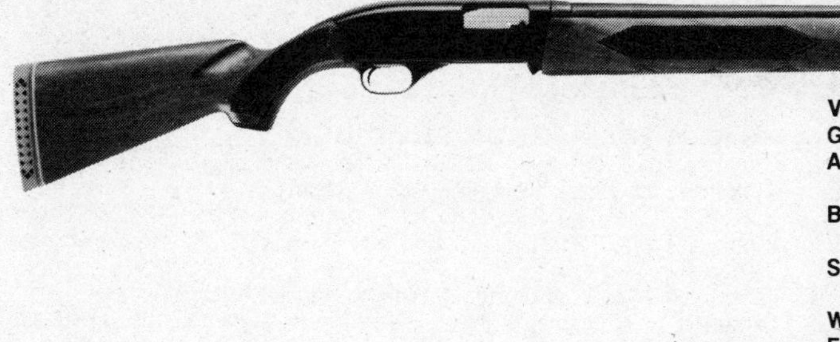

WINCHESTER 1400 AUTOMATIC MARK II

Gauge: 12, and 20 (3-shot).
Action: Gas operated autoloader. Front-locking 4-lug rotating bolt locks in bbl. Alloy receiver. Push button action release.
Barrel: 26″ (Imp. Cyl.), 28″ (Mod., Full), 30″ (Full, 12 ga. only). Metal bead front sight.
Stock: 14″x1½″x2⅜″. American walnut, new-design checkered p.g. and fore-end; fluted comb, p.g. cap, recoil pad.
Weight: With 26″ bbl., 20 ga. 6½ lbs., 16, 12 ga. 6¾ lbs.; 46⅝″ over-all.
Features: Self-compensating valve adjusts for std. or magnum loads. Bbls. interchangeable without fitting. Crossbolt safety in front of trigger guard.
Price: .... **$164.95** With vent. rib **$184.95**

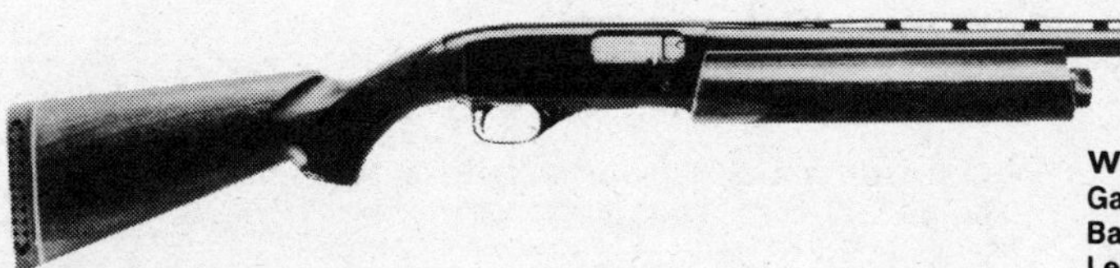

WINCHESTER SUPER-X MODEL 1 AUTO SHOTGUN

Gauge: 12 or 20, 4-shot.
Barrel: 26″ (Imp. Cyl.), 28″ (Mod., Full), 30″ (Full).
Length: 46″ over-all (26″ bbl.)
Stock: American walnut with cut-checkered p.g. and fore-end, 14″x1½″x2½″ (Field).
Sights: Metal bead front.
Features: Receiver and all metal parts made of machined steel. Straight-line, 3-piece bolt, short-stroke gas system, all steel trigger assembly, steel shell carrier.
Price: Plain barrel **$255.00**
Price: Vent. rib **$275.00**

Winchester Super-X Model 1 Trap and Skeet Models
Same as Field model except: Trap has 30″ bbl., vent. rib (Mod. or Full) and regular or Monte Carlo stock. Engraved receiver, red bead front sight, black rubber recoil pad with white spacer—**$305.00.** for regular stock, **$310.00** for Monte Carlo. Skeet model has 26″ vent. rib barrel (Skeet), otherwise same as trap gun—**$305.00.**

Winchester Super-X Model 1 Deer Gun
Same as Field model except: 12 ga. only, 22″ barrel, Cylinder choke, iron sights.
Price: **$265.00**

U.S. SHOTGUNS — SLIDE ACTION

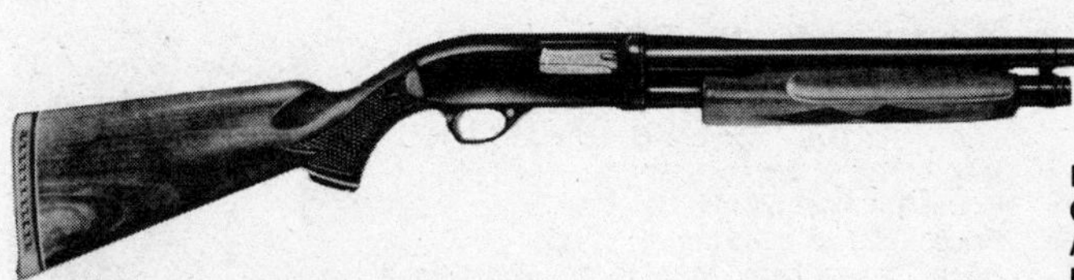

HI-STANDARD FLITE-KING DELUXE PUMP GUNS

Gauge: 12, 20, 28, and 410 (6 shots; 3-shot plug furnished).
Action: "Free-falling" slide action.
Barrel: 12 ga., 30″ (Full); 12, 20 ga., 28″ (Mod. or Full), 26″ (Imp. Cyl.); 410, 26″ (Full). 12 ga. barrels interchangeable.
Stock: 14″x1½″x2½″. Walnut, checkered p.g. and fore-end. Recoil pad except: 410 & Skeet guns.
Weight: 12 ga. 7¾ lbs., 20, 410 ga. 6½ lbs.
Features: Side ejection.
Price: Field **$134.95**
Price: 12 ga., with adj. choke, 27″ bbl **$159.95**
Price: De Luxe Rib, with vent. rib, w/o adj. choke **$154.95**
Price: 12 and 20 ga., as above with adj. choke **$159.95**
Price: Brush, 12 ga. only with 20″ cyl. bbl., grooved fore-end, adj. rifle sights. Stock (14¼″x1½″x1⅞″) 39¾″ over-all **$154.95**

Hi-Standard Flite-King Trap
Same features as Flite-King Skeet except: 30″ full choke; Monte Carlo stock with recoil pad. About 8¼ lbs. 12 ga. only **$179.95**

Hi-Standard Flite-King Skeet
Same as Flite-King DeLuxe except: Vent. rib, no recoil pad; 26″ Skeet choke bbl.; all external parts high polished; internal parts super finished; better grade American walnut stock (14″x1½″x2½″) and fore-end with cabinet finish. Wgt. 12 ga. 7½ lbs., 20, 6¼ lbs., 28 and 410 ga. 6¼ lbs. **$169.95**

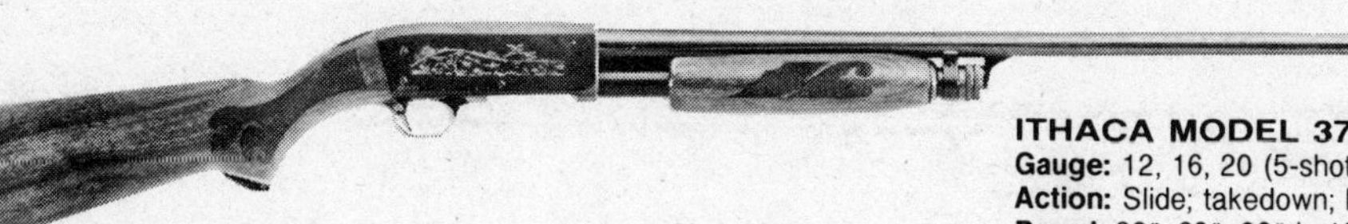

ITHACA MODEL 37 FEATHERLIGHT

Gauge: 12, 16, 20 (5-shot; 3-shot plug furnished).
Action: Slide; takedown; bottom ejection.
Barrel: 26″, 28″, 30″ in 12 ga. 26″ or 28″ in 16 or 20 ga. (Full, Mod. or Imp. Cyl.).
Stock: 14″x1⅝″x2⅝″. Checkered walnut capped p.g. stock and fore-end.
Weight: 12 ga. 6½ lbs., 16 ga. 6 lbs., 20 ga. 5¾ lbs.
Features: Ithaca Raybar front sight; decorated receiver; crossbolt safety; action release for removing shells.
Price: **$144.95**
Price: With vent. rib stock (14″x1½″x2½″) **$169.95**

Ithaca Model 37 De Luxe Featherlight
Same as Model 37 except: checkered stock with p.g. cap; beavertail fore-end; recoil pad. Wgt. 12 ga. 6¾ lbs.
Price: .... **$149.95** With vent. rib **$174.95**

Ithaca Model 37 Supreme
Same as Model 37 except: hand checkered beavertail fore-end and p.g. stock, Ithaca recoil pad and vent. rib **$274.95**
37 Supreme also with Skeet (14″x1½″x2½″) or Trap (14½″x1½″x1⅞″) stocks at no extra charge. Other options available at extra charge.

Ithaca Model 37 Deerslayer
Same as Model 37 except: 26″ or 20″ bbl. designed for rifled slugs; sporting rear sight, Raybar front sight; rear sight ramp grooved for Redfield long eye relief scope mount. 12, 16, or 20 gauge. With checkered stock, beavertail fore-end and recoil pad.
Price: **$159.95**
Price: As above with special select walnut stock **$179.95**

U.S. SHOTGUNS—SLIDE ACTION

MARLIN 120 MAGNUM PUMP GUN

Gauge: 12 ga. (2¾" or 3" chamber) 5-shot; 3-shot plug furnished.
Action: Hammerless, side ejecting, slide action.
Barrel: 26" (Imp. Cyl.), 28" (Mod.), 30" (Full), with vent. rib. or 40" MXR plain.
Stock: (14"x1½"x2⅜"). Checkered walnut, capped p.g., semi-beavertail checkered fore-end.
Length: 50½" over-all (30" bbl.). **Weight:** About 7¾ lbs.
Features: Interchangeable bbls., slide lock release; large button cross-bolt safety.
Price: **$158.95**
Price: Extra barrels **$50.00**

Marlin 120 Trap Gun

Same as 120 Magnum except: Monte Carlo stock and full fore-end with hand-cut checkering. Stock dimensions are 14¼"x1¼"x1¾". Available with 30" Full choke barrel with vent. rib. **$234.95**

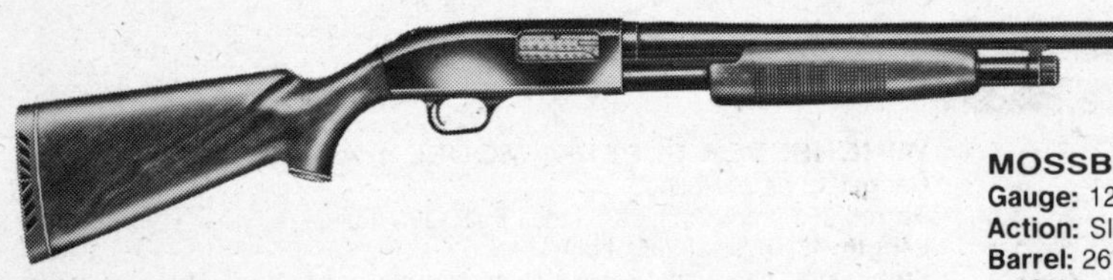

MOSSBERG MODEL 500 PUMP GUN

Gauge: 12, 16 (2¾"), 20; 3" (6-shot, 3-shot plug furnished).
Action: Slide, takedown; safety on top of receiver.
Barrel: 26" (Imp. Cyl.) 28" (Full or Mod.), 30" (Full), 12 ga. only. Also 12 ga. 18½" cylinder, for police only).
Stock: 14"x1½"x2½". Walnut p.g., extension fore-end. Recoil pad. 13 oz. steel plug furnished for use with Magnum barrel.
Weight: 12 ga. 6¾ lbs., 45¼" over-all (26" bbl.).
Features: Easy interchangeability of barrels; side ejection; disconnecting trigger makes doubles impossible; straight-line feed.
Price: Standard barrel **$124.60**
Price: With C-Lect Choke, 3" Mag., or 24" Slugster bbls. **$129.70**
Price: Extra barrel, 2¾" chamber **$35.60**
Price: Extra Magnum, C-Lect Choke or Slug, bbl. **$35.60**

Mossberg Model 500 Super Grade

Similar to the Model 500 except: vent. rib bbls. in 12 ga. (2¾") or 20 ga. (3"); 26" (Skeet), 28" (Mod., Full), and 30" Full (12 ga. only) 2¾" or 3" mag. Checkered p.g. and fore-end stock with fluted comb and recoil pad (14"x1½"x2½").
Price: 12 or 20 ga. **$143.25**
Price: 12 ga. 3" Magnum or C-Lect Choke 12 and 20 ga. **$151.20**

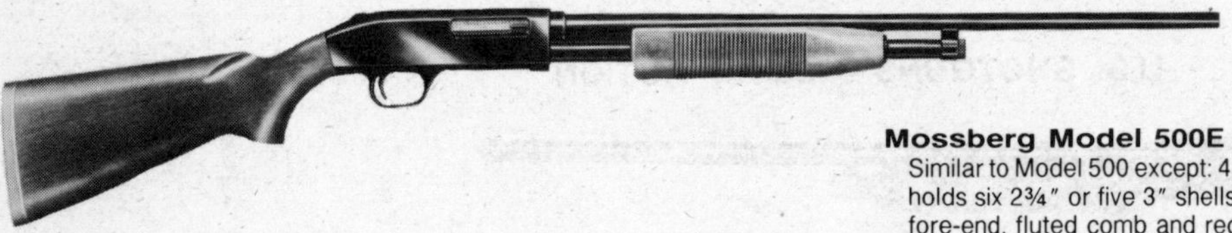

Mossberg Model 500E

Similar to Model 500 except: 410 bore only, 26" bbl. (Full, Mod. or Imp. Cyl.); holds six 2¾" or five 3" shells. Walnut stock with smooth p.g. and grooved fore-end, fluted comb and recoil pad (14"x1¼"x2½").
Weight: About 5¾ lbs., length over-all 46".
Price: Standard barrels **$124.60**
Price: C-Lect Choke barrel **$143.25**
Price: Super Grade, 26" Full, Mod., or Skeet bbl., vent. rib **$174.95**

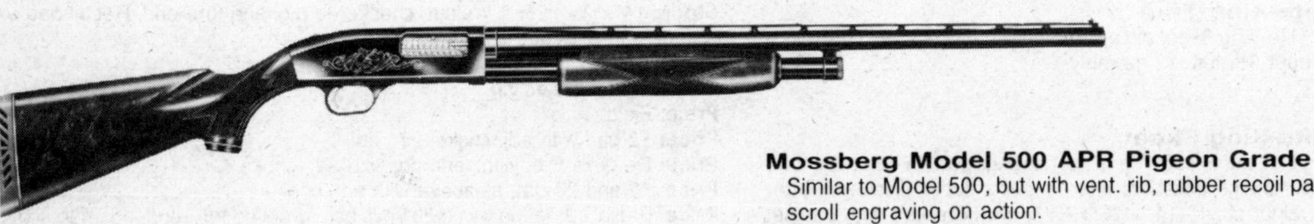

Mossberg Model 500 APR Pigeon Grade

Similar to Model 500, but with vent. rib, rubber recoil pad, hand checkering, scroll engraving on action.
Price: **$174.95**
Price: 500 APTR trap gun 30" full choke barrel, M.C. stock, 14½"x1½"x2", additional barrels available. **$181.80**

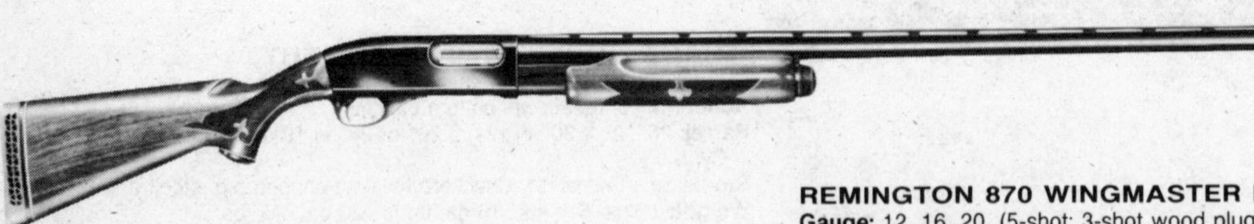

REMINGTON 870 WINGMASTER PUMP GUN

Gauge: 12, 16, 20, (5-shot; 3-shot wood plug).
Action: Takedown, slide action.
Barrel: 12, 16, 20, ga., 26" (Imp. Cyl.); 28" (Mod. or Full); 12 ga., 30" (Full).
Stock: 14"x1⅝"x2½". Checkered walnut, p.g.; fluted extension fore-end; fitted rubber recoil pad.
Weight: 7 lbs., 12 ga. (7¾ lbs. with Vari-Weight plug); 6¾ lbs., 16 ga.; 6½ lbs., 20 ga. 48½" over-all (28" bbl.).
Features: Double action bars, crossbolt safety. Receiver machined from solid steel. Hand fitted action.
Price: Plain bbl. .... **$139.95** Vent. rib **$164.95**
Price: Riot gun, 18" or 20" Riot bore, (12 ga. only) **$124.95**
Price: Riot gun, 20" Imp. Cyl., rifle sights **$134.95**
Price: Left hand, vent. rib., 12 and 20 ga. **$169.95**

REMINGTON 870 ALL AMERICAN

Gauge: 12 only.
Barrel: 30" full choke.
Weight: 7 lbs.
Stock: Select walnut, fluted extension fore end, cut checkered.
Features: Receiver, trigger quard and breech fully engraved. Special "All American" shield fitted to left side of receiver. RK-W finished wood. Pistol grip cap has gold plate for initials. Supplied with luggage type, foam lined case.
Price: Standard or Monte Carlo stock **$555.00**

U.S. SHOTGUNS—SLIDE ACTION

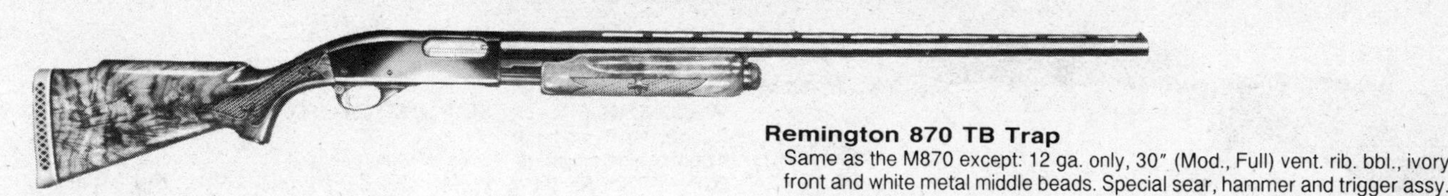

Remington 870 Magnum
Same as the M870 except 3″ chamber, 12 ga. 30″ bbl. (Mod. or Full), 20 ga. 28″ bbl. (Mod. or Full). Recoil pad installed. Wgt., 12 ga. 8 lbs., 20 ga. 7½ lbs.
Price: Plain bbl. .... **$159.95** Vent. rib bbl. **$184.95**
Price: Left hand model, vent rib. bbl. **$189.95**

Remington Model 870 Brushmaster Deluxe
Carbine version of the M870 with 20″ bbl. (Imp. Cyl.) for rifled slugs. 40½″ over-all, wgt. 6½ lbs. Recoil pad. Adj. rear, ramp front sights. 12 or 20 ga. Deluxe **$159.95**

Remington 870D Tournament
Same as 870 except: better walnut, hand checkering, Engraved reciver & bbl. Vent.-rib. Stock dimensions to order **$660.00**

Remington 870 Small Gauges
Exact copies of the large ga. Model 870, except that guns are offered in 20, 28 and 410 ga. 25″ barrel (Full, Mod., Imp. Cyl.).
Plain barrel **$149.95**
D and F grade prices same as large ga. M870 prices.
Price: With vent. rib barrel **$174.95**
Price: Lightweight Magnum, 20 ga. plain bbl. (5¾ lbs.) **$169.95**
Price: Lightweight Magnum, 20 ga., vent. rib bbl. **$194.95**

Remington 870 TB Trap
Same as the M870 except: 12 ga. only, 30″ (Mod., Full) vent. rib. bbl., ivory front and white metal middle beads. Special sear, hammer and trigger assy. 14⅜″x1½″x1⅞″ stock with recoil pad. Hand fitted action and parts. Wgt. 8 lbs. **$204.95**
Price: With Monte Carlo stock **$214.95**
Price: Add **$5.00** for left hand model

Remington 870 SA Skeet
Same as the M870 except: 26″ bbl. Skeet bored. Vent. rib with ivory front and white metal middle beads. 14″x1⅝″x2½″ stock with rubber recoil pad, 12 or ga. only **$169.95**
Price: Add for Cutts comp. **$25.00**
Price: 28 and 410 ga., 25″ bbl., no recoil pad **$179.95**

Remington 870 Extra Barrels
Plain **$39.95.** Vent. rib **$64.95.** Vent. rib Skeet **$69.95.** Vent. rib Trap **$69.95.** 34″ Trap **$74.95.** With rifle sights **$50.95.** Available in the same gauges and chokes as shown on guns.

Remington 870F Premier
Same as M870, except select walnut, better engraving **$1,350.00**

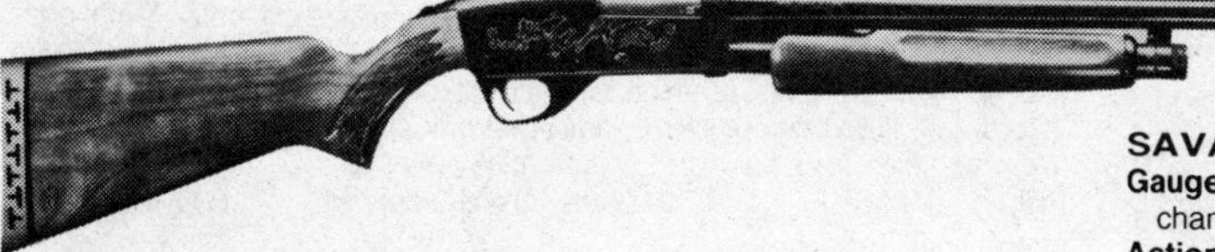

Savage Model 30 Slug Gun
Same as the Model 30 Field Grade but with 22″ bbl., 12 or 20 ga. only, with rifle sights **$109.90**

Savage Model 30 Field Grade
Same as Model 30 except plain bbl. and receiver, hard rubber buttplate.
Price: **$104.60**

SAVAGE MODEL 30-D PUMP GUN
Gauge: 12, 20, and 410, 5-shot (410, 4-shot) 3-shot plug furnished. All gauges chambered for 3″ Magnum shells.
Action: Slide, hammerless, take-down; side ejection; top tang safety.
Barrel: Vent. rib. 12, 20 ga. 26″ (Imp. Cyl.); 28″ (Mod. or Full); 12 ga., 30″ (Full); 410, 26″ (Full).
Stock: 14″x1½″x2½″. Walnut, checkered p.g., grooved extension fore-end, recoil pad.
Weight: 7 lbs. (410, 6¼ lbs.). Over-all 49½″ (30″ bbl.).
Features: Decorated lightweight receiver; plated trigger.
Price: **$125.55**

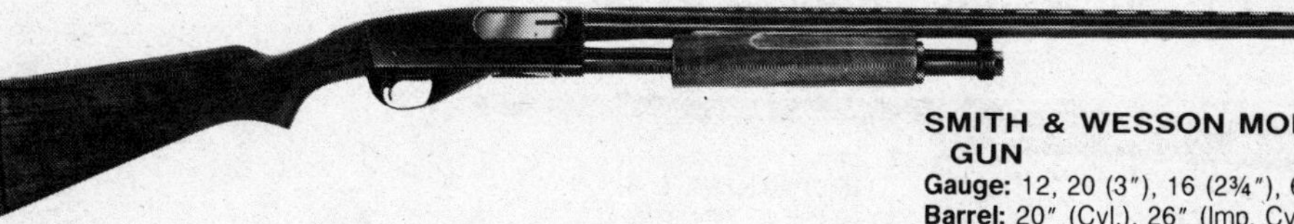

SMITH & WESSON MODEL 916 EASTFIELD PUMP GUN
Gauge: 12, 20 (3″), 16 (2¾″), 6-shot (3-shot plug furnished).
Barrel: 20″ (Cyl.), 26″ (Imp. Cyl.), 28″ (Mod., Full or adj. choke) 30″ (Full), plain. Vent. rib 26″, 28″, 30″.
Weight: 7¼ lbs. (28″ plain bbl.).
Stock: 14″x2½″x1⅝″, American walnut, fluted comb, finger-grooved fore-end.
Features: Vent. rib, vent. recoil pad, adj. choke available as options. Satin finish steel receiver with non-glare top.
Price: Plain bbl., no recoil pad **$104.95**
Price: Plain bbl. with recoil pad **$109.95**
Price: Vent. rib and recoil pad (illus.) **$125.95**

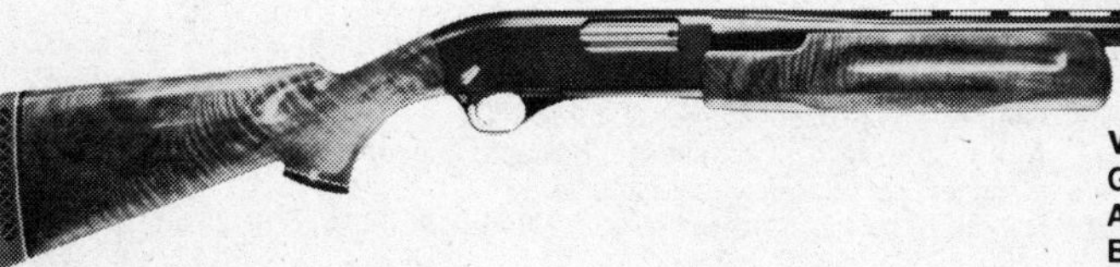

WEATHERBY PATRICIAN PUMP
Gauge: 12 only, 2¾″ chamber.
Action: Short stroke slide action.
Barrel: 26″ (Mod. Imp. Cyl, Skeet), 28″ (Full, Mod.), 30″ (Full) Vent. Rib.
Weight: About 7½ lbs. **Length:** 48⅛ (28″ bbl.)
Stock: Walnut hand checkered p.g. and fore-end, white line spacers at p.g. cap and recoil pad.
Features: Short stroke action, hidden magazine cap, crossbolt safety. Extra interchangeable bbls. **$79.95**
Price: Field or Skeet grade **$229.50** Trap grade **$259.50**

U.S. SHOTGUNS—SLIDE ACTION

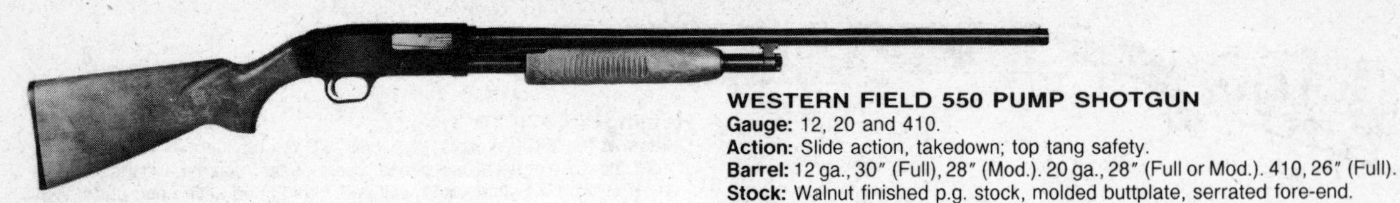

WINCHESTER 12 FIELD PUMP SHOTGUN
Gauge: 12 only, 6-shot (3-shot plug installed).
Barrel: 26″ (Imp. Cyl.), 28″ (Mod.), 30″ (Full), 2¾″ only.
Length: 45¾″ (26″ bbl.). **Weight:** 7¾ lbs.
Stock: 14″x1½″x2½″. Semi-fancy walnut, checkered p.g. and fore-end.
Features: Ventilated rib, hand checkered, engine turned bolt.
Price: **$399.95**

WESTERN FIELD 550 PUMP SHOTGUN
Gauge: 12, 20 and 410.
Action: Slide action, takedown; top tang safety.
Barrel: 12 ga., 30″ (Full), 28″ (Mod.). 20 ga., 28″ (Full or Mod.). 410, 26″ (Full).
Stock: Walnut finished p.g. stock, molded buttplate, serrated fore-end.
Weight: 8½ lbs.
Features: Straight-line feed, interchangeable bbls., trigger disconnector prevents doubling.
Price: .... **$92.00** 410 .... **$98.00**
As above, but with variable choke in 12, 16 or 20 ga. **$115.00**
Slug gun with 24 bbl. without choke **$115.00**
Magnum 12 ga., 30″ bbl. (Full Choke) **$102.99**
Vent. rib models available, fixed or variable choke **$130.00**
to **$138.00**

Winchester 12 Skeet
Same as Model 12 except available only with 26″ Skeet bored bbl. 14″x1½″x2½″ stock with recoil pad **$424.95**

Winchester 12 Trap
Same as Model 12 except: 30″ full choke vent. rib bbl. only. 49¾″ overall. 14⅜″x1⅜″x1⅞″ stock w/recoil pad **$424.95**
With Monte Carlo stock, 14⅜″x1½″x2⅛″ **$434.95**

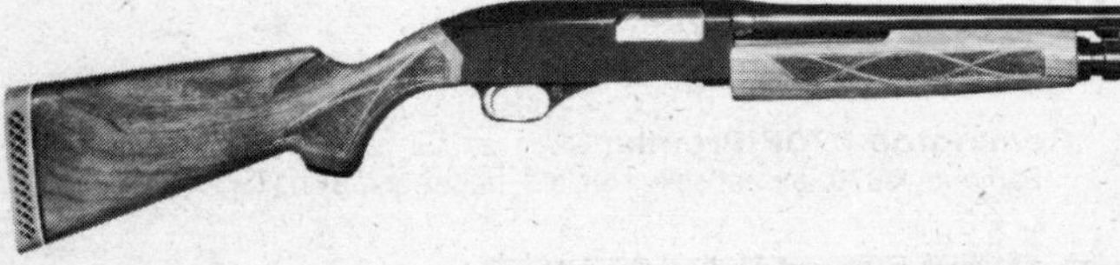

WINCHESTER 1200 FIELD PUMP GUN
Guage: 12 and 20 (5-shot; 3-shot plug installed).
Action: Slide; front locking 4-lug rotating bolt locks into bbl. Alloy receiver, cross-bolt safety in front of trigger guard. Take-down.
Barrel: 26″ (Imp. Cyl.), 28″ (Mod., Full) and 30″ Full (12 ga. only). Metal bead front sight.
Stock: 14″x1⅜″x2⅜″. American walnut with new-design checkered p.g. and fore-end; fluted comb, recoil pad. Steel p.g. cap.
Weight: 12 ga. 6½ lbs. with 26″ bbl. 46⅝″ over-all.
Price: .... **$129.95** With vent. rib **$149.95**

Winchester 1200 Deer Gun
Same as M1200 except: 12 ga. only, 22″ bbl. bored for rifled slugs; rifle-type sights, rear adj. for e. only **$138.95**
Winchester 1200 Extra Barrels: Field w/o sights, 12, 20 ga. **$42.95.** Field with vent. rib, 12, 20 ga. **$62.95**
Winchester 1200 with interchangeable choke tubes which are screwed into the barrel and tightened with supplied wrench. Available in 12, 16, and 20 ga. (28″) Mod. tube. Price: Field **$129.95** vent. rib **$149.95.** Extra tubes in Full, Mod. or Imp. Cyl. **$4.95.** Wrench **$1.25.**

Winchester 1200 Field 3″ Magnum
Same as 1200 except: 12 and 20 ga. only, 2¾″ or 3″ shells, 28″ and 30″ full choke bbls., 3 lbs. with 38″ bbl., 48⅝″ over-all.
Price: .... **$139.95** With vent. rib **$159.95**

U.S. SHOTGUNS — DOUBLE BARREL

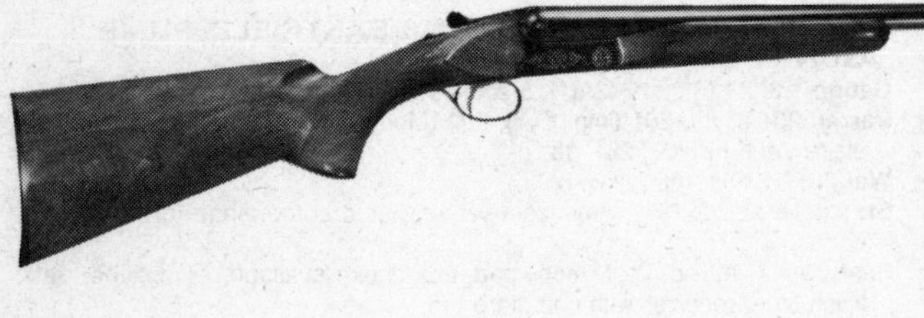

BROWNING B-SS
Gauge: 12 (2¾″), 20 (3″).
Action: Top lever break-open action, top tang safety, single trigger.
Barrel: 26″ (Mod. and Full or Imp. Cyl. and Mod.), 28″ (Mod. and Full).
Weight: 6¾ lbs. (26″ bbl.); 7 lbs. (28″ bbl.).
Stock: 14¾″x1⅝″x2½″. Walnut, hand checkered. Full p.g., full beavertail fore-end.
Features: Automatic safety, automatic ejectors. Hand engraved receiver, mechanical trigger.
Price: **$274.50**

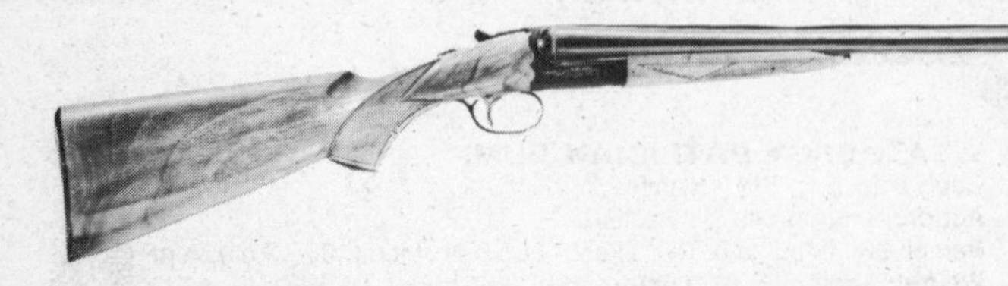

ITHACA SKB 100 FIELD GRADE DOUBLE
Gauge: 12 (2¾″ chambers) and 20 (3″).
Action: Top lever, hammerless, boxlock, automatic safety, single selective trigger, non-automatic extractor.
Barrel: 12 ga. 26″ (Imp. Cyl., Mod.). 28⅛ or 30″ (Mod., Full). 20 ga. 28″ (Mod., Full). 25″ (Imp. Cyl., Mod.).
Stock: 14″x1½″x2⅝″. Walnut, hand checkered p.g. and fore-end, p.g. cap, fluted comb.
Weight: 7 lbs. (12 ga.); 6 lbs. (20 ga.).
Features: Automatic safety. Chrome lined action and barrels, hand engraved receiver.
Price: **$249.95**

Ithaca SKB Model 150
Same as SKB 100 except: Beavertail fore-end and extensively etched scrollwork frame.
Price: **$274.95**

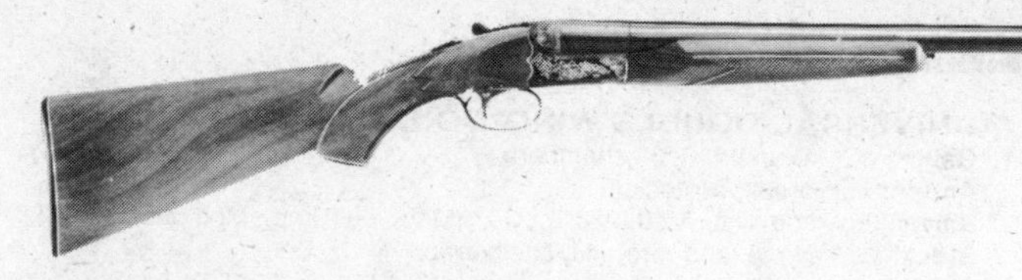

Ithaca SKB 200E Field Grade Double

Same as 100 Field Grade except: automatic selective ejectors, bead middle sight and scroll engraving on receiver, beavertail fore-end. White line spacers. Gold plated trigger and nameplate **$329.95**

Ithaca SKB 200E Skeet Grade

Same as 200E Deluxe Field Grade except: recoil pad, non-auto. safety. Bbls. 26″ 12 ga. or 25″ 20 ga. (Skeet, Skeet). Wgt. 7¼ and 6¼ lbs.
Price: **$339.95**

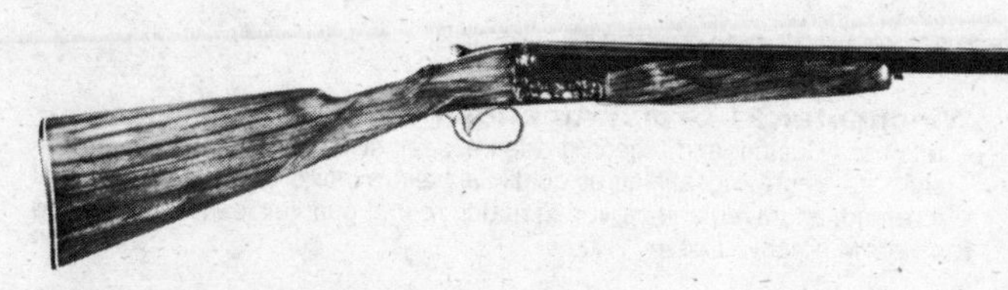

Ithaca-SKB Model 280 Quail Double
Gauge: 20 only, 3″ chambers.
Barrel: 25″ (I.C. & I.C.).
Weight: 6½ lbs.
Stock: 14″x1½″x2⅝″, English style.
Features: Designed for quail and upland game shooting. Straight stock, wrap-around checkering, scroll game scene on frame, semi-beavertail fore-end. Auto. selective ejectors, single trigger.
Price: **$344.95**

ITHACA SKB 280 ENGLISH DOUBLE
Gauge: 12 ga. (2¾″), 20 ga. (3″).
Barrel: 25″, 26″ (Mod. & I.C.), 28″ (Full & Mod.).
Weight: 6½ to 7⅛ lbs.
Stock: English style straight grip. 14″x1½″x2⅝″.
Features: Wrap-around checkering, semi-beavertail fore-end. Receiver hand engraved with quail and English scroll. Simulated oil finish stock.
Price: **$344.95**

PEDERSEN 2000 SERIES DOUBLE, GRADE I
Gauge: 12 or 20 ga.
Action: Boxlock.
Weight: To customer's specs. **Length:** To customer's specs.
Stock: Dimensions to customer's specs. Walnut, hand checkered p.g. and fore-end.
Features: Automatic selective ejectors, barrel selector/safety, gold filled engraving, automatic safety, single selective trigger. Gun is made entirely to customer specifications.
Price: Grade I **$1,800.00**

Pedersen 2000 Series Double, Grade II

Same as Grade I except: standard stock dimensions (14″x2½″x1½″), different receiver engraving, less fancy wood.
Price: 12 or 20 ga. **$1,400.00**

Pedersen 2500 Grade III Double

Field gun version of Series 2000. No receiver engraving, standard stock dimensions. European walnut stock, hand checkered p.g. and beavertail fore-end.
Price: 12 or 20 ga. **$295.00**

SAVAGE FOX MODEL B-SE Double
Gauge: 12, 20, 410 (20, 2¾″ and 3″; 410, 2½″ and 3″ shells).
Action: Hammerless, takedown; non-selective single trigger; auto. safety. Automatic ejectors.
Barrel: 12, 20 ga. 26″ (Imp. Cyl., Mod.); 12 ga. (Mod., Full); 410, 26″ (Full, Full). Vent. rib on all.
Stock: 14″x1½″x2½″. Walnut, checkered p.g. and beavertail fore-end.
Weight: 12 ga. 7 lbs., 16 ga. 6¾ lbs., 20 ga. 6½ lbs., 410 ga. 6¼ lbs.
Features: Decorated, case-hardened frame; white bead front and middle sights.
Price: **$173.20**
Also available with double triggers, case hardened frame, without white line spacers and auto. ejectors as Model B **$146.95**

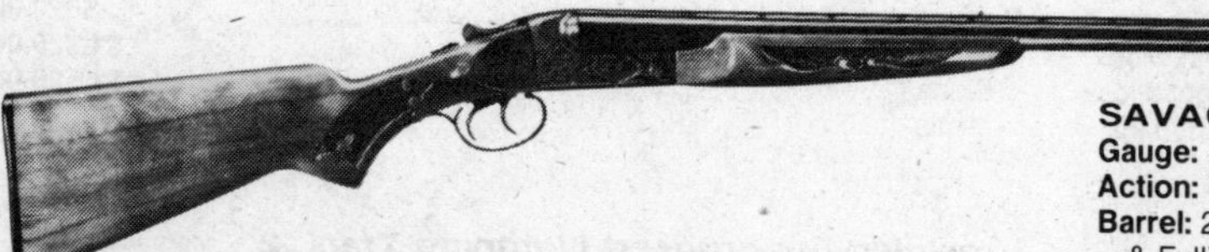

SAVAGE/FOX B 24″ LIGHTWEIGHT
Gauge: 12, 20, 2¾″ & 3″ chamber.
Action: Hammerless, top lever, double triggers.
Barrel: 24″, 12 & 20 ga. (Imp. Cyl. & Mod.), 26″ (Imp. Cyl. & Mod.), 28″ (Mod. & Full), 30″ (Mod. & Full, 12 ga. only), 26″, 410 ga. (Full & Full).
Weight: 7 to 8 lbs.
Stocks: 14″x1½″x2½″, select walnut. Checkered p.g. and fore-end.
Features: Color case-hardened frame, beavertail fore-end, vent. rib.
Price: **$146.95**

SAVAGE-STEVENS MODEL 311 DOUBLE
Gauge: 12, 16, 20, 410 (12, 20 and 410, 3″ chambers).
Action: Top lever, hammerless; double triggers, auto top tang safety.
Barrel: 12, 16, 20 ga. 36″ (Imp. Cyl., Mod.); 12 ga. 28″ (Mod., Full); 12 ga. 30″ (Mod., Full); 410 ga. 26″ (Full, Full).
Length: 45¾″ over-all. **Weight:** 7-8 lbs. (30″ bbl.).
Stock: 14″x1½″x2½″. Walnut finish, p.g., fluted comb.
Features: Box type frame, case-hardened finish.
Price: **$115.45**

U.S. SHOTGUNS—DOUBLE BARREL

UNIVERSAL DOUBLE WING DOUBLE

Gauge: 12, 20 and 410, 3″ chambers
Action: Top break, boxlock.
Barrel: 26″ (Imp. Cyl., Mod.); 28″ or 30″ (Mod., Full; Imp., Mod.; Full & Full).
Stock: Walnut p.g. and fore-end, checkered.
Weight: About 7 lbs.
Features: Double triggers; Recoil pad. Beavertail style fore-end.
Price: **$189.95**
Price: 10 ga. 3½″ chamber 32″ Full and Full (M2030) **$205.95**

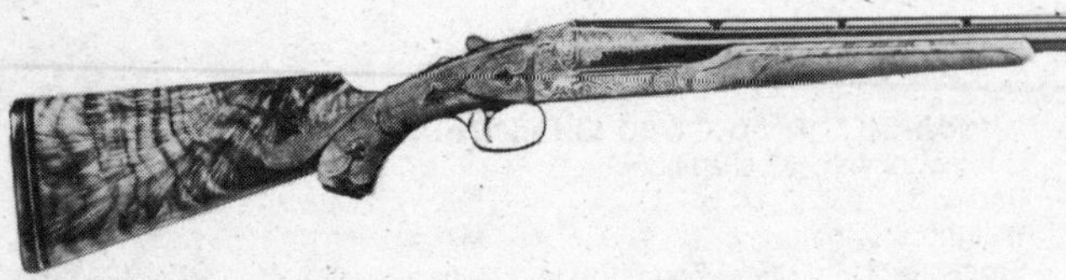

WINCHESTER 21 CUSTOM DOUBLE GUN

12, 16 or 20 ga. Almost any choke or bbl. length combination. Matted rib, 2¾″ chambers, rounded frame, stock of AA-grade full fancy American walnut to customer's dimensions; straight or p.g., cheekpiece, Monte Carlo and/or offset; field. Skeet or trap fore-end.
Full fancy checkering, engine-turned receiver parts, gold plated trigger and gold oval name plate (optional) with three initials **$2,985.00**

Winchester 21 Grand American

Same as Custom and Pigeon grades except: style "B" stock carving, with style "6" engraving, all figures gold inlaid; extra pair of bbls. with beavertail fore-end, engraved and carved to match rest of gun; full leather trunk case or all, with canvas cover **$5,900.00**

Winchester 21 Pigeon grade

Same as Custom grade except: 3″ chambers, available in 12 and 20 ga.; matted or vent. rib, leather covered pad (optional); style "A" stock carving and style "6" engraving (see Win. catalog); gold inlaid p.g. cap, gold nameplate or 3 gold initials in guard **$4,300.00**

U.S. SHOTGUNS — OVER UNDER

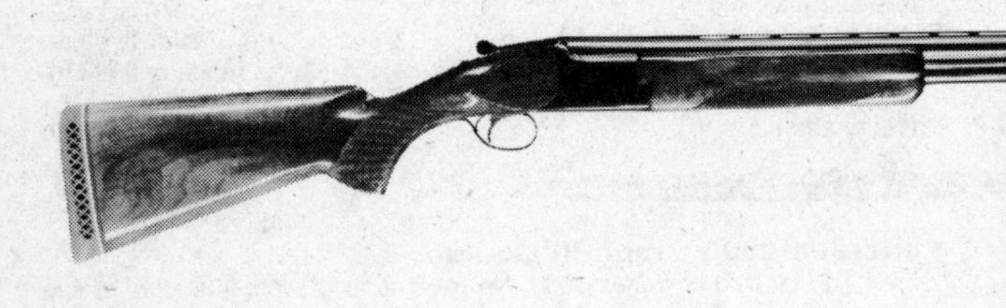

BROWNING CITORI O/U SHOTGUN

Gauge: 12 and 20 ga.
Barrel: 26″, 28″ (Mod. & Full, Imp. Cyl. & Mod.), 30″ (Mod. & Full, Full & Full) in 12 ga., 26″ or 28″ in 20 ga., same chokes.
Weight: 7½ lbs. (26″, 12 ga.) 6¾ lbs. (26″, 20 ga.)
Length: 43″ over-all (26″ bbl.).
Stock: Dense walnut, hand checkered, full pistol grip. Beavertail fore-end. Recoil pad on 12 ga. field guns and Trap and skeet models.
Sights: Medium raised sights, German nickel silver.
Features: Barrel selector integral with safety, auto. ejectors, three-piece take-down.
Price: Field Model (12 or 20 ga.) **$325.00**
Price: Trap Model, 12 ga. only (30″ bbl. only) **$335.00**
Price: Skeet Model, 12 ga. only (26″ & 28″ bbls.) **$330.00**

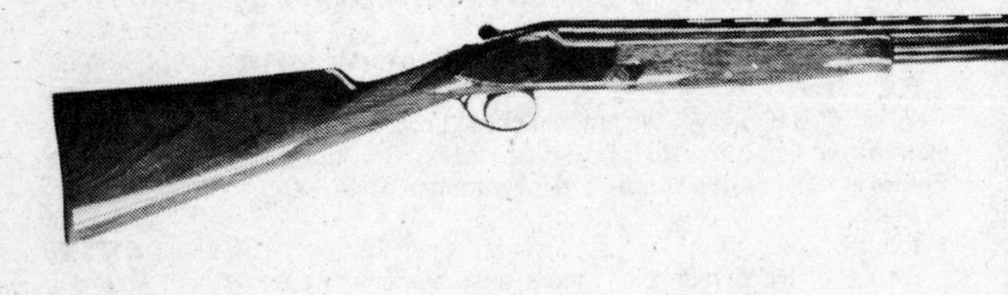

BROWNING SUPERPOSED SUPER-LIGHT

Gauge: 12, & 20 2¾″ chamber.
Action: Boxlock, top lever, single selective trigger. Bbl. selector combined with manual tang safety.
Barrels: 26½″ (Mod. & Full, or Imp. Cyl. & Mod.)
Stock: Straight grip (14¼″ x 1⅝″ x 2½″) hand checkered (fore-end and grip) select walnut.
Weight: 6⅜ lbs., average.
Features: Slender, tapered vent. rib. Hand rubbed finish, engraved receiver.
Price: Grade 1 .... **$820.00**
Pigeon **$1,220.00**
Diana **$1,520.00**
Midas **$2070.00**

Browning Superposed Magnum 12

Browning Superposed 3″ chambers; 30″ (Full and Full or Full and Mod.) barrels, Stock, 14¼″x1⅝″x2½″ with factory fitted recoil pad. Weight 8 lbs. Grade 1, **$780.00,** Pigeon **$1,150.00,** Diana **$1,450.00,** Midas **$2,000.00.**

Browning Superposed All-Gauge Skeet Set

Consists of four matched sets of barrels in 12, 20, 28 and 410 ga. Available in either 26½″ or 28″ length. Each bbl. set has a ¼″ wide vent. rib with two ivory sight beads. Grade 1 receiver is hand engraved and stock and fore-end are checkered. Weight 7 lbs., 10 oz. (26½″ bbls.), 7 lbs., 12 oz. (28″ bbls.). Grade 1 **$2,400.00,** Pigeon **$3,100.00,** Diana **$3,600.00,** Midas **$4,700.00.**

Browning Superposed Lightning Skeet

Same as Standard Skeet except: 12 and 20 ga. only. Wgt. 6½-7¾ lbs. Grade 1 **$800.00,** Pigeon **$1,170.00,** Diana **$1,470.00,** Midas **$2,020.00.**

Browning Superposed Lightning Trap 12

Same as Browning Lightning Superposed except: semi-beavertail fore-end and ivory sights; stock, 14⅜″x1 7/16″x1⅝″. 7¾ lbs. 30″ (Full & Full, Full & Imp. Mod. or Full and Mod.) Grade 1 **$800.00,** Pigeon **$1,170.00,** Diana **$1,470.00,** Midas **$2,020.00.**

Browning Superposed Lightning

7-7¼ lbs. in 12 ga. 6-6¼ lbs. in 20 ga. Grade 1 **$780.00,** Pigeon **$1,150.00,** Diana **$1,450.00,** Midas **$2,000.00.**

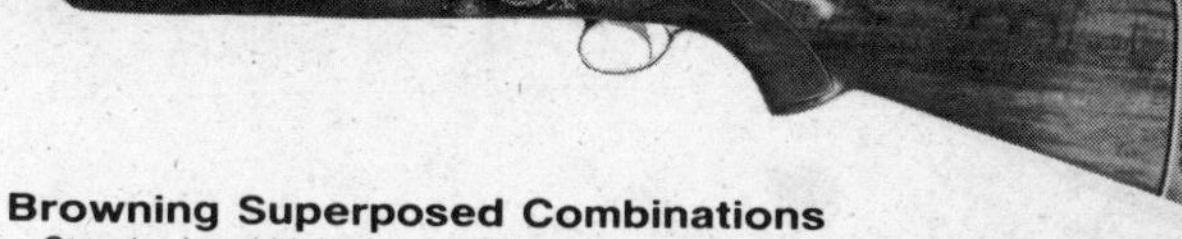

Superposed Broadway Trap 12
Same as Browning Lightning Superposed except: ⅝″ wide vent. rib; stock, 14⅜″x1$^{7}/_{16}$″x1⅝″. 30″ or 32″ (Imp. Mod, Full; Mod., Full; Full, Full). 8 lbs. with 32″ bbls. Grade 1 **$820.00,** Pigeon **$1,220.00,** Diana **$1,520.00,** Midas **$2,070.00.**

Browning Superposed Combinations
Standard and Lightning models are available with these factory fitted extra barrels: 12 and 20 ga., same gauge bbls.; 12 ga., 20 ga. bbls.; 20 ga., extra sets 28 and/or 410 gauge; 28 ga., extra 410 bbls. Extra barrels may be had in Lightning weights with Standard models and vice versa. Prices range from **$1,250.00** (12, 20 ga., one set extra bbls. same gauge) for the Grade 1 Standard to about **$3,070.00** for the Midas grade in various combinations, all as cased sets.

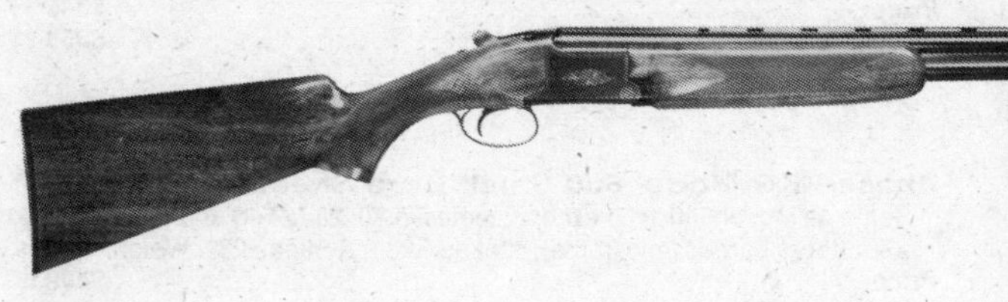

BROWNING "LIEGE" O/U
Gauge: 12 only (2¾″ or 3″ mag.).
Action: Boxlock, top lever, single selective trigger.
Barrels: 26½″, 2¾″ (Full & Full, Mod. & Full. or Imp. Cyl. & Mod.); 28″ 2¾″ (Full & Full, Mod. & Full, Imp. Cyl. & Mod.); 30″, 3″ Mag. (Full & Full or Mod. & Full).
Stock: 14¼″x1⅝″x2½″. Select walnut, hand rubbed finish, hand checkered p.g. & fore-end.
Weight: 7¼ lbs. to 7¾ lbs.
Features: Mechanical trigger, manual safety with bbl. selector, 3-piece assembly, fore-end detaches for disassembly.
Price: **$497.50**

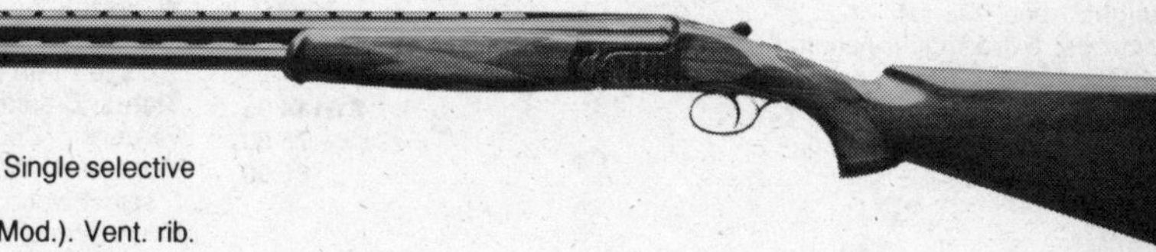

ITHACA MIRAGE O/U
Gauge: 12 only (2¾″ chambers).
Action: Boxlock type, interchangeable hammer-trigger group. Single selective trigger, specify choice of firing order.
Barrel: 28″, 30″, or 32″ (Skeet and Skeet or Extra-Full and Mod.). Vent. rib.
Weight: 8¼ lbs. **Length:** 44″ over-all.
Stock: Walnut, hand checkered with schnabel fore-end, 1½″x2⅜″x14″. Rubber recoil pad.
Price: Trap model **$1,674.95**
Price: Skeet model **$1,674.95**

ITHACA MX-8 TRAP GUN
Gauge: 12 only, 2¾″ chambers.
Action: Boxlock type, single non-selective trigger; interchangeable trigger-hammer group offers choice of firing order.
Barrel: 30″ or 32″, especially bored for international clay target shooting. High concave vent rib has 5″ ramp.
Stock: Custom, finely checkered (oiled or lacquer finish) European walnut, interchangeable with other models, 9 available including Monte Carlo.
Weight: About 8 lbs.
Features: Ventilated middle rib has additional vent ports for maximum heat dissipation, better balance and smoother swing.
Price: **$1,674.95**
Extra trigger-hammer group **75.00**
Extra stock **85.00**

Ithaca MX-8 Combination
Same as MX-8 Trap Gun except comes with interchangeable single barrel (32″ or 34″).
Price: **$2,234.95**

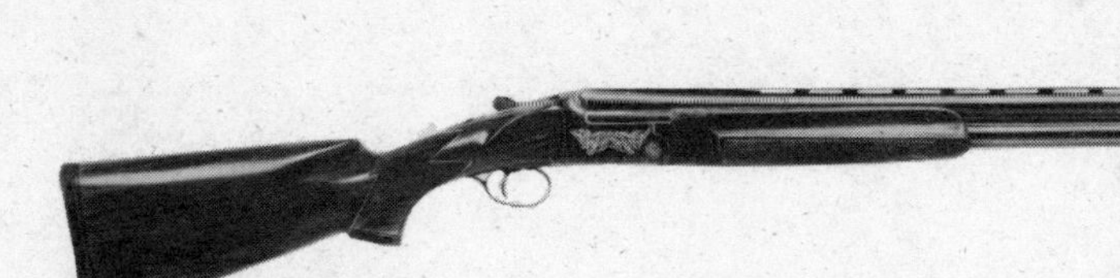

ITHACA COMPETITION I SKEET O/U
Gauge: 12 only, 2¾″ chambers.
Action: Boxlock type, interchangeable hammer-trigger group. Single non-selective trigger.
Barrel: 26¾″ (Skeet & Skeet). Vent rib has concave surface with deep cuts.
Stock: 14½″x1½″x2⅜″, interchangeable walnut, custom stocks available.
Weight: About 7¾ lbs.
Features: Extra trigger-hammer groups to change firing order and/or weight of pull. Leather faced recoil pad has bevelled heel that will not catch. Extra stocks interchange for different style and dimension.
Price: **$1,114.95**
Extra trigger-hammer group **75.00**

Ithaca-SKB Model 680 English O/U
Gauge: 12 or 20 ga.
Action: Boxlock.
Barrel: 26″ or 28″ (Full & Mod., Mod. & I.C.).
Weight: 7 lbs.
Stock: 14″x1½″x2⅝″, straight grip, walnut, wrap-around checkering.
Features: Auto. selective ejectors, Bradley-type sights on target grades. Single selective trigger, chrome lined barrels with black chrome exteriors.
Price: **$419.95**

Ithaca SKB 600 Trap Grade O/U

Same as 500 Field Grade except 30″ bbl. (Imp. Mod., Full, or Full, Full), fine scroll engraved receiver; bead middle sight; Monte Carlo stock (14½″x1½″x1½″x2″), p.g. white line spacer and recoil pad.

Price: **$399.95**

Field Grade 600, on recoil pad or Monte Carlo **$394.95**

Trap Grade 700, features select walnut oil finished stock and band engraved receiver **$499.95**

ITHACA COMPETITION I TRAP O/U

Gauge: 12 only, 2¾″ chambers.

Action: Boxlock type, interchangeable hammer-trigger group. Single non-selective trigger, specify choice of firing order.

Barrel: 30″ or 32″, upper Full; lower, Imp.-Mod., vent rib has concave surface with deep cuts.

Stock: Interchangeable, 6 standard (1³⁄₁₆″ to 1½″ at comb x1⅜″ to 1⅞″ at heel) and 3 Monte Carlo (1⅜″ to 1⁹⁄₁₆″x1⅜″ to 1⁹⁄₁₆″) of walnut; all have 14½″ pull. Fore-end has slight taper and finger groove for firm grip.

Weight: About 7¾ lbs.

Features: Extra trigger-hammer groups are available to change firing sequence and/or trigger pull. Custom stocks also available.

Price: **$1,114.95**

Extra trigger-hammer group **75.00**

Extra stock **85.00**

ITHACA-SKB MODEL 880 CROWN GRADE O/U

Gauge: 12 or 20.

Action: Boxlock with sideplates.

Barrel: Trap 30″ or 32″ (Full & Imp. Mod.), Skeet 26″ (Skeet & Skeet), 20 ga. Skeet 28″ (Skeet & Skeet).

Weight: 7 lbs. (Skeet), 8 lbs. (Trap).

Stock: 14½″x2″x1½″x1½″ Trap with M.C., 14″x2½″x1½″ Skeet. Full fancy French walnut.

Sights: Bradley-type.

Features: Hand-honed action, extensive engraving and checkering. Gold-inlaid "crown" on bottom of frame.

Price: **$999.95**

ITHACA SKB 500 FIELD GRADE O/U

Gauge: 12 (2¾″ or 3″ chambers), 20 (3″).

Action: Top lever, hammerless, boxlock; gold-plated single selective trigger; automatic ejectors, non-auto safety.

Barrel: 26″ vent. rib (Imp. Cyl., Mod.); 28″ (Imp. Cyl., Mod. or Mod., Full); 30″ (Mod., Full); 12 ga., 2¾″ chambers. 26″ (Imp. Cyl., Mod.); 28″ (Mod., Full); 20 ga., 3″ chambers.

Stock: 14″x1½″x2⅝″. Walnut, checkered p.g. and fore-end, p.g. cap, fluted comb.

Weight: 7½ lbs. (12); 6½ lbs. (20).

Features: Border scroll engraved receiver. Chrome lined bbls. and action. Raybar front sight.

Price: **$349.95**

Price: Magnum model **$359.95**

Ithaca-SKB Model 600 Small Bore Skeet

Same as Model 600 Trap except: comes in 20, 28 (2¾″) and 410 (2½″) as a set (three barrels, one frame), choked Skeet & Skeet, 28″. Weight 7¼ lbs.

Price: **$409.95**

ITHACA-SKB TRAP DOUBLES MODEL 600, 700 O/U

Gauge: 12, 2¾″.

Barrel: 30″ or 32″, special bore.

Weight: 8 lbs.

Stocks: 14″x1½″x1⅞″, American walnut, hand fitted, hand checkered, curved trap pad. Available with M.C. stock.

Sights: Bradley-type.

Features: Double locking lugs, non-automatic safety. Built expressly for shooting doubles and Continental/International style trap. Model 700 has select wood, extra-wide rib, more detailed scroll work on frame.

Price: Model 600 .... **$399.95**

Price: Model 700 (deluxe version of 600) **$499.95**

Ithaca SKB 600 Skeet Grade O/U

Same as 600 Trap except: 26″ or 28″ bbls. (Skeet, Skeet), stock (14″x1½″x2⅝″), standard buttplate and whiteline spacer. Weight 7½ lbs.

Price: **$399.95**

Skeet Grade 700, select walnut oil finished stock and band engraved receiver **$499.95**

ITHACA LIGHT GAME MODEL

Gauge: 12 only (2¾″ chambers).

Action: Boxlock type interchangeable hammer-trigger group. Offers choice of firing order. Single non-selective trigger.

Barrel: 27⅝″ (Mod. and Full, Imp. Cyl. and Full, Imp. Cyl. and Mod.) Vent. rib.

Weight: 6¾ lbs. **Length:** 44½ overall.

Stock: French walnut. Hand checkered p.g., fore-end and butt, schnabel fore-end, 1½″x2⅜″x14″.

Features: Hand engraved, case hardened frame.

Price: **$1,114.95**

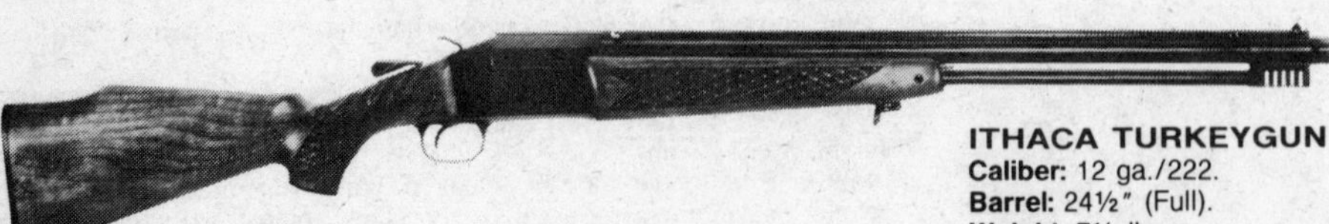

ITHACA TURKEYGUN

Caliber: 12 ga./222.

Barrel: 24½″ (Full).

Weight: 7½ lbs.

Stock: 14″x1⅝″x1⅞″x2¼″, walnut.

Sights: Ramp front, folding leaf rear.

Features: Detachable choke tubes (Full choke supplied, Mod., Imp. Cyl. available), rifle barrel, sling swivels, grooved for scope mounts. Imported by Ithaca.

Price: **$259.95**

PEDERSEN 1000 SERIES CUSTOM O/U
Gauge: 12 or 20 ga.
Action: Boxlock.
Barrel: To customer specs.
Weight: To customer specs. **Length:** To customer specs.
Stock: Dimensions to customer specs. American walnut, hand checkered p.g. and fore-end, rubber recoil pad.
Features: Vent. rib, single selective trigger, automatic ejectors, gold filled, hand engraved receiver, gun made entirely to customer specifications.
Price: 12 or 20 ga. **$1,800.00**
Price: Trap or Skeet models **$1,800.00**

Pedersen 1000 Series O/U, Grade II
Same as Grade I except: standard stock dimensions (14"x2½"x1½"x2"), less fancy wood, different receiver engraving.
Price: 12 or 20 ga. **$1,400.00**
Price: Trap model (with trap dimensions) **$1,425.00**
Price: Skeet model **$1,410.00**

Pedersen 1000 Series O/U, Grade III
Same as Grade I except: standard stock dimensions (14"x2½"x1½"x2"), no receiver engraving. Gold plated trigger and fore-end release.
Price: 12 or 20 ga. **$1,200.00**
Price: Trap model **$1,225.00**
Price: Skeet model **$1,210.00**

PEDERSEN 1500 O/U
Gauge: 12 only.
Action: Boxlock.
Barrel: 26" to 32".
Weight: 7 to 7½ lbs. **Length:** 44" over-all (26" bbl.).
Stock: 14"x2½"x1½"x2". European walnut, hand checkered p.g. and fore-end, rubber recoil pad.
Features: Field gun version of Series 1000. Automatic selective ejectors, vent. rib, choice of sights on target guns, Field model has Raybar type.
Price: 12 ga., Field **$450.00**
Price: Trap (has M.C. stock and pad) **$470.00**
Price: Skeet (skeet chokes) **$460.00**

REMINGTON 3200 O/U
Gauge: 12, 2¾" chambers.
Action: Top lever, break open. Single selective trigger.
Barrel: 26" (Imp. Cyl. & Mod., Skeet & Skeet), 28" (Mod. & Full, Skeet & Skeet), 30" (Mod. & Full, Full & Full, Imp. Mod. & Full). Vent. rib.
Weight: 7¾ lbs. (26" bbl.).
Stock: 14"x1½"x2⅛", American walnut. Checkered p.g. and fore-end. Modified beavertail fore-end on field model, full on trap and Skeet.
Features: Super-fast lock time, separated barrels, engraved receiver, unbreakable firing pins, combination barrel selector/safety, wide trigger, shield-covered breech.
Price: Field (illus.) .... **$485.00** Skeet **$530.00**
Price: Trap .... **$550.00** Special Trap **$660.00**
Price: "One of 1,000" Skeet **$1,050.00**

SAVAGE MODEL 24-C O/U
Caliber: Top bbl. 22 S, L, LR; bottom bbl. 20 gauge cyl. bore.
Action: Take-down, low rebounding visible hammer. Single trigger, barrel selector spur on hammer.
Barrel: 20" separate barrels.
Weight: 5¾ lbs. **Length:** 35" (taken down 20").
Stock: Walnut finished hardwood, straight grip.
Sight: Ramp front, rear open adj. for e.
Features: Trap door butt holds two shotshells and ten 22 cartridges, comes with special carrying case. Measures 5"x22" when in case.
Price: **$78.70**

Savage Model 24-D O/U
Caliber: Top bbl. 22 S, L, LR or 22 Mag.; bottom bbl. 20 or 410 gauge.
Action: Two-way top lever opening, low rebounding visible hammer, single trigger, barrel selector spur on hammer, separate extractors, color case-hardened frame.
Barrel: 24", separated barrels.
Weight: 6¾ lbs. **Length:** 40".
Stock: Walnut, checkered p.g. and fore-end (14"x1½"x2½").
Sights: Ramp front, rear open adj. for e.
Features: Receiver grooved for scope mounting.
Price: **$83.95**

SAVAGE MODEL 24-F.G. O/U

Same as Model 24-D except: color case hardened frame, stock is walnut finished hardwood, no checkering or M.C.

Price: **$70.25**

Savage Model 24-V

Same as Model 24-DL except: 222 Rem. or 30-30 and 20 ga. only; color case-hardened frame; barrel; band; folding leaf rear sight; rec. tapped for scope **$104.95**

SAVAGE 333 O/U

Gauge: 12, 20 (2¾" & 3" chambers).
Action: Top lever, break open.
Barrel: 26" (Skeet & Skeet or Imp. Cyl. & Mod.), 28" (Mod. & Full), 30" (Mod. & Full, 12 ga. only).
Weight: 6¼ to 7¼ lbs.
Stock: 14"x1½"x2½", French walnut. Fleur-de-lis checkering.
Features: Single selective trigger, auto. safety, ejectors, cocking indicators. Engraved steel receiver.
Price: **$339.50**

Savage Model 330 O/U Set

Identical to the Model 330 but with two sets of barrels, one in 12 ga. the other in 20 (Mod. & Full). Same fore-end fits both sets of bbls. Comes with padded case with pocket for extra bbl.

Price: Factory fitted **$368.50**

SAVAGE MODEL 330 O/U

Gauge: 12, 2¾" chambers, 20 ga. 3" chambers.
Action: Top lever, break open. Selective single trigger, auto top tang safety locks trigger, coil springs.
Barrel: 26" (Mod. & Imp. Cyl.), 28" or 30" (Mod. & Full).
Stock: 14"x1½"x2½"). Walnut, checkered p.g. and fore-end, hard rubber plate.
Weight: About 7 lbs., 46½" (30" bbl.) over-all.
Features: Monoblock locking rails are engaged by locking shield that snaps forward as gun is closed. This shield overlaps the breech for added strength.
Price: **$269.50**

SAVAGE 333-T

Same specifications as Model 330 except has trap specifications and features: 30" bbl. choked Imp. Mod. and Full, manually operated top tang safety (disconnects trigger from sears), stock measures 14½"x1½"x1½" at Monte Carlo, 2½" heel. Over-all length 47", taken down 30", weight 7¾ lbs. Has extra-wide ventilated rib, extractors, recoil pad.

Price: **$340.00**

UNIVERSAL OVER WING O/U SHOTGUN

Gauge: 12, 20. 3" chamber.
Action: Top lever, hammerless, box lock, double triggers.
Barrel: 26" vent. rib (Imp. Cyl., & Mod.); 28" or 30" (Mod. & Full). Front & middle sights.
Stock: 14"x1½"x2⅝". Walnut, checkered p.g. and fore-end. Recoil Pad.
Weight: 7½ lbs. (12); 6½ lbs. (20).
Price: **$289.95**

WEATHERBY REGENCY O/U SHOTGUN

Gauge: 12 ga. (2¾" chambers), 20 ga. (3" chambers).
Action: Boxlock (simulated side-lock) top lever break-open. Selective auto ejectors, single selective trigger (selector inside trigger guard).
Barrel: 28" with vent rib and bead front sight, Full & Mod., Mod. & Imp. Cyl. or Skeet & Skeet.
Stock: American walnut, checkered p.g. and fore-end (14¼"x1½"x2½").
Weight: 12 ga. 7⅜ lbs., 20 ga. 6⅞ lbs.
Features: Mechanically operated trigger. Top tang safety, Greener cross-bolt, fully engraved receiver, recoil pad installed.
Price: 12 or 20 ga. Field and Skeet **$599.00**
Price: 12 ga. Trap Model **$649.50**

U.S. SHOTGUNS—OVER-UNDER

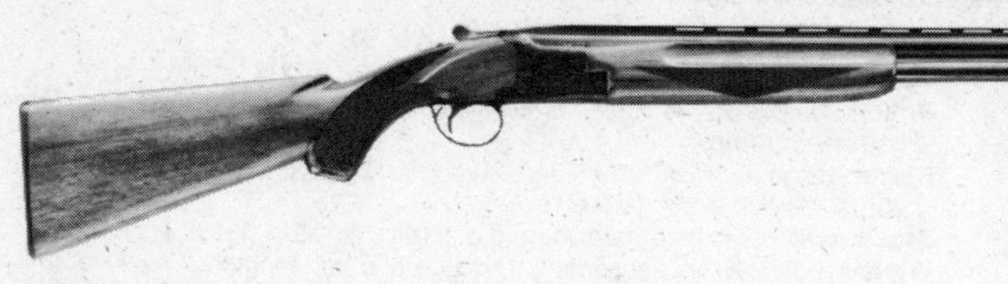

WINCHESTER 101 OVER/UNDER Field Gun

Gauge: 12 and 28, 2¾"; 20 and 410, 3".
Action: Top lever, break open. Manual safety combined with bbl. selector at top of receiver tang.
Barrel: Vent. rib 26" 12, 26½", 20 and 410 (Imp. Cyl., Mod.), 28" (Mod & Full), 30" 12 only (Mod. & Full). Metal bead front sight. Chrome plated chambers and bores.
Stock: 14"x1½"x2½". Checkered walnut p.g. and fore-end; fluted comb.
Weight: 12 ga. 7¾ lbs. Others 6¼ lbs. **Length:** 44¾" over-all (28" bbls.).
Features: Single selective trigger, auto ejectors. Hand engraved receiver.
Price: 12 or 20 ga **$425.00**
Price: 28 or 410 ga. **$455.00**

Winchester 101 Magnum Field Gun

Same as 101 Field Gun except: chambers 3" Magnum shells; 12 & 20 ga. 30" (Full & Full or Mod. & Full); hand-engraved receiver, select French walnut stock with fluted comb, hand-checkered pistol grip and beavertail fore-end with recoil pad **$435.00**

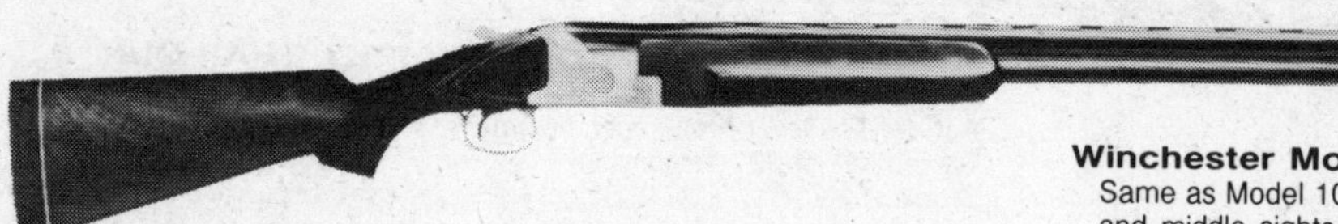

Winchester Model 101 Pigeon Grade Trap Gun

Same as Model 101 Field except has new-design vent. rib with bead front and middle sights, hand-engraved satin finish receiver, knurled, non-slip trigger. Stock and fore-end of fancy French walnut, hand checkered p.g. and fore-end. 12 ga. only, 2¾" chambers, 30" or 32" (I.M. & Full). Stock measures 14⅜"x1⅜"x1⅞". Weighs 8¼ lbs.
Price: Standard trap stock **$665.00**
Price: Monte Carlo stock **$675.00**

Winchester 101 Skeet

Same as M-101 except: 12 ga., 26" bbls., 20, 26½", 28 & 410, 28". Bored Skeet and Skeet only, 12 or 20 ga. **$465.00**
M101 in 28 or 410 .... **$495.00**

Winchester 101 Combination Skeet Set

Same as 101 20 ga. Skeet except: Includes Skeet bbls. in 410 & 28 ga. Vent. ribs match 20 ga. frame. With fitted trunk case **$1,080.00**

U.S. SHOTGUNS—SINGLE BARREL

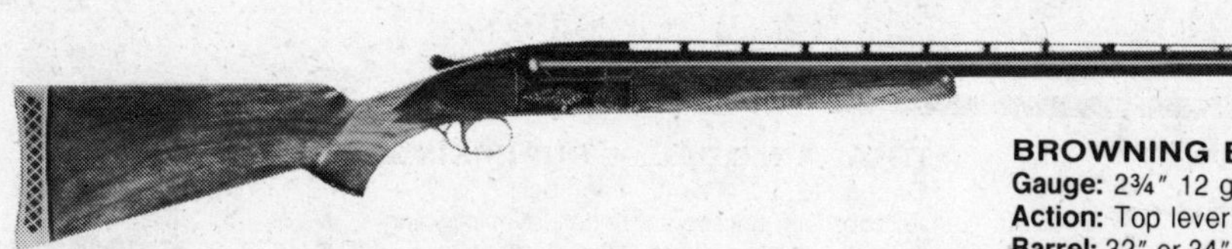

BROWNING BT-99 SINGLE BARREL TRAP

Gauge: 2¾" 12 gauge only.
Action: Top lever break-open hammerless, engraved.
Barrel: 32" or 34" (Mod., Imp. Mod. or Full) with 1 1/32" wide, high post floating vent rib.
Stock: French walnut, hand checkered full p.g. and beavertail fore-end, factory fitted recoil pad (14⅜"x1 7/16"x1⅝").
Weight: 8 lbs. (32" bbl.), 8⅛ lbs. (34" bbl.).
Features: Automatic ejector, gold plated trigger has about 3½ lb. pull, no safety.
Price: **$350.00**

CLERKE FALLING BLOCK SHOTGUN

Gauge: 12, 20, 410 (2¾" or 3" magnums).
Weight: 6¼ lbs. (12 ga.). **Length:** 42" to 52" (12 ga.).
Stock: Walnut finish stock and fore-end. Full pistol grip.
Features: Exposed rebounding hammer, falling block side lever action, color case hardened frame. Vent. rib, trap grade stock and rubber recoil pad available as options.
Price: **$49.95**

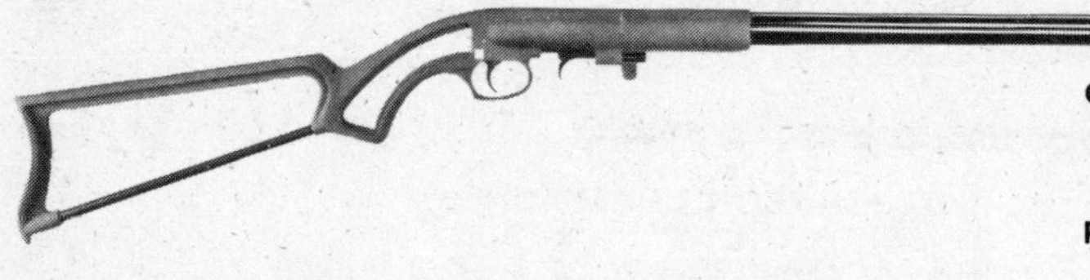

GARCIA BRONCO 410 SHOTGUN

Lightweight single shot (3" chamber), featuring swing-out chamber, skeletonized 1-pc. receiver and p.g. stock, push-button safety, 3½ lbs., instant take-down.
Price: Approx. **$40.00**

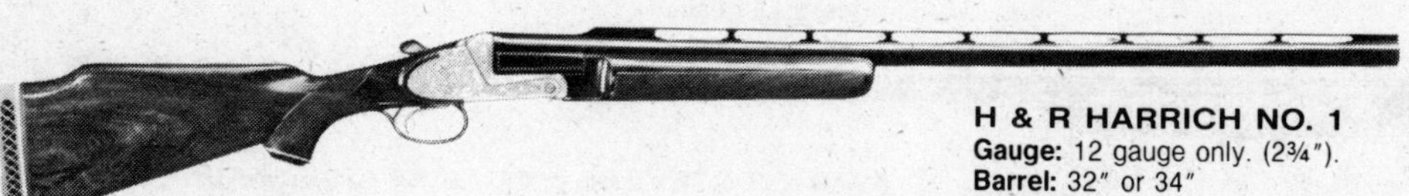

H & R HARRICH NO. 1

Gauge: 12 gauge only. (2¾").
Barrel: 32" or 34"
Weight: 8½ lbs.
Stock: Select walnut, checkered p.g. and beavertail fore-end 14¾"x1¼"x1¼"x2".
Features: Anson & Deeley type locking system with Kersten top locks and double under-locking lugs. Full length high line vent. rib. Hand engraved side locks.
Price: **$1,600.00**

U.S. SHOTGUNS—SINGLE BARREL

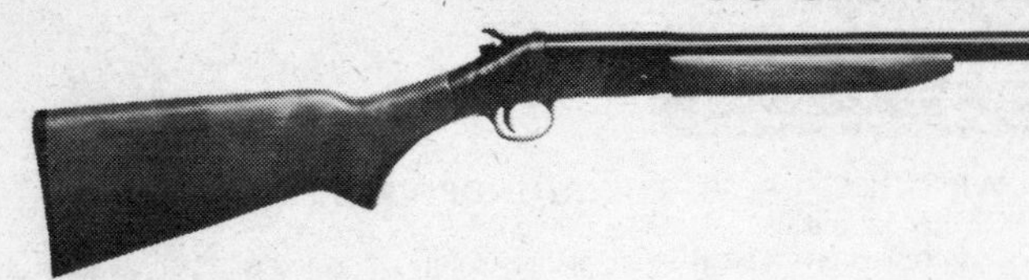

H & R TOPPER MODELS 58 and 98

Gauge: 12, 20 and 410. (2¾" or 3" chamber), 16 (2¾" only).
Action: Takedown. Side lever opening. External hammer, auto ejection. Case hardened frame.
Barrel: 12 ga., 28", 30", 32", 36"; 20 and 410 ga., 28". (Full choke). 12, 16, 20 ga. available 28" (Mod.).
Stock: Walnut finished hardwood; p.g., (14"x1¾"x2½").
Weight: 5 to 6½ lbs., according to gauge and bbl. length.
Features: Self-adj. bbl. lock; coil springs throughout; auto. rebound hammer.
Price: M58 .... **$46.00**
Model 98, Topper Deluxe Chrome frame, ebony finished stock. 20 ga. and 410, 28" bbl. **$52.00**

H & R Topper Jr. Model 490
Like M158 except ideally proportioned stock for the smaller shooter. Can be cheaply changed to full size. 20 ga. (Mod.) or 410 (Full) 26" bbl. Weight 5 lbs., 40½" over-all **$49.00**

H & R Topper Buck Model 162
Same as M158 except 12 ga. 24" cyl. bored bbl., adj. Lyman peep rear sight, blade front, 5½ lbs.; over-all 40". Cross bolt safety: push-button action release **$53.00**

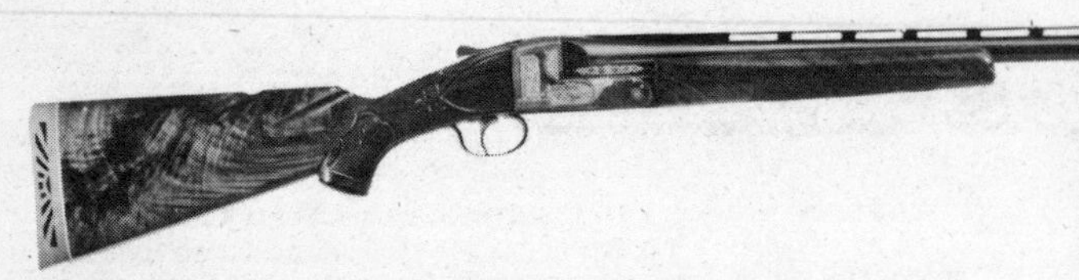

ITHACA 4E GRADE SINGLE BARREL TRAP GUN

Gauge: 12 only.
Action: Top lever break open hammerless, dual locking lugs.
Barrel: 30" or 32", rampless rib.
Stock: (14½"x1½"x1⅞"). Select walnut, checkered p.g. and beavertail fore-end, p.g. cap, recoil pad, Monte Carlo comb, cheekpiece, Cast-on, cast-off or extreme deviation from standard stock dimensions $100 extra. Reasonable deviation allowed without extra charge.
Features: Frame, top lever and trigger guard engraved. Gold name plate in stock.
Price: Custom made: **$2,250.00**

Ithaca 5E Grade Single Barrel Trap
Same as 4E except: Vent. rib bbl., better wood, more extensive engraving, and gold inlaid figures. Custom made: **$3,000.00**

ITHACA-SKB CENTURY SINGLE BARREL TRAP

Gauge: 12 only, 2¾".
Barrel: 32" or 34" (Full).
Weight: 8 lbs.
Stock: 14½"x1½"x1⅞" (Trap). French walnut, hand checkered, curved pad, full beavertail fore-end. M.C. stock available.
Sights: Bradley-type front, middle bead.
Features: Scroll-engraved silver-finish frame, chrome lined barrel, semi-wide vent. rib, auto. ejector.
Price: **$454.95**
Price: Monte Carlo stock **$464.95**

ITHACA PERAZZI SINGLE BARREL

Gauge: 12 (2¾" chamber)
Action: Top lever, break open, top tang safety.
Barrel: 32" or 34"; custom choking; ventilated rib.
Stock: Custom fitted European walnut in lacquered or oil finish.
Weight: About 8½ lbs.
Features: Hand-engraved receiver; interchangeable stocks available with some fitting.
Price: **$995.00**

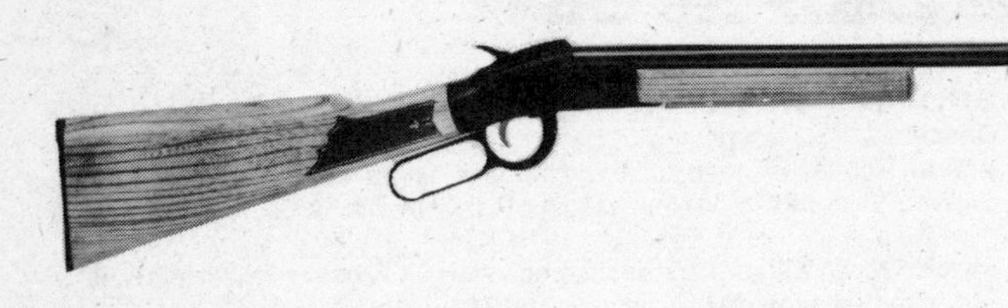

ITHACA MODEL 66 SUPERSINGLE

Gauge: 12, 20, 410 (3" chamber).
Action: Non-takedown; under lever opening.
Barrel: 12, 20 ga. 28" (Mod., Full); 12 ga., 30" (Full), 410, 26" (Full).
Stock: Straight grip walnut-finish stock and fore-end.
Weight: About 7 lbs.
Features: Rebounding hammer independent of the lever.
Price: **$49.95**
With vent. rib, 20 ga. only **$59.95**

Ithaca Model 66 Supersingle Youth
Same as the 66 Standard except: 20 (26" Bbl., Mod.) and 410 ga. (26" Bbl., Full) shorter stock with recoil pad **$54.95**
With vent. rib, 20 ga. only **$64.95**

Ithaca Model 66 RS Supersingle Buckbuster
Same as the Model 66 Standard except: 12 and 20 ga. only, 22" bbl. with rifle sights, designed to shoot slugs **$59.95**
Heavy bbl. (12 ga. only) **$59.95**

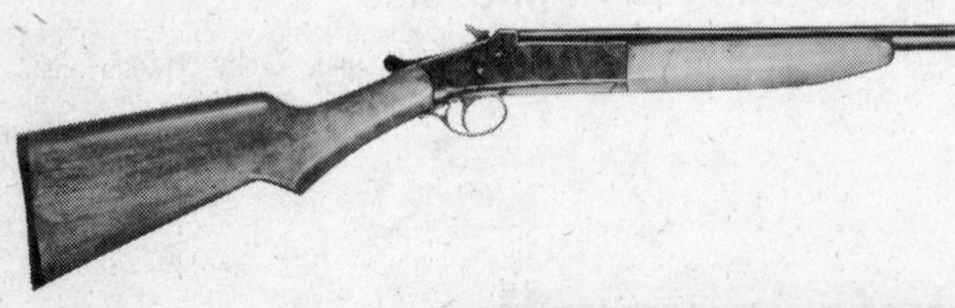

IVER JOHNSON CHAMPION

Gauge: 12, 20 or 410 (3" chamber).
Barrel: 12 gauge, 28" or 30"; 20 gauge, 28"; 410, 26"; full choke.
Stock: Walnut finish, trap style fore-end.
Features: Takedown action, automatic ejection.
Price: Either gauge **$44.95**

SAVAGE-STEVENS MODEL 94-C Single Barrel Gun

Gauge: 12, 16, 20, 410 (12, 20 and 410, 3" chambers).
Action: Top lever break open; hammer; auto. ejector.
Barrel: 12 ga. 28", 30", 32", 36"; 16, 20 ga. 28"; 410 ga. 26". Full choke only.
Stock: 14"x1½"x2½". Walnut finish, checkered p.g. and fore-end.
Weight: About 6 lbs. Over-all 42" (26" bbl.).
Features: Color case-hardened frame, low rebounding hammer.
Price: 26" to 32" bbls. .... **$45.55** 36" bbl. **$46.95**

Stevens M94-Y Youth's Gun
Same as Model 940 except: 26" bbl., 20 ga. Mod. or 410 Full, 12½" stock with recoil pad. Wgt. about 5½ lbs. 40½" over-all. **$46.95**

U.S. SHOTGUNS — SINGLE BARREL

WINCHESTER 37A SINGLE SHOT

Gauge: 12, 20, 410 (3″ chamber), 16, 28 (2¾″ chamber).
Action: Top lever break-open, exposed hammer.
Barrel: 26″, 410 ga. (Full), 28″, 20 & 28 ga. (Full), 30″, 16 ga. (Full), 30″, 32″ 36″, 12 ga. (Full).
Length: 42¼″ over-all (26″ bbl.). **Weight:** 5½ to 6¼ lbs.
Stock: 14″x1⅜″x2⅜″, walnut finish.
Sights: Metal bead front.
Features: Checkered p.g. and fore-end bottom, gold plated trigger, engraved receiver, concave hammer spur. Grip cap and buttplate have white spacers. Auto. ejector. Top lever opens right or left.
Price: Standard Model, 12 ga. **$53.45**
Price: 16, 20, 28 410 ga. **$52.45**

Winchester 37A Youth Model
Same as std. 37A except: shorter 26″ bbl., youth-size stock (12½″ pull), 40¾″ over-all length. Rubber recoil pad. Available only in 20 ga. (Imp. Mod.) or 410 (Full). **$53.45**

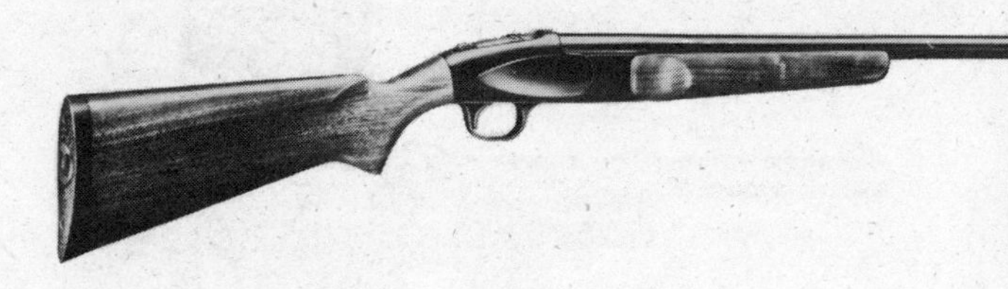

WESTERN FIELD 100 Single Barrel Gun

Gauge: 12, 16, 20, 410 (410, 3″ chamber).
Action: Hammerless; thumb slide break open.
Barrel: 12 ga., 30″; 16, 20 ga., 28″; 410 ga., 26″. All Full choke.
Stock: Walnut finished, p.g., recoil pad.
Weight: 6¼ to 7 lbs.
Features: Automatic safety, auto ejector.
Price: **$48.99**
Also available as Youth's Model. 26″ barrel, 20 or 410 gauge. Wgt. 6 lbs., 41″ over-all **$49.99**

U.S. SHOTGUNS — BOLT ACTION

MARLIN GOOSE GUN BOLT ACTION

Gauge: 12 only, 2-shot (3″ mag. or 2¾″).
Action: Bolt action, thumb safety, detachable clip.
Barrel: 36″, Full choke.
Stock: Walnut, p.g., recoil pad, leather strap & swivels.
Weight: 7¼ lbs., 57″ over-all.
Features: Tapped for receiver sights. Swivels and leather carrying strap. Gold-plated trigger.
Price: **$69.95**

Marlin 55S Slug Gun
Same as Goose Gun except: 24″ barrel, iron sights (rear adj.), drilled and tapped for scope mounting. Comes with carrying strap and swivels. Weight is 7 lbs., over-all length 45″. **$74.95**

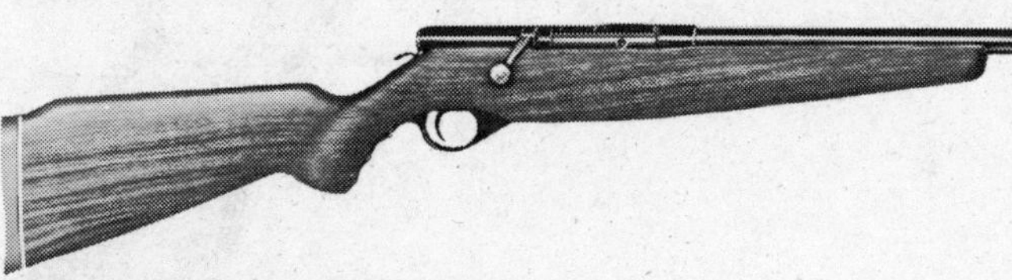

MOSSBERG MODEL 395K BOLT ACTION

Gauge: 12, 3-shot (3″ chamber).
Action: Bolt; takedown; detachable clip.
Barrel: 28″ with C-Lect-Choke.
Stock: Walnut finish, p.g. Monte Carlo comb; recoil pad.
Weight: 6¾ lbs. 47½″ over-all.
Features: Streamlined action; top safety; grooved rear sight.
Price: **$73.25**
Also available in 20 ga. 3″ chamber 28″ bbl. 6¼ lbs., as M385K, **$68.10**, and in 16 ga. 28″ bbl., 6¾ lbs., as M390K **$71.65**

MOSSBERG MODEL 183K BOLT ACTION

Gauge: 410, 3-shot (3″ chamber).
Action: Bolt; top-loading mag.; thumb safety.
Barrel: 25″ with C-Lect-Choke.
Stock: Walnut finish, p.g., Monte Carlo comb., rubber recoil pad w/spacer.
Weight: 6¾ lbs. **Length:** 43½″ over-all.
Features: Moulded trigger guard with finger grooves, gold bead front sight.
Price: **$61.40**
Price: As 183T without choke **$57.35**

Mossberg Model 395S Bolt Action
Same as Model 395K except 24″ barrel with adjustable folding leaf rear sight and ramp front, for use with slugs. Sling supplied **$63.60**

SAVAGE-STEVENS 58 BOLT ACTION SHOTGUN

Gauge: 410 ga., 2½″ and 3″ chambers, 3-shot clip.
Action: Self-cocking bolt; double extractors; thumb safety.
Barrel: 24″, Full choke.
Stock: Walnut finish, checkered fore-end and p.g., recoil pad.
Weight: 5½ lbs. **Length:** 43″ over-all.
Features: Crisp trigger pull, Electro-Cote stock finish.
Price: **$50.95**

WESTERN FIELD 172 BOLT ACTION SHOTGUN

Gauge: 12 (3″ chamber).
Action: Self-cocking bolt. Thumb safety, double locking lugs, detachable clip.
Barrel: 28″ adj. choke, shoots rifled slugs.
Stock: Walnut, Monte Carlo design, p.g., recoil pad.
Features: Quick removable bolt with double extractors, grooved rear sight.
Price: **$60.00**
M175 Similar to above except 20 ga., **$59.00.** Without recoil pad and adj. choke (M160) **$55.00**

WESTERN FIELD 150C BOLT ACTION SHOTGUN

Gauge: 410 (3″ chamber).
Action: Self cocking, bolt action. Thumb safety. 3-shot magazine.
Barrel: 24″, full choke.
Weight: 5½ lbs. **Length:** 44½″ over-all.
Stock: Hardwood, Monte Carlo design.
Features: Top loading.
Price: **$50.00**

IMPORTED HANDGUNS—AUTOLOADERS

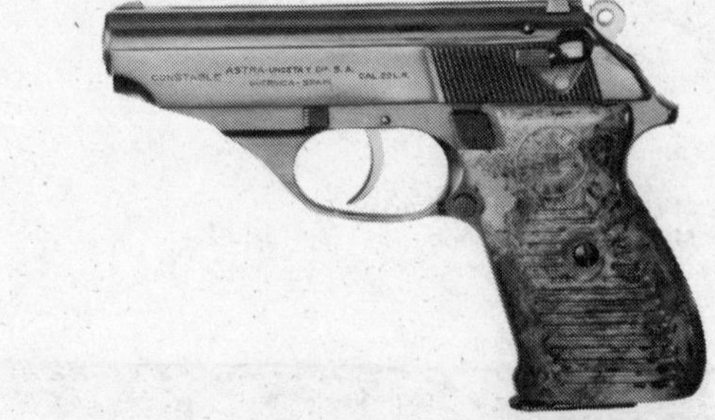

ASTRA CONSTABLE AUTO PISTOL

Caliber: 22 LR, 10-shot; 32 ACP, 8-shot; and 380 ACP, 7-shot.
Barrel: 3½".
Weight: 26 oz.
Stocks: Moulded plastic.
Sights: Adj. rear.
Features: Double action, quick no-tool takedown, non-glare rib on slide. 380 available in blue or chrome finish. Imported from Spain by Garcia.
Price: **$125.00**

BERETTA MODEL 70T AUTO PISTOL

Caliber: 32 ACP, 9-shot magazine.
Barrel: 6".
Weight: 19 oz. **Length:** 9½".
Stocks: Checkered plastic wrap-around.
Sights: Fixed front, adj. rear.
Features: External hammer, target-length bbl., slide stays open after last shot. Imported from Italy by Garcia.
Price: **$149.00**

BERETTA MODEL 101 AUTO PISTOL

Same as Model 70T except 22 LR, 10-round magazine. Imported from Italy by Garcia.
Price: **$149.00**

BERETTA MODEL 76 AUTO PISTOL

Caliber: 22 LR, 10-shot magazine.
Barrel: 6".
Weight: 35 oz. **Length:** 9½".
Stocks: Checkered plastic wrap-around.
Sights: Interchangeable blade front, adj. rear.
Features: Competition-type, non-glare ribbed heavy bbl., external hammer. Imported from Italy by Garcia.
Price: **$155.00**

BERETTA MODEL 70S AUTO PISTOL

Caliber: 380 ACP, 7-shot magazine.
Barrel: 3⅝".
Weight: 23¼ oz. **Length:** 6¼".
Stocks: Checkered plastic wrap-around.
Sights: Fixed front and rear.
Features: External hammer. Imported from Italy by Garcia.
Price: **$125.00**

BERETTA MODEL 90 AUTO PISTOL

Caliber: 32 ACP, 8-shot magazine.
Barrel: 3⅝".
Weight: 19½ oz. **Length:** 6¾".
Stocks: Moulded plastic wrap-around.
Sights: Fixed.
Features: Double action, chamber loaded indicator, sighting rib on slide, external hammer, stainless steel bbl. Imported from Italy by Garcia.
Price: **$185.00**

BERETTA MODEL 951 AUTO PISTOL

Caliber: 9mm Para., 8-shot magazine.
Barrel: 4½".
Weight: 31 oz. **Length:** 8".
Stocks: Moulded plastic.
Sights: Fixed.
Features: Crossbolt safety, external hammer, slide stays open after last shot. Imported from Italy by Garcia.
Price: **$199.00**

BERNARDELLI MODEL 60 AUTO PISTOL
Caliber: 22 LR, 10-shot; 32 ACP, 8-shot; and 380, 7-shot.
Barrel: 3½".
Weight: 26 oz. **Length:** 6⅓".
Stocks: Checkered plastic.
Sights: Post front, click adj. rear.
Features: Manual and magazine safeties. Optional thumb rest grips, $10.00. Imported from Italy by Kleingunther's, Liberty.
Price: **$90.00**

ERMA KGP 68 AUTO PISTOL
Caliber: 32 ACP, 6-shot; 380 ACP, 5-shot.
Barrel: 3½".
Weight: 22½ oz. **Length:** 6¾".
Stocks: Checkered walnut.
Sights: Fixed rear, adj. blade front.
Features: Sidelock manual safety. Imported from Germany by R. G. Industries.
Price: **$83.95**

ERMA KGP 69 AUTO PISTOL
Caliber: 22 LR, 8-shot magazine.
Barrel: 4".
Weight: 29 oz. **Length:** $7\frac{5}{16}$".
Stocks: Checkered walnut.
Sights: Fixed rear, adj. front.
Features: Stays open after last shot. Imported from Germany by R. G. Industries.
Price: **$81.95**

HAMMERLI STANDARD, MODELS 208 & 211
Caliber: 22 LR.
Barrel: 5.9", 6-groove.
Weight: 37.6 oz. (45 oz. with extra heavy barrel weight). **Length:** 10".
Stocks: Walnut. Adj. palm rest (208), 211 has thumbrest grip.
Sights: Match sights, fully adj. for w. and e. (click adj.). Interchangeable front and rear blades.
Features: Semi-automatic, recoil operated. 8-shot clip. Slide stop. Fully adj. trigger (2¼ lbs. and 3 lbs.). Extra barrel weight available. Gil Hebard, importer.
Price: Model 208, approx. **$320.00** Model 211 approx. **$395.00**

HAMMERLI MODEL 230 RAPID FIRE PISTOL
Caliber: 22 S.
Barrel: 6.3", 6-groove.
Weight: 43.8 oz. **Length:** 11.6".
Stocks: Walnut. Standard grip w/o thumbrest (230-1), 230-2 has adj. grip.
Sights: Match type sights. Sight radius 9.9". Micro rear, click adj. Interchangeable front sight blade.
Features: Semi-automatic. Recoil-operated, 6-shot clip. Gas escape in front of chamber to eliminate muzzle jump. Fully adj. trigger from 5¼ oz. to 10½ oz. with three different lengths available. Designed for International 25 meter Silhouette Program. Gil Hebard, importer.
Price: Model 230-1 .... **$425.00**
Price: Model 230-2 .... **$450.00**

LLAMA MODELS VIII, IXA AUTO PISTOLS
Caliber: Super 38 (M. VIII), 45 ACP (M. IXA).
Barrel: 5".
Weight: 30 oz. **Length:** 8½".
Stocks: Checkered walnut.
Sights: Fixed.
Features: Grip and manual safeties, ventilated rib. Engraved, chrome engraved or gold damascened finish available at extra cost. Imported from Spain by Stoeger Arms.
Price: **$129.95**

LLAMA XI AUTO PISTOL
Caliber: 9mm Para.
Barrel: 5".
Weight: 38 oz. **Length:** 8½".
Stocks: Moulded plastic.
Sights: Fixed front, adj. rear.
Features: Also available with engraved, chrome engraved or gold damascened finish at extra cost. Imported from Spain by Stoeger Arms.
Price: **$129.95**

The product prices mentioned in these catalog pages were correct at presstime, but may be higher when you read this.

LLAMA MODELS XV, XA, IIIA AUTO PISTOLS
Caliber: 22 LR, 32 ACP and 380.
Barrel: 3¹¹⁄₁₆".
Weight: 23 oz. **Length:** 6½".
Stocks: Checkered plastic, thumb rest.
Sights: Fixed front, adj. notch rear.
Features: Ventilated rib, manual and grip safeties. Model XV is 22 LR, Model XA is 32 ACP, and Model IIIA is 380. Models XA and IIIA have loaded indicator; IIIA is locked breech. Imported from Spain by Stoeger Arms.
Price: **$99.95**

MAUSER PARABELLUM P-08
Caliber: 30 Luger, 9mm Parabellum, 8-shot clip.
Barrel: 6" in 30 Luger, 4" and 6" in 9mm Parabellum
Weight: 32 oz. **Length:** 4" bbl—8.66"; 6" bbl—10.63".
Stocks: Checkered Walnut.
Sights: Fixed.
Features: Differs from current '06 with classic '08 details, including different take-down lever, trigger, safety and curved front strap. Limited production marked with American eagle over chamber and Mauser banner on the toggle. Imported by Interarms.
Price: **$350.00**

MAUSER PARABELLUM AUTO PISTOL
Caliber: 30 Luger, 9mm Para., 8-shot.
Barrel: 4" (9mm), 4" and 6" (30 Luger).
Weight: 32 oz. **Length:** 8⅔" (4" bbl.).
Stocks: Checkered walnut.
Sights: Fixed.
Features: Manual and grip safeties, American eagle over chamber. Imported from Germany by Interarms.
Price: **$249.00**

MAUSER HSc AUTO PISTOL
Caliber: 32 ACP, 380 ACP, 7-shot.
Barrel: 3⅜".
Weight: 23 oz. **Length:** 6.05".
Stocks: Checkered walnut.
Sights: Fixed.
Features: Double action, manual and magazine safeties. Imported from Germany by Interarms.
Price: .... **$136.00** Nickel plated **$152.00**

MKE MODEL TPK AUTO PISTOL
Caliber: 32 ACP, 8-shot; 380, 7-shot.
Barrel: 4".
Weight: 23 oz. **Length:** 6½".
Stocks: Checkered black plastic.
Sights: Fixed front, adj. notch rear.
Features: Double action with exposed hammer; safety blocks firing pin and drops hammer. Chamber loaded indicator pin. Imported from Turkey by Firearms Center.
Price: **$120.00**
Price: With Armaloy finish **$150.00**

STAR MODEL FM AUTO PISTOL
Caliber: 22 LR, 10-shot magazine
Barrel: 4¼".
Weight: 30 oz.
Stocks: Checkered plastic.
Sights: Fixed front, adj. rear.
Features: Blue or chrome finish. External hammer, manual safety. Imported from Spain by Garcia.
Price: Blue **$94.00**
Price: Chrome **$99.00**

STAR BKS STARLIGHT AUTO PISTOL
Caliber: 9mm Para., 8-shot magazine.
Barrel: 4¼".
Weight: 25 oz.
Stocks: Checkered plastic.
Sights: Fixed.
Features: Blue or chrome finish. Magazine and manual safeties, external hammer. Imported from Spain by Garcia.
Price: Blue **$140.00**
Price: Chrome **$150.00**

STAR FRS AUTO PISTOL
Caliber: 22 LR, 10-shot magazine.
Barrel: 6".
Weight: 30 oz.
Stocks: Checkered plastic.
Sights: Fixed front, adj. rear.
Features: External hammer, manual safety. Available in blue or chrome (Model FRS-C). Alloy frame. Imported from Spain by Garcia.
Price: Blue **$94.00**
Price: Chrome **$99.00**

STAR MODELS A, B AND P AUTO PISTOLS
Caliber: 38 Super (Model A), 9-shot; 9mm Para. (Model B), 9-shot; and 45 ACP (Model P), 7-shot.
Barrel: 5″.
Weight: 37½ oz. **Length:** 8½″.
Stocks: Checkered walnut.
Sights: Fixed.
Features: Blue or chrome finish. Magazine and manual safeties, wide-spur hammer. Imported from Spain by Garcia.
Price: Models A and B, blue .... **$140.00** Chrome **$150.00**
Price: Model P, blue ..... **$155.00** Chrome **$165.00**

STAR SUPER SM
Caliber: 380 ACP, 10-shot.
Barrel: 4″.
Weight: 22 oz. **Length:** 6⅝″ over-all.
Stocks: Plastic, checkered.
Sights: Blade front, adj. rear.
Features: Blue or chrome finish. Loaded chamber indicator, thumb safety. Imported from Spain by Garcia.
Price: Blue **$130.00**
Price: Chrome **$140.00**

WALTHER GSP MATCH PISTOL
Caliber: 22 LR, 32 S&W wadcutter (GSP-C), 5-shot.
Barrel: 4½″.
Weight: 44.8 oz. (22 LR), 49.4 oz. (32). **Length:** 11.8″ over-all.
Stock: Walnut, special hand-fitting design.
Sights: Fixed front, rear adj. for w. & e.
Features: Available with either 2.2 lb. (1000 gm) or 3 lb. (1360 gm) trigger. Spare mag., bbl. weight, tools supplied in Match Pistol Kit. Imported from Germany by Interarms.
Price: GSP **$379.00**
Price: GSP-C **$439.00**
Price: 22 cal. conversion unit for GSP-C **$209.00**

WALTHER OSP RAPID-FIRE PISTOL
Similar to Model GSP except 22 Short only, stock has adj. free-style hand rest.
Price: **$379.00**

WALTHER PP AUTO PISTOL
Caliber: 22 LR, 32 ACP, 8-shot; 380 ACP, 7-shot.
Barrel: 3.86″.
Weight: 23½ oz. **Length:** 6.7″.
Stocks: Checkered plastic.
Sights: Fixed, white markings.
Features: Double action, manual safety blocks firing pin and drops hammer, chamber loaded indicator on 32 and 380, finger rest extra magazine provided. Imported from Germany by Interarms.
Price: (22 LR) **$179.00**
Price: (32 and 380) **$169.00**
Price: Engraved models start at **$470.00**

Walther PPK/S Auto Pistol
Same as PP except bbl. 3.27″, length 6.1″ o.a.
Price: **$169.00**
Price: Engraved models start at **$470.00**

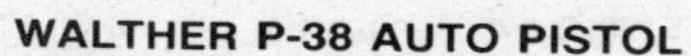

WALTHER P-38 AUTO PISTOL
Caliber: 22 LR, 30 Luger or 9mm Luger, 8-shot.
Barrel: 4$\frac{15}{16}$″ (9mm and 30), 5$\frac{1}{16}$″ (22 LR).
Weight: 28 oz. **Length:** 8½″.
Stock: Checkered plastic.
Sights: Fixed.
Features: Double action, safety blocks firing pin and drops hammer, chamber loaded indicator. Matte finish standard, polished blue, engraving and/or plating available. Imported from Germany by Interarms.
Price: (9mm) **$219.00**
Price: (22 LR, 30 Luger) **$249.00**
Price: 9mm polished blue finish **$229.00**
Price: Engraved models start at **$590.00**

IMPORTED HANDGUNS—REVOLVERS

ARMINIUS REVOLVERS

Caliber: 38 Special, 32 S&W Long (6-shot); 22 Magnum, 22 LR (8-shot).
Barrel: 4" (38 Spec., 32 S&W, 22 LR); 6" (38 Spec., 22 LR); 9½" (22 Mag. only).
Weight: 35 oz. (6" bbl.). **Length:** 11" (6" bbl. 38).
Stocks: Checkered plastic.
Sights: Ramp front, fixed rear on standard models, w. & e. adj. on target models.
Features: Ventilated rib, solid frame, swing-out cylinder. Interchangeable 22 Mag. cylinder available with 22 cal versions. Imported from West Germany by Firearms Import & Export.
Price: .... **$52.95** to **$94.95**

ASTRA 357 MAGNUM REVOLVER

Caliber: 357 Magnum, 6-shot.
Barrel: 3", 4", 6".
Weight: 40 oz. (6" bbl.). **Length:** 11¼" (6" bbl.).
Stocks: Checkered walnut. Magna-style on 3", target-type on 4" and 6".
Sights: Fixed front, rear adj. for w. and e.
Features: Swing-out cylinder with countersunk chambers, floating firing pin. Imported from Spain by Garcia
Price: **$140.00**

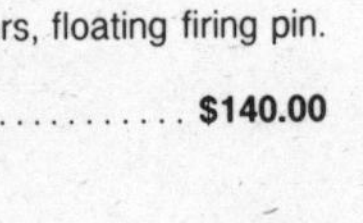

BISON SINGLE ACTION REVOLVER

Caliber: 22 LR.
Barrel: 4¾".
Weight: 20 oz.
Stocks: Imitation stag.
Sights: Fixed front, adj. rear.
Features: 22 WRM cylinder also available ($5.00 additional). Imported from Germany by Jana.
Price: **$40.00**

APACHE REVOLVERS

Caliber: 22 LR, 8 shot; 32 S&W, 7 shot; 38 Special, 6 shot.
Barrel: 4", 3" (available in 38 Special only).
Stocks: Checkered plastic.
Sights: Fixed front, rear adj. for w. & e.
Features: Ventilated rib on bbl. Imported from Germany by Jana.
Price: **$65.00**

DAKOTA SINGLE ACTION REVOLVER

Caliber: 22 S, L, LR, 22 Mag., 357 Mag., 44-40, 45 Colt.
Barrel: 4⅝", 5½", 7½".
Weight: 40 oz. (357 w/5½" bbl.). **Length:** 10¼" (4⅝" bbl.) over-all.
Stocks: One-piece walnut.
Sights: Blade front, notch rear.
Features: Blued barrel and cylinder, case hardened frame, brass trigger guard and backstrap. Imported by Intercontinental Arms.
Price: .... **$99.75** Engraved model **$175.00**

SUPER DAKOTA REVOLVER

Caliber: 41 Mag., 44 Mag.
Barrel: 5½", 7½".
Weight: 44 oz. **Length:** 11½" (5½ bbl.) over-all.
Stock: Walnut, one-piece.
Sights: Ramp front with matted and ribbed blade, integral ramp rear open notch adj. for w. & e.
Features: Flat-top single action. Brass trigger guard and backstrap, rest blued. Imported by Intercontinental Arms.
Price: **$117.50**

F.I.E. SHERIFF SINGLE ACTION REVOLVER

Caliber: 22 LR/22 Mag., 357 Mag., 44 Mag., 6-shot.
Barrel: 5½".
Weight: 42 oz. (357).
Stocks: Smooth walnut.
Sights: Fixed.
Features: Positive hammer block system. Brass backstrap and trigger guard. Case hardened frame. Imported from Argentina by F.I.E.
Price: **$95.00**

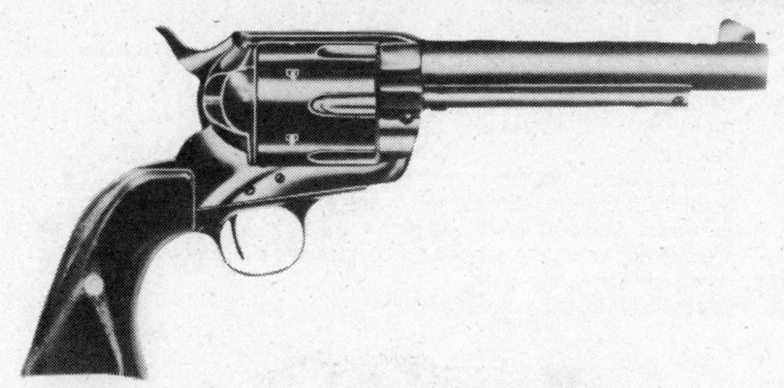

HAWES WESTERN MARSHAL REVOLVERS

Caliber: 357 Magnum, 44 Magnum, 45 Long Colt, 22 Magnum, 22 LR, 6-shot.
Barrel: 6″ (357 Mag., 44 Mag., 45) and 5½″ (22 Mag., 22 LR).
Weight: 44 oz. (big bore), 40 oz. (small bore). **Length:** 11¾″ and 11¼″.
Stocks: Rosewood (big bore), moulded stag (small bore).
Sight: Blade front.
Features: Single action. Interchangeable cyclinders available for 22 caliber guns: 22 LR with 22 Mag. Imported from West Germany by Hawes.
Price: 357 Mag., 44 Mag., 45 LC **$129.95**
Price: 22 LR **$84.95**
Price: 22 LR with 22 Mag. cylinder **$104.95**

Hawes Texas Marshal Revolver

Similar to Western Marshal except full nickel finish and black or white Pearlite grips.
Price: **$114.95**

Hawes Montana Marshal Revolver

Same as Western Marshal except with solid brass back strap and trigger guard.
Price: .... **$99.95** to **$157.45**

HAWES SILVER CITY MARSHAL REVOLVER

Caliber: 22 LR, 22 LR/22 WRM, 357, 44 Mag., 45 L.C.
Barrel: 6″ (357, 44, 45), 5½″ (22 cal.).
Weight: 44 oz. **Length:** 11¾″ over-all.
Stock: White Pearlite.
Sights: Fixed.
Features: Nickel plated frame, brass backstrap and trigger guard, blue barrel and cylinder. Imported by Hawes Firearms.
Price: .... **$105.95** to **$165.85**

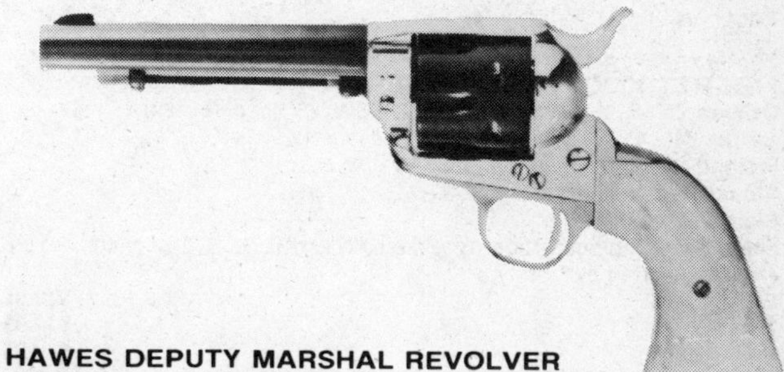

HAWES DEPUTY MARSHAL REVOLVER

Caliber: 22 LR, 22 LR/22 WRM.
Barrel: 5½″.
Weight: 34 oz. **Length:** 11″ over-all.
Stock: Black, white or wood.
Sights: Fixed.
Features: Available in std. blue finish with black grips, with brass backstrap and trigger guard and wood grips, with completely chromed finish and white grips, or with chrome frame, brass backstrap and trigger guard, blue cylinder and barrel and white grips. Imported by Hawes Firearms.
Price: .... **$49.95** to **$68.95**

HAWES FEDERAL MARSHAL REVOLVER

Caliber: 357, 44 Mag., 45 L.C.
Barrel: 6″.
Weight: 44 oz. **Length:** 11¾″ over-all.
Stock: Smooth walnut.
Sights: Blade front, fixed rear.
Features: Color case hardened frame, brass backstrap and trigger guard. Imported by Hawes Firearms.
Price: **$156.95**

HAWES CHIEF MARSHAL REVOLVER

Caliber: 357 Magnum, 44 Magnum, 45 Long Colt; 6-shot.
Barrel: 6″.
Weight: 48 oz. **Length:** 11¾″.
Stocks: Extra large smooth rosewood.
Sights: Ramp target front, rear adj. for w. & e.
Features: Single action. Extra heavy frame. Imported from West Germany by Hawes.
Price: **$156.95**

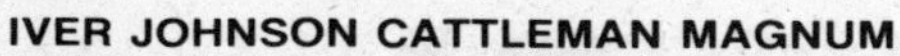

IVER JOHNSON CATTLEMAN MAGNUM

Caliber: 357, 44 Mag., 45 LC, 6-shot.
Barrel: 4¾″, 5½″ or 7½″. 44 Mag. avail. with 6″, 6¼″ or 7½″.
Weight: 2½ lbs.
Stocks: Smooth walnut.
Sights: Fixed.
Features: Case-hardened frame, single action, blued barrel, brass backstrap and trigger guard. Imported by Iver Johnson.
Price: 357, 45 LC .... **$99.95** 44 Mag. **$115.95**

IVER JOHNSON CATTLEMAN TRAILBLAZER

Caliber: 22 S, L, LR, 22 Mag.
Barrel: 5½″ or 6½″.
Weight: 2½ lbs.
Stocks: Smooth walnut.
Sights: Ramp front, rear adj. for w. and e.
Features: Comes with interchangeable magnum cylinder. Single action. Case-hardened frame, brass backstrap and trigger guard. Imported by Iver Johnson.
Price: **$104.35**

I. J. CATTLEMAN BUCKHORN MAGNUM
Caliber: 357, 38 Spec., 44 Mag., 45 LC.
Barrel: 6½", 7½" (44 Mag.), 5¾" or 7½" (357, 38, 45).
Weight: 2¾ lbs.
Stocks: Smooth walnut.
Sights: Ramp front, rear adj. for w. and e.
Features: Single action. Blued barrel, case-hardened frame, brass backstrap and trigger guard. Imported by Iver Johnson.
Price: 357, 45 LC **$131.95**
Price: 44 Mag. **$151.15**

LIBERTY MUSTANG
Caliber: 22 LR, 22 Mag. or combination, 8-shot.
Barrel: 5".
Weight: 34 oz. **Length:** 10¼" over-all.
Stocks: Smooth rosewood.
Sights: Blade front, adj. rear.
Features: Single action, slide ejector rod. Imported by Liberty.
Price: With one cylinder **$36.95**
Price: With two cylinders **$44.95**

LIBERTY KODIAK REVOLVER
Caliber: 22 LR, 22 MWR (8-shot), 32 S&W, 38 Spec. (6-shot).
Barrel: 24", 4".
Weight: 27 oz. (2" bbl.). **Length:** 6¾" (2" bbl.).
Stocks: Smooth wood.
Sights: Fixed.
Features: Swing-out cylinder. Blue finish (22 and 32 cals.), blue or chrome (38 cal.). Imported by Liberty.
Price: 22 cal. **$39.95**
Price: 32 cal. **$44.95**
Price: 38 cal. **$49.95**

LLAMA "MARTIAL" REVOLVERS
Caliber: 22 LR, 22 RFM, 38 Special.
Barrel: 6", 4" (except 22 LR).
Weight: 22 LR 24 oz., 38 Special 31 oz. **Length:** 9¼" (4" bbl.).
Stocks: Checkered walnut.
Sights: Fixed blade front, rear adj. for w. & e.
Features: Ventilated rib, wide spur hammer. Chrome plating, engraved finishes available. Imported from Spain by Stoeger Arms.
Price: **$119.95**

RG 38S REVOLVER
Caliber: 38 Special, 6-shot.
Barrel: 3" and 4".
Weight: 3", 31 oz.; 4", 34 oz. **Length:** 3", 8½"; 4", 9¼".
Stocks: Checkered plastic.
Sights: Fixed front, rear adj. for w.
Features: Swing out cylinder with spring ejector, choice of blue or nickel finish. Imported from Germany by R. G. Industries.
Price: Blue **$53.95**
Price: Nickel **$64.95**

RG30 REVOLVER
Caliber: 22 LR and 32, 6-shot.
Barrel: 4".
Weight: 30 oz. **Length:** 9".
Stocks: Checkered plastic.
Sights: Fixed front, rear adj. for w.
Features: Swing-out cylinder, choice of blue or nickel ($8.00 additional) finish. Imported from Germany by R. G. Industries.
Price: (22) .... **$47.95** (32) **$47.95**

RG 57 REVOLVER
Caliber: 357 Magnum.
Barrel: 4".
Weight: 44 oz. **Length:** 9½".
Stocks: Checkered plastic.
Sights: Fixed rear.
Features: Swing out cylinder, spring ejector, steel frame. Imported from Germany by R. G. Industries.
Price: **$97.95**

IVER JOHNSON CATTLEMAN BUNTLINE BUCKHORN MAGNUM
Caliber: 357, 38 Spec., 44 Mag., 45 LC, 6-shot.
Barrel: 18".
Weight: 3½ lbs.
Stocks: Smooth walnut.
Sights: Ramp front, rear adj. for w. and e.
Features: Single action. Blued barrel, case-hardened frame, brass trigger guard and backstrap. Comes with detachable shoulder stock. Imported by Iver Johnson
Price: 357, 45 LC .... **$252.00** 44 Mag. **$264.00**

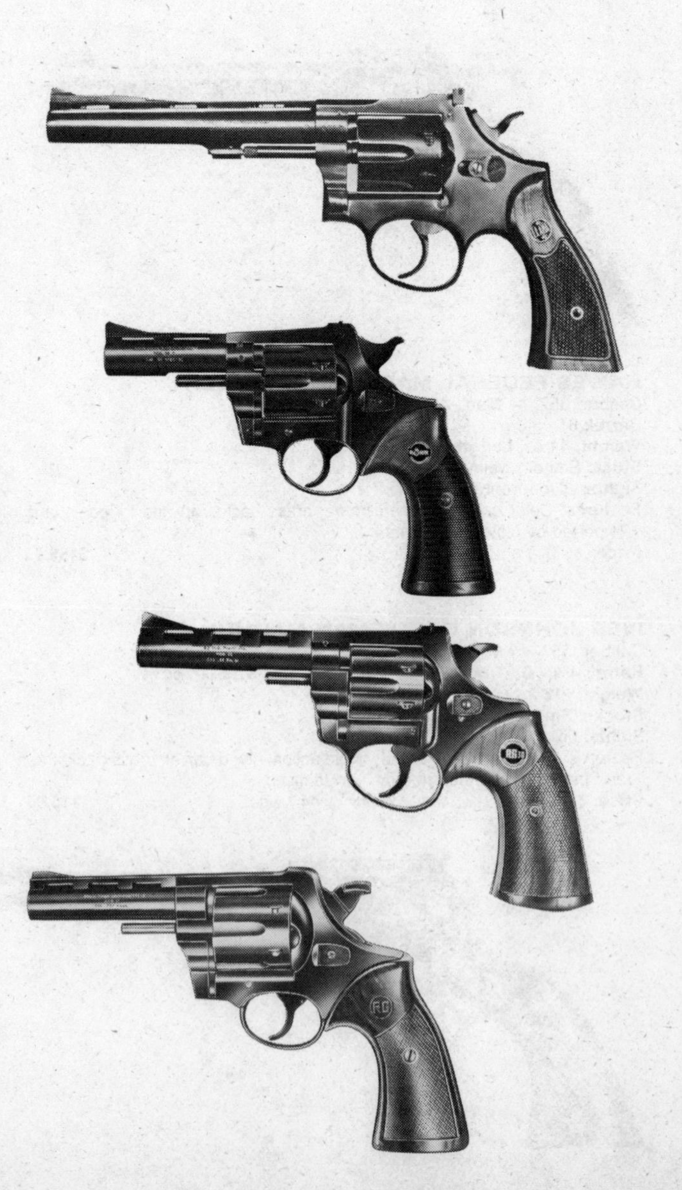

IMPORTED HANDGUNS—REVOLVERS

RG63 WESTERN STYLE REVOLVER

Caliber: 22 LR & 22 Mag., 8-shot; 32 S&W & 38 Spec., 6-shot.
Barrel: 5".
Weight: 34-36 ozs. **Length:** 10¼".
Stocks: Checkered plastic.
Sights: Fixed.
Features: Slide ejector rod, choice of blue or nickel. Model 63M is combo set with both 22 LR and 22 Mag. cylinders. Imported from Germany by R. G. Industries.
Price: Blue (22) .... **$39.95** (22M, 38) **$47.95**

RG 66 SUPER SINGLE ACTION REVOLVER

Caliber: 22 LR, 22 Mag., 6-shot.
Barrel: 4¾".
Weight: 32 oz. **Length:** 10".
Stocks: Checkered plastic.
Sights: Fixed front, rear adj.
Features: Slide ejector rod, choice of blue or nickel finish. Model 66M is combo set with both 22 LR and 22 mag. cylinders. Imported from Germany by R. G. Industries.
Price: Blue .... **$39.95**; (Model 66M) **$45.95**
Price: Nickel .... **$43.95**; (Model 66M) **$53.95**
Price: Blue (6") .... **$42.95**; Magnum **$48.95**
Price: Blue (9") .... **$43.95**; Magnum **$49.95**

ROSSI REVOLVERS

Caliber: 22 LR, 22 Mag., 32 S&W Long (6-shot), 38 Spec. (5-shot).
Barrel: 3", 6" (22 Mag. only).
Weight: 22 oz.
Stocks: Smooth wood.
Sights: Ramp front, adj. rear.
Features: Full length barrel rib. Blue or nickel finish. Imported by Garcia.
Price: 3" bbl., blue **$75.00**
Price: 3" bbl., nickel **$80.00**
Price: 6" bbl., blue **$80.00**

TAURUS MODEL 74 SPORT REVOLVER

Caliber: 32 S&W Long, 6-shot.
Barrel: 3".
Weight: 22 oz. **Length:** 8¼" over-all.
Stocks: Oversize target-type, checkered Brazilian walnut.
Sights: Serrated ramp front, rear adj. for w. and e.
Features: Imported from Brazil by International Distributers.
Price: Blue **$70.00**
Price: Nickel **$72.00**

TAURUS MODEL 80 STANDARD REVOLVER

Caliber: 38 Spec., 6-shot.
Barrel: 3" or 4".
Weight: 31 oz. (4" bbl.). **Length:** 9¼" over-all (4" bbl.).
Stocks: Checkered Brazilian walnut.
Sights: Serrated ramp front, square notch rear.
Features: Imported from Brazil by International Distributors.
Price: Blue **$63.00**
Price: Nickel **$65.00**

TAURUS MODEL 82 HEAVY BARREL REVOLVER

Caliber: 38 Spec., 6-shot.
Barrel: 3" or 4", heavy.
Weight: 33 oz. (4" bbl.). **Length:** 9¼" over-all (4" bbl.).
Stocks: Checkered Brazilian walnut.
Sights: Serrated ramp front, square notch rear.
Features: Imported from Brazil by International Distributors.
Price: Blue **$65.00**
Price: Nickel **$68.00**

IMPORTED HANDGUNS — REVOLVERS

TAURUS MODEL 86 TARGET MASTER REVOLVER

Caliber: 38 Spec., 6-shot.
Barrel: 6" only.
Weight: 41 oz. **Length:** 11¼" over-all.
Stocks: Over size target-type, checkered Brazilian walnut.
Sights: Patridge front, micro. click rear adj. for w. and e.
Features: Blue finish with non-reflective finish on barrel. Imported from Brazil by International Distributors.
Price: **$105.00**
Price: Model 96 Scout Master, same except in 22 cal **$105.00**

TAURUS MODEL 94 SPORT REVOLVER

Caliber: 22, 6-shot.
Barrel: 4".
Weight: 23 oz. **Length:** 9¼" over-all.
Stocks: Oversize target-type, checkered Brazilian walnut.
Sights: Serrated ramp front, rear adj. for w. and e.
Features: Imported from Brazil by International Distributors.
Price: Blue **$70.00**
Price: Nickel **$72.00**

TAURUS MODEL 84 SPORT REVOLVER

Caliber: 38 Spec., 6-shot.
Barrel: 4".
Weight: 30 oz. **Length:** 9¼" over-all.
Stocks: Checkered Brazilian walnut.
Sights: Serrated ramp front, rear adj. for w. and e.
Features: Imported from Brazil by International Distributors.
Price: Blue **$70.00**
Price: Nickel **$72.00**

THE VIRGINIAN SINGLE ACTION REVOLVER

Caliber: 357 Mag., 45 Colt, 6-shot.
Barrel: 4⅝", 5½", 7½".
Weight: 2½ lbs. (357 w/5½" bbl.). **Length:** 11" over-all (5½" bbl.).
Stocks: One-piece walnut.
Sights: Blade front, fixed notch rear.
Features: Chromed trigger guard and back strap, blue barrel, color case-hardened frame, unique safety system. Made by Hammerli. Imported by Interarms.
Price: **$199.00**

IMPORTED HANDGUNS — SINGLE SHOT

HAMMERLI MODEL 120 TARGET PISTOL

Caliber: 22 LR.
Barrel: 10", 6-groove.
Weight: 44.1 oz. **Length:** 14.8".
Stocks: Walnut. Standard grip with thumb rest (120-1), adjustable grip on 120-2.
Sights: Fully adj. micro click rear (match type), sight radius is 9.9" or 14.6". Interchangeable front sight blade.
Features: Single shot with new action operated by lateral lever. Bolt fully encloses cartridge rim. Target trigger adj. from 1.8 oz. to 12 oz. Trigger position adj. Gil Hebard, importer.
Price: Model 120-1 .... **$200.00**
Price: Model 120-2 .... **$225.00**
Price: Model 120-2 Heavy Barrel (5.7", 41 oz.) **$225.00**

HAMMERLI MODEL 150 FREE PISTOL

Caliber: 22 LR.
Barrel: 11.4", 6-groove. Free floating.
Weight: 42.4 oz. Up to 49.4 oz. with weights. **Length:** 15.4".
Stocks: Walnut. Special anatomical design with adj. palm shelf.
Sights: Match sights. Sight radius 14.6". Micro-click rear with interchangeable blade.
Features: Single shot Martini-type action operated by a lateral lever. Straight line hammerless ignition is vibration-free with an ignition time of 0.0016 sec. New set-trigger design fully adj. Low barrel and sight line. Extra weights availabe. Gil Hebard, importer.
Price: Including fitted case **$570.00**

ROLLING BLOCK SINGLE SHOT PISTOL

Caliber: 22 LR, 22 WRM, 5mm Rem. Mag., 357 mag.
Barrel: 8".
Weight: 2 lbs. **Length:** 12".
Stock: Walnut.
Sights: Front adj. for w., buckhorn adj. for e.
Features: Polished brass trigger guard. Supplied with wooden display box. Imported by Navy Arms.
Price: **$125.00**

HAWES FAVORITE SINGLE SHOT PISTOL

Caliber: 22 S, L, LR.
Barrel: 8".
Weight: 20 oz. **Length:** 12".
Stocks: Laminated wood or plastic.
Sights: Fixed front, adj. rear.
Features: Tilt up action, blued bbl., chromed frame. Imported by Hawes Firearms.
Price: **$52.95**

The product prices mentioned in these catalog pages were correct at presstime, but may be higher when you read this.

IMPORTED CENTERFIRE RIFLES — AUTOLOADING & LEVER ACTION

CLASSIC 1873 LEVER ACTION RIFLE

Caliber: 357 Magnum, 44-40.
Barrel: 20″.
Weight: 7 lbs. **Length:** 39″.
Stock: Walnut, straight grip, carbine buttplate.
Sights: Fixed front, adj. rear.
Features: Exact copy of 1873 Winchester, with full length tubular mag., center hammer, top ejection. Imported from Italy by Jana.
Price: **$225.00**

NAVY ARMS "1873" MODEL RIFLE

Caliber: 357 Mag., 44-40.
Barrel: 24″ (rifle, octagon); 20″ (carbine, round), 16½″ (trapper).
Weight: 9 lbs. (rifle); 7½ lbs. (carbine).
Stock: Walnut.
Sights: Blade front, step adj. rear.
Features: Available in blue, case-hardened or nickel (44-40 only) finish. Sliding dust cover, lever latch. Imported by Navy/Replica.
Price: Rifle **$210.00**
Price: Carbine **$210.00**
Price: Trapper **$210.00**
Price: Model 1001 .... **$1,000.00**

SAKO MODEL 73 LEVER ACTION RIFLE

Caliber: 243, 308.
Barrel: 23″.
Weight: 6¾ lbs. **Length:** 42½″.
Stock: Hand-checkered European walnut, Monte Carlo, one-piece.
Sights: Hooded front, dovetail blocks rear for tip-off scope mount or iron sights.
Features: Hammerless, short-throw lever, solid top, side ejection, 3-shot detachable mag. Imported from Finland by Garcia.
Price: **$260.00**

VALMET M-72S

Caliber: 223, 15- and 30-shot detachable magazines.
Barrel: 16⅝″.
Weight: 8¾ lbs. **Length:** 36⅝″ over-all.
Stock: Wood or reinforced resin (ABS).
Sights: Open tangent rear sight adjustable for elevation. Post front sight with protectors, adjustable for windage.
Features: Finnish semi-automatic version of AK-47. Imported by Interarms.
Price: ABS Stock **$309.00**
Price: Wood Stock **$319.00**

VALMET M-62/S RIFLE

Caliber: 7.62x39mm, 15- and 30-shot detachable box magazines.
Barrel: 16⅝″.
Weight: 8¾ lbs. **Length:** 36⅝″ over-all.
Stock: Fixed metal tube. Walnut optional.
Sights: Hooded post front adj. for w., tangent peep rear adj. for e.
Features: Finnish semi-automatic version of the AK-47. Basic Kalashnikov design (gas piston operating a rotating bolt assy.). Imported by Interarms.
Price: Metal stock version **$289.00**
Price: Wood stock version **$299.00**

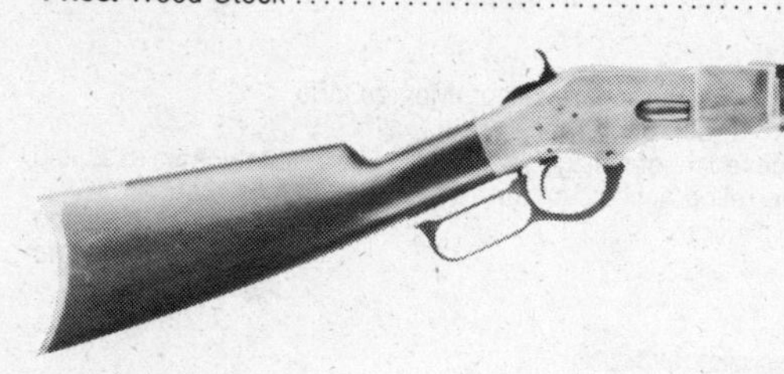

NAVY ARMS MODEL 66 LEVER ACTION RIFLE

Caliber: 22 LR, 38 Special, 44-40.
Barrel: 16½″, 19″, 24″.
Weight: 9¼ lbs. **Length:** 39½″.
Stock: Walnut.
Sights: Fixed front, folding rear.
Features: Replica of Winchester Model 1866 "Yellowboy." Available with three grades of engraving, selected stock and fore-end at additional cost. 22 LR also available with 16″ bbl. (Trapper's Model). Imported by Navy Arms.
Price: **$185.00**
Price: 24″ octagon bbl. **$210.00**

IMPORTED CENTERFIRE RIFLES — BOLT ACTION

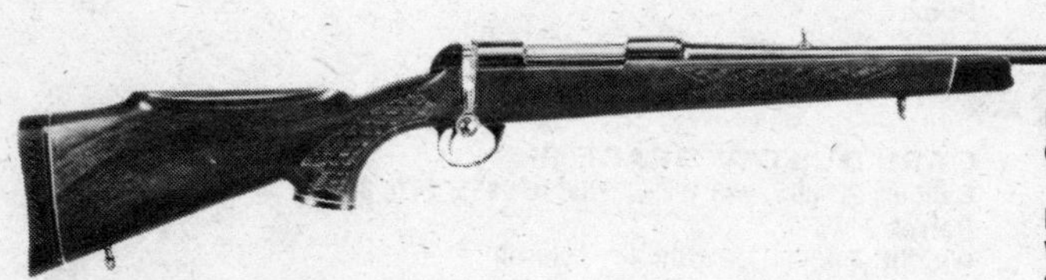

BSA MONARCH BOLT ACTION RIFLE

Caliber: 22-250, 222 Rem., 243 Win., 270 Win., 308 Win., 30-06, 7mm Rem. Mag., 300 Win. Mag.
Barrel: 22″.
Weight: 7 lbs.
Stock: Hand checkered European walnut, Monte Carlo, white line spacers on p.g. cap, fore-end tip and recoil pad.
Sights: Hooded ramp front, flip up rear.
Features: Adj. trigger, hinged mag. floor plate, silent sliding safety locks bolt and trigger. Imported from England by Galef.
Price: **$198.20**

IMPORTED CENTERFIRE RIFLES — BOLT ACTION

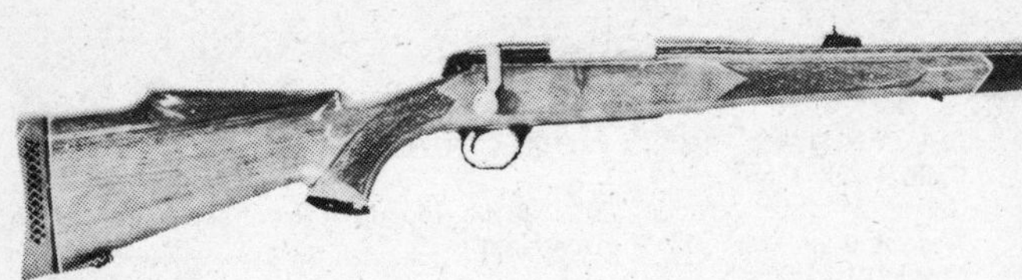

BSA/KASSNAR CF-2 RIFLE

Caliber: 222, 22-250, 243, 7x57, 7x64, 7mm Rem. Mag., 308, 30-06, 300 Win. Mag.
Barrel: 23½".
Weight: 7¼ lbs.
Stock: Hand checkered walnut. Roll over Monte Carlo cheekpiece. Rosewood fore-end tip and p.g. cap. Rubber recoil pad.
Sights: Williams hooded front, rear adj. for w. and e.
Features: Adjustable trigger, side safety. Enclosed bolt face. Drilled and tapped for scope mounts. Hinged floorplate. Imported by Kassnar Imports.
Price: **$210.00**

CHURCHILL "ONE OF ONE THOUSAND"

Caliber: 270, 308, 30-06, 7mm Rem. Mag., 300 Win. Mag., 375 H&H, 458 Win.
Barrel: 24" (average).
Weight: 8 lbs. (30-06). **Length:** 44" (24" bbl.).
Stock: Select European walnut.
Sights: Hooded gold bead ramp front, 3-leaf folding rear.
Features: Commercial Mauser action, adj. trigger, hinged floorplate swivel-mounted rubber recoil pad with cartridge trap, p.g. cap recess holds extra front sight, bbl. mounted sling swivel. Lifetime guarantee. Only 1,000 rifles being produced. Fitted leather case available. By Churchill (Gunmakers) Ltd., imported by Interarms.
Price: **$1,000.00**

DUMOULIN BOLT ACTION RIFLE

Caliber: All commercial calibers.
Barrel: 25".
Weight: 7 lbs. **Length:** 43".
Stock: French walnut with rosewood p.g. cap and fore-end tip, standard or skip line checkering, recoil pad.
Sights: Optional, available at extra cost.
Features: Made to customer requirements using Sako or FN action, with or without engraving (3 grades available). Imported from Belgium by Firearms Center.
Price: .... from **$575.00**

FN MAUSER BOLT ACTION RIFLE

Caliber: 243, 7x57mm, 270, 308, 30-06, 264 Mag., 7mm Mag., 300 Win. Mag.
Barrel: 24".
Weight: 8½ lbs.
Stock: Hand-checkered European walnut, Monte Carlo.
Sights: Hooded front, adj. peep rear.
Features: Adj. grooved trigger, hinged floorplate, sliding safety. Also available as actions or barrelled actions. Imported from Belgium by Garcia.
Price: Standard calibers **$430.00**
Price: Magnums **$445.00**

CARL GUSTAV GRADE II

Caliber: 22-250, 243 Win., 25-06, 6.5x55, 270, 30-06, 308, 5-shot.
Barrel: 23½".
Weight: 7⅛ lbs. **Length:** 44" over-all.
Stock: European walnut, hand checkered.
Sights: Hooded ramp front, folding leaf rear.
Features: Externally adj. trigger, silent safety, 80° bolt lift, enclosed bolt face, hinged floor plate. Also available in left hand version. Imported from Sweden by Stoeger Industries.
Price: **$299.95**

Carl Gustav Grade II Magnum
Same as Grade II except: has rubber recoil pad. Available in 7mm Rem., 300 Win.
Price: **$299.95**

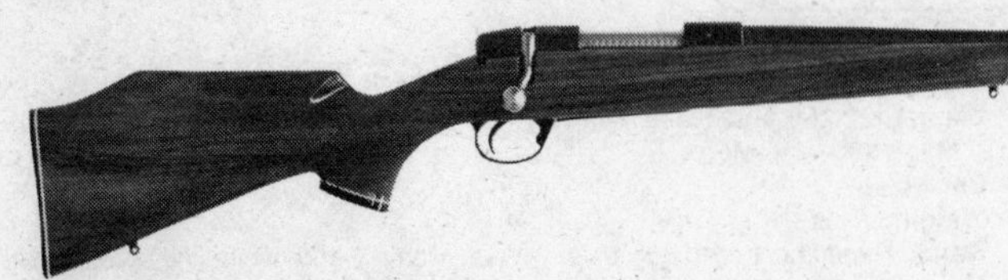

CARL GUSTAV GRADE III

Caliber: 22-250, 243 Win., 25-06, 6.5x55, 270, 30-06, 308, 5-shot.
Barrel: 23½".
Weight: 7⅛ lbs. **Length:** 44" over-all.
Stock: French walnut, hand checkered.
Sights: None furnished.
Features: Engraved floor plate, detachable swivels, jeweled bolt. Also available in left-hand version. Imported from Sweden by Stoeger Industries.
Price: **$399.95**
Price: Left-hand **$349.95**

Carl Gustav Grade III Magnum
Same as Grade III except: has recoil pad and internal modifications to handle magnum calibers. Also available in left-hand version.
Price: **$399.95**
Price: Left-hand, all std. cals. **$349.95**

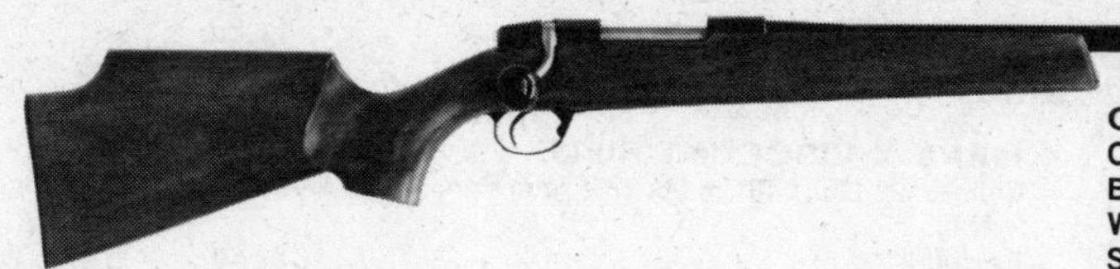

CARL GUSTAV V-T
Caliber: 222 Rem., 6.5x55.
Barrel: 27". Bbl. diameter .850".
Weight: 9½ lbs. **Length:** 47½" over-all.
Stock: European walnut.
Sights: None furnished. Drilled and tapped for scope mounts.
Features: Wundhammer p.g., full-floating barrel, externally adj. trigger, large bolt handle. Imported from Sweden by Stoeger Industries.
Price: **$309.95**

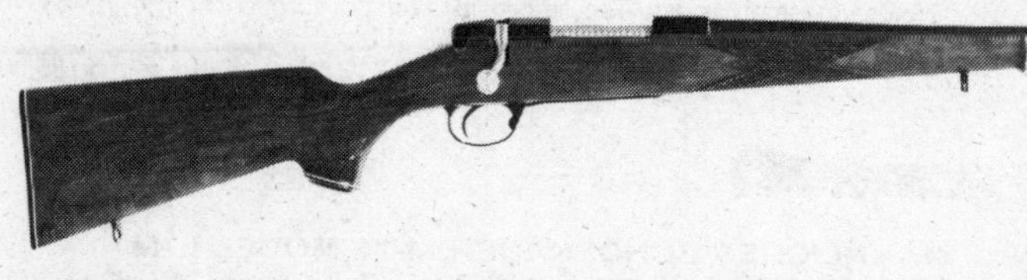

Carl Gustav "Swede"
Can be had in standard or deluxe versions utilizing the Grade II or Grade III barreled actions. Choice of either Monte Carlo design or sloping comb with schnabel fore-end. Same calibers as Grade II.
Price: Standard **$279.95**
Price: Deluxe **$329.95**

HERTER'S MARK J9 RIFLE
Caliber: 22-250, 25-06, 243, 6mm, 270, 308, 30-06, 264, 7mm mag., 300 Win. Mag.
Barrel: 23½".
Weight: 8 lbs. **Length:** 42½".
Stock: Black walnut, rollover cheek piece, ebonite p.g. cap and butt plate.
Sights: Ramp front, rear adj. for w. and e.
Features: Also available w/o sights, with Mannlicher or beavertail style stocks. Three grades (Hunter's, Supreme, Presentation) differ stock finish, style. Also available as actions or barreled actions. Imported from Yugoslavia by Herter's.
Price: Hunter's Grade **$93.80**
Price: Supreme Grade **$104.70**
Price: Presentation Grade **$118.70**

HERTER'S MARK U9 RIFLE
Caliber: 222, 222 mag., 223, 22-250, 25-06, 243, 6mm, 284, 308, 270, 30-06, 264, 7mm mag., 300 Win.
Barrel: 23½".
Weight: 6¼ lbs. **Length:** 42½".
Stock: American walnut, Monte Carlo, p.g.
Sights: Ramp front, rear adj. for w. and e.
Features: Also available less sights, with Mannlicher style stock, Douglas barrels (338 and 458 mag. plus above cals.). Three grades (Hunter's, Supreme, Presentation) differ in stock finish, style. Also available as actions or bbld. actions, bench rest, target or varmint versions. Imported from England by Herter's.
Price: Hunter's Grade **$120.90**
Price: Supreme Grade **$129.70**
Price: Presentation Grade **$144.70**

KLEINGUENTHER K-14 INSTA-FIRE RIFLE
Caliber: 243, 25-06, 270, 7x57, 7mm Rem. Mag., 30-06, 300 Win. Mag., 308 Win., 308 Norma, 375 H&H.
Barrel: 24", 26".
Weight: 7⅛ lbs. **Length:** 43½" over-all.
Stock: Available in light, medium or dark walnut. Monte Carlo, hand checkered, cheekpiece, rosewood fore-end tip, rosewood p.g. cap with diamond inlay.
Sights: None furnished. Drilled and tapped for scope mounts.
Features: Ultra fast lock/ignition time. Rubber recoil pad, hidden clip, external trigger adj., recessed bolt face, 60° bolt lift. Imported from Germany by Kleinguenther's.
Price: Std. cals. .... **$335.00** Mag. cals. **$335.00**

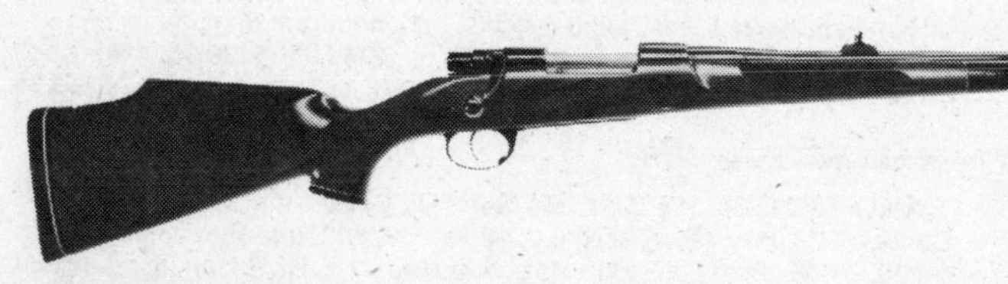

MARK X RIFLE
Caliber: 22-250; 243, 270, 308 Win.; 30-06; 25-06; 7 mm Rem. Mag; 300 Win. Mag.
Barrel: 24".
Weight: 7½ lbs. **Length:** 44".
Stock: Hand checkered walnut, Monte Carlo, white line spacers on p.g. cap, buttplate and fore-end tip.
Sights: Ramp front with removable hood, open rear adj. for w. and e.
Features: Sliding safety, quick detachable sling swivels, hinged floorplate. Adj. trigger available ($10.00 additional). Also available as actions or bbld. actions. Imported from Europe by Interarms.
Price: .... **$198.00** With adj. trigger **$208.00**

MARK X CAVALIER RIFLE
Caliber: 22-250; 243; 25-06; 270; 7mm Rem. Mag.; 308 Win.; 30-06; 300 Win. Mag.
Barrel: 24".
Weight: 7½ lbs. **Length:** 44".
Stock: Checkered Walnut with Rosewood fore-end tip and pistol grip cap, Monte Carlo cheek piece and recoil pad.
Sights: Ramp front with removable hood, open rear adjustable for windage and elevation.
Features: Contemporary-styled stock with sculptured accents; roll over cheek piece and flat bottom fore-end. Adjustable trigger with quick detachable sling swivels, standard. Receiver drilled and tapped for receiver sights and scope mounts. Also available without sights. Imported by Interarms.
Price: **$256.00**

MARK X VISCOUNT RIFLE
Caliber: 22-250; 243; 25-06; 270; 7mm Rem. Mag.; 308 Win.; 30-06; 300 Win. Mag.
Barrel: 24".
Weight: 7½ lbs. **Length:** 44".
Stock: Genuine Walnut stock, hand checkered with 1" sling swivels.
Sights: Ramp front with removable hood, open rear sight ajustable for windage and elevation.
Features: One piece trigger guard with hinged floor plate, drilled and tapped for scope mounts and receiver sight, hammer-forged chrome vanadium steel barrel. Imported by Interarms.
Price: **$185.00**

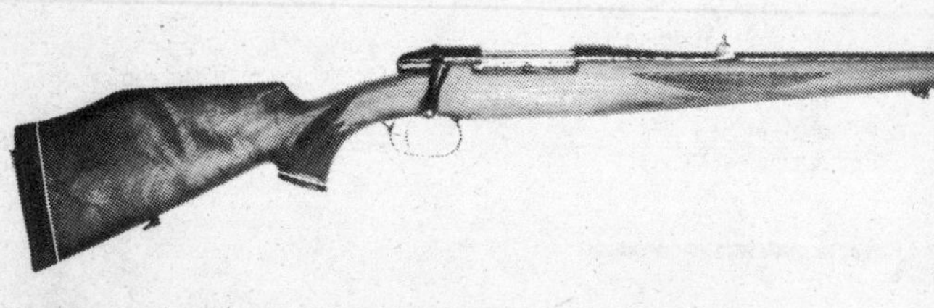

MANNLICHER-SCHOENAUER M-72 MODEL S
Caliber: 6.5x68, 7mm Rem. Mag., 8x68S, 9.3x64, 375 H&H Mag.
Barrel: 25½".
Weight: 8½ lbs. **Length:** 46" over-all.
Stock: Walnut half-stock style, varnished or oil finish. Rubber recoil pad, hand checkered. Monte Carlo cheekpiece.
Sights: Hooded ramp front, U-notch open rear.
Features: 6 forward locking lugs. 60° bolt throw. Wing-type safety. Choice of interchangeable single or double set triggers. Drilled and tapped for scope mounts. Custom engraving and stock carving avail. Imported by L.E.S.
Price: **$600.00**

MANNLICHER-SCHOENAUER M-72 MODEL L/M
Caliber: 22-250, 5.6x57, 6mm Rem. 243, 6.5x57, 270, 7x57, 7x64, 30-06, 308 Win.
Barrel: 20" (full stock), 23½" (half stock).
Weight: 7¼ lbs. (full stock). **Length:** 40" over-all (full stock).
Stock: Full Mannlicher or standard half stock, oil or varnish finish. Rubber recoil pad, hand checkered walnut, Monte Carlo cheekpiece.
Sights: Ramp front, open U-notch rear.
Features: 6 forward locking lugs. 60° bolt throw, wing-type safety. Choice of interchangeable single or double set triggers. Drilled and tapped for scope mounting. Imported by L.E.S.
Price: **$525.00**

MANNLICHER-SCHOENAUER M-72 MODEL T
Same as Model S except weighs 9¼ lbs., available in 9.3x64, 375 H&H Mag., and 458 Win. Mag. only **$650.00**

NAVY ARMS MODEL 1875 REVOLVING RIFLE
Caliber: 38 Special, 44-40.
Barrel: 20".
Weight: 5 lbs. **Length:** 38".
Stock: Walnut, brass butt plate.
Sights: Front blade adj. for w., buckhorn rear adj. for e.
Features: Action resembles Remington Model 1875 revolver. Polished brass trigger guard. Imported by Navy/Replica.
Price: **$175.00**

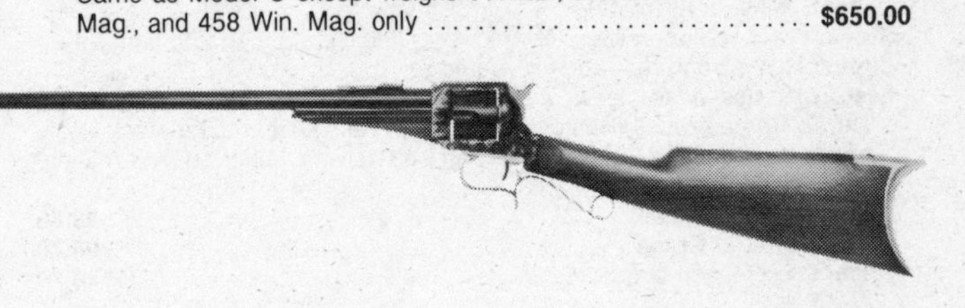

PARKER-HALE SUPER 1200 BOLT ACTION RIFLE
Caliber: 22-250, 243 Win., 6mm Rem., 25-06, 270 Win., 30-06, 308 Win., 7mm Rem. Mag., 300 Win. Mag.
Barrel: 24".
Weight: 7¼ lbs. **Length:** 45".
Stock: 13.5" x 1.8" x 2.3". Hand checkered walnut, rosewood p.g. and fore-end caps, fitted rubber recoil pad with white line spacers.
Sights: Bead front, folding adj. rear. Receiver tapped for scope mounts.
Features: 3-way side safety, single-stage adj. trigger, hinged mag. floorplate. Model 1200P has scroll engraved action, trigger guard and mag. floorplate, detachable swivels, no sights; avail. only in 243, 30-06. Varmint Model (1200V) has glass-bedded action, free-floating bbl., avail. in 22-250, 6mm Rem., 25-06, 243 Win., without sights. Imported from England by Jana.
Price: .... **$189.95** (**$199.95**, mag. cals.)
Price: 1200P .... **$239.95** 1200V **$199.95**

Sako Model 74 Deluxe Sporter
Same action as M-74 except has select wood, Rosewood p.g. cap and fore-end tip. Fine checkering on top surfaces of integral dovetail bases, bolt sleeve, bolt handle root and bolt knob. Vent. recoil pad, skip-line checkering, mirror finish bluing.
Price: 222 or 223 cals. **$385.00**
Price: 22-250, 243 or 308 .... **$410.00**
Price: 25-06, 270, 30-06 .... **$435.00**
Price: 338 Mag., 7mm Rem. Mag. 375 H&H **$440.00**

SAKO MODEL 74 SUPER SPORTER
Caliber: 222, 223, (short action); 22-250, 243, 308, (medium action); 25-06, 270, 30-06, 7mm Mag., 300 Mag., 338 Mag., 375 H&H Mag. (long action).
Barrel: 23" (222, 223, 22-250, 243 and 308), 24" (other cals.).
Weight: 6½ lbs. (short); 6¾ lbs. (med.); 8 lbs. (long).
Stock: Hand-checkered European walnut.
Sights: None furnished.
Features: Adj. trigger, hinged floorplate. 222 and 223 have short action, 22-250, 243 and 308 medium action, others are long action. Imported from Finland by Garcia.
Price: Short action **$255.00**
Price: Medium action **$265.00**
Price: Long action **$275.00**
Price: Magnum cals. **$285.00**

IMPORTED CENTERFIRE RIFLES — BOLT ACTION

Sako Heavy Barrel

Same as std. Super Sporter except has beavertail fore-end; available in 222, 223 (short action), 22-250, 243, 308 (medium action), 25-06 (long action). Weight from 8¼ to 9 lbs. 5-shot magazine capacity.

Price: 222, 223 (short action) **$285.00**
Price: 22-250, 243, 308 (medium action) **$285.00**
Price: 25-06 (long action) **$285.00**

Sako Golden Anniversary Model

Same as std. M-74 except stocked with fancy grade wood, hand carved and checkered; gold oak leaf inlays on receiver, trigger guard and floor plate. Serially numbered 1 to 1,000. In 7mm Rem. Mag. only, 24″ bbl., 8 lbs.

Price: **$770.00**

STEYR-MANNLICHER TARGET RIFLE—MODEL MATCH

Caliber: 308 Win.
Barrel: 25½″.
Weight: 9½ lbs. **Length:** 44½″ over-all.
Stock: Walnut or synthetic.
Sights: Hooded blade front, folding leaf rear or Walther diopter match sight.
Features: Extra magazine included with rifle. 6 rear locking lugs, 60° bolt throw. Adj. trigger. Optional 10-shot magazine available. Imported by L.E.S.
Price: Synthetic stock **$575.00**
Price: Walnut stock **$600.00**

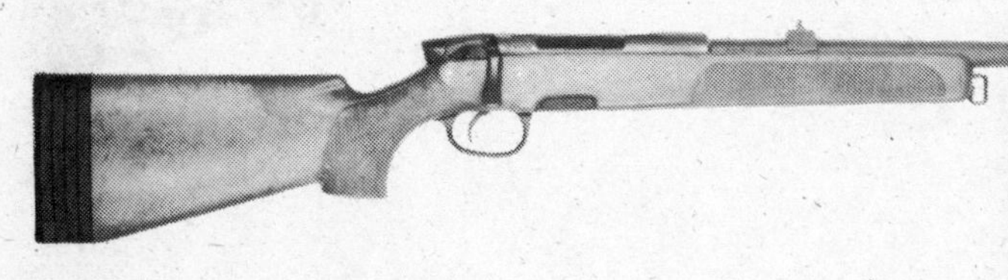

STEYR-MANNLICHER MODEL SSG

Caliber: 308 Win.
Barrel: 25½″.
Weight: 8½ lbs. **Length:** 44½″ over-all.
Stock: Walnut or synthetic.
Sights: Hooded blade front, folding leaf rear or Walther diopter match sight.
Features: Extra magazine included with rifle. 6 rear locking lugs, 60° bolt throw. Adj. trigger. Optional 10-shot magazine available. Imported by L.E.S.
Price: Synthetic stock **$425.00**
Price: Walnut **$475.00**

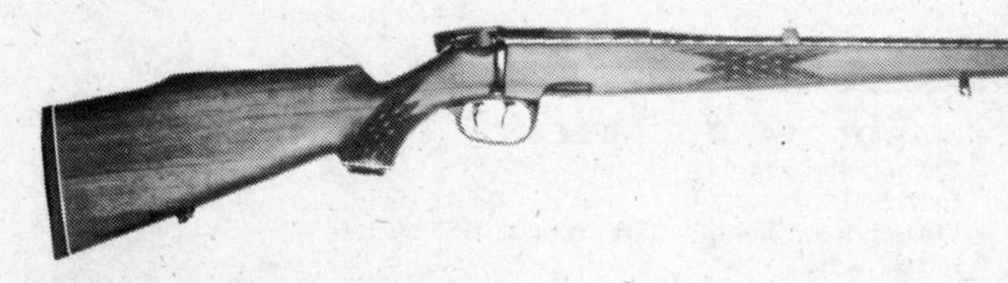

STEYR-MANNLICHER MODEL SL

Caliber: 222, 222 Rem. Mag., 223, 5.6x50 Mag.
Barrel: 20″ (full stock), 23½″ (half stock).
Weight: 5½ lbs. **Length:** 38¼″ over-all (20″ bbl.).
Stock: Hand checkered walnut with Monte Carlo cheekpiece. Either full Mannlicher or half stock.
Sights: Ramp front, open U-notch rear.
Features: Choice of interchangeable single or double set triggers. Extra magazine included. Detachable "Makrolon" rotary magazine. 6 rear locking lugs. Drilled and tapped for scope mounts. Custom hand engraving and stock carving avail. Imported by L.E.S.
Price: **$375.00**

Steyr-Mannlicher Model S

Same as Model SL except available in 6.5x68, 257 Weatherby Mag., 264 Win. Mag., 7mm Rem. Mag., 300 H&H, 308 Norma Mag., 8x68S, 338 Win. Mag., 9.3x64, 375 H&H Mag. Avail. only with half-stock. Extra magazine fits in buttstock recess **$525.00**

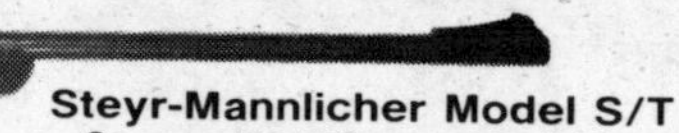

Steyr-Mannlicher Model S/T

Same as Model S except available only in 9.3x64, 375 H&H, 458 Win. Mag., has 23½″ barrel (458 has 23½″). Choice of interchangeable single or double set triggers. Detachable 4-shot Makrolon rotary magazine. Extra magazine (included) fits in recess in buttstock **$550.00**

STEYR-MANNLICHER MODEL M

Caliber: 6.5x55, 270, 7x57, 7x64, 30-06, 8x57JS, 9.3x62, 5-shot.
Barrel: 20″ (full stock).
Weight: 6½ lbs. (full stock). **Length:** 39″ over-all (full stock).
Stock: Full Mannlicher or standard half stock. Rubber recoil pad, hand checkered walnut. Monte Carlo cheekpiece.
Sights: Ramp front, open U-notch rear.
Features: Extra magazine included. Choice of interchangeable double set or single trigger. Detachable 5-shot rotary magazine. 6 rear locking lugs. Drilled and tapped for scope mounting. Imported by L.E.S.
Price: **$450.00**

Steyr-Mannlicher Model L

Same as Model M except available only in 22-250, 5.6x57, 6mm Rem., 243, 308 Win. Custom hand engraving and stock carving as well as heavy barrel varmint version available **$400.00**

TRADEWINDS HUSKY MODEL 5000 BOLT RIFLE

Caliber: 270, 30-06, 308, 243, 22-250.
Barrel: 23¾″.
Weight: 6 lbs. 11 oz.
Stock: Hand checkered European walnut, Monte Carlo, white line spacers on p.g. cap, fore-end tip and butt plate.
Sights: Fixed hooded front, adj. rear.
Features: Removeable mag., fully recessed bolt head, adj. trigger. Imported by Tradewinds.
Price: **$295.00**

IMPORTED CENTERFIRE RIFLES — BOLT ACTION

WALTHER KKJ BOLT ACTION RIFLE
Caliber: 22 Hornet, 5 shot.
Barrel: 22½".
Weight: 5½ lbs. **Length:** 41½".
Stock: Hand checkered walnut, p.g., cheek piece.
Sights: Hooded ramp front, adj. rear; dove tailed for slide-on scope mounts.
Features: Double set triggers available. Imported from Germany by Interarms.
Price: .... **$299.00** With dobule set trigger ... **$319.00**

TYROL CUSTOM CRAFTED RIFLE
Caliber: 243, 25-06, 308, 30-06, 7mm, 300 Win.
Barrel: 24".
Weight: 7 lbs. **Length:** 42½" over-all.
Stock: Hand checkered walnut, rosewood fore-end and p.g. cap, rubber recoil pad and detachable swivels.
Sights: Hooded ramp front, 100 and 200 yd. rear. Drilled and tapped for scope mounting.
Features: Shotgun-type tang safety, adj., trigger. Imported from Austria by Firearms Center, Inc.
Price: **$220.95**

WHITWORTH EXPRESS RIFLE
Caliber: 375 H&H; 458 Win. Mag.
Barrel: 24".
Weight: 7½-8 lbs. **Length:** 44".
Stock: Classic English Express rifle design of hand checkered, select European Walnut.
Sights: Three leaf open sight calibrated for 100, 200, 300 yards, ramp front with removable hood.
Features: Solid rubber recoil pad, barrel mounted sling swivel, adjustable trigger, hinged floor plate, solid steel recoil cross bolt. Imported by Interarms.
Price: **$360.00**

IMPORTED CENTERFIRE RIFLES — REPLICAS

MARTINI TARGET RIFLES
Caliber: 45-70 or 444.
Barrel: 18", 26" or 30".
Weight: 9 lbs. **Length:** 35½" over-all (18" bbl.).
Stock: Walnut.
Sights: Blade front, U-notch middle, fully adj. vernier tang peep.
Features: Action color case hardened. Half-round half-octagon barrel, p.g. stock, schnabel fore-end, long cocking lever. Imported by Navy Arms.
Price: **$195.00**

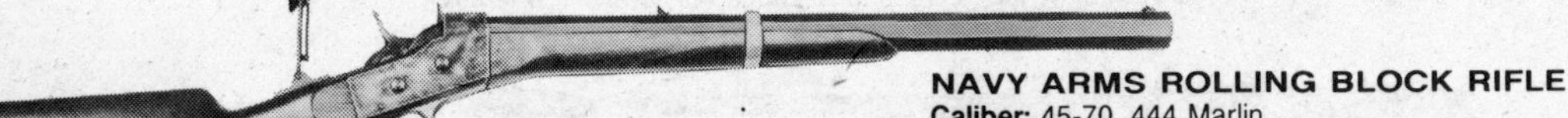

NAVY ARMS ROLLING BLOCK RIFLE
Caliber: 45-70, 444 Marlin.
Barrels: 26½".
Stock: Walnut finished.
Sights: Fixed front, adj. rear.
Features: Reproduction of classic rolling block action. Available in Buffalo Rifle (octagonal bbl.) and Creedmore (half round, half octagonal bbl.) models. Imported by Navy Arms.
Price: **$150.00**
Price: Creedmore Model **$175.00**

ROLLING BLOCK BABY CARBINE
Caliber: 22 LR, 357 Mag., 44-40.
Barrel: 20", octagon.
Weight: 4¾ lbs. **Length:** Approx. 35" over-all.
Stock: Walnut.
Sights: Blade front, rear adj. for e.
Features: Small rolling block action is color case hardened with blue barrel. Trigger guard and buttplate polished brass. Imported by Navy/Marietta Replica Arms.
Price: **$135.00**

STAR ROLLING BLOCK CARBINE
Caliber: 30-30, 357 Mag., 44 Mag.
Barrel: 20".
Weight: 6 lbs. **Length:** 35" over-all.
Stock: Walnut, straight grip.
Sights: Square bead ramp front, folding leaf rear.
Features: Color case-hardened receiver, crescent buttplate. Forged steel receiver. Imported by Garcia.
Price: Approx. **$150.00**

IMPORTED RIMFIRE RIFLES — AUTOLOADING & LEVER ACTION

AMERICAN 180 AUTO CARBINE

Caliber: 22 LR, 177-round magazine.
Barrel: 16½".
Weight: 5¾ lbs. (empty), 10 lbs. (loaded). **Length:** 33¼" over-all.
Stock: High impact plastic stock and fore-end.
Sights: Blade front, peep rear adj. for w. and e.
Features: Available in selective fire version for law enforcement or semi-auto only for civilians. Laser-Lok laser beam sight available at extra cost. Imported from Austria by American International.
Price: **$295.00**
Price: Laser-Lok sight system **$395.00**
Price: Extra magazine **$35.00**

AP-15 AUTO RIFLE

Caliber: 22 LR, 32 ACP, 15 shot magazine.
Barrel: 20" including flash reducer.
Weight: 6½ lbs. **Length:** 38½" over-all.
Stock: Black plastic.
Sights: Ramp front, adj. peep rear.
Features: Pivotal take-down, easy disassembly. AR-15 look-alike. Sling and sling swivels included. Imported by Kassnar Imports.
Price: **$99.95**

ERMA EM1 22 AUTOLOADING CARBINE

Caliber: 22 LR, 10-shot.
Barrel: 17¾".
Weight: 5¾ lbs. **Length:** 35⅜".
Stock: Walnut, semi p.g.
Sights: Fixed front, rear adj. for w. & e., grooved for scope mts. Looks and operates like U.S. M1 carbine. 15-shot mag. also available. Imported from Germany by R.G. Industries.
Price: **$83.95**

ERMA EG71 LEVER ACTION RIFLE

Caliber: 22 LR, 15-shot.
Barrel: 18½".
Weight: 5 lbs., 5 ozs. **Length:** 35⅞".
Stock: Walnut.
Sights: Fixed front, adj. rear, receiver grooved for scope mts.
Features: Looks and operates like traditional 30-30. Imported from Germany by R. G. Industries.
Price: **$82.95**

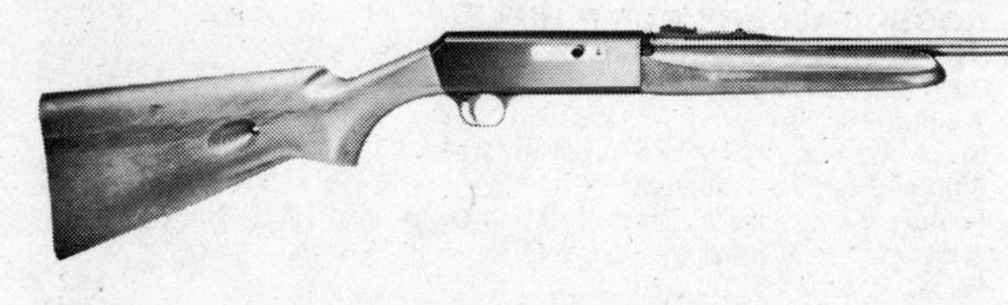

FRANCHI CENTENNIAL AUTO RIFLE

Caliber: 22 LR. (11-shot).
Barrel: 21".
Weight: 5 lbs. 2 oz. **Length:** 39⅛".
Stock: Epoxy-finished walnut.
Sights: Gold bead front, adj. rear.
Features: Quick takedown, cross-bolt safety, receiver grooved for tip-off scope mounts. Available in standard and deluxe (engraved action) grades. Imported from Italy by Stoeger Arms.
Price: **$165.95**

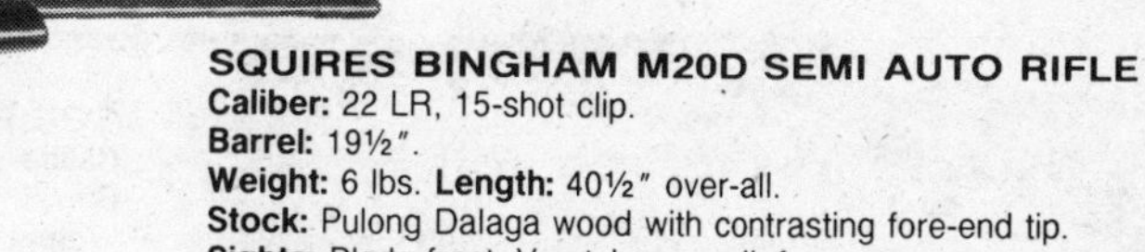

SQUIRES BINGHAM M20D SEMI AUTO RIFLE

Caliber: 22 LR, 15-shot clip.
Barrel: 19½".
Weight: 6 lbs. **Length:** 40½" over-all.
Stock: Pulong Dalaga wood with contrasting fore-end tip.
Sights: Blade front, V-notch rear adj. for e.
Features: Positive sliding thumb safety. Receiver grooved for tip-off scope mount. Flash suppressor/muzzle brake. Imported by American Import.
Price: **$66.95**

SQUIRES BINGHAM M16 SEMI AUTO RIFLE

Caliber: 22 LR, 15-shot clip.
Barrel: 16½".
Weight: 6 lbs. **Length:** 38½" over-all.
Stock: Black painted mahogany.
Sights: Post front, rear adj. for e.
Features: Box magazine, muzzle brake/flash suppressor. Imported by American Import.
Price: **$89.95**

TRADEWINDS MODEL 260-A AUTO RIFLE

Caliber: 22 LR, 5-shot (10-shot mag. avail.).
Barrel: 22½".
Weight: 5¾ lbs. **Length:! 41½".**
Stock: Walnut, with hand checkered p.g. and fore-end.
Sights: Ramp front with hood, 3-leaf folding rear, receiver grooved for scope mt.
Features: Double extractors, sliding safety. Imported by Tradewinds.
Price: **$165.00**

IMPORTED RIMFIRE RIFLES — BOLT ACTION

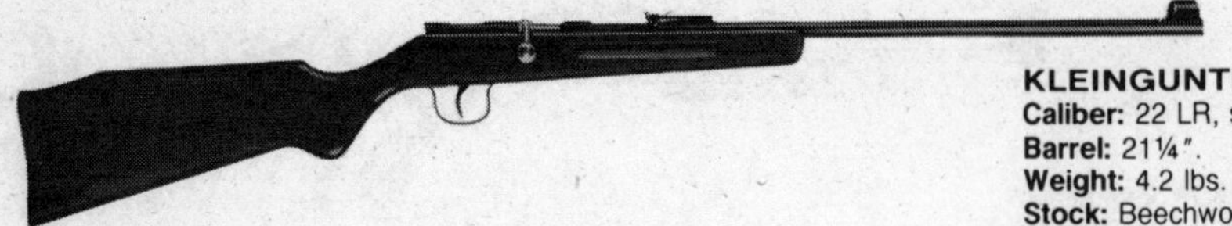

KLEINGUNTHER K-10 BOLT ACTION RIFLE
Caliber: 22 LR, single shot.
Barrel: 21¼″.
Weight: 4.2 lbs. **Length:** 38¼″.
Stock: Beechwood, walnut stained.
Sights: Hooded front, Mauser type tangent rear.
Features: Mauser type thumb safety locks firing pin. Imported from Europe by Kleingunther
Price: $39.00

KLEINGUNTHER K-12 BOLT ACTION RIFLE
Caliber: 22 LR, 5-shot or 10-shot.
Barrel: 21¼″.
Weight: 5.7 lbs. **Length:** 40″.
Stock: Hand checkered walnut, p.g., rosewood fore-end tip.
Sights: Hooded front, 2 leaf folding rear. Receiver grooved for scope mts.
Features: Adj. trigger, thumb lever safety. Imported from Europe by Kleingunther
Price: $86.00

Kleingunther K-13 Bolt Action Rifle
Same as K-12 except chambered for 22 WMR, weight 5.9 lbs.
Price: $128.00

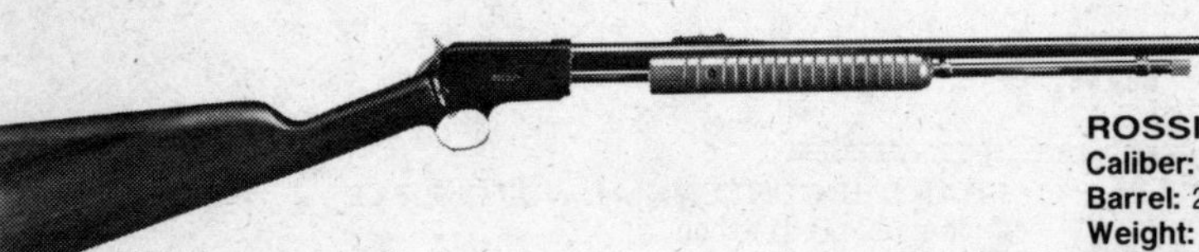

ROSSI GALLERY PUMP RIFLE
Caliber: 22 S, L or LR (Standard), 22 RFM (Magnum).
Barrel: 22½″.
Weight: 5¼ lbs.
Stock: Walnut, straight grip, grooved fore-end.
Sights: Fixed front, adj. rear.
Features: Capacity 20 Short, 16 Long or 14 Long Rifle. Quick takedown. Imported from Brazil by Garcia.
Price: Standard $90.00
Price: Magnum $105.00

TRADEWINDS MODEL 311-A BOLT ACTION RIFLE
Caliber: 22 LR, 5-shot (10-shot mag. avail.).
Barrel: 22½″.
Weight: 6 lbs. **Length:** 41¼″.
Stock: Walnut, Monte Carlo with hand checkered p.g. and fore-end.
Sights: Ramp front with hood, folding leaf rear, receiver grooved for scope mt.
Features: Sliding safety locks trigger and bolt handle. Imported by Tradewinds.
Price: $150.00

The product prices mentioned in these catalog pages were correct at presstime, but may be higher when you read this.

SQUIRES BINGHAM M14D BOLT ACTION RIFLE
Caliber: 22 S, L, LR, 5-shot clip.
Barrel: 19½″.
Weight: 6 lbs. **Length:** 41″ over-all.
Stock: Pulong Dalaga wood with contrasting fore-end tip. Monte Carlo cheekpiece.
Sights: Hooded ramp front, V-notch rear adjustable for e.
Features: Positive sliding thumb safety, receiver grooved for tip-off scope mount. Also available in 22 mag. as model 15. Imported by American Import.
Price: Model 14D $63.95
Price: Model 15 .... $99.95

WALTHER KKJ RIMFIRE RIFLE
Caliber: 22 LR, 5 or 8 shot; 22 WRM, 5 shot.
Barrel: 22½″.
Weight: 5½ lbs. **Length:** 41½″.
Stock: Hand checkered walnut, p.g., cheek piece.
Sights: Hooded ramp front, adj. rear; dove tailed for slide-on scope mounts.
Features: Double set triggers available. Imported from Germany by Interarms.
Price: 22 LR $279.00
Price: 22 WRM $299.00
Price: 22 LR with double set trigger $299.00
Price: 22 WRM with double set trigger $319.00

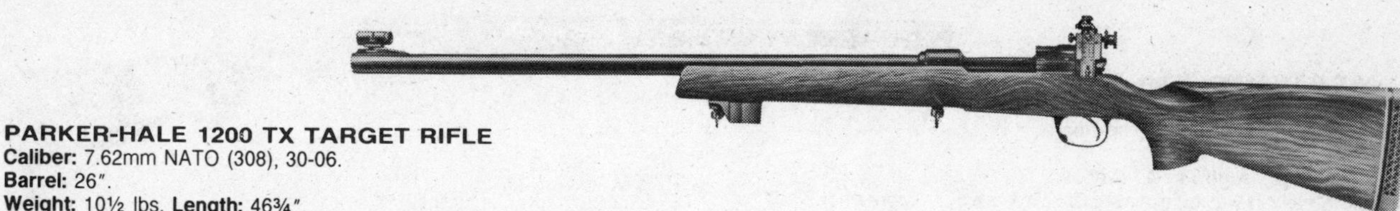

PARKER-HALE 1200 TX TARGET RIFLE
Caliber: 7.62mm NATO (308), 30-06.
Barrel: 26".
Weight: 10½ lbs. **Length:** 46¾".
Stock: 13³⁄₁₆" x 1¹¹⁄₁₆" x 1¹⁵⁄₁₆". Oil finish, full beavertail, p.g., vent. rubber butt pad.
Sights: Micro adj. ¼" click rear, interchangeable element tubular front.
Features: Full floating bbl., epoxy bedded action, fully adj. trigger, selected bbl. Imported from England by Jana.
Price: **$249.95**

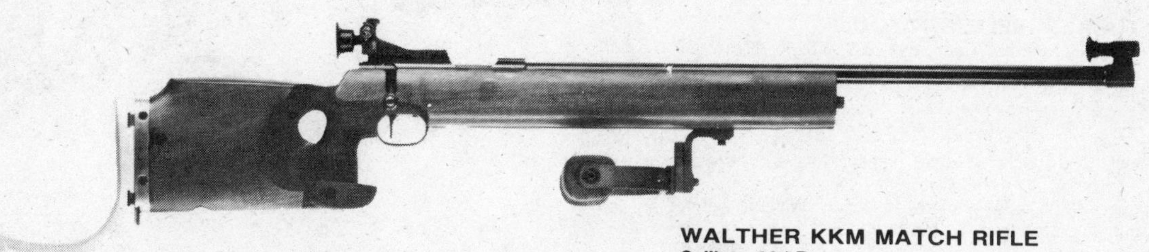

WALTHER KKM MATCH RIFLE
Caliber: 22 LR.
Barrel: 28".
Weight: 15½ lbs. **Length:** 46".
Stock: Walnut, with fully adj. hook butt plate, hand shelf and selection of ball-type offset yoke palm rest.
Sights: Olympic front with post and aperture inserts, micrometer rear click adj. for w. & e.
Features: Fully adj. match trigger. Imported from Germany by Interarms.
Price: **$469.00**

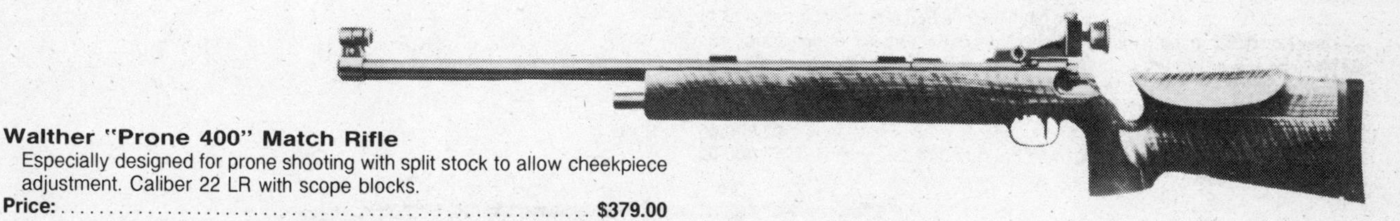

Walther "Prone 400" Match Rifle
Especially designed for prone shooting with split stock to allow cheekpiece adjustment. Caliber 22 LR with scope blocks.
Price: **$379.00**

WALTHER U.I.T. MATCH RIFLE
Caliber: 22 LR.
Barrel: 25½".
Weight: 10 lbs., 3 oz. **Length:** 44¾".
Stock: Walnut, adj. for length and drop; fore-end guide rail for sling or palm rest.
Sights: Interchangeable post or aperture front, micro adj. rear.
Features: Conforms to both NRA and U.I.T. requirements. Fully adj. trigger. Left hand stock available on special order. Imported from Germany by Interarms.
Price: **$339.00**

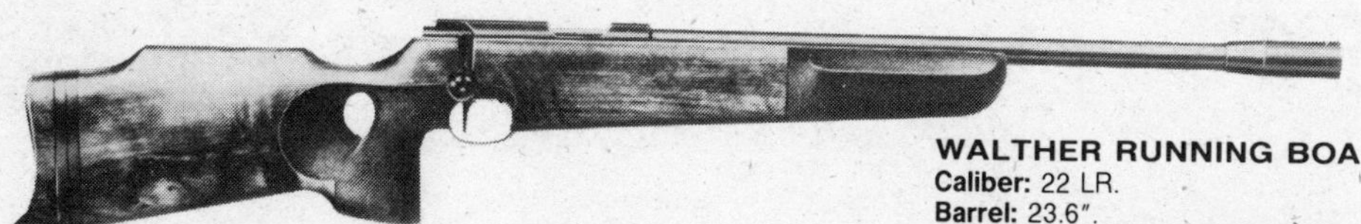

WALTHER RUNNING BOAR MATCH RIFLE
Caliber: 22 LR.
Barrel: 23.6".
Weight: 8 lbs. 5 oz. **Length:** 42" over-all.
Stock: Walnut thumb-hole type. Fore-end and p.g. stippled.
Sights: Globe front, micro adj. rear.
Features: Especially designed for running boar competition. Receiver grooved to accept dovetail scope mounts. Adjustable cheekpiece and butt plate. 1.1 lb. trigger pull. Imported by Interarms.
Price: **$319.00**

IMPORTED DRILLINGS, DOUBLE & COMBO RIFLES

COLT SAUER DRILLING

Caliber: 12 ga., 12 ga., over 30-06.
Action: Top lever, cross bolt, box lock.
Barrel: 25″ (Mod. & Full).
Weight: 8 lbs. **Length:** 41¾″ over-all.
Stock: American walnut, oil finish. Checkered p.g. and fore-end. Black p.g., cap, recoil pad. 14¼″x2″x1½″.
Sights: Blade front with brass bead, folding leaf rear.
Features: Cocking indicators, tang barrel selector, automatic sight positioner, set rifle trigger, side safety. Blue finish with bright receiver engraved with animal motifs and European-style scrollwork. Imported by Colt.
Price: **$1,650.00**

FERLACH O/U TURKEY RIFLE/SHOTGUN

Gauge: 12, 16, 20, and 22 Hornet, 222 Rem., 243, 257, 6.5x55, 270, 7x57, 30-06.
Action: Anson & Deeley boxlock.
Barrel: 22″ or 24″.
Weight: 6½ lbs.
Stock: Circassian walnut, hand checkered at p.g. and split fore-end, horn p.g. cap and buttplate.
Features: Double triggers, auto safety, engraved action. With or without cheekpiece, recoil pad. Imported from Austria by Flaig's.
Price: **$950.00**

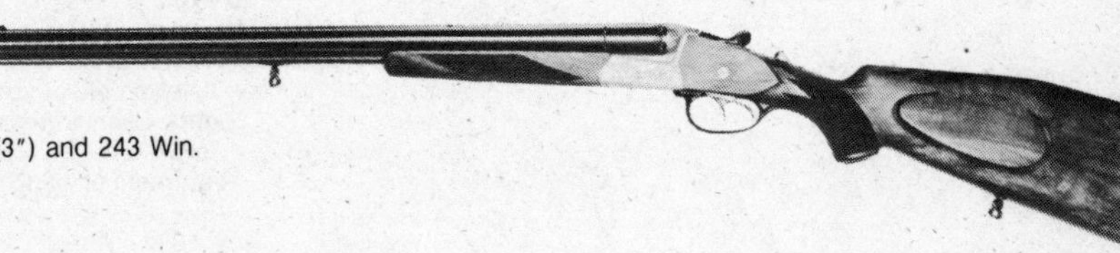

KRIEGHOFF TRUMPF DRILLING

Caliber: 12 and 12 ga. (2¾″) and 30-06, 20 and 20 (3″) and 243 Win.
Action: Sidelock or boxlock.
Barrel: 25″, solid rib.
Weight: 7½ lbs. **Length:** 41″ over-all.
Stock: 14¼″x1¼″x2¼″, European walnut.
Sights: Sourdough front, express rear.
Features: Shot barrel locks cock on opening, rifle barrel cocked and rear sight raises by action of tang mounted slide. Split extractors. American scope can be mounted at factory with claw mounts. Imported by Unordco.
Price: Boxlock action with optional engraving coverage and special stock features **$1,560.00**
Price: Sidelock version (Neptun) **$2,600.00**
Price: Deluxe Neptun (engraved) with hand-detachable locks **$3,300.00**

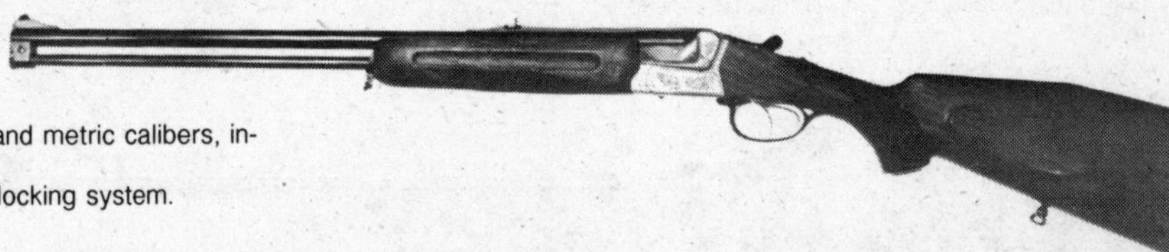

KRIEGHOFF "TECK" DOUBLE RIFLE

Caliber: All standard rimless and rimmed American and metric calibers, including 375 H & H and 458 Win. Mag.
Action: Kersten double cross bolt, double under-lug locking system.
Barrel: 25″, separated, free-floating.
Weight: From 8 lbs. **Length:** 41″ over-all.
Stock: 14¼″x1¼″x2¼″, European walnut.
Sights: Sourdough front, express rear.
Features: Imported by Unordco.
Price: Std. cals. **$1,680.00**
Price: Belted magnum cals. **$1,920.00**
Price: Model Ulm (sidelocks) **$3,060.00**
Price: Model Ulm (engraved, hand-detachable sidelocks) **$3,300.00**
Price: Interchangeable o/u shotgun barrel **$480.00**
Price: Interchangeable o/u rifle barrel **$990.00**

KRIEGHOFF RIFLE-SHOTGUN COMBO

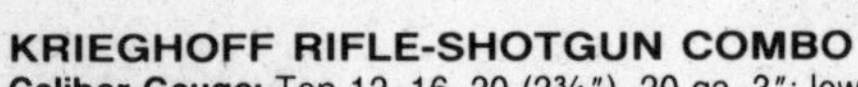

Caliber Gauge: Top-12, 16, 20 (2¾″), 20 ga. 3″; lower-all popular U.S. and metric cartridges, rimless and rimmed.
Action: Boxlock.
Barrel: 25″, solid rib.
Weight: 6¼ lbs. **Length:** 41″ over-all.
Stock: 14¼″x1¼″x2¼″, European walnut.
Sights: Sourdough front, express rear.
Features: Interchangeable rifle barrels in 22 Hornet, 222 Rem., 222 Rem. Mag. priced at $175.00. Scope optional. Imported by Unordco.
Price: 12 ga./30-06 or 222 Rem. **$1,440.00**
Price: Sidelock Ulm model **$2,200.00**
Price: Ulm Primus (deluxe) **$2,800.00**
Price: 12 ga. double barrels (only) with ejectors **$480.00**

IMPORTED SHOTGUNS—PUMP & AUTOLOADING

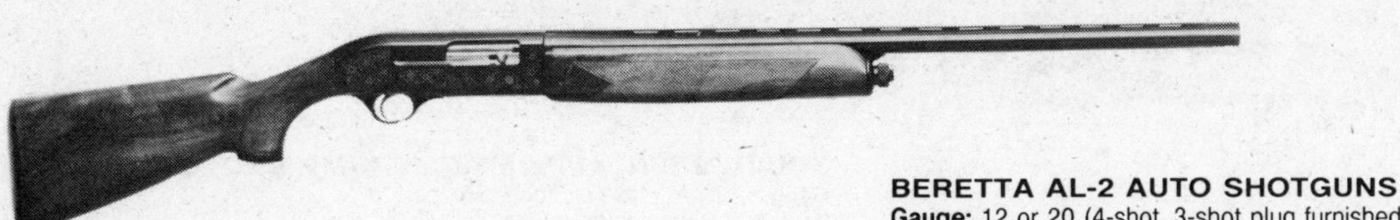

BENELLI AUTOLOADING SHOTGUN

Gauge: 12 only (5-shot).
Barrel: 26″ (Imp. Cyl., Mod.); 28″ (Full, Imp. Mod., Mod.). Vent. rib.
Weight: 6¾ lbs.
Stock: European walnut. 14″x1½″x2½″. Hand checkered p.g. and fore-end.
Sights: Metal bead front.
Features: Quick interchangeable barrels. Cross-bolt safety. Hand engraved on higher grades. Imported from Italy by Diana Import Co.
Price: Standard model **$335.00**
Price: Engraved **$475.00**

BERETTA AL-2 AUTO SHOTGUNS

Gauge: 12 or 20 (4-shot, 3-shot plug furnished). 2¾″ or 3″ chambers.
Action: Gas-operated autoloader.
Barrel: 12 ga., 30″ or 28″ (Full), 28″ (Mod.), 26″ (Imp. Cyl.); 20 ga., 28″ (Full or Mod.), 26″ (Imp. Cyl.); 12 ga. Trap, 30″ (Full); 12 or 20 ga. Skeet, 26″ (Skeet); 12 ga., 3″ mag. 30″ (Full), 28″ (Mod.).
Weight: 12 ga. 7 lbs., 20 ga. 6½ lbs., Trap 7½ lbs.
Stock: Hand checkered European walnut, p.g. Monte Carlo on trap models.
Features: AL-2 has hand-engraved receiver and ventilated rib. Crossbolt safety. Imported from Italy by Garcia.
Price: AL-2 .... **$285.00**
Price: AL-2 Trap or Skeet **$320.00**
Price: AL-2 3″ Magnum **$305.00**

CHARLES DALY AUTO SHOTGUN

Gauge: 12 (2¾″ chamber).
Action: Recoil-operated semi-auto.
Barrel: 26″ (I.C.), 28″ (Mod. or Full), 30″ (Full), vent. rib.
Stock: Hand-checkered walnut, p.g.
Features: Button safety, 5-shot capacity (3-shot plug furnished). Imported by Sloan's.
Price:.................. **$255.00** Extra barrels **$85.00**

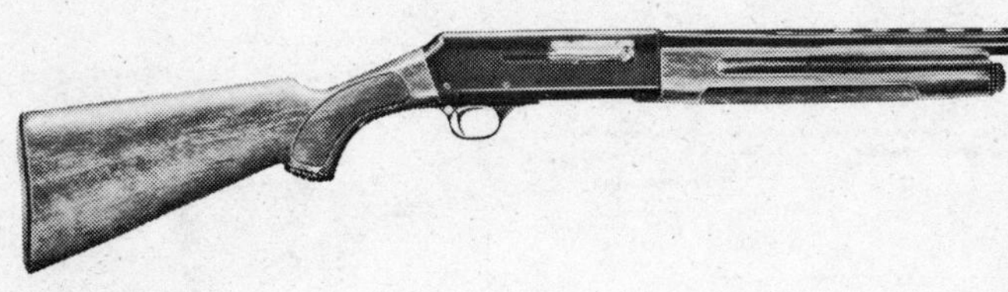

FRANCHI STANDARD AUTO SHOTGUN

Gauge: 12, 20 or 28, 5-shot. 2¾″ or 3″ chamber.
Action: Recoil-operated automatic.
Barrel: 24″ (Imp. Cyl. or Cyl.); 26″ (Imp. Cyl. or Mod.); 28″ (Skeet, Mod. or Full); 30″, 32″. (Full).
Weight: 12 ga. 6¼ lbs., 20 ga. 5 lbs. 2 oz.
Stock: Epoxy-finished walnut.
Features: Chrome-lined bbl., easy takedown, 3-round plug provided. Available with plain round or ventilated rib barrel. Imported from Italy by Stoeger Arms.
Price: Plain bbl. 12 or 20 ga. **$229.95**
Price: Vent. rib 12 or 20 ga. **$274.95**
Price: Hunter model (engraved, 12 or 20) **$314.95**
Price: "EL Dorado" Model **$374.95**

FRANCHI MAGNUM AUTO SHOTGUN

Gauge: 12 or 20, 3-inch shells.
Action: Recoil-operated automatic.
Barrel: 32″, 12 ga.; 28″, 20 ga., both Full.
Weight: 12 ga. 8¼ lbs., 20 ga. 6 lbs.
Stock: Epoxy-finished walnut with recoil pad.
Features: Chrome-lined bbl., easy takedown. Available with ventilated rib barrel. Imported from Italy by Stoeger Arms.
Price:.. **$314.95**

Franchi Slug Gun

Same as Standard automatic except 22″ cylinder bored bbl., adj. rear sight, sling swivels.
Price:.. **$274.95**

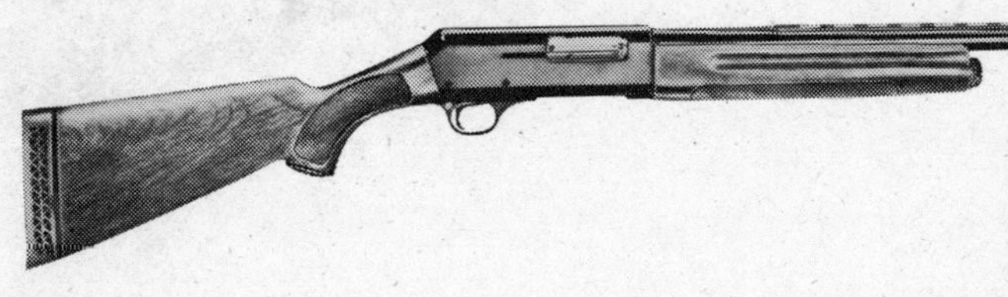

TRADEWINDS H-170 AUTO SHOTGUN

Gauge: 12 only, 2¾″ chamber.
Action: Recoil-operated automatic.
Barrel: 26″, 28″ (Mod.) and 28″ (Full), chrome lined.
Weight: 7 lbs.
Stock: Select European walnut stock, p.g. and fore-end hand checkered.
Features: Light alloy receiver, 5-shot tubular magazine, ventilated rib. Imported by Tradewinds.
Price:.. **$259.50**

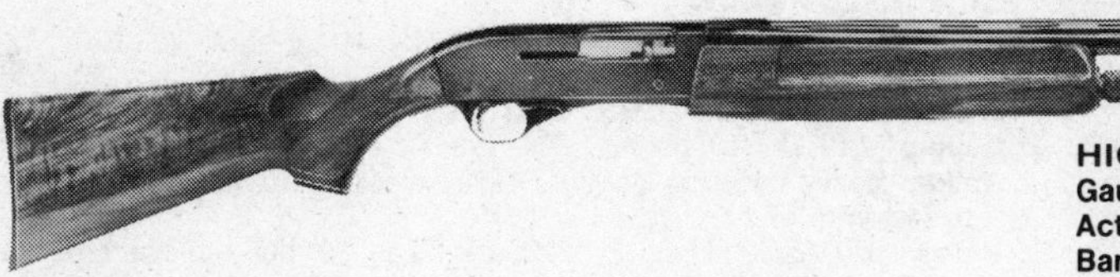

HIGH STANDARD SHADOW AUTO SHOTGUN

Gauge: 12 or 20 (2¾″ and 3″ chambers).
Action: Gas operated
Barrel: 26″ (Imp., Skeet), 28″ (Imp. Mod., Mod., Full), 30″ (Full, Trap). Full airflow rib.
Weight: 7 lbs.
Stock: American walnut. Hand checkered p.g. and wide fore-end.
Sights: Metal bead front.
Features: Self-cleaning gas system. Highly polished octagonal bolt. Takedown, interchangeable barrels, p.g. cap on all models, recoil pad available on 3″ mag. models. Crossbolt safety. Imported by High Standard.
Price:.. **$264.00**

IMPORTED SHOTGUNS — PUMP & AUTOLOADING

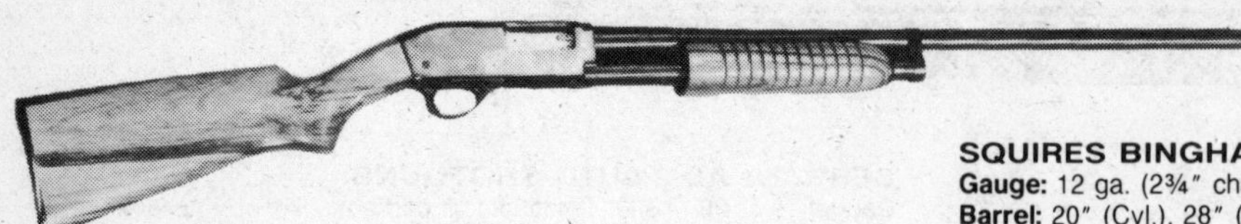

SQUIRES BINGHAM M30/28 PUMP SHOTGUN

Gauge: 12 ga. (2¾" chamber), 5-shot.
Barrel: 20" (Cyl.), 28" (Mod.), 30" (Full).
Weight: 7 lbs. **Length:** 49¾" over-all.
Stock: Pulong Dalaga wood.
Sights: Brass bead front.
Features: Blued frame and barrel. Cross-bolt safety. Damascene bolt. 5-shot capacity, plugged for 3. Imported from the Philippines by American Import.
Price: **$99.95**

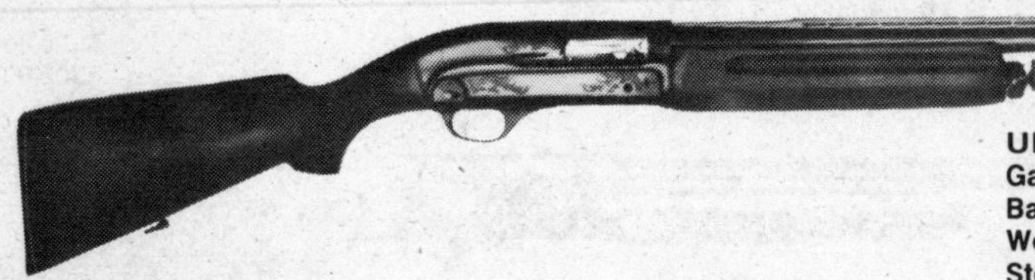

UNIVERSAL BAIKAL MC-21 AUTO SHOTGUN

Gauge: 12 ga., 2¾" chamber. 5-shot.
Barrel: 26" (Imp. Cyl.), 28" (Mod.), 30" (Full). Vent. rib.
Weight: 7½ lbs.
Stock: Hand checkered walnut with cheekpiece. White spacers at p.g. and buttplate. Hand rubbed finish.
Features: Chrome barrel and chamber. Reversible safety. Instant take-down including trigger housing. Interchangeable barrels. Target grade trigger. Magazine cut-off. Imported by Universal Sporting Goods.
Price: **$350.00**

IMPORTED SHOTGUNS—DOUBLE BARREL

AYA MODELS 56 & 53E DOUBLE BARREL SHOTGUNS

Gauge: 12, 20 (2¾" chambers standard, 3" on request).
Action: Heavy Competition sidelock frame, triple bolting.
Barrel Up to 30" (length and choke customer specified).
Stock: Made to customer specifications.
Features: Auto safety and ejectors, loading indicators, matted rib, gas escape valves, folding front trigger, engraved frame. Made to customer requirements, 10-12 month delivery. Model 53-E same except has hand detachable locks, concave rib. Imported from Spain by JBL Arms.
Price: 56 .... **$938.00**
Price: 53E **$808.00**

Aya XXV/SL Double Barrel Shotgun

Same as 56 except 12 ga., 2¾" chamber only, narrow top rib, 25" bbl.
Price: **$771.00**

Aya No. 1 Double Barrel Shotgun

Same as 56 except lightweight frame, concave rib, double bolting, 2¾" chambers only.
No. 2 similar to No. 1 except without loading indicators or folding front trigger.
Price: No. 1 .... **$938.00**
Price: No. 2 .... **$671.00**

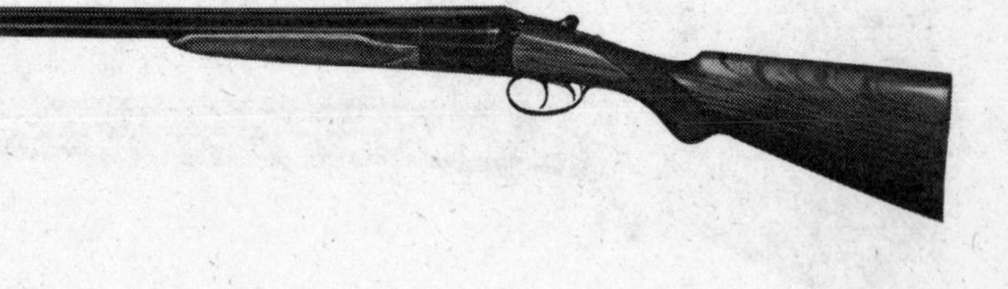

BERETTA GR DOUBLE BARREL SHOTGUNS

Gauge: 12 (2¾" chambers), 20 (3" chambers).
Action: Improved Greener action.
Barrel: 12 ga. 30" or 28" (Mod., Full), 26" (Imp. Cyl., Mod.) 20 ga. 28" (Mod., Full), 26" (Imp. Cyl., Mod.)
Weight: 12 ga. 7 lbs., 20 ga. 6½ lbs., 12 ga. Mag. 8 lbs.
Stock: 14" x 1½" x 2½" hand checkered European walnut stock and semi-beavertail fore-end.
Features: Ventilated rib. Model GR-2 has double triggers; GR-3 has single selective trigger; GR-4 has single selective trigger, auto ejectors, engraved action and select wood. Imported from Italy by Garcia.
Price: .... **$475.00**(GR-2) to **$650.00**(GR-4)

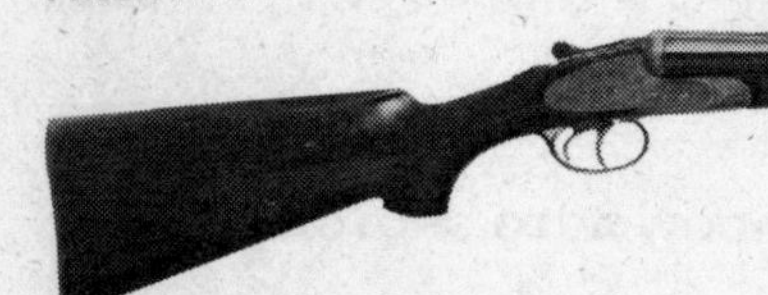

CENTURY FOLDING DOUBLE BARREL SHOTGUN

Gauge: 410 (3" chambers).
Action: Hammer, side lever to open action.
Barrel: 27¾" (Full & Full).
Weight: 4¾ lbs.
Stock: Hand checkered walnut, semi p.g.
Features: Depressing button on frame allows gun to be folded for carrying or storage. Imported from Spain by Century Arms.
Price: **$34.50**

BERETTA SO DOUBLE BARREL SHOTGUNS

Gauge: 12 (2¾" chambers).
Action: Heavy underlug locking. Single selective or double triggers, gold plated on SO-7.
Barrel: 28" (Mod. and Full), 26" (I.C. and Mod.); 30" bbl. and different choke combos available.
Weight: 7 to 7¼ lbs.
Stock: Select European walnut, 14⅛" x 1½" x 2½" or custom fitted, p.g. or straight grip.
Features: Made to order to customer's specifications. SO-7 has more ornamentation. Auto safety on Field models, manual on Skeet and Trap. Imported from Italy by Garcia.
Price: SO-6, SO-7 .... On request only.

IMPORTED SHOTGUNS—DOUBLE BARREL

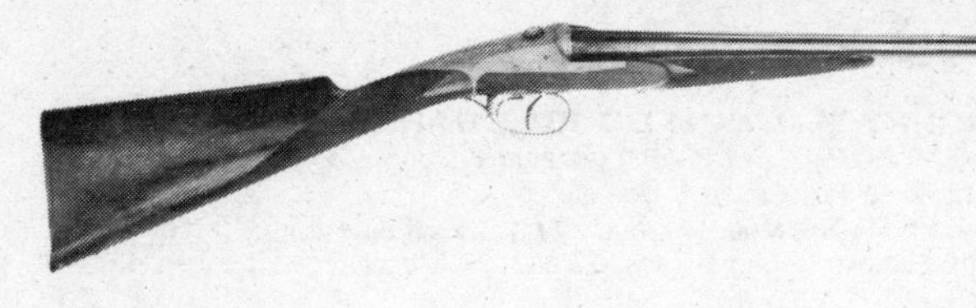

DARNE SLIDING BREECH DOUBLE
Gauge: 12, 16, 20 or 28.
Action: Sliding breech.
Barrel: 25½" to 27½", choice of choking.
Weight: 5½ to 6½ lbs.
Stock: European walnut, hand checkered p.g., and fore-end. English style or semi-p.g.
Features: Double triggers, selective ejectors, plume or raised rib, case-hardened or engraved receiver. Available in 8 grades, stock or custom made. Imported from France by Firearms Center, Inc.
Price: from **$475.00**

DIXIE HAMMER DOUBLE BARREL SHOTGUN
Gauge: 12, 28 ga. regular.
Action: Front and back action.
Barrel: 28" to 32" barrels.
Stock: Straight, semi-pistol or full pistol-grip halfstocks, some with checkered grip and fore-end, some smooth.
Weight: Varies.
Features: Proofed for heaviest smokeless powder loads. Case-hardened frames with modest engraving. Imported from Belgium by Dixie Gun Works.
Price:...**$125.00** to **$140.00**

DAVIDSON MODEL 63B DOUBLE BARREL SHOTGUN
Gauge: 12, 16, 20, 28 (2¾" chambers); 410 (3" chambers).
Action: Anson & Deeley with crossbolt (no crossbolt on 28 and 410).
Barrel: 30" 12 (Mod. & Full); 26" (I.C. & Mod.) and 28" (Mod. & Full) all except 410; 410, 25" (Full & Full) only.
Weight: 12 ga., 7 lbs.; 16, 20, 28 ga., 6½ lbs.; 410 ga., 5 lbs. 11 oz.
Stock: Hand finished checkered European walnut, white line spacers on p.g. cap and butt plate.
Features: Auto safety, manual extractors, gold-plated double triggers, engraved nickel-plated frame. Imported by Davidson.
Price:.. **$169.95**

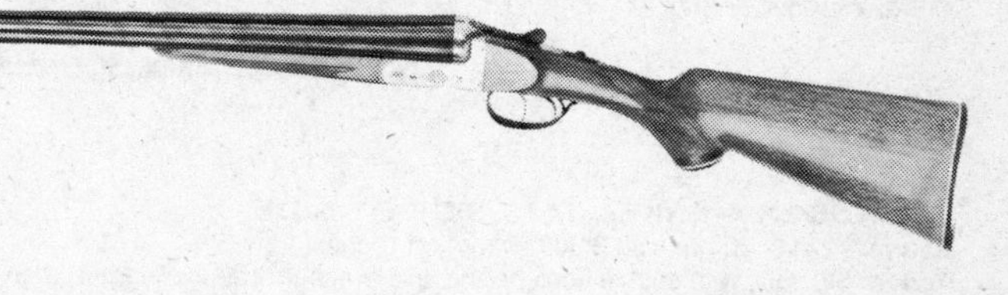

DAVIDSON 63B MAGNUM DOUBLE SHOTGUN
Gauge: 10 (3½" chambers), 12 and 20 (3" chambers) magnum.
Barrel: 32" 10 (Full & Fyll), 30" 12 (Mod. & Full), 28" 20 (Mod. & Full).
Weight: 10 ga., 10 lbs. 10 oz.; 12 ga., 7½ lbs.; 20 ga. 6¾ lbs.
Stock: Hand finished checkered European walnut, beavertail fore-end, white line spacers on p.g. cap and recoil pad.
Features: Auto safety, manual extractors, gold-plated double triggers (front hinged), engraved nickel-plated action. Imported from Europe by Davidson.
Price: 12, 20 ga.. **$189.95**
Price: 10 ga. **$209.95**

FALCON GOOSE DOUBLE BARREL SHOTGUN
Gauge: 10 (3½-inch chambers).
Action: Anson & Deeley with Holland type extractors, double triggers.
Barrel: 32" (Full and Full).
Weight: 11 lbs.
Stock: Hand checkered walnut, plastic p.g. cap and rubber recoil pad with white spacers.
Features: Auto safety, rubber recoil pad, engraved action. Imported from Spain by American Import.
Price:... **$239.00**

F.I.E. DOUBLE BARREL SHOTGUN
Gauge: 12, 20, 410.
Action: Boxlock.
Barrel: 30" 12 only (Full & Full); 28" all exc. 410 (Mod.& Full); 26" all exc. 410 (I.C.& Mod.); 26" 410 (Mod.& Full or Full & Full).
Stock: Hand checkered walnut, beavertail fore-end, white line spacers on p.g. cap and butt plate.
Features: Raised matted rib, double triggers, engraved case hardened receiver. Imported from Brazil by Firearms Import & Export.
Price:... **$109.95**

KLEINGUENTHER'S BRESCIA SHOTGUN
Gauge: 12, 20 (2¾" chambers).
Action: Anson & Deeley.
Barrel: 28" (Full & Mod. or I.C. & Mod.), chrome lined.
Weight: 6½ lbs.
Stock: Hand checkered walnut, p.g. or straight, recoil pad.
Features: Double triggers, engraved action. Imported from Italy by Kleingunther.
Price:... **$216.20**

LOYOLA MAGNUM DOUBLE BARREL SHOTGUN
Gauge: 10 (3½ chambers); 12, 20 and 410 (all 3" chambers).
Action: Hammerless, double trigger, auto. safety.
Barrel: 12, 20 ga. 26" (Imp. Cyl., Mod.), 28" (Full, Mod.); 10, 12 ga. 30" (Full, Mod.); 10 ga. 32", 12 ga. 30" and 410 ga. 26" (Full, Full).
Stock: Checkered walnut, p.g., fitted rubber recoil pad.
Features: Available with solid or vent. rib. ($20.00 additional). Imported from Spain by Jana.
Price:...................... **$140.00** (12, 20, 410 ga.), **$175.00** (10 ga.)

IMPORTED SHOTGUNS—DOUBLE BARREL

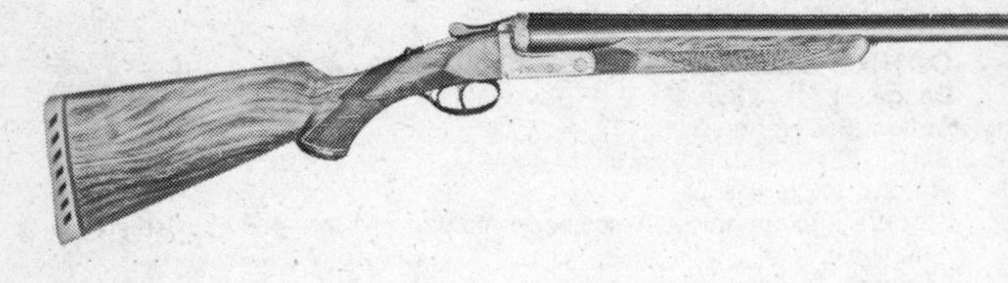

MERCURY MAGNUM DOUBLE BARREL SHOTGUN
Gauge: 10 (3½"), 12 or 20 (3") magnums.
Action: Triple-lock Anson & Deeley type.
Barrel: 28" (Full & Mod.), 12 and 20 ga.; 32" (Full & Full), 10 ga.
Weight: 7¼ lbs. (12 ga.); 6½ lbs. (20 ga.); 10⅛ lbs. (10 ga.). **Length:** 45" (28" bbls.).
Stock: 14" x 1⅝" x 2¼" walnut, checkered p.g. stock and beavertail fore-end, recoil pad.
Features: Double triggers, front hinged, auto safety, extractors; safety gas ports, engraved frame. Imported from Spain by Tradewinds.
Price: .... **$198.50** (12, 20 ga.)
Price: .... **$249.50** (10 ga.)

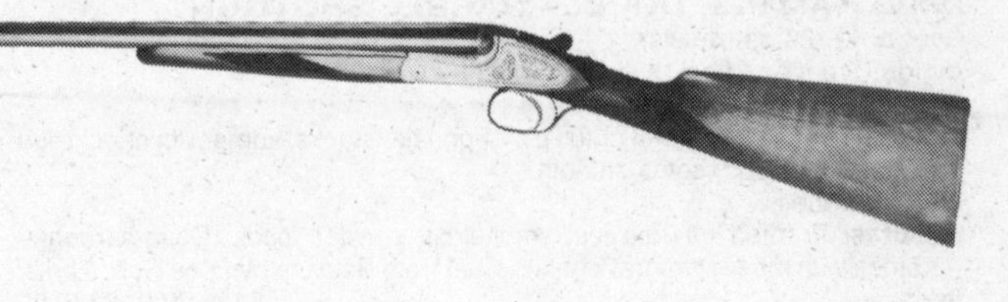

GEBRUDER MERKEL 47S SIDE-BY-SIDE
Gauge: 12, 16, 20, 3" chambers on request.
Action: Sidelock with double hook bolting and Greener breech.
Barrel: To customer's specs., choice of chokes.
Weight: 6¼ to 6¾ lbs.
Stock: To customer's specs. Walnut with p.g. or English style.
Features: Double, single or single selective trigger. Cocking indicators. English arabesque engraving. Imported by Champlin Firearms.
Price: With double trigger **$825.00**

GEBRUDER MERKEL 147S SIDE-BY-SIDE
Gauge: 12, 16, 20 ga. with 3" chambers on request.
Action: Sidelock with double hook bolting and Greener breech. Trigger catch bar.
Barrel: To customer's specs, choice of chokes.
Weight: 6½ to 6¾ lbs.
Stock: Walnut finish. English style or p.g., to customer's specs.
Features: 30% faster trigger than conventional lock design. Hunting scene engraving. Highest grade side-by-side Merkel. Double, single or single selective trigger. Imported by Champlin Firearms.
Price: With double trigger **$1,000.00**

GEBRUDER MERKEL 147E SIDE-BY-SIDE
Gauge: 12, 16, 20, 3" chambers on request.
Action: Anson-Deeley with double hook bolting and Greener breech.
Barrel: To customer's specs, choice of chokes.
Weight: 6¼ to 6½ lbs.
Stock: Walnut. English style or p.g., to customer's specs.
Features: Hunting scene engraving. Double, single or single selective trigger. Imported by Champlin Firearms.
Price: With double triggers **$525.00**

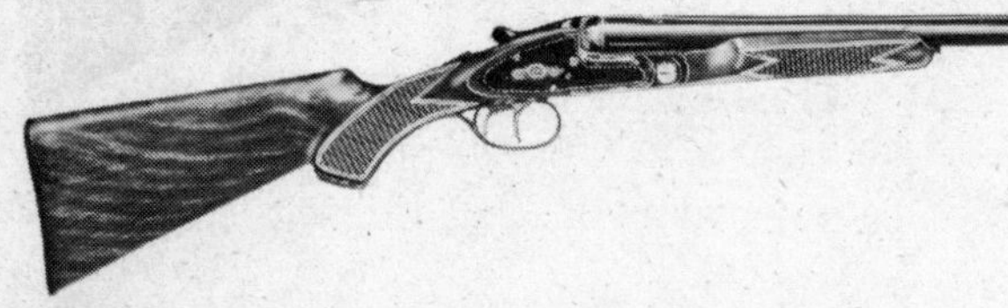

Premier Continental Double Hammer Shotgun
Same as Ambassador except outside hammers, not avail. in 410.
Price: **$190.40**

PREMIER AMBASSADOR DOUBLE BARREL SHOTGUN
Gauge: 12, 16 (2¾"); 20, 410 (3").
Action: Triple Greener crossbolt, Purdey avail. on 410; side locks.
Barrels: 22" exc. 410; 26" all (Mod. & Full).
Weight: 7¼ lbs. (12) to 6¼ lbs. (410). **Length:** 44½".
Stock: 14" x 1⅝" x 2½" checkered walnut, p.g., beavertail fore-end.
Features: Cocking indicators, double triggers, auto safety. Imported from Europe by Premier.
Price: **$209.40**

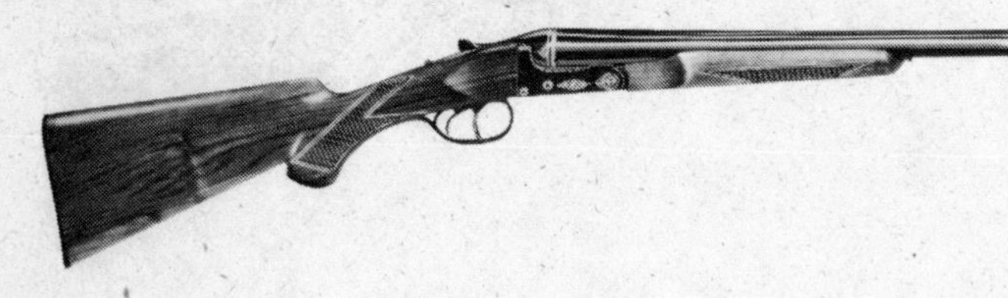

PREMIER REGENT DOUBLE BARREL SHOTGUN
Gauge: 12, 16, 28 (2¾" chambers); 20, 410 (3" chambers).
Action: Triple Greener crossbolt; Purdey optional on 28, 410.
Barrels: 26" (I.C. & Mod.) exc. 28 and 410 only (Mod. & Full); 28" (Mod. & Full); 30" 12 only (Mod. & Full).
Weight: 7¼ lbs. (12) to 6⅛ lbs. (410). **Length:** 42½" (26" bbls.).
Stock: 14" x 1⅝" x 2½" checkered walnut, p.g. and fore-end.
Features: Matted tapered rib, double triggers, auto safety. Extra bbl. sets avail. Imported from Europe by Premier.
Price: **$154.50**

Premier Brush King Double Barrel Shotgun
Same as Regent except 12 and 20 ga. only, 22" bbls. (I.C. & Mod.), weight 6¼ lbs. (12), 5¾ lbs. (20).
Price: **$165.75**

Premier Magnum Double Barrel Shotgun
Similar to Regent except 10 ga. (3½" chambers) 32" or 12 ga. (3" chambers) 30", both Full & Full. Recoil pad, beavertail fore-end.
Price: 12 ga. **$173.60**
Price: 10 ga. **198.00**

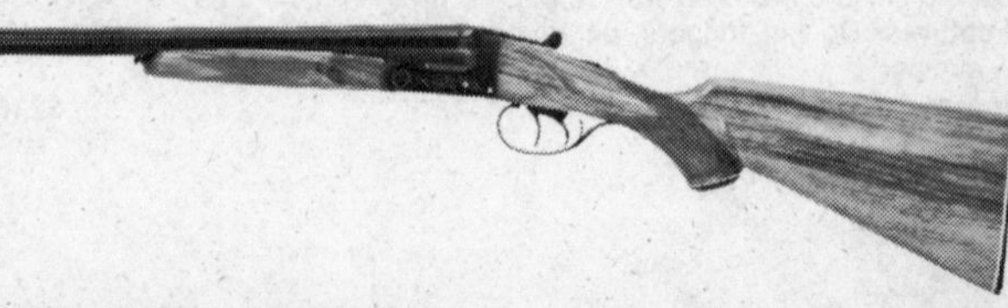

SLOAN'S P-O-S DOUBLE BARREL SHOTGUN
Gauge: 10, 12, 20 or 410 (3" chambers except 10, 3½"; 28, 2¾").
Action: Hammerless, double triggers.
Barrel: 32" 10, 30" 12 (Full & Full); 30" 12, 28" 12 or 20, 26" 28 or 410 (Mod. & Full); 26" 12 or 20 (I.C. & Mod.).
Stock: Checkered walnut, p.g. cap and buttplate with white line spacers.
Features: Imported from Spain by Charles Daly.
Price: 12, 20, 28, 410 ga. **$100.00**
Price: 10 ga. **$150.00**

Sloan's P-O-S Coach Gun
Similar to standard P-O-S except has exposed hammers, 12 or 20 ga. only with 20" barrels **$105.00**

IMPORTED SHOTGUNS—DOUBLE BARREL

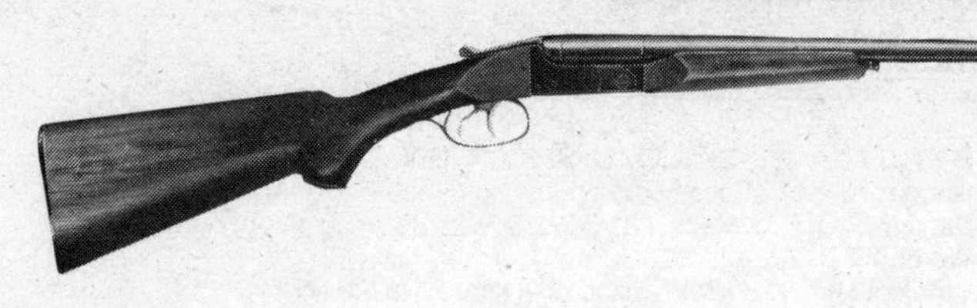

ROSSI HAMMERLESS
Gauge: 12, 20, 3″ chambers.
Action: Greener crossbolt, top lever, break-open.
Barrel: 12 and 20 ga. 28″ (Mod., Full).
Weight: 6 to 7¾ lbs.
Stock: Brazilian hardwood, walnut finish.
Features: Double triggers, raised matted rib with bead front, beavertail fore-end, extractors. Imported from Brazil by Garcia.
Price: **$170.00**

UGARTECHEA DOUBLE BARREL SHOTGUN
Gauge: 12 (Model 1302), 20 (Model 1303), 28 (Model 1304), 410 (Model 1305). All 3-inch chambers except 28 ga.
Action: Anson & Deeley, gold plated double triggers.
Barrel: 30″ (Mod. and Full) 12 ga., 28″ (Mod. and Full) 12 and 20 ga., 26″ (Imp. Cyl. and Mod.) 12 and 20 ga., (Mod. and Full) 28 ga., (Full and Full) 410 ga.
Stock: Hand checkered walnut, ebonite p.g. cap and butt plate with white spacers, beavertail fore-end.
Features: Scroll engraving. Imported from Spain by American Import.
Price: **$179.50**

ROSSI OVERLAND DOUBLE BARREL SHOTGUN
Gauge: 12, 20 (3-in. chambers).
Action: Sidelock with external hammers; Greener crossbolt.
Barrel: 12 ga., 20″ (Imp. Cyl., Mod.) 20 ga., 20″ (Mod., Full).
Weight: 6½ to 7 lbs.
Stock: Walnut p.g. with beavertail fore-end.
Features: Solid raised matted rib. Imported from Brazil by Garcia.
Price: **$160.00**

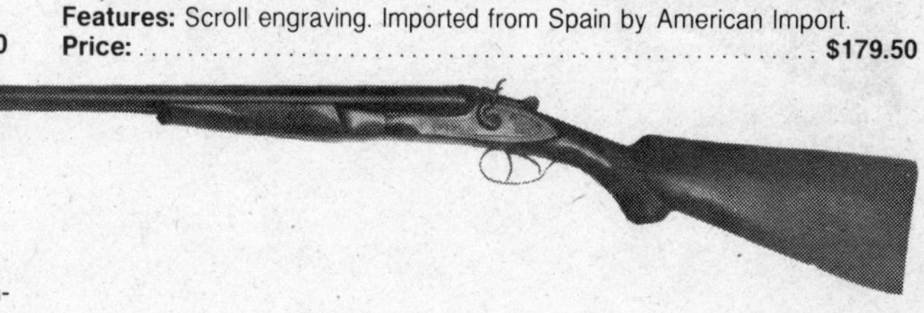

UNIVERSAL BAIKAL TOZ-66 SIDE-BY-SIDE
Gauge: 12 ga., 2¾″ chambers.
Barrel: 20″ (Imp. Cyl. & Mod.), 28″ (Mod. & Full).
Weight: 6¼-6½ lbs.
Stock: Walnut. Hand checkered p.g. and beavertail fore-end.
Features: Exposed hammers. Chrome barrels and chambers. Fore-end center latch. Hand engraved receiver. Extractors. Imported by Universal Sporting Goods.
Price: **$139.95**

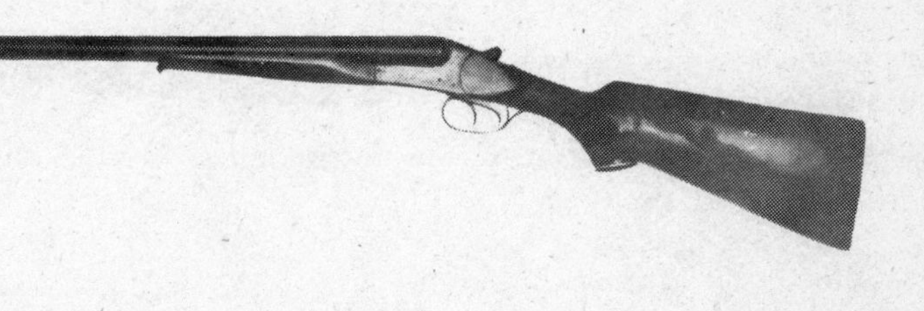

UNIVERSAL BAIKAL IJ-58M SIDE-BY-SIDE
Gauge: 12 ga., 2¾″ chambers.
Barrel: 26″ (Imp. Cyl. & Mod.), 28″ (Mod. & Full).
Weight: 6¾ lbs.
Stock: Walnut. Hand checkered p.g. and beavertail fore-end.
Features: Hinged front double trigger. Chrome barrels and chambers. Fore-end center latch. Hand engraved receiver. Extractors. Imported by Universal Sporting Goods.
Price: **$169.95**

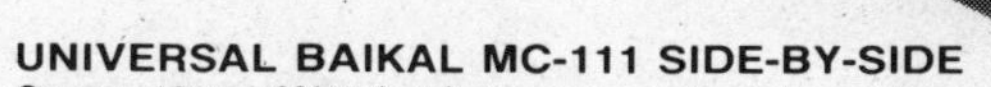

UNIVERSAL BAIKAL MC-10 SIDE-BY-SIDE
Gauge: 12 or 20 ga., 2¾″ chambers.
Barrel: 12 ga. 28″ (Mod. & Full), 20 ga. 26″ (Imp. Cyl. & Mod.).
Weight: 6 lbs. (20 ga.), 6¾ lbs. (12 ga.).
Stock: Fancy walnut. Hand checkered p.g. and fore-end. Choice of full p.g. or straight stock. Semi-beavertail fore-end.
Features: Fully engraved receiver with animal and bird scenes. Engraved trigger guard and tang. Double trigger. Chrome barrels, chambers and internal parts. Raised solid rib. Extractors or selective ejectors. Auto. safety, sling swivels. Imported by Universal Sporting Goods.
Price: **$700.00**

UNIVERSAL BAIKAL MC-111 SIDE-BY-SIDE
Gauge: 12 ga., 2¾″ chambers.
Barrel: To customer's specifications, choice of chokes.
Weight: 7 lbs.
Stock: Fancy walnut. Choice of p.g. or straight stock. Gold and silver inlays in butt. Semi-beavertail fore-end. Monte Carlo. To customer's specifications.
Features: Handmade sidelock shotgun. Removable sideplates. Chrome barrels, chambers and internal parts. Selective ejectors, single selective trigger, hammer interceptors, cocking indicators. Hand chiseled scenes on receiver to customer specs. Gold inlays as requested. Sling swivels on barrel and butt. Imported by Universal Sporting Goods.
Price: Special order only **$1,800.00**

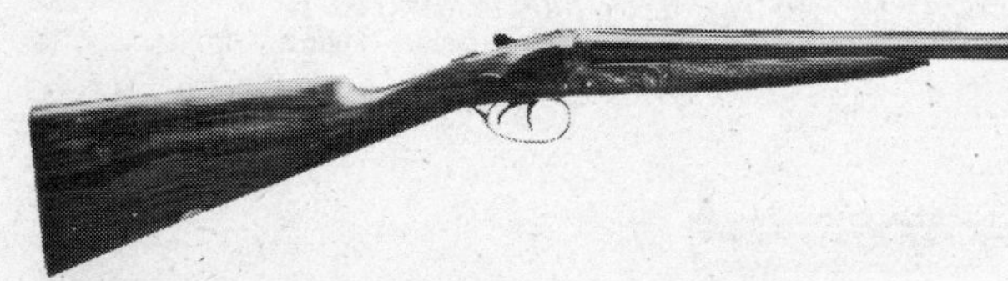

ZABALA DOUBLE BARREL SHOTGUN
Gauge: 10 (3½″); 12, 20, 410 (3″); 16, 20 (2¾″).
Action: Modified Anson & Deeley boxlock.
Barrels: 32″ 10, 12 only (Full & Full); 30″ 12 only (Mod.& Full); 28″ all exc. 410 (Mod.& Full); 26″ 12, 20, 28 (I.C.&Mod.); 26″ 410 only (Mod.& Full); 22″ 12 only (I.C.& I.C.).
Weight: 10½ lbs.(10), 7¾ lbs.(12) to 6 lbs.(410).
Stock: Hand checkered European walnut, p.g., beavertail fore-end, rubber recoil pad. Dimensions vary with gauge.
Features: Auto safety, plain extractors. Imported from Spain by Galef.
Price: 10 ga. .... **$175.95** 12 - 410 .... **$142.95**

WEBLEY & SCOTT SIDE-BY-SIDE SHOTGUNS
Gauge: 20 ga., 3″ chambers, 28 ga., 2¾″ chambers.
Action: Boxlock.
Barrel: 26″ (Imp. & Imp. Mod.), 28 ga., 25″ (Imp. & Imp. Mod.).
Weight: 6 lbs. (20 ga.), 5½ lbs. (28 ga.).
Stock: Walnut, straight grip. 14⅝″x1½″x2¼″.
Features: Engine-turned flat rib. Engraved action. Checkered p.g. and fore-end. Comes with fitted leather case, snap caps, complete cleaning equipment. Imported by Harrington & Richardson.
Price: Model 720 (20 ga.) **$1,400.00**
Price: Model 728 (28 ga.) **$1,400.00**

IMPORTED SHOTGUNS—OVER-UNDER

BERETTA BL-2/S O/U SHOTGUN

Gauge: 12 ga., 3" chambers on magnum model.
Barrel: 26" (I.C. & Mod.); 28" (Mod. & Full); 30" mag. (Mod. & Full). Vent. rib.
Weight: 7 to 7¼ lbs.
Stock: 14⅛"x1½"x2½". Hand checkered, walnut finish.
Sights: Metal bead front.
Features: Selective "Speed-Trigger"—pull top part of trigger for more open-choked (lower) barrel, bottom part for upper (tighter-choked) barrel, or reverse order.
Price: 3" Mag. **$395.00**
Price: Field, 28" bbl. **$380.00**
Price: Field, 26" bbl. **$380.00**

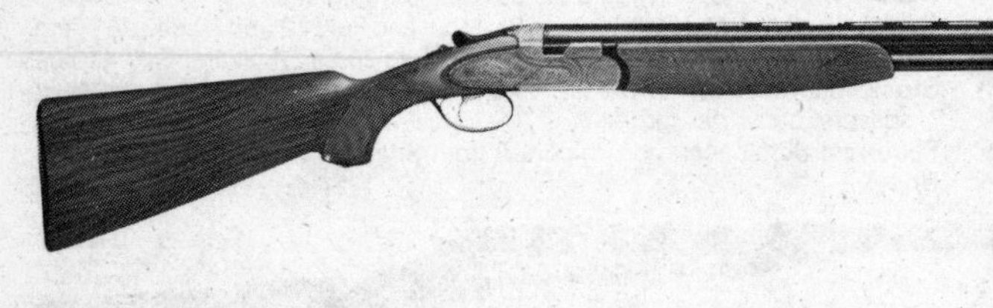

BERETTA BL O/U SHOTGUNS

Gauge: 12, 28 (2¾" chambers); 12 mag., 20 (3" chambers).
Action: Hammerless boxlock with gold-plated single-selective trigger. BL-6 has sideplates.
Barrel: 12 ga., 30" or 28" (Mod., Full), 26" (Imp. Cyl., Mod.); 20 ga., 28" (Mod., Full), 26" (Mod., Full); 28 ga., 28" (Mod., Full), 26" (Imp. Cyl, Mod.); 12 ga. Trap, 30" (Imp. Mod., Full); 12 or 20 ga. Skeet, 26" (Skeet, Skeet).
Weight: 7¼ lbs. (12 ga.), 6 lbs (20 and 28 ga.), 7½ lbs (Trap and 12 ga. Mag.).
Stock: 14⅛"x1½"x2½" (Standard), 14⅜"x1⅜"x1¾" (Trap), hand-checkered European walnut, p.g.
Features: Hand-engraved receivers, ventilated rib. BL-4 has more engraving and checkering than BL-3, is available with two sets of barrels. BL-6 has additional hand-engraved sideplates, specially selected wood. Imported from Italy by Garcia.
Price: .... From **$395.00** (BL-3) to **$840.00** (BL-6 Trap or Skeet)

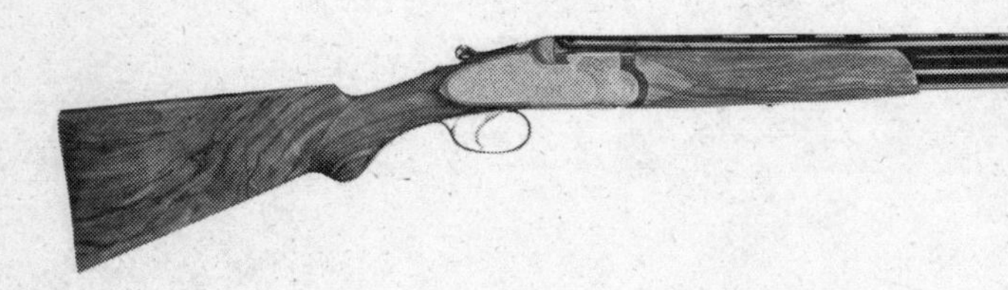

BERETTA SO SERIES O/U SHOTGUNS

Gauge: 12 (2¾" chambers).
Action: Sidelock, with modified Greener crossbolt, hand-detachable on SO-4 and 5. Single selective or double triggers, gold plated on SO-5 only.
Barrel: 28" (Mod. and Full), 26" (I.C. and Mod.). 30" and different choke combos available.
Weight: 7 to 7¼ lbs.
Stock: Select European walnut, 14⅛"x1½"x2½" or custom fitted, p.g. or straight grip.
Features: Made to order to customer's specifications. Ornamentation varies with grade, SO-2 through SO-5. Imported from Italy by Garcia.
Price: .... On request only.

CHARLES DALY VENTURE GRADE O/U SHOTGUNS

Gauge: 12 (2¾" chambers), 20 (3" chambers).
Action: Box lock, single selective inertia trigger.
Barrel: 26" (I.C. and Mod., Skeet and Skeet), 28" (Mod. and Full), 30" (Imp. Mod. and Full) 12 only.
Weight: 12 ga., 7 lbs.; 20 ga., 6 lbs. 5 oz.
Stock: 14"x1½"x2½" checkered walnut, p.g.
Features: Ventilated rib, manual safety, auto ejectors. Imported from Japan by Sloan's.
Price: **$415.00**
Price: 30", Monte Carlo **$420.00**

CHARLES DALY FIELD GRADE O/U SHOTGUNS

Gauge: 12, 20 (2¾" chambers).
Action: Boxlock, single selective inertia trigger, auto safety (exc. Skeet).
Barrel: 30" 12 (Full & Full); 28" 12, 20 (Mod. & Full); 26" 12, 20, (Skeet & Skeet, I.C. & Mod.).
Weight: 12 ga.. 7 lbs.; others, about 6¼ lbs.
Stock: 14"x1½"x2½" walnut, p.g. 12 Mag. has recoil pad.
Features: Ventilated rib, selective auto ejectors. Imported from Japan by Sloan's.
Price: 12 and 20 ga. **$450.00**

CHARLES DALY SUPERIOR GRADE O/U SHOTGUN

Gauge: 12, 20 (2¾" chambers except 20. Field models, 3")
Action: Boxlock, single selective inertia trigger.
Barrel: Same as Field Grade plus 28" 12, 20 (Skeet & Skeet).
Weight: 12 ga., 7¼ lbs.; others, 6 lbs. 10 oz.
Stock: 14"x1½"x2½" checkered walnut, p.g., beavertail fore-end.
Features: Ventilated rib. "Selexor" permits shooter to select auto ejection or merely extraction. Imported from Japan by Sloan's.
Price: .... **$500.00** to **$525.00**
Price: Superior Grade Trap .... **$500.00** to **$595.00**
Price: Diamond Grade International **$895.00**

IMPORTED SHOTGUNS—OVER-UNDER

FRANCHI FALCONET O/U SHOTGUN

Gauge: 12, 16, 20, 28 and 410.
Action: Hammerless with overhead-sear trigger and auto. safety.
Barrel: 24″, 12 or 20 ga. (Cyl. & Imp. Cyl.); 26″, all except 410 (Imp. Cyl. & Mod.), 410 (Mod. & Full); 28″, all (Mod. & Full); 30″, 12 ga. (Mod. & Full); 26″, all except 16 ga. (Skeet 1-Skeet 2); 30″ 12 ga. Trap (Mod. & Full).
Weight: 6 lbs. (approx.) except Skeet 7½ lbs. and Trap 8¼ lbs.
Stock: Epoxy finished walnut.
Features: Chrome-lined barrels, selective single trigger, auto ejectors. Available with "Buckskin" or "Ebony" (Blue) colored Frames. Skeet and Trap models have 10mm rib, middle sight, non-auto safety. Imported from Italy by Stoeger Arms.
Price: Ebony 12 & 20 ga. **$419.95**
Price: Buckskin **$419.95**
Price: Model 2002 Trap or Skeet **$949.95**
Price: Model 3003 Trap or Skeet **$1,800.00**
Price: Silver **$459.95**
Price: Super Falconet, Ebony, Buckskin **$549.95**
Price: Super Silver **$629.95**

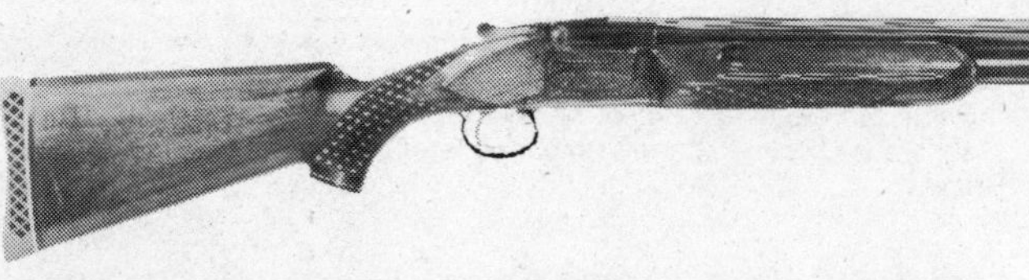

HIGH STANDARD SHADOW SEVEN O/U SHOTGUN

Gauge: 12 (2¾″ chambers).
Action: Boxlock.
Barrel: 27½″ (Skeet & Skeet, Mod. & Imp., Full & Mod.); 29¾″ (Full & Full, Imp. Mod. & Full).
Weight: 8 lbs. (29¾″ bbl.)
Stock: American walnut. Hand checkered p.g. and fore-end. Field & Skeet: 14″x1⅜″1⅞″; Trap: 14⅜″x1⅜″x1⅞″.
Sights: Metal bead front.
Features: Solid frame. Single selective gold-plated trigger, automatic selective ejectors. Manual safety. Vent. rib. Imported by High Standard.
Price: **$499.95**

HIGH STANDARD SHADOW INDY O/U SHOTGUN

Gauge: 12 (2¾″ chambers).
Action: Boxlock with 4 locks.
Barrel: 27½″ (Skeet & Skeet), 29¾″ (Full & Full, Imp. Mod. & Full).
Weight: 8 lbs., 2 oz. (29¾″ bbl.).
Stock: American walnut. Skip-line checkered p.g. and fore-end. Air ducting fore-end. Vent. rubber recoil pad. Field & Skeet: 14″x1½″x2½″; Trap: 14⅜″x1⅜″x1⅞″.
Sights: Metal bead center and front.
Features: Wide aluminum airflow rib. Hand engraved frame. Single selective trigger, selective auto. ejectors. White spacers at p.g. and recoil pad. Chrome plated bores. Highly polished and damascened action. Imported by High Standard.
Price: **$595.00**

KASSNAR/FIAS SK-1 O/U SHOTGUN

Gauge: 12 or 20 ga., 3″ chambers.
Action: Top lever break open, box lock, Greener cross bolt.
Barrel: 26″ (Imp. Cyl. & Mod.), 28″ (Mod. & Full), 30″ (Mod. & Full), 32″ (Full & Full).
Weight: 6-6½ lbs.
Stock: Select European walnut. 14″x2¼″x1¼″.
Features: Double triggers and non-automatic extractors. Checkered p.g. and fore-end. Imported by Kassnar Imports.
Price: **$249.95**

IVER JOHNSON SILVER SHADOW O/U SHOTGUN

Gauge: 12 ga. only.
Barrel: 28″ (Mod. & Full). Vent. rib.
Weight: 8¼ lbs.
Stock: Walnut. Checkered p.g. and fore-end.
Sights: Metal bead front.
Features: Single or double trigger. Imported from Italy by Iver Johnson.
Price: Single trigger **$229.95**
Price: Double trigger **$247.50**

Kassnar/Fias SK-3 O/U Shotgun

Same as SK-1 except has single selective trigger **$275.00**

Kassnar/Fias SK-4D O/U Shotgun

Same as SK-4 except has deluxe receiver engraving, sideplates, better wood **$389.95**

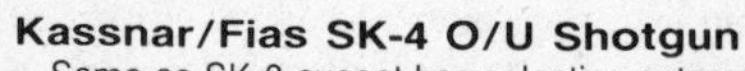

Kassnar/Fias SK-4 O/U Shotgun

Same as SK-3 except has selective automatic ejectors, select wood, beavertail fore-end. Trap model (SK-4T) has wide tapered rib **$349.95**

KLEINGUENTHER'S CONDOR O/U SHOTGUN

Gauge: 12, 20 (2¾″ or 3″ chambers).
Action: Purdey type double lock.
Barrel: 26″ (I.C. & Mod., Skeet & Skeet); 28″ (Full & Mod., I.M.& Mod.); 30″ (Full & Full, Full & Mod.) 12 mag. only.
Weight: 6½ lbs. (26″20) to 7 lbs.3oz. (30″12).
Stock: 14″x1½″x2½″ handcheckered walnut, p.g. and fore-end, recoil pad.
Features: Single selective trigger, auto ejectors, manual tang safety, vent. rib. Skeet Grade has extra wide rib. Imported from Italy by Kleingunther.
Price: Field grade **$367.00**
Price: Skeet **$387.83**

Kleinguenther's Condor Trap O/U Shotgun

Same as Field Grade except wide rib, Monte Carlo stock, 12 ga. only, 28″ (Full & Mod.); 30″ or 32″ (I.M.& Full, Full & Full), weight 7 lbs.7oz.
Price: **$397.40**

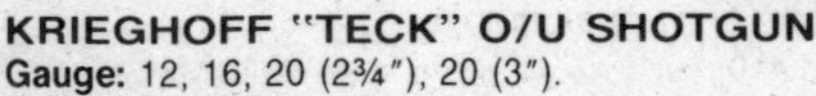

KRIEGHOFF "TECK" O/U SHOTGUN

Gauge: 12, 16, 20 (2¾"), 20 (3").
Action: Boxlock.
Barrel: 28½" (Full & Mod.), vent. rib.
Weight: 7 lbs. **Length:** 44" over-all.
Stock: 14¼"x1¼"x2¼", European walnut.
Features: Kersten double crossbolt system. Interchangeable barrels. Imported from Germany by Unordco.
Price: With ejectors **$1,440.00**
Price: Interchangeable double rifle barrels up to 7mm Rem. Mag. **$990.00**
Price: Double rifle barrels, 7mm, 375, 458 Win. Mag. **$1,200.00**
Price: Interchangeable shotgun-rifle barrel combination **$660.00**
Price: Model Ulm with sidelocks **$2,160.00**
Price: Model Ulm with hand-detachable engraved sidelocks **$2,820.00**

KRIEGHOFF MODEL 32 O/U SHOTGUN

Gauge: 12, 20, 28 & 410.
Action: Boxlock.
Barrel: 28", 30", 32", 34".
Stock: Hand checkered walnut, p.g., beavertail fore-end.
Features: Three-way safety (manual, auto or inoperative). Selective single trigger, ejectors and ventilated rib. Other barrel lengths, chokes to order. Available with fancier walnut and relief engraving and silver and gold inlays. Extra barrels available. Imported from Germany by Krieghoff Gun Co.
Price: .... **$1,295.00** to **$11,000.00**

LAURONA MODEL 71-G O/U SHOTGUN

Gauge: 12 (3" chambers).
Action: Hammerless, gold-plated double selectable triggers, auto. safety.
Barrel: 26" (Imp. Cyl. & Mod.); 28" (Full & Mod.); 30" (Full & Full), 30" (Full & Mod.), vent. rib.
Stock: Hand-checkered walnut, p.g., vent. rubber recoil pad.
Feature: Chromed bores, vent. rib. Imported from Spain by Jana.
Price: **$250.00**

LAMES FIELD MODEL O/U

Gauge: 12 only, 3" chambers.
Barrel: 26" (Imp. Cyl. & Mod.), 28" (Mod. & Full), 30" (Mod. & Full or Full & Full).
Weight: 8½ lbs.
Stock: Walnut, checkered p.g. and fore-end, rubber recoil pad.
Features: Vent. rib with front bead, engraved receiver, auto. ejectors, single selective trigger. Imported from Italy by Jana.
Price: **$310.00**

Lames California Trap

Same as Standard Trap except: double vent. ribs, M.C. stock, luminous front and center sights.
Price: **$675.00**

Laurona Model 71-G-EX O/U Shotgun

Same as Model 67-G except supplied with both 12 and 20 ga. bbls., 28" (Full & Mod.).
Price: **$400.00**

Lames Double Vent. Rib Model

Same as Field Model except: has conventional top vent. rib plus ventilated separation between barrels. Imported from Italy by Jana.
Price: **$350.00**

Lames Std. Trap "Monte Carlo"

Same as Field Model except: M.C. type stock, checkered semi-beavertail fore-end, wide vent. rib, front and center bead sights. 2¾" chambers. 30" (Full & Full or Imp. Mod. & Full), 32" (Imp. Mod. & Full).
Price: .... **$400.00** With standard stock design **$380.00**

Lames Skeet Model

Same as Field Model except: semi-beavertail fore-end with wrap-around checkering, stock with Skeet dimensions, double vent. ribs, 2¾" chambers, 26" (Skeet & Skeet).
Price: **$370.00**

GEBRUDER MERKEL 201E O/U

Gauge: 12, 16, 20, 28, 3" chambers on request.
Action: Kersten double crossbolt.
Barrel: To customer's specs with choice of chokes.
Weight: 6¾ lbs.
Stock: To customer's specs. Walnut with p.g. or English style.
Features: Double, single or single selective trigger, cocking indicators. Fine hunting scene engraving. Imported by Champlin Firearms.
Price: With single selective trigger **$1,200.00**

Gebruder Merkel 200E O/U

Similar to 201E except: English arabesque engraving and color case-hardening.
Price: With single non-selective trigger **$960.00**

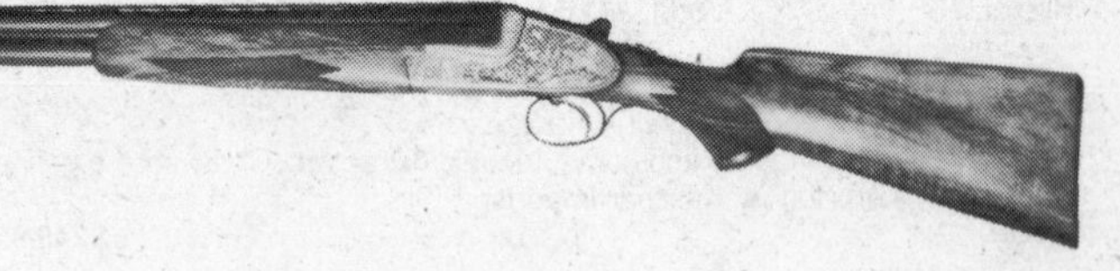

GEBRUDER MERKEL MODEL 203E O/U

Gauge: 12, 16, 20, 28, 3" chambers on request.
Action: Merkel H&H hand-detachable side locks with double sears. Double crossbolt breech.
Barrel: To customer's specs, choice of chokes.
Weight: 7 lbs.
Stock: Deluxe walnut with p.g. or English style. To customer's specs.
Features: Double, single or single selective trigger. Cocking indicators. Choice of arabesque or fine hunting scene engraving. Imported by Champlin Firearms.
Price: With single selective trigger **$2,000.00**

Gebruder Merkel Model 303E O/U

Similar to Model 203E except: double hook-bolting in conjunction with double crossbolt breech. Finer quality.
Price: **$3,000.00**

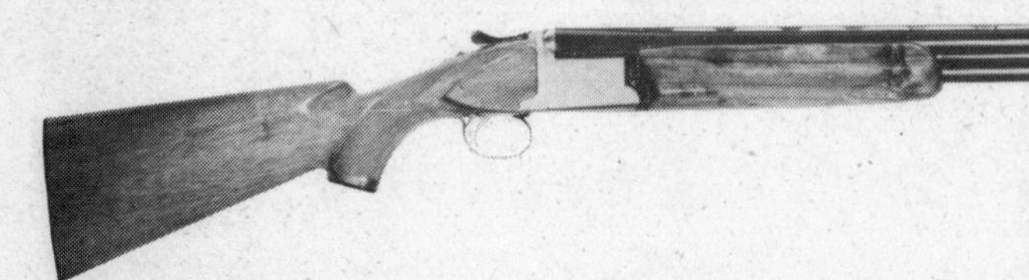

Miida Model 2100 Skeet

Same as Model 612 except: 27" bbl. bored Skeet & Skeet, 50% engraving coverage, weighs 7¾ lbs., length is 43¾". White line spacers at buttplate and p.g. cap.
Price: **$445.00**

MIIDA MODEL 612 O/U

Gauge: 12 only.
Action: Boxlock-type.
Barrels: 28" (Full & Mod.), 26" (Mod. & Imp. Cyl.). Vent. rib.
Weight: 6¾ lbs. **Length:** 42¾" (26" bbl.).
Stock: French walnut (14"x1½"x2½"), hand checkered. Black buttplate & p.g. cap.
Features: Automatic selective ejectors, single selective trigger, tang safety. Chrome-plated bores. Blued bbls., trigger guard and locking lever, silver, engraved receiver. Imported from Japan by Marubeni America Corp.
Price: Field Grade **$395.00**

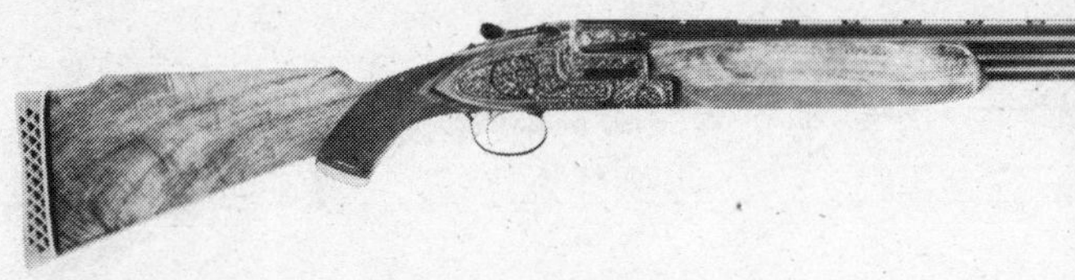

Miida Model 2200 Trap & Skeet
Same as Model 612 except: white line spacers at buttplate and p.g. cap, bbls. 29¾" (Full & Imp. Mod.) or 27" (Skeet & Skeet), wide rib, 60% engraving coverage, gold plated trigger, Skeet or Trap stock dimensions. Trap model has Pachmayr pad.
Price: Trap .... **$510.00** Skeet **$485.00**

MIIDA MODEL GRANDEE TRAP & SKEET

Gauge: 12 only.
Action: Boxlock type.
Barrel: 29" (Full & Full), 26" (Skeet & Skeet).
Weight: 7¾ lbs. **Length:** 42¾" over-all (Skeet).
Stock: 14⅜"x1⅜"x2⅛"x1⅜" (Trap), 14"x1½"x2½" (Skeet). Super fancy French walnut. Deep fluted comb. Trap model has Pachmayr pad. Semi-beavertail fore-end. Fine checkering.
Features: Ivory p.g. cap, outer surfaces of breech block, ejectors, and locking levers engine-turned, wide vent. rib. Frame, bbl. (breech end), trigger guard, locking lever fully hand engraved with gold inlays. Imported by Marubeni.
Price: Skeet or Trap **$1,195.00**

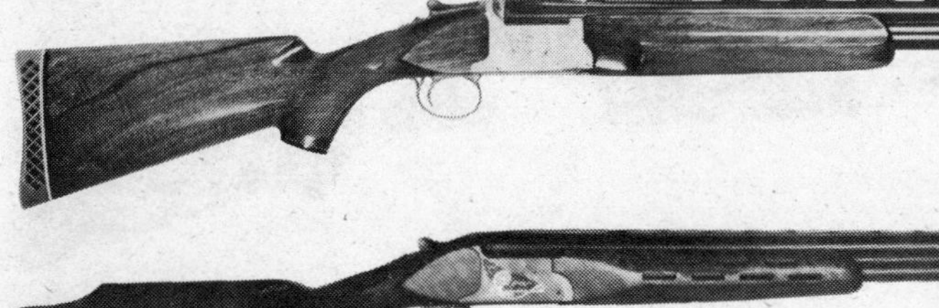

Miida Model 2300 Trap & Skeet
Same as Model 2200 except: 70% engraving coverage, fancy French walnut, semi-beavertail fore-end. Imported by Marubeni.
Price: Trap model .... **$550.00** Skeet model **$525.00**

Universal Baikal IJ-27 O/U
Same as IJ-25 except has double triggers, auto safety, non-selective ejectors. From Universal **$269.95**
IJ-27E is same as IJ-27 except has selective ejectors **$289.95**

UNIVERSAL BAIKAL IJ-25 O/U

Gauge: 12 ga., 2¾" chambers.
Barrel: 26" (Skeet & Skeet), 28" (Mod. & Full), 30" (Imp. Mod. & Full).
Weight: 7¾-8¼ lbs.
Stock: Hand checkered walnut, rubber recoil pad. Ventilated fore-end. White spacers at p.g. and recoil pad.
Features: Single non-selective trigger. Chrome barrels, chambers and internal parts. Hand-fitted vent. rib. Hand engraved and silver inlayed receiver, trigger guard and fore-end latch. Target grade trigger. Imported by Universal Sporting Goods.
Price: **$475.00**

UNIVERSAL BAIKAL MC-8 O/U

Gauge: 12 ga., 2¾" chambers.
Barrel: 26" special parabolic Skeet, 28" (Mod. & Full). Available in 2 bbl. sets.
Weight: 7¾ lbs.
Stock: Fancy walnut. Beavertail fore-end permanently attached to barrels. Hand checkered p.g. and fore-end. Monte Carlo.
Features: Handmade competition shotgun. Blued, engraved receiver. Double triggers, extractors. Chrome barrels, chambers and internal parts. Hand fitted vent. rib. Available with single selective trigger and selective ejectors at customer's request. Imported by Universal Sporting Goods.
Price: **$650.00**

UNIVERSAL BAIKAL MC-5 O/U

Gauge: 20 ga., 2¾" chambers.
Barrel: 26" (Imp. Cyl. & Mod., Skeet & Skeet).
Weight: 5¾ lbs.
Stock: Fancy hand checkered walnut. Choice of p.g. or straight stock, with or without cheekpiece. Fore-end permanently attached to barrels.
Features: Fully engraved receiver. Double triggers, extractors. Chrome barrels, chambers and internal parts. Hand-fitted solid rib. Hammer interceptors. Imported by Universal Sporting Goods.
Price: MC-5 .... **$525.00**
Price: MC-6 (as Skeet gun, single non-selective trigger, raised rib, weighs 7½ lbs.) **$825.00**

UNIVERSAL BAIKAL MC-7 O/U

Gauge: 12 or 20 ga., 2¾" chambers.
Barrel: 12 ga. 28" (Mod. & Full), 20 ga. 26" (Imp. Cyl. & Mod.).
Weight: 7 lbs. (12 ga.), 6¾ lbs. (20 ga.)
Stock: Walnut. Hand checkered with or without p.g. and cheekpiece. Beavertail fore-end.
Features: Fully chiseled and engraved receiver. Chrome barrels, chambers and internal parts. Double trigger, selective ejectors. Solid raised rib. Single selective trigger available. Imported by Universal Sporting Goods.
Price: **$1,525.00**

UNIVERSAL BAIKAL MC-9-01 O/U

Gauge: 12 ga., 2¾" chambers.
Barrel: 28" (Mod. & Full), 30" (Imp. Mod. & Full). Special parabolic chokes.
Weight: 8 lbs.
Stock: Fancy walnut. Hand checkered p.g. with cheekpiece. Rubber recoil pad with white spacers. Monte Carlo. Ventilated fore-end.
Features: Handmade sidelock competition shotgun. Removable sideplates. Chrome barrels, chambers and internal parts. Single selective target trigger, selective ejectors, cocking indicators. Hand engraved receiver and trigger guard. Hand fitted vent. rib. Imported by Universal Sporting Goods.
Price: Special order only **$1,160.00**

UNIVERSAL BAIKAL MC-109 O/U

Gauge: 12 ga., 2¾" chambers.
Barrel: To customer's specifications. Choice of chokes.
Weight: 7¼ lbs.
Stock: Fancy walnut. Choice of p.g. or straight stock, with or without cheekpiece. Beavertail fore-end. Hand carved and checkered to customer's specs.
Features: Handmade sidelock shotgun. Removable sideplates. Chrome barrels, chambers and internal parts. Single selective trigger, selective ejectors, cocking indicators, hammer interceptors. Hand chiseled scenes on receiver to customer specs. Gold inlays to customer specs. Imported by Universal Sporting Goods.
Price: Special order only **$2,350.00**

IMPORTED SHOTGUNS—OVER-UNDER

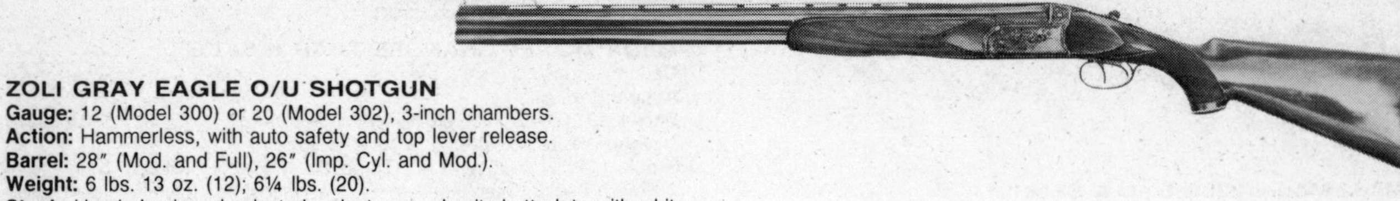

ZOLI GRAY EAGLE O/U SHOTGUN

Gauge: 12 (Model 300) or 20 (Model 302), 3-inch chambers.
Action: Hammerless, with auto safety and top lever release.
Barrel: 28″ (Mod. and Full), 26″ (Imp. Cyl. and Mod.).
Weight: 6 lbs. 13 oz. (12); 6¼ lbs. (20).
Stock: Hand checkered selected walnut, p.g., ebonite butt plate with white spacer.
Features: Ventilated rib, chrome plated bore. Imported from Italy American Import.
Price: **$275.00**

ZOLI SILVER SNIPE O/U SHOTGUN

Gauge: 12, 20 (3″ chambers).
Action: Purdey type double boxlock, crossbolt.
Barrels: 26″ (I.C.& Mod.), 28″ (Mod.&Full), 30″, 12 only (Mod.& Full); 26″ Skeet (Skeet & Skeet), 30″ Trap (Full & Full).
Weight: 6½ lbs. (12 ga.).
Stock: Hand checkered European walnut, p.g. and fore-end.
Features: Auto safety (exc. Trap and Skeet), vent rib, single trigger, chrome bores. Imported from Italy by Galef.
Price: Field .... **$325.00** Skeet and Trap **$382.95**

Zoli Golden Snipe O/U Shotgun

Same as Silver Snipe except selective auto ejectors.
Price: Field .... **$375.65** Skeet and Trap **$448.20**

IMPORTED SHOTGUNS—SINGLE BARREL

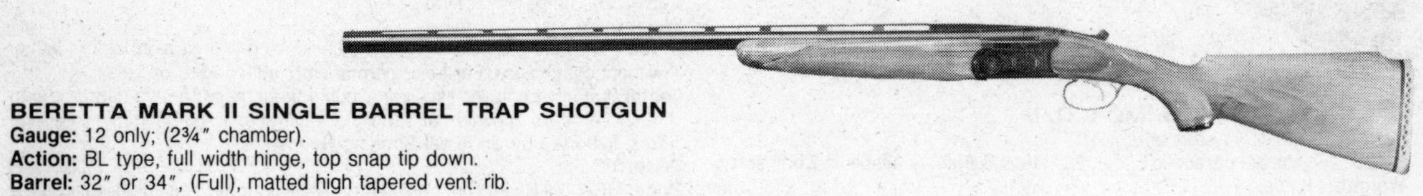

BERETTA MARK II SINGLE BARREL TRAP SHOTGUN

Gauge: 12 only; (2¾″ chamber).
Action: BL type, full width hinge, top snap tip down.
Barrel: 32″ or 34″, (Full), matted high tapered vent. rib.
Weight: 8¼ lbs.
Stock: 14⅜″ x 1⅜″ x 1¾″. Hand checkered European walnut, p.g.; rubber recoil pad, beavertail fore-end, Monte Carlo.
Features: Hand engraved receiver. Imported from Italy by Garcia.
Price: **$435.00**

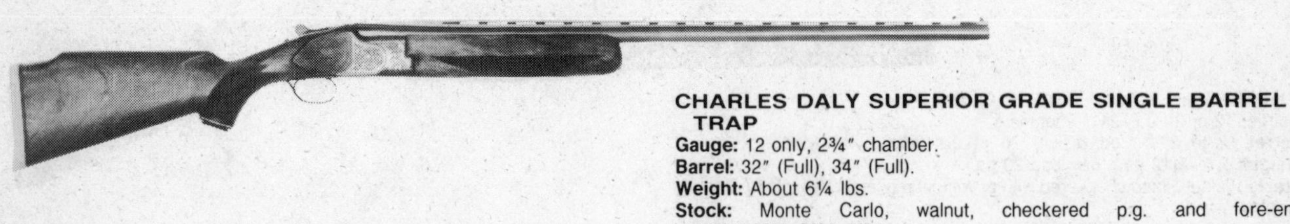

CHARLES DALY SUPERIOR GRADE SINGLE BARREL TRAP

Gauge: 12 only, 2¾″ chamber.
Barrel: 32″ (Full), 34″ (Full).
Weight: About 6¼ lbs.
Stock: Monte Carlo, walnut, checkered p.g. and fore-end. 14⅜″x1½″x2½″x1½″.
Features: Special nickel-finish receiver, scroll engraving.
Price: **$450.00**

F.I.E. SINGLE BARREL SHOTGUN

Gauge: 12, 20, 410.
Barrel: 12 & 20 ga. 28″ (Full); 410 ga. (Full).
Weight: 6½ lbs.
Stock: Walnut stained hardwood. Checkered p.g. and fore-end.
Sights: Metal bead front.
Features: Trigger guard is pulled to open action. Imported from Brazil by F.I.E.
Price: **$34.95**

GALEF COMPANION SINGLE BARREL SHOTGUN
Gauge: 12, 20, 410 (3″); 16, 28 (2¾″).
Action: Folding boxlock.
Barrel: 28″ exc. 12 (30″) and 410 (26″), all Full.
Weight: 5½ lbs. (12) to 4½ lbs. (410).
Stock: 14″x1½″x2⅝″ hand checkered walnut, p.g.
Features: Non-auto safety, folds. Vent. rib $5.00 additional. Imported from Italy by Galef.
Price: Plain bbl. .... **$62.75** Vent. rib **$68.80**

KLEINGUENTHER'S DAINO SINGLE BARREL SHOTGUN
Gauge: 12, 20.
Action: Folding, underlever.
Barrel: 27½″ (Full).
Weight: 5½ lbs. **Length:** 44½″.
Stock: Hand checkered walnut, semi p.g.
Features: Folds to 27½″, choice of plain or vent rib ($5.25 additional) barrel, engraved action. Imported by Kleingunther
Price: **$68.50**

KRIEGHOFF SINGLE BARREL TRAP SHOTGUN
Gauge: 12.
Action: Boxlock, short hammer fall.
Barrel: 32″ or 34″ (Full).
Weight: About 8½ lbs.
Stock: Monte Carlo with checkered p.g. and grooved beavertail fore-end.
Features: Thumb safety, vent. rib. Extra bbls. available **$445.00.** Available with various grades of decoration, wood. Imported from Germany by Krieghoff Gun Co.
Price: Standard ....**$1,295.00** San Remo **$2,695.00**
Monte Carlo Grade ......**$5,295.00** Crown **$5,695.00**
Super Crown Grade **$6,695.00**

KRIEGHOFF VANDALIA TRAP MODEL
Gauge: 12 only.
Action: Boxlock.
Barrel: 30″, 32″, 34″. Available as either single or over/under.
Stock: Hand checkered walnut, p.g., beavertail fore-end.
Weight: About 9 lbs.
Features: Three-way safety (manual, auto or inoperative). Selective single trigger, ejectors and full length vent. rib. Other bbl. lengths, chokes to order. Available with fancier walnut and relief engraving and silver and gold inlays. Extra bbls. available. Imported from Germany by Krieghoff Gun Co.
Price: ....**$1,695.00** to **$6,995.00**

MONTE CARLO SINGLE BARREL SHOTGUN
Gauge: 12 (2¾″ chamber).
Action: Monte Carlo, bottom release.
Barrel: 32″ (Trap).
Weight: 8¼ lbs.
Stock: 14½″x1⅛″x1⅝″ hand checkered walnut, p.g., beavertail fore-end, recoil pad.
Features: Auto ejector, slide safety, gold plated trigger. Imported from Italy by Galef.
Price: **$169.95**

PRIDE OF BRAZIL SINGLE BARREL SHOTGUN
Gauge: 12, 20, 410.
Barrel: 12 & 20 ga. 28″ (Full); 410 ga. 26″ (Full).
Weight: 6½ lbs.
Stock: Walnut stained hardwood.
Sights: Metal bead front.
Features: Button on front of trigger guard opens action. Exposed hammer. Automatic extractor. Imported from Brazil by F.I.E.
Price: **$41.95**

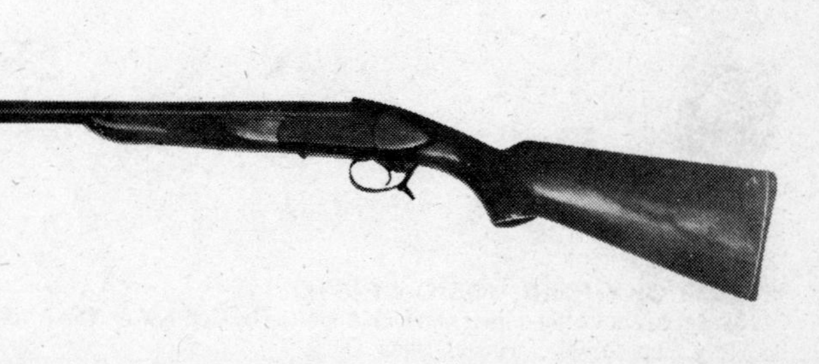

UNIVERSAL BAIKAL IJ-18 SINGLE BARREL
Gauge: 12 or 20 ga., 2¾″ chambers.
Barrel: 12 ga. 28″ (Mod.), 30″ (Full), 20 ga. 26″ (Mod.).
Weight: 5¾ lbs.
Stock: Walnut. Hand checkered p.g. and fore-end. White spacers at p.g. and plastice buttplate.
Features: Chrome barrel and chamber. Cross-bolt safety in trigger guard. Cocking indicator. Extractor. Imported by Universal Sporting Goods.
Price: **$49.95**

BLACK POWDER GUNS

The following pages catalog the black powder arms currently available to U.S. shooters. These range from quite precise replicas of historically significant arms to totally new designs created expressly to give the black powder shooter the benefits of modern technology.

Most of the replicas are imported, and many are available from more than one source. Thus examples of a given model such as the 1860 Army revolver or Zouave rifle purchased from different importers may vary in price, finish and fitting. Most of them bear proof marks, indicating that they have been test fired in the proof house of their country of origin.

A list of the importers and the retail price range are included with the description for each model. Many local dealers handle more than one importer's products, giving the prospective buyer an opportunity to make his own judgment in selecting a black powder gun. Most importers have catalogs available free or at nominal cost, and some are well worth having for the useful information on black powder shooting they provide in addition to their detailed descriptions and specifications of the guns.

A number of special accessories are also available for the black powder shooter. These include replica powder flasks, bullet moulds, cappers and tools, as well as more modern devices to facilitate black powder cleaning and maintenance. Ornate presentation cases and even detachable shoulder stocks are also available for some black powder pistols from their importers. Again, dealers or the importers will have catalogs.

The black powder guns are arranged in four sections: Single Shot Pistols, Revolvers, Muskets & Rifles, and Shotguns. The guns within each section are arranged by date of the original, with the oldest first. Thus the 1847 Walker replica leads off the revolver section, and flintlocks precede precussion arms in the other sections.

BLACK POWDER SINGLE SHOT PISTOLS—FLINT & PERCUSSION

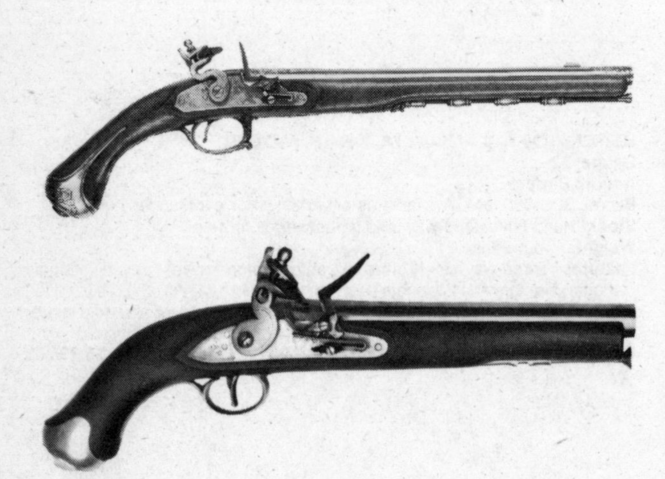

DIXIE FLORENTINE HOLSTER PISTOL

Caliber: 50.
Barrel: 13", smoothbore.
Weight: 2¾ lbs. **Length:** 21" over-all.
Stock: Walnut.
Sights: Fixed.
Features: Ornamental sideplate, butt cap, lower thimble and trigger guard. All furniture except sideplate has antique silver plate finish.
Price: **$209.50**

TOWER FLINTLOCK PISTOL

Caliber: 45, 69.
Barrel: 8¼".
Weight: 40 oz. **Length:** 14" over-all.
Stock: Walnut.
Sights: Fixed.
Features: Engraved lock, brass furniture. Specifications, including caliber, weight and length may vary with importers. Available as flint or percussion. Imported by The Armoury, F.I.E., Hawes, C.V.A., Centennial, Dixie, Navy/Replica.
Price: .... **$23.00** to **$51.95.**

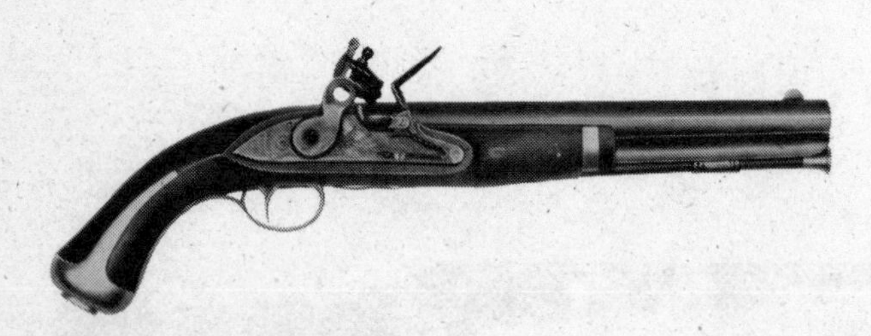

HARPER'S FERRY 1806 PISTOL

Caliber: 54.
Barrel: 10".
Weight: 40 oz. **Length:** 16" over-all.
Stock: Walnut.
Sights: Fixed.
Features: Case hardened lock, brass mounted browned bbl. Replica of the first U.S. Gov't.-made flintlock pistol. Imported by Navy/Replica.
Price: **$95.00**

KENTUCKY FLINTLOCK PISTOL

Caliber: 44, 45.
Barrel: 10⅛".
Weight: 32 oz. **Length:** 15½" over-all.
Stock: Walnut.
Sights: Fixed.
Features: Case hardened lock, blued bbl.; available also as brass bbl. flint Model 1821 ($95.00, Navy). Imported by Navy/Replica, The Armoury, Century, Centennial, F.I.E., Jana, Dixie, C.V.A.
Price: .... **$40.95** to **$89.95**
Price: In kit form **$39.75**

KENTUCKY PERCUSSION PISTOL

Similar to above but percussion lock. Imported by Centennial, The Armoury, Navy/Replica, F.I.E., Hawes, Jana, C.V.A.
Price: .... **$26.95** to **$85.00**
Price: In kit form **$35.95**

BLACK POWDER SINGLE SHOT PISTOLS—FLINT & PERCUSSION

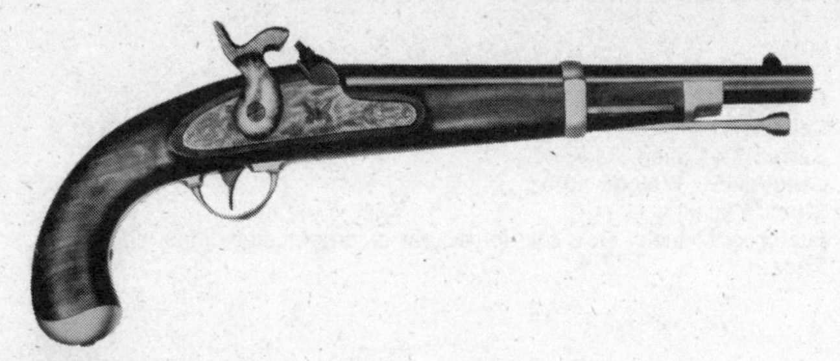

HARPER'S FERRY MODEL 1855 PERCUSSION PISTOL
Caliber: 58.
Barrel: 11¾", rifled.
Weight: 56 oz. **Length:** 18" over-all.
Stock: Walnut.
Sights: Fixed.
Features: Case hardened lock and hammer; brass furniture; blued bbl. Shoulder stock available, priced at $35.00. Imported by Navy/Replica.
Price: **$95.00**
Price: With detachable shoulder stock **$125.00**

KENTUCKY BELT PERCUSSION PISTOL
Caliber: 45.
Barrel: 7", rifled.
Weight: 29 oz. **Length:** 12" over-all.
Stock: Walnut.
Sights: Fixed.
Features: Engraved lock, brass furniture, steel ramrod. Available as flint or percussion. Imported by The Armoury, C.V.A., Hawes.
Price: .... **$22.95** to **$33.95.**

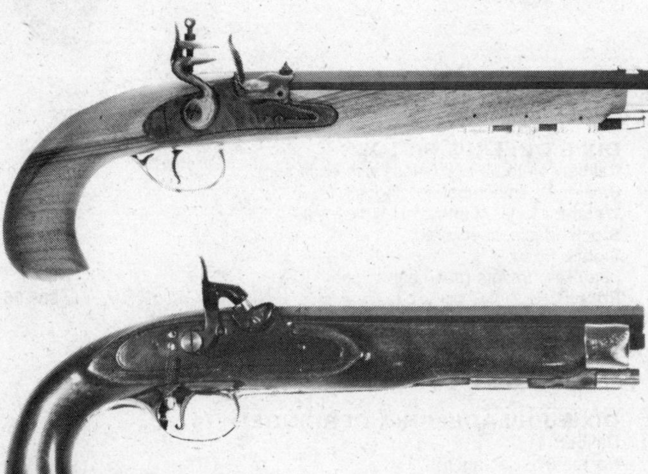

ENGLISH BELT PISTOL
Caliber: 44 (.451" bore).
Barrel: 7", octagonal, rifled.
Length: 12" over-all.
Stock: Walnut.
Features: Case-hardened lock, brass furniture, fixed sights. Available in either flint or percussion. Imported by CVA.
Price: Percussion **$32.95**
Price: Flint **$36.45**
Also available in kit form, either flint or percussion. Stock 90% inletted.
Price: .... **$19.95** to **$25.95**

RIPOLL BOOT PISTOL
Caliber: 45.
Barrel: 4", rifled.
Length: 8¼" over-all. **Weight:** 17 oz.
Stock: Walnut.
Features: Miquelet lock, cold-forged barrel, proof tested. Imported by CVA.
Price: **$79.95**

KENTUCKIAN PISTOL
Caliber: 44.
Barrel: 9½".
Weight: 40 oz. **Length:** 15" over-all.
Stock: Select walnut.
Sights: Dovetailed brass blade front, open notch rear.
Features: Brass trigger guard, side plate, barrel cap. Case hardened action with engraved lockplate. Imported by Intercontinental Arms.
Price: Flint or Percussion **$59.95**
Price: Cased set (includes fitted case, flask, mould, wrench and tool) **$99.50**

MOWREY KENTUCKY PISTOL
Caliber: 45 or 50.
Barrel: 8".
Weight: 3½ lbs. **Length:** 15" over-all.
Stock: Walnut.
Sights: Bead front.
Features: Percussion only. Brass stock furniture. Also available in kit form.
Price: Complete .... **$120.45** Kit **$97.85**

RENEGADE PISTOL
Caliber: 44 or 36.
Barrel: 8¼".
Weight: Approx. 31 oz. **Length:** 13¼" over-all.
Stock: Walnut.
Sights: Bead front.
Features: Double barrel, double trigger percussion pistol with rifled barrels. Engraved side plates and hammers. Engraved brass trigger guard and butt cap. Steel ramrod with brass tip. Imported by Intercontinental Arms.
Price: Pistol only **$49.95**
Price: Cased set (includes fitted case, pistol, powder flask, bullet mould, wrench, and tool) **$89.50**

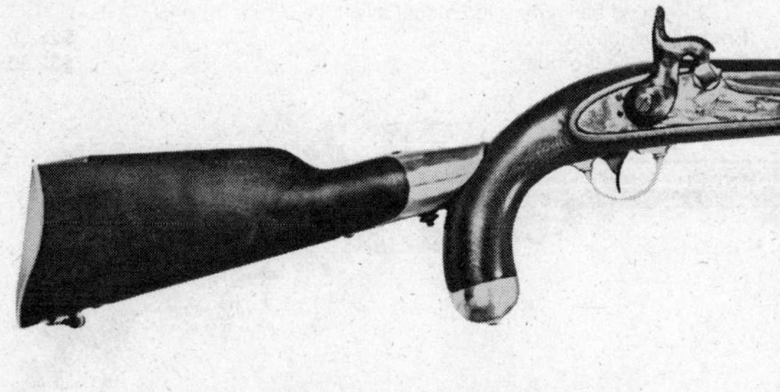

DRAGOON REPLICA PERCUSSION PISTOL
Caliber: 58.
Barrel: 11¾".
Weight: 5½ lbs. **Length:** 29" over-all (with stock).
Stock: Walnut finish.
Sights: Dual folding leaf rear, post front.
Features: Comes complete with detachable extension stock. Sling swivels, brass fittings. Imported by American Import.
Price: **$125.00**

DIXIE OVERCOAT PISTOL
Caliber: 39.
Barrel: 4", smoothbore.
Weight: 13 oz. **Length:** 8" over-all.
Stock: Walnut-finish hardwood. Checkered p.g.
Sights: Fixed.
Features: Shoots .380" balls. Breech plug and engraved lock are burnished steel finish; barrel and trigger guard blued.
Price: Plain model **$26.95**
Price: Engraved model **$34.50**

BLACK POWDER SINGLE SHOT PISTOLS—FLINT & PERCUSSION

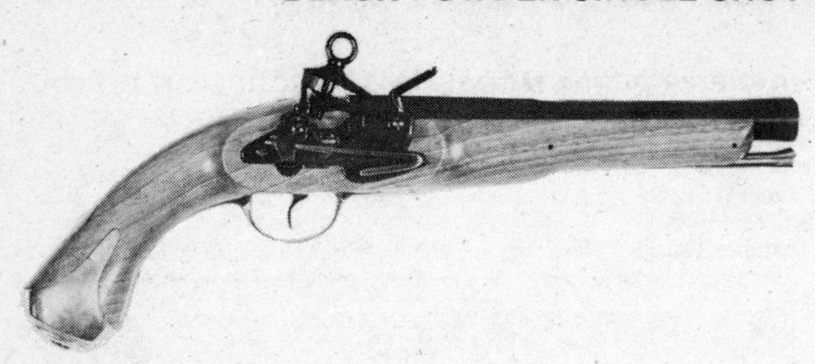

RIPOLL BELT PISTOL
Caliber: 61.
Barrel: 8¾" rifled.
Length: 15". **Weight:** 40 oz.
Stock: Walnut.
Features: Miquelet lock, cold-forged barrel, proof tested. Imported by CVA.
Price: **$84.95**

HOPKINS & ALLEN M-L BOOT PISTOL
Caliber: 36 or 45, single shot percussion.
Barrel: 6 inch octagonal, regular or gain twist.
Length: 13". **Weight:** 34 oz.
Stocks: Smooth walnut, birdshead style.
Sights: Fixed blade front, adj. rear.
Features: Underhammer lockwork, match trigger. From High Standard.
Price: **$39.95**

DIXIE DUELING PISTOL
Caliber: 44 to 50 cal. (varies with each gun).
Barrel: 9", smoothbore, octagon.
Weight: 1¼ lbs. **Length:** 15¼" over-all.
Stock: Maple, checkered.
Sights: Fixed.
Features: Shoots round ball or shot.
Price: **$69.95**

PHILADELPHIA DERRINGER PERCUSSION PISTOL
Caliber: 41.
Barrel: 3⅛".
Weight: 14 oz. **Length:** 7" over-all.
Stock: Walnut, checkered grip.
Sights: Fixed.
Features: Engraved wedge holder and bbl. Also available in flintlock version (Armoury, $29.95). Imported by C.V.A., Century, The Armoury, Hawes.
Price: .... **$18.37** to **$27.95**

DIXIE PHILADELPHIA DERRINGER
Caliber: 41.
Barrel: 3½", octagon.
Weight: 8 oz. **Length:** 5½" over-all.
Stock: Walnut, checkered p.g.
Sights: Fixed.
Features: Barrel and lock are blued; brass furniture. From Dixie Gun Works.
Price: **$27.95**

DIXIE BRASS FRAME DERRINGER
Caliber: 41.
Barrel: 2½".
Weight: 7 oz. **Length:** 5½" over-all.
Stock: Walnut.
Features: Brass frame, color case hardened hammer and trigger. Shoots .395" round ball. Engraved model available. From Dixie Gun Works.
Price: Plain model **$25.50**
Price: Engraved model **$32.50**

BUCCANEER DOUBLE BARREL PISTOL
Caliber: 36 or 44 cal.
Barrel: 9½".
Weight: 40 oz. **Length:** 15½" over-all.
Stock: Walnut, one piece.
Sights: Fixed.
Features: Case hardened and engraved lockplate, solid brass fittings. Percussion or flintlock. Imported by Hawes Firearms, The Armoury.
Price: .... **$82.95** to **$89.50**

SINGLE SHOT PERCUSSION TARGET PISTOL
Caliber: 44.
Barrel: 9" octagonal.
Weight: 42 oz.
Stocks: Walnut.
Sights: Bead front, rear adj. for w. and e.
Features: Engraved scenes on frame sides; brass backstrap and trigger guard; case hardened frame and hammer. Imported by Navy/Replica.
Price: .... **$64.95** to **$70.00**

BLACK POWDER SINGLE SHOT PISTOLS — FLINT & PERCUSSION

DIXIE TROPHY WINNER 44

Similar to standard target pistol except has 10″ barrel. Interchangeable shotgun barrel available.

Price: **$49.50**
Price: 28 ga. shotgun barrel **$12.95**

TINGLE BLACK POWDER M1960 PISTOL

Caliber: 40, single shot, percussion.
Barrel: 8″, 9″, 10″, or 12″ octagon.
Length: 11¾ inches. **Weight:** 33 oz. (8″ bbl.).
Stocks: Walnut, one piece.
Sights: Fixed blade front, w. adj. rear.
Features: 6-groove bbl., easily removable for cleaning; 1-in-30 twist.
Price: **$64.95**

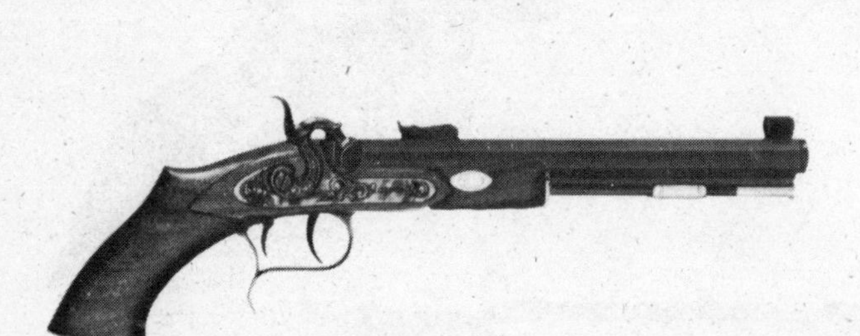

THOMPSON/CENTER PATRIOT PERCUSSION PISTOL

Caliber: 45.
Barrel: 9¼″.
Weight: 36 oz. **Length:** 16″ over-all.
Stock: Walnut.
Sights: Patridge-type. Rear adj. for w. and e.
Features: Hook breech system; ebony ramrod; double set triggers; coil mainspring. From Thompson/Center Arms.
Price: **$125.00**
With accessory pack (bullet mould T/C patches, adj. powder measure, short starter, extra nipple and nipple wrench).
Price: **$148.95**

BLACK POWDER REVOLVERS

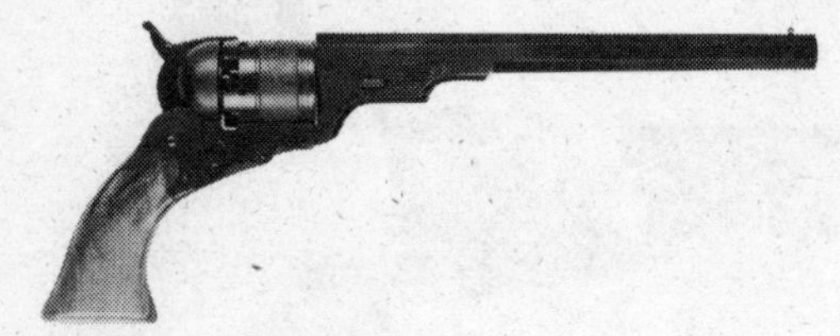

DIXIE PATERSON REVOLVER

Caliber: 36, 5-shot.
Barrel: 9″, octagon.
Weight: 2¾ lbs. **Length:** 14¼″ over-all.
Stocks: Walnut.
Sights: Fixed.
Features: Uses .377″ ball. All metal parts blued.
Price: **$99.50**

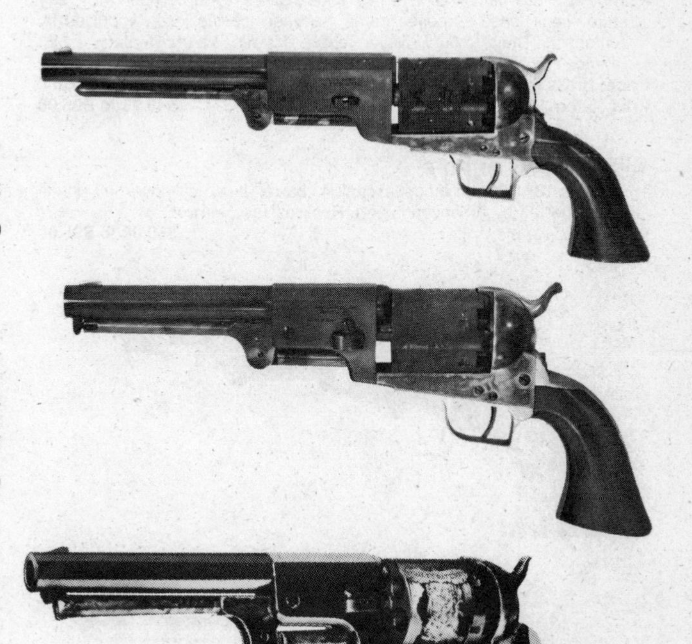

WALKER 1847 PERCUSSION REVOLVER

Caliber: 44, 6-shot.
Barrel: 9″.
Weight: 72 oz. **Length:** 15½″ over-all.
Stocks: Walnut.
Sights: Fixed.
Features: Case hardened frame, loading lever and hammer; iron backstrap; brass trigger guard; engraved cylinder. Imported by Navy/Replica, Jana.
Price: .... **$100.00** to **$115.00**

SECOND MODEL DRAGOON 1848 REVOLVER

Caliber: 44, 6-shot.
Barrel: 7½″.
Weight: 64 oz. **Length:** 14″ over-all.
Stocks: One piece walnut.
Sights: Fixed.
Features: Case hardened frame, loading lever and hammer; engraved cylinder scene; safety notches on hammer, safety pin in cylinder. Imported by Navy/Replica. First and Third Models also available.
Price: .... **$90.00** to **$110.00**

COLT 3RD MODEL DRAGOON REVOLVER

Caliber: 44 (for .457″ round ball), 6-shot.
Barrel: 7½″.
Weight: 4 lbs., 2 oz. **Length:** 14″ over-all.
Stock: Oiled walnut, one piece.
Sights: Blade front, fixed V-notch rear.
Features: Brass backstrap and trigger guard. Color case hardened frame, hammer and loading lever. Blue barrel and cylinder engraved with original Ranger and Indian scene. Serial numbers resume at 20,901 where manufacture stopped in 1860. From Colt.
Price: **$185.00**

BLACK POWDER REVOLVERS

BABY DRAGOON 1848 PERCUSSION REVOLVER

Caliber: 31, 5-shot.
Barrel: 4", 5", 6".
Weight: 24 oz. (6" bbl.). **Length:** 10½" (6" bbl.).
Stocks: Walnut.
Sights: Fixed.
Features: Case hardened frame; safety notches on hammer and safety pin in cylinder; engraved cylinder scene; octagonal bbl. Imported by Navy/Replica, F.I.E., Jana.
Price: .... **$38.15** to **$76.25**

1849 WELLS FARGO PERCUSSION REVOLVER

Caliber: 31, 5-shot.
Barrel: 3", 4", 5", 6".
Weight: 22 oz.
Stocks: Walnut.
Sights: Fixed.
Features: No loading lever; square-back trigger guard; case hardened frame and hammer; engraved cylinder; brass trigger guard and back-strap. Imported by Navy/Replica, Jana. Bbl. lengths may vary with importer.
Price: .... **$60.00** to **$75.00**

COLT 1851 NAVY PERCUSSION REVOLVER

Caliber: 36, 6-shot.
Barrel: 7½".
Weight: 40½ oz. **Length:** 13" over-all.
Stocks: Black walnut.
Sights: Fixed.
Features: Color case hardened frame; barrel and cylinder blued. Silver plated trigger guard and backstrap. Naval Scene engraving by W. L. Ormsby on cylinder. From Colt.
Price: **$166.50**

NAVY MODEL 1851 PERCUSSION REVOLVER

Caliber: 36 or 44, 6-shot.
Barrel: 7½".
Weight: 42 oz. **Length:** 13" over-all.
Stocks: Walnut finish.
Sights: Fixed.
Features: Brass backstrap and trigger guard; engraved cylinder with navy battle scene; case hardened frame, hammer, loading lever. Imported by Centennial, The Armoury, Navy/Replica, Hawes, Valor, Century, F.I.E., American Import, Jana, Dixie.
Price: Brass frame .... **$31.50** to **$55.00**
Price: Steel frame .... **$40.95** to **$95.00**

1851 NAVY-SHERIFF

Same as 1851 Sheriff model except: 4" barrel, fluted cylinder, belt ring in butt. Imported by American Import, Replica/Navy, Hawes.
Price: .... **$50.00** to **$95.00**

POCKET MODEL 1849 PERCUSSION REVOLVER

Caliber: 31, 5-shot.
Barrel: 4", 6".
Weight: 26 oz.
Stocks: Walnut finish.
Sights: Fixed.
Features: Round trigger guard; Colt stagecoach hold-up scene on cylinder. Imported by Navy/Replica.
Price: **$75.00**

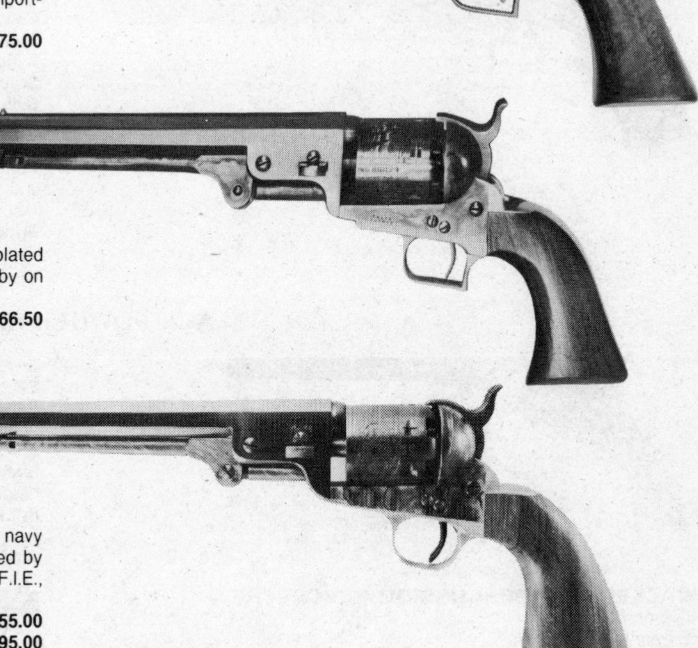

LYMAN 1851 NAVY

Same as standard model except has square-back trigger guard **$109.95**
Gun and kit (includes single cavity round ball mould with handles, six spare nipples with wrench, Hodgdon's "Spit Ball" and Lyman's "Black Powder Basics" book) **$119.95**

1851 SHERIFF MODEL PERCUSSION REVOLVER

Caliber: 36, 44, 6-shot.
Barrel: 5".
Weight: 40 oz. **Length:** 10½" over-all.
Stocks: Walnut.
Sights: Fixed.
Features: Brass back strap and trigger guard; engraved navy scene; case hardened frame, hammer, loading lever. Available with brass frame from some importers at slightly lower prices. Imported by Centennial, The Armoury, Navy/Replica, Hawes.
Price: Steel frame .... **$41.95** to **$95.00**
Price: Brass frame .... **$34.95** to **$54.95**

ARMY 1851 PERCUSSION REVOLVER

Caliber: 44, 6-shot.
Barrel: 7½".
Weight: 45 oz. **Length:** 13" over-all.
Stocks: Walnut finish.
Sights: Fixed.
Features: 44 caliber version of the 1851 Navy. Imported by Valor, The Armoury, Jana.
Price: .... **$33.50** to **$65.00**

BLACK POWDER REVOLVERS

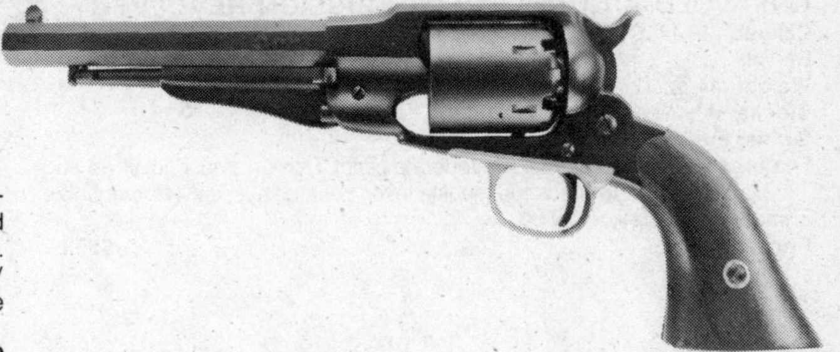

NEW MODEL 1858 ARMY PERCUSSION REVOLVER

Caliber: 36 or 44, 6-shot.
Barrel: 6½" or 8".
Weight: 40 oz. **Length:** 13½" over-all.
Stocks: Walnut.
Sights: Fixed.
Features: Replica of Remington Model 1858. Also available from some importers as Army Model Belt Revolver in 36 cal., shortened and lightened version of the 44. Target Model (Centennial, Navy/Replica) has fully adj. target rear sight, target front, 36 or 44 ($74.95-$125.00). Imported by Navy/Replica, Century, F.I.E., Hawes, C.V.A., Valor, American Import, Jana, The Armoury, Centennial.
Price: .... **$49.95** to **$95.00**

LYMAN 36 NEW MODEL NAVY REVOLVER

Caliber: 36, 6-shot.
Barrel: 6½".
Weight: 42 oz. **Length:** 12¼" over-all.
Stock: Walnut.
Sights: Fixed.
Features: Replica of 1860 Remington. Brass trigger guard. Solid frame with top strap. Heavy duty nipples. From Lyman Gunsight Corp.
Price: **$109.95**

LYMAN 44 NEW MODEL ARMY REVOLVER

Caliber: 44, 6-shot.
Barrel: 8".
Weight: 40 oz. **Length:** 13½" over-all.
Stock: Walnut.
Sights: Fixed.
Features: Replica of 1858 Remington. Brass trigger guard. Solid frame with top strap. Heavy duty nipples. From Lyman Gunsight Corp.
Price: **$109.95**

1860 ARMY PERCUSSION REVOLVER

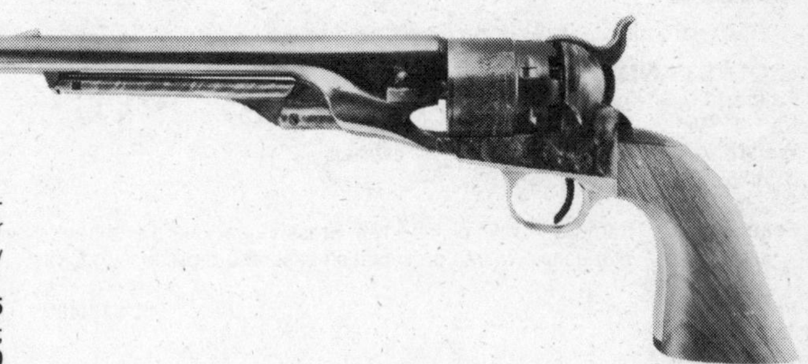

Caliber: 44, 6-shot.
Barrel: 8".
Weight: 40 oz. **Length:** 13⅝" over-all.
Stocks: Walnut.
Sights: Fixed.
Features: Engraved navy scene on cylinder; brass trigger guard; case hardened frame, loading lever and hammer. Some importers supply pistol cut for detachable shoulder stock, have accessory stock available. Imported by Navy/Replica, Centennial, The Armoury, Hawes, Jana, Dixie, Lyman.
Price: .... **$44.95** to **$114.95**
1861 Navy: Same as Army except 36 cal., 7½" bbl., wt. 41 oz., cut for stock; round cylinder (fluted avail.), from Navy/Replica **$95.00**
Lyman 1860 Army gun and kit (includes single cavity round ball mould with handles, six spare nipples, nipple wrench, Hodgdon's "Spit Ball" and Lyman's "Black Powder Basics" book). **$126.95**

1861 NAVY MODEL REVOLVER

Caliber: 36, 6-shot.
Barrel: 7½".
Weight: 2½ lbs. **Length:** 13" over-all.
Stocks: One piece smooth walnut.
Sights: Fixed.
Features: Shoots .380" ball. Case-hardened frame, loading lever and hammer. Cut for shoulder stock. Non-fluted cylinder. From Navy/Replica Arms.
Price: **$95.00**
Price: With full fluted cyl. **$95.00**

1862 POLICE MODEL PERCUSSION REVOLVER

Caliber: 36, 5-shot.
Barrel: 4½", 5½", 6½".
Weight: 26 oz. **Length:** 12" (6½" bbl.).
Stocks: Walnut.
Sights: Fixed.
Features: Half-fluted and rebated cylinder; case hardened frame, loading lever and hammer; brass trigger guard and back strap. Imported by Navy/Replica.
Price: **$95.00**
Price: Cased with accessories **$119.95**

1862 POCKET NAVY MODEL REVOLVER

Caliber: 36, 6-shot.
Barrel: 4½", 5½", 6½".
Weight: 26 oz. **Length:** 12" over-all (6½" bbl.).
Stocks: Smooth walnut.
Sights: Fixed.
Features: Shortened version of std. Navy model. Case hardened frame, hammer and loading lever; brass backstrap and trigger guard. Imported by Navy/Replica Arms.
Price: **$95.00**

BLACK POWDER REVOLVERS

GRISWOLD & GUNNISON PERCUSSION REVOLVER

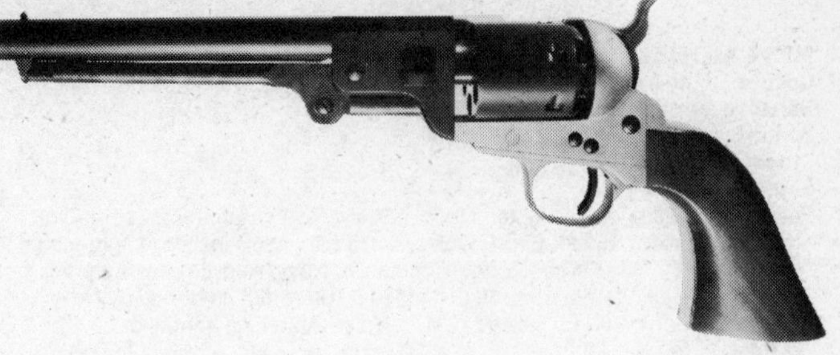

Caliber: 36, 44, 6-shot.
Barrel: 7½".
Weight: 44 oz. (36 cal.). **Length:** 13" over-all.
Stocks: Walnut.
Sights: Fixed.
Features: Replica of famous Confederate pistol. Brass frame, backstrap and trigger guard; case hardened loading lever; rebated cylinder (44 cal. only). Imported by Navy/Replica.
Price: **$55.00**

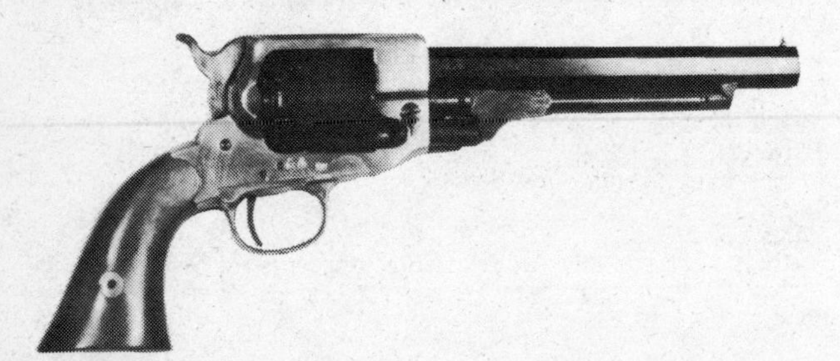

DIXIE SPILLER & BURR REVOLVER

Caliber: 36.
Barrel: 7", octagon.
Weight: 2½ lbs. **Length:** 12½" over-all.
Stock: Two-piece walnut.
Sights: Fixed.
Features: Reproduction of the C.S.A. revolver. Brass frame and trigger guard. Also available as a kit.
Price: **$69.95**
Price: Kit form **$39.95**

HIGH STANDARD LEECH & RIGDON REVOLVER

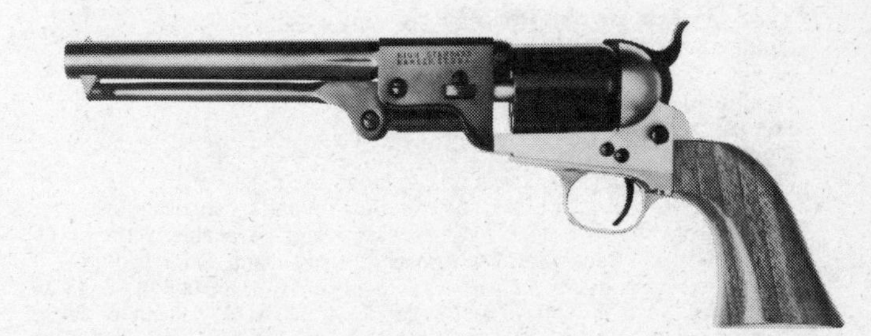

Caliber: 36, 6-shot.
Barrel: 7½".
Weight: Approx. 40 oz. **Length:** 13¼" over-all.
Stocks: Smooth walnut.
Sights: Fixed.
Features: Steel frame with satin nickel finish. Brass trigger guard and backstrap. Comes with deluxe walnut presentation case and reproduction Civil War belt buckle.
Price: **$139.00**

HIGH STANDARD GRISWOLD & GUNNISON REVOLVER

Caliber: 36, 6-shot.
Barrel: 7½".
Weight: Approx. 40 oz. **Length:** 13¼" over-all.
Stocks: Smooth walnut.
Sights: Fixed.
Features: Brass frame and trigger guard, rest blued. Reproduction of Confederate versions of Colt 1851 Navy. Comes with Georgia White Pine presentation case and brass plate depicting Georgia state seal.
Price: **$139.00**

RUGER 44 OLD ARMY PERCUSSION REVOLVER

Caliber: 44, 6-shot. Uses .457" dia. lead bullets.
Barrel: 7½" (6-groove, 16" twist).
Weight: 46 oz. **Length:** 13½" over-all.
Stock: Smooth walnut.
Sights: Ramp front, rear adj. for w. and e.
Features: Stainless steel standard size nipples, chrome-moly steel cylinder and frame, same lockwork as in original Super Blackhawk. Made in USA. From Sturm, Ruger & Co.
Price: Blued **$115.00**
Price: With brass Dragoon-style grip frame and wide trigger **$130.00**

BLACK POWDER MUSKETS & RIFLES

FLINTLOCK BLUNDERBUSS

Caliber: 70.
Barrel: 15½".
Weight: 6¼ lbs. **Length:** 30".
Stock: Walnut finish, hand rubbed.
Sights: None.
Features: Brass barrel and fittings, steel lock from Navy; others have steel bbl., brass fittings. Imported by Navy/Replica, The Armoury, Dixie.
Price: .... **$37.95** to **$135.00**

BLACK POWDER MUSKETS & RIFLES

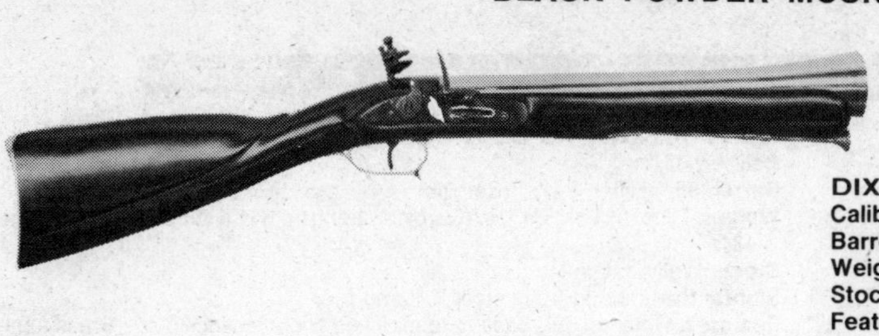

DIXIE FLINT COACH GUARD BLUNDERBUSS
Caliber: 95.
Barrel: 13⅝".
Weight: 5¼ lbs. **Length:** 27½" over-all.
Stock: Ebony-finish hardwood.
Features: Muzzle bell measures 1 14/16". Proofed in Belgium. Shoots shot or ball. Brass trigger guard, buttplate, thimbles. Steel barrel. From Dixie Gun Works.
Price: **$135.00**

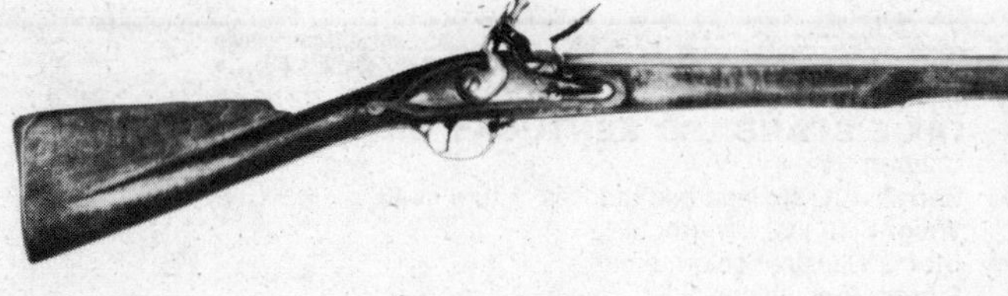

BROWN BESS FLINTLOCK MUSKET
Caliber: 70, 75.
Barrel: 42".
Weight: 10½ lbs. **Length:** 59" over-all.
Stock: Walnut.
Sights: Fixed.
Features: Replica of Revolutionary War period model. Replica bayonet ($12.00) available. Carbine version (30½" bbl., 7¾ lbs.) also available. Can be purchased as kit ($175.00). Imported by Navy/Replica, Lyman.
Price: **$295.00**

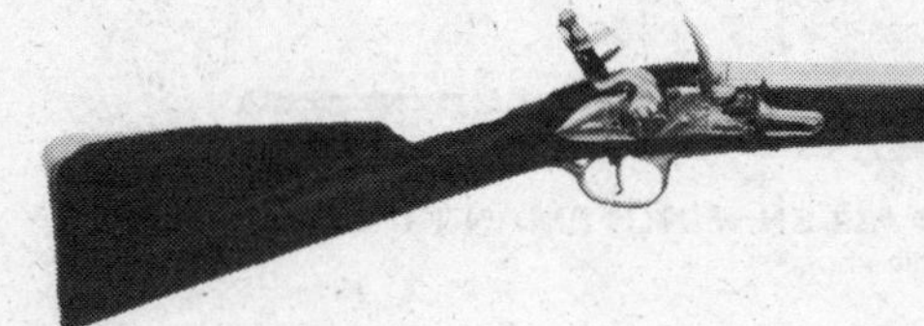

DIXIE SECOND MODEL BROWN BESS
Caliber: 75.
Barrel: 41¾" smoothbore.
Weight: 9½ lbs. **Length:** 57¾".
Stock: Walnut-finish hardwood.
Sights: Fixed.
Features: All metal finished bright. Brass furniture. Lock marked "Tower" and has a crown with "GR" underneath. From Dixie Gun Works.
Price: **$225.00**

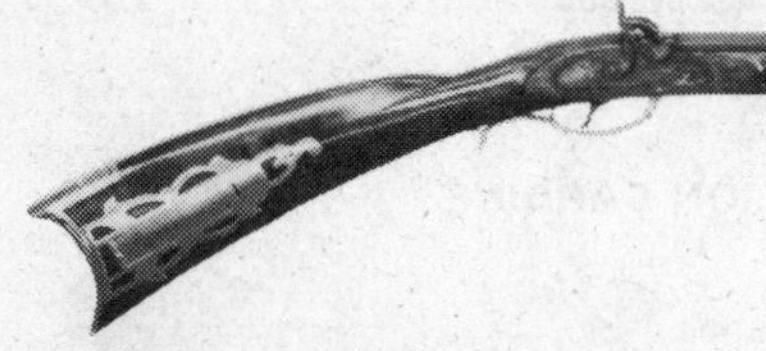

PENNSYLVANIA LONG RIFLE
Caliber: 36 or 45.
Barrel: 39" octagonal.
Weight: 10½ lbs. **Length:** 55" over-all.
Stock: Full-length tiger striped maple, traditional Pennsylvania form.
Sights: Brass blade front, open notch rear.
Features: Solid brass engraved furniture (crescent buttplate, patch box, fore-end cap, etc.) From High Standard.
Price: Flint or percussion form **$179.95**

DIXIE PENNSYLVANIA PERCUSSION RIFLE
Caliber: 45.
Barrel: 40", octagon.
Weight: 10 lbs. **Length:** 55".
Stock: Maple, Roman nose comb.
Sights: Fixed, Kentucky open-type.
Features: Brass patchbox, wide buttplate, color case hardened lock, blue barrel. From Dixie Gun Works.
Price: Flint or percussion **$209.95**

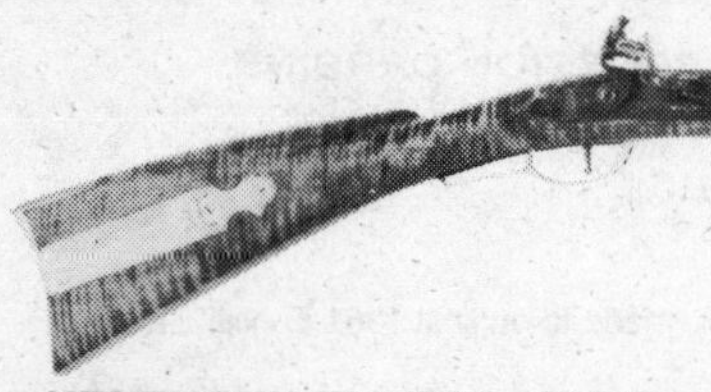

KENTUCKY FLINTLOCK RIFLE
Caliber: 44.
Barrel: 35".
Weight: 7 lbs. **Length:** 50" over-all.
Stock: Walnut stained, brass fittings.
Sights: Fixed.
Features: Available in Carbine model also, 28" bbl. Some variations in detail, finish. Kits also available from some importers. Imported by Navy/Replica, Centennial, The Armoury, Intercontinental, Century, Dixie and Challenger.
Price: .... **$72.50 to $165.00**

Kentucky Percussion Rifle
Similar to above except percussion lock. Finish and features vary with importer. Imported by Jana, Centennial, Navy/Replica, Firearms Import & Export, The Armoury, Century, Challenger, Dixie, Connecticut Valley, Valor.
Price: .... **$65.00 to $229.95**

MOWREY PENNSYLVANIA RIFLE
Caliber: 45.
Barrel: 42".
Weight: 7¾ lbs. **Length:** 56" over-all.
Stock: Maple.
Sights: Open, fixed.
Features: Available in either flint or percussion. 12-coat hand rubbed oil finish. Hand made by Mowrey Gun Works.
Price: Percussion .... **$365.00** Kit **$233.60**
Price: Flint .... **$375.00** Kit **$240.00**

CVA KENTUCKY RIFLE
Caliber: 44 (.451" bore).
Barrel: 34½", rifled, octagon (⅞" flats).
Length: 50" over-all.
Stock: Dark polished walnut.
Sights: Brass Kentucky blade type front. dovetail open rear.
Features: Available in either flint or percussion. Nipple wrench included. Imported by CVA.
Price: Percussion **$86.95**
Price: Flint **$89.95**

BLACK POWDER MUSKETS & RIFLES

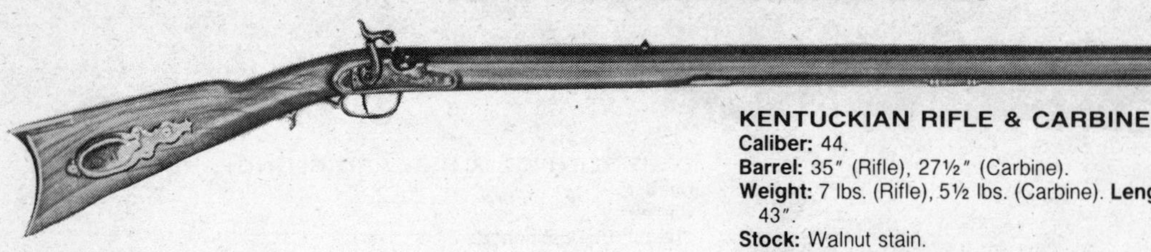

KENTUCKIAN RIFLE & CARBINE

Caliber: 44.
Barrel: 35″ (Rifle), 27½″ (Carbine).
Weight: 7 lbs. (Rifle), 5½ lbs. (Carbine). **Length:** 51″ (Rifle) over-all, carbine 43″.
Stock: Walnut stain.
Sights: Brass blade front, steel V-Ramp rear.
Features: Octagon bbl., case-hardened and engraved lock plate. Brass furniture. Imported by Intercontinental Arms, Dixie.
Price: Rifle (illus.) or carbine, flint or percussion ...... **$135.00** to **$145.00**

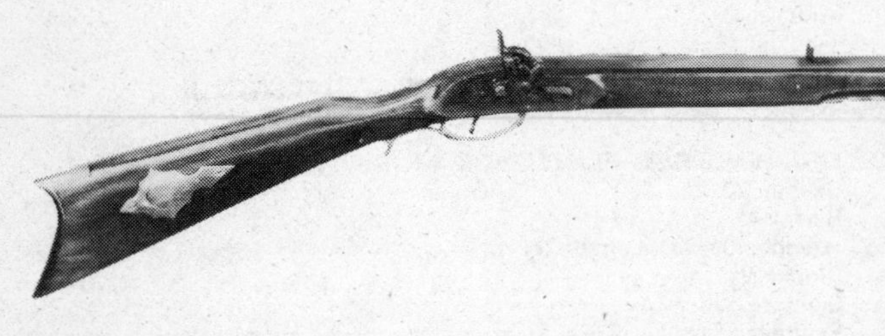

DIXIE STANDARD KENTUCKY RIFLE

Caliber: 45.
Barrel: 40″, six land and grooves, 1 turn in 48″.
Weight: 10 lbs. **Length:** 56½″.
Stock: Chestnut colored maple.
Sights: Brass blade front, Kentucky-type rear.
Features: Trigger guard, buttplate, patchbox and thimbles are brass. Double set triggers available ($8.50 extra). Color case hardened lock. From Dixie Gun Works.
Price: Percussion **$179.95**
Price: Flintlock **$189.95**

HOPKINS AND ALLEN MINUTEMAN RIFLE

Caliber: 36, 45, single-shot.
Barrel: 39″.
Weight: 9½ lbs. **Length:** 55″ over-all.
Stock: Maple.
Sights: Fixed.
Features: Brass furniture, patch box. Available in either flint or percussion. From High Standard.
Price: Either caliber, either ignition system **$179.95**

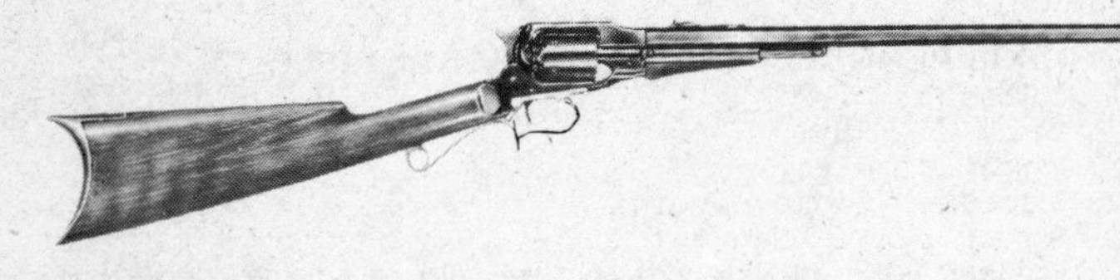

REVOLVING PERCUSSION CARBINE

Caliber: 44, 6-shot.
Barrel: 18″, 20″.
Weight: 5 lbs. **Length:** 38″ over-all.
Stock: Walnut, brass butt plate.
Sights: Blade front adj. for w., buckhorn rear adj. for e.
Features: Action based on 1858 Remington revolver. Brass trigger guard. Imported by Navy/Replica.
Price: **$150.00**

ENFIELD PATTERN 1858 NAVAL RIFLE

Caliber: .577″.
Barrel: 33″.
Weight: 8½ lbs. **Length:** 48½″ over-all.
Stock: European walnut.
Sights: Blade front, step adj. rear.
Features: Two-band Enfield percussion rifle with heavy barrel. 5-groove progressive depth rifling, solid brass furniture. All parts made exactly to original patterns. Imported from England by Jana.
Price: **$225.00**

CVA ZOUAVE RIFLE KIT

Caliber: 58.
Barrel: 33¼″, rifled.
Weight: About 9½ lbs. **Length:** 49″ over-all.
Stock: Walnut.
Sights: Fixed front, rear adj. for e.
Features: Cold forged rifled bbl., authentic lock, solid brass hardware. Imported by CVA.
Price: **$89.95**

ENFIELD MODEL 1861 PERCUSSION CARBINE

Caliber: 577.
Barrel: 24″.
Weight: 7½ lbs. **Length:** 40¼″ over-all.
Stock: Walnut.
Sights: Fixed front, adj. rear.
Features: Percussion muzzle loader, made to original 1861 English patterns. Imported from England by Jana.
Price: **$225.00**

BUGGY RIFLE CASED SET

Caliber: 45.
Barrel: 16″.
Stock: Detachable butt stock with brass furniture.
Sights: Tube sight with interchangeable apertures. Not a telescope.
Features: Cased set contains false muzzle, concentric bullet starter, ramrod, cleaning equipment, bullet mould and swage, powder flask and measure, funnel, nipple wrench, oil bottle, bullet and patch block. Rifle has brass frame and p.g. cap, blued octagon bbl. Imported by Intercontinental Arms.
Price: Cased set complete **$500.00**

BLACK POWDER MUSKETS & RIFLES

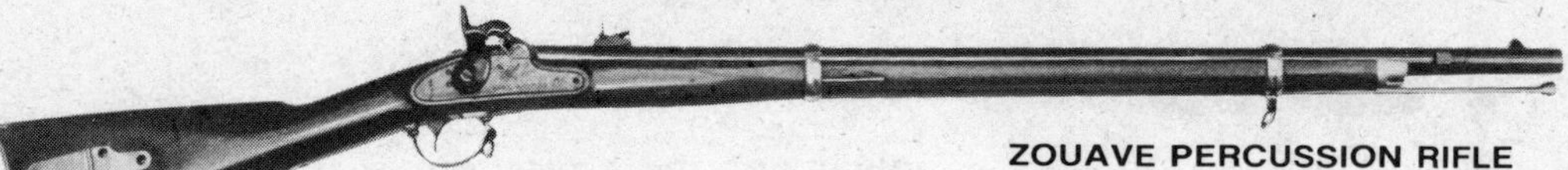

ZOUAVE PERCUSSION RIFLE

Caliber: 58.
Barrel: 32½".
Weight: 9½ lbs. **Length:** 48½" over-all.
Stock: Walnut finish, brass patch box and butt plate.
Sights: Fixed front, rear adj. for e.
Features: Also available from Navy Arms as carbine, with 22" bbl. Extra 20 ga. shotgun bbl. $45.00. Imported by Navy/Replica, Centennial, The Armoury, Lyman, F.I.E.
Price: .... **$88.95** to **$160.00**
Lyman rifle and kit (includes 58 minie ball mould and handles, spare nipple and wrench, Hodgdon's "Minie Lube" and Lyman's "Black Powder Basics" book). **$175.00**

MISSISSIPPI MODEL 1841 PERCUSSION RIFLE

Similar to Zouave Rifle but patterned after U.S. Model 1841. Imported by Navy/Replica.
Price: **$145.00**

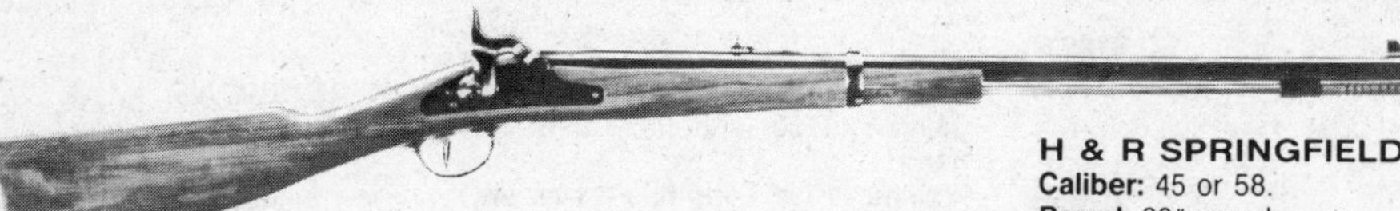

H & R SPRINGFIELD STALKER

Caliber: 45 or 58.
Barrel: 28" round.
Weight: 8 lbs. (45 cal.), 7½ lbs. (58 cal.). **length:** 43" over-all.
Stock: American walnut.
Sights: Blade front, rear open adj. for w. and e.
Features: Action similar to Civil War Springfield. Supplied with solid brass ramrod with hardwood handle and nipple wrench. Blue-black finish.
Price: **$175.00**

H & R DELUXE SPRINGFIELD STALKER

Same as standard model except has hand checkered p.g. and fore-end, better wood, hand polished American walnut stock **$250.00**

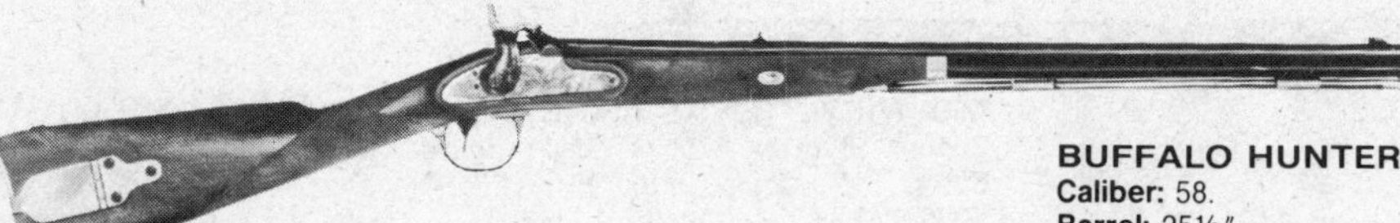

BUFFALO HUNTER PERCUSSION RIFLE

Caliber: 58.
Barrel: 25½".
Weight: 8 lbs. **Length:** 41½" over-all.
Stock: Walnut finished, hand checkered, brass furniture.
Sights: Fixed.
Features: Designed for primitive weapons hunting. 20 ga. shotgun bbl. also available **$45.00.** Imported by Navy/Replica.
Price: **$150.00**

DICKSON BUFFALO HUNTER RIFLE/SHOTGUN

Similar to standard Buffalo Hunter except: over-all length 42", no checkering, 26" bbl, 58 caliber, imported by American Import.
Price: **$159.00**

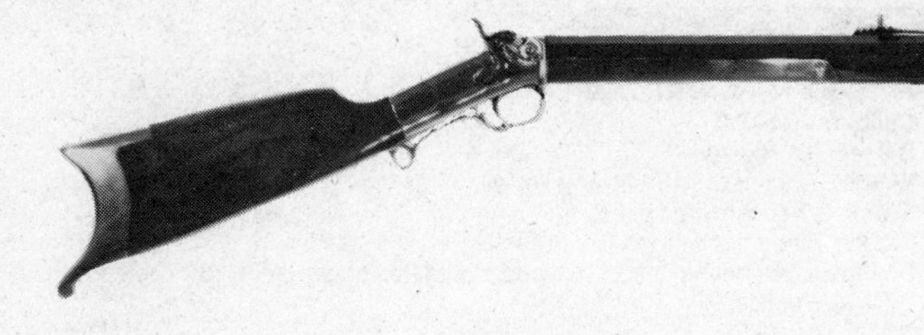

MOWREY ALLEN & THURBER REPLICA

Caliber: 45, 50, 54 or 58.
Barrel: 32", 8-groove rifling, octagon.
Weight: 10¼ lbs. **Length:** 48" over-all.
Stock: Walnut with curved brass butt plate.
Sights: Open, adj. for w. & e.
Features: Polished brass furniture, brass fore-end, ramrod. Also available in kit form.
Price: Complete .... **$175.45** Kit **$119.54**

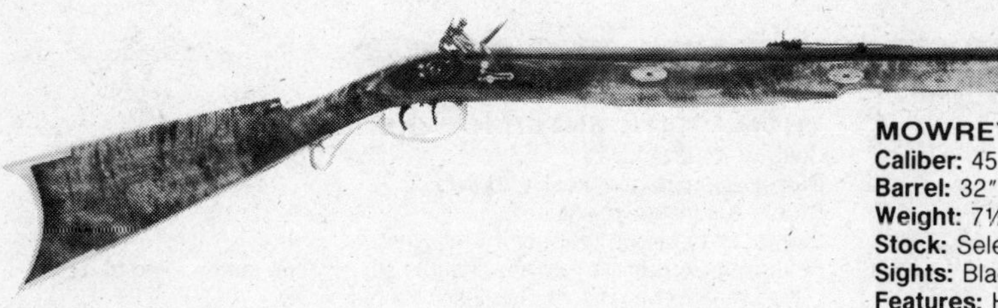

MOWREY HAWKEN FULL STOCK

Caliber: 45, 50, 54, 58.
Barrel: 32"
Weight: 7½ lbs. **Length:** 50" over-all.
Stock: Select maple. Hand rubbed oil finish, brass furniture.
Sights: Blade front, step adj. rear.
Features: Hawken replica, fullstock design. Double set triggers. Also available in kit form.
Price: Percussion .... **$313.50** Flint **$324.50**

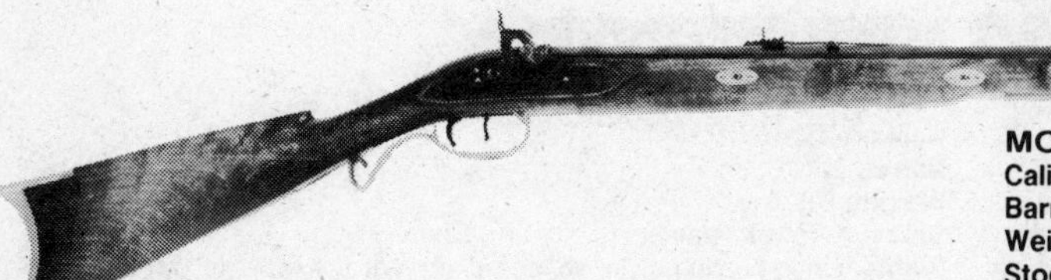

MOWREY HAWKEN FULL STOCK CARBINE

Caliber: 45, 50, 54, 58.
Barrel: 20".
Weight: 7 lbs. **Length:** 38" over-all.
Stock: Maple.
Sights: Open, adj.
Features: Shortened version of Hawken full stock. 10 coat hand rubbed stock finish. From Mowrey Gun Works.
Price: Percussion .... **$285.00** Kit **$182.40**
Price: Flint .... **$295.00** Kit **$188.80**

BLACK POWDER MUSKETS & RIFLES

MOWREY ALLEN & THURBER SPECIAL
Caliber: 45, 50, 54 or 58.
Barrel: 32″ octagonal.
Weight: 10 lbs. **Length:** 48″ over-all.
Stock: Walnut with curved brass buttplate, walnut fore-end.
Sights: Open, fully adj.
Features: Same design as A&T Replica except has walnut fore-end. Polished brass furniture. Also available in kit form.
Price: Complete .... **$180.95** Kit **$126.80**

MOWREY HAWK
Caliber: 45, 50 54 or 58.
Barrel: 32″.
Weight: 9½ lbs. **Length:** 49″ over-all.
Stock: Walnut, sporter-type with cheek-piece, walnut fore-end.
Sights: Open, fully adj. for w. and e.
Features: Hawkins-type buttplate and action housing of brass. Adj. trigger. Also available in kit form.
Price: Complete .... **$191.95** Kit **$130.32**

MOWREY GEORGIA TREE GUN
Caliber: 45, 50, 54, 58.
Barrel: 22″.
Weight: 7¼ lbs. **Length:** 38″ over-all.
Stock: Walnut.
Sights: Blade front, step adj. rear.
Features: Shortened version of Allen & Thurber rifle especially suited for tree stand shooting.
Price: Complete gun **$180.95**
Price: Kit **$126.80**

MOWREY HAWKEN HALF STOCK REPLICA
Caliber: 45, 50, 54 or 58.
Barrel: 27½″.
Weight: 11 lbs. **Length:** 50″ over-all.
Stock: Select maple with brass furniture. Hand rubbed oil finish.
Sights: Open, fully adj. for w. & e.
Features: Available in flint or percussion. Double set trigger. Built in limited quantities.
Price: Percussion .... **$275.00** Kit **$175.45**
Price: Flint .... **$286.00** Kit **$181.50**

MOWREY "TEXAS CARBINE"
Caliber: 58, takes .575″ mini-ball or round ball.
Barrel: 24″ octagon, 4-groove.
Weight: 8 lbs. **Length:** 39″ over-all.
Stock: Dark maple (walnut optional).
Sights: Adjustable front and rear.
Features: "1 of 100" inscribed on first 100, "1 of 1000" on remaining 1000. Saddle ring with leather thong and Texas seal imbedded in stock. Distributed by Trail Guns Armory.
Price: **$189.50**

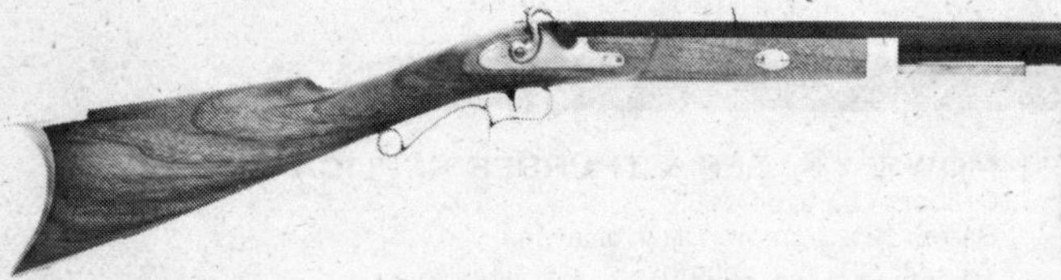

HAWKEN HURRICANE
Caliber: 45 or 50.
Barrel: 28″, octagon.
Weight: 6 lbs. **Length:** 44¾″ over-all.
Stock: American walnut.
Sights: Blade front, open fixed rear.
Features: American made. Curved buttplate, brass stock furniture. From Navy/Replica.
Price: **$175.00**
Price: Hawken Hunter (58 cal.) **$175.00**

THOMPSON/CENTER HAWKEN RIFLE
Caliber: 45 or 50.
Barrel: 28″ octagon, hooked breech.
Stock: American walnut.
Sights: Blade front, rear adj. for w. & e.
Features: Solid brass furniture, double set triggers, button rifled barrel, coil-type main spring. From Thompson/Center Arms.
Price: Percussion Model .. **$195.00** Flintlock Model **$205.00**

THOMPSON/CENTER SENECA RIFLE
Caliber: 36, 45.
Barrel: 27″.
Weight: 6½ lbs.
Stock: American walnut.
Sights: Open hunting style, square notch rear fully adj. for w. and e.
Features: Coil spring lock, octagon bbl. measures 13/16″ across flats, brass stock furniture.
Price: Rifle **$195.00**
Price: Rifle with accessory kit (includes bullet mould, patches, powder measure, short starter, extra nipple & nipple wrench) **$218.95**

BLACK POWDER MUSKETS & RIFLES

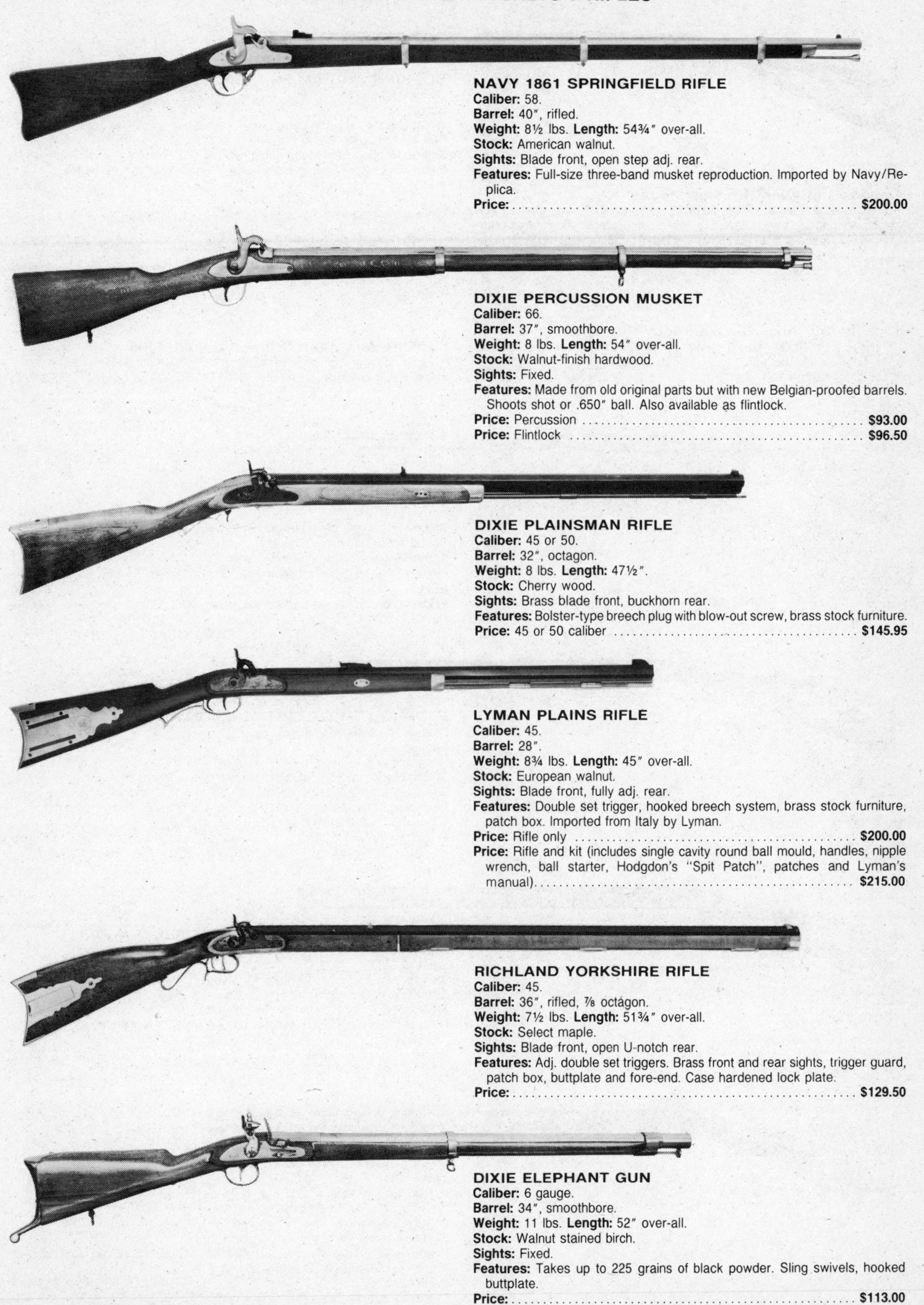

NAVY 1861 SPRINGFIELD RIFLE

Caliber: 58.
Barrel: 40", rifled.
Weight: 8½ lbs. **Length:** 54¾" over-all.
Stock: American walnut.
Sights: Blade front, open step adj. rear.
Features: Full-size three-band musket reproduction. Imported by Navy/Replica.
Price: $200.00

DIXIE PERCUSSION MUSKET

Caliber: 66.
Barrel: 37", smoothbore.
Weight: 8 lbs. **Length:** 54" over-all.
Stock: Walnut-finish hardwood.
Sights: Fixed.
Features: Made from old original parts but with new Belgian-proofed barrels. Shoots shot or .650" ball. Also available as flintlock.
Price: Percussion $93.00
Price: Flintlock $96.50

DIXIE PLAINSMAN RIFLE

Caliber: 45 or 50.
Barrel: 32", octagon.
Weight: 8 lbs. **Length:** 47½".
Stock: Cherry wood.
Sights: Brass blade front, buckhorn rear.
Features: Bolster-type breech plug with blow-out screw, brass stock furniture.
Price: 45 or 50 caliber $145.95

LYMAN PLAINS RIFLE

Caliber: 45.
Barrel: 28".
Weight: 8¾ lbs. **Length:** 45" over-all.
Stock: European walnut.
Sights: Blade front, fully adj. rear.
Features: Double set trigger, hooked breech system, brass stock furniture, patch box. Imported from Italy by Lyman.
Price: Rifle only $200.00
Price: Rifle and kit (includes single cavity round ball mould, handles, nipple wrench, ball starter, Hodgdon's "Spit Patch", patches and Lyman's manual).. $215.00

RICHLAND YORKSHIRE RIFLE

Caliber: 45.
Barrel: 36", rifled, ⅞ octagon.
Weight: 7½ lbs. **Length:** 51¾" over-all.
Stock: Select maple.
Sights: Blade front, open U-notch rear.
Features: Adj. double set triggers. Brass front and rear sights, trigger guard, patch box, buttplate and fore-end. Case hardened lock plate.
Price: $129.50

DIXIE ELEPHANT GUN

Caliber: 6 gauge.
Barrel: 34", smoothbore.
Weight: 11 lbs. **Length:** 52" over-all.
Stock: Walnut stained birch.
Sights: Fixed.
Features: Takes up to 225 grains of black powder. Sling swivels, hooked buttplate.
Price: $113.00

BLACK POWDER MUSKETS & RIFLES

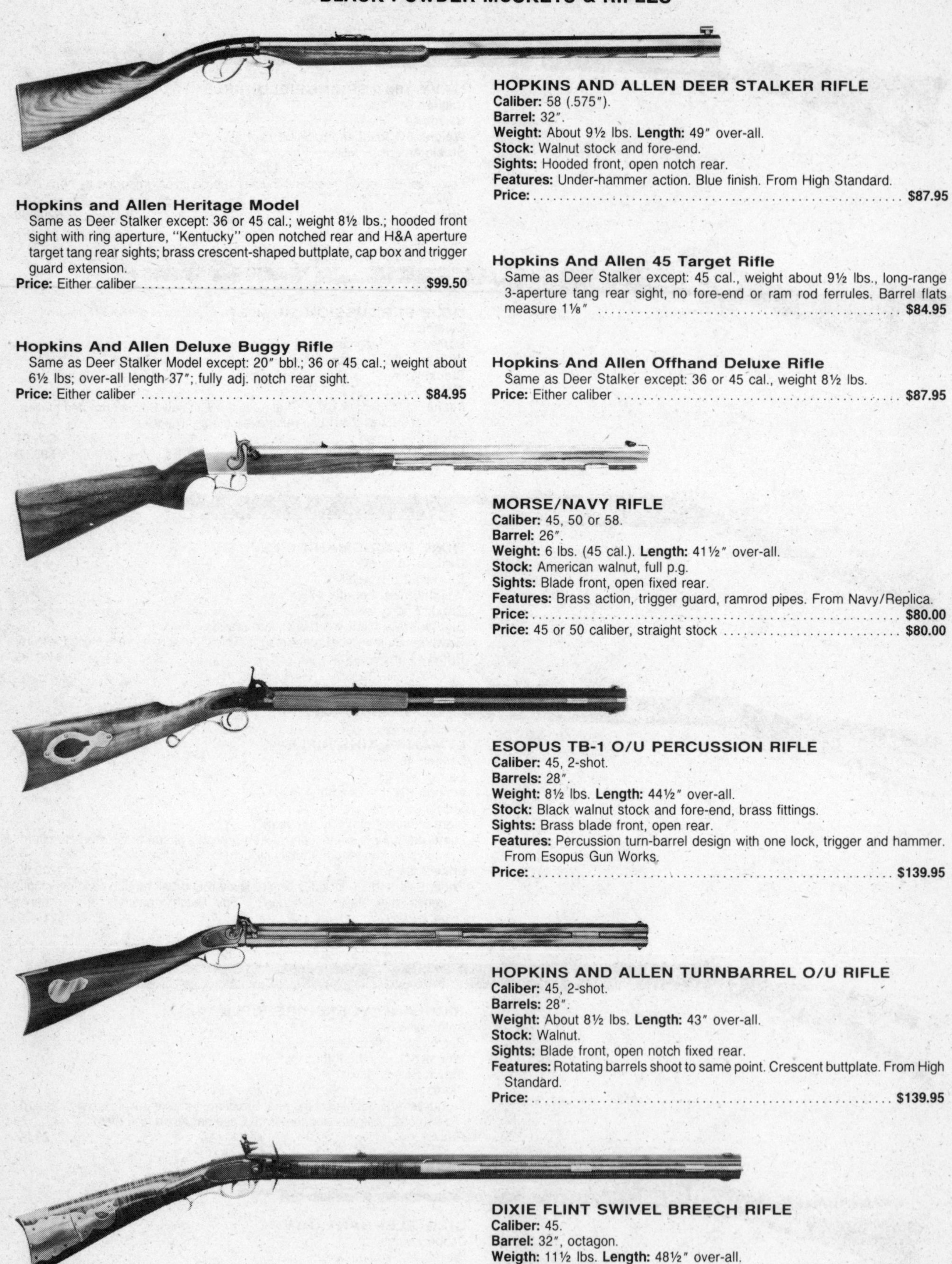

HOPKINS AND ALLEN DEER STALKER RIFLE

Caliber: 58 (.575").
Barrel: 32".
Weight: About 9½ lbs. **Length:** 49" over-all.
Stock: Walnut stock and fore-end.
Sights: Hooded front, open notch rear.
Features: Under-hammer action. Blue finish. From High Standard.
Price: **$87.95**

Hopkins and Allen Heritage Model

Same as Deer Stalker except: 36 or 45 cal.; weight 8½ lbs.; hooded front sight with ring aperture, "Kentucky" open notched rear and H&A aperture target tang rear sights; brass crescent-shaped buttplate, cap box and trigger guard extension.
Price: Either caliber **$99.50**

Hopkins And Allen 45 Target Rifle

Same as Deer Stalker except: 45 cal., weight about 9½ lbs., long-range 3-aperture tang rear sight, no fore-end or ram rod ferrules. Barrel flats measure 1⅛" **$84.95**

Hopkins And Allen Deluxe Buggy Rifle

Same as Deer Stalker Model except: 20" bbl.; 36 or 45 cal.; weight about 6½ lbs; over-all length 37"; fully adj. notch rear sight.
Price: Either caliber **$84.95**

Hopkins And Allen Offhand Deluxe Rifle

Same as Deer Stalker except: 36 or 45 cal., weight 8½ lbs.
Price: Either caliber **$87.95**

MORSE/NAVY RIFLE

Caliber: 45, 50 or 58.
Barrel: 26".
Weight: 6 lbs. (45 cal.). **Length:** 41½" over-all.
Stock: American walnut, full p.g.
Sights: Blade front, open fixed rear.
Features: Brass action, trigger guard, ramrod pipes. From Navy/Replica.
Price: **$80.00**
Price: 45 or 50 caliber, straight stock **$80.00**

ESOPUS TB-1 O/U PERCUSSION RIFLE

Caliber: 45, 2-shot.
Barrels: 28".
Weight: 8½ lbs. **Length:** 44½" over-all.
Stock: Black walnut stock and fore-end, brass fittings.
Sights: Brass blade front, open rear.
Features: Percussion turn-barrel design with one lock, trigger and hammer. From Esopus Gun Works.
Price: **$139.95**

HOPKINS AND ALLEN TURNBARREL O/U RIFLE

Caliber: 45, 2-shot.
Barrels: 28".
Weight: About 8½ lbs. **Length:** 43" over-all.
Stock: Walnut.
Sights: Blade front, open notch fixed rear.
Features: Rotating barrels shoot to same point. Crescent buttplate. From High Standard.
Price: **$139.95**

DIXIE FLINT SWIVEL BREECH RIFLE

Caliber: 45.
Barrel: 32", octagon.
Weigth: 11½ lbs. **Length:** 48½" over-all.
Stock: Curly maple.
Sights: Fixed.
Features: Wood panelled barrels rotate for second shot. Single trigger. Brass furniture. From Dixie Gun Works.
Price: Flintlock **$450.00**
Price: Percussion **$325.00**

BLACK POWDER MUSKETS & RIFLES

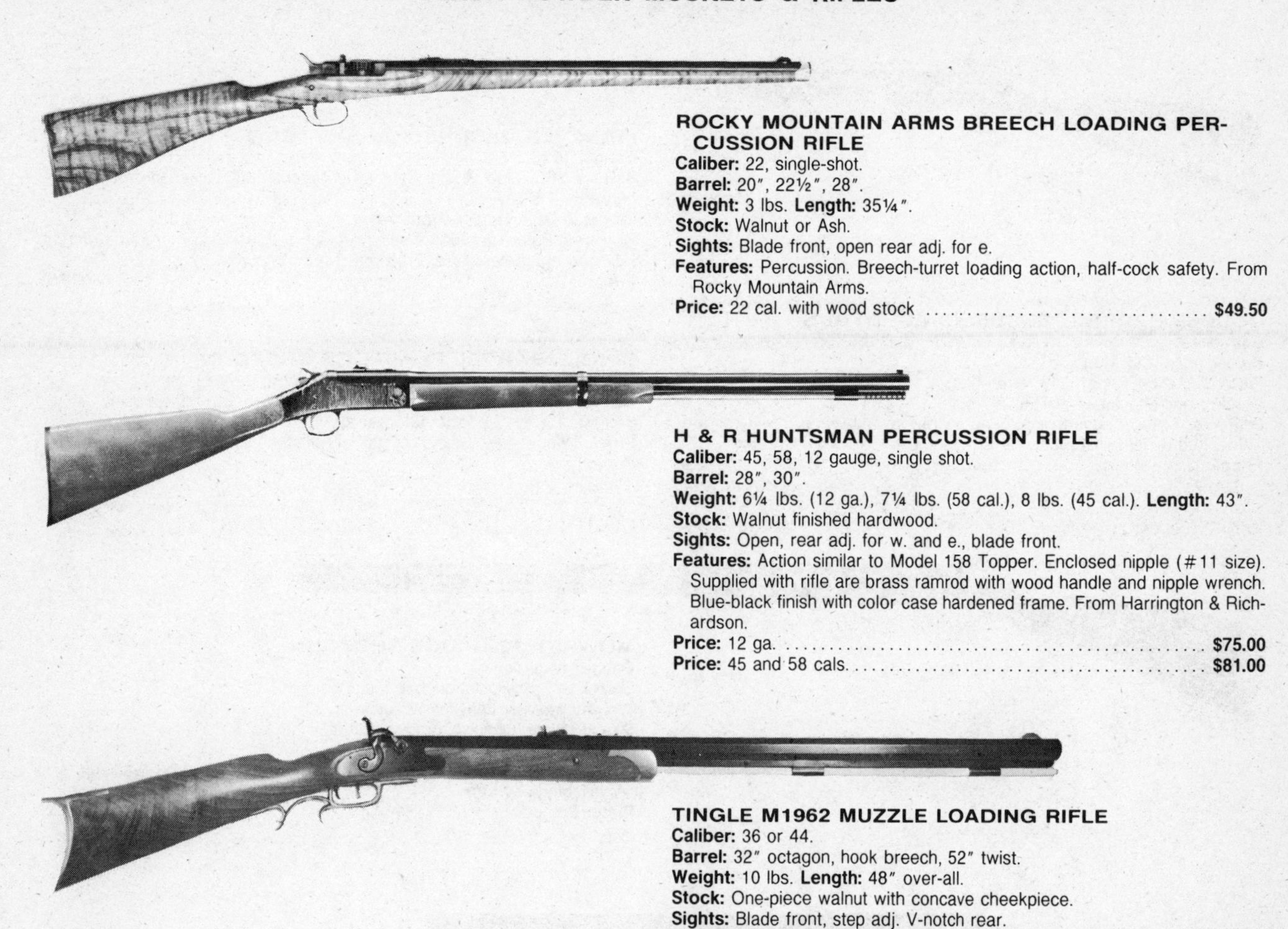

ROCKY MOUNTAIN ARMS BREECH LOADING PERCUSSION RIFLE
Caliber: 22, single-shot.
Barrel: 20″, 22½″, 28″.
Weight: 3 lbs. **Length:** 35¼″.
Stock: Walnut or Ash.
Sights: Blade front, open rear adj. for e.
Features: Percussion. Breech-turret loading action, half-cock safety. From Rocky Mountain Arms.
Price: 22 cal. with wood stock **$49.50**

H & R HUNTSMAN PERCUSSION RIFLE
Caliber: 45, 58, 12 gauge, single shot.
Barrel: 28″, 30″.
Weight: 6¼ lbs. (12 ga.), 7¼ lbs. (58 cal.), 8 lbs. (45 cal.). **Length:** 43″.
Stock: Walnut finished hardwood.
Sights: Open, rear adj. for w. and e., blade front.
Features: Action similar to Model 158 Topper. Enclosed nipple (#11 size). Supplied with rifle are brass ramrod with wood handle and nipple wrench. Blue-black finish with color case hardened frame. From Harrington & Richardson.
Price: 12 ga. **$75.00**
Price: 45 and 58 cals. **$81.00**

TINGLE M1962 MUZZLE LOADING RIFLE
Caliber: 36 or 44.
Barrel: 32″ octagon, hook breech, 52″ twist.
Weight: 10 lbs. **Length:** 48″ over-all.
Stock: One-piece walnut with concave cheekpiece.
Sights: Blade front, step adj. V-notch rear.
Features: Solid brass furniture, double-set trigger with adj. pull, percussion lock.
Price: **$139.95**

BLACK POWDER SHOTGUNS

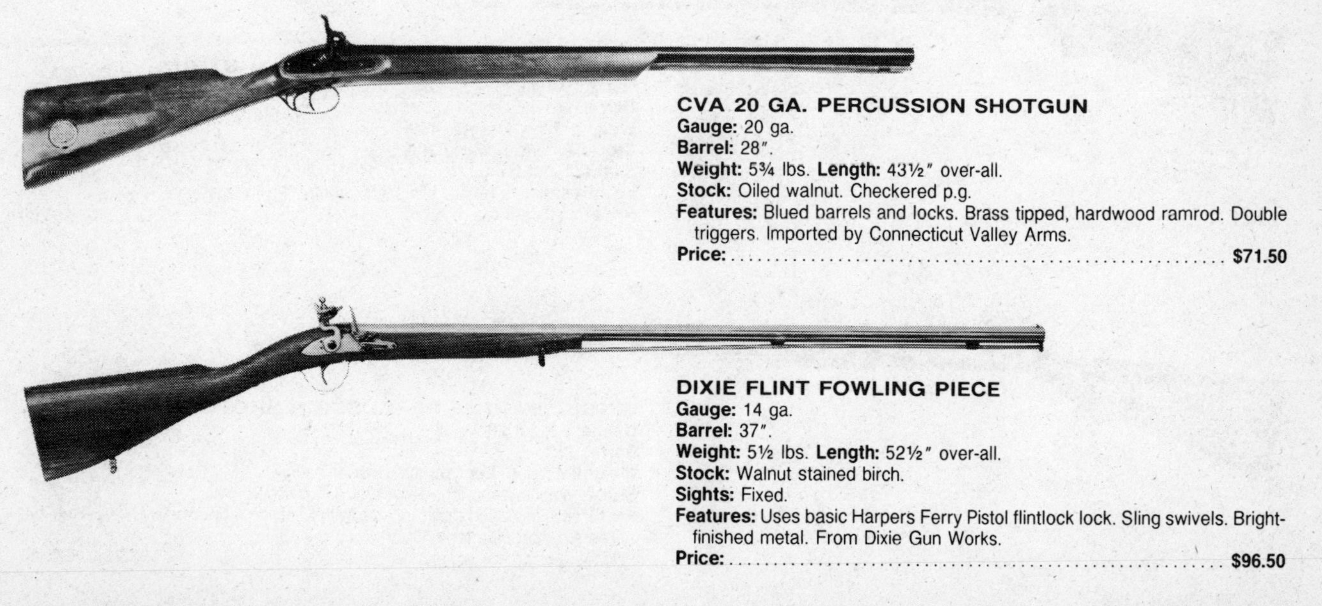

CVA 20 GA. PERCUSSION SHOTGUN
Gauge: 20 ga.
Barrel: 28″.
Weight: 5¾ lbs. **Length:** 43½″ over-all.
Stock: Oiled walnut. Checkered p.g.
Features: Blued barrels and locks. Brass tipped, hardwood ramrod. Double triggers. Imported by Connecticut Valley Arms.
Price: **$71.50**

DIXIE FLINT FOWLING PIECE
Gauge: 14 ga.
Barrel: 37″.
Weight: 5½ lbs. **Length:** 52½″ over-all.
Stock: Walnut stained birch.
Sights: Fixed.
Features: Uses basic Harpers Ferry Pistol flintlock lock. Sling swivels. Bright-finished metal. From Dixie Gun Works.
Price: **$96.50**

BLACK POWDER SHOTGUNS

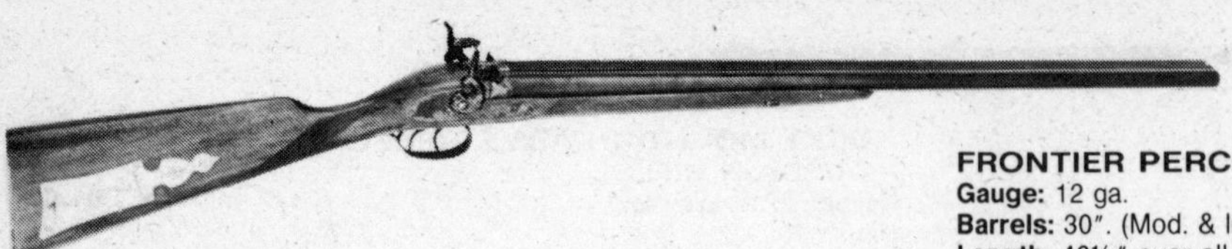

FRONTIER PERCUSSION SHOTGUN
Gauge: 12 ga.
Barrels: 30". (Mod. & Imp. Cyl.). Patent breech with threaded breech plugs.
Length: 46½" over-all.
Stock: Walnut. Length of pull 14".
Features: Patent breech for easy cleaning & disassembly. Front bead sight. Engraving on hardware. Brass patch box. Imported by CVA.
Price: **$99.95**

DOUBLE BARREL PERCUSSION SHOTGUN
Gauge: 12.
Barrel: 30" (I.C.& Mod.).
Weight: 6¼ lbs. **Length:** 45" over-all.
Stock: Hand checkered walnut, 14" pull.
Features: Double triggers, light hand engraving. Details vary with importer. Imported by Navy/Replica, The Armoury, Century, Dixie, C.V.A.
Price: .... **$125.00** to **$140,95**

SINGLE BARREL FLINTLOCK SHOTGUN
Gauge: 28.
Barrel: 28".
Weight: 4½ lbs. **Lenght:** 43" over-all.
Stock: Walnut finish, choice of half or full stock. Imported by The Armoury.
Price: **$37.95**

MOWREY 12 GAUGE SHOTGUN
Gauge: 12 ga. only.
Barrel: 32", half octagon, half round.
Weight: 7½ lbs. **Length:** 48" over-all.
Stock: Maple, oil finish, brass furniture.
Sights: Bead front.
Features: Available in percussion only. Uses standard 12 ga. wadding. Also available in kit form.
Price: Complete .... **$164.45** Kit **$112.28**

TINGLE PERCUSSION SINGLE BARREL SHOTGUN
Gauge: 12 only.
Barrel: 30" straight bored, no choke.
Weight: 5 lbs.
Stock: Lacquered walnut.
Features: Mule ear side hammer lock, iron trigger guard, rubber recoil pad.
Price: Blued **$99.75**

MORSE/NAVY SINGLE BARREL SHOTGUN
Gauge: 12 ga.
Barrel: 26".
Weight: 5 lbs. **Length:** 41½" over-all.
Stock: American walnut, full p.g.
Sights: Front bead.
Features: Brass receiver, black buttplate. From Navy/Replica.
Price: **$80.00**

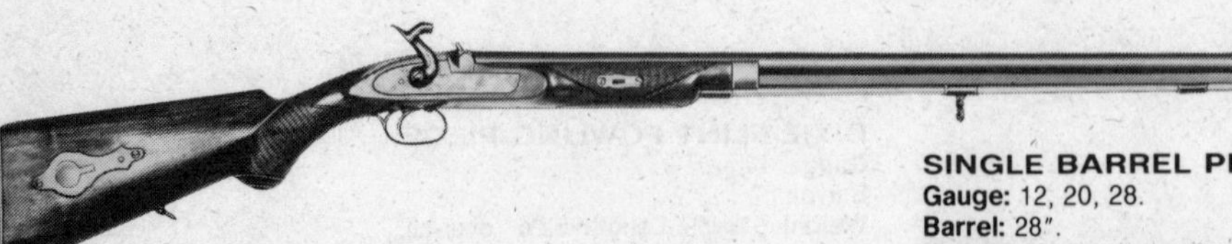

SINGLE BARREL PERCUSSION SHOTGUN
Gauge: 12, 20, 28.
Barrel: 28".
Weight: 4½ lbs. **Length:** 43" over-all.
Stock: Walnut finish, choice of half or full stock.
Features: Finish and features vary with importer. Imported by Navy/Replica, The Armoury, Century, Dixie.
Price: .... **$32.95** to **$65.00**

PELLET GUNS—HANDGUNS

Guns in this section are powered by: A) disposable CO^2 cylinders, B) hand-pumped compressed air released by trigger action, C) air compressed by a spring-powered piston released by trigger action. Calibers are generally 177 (BB or pellet) and 22 (ball or pellet); a few guns are made in 20 or 25 caliber. Pellet guns are usually rifled, those made for BB's only are smoothbore.

AMPELL CO^2 PISTOL KIT

Caliber: BB, 177 or 22. (BB only has 80-shot mag., others single shot.)
Barrel: 8½″, rifled.
Length: 11¾″. **Weight:** 36 oz.
Sights: Sq. notch rear adj. for w. and e., blade front.
Power: Standard CO$_2$ cylinder.
Features: Up to 365 f.p.s. M.V.; 2-lb. trigger pull. Kit includes pistol, 250 pellets, Ampow'r CO^2. BB kit includes pistol, 1200 BB's and Ampow'r CO^2.
Price: **$23.50**

BENJAMIN SUPER S. S. TARGET PISTOL SERIES 130

Caliber: BB, 22 and 177; single shot.
Barrel: 8 inches; BB smoothbore; 22 and 177, rifled.
Length: 11″. **Weight:** 2 lbs.
Power: Hand pumped.
Features: Bolt action; fingertip safety; adj. power.
Price: M130, BB **$42.90**
Price: M132, 22 .... **$42.90** M137, 177 .... **$42.90**

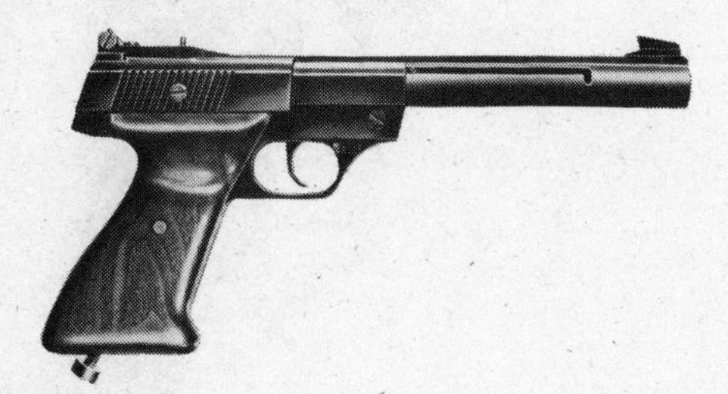

CROSMAN 454 BB PISTOL

Caliber: BB, 16-shot.
Length: 11″ over-all. **Weight:** 30 oz.
Power: Standard CO^2.
Stocks: Contoured with thumb-rest.
Sights: Patridge-type front, fully adj. rear.
Features: Gives about 80 shots per powerlet, slide-action safety, steel barrel, die-cast receiver.
Price: **$24.30**

CROSMAN PEACEMAKER "44"

Caliber: 22, 6 shot.
Barrel: 4¾″, button rifled.
Length: 10⅜″. **Weight:** 34 oz.
Power: Crosman CO^2 Powerlet
Features: Revolving cylinder, walnut finished grips. Simulated gold hammer and trigger, positive valve design. Single-action.
Price: **$27.25**

CROSMAN FRONTIER "36"

Caliber: BB, 18-shot.
Barrel: 4¾″, smoothbore.
Length: 10⅜″. **Weight:** 34 oz.
Power: Crosman CO^2 Powerlet
Features: Single-action, steel barrel, revolving cylinder. Walnut finish grips.
Price: **$27.75**

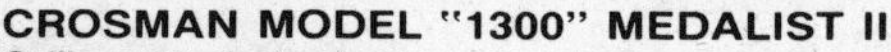

CROSMAN MODEL "1300" MEDALIST II

Caliber: 22, single shot.
Barrel: 8″, button rifled.
Length: 11¾″. **Weight:** 37 oz.
Power: Hand pumped.
Features: Moulded plastic grip, hand size pump forearm. Cross bolt safety, self-cocking.
Price: **$32.20**

CROSMAN MARK I TARGET PISTOL

Caliber: 22, single shot.
Barrel: 7¼″, button rifled.
Length: 11″. **Weight:** 42 oz.
Power: Crosman Powerlet CO^2 cylinder.
Features: New system provides same shot-to-shot velocity, adj. from 300- to 400 fps. Checkered thumbrest grips, right or left. Patridge front sight, rear adj. for w. & e. Adj. trigger.
Price: 22 or 177 .... **$30.20**

Crosman Mark II Target Pistol

Same as Mark I except 177 cal. **$30.20**

CROSMAN 38 TARGET REVOLVER M9
Caliber: 22, 6-shot.
Barrel: 6", rifled.
Length: 11 inches. **Weight:** 43 oz.
Power: CO^2 Powerlet cylinder.
Features: Double action, revolving cylinder. Adj. rear sight.
Price: **38.15**

Crosman 38 Combat Revolver
Same as 38 Target except 3½" BBL., 38 oz. **$38.15**

DAISY 179 SIX GUN
Caliber: BB, 12-shot.
Barrel: Steel lined, smoothbore.
Length: 11½". **Weight:** NA
Power: Spring.
Features: Forced feed from under-barrel magazine. Single action, molded wood grained grips.
Price: **$11.25**

DAISY CO^2 200 SEMI-AUTO PISTOL
Caliber: BB, 175-shot semi-auto.
Barrel: 7½", steel-lined, smoothbore.
Length: 11⅞", sight radius 9". **Weight:** 24 oz.
Power: Daisy CO^2 cylinders, 8½ grams (100 shots) or 12 grams (160 shots).
Features: 175-shot magazine; constant full power; valve system eliminates gas leakage; checkered thumbrest stocks; undercut ramp front sight and adjustable rear.
Price: **$30.00**

DAISY 5679 TEXAS RANGER COMMEMORATIVE PISTOLS
Caliber: BB, 12-shot.
Barrel: Steel. Coined with "1823-The Texas Rangers-1973".
Length: 11½" over-all. **Weight:** 2½ lbs.
Stock: Wood grained, molded grips, mounted with Texas Ranger commemorative seal miniature and on the reverse a miniature of the Ranger badge.
Features: Matched set. "Spittin' image" of the Western Peacemaker. Exclusive case-hardened plating on receiver. Comes with 48-page history of the Texas Rangers.
Price: Per pair **$27.50**

DAISY 177 BB PISTOL
Caliber: BB, 150-shot.
Barrel: Formed steel, smoothbore.
Length: 11¼". **Weight:** NA.
Power: Spring.
Features: Gravity feed, adjustable rear sight, molded plastic thumbrest grips.
Price: **$11.25**

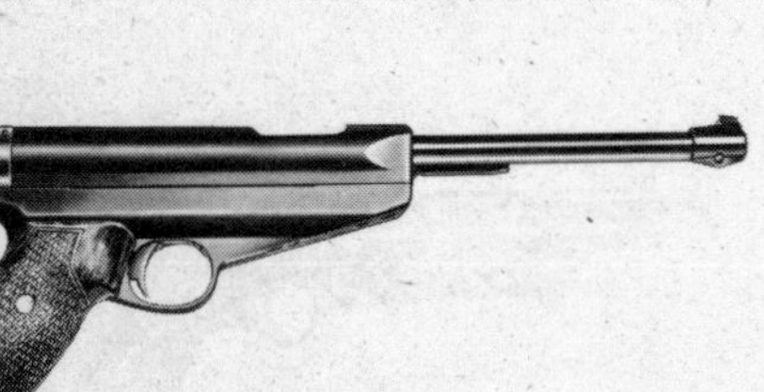

DAISY/FWB 65 TARGET PISTOL
Caliber: 177, single shot.
Barrel: 7½", rifled, fixed to receiver.
Length: 15½". **Weight:** 42 oz.
Power: Spring, cocked by left-side lever.
Features: Recoiless operation, may be set to give recoil; Micro. rear sight, 14" radius. Adj. trigger; normal 17.6 oz. pull can be raised to 48 oz. for training. Checkered, thumbrest target grips. Air Rifle Hdqtrs. or Daisy, importer.
Price: **$250.00**

FEINWERKBAU F-65 AIR PISTOL
Caliber: 177.
Barrel: 7½".
Length: 14½" over-all. **Weight:** 42 oz.
Power: Spring, sidelever cocking.
Stock: Walnut, stippled thumb-rest.
Sights: Front, interchangeable post element system, open rear, click adj. for w. & e. and for sighting notch width.
Features: Cocking effort 9 lbs. 2-stage trigger, 4 adjustments. Programs instantly for recoil or recoiless operation. Permanently lubricated. Special switch converts trigger from 17.6 oz. pull to 42 oz. let-off. Imported by Air Rifle Hdq., Beeman's
Price: .... **$218.50** to **$268.50**

Feinwerkbau Model 65 International Match Pistol
Same as FWB 65 pistol except: new adj. wood grips to meet international regulations, optional 3 oz. barrel sleeve weight. Imported by A.R.H., Beeman's.
Price: .... **$265.00** to **$324.50**

PELLET GUNS—HANDGUNS

HAMMERLI "MASTER" CO^2 TARGET PISTOL
Caliber: .177 waisted pellets.
Barrel: 6.4″, 12-groove.
Length: 16″. **Weight:** 38.4 oz.
Stocks: Plastic with thumbrest and checkering.
Sights: Ramp front, micro rear, click adj. Adj. sight radius from 11.1″ to 13.0″.
Features: Single shot, manual loading. Residual gas vented automatically. 5-way adj. trigger. Imported by HY-SCORE, Gil Hebard.
Price: Approx. **$74.95**

HAMMERLI "SINGLE" CO^2 TARGET PISTOL
Caliber: .177 waisted pellets.
Barrel: 4.5″, 12-groove.
Length: 12″. **Weight:** 33 oz.
Stocks: Plastic with thumb rest and checkering.
Sights: Ramp front, micro-click rear. Adj. sight radius from 11.1″ to 13.0″.
Features: Single shot, easy manual loading, 4-way adj. trigger. Imported by HY-SCORE, Gil Hebard.
Price: Approx. **$64.95**

HEALTHWAYS SHARPSHOOTER
Caliber: 175 (BB), 50-shot.
Barrel: 6¼″.
Weight: 28 oz.
Power: Spring (barrel cocking).
Features: Easy cocking action. Loading pocket speeds and simplifies loading. Spring mechanism housed in grip.
Price: **$14.00**

HEALTHWAYS ML 175 CO^2 AUTOMATIC PISTOL
Caliber: BB, 100-shot repeater.
Barrel: 5¾″, smooth.
Length: 9½″. **Weight:** 28 oz.
Power: Standard CO^2 cylinder.
Features: 3 position power switch. Auto. ammunition feed. Positive safety.
Price: **$21.00**

HY-SCORE 814 JUNIOR PISTOL
Caliber: 177 darts BBs, single shot.
Barrel: Smoothbore.
Length: About 10″. **Weight:** NA.
Power: Spring, compressed by screwing in breech plug.
Features: Checkered wooden grips.
Price: Blued **$5.95**

HY-SCORE 815 Target Pistol
Same as Hy-Score M816 except: without recoil-less system; is slightly lighter; has fixed aperture front sight. In plastic case. Also in 22 cal. **$44.95**

HY-SCORE 816 M TARGET PISTOL
Caliber: 177, single shot.
Barrel: 7″ precision rifled.
Length: 16″. **Weight:** 50 oz.
Power: Spring, bbl. cocking.
Features: Recoil-less firing, adj. trigger. Hooded front sight with 3 apertures, click adj. rear with 4 apertures. Plastic thumbrest target grips.
Price: In plastic case **$69.95**

MARKSMAN REPEATER PISTOL
Caliber: 177, 20-shot repeater.
Barrel: 2½″, smoothbore.
Length: 8¼″. **Weight:** 24 oz.
Power: Spring.
Features: Thumb safety. Uses BBs, darts or pellets. Repeats with BBs only.
Price: Black finish **$11.95**

ROGER CO^2 BB PISTOL
Caliber: BB, 100-shot.
Barrel: 4¼″, smooth.
Length: 10¼″ over-all. **Weight:** 22 oz. **Sights:** Blade front, adj. rear.
Power: Standard CO^2 cartridge.
Features: Semi-automatic. Checkered plastic thumbrest target grips. Precise Imports, importer.
Price: **$29.00**

PELLET GUNS—HANDGUNS

SMITH & WESSON MODELS 78G & 79G

Caliber: 22 cal. pellet (78G), 177 cal. pellet (79G), single-shot.
Barrel: 8½", rifled steel.
Weight: 42 oz.
Power: 12.5 gram CO^2 cartridge.
Stocks: Simulated walnut, checkered. Thumb rest. Left or right hand.
Sights: Patridge front, fully adj. rear with micro. click windage adjustment.
Features: Pull-bolt action, crossbolt safety, double sear trigger with adj. engagement. High-low power adjustment. Gun blue finish.
Price: **$37.50**

WALTHER MODEL LP-3

Caliber: 177, single shot.
Barrel: 9⅜", rifled.
Length: 13³⁄₁₆". **Weight:** 45½ oz.
Power: Compressed air, lever cocking.
Features: Recoiless operation, cocking in grip frame. Micro-click rear sight, adj. for w. & e., 4-way adj. trigger. Plastic thumbrest grips. Imported by Interarms.
Price: **$155.00**

Walther Model LP-3 Match Pistol

Same specifications as LP-3 except for grips, frame shape and weight. Has adjustable walnut grips to meet international shooting regulations. Imported by Interarms.
Price: **$185.00**

WALTHER MODEL LP-53 PISTOL

Caliber: 177, single shot.
Barrel: 9⅜".
Length: 12⅜" over-all. **Weight:** 40.5 oz.
Power: Spring air.
Features: Micrometer rear sight. Interchangeable rear sight blades. Target grips. Bbl. weight available at extra cost. Interarms, Alexandria, Va.
Price: **$93.00**

WEBLEY AIR PISTOLS

Model:	**Junior**	**Premier**
Caliber:	177	177 or 22
Barrel:	6⅛"	6½"
Weight:	23¼ oz.	37 oz.
Power:	Spring, barrel cocking	Same
Sights:	Adj. for w.	Adj. for w.&e.
Trigger:	Fixed	Adj.
Price:	**$44.50**	**$49.95**

Features: Single stroke cocking, heavy steel construction, blued. Imported by A.R.H., Beeman's, Fanta.

WEIHRAUCH HW-70 AIR PISTOL

Caliber: 177, single shot.
Barrel: 6¼", rifled.
Length: 12¾" over-all. **Weight:** 38 oz.
Sights: Hooded post front, square notch rear adj. for w. and e.
Power: Spring, barrel cocking.
Features: Adj. trigger. 24-lb. cocking effort, 365 f.p.s. M.V.; automatic safety. Air Rifle HQ, Beeman's, importers.
Price: .... **$49.95** to **$58.50**

WINCHESTER 363 TARGET PISTOL

Caliber: 177, single shot.
Barrel: 7" rifled.
Length: 16". **Weight:** 3 lbs.
Power: Spring, barrel cocking.
Features: Recoil-less firing, adj. double pull type trigger, hooded front sight with 3 apertures, click adj. rear sight. Plastic thumbrest target grips. M.V. 378 fps.
Price: **$55.95**

PELLET GUNS—HANDGUNS

WINCHESTER 353 TARGET PISTOL

Caliber: 177 or 22, single shot.
Barrel: 7″ rifled.
Length: 16″. **Weight:** 2 lbs. 11 oz.
Power: Spring, barrel cocking.
Features: Plastic thumbrest target grips. Adj. double pull trigger, Micro rear sight, detachable bead front with hood. M.V. 378 fps.
Price: 22 cal. **$41.95**
Price: 177 cal. **$48.95**

WISCHO CUSTOM MATCH PISTOL

Caliber: 177, single shot.
Barrel: 7″ rifled.
Length: 15.8″ over-all. **Weight:** 45 oz.
Stocks: Walnut with thumbrest.
Sights: Hooded bead front, rear adj. for w. and e.
Power: Spring, barrel cocking.
Features: Cocking effort of 17 lbs.; M.V. 450 f.p.s.; adj. trigger. Optional scope and mount available from A.R.H. (**$54.50** installed). Air Rifle HQ, Beeman's importers.
Price: .... **$59.95** to **$88.50**

PELLET GUNS—LONG GUNS

AMPELL BB MAGNUM RIFLE

Caliber: BB, 48-shot magazine.
Length: 38″ over-all. **Weight:** 4¼ lbs.
Sights: Blade front, rear square notch adj. for w. and e.
Power: Spring, Pump cocking
Features: Hardwood stock, cross-bolt safety, 4-5 lb. trigger pull.
Price: **$26.50**

ANSCHUTZ 335 RIFLE

Caliber: 177, single-shot.
Barrel: 18½″, 12-groove, rifled.
Length: 43″ over-all. **Weight:** 7 lbs.
Power: Spring, barrel-cocking.
Stock: Checkered M.C. Stock with cheekpiece and white line spacer buttplate.
Sights: Tunnel front with blade, open rear adj. for w. & e.
Features: Special safety latch to prevent barrel backlash when breech is open. Imported by Beeman's.
Price: With open sight **$89.95**
Price: With #6706 match aperture sight **$119.95**

ANSCHUTZ 250 TARGET RIFLE

Caliber: 177, single shot.
Barrel: 18½″, rifled, one piece with receiver.
Length: 45″. **Weight:** 11 lbs. with sights.
Power: Spring, side-lever cocking, 17 lb. pull.
Features: Recoil-less operation. Two-stage adj. trigger. Checkered walnut p.g. stock with Monte Carlo comb & cheekpiece; adj. buttplate; accessory rail. Imported by Beeman's.
Price: Without sights **$179.50**
With #6723 match sight set **$204.50**

ANSCHUTZ 275 REPEATER AIR RIFLE

Caliber: 173 (4.4 mm) lead balls, 6-shot clip.
Length: 41.3″ over-all. **Weight:** 5.7 lbs.
Stock: Walnut finished hardwood.
Power: Spring air; piston cocked by bolt like Haenel or Mauser trainers.
Sights: Open, fixed.
Features: Approx. 450 fps. Rigid barrel/receiver unit. Imported by Beeman's.
Price: **$137.50**

BENJAMIN 3030 CO^2 REPEATER

Caliber: BB only.
Barrel: 25½″, smoothbore, takedown.
Length: 36″. **Weight:** 4 lbs.
Power: Standard CO^2 cylinder.
Features: Hammer lock safety. 30-shot repeater with permanent-magnet shot-holder ammo feed.
Price: **$31.75**

PELLET GUNS—LONG GUNS

BENJAMIN SERIES 3100 SUPER REPEATER RIFLES

Caliber: BB, 100-shot; 22, 85-shot.
Barrel: 23″, rifled or smoothbore.
Length: 35″. **Weight:** 6¼ lbs.
Power: Hand pumped.
Features: Bolt action. Piggy back full view magazine. Bar V adj. rear sight. Walnut stock and pump handle.
Price: M3100, BB .... **$50.00** M3120, 22 rifled **$50.00**

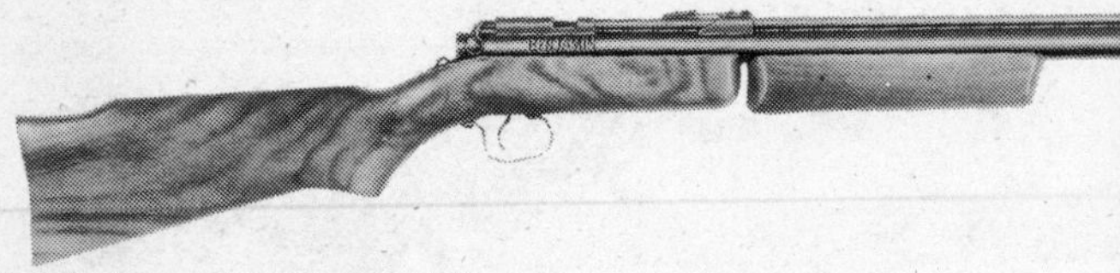

BENJAMIN SERIES 340 AIR RIFLE

Caliber: 22 and 177 pellets or BB; single shot.
Barrel: 23″, rifled and smoothbore.
Length: 35″. **Weight:** 6 lbs.
Power: Hand pumped.
Features: Bolt action, walnut Monte Carlo stock and pump handle. Ramp-type front sight, adj. leaf type rear. Push-pull safety.
Price: M340, BB **$48.95**
Price: M342, 22 .... **$48.95** M347, 177 .... **$48.95**

BSF S-54 AIR RIFLES

Model:	S-54 Std.	S-54 Match	S-54 Bayern
Caliber:	177	177	177
Barrel:	19⅜″	19⅜″	19⅜″
Rifled:	Yes	Yes	Yes
Weight:	7¾ lbs.	8¾ lbs.	8 lbs.
MV:	669	669	669
Sights:	Adj.	Adj.	Adj.
Price:	**$110.00**	**$130.00**	**$120.00**

Features: Spring powered, under lever cocking. Adj. 2-stage triggers. All three models are mechanically identical. Bayern and Match have select walnut stocks with checkered p.g. and fore-end. Match has polished, semi-curved aluminum buttplate. Standard has polished beech stock. Walnut optional at $4.00 extra. Beeman's imports only S-54 Match. Fanta imports all three.

BSF AIR RIFLES

Model:	Junior	Bavaria 30	Media 45
Caliber:	177	177	177 or 22
Barrel:	15¼″	13½″	16″
Rifled:	Yes	Yes	Yes
Length:	38⅛″	34½″	39½″
Weight:	4½ lbs.	3½ lbs.	5¾ lbs.
MV:	561 fps.	465 fps.	682, 560 fps.
Sights:	Adj.	Adj.	Adj.
Price:	**$51.00**	**$42.00**	**$66.00**

Features: Spring powered, barrel cocking. Polished beech stocks. Adj. triggers. Blued metal parts. Bavaria 30, Junior, Media 45 available from Fanta. Beeman's imports only the Model Media 45.

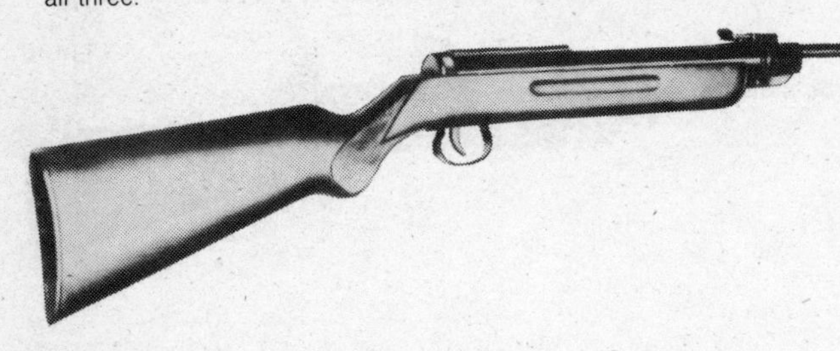

BSF 55, S-60, S-70 RIFLES

Model:	Bavaria 55	S-60 (illus.)	S-70
Caliber:	177 or 22	177 or 22	177
Barrel:	16″	19″	19″
Rifled:	Yes	Yes	Yes
Length:	40½″	43½″	43¾″
Weight:	6¼ lbs.	6½ lbs.	6½ lbs.
MV:	763, 605	763, 605	763
Sights:	Elev. only	w. & e.	w. & e.
Price:	**$93.00**	**$95.00**	**$107.00**

Features: Spring powered, barrel cocking. Blued metal. Adj. 2-stage triggers. Beech stocks on B-55 and S-60. walnut stocks (optional) have checkered p.g. S-70 mechanically identical to S-60, Beech, checkered p.g. and fore-end. Raised cheek pad, curved rubber buttplate. Beeman's imports only Bavaria 55, Fanta imports all three.

CROSMAN MODEL 70 CO^2 BOLT ACTION RIFLE

Caliber: 177 pellet, single-shot.
Barrel: 23¾″, rifled steel.
Length: 41″ over-all. **Weight:** 5¾ lbs.
Stock: Full-size hardwood, walnut finish, Monte Carlo-style.
Sights: Blade front, rear adjustable for w. and e.
Features: Average velocity 650 fps. Full sized gun. Cross bolt safety. Each powerlet (12.5 grams) gives an average of 40 shots. Crosman 4X Superscope and mounts available separately ($13.00).
Price: **$39.95**
Price: With scope and mounts **$52.95**

CROSMAN POWERMATIC "500"

Caliber: BB, 50-shot semiautomatic.
Barrel: 18″, smoothbore steel.
Length: 37¾″. **Weight:** 4½ lbs.
Power: Crosman CO^2 Powerlet.
Features: Positive safety, over 100 shots from one Powerlet. Walnut finished stock, grooved receiver for optional scope or peep sight. Rear sight is adjustable for windage and elevation.
Price: **$27.75**

CROSMAN M-1 CARBINE

Caliber: BB, 270-shot.
Barrel: Smoothbore, steel.
Length: 35⅝″. **Weight:** 4½ lbs.
Power: Spring.
Features: Patterned after U.S. M1 carbine, uses slide action cocking, military type adj. sights. Hardwood stock.
Price: **$22.15**

PELLET GUNS—LONG GUNS

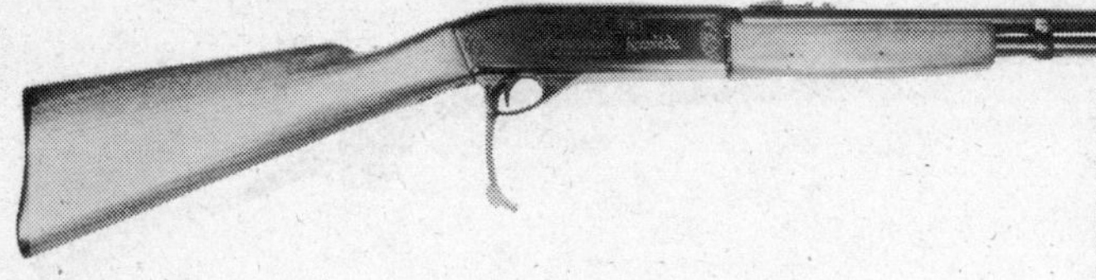

CROSMAN RAWHIDE 125 PUMP RIFLE

Caliber: BB only, 35-shot magazine.
Barrel: 20¼".
Length: 36" over-all. **Weight:** 5 lbs.
Stock: Wood grain high impact plastic stock and fore-end.
Sights: Blade front, step adj. rear for w. and e.
Features: Average velocity 300 fps. Short stroke single pump pneumatic action. Engraved die-cast receiver, solid steel barrel. Force feed magazine. Crossbolt safety. Comes with leather thong and saddle ring.
Price: $20.00

CROSMAN MODEL 3500 SLIDEMASTER

Caliber: BB, 22-shot slide action.
Barrel: 18", smoothbore steel.
Length: 35½". **Weight:** 4 lbs.
Power: High compression spring.
Features: Fast and easy cocking, hooded post front sight and fully adjustable rear sight. Scope and mount optional. High comb Monte Carlo stock.
Price: $19.30

CROSMAN 761XL PUMP RIFLE

Caliber: BB, 180-shot or 177 cal. pellet (single-shot).
Power: Hand pumped.
Barrel: 19", button rifled.
Length: 36" over-all. **Weight:** 4¾ lbs.
Stock: Full-size, walnut.
Sights: Hooded front, step adj. rear for w. & e.
Features: Receiver grooved for scope mounting, gold-colored receiver, cross-bolt safety.
Price: $36.40
Price: $10.95

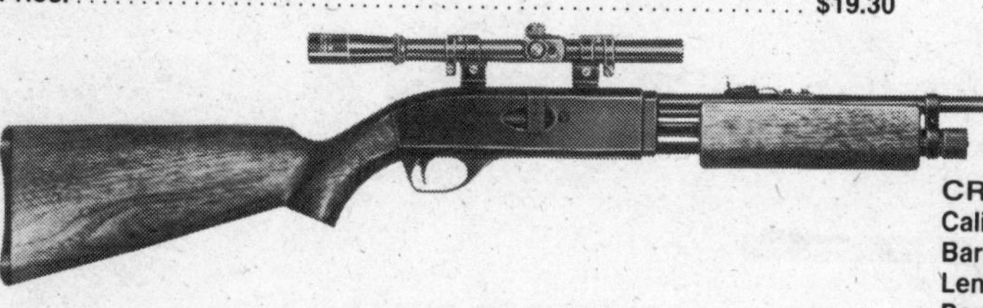

CROSMAN 622 PELL-CLIP REPEATER

Caliber: 22, 6-shot rotating, clip
Barrel: 23"
Length: 40". **Weight:** 6½ lbs.
Power: Crosman CO^2 Powerlet, pump action
Features: Removable 6-shot pell clip. Adjustable rear sight. Scope and mount extra.
Price: $39.75

CROSMAN MODEL 760 POWERMASTER

Caliber: BB, 180 shot.
Barrel: 19½", smoothbore steel.
Length: 35". **Weight:** 4⅛ lbs.
Power: High compression spring.
Features: Short stroke, power determined by number of strokes. Walnut finished checkered stock and forearm. Post front sight and adjustable rear sight. Cross-bolt safety. Scope and mount optional.
Price: $27.75

CROSMAN 1400 RIFLE

Caliber: 22, single shot.
Barrel: 19½", rifled steel.
Length: 35½". **Weight:** About 6 lbs.
Power: Hand pumped.
Features: Bolt action. Air-Trol valve prevents air lock from over-pumping. Adj. trigger, left or right hand safety. Scope and mount optional.
Price: $40.20

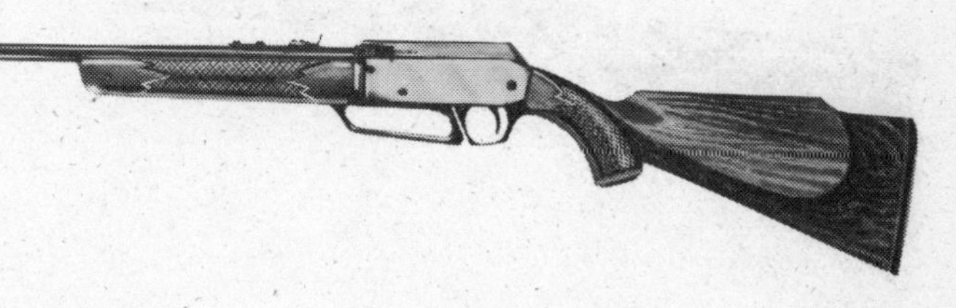

DAISY POWER-LINE 881 PUMP-UP AIR GUN

Caliber: 177 pellets, BB
Barrel: Decagon rifled.
Length: 37¾" over-all. **Weight:** 6 lbs.
Power: Spring air.
Stock: Wood grain moulded plastic with Monte Carlo cheekpiece.
Sights: Ramp front, step-adj. rear for e.
Features: Accurized version of Model 880. Checkered fore-end and p.g.
Price: $39.00

DAISY MODEL 450

Caliber: 177, 5-shot.
Barrel: 11", rifled.
Length: 37". **Weight:** 3⅛ lbs.
Stock: Monte Carlo design wood stock, beavertail fore-end.
Sights: Post-ramp front, rear adj. for w. and e.
Power: Spring, lever cocking.
Features: Automatic safety, removable "Rota-Clip" magazine.
Price: $26.00
Price: Model 400 (feather-weight version, weighs 2½ lbs.) $18.25
Price: Model 452 (better sights) about $27.00

DAISY 5694 TEXAS RANGER COMMEMORATIVE CARBINE

Caliber: BB, 40-shot.
Barrel: 17½". Coined with "1823-The Texas Rangers-1973".
Length: 38⅜" over-all. **Weight:** 3¾ lbs.
Stock: Molded plastic, with mounted Texas Ranger commemorative seal.
Sights: Post ramp front, adjustable open rear.
Features: "Spittin' image" carbine. Exclusive case-hardened plating on receiver. Replica of Texas Ranger badge mounted on receiver. 2-way lever cocking, side-loading port. In special commemorative package including a 48-page history of the Texas Rangers.
Price: $27.50

DAISY POWER-LINE 880 PUMP-UP AIR GUN
Caliber: 177 pellets, BB.
Barrel: Smoothbore, steel.
Length: 37¾″ over-all. **Weight:** 6 lbs.
Power: Spring air.
Stock: Wood grain moulded plastic.
Sights: Ramp front, open rear adj. for e.
Features: Variable power (velocity and range) increase with pump strokes. 10 strokes for maximum power. 100-shot BB magazine. Cross-bolt trigger safety. Positive cocking valve.
Price: **$33.00**

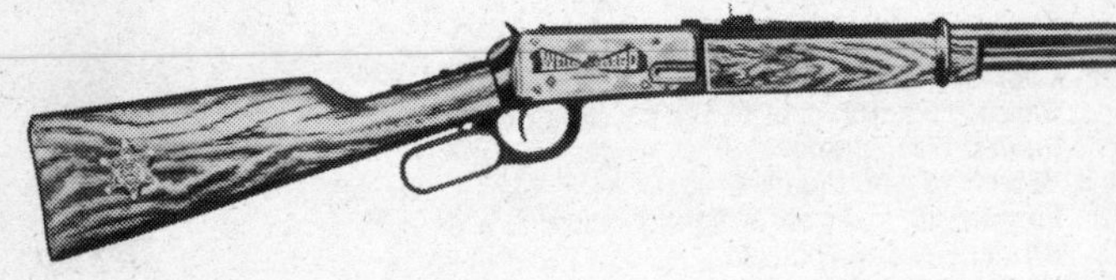

DAISY MODEL 5994 WELLS FARGO COMMEMORATIVE
Caliber: BB only.
Barrel: Smoothbore.
Length: 38⅜″ over-all. **Weight:** 3 lbs.
Power: Spring air.
Stock: Wood grain moulded plastic with replica Wells Fargo agent's star.
Sights: Post ramp front, step adj. rear for e.
Features: Antiqued gun metal receiver with Wells Fargo design. Side loading port. 40-shot magazine.
Price: **$27.50**

DAISY CO² 300 REPEATER
Caliber: BB, 5-shot semi-auto.
Barrel: 22″, smoothbore.
Length: 37¼″. **Weight:** 2 lbs. 14 oz.
Power: Daisy 8.5 or 12 gram CO² cylinder.
Features: Free-style stock, cross-bolt safety, 200 shot magazine capacity, blade front, adj. open rear sights, receiver grooved for scope.
Price: **$39.00**

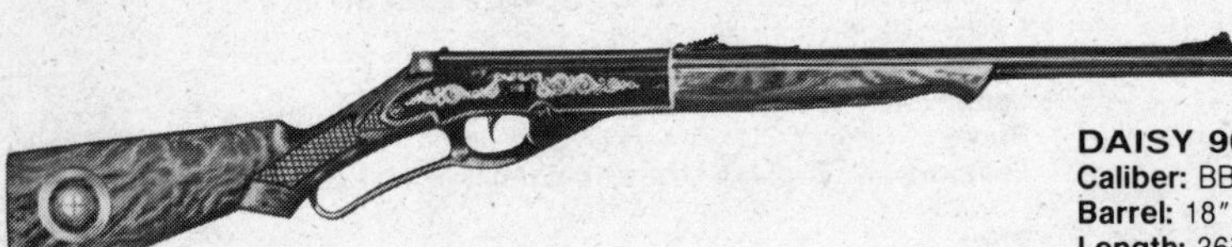

DAISY 90 SPORTSTER BB RIFLE
Caliber: BB, 700-shot repeater action.
Barrel: 18″, smoothbore.
Length: 36¾″ over-all. **Weight:** 3 lbs.
Stock: Molded plastic.
Sights: Post ramp front, open rear.
Features: Modern sports styling. Lever cocking. Simulated gold engraving on receiver section. Automatic safety. Steel receiver.
Price: **$17.00**

DAISY 25 PUMP GUN
Caliber: BB, 50-shot.
Barrel: 18″, smoothbore.
Length: 37¼″. **Weight:** NA.
Power: Pump cocking spring.
Features: Ramp front and adj. rear sights. BBs are spring-force fed.
Price: **$21.00**

DAISY MODEL 86/70 SAFARI MK. I
Caliber: BB, 240-shot.
Barrel: 11″ smooth.
Length: 34¼″. **Weight:** 2 lbs.
Sights: Ramp front, V-notch rear.
Features: Plastic stock and fore-end, force-feed magazine. Trigger-guard cocking action with cross-bolt safety.
Price: **$15.75**

DAISY HIGH POWER RIFLES

Model:	**160**	**225**	**230**	**250**
Caliber:	177 & BB	177	22	22
Barrel:	12″	15¾″	15¾″	15¾″
Rifled:	No	Yes	Yes	Yes
Length:	33½″	5 lbs.	37½″	39″
Weight:	3 lbs.	37½″	5 lbs.	5½ lbs.
Power:	Spring	Spring	Spring	Spring
Price:	**$22.75**	**$38.75**	**$40.50**	**$48.50**

Features: All are barrel cocking with beechwood stocks. 160 and 220 have bead front and adj. rear sights. 230 and 250 have blade front and adj. rear target sights.

The product prices mentioned in these catalog pages were correct at presstime, but may be higher when you read this.

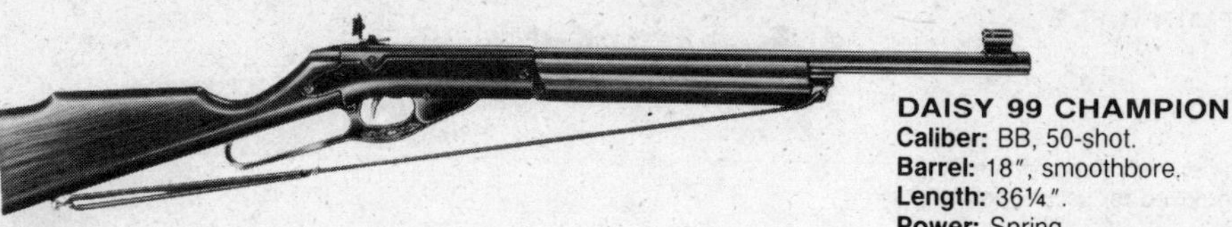

DAISY 99 CHAMPION
Caliber: BB, 50-shot.
Barrel: 18″, smoothbore.
Length: 36¼″.
Power: Spring.
Features: Wood stock, beavertail fore-end; sling; hooded front sight with four insert apertures, adj. aperture rear, stock medallion.
Price: **$25.00**

DAISY/FWB 4300
Caliber: 177, single shot.
Barrel: 29¼″, rifled.
Length: 45″. **Weight:** 11 lbs.
Stock: Walnut, Monte Carlo cheekpiece, checkered palmswell p.g.
Sights: Globe front with inserts, micro. adj. peep rear.
Power: Spring, barrel cocking.
Features: Adj. trigger, adj. buttplate.
Price: **$325.00**

DAISY RIFLES

Model:	**95**	**102**	**104**	**111**
Caliber:	BB	BB	BB	BB
Barrel:	18″	13½″	13½″	18″
Length:	35″	30¼″	30½″	35″
Power:	Spring	Spring	Spring	Spring
Capacity:	700	350	350	700
Price:	**$16.00**	**$11.30**	**$13.00**	**$15.00**

Features: 95 stock is wood, fore-end plastic; 111 and 104 have plastic stocks; 102 has wood stock; 104 has sighting tube w/aperture and is gold finished.

DAISY MODEL 7404 PELLET RIFLE
Caliber: 177.
Barrel: Smoothbore.
Length: 35½″ over-all. **Weight:** 4¼ lbs.
Power: Spring air.
Stock: Stained hardwood with Monte Carlo cheekpiece.
Sights: Post ramp front, step adj. rear for e.
Features: 5-shot repeater with removeable "Rota-Clip" pellet cylinder. Auto. trigger block safety. Model 7454 has rifled barrel.
Price: Model 7454 .... **$27.25**
Price: Model 7404 .... **$18.25**

DAISY 1894 SPITTIN' IMAGE CARBINE
Caliber: BB, 40-shot.
Barrel: 17½″, smoothbore.
Length: 38⅜″.
Power: Spring.
Features: Cocks halfway on forward stroke of lever, halfway on return.
Price: **$24.50**

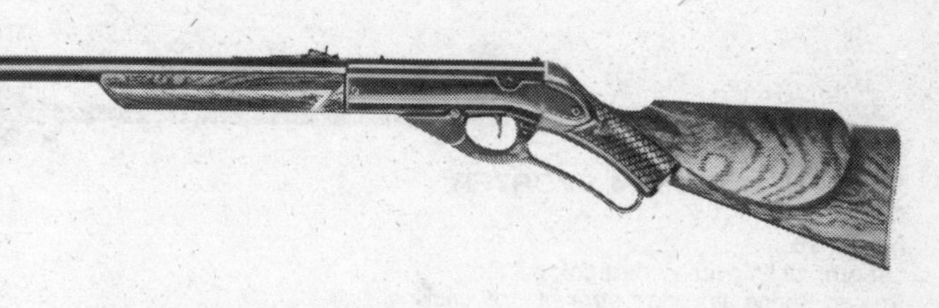

DAISY MODEL 98 MONTE CARLO BB RIFLE
Caliber: BB only.
Barrel: Smoothbore.
Length: 36″ over-all. **Weight:** 4 lbs.
Power: Spring air.
Stock: Wood grain moulded plastic with Monte Carlo cheekpiece.
Sights: Post ramp front, open rear adj. for e.
Features: Lever cocking, gravity feed. 700-shot magazine. Auto. trigger block safety.
Price: **$22.00**

DAISY 7938 RED RYDER COMMEMORATIVE BB CARBINE
Caliber: BB, 700-shot repeating action.
Barrel: Sturdy steel, under-barrel loading port.
Length: 35″ over-all. **Weight:** 3½ lbs.
Stock: Wood stock burned with Red Ryder lariat signature.
Sights: Post front, adjustable V-slot rear.
Features: Wood fore-end. Saddle ring with leather thong. Lever cocking. Gravity feed. Controlled velocity. Commemorates one of Daisy's most popular guns, the Red Ryder of the 1940s and 1950s.
Price: **$20.50**

EL GAMO REPEATER AIR RIFLE
Caliber: 177, 25-shot.
Barrel: 17½″, 12 groove rifling.
Length: 37½″. **Weight:** 6½ lbs.
Power: Spring, barrel cocking.
Features: M.V. 675 fps. Micro, adj. target sights, adj. trigger; target type recoil pad, M.C. comb and cheekpiece. Precise Imports, importer.
Price: **$90.00**

El Gamo Single Shot Rifle
Same as repeater version except: available in either 177 or 22 cal.; over-all length 41″, weight 5¼ lbs.
Price: **$64.00**

PELLET GUNS—LONG GUNS

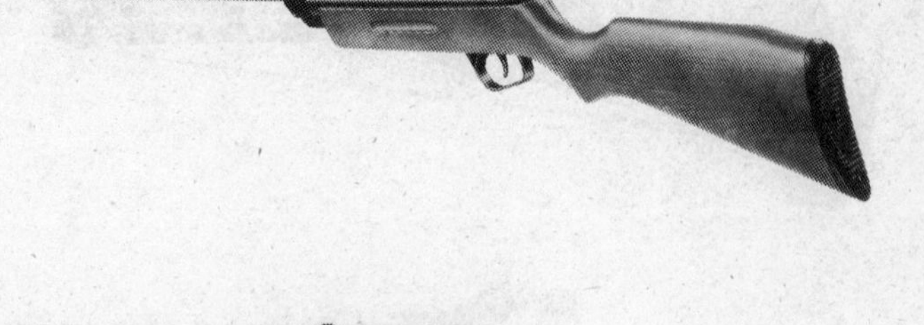

PRECISE/EL GAMO TOURNAMENT AIR RIFLE

Caliber: 177, 22, single shot.
Barrel: 18". 12-groove rifling.
Length: 43" over-all. **Weight:** 6¾ lbs.
Power: Spring, barrel cocking.
Features: Micro. adj. rear sight, hooded front. Walnut finish stock; Monte Carlo comb with cheek piece, recoil pad. Receiver grooved for scope mounting. Precise Imports, importer.
Price: **$50.00**

Precise/El Gamo Carbine Air Rifle
Same as Tournament model except has plain stock without Monte Carlo comb, cheekpiece **$28.00**

FEINWERKBAU 300-S TYROLEAN MATCH RIFLE

Caliber: 177, single shot.
Barrel: 19.9".
Length: 42.8" over-all. **Weight:** 9.5 lbs.
Power: Spring air, sidelever.
Stock: Walnut. High Tyrolean cheekpiece, medium-weight fore-end.
Sights: Globe front with inserts, micro. adj. rear aperture.
Features: Barrel and receiver recoil together to eliminate felt recoil. 4-way adj. trigger. Muzzle velocity 640 fps. Optional 12 oz. bbl. sleeve. Imported by A.R.H. and Beeman's.
Price: .... **$294.50** to **$428.00**

Feinwerkbau 200 Rifle
Same as F'bau 300 except: has slight recoil effect; 20" bbl., 640 fps. M.V. Imported by Daisy.
Price: **$144.50**

FEINWERKBAU 300-S SERIES MATCH RIFLES

Caliber: 177.
Barrel: 19.9", fixed solid with receiver.
Length: 42.8" over-all. **Weight:** Approx. 10 lbs. with optional bbl. sleeve.
Power: Single stroke sidelever, spring piston.
Stock: Match model—walnut, deep fore-end, adj. buttplate. Std. model—walnut finish, lighter weight, regular fore-end, lacks p.g. cap.
Sights: Globe front with interchangeable inserts. Click micro. adj. match aperture rear.
Features: Recoilless, vibration-free. Grooved for scope mounts. Permanent lubrication and seals. cocking effort 9 lbs. Optional 10 oz. bbl. sleeve. Imported by A.R.H. and Beeman's.
Price: Standard **$258.50**
Price: 300-S Match .... **$278.50** to **$378.50**

FEINWERKBAU 124 SPORTER

Caliber: 177.
Barrel: 18.3".
Length: 43.5" over-all. **Weight:** 6.3 lbs.
Power: Spring air; single stroke barrel cocking.
Stock: Walnut finished hardwood.
Sights: Tunnel front, fully adj. open rear.
Features: Velocity over 780 fps. Cocking effort 19 lbs. Automatic safety, adj. trigger. Standard model has no checkering or cheekpiece. Deluxe has checkered p.g. and fore-end, high comb cheekpiece, sling swivels. Imported by A.R.H. and Beeman's.
Price: Standard model **$139.50**
Price: Deluxe model (illus. below) **$154.50**
Price: Deluxe left-hand **$159.50**

Feinwerkbau 124 Custom Sporter
Same as Standard 124 except assembled in U.S. with select American walnut stock with rollover cheekpiece, rosewood p.g. cap, white line spacers, rubber buttplate, choice of super gloss or semi-gloss finish. Velocity approx. 790 fps, cocking effort 18 lbs. Special thumbhole stock. Accurized version of 124. Imported and assembled by Beeman's **$264.50**

HY-SCORE 809M TARGET RIFLE

Caliber: 22, single shot.
Barrel: 19" rifled.
Length: 44". **Weight:** 7 pounds.
Power: Spring, bbl. cocking.
Features: Adj. target receiver sight, aperture front with 4 inserts, in addition to open adj. middle sight also with 4 apertures.
Price: **$64.95**

The product prices mentioned in these catalog pages were correct at presstime, but may be higher when you read this.

HY-SCORE 810M OLYMPIC INTERNATIONAL RIFLE

Caliber: 177, single shot.
Barrel: 19¼" 12-groove rifled.
Length: 44". **Weight:** 9½ lbs.
Power: Spring (barrel cocking).
Features: Full cheekpiece, Monte Carlo stock, hand checkered; grooved fore-end, curved rubber buttplate. Adj. target receiver sight (includes 4 apertures), hooded front sight (includes 4 inserts).
Price: **$99.95**

M810SM Super Match

As above but with weight increased to 14 lbs., bbl. locking device, adj. stock, replaceable mainspring, MV 580 fps, accuracy tested: ¼" spread at 33'
Price: **$169.95**

HY-SCORE RIFLES

Model:	**801**	**806**	**807**	**808**	**813**
Caliber:	22	177	22	177	22
Barrel:	15¾"	14½"	17⅜"	12"	14¼"
Rifled:	Yes	Yes	Yes	No	Yes
Length:	38½"	36½"	41¾"	33"	36½"
Weight:	5 lbs.	3¾ lbs.	5 lbs. 14 oz.	3 lbs.	4 lbs.
Power:	Spring	Spring	Spring	Spring	Spring
Price:	**$29.95**	**$19.95**	**$39.95**	**$14.95**	**$25.95**

Features: All are barrel cocking. All have adj. sights and regular triggers except 807, which has an adj. trigger. Staeble 2.2X scope and mt. available for all but 808, **$14.95.**
M813 and scope available at a combination price of **$33.40**
M801 available as 801M with click adj. receiver sight **$49.95**

ITHACA BSA METEOR & MECURY RIFLES

Caliber: 177 or 22.
Barrel: 18½" rifled.
Length: 42" over-all. **Weight:** 6 lbs. (Meteor), 7 lbs. (Mercury)
Stock: European hardwood. Mercury has Monte Carlo.
Sights: Blade front, micro. adj. rear (Meteor). Mecury has hooded front.
Features: Meteor—barrel cocking action. Adjustable single stage trigger, 3-5 lb. pull. Receiver dovetailed for standard scope mounts. 650 fps (177 cal.); 500 fps (22 cal.). Mercury—700 fps (177), 550 fps (22), comes with pellets, target, target holder and lubricant. Imported by Ithaca.
Price: Meteor **$34.95**
Price: Mercury **$74.95**

MARKSMAN 740 AIR RIFLE

Caliber: 177, 400-shot.
Barrel: 15½", smoothbore.
Length: 36½". **Weight:** 4 lbs., 2 oz.
Power: Spring, barrel cocking.
Features: Automatic safety; fixed front, adj. rear sights; shoots 177 cal. BB's pellets and darts.
Price: **$19.95**
Also available as Model 742 "shorty" with 10" bbl. and o.a. length of 31".
Price: **$19.95**

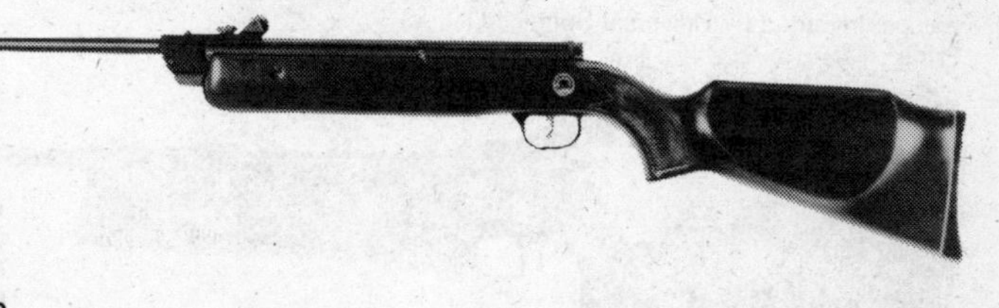

MARKSMAN MODEL 746 RIFLE

Caliber: 177 or 22, single-shot.
Barrel: 15".
Length: 42" over-all. **Weight:** 6½ lbs.
Stock: Beech. Monte Carlo cheekpiece, checkered p.g.
Sights: Hooded post front, micro rear adj. for w. and e.
Features: Velocity of 580 fps; 3½ lb. trigger pull; cocking effort of 22 lbs. Metal parts blued. Receiver grooved for scope mounting.
Price: Approx. **$75.00**

NATIONAL "VOLCANIC" SHOTGUN/RIFLE #730

Caliber: 25, single-shot, shot or pellet.
Barrel: 20", interchangeable smoothbore and rifled barrels.
Length: 37" over-all. **Weight:** 6½ lbs.
Power: Hand pumped, swinging fore-end.
Sights: Blade front, open rear adj. for e.
Features: Use rifled bbl. for heavy 25 cal. lead balls or pellets or quickly install smoothbore bbl. for use of refillable plastic cartridges containing from 4 to 100 #8 birdshot. Available from Beeman's.
Price: With rifle and shotgun barrels. **$89.95**

PIC CO^2 BOBCAT BOLT ACTION RIFLE

Caliber: 177, 22, single-shot.
Barrel: 19¼".
Length: 35" over-all. **Weight:** 4¾ lbs.
Power: Standard CO^2 cartridges.
Features: Walnut finish stock; receiver grooved for scope mounting. Precise Imports, importer.
Price: **$38.00**

PRECISE/SLAVIA MODEL 624

Caliber: 177, single-shot.
Barrel: 16", rifled.
Length: 38" over-all. **Weight:** 3¾ lbs.
Stock: Walnut finish hardwood, p.g., no buttplate or p.g. cap.
Sights: Hooded front, open leaf rear.
Features: Muzzle velocity 371 fps, barrel-cocking action. Imported by Precise Imports.
Price: **$30.00**

SMITH & WESSON MODEL 77A

Caliber: 22, single shot.
Barrel: 22", rifled.
Length: 40" over-all. **Weight:** 6½ lbs.
Power: Hand pumped, swinging fore-end.
Stock: Hardwood, p.g., M.C., walnut finish.
Sights: Blade front, adj. notch rear.
Features: Automatic safety, receiver grooved for scope mounting.
Price.. **$42.50**

SHERIDAN BLUE AND SILVER STREAK RIFLES

Caliber: 5mm (20 cal.), single shot.
Barrel: 18½", rifled.
Length: 37". **Weight:** 5 lbs.
Power: Hand pumped (swinging fore-end).
Features: Rustproof barrel and piston tube. Takedown. Thumb safety. Mannlicher type walnut stock. Left-hand models same price.
Price: Blue Streak .... **$53.25** Silver Streak **$54.25**
Sheridan accessories: Intermount, a base for ⅜" Tip-Off scope mounts, **$6.75**; Sheridan-Williams 5DSH receiver sight, **$7.25** Sheridan Pelletrap, **$15.50**; Model 222 Targetrap **$39.25**; Model 333 Targetrap **$22.50**; Sheridan 5mm pellets, **$2.75** for 500. Weaver 4 x scope and Intermount installed **$17.70 (extra).**

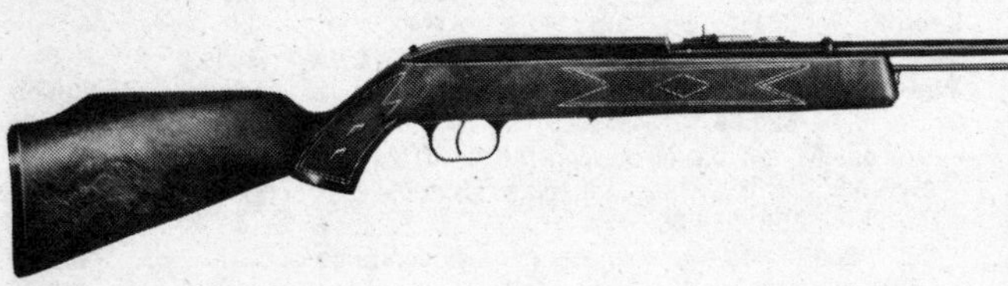

SMITH & WESSON MODEL 80 AUTO BB RIFLE

Caliber: BB, 50-shot tube magazine.
Barrel: 22".
Length: 39" over-all. **Weight:** 3¼ lbs.
Power: Standard CO^2 cylinder.
Stock: Walnut color, checkered, wood grain finish.
Sights: Ramp front, fully adj. rear.
Features: Top tang safety, receiver grooved for scope mounting, gas cut-off, fast CO^2 cartridge loading.
Price:.. **$27.95**

UNIVERSAL BAIKAL IJ-22 AIR RIFLE

Caliber: 177, single-shot.
Barrel: 18", 12-groove rifling.
Weight: 5 lbs.
Stock: Walnut with full p.g. Plastic buttplate and p.g. cap.
Sights: Blade front, rear adj. for w. and e.
Power: Spring air, barrel cocking.
Features: Safety interlock mechanism prevents firing unless completely closed. 775 fps. Comes with cleaning rod, replacement springs and piston cups. Imported by Universal Sporting Goods.
Price:.. **$39.95**

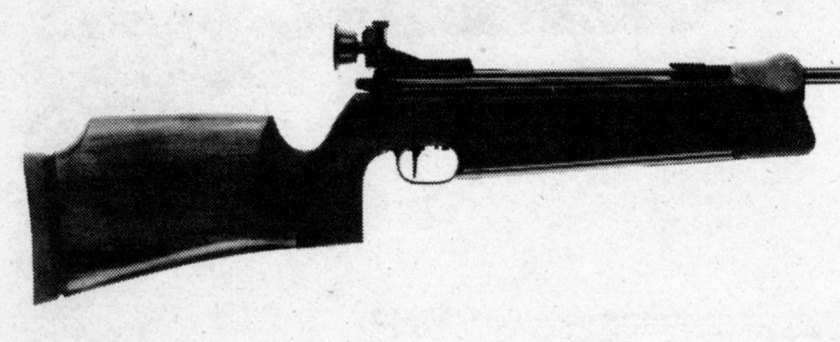

WALTHER LGR RIFLE

Caliber: 177, single-shot.
Barrel: 19½", rifled.
Length: 44¼" over-all. **Weight:** 10.2 lbs.
Power: Side lever cocking, compressed air.
Stock: French walnut.
Sights: Replaceable insert hooded front, Walther micro. adjustable rear.
Features: Recoilless operation. Trigger adj. for weight, pull and position. High comb stock with broad stippled fore-end and p.g. Imported by Interarms.
Price:.. **$290.00**

WALTHER LGV SPECIAL

Caliber: 177, single shot.
Barrel: 16", rifled.
Length: 41⅜". **Weight:** 11¼ lbs.
Power: Spring air (barrel cocking).
Features: Micro. click adj. aperture receiver sight; Adj. trigger. Walnut match stock, adj. buttplate. Double piston provides vibration-free shooting. Easily operated bbl. latch. Removable heavy bbl. sleeve. 5-way adj. trigger. Imported by Interarms.
Price:.. **$235.00**

WEBLEY U/L AIR RIFLES

Model:	Mark III	Mark III Supertarget
Caliber:	177 or 22	177
Barrel:	18½"	18½" heavy
Rifled:	Yes	Yes
Sights:	Open, adj.	Parker Hale peep
Weight:	7¼ lbs.	8¼ lbs.
Power:	Spring air	Spring air
Price:	**$125.00**	**$175.00**

Features: High luster blue finish. Adjustable triggers. Supertarget has six hole aperture sight and stock holds interchangeable front sight elements. Imported by Fanta Air Rifles, Universal Sporting Goods.

PELLET GUNS—LONG GUNS

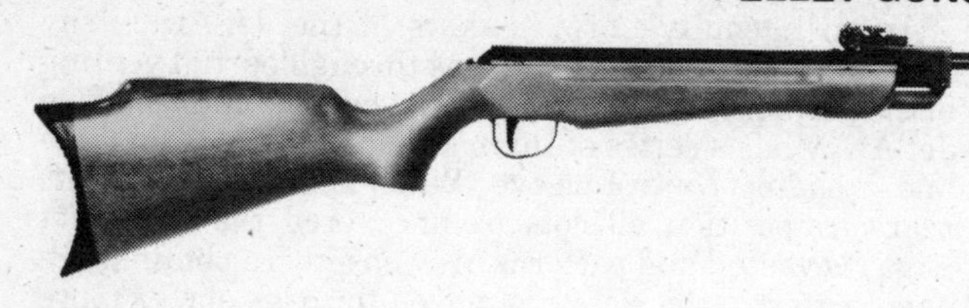

WISCHO 70 SPORTING RIFLE

Caliber: 177 or 22, single shot.
Barrel: 16¼", rifled.
Length: 41". **Weight:** 6¼ lbs.
Power: Spring (barrel cocking).
Features: High velocity (750 fps in 177) and accuracy combined with rapid loading, can be reloaded in 5 seconds. Stock is walnut finished with checkered p.g. and buttplate. Open rear, bead front sights; receiver grooved for scope mounting. Trigger is adjustable. Air Rifle Headquarters, Beeman's, importers.
Price: . . . . **$104.50** to **$158.50**

WEIHRAUCH 30 & 50 SERIES RIFLES

Model:	30 M-II	30S	50S	50E
Caliber:	177	177	177	177
Barrel:	16⅞"	16⅞"	18½"	18½"
Trigger:	fixed	fixed	adj.	adj.
Length:	40"	40"	43½"	43½"
Wgt., lbs.:	5½	5½	7	7¼
Price:	$68.50	$79.50 to $86.50	$98.50	$108.50 to $124.50

Features: All are rifled and spring-operated by single stroke cocking. Post and ramp front sights (except 50S and 50E have globe fronts with 4 inserts). Open click rear sights, adj. for w. & e., except 30 Mk-11 has lock-screw windage. Walnut finished stocks. 50E has cheek-piece, checkering, ¾" sling swivels. MV of all 660-67 fps. Models 30M-11 and 50S available from Beeman's only. Air Rifle Hdqtrs., Beeman's, importers.

WEIHRAUCH 55 TARGET RIFLES

Model:	55MM	55MM-L	55T
Caliber:	177	177	177
Barrel:	18½"	18½"	18½"
Length:	43½"	43½"	43½"
Wgt. lbs.:	8	8	8
Rear sight:	aperture	aperture	aperture
Front sight:	All with globe and 4 interchangeable inserts.		
Power:	All with spring (bbl. cocking) .600 fps		
Price:	$194.50 to $198.50	$194.50 to $218.50	$198.50 to $218.50

Features: Trigger fully adj. and removable. Micrometer rear sight adj. for w. and e. on all. P.g. high comb stock with beavertail fore-end, walnut finish stock on 55SM. Walnut stock on 55MM, Tyrolean stock on 55T. Model 55SM available only from Beeman's ($178.50). Air Rifle Hdqtrs., Beeman's, importers.

WINCHESTER HIGH POWER AIR RIFLES

Model:	333	427	435	450
Caliber:	177	22	177	177
Length:	43¼"	42"	44"	44½"
Wgt. lbs.:	9½	6	6½	7¾
Velocity, fps:	576	660	693	693
Price:	$195.95	$60.95	$70.95	$123.95

Features: All are rifled, except 416 (smoothbore), and spring operated by single stroke cocking. **Triggers:** 416, 422 & 423—double pull type triggers. 425, 427 & 435—adjustable double pull type triggers. 333—two stage trigger adj. for wgt., pre-travel & sear-off. **Front sights:** 416 & 422—bead post front sights; 423—blade front sight with ramp. 425 & 427—hooded front sights; 450 & 333—interchangeable front sight assemblies. **Rear Sights:** 416, 422 & 423—adj. screw, 425, 427, 435 & 450—Adj. micro., 333—Adj. diopter. Also, 425, 427, 435 & 450 have dovetail bases for scope mounting. 435, 450 & 333 have rubber butt pads, cheekpieces & checkered p.g. areas. 333 has an auto. safety, when bbl. is open and red indicator when bbl. is closed.

WEBLEY HAWK MK II AIR RIFLE

Caliber: 177 (650 fps), 22 (550 fps).
Barrel: 17⅛", rifled steel.
Length: 42¼" over-all. **Weight:** 6½ lbs.
Power: Spring air, barrel cocking.
Stock: Walnut, full p.g., Monte Carlo, rubber buttplate.
Sights: Hooded post front, fully adj. micro. rear.
Features: Consistent velocity. Adj. trigger, auto. safety. Comes with 2 interchangeable barrels. Imported by Fanta Air Rifles, Universal Sporting Goods.
Price: **$79.50**

WISCHO/BSF S54 RIFLE

Caliber: 177, single shot.
Length: 45½" over-all. **Weight:** 8¼ lbs.
Stock: Walnut finish on std. model. Walnut with checkering and cheepiece on Bayern.
Power: Spring air, underlever.
Sights: Open, adj. on std. and Bayern, aperture on Match model.
Features: Velocity 630 fps, rotating loading tap. Available in three grades. Match model has walnut stock with checkering and Swiss-type cheekpiece. Imported by Beeman's.
Price: Standard model **$115.00**
Price: Bayern model **$129.50**
Price: Match model **$149.50**

WEIHRAUCH 35 TARGET RIFLES

Model:	35/S	35L
Caliber:	177	177
Barrel:	19½"	19½"
Length:	43½"	43½"
Wgt. lbs.:	7.9	8
Rear sight:	open	open
Front sight:	All with globe and 4 interchangeable inserts.	
Power:	All with spring (barrel cocking).	
Price:	$118.50	$128.50 to $139.95

Features: Trigger fully adj. and removable. Open rear sight click adj. for w. and e. P.g. high comb stock with beavertail fore-end, walnut finish, except 35E has checkered walnut with standard cheekpiece. 35L has Tyrolean cheekpiece stock. Model 35S available from Beeman's only. Air Rifle Hdqtrs., Beeman's, importers.

WINCHESTER AIR RIFLES

Model:	416	422	423	425
Calibers:	177	177	177	22
Length:	33"	36"	36"	38"
Wgt. lbs.:	2¾	3¾	4	5
Velocity, fps:	363	480	480	543
Price:	$23.95	$33.95	$36.95	$54.95

YEWHA TRIPLE B "DYNAMITE" SHOTGUN/RIFLE

Caliber: 25, single-shot.
Barrel: 23", smoothbore.
Length: 41" over-all. **Weight:** 6¾ lbs.
Power: Hand pumped, plunger.
Stock: Hardwood.
Sights: Post front, open rear.
Features: Use as rifle to fire lead balls or pellets (up to 950 fps. MV) or as unusually powerfull air shotgun with refillable plastic cartridges containing from 4-to-100 #9 birdshot. Patterns about 12" at 50 feet with #8 shot. Imported by Beeman's Precision Airguns.
Price: With accessory kit **$59.95**

Chokes & Brakes

Contra-Jet Muzzle Brake

The steel tube on body of the C-J device has 48 intersecting slots that dissipate energy via the mutual interference of the emerging gases. Recoil energy is reduced nearly 38% (in cal. 308), accuracy is enhanced through lessened muzzle jump and flinching, yet no increase in muzzle blast occurs. Readily fitted by a competent gunsmith, the 3″ long, 3½ oz. Contra-Jet is available in 25, 28, 30, 35, 37 and 45 calibers. Cost is from $29.50 to $37.50, installation not included.

Cutts Compensator

The Cutts Compensator is one of the oldest variable choke devices available. Manufactured by Lyman Gunsight Corporation, it is available with either a steel or aluminum body. A series of vents allows gas to escape upward and downward, reducing recoil without directing muzzle blast toward nearby shooters. For the 12-ga. Comp body, six fixed-choke tubes are available: the Spreader—popular with Skeet shooters; Improved Cylinder; Modified; Full; Superfull, and Magnum Full. Full, Modified and Spreader tubes are available for 12, 16, 20, 28, and 410, and an Adjustable Tube, giving Full through Improved Cylinder chokes, is offered in 12, 16, 20 and 28 gauges. Barrel adaptors in various internal diameters are available at $1.75 to permit exact fitting of Cutts Expansion Chambers. Cutts Compensator installed complete with wrench and any single tube $22.50; with the adjustable tube $30.00, installed. All single choke tubes $5.50 each; adjustable tubes $14.50.

Dahl Muzzle Blast Controller

Only 1⅞″ long by ¾″ in diameter, this device is claimed to reduce recoil up to 30%. An outer sleeve, threaded onto the gun muzzle, is threaded on the inside to accept a machined plug which is bored through for bullet passage. Gas behind the bullet is bled off through slots in the plug, swirled through a number of tiny passages while contained by the sleeve, and then vented upward, this final action somewhat offsetting muzzle jump. Price is $25.00, installed.

Emsco Choke

E. M. Schacht of Waseca, Minn., offers the Emsco, a small diameter choke which features a precision curve rather than a taper behind the 1½″ choking area. 9 settings are available in this 5 oz. attachment. Its removable recoil sleeve can be furnished in dural if desired. Choice of three sight heights. For 12, 16 or 20 gauge. Price installed, $21.95. Not installed, $16.50.

Herter's Rifle Recoil Eliminator

The Recoil Eliminator is a metal tube—1¹⁵⁄₁₆″ long and ⅞″ diam. in the standard model, same length and 1⅛″ diam. in target type—which is screwed to the muzzle. Angled ports direct escaping gas upward and rearward, reducing recoil and muzzle jump. The target model has a shield to prevent muzzle blast from annoying nearby shooters. Weights are 2 oz. and 3 oz. respectively. Made for calibers 25 to 32. Price for standard, $3.00, $6.50 installed. Target, $4.50 and $8.00.

Vari-Choke

Herter's, Inc., supplies the Vari-Choke, which features a ball-bearing micro-click adjustment of the pattern sleeve, rather than the spring system used by others. This model has 8 choke settings, from Full to Improved Cylinder. With Recoil Eliminator, price is $18.97 installed; without Eliminator, $14.47.

Jet-Away Choke

Arms Ingenuity Corp., makers of the Jet-Away, say that this device controls patterns through partial venting of the powder gases which normally enlarge patterns. The Jet-Away has a series of three slots in the top of the tube and a sliding control sleeve. When the sleeve is in its rearward position, all slots are uncovered, the maximum of gas is vented and patterns are densest. To obtain more open patterns, the sleeve is moved to cover one or more slots. In 12 or 20 gauge only, the Jet-Away is made of aluminum, weighs 3 ozs. $24.95 installed.

Lyman CHOKE

The Lyman CHOKE is similar to the Cutts Comp in that it comes with fixed-choke tubes or an adjustable tube, with or without recoil chamber. The adjustable tube version sells for $20.00 with recoil chamber, $17.25 without, in 12, 16 or 20 gauge. Lyman also offers a Single-Choke Adaptor at $8.25 installed. This device may be used with or without a recoil-reduction chamber; cost of the latter is $3.25 extra.

Mag-Na-Port

EDM is the process to "install" this muzzle brake on any firearm except those having shrouded barrels. EDM is a metal-erosion technique using carbon electrodes that control the area to be processed. The Mag-Na-Port brake utilizes small trapezoidal openings that go into and through the barrel that direct powder gases upward and outward to reduce recoil.

The resultant opening made by the EDM process is smoothly and cleanly made, with no burring in or out. No effect is had on bluing or nickeling outside the Mag-Na-Port area so no refinishing is needed. Cost for the Mag-Na-Port treatment is $29.50, plus transportation both ways.

Single barrel shotguns can be ported with four ports on both sides of the barrel for $39.50. Over-under shotguns are ported on both barrels, cost is $75.00.

Pendleton Dekicker

This Dekicker is unusual in that it is not a separate tube added onto a rifle muzzle but is machined into the barrel itself. Obviously, it cannot be installed by the customer. It must be sent to J. F. Mutter's Pendleton Gunshop, where a section of the bore a short distance behind the muzzle is relieved into an expansion chamber. Exit holes drilled at precise locations vent gas to lower apparent kick. Because metal is removed instead of being added, there is a small decrease in gun weight. Installation, including barrel polishing, is $50.00 for all calibers.

Poly-Choke

Poly-Choke Co., Inc., now is offering the Delux Signature Poly-Choke. It provides 9 choke settings (marked in 24 karat gold) to cover the complete pattern range as well as handle rifled slugs. It comes in two versions, the standard at $27.95, and the ventilated model at $29.95 installed. Fits 12, 16, 20 or 28 gauge. The Poly-Choke has been on the market for more than 40 years and is still gaining popularity.

Micrometer Receiver Sight

Receiver Sights

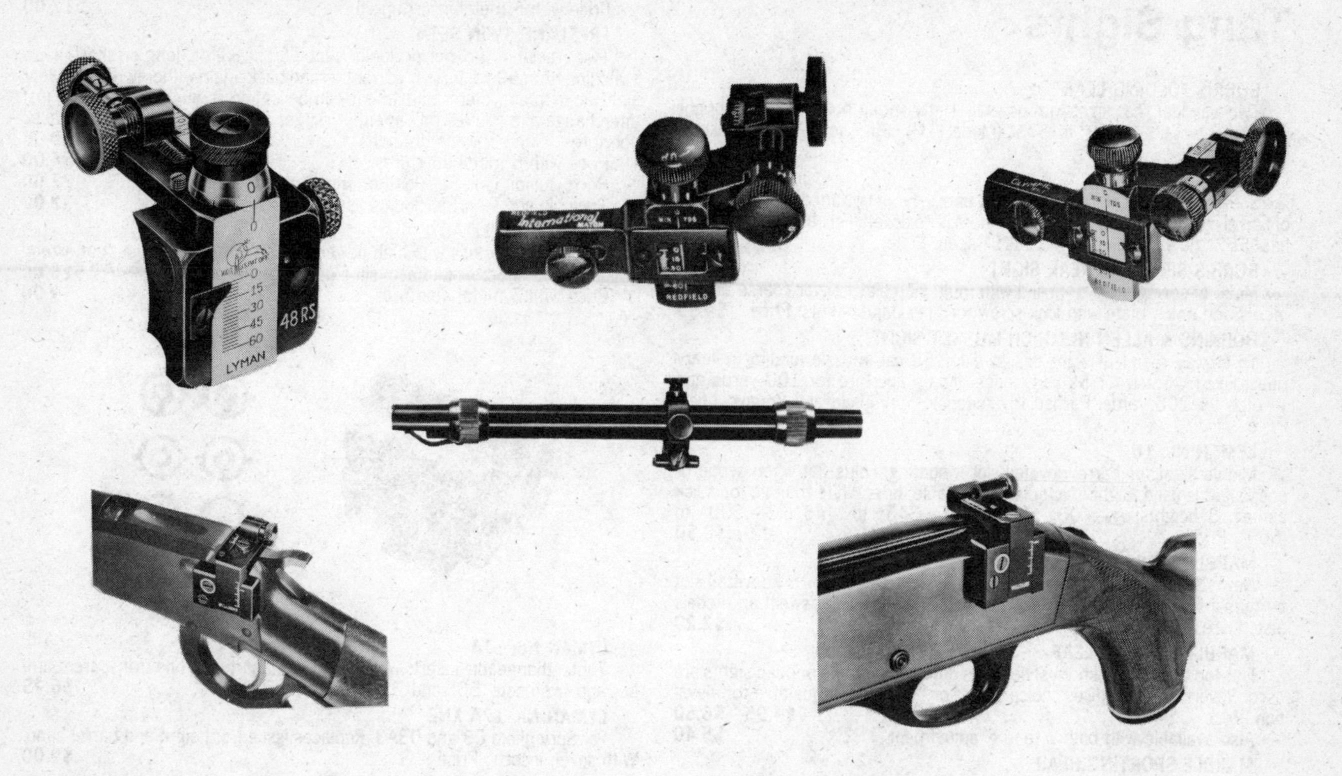

LYMAN No. 48
¼-min. clicks for w. & e. Any disc. Target or Stayset (hunting) knobs. Quick release slide, adjustable zero scales. Made for almost all modern big-game rifles. Price: **$20.50** With long slide **$22.50**

LYMAN No. 57
¼-min. clicks. Target or Stayset knobs. Quick release slide, adjustable zero scales. Made for almost all modern rifles. Price **$16.00**

LYMAN No. 60
¼-min. clicks for w. and e. Extension arm permits choice of 3 positions of eye relief. Designed for use on medium-weight, small bore target rifles. Price **$18.00**

LYMAN No. 66
Fits close to the rear of flat-sided receivers, furnished with target or Stayset knobs. Quick release slide, ¼-min. adj. For most lever or slide action or flat-sided automatic rifles. Price **$16.00**

REDFIELD No. 75
For Junior Target rifles. ¼-min. clicks for w. and e. Quick detachable extension, adj. to two positions. Available in two heights, scope or standard. For 75HW—Win. 75: 75HG and SG—Sav. 19; 75HV and SV—Stev. 416, Sears Ranger; 75HM and SM—Mossberg, master actions; 75HB and SB—Ballard; 75HR and SR—Win. SS, High Wall action only; Walnut Hill and 417; 75RT—Rem. 513T; 75RS—Rem. 513S; 75RX—Rem. 521. Price . **$19.00**

REDFIELD INTERNATIONAL MATCH
Spring loaded windage and elevation adjustments eliminate lost motion or backlash. Large adjusting screws. ¼-min. click values. Base and ⅞" disc. Fits same base as Olympic. Price **$38.00**
With base and "Sure-X" disc (see Sight Attachments). Price .. **$47.00**

REDFIELD INTERNATIONAL MARK 8
⅛-min. click adj. for windage and elevation distinguishes the Mark 8 which has all of the refinements of Redfield's International Match. Equipped with standard base and ⅞" disc. Price **$44.00**
With base and Sure-X disc (see Sight Attachments). Price **$55.00**

REDFIELD OLYMPIC
Elevation, windage, and extension adjustments. New elevation compensation. ¼-min. click. Base and ⅞" disc. Made for practically all target rifles. Price **$29.00**
Extra bases. Price **$4.80**
With base and Sure-X disc (see Sight Attachments). Price **$38.00**

WILLIAMS "FOOLPROOF"
Internal click adjustments. Positive locks. For virtually all rifles, plus Win., Rem. and Ithaca shotguns. Price **$13.75**
Add .50 for Twilight aperture. Extra shotgun aperture **2.00**

B-SQUARE SMLE (LEE-ENFIELD)
For No. 4 and Jungle carbine. No drilling or tapping required. 3/32" disc furnished. Price **$3.95**

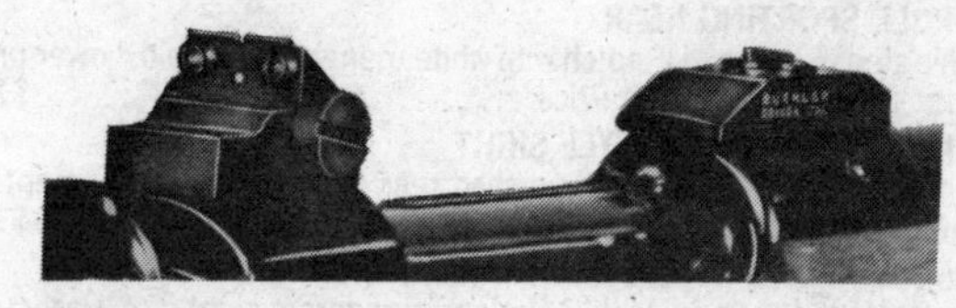

BUEHLER
"Little Blue Peep" auxiliary sight used with Buehler and Redfield scope mounts. Price **$3.35**
Mark IV front sight for above .... **.95**

FREELAND TUBE SIGHT
Uses Unertl 1" micrometer mounts. Complete with bases for 22-cal. target rifles, inc. 52 Win., 37, 40X Rem. and BSA Martini. Price **$53.50**

KUHARSKY AUXILIARY
Fits onto B&L or Kuharsky mounts to give emergency sighting. Includes peep rear and post front sights; extension rail slides forward for increased sight radius. Price **$9.95**

LYMAN No. 53
Shotgun receiver sight, mounts compactly near rear of receiver. For most Win., Rem., Sav., Marlin, Mossberg, J. C. Higgins and Ithaca shotguns. Price **$7.00**

WILLIAMS 5-D SIGHT
Low cost sight for shotguns, 22's and the more popular big game rifles. Adjustment for w. and e. Fits most guns without drilling or tapping. Also for Br. SMLE. Price **$8.00**

WILLIAMS GUIDE
Receiver sight for 30 M1 Car., M1903A3 Springfield, Savage 24's, Savage-Anschutz rifles and Wby. XXII. Utilizes military dovetail; no drilling. Double-dovetail W. adj., sliding dovetail adj. for E. Price **$7.60**

Sporting Leaf and Tang Sights

BURRIS FOLDING LEAF
Two-way leaf rear sight with dovetail. Hefty spring holds sight in upright position. 2 heights—.450" to .575" (Model FLH), .350" to .475" (Model FLL. Price $3.95

BURRIS LEAF BASE
Screw-attaches with two screws into barrel. From bottom of dovetail to top of barrel measures .080". Use where there is no dovetail in barrel. Model FLBA has .562" hole span, FLBB has .625" span. Price $1.95

BURRIS SPORTING REAR SIGHT
Made of spring steel, supplied with multi-step elevator for coarse adjustments and notch plate with lock screw for finer adjustments. Price .. $4.95

HOPKINS & ALLEN NUMRICH MUSKET SIGHT
Three-way rear leaf sight designed for 58 cal. muzzle loading military rifles. Fixed V-notch for 50-yard range, flip-up aperture for 100 yards and V-notch for 200 yards. Particularly suited to Springfield and Zouave rifles. Price $4.95

LYMAN No. 16
Middle sight for barrel dovetail slot mounting. Folds flat when scope or peep sight is used. Sight notch plate adjustable for e. White triangle for quick aiming. 3 heights; A—.400" to .500", B—.345" to .445", C—.500" to .600". Price $3.50

MARBLE FALSE BASE
New screw-on base for most rifles replaces factory base. ⅜" dovetail slot permits installation of any Marble rear sight. Can be had in sweat-on models also. Price $2.20

MARBLE FOLDING LEAF
Flat-top or semi-buckhorn style. Folds down when scope or peep sights are used. Reversible plate gives choice of "U" or "V" notch. Adjustable for elevation. Price .... $4.95—$6.50
Also available with both w. and e. adjustment $5.40

MARBLE SPORTING REAR
With white enamel diamond, gives choice of two "U" and two "V" notches of different sizes. Adjustment in height by means of double step elevator and sliding notch piece. For all rifles; screw or dovetail installation. Price $4.75—$6.00

MARBLE SPORTING REAR
Single step elevator. "U" notch with white triangle aiming aid. Lower priced version of double step model. Price $2.50

NUMRICH KENTUCKY STYLE SIGHT
Standard dovetail, traditional notched rear sight. ¼" high. For Kentucky and Hawken type rifles. Price $2.75

NUMRICH LONG RANGE REAR TARGET SIGHT
Adjustable for w. and e. with 3-size aperture target sight disc. Particularly suited for H&A Underhammer rifles. Price $5.95

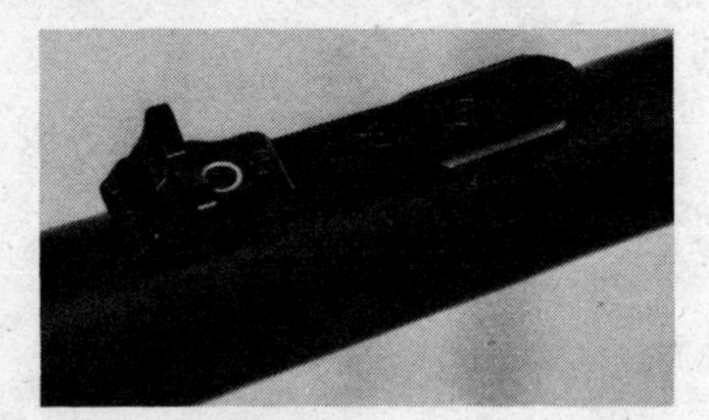

WILLIAMS DOVETAIL OPEN SIGHT
Open rear sight with w. and e. adjustment. Furnished with "U" notch or choice of blades. Slips into dovetail and locks with gib lock. Heights from .281" to .531". Price with blade $4.45

WILLIAMS GUIDE
Open rear sight with w. and e. adjustment. Bases to fit most military and commercial barrels. Choice of square "U" or "V" notch blade, 3/16", ¼", 5/16", or ⅜" high $5.50
Extra blades, each $1.55

Globe Target Front Sights

FREELAND SUPERIOR
Furnished with six 1" plastic apertures. Available in 4½"-6½" lengths. Made for any target rifle. Price with base $16.00
Price with 6 metal insert apertures 19.00

FREELAND JR
Same as above except standard dovetail mounting, various heights.
Price with base and 6 plastic apertures $14.00
Price with 6 metal insert apertures 17.00

FREELAND TWIN SET
Two Freeland Superior or Junior Globe Front Sights, long or short, allow switching from 50 yd. to 100 yd. ranges and back again without changing rear sight adjustment. Sight adjustment compensation is built into the set; just interchange and you're "on" at either range. Set includes base and 6 plastic apertures. Twin set (long or short) $30.00
Price with 6 metal apertures 34.00
Price, Junior Twin Set (long or short) plastic apertures 27.00
Price, Junior Twin Set (long or short) metal apertures 32.00

FREELAND MILITARY
Short model for use with high-powered rifles where sight must not extend beyond muzzle. Screw-on base; six plastic apertures. Price $16.00
Price with 6 metal apertures 19.00

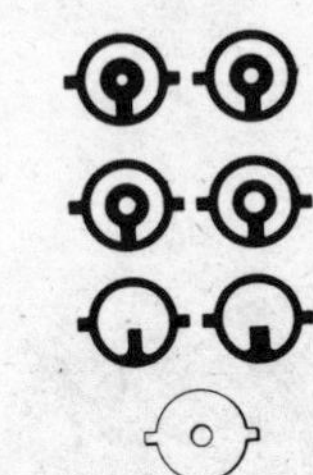

LYMAN No. 17A
7 interchangeable inserts which include 4 apertures, one transparent amber and two posts .50" and .100" in width. Price $6.25

LYMAN No. 17A XNB
For Springfield 03 and 03A3. Replaces issue front sight and barrel band. With seven inserts. Price $9.00

LYMAN 77
Similar to M17A, except mounts to a separate base, is quickly detachable. Base **$2.00** Sight $6.50

REDFIELD Nos. 63 and 64
For rifles specially stocked for scopes where metallic sights must be same height as scopes. Instantly detachable to permit use of scope. Two styles and heights of bases. Interchangeable inserts. No. 64 is ¼" higher. With base, Price $7.40

REDFIELD No. 65
1" long, ⅝" diameter. Standard dovetail base with 7 aperture or post inserts which are not reversible. For any rifle having standard barrel slot. 13/32" height from bottom of base to center of aperture. No. 65NB same as above with narrow base for Win. 64 N.R.A., 70, and Savage 40, 45, and 99 with ramp front sight base. Price $7.40

REDFIELD No. 66
Replaces entire removable front sight stud, locked in place by screw in front of barrel band. ¾" from bottom of base to center of aperture. For Spgfld. 1903. Price $7.40

REDFIELD No. 68
For Win. 52, heavy barrel, Sav. 19 and 33, and other rifles requiring high front sight. 17/32" from bottom of base to center of aperture. Standard dovetail size only. Price $7.40

REDFIELD OLYMPIC
Detachable. 10 inserts—5 steel, sizes .090", .110", .120", .140", .150"; one post insert, size .100"; four celluloid, sizes .090", .110", .120", .140". Celluloid inserts in clear, green, or amber, with or without cross hairs. For practically all rifles and with any type rear sight. Fits all standard Redfield, Lyman, or Fecker scope blocks. With base, Price $15.00

REDFIELD INTERNATIONAL SMALLBORE FRONT (Illustrated)
Similar to Olympic. Drop-in insertion of eared inserts. Outer sleeve prevents light leakage. Comes complete with 6 clear inserts and 6 skeleton inserts $22.00

REDFIELD INTERNATIONAL MILITARY BIG BORE
Same as International Match except tube only 2¼" long. For 30 cal. use Price $21.00

Ramp Sights

Williams Streamlined Ramp

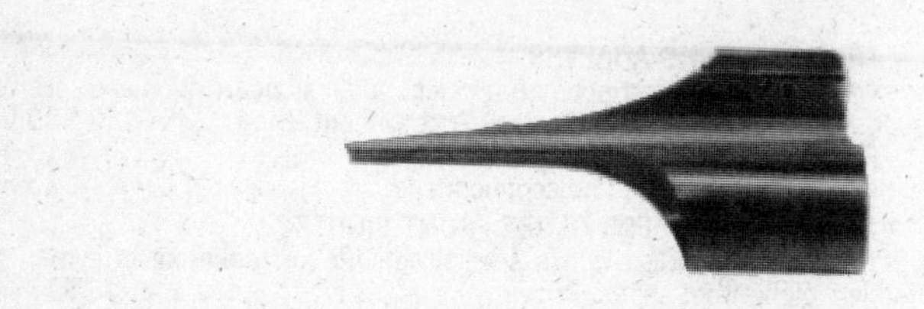

Burris Ramps.

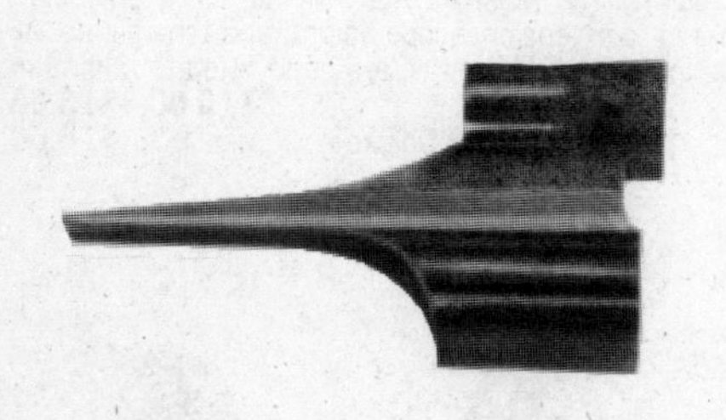

BURRIS
Top ramps, screw- and sweat-on ramps with 3/8" dovetail. Accepts .250" width (N) front sight. 8 heights available from .200" to .500". Price **$3.95**
Hoods for above ramps .... **.95**

BURRIS BAND RAMPS
Tapered to slip over the barrel and be driven on until snug. Set screw locks ramp in place. 7 heights available, 7 barrel diameters. Price **$9.95**
Hoods for above ramps .... **.95**

LYMAN SLIP-ON RAMP AND FRONT SIGHT
No soldering or brazing necessary, has tapered hole. Inside dia. .550" to .640". Removable hood. Price for ramp, sight and hood **$11.50**

LYMAN SCREW-ON RAMP AND SIGHT
Used with 8-40 screws but may also be brazed on. Heights from .10" to .350". Price with sight **$8.00**

MARBLE CONTOUR RAMP
For late model Rem. 725, 740, 760, 742. 9/16" between mounting screws. Price **$4.95**

MARBLE RAMPS
Available in either screw-on or sweat-on style. 5 heights; 3/16", 5/16", 3/8", 7/16", 9/16". Standard 3/8" dovetail slot. Price **$4.65**
Hoods for above ramps **$1.10**

PEDERSON "REX"
Offered as the "Rex" ramp, this is a hoodless type without barrel band. Heights available are 1/4" to 9/16". Blued or in the white, and without sights. Price **$2.95**

WILLIAMS SHORTY RAMP
Companion to "Streamlined" ramp, about 1/2" shorter. Screw-on or sweat-on. It is furnished in 1/8", 3/16", 9/32", and 3/8" heights without hood only. Price **$3.90**

WILLIAMS STREAMLINED RAMP
Hooded style in screw-on or sweat-on models. Furnished in 9/16", 7/16", 3/8", 5/16", 3/16" heights. Price with hood **$6.00**
Price without hood **$5.00**

WILLIAMS SHOTGUN RAMP
Designed to elevate the front bead for slug shooting or for guns that shoot high. Diameters to fit most 12, 16, 20 ga. guns. Fastens by screw-clamp, no drilling required. Price, with Williams gold bead **$3.50**
Price, without bead **2.75**

Front Sights

Lyman ramp and front sight

Burris Patridge.

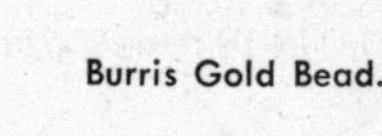

Burris Gold Bead.

Burris Ivory Bead.

BURRIS FRONT SIGHTS
Three styles: Patridge, gold or ivory bead. Widths are .250", .340", .500" and Mauser .310"................................from **$2.50** to **$3.75**

LYMAN BLADE & DOVETAIL SIGHTS
Made with gold, silver or red beads 1/16" to 3/32" wide and in varying heights for most military and commercial rifles. Price **$3.50**

LYMAN No. 22
Ivory bead front sight for Savage 24 series O-U. Price **$3.50**

MARBLE STANDARD
Ivory, red, or gold bead. For all American made rifles. 1/16" wide bead with semi-flat face which does not reflect light. Specify type of rifle when ordering **$2.10**

MARBLE-SHEARD "GOLD"
Show up well even in darkest timber. Shows same color on different colored objects; sturdily built. Medium bead. Various models for different makes of rifles so specify type of rifle when ordering. Also made for 30 or 9 mm Lugers, Colt's Single Action Army, Bisley Model, with plain sight or any other Colt's or S & W revolver with stationary front sight. Price **$3.50**

MARBLE CONTOURED
Same contour and shape as Marble-Sheard but uses standard 1/16" or 3/32" bead, ivory, red or gold. Specify rifle type **$2.50**

NUMRICH MUSKET FRONT SIGHT
Traditional 58 cal. front sight. Can be used for 58 caliber Springfield or Zouave replacement barrels., or '41 Mississippi barrel. Price **$1.95**

NUMRICH SILVER BLADE FRONT SIGHT
Same sight as used on H&A "Minuteman" rifle and Rolling Block "Buffalo Rifle." Suited for most ML and black powder cartridge guns. Price .. **$3.45**

WILLIAMS GUIDE BEAD SIGHT
Fits all shotguns. 1/8" ivory, red or gold bead. Screws into existing sight hole. Various thread sizes and shank lengths **$1.75**
Cultured Pearl Guide Bead **$4.50**

Handgun Sights

MMC Number 1 sight.

Micro handgun sight.

MMC Number 5 sight.

BO-MAR DE LUXE
Gives 3⁄8" w. and e. adjustment at 50 yards on Colt Gov't 45, sight radius under 7". For Colt, Hi-Standard, Ruger and S&W autos. Uses existing dovetail slot. Has shield-type rear blade **$17.75**

BO-MAR HIGH STANDARD RIB
Full length, 8¾" sight radius, for all bull barrels and military. Slide alteration required **$32.00**

BO-MAR LOW PROFILE RIB
Streamlined rib with front and rear sights; 7⅛" sight radius. Brings sight line closer to the bore than standard or extended sight and ramp. Weighs 4 oz. Made for Colt Gov't 45, Super 38, and Gold Cup 45 and 38 . **$32.00**
With extended sight and ramp, 8⅛" radius, 5¾ oz. **34.00**
Rib & tuner—inserted in Low Profile Rib—accuracy tuner. Adjustable for barrel positioning **$45.95**

BO-MAR FRONT SIGHTS
⅛" tapered post, made for Colt, Hi-Standard, Ruger and S&W autos. **$3.00**

BO-MAR COMBAT RIB
For S&W Model 19 revolver with 4" barrel. Sight radius 5¾"; weight 5½ oz. **$28.00**

BO-MAR MINI RIB
Shortened version of the full-length rib with barrel positioner. Weight 2½ oz. For Colt Gov't 45 and Super 38 .... **$28.00**
Undercut ramp front sight **$4.00**

BO-MAR FAST DRAW RIB
Streamlined full length rib with integral Bo-Mar micrometer sight and serrated fast draw sight. For Browning 9mm, S&W 39, Colt Commander 45, Super Auto and 9mm **$28.00**

MICRO
Click adjustable w. and e. rear with plain or undercut front sight in 1⁄10", ⅛", or 5⁄32" widths. Standard model available for 45, Super 38 or Commander autos. Low model for above pistols plus Colt Service Ace. Also for Ruger with 4¾" or 6" barrel. Price for sets **$17.50**
Price with ramp front sight **$20.50**
Adjustable rear sight only **$14.50**
Front ramp only, with blade **$8.00**

MMC COMBAT DESIGN
Available specifically for Colt M1911 and descendants, High Standard autos, Ruger standard autos. Adaptable to other pistols. Some gunsmithing required.
Price, less leaf **$13.00**
Plain leaf **$3.75**
White outline leaf **$5.60**

MMC NO. 5
Fully adjustable and replaces the factory sight for S&W M39 and M59. Supplied assembled, no gunsmithing required. ⅛" wide notch, white outline or plain.
Complete, plain **$33.70**
White outline **$35.65**
Extra for nickel **$4.45**

Shotgun Sights

FOR DOUBLE BARREL SHOTGUNS (PRESS FIT)
Marble 214—Ivory front bead, 11⁄64" ... **$1.10; 215**—same with .080" rear bead and reamers ... **$3.25. Marble 220**—Bi-color (gold and ivory) front bead, 11⁄64" and .080 rear bead, with reamers ... **$4.35; Marble 221**—front bead only ... **$2.10. Marble 223**—Ivory rear .080 ... **$1.10. marble 224**—Front sight reamer for 214-221 beads ... **$0.85; Marble 226**—Rear sight reamer for 223 .... **$0.85**

FOR SINGLE OR DB SHOTGUNS (SCREW-ON FIT)
Marble 217—Ivory front bead 11⁄64" ... **$1.30; Marble 216$2.75 Marble 218**—Bi-color front, 11⁄64" ... **$1.75; Marble 219** ... **$3.35 Marble 223T**—Ivory rear .080 ... **$1.75**; with tap and wrench ... **$3.35**
Marble Bradley type sights 223BT—⅛", 5⁄64" and 11⁄64" long. Gold, Ivory or Red bead **$1.75**

SLUG SITE
A combination V-notch rear and bead front sight made of adhesive-backed formed metal approx. 7" over-all. May be mounted, removed and re-mounted as necessary, using new adhesive from the pack supplied **$5.00**

Sight Attachments

FREELAND LENS ADAPTER
Fits 1⅛" O.D. prescription ground lens to all standard tube and receiver sights for shooting without glasses. Price without lens **$20.00**
Price clear lens ground to prescription **$13.50**
Price, yellow or green prescription lens **15.50**

MERIT ADAPTER FOR GLOBE FRONT SIGHTS
An Iris Shutter Disc with a special adapter for mounting in Lyman or Redfield globe front sights. Price **$11.00**

MERIT IRIS SHUTTER DISC
Eleven clicks gives 12 different apertures. No. 3 and Master, primarily target types, .022" to .125"; No. 4, ½" dia. hunting type, .025" to .155". Available for all popular sights. The Master Disc, with flexible rubber light shield, is particularly adapted to extension, scope height, and tang sights. All Merit Deluxe models have internal click springs; are hand fitted to minimum tolerance. Price .... **$10.00—$13.00**
Master .... **$12.00** Master Deluxe **$15.00**

Merit Master Target Disc

Merit Hunting Disc #4

Merit Deluxe Lens Disc

MERIT LENS DISC
Similar to Merit Iris Shutter (Model 3 or Master) but incorporates provision for mounting prescription lens integrally. Lens may be obtained locally, or prescription sent to Merit. Sight disc is 7⁄16" wide (Mod. 3), or ¾" wide (Master). Lens, ground to prescription,**$9.60** Standard tints, **$11.10.** Model 3 Deluxe **$16.00**
Master Deluxe **$19.00**

REDFIELD SURE-X SIGHTING DISC
Eight hole selective aperture. Fits any Redfield target sight. Each click changes aperture .004". Price **$9.00**

REDFIELD SIGHTING DISCS
Fit all Redfield receiver sights. .046" to .093" aperture. ⅜", ½" and ⅞" O.D. Price, each **$2.00**

WILLIAMS APERTURES
Standard thread, fits most sights. Regular series ⅜" to ⅝" O.D., .050" to .125" hole. "Twilight" series has white reflector ring. .093" to .125" inner hole. Price, regular series ... **$1.00.** Twilight series **$1.50**
New wide open 5⁄16" aperture for shotguns fits 5-D and Foolproof sights. Price **$2.00**

MERIT OPTICAL ATTACHMENT
For revolver and pistol shooters. Instantly attached by rubber suction cup to regular or shooting glasses. Any aperture .020" to .156". Price, **$10.00.**
Deluxe (swings aside) **$12.00**

SCOPES & MOUNTS

HUNTING, TARGET* AND VARMINT* SCOPES

Maker and Model	Magn.	Field at 100 Yds. (feet)	Relative Bright-ness	Eye Relief (in.)	Length (in.)	Tube Diam. (in.)	W&E Adjust-ments	Weight (ozs.)	Other Data	Price
American Import Co.										
Dickson 25P	2½	35	158	3	—	1	Int.	—	Adj. under protective ring at rear. 4-post reticle in all. Half-MOA adj. in straight powers, 1 MOA in variables.	$43.75
Dickson 40P	4	31½	64	3	—	1	Int.	—		43.75
Dickson 44P	4	31½	100	3	—	1	Int.	—		46.45
Dickson 64P	6	20½	44	3	—	1	Int.	—		47.50
Dickson N15420	1½-4	71-24	169-16	3	—	1	Int.	—		59.50
Dickson N3933	3-9	31-12	122-12	3	—	1	Int.	—		61.00
Dickson N3942	3-9	31-12	177-19	3	—	1	Int.	—		67.25
Bausch & Lomb										
Custom Baltur A	2½	43	64	3¼	12¼	1	Ext.	9½	Custom models must be used with B&L or other adj. mount. Trophy models have internal ½ MOA adj. Custom variables have tapered CH. Straight powers have CH, Post $5, dot $10. Balfor B has CH; post, tapered CH, dual-ine, taper-dot $5, dot $10. Balvar 8B has CH; post, tapered CH, RF, dualine, taper-dot $5, dot $10.	59.95
Custom Balfor A	4	30	56	3¼	12¼	1	Ext.	9		69.95
Custom Balvar 5	2½-5	40-20	164-41	3½	12¾	1	Ext.	9½		79.95
Custom Balvar 8B	2½-8	40-12½	256-25	3½	12¾	1	Ext.	10½		114.50
Trophy Baltur B	2½	42	164	3	12⅛	1	Int.	11		68.50
Trophy Balfor B	4	30	64	3	11⅞	1	Int.	11		79.50
Trophy Balsix B	6	20	36	3	11⅞	1	Int.	10¾		79.95
Trophy Balvar 8B	2½-8	40-12½	207-20	3½	11⅞	1	Int.	12½		104.95
Browning										
22 Scope	4	24½	25	3	9½	.75	Int.	6	W/mt. $43.45 - $47.95.	31.95
Wide Angle	4	37	49	3¼	11½	1	Int.	12	Dot reticle $10 extra.	74.95
Wide Angle	2-7	50-20	81-23	3¼	11¾	1	Int.	14½		99.95
Wide Angle	3-9	39-15	72-17	3¼	16½	1	Int.	15		104.95
Bushnell										
Scopechief IV	2¾	43	58	4	10	1	Int.	8½	Scopechief models have Command Post reticle with Magnetic Control Ring. Constantly centered reticles in Scopechiefs, Customs and Banners. Integral mounts $5 extra on Scopechiefs. Phantoms intended for handgun use.	64.50
Scopechief IV	4	32	64	3¾	11¾	1	Int.	10½		75.50
Scopechief IV	6	20	40	4	12½	1	Int.	11½		83.50
Scopechief IV	1½-4½	78-26	216-23	4¼-3¼	9¼	1	Int.	7¾		92.50
Scopechief IV	2½-8	44-15	160-16	4-3¼	11	1	Int.	11		97.50
Scopechief IV	3-9	39-13	160-18	3¾-3¼	11½	1	Int.	12¼		110.50
Scopechief 22	3-8	30-12	55-6	2½	11	⅞	Int.	7½	Mount rail. Similar 4x at $29.95.	36.85
Scopechief V	4	30	96	3½	12¼	1	Int.	10¾	Battery powered Lite-Site reticles in Scopechief V models.	75.50
Scopechief V	1½-4	76-27½	213-27	4¼-3¼	10¾	1	Int.	12		92.50
Scopechief V	3-9	34-12½	169-27	3¾-3	12⅞	1	Int.	14		110.50
Custom 22	3-7	29-13	28-5	2	10	⅞	Int.	6½	Similar 4x at $19.95.	23.95
Banner	2½	45	64	4¼	10½	1	Int.	8		41.95
Banner	4	30	64	4	11¾	1	Int.	10		49.95
GP Wide Angle	4	35½	100	2¾	12¼	1	Int.	12		69.95
Banner	6	19½	29	3¾	13¼	1	Int.	10½		54.95
Banner	10	12	26	3½	14¼	1	Int.	14½	Obj. focuses for range.	69.95
Banner	1½-4	63-28	169-25	4¼-3¼	10	1	Int.	10¼		62.95
Banner	3-9	39-13	115-13	3¾-3	11¼	1	Int.	12	With 40mm obj. $74.95.	69.95
AP Wide Angle	3-9	43-14	150-18	3	12¼	1	Int.	14		89.95
Banner	4-12	29-10	181-18	3¼	13¼	1	Int.	15½	Obj. focuses for range.	79.95
Phantom	1⅓	24	441	6-17	7⅝	⅞	Int.	5		39.50
Phantom	2½	10	100	7-16	9¼	⅞	Int.	5½		49.50
Shotgun	1	92	337	6	9⅞	1	Int.	11½		72.50
Davis Optical										
Spot Shot 1½"	10, 12, 15, 20, 25, 30	10-4		2	25	.75	Ext.		Focus by moving non-rotating obj. lens unit. Ext. mounts included. Recoil spring $3.50 extra.	89.50
Spot Shot 1¼"	10, 12, 15, 20,	10-6		2	25	.75	Ext.			69.50
Herter's										
Perfect	1	100	256	3-5	9¾	1	Int.	10¼	A variety of reticles including dots and rangefinders available in different scopes at small price increase. Hudson Bay rimfire 4x, $19.95.	33.95
Mark II	2¾	44	58	3½	10¼	1	Int.	8½		19.95
Mark IV	4	30	64	3½	11½	1	Int.	9½		32.95
Mark XI	1½-4½	52-27	177-25	3½	9¼	1	Int.	—		33.95
Mark IA	3-9	14-41	157-18	3½	12½	1	Int.	14½		56.97
Mark XXI	4-12	11½-34	100-14	3½	13¼	1	Int.	12½		56.97
Hutson										
Handgunner	1	9	—	25	5¼	—	Ext.	3	CH. ⅞" obj. lens. Adj. in mount, $14.95.	45.00
Hy-Score										
Gold Dot 471 UV	2½	42	96	3¾	11	1	Int.	7¾	Alloy tubes, rubber eyebrow guards, nitrogen filled. CH, dual CH or post and CH.	39.95
Gold Dot 475UV	4	27	96	3½	12	1	Int.	9½		42.95
Gold Dot 473UV	6	19½	50	3	13¼	1	Int.	10		47.95
Gold Dot 477UV	3-9	36-12	166-19	3	11½	1	Int.	11		64.95
Gold Dot 476UV	3-9	33-12	265-29	3¼	12½	1	Int.	13¼		69.95
Red Dot 489UV	4	30	96	3¾	11½	1	Int.	10½		69.95
Red Dot 487UV	3-9	39-13	241-27	3½	12¼	1	Int.	12¼		99.95

SCOPES & MOUNTS

Hunting, Target and Varmint Scopes—Continued

Maker and Model	Magn.	Field at 100 Yds. (feet)	Relative Bright-ness	Eye Relief (in.)	Length (in.)	Tube Diam. (in.)	W&E Adjust-ments	Weight (ozs.)	Other Data	Price
Jana										
Jana 4x	4	29	—	3½	12	1	Int.	9		27.50
Economy 4x	4	29	—	3½	12	1	Int.	9	Deluxe model offers choice of dot or Dual-X reticle. Zoom offers choice of crosshair or Dual-X. Others have constantly centered reticles.	24.95
Deluxe	4	32	—	3½	12	1	Int.	9		29.95
Super	4	32	—	3½	12	1	Int.	—		34.50
JA-2	2½	32	—	—	12	1	Int.	9⅛		24.95
JA-6	6	17½	—	3⅛	12	1	Int.	9		28.95
Zoom	3-9	35-12	—	—	12½	1	Int.	13½		47.95
JA-420	4	15½	—	—	11	¾	Int.	5¼		10.95
JA-37	3-7	23-10	—	2½-3	11⅓	⅞	Int.	9½		19.95
Jason										
860	4	27¼	64	3½	12	1	Int.	9	Constantly centered reticles, ball-bearing click stops, nitrogen filled tubes, coated lenses.	31.50
861	3-9	31½-12	112-12	3	13¼	1	Int.	13¾		49.95
865	3-9	31½-12	177-19	3	13½	1	Int.	15¼		53.50
Leupold										
M8	2	25	100	8.18	8.45	1	Int.	7.25		53.50
M8	3	43	45	3.85	10.13	1	Int.	8.25	Constantly centered reticles; in addition to the crosshair reticle the post, tapered (CPC), post and duplex, and duplex reticles are optional at no extra cost. Dot reticle $10.00 extra. 2x suitable for handguns and Win. 94.	68.50
M8	4	30	50	3.85	11.50	1	Int.	9.00		74.50
M8	6	18		3.85	11.7	1	Int.	10.3		84.50
M8 AO	7½	14	32	3.60	12.60	1	Int.	12.75		102.50
M8 AO	10	10	16	3½	13	1	Int.	13¾		104.50
M8 AO	12	9	11	3½	14½	1	Int.	14		107.50
M8 AO	24	4½	—	3½	15¼	1	Int.	15½	Mounts solidly on action. ¼ MOA clicks. Crosshair or dot.	169.50
Vari-X II	1-4	70-28	—	4¼-3½	9½	1	Int.	9½		94.50
Vari-X II	2-7	42-18	144-17	3.7-4.12	11.00	1	Int.	10.75		102.50
Vari-X II	3-9	30.5-13	208-23	3.5-4.12	12.60	1	Int.	13.75	With adj. obj. — $115.50	112.50
Vari-X III	1½-5	64-23	—	4½-3½	9¾	1	Int.	9¾		119.50
Vari-X III	2½-8	36-12½	—	4¼-3½	11¾	1	Int.	11½		129.50
Vari-X III	3½-10	29½-10½	—	4-3½	12¾	1	Int.	12¾		139.50
Lyman										
All-American	2½	43		3¼	10½	1	Int.	8¾	2, 3, or 4 minute dot reticle $10 extra. Choice of standard CH, tapered post, or tapered post and CH reticles. All-weather reticle caps. All Lyman scopes have new Perma-Center reticle which remains in optical center regardless of changes in W. & E.	59.95
All-American	3	35		3¼	11	1	Int.	9		59.95
All-American	4	30		3¼	12	1	Int.	10		65.95
All-American	6	20		3¼	13⅞	1	Int.	12¼		72.95
All-American 6x-P	6	20	—	3¼	14	1	Int.	14		89.50
◆ All-American	8	14		3¼	14⅜	1	Int.	13		99.95
◆ All-American	10	12		3¼	15½	1	Int.	13½	Adj. for parallax.	99.95
All-American	1¾-5	47-18	—	3	12¼	1	Int.	12¼		99.50
All-American	3-9	39-13	—	3½	12	1	Int.	14		109.50
◆ L.W.B.R.	20	5.5		2¼	17⅛	1	Int.	15¼	⅛ or ¼ MOA clicks.	124.95
◆ All-American	3-9	39-13	—	3¾-3¼	10½	1	Int.	14		109.95
◆ Super Targetspot	10, 12, 15, 20, 25, 30	12, 9.3, 8.9, 5.6, 4.3, 4	86	2-1⅞	24-24⅜	.75	Ext.	24¼-25	Non-rotating objective lens focusing. ¼ MOA click adjustments. Sunshade, $4 extra. Steel case, $12.00 extra. 5 different dot reticles, $12.50 extra.	164.95
Marble										
A-2.5	2¾	43	164	3½	11¾	1	Int.	10¾	Duralumin tubes, nitrogen filled. Post, CH, dot or 3-post reticle. Variables have ½ MOA adj.	39.50
A-4.0	4	30	64	3½	11¾	1	Int.	10¾		39.50
VL-3.9	3-9	38½-12½	177-19	3¼	13½	1	Int.	15½		68.50
VS-3.9	3-9	37-10½	114-12	3¼	13½	1	Int.	13½		69.50
Marlin										
300	4	23	25	1½	11¾	⅞	Int.	9	Coated lenses, non-magnifying reticles. Tri-Post reticle.	17.95
500	3-7	24-10	49-16	1¾	12	⅞	Int.	9½		19.95
425	4	28	64	3½	—	1	Int.	—	A 4x Glenfield M200, suitable for 22 rifles, and with ½-minute adj., is $8.00.	31.95
825	3-9	34-11	—	3	—	1	Int.	—		49.95
Glenfield 400	4	28	64	3½	12	1	Int.	9		20.00
Nickel										
Supralyt	2½	42	64	3½	11½	1.024	Int.	7½		130.00
Supralyt	4	33	25	3½	11½	1.024	Int.	8		130.00
Supra	4	32	81	3½	11¼	1.024	Int.	9	¼ MOA click adjustments. Steel or alloy tubes. Weatherproof reticle caps. Crosshair, post and c.h. or post and crosshair reticles are standard. New "Diflex" coated lenses. Continental Arms Co.	145.00
Supra	6	21	36	3½	12½	1.024	Int.	9		145.00
◆ Supra Varminter	6	24	49	3¼-5	12¼	1.024	Int.	11½		160.00
Supra Vari-Power	1-4	66.5-27.3	153-28	3½	10½	1.024	Int.	13.1		180.00
Supra Vari-Power	1½-6	60-21.6	176-36	3½	12	1.181	Int.	14.8		225.00
Supra Vari-Power	2½-7	38-21	125-36	3½	11¾	1.024	Int.	11		190.00
Supra Vari-Power	2½-9	42-15.6		3½	14½	1.181	Int.	17.3		250.00
Supra Vari-Power	3-10	30-12	100-18.5	3½	12½	1.024	Int.	12½		225.00
Normark										
Singlepoint	1	—	—		6¾	1	Int.	7½	Usable on rifles, shotguns ($9.95), handguns.	24.95
Precise Imports										
20241	4	23	14	2	11	.75	Int.	6¾		11.00
20257	3-7	23-13	43-8	3	11½	.75	Int.	7½	Price with mount.	27.00
20265	2½	32	164	3¾	12	1	Int.	9.6	All scopes have constantly centered reticle.	20.00
20244	4	29	64	3½	12	1	Int.	9		31.00
20249	3-9	36-13	177-19	3	13⅓	1	Int.	15		52.00
20260	10	12.2	16	3	12½	1	Int.	10½		37.50
Leatherwood Bros.										
Auto/Range	6	20	38	3-5	14⅝	1	Int.	18	Supplied with special mounts and range cams for most popular rifles and calibers.	119.50
Auto/Range	4	31	73	3-5	11	1	Int.	17		119.50
Auto/Range	1½-4½	65-26	225-49	3-5	12¼	1	Int.	17		129.50
Auto/Range	3-9	34-12	144-16	3-5	12¾	1	Int.	17		129.50

SCOPES & MOUNTS

Hunting, Target and Varmint Scopes—Continued

Maker and Model	Magn.	Field at 100 Yds. (feet)	Relative Bright-ness	Eye Relief (in.)	Length (in.)	Tube Diam. (in.)	W&E Adjust-ments	Weight (ozs.)	Other Data	Price
Redfield										
Traditional	4	24½	27	3½	9⅜	.75	Int.		Traditionals have round lenses. 4-Plex reticle is standard. 10x and 12x have QD target knobs, parallax adj.	32.70
Traditional	2½	43	64	3½	10¼	1	Int.	8½		54.30
Traditional	4	28½	56	3½	11⅜	1	Int.	9¾		61.40
Traditional	10	11½	18	3½	14⅞	1	Int.	13		105.00
Traditional	12	10	14	3½	14⅞	1	Int.	13	Accu-Range reticle avail. on most variables at extra cost.	120.00
Traditional	2-7	42-14	207-23	3½	11¼	1	Int.	12		84.50
Traditional	3-9	34-11	163-18	3½	12½	1	Int.	13		99.60
Traditional	4-12	26-9	112-14	3½	13⅞	1	Int.	14		130.00
Traditional	6-18	18-6	50-6	3½	13-15/16	1	Int.	18		141.00
Widefield	2-¾	55½	69	3½	10½	1	Int.	8	Dot about $10 extra in Widefields.	67.60
Widefield	4	37½	84	3½	11½	1	Int.	10		77.60
Widefield Low Profile	4	37½	84	3½	11½	1	Int.	10		—
Widefield	6	24	54	3½	12¾	1	Int.	11		88.00
Widefield	1¾-5	70-27	136-21	3½	10¾	1	Int.	11½		98.80
Widefield	2-7	49-19	144-21	3½	11¾	1	Int.	13		112.00
Widefield	3-9	39-15	112-18	3½	12½	1	Int.	14		122.80
3200 Target	12, 16, 20, 24	6½, 5¼, 4, 3¾	9, 6, 3¼, 2¼	2½	23¼	1	Int.	21	Mounts solidly.	186.90
6400 Target	16, 20, 24	6½, 5, 4½	5¾, 3½, 2½	3	17	1	Int.	18	Mounts on receiver. CH or dot.	225.00
Sanders										
Bisley 2½x20	2½	42	64	3	10¾	1	Int.	8¼	Alum. alloy tubes, ¼" adj., coated lenses.	38.50
Bisley 4x33	4	28	64	3	12	1	Int.	9	Two other scopes are also offered: a 3-9x at $56.50, and a 6x45 at $42. Rubber lens covers (clear plastic) are $2.50.	44.50
Bisley 6x40	6	19	45	3	12½	1	Int.	9½		46.50
Bisley 8x40	8	18	25	3¼	12½	1	Int.	9½		48.50
Bisley 10x40	10	12½	16	2½	12½	1	Int.	10¼	Choice of reticles in CH, PCH, 3-post.	50.50
Bisley 5-13x40	5-13	29-10	64-9	3	14	1	Int.	14		66.50
Southern Precision										
562	2½	40	144	3½	12	1	Int.	9¼	Centered reticles, CH or post. All elements sealed.	33.95
564	4	30	64	3½	12	1	Int.	9¼		33.95
567D	6	21	28	3¼	12	1	Int.	9¼		47.25
Swift										
Stag	4	28½	64	3	11.7	1	Int.	8.5	Dot, tapered post & CH or Rangefinder reticles available on all but Zoom & Game, $2.50 extra. Rangefinder optional on Zoom & Game. All have self-centering reticles.	39.95
Aerolite	4	28½	64	3	11¾	1	Int.	9½		29.95
Aerolite	2½-8	32-13	164-16	3	13¼	1	Int.	11¼		40.00
Yukon	2½-8	32½-13	164-16	3	13¼	1	Int.	11.3		55.00
Tasco										
Pistol Scope	1¾	23	104	19	8⅝	⅞	Int.	7½	Lens covers furnished. Constantly centered reticles. Write the importer, Tasco, for data on complete line.	39.95
Sniper	2-5	58-19	100-16	3	11¼	1	Int.	10		79.95
Super Marksman	3-9	35-14	177-19	3½	12⅜	1	Int.	14		95.95
Omni-View	3-9	42-15	177-19	3	12⅛	1	Int.	12¼		139.95
Tops										
4X	4	28½	64	3	11½	1	Int.	9½	Hard-coated lenses, nitrogen filled, shock-proof tested. Write Ed Paul, importer, for data on complete line.	23.95
8X	8	14½	16	3	13	1	Int.	10		29.95
3X-9X	3-9	33-15	175-19	3	12¾	1	Int.	14		39.95

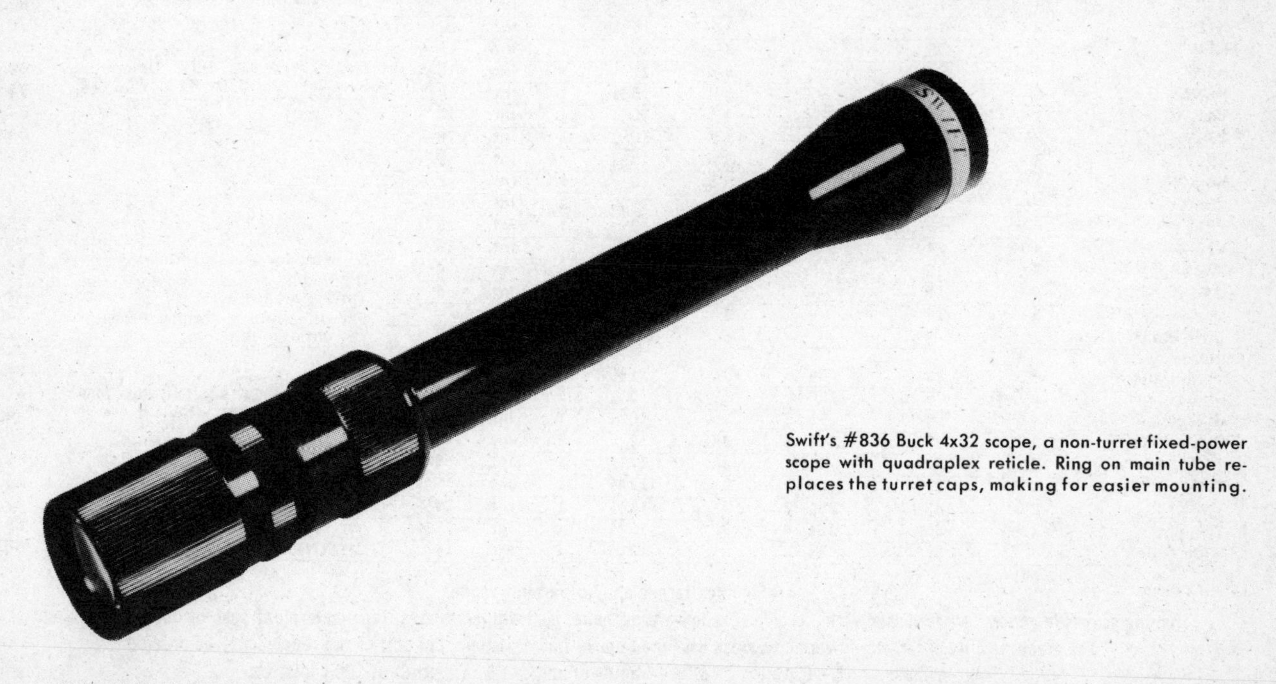

Swift's #836 Buck 4x32 scope, a non-turret fixed-power scope with quadraplex reticle. Ring on main tube replaces the turret caps, making for easier mounting.

SCOPES & MOUNTS

Hunting, Target and Varmint Scopes—Continued

Maker and Model	Magn.	Field at 100 Yds. (feet)	Relative Bright-ness	Eye Relief (in.)	Length (in.)	Tube Diam. (in.)	W&E Adjust-ments	Weight (ozs.)	Other Data	Price
United										
Golden Hawk	4	30	64		11⅞	—	Int.	9½	Anodized tubes, nitrogen filled. Write United for data on complete line.	44.50
Golden Grizzly	6	18½	44		11⅞	1	Int.	11		55.00
Golden Falcon	4-9	29½-14	100-20		13½	1	Int.	12¼		89.50
Golden Plainsman	3-12	33-12½	169-11		13½	1	Int.	12¾		110.00
Unertl										
Falcon	2¾	40	75.5	4	11	1	Int.(1′)	10	Black dural tube in hunting models. (2 oz. more with steel tube.)	61.00
Hawk	4	34	64	4	11¾	1	Int.(1′)	10.5		66.00
Condor	6	17	40	3-4	13½	1	Int.(1′)	12		83.00
◆1″ Target	6,8,10	16-10	17.6-6.25	2	21½	.75	Ext.	21	Dural ¼ MOA click mounts. Hard coated lenses. Non-rotating objective lens focusing.	89.00
◆1¼″ Target	8,10,12,14	12-6	15.2-5	2	25	.75	Ext.	25		120.00
◆1½″ Target	8,10,12,14 16,18,20,24	11.5-3.2		2¼	25½	.75	Ext.	31		140.00
◆2″ Target	8,10,12,14 16,18,24 30,36		22.6-2.5	2¼	26¼	1	Ext.	44		188.00
◆Varmint, 1¼″	6,8,10,12	14.1-7	28.7-1	2½	19½	.875	Ext.	26	¼ MOA dehorned mounts. With target mounts.	118.00 122.00
◆Ultra Varmint, 2″	8,10 12,15	12.6-7	39.7-11	2½	24	1	Ext.	34	With dehorned mount. With calibrated head.	153.00 170.00
◆Small Game	4,6	25-17	19.4-8.4	2¼	18	.75	Ext.	16	Same as 1″ Target but without objective lens focusing.	66.00
◆Vulture	8 10	11.2 10.9	29 18½	3-4	15⅝ 16⅛	1	E or I	15½	Price with internal adj. Price with ¼ MOA click mounts.	108.00 133.00
◆Programer 200	8,10,12,14 16,18,20,24 30,36	11.3-4	39-1.9		26½	1	Ext.	45	With new Posa mounts.	234.00
◆BV-20	20	8	4.4	4.4	17⅞	1	Ext.	21¼	Range focus unit near rear of tube. Price is with Posa mounts. Magnum clamp. With standard mounts and clamp ring, $156.00.	166.00
Universal										
Deluxe UC	2½	32	172	3½	12	1	Int.	9¼	Aluminum alloy tubes, centered reticles, coated lenses. Similar Standard series available at lower cost.	34.95
Deluxe UE	4	29	64	3½	12	1	Int.	9		35.95
Deluxe UL	3-9	34-12	177-18	3	12¾	1	Int.	15¼		57.95
Weatherby										
Mark XXII	4	25	50	2½-3½	11¾	⅞	Int.	9¼	Focuses in top turret.	34.50
Premier Standard	2¾	45	212	3½	11¾	1	Int.	12¼	Centered, non-magnifying reticles. Binocular focusing. Lumi-Plex or Open Dot, $5 extra.	69.50
Premier Standard	4	31	100	3½	12¾	1	Int.	12¼		79.50
Premier Standard	3-9	43½-14½	177-19	3	12	1	Int.	14¾		94.50
Premier Wide Angle	4	35-¾	100	3	11¾	1	Int.	14		99.50
Premier Wide Angle	3-9	43½-14¾	177-19	3	12	1	Int.	14¾		109.50
Weaver										
K1.5	1½	56		3-5	9¾	1	Int.	7		29.95
K2.5	2½	43		3-6	10⅜	1	Int.	8½		39.95
K3	3	37		3-6	10⅜	1	Int.	8½		44.95
K4	4	31		3-5½	11¼	1	Int.	9½		54.95
K6	6	20		3-5	13⅝	1	Int.	11		59.95
K8	8	15		3-5	15⅜	1	Int.	12¼	Crosswires, post, rangefinder or Dual X reticle optional on all K and V scopes (except no RF in K1½, post in K8, 10, 12, or RF in V22). Dot $7.50 extra in K and V models only. Objective lens on K8, K10, K12, V9, V12 and V9-W focuses for range.	64.95
K10	10	12		3-5	15½	1	Int.	12½		69.95
K12	12	10		3-5	15¾	1	Int.	12½		79.95
K3-W	3	55	—	3¾	10¾	1	Int.	12½		59.95
K4-W	4	37½	—	3¾	12	1	Int.	13¼		69.95
K6-W	6	25	—	3¾	13¾	1	Int.	14¼		74.95
V4.5-W	1½-4½	70-26	—	4	10¾	1	Int.	14		74.95
V7-W	2½-7	53-20	—	3¾	12½	1	Int.	16		84.95
V9-W	3-9	41-16	—	3¾	13¾	1	Int.	19¾		94.95
V4.5	1½-4½	54-21		3-5	10	1	Int.	8½		59.95
V7	2½-7	40-15		3-5	11⅝	1	Int.	10½		69.95
V9	3-9	33-12		3-5	13	1	Int.	13		79.95
V12	4-12	24-9		4	13		Int.	13		89.95
V22	3-6	30-16		2	12½	.875	Int.	4½	$1 extra for Dual X reticle.	16.95
D4	4	28	—	2	11⅝	.875	Int.	4	D model prices include N or Tip-Off mount.	11.95
D6	6	18	—	2	12	.875	Int.	4		13.95
Qwik-Point	1	—	—	6	—	—	Int.	8	For rifles and shotguns. Projects red dot aiming point.	39.95
Williams										
Guide Line	4	29½	64	3¾	11¾	1	Int.	9½	Coated lenses, nitrogen filled tubes, ½ MOA adj. CH, dot, TNT or Guide reticle. Dot covers 3 MOA at 4x in all models.	88.50
Guide Line	1½-4½	78-26	196-22	4⅓-3¼	9½	1	Int.	7¾		118.50
Guide Line	2-6	60-20	169-18	3¼	10¼	1	Int.	10		118.50
Guide Line	3-9	39-13	161-18	3¾-3¼	12	1	Int.	14½		130.00
Twilight	2½	32	64	3¾	11¼	1	Int.	8½	$5.50 more for TNT reticle.	40.00
Twilight	4	29	64	3½	11¾	1	Int.	9½		44.50
Twilight	2-6	45-17	256-28	3	11½	1	Int.	11½		62.50
Twilight	3-9	36-13	161-18	3	12¾	1	Int.	13½		69.50
Wide Guide	4	35	64	3¼	12¼	1	Int.	14	CH, TNT or Guide reticle.	88.50

◆Signifies target and/or varmint scope.

Hunting scopes in general are furnished with a choice of reticle—cross hairs, post with crosshairs, tapered or blunt post, or dot crosshairs, etc.

The great majority of target and varmint scopes have medium or fine crosshairs but post or dot reticles may be ordered.

W—Windage E—Elevation MOA—Minute of angle or 1″ (approx.) at 100 yards, etc.

SCOPES & MOUNTS

TELESCOPE MOUNTS

Maker, Model, Type	Adjust.	Scopes	Suitable for	Price
Browning				
One Piece (T)	W only	1″ split rings	Browning, Winchester, Remington, Savage, Marlin.	22.00
One Piece (T)	No	¾″ split rings	Browning 22 semi-auto.	5.00
One Piece Barrel Mount Base	No	Groove mount	22 rifles with grooved receiver.	6.50
Two Piece	No	¾″ ring mount.	For Browning T-bolt 22.	9.50
B-Square Co.				
Mono-Mount	No	Leupold M8-2x (mounts ahead of action)	M94 Win. M1 Carbine.	12.20 10.20
Buehler				
One Piece (T)	W only	¾″ or 1″ solid rings; ⅞″, 1″ or 26mm split rings. 4″ or 5″ spacing.	All popular models.	**Solid rings—24.00** **Split rings—29.50**
One Piece "Micro-Dial" Universal	Yes	Same. 4″ ring spacing only.	Most popular models.	**Solid—31.00 Split—36.50**
Two Piece (T)	W only	Same. Rings for 26.5—27 mm adjust to size by shims.	Rem. 700, 721, 722, 725; Win. 70, 52; FN; Rem. 37; Mathieu; Schultz & Larsen; Husq.	**Solid—24.00** **Split—29.50**
One Piece Pistol Base	W only	Uses any Buehler rings.	S&W K. Colt, Ruger, Thompson	**Bases only—12.50**
One Piece (T)	W only	Same.	Rem. XP100 pistol.	**Base only—12.50**
Burris				
Supreme One Piece (T) Trophy Two Piece (T)	W only W only	1″ split rings, 3 heights 1″ split rings, 3 heights	Most popular rifles.	**Rings—17.95** **1 piece base—10.95** **2 piece base— 9.95**
Bushnell				
Detachable (T)	No	1″ only, 2 heights.	Most popular rifles.	**Rings— 8.75** **Bases— 1.50** **1 pc. bridge base— 1.50**
Pivot (T)	No	1″ only.	Most popular rifles.	11.45
All Purpose	No	Phantom	V-block bottoms lock to chrom-moly studs seated into two 6-48 holes.	7.50
Rigid	No	Phantom	Heavy loads in Colt, S&W, Ruger revolvers, Rem. XP100, Ruger Hawkeye.	6.00
94 Win.	No	Phantom	M94 Win., end of bbl. clamp or center dovetail.	7.50
Clearview	No	1″	Most popular rifles. Uses Weaver bases.	13.50
Conetrol				
One Piece (T) Two Piece (T)	W only W only	1″ solid or split rings. Same.	Most popular rifles.	**Huntur** 17.85-22.85 **Gunnur** 21.85-27.85 **Custum** 27.85-34.85
Griffin & Howe				
Standard Double Lever (S)	No	All standard models.	All popular models. (Garand $37.50; Win. 94 $30.00).	30.00
E. C. Herkner Echo (S)	No	All standard models.	All popular models. Solid or split rings.	27.50
Holden				
Ironsighter (T)	No	1″ split rings.	Many popular rifles. Rings have oval holes to permit use of iron sights. For 22 rimfire grooved receivers, ¾, ⅞ or 1 inch tubes, $6.95. For long eye relief scopes on M94, $19.95.	14.95
International Guns Inc. handles the complete line of Parker-Hale (British) Roll-Over and other scope mounts.				
Jaeger				
QD, with windage (S)	W only	1″, 26mm; 3 heights.	All popular models.	42.00
Jaguar				
QD Dovetail (T)	No	1″, 26mm and 26½mm rings.	For BSA Monarch rifle (Galef, importer).	16.95
Kesselring				
Standard QD (T)	W only	¾″, ⅞″, 1″, 26mm—30 mm split or solid rings.	All popular rifles, one or two piece bases.	19.50
See-Em-Under (T)	W only	Same.	Rem. 760, 740, 788, Win. 100, 88, Marlin 336	22.00
QD Dovetail (T)	W only	1″, 26mm.	Steyr 22, Sako, BSA, Brno, Krico	19.50
Kwik-Site (T)	No	1″ split rings	Wider-View, $15.75. Mounts scope high to permit iron sight use. Offset base for 94 Win.	14.75 19.95

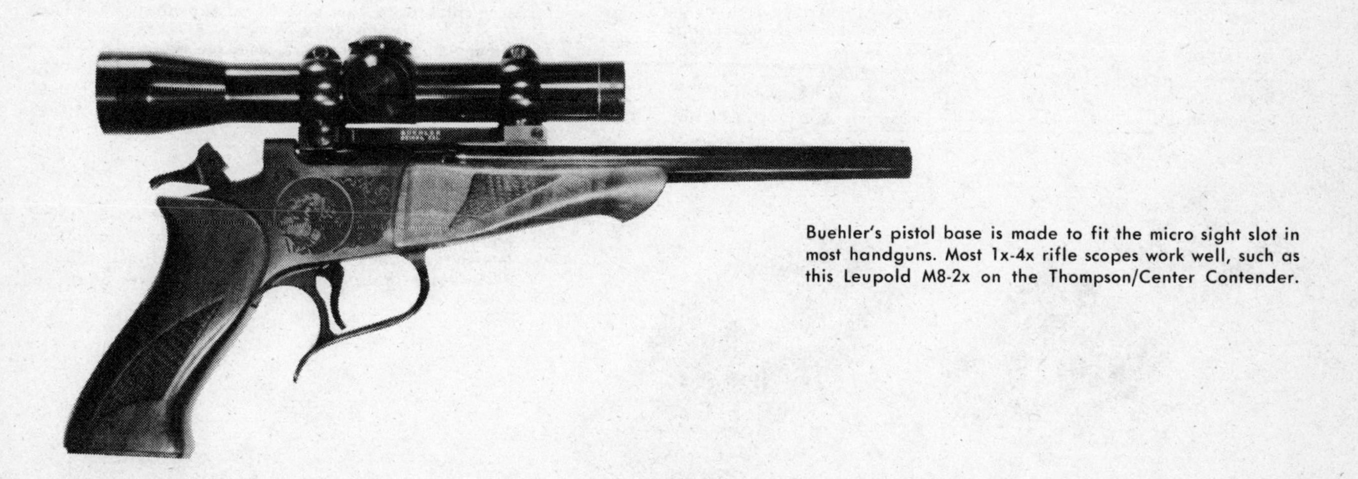

Buehler's pistol base is made to fit the micro sight slot in most handguns. Most 1x-4x rifle scopes work well, such as this Leupold M8-2x on the Thompson/Center Contender.

SCOPES & MOUNTS

TELESCOPE MOUNTS—Continued

Maker, Model, Type	Adjust.	Scopes	Suitable for	Price
Leupold STD (T)	W only	1″ only, 3 heights. Interchange with Redfield Jr. and Sr. components.	Most popular rifles.	Rings—16.70 Base—10.50
Lyman All-American Tru-lock (T)	No	¾″, ⅞″, 1″, 26mm, split rings.	All popular post-war rifles, plus Savage 99, 98 Mauser. One or two piece bases.	11.00
Marble Game Getter (T)	No	1″ only.	Many popular rifles. Has see-through base to permit use of iron sights.	14.95
Game Getter (S)	No	1″ only.	Win. 64, 94.	
Marlin One Piece QD (T)	No	1″ split rings.	Most popular models. Glenfield model. 5.00.	6.95
Numrich Side mount	No	1″ split rings.	M-1 carbine.	7.95
Pachmayr Lo-Swing (S)	Yes	¾″, ⅞″, 1″, 26mm solid or split loops.	All popular rifles. Scope swings aside for instant use of iron sights.	25.00
Lo-Swing (T)	Yes	¾″, ⅞″, 1″, 26mm split rings.	Adjustable base. Win. 70, 88; Rem. 721, 722, 725, 740, 760; Mar. 336; Sav. 99.	30.00
Parker-Hale Roll-Off	No	1″ and 26mm.	Most popular rifles.	13.95
Precise Imports M-21 (rings only)	No	1″ tube; not over 32mm obj.	Fit Weaver bases.	3.95
M-22 (rings only)	No	1″ tube; 40mm obj. scopes.		3.95
Leatherwood Bros. V lock QD (T)	No	1″ split rings.	Most popular rifles.	13.00
Redfield JR-SR (T)	W only	¾″, 1″, 26mm.	Low, med. & high, split rings. Reversible extension front rings for 1″. 2-piece bases for Mannlicher-Schoenauer and Sako. Colt Sauer bases.	27.20-50.00 18.00
Swing-Over (T) base only	No	1″. (Not for variables.)	Standard height split rings. Also for shotguns.	19.60
Ring (T)	No	¾″ and 1″.	Split rings for grooved 22's.	8.80-11.20
Frontier (T) bases	No	Takes ¾″ or 1″ rings.	See-thru bases $5.40; shotgun model $6.40. Rings $11.20.	2.40
S&K Insta-Mount (T) base only	No	Most take S&K or Weaver rings.	M1903, A3, M1 Carbine, Lee Enfield #3, #4 #5, P14, M1917, M98 Mauser, FN Auto, AR-15. For M1 Garand, steel rings. Bases—M94, 64.	7.50-30.00 42.80
Conventional rings and bases	No	1″ split rings.	Most popular rifles. For "see through underneath" risers, add $4.15.	24.20
Sako QD Dovetail (T)	W only	1″ or 26mm split rings.	Sako, or any rifle using Sako action. 3 heights and extension rings available. Garcia, importer.	32.00
Savage No. 40 (S)	No	1″	For Savage 340.	3.25
Tasco 700(T) and 800(S) series	No	1″ split rings, regular or high.	Many popular rifles. Swing mount, $19.95.	9.40-15.90
M722	No	Split rings.	For 22s with grooved receivers.	5.95
Unertl Posa (T)	Yes	¾″, ⅞″, 1″ scopes	Unertl target or varmint scope.	30.00-35.00
¼ Click (T)	Yes	¾″, 1″ target scopes	Any with regular dovetail scope bases.	27.00-32.00
Dehorned Varmint (T)	Yes	¾″, ⅞″, 1″ scopes	Add $3 for Posa.	29.00-32.00
Weaver Detachable Mount (T & S)	No	¾″, ⅞″, 1″, 26mm.	Nearly all modern rifles. Extension rings, 1″ $11.95.	9.95
Type N (S)	No	¾″ scopes only.	Same. High or low style mounts.	2.00
Pivot Mount (T)	No	¾″, 1″.	Most modern big bore rifles.	12.95
Tip-Off (T)	No	¾″, ⅞″.	22s with grooved receivers.	3.95
Tip-Off (T)	No	1″, two-piece	Same. Adapter for Lee Enfield—$2.00.	9.95
Williams Offset (S)	No	¾″, ⅞″, 1″, 26mm solid, split or extension rings.	Most rifles (with over-bore rings, $20.50). Br. S.M.L.E. (round rec.) $6.60 extra.	17.85
QC (T)	No	Same.	Same. Add $8.65 for micro. windage ring.	17.85
QC (S)	No	Same.	Most rifles.	17.85
Sight-Thru	No	1″, ⅞″ sleeves $1	Many modern rifles.	15.00

(S)—Side Mount (T)—Top Mount 22mm = .866″ 25.4mm = 1″ 26mm = 1.024″ 26.5mm = 1.045″ 30mm = 1.181″

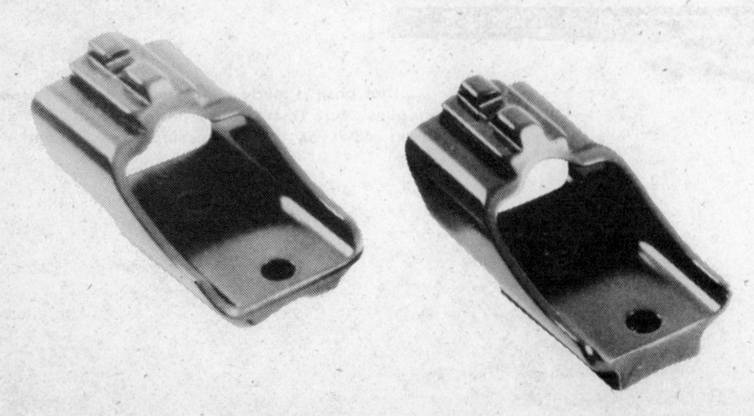

Redfield's FR See-Thru mounts feature the same locking lug as their regular FR bases. The two-piece design allows interchangeability of the FR rings to See-Thru or regular FR bases without the cost of an extra set of rings.

SPOTTING SCOPES

BAUSCH & LOMB BALSCOPE Sr.—60mm objective, 20X. Field at 100 yds. 11.1 ft. Relative brightness, 9. Wgt., 48 oz. Length closed, 16 7/16". Rapid prismatic focusing **$164.50**
Also 15X, 20X, 25X, 40X, 60X eyepieces, each **$29.50**
20X wide angle eyepiece **$39.50**

BAUSCH & LOMB BALSCOPE ZOOM—15X to 60X variable power. 60mm objective. Field at 1000 yds. 150 ft. (15X) to 37½ feet (60X). Relative brightness 16 (15X) to 1 (60X). Wgt., 48 oz., 16 11/16" overall. Integral tripod lug. Straight eyepiece **$199.50**
With 45° eyepiece **$229.50**

BAUSCH & LOMB BALSCOPE 20—40mm objective. 20X. Field at 100 yds., 7.5 ft. 15⅜" over-all, Wgt., 22 oz. **$36.50**

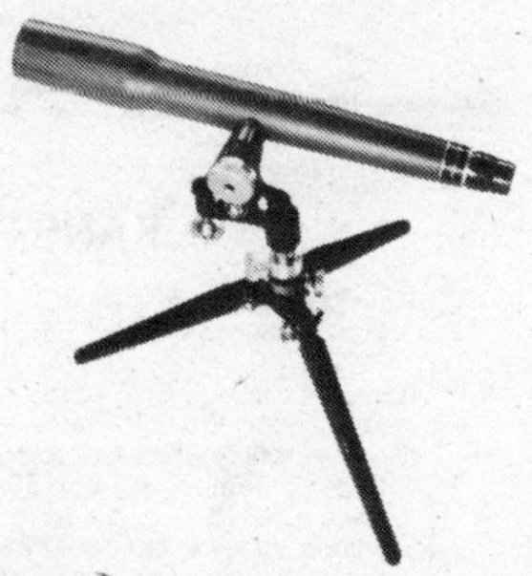

BAUSCH & LOMB BALSCOPE 10—30mm objective. 10X. Field at 100 yds. 7.5 ft. 10¼" over-all, weight, 9 oz. **$14.95**

BUSHNELL SPACEMASTER—60mm objective, 25X. Field at 100 yds., 10.5 ft. Relative brightness, 5.76. Wgt., 39 oz. Length closed, 15¼". Prism focusing, sliding sunshade **$142.50**
15X, 20X, 25X, 40X and 60X eyepieces, each **$29.50**
20X wide angle eyepiece **$39.50**

BUSHNELL SPACEMASTER 45°—Same as above except: Wgt., 43 oz., length closed 16¼". Eyepiece at 45° **$157.50**

BUSHNELL SPACEMASTER II—20X-45X zoom. 60mm objective. Field at 100 yards 12-7.2 ft. Relative brightness 9-1.7. Wgt. 36 oz., length 11⅝" Price **$165.50**

BUSHNELL SENTRY II—20X. 50mm objective. Field at 100 yards 12 ft. Relative brightness 6.25 .... **$86.50**
Also 32X and 48X eyepieces, each **$25.00**

BUSHNELL ZOOM SPOTTER—40mm objective. 9X-30X var. power Price **$45.50**

HUTSON CHROMATAR 60—63.4mm objective. 22.5X eyepiece at 45D. Wgt. 24 oz. 8" over-all. 10½" foot field at 100 yards. **$119.00**
15X or 45X eyepieces, each **22.00**

HY-SCORE MODEL 460—60mm objective. 15X, 20X, 25X, 40X and 60X eyepieces included. Field at 100 yds. 15.8 to 3.2 ft. Length closed 11". Wgt., 35 oz. With tripod and case **$129.95**
Zoom—20X to 40X **$144.95**

PRECISE IMPORTS, 21285—60mm objective, 15X to 30X zoom scope. About 15" long, weighs approximately 6 lbs. with adj. tripod... **$100.00**

PRECISE IMPORTS, 21287—60mm objective, interchangeable eyepieces of 15X, 20X, 30X, 40X, 60X. Sliding sunshade. Weighs about 6 lbs. with adj. tripod **$132.00**

REDFIELD FIFTEEN-SIXTY—15X-60X zoom. 60mm objective. Field at 100 yards 15.6-3.7 ft. Relative brightness 16-1. Wgt. 48 oz., length 16¾" **$225.00**
Tripod stand **$33.50**
Bipod stand **$33.50**
Carrying case **$44.00**
Window mount **$7.00**

REDFIELD FIFTEEN-FORTY-FIVE—Similar to above but power range is 15X-45X **$170.00**

SOUTHERN PRECISION MODEL 549—60mm objective and 5 eyepieces from 15X to 60X; extensible sunshade and folding tripod. Closed, 14¾", Wgt., 4¼ lbs. **$86.50**

SOUTHERN PRECISION ZOOM MODEL 547—60mm objective, 25X to 50X; ext. sunshade folding tripod. Closed, 18", wgt. 4½ lbs. with tripod (included) **$103.00**

SOUTHERN PRECISION MODEL 546—50mm objective, 25X. Folding tripod, leather case included. Closed, 13", wgt. 3 lbs. **$48.00**

SWIFT TELEMASTER M841—60mm objective. 15X to 60X variable power. Field at 1000 yards 160 feet (15X) to 40 feet (60X). Wgt. 3.4 lbs. 17.6" over-all **$210.00**
Tripod for above **$46.50**
Photo adapter **$12.95**
Case for above **$32.95**

SWIFT MODEL 821—60mm objective. 15X, 20X, 30X, 40X and 60X eyepieces included. Field at 100 yds., 158 to 32 ft. Length 13½" (without sunshade). 6 lbs. **$154.50**

TASCO ZOOM—60mm objective. 20X to 60X variable power. Field at 1000 yards 158 feet (16X) to 40 feet (50X). Wgt. 4½ lbs. 18" overall . **$119.95**

TASCO 28T ANGLEVIEW—60mm objective. 25X, resolves to 2 sec. at 100 yds. Rapid focus knob. Table top tripod with adj. elevation leg. Camera tripod adapter, extending sun shade. Wgt., 6 lbs., length 16½". Complete with lens covers **$199.95**

TASCO 8T SPOTTING 60—60mm objective, 4 par-focal, variable power eye-lenses 15X, 30X, 40X and 60X. Resolves 2.8 sec. at 100 yds. Wgt., 4 lbs., length 16½" **$149.95**

UNERTL RIGHT ANGLE—63.5mm objective. 24X. Field at 100 yds., 7 ft. Relative brightness, 6.96. Eye relief, ½". Wgt., 41 oz. Length closed, 19". Push-pull and screw-focus eyepiece. 16X and 32X eyepieces $18 each. Price **$139.00**

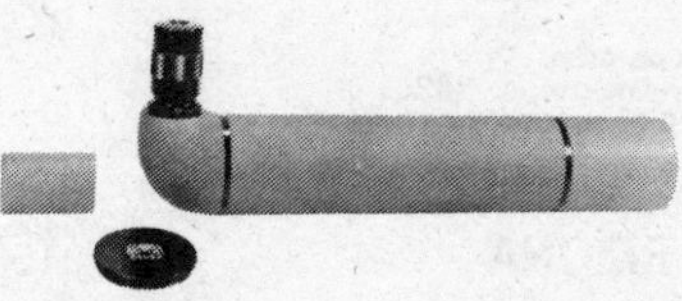

UNERTL STRAIGHT PRISMATIC—Same as Unertl Right Angle except: straight eyepiece and Wgt. of 40 oz. **$119.00**

UNERTL 20X STRAIGHT PRISMATIC—54mm objective. 20X. Field at 100 yds., 8.5 ft. Relative brightness, 6.1. Eye relief, ½". Wgt., 36 oz. Length closed, 13½". Complete with lens covers **$99.00**

UNERTL TEAM SCOPE—100mm objective. 15X, 24X. 32X eyepieces. Field at 100 yds. 13 to 7.5 ft. Relative brightness, 39.06 to 9.79. Eye relief, 2" to 1½". Weight, 13 lbs. 29⅞" overall. Metal tripod, yoke and wood carrying case furnished (total weight, 80 lbs.) **$485.00**

WEATHERBY—60mm objective, 20X-45X zoom **$150.00**
Tripod for above **$24.50**

SCOPE ATTACHMENTS

DAVIS TARGETEER—Objective lens/tube units that attach to front of low power scopes, increase magnification to 8X. 1¼" lens, **$25**, 1½" lens **$29.50**

HERMANN DUST CAPS—Connected leather straps, hand made, natural color. For all popular scopes. **$4.00**

LEE TACKHOLE DOTS—Various size dots for all scopes. Price **$7.50—$17.50**

LYMAN HAZE FILTER—For morning and late afternoon hunting. Filters out blue and violet rays allowing only the best part of the spectrum to transmit through your telescope lenses. For all riflescopes **$2.75**

PGS SCOPE SHIELDS—Flexible rubber, usable at front and rear, protect scopes from snow or rain. Made for all scopes. **$3.95**

PREMIER RETICLES—Various size dots for all scopes, also special reticles to order. Price—**$7.00** to **$18.50. PREMIER WEATHER CAPS**— transparent, high light transmission. For all popular scopes. Price **$3.50** Special sizes **$5.00**

W. P. SIEBERT—Converts Lyman, Leupold and Weaver K model varmint scopes to 15X-24X **$30.00**

STORM KING LENS CAPS—A hinged glass-and-rubber protector set (2), made in various sizes for all scopes. May be unhinged or sighted through. Anderson Gun Shop. Per pair **$3.95**

SUPREME LENS COVERS—Hinged protectors for most scope models, front and rear lenses shielded. Butler Creek Corp. Per pair, postpaid. **$7.50**

SPOTTING SCOPE STANDS

DAVIDSON MARK 245—Bipod adjustable for elevation, 9½"-14½". Side mount with two straps. Black crinkle finish. Length folded 16½". Price **$23.95**

FREELAND ALL ANGLE—Tripod adjustable for elevation. Left or right side mount with worm drive clamp. Folding legs. Clamps available for any scope tube size. Black, gray, or green crinkle finish. Price **$22.75**
Also 12" 18", 24" extensions available **$3.00-5.00**

FREELAND OLYMPIC—Bipod adjustable for elevation. All angle mount with padded worm drive clamp. Folding legs. Clamps available for any scope tube size. Black, grey, or green crinkle finish. Price **$24.75**
Also 12", 18", 24" extensions available **$3.00-5.00**
Zoom head for tripod or bipod **$11.00**

FREELAND REGAL BIPOD—Choice of saddle or zoom head. All adjustment knobs are oversize for easy adjusting. Large "ball" carrying knob. Gray or green finish **$26.75**
Above with stability weight **34.25**
Extensions 12"-24" **$3.00-5.00**

ARMS ASSOCIATIONS IN AMERICA AND ABROAD

UNITED STATES

ALABAMA

Alabama Gun Collectors Assn.
P.O. Box 2131, Birmingham, AL 35201
North Alabama Gun Coll. Assn.
P.O. Box 564, Huntsville, Ala. 35804

ARIZONA

Arizona Gun Collectors Assn., Inc.
Miles S. Vaughn, 1129 S. 6th Ave., Tucson, Ariz. 85701
International Cartridge Coll. Assn., Inc.
A. D. Amesbury, 4065 Montecito Ave., Tucson, Ariz. 85711

ARKANSAS

Ft. Smith Dealers & Coll. Assn.
Tony Smith, 1407 57 Terrace, Ft. Smith, Ark. 72901

CALIFORNIA

Calif. Hunters & Gun Owners Assoc.
V. H. Wacker, 2309 Cipriani Blvd., Belmont, Cal. 94002
Greater Calif. Arms & Collectors Assn.
Donald L. Bullock, 8291 Carburton St., Long Beach, Cal. 90808
Los Angeles Gun & Ctg. Collectors Assn.
F. H. Ruffra, 20810 Amie Ave., Torrance, CA 90503
Northern California Historical Arms Coll. Assn.
Julia Lundwall, 25 Mizpah St., San Francisco Ca. 94131
San Bernardino Valley Arms Collectors, Inc.
F. Schaperkotter, 2075 W. Rialto Ave., Space 48, San Bernadino, Cal. 92410
Santa Barbara Antique Arms Coll. Assn., Inc.
P.O. Box 6291, Santa Barbara, CA. 93111
Southern California Arms Collectors Assn.
Frank E. Barnyak, 4204 Elmer Ave., No. Hollywood, Cal. 91602

COLORADO

Arapahoe Gun Collectors
Bill Rutherford, 2968 S. Broadway, Englewood, Colo. 80110
Colorado Gun Collectors Assn.
Arnie Dowd, 5970 Estes Ct., Arvada, Colo. 80002
Pikes Peak Gun Collectors Guild
Charles Cell, 406 E. Uintah St., Colorado Springs, Colo. 80903

CONNECTICUT

Antique Arms Coll. Assn. of Conn.
T. N. Reiley, 17 Philip Rd., Manchester, Conn. 06040
National Shooting Sports Fdtn., Inc.
Warren Page, President, 1075 Post Rd., Riverside, Conn. 06878
Stratford Gun Collectors Assn., Inc.
P.O. Box 721, Stratford, CT 06497
Ye Conn. Gun Guild, Inc.
Rob. L. Harris, P.O. Box 67, Cornwall Bridge, Conn. 06754

DELAWARE

Delaware Antique Arms Collectors
C. Landis, 2408 Duncan Rd., Wilmington, Del. 19808

DISTRICT OF COLUMBIA

American Defense Preparedness Assn.
819 Union Trust Bldg., Washington, D.C. 20005
American Military Inst.
Box 568, Washington, D.C. 20044
National Rifle Assn.
1600 Rhode Island Ave., Washington, D.C. 20036

FLORIDA

American Police Pistol & Rifle Assn.
1100 N.E. 125th St., No. Miami, Fl. 33161 (law enforcement members and gun enthusiasts).
Florida Gun Collectors Assn.
Bob Marvin, P.O. Box 470, Jasper, Fla. 32052
National Police Officers Assn. of America
Natl. Police Hall of Fame Bldg., Venice, Fla. 33595

GEORGIA

Georgia Arms Collectors
Aubrey C. Oliveros, P.O. Box 450, Atlanta, Ga. 30301

ILLINOIS

American Single Shot Rifle Assn.
Dennis Hrusosky, 411 David Ave., Joliet, Ill. 60433
Central Illinois Gun Collectors Assn., Inc.
Donald E. Bryan, 20 Book Lane, Jacksonville, Ill. 62650
Fox Valley Arms Fellowship, Inc.
P.O. Box 301, Palatine, Ill. 60067
Illinois State Rifle Assn.
2800 N. Milwaukee Ave., Chicago, Ill. 60618
Illinois Gun Collectors Assn.
P. E. Pitts, P.O. Box 1524, Chicago, Ill. 60690
Little Fort Gun Collectors Assn.
Ernie Robinson, P.O. Box 194, Gurney, Ill. 60031
Mississippi Valley Gun & Cartridge Coll. Assn.
Mel Sims, Box 426, New Windsor, Ill. 61465
National Assn. of Federally Licd. Firearms Dealers
Andrew Molchan, 7001 N. Clark St., Chicago, IL 60625
Sauk Trail Gun Collectors
L. D. Carlock, Rte. 1, Box 169, Prophetstown, Ill. 61277
Wabash Valley Gun Collectors Assn., Inc.
Mrs. Betty Baer, 1002 Lincoln Pk. Ave., Danville, Ill. 61832

INDIANA

Crawfordsville Gun Club, Inc.
Rob. J. K. Edmonds, R.R. 2, Crawfordsville, Ind. 47933
Midwest Gun Traders Inc.
c/o Glen Whittenberger, 4609 Oliver St., Ft. Wayne, IN 46806
National Muzzle Loading Rifle Assn.
Box 67, Friendship, Ind. 47021
Northern Indiana Gun Collectors Assn.
Joe Katona, 16150 Ireland Rd., Mishawaka, IN 46544
Southern Indiana Gun Collectors Assn., Inc.
Harold M. McClary, 509 N. 3rd St., Boonville, Ind. 47601

IOWA

Cedar Valley Gun Collectors
R. L. Harris, 1602 Wenig Rd. N.E., Cedar Rapids, IA 52402
Central States Gun Collectors Assn.
Avery Giles, 1104 S. 1st Ave., Marshtown, IA 50158

KANSAS

Four State Collectors Assn.
M. G. Wilkinson, 915 E. 10th, Pittsburgh, Kan. 66762
Kansas Cartridge Coll. Assn.
Bob Linder, Box 84, Plainville, Kans. 67663
Missouri Valley Arms Collectors Assn.
Chas. F. Samuel, Jr., Box 8204, Shawnee Mission, Kans. 66208
Solomon Valley Gun Collectors
Frank Wheeler, Box 230, Osborne, Kan. 67473

KENTUCKY

John Hunt Morgan Gun Coll. Inc.
P.O. Box 525, Paris, Ky. 40361
Kentuckiana Arms Coll. Assn.
Charles R. Phelps, Box 1776, Louisville, Ky. 40201
Kentucky Gun Collectors Assn., Inc.
J. A. Smith, Box 64, Owensboro, Ky. 42301

LOUISIANA

Ark-La-Tex Gun Collectors Assn.
Ray Franks, 1521 Earl St., Shreveport, La. 71108
Bayou Gun Club
Dave Dugas, c/o Le Petit Soldier Shop, 528 Rue Royale, New Orleans, La. 70130
Pelican Arms Collectors
8681 Sharon Hills Blvd., Baton Rouge, LA 70811

MARYLAND

Baltimore Antique Arms Assn.
Stanley I. Kellert, R.D. 1, Box 256, Lutherville, MD 21093

MASSACHUSETTS

Bay Colony Weapons Collectors Inc.
Ronald B. Santurjian, 47 Homer Rd., Belmont, Mass. 02178
Massachusetts Arms Collectors
John J. Callan, Jr., P.O. Box 1001, Worcester, Mass. 01613
U. S. Revolver Assn.
Stanley A. Sprague, 59 Alvin St., Springfield, Mass. 01104

MICHIGAN

Michigan Antique Arms Coll., Inc.
W. H. Heid, 8914 Borgman Ave., Huntington Woods, Mich. 48070
Michigan Rifle & Pistol Assn.
Betty Swarthout, 8384 Perrin, Westland, Mich. 48185
Royal Oak Historical Arms Collectors, Inc.
Nancy Stein, 25487 Hereford, Huntington Woods, Mich. 48070

MINNESOTA

Minnesota Weapons Coll. Assn., Inc.
Box 662, Hopkins, MN 55343
Twin Ports Weapons Collectors
Jack Puglisi, 6504 Lexington St., Duluth, MN. 55807

MISSOURI

Edwardsville, Ill. Gun Collectors
A. W. Stephensmeier, 1055 Warson Woods Dr., St. Louis, MO 63122
Mineral Belt Gun Coll. Assn.
G. W. Gunter, 1110 E. Cleveland Ave., Monett, Mo. 65708

MONTANA

Montana Arms Collectors Assn.
Lewis E. Yearout, 308 Riverview Dr. East, Great Falls, MT 59404

NEBRASKA

Nebraska Gun & Cartridge Collectors
E. M. Zalud, 710 West 6th St., North Platte, Neb. 69101
Pine Ridge Gun Coll.
Loren Pickering, 509 Elm St., Crawford, NB 69339

NEW HAMPSHIRE

Maple Tree Gun Coll. Assn.
E. P. Hector, Meriden Rd., Lebanon, N.H. 03766
New Hampshire Arms Collectors Inc.
Frank H. Galevciz, Rt. 28, Windham, N.H. 03087

NEW JERSEY

Experimental Ballistics Associates
Ed Yard, 110 Kensington, Trenton, N.J. 08618
Jersey Shore Antique Arms Collectors
Joe Sisia, P.O. Box 100, Bayville, NJ 08721
New Jersey Arms Collectors Club, Inc.
Joseph S. Rixon, 230 Morris St., Morristown, N.J. 07960

NEW MEXICO

New Mexico Gun Collectors Assn.
P.O. Box 14145, Albuquerque, NM. 87111

NEW YORK

Armor & Arms Club
J. K. Watson, Jr., 25 Broadway, New York, NY 10004
Hudson-Mohawk Arms Collectors Assn., Inc.
Bennie S. Pisarz, 108 W. Main St., Frankfort, N.Y. 13340
International Benchrest Shooters
Donalee Sterl, R.D. 1, Robinson Rd., Mowhawk, N.Y. 13407
Iroquois Arms Collectors Assn.
Dennis Freeman, 12144 McNeeley Rd., Akron, N.Y. 14001
Mid-State Arms Coll. & Shooters Club
Bennie S. Pisarz, 108 W. Main St., Frankfort, N.Y. 13340
New York State Arms Collectors Assn., Inc.
Marvin Salls, R. D. 1,Ilion, N.Y. 13357
Sporting Arms and Ammunition Mfrs.' Inst., Inc.
420 Lexington Ave., N.Y., N.Y. 10017
Westchester Arms Collectors Club, Inc.
F. E. Falkenbury, Secy., 79 Hillcrest Rd., Hartsdale, N.Y. 10530

NORTH CAROLINA

Carolina Gun Collectors Assn.
Morris Lawing, 1020 Central Ave., Charlotte, NC 28205

OHIO

Amateur Trap Shooting Assn.
P.O. Box 246, Vandalia, O. 45377
American Society of Arms Collectors, Inc.
Rob. F. Rubendunst, 6550 Baywood Ln., Cincinnati, O. 45224
Barberton Gun Collectors Assn.
R. N. Watters, 1108 Bevan St., Barberton, O. 44203
Central Ohio Gun and Indian Relic Coll. Assn.
Coyt Stookey, 134 E. Ohio Ave., Washington C.H., O. 43160
Maumee Valley Gun Collectors Assn.
A. Kowalka, 3203 Woodville Rd., Northwood, OH 43616
National Bench Rest Shooters Assn., Inc.
Bernice McMullen, 607 W. Line St., Minerva, O. 44657
Ohio Gun Collectors, Assn., Inc.
Mrs. C. D. Rickey, 130 S. Main St., Prospect, O. 43342
The Stark Gun Collectors, Inc.
Russ McNary, 147 Miles Ave., N.W., Canton, O. 44708
Tri-State Gun Collectors
Doyt S. Gamble, 1115 N. Main St., Lima, OH 45801

OKLAHOMA

Indian Territory Gun Collectors Assn.
P.O. Box 4491, Tulsa, Okla. 74104

OREGON

National Reloading Mfrs. Assn., Inc.
1220 Morrison St., S.W., Portland, OR 97205
Oregon Cartridge Coll. Assn. Inc.
Dick Hamilton, P.O. Box 1015, Corvallis, OR, 97330
Oregon Arms Coll. Assn., Inc.
Ted Dowd, P.O. Box 25103, Portland, OR 97225
Willamette Valley Arms Coll. Assn.
K. Gardner, Rt. 3, Box 283, Springfield, OR 97477

PENNSYLVANIA

Boone & Crockett Club
C/O Carnegie Museum, 4400 Forbes Ave., Pittsburgh, Pa. 15213
Central Penn Antique Arms Assn.
Geo. Smithgall, 549 W. Lemon St., Lancaster, PA 17603
Forks of the Delaware Weapons Assn., Inc.
John F. Scheid, 348 Bushkill St., Easton, Pa. 18042
Lancaster Muzzle Loading Assn.
James H. Frederick, RD 1, Box 447, Columbia, PA 17512
Pennsylvania Gun Collectors Assn.
Arch Waugh, 37 Woodside Dr., Washington, PA 15301
Presque Isle Gun Coll. Assn.
James Welch, 156 E. 37 St., Erie, PA 16506
Somerset Sportsmen & Rifle Club
Clifford Dunmyer, Rt. 1, Somerset, PA 15501
Two Lick Valley Gun Collectors
Carl Steel II, 158 N. 14th St., Indiana, PA 15701

SOUTH CAROLINA

Belton Gun Club Inc.
J. K. Phillips, P.O. Box 605, Belton S.C. 29627
South Carolina Arms Coll. Assn.
J. W. McNelley, 3215 Lincoln St., Columbia, S.C. 29201

SOUTH DAKOTA

Dakota Territory Gun Coll. Assn., Inc.
Jim Aplan, Box 474, Onida, SD 57564

TENNESSEE

Memphis Antique Weapons Assn.
Nelson T. Powers, 4672 Barfield Rd., TN 38138
Tennessee Gun Collectors Assn., Inc.
M. H. Parks, 3556 Pleasant Valley Rd., Nashville, Tenn. 37204

TEXAS

Alamo Arms Collectors
Bill Brookshire, 410 Rector, San Antonio, Tex. 78216
Houston Gun Collectors Assn.
P.O. Box 53435, Houston, TX 77052
National Skeet Shooting Assn.
James M. Leer, Jr., P.O. Box 28188, San Antonio, TX 78228
Paso Del Norte Gun Collectors Inc.
Robert L. Bullard, 5910 Falcon St., El Paso, Tex. 79924
Permian Basin Rifle & Pistol Club, Inc.
E. L. Good, Box 459, Midland, Tex. 79701
Sabine Gun Collectors Club
Mrs. Irene Vivier, 1042 Iowa, Beaumont, Tex. 77705
Texas State Rifle Assn.
Lafe R. Pfeifer, P.O. Drawer 34809, Dallas TX 75234
Waco Gun Collectors
C. V. Pruitt, 4021 N. 26th, Waco, Tex. 76708

UTAH

Utah Gun Collectors Assn.
S. Gerald Keogh, 875 20th St., Ogden, Utah 84401

VIRGINIA

North-South Skirmish Assn., Inc.
John L. Rawls, Rt. 2, Box 245A, Winchester, VA 22601
Shenandoah Valley Gun Coll. Assn.
Daniel E. Blye, P.O. Box 926, Winchester, Va. 22601
Virginia Arms Collectors & Assn.
W. H. Bacon, 4601 Sylvan Rd., Richmond, Va. 23225

WASHINGTON

Washington Arms Collectors, Inc.
Don Zwicker, 446 Pelly Ave., Renton, WA 98055

WISCONSIN

Chippewa Valley Weapons Collectors
J. M. Sullivan, 504 Ferry St., Eau Claire, Wis. 54701
Great Lakes Arms Coll. Assn., Inc.
E. Warnke, 1811 N. 73rd St. Wauwatosa, WI 53213
Miniature Arms Collectors/Makers Society Ltd.
Joseph J. Macewicz, 104 White Sand Ln., Racine, WI 53402
Wisconsin Gun Collectors Assn., Inc.
Rob. Zellmer, W180N8996 Leona Lane, Menomonee Falls, WI. 53051

WYOMING

Wyoming Gun Collectors
Bob Funk, 224 N. 2W., Riverton, Wyo. 82501

AUSTRALIA

Nat'l. Sporting Shooters' Assn. of Australia
Mrs. O. H. Francis, Box 1064, G.P.O., S.A. 5001 Australia

CANADA

ALBERTA

Canadian Historical Arms Society
P.O. Box 901, Edmonton, Alb., Canada T5J 2L8

ONTARIO

Oshawa Antique Gun Coll. Inc.
Gordon J. Dignem, 613 Rosmere St., Oshawa, Ont., Canada

QUEBEC

Lower Canada Arms Collectors Assn.
Secretary, P.O. Box 1162, St. B. Montreal 101, Quebec, Can.

EUROPE

ENGLAND

Arms and Armour Society of London
F. Wilkinson, 40 Great James St., Holborn, London, N. 3HB W.C.1.
Historical Breechloading Smallarms Assn.
D. J. Penn, M.A., Imperial War Museum, Lambeth Rd., London SE1 6HZ, England. A biennial Journal is $7 a yr.
Muzzle Loaders' Assn. of Great Britain
Membership Records, 12 Francis Rd., Baginton, Coventry, England
National Rifle Assn. (British)
Bisley Camp, Brookwood, Woking, Surrey, England

FRANCE

Les Arquebusiers de France,
Mme, Marckmann, 70 Rue des Chantiers, 78-Versailles, France

NEW ZEALAND

New Zealand Deerstalkers Assn.
J. M. Murphy, P.O. Box 263, Wellington, New Zealand

SOUTH AFRICA

Historical Firearms Soc. of South Africa
"Minden" 11 Buchan Rd., Newlands, Cape Town, South Africa

PERIODICAL PUBLICATIONS

ALASKA Magazine
Alaska Northwest Pub. Co., Box 4-EEE, Anchorage, Alaska 99509. $9.00 yr. Hunting and fishing articles.

The American Blade*
Southern House Publications, Inc., 120 Alden Ave., N.W., Suite E-1, Atlanta, GA 30309. $5 yr. Add $1 f. foreign subscription. A magazine for all enthusiasts of the edged blade.

American Field†
222 W. Adams St., Chicago, Ill. 60606. $10.00 yr. Field dogs and trials, occasional gun and hunting articles.

American Firearms Industry
American Press-Media Assn. Inc., 7001 No. Clark St., Chicago, IL 60626. $6 yr. A relatively new publication, oriented to the gun trade.

The American Hunter (M)
Natl. Rifle Assn., 1600 Rhode Island Ave. N.W., Washington, DC 20036. $5.00 yr.

The American Rifleman (M)
National Rifle Assn., 1600 Rhode Island Ave., N.W., Wash., D.C. 20036. $10.00 yr. Firearms articles of all kinds.

The American Shotgunner
P.O. Box 3351, Reno, NV 89505. $6.50 yr. Shotgun articles of all kinds.

The American West*
American West Publ. Co., 599 College Ave., Palo Alto, Ca. 94306. $9.00 yr.

Argosy
Popular Publ., Inc., 420 Lexington Ave., New York, N.Y. 10017. $7.00 yr.

Arms Gazette
Wallace Beinfeld Publications, Inc., 2310 So. Sepulveda Blvd., Los Angeles, CA 90064. $8 yr. Excllent brief articles for the collector of antique and modern firearms.

Army (M)
Assn of the U.S. Army, 1529 18th St. N.W., Wash., D.C. 20036. $10.00 yr. Occasional articles on small arms

Australian Shooters' Journal
P.O. Box 12, Elizabeth, South Australia 5112, Australia. $5.50 yr. locally; $7.50 yr. overseas. Hunting and shooting articles.

Canadian Journal of Arms Collecting (Q)
Museums Restoration Service P.O. Box 2037, Sta. D, Ottawa, Ont., Canada KIP 5W3. $4.00 yr.

Deutsches Waffen Journal
Journal-Verlag Schwend GmbH, Postfach 340, D7170 Schwabisch Hall, Germany. $17.50 yr. Antique and modern arms, their history, technical aspects, etc. German text.

Ducks Unlimited, Inc. (M)
P.O. Box 66300, Chicago, Ill. 60666.

Enforcement Journal (Q)
Natl. Police Officers Assn., 1890 S. Tamiami Trail, Venice, Fla. 33595. $6.00 yr.

The Field†
The Harmsworth Press Ltd., 8 Stratton St., London W.I., England. $33.80 yr. Hunting and shooting articles.

Field & Stream
CBS Publications, 383 Madison Ave., New York, N.Y. 10017. $5.95 yr. Articles on firearms plus hunting and fishing.

Fur-Fish-Game
A. R. Harding Pub. Co., 2878 E. Main St., Columbus, Ohio 43209. $4.00 yr. "Gun Rack" column by M. H. Decker.

The Gun Report
World Wide Gun Report, Inc., Box 111, Aledo, Ill. 61231. $7.00 yr. For the gun collector.

Gunsport & Gun Collector
Leisure Publ., Inc., 711 Penn Ave., Pittsburgh, PA 15222. $7.50 yr.

Gun Week†
Amos Press, Inc., P.O. Box 150, Sidney, Ohio 45365. $5.00 yr. U.S. and possessions; $6.00 yr. Canada; $7.00 yr. foreign. Tabloid paper on guns, hunting, shooting.

Gun World
Gallant Publishing Co., 34249 Camino Capistrano, Capistrano Beach, CA 92624. $7.50 yr. For the hunting, reloading and shooting enthusiast.

Guns & Ammo
Petersen Pub. Co., 8490 Sunset Blvd., Los Angeles, Calif. 90069. $7.50 yr. Guns, shooting, and technical articles.

Guns
Guns Magazine, 8150 N. Central Park Ave., Skokie, Ill. 60076. $9.00 yr. Articles for gun collectors, hunters and shooters.

Guns Review
Ravenhill Pub. Co. Ltd., Standard House, Bonhill St., London E.C. 2A 4DA, England. $10.20 yr. For collectors and shooters.

The Handgunner (M)
U.S. Revolver Assn., 59 Alvin St., Springfield, Mass. 01104. $5.00 yr. General handgun and competition articles

Handloader*
Dave Wolfe Pub. Co., Box 3030, Prescott, Ariz. 86301 $6.50 yr. The journal of ammunition reloading.

Hobbies
Lightner Pub. Co., 1006 S. Michigan Ave., Chicago, Ill. 60605. $6.00 yr.; Canada $7.00; foreign $7.50. Collectors departments.

International Shooting Sport*
Union Internationale de Tir, 62 Wiesbaden-Klarenthal, Klarenthalerstr., Germany. $7.20 yr., p.p. For the International target shooter.

The Journal of the Arms & Armour Society (M)
F. Wilkinson (Secy.), 40 Great James St., Holborn, London WC1, N 3HB, England. $4.00 yr. Articles for the collector.

Journal of the Historial Breechloading Smallarms Assn.
Publ. twice a year, Imperial War Museum, Lambeth Road, London SE1 6HZ, England. $7 yr. Articles for the collector.

Law and Order
Law and Order Magazine, 37 W. 38th St., New York, N.Y. 10018. $7.00 yr. Articles on weapons for law enforcement.

The Luger Journal
Robt. B. Marvin, Publ., P.O. Box 326, Jasper, FL 32052. $6.00 yr.

Muzzle Blasts (M)
National Muzzle Loading Rifle Assn. P.O. Box 67, Friendship, Ind. 47021. $8.00 yr. For the black powder shooter.

National Defense (M)
American Defense Preparedness, 819 Union Trust Bldg., Wash., D.C. 20005. $8.00 yr. Articles on small arms, military equipment, and related subjects.

National Rifle Assn. Journal (British)
Natl. Rifle Assn. (BR.), Bisley Camp, Brookwood, Woking, Surrey, England. Gu24 OPB.

National Wildlife*
Natl. Wildlife Fed. Inc., 1412 16th St. N.W., Washington, D.C. $7.50 yr. World/Assoc. membership *includes Intl. Wildlife;* 12 issues $12.50.

New Zealand Wildlife (Q)
New Zealand Deerstalkers Assoc. Inc., P.O. Box 263, Wellington, N.Z. $2.00 U.S. and Canada, elsewhere on application. Hunting and shooting articles.

Outdoor Life
Times Mirror Magazines, Inc., 380 Madison Ave., New York, N.Y. 10017. $6.00 yr. Shooting column by Jim Carmichel, trap and Skeet by Bob Rodale.

Outdoor World (Q)
Country Beautiful Corp., 24198 W. Bluemound Rd., Waukesha, Wis. 53186. $5.00 yr. Conservation and wildlife articles.

Police Times (M)
1100 N.E. 125th St., No. Miami, Fla. 33161.

Popular Mechanics
Hearst Corp., 224 W. 57th St., New York, N.Y. 10019. $5.97 yr., $7.97 Canada, $9.97 foreign. Hunting and shooting articles.

Precision Shooting
Precision Shooting, Inc., Box 6, Athens, PA 18810. $5.00 yr. Journal of the International Benchrest Shooters.

The Rifle Magazine*
Dave Wolfe Publishing Co., Box 3030, Presott, Ariz. 86301. $6.50 yr. Journal of the NBRSA.

The Rifleman (Q)
National Smallbore Rifle Assoc., 113 Southwark St., London, S. E. 1, England. $9.00 (5 yrs.). Data on British Matches and International Matches, and technical shooting articles.

Rod and Gun in Canada
Rod and Gun Pub. Corp., 1219 Hotel deVille, Montreal 129, P.Q. Canada. $3.00 yr., $5.00 2 yrs., out of Canada, postage $1.00 p. yr. extra. Regular gun and shooting articles.

Saga
Gambi Public., 333 Johnson Ave., Brooklyn, N.Y. 11026. $6.00 yr. U.S., $6.50 Canada.

The Shooting Industry
Publisher's Dev. Corp., 8150 N. Central Pk., Skokie, Ill. 60076. $7.00 yr.

The Shooting Times & Country Magazine (England) †
Cordwallis Estate, Clivemont Rd., Maidenhead, Berksh., England. $24 yr. Game shooting, wild fowling, hunting and firearms articles.

Shooting Times
PJS Publications, News Plaza, Peoria, Ill. 61601 $5.85 yr. Guns, shooting, reloading; articles on every gun activity.

The Shotgun News‡
Snell Publishing Co., Box 1147, Hastings, NB 68901. $5.00 yr. Sample copy 75¢. Gun ads of all kinds.

The Skeet Shooting Review
National Skeet Shooting Assn., P.O. Box 28188, San Antonio, TX 78228. $9.00 yr. (Assn. membership of $10.00 includes mag.) Scores, averages, skeet articles.

Sporting Goods Business
Gralla Publications, 1501 Broadway, New York, NY 10036, Trade journal.

The Sporting Goods Dealer
1212 No. Lindbergh Blvd., St. Louis, Mo. 63166. $4.00 yr. The sporting goods trade journal.

Sports Afield
The Hearst Corp., 250 W. 55th St., New York, N.Y. 10019. $5.00 yr. Pete Brown on firearms plus hunting and fishing articles.

Sports Illustrated†
Time, Inc., 541 N. Fairbanks Court, Chicago, Ill. 60611. $14.00 yr. U.S. Poss. and Canada; $18.00 yr. all other countries. Articles on the current sporting scene.

Trap & Field
1100 Waterway Blvd., Indianapolis, Ind. 46202. $8.00 yr. Official publ. Amateur Trapshooting Assn. Scores, averages, trapshooting articles.

True
Fawcett Publ., Inc., Fawcett Bldg., Greenwich, Conn. 06830. $7.00 yr. U.S. Poss., and Canada; $10.00 yr. all other countries.

Wildlife Review (Q)
Dep't of Rec. and Conservation, Parliament Bldgs., Victoria, B.C., Canada $1.00 yr.

* Published bi-monthly
† Published weekly
‡ Published twice per month.

M Membership requirements; write for details.
Q Published Quarterly.
All others are published monthly.

Directory of the Arms Trade

Zip Code Abbreviations

State	Abbr.	State	Abbr.	State	Abbr.
Alaska	AK	Kentucky	KY	North Dakota	ND
Alabama	AL	Louisiana	LA	Ohio	OH
Arizona	AZ	Maine	ME	Oklahoma	OK
Arkansas	AR	Maryland	MD	Oregon	OR
California	CA	Massachusetts	MA	Pennsylvania	PA
Canal Zone	CZ	Michigan	MI	Puerto Rico	PR
Colorado	CO	Minnesota	MN	Rhode Island	RI
Connecticut	CT	Mississippi	MS	South Carolina	SC
Delaware	DE	Missouri	MO	South Dakota	SD
District of Columbia	DC	Montana	MT	Tennessee	TN
Florida	FL	Nebraska	NB	Texas	TX
Georgia	GA	Nevada	NV	Utah	UT
Guam	GU	New Hampshire	NH	Vermont	VT
Hawaii	HI	New Jersey	NJ	Virginia	VA
Idaho	ID	New Mexico	NM	Virgin Islands	VI
Illinois	IL	New York	NY	Washington	WA
Indiana	IN	North Carolina	NC	West Virginia	WV
Iowa	IA			Wisconsin	WI
Kansas	KS			Wyoming	WY

AMMUNITION (Commercial)

Alcan Shells, (See: Smith & Wesson Ammunition Co.)
Cascade Cartridge Inc., (See Omark)
DWM (see RWS)
Dynamit Nobel of America, Inc., 105 Stonehurst Ct., Northvale, NJ 07647 (DWM, RWS)
Federal Cartridge Co., 2700 Foshay Tower, Minneapolis, Minn. 55402
Frontier Cartridge Co., Inc., Box 1848, Grand Island, Neb. 68801
Omark-CCI, Inc., Box 856, Lewiston, Ida. 83501
RWS (see Dynamit Nobel)
Remington Arms Co., Bridgeport, Conn. 06602
Service Armament, 689 Bergen Blvd., Ridgefield, N.J. 07657
Smith & Wesson Ammunition Co., 3640 Seminary Rd., Alton, IL 62002
Super-Vel Cartridge Co., Box 40, Shelbyville, Ind. 46176
Weatherby's, 2781 E. Firestone Blvd., South Gate, Calif. 90280
Winchester-Western, East Alton, Ill. 62024

AMMUNITION (Custom)

Ed Agramonte, Inc., 41 Riverdale Ave., Yonkers, NY 10701
Ammodyne, Box 1589, Los Angeles, Calif. 90053
Bill Ballard, P.O. Box 656, Billings, MT 59103 (ctlg. 25¢)
Russell Campbell, 219 Leisure Dr., San Antonio, Tex. 78201
Collectors Shotshell Arsenal, 365 S. Moore, Lakewood, CO 80226
Cumberland Arms, 1222 Oak Dr., Manchester, Tenn. 37355
Custom Ammo & Gunsmithing, 2325 E. 15th St., Farmington, NM 87401
J. Dewey Gun Co., Clinton Corners, N.Y. 12514
E. W. Ellis Sport Shop, RFD 1, Box 139, Corinth, N.Y. 12822
Ellwood Epps (Orillia) Ltd., Hwy. 11 North, Orillia, Ont., Canada
David J. Gaida, 1109 S. Millwood, Wichita, KS 67203
Gussert Bullet & Cartridge Co., 1868 Lenwood Ave., Green Bay, WI 54303
J-4, Inc., P.O. Box 979, Tustin, CA 92680 (custom bullets)
R. H. Keeler, 1304 S. Oak, Port Angeles, Wash. 98362
KTW Inc., 710 Foster Park Rd., Lorain, OH 44053 (bullets)
Dean Lincoln, P.O. Box 1886, Farmington, NM 87401
Lomont Precision Bullets, 4421 S. Wayne Ave., Ft. Wayne, IN 46807 (custom bullets)
Pat B. McMillan, 1828 E. Campo Bello Dr., Phoenix, Ariz. 85022
Mansfield Gunshop, Box 83, New Boston, N.H. 03070
Man-Tol Shells, Box 134, Bunnell, Fla. 32010
Numrich Arms Corp., 203 Broadway, W. Hurley, N.Y. 12491
Robert Pomeroy, Morison Ave., Corinth, ME 04427 (custom shells)
A. F. Sailer, 707 W. 3d St., Owen, WI 54460
Sanders Cust. Gun Serv., 2358 Tyler Lane, Louisville, Ky. 40205
David Schneider, P.O. Box 895, Montebello, CA 90640
Shooter's Service & Dewey, Inc., Clinton Corners, N.Y. 12514
Geo. Spence, P.O. Box 222, Steele, MO 63877 (box-primed cartridges)
James C. Tillinghast, Box 568, Marlow, N.H. 03456
Whitney Cartridge Co., P.O. Box 608, Cortez, CO 81321 (shotshells)
H. Winter Cast Bullets, 422 Circle Dr., Clarksville, TN 37040

AMMUNITION (Foreign)

Abercrombie & Fitch, Madison at 45th St., New York, N.Y. 10017
Canadian Ind. Ltd. (C.I.L.), Box 10, Montreal, Que., Canada
C-I-L Ammunition Inc., P.O. Box 831, Plattsburgh, N.Y. 12901
Colonial Ammunition Co., Box 8511, Auckland, New Zealand
DWM, Speer Prods. Inc., Box 896, Lewiston, Ida. 83501
Dynamit Nobel of America, Inc., 105 Stonehurst Court, Northvale, NJ 07647 (RWS)
Gevelot of Canada, Box 1593, Saskatoon, Sask., Canada
Hy-Score Arms Co., 200 Tillary, Brooklyn, N.Y. 11201
Paul Jaeger Inc., 211 Leedom St., Jenkintown, Pa. 19046
S. E. Laszlo, 200 Tillary, Brooklyn, N.Y. 11201
L.E.S., 3640 Dempster, Skokie, IL 60076 (Hirtenberg)
NORMA-Precision, South Lansing, N.Y. 14882
Oregon Ammo Service, Box 19341, Portland, Ore. 97219
RWS (Rheinische-Westfalische Sprengstoff) see: Stoeger
Stoeger Arms Corp., 55 Ruta Ct., So. Hackensack, N.J. 07606 (RWS)
James C. Tillinghast, Box 568, Marlow, N.H. 03456

AMMUNITION COMPONENTS—BULLETS, POWDER, PRIMERS

Alcan, (see: Smith & Wesson Ammunition Co.)
Ammo-O-Mart, P.O. Box 66, Hawkesbury, Ont., Canada (Curry bullets)
Austin Power Co. (see Red Diamond Dist. Co.)
Bahler Die Shop, Rte. 1, 412 Hemlock St., Florence, OR 97439 (17 cal. bull.)
Lee Baker, 10314 Langmuir Ave., Sunland, CA 91040 (17 cal. bull.)
Joe J. Balickie, 6108 Deerwood Pl., Raleigh, NC 27607
Ballistic Research Industries, see: S & W-Fiocchi (12 ga. Sabot bullets)
Bitterroot Bullet Co., Box 412, Lewiston, Ida. 83501
The Bullet Boys, Box 367, Jaffrey, NH 03452 (cast bullets)
Centrix, 2116 N. 10th Ave., Tucson, Ariz. 85705
Kenneth E. Clark, 18738 Highway 99, Madera, CA 93637 (Bullets)
Colorado Custom Bullets, Rt. 1, Box 507-B, Montrose, Colo. 81401
Curry Bullets Canada, P.O. Box 66, Hawkesbury, Ont., Canada
Division Lead, 7742 W. 61 Pl., Summit, Ill. 60502
DuPont, Explosives Dept., Wilmington, Del. 19898
Elk Mountain Shooters Supply, 1719 Marie, Pasco, WA 99301 (Alaskan bullets)
Farmer Bros. Mfg. Co., 1102 Washington St., Eldora, IA 50627 (Lage shotshell wads)
Forty Five Ranch Enterprises, 119 S. Main, Miami, Okla. 74354
Godfrey Reloading Supply, R.R. 1, Box 688, Brighton, Ill. 62012 (cast bullets)
Lynn Godfrey, see: Elk Mtn. Shooters Supply
G. J. Godwin Firearm & Accessories, 455 Fox Lane, Orange Park, FL 32073 (cast bullets)
Green Bay Bullets, 233 No. Ashland, Green Bay, Wis. 54303 (lead)
Gussert Bullet & Cartridge Co., 1868 Lenwood Ave., Green Bay, WI 54303
Hercules Powder Co., 910 Market St., Wilmington, Del. 19899
Herter's Inc., Waseca, Minn. 56093
Hi-Precision Co., 109 Third Ave., N.E., Orange City, Ia. 51041
B. E. Hodgdon, Inc., 7710 W. 50th Hwy., Shawnee Mission, Kans. 66202
Hornady Mfg. Co., Box 1848, Grand Island, Neb. 68801
N. E. House Co., Middletown Rd., E. Hampton, Conn. 06424 (zinc bases only)
J-4, Inc., P.O. Box 979, Tustin, CA 92680 (custom bullets)
Jurras Munition Corp., Box 140, Shelbyville, Ind. 46176
Kush Plastics, P.O. Box 366, Palatine, IL 60067 (shotshell wads)
L. L. F. Die Shop, 1281 Highway 99 North, Eugene, Ore. 97402
LAGE wads, see Farmer Bros.

Lee's Precision Bullets, 10314 Langmuir Ave., Sunland, CA 91040 (17 cal.)
Ljutic Ind., Inc., Box 2117, Yakima, WA 98902 (Mono-wads)
Lomont Precision Bullets, 4421 S. Wayne Ave., Ft. Wayne, IN 46807
Lyman Gun Sight Products, Middlefield, Conn. 06455
Markell, Inc., 4115 Judah St., San Francisco, Calif. 94112
Meyer Bros. Mfgrs., Wabasha, Minn. 55981 (shotgun slugs)
Michael's Antiques, Box 233, Copiague, L.I., NY 11726 (Balle Blondeau)
Miller Trading Co., 20 S. Front St., Wilmington, N.C. 28401
Norma-Precision, So. Lansing, N.Y. 14882
Northridge Bullet Co., P.O. Box 1208, Vista, Ca. 92083
Nosler Bullets, P.O. Box 688, Beaverton, OR 97005
Oregon Ammo Service, Box 19341, Portland, Ore. 97219
Pattern Perfect, P.O. Box 366, Palatine, IL 60067 (shotshell wads)
Robert Pomeroy, Morison Ave., East Corinth, ME 04427
Red Diamond Distributing Co., 1304 Snowdon Dr., Knoxville, TN 37912 (black powder)
Remington-Peters, Bridgeport, Conn. 06602
Sanderson's, 724 W. Edgewater, Portage, Wis. 53901 (cork wad)
Sierra Bullets Inc., 421 No. Altadena Dr., Pasadena, Ca. 91107
Sisk Bullet Co., Box 874, Iowa Park, TX 76367
Smith & Wesson Ammunition Co., 3640 Seminary Rd., Alton, IL 62002
Speedy Bullets, Box 1262, Lincoln, Neb. 68501
Speer Products Inc., Box 896, Lewiston, Ida. 83501
C. H. Stocking, Rte. 3, Hutchinson, Minn. 55350 (17 cal. bullet jackets)
Super-Vel Cartr. Corp., 129 E. Franklin St., Shelbyville, Ind. 46176
Taylor Bullets, P.O. Box 21254, San Antonio, Tex. 78221
James C. Tillinghast, Box 568, Marlow, N.H. 03456
Vitt & Boos, Sugarloaf Dr., Wilton, Conn. 06897
Winchester-Western, New Haven, Conn. 06504
F. Wood, Box 386, Florence, Ore. 97439 (17 cal.)
Xelex Ltd., Hawksbury, Ont., Canada (powder, Curry bullets)
Zero Bullet Co., P.O. Box 1012, Cullman, AL 35055

ANTIQUE ARMS DEALERS

Robert Abels, P.O. Box 428, Hopewell Junction, NY 12533 (Catalog $1.00)
Ed Agramonte, Inc., 41 Riverdale Ave., Yonkers, NY 10701
F. Bannerman Sons, Inc., Box 126, L.I., Blue Point, NY 11715
Wm. Boggs, 1243 Grandview Ave., Columbus, Ohio 43212
Ed's Gun House, 1626 W. 9th St., Winona, MN 55987
Ellwood Epps (Orillia) Ltd., Hwy. 11 North, Orillia, Ont., Canada
Farris Muzzle Guns, 1610 Gallia St., Portsmouth, Ohio 45662
A. A. Fidd, Diamond Pt. Rd., Diamond Pt., N.Y. 12824
N. Flayderman & Co., Squash Hollow, New Milford, Conn. 06776
Fulmer's Antique Firearms, P.O. Box 792, Detroit Lakes, MN 56501
Herb Glass, Bullville, N.Y. 10915
Goergen's Gun Shop, 707 8th St. S.E., Austin, MN 55912
Goodman's for Guns, 1101 Olive St., St. Louis, Mo. 63101
Griffin's Guns & Antiques, R.R. 4, Peterboro, Ont., Canada K9J 6X5
The Gun Shop, 6497 Pearl Rd., Cleveland, O. 44130
Hansen & Company, 244 Old Post Rd., Southport, CT 06490
Heritage Firearms Co., P.O. Box 69, Rte. 7, Wilton, CN 06897
Holbrook Arms Museum, 12953 Biscayne Blvd., N. Miami, Fla. 33161
Ed Howe, 2 Main, Coopers Mills, Me. 04341
Jackson Arms, 6209 Hillcrest Ave., Dallas, Tex. 75205
Jerry's Gun Shop, 9220 Ogden Ave., Brookfield, Ill. 60513
Kenfix Co., 3500 E. Hillsborough Ave., Tampa, FL 33610
Lever Arms Serv. Ltd., 771 Dunsmuir St., Vancouver, B.C., Canada V6C 1M9
John J. Malloy, Briar Ridge Rd., Danbury, CT 06810
Montana Outfitters, 308 Riverview Dr. E., Great Falls, MT 59404
Charles W. Moore, R.D. 2, Schenevus, N.Y. 12155
Museum of Historical Arms, 1038 Alton Rd., Miami Beach, Fla. 33139
National Gun Traders, Inc., 225 S.W. 22nd Ave., Miami, Fla. 33135
New Orleans Arms Co., Inc., 240 Chartres St., New Orleans, La. 70130
Old West Gun Room, 3509 Carlson Blvd., El Cerrito, Cal. 94530 (write for list)
Pioneer Guns, 5228 Montgomery, Cincinnati (Norwood), OH 45212
Powell & Clements Sporting Arms, 210 E. 6th St., Cincinnati, O. 45202
Glode M. Requa, Box 35, Monsey, N.Y. 10952
Martin B. Retting Inc., 11029 Washington, Culver City, Calif. 90230
Ridge Guncraft, Inc., 234 N. Tulane Ave., Oak Ridge, Tenn. 37830
S.G. Intl., P.O. Box 702, Hermosa Beach, CA. 90254
Safari Outfitters Ltd., 71 Ethan Allen Highway, Ridgefield, CT 06877
San Francisco Gun Exch., 124 Second St., San Francisco, Calif. 94105
Santa Ana Gunroom, P.O. Box 1777, Santa Ana, Calif. 92702
Ward & Van Valkenburg, 402-30th Ave. No., Fargo, N. Dak. 58102
M. C. Wiest, 234 N. Tulane Ave., Oak Ridge, Tenn. 37830
Yale's Gun Shop, R.D. 1, Box 133, Bel Air, MD 21014
Yeck Antique Firearms, 579 Tecumseh, Dundee, Mich. 48131

BOOKS (ARMS), Publishers and Dealers

CB Press, Box 4087, Bartonville, IL 61607
Digest Books, Inc., 540 Frontage Rd., Northfield, IL 60093
Norm Flayderman, RFD 2, Squash Hollow, New Milford, CT 06776
Fortress Publications Inc., P.O. Box 241, Stoney Creek, Ont. L8G 3X9, Canada
Handgun Press, 5832 S. Green, Chicago, IL 60621
Normount Technical Publications, P.O. Drawer N-2, Wickesburg, AZ 85358
Personal Firearms Record Book, Box 201, Park Ridge, IL 60068
Ray Riling Arms Books Co., 6844 Gorsten St., Philadelphia, PA 19119
Rutgers, Mark Aziz, 127 Raritan Ave., Highland Park, NJ 08904

BULLET & CASE LUBRICANTS

Alpha-Molykote, Dow Corning Corp., 45 Commerce Dr., Trumbull, Ct. 06601
Birchwood-Casey Co., Inc., 7900 Fuller Rd., Eden Prairie, Minn. 55343 (Anderol)
Chopie Mfg. Inc., 531 Copeland, La Crosse, Wis. 54601 (Black-Solve)
Cooper-Woodward, Box 972, Riverside, Cal. 92502 (Perfect Lube)
Green Bay Bullets, 233 N. Ashland, Green Bay, Wis. 54303 (EZE-Size case lube)
Gussert Bullet & Cartridge Co., 1868 Lenwood Ave., Green Bay, WI 54303 (Super Lube)
Herter's, Inc., Waseca, Minn. 56903 (Perfect Lubricant)
IPCO (Industrial Products Co.), Box 14, Bedford, MA 01730
Javelina Products, Box 337, San Bernardino, Cal. 92402 (Alox beeswax)
Jet-Aer Corp., 100 Sixth Ave., Paterson, N.J. 07524
Lenz Prod. Co., Box 1226, Sta. C, Canton, O. 44708 (Clenzoil)
Lyman Gun Sight Products, Middlefield, Conn. 06455 (Size-Ezy)
Micro Shooter's Supply, Box 213, Las Cruces, N. Mex. 88001 (Micro-Lube)
Mirror Lube, P.O. Box 693, San Juan Capistrano, CA 92675
Nutec, Box 1187, Wilmington, Del. 19899 (Dry-Lube)
Pacific Tool Co., P.O. Drawer 2048, Ordnance Plant Rd., Grand Island, NB 68801
Phelps Rel. Inc., Box 4004, E. Orange, N.J. 07019
RCBS, Inc., Box 1919, Oroville, Calif. 95965
SAECO Rel. Inc., P.O. Box 778, Carpinteria, CA 93103
Scientific Lubricants Co., 3753 Lawrence Ave., Chicago, Ill. 60625
Shooters Accessory Supply (SAS), Box 250, N. Bend, Ore. 97459
Sports Distr. Co., Rte. 1, Rapid City, S.D. 57701 (Reloader No. 7)
Testing Systems, Inc., 2832 Mt. Carmel, Glenside, PA 19038

BULLET SWAGE DIES AND TOOLS

Bahler Die Shop, Box 386/412 Hemlock St., Florence, OR 97439
Belmont Products, Rte. #1, Friendsville, TN 37737
C-H Tool & Die Corp., P.O. Box L, Owen, WI 54460
Clymer Mfg. Co., 14241 W. 11 Mile Rd., Oak Park, MI 48237
Lester Coats, 416 Simpson St., North Bend, OR 97459 (lead wire cutter)
Herter's Inc., Waseca, MN 56093
Hollywood, Whitney Sales Inc., P.O. Box 875, Reseda, CA 91335
Independent Machine & Gun Shop, 1416 N. Hayes, Pocatello, ID 83201 (TNT)
L.L.F. Die Shop, 1281 Highway 99 North, Eugene, OR 97402
Rorschach Precision Products, P.O. Box 1613, Irving, TX 75060
SAS Dies, P.O. Box 250, North Bend, OR 97459
Robert B. Simonson, Rte. 2, 2129 Vanderbilt Rd., Kalamazoo, MI 49002
TNT (see Ind. Mach. & Gun Shop)

CARTRIDGES FOR COLLECTORS

Antique Arsenal, 365 So. Moore St., Lakewood, Colo. 80226
J. A. Belton, 52 Sauve Rd., Mercier, Chateauguay Cty, Quebec, Canada
Peter Bigler, 291 Crestwood Dr., Milltown, N.J. 08850 (ctlg. $1.50)
Geo. Blakeslee, 3135 W. 28th St., Denver, CO 80211
Cameron's, 16690 W. 11th Ave., Golden, Colo. 80401
Carter Gun Works, 2211 Jefferson Pk. Ave., Charlottesville, Va. 22903
Gerry Coleman, 163 Arkell St., Hamilton, Ont., Canada
Chas. E. Duffy, Williams Lane, West Hurley, N.Y. 12419
Tom M. Dunn, 1342 So. Poplar, Casper, Wyo. 82601
Ellwood Epps (Orillia) Ltd., Hwy. 11 North, Orillia, Ont., Canada
Ed Howe, 2 Main St., Coopers Mills, Me. 04341
Walt Ireson, 47 Chedoke Ave., Hamilton 12, Ont., Canada
Jackson Arms, 6209 Hillcrest Ave., Dallas, Tex. 75205
George Kass, 30 Ivy Circle, West Haven, CT 06516 (ctlg. $1)
Montana Outfitters, 308 Riverview Dr. E., Great Falls, MT 59404
Oregon Ammo Service, Box 19341, Portland, Ore. 97219 (catlg. $2.00)
Powder Horn, 3135 W. 28th, Denver, CO 80211
Martin B. Retting Inc., 11029 Washington, Culver City, Calif. 90230
San Francisco Gun Exchange, 124 Second St., San Francisco, CA 94105
Perry Spangler, 519 So. Lynch, Flint, Mich. 48503 (list 50¢)
Ernest Tichy, 365 S. Moore, Lakewood, Colo. 80226
James C. Tillinghast, Box 568, Marlow, N.H. 03456 (list 50c)

CASES, CABINETS AND RACKS—GUN

Alco Carrying Cases Inc., 601 W. 26th St., New York, N.Y. 10001
Artistic Wood Specialties, 923-29 W. Chicago Ave., Chicago, Ill. 60622
Morton Booth Co., Box 123, Joplin, Mo. 64801
Boyt Co., Div. of Welsh Sportg. Gds., Box 1108, Iowa Falls, Ia. 50126
Browning, Rt. 4, Box 624-B, Arnold, MO 63010
Cap-Lex Gun Cases, Capitol Plastics of Ohio, Inc., 333 Van Camp Rd., Bowling Green, OH 43402
Castle Westchester Prods. Co., Inc., 498 Nepperhan Ave., Yonkers, N.Y. 10701
Challanger Mfg. Co., 118 Pearl St., Mt. Vernon, NY 10550
Coladonato Bros., Box 156, Hazleton, Pa. 18201
Do-All Mfg. Co., 3206 Plant Dr., Boise, ID 83703
E & C Enterprises, P.O. Box 823, So. Pasadena, CA 91030 (gun socks)
East-Tenn Mills, Inc., Box 1030, Johnson City, TN 37601 (gun socks)
Ellwood Epps (Orillia) Ltd., Hwy. 11 North, Orillia, Ont., Canada
Farber Bros., Inc., 821 Linden Ave., Memphis, Tenn. 38101 (truck pouch)
Ferrell Co., Rte. 3, Gallatin, Tenn. 37066 (Redi-Rack)
Flambeau Plastics Corp., 801 Lynn, Baraboo, Wis. 53913
Gun-Ho Case Mfg. Co., 110 East 10th St., St. Paul, Minn. 55101
Gun Racks, Inc., P.O. Box 22675, Houston, Tex. 77027
Harbor House Gun Cabinets, 12508 Center St., South Gate, CA 90280
B. E. Hodgdon, Inc., 7710 W. 50 Hiway, Shawnee-Mission, Kans. 66202
Ithaca Gun Co., Terrace Hill, Ithaca, N.Y. 14850
J-K Imports, Box 403, Novato, Cal. 94947 (leg 'o mutton case)
Jumbo Sports Prods., P.O. Box 280-Airport Rd., Frederick, MD 21701
Kolpin Bros. Co., Inc., Box 231, Berlin, Wis. 54923
Marble Arms Corp., 420 Industrial Park, Gladstone, Mich. 49837

W. A. Miller Co., Inc. (Wamco), Mingo Loop, Oguossoc, ME 04964 (wooden handgun cases)
National Sports Div., 19 E. McWilliams St., Fond du Lac, Wis. 54935
Nortex Co., 2821 Main St., Dallas, Tex. 75226 (automobile gun rack)
North Star Devices, Inc., P.O. Box 2095, North St., Paul, MN 55109 (Gun-Slinger portable rack)
Paul-Reed, Inc., P.O. Box 227, Charlevoix, Mich. 49720
Penguin Industries, Inc., Box 97, Parkesburg, Pa. 19365
Pistolsafe, Dr. L., N. Chili, NY 14514 (handgun safe)
Precise Imp. Corp., 3 Chestnut, Suffern, N.Y. 10901
Protecto Plastics, Inc., 201 Alpha Rd., Wind Gap, Pa. 18091 (carrying cases)
Richland Arms Co., 321 W. Adrian, Blissfield, Mich. 49228
Saf-T-Case, Box 10592, Dallas, Tex. 75207
San Angelo Die Castings, Box 984, San Angelo, Tex. 76901
Buddy Schoellkopf, 4100 Platinum Way, Dallas, Tex. 75237
Security Gun Chest, Div. of Tread Corp., P.O. Box 5497, Roanoke, VA 24012
Sile Distr., 7 Centre Market Pl., New York, N.Y. 10013 (leg o'mutton case)
Stearn Mfg. Co., Div. & 30th St., St. Cloud, Minn. 56301
Sundance Prods., 255 W. 200 S., Salt Lake City, UT 84101
Tread Corp., P.O. Box 5497, Roanoke, VA 24012 (security gun chest)
Western Holder Co., Box 33, Menomonee Falls, Wis. 53051
Woodstream Corp., Box 327, Lititz, Pa. 17543
Yield House, Inc., RFD, No. Conway, N.H. 03860

CHOKE DEVICES & RECOIL ABSORBERS

Arms Ingenuity Co., Box 1, Weatogue, Conn. 06089 (Jet-Away)
Contra-Jet, 7920 49th Ave. So., Seattle, Wash. 98118
Dahl's Gun Shop, Rt. 2, Billings, Mont. 59101
Diverter Arms, Inc., 6520 Rampart St., Houston, TX 77036 (shotgun diverter)
Edwards Recoil Reducer, 269 Herbert St., Alton, Ill. 62002
Emsco Chokes, 101 Second Ave., S.E., Waseca, Minn. 56093
Herter's Inc., Waseca, Minn. 56093. (Vari-Choke)
Lyman Gun Sight Products, Middlefield, Conn. 60455 (Cutts Comp.)
Mag-Na-Port Arms, Inc., 16746 14 Mile Rd., Fraser, MI 48026 (muzzle-brake system)
Pendleton Dekickers, 1210 S. W. Hailey Ave., Pendleton, Ore. 97801
Poly-Choke Co., Inc., Box 296, Hartford, Conn. 06101

CHRONOGRAPHS AND PRESSURE TOOLS

Avtron, 10409 Meech Ave., Cleveland, Ohio, 44105
B-Square Co., Box 11281, Ft. Worth, Tex. 76110
Chronograph Specialists, P.O. Box 5005, Santa Ana, Calif. 92704
Display Electronics, Box 1044, Littleton, CO 80120
Diverter Arms, Inc., 6520 Rampart St., Houston, TX 77036 (press. tool)
Herter's, Waseca, Minn. 56093
Micro-Sight Co., 242 Harbor Blvd., Belmont, Calif. 94002 (Techsonic)
Oehler Research, P.O. Box 9135, Austin, Tex. 78756
Scharon Fabricators, Box 11834, Clayton, MO 63105
Sundtek Co., P.O. Box 744, Springfield, Ore. 97477
Telepacific Electronics Co., Inc., 3335 W. Orange Ave., Anaheim, CA 92804
M. York, 19381 Keymar Way, Gaithersburg, MD 20760 (press. tool)

CLEANING & REFINISHING SUPPLIES

ADSCO, Box 191, Ft. Kent, Me. 04743 (stock finish)
A 'n A Co., Box 571, King of Prussia, PA 19406 (Valet shotgun cleaner)
Allied Products Co., 734 N. Leavitt, Chicago, Ill. 60612 (Cor-O-Dex)
Armite Labs., 1845 Randolph St., Los Angeles, CA 90001 (pen oiler)
Armoloy, 206 E. Daggett St., Ft. Worth, TX 76104
Backus Co., 411 W. Water St., Smethport, Pa. 16749 (field gun-cleaner)
Ber Big Enterprises, P.O. Box 291, Huntington, CA 90255 (gunsoap)
Birchwood-Casey Chem. Co., 7900 Fuller Rd., Eden Prairie, Minn. 55343 (Anderol, etc.)
Bisonite Co., Inc., 2250 Military Rd., Tonwanda, NY 14150
Jim Brobst, 299 Poplar St., Hamburg, Pa. 19526 (J-B Compound)
GB Prods. Dept., HRR, Inc., Industrial Rowe, Gardner, MA 01440
Browning Arms, Rt. 4, Box 624-B, Arnold, Mo. 63010
J. M. Bucheimer Co., Airport Rd., Frederick, MD 21701
Burnishine Prod. Co., 8140 N. Ridgeway, Skokie, Ill. 60076 (Stock Glaze)
C & R Distr. Corp., 449 E. 21st So., Salt Lake City, Utah 84115
Caddie Products Corp., Div. of Jet-Aer, Paterson, NJ 07524 (the Cloth)
Cherry Corners Mfg. Co., 11136 Congress Rd., Lodi, Ohio 44254 (buffing compound)
Chopie Mfg. Inc., 531 Copeland, La Crosse, Wis. 54601 (Black-Solve)
Clenzoil Co., Box 1226, Sta. C, Canton, O. 44708
Clover Mfg. Co., 139 Woodward Ave., Norwalk, CT 06856 (Clover compound)
Craftsman Wood Serv. Co., 2729 S. Mary, Chicago, Ill. 60608 (ctlg. 50¢)
Dex-Kleen, Box 509, Des Moines, Ia. 50302 (gun wipers)
J. Dewey Gun Co., Clinton Corners, N.Y. 12514
Dri-Slide, Inc., Industrial Park, Fremont, Mich. 49412
Forty-Five Ranch Enterpr., 119 S. Main St., Miami, Okla. 74354
Garcia Sptg. Arms Corp., 329 Alfred Ave., Teaneck, N.J. 07666
Gun-All Products, Box 244, Dowagiac, Mich. 49047
Percy Harms Corp., 7349 N. Hamlin, Skokie, Ill. 60076
Frank C. Hoppe Div., P.O. Box 97, Parkesburg, Pa. 19365
Hunting World, 247 E. 50th St., N.Y. 10022 (P-H Safari Kit)
J & G Rifle Ranch, Box 80, Turner, MT 59542
Jet-Aer Corp., 100 Sixth Ave., Paterson, N.J. 07524 (blues & oils)
K.W. Kleinendorst, 48 Taylortown Rd., Montville, N.J. 07045 (rifle clg. rods)
Knox Laboratories, 2335 S. Michigan Ave., Chicago, Ill. 60616
LPS Res. Labs. Inc., 2050 Cotner Ave., Los Angeles, Calif. 90025
Carl Lampert Co., 2639 So. 31st St., Milwaukee, Wis. 53215 (gun bags)
LEM Gun Spec., Box 31, College Park, Ga 30337 (Lewis Lead Remover)
Liquid Wrench, Box 10628, Charlotte, N.C. 28201 (pen. oil)
Lynx Line Gun Prods. Div., Protective Coatings, Inc., 20626 Fenkell Ave., Detroit, MI 48223
Marble Arms Co., 420 Industrial Pk., Gladstone, Mich. 49837
Micro Sight Co., 242 Harbor Blvd., Belmont, Ca. 94002 (bedding)
Mill Run Prod., 1360 W. 9th, Cleveland, O. 44113 (Brite-Bore Kits)
Mint Luster Cleaners, 1102 N. Division, Appleton, Wis. 54911
Mirror-Lube, P.O. Box 693, San Juan Capistrano, CA 92675
Mistic Metal Mover, Inc., R.R. 2, P.O. Box 336, Princeton, Ill. 61356
Mitchell Chemical Co., Wampus Lane, Milford, CT 06460 (Gun Guard)
New Method Mfg. Co., Box 175, Bradford, Pa. 16701 (gun blue)
Northern Instruments, Inc., 4643 No. Chatsworth St., St. Paul, MN 55112 (Stor-Safe rust preventer)
Numrich Arms Co., West Hurley, N.Y. 12491 (44-40 gun blue)
Nutec, Box 1187, Wilmington, Del. 19899 (Dry-Lube)
Outers Laboratories, Box 37, Onalaska, Wis. 54650 (Gunslick kits)
Radiator Spec. Co., 1400 Independence Blvd., Charlotte, N.C. 28201 (liquid wrench)
Realist Inc., N. 93 W. 16288 Megal Dr., Menomonee Falls, Wis. 53051
Reardon Prod., 323 N. Main St., Roanoke, Ill. 61561 (Dry-Lube)
Reese Arms Co., R.R. 1, Colona, IL 61241 (Dry-film lube)
Rice Dry Film Gun Coatings, 1521-43rd St., West Palm Beach, FL 33407
Riel & Fuller, 423 Woodrow Ave., Dunkirk, N.Y. 14048 (anti-rust oil)
Rig Products Co., Box 279, Oregon, Ill. 61061 (Rig Grease)
Rocket Chemical Co., Inc., 5390 Napa St., San Diego, Calif. 92110 (WD-40)
Rusteprufe Labs., 605 Wolcott St., Sparta, Wis. 54656
Saunders Sptg. Gds., 338 Somerset, No. Plainfield, NJ 07060 (Sav-Bore)
Schultea's Gun String, 67 Burress, Houston, TX 70022
Service Armament, 689 Bergen Blvd., Ridgefield, N. J. 07657 (Parker-Hale)
Sheldon's Inc., Box 508, Antigo, Wis. 54409 (shotgun brushes)
Shooter's Serv. & Dewey (SS&D), Clinton Corners, N.Y. 12514
Silicote Corp., Box 359, Oshkosh, Wis. 54901 (Silicone cloths)
Silver Dollar Guns, P.O. Box 489, Franklin NH 03235 (Silicone oil)
A. D. Soucy, Box 191, Ft. Kent, Me. 04743 (ADSCO stock finish)
Southeastern Coatings, Ind., (SECOA), Bldg. 132, P.B.I. Airport, W. Palm Beach, Fla. 33406 (Teflon Coatings)
Sportsmen's Labs., Inc., Box 732, Anoka, Minn. 55303 (Gun Life lube)
Surcon, Inc., P.O. Box 277, Zieglerville, Pa. 19492
Taylor & Robbins, Box 164, Rixford, Pa. 16745 (Throat Saver)
Testing Systems, Inc., 2832 Mt. Carmel, Glenside, PA 19038 (gun lube)
Texas Platers Supply Co., 2453 W. Five Mile Parkway, Dallas, TX 75233 (plating kit)
C. S. Van Gorden, 120 Tenth Ave., Eau Claire, Wis. 54701 (Instant Blue)
WD-40 Co., 1061 Cudahy Pl., San Diego, CA 92110
West Coast Secoa, Inc., Rt. 5, Box 138, Lakeland, FL 33801 (Teflon coatings)
Williams Gun Sight, 7389 Lapeer Rd., Davison, Mich. 48423 (finish kit)
Winslow Arms Co., P.O. Box 578, Osprey, Fla. 33595 (refinishing kit)
Wisconsin Platers Supply Co., see: Texas Platers Supply Co.
Woodstream Corp., P.O. Box 327, Lititz, Pa. 17543 (Mask)

CUSTOM GUNSMITHS

W. S. Abe, Abe's Gun Shop, 5124 Huntington Dr., Los Angeles, CA 90032
Franz Achleithner, Main St., Margaretville, NY 12455
P. O. Ackley, 2235 Arbor Lane, Salt Lake City, UT 84117
Ed Agramonte, Inc., 41 Riverdale Ave., Yonkers, NY 10701
Ahlman Cust. Gun Shop, R.R. 1, Box 20, Morristown, Minn. 55052
Anderson's Guns, 706 S. 23rd St., Laramie, WY 82070
Dale P. Andrews, 3572 E. Davies, Littleton, CO 80122
R. J. Anton, 1016 Riehl St., Waterloo, Ia. 50703
Arms Divs., M. R. Co., 5920 Smith Ave., Baltimore MD 21209
Atkinson Gun Co., P.O. Box 512, Prescott, AZ 86301
Bacon Creek Gun Shop, Cumberland Falls Rd., Corbin, Ky. 40701
Bain and Davis Sptg. Gds., 599 W. Las Tunas Dr., San Gabriel, Calif. 41776
Joe J. Balickie, 6108 Deerwood Pl., Raleigh, N.C. 27607
Wm. G. Bankard, 4211 Thorncliff Rd., Baltimore, MD 21236 (Kentuckys)
Barta's, Rte. 1, Box 129-A, Cato, Wis. 54206
Bayer's Gun Shop, 213 S. 2nd, Walla Walla, Wash. 99362
Bennett Gun Works, 561 Delaware Ave., Delmar, N.Y. 12054
Irvin L. Benson, Saganaga Lake, Pine Island Camp, Ontario, Canada
Gordon Bess, 708 River St., Canon City, Colo. 81212
Bruce Betts Gunsmith Co., 26 Rolla Gardens Dr., Rolla, Mo. 65401
Stephen L. Billeb, Rte. 3, Box 163, Bozeman, MT 59715
John Bivins, Jr., 446 So. Main St., Winston-Salem, N.C. 27101
Edwin T. Blackburn, Jr., 474 E. McKinley, Sunnyvale, CA 94086 (precision metal work)
Boone Mountain Trading Post, Averyville Rd., St. Marys, Pa. 15857
T. H. Boughton, 410 Stone Rd., Rochester, N.Y. 14616
Kay H. Bowles, Pinedale, Wyo. 82941
Breckheimers, Parish, NY 13131
L. H. Brown, Rte. 2, Airport Rd., Kalispell, Mont. 59901
Lenard M. Brownell, Box 25, Wyarno, WY 82845
George Bunch, 7735 Garrison Rd., Hyattsville, Md. 20784
Samuel W. Burgess, 25 Squam Rd., Rockport, MA 01966 (bluing repairs)
Tom Burgess, Rte. 3, Box 124, Kalispell, MT 59901 (metalsmithing only)
Leo Bustani, P.O. Box 8125, W. Palm Beach, Fla. 33407
Gus Butterowe, 10121 Shoreview Rd., Dallas, TX 75238
Cameron's Guns, 16690 W. 11th Ave., Golden, Colo. 80401
Carpenter's Gun Works, Gunshop Rd., Box C, Plattekill, N.Y. 12568
Carter Gun Works, 2211 Jefferson Pk. Ave., Charlotteville, Va. 22903
Cassell Gun Shop, 403 West Lane, Worland, Wyo. 82401
Ray Chalmers, 18 White Clay Dr., Newark, Del. 19711
N. C. Christakos, 2832 N. Austin, Chicago, IL 60634
Kenneth E. Clark, 18738 Highway 99, Madera, Calif. 93637

Cloward's Gun Shop, 4023 Aurora Ave. N., Seattle, WA 98102
Crest Carving Co., 14849 Dillow St., Westminster, Ca. 92683
Philip R. Crouthamel, 817 E. Baltimore, E. Lansdowne, Pa. 19050
Custom Rifle Shop, 4550 E. Colfax Ave., Denver, Colo. 80220
Jim Cuthbert, 715 S. 5th St., Coos Bay, Ore. 97420
DS Antique Arms Co., 1110 Cleveland Ave., Monett, MO 65708 (Hawken copies)
Dahl's Gunshop, Rt. 2, Billings, Mont. 59101
Davis Gun Shop, 7213 Lee Highway, Falls Church, VA 22046
Dee Davis, 5658 So. Mayfield, Chicago, Ill. 60638
Jack Dever, 8520 N.W. 90, Okla. City, OK 73132 (S. S. Work)
J. Dewey Gun Co., Clinton Corners, N.Y. 12514
Dominic DiStefano, 4303 Friar Lane, Colorado Springs, CO 80907
Drumbore Gun Shop, 119 Center St., Lehigton, PA 18235
Charles Duffy, Williams Lane, W. Hurley, N.Y. 12491
Gerald D. Eisenhauer, Rte. #3, Twin Falls, Ida. 83301
Bill English, 4411 S. W. 100th, Seattle, Wash. 98146
Ken Eyster, Heritage Gunsmiths Inc., 6441 Bishop Rd., Centerburg, O. 43011
N. B. Fashingbauer, Box 366, Lac Du Flambeau, Wis. 54538
Ted Fellowes, Beaver Lodge, 9245-16th Ave., S.W., Seattle, Wa. 98106 (muzzle loaders)
The Fergusons, Temple Rd., New Ipswich, NH 03071
H. J. and L. A. Finn, 12565 Gratiot Ave., Detroit, MI 48205
Loxley Firth Firearms, 8563 Oswego Rd., R. D. 4, Baldwinsville, N.Y. 13027
Marshall F. Fish, Westport, N.Y. 12993
Jerry Fisher, 1244—4th Ave. West, Kalispell, Mont. 59901
Flagler Gun Clinic, Box 8125, West Palm Beach, Fla. 33407 (Win. 92 & 94 Conv.)
Frazier's Custom Guns, Box 3, Tyler, WA 99035
Clark K. Frazier/Matchmate, RFD 1, Rawson, OH 45881
Freeland's Scope Stands, 3737—14th Ave., Rock Island, Ill. 61201
Fred's Gun Shop, Box 725, Juneau, Alaska 99801
Frederick Gun Shop, 10 Elson Drive, Riverside, R.I. 02915
Frontier Arms, Inc., 420 E. Riding Club Rd., Cheyenne, Wyo. 82001
Fuller Gunshop, Cooper Landing, Alas. 99572
Geo. M. Fullmer, 2499 Mavis St., Oakland, Cal. 94501 (metal work, precision chambering only)
Georgia Gun & Smith, 5170 Thistle Rd., Smyrna, GA 30080
Ed Gillman, 116 Upper High Crest Rd., Butler, NJ 07405
Dale Goens, Box 224, Cedar Crest, NM 87008
A. R. Goode, R.D. 1, Box 84, Thurmont, MD 21788
G. T. Gregory, P.O. Box 162, Plymouth, CA 95669 (saddle rifles)
Griffin & Howe, 589-8th Ave., New York, N.Y. 10017
Dale M. Guise, Rt. 2, Box 239, Gardners, Pa. 17324 (Rem. left-hand conversions)
The Gunshop, Inc., Jack First, 44633 Sierra Highway, Lancaster, CA 93534
H & R Custom Gun Serv., 68 Passaic Dr., Hewitt, N.J. 07421
Paul Haberly, 2364 N. Neva, Chicago, IL 60635
Chas. E. Hammans, Box 788, Stuttgart, AR 72160
Harkrader's Cust. Gun Shop, 111 No. Franklin St., Christiansburg, Va. 24073
Rob't W. Hart & Son, 401 Montgomery St., Nescopeck, Pa. 18635 (actions, stocks)
Hal Hartley, Box 147, Blairs Fork Rd., Lenoir, N.C. 28654
Hubert J. Hecht, 55 Rose Mead Circle, Sacramento, CA 95831
Edw. O. Hefti, 300 Fairview, College Sta., Tex. 77840
Iver Henriksen, 1211 So. 2nd, Missoula, Mont. 59801
Wm. Hobaugh, Box 657, Philipsburg, Mont. 59858
Richard Hodgson, 9081 Tahoe Lane, Boulder, Colo. 80301
Hoenig-Rodman, 853 So. Curtis Rd., Boise, ID 83705
Hollis Gun Shop, 917 Rex St., Carlsbad, N.M. 88220
Hurt's Specialty Gunsmithing, Box 1033, Muskogee, Okla. 74401
Hyper-Single Precision SS Rifles, 520 E. Beaver, Jenks, OK 74037
Independent Machine & Gun Shop, 1416 N. Hayes, Pocatello, Ida. 83201
Jackson's, Box 416, Selman City, TX 75689
Paul Jaeger, 211 Leedom, Jenkintown, Pa. 19046
J. J. Jenkins, 462 Stanford Pl., Santa Barbara, CA 93105
Jerry's Gun Shop, 9220 Ogden Ave., Brookfield, Ill. 60513
Johnson Automatics Assoc., Inc., Box 306, Hope Valley, R.I. 02832
Johnson's Gun Shop, 1316 N. Blackstone, Fresno, Calif. 93703
Kennedy Gun Shop, Rt. 6, Clarksville, Tenn. 37040
Monte Kennedy, P.O. Box 214, Kalispell, MT 59901
Kennon's Custom Rifles, 5408 Biffle, Stone Mtn., Ga. 30083
Kerr Sport Shop, Inc., 9584 Wilshire Blvd., Beverly Hills, Calif. 90212
Kess Arms Co., 12515 W. Lisbon Rd., Brookfield, Wis. 53005
Kesselring Gun Shop, 400 Pacific Hiway 99 No., Burlington, Wash. 98233
Knights Gun Store, Inc., 103 So. Jennings, Ft. Worth, Tex. 76104
Ward Koozer, Box 18, Walterville, Ore. 97489
R. Krieger & Sons, 34923 Gratiot, Mt. Clemens, Mich. 48043
Lacy's Gun Service, 1518A West Blvd., Charlotte, N.C. 28208
Sam Lair, 520 E. Beaver, Jenks, OK 74037
R. H. Lampert, Rt. 1, Box 61, Guthrie, MN 56451 (metalsmithing only)
LanDav Custom Guns, 7213 Lee Highway, Falls Church, VA 22046
Harry Lawson Co., 3328 N. Richey Blvd., Tucson, Ariz. 85716
John G. Lawson, 1802 E. Columbia, Tacoma, Wa. 98404
Gene Lechner, 636 Jane N.E., Albuquerque, NM 87123
LeDel, Inc., Main and Commerce Sts., Cheswold, Del. 19936
Art LeFeuvre, 1003 Hazel Ave., Deerfield, Ill. 60015
LeFever Arms Co., R.D. 1, Lee Center, N.Y. 13363
Max J. Lindauer, R.R. 1, Box 114, Washington, Mo. 63090
Robt. L. Lindsay, 9416 Emory Grove Rd., Gaithersburg, Md. 20760 (services only)
Ljutic Ind., Box 2117, Yakima, WA 98902 (Mono-Wads)
Llanerch Gun Shop, 2800 Township Line, Upper Darby, Pa. 19083
McCormick's Gun Bluing Service, 4936 E. Rosecrans Ave., Compton, Calif. 90221
Harry McGowen, Momence, IL 60954
Bill McGuire, Inc., 10324 Valmay Ave., Seattle, WA 98177
Pat B. McMillan, 1828 E. Campo Bello Dr., Phoenix, Ariz. 85022
R. J. Maberry, 511 So. K, Midland, Tex. 79701
Harold E. MacFarland, Star Route, Box 84, Cottonwood, Ariz. 86326
Marquart Precision Co., Box 1740, Prescott, AZ 86301
E. H. Martin, 937 S. Sheridan Blvd., Denver, CO 80226
Maryland Gun Exchange, RD 5, Rt. 40 W., Frederick, MD 21701
Mashburn Arms Co., 1020 N.W. 6th St., Oklahoma City, OK 73102
Seely Masker, 261 Washington Ave., Pleasantville, NY 10570
Mathews & Son, 10224 S. Paramount Blvd., Downey, Calif. 90241
Maurer Arms, 2366 Frederick Dr., Cuyahoga Falls, Ohio 44221 (muzzleloaders)
Middaugh's Nodak, 318 2nd St., Bismarck, N.D. 58501
C.D. Miller Guns, St. Onge, SD 57779
Earl Milliron, 1249 N.E. 166th Ave., Portland, Ore. 97230
Mills (D.H.) Custom Stocks, 401 N. Ellsworth, San Mateo, Calif. 94401
Mitchell's Gun Repair, Rt. 1, Perryville, Ark. 72126
Thurman Nation, Rte. 1, Box 236, Clovis, NM 88101
Natl. Gun Traders, Inc., 225 S.W. 22nd Ave., Miami, Fla. 33135
Clayton N. Nelson, 1725 Thompson Ave., Enid, Okla. 73701
Newman Gunshop, 119 Miller Rd., Agency, Ia. 52530
Nu-Line Guns, Inc., 3727 Jennings Rd., St. Louis, Mo. 63121
Oak Lawn Gun Shop, Inc., 9618 Southwest Hwy., Oak Lawn, Ill. 60453
O'Brien Rifle Co., 324 Tropicana No. 128, Las Vegas, Nev. 89109
Pachmayr Gun Works, 1220 S. Grand Ave., Los Angeles, Calif. 90015
Harry Pagett Gun Shop, 125 Water St., Milford, Ohio 45150
Charles J. Parkinson, 116 Wharncliffe Rd. So., London, Ont., Canada N6J2K3
Pendleton Gunshop, 1210 S. W. Haley Ave., Pendleton, Ore. 97801
C. R. Pedersen & Son, Ludington, Mich. 49431
Al Petersen, Box 8, Riverhurst, Sask., Canada S0H3P0
A. W. Peterson Gun Shop, 1693 Old Hwy. 441 No., Mt. Dora, FL 32757 (ML rifles, also)
Gene Phipps, 10 Wood's Gap Rd., Floyd, Va. 24091
Purcell's Gunshop, 915 Main St., Boise, Idaho 83702
Ready Eddie's Gun Shop, 501 Van Spanje Ave., Michigan City, IN 46360
Marion Reed Gun Shop, 1522 Colorado, Bartlesville, Okla. 74003
R. Neal Rice, Box 12172, Denver, CO 80212
Ridge Guncraft, Inc., 234 N. Tulane, Oak Ridge, Tenn. 37830
Riedl Rifles, P.O. Box 308, San Juan Capistrano, CA 92675 (S.S.)
Rifle Shop, Box 657, Philipsburg, Mont. 59858
Riflemen's Hdqs., Rte. 3, RD 550-E, Kendallville, IN 46755
Carl Roth, P.O. Box 2593, Cheyenne, WY 82001
Royal Arms, Inc., 10064 Bert Acosta, Santee, Calif. 92071
Murray F. Ruffino, Rt. 2, Milford, ME 04461
Rush's Old Colonial Forge, 106 Wiltshire Rd., Baltimore, MD 21221 (Ky.-Pa. rifles)
Sanders Custom Gun Serv., 2358 Tyler Lane, Louisville, Ky. 40205
Sandy's Custom Gunshop, Rockport, Ill. 62370
Saratoga Arms Co., R.D. 3, Box 387, Pottstown, Pa. 19464
Roy V. Schaefer, 965 W. Hilliard Lane, Eugene, Ore. 97402
George Schielke, Washington Crossing, Titusville, N.J. 08560
N.H. Schiffman Cust. Gun Serv., 963 Malibu, Pocatello, ID 83201
Schuetzen Gun Works, 1226 Prairie Rd., Colorado Springs, Colo. 80909
Schumaker's Gun Shop, 208 W. 5th Ave., Colville, Wash 99114
Schwab Gun Shop, 1103 E. Bigelow, Findlay, O. 45840
Schwartz Custom Guns, 9621 Coleman Rd., Haslett, Mich. 48840
Schwarz's Gun Shop, 41-15th St., Wellsburg, W. Va. 26070
Jim Scott, Hiway 2-East, Leon, IA 50144
Scotty's Gun Shop, Second and Rancier, Killeen, TX 76541
Joseph M. Sellner, 1010 Stelton Rd., Piscataway, N.J. 08854
Shaw's, 1655 S. Euclid Ave., Anaheim, Calif. 92802
Shell Shack, Box 44, Laurel, MT 59044
George H. Sheldon, P.O. Box 489, Franklin, NH 03235 (45 autos only)
Shilen Rifles, Inc., 205 Metropark Blvd., Ennis, TX 75119
Harold H. Shockley, Box 355, Hanna City, Ill. 65126 (hot bluing & plating)
Shooters Service & Dewey Inc., Clinton Corner, N.Y. 12514
Walter Shultz, R.D. 3, Pottstown, Pa. 19464
The Sight Shop, 1802 E. Columbia Ave., Tacoma, Wa. 98404
Silver Dollar Guns, P.O. Box 489, Franklin, NH 03235
Simmons Gun Spec., 700 Rogers Rd., Olathe, Kans. 66061
Simms Hardward Co., 2801 J St., Sacramento, Calif. 95816
Skinner's Gun Shop, Box 30, Juneau, Alaska 98801
Markus Skosples, c/o Ziffren Sptg. Gds., 124 E. Third St., Davenport, IA 52801
Jerome F. Slezak, 1290 Marlowe, Lakewood (Cleveland), OH 44107
Small Arms Eng., P.O. Box 306, Des Plaines, IL 60018 (restorations)
John Smith, 912 Lincoln, Carpentersville, Ill. 60110
Smitty's Gunshop, 308 S. Washington, Lake City, Minn. 55041
Snapp's Gunshop, 6911 E. Washington Rd., Clare, Mich. 48617
R. Southgate, Rt. 2, Franklin, Tenn. 37064 (new Kentucky rifles)
Sport Service Center, 2364 N. Neva, Chicago, IL 60635
Sportsman's Den, 1010 Stelton Rd., Piscataway, N.J. 08854
Sportsmens Equip. Co., 915 W. Washington, San Diego, Calif. 92103
Jess L. Stark, 12051 Stroud, Houston, TX 77072
Ikey Starks, 1058 Grand Ave., So. San Francisco, Calif. 94080
Keith Stegall, Box 696, Gunnison, Colo. 81230
W. C. Strutz, Rte. 1, Eagle River, WI 54521
Suter's House of Guns, 332 N. Tejon, Colorado Springs, Colo. 80902
Swanson Custom Firearms, 1051 Broadway, Denver, Colo. 80203
A. D. Swenson's 45 Shop, P.O. Box 884, Lawndale, CA 90260
T-P Shop, 212 E. Houghton, West Branch, Mich. 48661
Talmage Ent., 1309 W. 12th St., Long Beach, Calif. 90813
Taylor & Robbins, Box 164, Rixford, Pa. 16745
Daniel Titus, 119 Morlyn Ave., Bryn Mawr, PA 19010
Tom's Gunshop, 600 Albert Pike, Hot Springs, Ark. 71901
Dave Trevallion, 3442 S. Post Rd., Indianapolis, IN 46239
Trinko's Gun Serv., 1406 E. Main, Watertown, Wis. 53094
Herb. G. Troester's Accurizing Serv., Cayuga, ND 58013
C. Hunt Turner, 618 S. Grove, Webster Groves, Mo. 63119 (shotguns only)

Upper Missouri Trading Co., Inc., Box 181, Crofton, MO 68730
Roy Vail, R. 1, Box 8, Warwick, N.Y. 10990
J. W. Van Patten, Box 145, Foster Hill, Milford, Pa. 18337
Herman Waldron, Box 475, Pomeroy, WN 99437 (metalsmithing)
Walker Arms Co., R. 2, Box 38, Selma, Ala. 36701
Harold Waller, 1288 Camillo Way, El Cajon, CA 99347
R. A. Wardrop, Box 245, Mechanicsburg, Pa. 17055
Weatherby's, 2781 Firestone Blvd., South Gate, Calif. 90280
Wells Sport Store, 110 N. Summit St., Prescott, Ariz. 86301
R. A. Wells, 3452 N. 1st, Racine, Wis. 53402
Robert G. West, 6626 S. Lincoln, Littleton, Colo. 80120
Western Stocks & Guns, 2206 E. 11th, Bremerton, Wash. 98310
M. C. Wiest, 234 N. Tulane Ave., Oak Ridge, Tenn. 37830
W. C. Wilber, 400 Lucerne Dr., Spartanburg, SC 29302
Williams Gun Sight Co., 7389 Lapeer Rd., Davison, Mich. 48423
Bob Williams, c/o Hermans-Atlas Custom Guns, 800 E St. N.W., Washington, DC 20004
Lou Williamson, 129 Stonegate Ct., Bedford, TX 76021
Wilson Gun Store Inc., R.D. 1, Rte. 225, Dauphin, Pa 17018
Robert M. Winter, Box 484, Menno, SD 57045
Lester Womack, Box 17210, Tucson, AZ 85710
York County Gun Works, RR 4, Tottenham, Ont., Canada (muzzle loaders)
Russ Zeeryp, 1601 Foard Dr., Lynn Ross Manor, Morristown, TN 37814
R. E. Zellmer, W180 N8996 Leona Ln., Menomonee Falls, WI 53051

DECOYS

Carry-Lite, Inc., 3000 W. Clarke, Milwaukee, WI 53245
Deeks, Inc., P.O. Box 2309, Salt Lake City, UT 84114
G & H Decoy Mfg. Co., P.O. Box 937, Henryetta, OK 74437
Tex Wirtz Ent., Inc., 1925 Hubbard St., Chicago, IL 60622
Woodstream Corp., P.O. Box 327, Lititz, PA 17543

ENGRAVERS, ENGRAVING, TOOLS

Emma Achleithner, Main St., Margaretville, NY 12455
Ralph O. Alpen, 39 Horseshoe Rd., Gilford, CT 06437
Austrian Gunworks Reg'd., P.O. Box 136, Eastman, Que., Canada
E. Averill, Rt. 1, 60 Chestnut St., Cooperstown, N.Y. 13326
Joseph Bayer, Sunset Ave., Sunset Hill, RD 1, Princeton, N.J. 08540
Sid Bell, R.D. 2, Tully, NY 13159
John T. Bickett, 401 Westmark Ave., Colorado Springs, CO 80906
Weldon Bledsoe, 6812 Park Place Dr., Fort Worth, Tex. 76118
Henry D. Bonham, Box 656 (Main St.), Brownville, Me. 04414
Ray Bossi, 3574 University Ave., San Diego, CA 92104
Max E. Bruehl, 781 No. 9th Ave., Canton, IL 61520
Burgess Vibrocrafters (BVI), Rt. 83, Grayslake, Ill. 60030
Winston Churchill, 55 High St., Ludlow, VT 05149
Joe Condon, 2983 E. Fremont, Las Vegas, NV 89104
Carl E. Courts, 2421 E. Anaheim St., Long Beach, Cal. 90804
Creative Carvings Inc., R.D. 2, Tully, N.Y. 13159
Bill Dyer, P.O. Box 75255, Oklahoma City, Okla. 73107
Ken Eyster, Heritage Gunsmiths Inc., 6441 Bishop Rd., Centerburg, O. 43011
Ken Flood, 63 Homestead, Stratford, Conn. 06497
H. H. Frank, #1 Mountain Meadows, Whitefish, MT 59937
Jos. Fugger, c/o Griffin & Howe, 589-8th Ave., N.Y., N.Y. 10017
Ed F. Giles, 3 Arnold St., Attleboro, MA 02703
Donald Glaser, 1520 West St., Emporia, Kans. 66801
Howard V. Grant, P.O. Box 396, Lac Du Flambeau, WI 54538
Griffin & Howe, 589-8th Ave., N.Y., N.Y. 10017
F. R. Gurney, Engraving Methods Ltd., #205 Birks Building, Edmonton, Alberta, Can.
Bryson J. Gwinnell, 2895 Seneca St., Buffalo, NY 14224
Neil Hartliep, Box 733, Fairmont, Minn. 56031
Frank E. Hendricks, Rt. 2, Box 189J, San Antonio, Tex. 78228
Heide Hiptmayer, P.O. Box 136, Eastman, Que., Canada
Ken Hurst, Box 21, Warrentown, VA 22186
Bob Izenstark, 101 Wolpers Rd., Park Forest, IL 60466
Paul Jaeger, 211 Leedom, Jenkintown, Pa. 19046
Robert C. Kain, R.F.D. Rte. #30, Newfane, Vermont 05345
T. J. Kaye, 4745 Dellwood, Beaumont, TX 77706
Lance Kelly, P.O. Box 1072, Pompana Beach, Fla. 33061
Kleinguenther's, P.O. Box 1261, Seguin, TX 78155
John Kudlas, 622 14th St. S.E., Rochester, MN 55901
N. Lewis, 17 S. Side Dr., Wallingford, CT 06492
Lynton S.M. McKenzie, 240 Chartres St., New Orleans, La. 70130 (booklet $3.00)
Wm. H. Mains, 2895 Seneca St., Buffalo, N.Y. 14224
Rudy Marek, Rt. 1, Box 1A, Banks, Ore. 97106
Franz Marktl, c/o Davis Gun Shop, 7211 Lee Hwy., Falls Church, VA 22046
S. A. Miller, Central P.O. Box 619, Naha, Okinawa, Japan
Frank Mittermeier, 3577 E. Tremont Ave., New York, N.Y. 10465
New Orleans Jewelers Supply, 206 Chartres St., New Orleans, LA 70130
Albin Obiltschnig, Ferlach, Austria
Tom Overbey, 612 Azalea Ave., Richmond, VA 23227
Pachmayr Gun Works, Inc., 1220 S. Grand Ave., Los Angeles, Calif. 90015
Hans Pfeiffer, 286 Illinois St., Elmhurst, IL 60126
Wayne E. Potts, 912 Poplar St., Denver, CO 80220
E. C. Prudhomme, 302 Ward Bldg., Shreveport, La. 71101
John R. Rohner, Sunshine Canyon, Boulder, Colo. 80302
Robert P. Runge, 94 Grove St., Ilion, N.Y. 13357
Shaw-Leibowitz, Rt. 1, Box 421, New Cumberland, W.Va. 26047 (etchers)
Russell J. Smith, 231 Springdale Rd., Westfield, Mass. 01085
Robt. Swartley, 2800 Pine St., Napa, Calif. 94559
Ray Viramontez, 4348 Newberry Ct., Dayton, OH 45432
Floyd E. Warren, Rt. 3, Box 87, Cortland, O. 44410
John E. Warren, P.O. Box 72, Eastham, Mass. 02642
A. A. White Engr., Inc., P.O. Box 68, Manchester, Conn. 06040

GAME CALLS

Black Duck, 1737 Davis, Whiting, Ind. 46394
Burnham Bros., Box 100-C, Marble Falls, Tex. 78654
Electronic Game Calls, Inc., 210 W. Grand, Wisconsin Rapids, Wis. 54494
Faulk's, 616 18th St., Lake Charles, La. 70601
Lohman Mfg. Co., 320 E. Spring, Neosho, Mo. 64850
M. L. Lynch, 306 Edgewood Blvd., Birmingham, Ala. 35209
Mallardtone, 2901 16th St., Moline, Ill. 61265
Edward J. Mehok, 1737 Davis Ave., Whiting, IN 46394
Phil. S. Olt Co., Box 550, Pekin, Ill. 61554
Penn's Woods Products, Inc., 19 W. Pittsburgh St., Delmont, Pa. 15626
Sport-Lore, Inc., 1757 Cherry St., Denver, Colo. 80220
Johnny Stewart Wildlife Calls, Box 7954, Waco, Tex. 76710
Thomas Game Calls, P.O. Box 336, Winnsboro, TX 75494
Weems Wild Calls, Box 7261, Ft. Worth, Tex. 76111
Wightman Electronics, Box 989, Easton, Md. 21601
Wildlife Prod. Inc., Prof. Bldg., 513 East Perkins Ave., Sandusky, Ohio 44870 (Lectro Hunter)
Tex Wirtz Ent., Inc., 1925 W. Hubbard St., Chicago, Ill 60622

GUNS (Foreign)

Abercrombie & Fitch, Madison at 45th, New York, N.Y. 10017
Alaskan Rifles, Box 30, Juneau, Alaska 99801
American Import Co., 1167 Mission St., San Francisco, Calif. 94103
American International, 103 Social Hall Ave., Salt Lake City, UT 84111
Armi Fabbri, Casella 206, Brescia, Italy 25100
Armi Famars, Via Cinelli 33, Gardone V.T. (Brescia), Italy 25036
Armoury Inc., Rte. 25, New Preston, Ct. 06777
Browning, Rt. 4, Box 624-B, Arnold, Mo. 63010
Centennial Arms Corp., 3318 W. Devon, Chicago, (Lincolnwood) Ill. 60645
Century Arms Co., 3-5 Federal St., St. Albans, Vt. 05478
Champlin Firearms, Inc., Box 3191, Enid, OK 73701 (Gebruder Merkel)
Connecticut Valley Arms Co., Candlewood Hill Rd., Higganum, CT 06441 (CVA)
Continental Arms Corp., 697 Fifth Ave., New York, N.Y. 10022
W. H. Craig, Box 927, Selma, Ala. 36701
Morton Cundy & Son, Ltd., 413 6th Ave. E., Kalispell, MT 59901
Daiwa, 14011 Normandie Ave., Gardena, CA 90247
Charles Daly (see: Sloan's Sptg. Gds.)
Davidson Firearms Co., 2703 High Pt. Rd., Greensboro, N.C. 27403 (shotguns)
Davis Gun Shop, 7213 Lee Highway, Falls Church, VA 22046 (Fanzoj, Ferlach; Spanish guns)
Diana Import Co., 411 Columbus Ave., San Francisco, CA 94133 (Benelli shotguns)
Dixie Gun Works, Inc., Hwy 51, South, Union City, Tenn. 38261 ("Kentucky" rifles)
Euroarms, Via Solferino 13/A, 25100 Brescia, Italy
J. Fanzoj, P.O. Box 25, Ferlach, Austria 9170
Ferlach (Austria) of North America, P.O. Box 143435, S. Miami, FL 33143
R. C. Fessler & Co., 1634 Colorado Blvd., Los Angeles, Calif. 90041
Firearms Center Inc. (FCI), 113 Spokane, Victoria, TX 77901
Firearms Imp. & Exp. Co., 2470 N.W. 21st St., Miami, Fla. 33142
Firearms International Corp., 515 Kerby Hill Rd., Washington, DC 20022
Flaig's Lodge, Millvale, Pa. 15209
Florida Firearms Corp., 5555 N.W. 36th Ave., Hialeah, FL 33142
Freeland's Scope Stands, Inc., 3737 14th Ave., Rock Island, Ill. 61201
J. L. Galef & Son, Inc., 85 Chambers, New York, N.Y. 10007
Garcia Sptg. Arms Corp., 329 Alfred Ave., Teaneck, N.J. 07666
Gevarm (see Blumenfeld Co.)
Gevelot of Can. Ltd., Box 1593, Saskatoon, Sask., Canada
Harrington & Richardson Arms Co., 320 Park Ave., Worcester, Mass. 01610 (HK pistol)
Hawes Firearms Co., 8224 Sunset Blvd., Los Angeles, Calif. 90046
Healthways, Box 45055, Los Angeles, Calif. 90061
Gil Hebard Guns, Box 1, Knoxville, IL 61448 (Hammerli)
A. D. Heller, Inc., Box 268, Grand Ave., Baldwin, NY 11510
Herter's, Waseca, Minn. 56093
Husqvarna, see FFV Sports Inc.
Interarmco, see: Interarms (Walther)
Interarms Ltd., 10 Prince St., Alexandria, Va. 22313 (Mauser)
Intercontinental Arms, 2222 Barry Ave., Los Angeles, Calif. 90064
Ithaca Gun Co., Terrace Hill, Ithaca, N.Y. 14850 (Perazzi)
Italguns, Via Leonardo da Vinci 36, 20090 Zingoni Di Trezzano, Milano, Italy
JBL Arms Co., 4315 Warren St., Davenport, IA 52806
J-K Imports, Box 403, Novato, Cal. 94947 (Italian)
Paul Jaeger Inc., 211 Leedom St., Jenkintown, Pa. 19046
Jana Intl. Co., Box 1107, Denver, Colo. 80201 (Parker-Hale)
J. J. Jenkins, 462 Stanford Pl., Santa Barbara, CA 93105
Guy T. Jones Import Co., 905 Gervais St., Columbia, S. Car. 29201
Kassnar Imports, P.O. Box 3895, Harrisburg, PA 17105
Kleinguenther's, P.O. Box 1261, Seguin, TX 78155
Knight & Knight, 5930 S.W. 48 St., Miami, FL 33155 (made-to-order only)
Krieghoff Gun Co., P.O. Box 48-1367, Miami, FL 33148
L. A. Distributors, 4 Centre Market Pl., New York, N.Y. 10013
Jos. G. Landmann, 2308 Preetz/Holstein, W. Germany (JGL)
S. E. Laszlo, 200 Tillary St., Brooklyn, N.Y. 11201
Lever Arms Serv. Ltd., 771 Dunsmuir, Vancouver, B.C., Canada V6C 1M9
Liberty Arms Organization, Box 306, Montrose, Calif. 91020
McKeown's Guns, R.R. 1, Pekin, Ill. 61554
McQueen Sales Co. Ltd., 1760 W. 3rd Ave., Vancouver, B.C., Canada V6J 1K5
Marietta Replica Arms Co., 706½ Mongomery St., Marietta, OH 45750
Marketing Unlimited, Inc., 1 Ranch Rite Rd., Yakima, WN 98901
Mars Equipment Corp., 3318 W. Devon, Chicago, Ill. 60645
Marubeni America Corp., 200 Park Ave., New York, NY 10017

Mauser-Bauer Inc., 34577 Commerce Rd., Fraser, MI 48026
Miida, see: Marubeni
Navy Arms Co., 689 Bergen Blvd., Ridgefield, N.J. 07657
Omnipol, Washingtonova 11, Praha 1, Czechoslovakia
Harry Owen, P.O. Box 774, Sunnyvale, Ca. 94088.
Pachmayr Gun Works, 1220 S. Grand Ave., Los Angeles, Calif. 90015 (Fabbri)
Pacific Intl. Merch. Corp., 2215 "J" St., Sacramento, CA 95816
Palmetto Imp., Inc., P.O. Box 4008, Columbia, SC 29204
Parker-Hale, Bisleyworks, Golden Hillock Rd., Sparbrook, Birmingham 11, England
Ed Paul Sptg. Goods, 172 Flatbush Ave., Brooklyn, N.Y. 11217 (Premier)
Precise Imp. Corp. (PIC), 3 Chestnut, Suffern, N.Y. 10901
Premier Shotguns, 172 Flatbush Ave., Brooklyn N.Y. 11217
RG Industries, Inc., 2485 N.W. 20th St., Miami, FL 33142 (Erma)
Richland Arms Co., 321 W. Adrian St., Blissfield, Mich. 49228
Sanderson's, 724 W. Edgewater, Portage, Wis. 53901
Savage Arms Corp., Westfield, Mass. 01085 (Anschutz)
Security Arms Co., 1815 No. Ft. Myer Dr., Arlington, VA 22209 (Heckler & Koch)
Service Armament, 689 Bergen Blvd., Ridgefield, N.J. 07657 (Greener Harpoon Gun)
Sherwood Dist., Inc., 18714 Parthenia St., Northridge, CA 91324
Simmons Spec., Inc., 700 Rogers Rd., Olathe, Kans. 66061
Skinner's Gun Shop (see Alaskan Rifles)
Sloan's Sprtg. Goods, Inc., 10 South St., Ridgefield, CT 06877
Solingen Cutlery, Box 306, Montrose, Calif. 91020
Spesco Corp., 3540 Browns Mill Rd. S.E., Atlanta, Ga. 30315
Sportex Intl. Ltd., 10389 W. Olympic Blvd, W. Los Angeles, CA 90064
Stoeger Arms Co., 55 Ruta Ct., S. Hackensack, N.J. 07606
Tradewinds, Inc., P.O. Box 1191, Tacoma, Wash. 98401
Twin City Sptg. Gds., 217 Ehrman Ave., Cincinnati, OH 45220
Universal Firearms Corp., 3746 E. 10th Ct., Hialeah, Fla. 33013
Universal Ordnance Co., Inc., P.O. Box 15723, Nashville, TN 37215 (Krieghoff combination guns)
Valor Imp. Corp., 5555 N.W. 36th Ave., Miami, FL 33142
Voere (see Marketing Unlimited)
Waffen-Frankonia, Box 380, 87 Wurzburg, W. Germany
Weatherby's, 2781 Firestone Blvd., So. Gate, Calif. 90280 (Sauer)
Dan Wesson Arms, 293 So. Main, Monson, Mass. 01057
Zavodi Crvena Zastava, 29 Novembra St., No. 12, Belgrade, Yugosl.

GUNS & GUN PARTS, REPLICA AND ANTIQUE

Antique Gun Parts, Inc., 569 So. Braddock Ave., Pittsburgh, Pa. 15221 (ML)
Armoury Inc., Rte. 25, New Preston, Conn. 06777
Artistic Arms, Inc., Box 23, Hoagland, IN 46745 (Sharps-Borchardt replica)
Bannerman, F., Box 126, Blue Point, Long Island, N.Y. 11715
Shelley Braverman, Athens, N.Y. 12015 (obsolete parts)
Carter Gun Works, 2211 Jefferson Pk. Ave., Charlottesville, Va. 22903
Cornwall Bridge Gun Shop, P.O. Box 67, Cornwall Bridge, CT 06754 (parts)
R. MacDonald Champlin, P.O. Box 74, Stanyan Hill, Wentworth, NH 03282 (replicas)
David E. Cumberland, 3509 Carlson Blvd., El Cerrito, CA 94530 (Replica Gatling guns)
Darr's Rifle Shop, 2309 Black Rd., Joliet, Ill. 60435 (S.S. items)
Dixie Gun Works, Inc., Hwy 51, South, Union City, Tenn. 38261
Federal Ordnance Inc., 9643 Alpaca St., So. El Monte, CA 91733
Kindig's Log Cabin Sport Shop, R.D. 1, P.O. Box 275, Lodi, Ohio 44254
Lever Arms Service Ltd., 771 Dunsmuir, Vancouver, B.C., Canada V6C 1M9
Edw. E. Lucas, 32 Garfield Ave., Old Bridge, N.J. 08857 (45-70)
Lyman Gun Sight Products, Middlefield, CT 06455
R. M. Marek, Rt. 1, Box 1-A, Banks Ore. 97106 (cannons)
Numrich Arms Co., West Hurley, N.Y. 12491
Replica Models, Inc., 610 Franklin St., Alexandria, VA 22314
Riflemen's Hdqs., Rt. 3, RD 550-E, Kendallville, IN 46755
S&S Firearms, 88-21 Aubrey Ave., Glendale, N.Y. 11227
C. H. Stoppler, 1426 Walton Ave., New York, NY 10452 (miniature guns)
C. H. Weisz, Box 311, Arlington, Va. 22210
W. H. Wescombe, P.O. Box 488, Glencoe, CA 95232 (Rem. R.B. parts)

GUN PARTS, U. S. AND FOREIGN

American Firearms Mfg. Co., Inc., 1200 Warfield, San Antonio, Tex. 78216 (clips)
Badger Shooter's Supply, Owen, Wisc. 54460
Shelley Braverman, Athens, N.Y. 12015
Philip R. Crouthamel, 817 E. Baltimore, E. Lansdowne, Pa. 19050
Charles E. Duffy, Williams Lane, West Hurley, N.Y. 12491
Federal Ordnance Inc., 9634 Alpaca St., So. El Monte, CA 91733
Greeley Arms Co., Inc., 223 Little Falls Rd., Fairfield, N.J. 07006
The Gunshop, Inc., 44633 Sierra Highway, Lancaster, CA 93534
Hunter's Haven, Zero Prince St., Alexandria, Va. 22314
International Sportsmen's Supply Co., Inc., Arapaho-Central Park, Suite 311, Richardson, TX 75080 (bbld. actions)
M. C. Matthews, Box 33095, Decatur, GA 30031 (ctlg. $1)
Numrich Arms Co., West Hurley, N.Y. 12491
Pacific Intl. Merch. Corp., 2215 "J" St., Sacramento, CA 95816
Potomac Arms Corp. (see Hunter's Haven)
Reed & Co., Shokan, N.Y. 12481
Martin B. Retting, Inc., 11029 Washington, Culver City, Cal. 90230
Ruvel & Co., 3037 N. Clark, Chicago, IL 60614
Sarco, Inc., 192 Central, Stirling, N.J. 07980
R. A. Saunders, 3253 Hillcrest Dr., San Antonio, Tex. 78201 (clips)
Sherwood Distr. Inc., 18714 Parthenia St., Northridge, CA 91324

Simms, 2801 J St., Sacramento, CA 95816
Clifford L. Smires, R.D., Columbus, N.J. 08022 (Mauser rifles)
Sporting Arms, Inc., 9643 Alpaca St., So. El Monte, CA 91733 (M-1 carb. access.)
N. F. Strebe, 4926 Marlboro Pike, S.E., Washington, D.C. 20027
Triple-K Mfg. Co., 568-6th Ave., San Diego, CA 92101

GUNS (Pellet)

Air Rifle Hq., 247 Court St., Grantsville, W. Va. 26147
AmPell Playtime Prods., Inc., 24 E. Main St., Honeoye, NY 14471
Beeman's Precision Airguns, P.O. Box 278, San Anselmo, CA 94960
Benjamin Air Rifle Co., 1525 So. 8th St., Louis, Mo. 63104
Continental Arms Corp., 697 5th Ave., New York, N.Y. 10022
Crosman Arms, a Coleman Co. Div., Fairport, NY 14450
Daisy Mfg. Co., Rogers, Ark. 72756 (also Feinwerkbau)
Fanta Air Rifles, Box 8122, La Crescenta, Calif, 91214
J. L. Galef & Son, Inc., 85 Chambers St., New York, N.Y. 10007 (B.S.A.)
H. F. Grieder, Box 487, Knoxville, IL 61448 (Hammerli)
Harrington & Richardson Arms Co., 320 Park Ave., Worcester, Mass. 01610 (Webley)
Healthways, Box 45055, Los Angeles, Calif. 90061
Gil Hebard Guns, Box 1, Knoxville, Ill. 61448
Hy-Score Arms Co., 200 Tillary St., Brooklyn, N.Y. 11201
Interarms, 10 Prince, Alexandria, Va. 22313 (Walther)
Kerrco, Inc., Box 368, Hastings, Nebr. 68901
Marksman Products, P.O. Box 2983, Torrance, CA 90509
Precise Imports Corp. (PIC), 3 Chestnut, Suffern, N.Y. 10901
Sears, Roebuck & Co., 825 S. St. Louis, Chicago, Ill. 60607
Service Armament, 689 Bergen Blvd., Ridgefield, N.J. 07657 (Webley, Jaguar)
Sheridan Products, Inc., 3205 Sheridan, Racine, Wis. 53403
Smith & Wesson, Inc., 7710 No. 30th St., Tampa, FL 33610
Solingen Cutlery, Box 306, Montrose, Calif. 91020
Stoeger Arms Corp., 55 Ruta Ct., S. Hackensack, N.J. 07606 (Peerless)
Stuart Distr. Co., 6 Riverside Dr., Baltimore, Md. 21221
Dan Wesson Arms, 293 S. Main, Monson, Mass. 01057

GUNS, SURPLUS PARTS AND AMMUNITION

Century Arms, Inc., 3-5 Federal St., St. Albans, Vt. 05478
W. H. Craig, Box 927, Selma, Ala. 36701
Cummings Intl. Inc., 41 Riverside Ave., Yonkers, N.Y. 10701
Eastern Firearms Co., 790 S. Arroyo Pkwy., Pasadena, Calif. 91105
Hunter's Lodge, 200 S. Union, Alexandria, Va. 22313
Lever Arms Serv. Ltd., 771 Dunsmuir St., Vancouver, B.C., Canada V6C IM9
Mars Equipment Corp., 3318 W. Devon, Chicago, Ill. 60645
National Gun Traders, 225 S.W. 22nd, Miami, Fla. 33135
Pacific Intl. Merch. Corp., 2215 "J" St., Sacramento, CA 95816
Plainfield Ordnance Co., Box 447, Dunellen, N.J. 08812
Potomac Arms Corp., Box 35, Alexandria, Va. 22313
Ruvel & Co., 3037 N. Clark St., Chicago, Ill. 60614
Service Armament Co., 689 Bergen Blvd., Ridgefield, N.J. 07657
Sherwood Distrib. Inc., 18714 Parthenia St., Northridge, CA 91324

GUNS, U.S.-made

Agawam Arms Co., 916 Suffield St., Agawam, Mass. 01001
American Firearms Mfg. Co., Inc., 1200 Warfield, San Antonio, Tex. 78216
ArmaLite, 118 E. 16th St., Costa Mesa, Calif. 92627
Apollo Custom Rifles, Inc., 1235 Cowles St., Long Beach, CA 90813
Artistic Arms, Inc., Box 23, Hoagland, IN 46745 (Sharps-Borchardt)
Bauer Firearms, 34750 Klein Ave., Fraser, MI 48026
Bortmess Gun Co., Inc., RD , Box 199A, Scenery Hill, PA 15360
Caraville Arms, P.O. Box 377, Thousand Oaks, CA 91360
Challanger Mfg. Corp., 118 Pearl St., Mt. Vernon, NY 10550 (Hopkins & Allen)
Champlin Firearms, Inc., Box 3191, Enid, Okla. 73701
Charter Arms Corp., 265 Asylum, Bridgeport, Conn. 06610
Clerke Products, 2219 Main St., Santa Monica, Ca. 90405
Colt's, 150 Huyshope Ave., Hartford, Conn. 06102
Commando Arms, Inc., Box 10214, Knoxville, Tenn. 37919
Cumberland Arms, 1222 Oak Dr., Manchester, Tenn 37355
Day Arms Corp., 7515 Stagecoach Ln., San Antonio, Tex. 78227
ESFAC Inc., P.O. Box 2028, Brownsville, TX 78520
Esopus Gun Works, Port Ewen, NY 12466 (muzzle loaders)
Falling Block Works, P.O. Box 22, Troy, MI 48084
Firearms Imp. & Exp. Co., 2470 N.W. 21st St., Miami, FL 33142 (FIE)
Firearms Intl. Corp., (see: Garcia)
Golden Age Arms Co., 657 High St., Worthington, O. 43085
Gyrojet (see Intercontinental Arms)
Harrington & Richardson, Park Ave., Worcester, Mass. 01610
A. D. Heller, Inc., Box 268, Grand Ave., Baldwin, NY 11510
High Standard Mfg. Co., 1817 Dixwell Ave., Hamden, Conn. 06514
Hopkins & Allen, see: High Standard
Indian Arms Corp., 13503 Joseph Campar, Detroit, MI 48212
Intercontinental Arms, Inc., 2222 Barry Ave., Los Angeles, Ca. 90064
Int'l. Sportsmen's Supply Co., Inc., Arapaho-Central Park, Suite 311, Richardson, TX 75080 (Santa Barbara bbld. actions)
Ithaca Gun Co., Ithaca, N.Y. 14850
Iver Johnson Arms & Cycle Works, Fitchburg, Mass. 01420
J & R carbine, (see: PJK Inc.)
Ljutic Ind., Inc., P.O. Box 2117, Yakima, WA 98902 (Mono-Gun)
MBAssociates (see Intercontinental Arms)
Manchester Arms, Inc., 6858 Manchester Rd., Rt. 2, Clinton, OH 44216
Marlin Firearms Co., 100 Kenna Dr., New Haven, Conn. 06473
Merrill Co. Inc., Box 187, Rockwell City, IA 50579

O. F. Mossberg & Sons, Inc., 7 Grasso St., No. Haven, Conn. 06473
W. L. Mowrey Gun Works, Inc., Box 28, Iowa Park TX 76367
Natl. Ordance Inc., 9643 Alpaca, S. El Monte, CA 91733
Navy Arms Co., 689 Bergen Blvd., Ridgefield, N.J. 07657
Norarmco, 41471 Irwin, Mt. Clemens, MI 48043 (D.A. 25 auto)
North Star Arms, R.2, Box 74A, Ortonville, MN 56278 (The Plainsman)
Numrich Arms Corp., W. Hurley, N.Y. 12491
Omega Arms Inc., 218 Austin St., Denton, TX 76201
PJK, Inc., 1527 Royal Oak Dr., Bradbury, Ca 91010 (J&R Carbine)
Pedersen Custom Guns, Div. of O. F. Mossberg & Sons, Inc., 7 Grasso Ave., North Haven, CT 06473
Plainfield Machine Co., Inc., Box 447, Dunellen, N.J. 08812
Plainfield Ordnance Co., P.O. Box 251, Middlesex, NJ 08846
Potomac Arms Corp., P.O. Box 35, Alexandria, Va. 22313 (ML replicas)
R G Industries, 2485 N.W. 20th SE., Miami, FL 33142
Ranger Arms Co., Box 704, Gainesville, Tex. 76240 (Texan Mag.)
Remington Arms Co., Bridgeport, Conn. 06602
Riedl Rifles, 15124 Weststate St., Westminster, CA 92683 (S.S.)
Rocky Mountain Arms Corp., Box 224, Salt Lake City, UT 84110
Savage Arms Corp., Westfield, Mass. 01085
Sears, Roebuck & Co., 825 S. St. Louis, Chicago, Ill. 60607
Seventrees Ltd., 315 W. 39th St., New York, N.Y. 10018
Smith & Wesson, Inc., 2100 Roosevelt Ave., Springfield, MA 01101
Sporting Arms, Inc., 9643 Alpaca St., So. El Monte, CA 91733 (M-1 carbine)
Sterling Arms Corp., 4436 Prospect St., Gasport, NY 14067
Sturm, Ruger & Co., Southport, Conn. 06490
T.D.E. Corp., 11609 Vanowen St., No. Hollywood, CA 91605 (Auto-Mag)
Thompson-Center Arms, Box 2405, Rochester, N.H. 03867 (Contender pistol)
Tingle, 1125 Smithland Pike, Shelbyville, Ind. 46176 (muzzleloader)
Trail Guns Armory, 2115 Lexington, Houston, TX 77006 (muzzleloaders)
Universal Firearms Corp., 3746 E. 10th Ct., Hialeah, Fla. 33013
Ward's, 619 W. Chicago, Chicago, Ill. 60607 (Western Field brand)
Weatherby's, 2781 E. Firestone Blvd., South Gate, Calif. 90280
Dan Wesson Arms, 293 So. Main St., Monson, Mass. 01057
Winchester Repeating Arms Co., New Haven, Conn. 06504
Winslow Arms Co., P.O. Box 578, Osprey, Fla. 33595

GUNSMITHS, CUSTOM (see Custom Gunsmiths)

GUNSMITHS, HANDGUN (see PISTOLSMITHS)

GUNSMITH SCHOOLS

Colorado School of Trades, 1545 Hoyt, Lakewood, CO 80215
Lassen Community College, Highway 139, Susanville, Calif. 96130
Oregon Institute of Technology, Klamath Falls, OR 97601
Penn. Gunsmith School, 812 Ohio River Blvd., Avalon, Pittsburgh, Pa. 15202
Trinidad State Junior College, Trinidad, Colo. 81082

GUNSMITH SUPPLIES, TOOLS, SERVICES

Alamo Heat Treating Co., Box 55345, Houston, Tex. 77055
Albright Prod. Co., P.O. Box 1027, Winnemucca, NV 89445 (trap buttplates)
Alley Supply Co., Carson Valley Industrial Park, Gardnerville, NV 89410
American Firearms Mfg. Co., Inc., 1200 Warfield, San Antonio, Tex. 78216 (45 Conversion Kit)
Anderson & Co., 1203 Broadway, Yakima, Wash. 98902 (tang safe)
Armite Labs., 1845 Randolph St., Los Angeles, Cal. 90001 (pen oiler)
B-Square Co., Box 11281, Ft. Worth, Tex. 76110
Jim Baiar, Rt. 1-B, Box 352, Columbia Falls, Mont. 59912 (hex screws)
Bonanza Sports Mfg. Co., 412 Western Ave., Faribault, Minn. 55021
Brookstone Co., 16 Brookstone Bldg., Vose Farm Rd., Peterborough, NH 03458
Brown & Sharpe Mfg. Co., Precision Pk., No. Kingston, R.I. 02852
Bob Brownell's, Main & Third, Montezuma, Ia. 50171
W. E. Brownell, 1852 Alessandro Trail, Vista, Calif. 92083 (checkering tools)
Maynard P. Buehler, Inc., 17 Orinda Hwy., Orinda, Calif. 94563 (Rocol lube)
Burgess Vibrocrafters, Inc. (BVI), Rte. 83, Grayslake, Ill. 60030
M. H. Canjar, 500 E. 45th, Denver, Colo. 80216 (triggers, etc.)
Centerline Prod., Box 14074, Denver, Colo. 80214
Chapman Mfg. Co., Rte. 17, Durham, CT 06422
Chase Chemical Corp., 3527 Smallman St., Pittsburgh, PA 15201 (Chubbs Multigauge)
Chicago Wheel & Mfg. Co., 1101 W. Monroe St., Chicago, Ill. 60607 (Handee grinders)
Choke Checker Co., 12505 Alpine St., Lynwood, CA 90262
Christy Gun Works, 875-57th St., Sacramento, Calif. 95819
Clover Mfg. Co., 139 Woodward Ave., Norwalk, CT 06856 (Clover compound)
Clymer Mfg. Co., 14241 W. 11 Mile Rd., Oak Park, Mich. 48237 (reamers)
Colbert Industries, 10107 Adella, South Gate, Calif. 90280 (Panavise)
A. Constantine & Son, Inc., 2050 Eastchester Rd., Bronx, N.Y. 10461 (wood)
Cougar & Hunter, 6398 W. Pierson Rd., Flushing, Mich. 48433 (scope jigs)
Dayton-Traister Co., P.O. Box 593, Oak Harbor, Wa. 98277 (triggers)
Dem-Bart Hand Tool Co., 7749 15th Ave. N.W., Seattle, WA 98117 (checkering tools)
Ditto Industries, 527 N. Alexandria, Los Angeles, Cal. 90004 (clamp tool)
Dixie Diamond Tool Co., Inc., 6875 S.W. 81st St., Miami, Fla. 33143 (marking pencils)
Dremel Mfg. Co., P.O. Box 518, Racine, Wis. 53401 (grinders)
Chas. E. Duffy, Williams Lane, West Hurley, N.Y. 12491
E-Z Tool Co., P.O. Box 3186, 25 N.W. 44th Ave., Des Moines, Ia. 50313 (lathe taper attachment)
Edmund Scientific Co., 101 E. Glouster Pike, Barrington, N.J. 08007
F. K. Elliott, Box 785, Ramona, Calif. 92065 (reamers)
Foredom Elec. Co., Rt. 6, Bethel, Conn. 06801 (power drills)
Forster Appelt Mfg. Co., Inc., 82 E. Lanark Ave., Lanark, Ill. 61046
Keith Francis, Box 343, Talent, Ore. 97540 (reamers)
Frantz Tools, 913 Barbara Ave., Placentia, Cal. 92670
G. R. S. Corp., Box 1157, Boulder, Colo. 80302 (Gravermeister)
Gager Gage and Tool Co., 27509 Industrial Blvd., Hayward, CA 94545 (speedlock triggers f. Rem. 1100 & 870 pumps)
Gilmore Pattern Works, 1164 N. Utica, Tulsa, Okla. 74110
Gold Lode, Inc., 181 Gary Ave., Wheaton, IL 60187 (gold inlay kit)
Grace Metal Prod., 115 Ames St., Elk Rapids, MI 49629 (screw drivers, drifts)
Gopher Shooter's Supply, Box 246, Faribault, Minn. 55021 (screwdrivers, etc.)
Gunline Tools Inc., 719 No. East St., Anaheim, CA 92805
H. & M. 24062 Orchard Lake Rd., Farmington, Mich. 48024 (reamers)
Half Moon Rifle Shop, Rt. 1B, Box 352, Columbia Falls, MT 59912 (hex screws)
Hartford Reamer Co., Box 134, Lathrup Village, Mich. 48075
O. Iber Co., 626 W. Randolph, Chicago, Ill. 60606
Paul Jaeger Inc., 211 Leedom St., Jenkintown, PA. 19046
Kasenite Co., Inc., 3 King St., Mahwah, N.J. 07430 (surface hrdng. comp.)
LanDav Custom Guns, 7213 Lee Highway, Falls Church, VA 22046
John G. Lawson, 1802 E. Columbia Ave., Tacoma, WA 98404
Lea Mfg. Co., 237 E. Aurora St., Waterbury, Conn. 06720
Lock's Phila. Gun Exch., 6700 Rowland Ave., Philadelphia, Pa. 19149
Marker Machine Co., Box 426, Charleston, Ill. 61920
Michaels of Oregon Co., P.O. Box 13010, Portland, Ore. 97213
Viggo Miller, P.O. Box 4181, Omaha, Neb. 68104 (trigger attachment)
Miller Single Trigger Mfg. Co., Box 69, Millersburg, Pa. 17061
Frank Mittermeier, 3577 E. Tremont, N.Y., N.Y. 10465
Moderntools Corp, Box 407, Dept. GD, Woodside, N.Y. 11377
N&J Sales, Lime Kiln Rd., Northford, Conn. 06472 (screwdrivers)
Karl A. Neise, Inc., 5602 Roosevelt Ave., Woodside, N.Y. 11377
P & S Sales, P.O. Box 45095, Tulsa, OK 74145
Palmgren, 8383 South Chicago Ave., Chicago, Ill. 60167 (vises, etc.)
C. R. Pedersen & Son, Ludington, Mich. 49431
Ponderay Lab., 210 W. Prasch, Yakima, Wash. 98902 (epoxy glass bedding)
Redford Reamer Co., Box 40604, Redford Hts. Sta, Detroit, MI 48240
Richland Arms Co., 321 W. Adrian St., Blissfield, Mich. 49228
Riley's Supply Co., 121 No. Main St., Avilla, Ind. 46710 (Niedner buttplates, caps)
Ruhr-American Corp., So. Hwy #5, Glenwood, Minn. 56334
A. G. Russell, 1705 Hiway 71N, Springdale, AR 72764 (Arkansas oilstones)
Schaffner Mfg. Co., Emsworth, Pittsburgh, Pa. 15202 (polishing kits)
Schuetzen Gun Works, 1226 Prarie Rd., Colo. Springs, Colo. 80909
Shaw's, 1655 S. Euclid Ave., Anaheim, Calif. 92802
A. D. Soucy Co., Box 191, Fort Kent, Me. 04743 (ADSCO stock finish)
L. S. Starrett Co., Athol, Mass. 01331
Technological Devices, Inc., P.O. Box 3491, Stamford, Conn. 06905 (Accu-Orb circle cutters)
Texas Platers Supply Co., 2453 W. Five Mile Parkway, Dallas, TX 75233 (plating kit)
Timney Mfg. Co., 5624 Imperial Hwy., So. Gate, Calif. 90280 (triggers)
Stan de Treville, Box 33021, San Diego, Calif. 92103 (checkering patterns)
Twin City Steel Treating Co., Inc., 1114 S. 3rd, Minneapolis, Minn. 55415 (heat treating)
R. G. Walters Co., 3235 Hancock, San Diego, Ca. 92110
Ward Mfg. Co., 500 Ford Blvd., Hamilton, O. 45011
Will-Burt Co., P.O. Box 160, Orrville, O. 44667 (vises)
Williams Gun Sight Co., 7389 Lapeer Rd., Davison, Mich. 48423
Wilson Arms Co., Box 364, Stony Creek, Branford, Conn. 06405
Wilton Tool Corp., 9525 W. Irving Pk. Rd., Schiller Park, Ill. 60176 (vises)
Wisconsin Platers Supply Co., see: Texas Platers
W. C. Wolff Co., Box 232, Ardmore, PA 19003 (springs)
Woodcraft Supply Corp., 313 Montvale, Woburn, MA 01801

HANDGUN ACCESSORIES

Baramie Corp., 6250 E. 7 Mile Rd., Detroit, MI 48234 (Hip-Grip)
Bar-Sto Precision Machine, 633 S. Victory Blvd., Burbank, CA 91502
B. L. Broadway, Rte. 1, Box 381, Alpine, CA 92001 (machine rest)
C'Arco, P.O. Box 2043, San Bernardino, CA 92406 (Ransom Rest)
Case Master, 4675 E. 10 Ave., Miami, Fla. 33013
Central Specialties Co., 6030 Northwest Hwy., Chicago, Ill. 60631
John Dangelzer, 3056 Frontier Pl., N.E., Albuquerque, N.M. 87106 (flasks)
Bill Dyer, 503 Midwest Bldg., Oklahoma City, Okla. 73102 (grip caps)
R. S. Frielich, 396 Broome St., New York, N.Y. 10013 (cases)
Hunt Eng., 121—17th St., Yucaipa, Calif. 92399 (Multi-Loader)
Jeffersontown Specty. Co., Inc., 9815 Taylorsville Rd., Jeffersontown, KY 40299 (pin pads)
R. G. Jensen, 16153½ Parthenia, Sepulveda, Calif. 91343 (auxiliary chambers)
Lee Prec. Mfg., 21 E. Wisconsin, Hartford, WI 53027 (pistol rest holders)
Los Gatos Grip & Specialty Co., P.O. Box 1850, Los Gatos, CA 95030 (custom-made)
Marcon, 1720 Marina Ct., Suite D, San Mateo, CA 94403 (Mellmark pistol safe)
Matich Loader, Box 958, So. Pasadena, Calif. 91030 (Quick Load)
J. McArthur, 1961 Overlook Ave., Youngstown, O. 44509 (sling)

W. A. Miller Co., Inc., Mingo Loop, Oguossoc, ME 04964 (cases)
No-Sho Mfg. Co., 10727 Glenfield Ct., Houston, TX 77035
Pachmayr, 1220 S. Grand, Los Angeles, Calif. 90015 (cases)
Pistolsafe, Dr. L., N. Chili, NY 14514 (handgun safe)
Platt Luggage, Inc., 2301 S. Prairie, Chicago, Ill. 60616 (cases)
Jules Reiver, 4104 Market St., Wilmington, Del. 19899 (cases)
Sportsmen's Equipment Co., 415 W. Washington, San Diego, Calif. 92103
M. Tyler, 1326 W. Britton, Oklahoma City, Okla. 73114 (grip adaptor)

HANDGUN GRIPS

Beckelhymer's, Hidalgo & San Bernardo, Laredo, Tex. 78040
Belmont Prods., Rte. #1, Friendsville, TN 37737
Cloyce's Gun Stocks, Box 1133, Twin Falls, Ida. 83301
Crest Carving Co., 8091 Bolsa Ave., Midway City, CA 92655
Custom Combat Grips, 148 Shepherd Ave., Brooklyn, N.Y. 11208
Fitz, Box 49797, Los Angeles, Calif. 90049
Herret's, Box 741, Twin Falls, Ida. 83301
Hogue Custom Pistol Grips, P.O. Box 1327, Cambria, CA 93428
J. R. Grips, 1601 Wilt Rd., Fallbrook, CA 92028
Mershon Co., Inc., 1230 S. Grand Ave., Los Angeles, Calif. 90015
Mustang Pistol Grips, P.O. Box 214, Temecula, CA 92390
Safety Grip Corp., Box 456, Riverside St., Miami, Fla. 33135
Sanderson Custom Pistol Stocks, 17695 Fenton, Detroit, Mich. 48219
Jay Scott, 81 Sherman Place, Garfield, N.J. 07026
Sile Dist., 7 Centre Market Pl., New York, N.Y. 10013
Sports Inc., P.O. Box 683, Park Ridge, IL 60068 (Franzite)

HEARING PROTECTORS

American Optical Corp., Mechanic St., Southbridge, Mass. 01550 (ear valve)
Bausch & Lomb, 635 St. Paul St., Rochester, N.Y. 14602
David Clark Co., 360 Franklin St., Worcester, Mass. 01604
Curtis Safety Prod. Co., Box 61, Webster Sq. Sta., Worcester, Mass. 01603 (ear valve)
Hodgdon, 7710 W. 50 Hiway, Shawnee Mission, Kans. 66202
Sigma Eng. Co., 11320 Burbank Blvd., No. Hollywood, Ca. 91601 (Lee-Sonic ear valve)
Safety Direct, P.O. Box 8907, Reno, NV 89507 (Silencio)
Smith & Wesson, 2100 Roosevelt Ave., Springfield, MA 01101
Vector Scientific, P.O. Box 21106, Ft. Lauderdale, FL 33315
Willson Prods Div., P.O. Box 622, Reading, Pa. 19603 (Ray-O-Vac)

HOLSTERS & LEATHER GOODS

American Sales & Mfg. Co., P.O. Box 677, Laredo, Tex. 78040
Andy Anderson, 6100 Vineland Ave., No. Hollywood, CA 91606 (Gunfighter Custom Holsters)
Berns-Martin, 1307 Spring St. N.W., Atlanta, GA 30309
Bianchi Holster Co., 100 Calle Cortez, Temecula, CA 92390
Boyt Co., Div. of Welch Sptg., Box 1108, Iowa Falls, Ia. 51026
Brauer Bros. Mfg. Co., 817 N. 17th, St. Louis, Mo. 63106
Browning, Rt. 4, Box 624-B, Arnold, MO 63010
J. M. Bucheimer Co., Airport Rd., Frederick, Md. 21701
Cathey Enterprises, P.O. Box 3545, Chula Vista, CA 92011
Clements Custom Leathercraft, 1245 S. Pennsylvania St., Denver, CO 80203 (Custom-made holsters)
Cole's Acku-Rite, Box 25, Kennedy, N.Y. 14747
Colt's, 150 Huyshope Ave., Hartford, Conn. 06102
Daisy Mfg. Co., Rogers, Ark. 72756
Eugene DeMayo & Sons, Inc., 2795 Third Ave., Bronx, N.Y. 10455
Ellwood Epps (Orillia) Ltd., Hwy. 11 North, Orillia, Ont., Canada
Filmat Enterpr., Inc., 200 Market St., East Paterson, N.J. 07407
Flintrop Arms Co., 4034 W. National Ave., Milwaukee, Wis. 53215
Goerg Ent., 3009 S. Laurel, Port Angeles, Wash. 98362
Gunfighter (See Anderson)
Hoyt Holster Co., P.O. Box 1783, Costa Mesa, Cal. 92626
Don Hume, Box 351, Miami, Okla. 74354
The Hunter Co., 3300 W. 71st Ave., Westminster, CO 80030
Jet Sports Corp., 4 Centre Market Pl., New York, N.Y. 10013
Jumbo Sports Prods., P.O. Box 280, Airport Rd., Frederick, MD 21701
George Lawrence Co., 306 S. W. First Ave., Portland, Ore. 97221
Leathercrafters, 710 S. Washington, Alexandria, VA 22314
MMGR Corp., 5710 12th Ave., Brooklyn, N.Y. 11219
S. D. Myres Saddle Co., Box 9776, El Paso, Tex. 79988
Alfonso Pineda, 4850 Lankershim Blvd., No. Hollywood, CA 91062 (custom holstermaker)
Pony Express Sport Shop, 17460 Ventura Blvd., Encino, Calif. 91316
Red Head Brand Co., 4100 Platinum Way, Dallas, Tex. 75237
Rickenbacker's, P.O. Box 532, State Ave., Holly Hill, SC 29059
R. E. Roseberry, 810 W. 38th, Anderson, Ind. 46014
Roy's Custom Leather Goods, Hwy. 132, Rt. 1, Box 245, Magnolia, AR 71753
Safariland Leather Products, 1941 Walker Ave., Monrovia, Calif. 91016
Safety Speed Holster, Inc., 910 So. Vail, Montebello, Calif. 90640
Saguaro Holsters, 1508 Del Carlo Circle, Seagoville, TX 75159 (custom)
Buddy Schoellkopf Products, Inc., 4100 Platinum Way, Dallas, Tex. 75237
Seventrees, Ltd., 315 W. 39 St., New York, N.Y. 10018
Sile Distr., 7 Centre Market Pl., New York, N.Y. 10013
Smith & Wesson Leather Co., 2100 Roosevelt, Springfield, Mass. 01101
Stein Holsters & Accessories, Inc., Drawer B, Wakefield Sta., Bronx, NY 10466
Swiss-Craft Co., Inc., 33 Arctic St., Worcester, MA 01604
Tandy Leather Co., 1001 Foch, Fort Worth, Texas 76107
Tayra Corp., 1529-19th St. N.W., Canton, O. 44709
Torel, Inc., 1053 N. South St., Yoakum, TX 77995 (gun slings)
Triple-K Mfg. Co., 568 Sixth Ave., San Diego, CA 92101
Whitco, Box 1712, Brownsville, Tex. 78520 (Hide-A-Way)
Woodland Sport and Gift Shop, Box 107, Mayfield, N.Y. 12117

HUNTING AND CAMP GEAR, CLOTHING, ETC.

Abercrombie & Fitch, 45th & Madison Ave., N.Y., N.Y. 10017
Action Sports, Box 1264, Wausau, WI 54401 (rain gear)
Eddie Bauer, 1737 Airport Way So., Seattle, Wash. 98134
L. L. Bean, Freeport, Me. 04032
Bear Archery Co., R.R. 1, Grayling, Mich. 49738 (Himalayan backpack)
Bernzomatic Corp., 740 Driving Pk. Ave., Rochester, N.Y. 14613 (stoves & lanterns)
Big Beam, Teledyne Co., 290 E. Prairie St., Crystal Lake, Ill. 60014 (lamp)
Thos. Black & Sons, 930 Ford St., Ogdensburg, N.Y. 13669 (ctlg. 25¢)
Bill Boatman & Co., So. Maple St., Bainbridge, OH 45612
Browning, Rte. 1, Morgan, Utah 84050
Camouflage Mfg. Co., P.O. Box 5437, Pine Bluff, AR 71601
Camp Trails, P.O. Box 14500, Phoenix, Ariz. 85031 (packs only)
Camp Ways, 415 Molino St., Los Angeles, CA 90013
Challanger Mfg. Co., Box 550, Jamaica, N.Y. 11431 (glow safe)
Coleman Co., Inc., 250 N. St. Francis, Wichita, Kans. 67201
Colorado Outdoor Sports Co., 5450 N. Valley Hwy., Denver, Colo. 80216
Converse Rubber Co., 1200 Kirk St., Elk Grove Village, IL 60007 (boots)
Corcoran, Inc., 2 Canton Street, Stoughton, Mass, 02072
Dana Safety Heater, J. L. Galef & Son, Inc., 85 Chamber St., N.Y. N.Y. 10007
DEER-ME Prod. Co., Box 345, Anoka, Minn. 55303 (tree steps)
Dunham's Footwear, RFD 3, Brattleboro, Vt. 05301 (boots)
Edmont-Wilson, 1300 Walnut St., Coshocton, O. 43812 (gloves)
Fabrico Mfg. Corp., 1300 W. Exchange, Chicago, Ill. 60609
Filmat Enterpr., Inc., 200 Market St., East Paterson, N.J. 07407 (field dressing kit)
Freeman Ind., Inc., 100 Marblehead Rd., Tuckahoe, N.Y. 10707 (Trak-Kit)
Game-Winner, Inc., 515 Candler Bldg., Atlanta, GA 30303 (camouflage suits)
Gander Mountain, Inc., Box 248, Wilmot, Wis. 53192
Gerry Mountain Sports, Inc. (see Colorado Sports)
Gokey, 94 E. 4th St., St. Paul, Minn. 55101
Gun Club Sportswear, Box 477, Des Moines, Ia. 50302
Gun-Ho Case Mfg. Co., 110 E. 10th St., St. Paul, Minn. 55101
Hawthorn Co., Div. of Kellwood Co., New Haven, Mo. 63068 (tents)
Herter's Inc., Waseca, Minn. 56093
Himalayan Back Packs, P.O. Box 5668, Pine Bluff, AR 71601
Bob Hinman, 1217 W. Glen, Peoria, Ill. 61614
Holubar Mountaineering, Box 7, Boulder, Colo. 80302
Kelty Pack, Inc., Box 3645, Glendale, Calif. 91201
Peter Limmer & Sons, Box 66, Intervale, N.H. 03845 (boots)
H. O. McBurnette, Jr., Rte. 4, Box 337, Piedmont, AL 36272 (camouflage suits)
Marble Arms Corp., 420 Industrial Park, Gladstone, Mich. 49837
National Sports Div., 19 E. McWilliams St., Fond du Lac, Wis. 54935
Nimrod & Wayfarer Trailers, 500 Ford Blvd., Hamilton, O. 45011
Charles F. Orvis Co., Manchester, Vt. 05254 (fishing gear)
Palco Prods., 15 Hope Ave., Worcester, MA 01603
Paulin Infra-Red Prod. Co., 30520 Lakeland Blvd., Willowick, OH 44094
Primus-Sievert, 354 Sackett Pt. Rd., No. Haven, CT 06473 (stoves)
Ranger Mfg. Co., Inc., P.O. Box 3676, Augusta, GA 30904
Red Head Brand Co., 4100 Platinum Way, Dallas Tex. 75237
Red Wing Shoe Co., Rte. 2, Red Wing, Minn. 55066
Refrigiwear, Inc., 71 Inip Dr., Inwood, L.I., N.Y. 11696
Reliance Prod. Ltd., 1830 Dublin Ave., Winnipeg 21, Man., Can. (tent peg)
W. R. Russell Moccasin Co., 285 S.W. Franklin, Berlin, WI 54923
Buddy Schoellkopf, Inc., 4100 Platinum Way, Dallas, Tex. 75237
Servus Rubber Co., 1136 2nd St., Rock Island, Ill. 61201 (footwear)
Snow Lion Corp., P.O. Box 9056, Berkeley, CA 94709 (sleeping bags and parkas)
Sportsgear, Inc., 4909 Fremont Ave. So., Minneapolis, Minn. 55409 (pack sack & port. chair)
Stearns Mfg. Co., Division & 30th St., St. Cloud, Minn. 56301
Sterno Inc., 105 Hudson St., Jersey City, N.J. 07302 (camp stoves)
Teledyne Co., Big Beam, 290 E. Prairie St., Crystal Lake, IL 60014
10-X Mfg. Co., 6185 Arapahoe, Boulder, CO 80303
Thermos Div., KST Co., Norwich, Conn. 06361 (Pop Tent)
Therm'x Corp., Inc., 1280 Columbus, San Francisco, Calif. 94133
Norm Thompson, 1805 N.W. Thurman St., Portland, Ore. 97209
Trailwise-The Ski Hut, 1615 University Ave., Berkeley, Calif. 94703
Ute Mountain Corp., Box 3602, Englewood, Colo. 80110 (Metal Match)
Utica Duxbak Corp., 815 Noyes St., Utica, N.Y. 13502
Visa-Therm Prod., Inc., P.O. Box 486, Bridgeport, Conn. 06601 (Astro/Electr. vest)
Waffen-Frankonia, Box 380, 87 Wurzburg, W. Germany
Ward Mfg. Co., 500 Ford Blvd., Hamilton, O. 45015 (trailers)
Weinbrenner Shoe Corp., Polk St., Merrill, WI 54452
Wenzel Co., 1280 Research Blvd., St. Louis, MO 63132
Wilson Certified Foods, Inc., Box 7345, Omaha, Neb. 68107
Wisconsin Shoe Co., 1039 So. Second, Milwaukee, Wis. 53204
Woods Bag & Canvas Co., Ltd., 16 Lake St., Ogdensburg, N.Y. 13669
Woodstream Corp., Box 327, Lititz, Pa. 17543 (Hunter Seat)
Woolrich Woolen Mills, Woolrich, Pa. 17779
Yankee Mechanics, Lacey Place, Southport, CT 06490 (hand winches)
Zeus Portable Generator Co., 500 Mildred, Primos, Ohio 19018

KNIVES, AXES, HATCHETS, KNIFEMAKER'S SUPPLIES—HUNTING

John Applebaugh, Box 68, Blackwell, OK 74631 (custom-knives)
Baker Forged Knives, P.O. Box 514, Hinsdale, IL 60521 (custom-made, folder $1)

L. L. Bean, Freeport, Maine 04032
Bear Archery Co., R.R. 1, Grayling, MI 49738
Lee Biggs, 3816 Via La Silva, Palo Verde, CA 92266 (custom-knives)
Ralph Bone Knife Co., 806 Avenue J, Lubbock, Tex. 79401
H. Gardner Bourne, 1252 Hope Ave., Columbus, O. 43212 (custom-knives)
Bowen Knife Co., P.O. Box 14028, Atlanta, GA 30324
L. E. "Red" Brown, 301 E. Neece St., Long Beach, CA 90805 (custom-knives)
Buck Knives, Inc., P.O. Box 1267, El Cajon, CA 92022
Busch Custom Knives, 940 Orion, Metairie, LA 70005
Pete Callan, 17 Sherline Ave., New Orleans, LA 70124 (custom-knives)
Camillus Cutlery Co., Camillus, NY 13031
W. R. Case Knives, 20 Russell Blvd., Bradford, Pa. 16701
Challanger Mfg. Co., 118 Pearl St., Mt. Vernon, NY 10550
Clements Custom Leathercraft, 1245 S. Pennsylvania St., Denver, CO 80203 (supplies)
Collins Brothers Div. (belt-buckle knife), see: Bowen Knife Co.
Cooper Knives, P.O. Box 1423, Burbank, CA 91505 (custom, ctlg. 50¢)
Custom Cutlery, 907 Greenwood Pl., Dalton, GA 30720
Custom Knifemaker's Supply, P.O. Box 11448, Dallas, TX 75223 (ctlg. 50¢)
Dan-D Custom Knives, Box 4479, Yuma, AZ 85364
Davis Custom Knives, North 1405 Ash, Spokane, WA 99201
Philip Day, Rte. 1, Box 465T, Bay Minetter, AL 36507 (custom-knives)
J. R. Dennard, 907 Greenwood Pl., Dalton, GA 30720 (custom-knives)
Chas. E. Dickey, 803 N.E. A St., Bentonville, AR 72712 (custom-knives)
T. M. Dowell, 139 St. Helen's Pl., Bend, OR 97701 (TMD custom-knives, ctlg. $1)
Draper Blade, Inc., 519 E. State Rd., American Fork, UT 84003 (custom knives, ctlg. 50¢)
John Ek, 1547 NW 119th St., No. Miami, FL 33167
Eze-Lap Diamond Prods., Box 2229, Westminster, CA 92683 (knife sharpeners)
Fischer Custom Knives, Rt. 1, Box 170-M, Victoria, TX 77901
H. H. Frank, #1 Mountain Meadows, Whitefish, MT 59937 (custom-knives)
James Furlow, 2499 Brookdale Dr. N.E., Atlanta, GA 30345 (custom-knives)
Garcia Sptg. Arms Corp., 329 Alfred Ave., Teaneck, NJ 07666
Gerber Legendary Blades, 14200 S.W. 72nd St., Portland, OR 99223
Gutman Cutlery Co., Inc., 900 S. Columbus Ave., Mt. Vernon, NY 10550
H & B Forge Co., Rte. 2, Shiloh, OH 44837 (tomahawks)
Hale Handmade Knives, Box 5988, Texarkana, TX 75501
Virgil W. Hartley, 1602 S. Hunter Rd., Indianapolis, IN 46239 (Bamsen knives)
C. M. (Pete) Heath, 119 Grant St., Winnecone, WI 54986 (custom-knives)
J. A. Henckels Twinworks, 1 Westchester Plaza, Elmsford, NY 10523
G. H. Herron, 920 Murrah Ave., Aiken, SC 29801 (custom-knives)
Chubby Hueske, 4808 Tamarisk Dr., Bellaire, TX 77401 (custom-knives)
Bill Imel (see Ramrod Knife & Gun Shop)
Indian Ridge Traders, P.O. Box X-50, Ferndale, MI 48220
Jet-Aer Corp., 100 Sixth Ave., Paterson, NJ 07524 (G96 knives)
LaDow (Doc) Johnston, 2322 W. Country Club Parkway, Toledo, OH 43614 (custom-knives)
KA-BAR Cutlery, Inc., 5777 Grant Ave., Cleveland, OH 44105
Jon W. Kirk, 800 N. Olive, Fayetteville, AR 72701 (custom-knives)
W. Kneubuhler, P.O. Box 327, Pioneer, OH 43554 (custom-knives)
Kustom Made Knives, 418 Jolee, Richardson, TX 75080
Lile Handmade Knives, Rte. 1, Box 56, Russellville, AR 72801
LocKnife, Inc., 11717 E. 23rd St., Independence, MO 64050
R. W. Loveless, P.O. Box 7836, Arlington Sta., Riverside, CA 92503 (custom-knives, ctlg. $1)
Bob Ludwig, 1028 Pecos Ave., Port Arthur, TX 77640 (custom-knives)
Marble Arms Corp., 420 Industrial Park, Gladstone, MI 49837
Joe S. Martin, Box 6652, Lubbock, TX 79413 (custom-knives)
John T. Mims, 620 S. 28th Ave., Apt. 327, Hattiesburg, MS 39401 (custom-knives)
Mitchell Knives, 511 Ave. B, So. Houston, TX 77587 (custom)
W. F. Moran, Jr., Rt. 5, Frederick, MD 21701 (custom-knives, ctlg. 50¢)
Morseth Sports Equip. Co., 1705 Hiway 71N, Springdale, AR 72764 (custom-knives)
Normark Corp., 1710 E. 78th St., Minneapolis, MN 55423
Ogg Custom Knives, Rt. 1, Box 230, Paris, AR 72855
Olsen Knife Co., Inc., 7 Joy St., Howard City, MI 49329
Ramrod Knife & Gun Shop, Route 5, State Road 3 North, Newcastle, IN 47362 (custom-knives)
Randall-Made Knives, Box 1988, Orlando, FL 32802 (ctlg. 25¢)
Razor Edge, Box 203, Butler, WI 53007 (knife sharpener)
F. J. Richtig, Clarkson, NB 68629 (custom-knives)
Rigid Knives, P.O. Box 460, Santee, CA 92071 (custom-made)
Ruana Knife Works, Box 574, Bonner, MT 59823 (ctlg. 50¢)
Sanders, 2358 Tyler Lane, Louisville, KY 40205 (Bahco)
Jack D. Schmier, 16787 Mulberry Ct., Fountain Valley, CA 92708 (custom-knives)
Bob Schrimsher, Custom Knifemaker's Supply, P.O. Box 11448, Dallas, TX 75223
John J. Schwarz, 41 Fifteenth St., Wellsburg, WV 26070 (custom-knives)
N. H. Schiffman Custom Knives, 963 Malibu, Pocatello, ID 83201
C. R. Sigman, Star Rte., Box 3, Red House, WV 25168
Skachet, (see: Gyrfalcon Inc.)
Smith & Wesson, 2100 Roosevelt Ave., Springfield, MA 01101
John T. Smith, 6048 Cedar Crest Dr., So. Haven, MS 38671 (custom-knives)
W. J. Sonneville, 1050 Chalet Dr. W., Mobile, AL 36608 (custom-knives)
Bernard Sparks, Box 32, Dingle, ID 83233 (custom-knives)
Stone Knives, 703 Floyd Rd., Richardson, TX 75080
Thompson/Center, P.O. Box 2405, Rochester, NH 03867
Track Knives, 1313 2nd St., Whitefish, MT 59937
Tru-Balance Knife Co., 2115 Tremont Blvd., Grand Rapids, MI 49504
True-Temper, 1623 Euclid, Cleveland, OH 44100 (handaxes and hatchets only)
Unique Inventions, Inc., 3727 W. Alabama St., Houston, TX 77027 (throwing knife)
W-K Knives, P.O. Box 327, Pioneer, OH 43554
Western Cutlery Co., 5311 Western Ave., Boulder, CO 80302
W. C. Wilber, 400 Lucerne Dr., Spartanburg, SC 29302 (custom knives)
Ronnie Wilson, P.O. Box 2012, Weirton, WV 26062 (custom-knives)
Don Zaccagaino, P.O. Box Zack, Pahokee, FL 33476 (custom-knives)

LABELS, BOXES, CARTRIDGE HOLDERS

Milton Brynin, Box 162, Fleetwood Station, Mount Vernon, NY 10552 (cartridge box labels)
E-Z Loader, Del Rey Products, P.O. Box 91561, Los Angeles, CA 90009
Jasco, J. A. Somers Co., P.O. Box 49751, Los Angeles, CA 90049 (cartridge box labels)
Llanerch Gun Shop, 2800 Township Line, Upper Darby, PA 19083 (cartridge boxes)
Peterson Label Co., P.O. Box 186, Redding Ridge, CT 06876 (cartridge box labels; Targ-Dots)
N. H. Schiffman, 963 Malibu, Pocatello, ID 83201 (cartridge carrier)
Shooters Supplies, 1251 Blair Ave., St. Paul, MN 55104 (cartridge and shotshell boxes)

LOAD TESTING & CHRONOGRAPHING

Carter Gun Works, 2211 Jefferson Pk. Ave., Charlottesville, Va. 22903
Custom Ballistics' Lab., 3354 Cumberland Dr., San Angelo, Tex. 76901
Horton Ballistics, North Waterford, Me. 04267
Hutton Rifle Ranch, Box 898, Topanga, CA 90290
Jurras Co., Box 163, Shelbyville, Ind. 46176
Kennon's, 5408 Biffle, Stone Mountain, Ga. 30083
Plum City Ballistics Range, Box 29C, Plum City, Wis. 54761
Shooters Service & Dewey, Inc., Clinton Corners, N.Y. 12514 (daily fee range also)
Gene West, 137 Baylor, Pueblo, Colo. 81005
H. P. White Lab., Box 331, Bel Air, Md. 21014

MISCELLANEOUS

Accurizing Service, Herbert G. Troester, Cayuaga, ND 58013
Adhesive Flannel, Forest City Prod., 722 Bolivar, Cleveland, OH 44115
Archery, Bear Co., R.R. 1, Grayling, Mich. 49738
Arms Restoration, J. J. Jenkins, 462 Stanford Pl., Santa Barbara, CA 93105
Barrel Band Swivels, Phil Judd, 83 E. Park St., Butte, Mont. 59701
Bedding Kit, Bisonite Co., 2250 Military Rd., Tonawanda, NY 14150
Bedding Kit, Fenwal, Inc., Resin Systems Div., 400 Main St., Ashland, Mass. 01721
Binocular/Camera Harness, Jack Worsfold Assoc., Box 25, Forest Hill, Md. 21050
Bootdryers, Baekgaard Ltd., 1855 Janke Dr., Northbrook, Ill. 60062
Breech Plug Wrench, Swaine Machine, 195 O'Connell, Providence, R.I. 02905
Cannons, South Bend Replicas Inc., 61650 Oak Rd., S. Bend, IN 46614 (ctlg. $1.50)
Case Gauge, Plum City Ballistics Range, Box 29C, Plum City, Wis. 54761
Chrome Brl. Lining, Marker Mach. Co., Box 426, Charleston, Ill. 61920
Color Hardening, Alamo Heat Treating Co., Box 55345, Houston, Tex. 77055
Crow Caller, Wightman Elec. Inc., Box 989, Easton, Md. 21601
Distress Flares, Marsh Coulter Co., P.O. Box 333, Tecumseh, MI 49286
Dog House, Canine Pal Sales, 421 E. 39th Ave., Gary, Ind. 46409 (portable)
Dryer, Thermo-Electric, Golden-Rod, (Phinney-Hale, Inc., Box 5286, Oxnard, CA 93030
E-Z Loader, Del Rey Prod., P.O. Box 91561, Los Angeles, CA 90009
Ear-Valv, Sigma Eng. Co., 11320 Burbank Blvd., N. Hollywood, Cal. 91601 (Lee-Sonic)
Emergency Food, Chuck Wagon, Micro Dr., Woburn, Mass. 01801
Fill N'File, Apsco Packaging Co., 9325 W. Bryon St., Schiller Park, IL 60176
Flares, Colt Industries, Huyshope Ave., Hartford, Conn. 06102
Flares, Intercontinental Arms, 2222 Barry Ave., Los Angeles, Ca. 90064 (MBA)
Flares, Smith & Wesson Chemical Co., 2399 Forman Rd., Rock Creek, OH 44084
Flat Springs, Alamo Heat Treating Co., Box 55345, Houston, Tex. 77055
Game Hoist, PIC, 3 Chestnut, Suffern, N.Y. 10901
Game Scent, Buck Stop, Inc., 3015 Grow Rd., Stanton, Mi 4888
Game Scent, Pete Rickard, R.D. 1, Carlisle Rd., Box 1002, Cobleskill, N.Y. 12043 (Indian Buck lure)
Gas Pistol, Penguin Ind., Inc., Box 97, Parkesburg, Pa. 19365
Golden-Rod, Phinney-Hale, Inc., P.O. Box 5286, Oxnard, CA 93030 (Thermo-Electric Dryers)
Gun Bedding Kit, Resin Systems Div., Fenwal, Inc., 400 Main St., Ashland, Mass. 01721
Gun Jewelry, Sid Bell Originals, R.D. 2, Tully, NY 13159
Gun Jewelry, Al Popper, 614 Turnpike St., Stoughton, Mass. 02072
Gun Lock, E & C Enterprises, P.O. Box 823, So. Pasadena, CA. 91030
Gun Sling, Kwikfire, Wayne Prods. Co., P.O. Box 247, Camp Hill, PA 17011
Gun Slings, Torel, Inc., 1053 N. South St., Yoakum, TX 77995
Hand-Plucks f. game birds, Hageman Corp., 102 5th St., Arbuckle, CA 95912
Hat Saver Co., Inc., P.O. Box 307, Rosenberg, TX 77471
Hollow Pointer, Goerg Ent., 3009 S. Laurel St., Port Angeles, Wash. 98362
Hugger Hooks, Roman Products, Box 891, Golden, Colo. 80401

Hunting Bag, Dan Barr, Rte. 1, Thornville, OH 43076
Insect Repellent, Armor, Div. of Buck Stop, Inc., 3015 Grow Rd., Stanton, Mich. 48888
Insert Barrels, (22 RF), H. Owen, P.O. Box 774, Sunnyvale, Calif. 94088
Lightnin-Loader, Hunter Mfg. Co., Box 2882, Van Nuys, Cal. 91404
Locks, Gun, Bor-Lok Prods., 105 5th St., Arbuckle, CA 95912
Magazine Clip (Colyer), Great Northern Trading Post, 13001 Hwy. 65 N.E., Rte. 4, Anoka, Minn. 55303
Magazine Clips, Amer. Firearms Mfg. Co., Inc., 1200 Warfield, San Antonio, Tex. 78216
Locks, Gun, Master Lock Co., 2600 N. 32nd St., Milwaukee, WI 53245
Military Museum, Lt. Col. E.H. Hoffman, 768 So. Main St., Woodstock, Va. 22664
Miniature Guns, C. H. Stoppler, 1426 Walton Ave., N.Y., N.Y. 10452
Monte Carlo Pad, Frank A. Hoppe Div., P.O. Box 97, Parkesburg, Pa. 19365
Muzzle-Top, Allen Assoc., 7502 Limekiln, Philadelphia, PA 19150 (plastic gun muzzle cap)
Pell Remover, A. Edw. Terpening, 838 E. Darlington Rd., Tarpon Springs, FL 33589
Personnel Armor, Second Chance, Box 638, Romulus, MI 48174
Powder Storage Magazine, C & M Gunworks, 2603 41st St., Moline, IL 61265
Pressure Testg. Machine, M. York, 19381 Keymar Way, Gaithersburg, MD 20760
Ransom Handgun Rests, C'Arco, P.O. Box 2043, San Bernardino, CA 92406
Retriev-R-Trainer, Scientific Prods. Corp., 426 Swann Ave., Alexandria, VA 22301
Rifle Slings, Bianchi, 212 W. Foothill Blvd., Monrovia, Cal. 91016
Rifle Sling, Ready Sling Co., P.O. Box 536, Delano, CA 93215
RIG, NRA Scoring Plug, Rig Prod. Co., Box 279, Oregon, Ill. 60161
Rubber Cheekpiece, W. H. Lodewick, 2816 N. E. Halsey, Portland, Ore. 97232
Safeties, Williams Gun Sight Co., 7389 Lapeer Rd., Davison, Mich. 48423
Salute Cannons, Naval Co., R.D. 2, Doylestown, PA 18901
Sav-Bore, Saunders Sptg. Gds., 338 Somerset St., N. Plainfield, NJ 07060
Scrimshaw Engraving, C. Milton Barringer, 217-2nd Isle N., Port Richey, FL 33568
Scrimshaw Engraving, A. Douglas Jacobs, Box 1236, Cutchogue, NY 11935
Sharpening Stones, Russell's Arkansas Oilstones, 1705 Hiway 71N., Springdale, AR 72764
Shell Shrinker Mfg. Co., Box 6143, Lubbock, Tex. 79413
Shok-Baton Co., 440 W. Nixon St., Savage, MN 55378
Shooting Bench/Porto, Seyferth's, Inc., 926 N. Memorial Dr., Racine, WI 53404
Shooting Coats, 10-X Mfg. Co., 6185 Arapahoe, Boulder, CO 80303
Shooting Ranges, Shooting Equip. Inc., 10 S. LaSalle, Chicago, IL 60603
Shotgun Sight, bi-ocular, Trius Prod., Box 25, Cleves, O. 45002
Silver Grip Caps, Bill Dyer, P.O. Box 75255, Oklahoma City, Okla. 73107
Snap Caps, Filmat, 200 Market, East Paterson, N.J. 07407
Snap Caps, G & S Engineering Co., Box 590, Clinton, MI 49236 (Practicaps)
Snowshoes, Sportsmen Prod. Inc., Box 1082, Boulder, Colo. 80302
Springfield Safety Pin, B-Square Co., P.O. Box 11281, Ft. Worth, Tex. 76110
Springs, W. Wolff Co., Box 232, Ardmore, Pa. 19003
Stock-Lo-Kater, Bill Matthews Co., 5004 Encinita Ave., Temple City, Ca. 91780
Supersound, Edmund Scientific Co., 101 E. Gloucester Pike, Barrington, NJ 08007 (safety device)
Swivels, Michaels, P.O. Box 13010, Portland, Ore. 97213
Swivels, Sile Dist., 7 Centre Market Pl., New York, N.Y. 10013
Swivels, Williams Gun Sight Co., 7389 Lapeer Rd., Davison, Mich. 48423
Trophies, L. G. Balfour Co., Attleboro, Mass. 02703
Trophies, Blackinton & Co., 140 Commonwealth, Attleboro Falls, Mass. 12763
Trophies, F. H. Noble & Co., 559 W. 59th St., Chicago, Ill. 60621
Universal 3-shot Shotgun Plug, LanDav Custom Guns, 7213 Lee Highway, Falls Church, VA 22046
World Hunting Info., Jack Atcheson & Sons, Inc., 3210 Ottawa St., Butte, MT 59701
World Hunting Info., Denver Jonas Bros., 1037 Broadway, Denver, CO 80203

MUZZLE-LOADING GUNS, BARRELS OR EQUIPMENT

Luther Adkins, Box 281, Shelbyville, Ind. 47176 (breech plugs)
Anderson & Co., 1203 Broadway, Yakima, WA 98902
Armoury, Inc., Rte. 25, New Preston, Conn. 06777
Dan Barr, Rte. 1, Thornville, OH 43076 (hunting bag)
John Bivins, Jr., 446 So. Main, Winston-Salem, N.C. 27101
G. S. Bunch, 7735 Garrison, Hyattsville, Md. 20784 (flask repair)
Caution Tool Co., Scout Rd., Southbury, CT 06488
Challanger Mfg. Co., 118 Pearl St., Mt. Vernon, NY 10550
Cherry Corners Mfg. Co., 11136 Congress Rd., Lodi, Ohio 44254
Chopie Mfg. Inc., 531 Copeland Ave., LaCrosse, WI 54601 (nipple wrenches)
Cornwall Bridge Gun Shop, P.O. Box 67, Cornwall Bridge, CT 06745
Earl T. Cureton, Rte. 6, 7017 Pine Grove Rd., Knoxville, Tenn. 37914 (powder horns)
John N. Dangelzer, 3056 Frontier Pl. N.E., Albuquerque, N. Mex. 87106 (powder flasks)
Ted Fellowes, Beaver Lodge, 9245 16th Ave. S.W., Seattle, Wash. 98106
Firearms Imp. & Exp. Corp., 2470 N.W. 21st St., Miami, Fla. 33142
Clark K. Frazier/Matchmate, RFD. 1, Rawson, OH 45881
Golden Age Arms Co., 657 High St., Worthington, Ohio 43085 (ctlg. $1)
Golden Strip Enterprises, Box 457, Simpsonville, SC 29681 (powder horns)
A. R. Goode, R.D. 1, Box 84, Thurmont, MD 21788
Green River Forge, 4326 120th Ave. S.E., Bellevue, WA 98006 (Forge-Fire flints)
Virgil W. Hartley, 1602 S. Hunter Rd., Indianapolis, IN 46239 (ML pouch)
House of Muzzle Loading, Box 4099, Downey, CA 90241
International M. L. Parts Co., 19453 Forrer, Detroit, MI 48235
JJJJ Ranch, Wm. Large, Rte. 1, Ironton, Ohio 45638
K & W Cap and Ball Dispenser, Rte. 2, 5073 Townsley Rd., Cedarville, OH 45314
Kindig's Log Cabin Sport Shop, R.D. 1, Box 275, Lodi, OH 44254
Art LeFeuvre, 1003 Hazel Ave., Deerfield, Ill. 60015 (antique gun restoring)
Les' Gun Shop (Les Bauska), Box 511, Kalispell, Mont, 59901
Lever Arms Serv. Ltd., 771 Dunsmuir, Vancouver 1, B.C., Canada
J. Lewis Arms Mfg., 3931 Montgomery Rd., Cincinnati, Ohio 45212 (pistol)
McKeown's Guns, R.R. 1, Pekin, IL 61554 (E-Z load rev. stand)
Judson E. Mariotti, Beauty Hill Rd., Barrington, NH 03825 (brass bullet mould)
Maryland Gun Exchange Inc., Rt. 40 West, RD 5, Frederick, MD 21701
Maurer Arms, 2366 Frederick Dr., Cuyahoga Falls, OH 44221 (cust. muzzleloaders)
Jos. W. Mellott, 334 Rockhill Rd., Pittsburgh, Pa. 15243 (barrel blanks)
W. L. Mowrey Gun Works, Inc., Box 28, Iowa Park, TX 76367
Numrich Corp., W. Hurley, N.Y. 12491 (powder flasks)
R. Paris & Son, R.D. 5, Box 61, Gettysburg, Pa. 17325 (barrels)
Penna. Rifle Works, 319 E. Main St., Ligonier, Pa. 15658 (ML guns, parts)
A. W. Peterson Gun Shop, 1693 Old Hwy. 441 N., Mt. Dora, FL 32757 (ML guns)
Rush's Old Colonial Forge, 106 Wiltshire Rd., Baltimore, MD 21221
H. M. Schoeller, 569 So. Braddock Ave., Pittsburgh, Pa. 15221
Shilo Ind., Inc., 173 Washington Pl., Hasbrouck Heights, NJ 07604 (4-cavity mould)
C. E. Siler, 181 Sandhill School, Asheville, N.C., 28806 (flint locks)
Ken Steggles, 77 Lower Eastern Green Lane, Coventry, CV5 7DT, England (accessories)
Upper Missouri Trading Co., Box 191, 2nd Harold St., Crofton, NB 68730
R. Watts, 826 Springdale Rd., Atlanta, GA 30306 (ML rifles)
Thos. F. White, 5801 Westchester Ct., Worthington, O. 43085 (powder horn)
Lou Williamson, 129 Stonegate Ct., Bedford, TX 76021
York County Gun Works, R.R. #4, Tottenham, Ont., Canada (locks)
R. E. Zellmer, W180 N8996 Leona Ln., Menomonee Falls, WI 53051 (Kentucky Fullstocks)

PISTOLSMITHS

Alamo Heat Treating, Box 55345, Houston, Tex. 77055
Allen Assoc., 7448 Limekiln Pike, Philadelphia, Pa. 19138 (speed-cock lever for 45 ACP)
Bain and Davis Sptg. Gds., 559 W. Las Tunas Dr., San Gabriel, Cal. 91776
Bar-Sto Precision Machine, 633 So. Victory Blvd., Burbank, CA 91502 (S.S. bbls. f. 45 Acp)
Behlert & Freed, Inc., 33 Herning Ave., Cranford. N.J. 07016 (short actions)
R. M. Champlin, P.O. Box 74, Stanyan Hill, Wentworth, NH 03282
F. Bob Chow, Gun Shop, 3185 Mission, San Francisco, Calif. 94110
J.E. Clark, Rte. 2, Box 22A, Keithville, LA 71047
Custom Gunshop, 33 Herning Ave., Cranford, N.J. 07016
Day Arms Corp., 7515 Stagecoach Lane, San Antonio, Tex. 78227
Alton S. Dinan, Jr., P.O. Box 6674, Canaan, Conn. 06018
Dominic DiStefano, 4303 Friar Lane, Colorado Springs, CO 80907 (accurizing)
Dan Dwyer, 915 W. Washington, San Diego, Calif. 92103
Giles' 45 Shop, Rt. 1, Box 47, Odessa, Fla. 33556
H. H. Harris, 1237 So. State, Chicago, Ill. 60605
Gil Hebard Guns, Box 1, Knoxville, Ill. 61448
Rudolf Marent, 9711 Tiltree, Houston, Tex. 77034 (Hammerli)
Maryland Gun Exchange, Inc., Rte. 40 W., RD 5, Frederick, MD 21701
Match Arms Co., 831 Mary St., Springdale, Pa. 15144
Pachmayr Gun Works, 1220 S. Grand Ave., Los Angeles, Calif. 90015
R. L. Shockey Guns, Inc., 1614 S. Choctaw, E. Reno, Okla. 73036
Silver Dollar Guns, 7 Balsam St., Keene, N.H. 03431 (45 auto only)
Sportsmens Equipmt. Co., 915 W. Washington, San Diego, Calif. 92103
A. D. Swenson's 45 Shop, P.O. Box 884, Lawndale, CA 90260
Dave Woodruff, 116 Stahl Ave., Wilmington Manor, DE 19720

REBORING AND RERIFLING

P.O. Ackley, 2235 Arbor Lane, Salt Lake City, UT 84117
Atkinson Gun Co., P.O. Box 512, Prescott, AZ 86301
Bain & Davis Sptg. Gds., 559 W. Las Tunas Dr., San Gabriel, Calif. 91776
Carpenter's Gun Works, Gunshop Rd., Box C, Plattekill, N.Y. 12568
Fuller Gun Shop, Cooper Landing, Alaska 99572
Ward Koozer, Box 18, Walterville, Ore. 97489
Les' Gun Shop, Box 511, Kalispell, Mont. 59901
Morgan's Cust. Reboring, 707 Union Ave., Grants Pass, OR 97526
Nu-Line Guns, 3727 Jennings Rd., St. Louis, Mo. 63121
Al Petersen, Box 8, Riverhurst, Saskatchewan, Canada S0H3P0
Schuetzen Gun Works, 1226 Prairie Rd., Colorado Springs, Colo. 80909
Siegrist Gun Shop, R.R. #1, Whittemore, MI 48770
Small Arms Eng., P.O. Box 306, Des Plaines, IL 60018
Snapp's Gunshop, 6911 E. Washington Rd., Clare, Mich. 48617
R. Southgate, Rt. 2, Franklin, Tenn. 37064 (Muzzleloaders)
J. W. Van Patten, Box 145, Foster Hill, Milford, Pa. 18337
Robt. G. West, 6626 So. Lincoln, Littleton, Colo. 80120

RELOADING TOOLS AND ACCESSORIES

Acme Ind. Inc., Box 101, Kaukauna, WI 54130 (loader & wingtraps)
Alcan, (See: Smith & Wesson Arms Co.)
Alpha-Molykote, Dow Corning Corp., 45 Commerce, Trumbull, Ct. 06601

Anchor Alloys, Inc., 966 Meeker Ave., Brooklyn, N.Y. 11222 (chilled shot)
Anderson Mfg. Co., Royal, Ia. 51357 (Shotshell Trimmers)
Aurands, 229 E. 3rd St., Lewistown, Pa. 17044
B-Square Eng. Co., Box 11281, Ft. Worth, Tex. 76110
Bahler Die Shop, Rte. 1, 412 Hemlock St., Florence, OR 97439
Bair Machine Co., Box 4407, Lincoln, Neb. 68504
Bill Ballard, P.O. Box 656, Billings, MT 59103 (ctlg. 25¢)
Belding & Mull, P.O. Box 428, Philipsburg, Pa. 16866
Belmont Prods., Rte. 1, Friendsville, TN 37737 (lead cutter)
Blackhawk SAA East, K2274 POB, Loves Park, Ill. 61111
Blackhawk SAA West, Box 285, Hiawatha, KS 66434
Bonanza Sports, Inc., 412 Western Ave., Faribault, Minn. 55021
Gene Bowlin, 3602 Hill Ave., Snyder, Tex. 79549 (arbor press)
Brown Precision Co., 5869 Indian Ave., San Jose, Calif. 95123 (Little Wiggler)
A. V. Bryant, 72 Whiting Rd., East Hartford, CT 06118 (Nutmeg Universal Press)
C-H Tool & Die Corp., Box L, Owen, Wis. 54460
Camdex, Inc., 18619 W. Seven Mile Rd., Detroit, Mich. 48219
Carbide Die & Mfg. Co., Box 226, Covina, CA 91724
Carter Gun Works, 2211 Jefferson Pk. Ave., Charlottesville, Va. 22903
Cascade Cartridge, Inc., (See Omark)
Clymer Mfg. Co., 14241 W. 11 Mile Rd., Oak Park, MI 48237 (½-jack. swaging dies)
Lester Coats, 416 Simpson St., No. Bend, Ore. 97459 (core cutter)
Cole's Acku-Rite Prod., P.O. Box 25, Kennedy, N.Y. 14747 (die racks)
Conevera's Reloading Supplies, 5064 Dialette Dr., Rockford, IL 61102
Container Development Corp., 424 Montgomery St., Watertown, WI 53094
Continental Kite & Key Co., Box 40, Broomall, PA 19008 (primer pocket cleaner)
Cooper-Woodward, Box 972, Riverside, Calif. 92502 (Perfect Lube)
J. Dewey Gun Co., Clinton Corners, N.Y. 12514 (bullet spinner)
Diverter Arms, Inc., 6520 Rampart St., Houston, TX 77036 (bullet puller)
Division Lead Co., 7742 W. 61st Pl., Summit, Ill. 60502
Eagle Products Co., 1520 Adelia Ave., So. El Monte, Cal. 91733
W. H. English, 4411 S. W. 100th, Seattle, Wash. 98146 (Paktool)
Farmer Bros. Mfg. Co., 1102 Washington St., Eldora, IA 50627 (Lage wads)
The Fergusons, Temple Rd., New Ipswich, NH 03071
Fitz, Box 49797, Los Angeles, Calif. 90049 (Fitz Flipper)
Flambeau Plastics, 801 Lynn, Baraboo, Wis. 53913
Forster-Appelt Mfg. Co., Inc., 82 E. Lanark Ave., Lanark, Ill. 61046
Gene's Gun Shop, 3602 Hill Ave., Snyder, Tex. 79549 (arbor press)
John R. Gillette, 4514 W. 123d Place, Alsip, IL 60658
Goerg Enterprises, 3009 S. Laurel, Port Angeles, WA 98362 (hollow pointer)
Gopher Shooter's Supply, Box 246, Faribault, Minn. 55021
Griffin Shooter's Supplies, 7801-A9 Hillmont, Houston, TX 77040 (Electric operator for MEC tools)
The Gun Clinic, 81 Kale St., Mahtomedi, Minn. 55115
Hart Products, 401 Montgomery St., Nescopeck, Pa. 18635
Ed Hart's Gun Supply, U.S. Rte. 15 No., Bath, NY 14810 (Meyer shotgun slugs)
Hensley & Gibbs, Box 10, Murphy, Ore. 97533
E. C. Herkner Co., Box 5007, Boise, Ida. 83702
Herter's Inc., RR1, Waseca, Minn. 56093
B. E. Hodgdon, Inc., 7710 W. 50 Hiway, Shawnee Mission, Kans. 66202
Hollywood Reloading, see: Whitney Sales, Inc.
Hulme Firearm Serv., Box 83, Millbrae, Calif. 94030 (Star case feeder)
Hunter Bradlee Co., 2800 Routh St., Dallas, TX 75201 (powder measure)
Independent Mach. & Gun Shop, 1416 N. Hayes, Pocatello, Ida. 83201
JASCO, Box 49751, Los Angeles, Calif. 90049
J & G Rifle Ranch, Box 80, Turner, MT 59542 (case tumblers)
Javelina Products, Box 337, San Bernardino, Cal. 92402 (Alox beeswax)
Kexplore, Box 22084, Houston, Tex. 77027
Kuharsky Bros. (see Modern Industries)
Kush Plastics, P.O. Box 366, Palatine, IL 60067 (shotshell wads)
Lachmiller Eng. Co., 11273 Goss St., Sun Valley, CA 91352
Lage universal shotshell wad, see: Farmer Bros.
LanDav, 7213 Lee Highway, Falls Church, VA 22046 (X-15 bullet puller)
Lee Engineering, 21 E. Wisconsin St., Hartford, Wis. 53027
Leon's Reloading Service, 3945 No. 11 St., Lincoln, Neb. 68521
L. L. F. Die Shop, 1281 Highway 99 N., Eugene, Ore. 97402
Dean Lincoln, P.O. Box 1886, Farmington, NM 87401 (mould)
Ljutic Industries, 918 N. 5th Ave., Yakima, Wash. 98902
Lock's Phila. Gun Exch., 6700 Rowland, Philadelphia, Pa. 19149
J. T. Loos, P.O. Box 41, Pomfret, CT. 06258 (primer pocket cleaner)
Lyman Gun Sight Products, Middlefield, Conn. 06455
McKillen & Heyer, Box 627, Willoughby, O. 44094 (case gauge)
Paul McLean, 2670 Lakeshore Blvd., W., Toronto 14, Ont., Canada (Universal Cartridge Holder)
Pat B. McMillan, 1828 E. Campo Bello Dr., Phoenix, Ariz. 85022
MTM Molded Prod., 5680 Webster St., Dayton, OH 45414
Magma Eng. Co., P.O. Box 881, Chandler, AZ 85224
Judson E. Mariotti, Beauty Hill Rd., Barrington, NH 03825 (brass bullet mould)
Marquart Precision Co., Box 1740, Prescott, AZ 86301 (precision case-neck turning tool)
Mayville Eng. Co., 715 South St., Mayville, Wis. 53050 (shotshell loader)
Merit Gun Sight Co., P.O. Box 995, Sequim, Wash. 98382
Minnesota Shooters Supply, 1915 E. 22nd St., Minneapolis, Minn. 55404
Modern Industries, Inc., 613 W-11, Erie, PA 16501 (primer pocket cleaner)
Murdock Lead Co., Box 5298, Dallas, Tex. 75222
National Lead Co., Box 831, Perth Amboy, N.J. 08861
Normington Co., Box 6, Rathdrum, ID 83858 (powder baffles)
Ohaus Scale Corp., 29 Hanover Rd., Florham Park, N.J. 07932
Omark-CCI, Inc., Box 856, Lewiston, Ida. 83501
Pacific Tool Co., P.O. Drawer 2048, Ordnance Plant Rd., Grand Island, NB 68801
Pak-Tool Co., 4411 S.W. 100th, Seattle, WA 98146
Pattern Perfect, P.O. Box 366, Palatine, IL 60067 (shotshell wads)
Perfection Die Co., 1614 S. Choctaw, El Reno, Okla. 73036
Personal Firearms Record Book, Box 201, Park Ridge, Ill. 60068
Ferris Pindell, R.R. 3, Box 205, Connersville, IN 47331 (bullet spinner)
Plum City Ballistics Range, Box 29C, Plum City, Wis. 54761
Ponsness-Warren, Inc., P.O. Box 861, Eugene, OR 97401
Potter Eng. Co., 1410 Santa Ana Dr., Dunedin, FL 33528 (electric pots only)
Marian Powley, 19 Sugarplum Rd., Levittown, Pa. 10956
RCBS, Inc., Box 1919, Oroville, Calif. 95965
Redding-Hunter, Inc., 114 Starr Rd., Cortland, N.Y. 13045
Remco, 1404 Whitesboro St., Utica, N.Y. 13502 (shot caps)
Rifle Ranch, Rte. 1, Prescott, Ariz, 86301
Rochester Lead Works, Rochester, N.Y. 14608 (leadwire)
Rorschach Precision Prods., P.O. Box 1613, Irving, Tex. 75060
Rotex Mfg. Co. (see Texan)
Ruhr-American Corp., So. East Hwy. 55, Glenwood, Minn. 56334
SAECO Rel. Inc., P.O. Box 778, Carpinteria, Calif. 93013
Sandia Die & Cartridge Co., Rte. 5, Box 5400, Albuquerque, NM 87123
Saunders Gun & Machine Shop, 145 Delhi Rd., Manchester, IA 52057 (primer feed tray)
Scientific Lubricants Co., 3753 Lawrence Ave., Chicago, Ill. 60625
Shilo IV, Inc., 173 Washington Pl., Hasbrouck Heights, NJ 07604 (4-cavity bullet mould)
Shoffstalls Mfg. Co., 740 Ellis Place, E. Aurora N.Y. 14052
Shooters Accessory Supply, Box 250, N. Bend, Ore. 97459 (SAS)
Shooters Serv. & Dewey, Inc., Clinton Corners, N.Y. 12514 (SS&D) (bullet spinner)
Sil's Gun Prod., 490 Sylvan Dr., Washington, Pa. 15301 (K-spinner)
Jerry Simmons, 713 Middlebury St., Goshen, Ind. 46526 (Pope de- & recapper)
Rob. B. Simonson, Rte. 7, 2129 Vanderbilt Rd., Kalamazoo, Mich. 49002
Smith & Wesson Ammunition Co., Inc., 3640 Seminary Rd., Alton, IL 62002
J. A. Somers Co., P.O. Box 49751, Los Angeles, CA 90049 (Jasco)
Star Machine Works, 418 10th Ave., San Diego, Calif. 92101
Sullivan Arms Corp., see: Anchor Plastics
Texan Reloaders, Inc., P.O. Box 5355, Dallas, Tex. 75222
VAMCO, Box 67, Vestal, N.Y. 13850
W. S. Vickerman, 505 W. 3rd Ave., Ellensburg, Wash. 98926
WAMADET, Silver Springs, Goodleigh, Barnstaple, Devon, England
Walker Mfg. Inc., 8296 So. Channel, Harsen's Island, MI 48028 (Berdan decapper)
Weatherby, Inc., 2781 Firestone Blvd., South Gate, Calif. 90280
Webster Scale Mfg. Co., Box 188, Sebring, Fla. 33870
Whitney Cartridge Co., P.O. Box 608, Cortez, CO 81321 (shotshells)
Whitney Sales, Inc., P.O. 875, Reseda, CA 91335 (Hollywood)
L. E. Wilson, Inc., Box 324, Cashmere, Wash. 98815
Xelex, Ltd., Hawksbury, Ont., Canada (powder)
Zenith Ent., RFD, Nordland, WA 98358
A. Zimmerman, 127 Highland Trail, Denville, N.J. 07834 (case trimmer)

RESTS—BENCH, PORTABLE, ETC.

Bill Anderson, 551 Fletcher, Wayne, PA 19087
Bausch & Lomb, 635 St. Paul St., Rochester, NY 14602 (rifle rest)
Gene Beecher Prods., 2155 Demington Dr., Cleveland Hgts., OH 44106
Jim Brobst, 299 Poplar St., Hamburg, PA 19526 (bench rest pedestal)
C'Arco, P.O. Box 2043, San Bernardino, CA 92401 (Ransom handgun rest)
Central Specialties Co., 630 Northwest Hwy., Chicago, IL 60631 (portable gun rest)
Cole's Acku-Rite Prod., Box 25, Kennedy, N.Y. 14747
F & H Machining, 4645 Cambio Ct., Fremont, CA 94536
The Fergusons, Temple Rd., New Ipswich, NH 03071 (rifle rests)
Frontier Arms, Inc., 420 E. Riding Club Rd., Cheyenne, Wyo. 82001
The Gun Case, 11035 Maplefield, El Monte, Cal. 91733
GVA Enterprises, P.O. Box 725, Garland, TX 75040 (Rif-L-Vise)
Harris Engr., Inc., Box 305, Fraser, Mich. 48026 (bipods)
Rob. W. Hart & Son, 401 Montgomery St., Nescopeck, Pa. 18635
North Star Devices, Inc., P.O. Box 2095, North St. Paul, MN 55109 (Gun Slinger)
Porto/Shooting bench, Seyferth's Inc., 926 N. Memorial, Racine, WI 53404
Rec. Prods, Res., Inc., 158 Franklin Ave., Ridgewood, N.J. 07450 (Butts Pi-pod)
Suter's, 332 Tejon, Colorado Springs, CO 80902
Basil Tuller, 29 Germania, Galeton, PA 16922 (Protecktor sandbags)
Walden Leisure Prods., 1040 Matley Lane, Bldg. 4, Reno, NV 89502 (bench rest accessory case; portable bench)

RIFLE BARREL MAKERS

P.O. Ackley, 2235 Arbor Lane, Salt Lake City, UT 84117
Apex Rifle Co., 7628 San Fernando, Sun Valley, Calif. 91352
Atkinson Gun Co., P.O. Box 512, Prescott, AZ 86301
Christy Gun Works, 875 57th St., Sacramento, Calif. 95819
Clerke Prods., 2219 Main St., Santa Monica, Calif. 90405
Cuthbert Gun Shop, 715 So. 5th, Coos Bay, Ore. 97420
Darr's Rifle Shop, 2309 Black Rd., Joliet, IL 60435
J. Dewey Gun Co., Clinton Corners, N.Y. 12514
Douglas Barrels, Inc., 5504 Big Tyler Rd., Charleston, W. Va. 25312
Douglas Jackalope Gun & Sport Shop, Inc., 1205 E. Richards St., Douglas, WY 82633
Federal Firearms Co., Inc., Box 145, Oakdale, Pa. 15071 (Star bbls., actions)
A. R. Goode, R.D. 1, Box 84, Thurmont, MD 21788
Hart Rifle Barrels, Inc., RD 2, Lafayette, N.Y. 13084
Wm. H. Hobaugh, Box 657, Philipsburg, Mont. 59858

Intern'l Casting Co., 19453 Forrer, Detroit, Mich. 48235
Johnson Automatics, Box 306, Hope Valley, R.I. 02832
Gene Lechner, 636 Jane N.E., Albuquerque, NM 87123
Les' Gun Shop, Box 511, Kalispell, Mont. 59901
McGowen Rifle Barrels, Rte. 3, St. Anne, Ill. 60964
D. M. Manley, 295 Main St., Brookville, PA 15825
Nu-Line Guns, Inc., 3727 Jennings Rd., St. Louis, Mo. 63121
Numrich Arms, W. Hurley, N.Y. 12491
R. Paris & Son, R.D. 5, Box 61, Gettysburg, Pa. 17325
Al Petersen, The Rifle Ranch, Box 8, Riverhurst, Sask., Canada SOH3PO
Rheinmetall (see John Weir)
SS & D, Inc., Clinton Corners, N.Y. 12514 (cold-formed bbls.)
Sanders Cust. Gun Serv., 2358 Tyler Lane, Louisville, Ky. 40205
Scotty's Gun Shop, Second & Rancier, Killeen, TX 76541
Sharon Rifle Barrel Co., P.O. Box 106, Kalispell, MT 59901
Ed Shilen Rifles, Inc., 205 Metropark Blvd., Ennis, TX 75119
W. C. Strutz, Rte. 1, Eagle River, WI 54521
Titus Barrel & Gun Co., Box 151, Heber City, Ut. 84032
John E. Weir, 3304 Norton Ave., Independence, Mo. 64052
Wilson Arms, Box 364, Stony Creek, Branford, Conn. 06405

SCOPES, MOUNTS, ACCESSORIES, OPTICAL EQUIPMENT

Alley Supply Co., Carson Valley Industrial Park, Gardnerville, NV 89410 (Scope collimator)
American Import Co., 1167 Mission, San Francisco, Calif. 94103
Anderson & Co., 1203 Broadway, Yakima, Wash. 98902 (lens cap)
Avery Corp., P.O. Box 99, Electra, TX 76360 (Mini-Light)
Ball-One Buck Scope Lens Cover, Box 426, Midway City, CA 92655
Bausch & Lomb Inc., 635 St. Paul St., Rochester, N.Y. 14602
Bennett, 561 Delaware, Delmar, N.Y. 12054 (mounting wrench)
Bridge Mount Co., Box 3344, Lubbock, Tex. 79410 (one-piece target mts.)
Browning Arms, Rt. 4, Box 624-B, Arnold, Mo. 63010
Maynard P. Buehler, Inc., 17 Orinda Highway, Orinda, Calif. 94563
Burris Co., 351 E. 8th St., Greeley, CO 80631
D. P. Bushnell & Co., Inc., 2828 E. Foothill Blvd., Pasadena, Calif. 91107
Kenneth Clark, 18738 Highway 99, Madera, Calif. 93637
Clearview Mfg. Co., Inc., 23702 Crossley Hazel Park, MI 48030 (mounts)
Clear View Sports Shields, P.O. Box 255, Wethersfield, CT 06107 (shooting/testing glasses)
Colt's, Hartford, Conn. 06102
Compass Instr. & Optical Co., Inc., 104 E 25th St., New York, N.Y. 10010
Conetrol, Hwy 123 South, Seguin, Tex. 78155
Continental Arms Corp., 697-5th Ave., New York, N.Y. 10022 (Nickel)
Davis Optical Co., P.O. Box 6, Winchester, Ind. 47934
M. B. Dinsmore, Box 21, Wyomissing, PA 19610 (shooting glasses)
Duo Mount see: Firearms Service
Eder Instrument Co., 5115 N. Ravenswood, Chicago, IL 60640 (borescope)
Flaig's, Babcock Blvd., Millvale, Pa. 15209
Freeland's Scope Stands, Inc. 3734 14th, Rock Island, Ill. 61201
Griffin & Howe, Inc., 589-8th Ave., New York, N.Y. 10017
E. C. Herkner Co., Box 5007, Boise, Idaho 83702
Herter's Inc., Waseca, Minn. 56093
J. B. Holden Co., Box 393, Plymouth, MI 48170
The Hutson Corp., P.O. 1127, Arlington, Tex. 76010
Hy-Score Arms Corp., 200 Tillary St., Brooklyn, N.Y. 11201
Paul Jaeger, 211 Leedom St., Jenkintown, Pa. 19046 (Nickel)
Jana Intl. Co., Box 1107, Denver, Colo. 80201
Jason Empire Inc., 9200 Cody, Overland Park, KS 66214
Kesselring Gun Shop, 400 Pacific Hiway 99 No, Burlington, Wash. 98283
Kuharsky Bros. (see Modern Industries)
Kwik-Site (rings) (see J. B. Holden Co.)
LanDav, 7213 Lee Highway, Falls Church, VA 22046 (steel leverlock side mt.)
T. K. Lee, Box 2123, Birmingham, Ala. 35201 (reticles)
E. Leitz, Inc., Rockleigh, N.J. 07647
Leupold & Stevens Inc., P.O. Box 688, Beaverton, Ore. 97005
Jake Levin and Son, Inc., 9200 Cody, Overland Park, KS 66214
W. H. Lodewick, 2816 N.E. Halsey, Portland, OR 97232 (scope safeties)
Lyman Gun Sight Products, Middlefield, Conn. 06455
Marble Arms Co., 420 Industrial Park, Gladstone, MI 49837
Marlin Firearms Co., 100 Kenna Dr., New Haven, Conn. 06473
Mitchell's Shooting Glasses, Box 539, Waynesville, MO 65583
Modern Industries, Inc., 613 W-11, Erie, PA 16501
O. F. Mossberg & Sons, Inc., 7 Grasso Ave., North Haven, Conn. 06473
Normark Corp., 1710 E. 78th St., Minneapolis, Minn. 55423 (Singlepoint)
Numrich Arms, West Hurley, N.Y. 12491
Nydar Div., Swain Nelson Co., Box 45, Glenview, Ill. 60025 (shotgun sight)
PGS, Peters' Inc., 622 Gratiot Ave., Saginaw, Mich. 48602 (scope shields)
Pachmayr Gun Works, 1220 S. Grand Ave., Los Angeles, Calif. 90015
Pacific Tool Co., P.O. Drawer 2048, Ordnance Plant Rd., Grand Island, NB 68801
Ed Paul's Sptg. Goods, Inc., 172 Flatbush Ave., Brooklyn, N.Y. 11217 (Tops)
Precise Imports Corp., 3 Chestnut, Suffern, N.Y. 10901 (PIC)
Ranging Inc., P.O. Box 9106, Rochester, N.Y. 14625
Ray-O-Vac, Willson Prod. Div., P.O. Box 622, Reading, PA 19603 (shooting glasses)
Realist, Inc., N. 93 W. 16288, Megal Dr., Menomonee Falls, Wis. 53051
Redfield Gun Sight Co., 5800 E. Jewell Ave., Denver, Colo. 80222
Rifleman's Bore Sighter Co., P.O. Box 1701, Saginaw, MI 48605
S & K Mfg. Co., Box 247, Pittsfield, Pa. 16340 (Insta-mount)
Sanders Cust. Gun Serv., 2358 Tyler Lane, Louisville, Ky. 40205 (MSW)
Saunders Gun & Machine Shop, 145 Delhi Rd., Manchester, IA 52057 (lens caps)
Savage Arms, Westfield, Mass. 01085
Sears, Roebuck & Co., 825 S. St. Louis, Chicago, Ill. 60607
W. H. Siebert, 22443 S.E. 56th Pl., Issaquah, Wn. 98027
Singlepoint (see Normark)
Southern Precision Inst. Co., 3419 E. Commerce St., San Antonio, TX 78219
Spacetron Inc., Box 84, Broadview, IL 60155 (bore lamp)
Stoeger Arms Co., 55 Ruta Ct., S. Hackensack, N.J. 07606
Supreme Lens Covers, Box GG, Jackson Hole, WY 83001 (lens caps)
Swift Instruments, Inc., 952 Dorchester Ave., Boston, Mass. 02125
Tasco, 1075 N.W. 71st, Miami, Fla. 33138
Thompson-Center Arms, P.O. Box 2405, Rochester, N.H. 03867 (handgun scope)
Tradewinds, Inc., Box 1191, Tacoma, Wash. 98401
John Unertl Optical Co., 3551-5 East St., Pittsburgh, Pa. 15214
United Binocular Co., 9043 S. Western Ave., Chicago, Ill. 60620
Universal Firearms Corp., 3746 E. 10th Ct., Hialeah, Fla. 33013
Vissing (see: Supreme Lens Covers)
H. P. Wasson, Box 15, Vacation Village, FL 33071 (eyeglass apertures)
Weatherby's, 2781 Firestone, South Gate, Calif. 90280
W. R. Weaver Co., 7125 Industrial Ave., El Paso, Tex. 79915
Wein Prods. Inc., 115 W. 25th St., Los Angeles, CA 90007 (Cronoscope)
Williams Gun Sight Co., 7389 Lapeer Rd., Davison, Mich. 48423
Willrich Precision Instrument Co., 37-13 Broadway, Rte. 4, Fair Lawn, NJ 07410 (borescope)
The Y Sight Inc., 1243 N.E. 4th Ave., Fort Lauderdale, FL 33304 (shotgun sight)
Carl Zeiss Inc., 444 Fifth Ave., New York, N.Y. 10018 (Hensoldt)

SIGHTS, METALLIC

B-Square Eng. Co., Box 11281, Ft. Worth, Tex. 76110
Bo-Mar Tool & Mfg. Co., Box 168, Carthage, Tex. 75633
Maynard P. Buehler, Inc., 17 Orinda Highway, Orinda, Calif. 94563
Christy Gun Works, 875 57th St., Sacramento, Calif. 95819
Cornwall Bridge Gun Shop, P.O. Box 67, Cornwall Bridge, CT 06754 (vernier)
E-Z Mount, Ruelle Bros., P.O. Box 114, Ferndale, MT 48220
Firearms Dev. Lab., Box 3, Lincoln, CA 95648
Freeland's Scope Stands, Inc., 3734-14th Ave., Rock Island, Ill. 61201
P. W. Gray Co., Fairgrounds Rd., Nantucket, Mass. 02554 (shotgun)
Paul T. Haberly, 2364 N. Neva, Chicago, IL 60635
Paul Jaeger, Inc., 211 Leedom St., Jenkintown, PA 19046
Lyman Gun Sight Products, Middlefield, Conn. 06455
Marble Arms Corp., 420 Industrial Park, Gladstone, Mich. 49837
Merit Gunsight Co., P.O. Box 995, Sequim, Wash. 98382
Micro Sight Co., 242 Harbor Blvd., Belmont, Calif. 94002
Miniature Machine Co., 212 E. Spruce, Deming, N.M. 88030
Modern Industries, Inc., 613 W-11, Erie, PA 16501
C. R. Pedersen & Son, Ludington, Mich. 49431
Poly Choke Co., Inc., P.O. Box 296, Hartford, CT 06101
Redfield Gun Sight Co., 5800 E. Jewell St., Denver, Colo. 80222
Schwarz's Gun Shop, 41 - 15th St., Wellsburg, W. Va. 26070
Simmons Gun Specialties, Inc., 700 Rodgers Rd., Olathe, Kans. 66061
Slug Site Co., 3810½ Douglas Ave., Des Moines, IA 50310
Sport Service Center, 2364 N. Neva, Chicago, IL 60635
Tradewinds, Inc., Box 1191, Tacoma, WA 98401
Williams Gun Sight Co., 7389 Lapeer Rd., Davison, Mich. 48423

STOCKS (Commercial and Custom)

W. S. Abe, Abe's Gunshop, 5124 Huntington Dr., Los Angeles, CA 90032
Adams Custom Gun Stocks, 13461 Quito Rd., Saratoga, CA 95070
Ahlman's Inc., R.R. 1, Box 20, Morristown, MN 55052
Anderson's Guns, 706 S. 23rd St., Laramie, WY 82070
Dale P. Andrews, 3572 E. Davies, Littleton, CO 80122
R. J. Anton, 1016 Riehl St., Waterloo, Ia. 50703
Austrian Gunworks Reg'd., P.O. Box 136, Eastman, Que., Canada
Jim Baiar, Rt. 1-B, Box 352, Columbia Falls, Mont. 59912
Joe J. Balickie, Custom Stocks, 6108 Deerwood Pl., Raleigh, N.C. 27607
Bartas, Rte. 1, Box 129-A, Cato, Wis. 54206
John Bianchi, 212 W. Foothill Blvd., Monrovia, Calif. 91016 (U. S. carbines)
Al Biesen, West 2039 Sinto Ave., Spokane, Wash. 99201
E. C. Bishop & Son Inc., Box 7, Warsaw, Mo. 65355
Nate Bishop, Box 334, Minturn, CO 81645
Kay H. Bowles, Pinedale, Wyo. 82941
Brown Precision Co., 5869 Indian Ave., San Jose, CA 95123
Lenard M. Brownell, Box 25, Wyarno, WY 82845
Calico Hardwoods, Inc., 1648 Airport Blvd., Windsor, Calif. 95492 (blanks)
Dick Campbell, 1445 So. Meade, Denver, Colo. 80219
Winston Churchill, 55 High St., Ludlow, VT 05149
Cloward's Gun Shop, 4023 Aurora Ave. N., Seattle, WA 98102
Mike Conner, Box 208, Tijeras, NM 87059
Crane Creek Gun Stock Co., 25 Shephard Terr., Madison, WI 53705
Crest Carving Co., 8091 Bolsa Ave., Midway City, CA 92655
Charles De Veto, 1087 Irene Rd., Lyndhurst, O. 44124
Custom Gunstocks, 1445 So. Meade, Denver, Colo. 80219
Reinhart Fajen, Box 338, Warsaw, Mo. 65355
N. B. Fashingbauer, Box 366, Lac Du Flambeau, Wis. 54538
Ted Fellowes, Beaver Lodge, 9245 16th Ave. S. W., Seattle, Wash. 98106
Clyde E. Fischer, Rt. 1, Box 170-M, Victoria, Tex. 77901
Jerry Fisher, 1244-4th Ave. W., Kalispell, MT 59901
Flaig's Lodge, Millvale, Pa. 15209
Horace M. Frantz, Box 128, Farmingdale, N.J. 07727
Freeland's Scope Stands, Inc., 3734 14th Ave., Rock Island, Ill. 61201
Aaron T. Gates, 3229 Felton St., San Diego, Calif. 92104
Dale Goens, Box 224, Cedar Crest, N.M. 87008
Gould's Myrtlewood, 1692 N. Dogwood, Coquille, Ore. 97423 (gun blanks)
Rolf R. Gruning, 315 Busby Dr., San Antonio, Tex. 78209
Gunstocks-Rarewoods, Haleiwa, Hawaii 97612 (blanks)

Gunwoods (N.Z.) Ltd., Box 18505, New Brighton, Christchurch, New Zealand (blanks)
Half Moon Rifle Shop, Rte. 1B, Box 352, Columbia Falls, MT 59912
Hank's Stock Shop, 1078 Alice Ave., Ukiah, Calif. 95482
Harper's Custom Stocks, 928 Lombrano St., San Antonio, Tex. 78207
Harris Gun Stocks, Inc., 12 Lake St., Richfield Springs, N.Y. 13439
Hal Hartley, Box 147, Blairsfork Rd., Lenoir, N.C. 28654
Hayes Gunstock Service Co., 914 E. Turner St., Clearwater, Fla. 33516
Hubert J. Hecht, 55 Rose Mead Circle, Sacramento, CA 95831
Edward O. Hefti, 300 Fairview, College Sta., Tex. 77840
Herter's Inc., Waseca, Minn. 56093
Klaus Hiptmayer, P.O. Box 136, Eastman, Que., Canada
Richard Hodgson, 9081 Tahoe Lane, Boulder, CO 80301
Hollis Gun Shop, 917 Rex St., Carlsbad, N.M. 88220
Jack's Walnut Woods, 10333 San Fernando Rd., Pacoima, CA 91331 (English and Claro blanks)
Jackson's, Box 416, Selman City, Tex. 75689 (blanks)
Paul Jaeger, 211 Leedom St., Jenkintown, Pa. 19046
I. D. Johnson, Rt. 1, Strawberry Point, Ia. 52076 (blanks)
Johnson's Gun Shop, 1316 N. Blackstone, Fresno, CA 93703
Monte Kennedy, P.O. Box 214, Kalispell, MT 59901
Leer's Gun Barn, Rt. 3, Sycamore Hills, Elwood, Ind. 46036
LeFever Arms Co., Inc., R.D. 1, Lee Center, N.Y. 13363
Bill McGuire, Inc., 7749 - 15th Ave. N.W., Seattle, WA 98117
Maryland Gun Exchange, Rd., 5, Rt. 40 W., Frederick MD 21701
Maurer Arms, 2366 Frederick Dr., Cuyahoga Falls, O. 44221
Leonard Mews, Spring Rd., Box 242, Hortonville, WI 54944
Robt. U. Milhoan & Son, Rt. 3, Elizabeth, W. Va. 26143
C. D. Miller Guns, St. Onge, S.D. 57779
Mills (D.H.) Custom Stocks, 401 N. Ellsworth Ave., San Mateo, Calif. 94401
Nelsen's Gun Shop, 501 S. Wilson, Olympia, Wash. 98501
Oakley and Merkley, Box 2446, Sacramento, CA 95811 (blanks)
Ernest O. Paulsen, Rte. 71, Box 11, Chinook, MT 59523 (blanks)
Peterson Mach. Carving, Box 1065, Sun Valley, Calif. 91352
Andrew Redmond, Inc., No. Anson, Me. 04958 (birchwood blanks)
R. Neal Rice, Box 12172, Denver, CO 80212
Richards Micro-Fit Stocks, P.O. Box 1066, Sun Valley, CA. 91352 (thumbhole)
Roberts Wood Prod., 1400 Melody Rd., Marysville, Calif. 95901
Carl Roth, Jr., P.O. Box 2593, Cheyenne, Wy. 82001
Royal Arms, Inc., 10064 Bert Acosta Ct., Santee, Calif. 92071
Sanders Cust. Gun Serv., 2358 Tyler Lane, Louisville, Ky. 40205 (blanks)
Saratoga Arms Co., R.D. 3, Box 387, Pottstown, Pa. 19464
Roy Schaefer, 965 W. Hilliard Lane, Eugene, Ore. 97402 (blanks)
Shaw's, 1655 S. Euclid Ave., Anaheim, Calif. 92802
Walter Shultz, R.D. 3, Pottstown, Pa. 19464
Sile Dist., 7 Centre Market Pl., New York, N.Y. 10013
Ed Sowers, 8331 DeCelis Pl., Sepulveda, Calif. 91343
Sportsmen's Equip. Co., 915 W. Washington, San Diego, Calif. 92103 (carbine conversions)
Keith Stegall, Box 696, Gunnison, Colo. 81230
Stinehour Rifles, Box 84, Cragsmoor, N.Y. 12420
Swanson Cust. Firearms, 1051 Broadway, Denver, Colo. 80203
Talmage Enterpr., 1309 W. 12 St., Long Beach, CA 90813
Trevallion Gunstocks, 3442 S. Post Rd., Indianapolis, IN 46239
Brent L. Umberger, R.R. 4, Cambridge, OH 43725
Roy Vail, Rt. 1, Box 8, Warwick, N.Y. 10990
Harold Waller, 1288 Camillo Way, El Cajon, CA 92021
Weatherby's, 2781 Firestone, South Gate, Calif. 90280
Western Stocks & Guns, Inc., 2206 E 11th, Bremerton, Wash. 98311
Joe White, Box 8505, New Brighton, Christchurch, N.Z. (blanks)
Bob Williams, c/o Hermans-Atlas Custom Guns, 800 E St. N.W., Washington, DC 20004
Lou Williamson, 129 Stonegate Ct., Bedford, TX 76021
Robert M. Winter, Box 484, Menno, S.D. 57045
Fred Wranic, 6919 Santa Fe, Huntington Park, Calif. 90255 (mesquite)
Paul Wright, 4504 W. Washington Blvd., Los Angeles, Calif. 90016

TAXIDERMY

D. Anderson, 140 E. 13800 South, Draper, UT 84020
Jack Atcheson & Sons, Inc., 3210 Ottawa St., Butte, MT 59701
Clearfield Taxidermy, 603 Hanna St., Clearfield, PA 16830
Jonas Bros., Inc., 1037 Broadway, Denver, CO 80203 (catlg. $2)
Knopp Bros., N. 6715 Division St., Spokane, WA 99208
Mac's Taxidermy, 1316 West Ave., Waukesha, WI 53186

TARGETS, BULLET & CLAYBIRD TRAPS

Black Products Co., 13513 Calumet Ave., Chicago, Ill. 60627
Caswell Target Carriers, Box 344, Anoka, Minn. 55303
Cole's Acku-Rite Prod., Box 25, Kennedy, N.Y. 14747 (Site Rite targets)
Detroit Bullet Trap Co., 2233 N. Palmer Dr., Schaumburg, Ill. 60172
Duncan Prods., P.O. Box 19036, Diamond Lake Sta., Minneapolis, MN 55419 (target holders)
Electro Ballistic Lab., P.O. Box 5876, Stanford, CA 94305 (Electronic Trap Boy)
Ellwood Epps (Orillia) Ltd., Hwy. 11 North, Orillia, Ont., Canada (hand traps)
Gopher Shooter's Supply, Box 246, Faribault, Minn. 55021 (Lok-A-Leg target holders)
Laporte S.A., B.P. 212, 06 Antibes, France (claybird traps)
Millard F. Lerch, Box 163, 10842 Front St., Mokena, Ill. 60448 (bullet target)
National Target Co., 4960 Wyaconda Rd., Rockville, Md. 20853
Outers Laboratories, Inc., Onalaska, Wis. 54650 (claybird traps)
Peterson Label Co., P.O. Box 186, Redding Ridge, CT 06876 (paste-ons)
Professional Tape Co., 355 E. Burlington Rd., Riverside, Ill. 60546 (Time Labels)
Ranger Arms Co., Box 704, Gainesville, Tex. 76240 (paper targets)
Recreation Prods. Res. Inc., 158 Franklin Ave., Ridgwood, N.J. 07450 (Butts bullet trap)
Remington Arms Co., Bridgeport, Conn. 06602 (claybird traps)
Scientific Prod. Corp., 426 Swann Ave., Alexandria, VA 22301 (Targetter)
Sheridan Products, Inc., 3205 Sheridan, Racine, Wis. 53403 (traps)
Shooting Equip. Inc., 2001 N. Parkside Ave., Chicago, Ill. 60639 (electric range)
Time Products Co. (See Prof. Tape Co.)
Trius Prod., Box 25, Cleves, O. 45002 (claybird, can thrower)
Winchester-Western, New Haven, Conn. 06504 (claybird traps)

TRAP & SKEET SHOOTERS EQUIP.

Creed Enterprises, P.O. Box 3029, Arcadia, CA 91006 (ammo pouch)
Filmat Ent., Inc., 200 Market St., East Paterson, NJ 07407 (shotshell pouches)
Laporte S.A., B.P. 212, 06 Antibes, France (traps, claybird)
Old Mill Trap & Skeet, 300 Mill Ridge Rd., Secaucus, NJ 07094 (Seymour shotshell catcher)
Outers Laboratories, Inc., P.O. Box 37, Onalaska, WI 54650 (trap, claybird)
Remington Arms Co., Bridgeport, CT 06602 (trap, claybird)
Safe-T-Shell, Inc., 4361 Woodhall Rd., Columbus, OH 43221 (shotgun)
Trius Products, Box 25, Cleves, OH 45002 (can thrower; trap, claybird)
Daniel Titus, 119 Morlyn Ave., Bryn Mawr, PA 19010 (hull bag)
Winchester-Western, New Haven, CT 06504 (trap, claybird)

TRIGGERS, RELATED EQUIP.

M. H. Canjar Co., 500 E. 45th Ave., Denver, CO 80216 (triggers)
Flaig's, Babcock Blvd. & Thompson Run Rd., Millvale, PA 15209 (trigger shoe)
Gager Gage & Tool Co., 27509 Industrial Blvd., Hayward, CA 94545 (speedlock triggers f. Rem. 1100 and 870 shotguns)
Michaels of Oregon Co., P.O. Box 13010, Portland, OR 97213 (trigger guards)
Ohaus Corp., 29 Hanover Rd., Florham Park, NJ 07932 (trigger pull gauge)
Pachmayr Gun Works, 1220 S. Grand Ave., Los Angeles, CA 90015 (trigger shoe)
Pacific Tool Co., P.O. Drawer 2048, Ordnance Plant Rd., Grand Island, NB 68801 (trigger shoe)
Richland Arms Co., 321 W. Adrian St., Blissfield, MI 49228 (trigger pull gauge)
Schwab Gun Shop, 1103 E. Bigelow, Findlay, OH 45840 (trigger release)
Sport Service Center, 2364 N. Neva, Chicago, IL 60635 (release triggers)
Melvin Tyler, 1326 W. Britton Ave., Oklahoma City, OK 73114 (trigger shoe)
L. H. Waltersdorf, 29 Freier Rd., Quakertown, PA 18951 (release trigger)
Williams Gun Sight Co., 7389 Lapeer Rd., Davison, MI 48423 (trigger shoe)

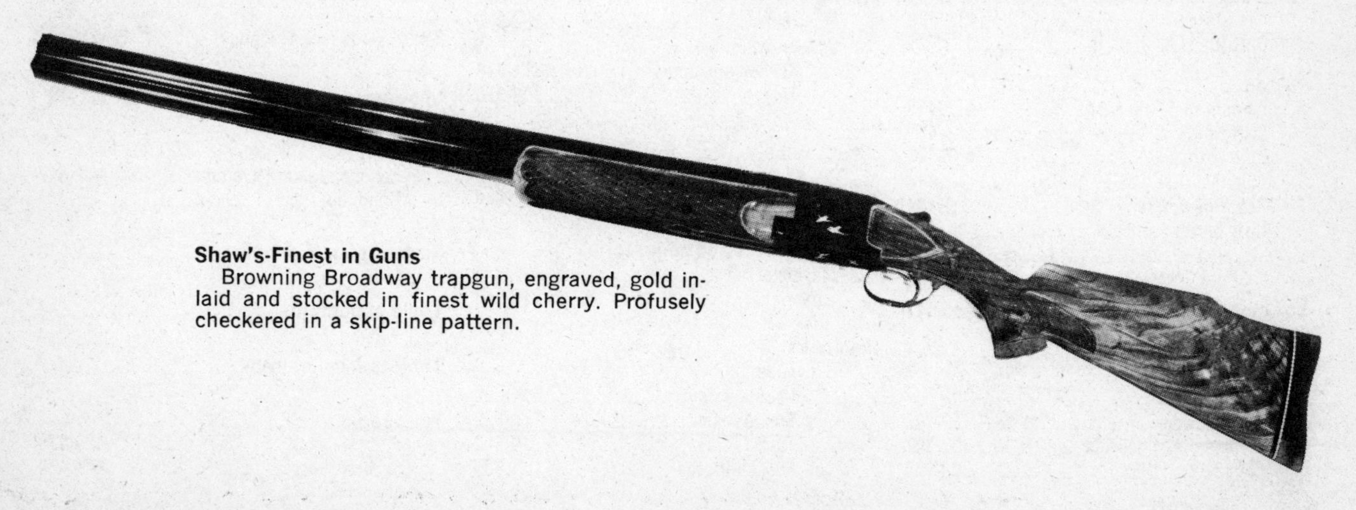

Shaw's-Finest in Guns
Browning Broadway trapgun, engraved, gold inlaid and stocked in finest wild cherry. Profusely checkered in a skip-line pattern.

INDEX

to the departmental and display pages of the GUN DIGEST *—29th Edition*